5.9₽

# BIOCHEMISTRY
Mechanisms of Metabolism

# BIOCHEMISTRY
## Mechanisms of Metabolism

**Earlene Brown Cunningham**

*Department of Biochemistry*
*Medical University of South Carolina*

**McGraw-Hill Book Company**

New York  St. Louis  San Francisco  Auckland  Bogotá  Düsseldorf
Johannesburg  London  Madrid  Mexico  Montreal  New Delhi
Panama  Paris  São Paulo  Singapore  Sydney  Tokyo  Toronto

**BIOCHEMISTRY**
Mechanisms of Metabolism

Copyright © 1978 by McGraw-Hill, Inc. All rights reserved.
Printed in the United States of America. No part of this publication may be reproduced, stored in a retrieval system, or transmitted, in any form or by any means, electronic, mechanical, photocopying, recording, or otherwise, without the prior written permission of the publisher.

1234567890 DODO 783210987

This book was set in Times Roman.
The editor was Donald C. Jackson;
the cover was designed by Joseph Gillians;
the production supervisor was Leroy A. Young.
The drawings were done by J & R Services, Inc.
R. R. Donnelley & Sons Company was printer and binder.

**Library of Congress Cataloging in Publication Data**

Cunningham, Earlene Brown, date
    Biochemistry: mechanisms of metabolism.

    Includes index.
    1. Biological chemistry.  2. Metabolism.
I. Title. [DNLM: 1. Biochemistry. 2. Metabolism.
QU120 C973b]
QP514.2.C86     574.1'92     77-24163
ISBN 0-07-014927-5

To those from whom I have learned

# CONTENTS

|  |  |  |
|---|---|---|
|  | Preface | ix |
| Chapter 1 | Introduction | 1 |
| Chapter 2 | Optical Activity | 62 |
| Chapter 3 | The Chemistry of Carbohydrates | 82 |
| Chapter 4 | The Chemistry of the Lipids | 112 |
| Chapter 5 | The Chemistry of the Amino Acids and the Proteins | 148 |
| Chapter 6 | The Chemistry of the Purines, Pyrimidines, and Nucleic Acids | 201 |
| Chapter 7 | Some Thermodynamic Aspects of Biochemical Systems: Bioenergetics | 259 |
| Chapter 8 | The Kinetics of Biochemical Reactions: Enzymes | 282 |
| Chapter 9 | Carbohydrate Metabolism | 330 |
| Chapter 10 | The Tricarboxylic Acid Cycle | 411 |
| Chapter 11 | Electron Transport and Energy Production | 442 |
| Chapter 12 | Lipid Metabolism | 474 |
| Chapter 13 | Metabolism of Purines, Pyrimidines, and Nucleic Acids | 543 |
| Chapter 14 | Metabolism of Amino Acids and Proteins | 611 |
|  | Index | 751 |

# PREFACE

Biochemical pathways comprise specific, fundamental bond-breaking and bond-making processes which are combined, arranged, and interdigitated in such a way as to allow a living organism to be produced and maintained. Perhaps for many of the same types of reasons that cause an inquisitive child to attempt to understand the way in which a toy works, the biochemist attempts to understand the way in which the living organism works. In the latter instance, the investigation frequently entails resolving intricate biochemical processes into familiar components which are more readily understood. One such component is the reaction mechanism and another is the kinetic mechanism. Thus, I have chosen to discuss the principal biochemical pathways in terms of their reaction mechanisms and kinetic mechanisms. For those who are less familiar with the structural, chemical, and physical characteristics of biochemical compounds, these are described within the first six chapters. Also included in this introductory material is a chapter on optical activity, which I believe is appropriate since in virtually all cases biochemical compounds are optically active. Following the first six chapters, and serving as a bridge between the description of the behavior of biochemical compounds in the flask and that in the living organism, are chapters that focus upon the thermodynamic and kinetic aspects of biochemical reactions. With this as background, carbohydrate, lipid, nucleic acid, and protein metabolism are discussed in some detail.

In my judgement, the reasons for discussing biochemical reactions from the perspective of their reaction mechanisms and their kinetic mechanisms are as follows. Reaction mechanisms readily illustrate that there are a relative few types of chemical conversions that occur and recur in all known biochemical pathways. Thus, these pathways can be dissected and recognized to comprise a sequence of familiar, simple bond-breaking and bond-making processes. It is, of course, reassuring to observe that the fundamental tenets of organic and inorganic reaction mechanisms pertain whether the reaction occurs in a living system or in the laboratory. Kinetic mechanisms, similarly, illustrate that the biochemical reactions which occur in living systems proceed according to prescribed patterns of behavior. Thus, in this instance, biochemical pathways can be dissected and recognized to comprise a sequence of reactions which each proceed according to one of a few familiar courses.

In summary, it is my wish to provide some insight into the processes that occur in living organisms by means of dissecting them and identifying the products of that dissection with familiar concepts. I believe that this is one way in which learning can be most efficient, most effective, and most enjoyable.

I also wish to express my sincerest gratitude to my colleagues in the Department of Biochemistry of the Medical University of South Carolina for encouragement and, in some instances, critical review during the time in which I was writing the book. In particular, I thank my department chairman, Bill Baggett. In addition, I also thank those at other institutions from whom I sought information, critical discussion, and also photographic prints to be reproduced for this text. The gracious assistance of all these persons made my task even more enjoyable.

*Earlene Brown Cunningham*

# BIOCHEMISTRY
Mechanisms of Metabolism

CHAPTER
# ONE

## INTRODUCTION

The study of biochemistry is an examination of the chemical reactions that occur in living organisms. The Greek word *bios*, from which the word biochemistry is derived, can be translated as "life" or "living organism." Thus, the word biochemistry means the chemistry of living organisms. Biochemistry includes aspects of organic chemistry, inorganic chemistry, physical chemistry, physics, and other basic disciplines. It is also interrelated with physiology, microbiology, pathology, and various clinical sciences.

Since biochemistry is concerned with the chemical reactions of living organisms, one might initially ask: What types of compounds participate in these reactions? What types of compounds are the constituents of living organisms? Four of the major types of compounds found in living organisms are the carbohydrates, the lipids, the proteins, and the nucleic acids. To a large extent, biochemical reactions are the reactions of these types of compounds and their supporting systems. As a point of departure, some of the structural characteristics of these compounds will be discussed, and subsequently, their reactions will be examined.

## CARBOHYDRATES

The carbohydrates are the most ubiquitous of all biochemical compounds. In fact, carbohydrates constitute a greater percentage of the total biochemical matter than all the other biochemical compounds combined. Carbohydrates are composed of carbon, hydrogen, and oxygen. Included in the category of carbohydrates are the glycogens, the starches, the celluloses, and the saccharides. In addition to the car-

## 2 MECHANISMS OF METABOLISM

bohydrates, per se, there are numerous naturally occurring complex polysaccharides, including the mucopolysaccharides, the lipopolysaccharides, the glycoproteins, and the glycolipids.

### Monosaccharides

The saccharides, or sugars, are the least complex of the carbohydrates. Saccharides are polyhydroxy aldehydes or polyhydroxy ketones. Monosaccharides are those with but one carbonyl group. Each of the remaining carbon atoms bears a hydroxyl group. When the monosaccharide has four carbon atoms one of which is the carbonyl carbon atom of an aldehyde group, the compound is referred to as an *aldotetrose*. The suffix *-ose* indicates that the compound is a saccharide. Similarly, a five-carbon monosaccharide containing a ketone group is a *ketopentose*, while a six-carbon monosaccharide with an aldehyde group is an *aldohexose*.

Although the monosaccharides are formally aldehydes or ketones, they exist in biochemical systems as cyclic hemiacetals or cyclic hemiketals. The hemiacetal forms of glucose and the hemiketal forms of fructose are shown below. The notations $\alpha$ and $\beta$ refer to the configuration at C(1) of the aldohexose or at C(2) of the ketohexose. When structures are written as shown for the naturally occurring saccharides, the hemiacetal carbon atom is of the $\alpha$ configuration when its hydroxyl group is "down," or below the plane of the ring. The configuration is $\beta$ when this hydroxyl group is "up," or essentially in the plane of the ring. Similarly, for the ketohexose, the hemiketal carbon atom is of the $\alpha$ configuration when the hydroxyl group is down and of the $\beta$ configuration when it is up.

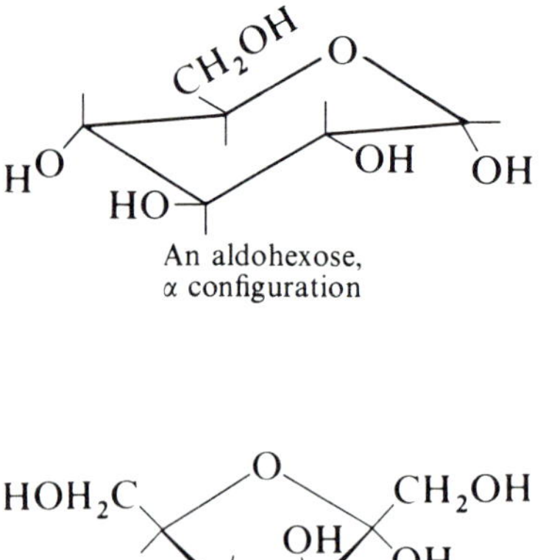

An aldohexose, $\alpha$ configuration

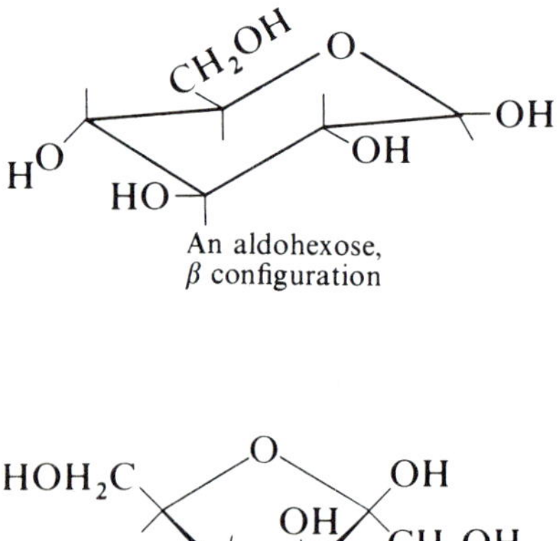

An aldohexose, $\beta$ configuration

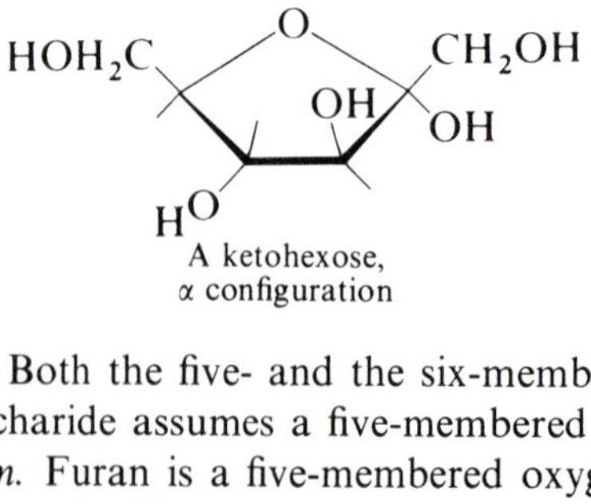

A ketohexose, $\alpha$ configuration

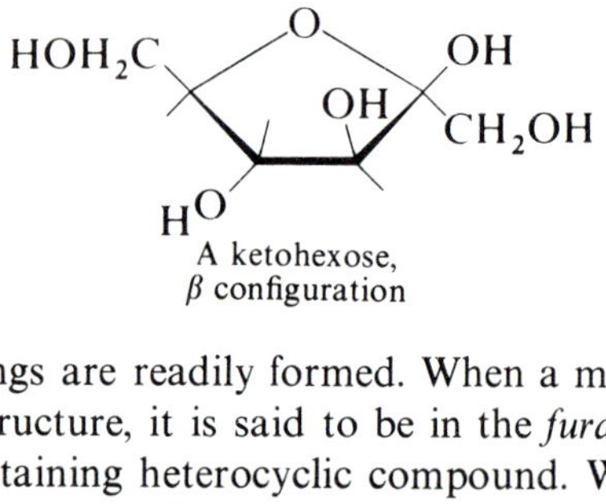

A ketohexose, $\beta$ configuration

Both the five- and the six-membered rings are readily formed. When a monosaccharide assumes a five-membered ring structure, it is said to be in the *furanose form*. Furan is a five-membered oxygen-containing heterocyclic compound. When the saccharide assumes a six-membered ring structure, it is said to be in the *pyranose form*. Pyran is the six-membered oxygen-containing heterocycle. The tendency for

**Table 1-1 Properties of carbocyclic ring structures**

| Number of carbon atoms per ring | Heat of combustion of cycloalkane per methylene group, kcal/mol | Strain per methylene group,* kcal/mol | Total strain per molecule,† kcal/mol |
| --- | --- | --- | --- |
| 3  | 166.6 | 9.2 | 27.6 |
| 4  | 164.0 | 6.5 | 26.4 |
| 5  | 158.7 | 1.3 | 6.5  |
| 6  | 157.4 | 0.0 | 0.0  |
| 7  | 158.3 | 0.9 | 6.3  |
| 8  | 158.6 | 1.2 | 9.6  |
| 9  | 158.8 | 1.4 | 12.6 |
| 10 | 158.6 | 1.2 | 12.0 |
| 11 | 158.4 | 1.0 | 11.0 |
| 12 | 157.7 | 0.3 | 3.6  |
| 13 | 157.8 | 0.4 | 5.2  |
| 14 | 157.4 | 0.0 | 0.0  |
| 15 | 157.5 | 0.1 | 1.5  |
| 16 | 157.5 | 0.1 | 1.6  |

* Strain per methylene group is an indication of the distortion of normal bond angles required to form the ring structure.

† Total strain per molecule is an indication, in part, of the energy requirements for ring closure.

five- and six-membered intramolecular rings to be formed, rather than rings of other sizes, is a result of the relative amounts of strain involved in achieving various cyclic structures. Data for a series of carbocyclic rings are shown in Table 1-1. The substitution of an oxygen atom for one of the carbon atoms does not alter the trend it shows.

Five-membered rings, including furanose structures, exist predominantly in puckered conformations, which allow the bulkier substituents to be staggered to some extent. Two such conformations are the *envelope form* and the *half-chair form*, which have greater symmetry than most other puckered conformations.

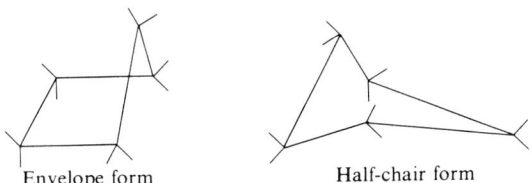

Envelope form            Half-chair form

Six-membered rings can exist in boat or chair conformations as well as in various intermediate twist forms, which are also puckered conformations. The *chair form* of six-membered rings is more stable than the twist forms by about 5 kcal/mol and more stable than the *boat form* by about 7 kcal/mol. In most instances six-membered rings exist almost exclusively in the chair conformation. Notice in Fig. 1-1 that half the bonds of the ring structure are oriented "up and down" while the other half are oriented essentially in the plane of the ring. Substituents linked by bonds oriented up

**4** MECHANISMS OF METABOLISM

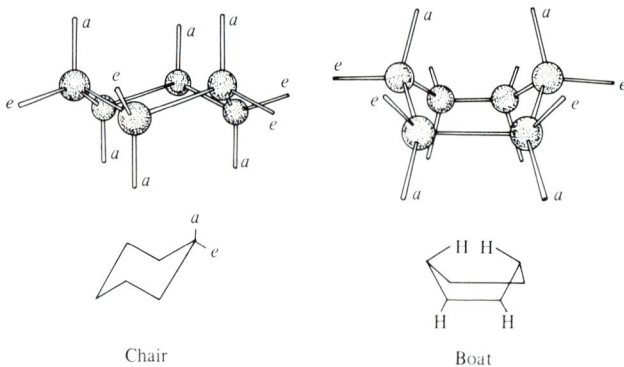

Figure 1-1 Chair and boat forms of cyclohexane; *a* stands for axial and *e* for equatorial.

or down are called *axial*, while those linked by bonds in the plane of the ring are called *equatorial*. When a six-membered ring is substituted, two different chair forms can be distinguished. In one chair form the substituents designated X are equatorial and those designated Y are axial. In the other, the substituents X are axial and the Y substituents are equatorial. In the pyranose form of the aldohexose represented below, the chair form on the left is referred to as the *normal* (N) conformation; that on the right is the *alternative* (A) conformation.

Normal conformation  Alternative conformation

Since the interconversion of the two chair forms of cyclohexane involves an activation energy of approximately 10 kcal/mol, the two conformational isomers cannot be separated at room temperature. (An activation energy of 16 to 20 kcal/mol or more is required to permit such a separation at room temperature.) Somewhat higher activation energies are involved in the chair-form interconversions of some of the pyranose forms of the monosaccharides, however. When one conformational isomer is much more stable than the other, the activation energy for the formation of the more unfavorable conformation may approach the energy permitting separation of the isomers. The principal factor that determines the stability of one conformational isomer with respect to the other is the extent of the van der Waals repulsion in the two forms. In these chair conformations there is van der Waals repulsion between substituents on adjacent carbon atoms plus that between transannular axial substituents. The distance between axial and equatorial substituents on adjacent carbon atoms is the same as that between two equatorial substituents on adjacent carbon atoms. In addition, two transannular axial substituents (not on adjacent carbon atoms) are also separated by this same distance.

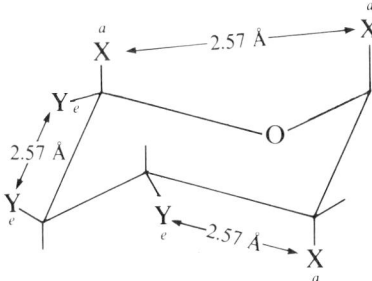

Therefore, there is repulsion between all substituents on neighboring carbon atoms; in addition, axial substituents not on adjacent carbon atoms interact with each other. Thus, the conformational isomer having more of its bulky substituents axial is the less stable, while the conformational isomer having more of its bulky substituents equatorial is the more stable.

Why are chair forms of six-membered rings favored thermodynamically over boat forms? Again, a major contributing factor is the extent of the van der Waals repulsion. In the chair forms, the torsion angle between atoms bonded to adjacent carbon atoms is $\pm 60°$. However, in the boat forms, the torsion angle between atoms bonded to some adjacent carbon atoms is virtually zero. In the latter case the substituents are said to be *synperiplanar* (in or nearly in the same plane), or *eclipsed*. The nomenclature for the various torsion angles is given in Fig. 1-2. The interaction

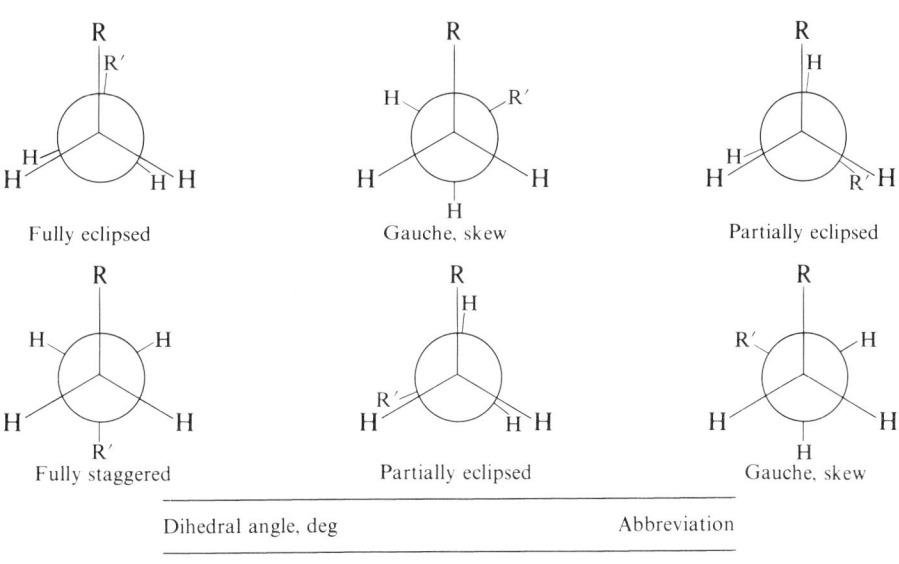

| Dihedral angle, deg | | Abbreviation |
|---|---|---|
| $0 \pm 30$ | $\pm$ synperiplanar | $\pm$ sp |
| $60 \pm 30$ | $+$ synclinal | $+$ sc |
| $120 \pm 30$ | $+$ anticlinal | $+$ ac |
| $180 \pm 30$ | $\pm$ antiperiplanar | $\pm$ ap |
| $-120 \pm 30$ | $-$ anticlinal | $-$ an |
| $-60 \pm 30$ | $-$ synclinal | $-$ sc |

**Figure 1-2** Torsion angles between atoms bonded to adjacent carbon atoms.

**6** MECHANISMS OF METABOLISM

energy associated with the synclinal and anticlinal conformations is several kilocalories less than that associated with synperiplanar conformations. Hence, chair conformations are favored with respect to boat conformations on this basis. In addition, in some boat conformations there is a strong van der Waals repulsion involving the substituents at the "bow" and "stern" of the boat. The interaction energy is over 8 kcal/mol in the boat form of cyclohexane, in which two hydrogen atoms repel each other. Substituents in these positions are separated by a distance of only 1.84 Å, while the sum of the van der Waals radii of the hydrogen atoms is 2.4 Å. Thus, boat conformations are further destabilized with respect to chair conformations.

## Disaccharides, Oligosaccharides, and Polysaccharides

Two monosaccharides can be linked together by an O-glycosidic bond to form a disaccharide. An O-glycosidic bond is an ether linkage derived from the hemiacetal or hemiketal hydroxyl group of one monosaccharide and a hydroxyl group that may or may not be derived from the carbonyl group of the second. An O-glycosidic bond can be designated as either an α or a β linkage. This notation again refers to the configuration at the hemiacetal or hemiketal carbon atom. As with the monosaccharides, the O-glycosidic linkage is of the α configuration when the hemiacetal or hemiketal oxygen atom is down, or below the plane of the ring in the structures shown.

Disaccharides:

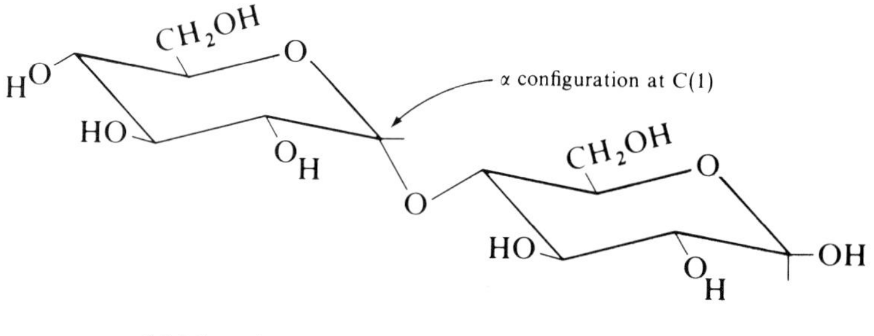

β-Maltose (4-O-α-D-glucopyranosyl-D-glucopyranose)

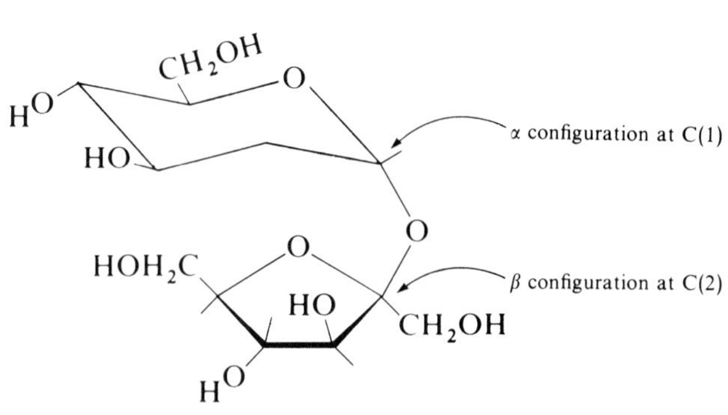

Sucrose
(α-D-glucopyranosyl-β-D-fructofuranoside)

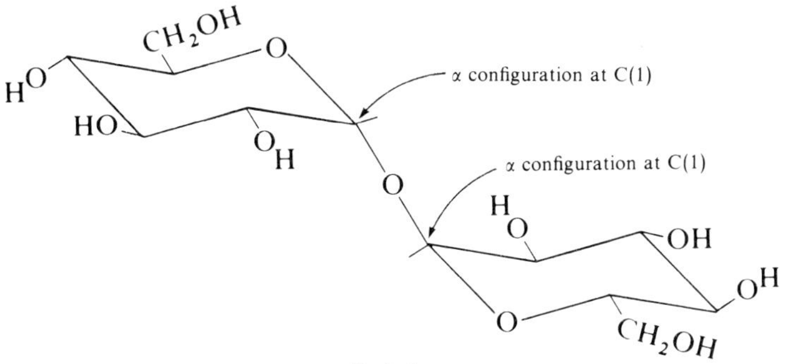

INTRODUCTION 7

Trehalose
(α-D-glucopyranosyl-α-D-glucopyranoside)

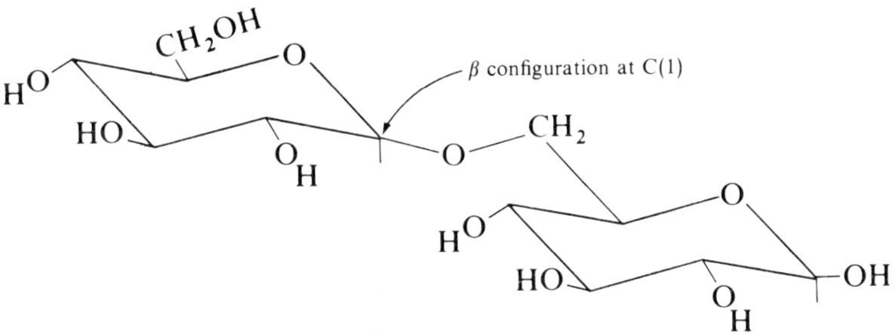

β-Gentiobiose
(6-O-β-D-glucopyranosyl-D-glucopyranose)

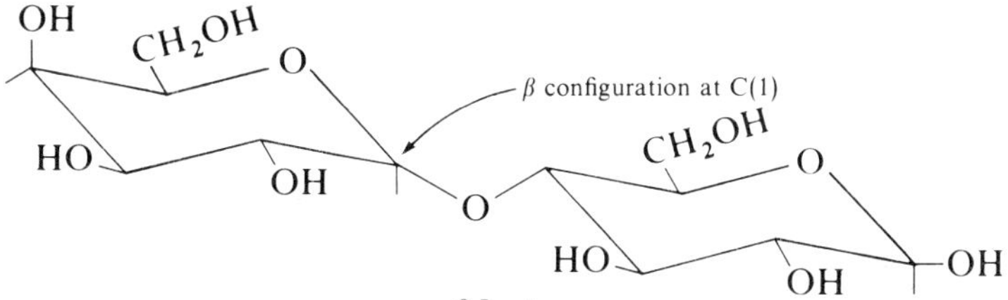

β-Lactose
(4-O-β-D-galactopyranosyl-D-glucopyranose)

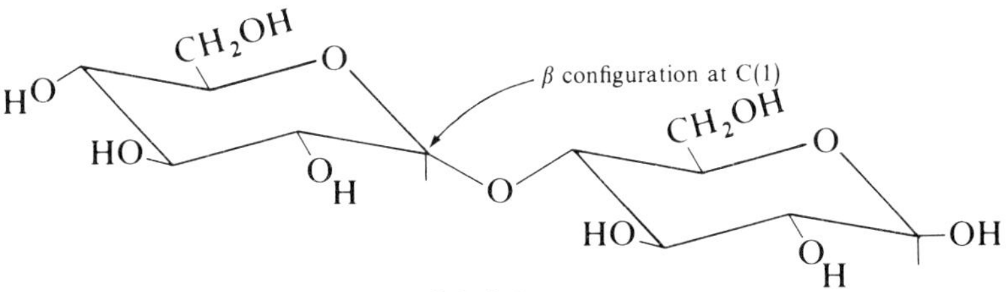

β-Cellobiose
(4-O-β-D-glucopyranosyl-D-glucopyranose)

**8** MECHANISMS OF METABOLISM

A trisaccharide:

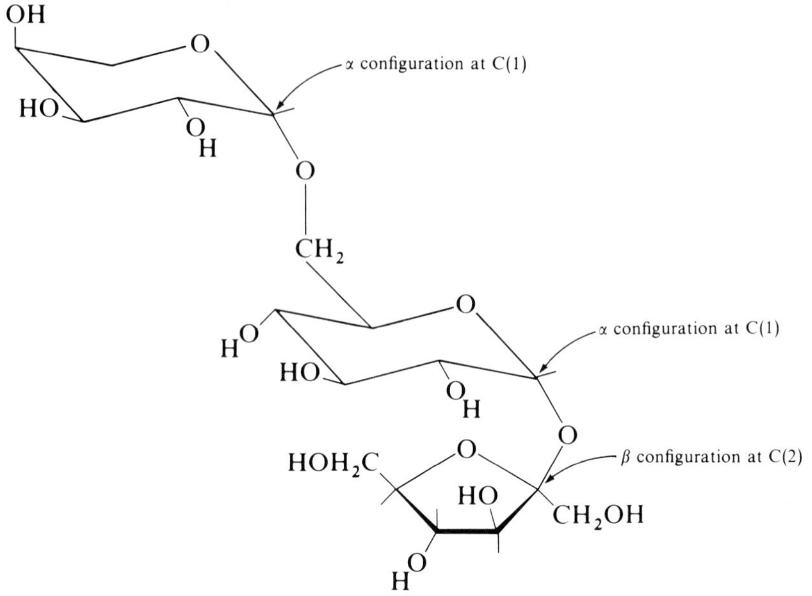

Raffinose
[O-α-D-galactopyranosyl-(1 → 6)-O-α-D-glucopyranosyl-(1 → 2)-β-D-fructofuranoside]

The configuration of this linkage is β when this oxygen is up, or essentially in or above the plane of the ring.

When three monosaccharides are linked together, a trisaccharide is formed, and when four are involved, a tetrasaccharide results. These molecules, each comprising several monosaccharide units, are referred to as *oligosaccharides*. (The Greek prefix *oligo-* means "few.")

Two common disaccharides are maltose, a degradation product of the polysaccharide starch, and sucrose, the sugar used to sweeten food. In maltose the O-glycosidic bond is of the α configuration and is derived from the hemiacetal hydroxyl group of one glucose molecule and the hydroxyl group at C(4) of the second glucose molecule. Sucrose also has an O-glycosidic bond of the α configuration, but in this case the bond is derived from the hydroxyl group of the glucose hemiacetal and the hydroxyl group of the fructose hemiketal. Other naturally occurring disaccharides include lactose, a sugar found in milk; cellobiose, a degradation product of cellulose; trehalose, a constituent of the body fluids of certain insects; and gentiobiose, a plant sugar occurring in bitter almond.

An example of a trisaccharide is found in a sugar obtained from beets, called *raffinose*. Another naturally occurring trisaccharide is *gentianose*, which consists of the gentiobiose structure with a fructofuranosyl moiety added. Naturally occurring trisaccharides are much less common than naturally occurring disaccharides.

Polysaccharides are macromolecules containing eight or ten to several thousand monosaccharide units joined by O-glycosidic bonds. Since polysaccharides are often referred to as *glycans*, those comprising a single monomeric unit are called *homo-*

*glycans* and those comprising two or more different monomeric units are called *heteroglycans.*

Cellulose, which is a plant polysaccharide, is the most abundant organic molecule on our planet. Cellulose is a homoglycan consisting of glucopyranose units joined by $\beta$ *O*-glycosidic bonds, as shown below. Cellulose is an essentially linear polymer for which molecular weights as high as $6 \times 10^6$ have been reported. Cellulose is also considered to be a structural polysaccharide; i.e., it is a component of the structures of living organisms. This is to be contrasted with the function of certain other polysaccharides which serve primarily as a source of nutrition.

In certain lower plants, including some fungi and algae, the polysaccharide chitin rather than cellulose is the principal structural element. Chitin is also a structural element in some lower animals such as arthropods (articulated or jointed animals) and annelids (segmented worms). (In higher animals, a protein called collagen is the corresponding structural material.) The structures of cellulose and chitin, which are somewhat similar, are shown below.

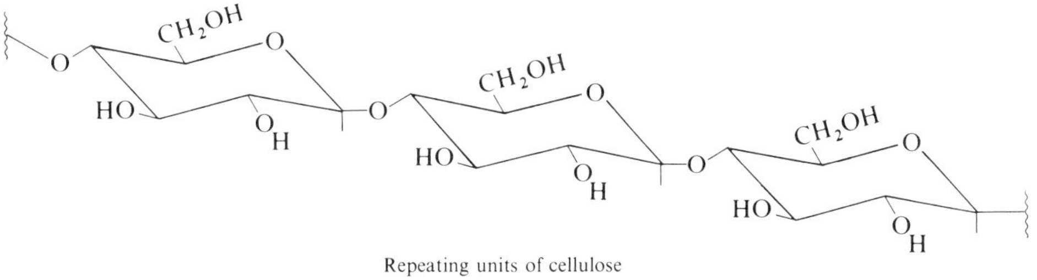

Repeating units of cellulose

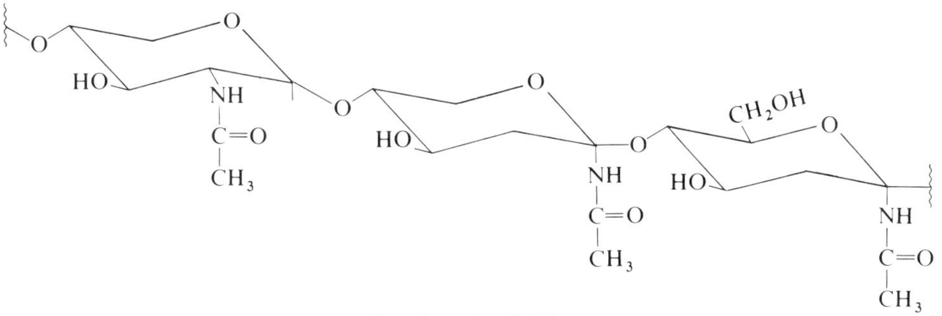

Repeating units of chitin

However, in chitin the monomeric unit is 2-acetamido-D-glucose, or *N*-acetylglucosamine, rather than D-glucose. In both cases the monomeric units are joined by *O*-glycosidic bonds of the $\beta$ configuration. Cellulose chains undergo aggregation as the result of the formation of interchain hydrogen bonds involving the equatorial hydroxyl groups of the glucopyranose units. This aggregation causes the polysaccharide molecules to form sheets (Fig. 1-3), which become the structural material. Chitin chains undergo a comparable aggregation as the result of the formation of interchain hydrogen bonds involving the acetamido groups. Again, sheets are formed. In chitin, three different arrangements of these sheets have been found, and three different types of chitin have been described (Fig. 1-4). Sheets of chitin associate

10 MECHANISMS OF METABOLISM

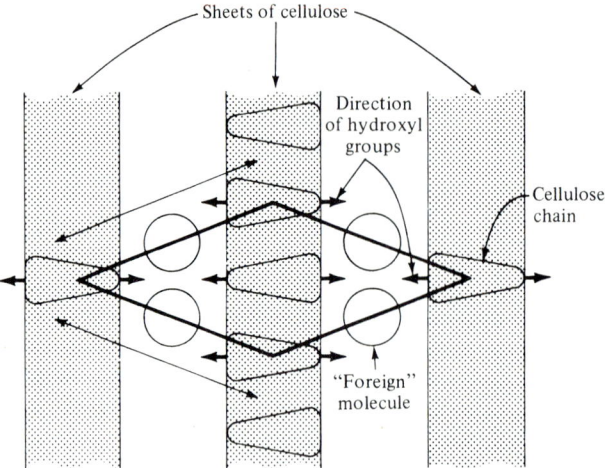

**Figure 1-3** Schematic representation of sheets of cellulose. Each cellulose chain is depicted as a ribbon having an oval cross section. The ribbon is viewed end on. The fiber (and also the polysaccharide-chain) axis is perpendicular to the plane of the page [*From Rees, D. A. (1969) Adv. Carbohydrate Chem.* **24**, 267–332 (*see p. 276*). *With permission.*]

with protein, unlike sheets of cellulose, and it is this chitin-protein complex that is the structural material.

The structural formula makes it clear that chitin contains nitrogen as well as carbon, hydrogen, and oxygen. Polysaccharides in which the monomeric units contain an amino group are called *mucopolysaccharides*.

Starch is a homoglycan that serves as a source of nutrition. Starch is composed of D-glucose units, just as cellulose is. However, in the starch macromolecule the *O*-glycosidic bond is of the α configuration. Some starches, called *amyloses*, are essentially linear polymers. Other starches, called *amylopectins*, are cross-linked. In amylopectins approximately 1 glucose unit in 25 or 30 is involved in cross-linking, entailing the formation of interchain *O*-glycosidic bonds between C(1) and C(6). These bonds are also of the α configuration.

Starch is a storage form of carbohydrate in plants. In grains, starch occurs in

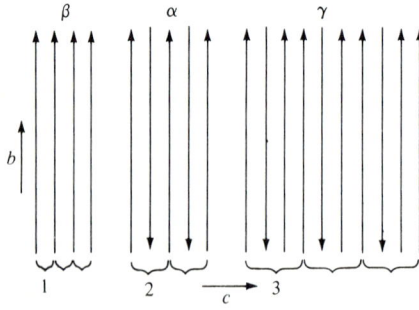

**Figure 1-4** Arrangement of sheets in α-, β-, and γ-chitin; the arrows show the direction of the chains in successive sheets. The fiber axis is given by *b*. The intersheet direction is indicated by *c*.

highly hydrated crystalline forms. Heating, however, expels some of the water of hydration, causing the starch to become amorphous.

Glycogen, also a homoglycan, is a storage form for carbohydrate in animals. Glycogen is likewise made up of D-glucose units joined by O-glycosidic bonds of the α configuration. Glycogen is also cross-linked, as is amylopectin. In fact the degree of cross-linking is even higher than it is in the starch. In glycogen, 1 glucose unit in 8 or 10 is cross-linked through the formation of an α(1→6) O-glycosidic bond.

Certain yeasts and bacteria contain dextrans, which are also homoglycans consisting of D-glucose units. In dextrans, however, the monomeric units are joined by α(1→6) O-glycosidic bonds primarily, with cross-linking occurring by means of the formation of α(1→2) and α(1→3) bonds.

Some yeasts also contain mannan, a homoglycan consisting of D-mannose units.

β-D-Mannose

In the yeast mannan, the monomeric units are linked by β(1 → 4) and β(1 → 3) O-glycosidic bonds, and the polysaccharide is highly cross-linked. Plant mannans, however, are not cross-linked, and the monomeric units are joined by β(1→4) bonds only.

Plants also contain the homoglycan xylan, which comprises D-xylose units joined by β(1→4) O-glycosidic bonds. In this case it has been shown that the pentose, xylose, is predominantly in the pyranose form rather than in the furanose form, as is true of many five-carbon monosaccharides.

Repeating units of xylan

**Homoglycans as antigens** Some cell membranes and biological fluids contains polysaccharides that function as antigens.† For example, certain meningococci (*Neisseria meningitides*) contain homoglycans that function as antigens. The antigenic polysaccharide of the group A meningococci is composed of D-mannosamine 1-phosphate units joined by phosphodiester bonds between C(1) of one monomer and C(6) of its

---

† An antigen is a factor that can induce an immune response in vivo and also react with the products of that response in vitro. The immune response includes the production of antibodies. An antibody is a specific protein produced in the lymphoid tissue in the human body (and at other sites in other living organisms) in response to the stimulation by the antigen. An antigen will combine with its specific antibody but not with other antibodies. The high degree of specificity involved in the antigen-antibody reaction is characteristic of this process. The antigenic determinant, sometimes called the *hapten*, cannot evoke the immune response by itself, but it can react in vitro with the product of the immune response. Whether a factor functions as a complete antigen or as a hapten depends upon several factors, including the species being immunized.

**12** MECHANISMS OF METABOLISM

neighbor. The antigenic polysaccharides of the group B and group C meningococci, on the other hand, are polymers of N-acetylneuraminate, a sialate. Notice that the six-membered ring is written in the alternative conformation, which allows the N-acetamido and propanetriol groups to be equatorial. The monomeric units of both of these polysaccharides are thought to be joined by 2 → 8 O-glycosidic bonds.†

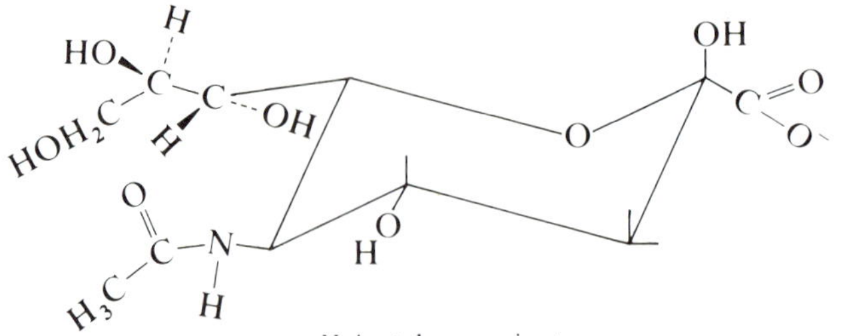

*N*-Acetylneuraminate

**Macromolecular structures of some homoglycans** The macromolecular structure of a given polysaccharide is determined on the basis of the relative potential-energy levels of the various conformations it can assume. The potential-energy level of a conformation can be computed by considering its nonbonded interaction energy (including van der Waals attraction and repulsion) plus its hydrogen-bond energy plus its torsional energy. This torsional energy can be described in terms of two torsion angles, $\phi$ and $\psi$, which as agreed at a symposium of the American Chemical Society in March in 1971, are defined as follows. For 1,4-linked monosaccharide units, the torsion angle $\phi$ is zero when the C(1)—O(1) bond is in the same plane as the C(4′)—H(4′) bond. On the other hand, the torsion angle $\psi$ is zero when the O(1)—C(4′) bond is in the same plane as the C(1)—H(1) bond.

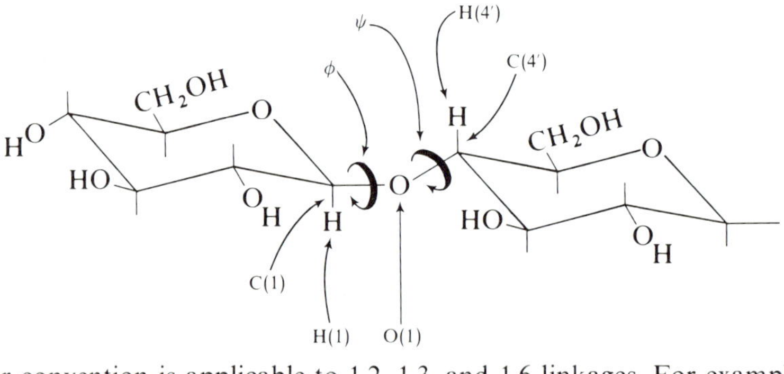

A similar convention is applicable to 1,2, 1,3, and 1,6 linkages. For example, in 1,6 linkages the torsion angle about the C(5′)—C(6) bond is denoted $\omega$ and considered to be zero when the O(1)—C(6′) bond is coplanar with respect to the C(4′)—C(5′) bond. In all cases, positive torsion angles are defined as the dihedral angle observed by looking at the bond on end when the substituent nearer the observer has been rotated counterclockwise with respect to the substituent behind. Frequently the potential energies corresponding to the various torsion angles are calculated and

† Liu, T. Y., Gotschlich, E. C., Dunne, F. T., and Jonssen, E. K. (1971) *J. Biol. Chem.* **246**, 4703–4712.

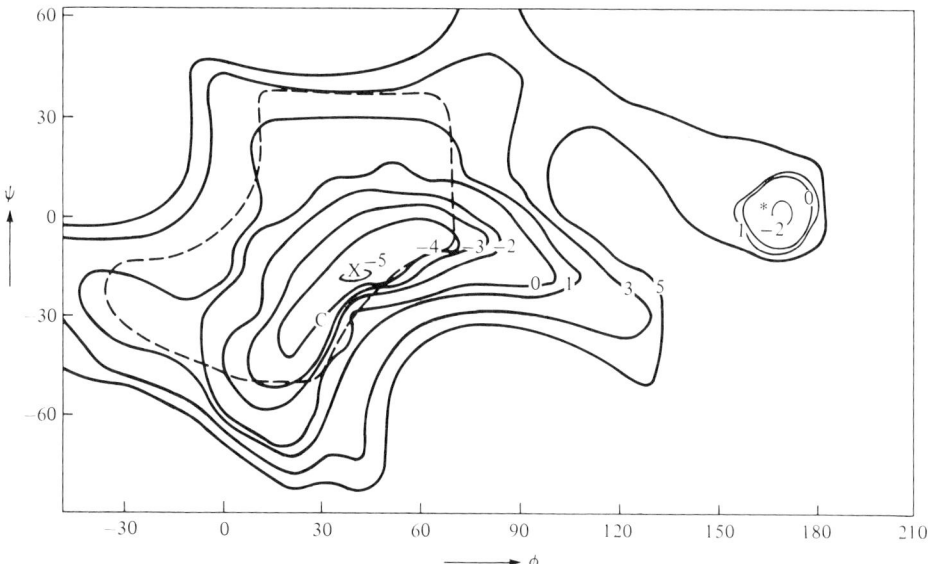

**Figure 1-5** Energy contour diagram (with energies in kilocalories per mole) derived for two β-D-glucose units joined by means of a β (1→4) glycosidic bond. The conformation having the minimum energy level is denoted by X. The point which represents the conformation that is actually found in the cellulose macromolecule is denoted by C. These data are based upon a different convention concerning $\phi$ and $\psi$, however. [*From Sathyanarayana, B. K., and Rao, V. S. R. (1971) Biopolymers* **10**, *1605–1615 (see p. 1609). With permission.*]

displayed in terms of a contour map. In such diagrams a given contour line represents a constant potential-energy value. An energy contour map relating to the possible torsion angles when two glucose units are joined by a β(1→4) glucosidic bond is shown in Fig. 1-5.

Energy contour maps relating to α-linked disaccharides have also been derived, and these indicate that the preferred conformations are those shown in Fig. 1-6.

## Some Naturally Occurring Heteroglycans

Among the many heteroglycans found in living organisms are the mucopolysaccharides hyaluronic acid, heparin, and chondroitin. Hyaluronic acid is the principal component of the ground substance of connective tissue. This heteroglycan is also found in vitreous humor, in synovial fluid, and in the umbilical cord. Hyaluronic acid is composed of N-acetylglucosamine units and glucuronate units. Glucuronic acid is a derivative of glucose in which the primary hydroxyl group at C(6) has been

Repeating units of hyaluronic acid

**14** MECHANISMS OF METABOLISM

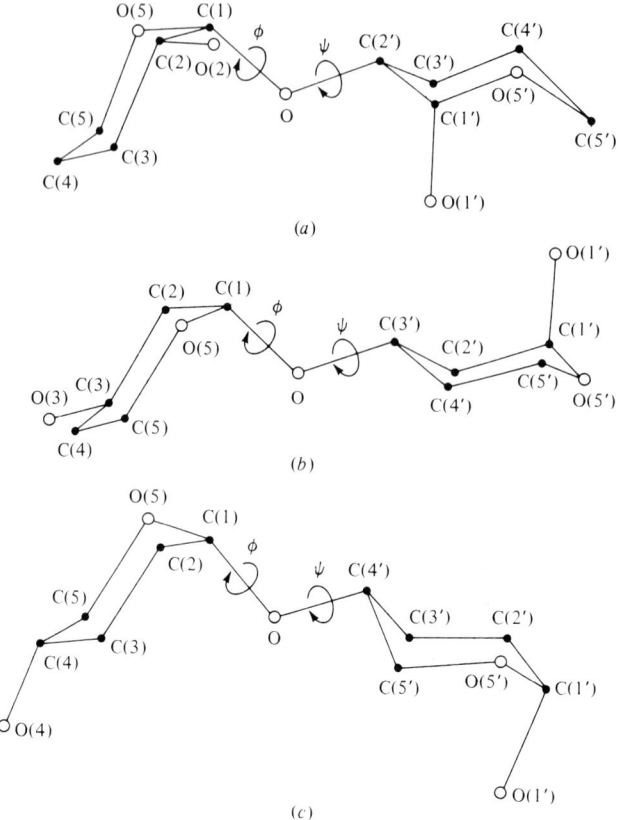

**Figure 1-6** Preferred conformations of two α-D-glucose units joined by means of (a) a 1→2, (b) a 1→3, and (c) a 1→4 glycosidic bond. [*From Sathyanarayana, B. K., and Rao, V. S. R. (1972) Biopolymers* **11**, *1379–1394 (see p. 1381). With permission.*]

oxidized to a carboxylic acid. In general, saccharide derivatives in which the terminal primary alcohol group has been converted to a carboxylic acid are named using the suffix *-uronic acid* or *-uronate*. Aldose derivatives in which the aldehyde moiety at C(1) has been oxidized to a carboxylic acid are named using the suffix *-onic acid* or *-onate*. When both C(1) and C(6) of an aldose have been oxidized to yield carboxylic acid functions, the saccharide is named using the suffix *-aric acid* or *-arate*. For example, the C(6), the C(1), and the C(1) plus C(6) oxidation of glucose yields glucuronate, gluconate, and glucarate, respectively.

Although hyaluronic acid is not usually cross-linked, it is a large macromolecule having a molecular weight of several million. Physiologically, hyaluronic acid is the substance that cements the tissue of living organisms and renders it impervious to foreign bodies (such as pathogenic bacteria) and also to some physiological components. However, hyaluronic acid can undergo enzymatic depolymerization, which removes this barrier to tissue permeation.

Heparin is a heteroglycan having a molecular weight of 17,000 to 20,000. Physiologically, heparin functions as a blood anticoagulant. Heparin also neutralizes hista-

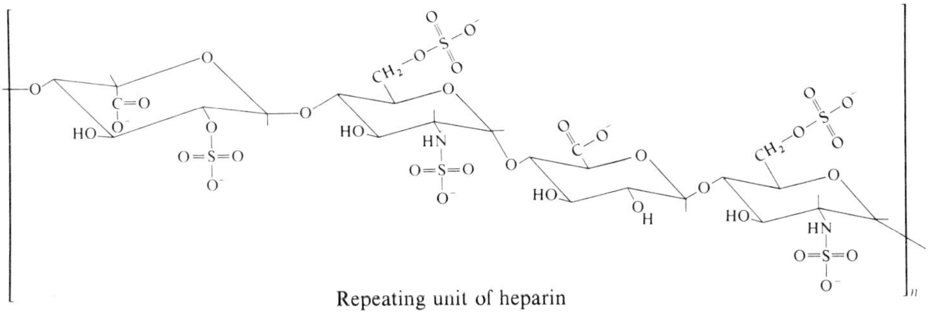

INTRODUCTION 15

Repeating unit of heparin

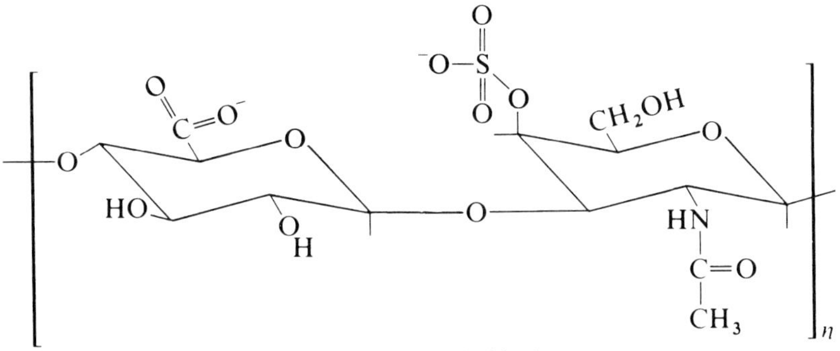

Repeating unit of chondroitin A

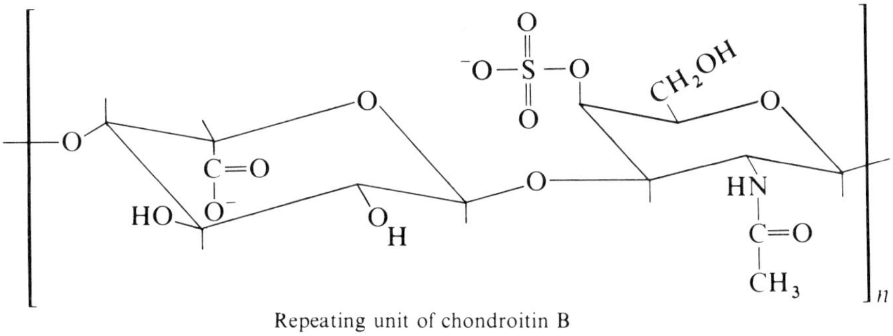

Repeating unit of chondroitin B

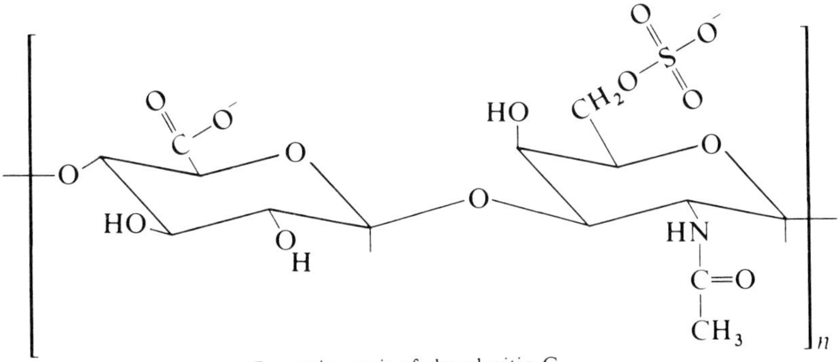

Repeating unit of chondroitin C

mine, a biochemical compound that participates in the allergic response. This mucopolysaccharide is composed of L-iduronate 2-sulfate units (iduronate is derived from the aldohexose idose), glucosesulfonamide 6-sulfate units, and glucuronate units.

Chondroitin, like hyaluronic acid, is a component of connective tissue; cartilage has the highest content of this mucopolysaccharide. Chondroitin C is composed of equimolar amounts of glucuronate and $N$-acetylgalactosamine 6-sulfate. Two other types of this heteroglycan have also been characterized, namely, chondroitin A, which consists of equimolar amounts of glucuronate and $N$-acetylgalactosamine 4-sulfate, and chondroitin B, comprising L-iduronate and $N$-acetylgalactosamine 4- or 6-sulfate.

**The blood-group antigens** In 1900 Karl Landsteiner, an Austrian physician, proposed the ABO system of human blood groups, which is based upon the antigenicity of human erythrocytes. The antigens involved are polysaccharide components of the cell envelope of the erythrocytes. Specifically, these antigens are heteroglycans. It is now known that in a large percentage of the human population these polysaccharide antigens also occur in various other body fluids, including saliva, gastric juice, ovarian-cyst fluid, and colonic mucus. These antigens are also present on the surface of some epithelial cells and even on the surface of some tumor cells. Three different polysaccharide components, the A antigen, the B antigen, and the H antigen, are responsible for the antigenic specificity exhibited. The H antigen is actually present on the surface of all erythrocytes that have the antigens of the ABO system, but in the erythrocytes of certain people this antigen is more fully exposed and more fully expressed. These people are said to belong to the type O blood group. On the other hand, the A antigen is the dominant antigenic component on the surface of the erythrocytes of people belonging to the type A blood group, and the B antigen is the dominant component in people belonging to the type B blood group. People whose erythrocytes bear both the A antigen and the B antigen belong to the AB blood group. Sera of people in the type O blood group contain both anti-A and anti-B isoagglutins, while sera of people in the type A blood group contain anti-B isoagglutins and sera of people in the type B blood group contain anti-A isoagglutins. Sera of people in the type AB group contain neither anti-A nor anti-B isoagglutins.

The erythrocytes of some people bear the antigens of the ABO system although their body fluids do not; however, the body fluids of these people contain the polysaccharide antigens of the Lewis system, designated Le$^a$ and Le$^b$. The antigens of the ABO blood groups and those of the Lewis blood groups have certain similarities. The polysaccharide chains in both cases are complexed with proteins. In fact these antigens are each a part of the blood-group macromolecule of the ABO and Lewis systems. This macromolecule is a large glycopeptide which is believed to have the structure shown in Fig. 1-7. Depending upon the specific antigens present, the macromolecule may have a molecular weight of from $2 \times 10^5$ to $1 \times 10^6$. It consists of about 85 percent carbohydrate and 15 percent protein, the carbohydrate moieties comprising D-galactose, L-fucose (L-6-deoxygalactose), D-glucosamine, and D-galactosamine. It has been shown that it is specifically the nonreducing termini, i.e., the termini not containing the aldehyde group, and the saccharide units linked to

# INTRODUCTION 17

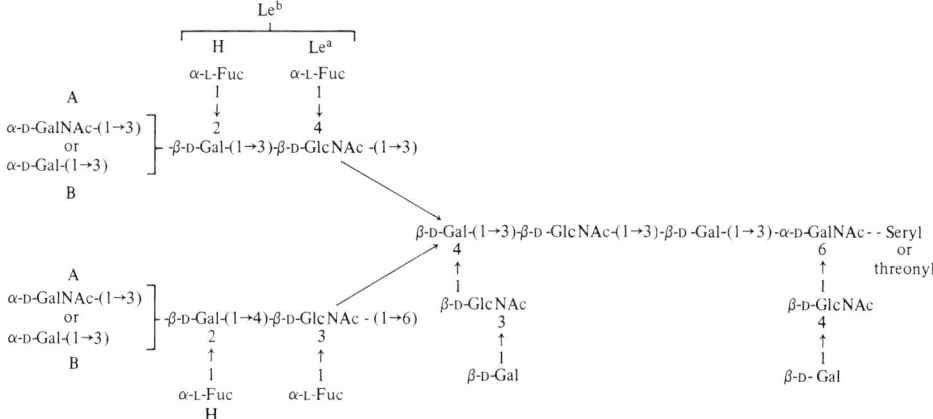

**Figure 1-7** Blood group macromolecule. The branched heteropolysaccharides project from a polypeptide backbone, of which the seryl or threonyl unit is indicated. The α(1→2)-fucosyl units, indicated by H, confer H antigenicity but if α(1→3)-*N*-acetylgalactosamine units (A) are also present on both branches of the heteropolysaccharide $A_1$ antigenicity is exhibited and H antigenicity is negligible. If an *N*-acetylgalactosamine unit is present only on the lower branch and the upper branch lacks a substituent, $A_2$ antigenicity is exhibited. On the other hand, if rather than acetylgalactosamine units α(1→3)-galactosyl units (B) are present, type B antigenicity is exhibited. H antigenicity is again masked although the fucosyl units are, again, still present. $Le^a$ activity is due to the α(1→4)-fucosyl unit indicated while $Le^b$ activity is thought to result from the presence of both the α(1→4)-fucosyl unit and the α(1→2)-fucosyl unit, as shown. [*From Vicari, G., and Kabat, E. A. (1970) Biochemistry,* **9,** *3414–3421 (see p. 3420). With permission.*]

**Table 1-2 Structures responsible for A, B, H, $Le^a$, and $Le^b$ specificities**

| | Structure | |
|---|---|---|
| Specificity | Type I | Type II |
| H | Gal-β-(1 → 3)-GlcNAc ···<br>2<br>↑<br>L-Fuc-α-1 | Gal-β-(1 → 4)-GlcNAc ···<br>2<br>↑<br>L-Fuc-α-1 |
| A | GalNAc-α-(1 → 3)-Gal-β-(1 → 3)-GlcNAc ···<br>2<br>↑<br>L-Fuc-α-1 | GalNAc-α-(1 → 3)-Gal-β-(1 → 4)-GlcNAc ···<br>2<br>↑<br>L-Fuc-α-1 |
| B | Gal-α-(1 → 3)-Gal-β-(1 → 3)-GlcNAc ···<br>2<br>↑<br>L-Fuc-α-1 | Gal-α-(1 → 3)-Gal-β-(1 → 4)-GlcNAc ···<br>2<br>↑<br>L-Fuc-α-1 |
| $Le^a$ | Gal-β-(1 → 3)-GlcNAc ···<br>4<br>↑<br>L-Fuc-α-1 | |
| $Le^b$ | Gal-β-(1 → 3)-GlcNAc ···<br>2    4<br>↑    ↑<br>L-Fuc-α-1  L-Fuc-α-1 | |

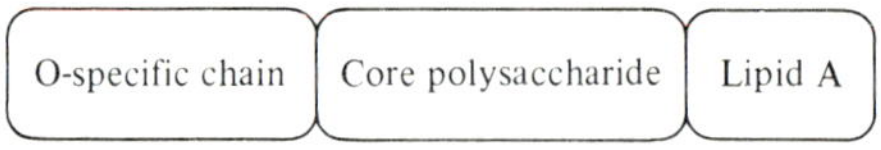

**18** MECHANISMS OF METABOLISM

| O-specific chain | Core polysaccharide | Lipid A |

**Figure 1-8** The three structural regions of the cell envelop of gram-negative bacteria.

them that are responsible for the antigenicity, and two types of nonreducing termini have been identified. The type I nonreducing terminus has a galactose unit linked to an $N$-acetylglucosamine unit by means of a $\beta(1\rightarrow 3)$ glycosidic bond. The type II nonreducing terminus has these units linked by a $\beta(1\rightarrow 4)$ glycosidic bond. The oligosaccharide moieties that are responsible for the A, B, H, Le$^a$, and Le$^b$ specificities are represented in Table 1-2.

In addition to the antigens of the ABO and Lewis systems, the antigens of the MNSs, Rh, and P blood-group systems are also mucopolysaccharides. These antigens bear some degree of structural similarity to each other and to the antigens of the systems discussed previously.

**Polysaccharides of the bacterial cell envelope and the bacterial capsule** The structure of the cell envelope of gram-negative bacteria can in many instances be represented diagrammatically as shown in Fig. 1-8. The outermost portion of the cell envelope consists of high-molecular-weight branched polysaccharides, which constitute the O antigen. The repeating units of various O antigens have been found to be composed of saccharide monomers including D-glucose, D-galactose, D-mannose, D-galactosamine, D-glucosamine, and also some of the less common monosaccharides such as L-fucose, L-rhamnose, abequose, colitose, paratose, and tyvelose.

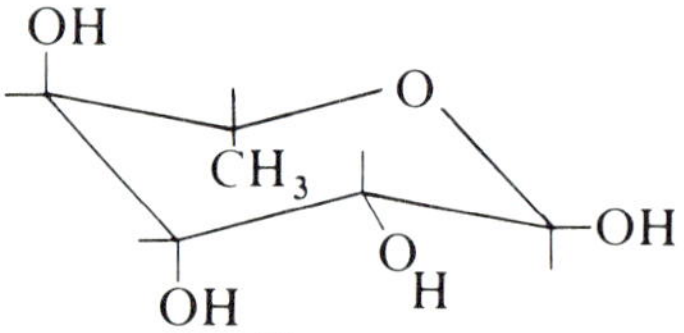

L-Rhamnose
(L-6-deoxymannose)

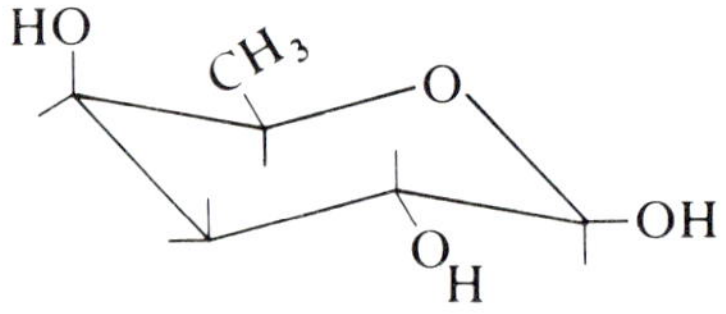

Abequose
(3,6-dideoxy-D-galactose)

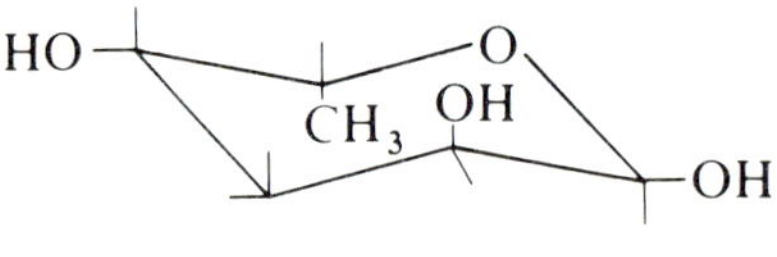

Colitose
(3,6-dideoxy-L-galactose)

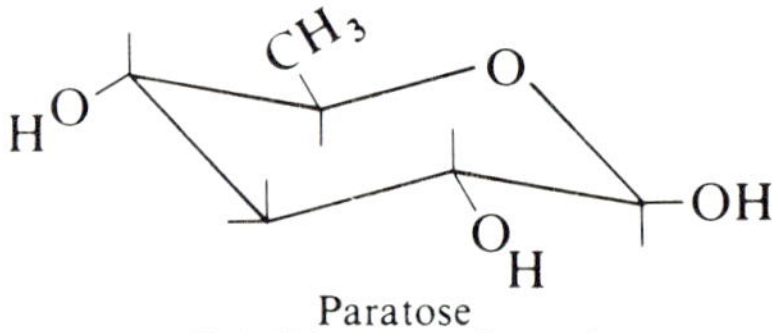

Paratose
(3,6-dideoxy-D-glucose)

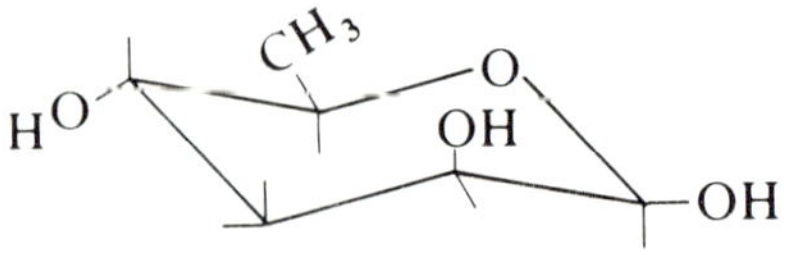

Tyvelose
(3,6-dideoxy-D-mannose)

The repeating unit of the O antigen of *Salmonella typhimurium* can be represented as

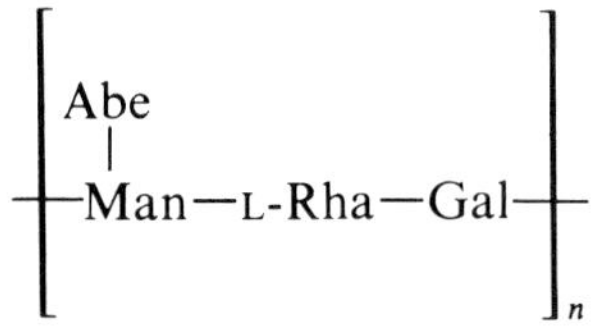

$$\left[ \begin{array}{c} \text{Abe} \\ | \\ -\text{Man}-\text{L-Rha}-\text{Gal}- \end{array} \right]_n$$

Generally, the O antigen of the cell envelope is linked to the outer core by means of glycosidic bonds. In *Salmonella typhimurium* this glycosidic bond involves C(1) of the terminal galactose unit of the O antigen and C(4) of the penultimate glucose unit of the outer core. In most *Salmonella* this linkage and the core itself can be represented as shown in Fig. 1-9. The inner core, or backbone, of the cell envelope

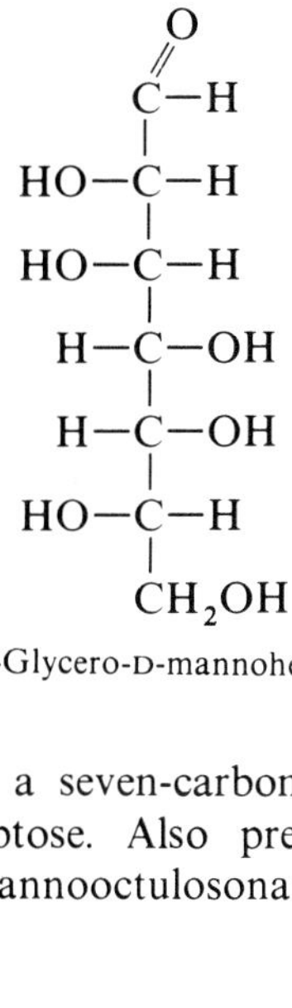

```
         O                              O
         ‖                              ‖
         C—H                            C—O⁻
         |                              |
    HO—C—H                              C=O
         |                              |
    HO—C—H                              CH₂
         |                              |
    H—C—OH                         HO—C—H
         |                              |
    H—C—OH                         HO—C—H
         |                              |
    HO—C—H                          HC—OH
         |                              |
       CH₂OH                          HC—OH
                                        |
                                       CH₂OH
  L-Glycero-D-mannoheptose       3-Deoxymannooctulosonate,
                              also called 2-oxo-3-deoxyoctanoate (KDO)
```

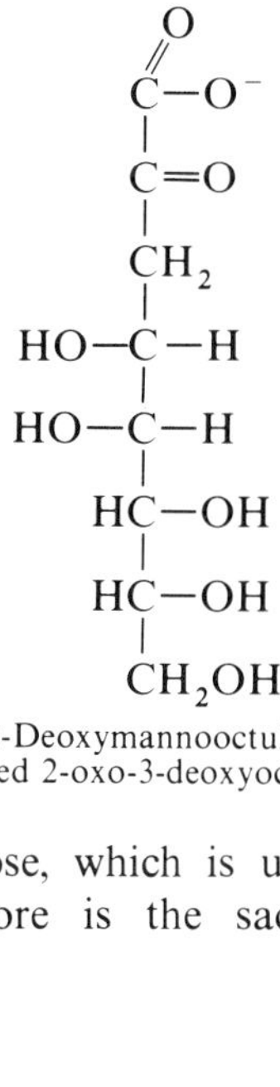

embodies a seven-carbon saccharide, or heptose, which is usually L-glycero-D-mannoheptose. Also present in the inner core is the saccharide derivative 3-deoxymannooctulosonate.

```
|–O-Antigen chain–| |–––Outer core–––| |–––Inner core or backbone–––| |–Lipid A–|
                          Gal
                           \
              GlcNAc        Glc – Hep – Hep – KDO – KDO →    ┌──────┐
                  \        /             |         |         │ GlcN │
                  Glc – Gal              PPEa      KDO       │  FA  │
 ┌──────────┐    /                                           │ PO₄  │
 │   Abe    │                                                └──────┘
 │    |     │
 │ Man-Rha-Gal │
 └──────────┘ₙ
```

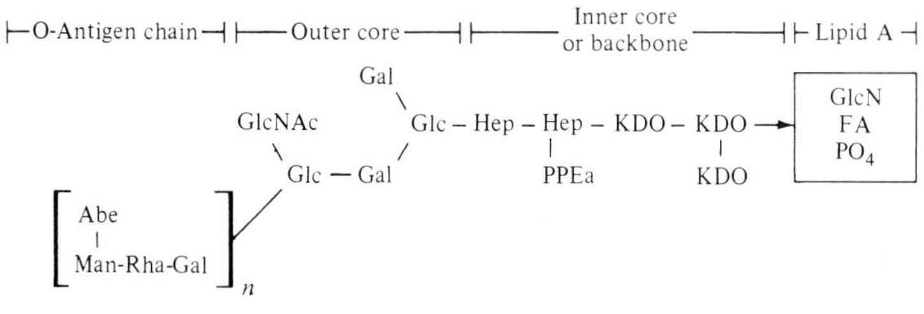

**Figure 1-9** Structure of the lipopolysaccharide of *Salmonella typhimurium*. Abe, abequose (3,6-dideoxy-D-galactose); Ea, ethanolamine; FA, fatty acid; P, phosphate. A number of such chains are cross-linked by phosphate bridges between the heptose residues and by pyrophosphate bridges between the glucosamine (GlcN) residues of lipid A.

In addition to their cell envelope, some gram-negative bacteria have a loosely bound capsule that is also polysaccharide in nature. These capsules are also antigenic, and among the virulent pneumococci approximately 75 different serological types have been distinguished. As examples, the pneumococcal capsular antigen S II is a heteroglycan having an estimated molecular weight of 240,000. It is composed of L-rhamnose (48 percent), D-glucuronate (16 percent), and D-glucose (35 percent), with the glucosyl units often situated at branch points in the molecule. The antigen S III is a polymer of cellobiuronate units linked by $1 \to 3$ O-glycosidic bonds. The repeating unit of the S VIII antigen, on the other hand, is a tetrasaccharide of glucose and glucuronate units, while that of the S XIV antigen consists of glucose, galactose, and N-acetylglucosamine units.

$\beta$-D-glucuronate$(1 \to 4)\beta$-D-glucose$(1 \to 4)\beta$-D-glucose$(1 \to 4)\beta$-D-glucose$(1 \to$

Proposed structure for pneumococcal antigen S VIII

$\beta$-D-galactose

$(1 \to 6)$

$\beta$-D-galactose$(1 \to 4)\beta$-N-acetyl-glucosamine$(1 \to 3)\beta$-D-galactose

$(1 \to 6)$

$\to 4)\beta$-D-glucose$(1 \to 4)\beta$-N-acetyl-D-glucosamine$(1 \to$

Structure of pneumococcal antigen S XIV

## LIPIDS

Lipids constitute another major category of biochemical compounds. Perhaps the simplest lipids are the saturated fatty acids, with the general formula $C_nH_{2n+1}COOH$. However, fatty acids per se are only minor constituents of biochemical systems. In general, both saturated and unsaturated fatty acids occur in biochemical systems in the form of esters or amides. When fatty acids have undergone esterification by glycerol, an acylglycerol (or glyceride) or in some cases an acylglycerol phosphate or phospholipid is formed. When a fatty acid undergoes amidation by sphingenine (sometimes called sphingosine), a sphingolipid is formed.

$$\begin{array}{c} \text{CH}_2-\text{O}-\overset{\overset{\displaystyle O}{\|}}{\text{C}}-\text{R} \\ | \\ \text{HO}-\text{CH} \\ | \\ \text{CH}_2-\text{OH} \end{array}$$

An acylglycerol
(a monoacylglycerol)

$$\begin{array}{c} \phantom{R'-}\text{CH}_2-\text{O}-\overset{\overset{\displaystyle O}{\|}}{\text{C}}-\text{R} \\ \overset{O}{\|}\phantom{XX} | \\ \text{R}'-\text{C}-\text{O}-\text{C}-\text{H} \\ | \\ \phantom{XXX}\text{CH}_2-\text{OH} \end{array}$$

An acylglycerol
(a diacylglycerol)

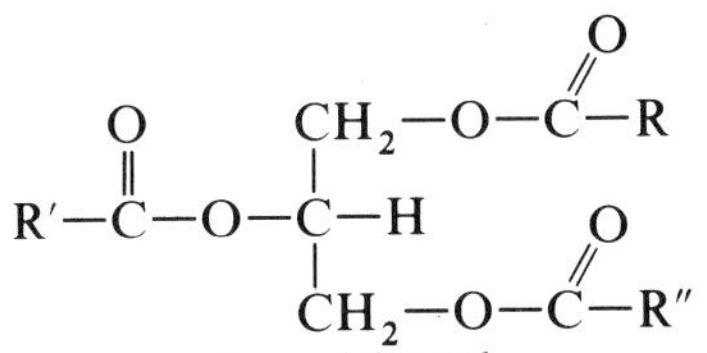

An acylglycerol
(a triacylglycerol)

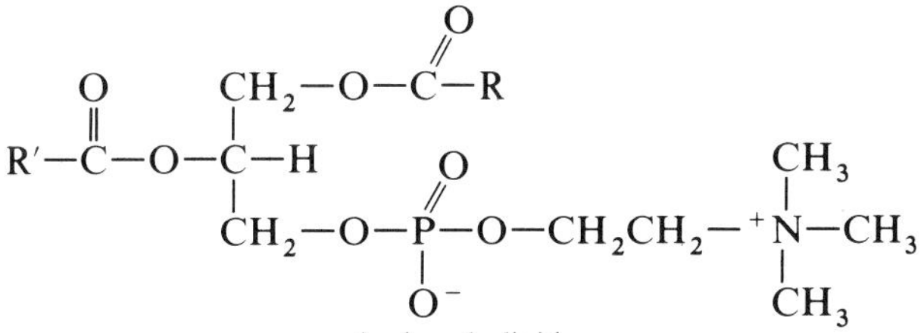

A phospholipid
(a phosphatidylcholine)

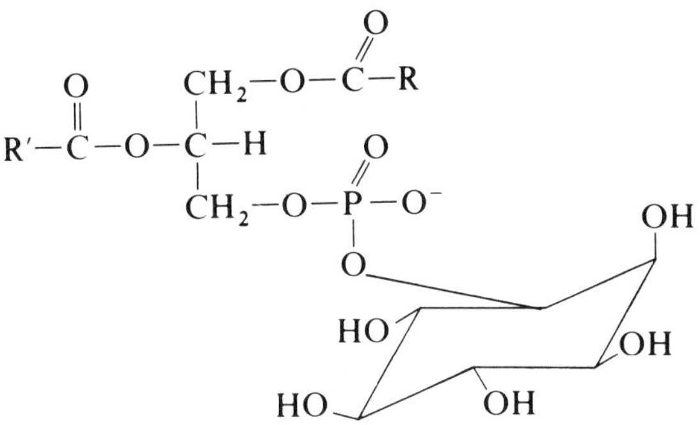

A phospholipid
(a phosphatidylinositol)

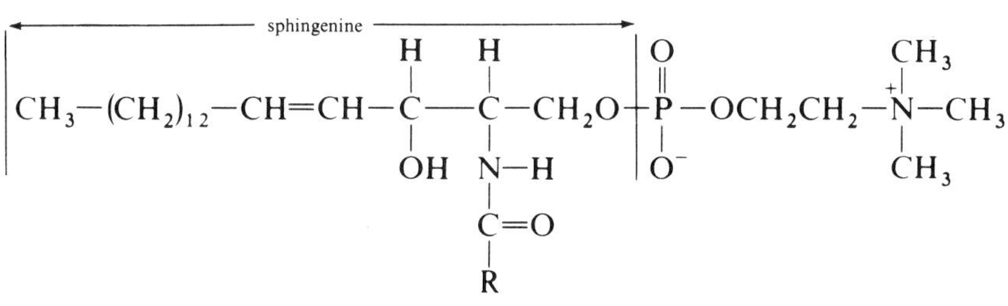

A sphingolipid
(a sphingomyelin)

## Acylglycerols

When all three of the hydroxyl groups of a glycerol molecule have undergone acylation by a fatty acid, a triacylglycerol, or triglyceride, is formed. Triacylglycerols are a principal storage form of lipid in man and in animals. Stored lipid, in the form of a triacylglycerol, can yield over twice as many calories per gram as stored carbohydrate, which is in the form of the extensively hydrated glycogen.

## 22 MECHANISMS OF METABOLISM

The fatty acids that undergo esterification by glycerol may be either saturated or unsaturated. The unsaturated acyl moieties generally have from one to six double bonds. Saturated and monounsaturated acyl groups generally tend to be at the 1 position of the glycerol moiety, while the more unsaturated acyl groups tend to occupy the 2 position.

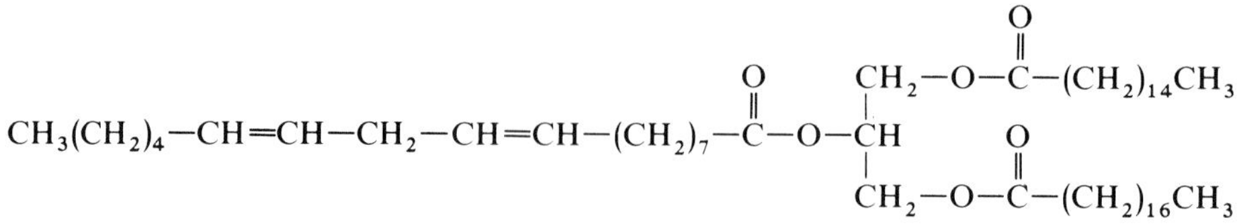

$$CH_3(CH_2)_4-CH=CH-CH_2-CH=CH-(CH_2)_7-\overset{O}{\underset{\|}{C}}-O-\underset{\underset{CH_2-O-\overset{O}{\underset{\|}{C}}-(CH_2)_{16}CH_3}{|}}{\overset{\overset{CH_2-O-\overset{O}{\underset{\|}{C}}-(CH_2)_{14}CH_3}{|}}{CH}}$$

Since enzymes that catalyze the deacylation and reacylation of glycerol are common in biochemical systems, diacylglycerols and monoacylglycerols are also present.

## Phospholipids

If one or two of the hydroxyl groups of glycerol are acylated by fatty acids while the third is acylated by orthophosphoric acid or by certain monoesters of orthophosphoric acid, an acylglycerol phosphate or phospholipid is formed. Several common phospholipids, in addition to phosphatidylcholine and phosphatidylinositol, are

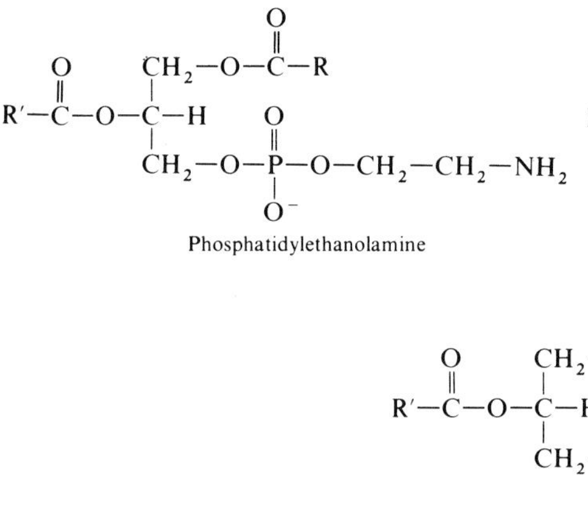

Phosphatidylethanolamine

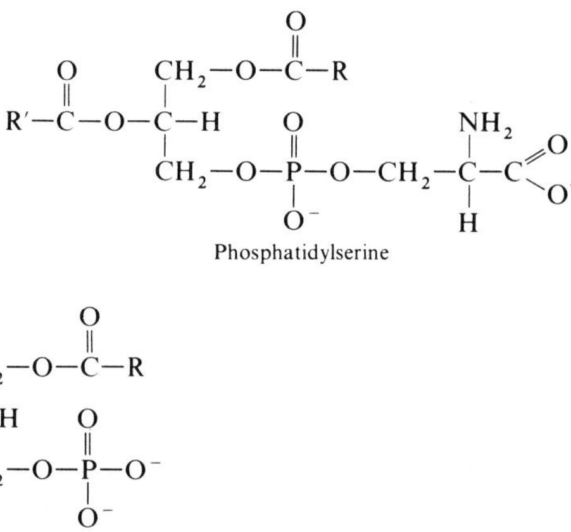

Phosphatidylserine

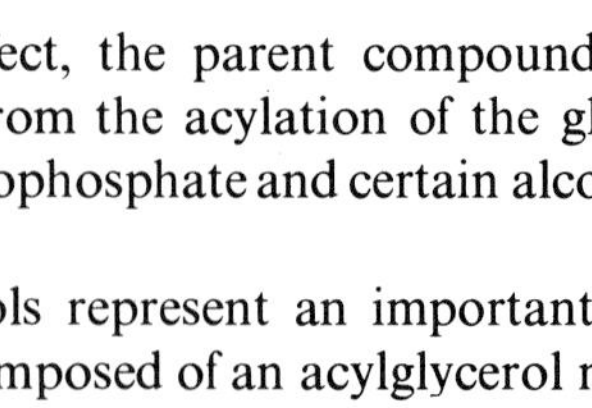

Phosphatidate

Phosphatidate is, in effect, the parent compound of the phospholipids. The other phospholipids result from the acylation of the glycerol hydroxyl group by a monoester derived from orthophosphate and certain alcohols including ethanolamine and serine.

The phosphatidylinositols represent an important category of phospholipids. Phosphatidylinositols are composed of an acylglycerol moiety, a phosphoryl moiety, and an inositol moiety. Inositols are hexahydroxycyclohexanes. There are nine distinguishable inositols, two of which are optically active. The remaining seven are meso forms. When inositol is mentioned without further qualification, particularly when mammalian systems are being considered, it is generally understood to mean myoinositol.

The C(4) and the C(5) hydroxyl groups of phosphatidylinositol can undergo phosphorylation with the result that phosphatidylinositol 4-phosphate or phosphatidylinositol 4,5-bisphosphate is formed.

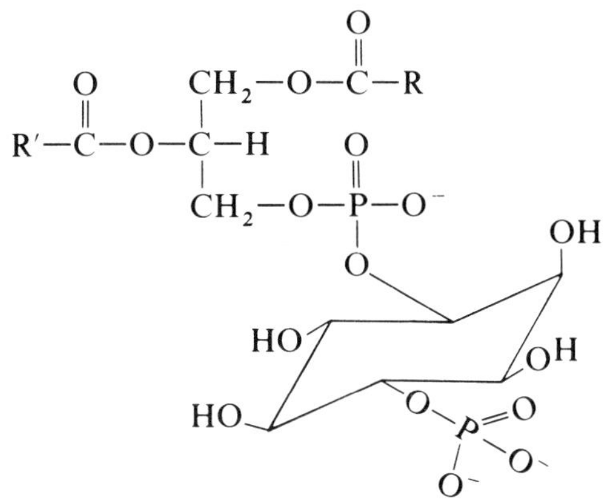

Phosphatidylinositol 4-phosphate

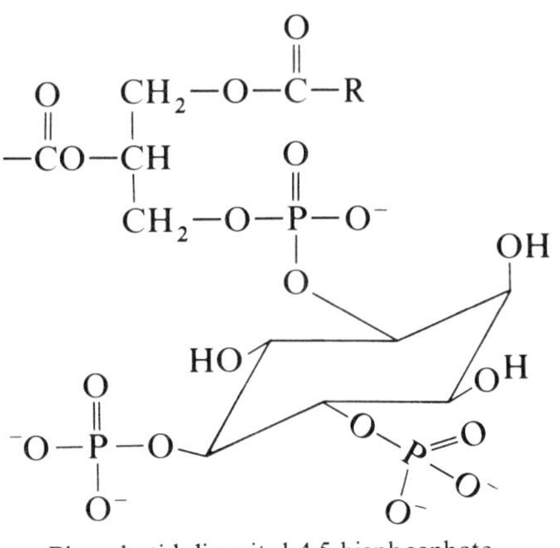

Phosphatidylinositol 4,5-bisphosphate

Yet another one of the phospholipids is bis(phosphatidyl)glycerol, sometimes called cardiolipin. Bis(phosphatidyl)glycerols have been shown to be components of the mitochondrion in man. Mitochondria are organelles contained in eukaryotic cells. The mitochondria are generally the second largest of these cell's organelles, the nucleus being the largest. The mitochondrion (discussed in more detail in subsequent chapters) has two membranes, i.e., an inner membrane and an outer membrane, composed of roughly 30 percent lipid (based on a dry weight), of which over 90 percent is phospholipid.

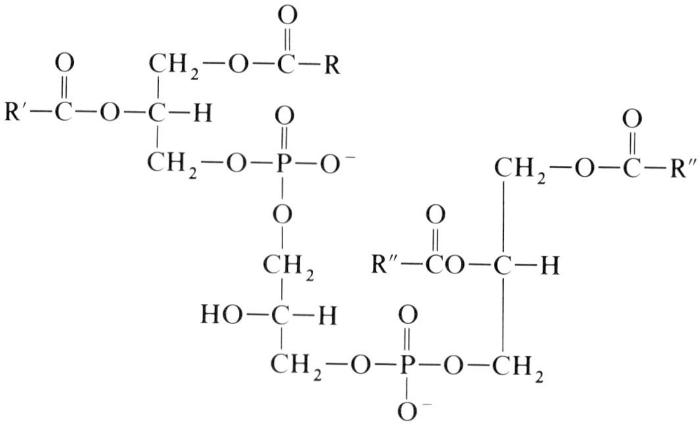

$$\text{R'}-\overset{\overset{O}{\|}}{C}-O-\overset{CH_2-O-\overset{\overset{O}{\|}}{C}-R}{\underset{CH_2-O-\overset{\overset{O}{\|}}{\underset{O^-}{P}}-O-CH_2-\underset{CH_2-O-\overset{\overset{O}{\|}}{\underset{O^-}{P}}-O-CH_2}{\overset{HO-C-H}{|}}-\overset{R''-CO-C-H}{|}-CH_2-O-\overset{O}{\overset{\|}{C}}-R''}{|}}}-H$$

A bis(phosphatidyl)glycerol

## Sphingolipids

The sphingolipids are derivatives of the amino diol sphingenine, or in some cases the amino diol eicosasphingenine, rather than the triol, glycerol. Furthermore, in this case the acyl moiety is bonded to the amino nitrogen atom rather than to a hydroxyl

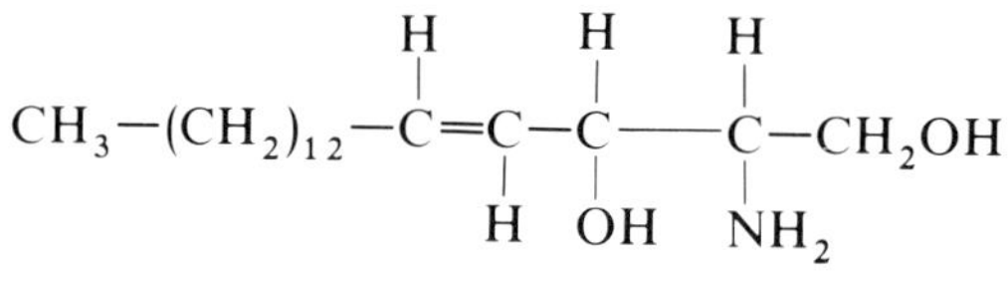

$$CH_3-(CH_2)_{12}-\underset{H}{\overset{H}{C}}=\underset{}{C}-\underset{OH}{\overset{H}{C}}-\underset{NH_2}{\overset{H}{C}}-CH_2OH$$

*trans*-D-Sphingenine
(*trans*-1,3-dihydroxy-2-aminooctadec-4-ene)

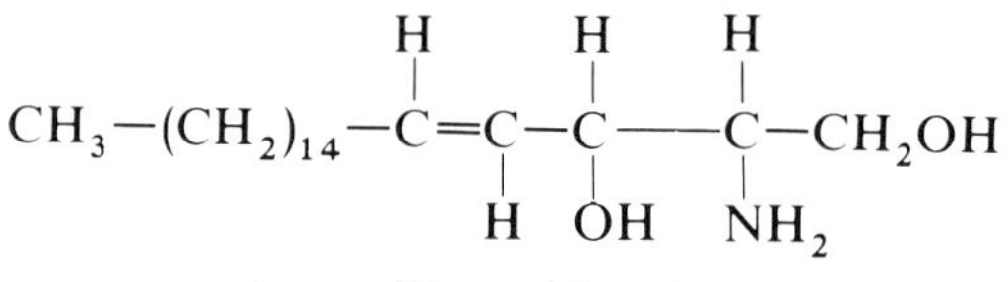

$$CH_3-(CH_2)_{14}-\underset{H}{\overset{H}{C}}=\underset{}{C}-\underset{OH}{\overset{H}{C}}-\underset{NH_2}{\overset{H}{C}}-CH_2OH$$

*trans*-D-Eicosasphingenine
(*trans*-1,3-dihydroxy-2-aminoeicos-4-ene)

oxygen atom. *N*-Acylsphingenines are called ceramides. When the C(1) hydroxyl group of a ceramide undergoes acylation by choline phosphate, sphingomyelin is formed. Sphingomyelin is found primarily in brain and in nerve cells, nearly 20 percent of the phospholipid of the white matter of the adult human brain being sphingomyelin. The acyl moiety of the sphingomyelin of the white matter generally consists of 24 or 26 carbon atoms. The gray matter of the adult human brain also contains sphingomyelin, but in this case the sphingolipid is frequently derived from eicosasphingenine and the acyl moiety is frequently the steroyl group.

Three classes of glycosphingolipids have been described. One of these is that of the neutral glycosphingolipids, or cerebrosides. In the cerebroside molecule a ceramide is joined to a galactose, a glucose, an *N*-acetylgalactose, or an *N*-acetylglucose moiety.

The linkage is by an *O*-glycosidic bond between C(1) of the sphingenine and C(1) of the saccharide or saccharide derivative. Cerebrosides are components of the human central nervous system and are also found in kidney, spleen, and blood plasma. The saccharide moiety of the cerebrosides of the central nervous system is usually galactose; glucose is found in the cerebrosides of human plasma.

Several subcategories of cerebrosides have been defined on the basis of the acyl moiety present in the molecule, e.g., the kerasines contain $C_{23}$, $C_{24}$, and $C_{25}$ acyl groups of the type illustrated by the lignoceroyl moiety. The nervons contain $C_{24}$, $C_{25}$, and $C_{26}$ acyl groups of the type illustrated by the nervonoyl moiety, while the cerebron fraction contains 2-hydroxyacyl groups such as the cerebronoyl moiety.

$$CH_3-(CH_2)_{22}-C\underset{OH}{\overset{O}{\diagup\hspace{-6pt}\diagdown}}$$

Lignoceric acid

$$CH_3-(CH_2)_7-CH=CH-(CH_2)_{13}-C\underset{OH}{\overset{O}{\diagup\hspace{-6pt}\diagdown}}$$

Nervonic acid

$$CH_3-(CH_2)_{21}-\underset{}{\overset{OH}{CH}}-C\underset{OH}{\overset{O}{\diagup\hspace{-6pt}\diagdown}}$$

Cerebronic acid

Cerebroside esters are also components of the human central nervous system. In these molecules the C(3) and/or C(6) hydroxyl groups of the galactose moiety or the C(3) hydroxyl group of the sphingenine are also acylated. This *O*-acyl group is usually a palmitoyl, a stearoyl, a palmitoleoyl, or an oleoyl moiety.

A second class of glycosphingolipids is characterized by the presence of an oligosaccharide moiety. These compounds generally occur as cell-membrane constituents. A major glycosphingolipid of the human erythrocyte membrane has the structure shown in Fig. 1-10.

A third category of glycosphingolipids is that of the gangliosides, which are composed of a ceramide moiety linked to a complex oligosaccharide embodying an *N*-acetyl- or *N*-glycolylneuraminate moiety. Gangliosides occur in the gray matter of the brain, as a component of the cell membranes. These glycosphingolipids are also found in the spleen, the kidney, and certain other organs.

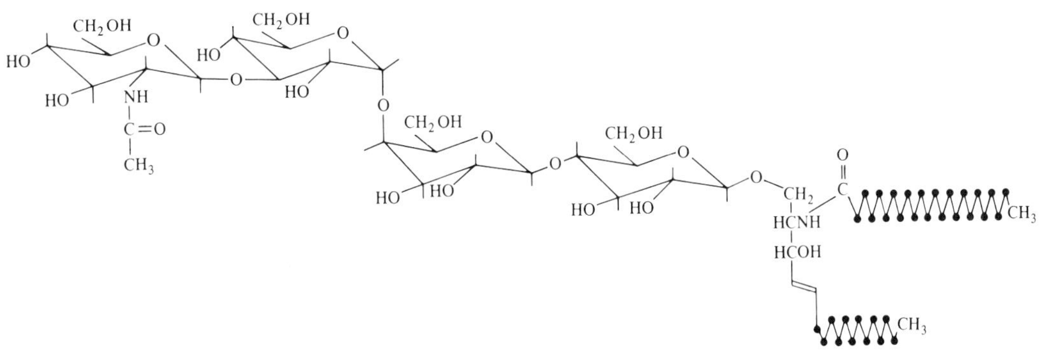

**Figure 1-10** A glycosphingolipid of the human erythrocyte membrane.

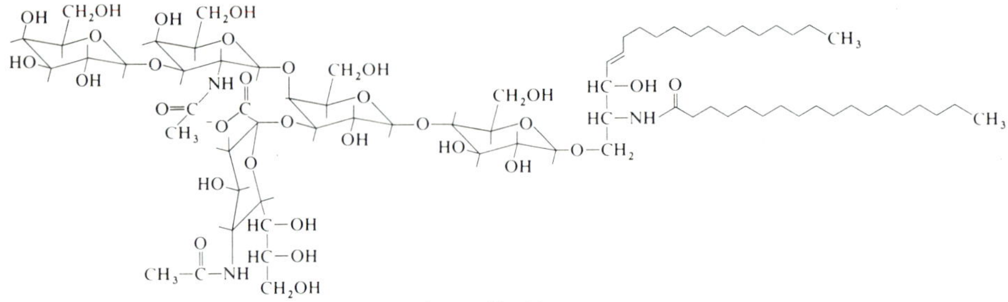

A ganglioside

## PROSTAGLANDINS

Certain long-chain polyenoic fatty acids can undergo cyclization and oxidation to yield members of a class of biochemically active compounds known as the prostaglandins. These compounds were initially identified in human seminal fluid and in extracts from ovine vesicular glands by the Swedish chemist U. S. von Euler in 1934. Their subsequent purification and structural characterization was carried out largely by S. Bergstrom, J. Sjovall, and B. Samuelsson, also in Sweden. The prostaglandins are cyclic, oxygen-containing $C_{20}$ fatty acids which can be considered to be derivatives of prostanoic acid. They function as biochemical regulators in certain systems. From a

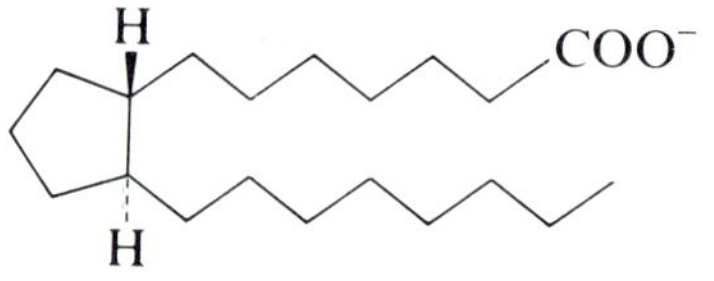

Prostanoate

pharmacological standpoint the prostaglandins can act as a vasodepressor, can induce the stimulation or the relaxation of smooth muscle, and can induce labor or abortion. Prostaglandins have been categorized chemically on the basis of the functional groups and the degree of saturation present in the molecule. The parent prostaglandins are considered to be those of the E series, which have an oxo group at C(9) and hydroxyl groups at C(11) and C(15). The members of the F series, by contrast, are trihydroxy compounds with a hydroxyl group at C(9) in addition to those at C(11) and C(15). In compounds of the E series the C(11) hydroxyl group can undergo elimination at a pH between 5 and 8, yielding a prostaglandin of the A series, in which a conjugated oxo group is present. Under alkaline conditions prostaglandins of the A series undergo rearrangement to yield prostaglandins of the B series. The members of each of these four series (E, F, A, and B) are placed in subseries on the basis of the degree of unsaturation and the stereochemistry of their structures.

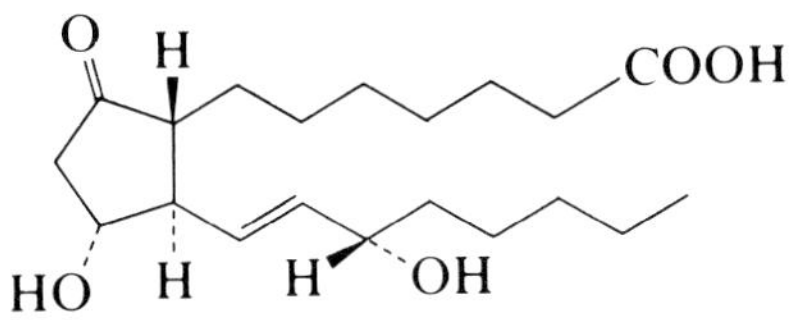

PGE₁ PGE₂

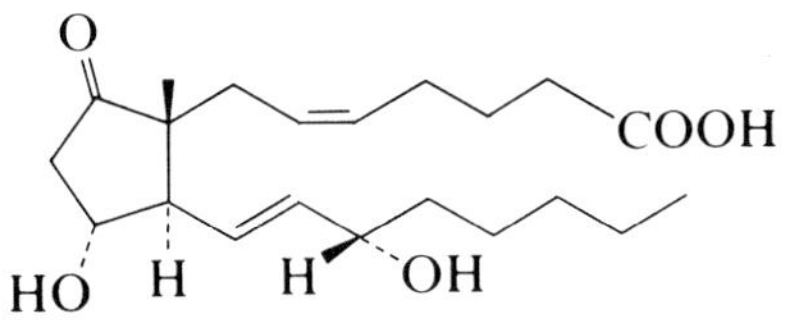

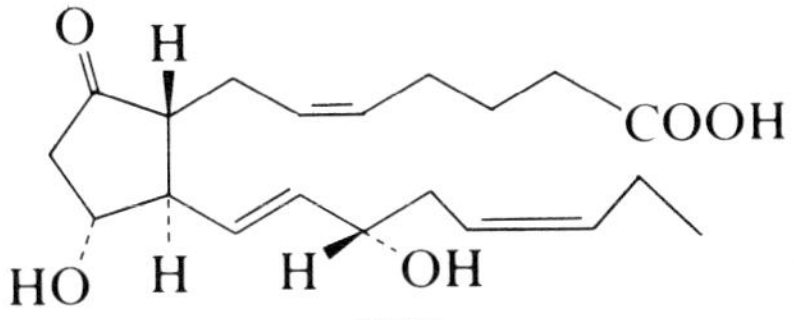

PGE₃

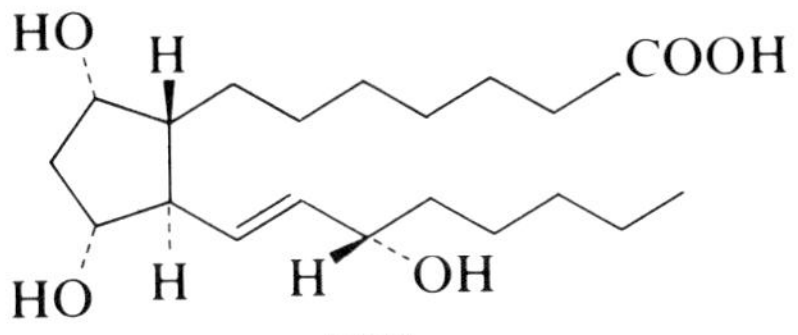

PGF₁α PGF₂α

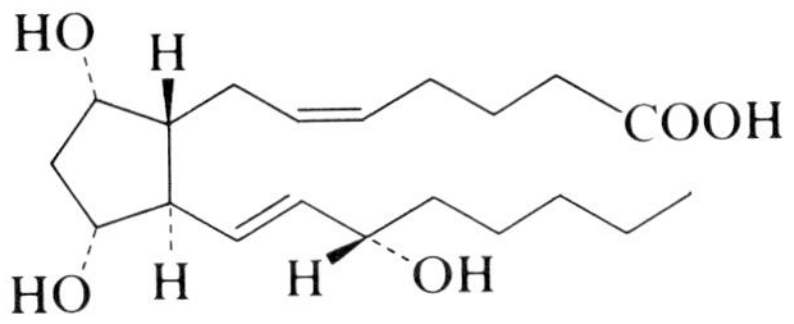

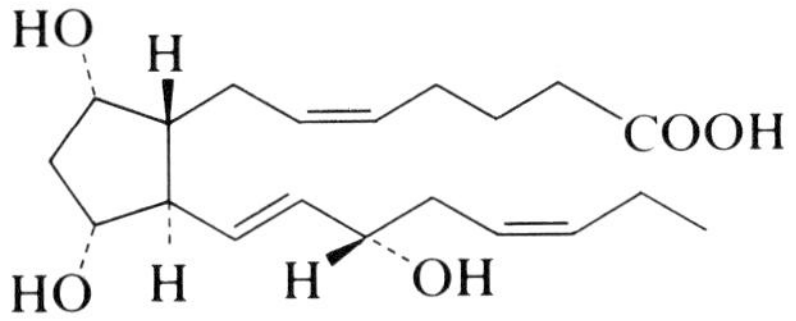

PGF₃α

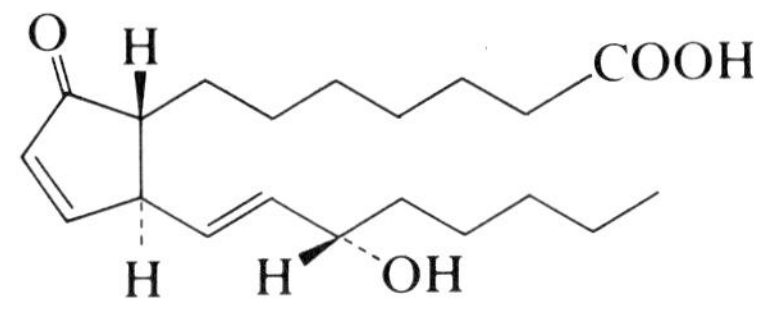

PGA₁ PGB₁

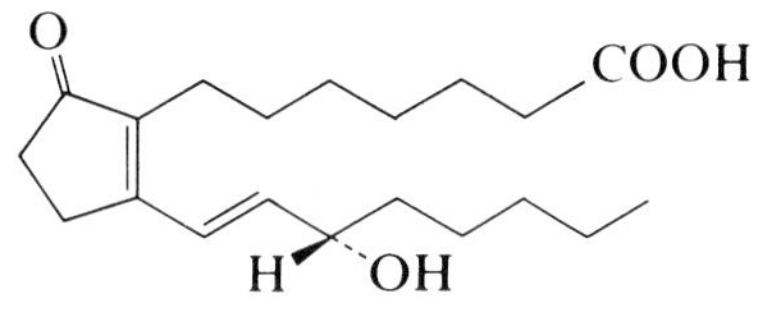

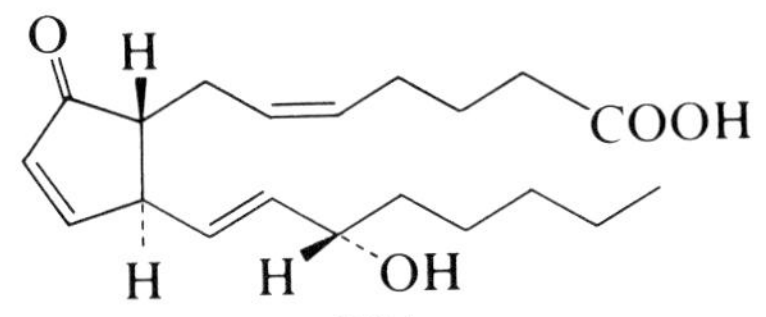

PGA₂ PGB₂

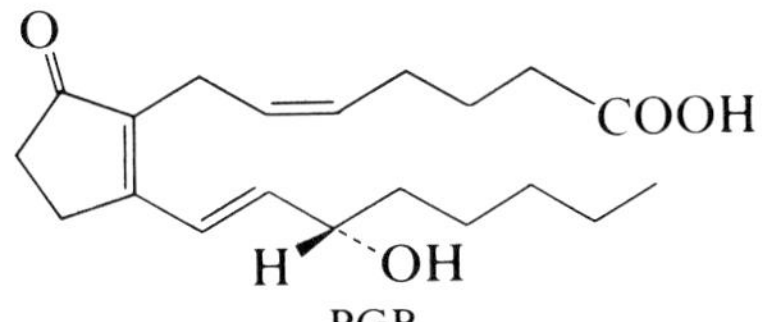

Structural differences between prostaglandins of the E, F, A, and B series:

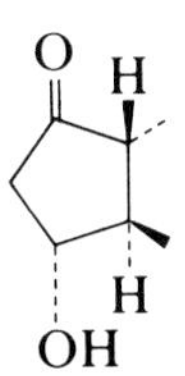

E   F$_\alpha$   F$_\beta$   A   B

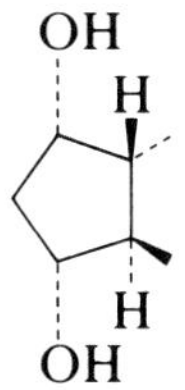

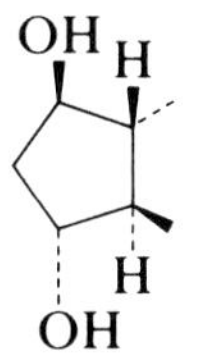

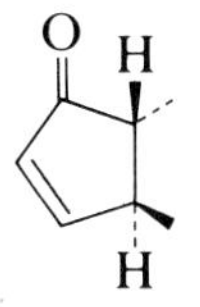

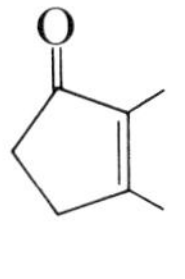

## Steroids

Steroids are lipoid compounds derived from perhydrocyclopentanophenanthrene. This fused-ring system consists of three six-membered rings, designated A to C, and a

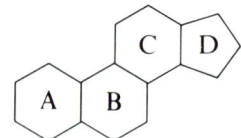

Perhydrocyclopentanophenanthrene

five-membered ring, the D ring. Each ring junction can be either cis or trans. Steroids in which the junction of the A and B rings is of the cis configuration are said to be of the *normal series*, while those with the trans configuration are of the *allo series*. In all the naturally occurring steroids, the junction of the B and C rings is of the trans configuration, as is the junction of the C and D rings in the case of the sterols and bile acids. However, in plant glycosides the junction of the C and D rings is cis.

Naturally occurring steroids are named as derivatives of the appropriate parent hydrocarbon; e.g., saturated steroids are named as derivatives of cholestane, cholane, pregnane, estrane, or androstane. Unsaturated steroids are named as derivatives of unsaturated parent hydrocarbons, e.g., estra-1,3,5(10)-triene, androsta-1,4-diene, or pregna-1,4-diene. Although the saturated six-membered rings assume chair forms in both the normal and the allo series, the introduction of unsaturations causes the six-membered rings to assume a half-chair conformation. In the half-chair conforma-

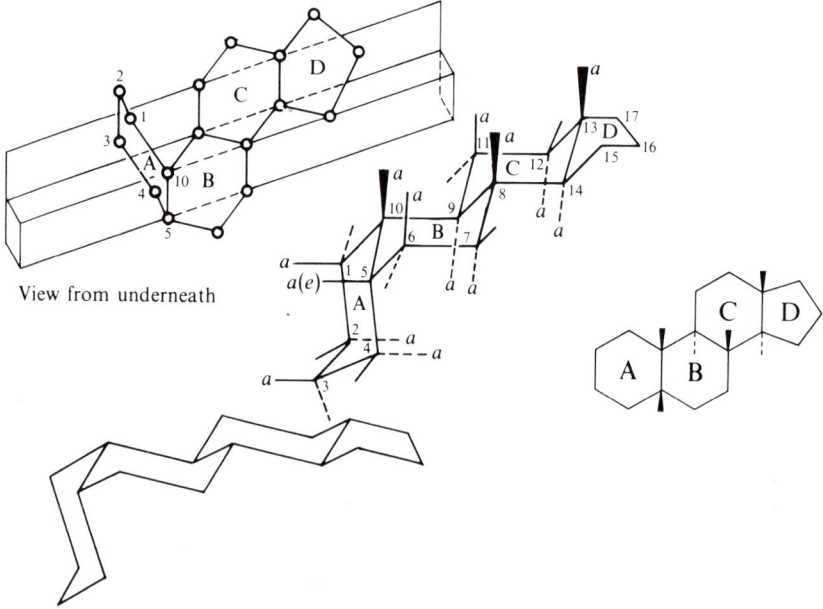

5-β (Normal) series, rings A/B cis

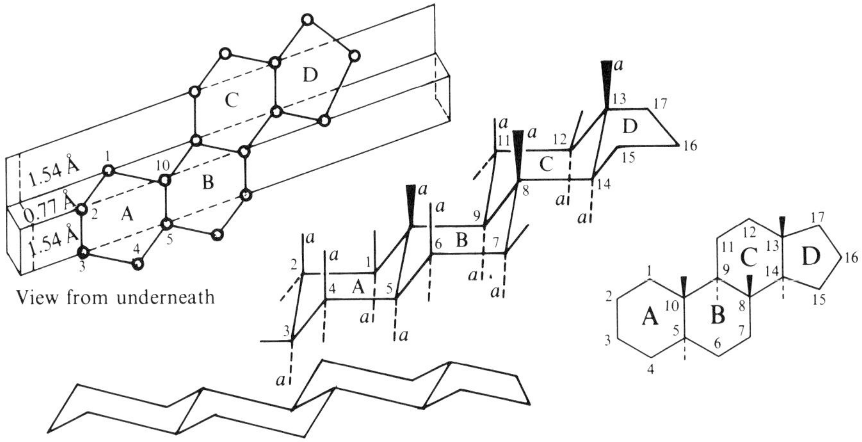

5-α (Allo) series, rings A/B trans

tion the two carbon atoms of the olefinic bond and the carbon atoms bonded to each of them lie in one plane while one of the two remaining carbon atoms occupies a position above that plane and the other a position below.

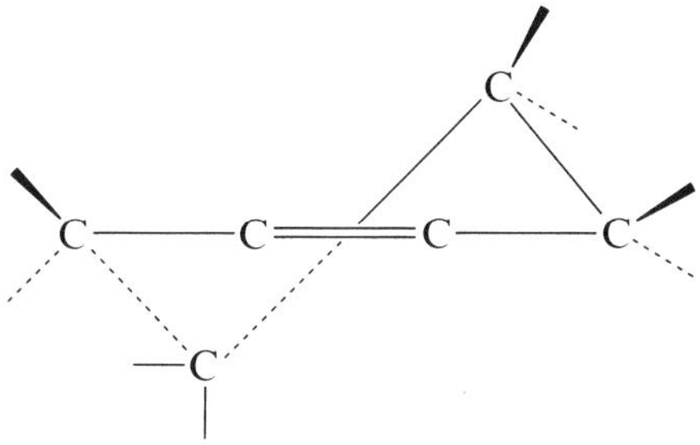

Axial ring substituents can project either above the plane of the ring or below. By convention, the bonds of axial ring substituents are represented by a wedge-shaped bond when the projection is above the plane of the ring. The substituent in this case is referred to as a β substituent. When the axial substituent projects below the plane of the ring, the bond is represented by a dashed line and the substituent is referred to as an α substituent.

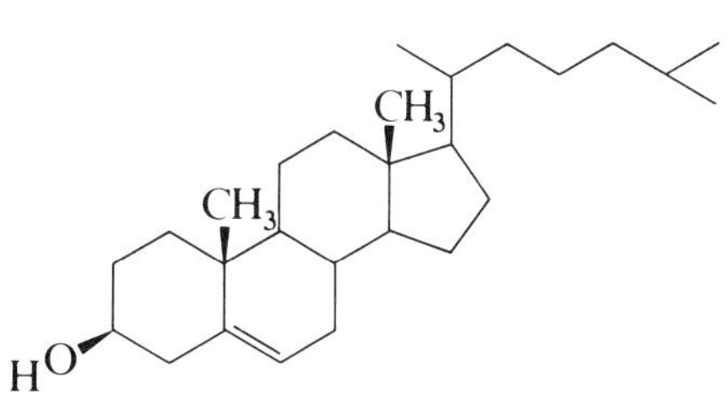

Cholesterol
(cholest-5-en-3β-ol)

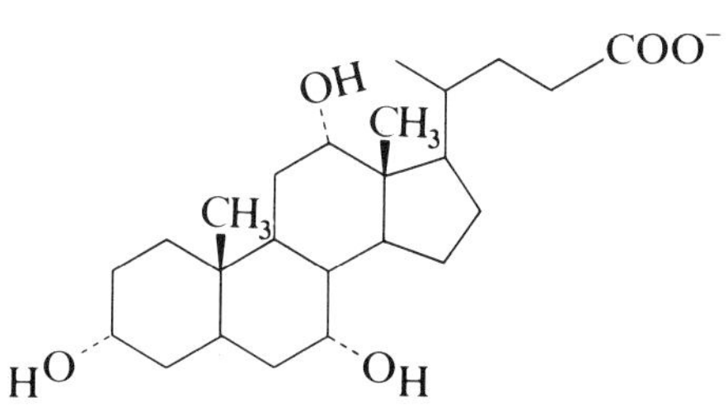

Cholate, a bile salt
(3α,7α,12α-trihydroxycholanate)

One of the more widely distributed steroids in mammalian systems is cholesterol (shown on page 29). Yeasts, on the other hand, contain primarily ergosterol, and higher plants contain primarily the phytosterols such as β-sitosterol.

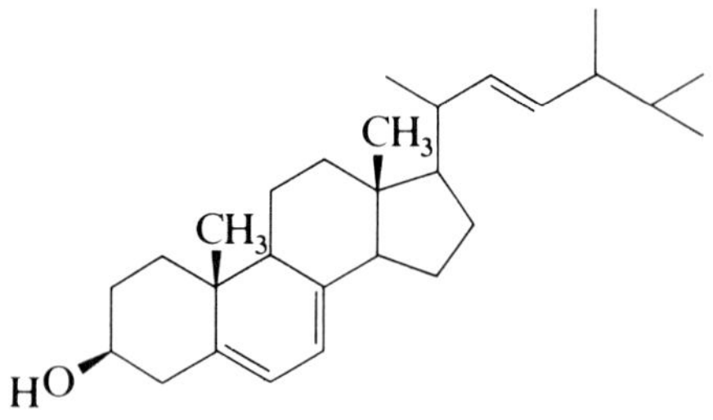

Ergosterol

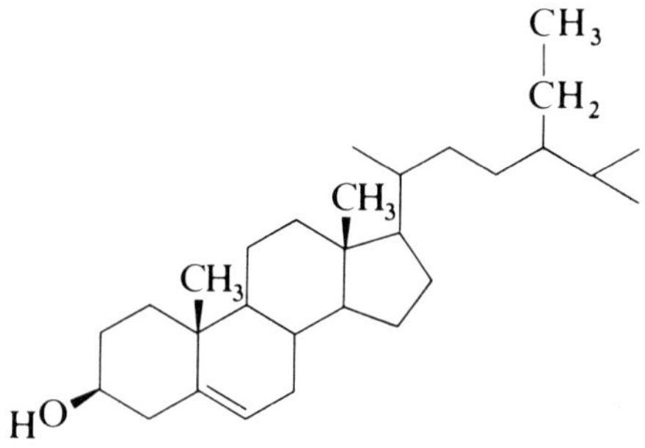

β-Sitosterol

**Cardiac glycosides** Certain plants, including digitalis, strophanthus, and the sea onion, contain glycolipids known as the cardiac glycosides or cardenolides. These cardiac glycosides are frequently isolated along with another class of plant glycosides called the saponins (discussed below). The cardiac glycoside molecule is composed of an aglycone moiety, which is a derivative of perhydrocyclopentanophenanthrene, plus an oligosaccharide moiety consisting of two to four monosaccharide units. Monosaccharides present in this oligosaccharide moiety include glucose, fucose, rhamnose, digitoxose, and cymarose. The oligosaccharide moiety is linked to the 3β-hydroxyl group of the steroid aglycone by a glycosidic bond. Structures of some of the steroid aglycone moieties of the cardiac glycosides follow. These structures embody, in addition to the A, B, C, and D rings, a fifth ring, which is a cyclic lactone.

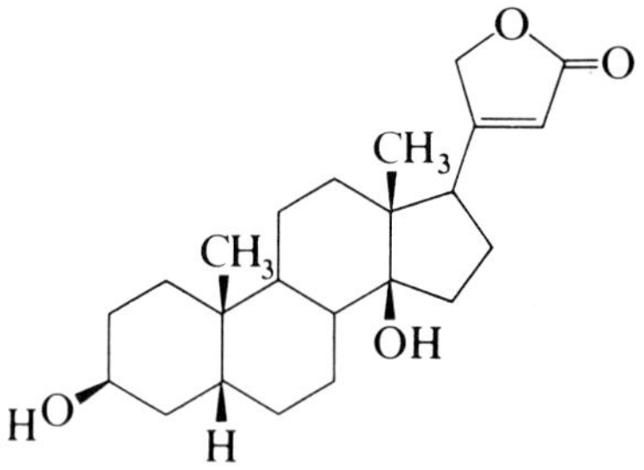

Digitoxigenin

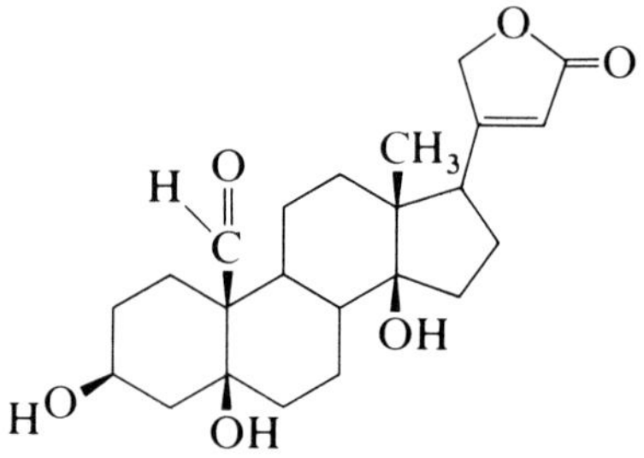

Strophanthidin

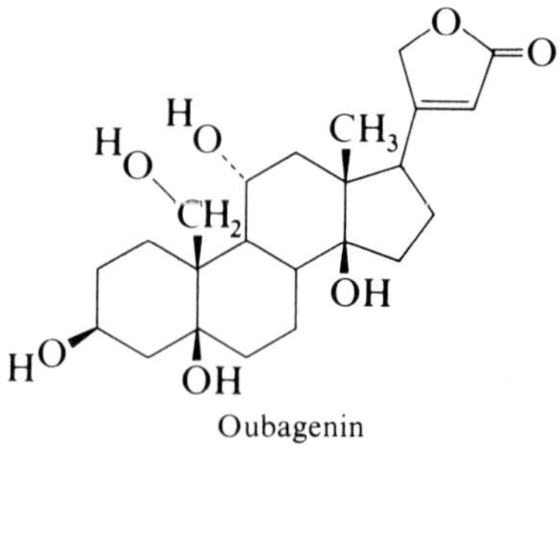

Oubagenin

The cardiac glycosides, which historically were used as arrow poisons, are used clinically today. The pharmacologically active portion of the molecule is the steroid aglycone, which causes an increase in the force of the systolic myocardial contraction resulting in increased cardiac output and decreased venous blood pressure. The cardiac glycosides are also useful for inducing diuresis.

**Steroid saponins** The steroid saponins are plant glycosides structurally somewhat similar to the cardiac glycosides. The steroid saponin molecule is also composed of a steroid aglycone moiety and an oligosaccharide moiety. The aglycone moiety, referred to as the sapogenin, consists of five fused rings, the A, B, and C six-membered rings, and the D and E five-membered rings. In addition, there is a sixth ring, the F ring, which is bonded to the E ring by a common atom, thus forming a spiro structure. The F ring is a pyran.

Digitogenin, a sapogenin

The saponin digitonin is composed of digitogenin plus an oligosaccharide consisting of two galactose units, two glucose units, and one xylose unit. Other steroid saponins have similar structures.

Saponins cause aqueous solutions to foam. These glycolipids function as detergents, forming oil-in-water emulsions. When injected into the bloodstream of animals, saponins cause the hemolysis of erythrocytes, which can be lethal. The steroid saponin digitonin can also be used as an analytical reagent since it forms an insoluble complex with cholesterol and most other $3\beta$-hydroxy steroids.

# Proteins

Proteins are polymers made up of amino acids bonded to each other by amide linkages involving the amino group of one monomer and the carboxyl group of the neighboring monomer. These amide linkages are referred to as *peptide bonds*. Approximately 20 specific amino acids serve as the monomeric units in the wide variety of proteins found in living systems. These proteins include macromolecules that constitute structural and contractile tissues; macromolecules that transport molecular oxygen, metal cations, and various other components; and also the hundreds of enzymes that catalyze a like number of biochemical reactions. Certainly a large number of structurally different macromolecules would seem to be required for such a wide spectrum of functions, and, indeed, this diversity is possible in the case of the proteins. If each protein molecule were to consist of only 250 aminoacyl units, the utilization of 20 different monomers would permit the formation of $10^{325}$ *different protein molecules!* In actuality, protein molecules frequently contain more than 250 amino acid units, and hence there is the possibility for an even greater number of different macromolecules.

Each of the different amino acids that serves as a monomeric unit in protein molecules has a different side chain. This side chain, which is not involved in the peptide-bond formation, frequently bears a functional group that can be a factor in determining the macromolecular structure and/or the function of the protein. Among the functional groups present as substituents of aminoacyl side chains are alcohol hydroxyl, phenol hydroxyl, amino, carboxylate, imidazolium, guanidinium, sulfhydryl, and thio ether groups.

$-CH_2OH$    $C_6H_4-OH$    $-NH_2$    $-C(=O)O^-$    imidazolium ring
Alcohol hydroxyl    Phenol hydroxyl    Amino    Carboxylate    Imidazolium

$-N(H)-C(=NH_2^+)-NH_2$    $-SH$    $-S-CH_3$
Guanidinium    Sulfhydryl    Thio ether

## Macromolecular Structure of Proteins

Although a protein consists of a series of amino acids linked by peptide bonds, the macromolecule is neither a rigid extended chain nor simply a tangled string: the protein macromolecule exhibits certain regular structural characteristics.

**α-Helical structure** One regular structure found in naturally occurring proteins is the α-helical structure. It can be generated by winding the protein chain about an imaginary axis so that there are 3.7 aminoacyl units per turn of the helix and an axial translation of 1.47 Å per unit. The pitch of such a helical structure is therefore 5.44 Å. The α helix (Fig. 1-11) is a thermodynamically favored structure because in this conformation each amide group can be planar with its bond angles essentially undistorted. Furthermore, each carbonyl oxygen atom and each hydrogen atom of each amide group can participate in hydrogen bonding in the α-helical conformation (Fig. 1-12).

An α-helical structure can be either right- or left-handed although in the left-handed α helix there usually are relatively unfavorable interactions between C(3) of one aminoacyl unit and the carbonyl oxygen atom of the neighboring aminoacyl unit. Hence, the right-handed α-helical structure is the more stable thermodynamically. An exception is found when prolyl or hydroxyprolyl units are involved, however. Because of the fixed orientation of the bond between C(2) and the nitrogen atom of the pyrrolidine ring, the right-handed α-helical structure is no longer favored thermodynamically. In proteins with an occasional prolyl or hydroxyprolyl unit an α-helical sequence if present is interrupted. In the homopolymer poly-L-proline

INTRODUCTION  33

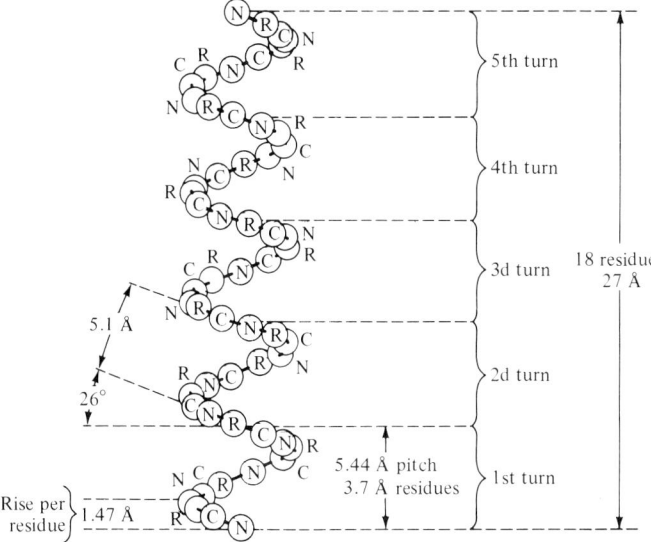

**Figure 1-11** A schematic representation of an α helix.

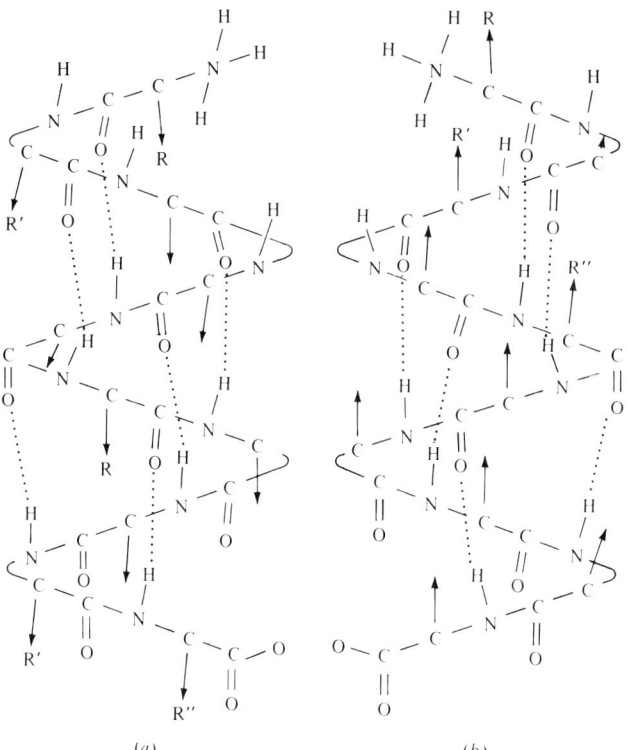

**Figure 1-12** Schematic representation of the hydrogen bonding that occurs in (a) a right-handed and (b) a left-handed α-helical structure.

(prepared in the laboratory) the macromolecule assumes a left-handed helical configuration. In such a homopolymer, there are three prolyl units per turn of the left-handed helical structure and an axial translation of 3.12 Å per aminoacyl unit under most conditions.

**Use of x-ray diffraction** X-ray diffraction has been used in demonstrating the presence of helixes and other structural characteristics of certain biopolymers, including proteins. The methods are based on the observation that when a parallel beam of monochromatic x-rays impinges upon a crystal or a fiber made up of a regular array of units, the light waves will be scattered by the electrons of the atoms of the crystal or fiber and characteristic diffraction patterns will be obtained. A crystal or a suitable fiber diffracts x-rays because each has a periodically repeating structure and because the period of this repeating structure is comparable in magnitude to the wavelength of x-rays (which is of the order of $10^{-8}$ cm = 1 Å). The period of the repeating structure in a crystal or fiber is the length of the unit cell.

The diffraction of x-rays by a crystal is analogous to the diffraction of visible light by a grating. Diffraction is observed because light waves scattered from a periodic object experience interference. This interference is dependent upon the phase relationships between the scattered waves. In a crystal or a fiber these phase relationships, in turn, depend upon the relative positions of the atoms in the molecules.

A useful, simplified interpretation of x-ray diffraction by a crystal was introduced by Sir William Henry Bragg, an English physicist. Bragg formulated an equation that expresses a relationship between the spacing of the lattice planes of a crystal $d$, the angle of the incident x-ray beam with respect to the lattice plane $\theta$, and the wavelength of the monochromatic x-ray beam $\lambda$ (see Fig. 1-13). The Bragg equation

$$2d \sin \theta = n\lambda \qquad (1\text{-}1)$$

states that in order for constructive interference or reinforcement to occur, the path difference between beams scattered from two successive lattice planes must be an integral number of wavelengths.

In actual practice when a monochromatic x-ray beam impinges upon a single unit cell of a crystal, the radiation that is scattered can be characterized by two parameters, its amplitude and its phase. The distribution of amplitude and phase for

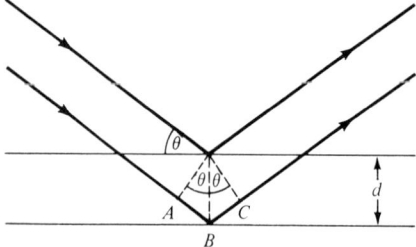

**Figure 1-13** Reflection from lattice planes.

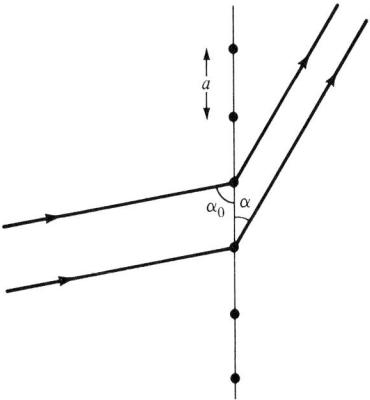

**Figure 1-14** Diffraction by a single row of lattice points.

all possible orientations for the incident x-ray beam is called the Fourier transform†
of the scattering object. In general, the Fourier transform of a single unit cell will be
continuous throughout a volume called *reciprocal space*. (The term is based on the
observation that the dimensions of the periodic object and the dimensions of the
diffraction pattern bear a reciprocal relationship to each other.) However, if instead
of a single unit cell the scattering object is a regular array of unit cells, the Fourier
transform of the scattering object will no longer be continuous. It will be finite only
at certain points in reciprocal space. This comes about as follows. A condition for
constructive interference is that the path differences between the x-ray beam diffracted from successive atoms which fall along a line parallel to a given crystal (or
fiber) axis must be an integral number of wavelengths (Fig. 1-14). An equation which
expresses this relationship is

$$a(\cos \alpha - \cos \alpha_0) = h\lambda \tag{1-2}$$

where $a$ = distance between two adjacent atoms
$\alpha, \alpha_0$ = angles of diffracted and incident beams, respectively
$h$ = integer

This equation defines a set of parallel planes in reciprocal space. Similar relationships
pertain with respect to successive atoms that fall along lines parallel to the other two
axes of the crystal, and similar sets of parallel planes are thus defined. The points at
which these three sets of planes intersect are the points in reciprocal space where
constructive interference occurs. At these points, known as *reciprocal lattice points*,
the Fourier transform of the crystal is finite.

Since constructive interference occurs only at certain points in reciprocal space, a
specific three-dimensional diffraction pattern is generated when an x-ray beam impinges upon a crystal. This diffraction pattern consists of spots, or *reflections*, as they
are called. An x-ray diffraction pattern derived from the heme-containing protein
cytochrome $c$ is shown in Fig. 1-15.

† A Fourier transform is a mathematical representation of a periodic function introduced by Jean
Baptiste Joseph Fourier, French mathematician and physicist.

**36** MECHANISMS OF METABOLISM

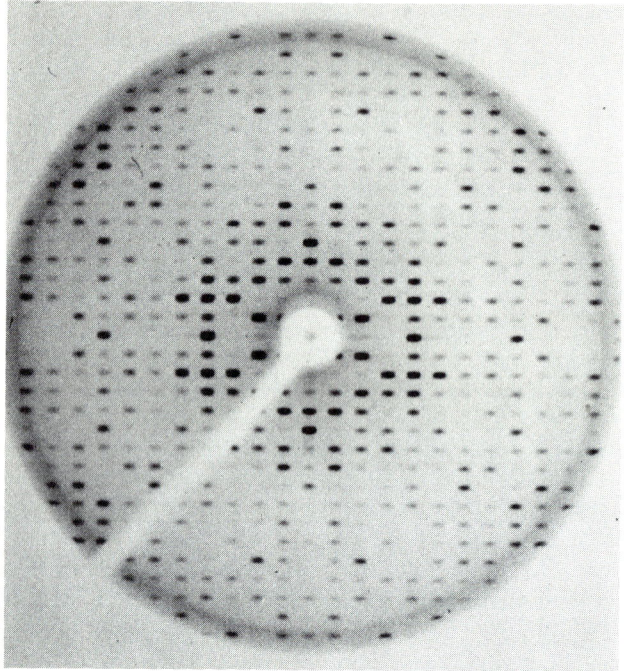

**Figure 1-15** X-ray diffraction pattern from a crystal of oxidized cytochrome c from equine heart. (*Courtesy of R. E. Dickerson.*)

How are these reflections used in the determination of the structural characteristics of a molecule? Since the structure of a crystal (or fiber) consists of repeating units, the electron density of these species can be described by a periodic function. However, as Fourier demonstrated, a periodic function can usually be treated as a superposition of a set of sinusoidal waves (Fig. 1-16). Therefore, the electron density of a crystal can conveniently be treated as a superposition of a set of sinusoidal waves. Each reflection in the x-ray diffraction pattern generated by a crystal corresponds to one of the component waves in the Fourier representation of the electron density of a crystal. When many (usually several thousand) such reflections are obtained and characterized, an approximation of the electron densities in the crystal can be derived by carrying out a Fourier synthesis.† As a result of this process a series

---

† To carry out the operation of Fourier synthesis both the amplitude (one-half the vertical distance from the crest to the trough of a wave) and the phase (the horizontal displacement of the wave maximum with reference to a common reference point) of a given component wave must be known. The amplitude is easily obtained since it is proportional to the square root of the intensity of the corresponding reflection. The phase is more difficult to determine, and a method such as that of isomorphous replacement must be used. This method is described in many books or chapters on x-ray diffraction, e.g., Wilson, H. R. (1966) *Diffraction of X-Rays by Proteins, Nucleic Acids, and Viruses*, Arnold, London, or Eisenberg, D. (1970) in *The Enzymes* (Boyer, P. B., ed.), 3d ed., vol. 1, pp. 1–89, Academic, New York.

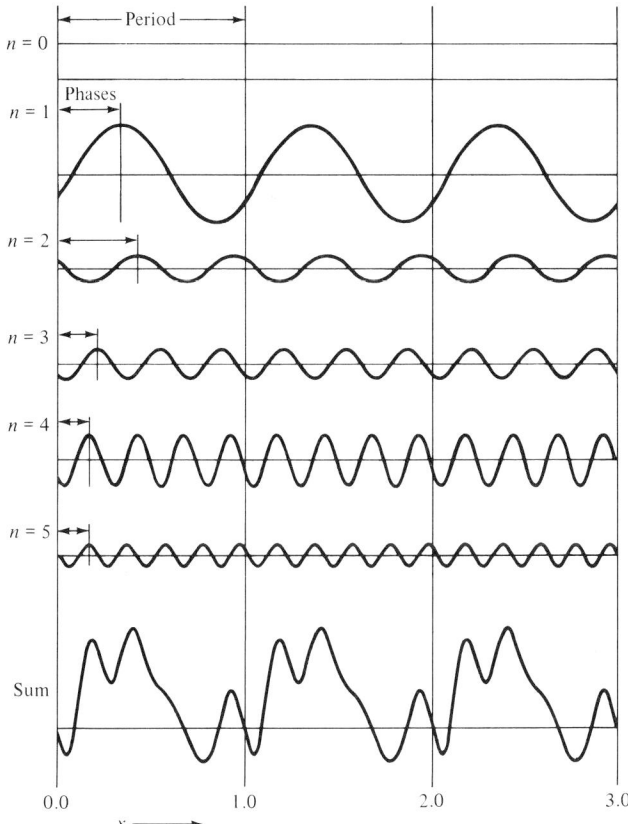

**Figure 1-16** Superposition of sinusoidal waves having the periodicity and phase indicated. The summation of these functions is shown at the bottom.

of electron-density diagrams can be obtained and used to construct three-dimensional representations of the electron densities in the molecule being examined. Such a representation is shown in Fig. 1-17.

As early as 1952 it was recognized that characteristic x-ray diffraction patterns are obtained from macromolecules that assume helical conformations. In these cases, the x-ray diffraction pattern generally has the form of an X, as illustrated by the diffraction pattern derived from the protein tropomyosin, which exists in an α-helical conformation (Fig. 1-18). A theoretical Fourier transform of a continuous helix is represented in Fig. 1-19. The characteristic x-ray diffraction patterns exhibited by proteins with helical structures have been useful in confirming the presence of these structures in some cases.

*β* **Structures** Another regular structure found in naturally occurring proteins is the *β* structure, three different types of which have been characterized and designated the

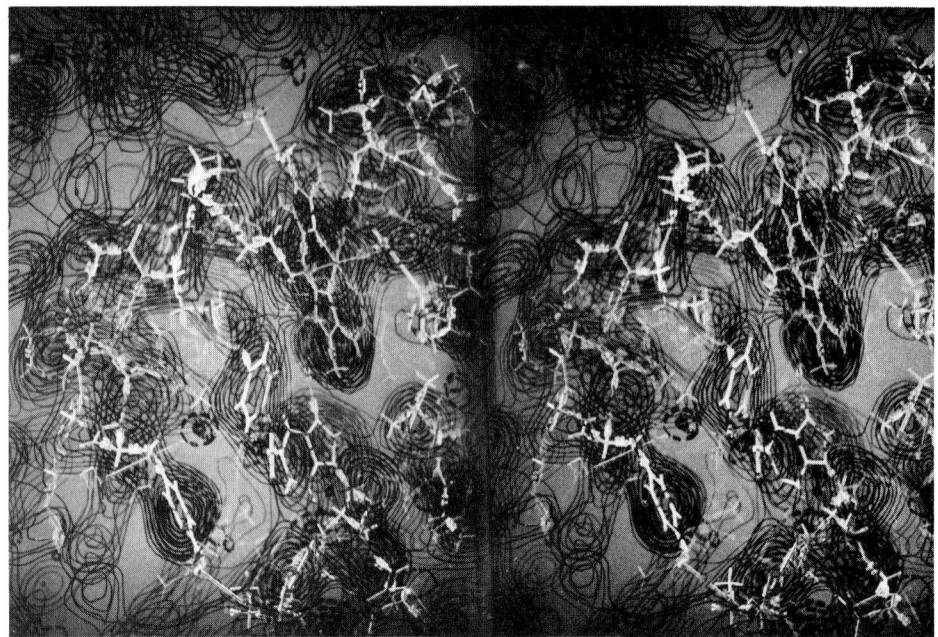

**Figure 1-17** Sections of the electron-density maps derived from x-ray diffraction data on oxidized cytochrome $c$. A reflection of the molecular model of the appropriate part of the macromolecule is superimposed upon the contour lines. [*From Dickerson, R. E., Takano, T., Eisenberg, D., Kallai, O. B., Samson, L., Cooper, A., and Margoliash, E. (1971) J. Biol. Chem.* **246,** *1511–1535 (see p. 1520). With permission.*]

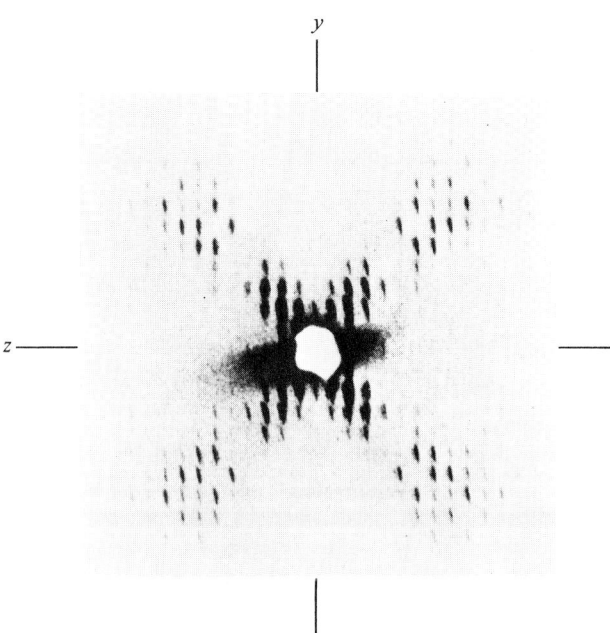

**Figure 1-18** X-ray diffraction pattern derived from a crystal of tropomyosin. [*From Cohen, C., Caspar, D. L. D., Parry, D. A. D., and Lucas, R. M. (1971) Cold Spring Harbor Sym. Quant. Biol.* **36,** *205–216 (see p. 207). With permission.*]

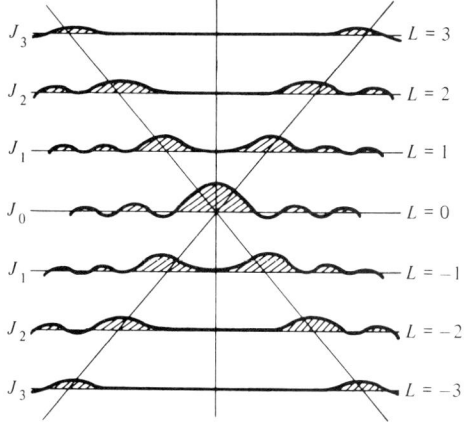

**Figure 1-19** Theoretical transform of a continuous helix.

*intermolecular antiparallel*, the *intramolecular antiparallel*, and the *parallel pleated-sheet conformations*. Each is represented in Fig. 1-20. The axial repeat distance in many of the parallel pleated-sheet conformations examined thus far is approximately 6.5 Å, while that in the antiparallel pleated-sheet conformations is approximately 7 Å. In a number of cases, interchain spacing between sheets is 4.7 Å, although it can vary from 3.5 to 8.0 Å, depending upon the nature of the amino acid side chains.

X-ray diffraction patterns from naturally occurring proteins that exist in pleated-sheet conformations are significantly different from those derived from naturally occurring proteins that exist predominantly in helical conformations, as illustrated in Fig. 1-21.

**The collagen helix** Collagen is a relatively insoluble protein found primarily in connective tissue. In man, collagen constitutes about 6 percent of the body weight. Collagen is characterized by a unique amino acid composition. Approximately 33 percent of the aminoacyl monomeric units are glycine, 10 percent are proline, and 8 percent are hydroxyproline. Sequences of the type Gly-Pro-X occur frequently throughout collagen, and the presence of these sequences imposes certain constraints upon the macromolecular structure of the protein. The high frequency of the inimo acids proline and hydroxyproline causes both right-handed α-helical and pleated-sheet conformations to be energetically unfavorable; instead, collagen exists in left-handed helical conformations in which three protein chains are intertwined. The collagen helix is represented by a space-filling model in Fig. 1-22. The x-ray diffraction pattern derived from collagen exhibits a faint suggestion of an X, but it is unlike patterns exhibited by right-handed α-helical structures (Fig. 1-23).

## Primary, Secondary, Tertiary, and Quaternary Structure

Polypeptides and proteins are composed of aminoacyl units joined by amide, or peptide, bonds. The unique sequence of these aminoacyl units that make up a particular polypeptide or protein chain is referred to as the *primary structure* of the

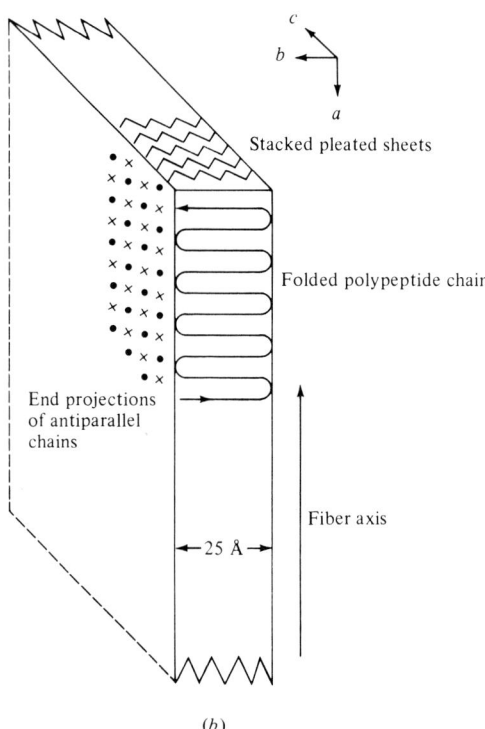

**Figure 1-20** (*a*) Chain arrangement in intermolecular antiparallel pleated-sheet (I) and parallel pleated-sheet (II) structures. (*b*) Schematic representation of the intramolecular antiparallel pleated-sheet structure (sometimes referred to as the *cross β structure*).

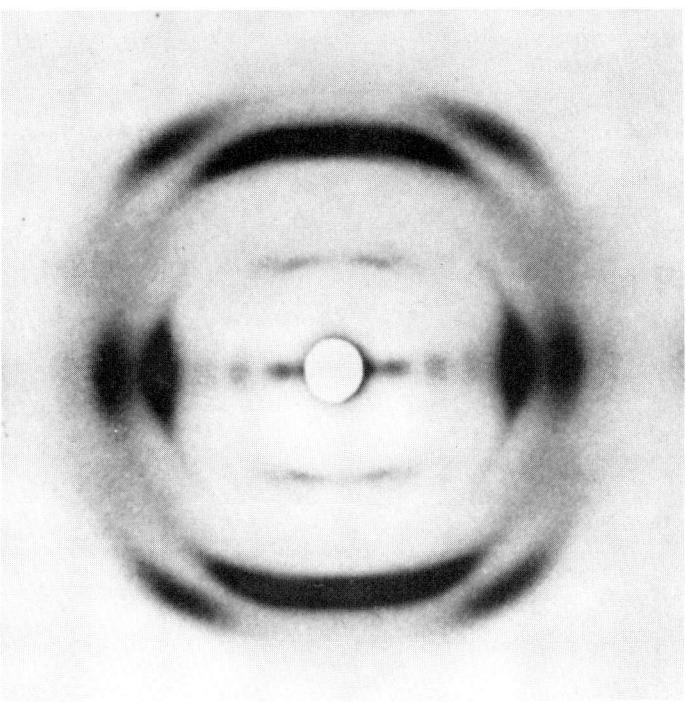

**Figure 1-21** X-ray diffraction pattern derived from a protein (the silk of the insect *Chrysopa flava*) that embodies predominantly the intramolecular antiparallel pleated-sheet structure. [*From Geddes, A. J., Parker, K. D., Atkins, E. D. T., and Brighton, E.* (1968) *J. Mol. Biol.* **32**, *343–358* (*see p. 345*). *With permission.*]

protein macromolecule. Polypeptide and protein molecules are extensively hydrogen-bonded, which helps determine the conformation of the macromolecule with respect to helical structures, pleated-sheet structures, and coiled structures. This aspect of the conformation of the polypeptide or protein is known as its *secondary structure*. In addition, most polypeptides and proteins have well-defined three-dimensional structure. It has been suggested that hydrophobic bonding participates in this aspect of the macromolecular structure, which is the *tertiary structure* of the polypeptide or protein. Finally, some proteins comprise subunits which are not covalently bonded to each other, although there are other interactions among them. This is called the *quarternary structure*.

## Conformations of Aminoacyl Units of Proteins

The bond joining the carbonyl carbon atom and the nitrogen atom of the amide moiety of proteins is somewhat rigid due to its double-bond character.

$$\begin{array}{c} \phantom{C(2)}-\text{N}-\text{H} \quad \text{O} \\ \phantom{C(2)}\phantom{-}| \phantom{-\text{H}} \quad \| \\ \phantom{C(2)}\phantom{-}\text{C}------\text{C}=\text{N}-\text{H} \\ \text{C(2)} \phantom{--}\text{C(1)} \phantom{-}| \\ \phantom{C(2)------C(1)--}\text{C} \\ \phantom{C(2)------C(1)--}\text{C(2)} \end{array}$$

**Figure 1-22** Model of the collagen triple helix based on the coordinates of Traub, W., Yonath, A., and Segal, D. M. (1969) *Nature*, **221**, 914–917. [*From Walton, A. G., and Blackwell, J. (1973) Biopolymers, pp. 407–463 (see p. 423), Academic, New York. With permission.*]

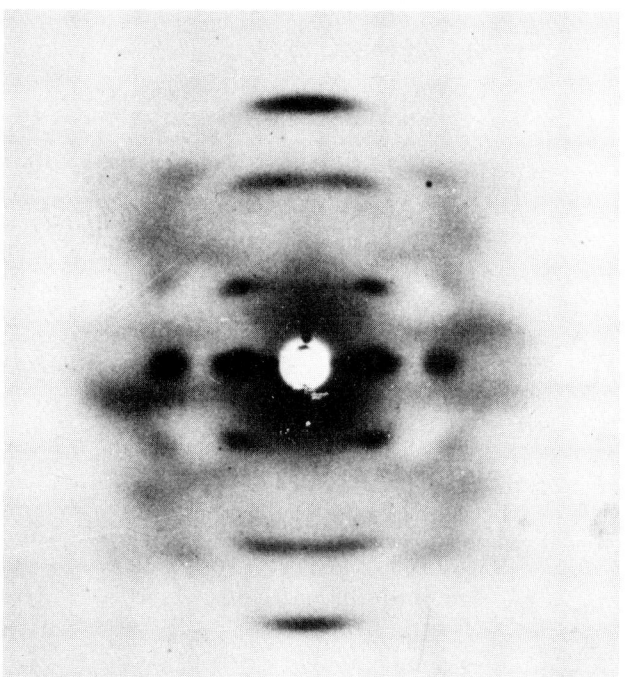

**Figure 1-23** X-ray diffraction pattern from collagen. (*Courtesy of A. C. T. North.*)

On the other hand, there is potentially free rotation about the bond joining C(2) and the carbonyl carbon atom, C(1), and also about the bond joining C(2) and the nitrogen atom. However, some of the torsion angles involved are energetically more favorable than others. In a manner parallel to that for the determination of the preferred conformations of the hexose units of polysaccharides, the preferred conformations of the aminoacyl units of proteins can be determined. With respect to the aminoacyl units, the torsion angle $\phi$ describes rotation about C(2) and the nitrogen atom while $\psi$ describes rotation about the bond joining C(1) and C(2). The torsion angle that described rotation about C(1) and the nitrogen atom of the adjacent aminoacyl unit is $\omega$. The dihedral angles $\phi$, $\psi$, and $\omega$ are zero when the two principal atoms involved lie in the same plane. Positive rotations are illustrated below.

Planar representation of the peptide backbone with $\psi$ and $\phi = 0°$

Table 1-3 gives values for the torsion angles $\phi$, $\psi$, and $\omega$ when the protein chain assumes the designated regular structure.

**44** MECHANISMS OF METABOLISM

**Table 1-3 Approximate torsion angles for some regular structures†**

|  | $\phi$, deg | $\psi$, deg | $\omega$, deg |
|---|---|---|---|
| Right-handed α helix [α-poly(L-alanine)] | −57 | −47 | 180 |
| Left-handed α helix | 57 | 47 | 180 |
| Parallel pleated sheet | −119 | 113 | 180 |
| Antiparallel pleated sheet [β-poly(L-alanine)] | −139 | 135 | −178 |
| Polyglycine II | −80 | 150 | 180 |
| Collagen | −51, −76, −45 | 153, 127, 148, | 180 |
| Poly(L-proline) I | −83 | 158 | 0 |
| Poly(L-proline) II | −78 | 149 | 180 |

† For a fully extended chain $\phi = \psi = \omega = +180°$.
*Source:* From the rules on nomenclature *J. Biol. Chem.* **245**, 6489–6497 (1970).

The energy associated with various rotational conformations can be estimated on the basis of the nonbonded, or van der Waals, interactions involved. Van der Waals interactions are frequently expressed using the Lennard-Jones potential

$$U = -\frac{A}{r^6} + \frac{B}{r^{12}} \qquad (1\text{-}3)$$

in which $r$ is the distance between two interacting atoms and $A$ and $B$ are constants for a given pair of atoms. The term $-A/r^6$ represents the forces of attraction, and $B/r^{12}$ represents the forces of repulsion involved. The Lennard-Jones potential is sometimes called the *6-12 function* since attraction varies with the inverse sixth power and repulsion varies with the inverse twelfth power of the distance between the atoms. Results of energy calculations for various proteins can be expressed in terms of potential-energy contour diagrams, just as for the polysaccharides.

## Structures of Specific Proteins

Three-dimensional structures of proteins and protein complexes have been determined through a combination of x-ray diffraction data, conformation data, and a knowledge of the amino acid sequence of the macromolecule. Among the proteins for which such structures have been detailed are hemoglobin, lysozyme, and carboxypeptidase A.

**Hemoglobin** Hemoglobin is a protein complex that binds oxygen and transports it to the various tissue sites throughout the body. Hemoglobin is made up of four iron porphyrin moieties, known as *heme moieties*, and a protein moiety, known as the *globin moiety*, which consists of two protein chains each with 141 aminoacyl units (the α chains) and two protein chains each with 146 aminoacyl units (the β chains). Each of these four protein chains is bonded to an iron porphyrin, or heme, moiety. A model of the hemoglobin macromolecule is shown in Fig. 1-24. The iron atoms of the heme moieties of hemoglobin are in the ferrous state both when oxygen is bound (in which case the macromolecule is designated as oxyhemoglobin) and when it is not (in which case the macromolecule is designated as deoxyhemoglobin). In deoxyhemoglobin the iron, which is in fact the central atom of a coordination complex, is high-spin† and five-coordinate, while in oxyhemoglobin it is low-spin and six-coordinate. In both deoxyhemoglobin and oxyhemoglobin the four nitrogen atoms of the porphyrin moiety provide four of the ligands of the iron coordination complex. (A porphyrin contains four pyrrole rings linked by methene groups.) The fifth ligand in each instance is the imidazolium moiety of a specific histidyl unit of the protein chain. This histidyl unit is referred to as the proximal histidyl unit and is aminoacyl unit F8 (see Fig. 1-25) in both the $\alpha$ chain and the $\beta$ chain. In the $\alpha$ chain aminoacyl unit F8 is His-87, and in the $\beta$ chain F8 is His-92. On the other side of the essentially planar heme moiety, the distal histidyl unit E7, that is, His-58 of the $\alpha$ chain or His-63 of the $\beta$ chain, and the valyl unit E11, that is, Val-62 of the $\alpha$ chain or Val-67 of the $\beta$ chain, in conjunction with the heme moiety itself, form a crevice into which the oxygen molecule fits. The oxygen molecule becomes the sixth ligand in oxyhemoglobin (Fig. 1-26).

The ligation of oxygen is, in fact, accompanied by changes in the conformation of the globin moiety in addition to the changes in the heme coordination complex. In deoxyhemoglobin each of the C-terminal aminoacyl units participates in the formation of interchain electrostatic bonds. The carboxyl group of Arg-141 of one $\alpha$ chain is electrostatically bonded to the amino group of Val-1 of the other $\alpha$ chain while the

---

† For an isolated atom which utilizes its $5d$ orbitals, such as iron, the energy levels of the orbitals are all equal. However, when such an atom becomes the central atom of a coordination complex, as in the iron atom of a heme moiety, the energy levels of all the $5d$ orbitals are no longer equal. Rather, these energy levels are split to yield a doublet and a triplet level when the coordination complex has octahedral symmetry. Thus, the $5d$ orbitals of the iron atom of the heme moiety of hemoglobin, which exhibits octahedral symmetry, are split to yield two orbitals designated as the $e_g$ orbitals and three designated as the $\tau_{2_g}$ orbitals. The former are at a higher energy level than the latter. It then follows that the six $d$ electrons of the iron atom of this heme moiety can be arranged in the available orbitals in more than one way. In fact, two arrangements are seen. In one of these the six $d$ electrons are paired in the three $\tau_{2_g}$ orbitals. Under these circumstances, the spins of the electrons are each paired, and the coordination complex is said to contain low-spin $d^6$ iron. In the other arrangement however, two of the six $d$ electrons are paired in one of the $\tau_{2_g}$ orbitals while the remaining four $d$ electrons occupy the remaining two $\tau_{2_g}$ orbitals and the two $e_g$ orbitals. In this case, the spins of only two of the six $d$ electrons are paired, and the coordination complex is said to contain high-spin $d^6$ iron. These two arrangements are

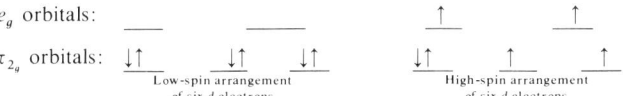

The low-spin $d^6$ iron is diamagnetic, and the high-spin $d^6$ iron is paramagnetic.

Determining whether a coordination complex contains a low-spin or a high-spin central atom depends, in part, upon the nature of the ligands involved. Ligands such as the chloride or bromide ion, which are known as *weak-field ligands*, generally promote the formation of complexes containing high-spin central atoms. Ligands such as ethylenediamine, ammonia, or the cyanide ion, which are known as *strong-field ligands*, generally promote the formation of complexes containing low-spin central atoms.

**Figure 1-24** Precision scale model of the hemoglobin molecule, constructed by Makio Murayama. [*From Nalbandian, R. M. (1971) Molecular Aspects of Sickle Cell Hemoglobin, Charles C Thomas, Springfield. With permission.*]

guanidinium group of Arg-141 is electrostatically bonded to the C(4) carboxylate group of Asp-126 of the other α chain. In addition, the carboxylate group of His-146 of one β chain is electrostatically bonded to the C(6) amino group of Lys-40 of an α chain while the imidazolium moiety of the His-146 unit interacts with the C(4) carboxyl group of Asp-94 of the same β chain. Furthermore, both the α chains and the β chains have penultimate tyrosyl units, which in deoxyhemoglobin are both

---

**Figure 1-25** (*a*) Representation and sequence of aminoacyl units of the α chain of human hemoglobin.
    (*b*) Representation and sequence of aminoacyl units of the β chain of human hemoglobin.
    Helical regions are designated by a single letter (e.g. A, B, C).
    Nonhelical regions are designated by two letters (e.g. AB, CD, EF). [*From Murayama, M. (1971) in Molecular Aspects of Sickle Cell Hemoglobin (Nalbandian, R. M., ed.), pp. 3-19 (see pp. 4-7), Charles C Thomas, Springfield. With permission.*]

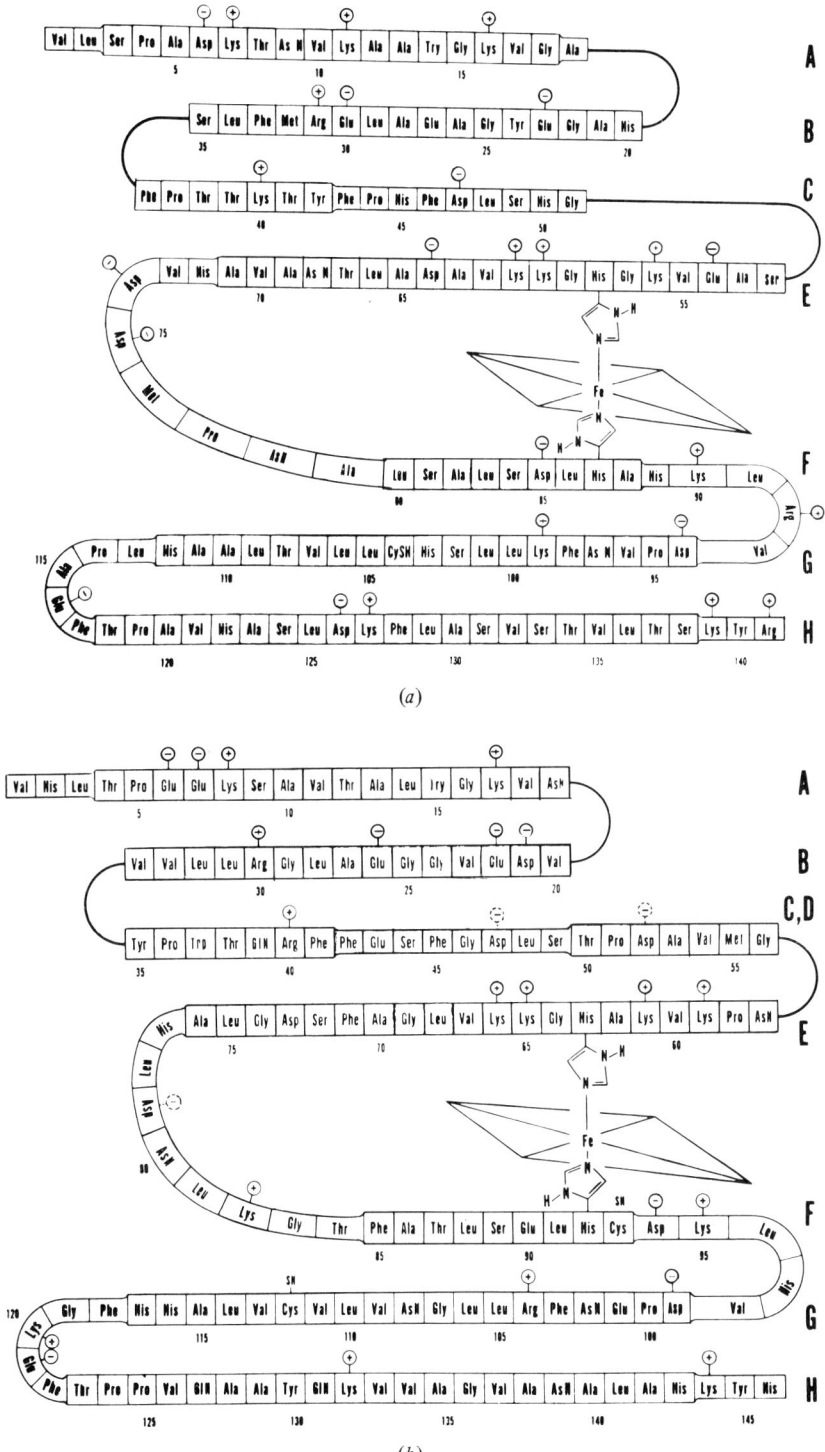

(a)

(b)

(a)

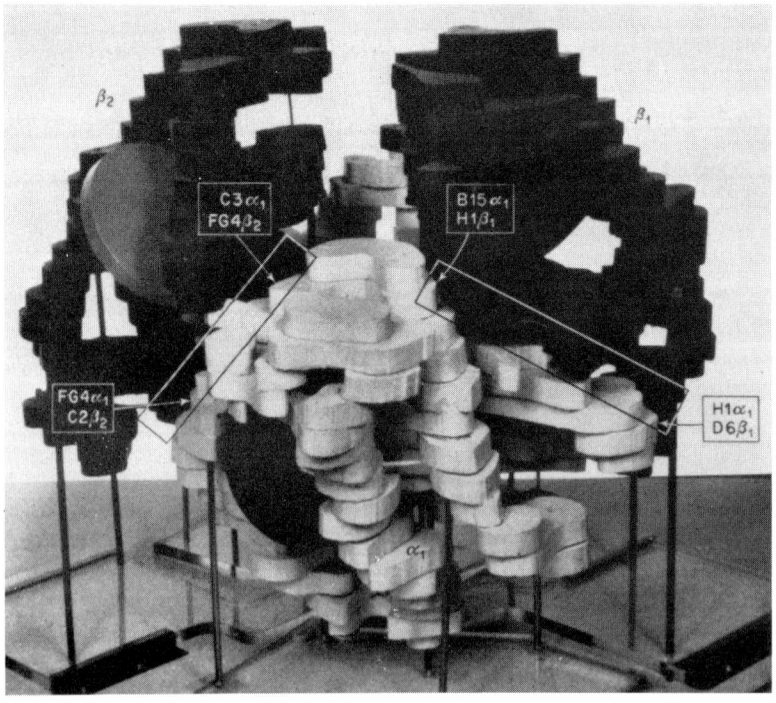

(b)

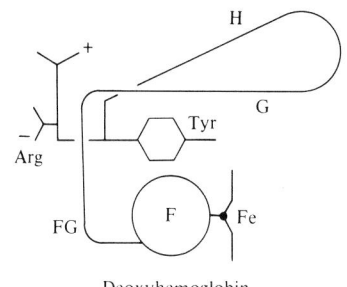

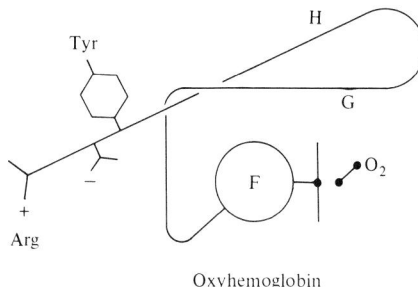

**Figure 1-27** Schematic representations of portions of the globin chains of hemoglobin in the vicinity of the heme moiety. Note the change in the position of the penultimate tyrosyl unit upon going from deoxyhemoglobin to oxyhemoglobin. The denotations F, H, and G refer to helical regions while FG denotes a nonhelical region, as indicated previously. [*From Perutz, M. F. (1970) Nature,* **228,** *726–734 (see p. 729). With permission.*]

confined in the crevice between the F and H helical regions as a result of the formation of the electrostatic bonds mentioned above. By contrast, the interchain electrostatic bonds are no longer present when oxygen is bound by the heme moiety, and hence the penultimate tyrosyl units are no longer confined. These changes are represented diagrammatically in Fig. 1-27.

**Abnormal hemoglobins** Screening of human blood samples has revealed over 100 different mutant hemoglobins. In many instances a *single one* of the 374 aminoacyl units is replaced by another, with the result that the properties of the hemoglobin macromolecule are drastically changed. Frequently, the presence of an abnormal hemoglobin is accompanied by specific clinical symptoms, e.g., inclusion body anemia (in which precipitated hemoglobin forms inclusion bodies within the erythrocyte, thus shortening its life), cyanosis, methemoglobinemia (in which the iron of the heme moiety is in the ferric state), hemolytic anemia, or polycthemia (in which there is an excess number of erythrocytes).

In the mutant designated hemoglobin S, Glu-6 of the $\beta$ chain is replaced by a valyl unit. A person who is homozygous for hemoglobin S generally exhibits a severe hemolytic anemia, splenic infarction, and repeated episodes of severe pain in the legs

---

**Figure 1-26** Models based on electron densities of (*a*) human deoxyhemoglobin and (*b*) human oxyhemoglobin. Rectangular areas indicate contacts between unlike globin chains. Arrows in (*b*) indicate reference points used to calculate the extent of the conformational changes that occurs as a concomitance of the conversion of oxyhemoglobin into deoxyhemoglobin. Disks represent ferroheme moieties. [*From Muirhead, H., Cox, J. M., Mazzarella, L., and Perutz, M. F. (1967) J. Mol. Biol.* **28,** *117–156 (see p. 130). With permission.*]

and abdomen. Such a person is said to have sickle-cell anemia. People who are heterozygous for hemoglobin S may be generally asymptomatic, but if they are exposed to an environment in which the partial pressure of oxygen is abnormally low, i.e., generally below 10 mmHg, they may experience certain clinical symptoms, including hematuria and, in some cases, splenic infarction. The clinical symptoms observed are apparently due to the transformation of a portion of the person's erythrocytes from the normal biconcave discoid form, which has a flexible cell membrane, to bizarre-shaped species with inflexible cell membranes. The latter are generally incapable of passing through the small blood vessels in the spleen, for example, and as a result they clog them and prevent normal circulation. The transfor-

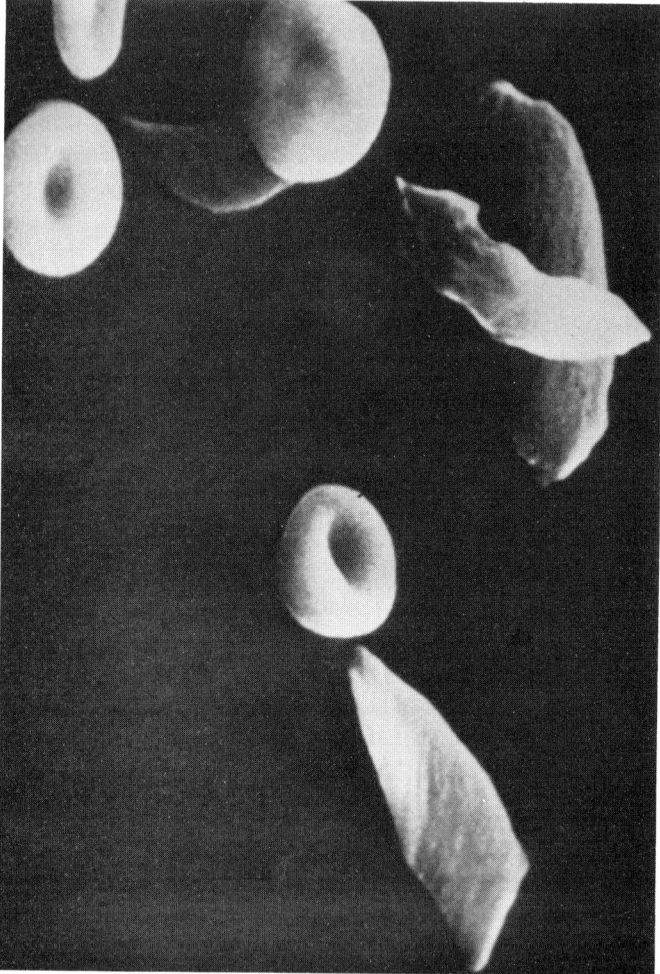

**Figure 1-28** Sickled cells along with "normal" biconcave discoid erythrocytes. [*From Barnhart, M. I. (1971) in Molecular Aspects of Sickle Cell Hemoglobin (Nalbandian, R. M., ed.), pp. 45–116 (see p. 74), Charles C Thomas, Springfield. With permission.*]

mation from the biconcave discoid form to the bizarre forms occurs when the erythrocyte contains a sufficient concentration of hemoglobin S which is specifically in the *deoxygenated* state. (It is for this reason that in the sickle-cell trait abnormally low partial pressures of oxygen initiate the symptomatology.) The bizarre forms that are generated are often crescent-shaped; hence the name sickle-cell anemia (Fig. 1-28).

In another hemoglobin mutant, called hemoglobin C, Glu-6 of the chain is replaced by a lysyl unit. People who are heterozygous for hemoglobin C are also generally asymptomatic, but people who are homozygous exhibit a mild hemolytic anemia. With respect to both hemoglobin S and hemoglobin C it has been suggested that the substitution of one aminoacyl unit for another results in a change in the solubility properties of the protein when this substitution takes place at a position on

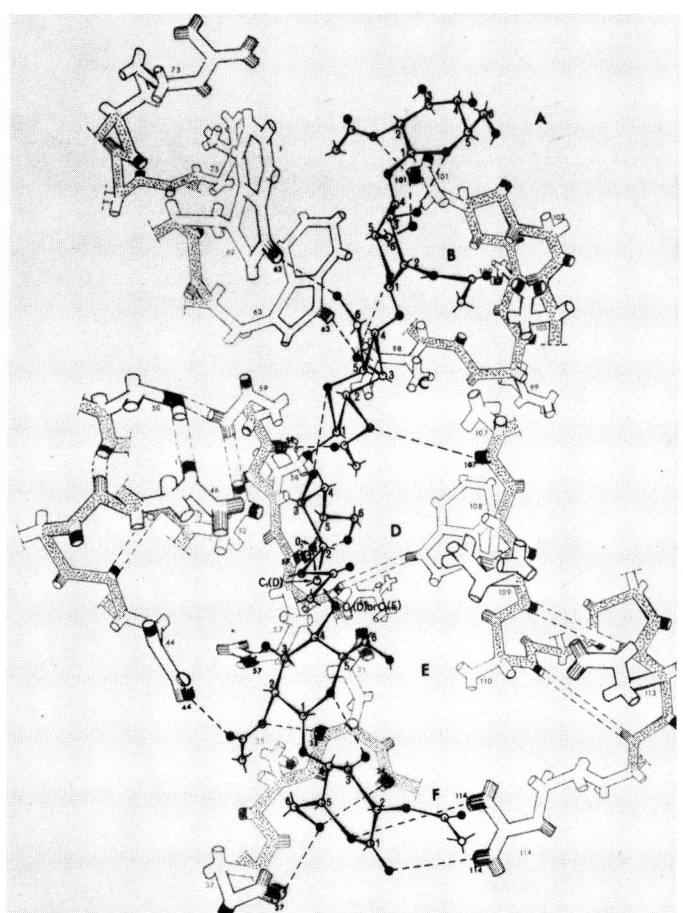

**Figure 1-29** Representation of the catalytic site of the enzyme lysozyme with a mucopolysaccharide molecule appropriately bound. Note the configuration of the fourth monosaccharide unit (D) which is in the half-chair form. [*From Blake, C. C. F., Johnson, L. N., Mair, G. A., North, A. C. T., Phillips, D. C., and Sarma, V. R. (1967) Proc. Roy. Soc. London* **167**, *378–388 (see p. 384). With permission.*]

**Figure 1-30** Representation of the protein chain of carboxypeptidase A. Note the zinc atom which is at the catalytic site. [*From Lipscomb, W. N., Reeke, G. N., Hartsuck, J. A., Quiocho, F. A., and Bethge, P. H. (1970) Phil. Trans. Roy. Soc. London* **B 257**, *177–214 (see p. 188). With permission.*]

the outer surface of the macromolecule. By contrast, substitutions in the interior regions of the macromolecules are frequently reflected by changes in the nature of the nonpolar contacts within the structure, and such changes have sometimes induced changes in the nature of the oxygen binding by the heme moiety. Examples are provided by several of the hemoglobins M, in which either the proximal or the distal histidyl unit is replaced by a tyrosyl unit. This alteration causes the heme iron atom to undergo oxidation, and since the ferriheme moiety binds oxygen less efficiently than the ferroheme moiety, cyanosis may result.

**Lysozyme** Lysozyme, an enzyme comprising 120 aminoacyl units, catalyzes the hydrolytic cleavage of the *O*-glycosidic bonds of certain mucopolysaccharides, including those which are components of certain bacterial cell walls. From a knowledge of the three-dimensional structure of this enzyme it has been proposed that the mucopolysaccharide to be cleaved binds in a specific crevice on the enzyme surface, and model building has indicated that three *N*-acetylhexosamine units of the mucopolysaccharide chain fit into one portion of this crevice while an additional three units fit into another portion provided that the conformation of the fourth of the six units is distorted. This distortion entails the assumption of a half-chair (rather than a chair) conformation by the fourth of the six *N*-acetylhexosamine units.

Although the half-chair conformation is thermodynamically less favorable than a chair form, in this case it appears that the former conformation is dictated by the requirements for binding at this locus on the enzyme. This is of particular interest since the half-chair conformation in fact promotes the reaction that takes place on the surface of the enzyme. The hydrolytic cleavage of the $O$-glycosidic bond proceeds by means of a transition state in which a carbonium ion is generated at C(1) and the resulting positive charge is delocalized by the presence of the neighboring oxygen atom. This delocalization is facilitated by the half-chair conformation (see Fig. 1-29).

**Carboxypeptidase A** Carboxypeptidase is an enzyme that catalyzes the cleavage of the C-terminal aminoacyl unit from a protein. This enzyme is, in fact, a metalloprotein. One zinc atom is tightly bound to the single protein chain of 307 aminoacyl units and participates in the binding of the protein reactant to the enzyme in that the carbonyl oxygen atom of the penultimate aminoacyl unit of the reactant becomes coordinated with the bound zinc (Fig. 1-30).

# NUCLEIC ACIDS AND THEIR COMPONENTS

The fourth major category of biochemical compounds is that of the nucleic acids. Unlike the carbohydrates, lipids, and proteins, the nucleic acids do not undergo degradation to yield small molecules utilized as a source of nutrition by the living organism. The primary function of the nucleic acids is to provide a means for the transfer of genetic information from generation to generation, which allows progeny to have the same characteristics as their parents.

## Purines and Pyrimidines

The nucleic acids are polymers consisting of nucleotide monomeric units. A nucleotide, in turn, is made up of a purine or a pyrimidine bonded to a pentose phosphate. Purines and pyrimidines are nitrogen-containing heterocyclic compounds. The principal purines occurring in the nucleic acids of higher organisms are adenine and guanine, and the principal pyrimidines are uracil, cytosine, and thymine.

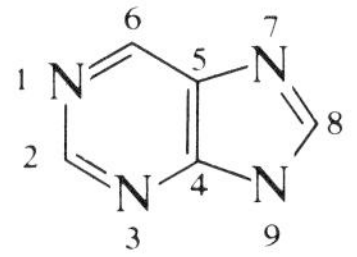

Purine

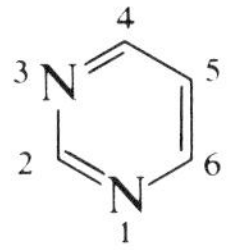

Pyrimidine

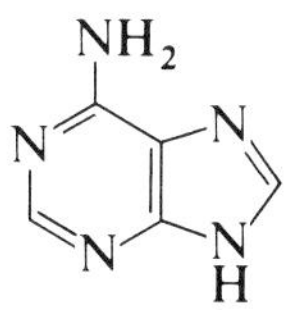

Adenine
(6-aminopurine)

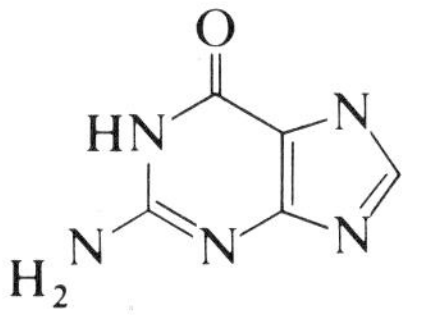

Guanine
(2-amino-6-oxopurine)

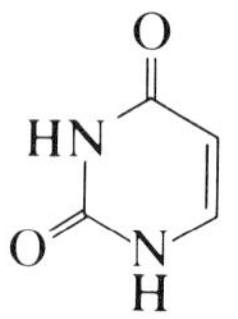

**54** MECHANISMS OF METABOLISM

Uracil
(2,4-dioxopyrimidine)

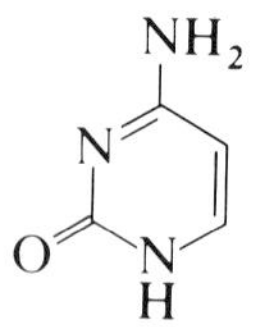

Cytosine
(2-oxo-4-aminopyrimidine)

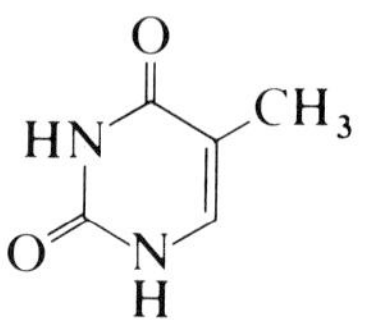

Thymine
(2,4-dioxo-5-methylpyrimidine)

Purines and pyrimidines exist in tautomeric forms. Generally, the oxo forms are more stable thermodynamically than the hydroxy forms, and the amine forms are more stable than the imine forms. Also, for the purine guanine it has been shown that the 7-H tautomer is more stable than the 9-H tautomer, while the reverse situation prevails with adenine.

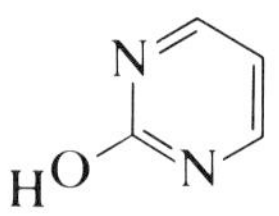

Hydroxyl tautomer 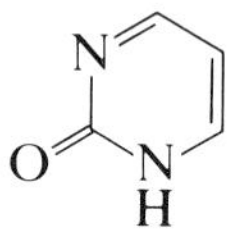    Oxo tautomer 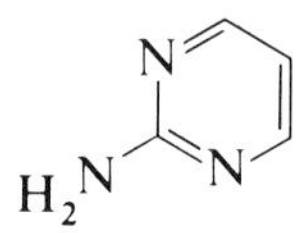    Amine tautomer 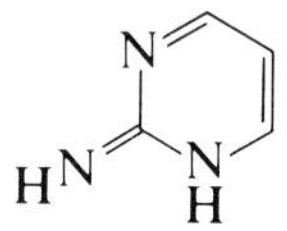    Imine tautomer

## Nucleosides and Nucleotides

A nucleoside is a purine or pyrimidine linked to a pentose (usually ribose or 2-deoxyribose) by means of an *N*-glycosidic bond. In general, this *N*-glycosidic bond involves N(1) of the pyrimidine moiety or N(9) of the purine moiety. When one or

Nucleosides:

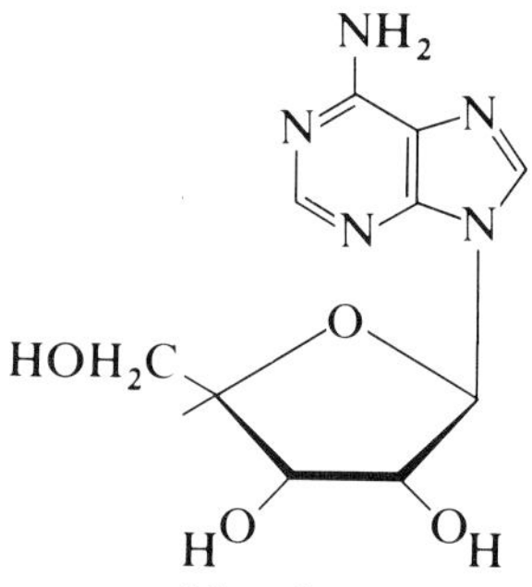

Adenosine

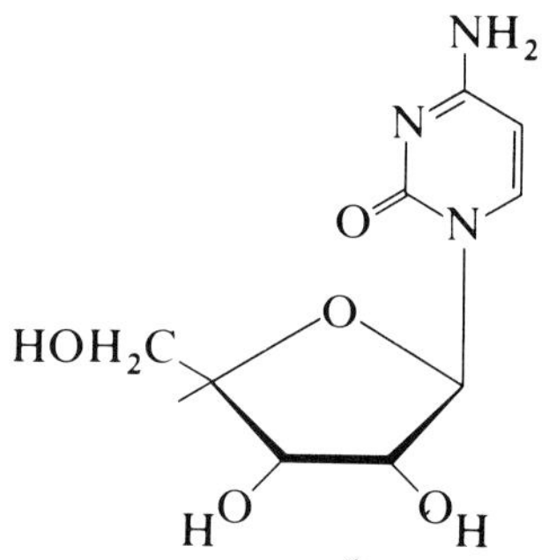

Cytidine

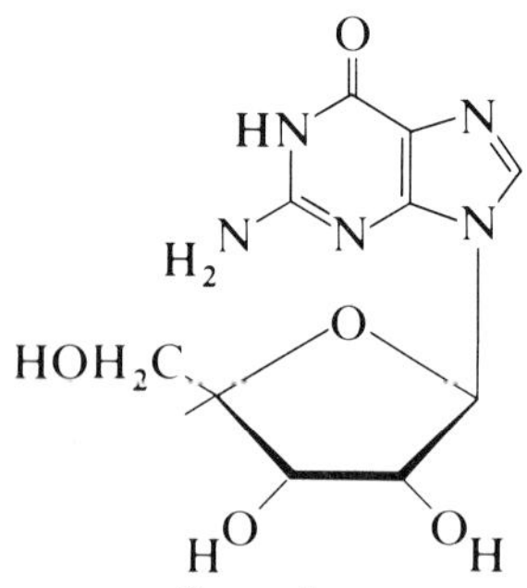

Guanosine

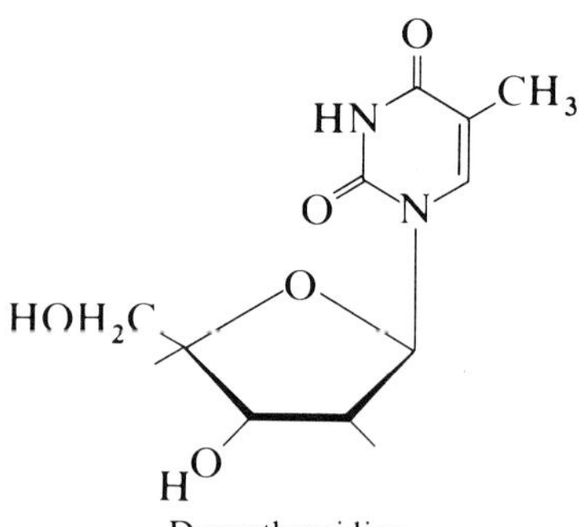

Deoxythymidine

Nucleotides:

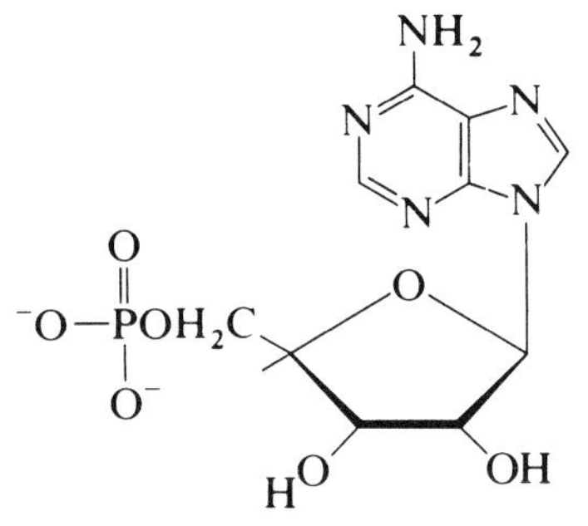

Adenosine 5'-monophosphate
(5'-AMP), an adenylate

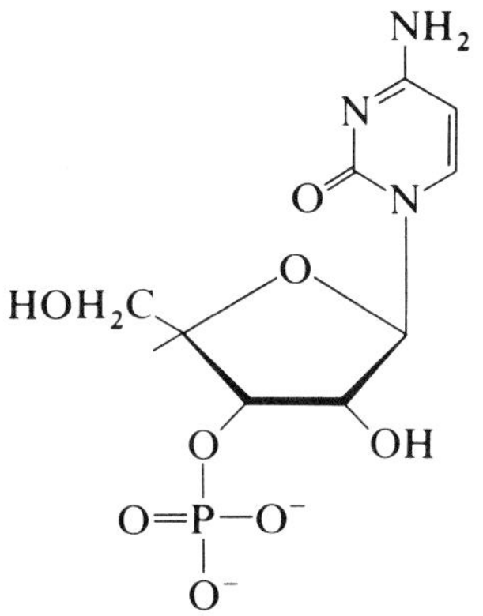

Cytidine 3'-monophosphate
(3'-CMP), a cytidylate

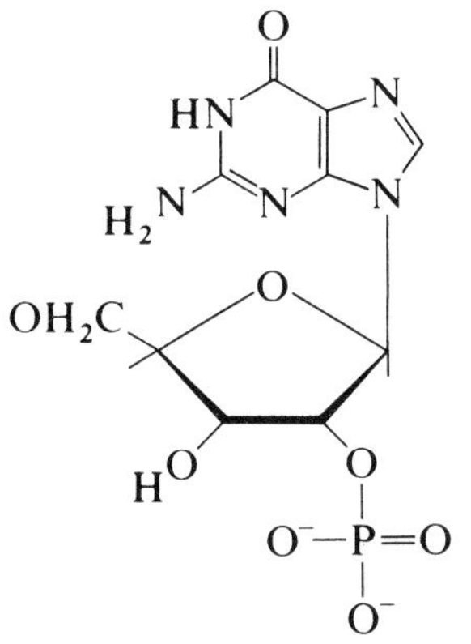

Guanosine 2'-monophosphate
(2'-GMP), a guanylate

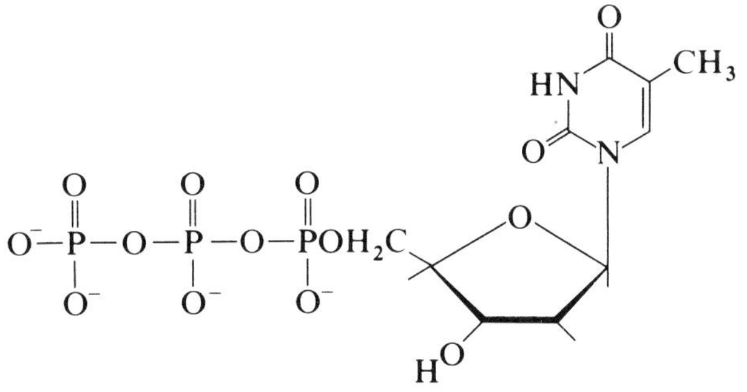

Deoxythymidine 5'-triphosphate
(5'-dTTP), a deoxythymidylate

more of the pentose hydroxyl groups has undergone phosphorylation, the resulting derivative is a nucleotide.

**Conformation about the *N*-glycosidic bond** Just as certain conformations about *O*-glycosidic bonds are thermodynamically preferred, certain conformations about the *N*-glycosidic bonds of nucleosides and nucleotides are similarly preferred. Consider the nucleotide represented in Fig. 1-31. The conformation of the *N*-glycosidic bond can be described in terms of the torsion angle $\chi$, while torsion angles $\phi$, $\psi$, and $\omega$ describe the conformations of the C—O, C—C, and O—P bonds, respectively. The zero positions for the dihedral angles involved are defined as those in which adjacent bonds are in the same plane. For the torsion angle $\chi$, which specifies the orientation of the purine or pyrimidine ring structure relative to the ribofuranose ring structure, the zero position is defined as that when the C(1')—O(4') bond of the pentose is in the same plane as the N(6)—C(1) bond of the pyrimidine or the N(9)—C(6) bond of the purine. If one views a particular bond end on, a positive torsion angle results

**56** MECHANISMS OF METABOLISM

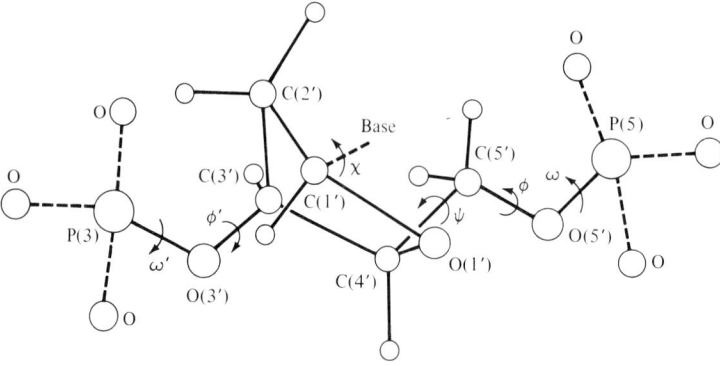

**Figure 1-31** Torsion angles about the N-glycosidic bond of a nucleotide. The pentose is represented by the five-membered ring structure. The base is the purine or pyrimidine to which the pentose is bonded.

when the more distant substituent is rotated counterclockwise with respect to the nearer substituent.

It has been determined that the conformation of the N-glycosidic bond is influenced by the conformation of the pentose moiety. Generally, the pentose moiety exists in a puckered furanoside form in which three of the ring atoms lie in a single plane while the remaining two ring atoms lie outside of this plane. On the basis of x-ray crystallographic studies at least four such puckered conformations exist, in which either C(2') or C(3') is most markedly displaced. When this displacement is on the same side of the ring plane as C(5'), the conformation is denoted *endo*. If it is on the opposite side, it is denoted *exo*. In nucleosides and nucleotides having β N-glycosidic bonds, the C(3') endo and C(2') endo pentose conformations are generally thermodynamically preferred. On the other hand, nucleosides and nucleotides having α N-glycosidic bonds generally have C(2') exo and C(3') exo pentose conformations.

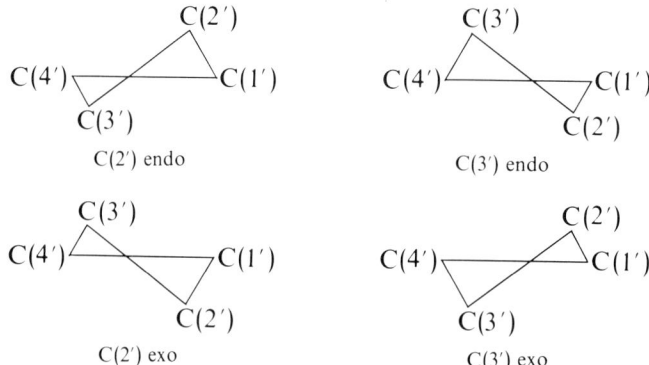

In addition, it is sometimes necessary to designate the spatial relationship between the purine or pyrimidine ring and the ribose ring. This is done by denoting the orientation about the N-glycosidic bond as either *syn* or *anti*. When the purine or pyrimidine ring is oriented away from the ribose ring, the conformation is anti.

Under the opposite circumstance, it is syn. In pyrimidine nucleosides having a $\beta$ $N$-glycosidic bond and a pentose with the C(2′) endo or C(3′) endo conformation, the anti conformation is more stable than the syn conformation by 1 to 2 kcal/mol.

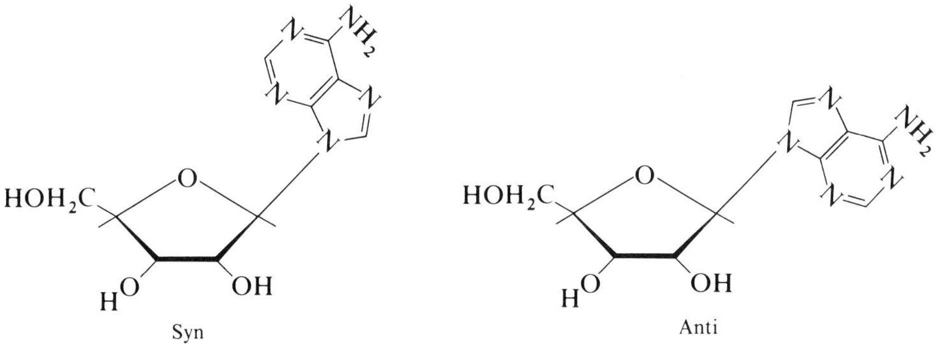

HOH$_2$C
O
HO
OH
NH$_2$
N
Syn
Anti


## Nucleic Acids

The nucleic acids are biopolymers composed of nucleotide monomers. The monomeric units of a given nucleic acid may each have ribose or 2-deoxyribose as the pentose moiety. If ribose is the pentose, the monomeric unit is a ribonucleotide and the nucleic acid is ribonucleic acid or RNA. If 2-deoxyribose is the pentose, the monomeric unit is a deoxyribonucleotide and the nucleic acid is deoxyribonucleic acid or DNA. DNA is made up of deoxyadenylyl, deoxyguanylyl, deoxycytidylyl, and

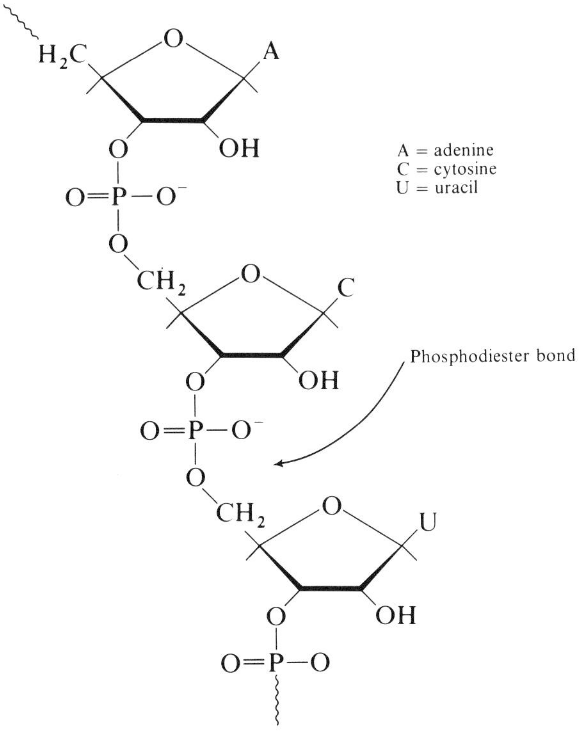

H$_2$C
O
A
OH
O=P—O$^-$
CH$_2$
C
U
A = adenine
C = cytosine
U = uracil
Phosphodiester bond

## Table 1-4 Molecular weights of some nucleic acids

|  | Molecular weight |
|---|---|
| Transfer RNA (yeast) | $2.64 \times 10^4$ |
| 5-S ribosomal RNA (*E. coli*) | $3.8 \times 10^4$ |
| 16-S ribosomal RNA (*E. coli*) | $5.6 \times 10^5$ |
| R17 bacteriophage RNA | $1.0 \times 10^6$ |
| 23 ribosomal RNA (*E. coli*) | $1.1 \times 10^6$ |
| $\phi$X174 bacteriophage DNA | $1.7 \times 10^6$ |
| 29-S ribosomal RNA (rat liver) | $1.75 \times 10^6$ |
| Poliomyelitis virus RNA | $2.0 \times 10^6$ |
| Tobacco mosaic virus DNA | $2.15 \times 10^6$ |
| Polyoma SV 40 virus DNA | $3.4 \times 10^6$ |
| Mitochondrial DNA (human) | $1.0 \times 10^7$ |
| T7 bacteriophage DNA | $2.43 \times 10^7$ |
| Newcastle disease virus RNA | $3.2 \times 10^7$ |
| Herpes simplex virus DNA | $7.0 \times 10^7$ |
| T2 bacteriophage DNA | $1.30 \times 10^9$ |
| Chromosomal DNA (*E. coli*) | $2.2 \times 10^9$ |

deoxythymidylyl units. On the other hand, RNA is made up of adenylyl, guanylyl, cytidylyl, and uridylyl units. The ribonucleotide units of RNA and the deoxyribonucleotide units of DNA are linked by phosphodiester bonds involving the C(5′) position of one unit and the C(3′) position of the adjacent unit.

Molecular weights of nucleic acids span a wide range. Some of the smaller nucleic acids, such as transfer RNA, a type of ribonucleic acid that participates in protein biosynthesis, have molecular weights of only 25,000 to 30,000. By contrast, some of the larger DNA molecules have molecular weights of over 20 million. Molecular weights of a variety of nucleic acids given in Table 1-4 illustrate the wide range that occurs.

**Macromolecular structure of nucleic acids** The macromolecular structure of the nucleic acids has been categorized in a manner paralleling that for proteins. Thus, the unique sequence of purine and pyrimidine nucleotides is referred to as the *primary structure* of the nucleic acid, the helical structure of these macromolecules is designated as its *secondary structure*, the coiling that is superimposed upon the helical structure in some of these macromolecules is the *tertiary structure*, and an interlocked, or catenated, arrangement of circular DNA is the *quaternary structure*.

**Macromolecular structure of transfer RNA** Transfer RNA, one of the smaller of the nucleic acids, exists as a single polynucleotide chain of approximately 75 ribonucleotidyl units. Portions of this chain are so coiled that specific purine and pyrimidine moieties can become hydrogen-bonded to each other. This type of bonding, which occurs in virtually all nucleic acids, is known as *base pairing* and takes place between specific purine and pyrimidine moieties, as discussed in Chap. 13. A transfer RNA molecule is represented schematically in Fig. 1-32.

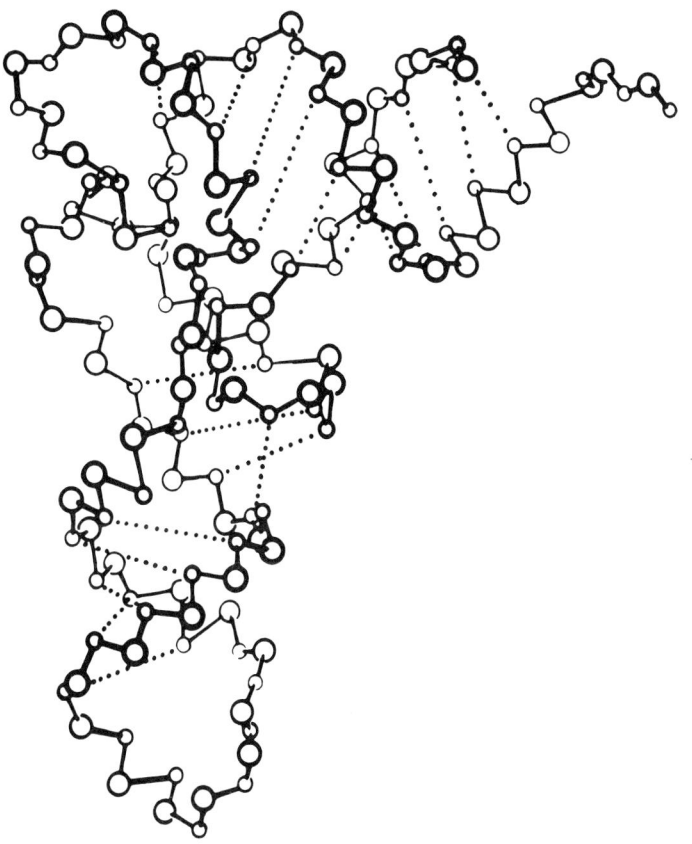

**Figure 1-32** Computer-generated representation of a transfer RNA molecule. Base pairing is indicated by dotted lines. [*From Kim, S. H., Suddaith, F. L., Quigley, G. J., McPherson, A., Sussman, J. L., Wang, A. H. J., Seeman, N. C., and Rich, A. (1974) Science* **185**, *435-440 (see p. 439). With permission.*]

**Macromolecular structure of viral RNA** Although RNA is generally single-stranded in mammalian cells, double-stranded RNA is found in certain viruses. One such virus, known as *reovirus* (an agent that affects the respiratory and intestinal tracts in man) has been found to contain double-stranded, helical conformations (similar to the conformations of DNA, discussed below). The helical structure of the reovirus RNA is thought to have 11 nucleotidyl units per turn, with an axial translation of 2.73 Å per unit. The plane of the purine or pyrimidine moieties is at an angle of 76° with respect to the axis of the helix, and the two polynucleotide chains of the duplex macromolecule interact by base pairing.

**Macromolecular structure of nuclear DNA** Although the RNA of mammals and other higher organisms is generally single-stranded, the nuclear DNA of these organisms is double-stranded and exists in defined helical conformations. Thus, as might be expected, x-ray diffraction patterns derived from DNA molecules exhibit the characteristic X, as illustrated in Fig. 1-33. In the conformation assumed by the DNA

**60** MECHANISMS OF METABOLISM

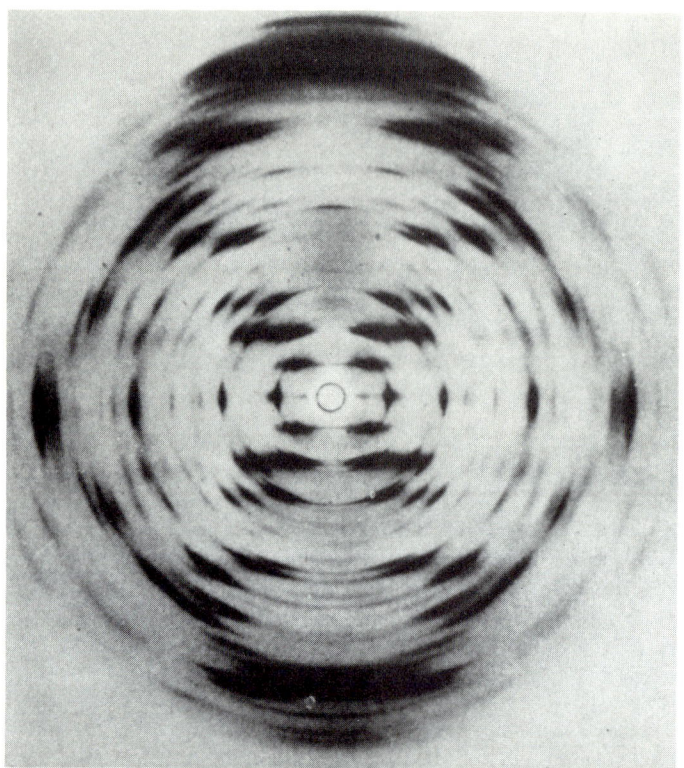

**Figure 1-33** X-ray diffraction pattern from a crystalline specimen of DNA. [*From Langridge, R., Wilson, H. R., Hooper, C. W., Wilkins, M. H. F., and Hamilton, L. D. (1960) J. Mol. Biol.* **2**, *19–37 (see p. 30). With permission.*]

macromolecule under most circumstances, i.e., that which produces the diffraction pattern shown, the helix is right-handed and has 10 nucleotidyl units per turn. The axial translation in this case is 3.4 Å per unit, and the plane of the purine and pyrimidine moieties is at an angle of 90° with respect to the axis of the helix. Figure 1-34 shows a schematic representation and a reproduction of a space-filling model of the DNA macromolecule in this conformation.

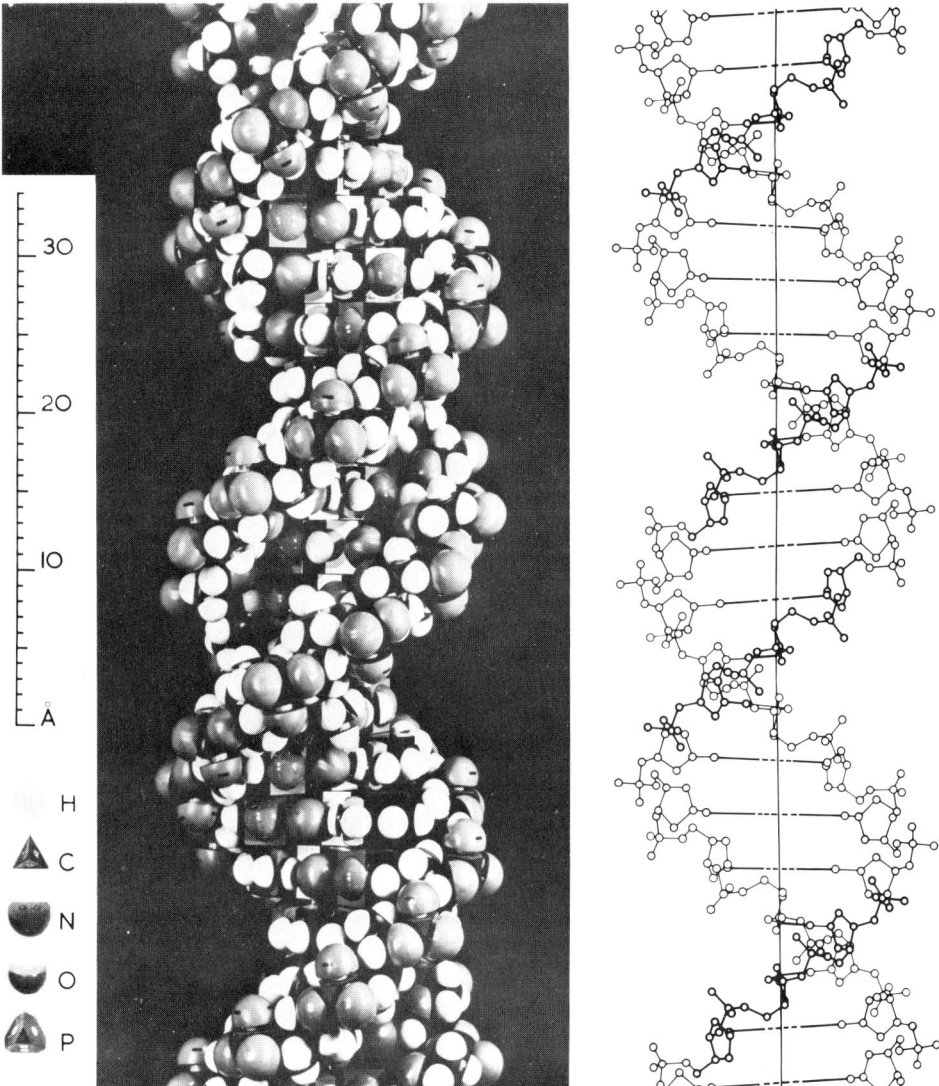

**Figure 1-34** Schematic representations of the DNA macromolecule. [*From Wilkins, M. H. F. (1963) Science* **140**, *941–950 (see p. 944). With permission.*]

CHAPTER
# TWO

## OPTICAL ACTIVITY

Most of the molecules that participate in biochemical reactions are optically active. Since optical activity is observed in the presence of polarized light, some of the principles concerning light, and in particular polarized light, will be reviewed in this chapter.

## POLARIZED LIGHT

Light can be considered as a transverse wave motion with two types of force fields associated with it, an electric field and a magnetic field (Fig. 2-1). The planes in which these two force fields oscillate and the plane of propagation of the light wave are mutually perpendicular. Light emitted by the sun or from an incandescent bulb is composed of waves oscillating in many different planes. Each wave has its associated electric field and its associated magnetic field. Therefore, there are electric fields and magnetic fields oscillating in many different planes. However, in 1809 Étienne Malus discovered a type of light characterized by associated electric fields oscillating in a single plane. Only the magnitude of these electric fields was found to vary. Since the projection of an oscillation in a single plane is a straight line that varies in length as a function of time, this type of light was designated as plane- (linearly) polarized light. Subsequently, in 1817 Augustin Fresnel observed another specific type of light, in which the magnitude of the associated electric fields remains constant while their direction varies. Since the periodic variation of such electric fields generates a circle, light of this type came to be known as circularly polarized light. Later it was recognized that plane-polarized light and circularly polarized light are special cases of a more general phenomenon, which can be described as follows.

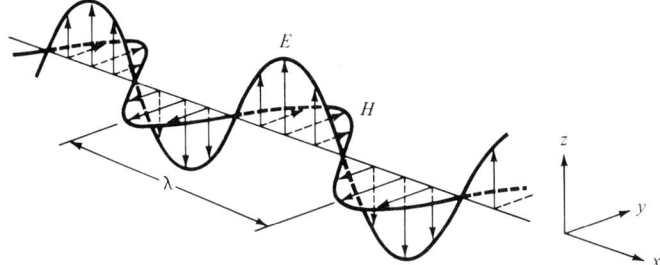

**Figure 2-1** A schematic representation of the electric field $E$ and the magnetic field $H$ associated with a light wave.

When natural light is passed through an anisotropic medium (one in which physical properties vary as a function of the direction in which the measurement is made), the incident light is separated into a reflected ray and *two* refracted rays rather than the usual one (Fig. 2-2). When the anisotropic medium is a calcite crystal, for example, one of these refracted rays oscillates in a plane perpendicular to the plane of the optic axis of the crystal. This ray is called the *ordinary ray*. The other refracted ray, which oscillates in the plane of the optic axis, is called the *extraordinary ray*. (The ordinary ray behaves according to the law of refraction,† whereas the extraordinary ray does not.) Each of these refracted rays is oscillating in a single plane, and therefore each is plane-polarized. Since the ordinary and extraordinary rays oscillate in mutually perpendicular planes, their associated electric fields oscillate in mutually perpendicular planes. Each of these electric fields can be represented by a sinusoidal function. These two sinusoidal functions have a constant phase difference with respect to each other. The resultant of two sinusoidal functions having a constant phase difference is an ellipse (Fig. 2-3). Therefore, light comprising two such mutually perpendicular rays is called elliptically polarized light. This is the general case. In the specific case where the phase difference between the two sinusoidal functions is $0, \pi, 2\pi, 3\pi, \ldots$, the resultant is an oscillation in a single plane, the projection of which is a straight line. This is the special case of linearly, or plane-polarized, light. In the special case in which the phase difference between the sinusoidal functions is $\pi/2$ (or some multiple of $\pi/2$) and their amplitudes are equal, the light is circularly polarized. When the phase difference is $\pi/2, 5\pi/2, 9\pi/2, \ldots$, the light is right circularly polarized, when the phase difference is $3\pi/2, 7\pi/2, 11\pi/2, \ldots$, the light is left circularly polarized (Fig. 2-4).

† The law of refraction, or Snell's law, states that the refracted ray lies in the plane of incidence and that the ratio of the sine of the angle of refraction and the sine of the angle of incidence is a constant.

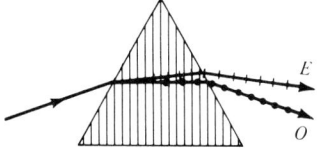

**Figure 2-2** The passage of light through a crystal such as calcite which separates the beam into two refracted rays, the ordinary ray $O$ and the extraordinary ray $E$.

**64** MECHANISMS OF METABOLISM

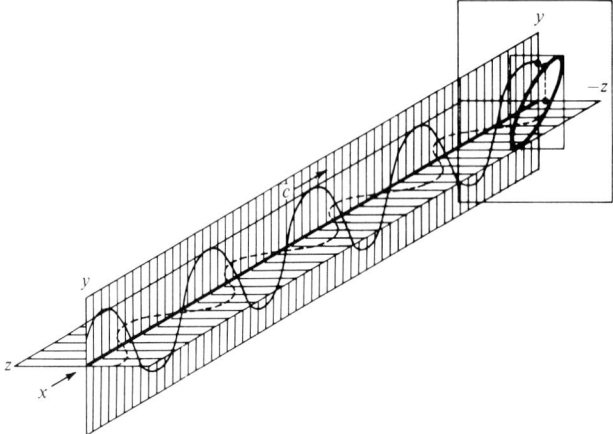

**Figure 2-3** The superposition of two sinusoidal waves which yields an ellipse.

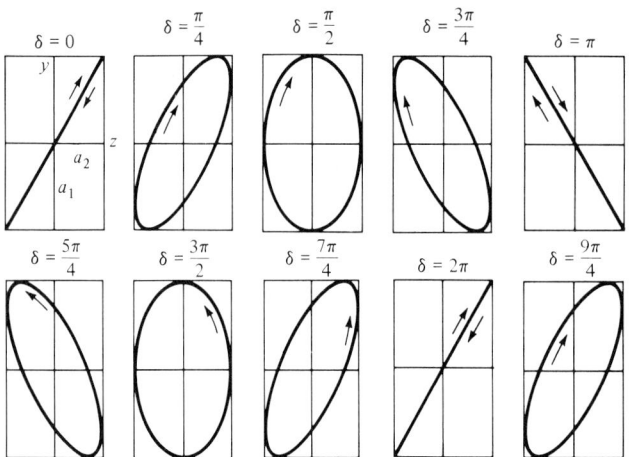

**Figure 2-4** The resultant of two harmonic motions, such as a sine wave, having the same frequency but not always the same phase. Phase difference is denoted by $\delta$.

## The Interaction of Polarized Light with a Dissymmetric Medium

When a molecule that lacks specific symmetry elements interacts with polarized light, the plane of this polarized light is rotated. In order for this to occur the molecule must lack a plane of symmetry or a center of symmetry or any other $n$-fold alternating axis of symmetry. A plane of symmetry is present when a plane can bisect a molecule into two halves that are mirror images of each other. A center of symmetry is present when rotation through $\pi$ rad (180°) about an axis generates the mirror image of the original structure. A plane of symmetry is actually a onefold alternating axis of symmetry, and a center of symmetry is actually a twofold alternating axis of symmetry. An $n$-fold alternating axis of symmetry is present if rotation through $2\pi/n$ rad followed by reflection in a plane perpendicular to the axis of rotation generates the original structure. (See Fig. 2-5.)

Why does the lack of an $n$-fold alternating axis of symmetry allow a molecule to rotate the plane of polarized light? When a molecule undergoes an electronic transition from a ground state to an excited state, there is a change in the electron distribution which is described by the electric-transition dipole moment. There is also an accompanying change in the magnetic field associated with this change in electron distribution. This is described by the magnetic-transition dipole moment. A quantity designated as the rotational strength $R_i$ is related to the electric-transition dipole moment $\mu_e^i$ and the magnetic-transition dipole moment $\mu_m^i$ as follows:

$$R_i = \mu_e^i \cdot \mu_m^i \tag{2-1}$$

This equation states that the rotational strength of the $i$th transition is given by the scalar product of the electric-transition dipole moment and the magnetic-transition dipole moment. When $R_i$ has a nonzero value, optical activity can be observed, while when $r_i$ is zero, no optical activity is observed. Because $R_i$ must be zero for all transitions when a molecule possesses an $n$-fold alternating-axis symmetry, only molecules devoid of this symmetry element can be optically active. The rationale is as follows.

When a molecule has an $n$-fold alternating axis of symmetry, the wave functions that describe the ground states and the excited states can be defined as being either odd functions or even functions. An odd function is one that changes sign when the sign of $x$ changes, i.e.,

$$f(x) = -f(-x) \tag{2-2}$$

(An example of an odd function is a sine function, and an example of an even function is a cosine function.) The equation for the electric-transition dipole moment is such that $\mu_e^i$ will be nonzero *only* if the product of the wave function that describes the ground state $\psi_g$ and the wave function that describes the excited state $\psi_e$ is an *odd* function. On the other hand, the equation for the magnetic-transition dipole moment is such that the product of $\psi_g$ and $\psi_e$ must be an *even* function in order for $\mu_m^i$ to be nonzero.† Therefore, when a molecule has an $n$-fold alternating axis of symmetry, either $\mu_m$ or $\mu_e$ must be zero for a given electronic transition. Hence, there are no conditions under which $R_i$ can be other than zero. In the absence of an $n$-fold alternating axis of symmetry the wave functions that describe the ground states and the excited states cannot be defined in terms of being either even or odd. Therefore, $R_i$ can have a nonzero value.

† The equations are

$$\mu_e = \int_{-\infty}^{+\infty} \psi_g e(\mathbf{i}x + \mathbf{j}y + \mathbf{k}z)\psi_e \, d\tau$$

and

$$\mu_m = \frac{eh}{4\pi mci} \int_{-\infty}^{+\infty} \psi_e \left[ \mathbf{i}\left(y\frac{\partial}{\partial z} - z\frac{\partial}{\partial y}\right) + \mathbf{j}\left(z\frac{\partial}{\partial x} - x\frac{\partial}{\partial z}\right) + \mathbf{k}\left(x\frac{\partial}{\partial y} - y\frac{\partial}{\partial x}\right) \right] \psi_g \, d\tau$$

where **i**, **j**, and **k** are vectors and $d\tau$ is a volume element.

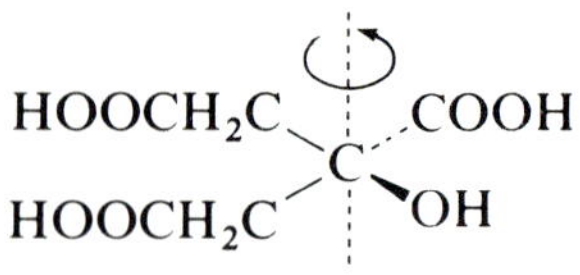
HOOCH$_2$C
COOH
C
HOOCH$_2$C
OH

Citric acid

(*a*)

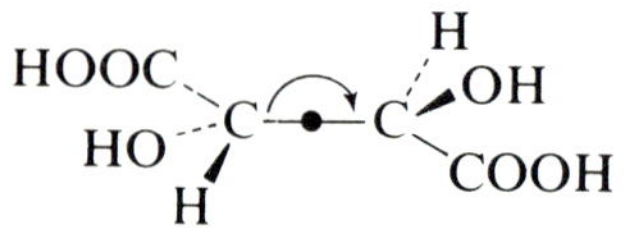
HOOC
H
OH
HO
C
C
COOH
H

*meso*-Tartaric acid

(*b*)

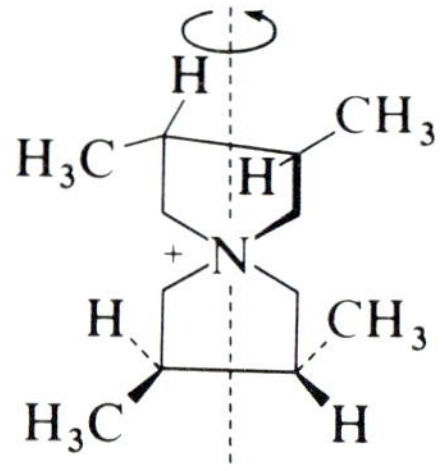
H
CH$_3$
H$_3$C
H
+
N
H
CH$_3$
H$_3$C
H

Bipyrrolidinium ion

(*c*)

**Figure 2-5** (*a*) Citric acid has a one-fold alternating axis of symmetry, i.e., a plane of symmetry. A plane perpendicular to the axis of rotation shown, bisecting the hydroxyl and carboxyl groups and passing between the two carboxymethylene groups, produces two halves of the molecule that are mirror images of each other. (*b*) *meso*-Tartaric acid has a two-fold alternating axis of symmetry, i.e., a center of symmetry. Rotation through 180° about the axis shown generates the mirror image of the original structure. (*c*) Bipyrrolidinium ion has a four-fold alternating axis of symmetry. Rotation through 90° and reflection in a plane that is perpendicular to the axis of rotation (while not bisecting the molecule) generates the original structure.

When considering the interaction between plane-polarized light and a medium, the plane-polarized beam can be considered to consist of two rays, one right circularly polarized and one left circularly polarized, of equal amplitude and in phase. (A simple harmonic motion along a straight line, e.g., a plane-polarized light beam, can be treated as the resultant of two opposing circular motions of equal amplitude and in phase.) When this plane-polarized beam passes through a medium containing molecules with an $n$-fold alternating axis of symmetry, the two circularly polarized components travel through the medium with the same velocity. However, when the plane-polarized beam passes through a medium containing molecules without this element of symmetry, one of the circularly polarized components will exhibit a greater velocity than the other component. The velocity with which a light ray passes through a medium determines the refractive index of the medium with respect to that particular type of light. Therefore, a dissymmetric medium will exhibit different refractive indices when the right and left circularly polarized rays of a plane-polarized beam are considered. Exhibiting different refractive indices in the presence of these right and left circularly polarized rays is known as *circular birefringence*. As a result of traveling at different velocities, the right and left circularly polarized rays emerge from the dissymmetric medium out of phase. Their resultant is still a plane-polarized beam, but the plane of polarization has been rotated. (This can perhaps be rationalized on an intuitive basis. If one is considering two rotating vectors and the velocity of one vector is diminished with respect to that of the other, the resultant of these two vectors will be displaced angularly rather than linearly.) The angular displacement $\alpha'$ is a function of the difference between the refractive index of the medium with respect to the left circularly polarized ray and that with respect to the right circularly polarized ray. This is stated by the Fresnel equation

$$\alpha' = \frac{\pi}{\lambda}(n_L - n_R) \tag{2-3}$$

where $\alpha'$ = angular displacement of plane of polarized light, rad per unit of length
$\lambda$ = wavelength of incident polarized light, same unit of length
$n_L, n_R$ = refractive indices of medium with respect to left and right circularly polarized components of plane-polarized beam

What happens when plane-polarized light instead of passing through a single dissymmetric molecule passes through a liquid phase containing many dissymmetric molecules? Since in the liquid phase or in solution the dissymmetric molecules are randomly oriented, one might expect the angular displacements induced as the plane-polarized beam passes through these molecules to cancel out. However, the interaction of the two rotating vectors at one end of the dissymmetric molecule is *not equal* and *opposite* to their interaction at the other end of the dissymmetric molecule.

When plane-polarized light interacts with a dissymmetric medium containing molecules which exhibit an absorption maximum at or near the wavelength of the light, one circularly polarized ray is absorbed to a greater extent than the other. Specifically, the circularly polarized ray for which the medium exhibits the larger refractive index (corresponding to the slower velocity within the medium) is also that which is absorbed to a greater extent. Greater absorption by the medium of one of the circularly polarized components of a plane-polarized beam is called *circular dichroism*. As a result of the unequal absorption of these component rays, the emergent beam is no longer plane-polarized but is now elliptically polarized. The difference between the absorption coefficients for the left and right circularly polarized rays can be related to a quantity known as the *angle of ellipticity* as follows:

$$\psi = \frac{\pi}{\lambda}(\kappa_L - \kappa_R) \tag{2-4}$$

where $\psi$ is the angle of ellipticity and $\kappa_L$ and $\kappa_R$ are the absorption coefficients for the left and right circularly polarized ray, respectively. (An absorption coefficient is related to the more common *molar extinction coefficient* $\epsilon$ by means of the approximation

$$\kappa = 2.303\epsilon c \tag{2-5}$$

where $c$ is the concentration of the absorbing species in moles per liter.) Specific ellipticity $[\psi]$ is given by

$$[\psi] = \frac{\psi}{lc} \tag{2-6}$$

where $l$ is the path length of the polarimeter cell in decimeters and $c$ is the concentration of the absorbing species in grams per cubic centimeter. Molecular ellipticity $[\theta]$, on the other hand, is defined by

$$[\theta] = \frac{[\psi]M}{100} \tag{2-7}$$

where $M$ is the molecular weight of the absorbing species.

Yet another characteristic of the interaction of plane-polarized light with a dissymmetric medium is that the observed optical rotation varies as a function of the wavelength of the polarized beam. This phenomenon is known as *optical rotatory dispersion*. One might intuitively sense that optical rotation will vary with wavelength since optical rotation is a function of refractive index [Eq. (2-3)] and refractive index is a function of wavelength. The latter relationship can be approximated by

$$n_\lambda = 1 + \sum_i n_i(\lambda) \tag{2-8}$$

where 1 is the index of refraction in a vacuum and $n_i$ is a partial refractive index which corresponds to a particular electronic transition. If optical rotation is observed as function of wavelength in a region that is not that of an absorption maximum of the molecules of the medium, the molar rotation† $[M]$ is approximated by

$$[M] = \sum_i \frac{a_i \lambda_i^2}{\lambda^2 - \lambda_i^2} \tag{2-9}$$

† Molar rotation $[M]$ is defined as

$$[M] = \frac{\alpha}{\rho l} \frac{\text{molecular weight}}{100}$$

where $\alpha$ is in degrees, $\rho$ is the concentration of the dissymmetric compound in grams per cubic centimeter, and $l$ is the path length of the polarimeter cell in decimeters.

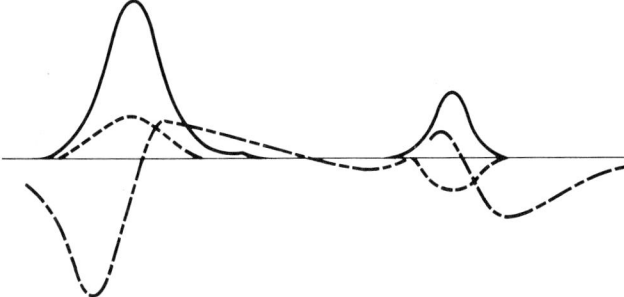

**Figure 2-6** Idealized circular-dichroism (---) and optical-rotatory-dispersion (— — —) curves shown in relation to the absorption bands exhibited by the molecule (———). The circular-dichroic effect associated with the absorption band at the left is positive, while that associated with the absorption at the right is negative. A positive Cotton effect is associated with the absorption band at the left, while a negative Cotton effect is associated with the absorption band at the right.

where $a_i$ is a constant for the $i$th transition and $\lambda_i$ is the mean wavelength of an absorption band of an absorbing molecule in the medium. The optical rotation is seen to increase in magnitude as the wavelength $\lambda$ decreases. However, in the region of an absorption band, the denominator of Eq. (2-9) approaches zero and thus $[M]$ approaches infinity. When, in fact, one observes the optical rotation of a compound in the region of one of its absorption bands, the rotation is seen to increase and then to decrease, both sharply. This phenomenon is known as a *Cotton effect* in recognition of the fact that Aimé Cotton, a French physicist, described such behavior in 1895. Idealized circular dichroism and optical-rotatory-dispersion curves in the region of an absorption band of the molecules of the medium are shown in Fig. 2-6.

## OPTICALLY ACTIVE MOLECULES

A simple and quite widespread circumstance that results in a molecule's lacking an $n$-fold alternating axis of symmetry is substitution on a tetrahedral carbon atom of four different substituents. On this basis, saccharides and polysaccharides are optically active. Acylglycerols are optically active provided that the two terminal carbon atoms of the glycerol moiety bear different substituents. All amino acids with the exception of glycine (and therefore all proteins) are optically active. When a molecule lacks an $n$-fold alternating axis of symmetry, it can exist in two forms that bear the relationship of mirror images with respect to each other. These two forms are *enantiomers*. If a molecule has more than one center of dissymmetry, it may exist in as many as $2^n$ forms, where $n$ represents the number of different dissymmetric centers present. In this case, there can be $2^n/2$ different enantiomeric pairs. Molecules of the group that are not enantiomers, i.e., mirror images of each other, are *diastereoisomers*. Although enantiomers generally exhibit identical physical properties when interaction with an electromagnetic field is not involved, diastereoisomers behave as distinctly different compounds. Because optical rotatory properties are often the basis for various biochemical studies, these properties will be mentioned and elaborated upon in subsequent chapters.

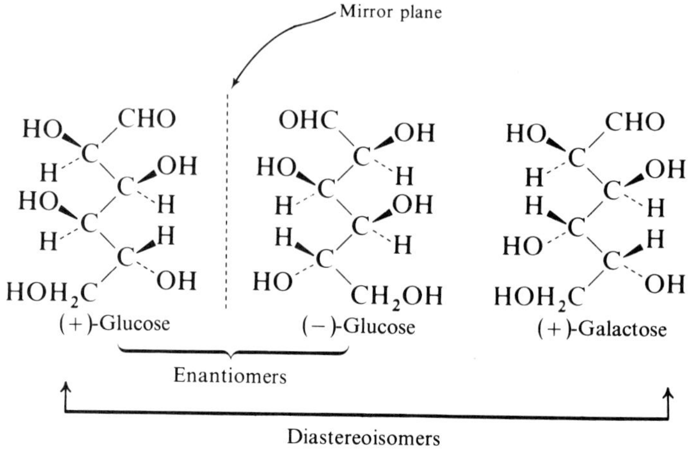

[Mirror plane diagram showing (+)-Glucose and (−)-Glucose as Enantiomers, and (+)-Galactose; the (+)-Glucose and (+)-Galactose pair are Diastereoisomers.]

## Nomenclature and Representation of Optically Active Molecules

To represent a three-dimensional model of an optically active compound in two dimensions a *Fischer projection formula* is often used. According to the convention introduced by Emil Fischer, when the dissymmetry of the molecule is due to tetrahedral carbon, all the tetrahedral apexes that connect dissymmetric carbon atoms lie in a straight line in the plane of the projection. The substituents that are at the "top" and the "bottom" of the tetrahedral carbon atom and in a plane behind it are also written along that straight line. The substituents to the "right" and the "left" of the tetrahedral carbon atom and in a plane in front of it shall be written on opposite sides of the straight line.

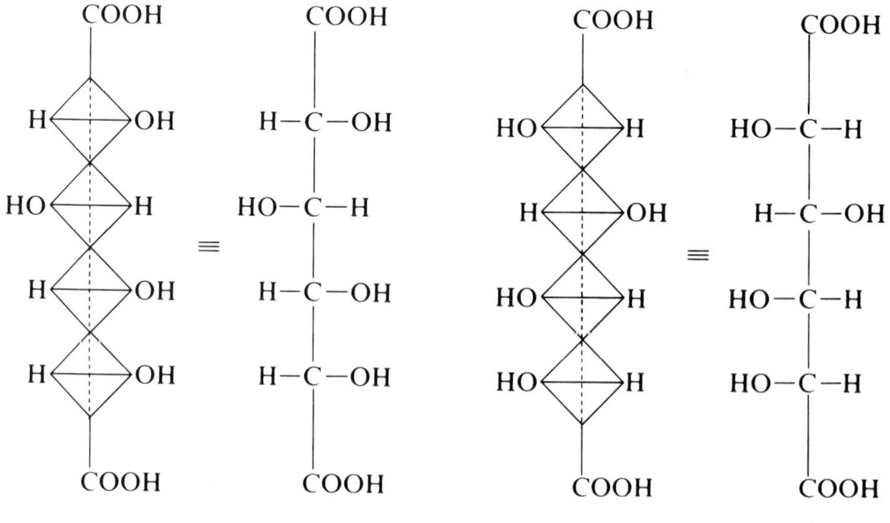

Since the Fischer projection formula is a two-dimensional representation of a three-dimensional object, it cannot be lifted out of the plane of the projection and turned over. Also, since the substituents connected to the dissymmetric carbon atom by vertical lines in the projection formula actually lie below the plane of that atom and those connected by horizontal lines actually lie above the plane of that atom, the Fischer projection cannot be rotated by 90 or 270°. It can be rotated by 180°, however. In addition, if one of the four substituents remains fixed and the other three are rotated in order about the central carbon atom, an equivalent structure is generated. Some of the allowed manipulations of a Fischer projection are

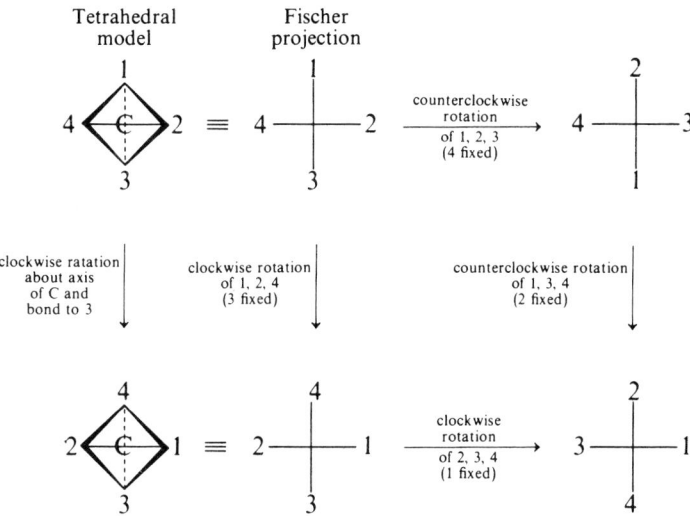

When one wishes to specify one of two enantiomers, this can be done by using either (+) or (−) before the name of the isomer and also by using either D or L before the name of the isomer. The symbols (+) and (−) stipulate the direction in which plane-polarized light is rotated by this particular enantiomer. If plane-polarized light is rotated in a clockwise manner (or to the "right"), the enantiomer is said to be *dextrorotatory* and the symbol (+) is used before its name. If plane-polarized light is rotated in a counterclockwise manner (or to the "left"), the enantiomer is *levorotatory* and (−) is used. The symbols D and L, on the other hand, designate the absolute configuration of an enantiomer. When the center of dissymmetry of a given enantiomer is of the form of D-glyceraldehyde or can be related to it, the name of the enantiomer is prefixed by D. When the center of dissymmetry of the enantiomer is of the opposite configuration, the name is prefixed by L. Most naturally occurring monosaccharides are of the D configuration at the penultimate carbon atom and, by convention, are designated as belonging to the D series. On the other hand, most naturally occurring amino acids have a configuration at C(2) which can be correlated with that at C(2) of L-glyceraldehyde and therefore belong to the L series.

```
    CHO              CHO               CHO                            COO⁻
    |                |            H ───┼─── OH                         |
H ──┼── OH      HO ──┼── H       HO ───┼─── H         H₂N ─────┼───── H
    |                |            H ───┼─── OH                         |
   CH₂OH           CH₂OH          H ───┼─── OH                        CH₃
                                       |
                                     CH₂OH

 D-Glyceraldehyde  L-Glyceraldehyde   D-Glucose                     L-Alanine
```

The convention for designating absolute configuration depends upon relating the substituents bonded to the dissymmetrically substituted carbon atom of the molecule under study to those similarly bonded in glyceraldehyde. This is not always easy. However, Robert S. Cahn and Christopher K. Ingold have introduced a system for placing the substituents of a dissymmetrically substituted atom in a prescribed order so that the chirality (right-handedness or left-handedness) of the molecule can readily be related to the reference compound.† According to this system, the four substituents bonded to a carbon atom are arranged in sequence based on specific priorities. The projection formula is then viewed from the side remote from the group having the lowest priority. It is now determined whether the sequence of *decreasing* priority proceeds in a clockwise or counterclockwise manner. If clockwise, the dissymmetric center is designated $R$ (for the Latin *rectus*, meaning "right"). If the sequence of decreasing priority proceeds counterclockwise, the center is designated $S$ (for the Latin *sinister*, meaning "left"). The rules for determining priority (in abbreviated form) are as follows:

1. Substituents are arranged on the basis of the atomic number of the atom attached to the dissymmetric carbon atom, the atom having the highest atomic number taking top priority.
2. When two or more substituents have the same atom attached to the dissymmetric carbon atom, the one with substitutions having atoms of the highest atomic number takes precedence. The following substituents are listed in order of decreasing priority:

$$-SH > -OH > -N-\overset{\overset{O}{\|}}{C}-CH_3 > -NH_2 > -\overset{\overset{O}{\|}}{C}-OR > -\overset{\overset{O}{\|}}{C}-OH >$$

$$-\overset{\overset{O}{\|}}{C}-H > -CH_2OH > -CH_3 > -T > -D > -H$$

The use of this convention is illustrated in Fig. 2-7.

Many biochemical molecules have more than one dissymmetrically substituted carbon atom, and in some cases two (or more) of these may be substituted identically. Under these circumstances there will be meso forms of the molecule. The

---

† Cahn, R. S., and Ingold, C. K. (1951) *J. Chem. Soc.* 612–622; Cahn, R. S., Ingold, C. K., and Prelog, V. (1956) *Experientia* **12**, 81–94.

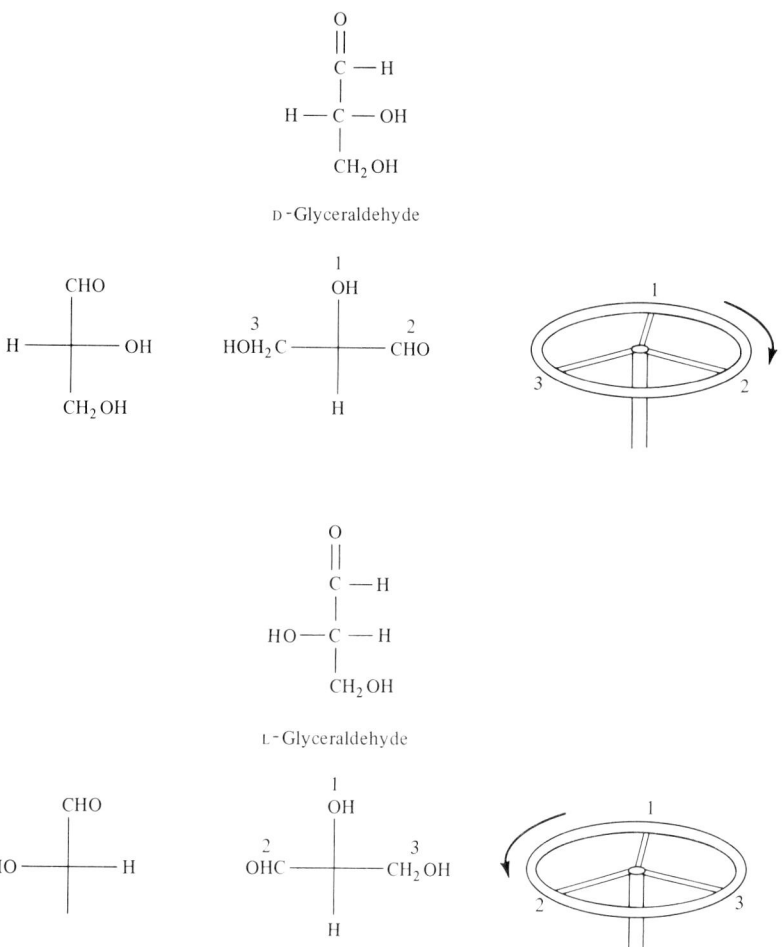

**Figure 2-7** According to the convention introduced by Cahn and Ingold, if four substituents have the ordered priority $a > b > c > d$, their spatial configuration is denoted by $R$ if the sequence $a \to b \to c$ proceeds in a clockwise manner when viewed from an external point beyond $d$, while it is denoted by $S$ if this sequence proceeds in a counterclockwise manner when viewed from beyond $d$. Here the order of substituents is $OH > CHO > CH_2OH$. The Fischer projection that represents the chemical formula is given on the left followed by an equivalent Fischer projection in which the substituent having the lowest priority is at the bottom. (The two projections are equivalent because the second is generated from the first as the result of an *even* number of exchanges of pairs of substituents. An odd number of such exchanges generates a projection that represents a molecule which has the opposite configuration as did the original.) Now if the bond joining the central carbon atom and the substituent having the lowest priority is considered to be the steering column and the other three substituents are considered to be the spokes of the steering wheel, as illustrated, the sequence $OH \to CHO \to CH_2OH$ proceeds in a clockwise manner in the case of D-glyceraldehyde and in a counterclockwise manner in the case of L-glyceraldehyde. Hence, D-glyceraldehyde has the $R$ configuration while L-glyceraldehyde has the $S$ configuration.

tartaric acids are a classical example of this situation. Meso forms are not optically active.

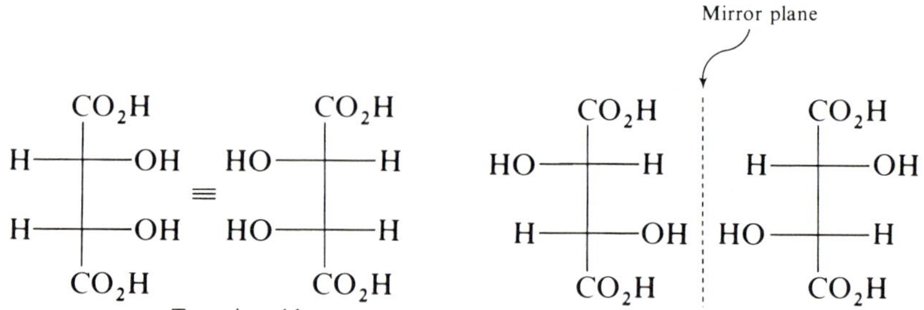

meso-Tartaric acid     D(−)-Tartaric acid     L(+)-Tartaric acid

When a molecule embodies two centers of dissymmetry, the terms *erythro* and *threo* can be used. When the Fischer projection formula is written, if two identical or similar substituents each bonded to dissymmetrically substituted carbon atoms are on the same side, as in erythrose, the isomer is said to be of the erythro form, and if the two identical or similar substituents are on opposite sides, as in threose, the isomer is of the threo form.

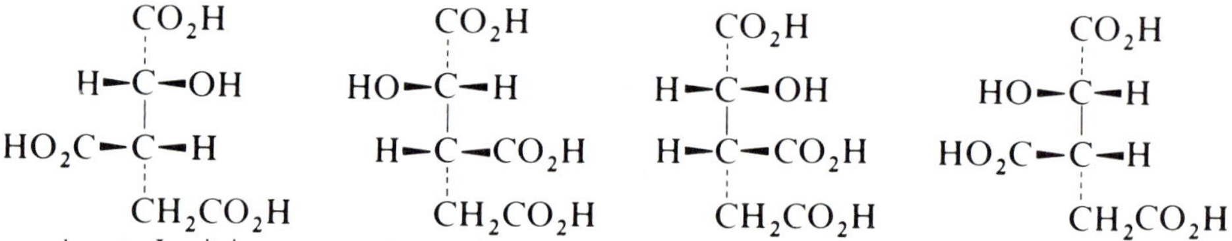

*threo*-$D_S$-Isocitric acid     *threo*-$L_S$-Isocitric acid     *erythro*-$D_S$-Isocitric acid     *erythro*-$L_S$-Isocitric acid

The five-, six-, and seven-carbon monosaccharides exist almost exclusively in the form of cyclic hemiacetals or hemiketals. The formation of these cyclic structures introduces another center of dissymmetry in addition to those already present in the molecule. The two diastereoisomers that result when a monosaccharide undergoes cyclization as a result of hemiacetal or hemiketal formation are called *anomers*, and the carbonyl carbon atom that becomes dissymmetrically substituted is frequently referred to as the *anomeric carbon atom*. Because hemiacetal and hemiketal formation is reversible (particularly when acid catalysis is provided), if one dissolves a given diastereoisomer, such as α-D-glucose, in an aqueous solution, an equilibrium mixture of the two diastereoisomers results. This interconversion between two such diastereoisomers is referred to as *mutorotation*. As a result of mutorotation a solution of either pure α-D-glucose or pure β-D-glucose approaches an equilibrium mixture in which there is 63.8 percent of the β anomer and 36.2 percent of the α anomer.

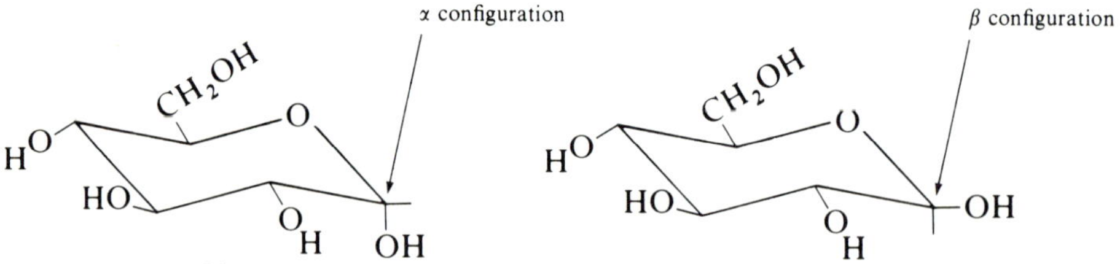

α-D-Glucose     β-D-Glucose
Diastereoisomers

# STEREOSELECTIVITY AND STEREOSPECIFICITY

If one carries out a reaction which can yield diastereoisomeric products, usually an unequal distribution of the diastereoisomers is obtained. (It should be remembered that diastereoisomers are distinct compounds.) A process in which one diastereoisomer is generated or destroyed preferentially when starting with a given enantiomer is said to be *stereoselective*. When it is the *kinetically determined* product of a stereoselective process that is obtained, the predominance of one diastereoisomer reflects the fact that the transition-state complex that collapses to yield this molecule is of lower energy than that which yields the other. These transition-state complexes are themselves diastereoisomeric, and the one of lower energy will be attained with greater frequency. On the other hand, when the *thermodynamically determined* product of a stereoselective process is obtained, the more stable diastereoisomer will be present in the greater concentration. The extent to which this diastereoisomer predominates reflects the relative ground-state levels of the two molecules. As an example of these types of processes, consider the reaction of the pentose xylose with methanol in the presence of hydrochloric acid. The initial, kinetically determined product is a mixture of the anomeric methyl xylofuranosides, in which the ratio of the $\alpha$ anomer to the $\beta$ anomer is 2.1 : 1. In time, however, this mixture is converted to the thermodynamically determined product, in which the ratio of the $\alpha$ anomer to the $\beta$ anomer is 1 : 1.2.

Under certain circumstances one of two geometric isomers, e.g., one of a pair of cis-trans isomers, undergoes a reaction which results in the formation of a given dissymmetrically substituted product while the same reaction carried out with the other geometric isomer yields an isomeric product. In this case the reaction is said to be *stereospecific*. A stereospecific process is one in which there is a relationship between the configuration of the reactant and that of the product. An example of a stereospecific reaction is the addition of the elements of water to the olefinic bond of fumarate. The fumarate molecule can be considered to have two faces, which can be distinguished using the priority rules introduced by Cahn and Ingold. If a trigonal carbon atom is substituted in such a manner that the sequence of decreasing priority proceeds clockwise, this face of the trigonal atom is designated as the *re* (derived from *rectus*) face. If this sequence proceeds in the opposite manner, this face of the trigonal atom is designated as the *si* (derived from *sinister*) face. When fumaric acid undergoes hydration in D₂O, the initial attack by D⁺ at either of the equivalent carbon atoms on the *re-re* face yields (2S),(3R)-malic acid. Similarly, attack by D⁺ at either of the equivalent carbon atoms on the *si-si* face results in the formation of (2R),(3S)-malic acid, the enantiomer of the product shown. On the other hand, hydration of the geometric isomer of fumaric acid, maleic acid, yields a racemic mixture of (2R),(3R)-malic acid and (2S),(3S)-malic acid, as shown.

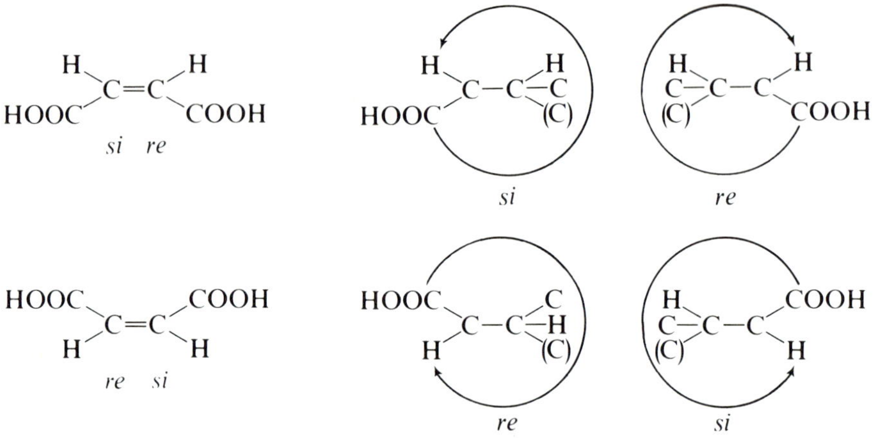

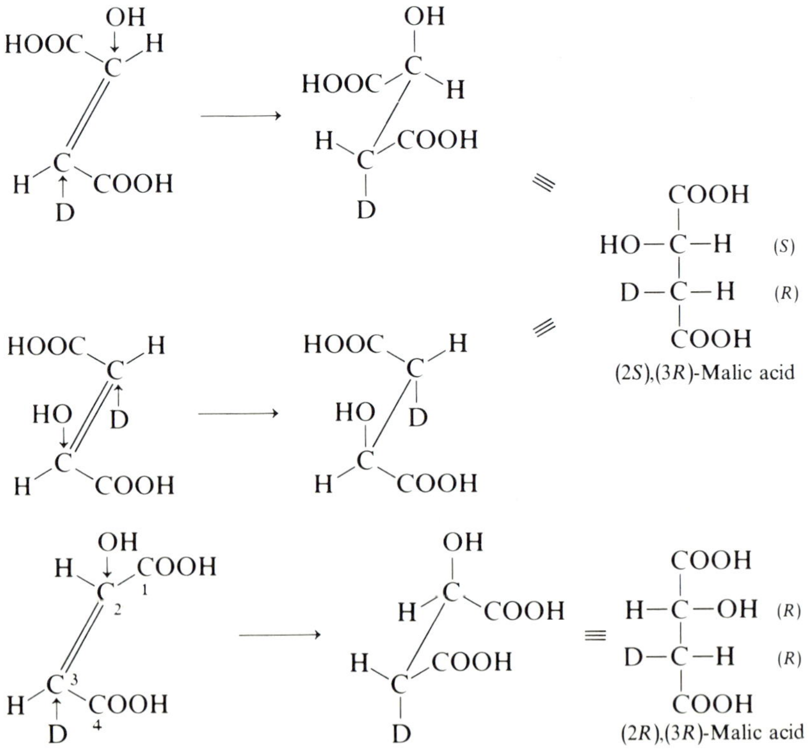

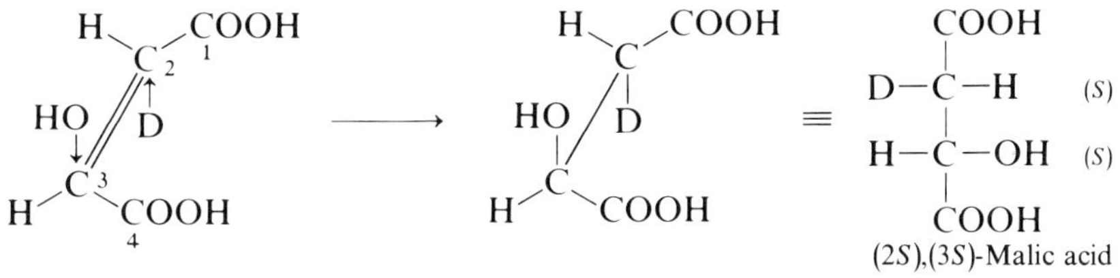

$$\underset{4}{\overset{H}{\underset{H}{\overset{|}{C}}}}\overset{COOH}{\underset{COOH}{\overset{|}{C_2}}}\phantom{xx}\longrightarrow\phantom{xx} \equiv \begin{array}{c}COOH\\D-C-H\phantom{x}(S)\\H-C-OH\phantom{x}(S)\\COOH\end{array}$$

(2S),(3S)-Malic acid

## ASYMMETRIC SYNTHESES

A process in which a new center of dissymmetry is created generally yields two diastereoisomers if one of the reactants is optically active. On the other hand, if the reactants are optically inactive, two enantiomers will be obtained if a new center of dissymmetry is created. However, in some instances one of these two diastereoisomers or one of these two enantiomers is obtained in excess of the other, a process referred to as *asymmetric synthesis*. As an example of an asymmetric synthesis in which one of the reactants is optically active, consider the aldol condensation of D-glyceraldehyde and dihydroxyacetone.

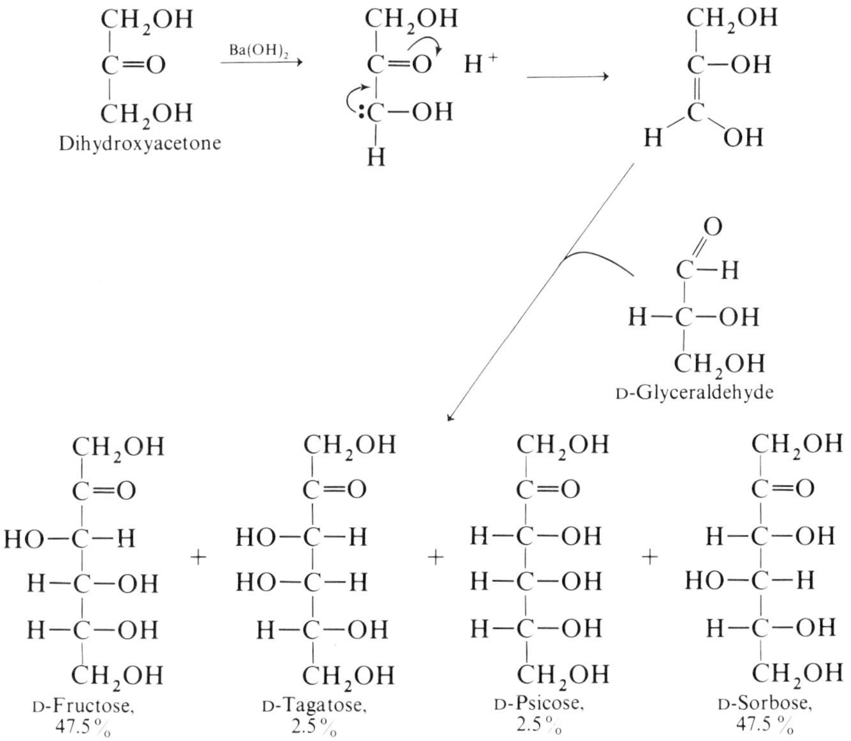

$$\begin{array}{c}CH_2OH\\|\\C=O\\|\\CH_2OH\end{array}\xrightarrow{Ba(OH)_2}\begin{array}{c}CH_2OH\\|\\C=O\\|\\:C-OH\\|\\H\end{array}\;H^+\longrightarrow\begin{array}{c}CH_2OH\\|\\C-OH\\\|\\C\\H\phantom{x}OH\end{array}$$

Dihydroxyacetone

$$\begin{array}{c}O\\\|\\C-H\\|\\H-C-OH\\|\\CH_2OH\end{array}$$

D-Glyceraldehyde

$$\begin{array}{c}CH_2OH\\|\\C=O\\|\\HO-C-H\\|\\H-C-OH\\|\\H-C-OH\\|\\CH_2OH\end{array}+\begin{array}{c}CH_2OH\\|\\C=O\\|\\HO-C-H\\|\\HO-C-H\\|\\H-C-OH\\|\\CH_2OH\end{array}+\begin{array}{c}CH_2OH\\|\\C=O\\|\\H-C-OH\\|\\H-C-OH\\|\\H-C-OH\\|\\CH_2OH\end{array}+\begin{array}{c}CH_2OH\\|\\C=O\\|\\H-C-OH\\|\\HO-C-H\\|\\H-C-OH\\|\\CH_2OH\end{array}$$

D-Fructose, 47.5%    D-Tagatose, 2.5%    D-Psicose, 2.5%    D-Sorbose, 47.5%

The principal products of this condensation are the diastereoisomers D-fructose and D-sorbose. Since *two* new centers of dissymmetry are created as a result of the condensation, *two pairs* of diastereoisomers are possible. One of each of these diastereoisomeric pairs is obtained in greater amount than the other member of that pair in each case. The diastereoisomers that predominate can be shown to be those favored on the basis of the configurations that are established at the new centers of dissymmetry. If the substituents that interact as a result of rotation about a carbon-carbon bond are designated as S (the smallest), M (the medium-sized), and L (the largest), the sinclinal conformations about that carbon-carbon bond can be represented as shown.

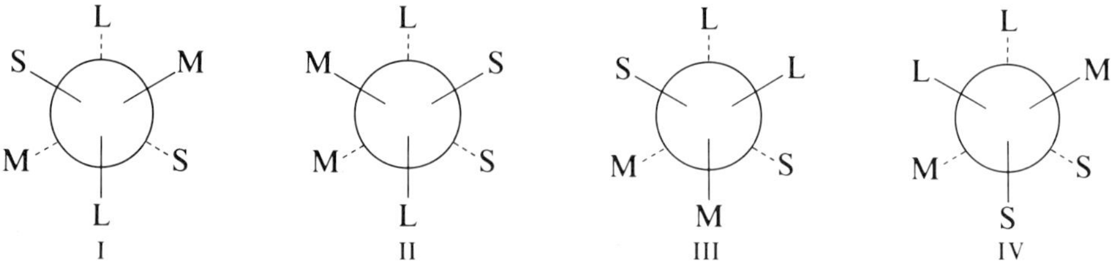

|  I  |  II  |  III  |  IV  |
|---|---|---|---|
| top: L, S–M, M–S, bottom: L | top: L, M–S, M–S, bottom: L | top: L, S–L, M–S, bottom: M | top: L, L–M, M–S, bottom: S |

Since interactions between two medium-sized groups are unfavorable and interactions between two large groups are *very* unfavorable, the conformation represented by I is the most favored thermodynamically particularly because the forces of repulsion between atoms vary with the inverse twelfth power of the interatomic distance and hence small differences in interatomic distances result in large differences in the interaction energies involved. When one considers the condensation reaction between dihydroxyacetone and D-glyceraldehyde, the conformations about the C(3)—C(4) carbon-carbon bond can be represented as follows:

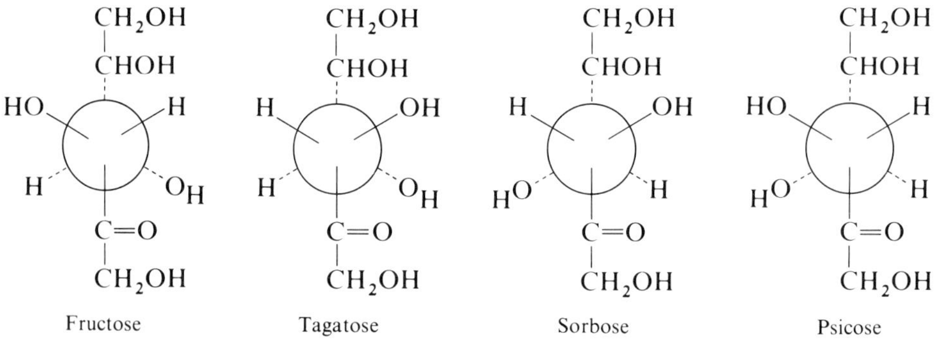

Fructose, Tagatose, Sorbose, Psicose

Thus it is seen that the conformations at the newly created dissymmetric centers are those which are thermodynamically favored.

The conversion of optically inactive reactants to optically active products requires the participation of an optically active chemical or physical agent. An optically active chemical agent that functions in this capacity is generally considered to be a catalyst. As an example of an asymmetric synthesis in which the reactants are optically inactive while an optically active catalyst is involved, consider the reaction of an aldehyde with HCN in the presence of the catalyst quinine. An initial complex formation between the aldehyde and the protonated base polarizes the carbonyl group, thus making the carbonyl carbon atom more electrophilic. The resulting complex, which is optically active, is then attacked by cyanide ion. This attack, which is the rate-determining step, can either be upon the *si* face or the *re* face of the trigonal carbon atom. However, the corresponding transition-state complexes are diastereoisomeric. Therefore, one will be of lower energy than the other, and hence one will be attained with greater frequency than the other. The corresponding products resulting from the collapse of these diastereoisomeric transition-state complexes will thus be obtained in unequal amounts.

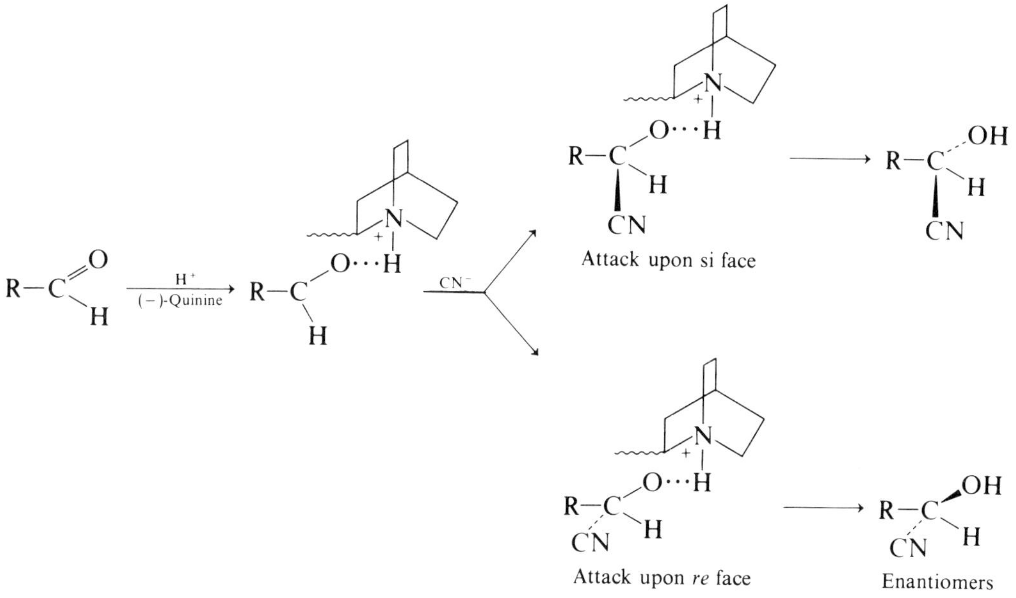

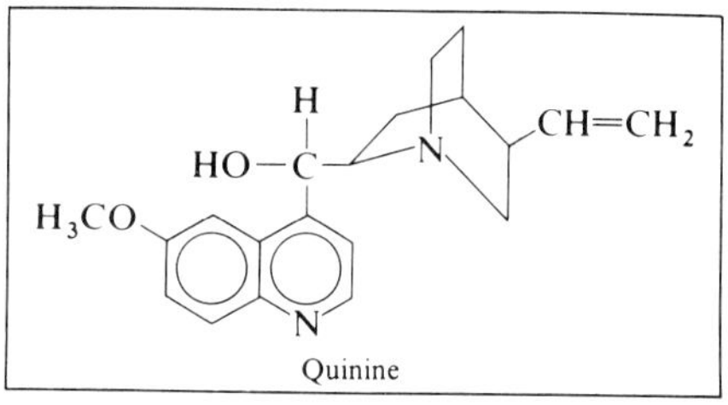

## DIASTEREOISOMERIC TRANSITION STATES IN ENZYMATIC REACTIONS

Diastereoisomeric transition states are also a factor in enzymatic reactions. Enzymes are the catalysts that participate in biochemical reactions. Since all enzymes are proteins, and since all proteins are optically active, an enzymatic reaction may yield a specific enantiomer even when the reactant is optically inactive.

Another situation involving diastereoisomeric transition states is that in which a reactant embodying two apparently identical substituents undergoes an enzymatic reaction in which a specific one of these substituents is acted upon while the other is not. Consider, for example, the dehydration of the metabolic intermediate citrate.

## 80 MECHANISMS OF METABOLISM

The citrate molecule, which is optically inactive, embodies two apparently identical carboxymethylene groups. However, citrate undergoes an enzymatic dehydration in which a specific one of the two hydrogen atoms of a specific one of the two carboxymethylene groups is eliminated as a proton. This type of specificity has, in fact, been observed in other enzymatic reactions. In order to rationalize such observations, certain criteria have been proposed for determining the circumstances under which two apparently identical substituents can be differentiated. According to one such proposal, which has been found to be quite useful, if a three-dimensional representation of a molecule containing two (or more) apparently identical groups, $a'$ and $a''$, can be repositioned in such a manner that $a'$ assumes the original position of $a''$ while $a''$ assumes the original position of $a'$ *and* this second arrangement is otherwise indistinguishable from the first, $a'$ and $a''$ *cannot* be differentiated using either optically active or optically inactive reagents or catalysts. However, if the three-dimensional representation of the molecule cannot be repositioned as described, $a'$

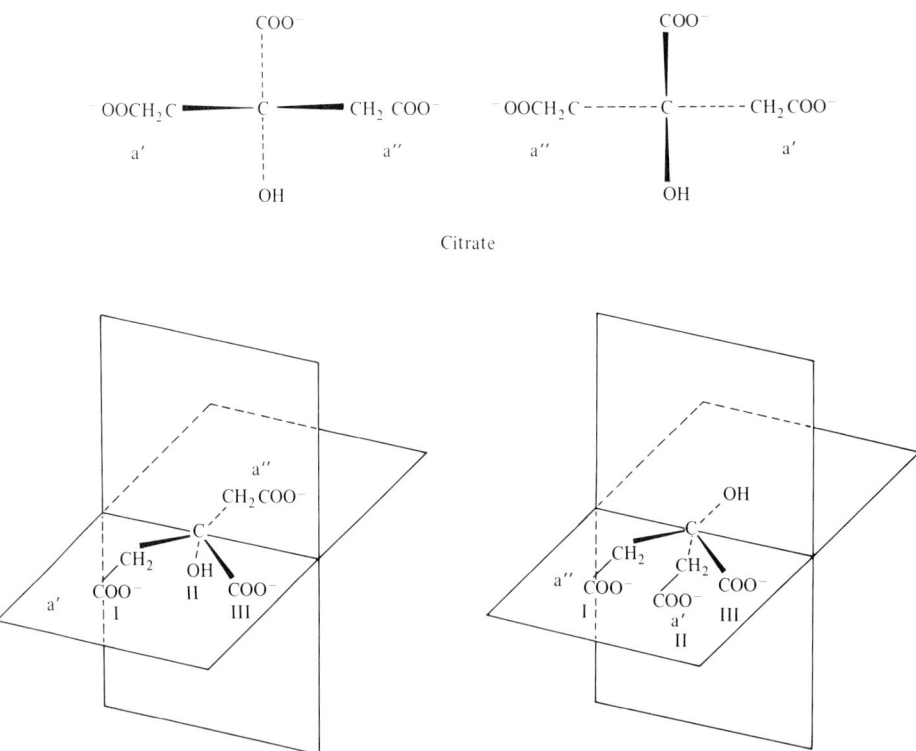

**Figure 2-8** If it is assumed that the functional groups of the citrate molecule must interact with binding sites I, II, and III on the enzyme surface, when the $a'$ carboxymethylene group is replaced by the $a''$ carboxylmethylene group, by means of counterclockwise rotation about the axis of the central carbon atom and the bond joining the carboxylate group, binding site II is no longer able to interact with the hydroxyl group, although binding site III can still interact with the carboxylate group. Thus, the repositioning of the citrate molecule (on the enzyme surface) does not yield an arrangement that is indistinguishable from the first.

and $a''$ can be differentiated using an optically active reagent or catalyst.† Differentiation is not possible using an optically inactive agent, however. The basis for differentiation using an optically active agent is that the interaction of $a'$ with the dissymmetric species produces a transition-state complex that is diastereoisomeric with respect to that resulting from the interaction of $a''$ with this molecule. This is illustrated for the case of citrate in Fig. 2-8, where it is seen that repositioning the molecule so that $a''$ assumes the original position of $a'$ yields an arrangement that is, in fact, distinguishable from the first arrangement. The two enzyme-citrate complexes are diastereomeric since they are dissymmetric but not mirror images of each other.

With respect to the two structures of citrate, at the top of Fig. 2-8 it is seen that functional group $a'$ can be made to assume the position originally assumed by $a''$ but an additional operation is required for the second arrangement to be indistinguishable from the first. The additional operation is reflection in a plane passing through the axis about which the original structure was rotated. When substituents can be interchanged only by the combined operations of rotation and reflection (rather than by rotation alone), they are said to be *enantiotopic*. Thus, the two carboxymethylene groups of citrate are enantiotopic.

With respect to the two methylene carbon atoms of a carboxymethylene group of citrate, it can be shown that rotations which allow one atom to assume the position originally occupied by the other again yield arrangements that are distinguishable. However, in this case not even rotation plus reflection in a plane passing through the axis of rotation can generate the original arrangement. Under such circumstances the substituents are called *diastereotopic*. In a reaction that could involve two (or more) diastereotopic substituents an optically active catalyst, or other agent, is not required for one substituent to react preferentially with respect to the other.

† Hirschmann, H. (1960) *J. Biol. Chem.* **235**, 2762–2767.

CHAPTER
# THREE

## THE CHEMISTRY OF CARBOHYDRATES

In this chapter some of the chemical characteristics of carbohydrates are discussed. In subsequent chapters it will be seen that many of these characteristics influence the behavior of the carbohydrates during their participation in various metabolic pathways. Following a listing of common aldopentoses and aldohexoses (Fig. 3-1), some of the procedures for the laboratory synthesis of carbohydrates are discussed.

Aldopentoses:

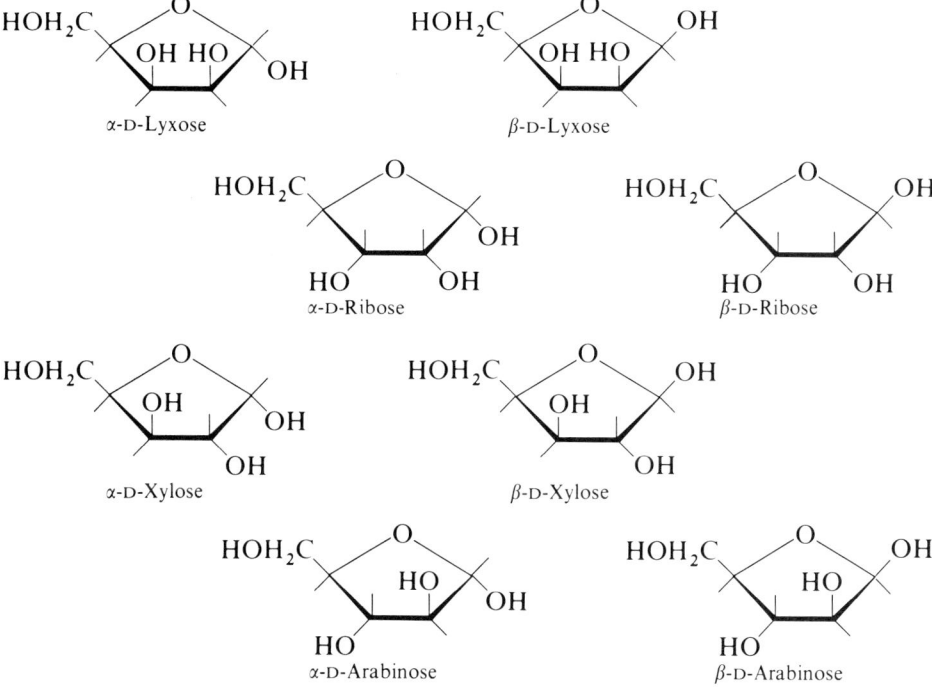

Aldohexoses:

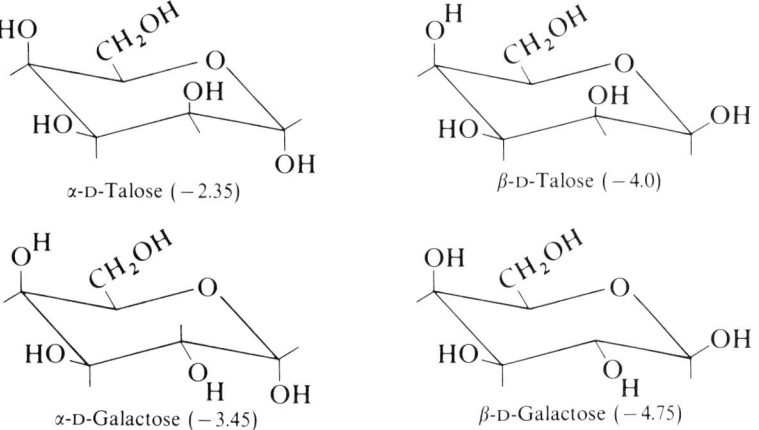

**Figure 3-1** The common aldopentoses and aldohexoses. The difference between the interaction energies of the normal and alternative conformations are given (in kilocalories per mole) for the aldohexoses. A negative value indicates that the normal conformation is the more stable. When the difference exceeds 2 kcal/mol only the more stable conformation is shown. [*Data from Capon, B. (1969) Chem. Rev.* **69**, 407–498.]

**84** MECHANISMS OF METABOLISM

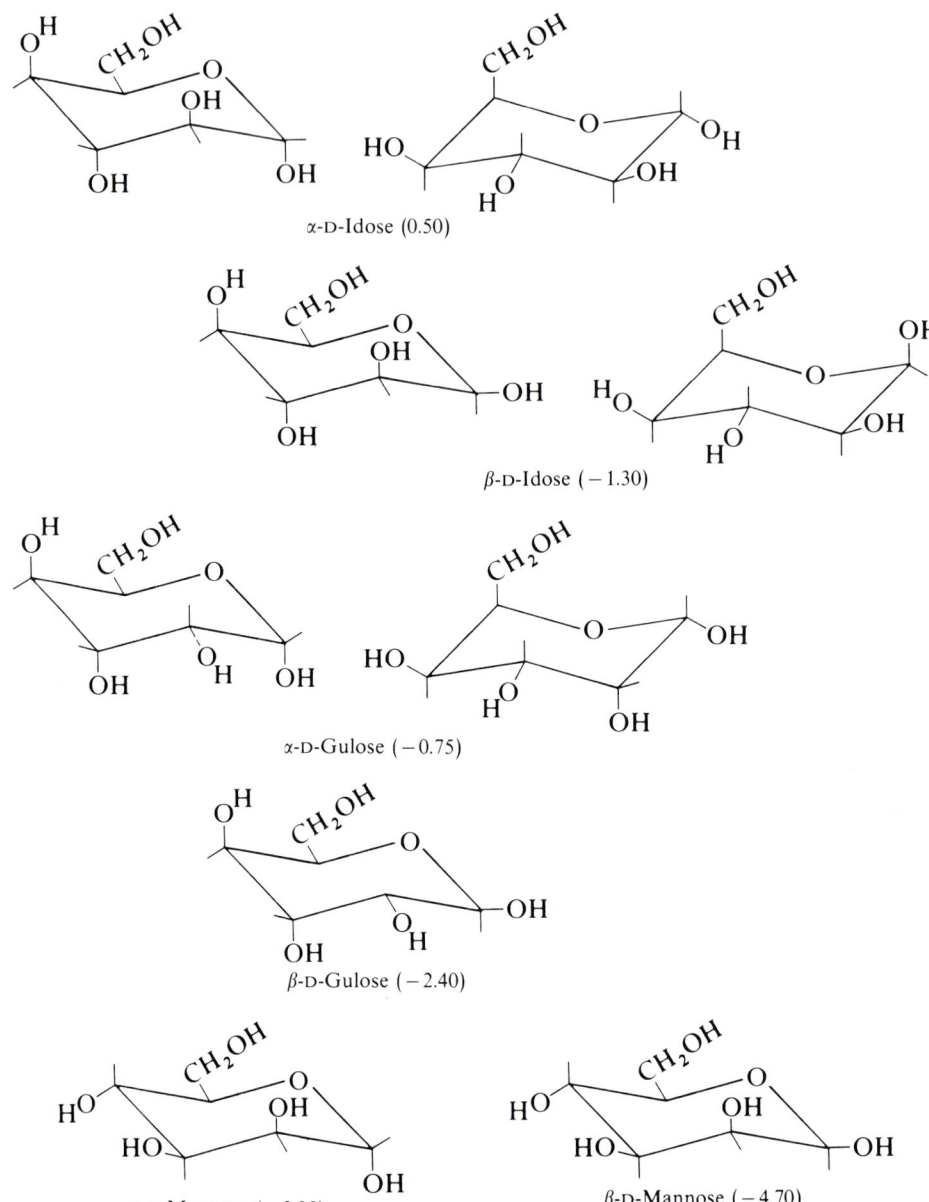

Figure 3-1 (*continued*)

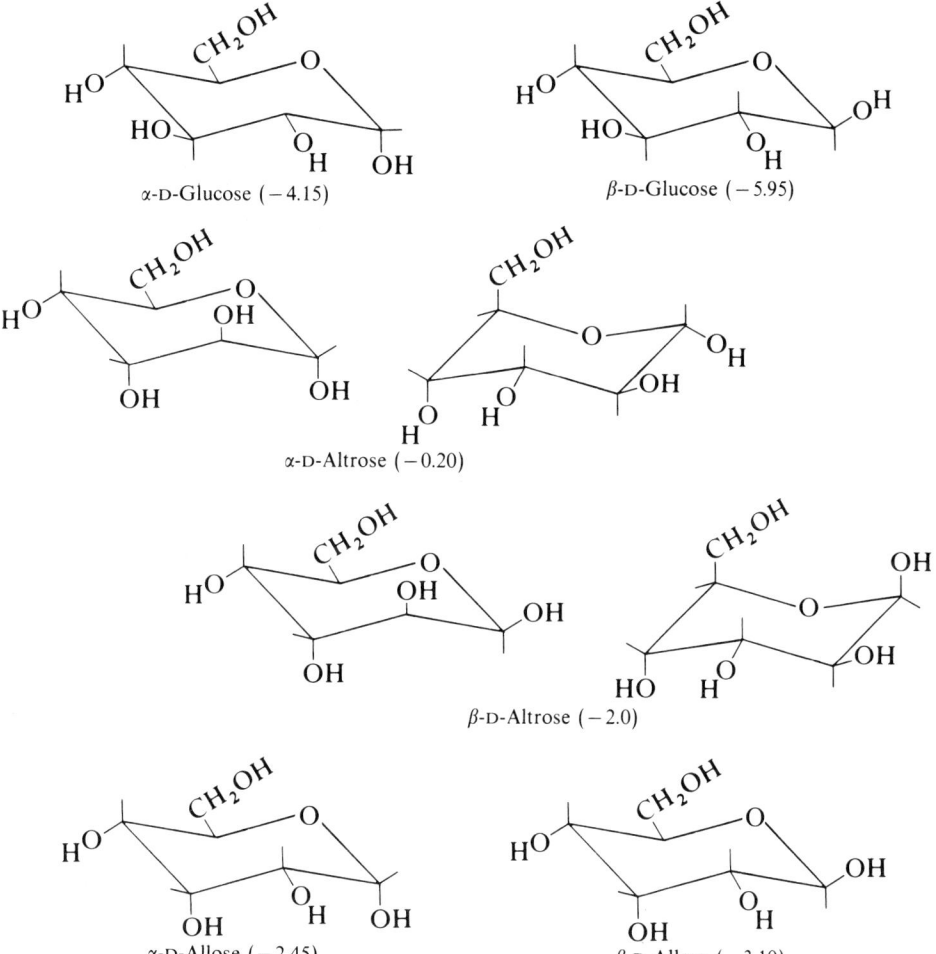

Figure 3-1 (continued)

## SYNTHESIS OF MONOSACCHARIDES

In 1885 Heinrich Kiliani reported the reaction of cyanide with a hydrolysate of inulin, a polysaccharide composed of D-fructose units. The product of this reaction was the cyanohydrin derived from fructose. When this cyanohydrin was hydrolyzed to yield the corresponding hydroxy acid and the carboxyl group was subsequently reduced to an aldehyde group, a monosaccharide with seven carbon atoms was obtained. This sequence consisting of cyanohydrin formation, hydrolysis of the nitrile, and reduction of the carboxyl group has since become known as the *Kiliani synthesis*. If the synthesis is begun with D-glyceraldehyde, all the aldotrioses, aldotetroses, aldopentoses, and aldohexoses of the D configuration can be obtained.

The reaction of cyanide ion with the carbonyl carbon atom of an aldehyde group is initiated by a nucleophilic attack by the carbon atom of this ion. Cyanide ion is an ambident species, and either the carbon atom or the nitrogen atom can be the reactive site. Generally, in reactions that proceed by means of unimolecular mechanisms cyanide ion undergoes reaction at the more electronegative nitrogen atom, while in bimolecular displacement reactions it is usually the carbon atom that attacks the electrophilic center (Fig. 3-2).

Monosaccharides can also be prepared by means of aldol condensation reactions. For example, the condensation of D-glyceraldehyde and dihydroxyacetone yields predominantly a mixture of D-fructose and D-sorbose, as discussed in Chap. 2.

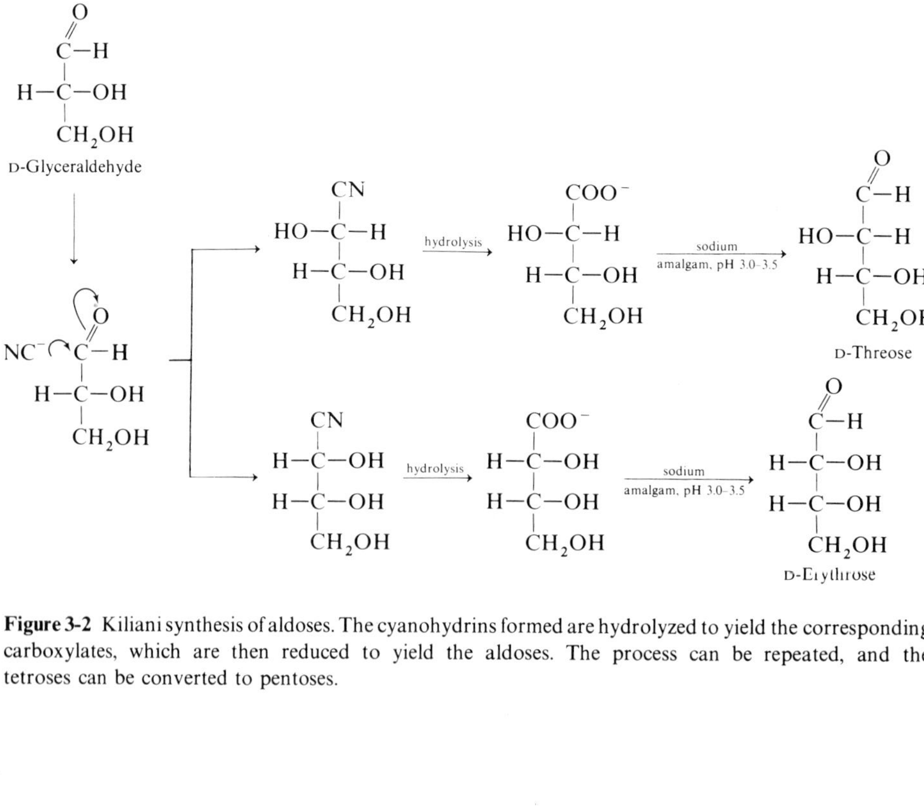

**Figure 3-2** Kiliani synthesis of aldoses. The cyanohydrins formed are hydrolyzed to yield the corresponding carboxylates, which are then reduced to yield the aldoses. The process can be repeated, and the tetroses can be converted to pentoses.

Another example of this procedure is found in the condensation of D-glyceraldehyde and glycolaldehyde. In this instance, the pentoses D-arabinose and D-xylose are obtained as the principal products.

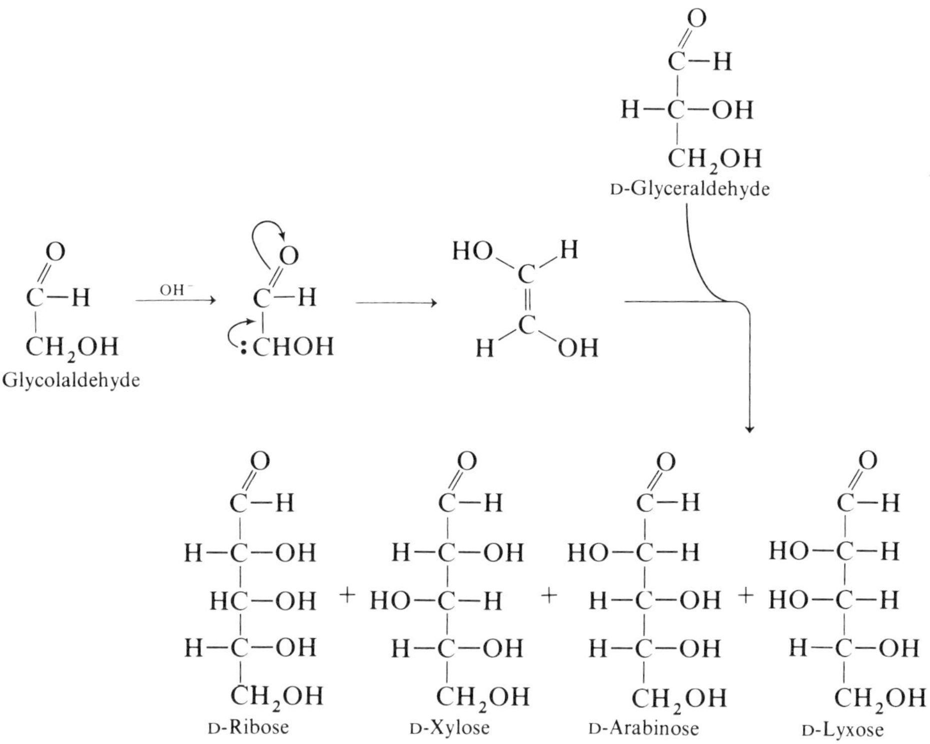

$$
\begin{array}{c}
\text{O} \\
\| \\
\text{C—H} \\
|\\
\text{CH}_2\text{OH} \\
\text{Glycolaldehyde}
\end{array}
\xrightarrow{\text{OH}^-}
\begin{array}{c}
\text{O} \\
\| \\
\text{C—H} \\
|\\
\text{:CHOH}
\end{array}
\longrightarrow
\begin{array}{c}
\text{HO}\quad\text{H} \\
\diagdown\;\diagup \\
\text{C} \\
\| \\
\text{C} \\
\diagup\;\diagdown \\
\text{H}\quad\text{OH}
\end{array}
$$

D-Glyceraldehyde:
$$
\begin{array}{c}
\text{O} \\
\| \\
\text{C—H} \\
|\\
\text{H—C—OH} \\
|\\
\text{CH}_2\text{OH}
\end{array}
$$

Products:

| D-Ribose | D-Xylose | D-Arabinose | D-Lyxose |
|---|---|---|---|
| CHO<br>H—C—OH<br>H—C—OH<br>H—C—OH<br>CH₂OH | CHO<br>H—C—OH<br>HO—C—H<br>H—C—OH<br>CH₂OH | CHO<br>HO—C—H<br>H—C—OH<br>H—C—OH<br>CH₂OH | CHO<br>HO—C—H<br>HO—C—H<br>H—C—OH<br>CH₂OH |

In addition, monosaccharides can be prepared by using reagents such as nitromethane, diazomethane, and ethynylmagnesium bromide, among others.

Nitromethane synthesis:

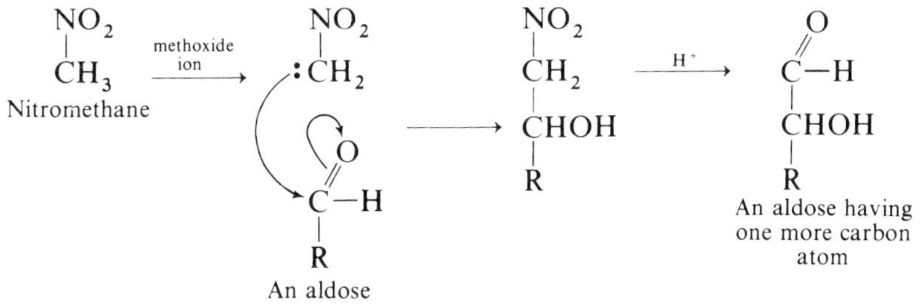

$$
\underset{\text{Nitromethane}}{\begin{array}{c}\text{NO}_2\\|\\ \text{CH}_3\end{array}}
\xrightarrow{\text{methoxide ion}}
\begin{array}{c}\text{NO}_2\\|\\ \text{:CH}_2\end{array}
+ \underset{\text{An aldose}}{\begin{array}{c}\text{O}\\\|\\ \text{C—H}\\|\\ \text{R}\end{array}}
\longrightarrow
\begin{array}{c}\text{NO}_2\\|\\ \text{CH}_2\\|\\ \text{CHOH}\\|\\ \text{R}\end{array}
\xrightarrow{\text{H}^+}
\underset{\substack{\text{An aldose having}\\ \text{one more carbon}\\ \text{atom}}}{\begin{array}{c}\text{O}\\\|\\ \text{C—H}\\|\\ \text{CHOH}\\|\\ \text{R}\end{array}}
$$

Diazomethane synthesis:

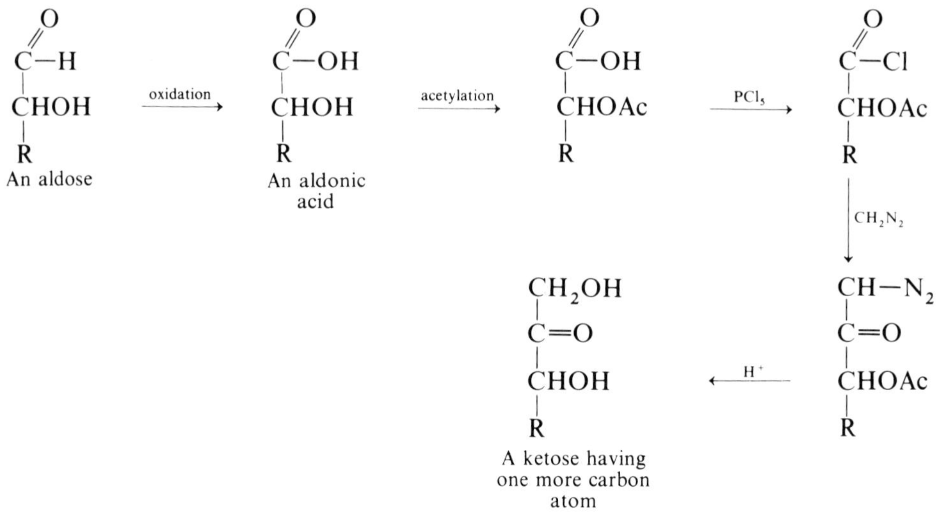

$$\underset{\text{An aldose}}{\overset{\text{O}}{\underset{\text{R}}{\overset{\|}{\text{C}}-\text{H}}}\atop\text{CHOH}} \xrightarrow{\text{oxidation}} \underset{\substack{\text{An aldonic}\\\text{acid}}}{\overset{\text{O}}{\underset{\text{R}}{\overset{\|}{\text{C}}-\text{OH}}}\atop\text{CHOH}} \xrightarrow{\text{acetylation}} \underset{\text{R}}{\overset{\text{O}}{\overset{\|}{\text{C}}-\text{OH}}\atop\text{CHOAc}} \xrightarrow{\text{PCl}_5} \underset{\text{R}}{\overset{\text{O}}{\overset{\|}{\text{C}}-\text{Cl}}\atop\text{CHOAc}}$$

$$\downarrow \text{CH}_2\text{N}_2$$

$$\underset{\substack{\text{A ketose having}\\\text{one more carbon}\\\text{atom}}}{\overset{\text{CH}_2\text{OH}}{\underset{\text{R}}{\text{C}=\text{O}}}\atop\text{CHOH}} \xleftarrow{\text{H}^+} \underset{\text{R}}{\overset{\text{CH}-\text{N}_2}{\text{C}=\text{O}}\atop\text{CHOAc}}$$

Ethynylmagnesium bromide synthesis:

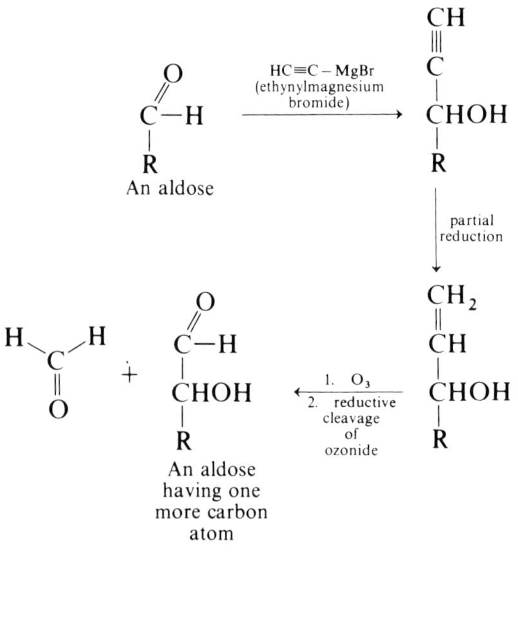

$$\underset{\text{An aldose}}{\overset{\text{O}}{\underset{\text{R}}{\overset{\|}{\text{C}}-\text{H}}}} \xrightarrow[\substack{\text{(ethynylmagnesium}\\\text{bromide)}}]{\text{HC}\equiv\text{C}-\text{MgBr}} \underset{\text{R}}{\overset{\text{CH}}{\underset{\|}{\text{C}}}\atop\text{CHOH}}$$

$$\downarrow \substack{\text{partial}\\\text{reduction}}$$

$$\underset{\substack{\text{An aldose}\\\text{having one}\\\text{more carbon}\\\text{atom}}}{\overset{\text{O}}{\underset{\text{R}}{\overset{\|}{\text{C}}-\text{H}}}\atop\text{CHOH}} + \overset{\text{H}}{\underset{\text{O}}{\overset{\diagdown}{\text{C}}\diagup\text{H}}} \xleftarrow[\substack{\text{2. reductive}\\\text{cleavage}\\\text{of}\\\text{ozonide}}]{\text{1. O}_3} \underset{\text{R}}{\overset{\text{CH}_2}{\underset{\|}{\text{CH}}}\atop\text{CHOH}}$$

## REACTIONS OF SACCHARIDES

The saccharides are hydroxy aldehydes or hydroxy ketones or their derivatives. Although these aldoses and ketoses exist predominantly in the form of internal hemiacetals or hemiketals, they readily react with the common carbonyl reagents.

## Reactions of Saccharides with Carbonyl Reagents

The carbonyl group of a saccharide can react with hydrazine (or a substituted hydrazine), hydroxylamine, or semicarbazide. In each instance, a nucleophilic nitrogen atom of the reagent attacks the carbonyl carbon atom of the saccharide, with the result that a carbinolamine is formed. The carbinolamine can in turn undergo dehydration to yield the corresponding Schiff base. Usually a plot of the pH of the reaction medium as a function of the rate of Schiff base formation exhibits a maximum. This is generally interpreted as indicating that a change in the rate-determining process occurs as the pH of the medium is varied. Such a change can be rationalized as follows. At a lower pH when the concentration of the nonprotonated nitrogen base is low, the rate-determining step of the overall process is the nucleophilic attack by the base upon the carbonyl carbon atom. However, at high pH the dehydration of the carbinolamine becomes rate-determining since this process is acid-catalyzed. In practice, it is found that the formation of the Schiff base occurs at the maximal rate when the pH of the medium is between 4 and 5.

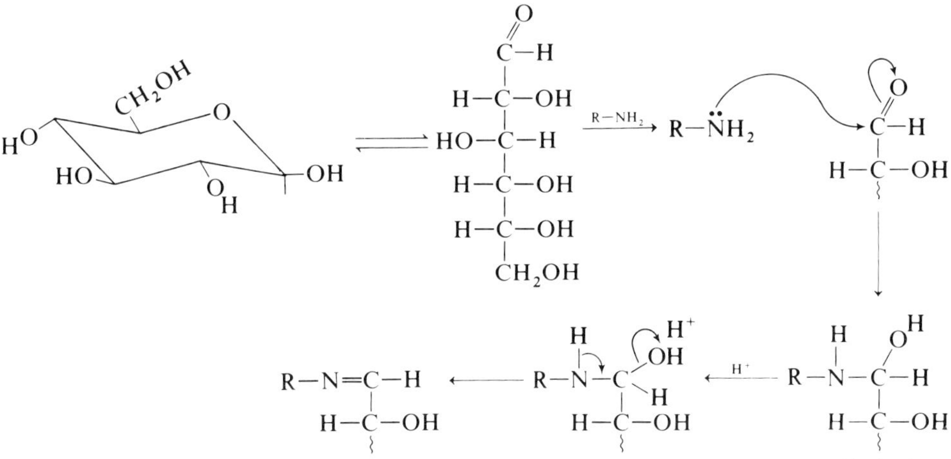

where R = $H_2N-$ = hydrazine

R = ⟨◯⟩$-NH-$ = phenylhydrazine

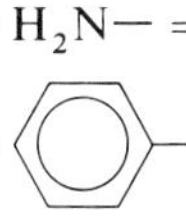

R = $HO-$ = hydroxylamine

R = $NH_2-N-C-$ (with H and O) = semicarbazide

When a saccharide reacts with a hydrazine, a hydrazone is formed. On the other hand, reaction of a saccharide and hydroxylamine yields an oxime, and a semicarbazone is formed as the result of the reaction of a saccharide and semicarbazide.

**Geometrical isomers of hydrazones, oximes, and semicarbazides** Each of these derivatives can exist in either a syn or an anti conformation although frequently a single isomer is obtained. Usually it is the isomer that is thermodynamically more stable, although in the formation of certain 2,4-dinitrophenylhydrazones the rate-determined product is generally isolated because equilibrium is attained very slowly.

$$\begin{array}{cc} \underset{R}{\overset{H}{\diagdown}}C=N\underset{}{\overset{}{\diagdown}}R' & \underset{R}{\overset{H}{\diagdown}}C=N\underset{}{\overset{R'}{\diagup}} \\ \text{Syn configuration} & \text{Anti configuration} \end{array}$$

Nuclear magnetic resonance (NMR) studies,† among others, have been used in an attempt to distinguish between syn and anti forms of the hydrazones, oximes, and semicarbazones. As an example of studies of this type it has been shown that in aldehyde derivatives the hydrogen atom that is bonded to the methenyl carbon atom achieves resonance at a higher magnetic field strength when the configuration is anti than when it is syn because the hydrogen atom concerned is more shielded in the anti configuration.

One of the most widely used derivatives of the aldoses and the ketoses is the osazone. Osazones are 1,2-bishydrazones. These derivatives are formed as a result of the reaction of the saccharide with at least three molar quantities of the hydrazine. The saccharide reacts initially with the first molecule of the hydrazine to form a hydrazone. Subsequently, a rearrangement similar to an Amadori rearrangement occurs. The question has been raised whether the saccharide reacts with a second molecule of the hydrazine before this rearrangement or after. Prior rearrangement is depicted in mechanism A, and subsequent rearrangement is depicted in mechanism B below. In either case, the carbonyl group thus generated, would react with the third molecule of the hydrazine to yield the 1,2-bishydrazone, or osazone.

---

† When an atom having a nucleus that has a magnetic moment is placed in a magnetic field, the nucleus tends to align itself with that field. Because the nucleus has spin angular momentum, it does not change its mean orientation with respect to the magnetic field; instead its spin axis precesses around the direction of the applied field. Reorientation of the precessing nucleus with respect to the magnetic field can be effected by allowing the nucleus to interact with a second magnetic field at right angles with the first magnetic field. This second magnetic field must be of the same frequency and phase as the precessional motion of the nucleus. When these conditions are fulfilled, the nucleus absorbs energy and reorients itself. The frequency that allows this absorption of energy and the reorientation is called the *resonance frequency*. The procedure by which this resonance frequency is determined is called NMR spectroscopy. NMR spectroscopy studies can be conducted on compounds containing hydrogen ($^1H$), phosphorus ($^{31}P$), fluorine ($^{19}F$), and the isotope $^{13}C$.

In order to examine a compound by NMR spectroscopy the sample is placed in a strong uniform magnetic field $H_0$. An electromagnetic frequency is then applied in such a way that its magnetic component $H_1$ is at an angle of 90° with respect to $H_0$. Now one of the magnetic fields is varied. In actual practice the electromagnetic frequency $H_1$ is held constant, and $H_0$ is swept over the desired range. When the sweeping field achieves the resonance frequency and the nucleus absorbs energy, this is detected by the spectrometer and an NMR signal is recorded.

The resonance frequency is a characteristic not only of the particular nucleus but also of the chemical environment of that nucleus. The electron density in the vicinity of the nucleus concerned is one of the several factors that dictates the resonance frequency. The electron density contributes to the magnitude of the magnetic screening of the nucleus. When a nucleus is highly screened, e.g., in an environment characterized by a high electron density, the nucleus is said to be *shielded*. Nuclei that are less screened are said to be *deshielded*. For the more shielded nucleus the resonance frequency occurs at a higher magnetic field.

Mechanism A:

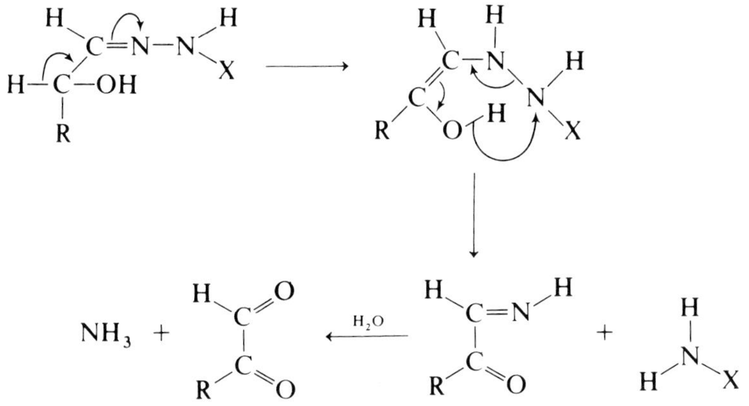

Mechanism B:

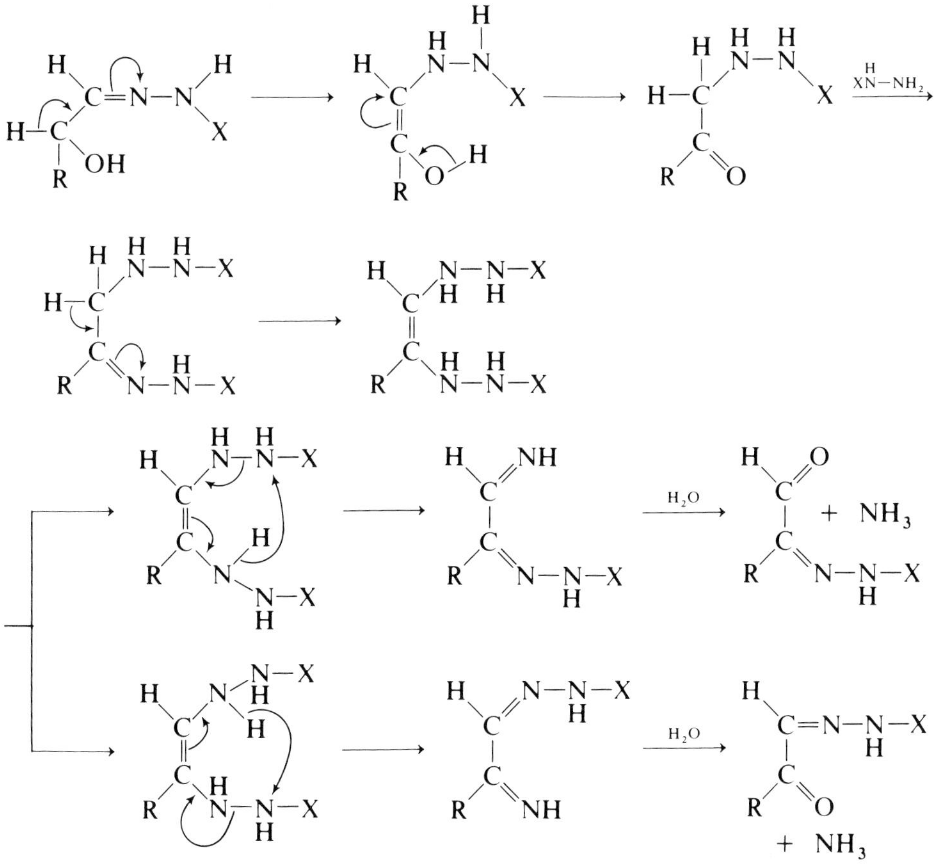

where X = H or a substituent such as 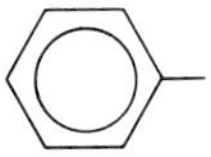

Several studies have been undertaken in an attempt to determine whether mechanism A or mechanism B is operative. One such study entailed the use of fructose *p*-nitrophenylhydrazone labeled with $^{15}N$. This derivative was then allowed to react with nonlabeled *p*-nitrophenylhydrazine. Under these conditions, if mechanism A were operative, the ammonia derived would be labeled and the osazone would not contain $^{15}N$. On the other hand, if mechanism B were operative, both the ammonia and the osazone would be labeled. When the products of this reaction were examined, it was found that virtually all the $^{15}N$ was contained in the ammonia, thus offering support for mechanism A.

NMR studies on phenylosazones have indicated that these molecules exist in intramolecularly hydrogen-bonded configurations like

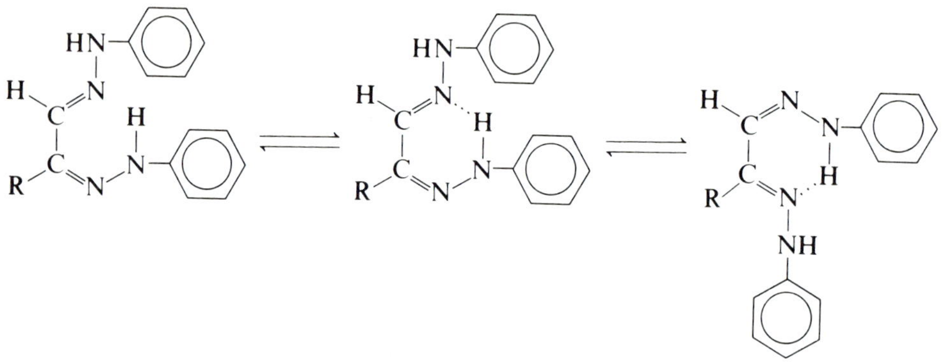

## The Periodate Oxidation of Saccharides

Since the saccharides embody vicinal hydroxyl groups, these molecules are cleaved by periodate. In the presence of the reagent $H_5IO_6$ the hydroxyl groups of the saccharide are oxidized to carbonyl groups, and, concomitantly, the periodate is reduced to iodate.

Studies on the mechanism of this reaction have shown that the major pathway involves the dehydrated species $IO_4^-$ rather than $H_5IO_6$. The reaction is formulated as an addition of the periodate monoanion to the saccharide to yield an intermediate similar to that formed in the cleavage of glycols by lead tetraacetate. In general, acyclic *threo*-diols are oxidized and cleaved more rapidly than corresponding *erythro*-diols.

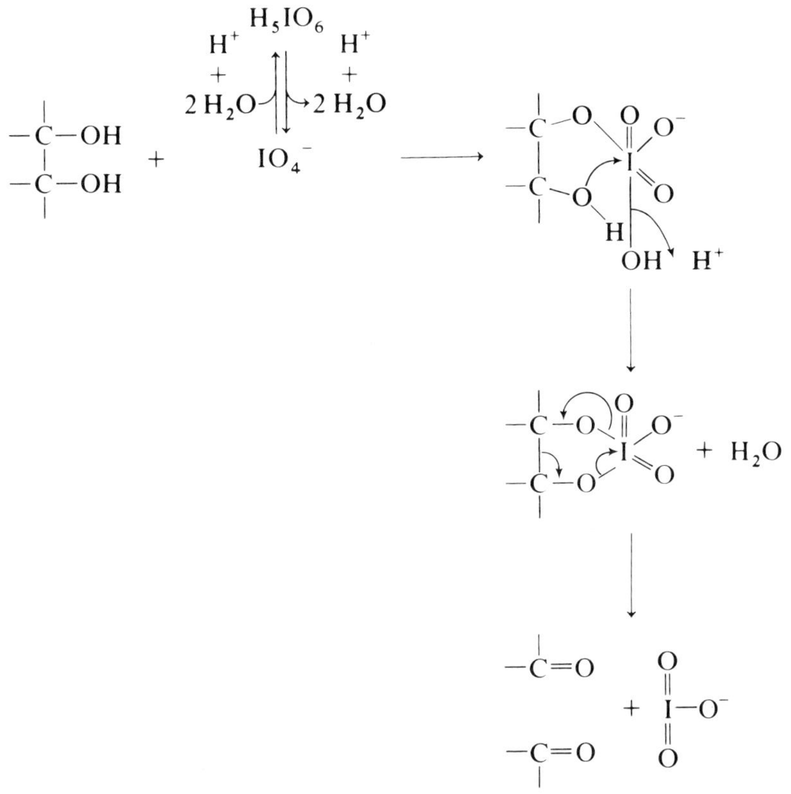

$$\begin{array}{c}-\overset{|}{\underset{|}{C}}-OH \\ -\overset{|}{\underset{|}{C}}-OH\end{array} + \begin{array}{c}H_5IO_6 \\ H^+ \quad \uparrow\downarrow \quad H^+ \\ +\quad \quad + \\ 2H_2O \rightleftharpoons 2H_2O \\ IO_4^-\end{array} \longrightarrow$$

[reaction scheme showing periodate cleavage of vicinal diol proceeding through cyclic intermediate to yield two carbonyl groups and $IO_3^-$]

## GLYCOSIDES

An *O*-glycosidic bond is derived from a hemiacetal hydroxyl group of one saccharide molecule and a hydroxyl group of another saccharide or, alternatively, the hydroxyl group of some other alcohol. Thus, *O*-glycosides are, in fact, hemiacetal or hemiketal ethers. In general, the *O*-glycosidic bonds in biochemical systems are those of oligo- and polysaccharides. In the laboratory, however, *O*-glycosides derived from a saccharide and an alcohol such as methanol are readily formed.

### Laboratory Synthesis of *O*-Glycosides

*O*-Glycosides, the hemiacetal or hemiketal ethers of saccharides, were originally synthesized in the laboratory by a reaction involving the formation of a carbonium ion at the carbonyl carbon atom. The carbonium ion was generated from a mesitoyl, acetyl, or halogen derivative of the saccharide. The carbonium ion formed is stabilized due to delocalization involving the adjacent heterocyclic oxygen atom. This carbonium ion can subsequently react with an alcohol or with the alcohol group of another saccharide to yield a simple *O*-glycoside or a compound carbohydrate, respectively.

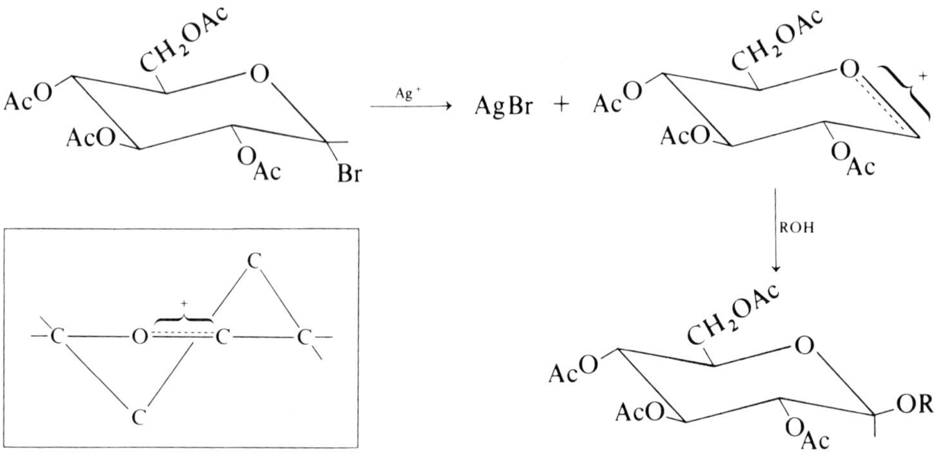

The carbonium ion derived from the saccharide is shown in the inset in the half-chair conformation. This conformation, although strained, allows the delocalization of the charge of the carbonium ion to be maximized.

Although this reaction has been shown to involve a carbonium-ion intermediate, it does not yield a random mixture of the two possible diastereomers. It has been suggested that the direction from which the alcohol component approaches and captures the carbonium ion is dictated by steric influences. For example, it was proposed that in the case of the reaction involving tetra-$O$-acetyl-$\alpha$-D-glucosyl-1-bromide the substituent at C(2) prevents the alcohol from approaching in the direction required for the formation of the $\alpha$ anomer and that for this reason the reaction proceeds with stereoselectivity to yield the $\beta$-glucoside.

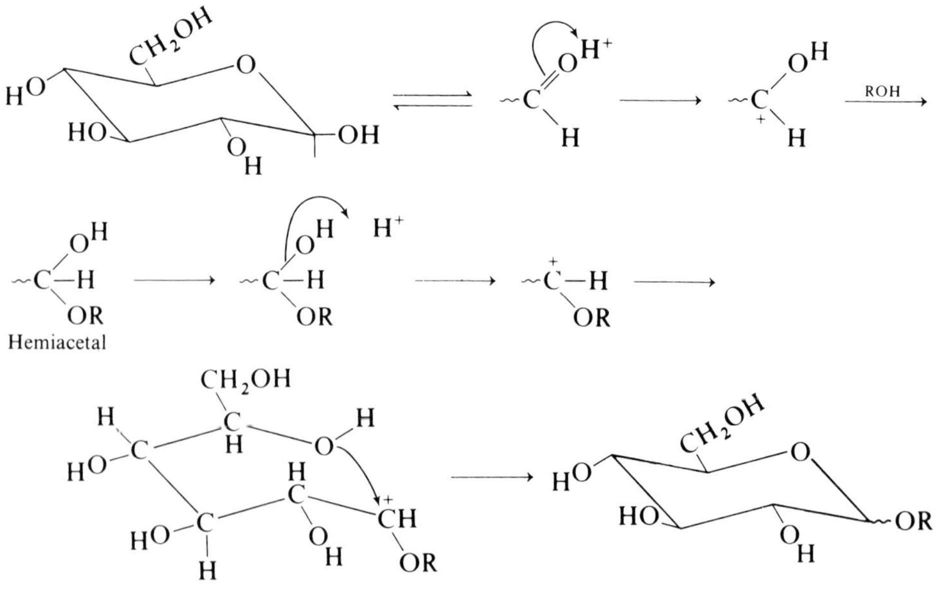

More recently the laboratory synthesis of $O$-glycosides has been accomplished by the Fischer glycoside synthesis. In this procedure the saccharide is allowed to react with the alcohol component in the presence of hydrochloric acid, a sulfonic acid, or a strong acid ion-exchange resin. Each provides a strongly acidic environment for the reaction. Although the mechanism of the synthesis has not been established unequivocally, it is generally thought to proceed by means of the formation of a hemiacetal intermediate. Hemiacetal (and also acetal) formation is known to be acid-catalyzed.

## Acid-catalyzed Hydrolysis of O-Glycosides

The acid-catalyzed hydrolysis of aldopyranosides has been shown to entail a monomolecular rate-determining step. Since the reaction is monomolecular, and since in the presence of the acid catalyst it can be considered that it is actually the conjugate acid of the glycoside that undergoes the rate-determining step, the hydrolysis can be said to proceed by means of an A1 mechanism.† Two possibilities can be envisaged, however, one involving the generation of a cyclic carbonium ion and the other, an acyclic carbonium ion. These alternatives are illustrated below.

Cyclic mechanism:

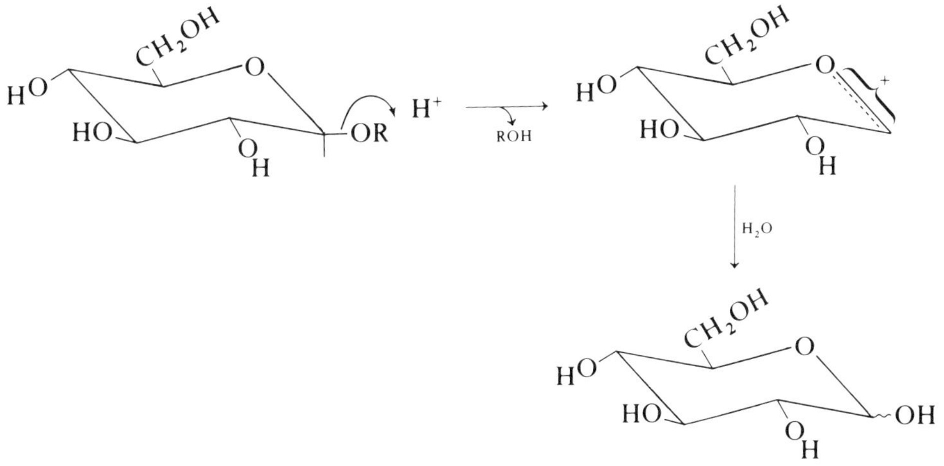

† Reactions have been classified mechanistically on the basis of the type of reaction and the molecularity of the reaction. For example, a substitution reaction that involves a nucleophilic component and is bimolecular is designated as an $S_N2$ reaction, i.e., substitution, nucleophilic, bimolecular. A substitution reaction that also involves the introduction of a nucleophilic substituent but is monomolecular is designated as an $S_N1$ reaction. In some nucleophilic substitution reactions where the leaving group must undergo protonation before its departure, the designation $S_N1cA$ or $S_N2cA$ is used (cA denotes conjugate acid). These abbreviations are usually further abbreviated to A1 or A2, respectively.

## 96 MECHANISMS OF METABOLISM

Acyclic mechanism:

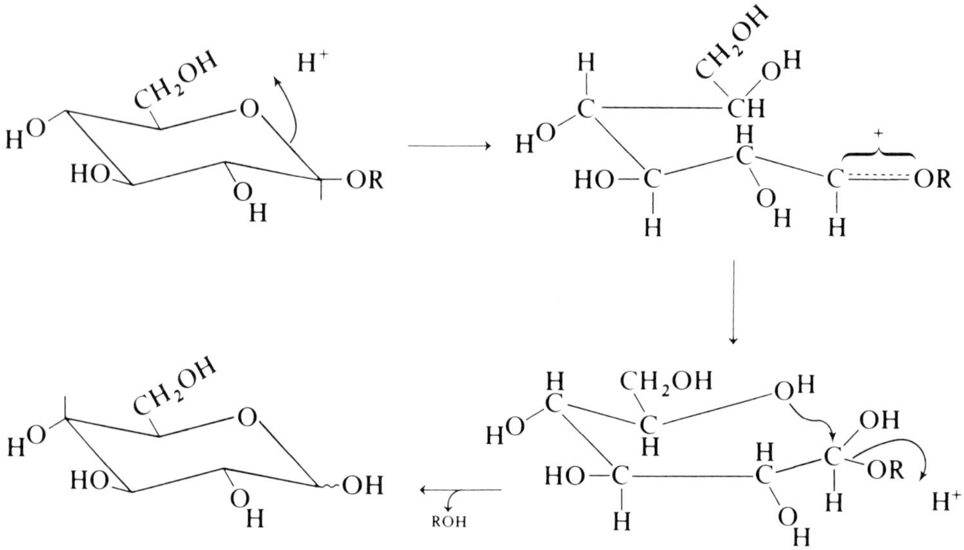

In an effort to decide between these two possibilities it was decided to determine whether or not there is a kinetic isotope effect† when the hydrolysis is conducted using a glycoside in which the glycosidic oxygen atom is labeled with $^{18}O$. If the

---

† A kinetic isotope effect is observed when an atom of a bond that is broken in the rate-determining step of a reaction is replaced by an isotope of that atom. In the presence of the isotope a different amount of energy is required to achieve the transition state. When the isotope has a greater mass than the ordinary atom, a greater amount of energy is required in order to achieve the transition state and this is reflected in a slower reaction rate. The kinetic isotope effect is usually expressed as the ratio of the reaction rate when the nonlabeled component is used and the reaction rate when the labeled component is used, i.e., $k_n/k_l$.

Consider the breaking of the C—H bond and the C—D bond. Since the zero-point energy level of the deuterium atom is lower than that of the hydrogen atom, the potential energies required for the breaking of the C—H and the C—D bonds are different. More specifically, that required for the breaking of the C—D bond is greater. In general, the magnitude of this energy difference reflects the ratio of the masses of the two isotopic atoms. Thus, one would expect that if a tritium atom rather than a deuterium atom were substituted for a hydrogen atom, a kinetic isotope effect of even greater magnitude would be observed. This has, in fact, been demonstrated and is illustrated by the listing of maximum kinetic isotope effects shown below.

**Estimated maximum kinetic isotope effects (25°C)**

| Isotopic forms | Rate, nonlabeled/labeled ($k_n/k_l$) |
|---|---|
| $^1H$ and $^3H$ | 60 |
| $^1H$ and $^2H$ | 18 |
| $^{12}C$ and $^{13}C$ | 1.25 |
| $^{16}O$ and $^{18}O$ | 1.19 |

*Source:* Laidler, K. J. (1965) *Chemical Kinetics*, p. 97, McGraw-Hill, New York, used by permission.

hydrolytic cleavage proceeds by means of the cyclic carbonium ion, the rate-determining event should be the C—O cleavage of the glycosidic bond and the rate of the reaction should be slower when a C—$^{18}$O bond must be broken. On the other hand, if the acyclic mechanism is operative, the breaking of the C—$^{18}$O glycosidic bond would not be expected to be rate-determining and one should not observe a kinetic isotope effect. When methyl-α-D-glucopyranoside appropriately labeled with $^{18}$O was hydrolyzed under acidic conditions, it was found that the rate of hydrolysis was slower than when the nonlabeled glycopyranose was employed, indicating that the breaking of the C—O glycosidic bond is rate-determining and that the reaction presumably proceeds by means of the cyclic intermediate.

In contrast to the aldopyranosides, aldofuranosides undergo acid-catalyzed hydrolysis by a bimolecular mechanism. More specifically, in this case there is evidence in support of an A2 mechanism which entails ring opening. Such a mechanism might be depicted as shown.

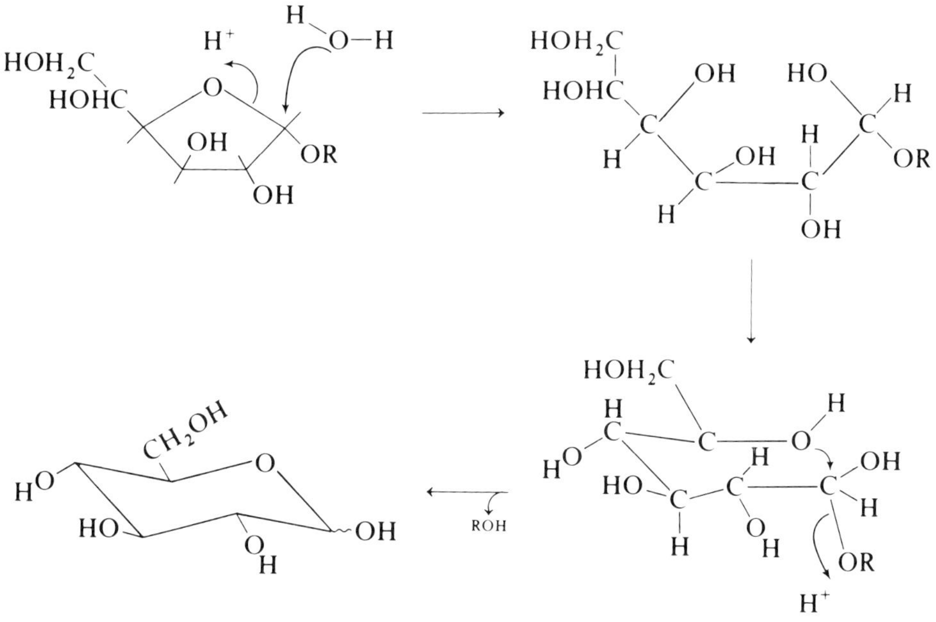

With respect to the acid-catalyzed hydrolysis of ketofuranosides it is indicated that the reaction proceeds by means of an A1 mechanism in which a tertiary carbonium ion is generated. The formation of a tertiary carbonium ion occurs with greater facility than that of a secondary carbonium ion, e.g., that which would be generated in the acid-catalyzed hydrolysis of aldopyranosides.

## Alkaline Hydrolysis of O-Glycosides

O-Glycosides are, in fact, not readily hydrolyzed in alkaline media. Furthermore, O-glycosides undergo isomerization and even fragmentation in alkaline media, and therefore it is relatively difficult to study the hydrolytic process under these conditions. However, it has been shown that in alkaline media hydrolysis is initiated by the removal of a proton from an appropriate hydroxyl group. Furthermore, it has also been shown that furanosides and pyranosides that have a hydroxyl group at C(2) which is trans with respect to the acetal ether —OR group undergo hydrolysis 2 to 10 times faster than when the relationship is cis. This difference in reactivity is attributed to neighboring-group participation, frequently referred to as *anchimeric assistance*. (The word *anchimeric* is derived from the Greek *anchi*, meaning "neighboring or adjacent," and *meros*, meaning "portion or part.") The alkaline hydrolysis of a

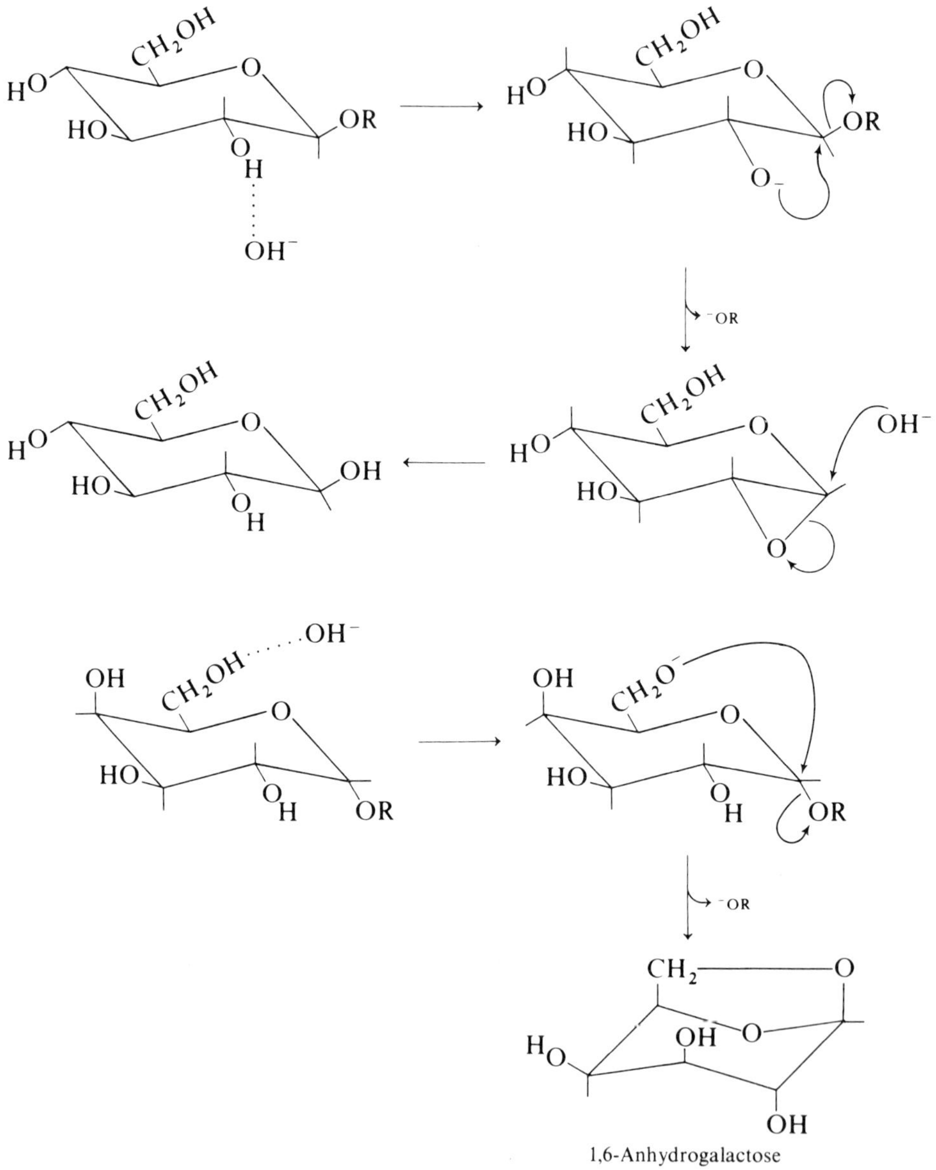

1,6-Anhydrogalactose

β-glucoside might therefore be depicted as shown. Here, because of the spatial relationship between the hydroxyl group at C(2) and the acetal ether group at C(1), formation of the epoxide intermediate is greatly facilitated. It might be mentioned at this point that under alkaline conditions an α-D-galactoside can be converted into a 1,6-anhydrogalactose.

## Laboratory Synthesis of *N*-Glycosides

*N*-Glycosides are compounds in which the hemiacetal or hemiketal oxygen atom of a saccharide is replaced by the nitrogen atom of an amine or some other nitrogen base. In the laboratory *N*-glycosides can be prepared by the reaction of an appropriately substituted glycosyl halide and an organometallic derivative of a nitrogen base. One example of such a procedure is the following reaction of the substituted ribosyl bromide and dithyminylmercury. Other organometallic derivatives, including silver salts of hydroxypyridines and chloromercury derivatives of certain purines, have been used in conjunction with various glycosyl halides.

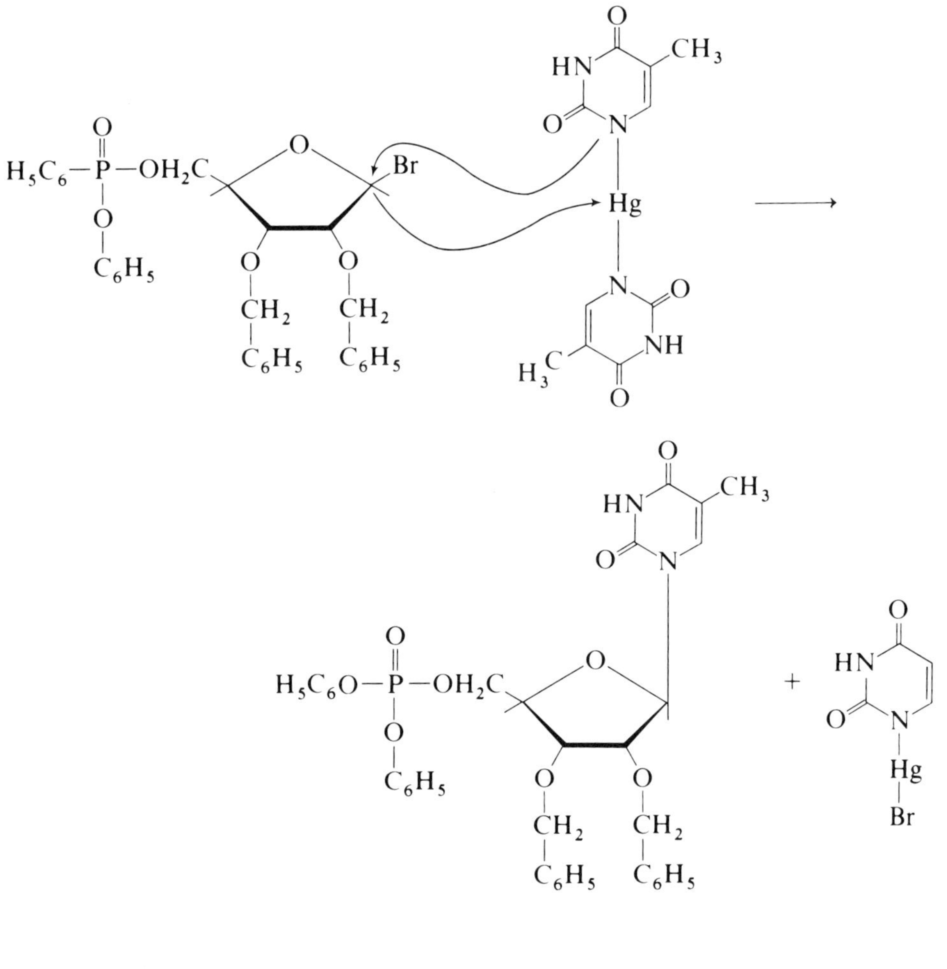

## Hydrolysis of N-Glycosides

The acid-catalyzed hydrolysis of the N-glycosidic bond of N-β-D-glucopyranosylpiperidine has been formulated as shown. In the hydrolytic cleavage of this N-glycoside a Schiff base intermediate is involved, and in the acidic reaction medium the rate-determining step in the reaction is the attack of the water molecule upon the methenyl carbon atom of the Schiff base.

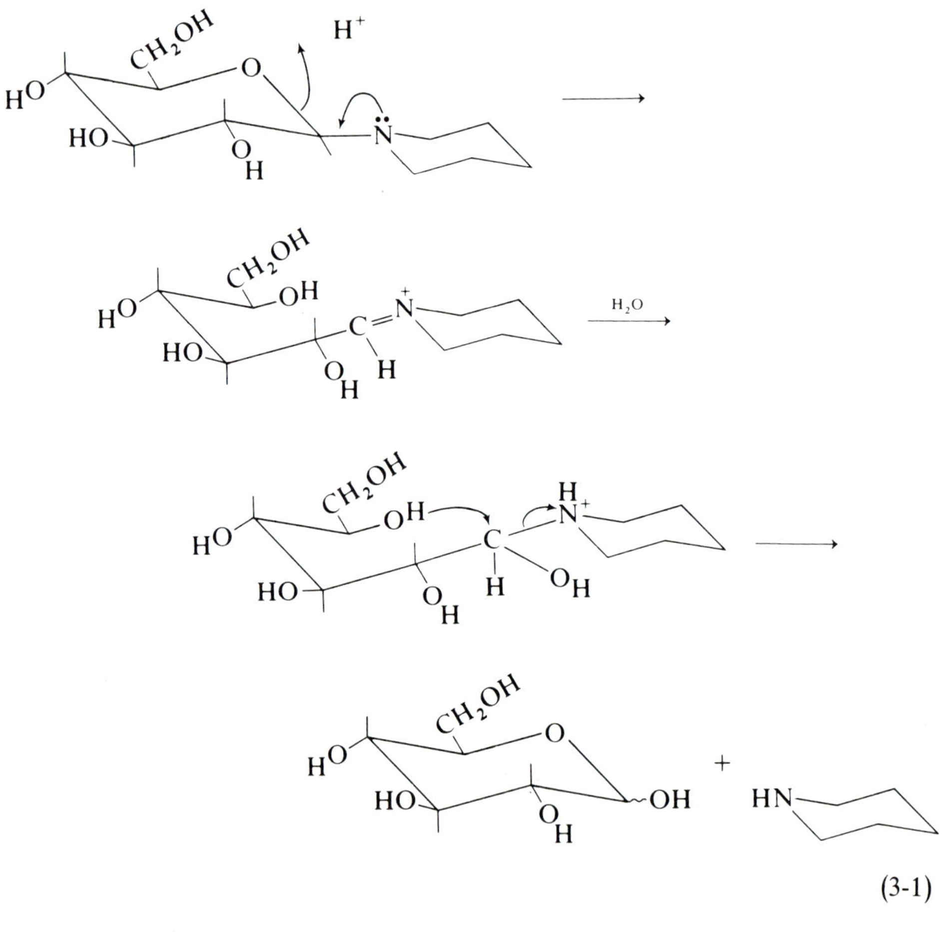

(3-1)

By contrast, the acid-catalyzed hydrolysis of the N-glycosidic bond of a nucleoside or a nucleotide is believed to entail the formation of a protonated form of the purine or pyrimidine moiety. A suggested mechanism involving such a protonated form follows.

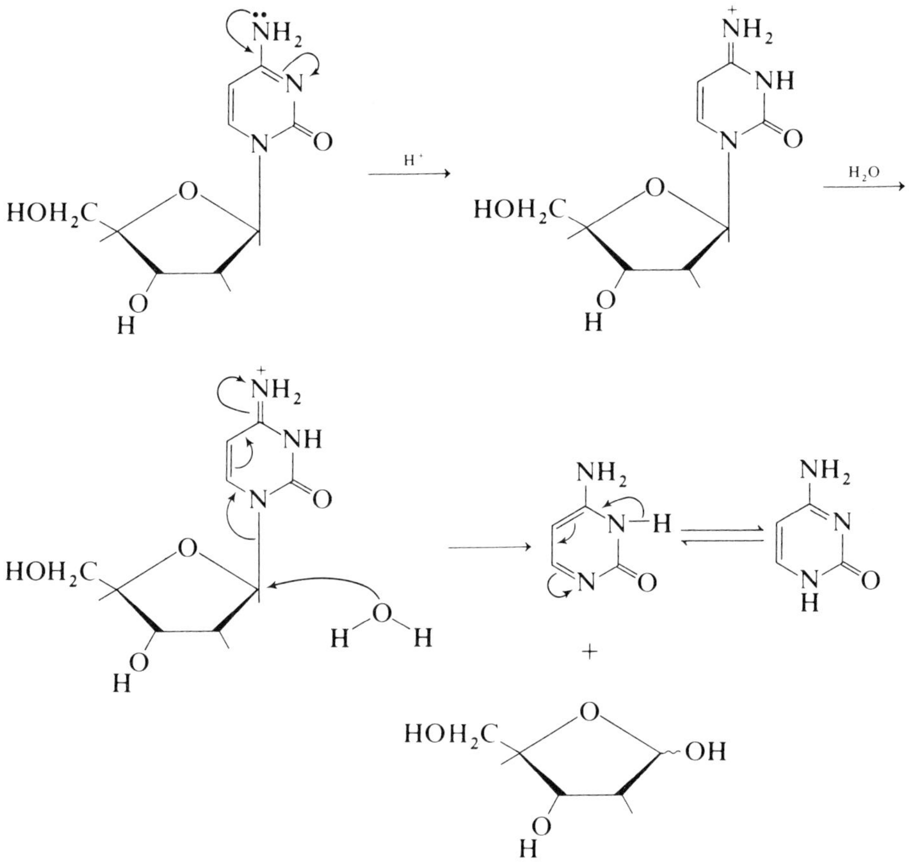

## PHOSPHORYL DERIVATIVES OF SACCHARIDES

Phosphoryl derivatives of monosaccharides participate in many biochemical reactions. Among the more common phosphoryl derivatives are glucose 1-phosphate, glucose 6-phosphate, ribose 5-phosphate, and deoxyribose 5-phosphate.

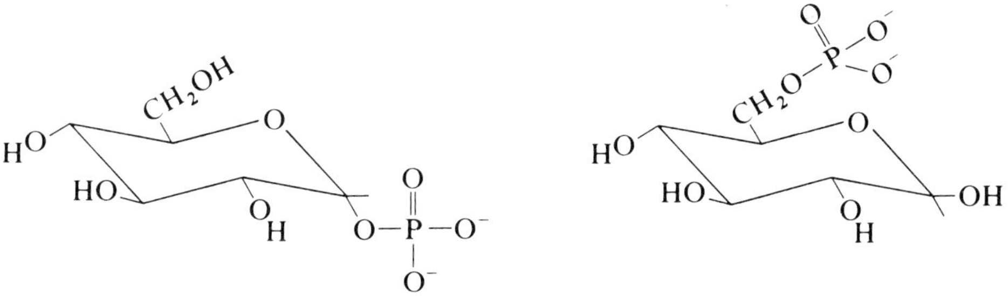

α-D-Glucose 1-phosphate

β-D-Glucose 6-phosphate

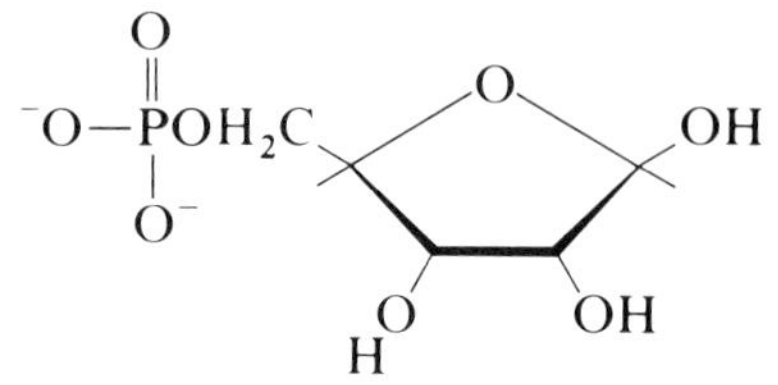

β-D-Ribose 5-phosphate

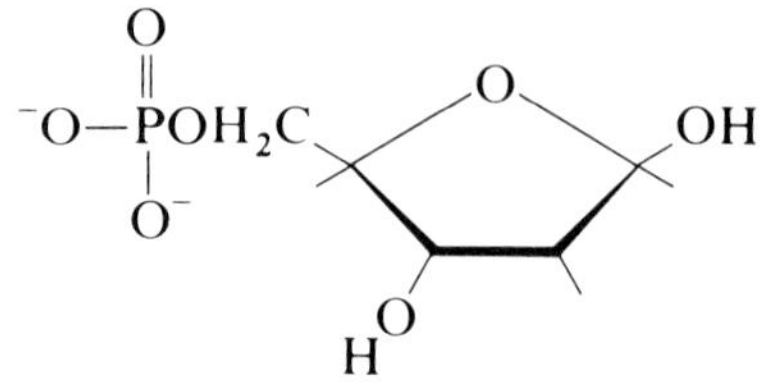

β-D-Deoxyribose 5-phosphate

## Laboratory Synthesis of Phosphoryl Derivatives of Saccharides

When phosphoryl derivatives of monosaccharides are prepared in the laboratory, one generally employs a phosphorylating agent such as a phosphorochloridate, a phosphoroamidate, or a substituted orthophosphate. As an example, the phosphorylation of a saccharide (derivative) in the presence of a phosphorochloridate is shown below. In such a procedure when only a specific hydroxyl group or groups are to undergo phosphorylation, the rest of the hydroxyl groups must be masked. In the example shown, 2,3-isopropylidene-D-ribose is allowed to react with dibenzylphosphorochloridate. Subsequently, the benzyl moieties can be removed by catalytic hydrogenation and the isopropylidine moiety by mild acid hydrolysis. An appropriately masked nucleoside can also be used in such a procedure and under these circumstances the nucleoside is converted into a nucleotide.

The phosphorylation of a saccharide in the presence of a phosphoroamidate parallels that shown above, with a phosphorochloridate as the phosphoryl donor.

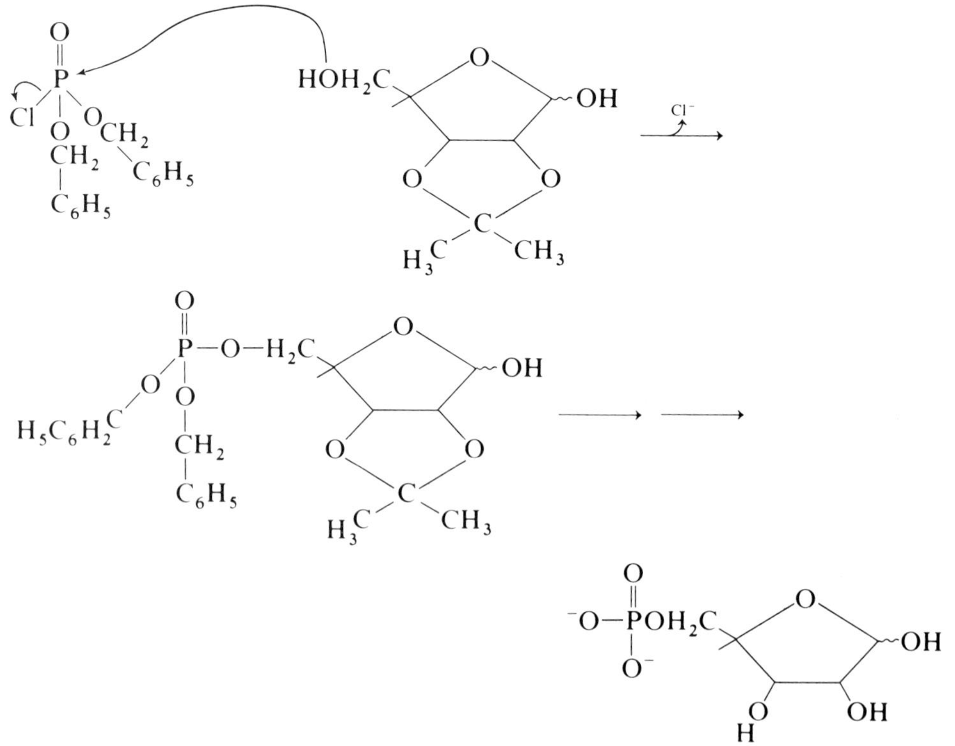

However, when a phosphoroamidate is used, the leaving group is ammonia rather than chloride ion.

In each of these instances the reaction entails a nucleophilic attack by a hydroxyl oxygen atom upon the electrophilic phosphoryl phosphorus atom. This process can be compared with the attack by a nucleophile upon a carbonyl carbon atom. In a nucleophilic attack upon the carbon atom of a planar carbonyl group a tetrahedral intermediate is generated. By contrast, in a nucleophilic attack upon the phosphorus atom of an essentially tetrahedral phosphoryl group a pentacovalent trigonal bipyramidal transition-state intermediate is generated. For a reaction between 2,3-isopropylidene-D-ribose and phosphoroamidate this intermediate is

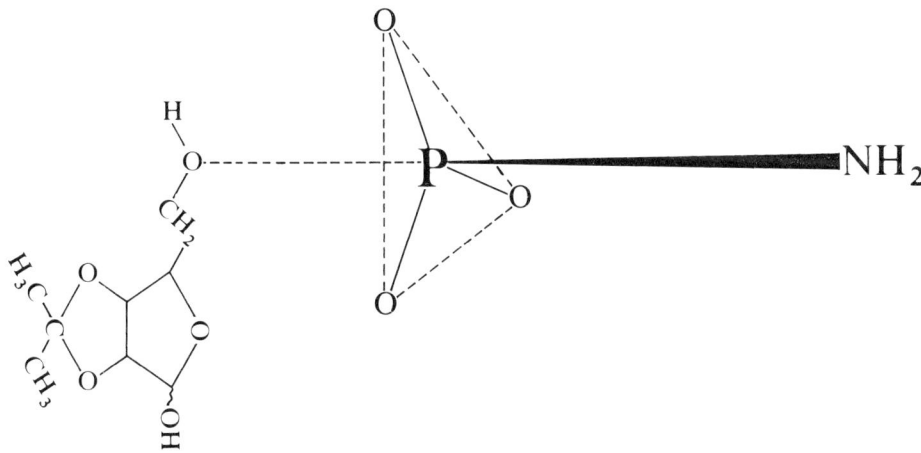

When a saccharide undergoes phosphorylation in the presence of a phosphorochloridate, the reaction proceeds by means of an $S_N2$ mechanism. On the other hand, with a phosphoroamidate as the phosphoryl donor the reaction has an A2 mechanism since the amino group of the phosphoroamidate must be protonated before it is expelled.

Derivatives of orthophosphate can serve as phosphoryl donors when the hemiacetal hydroxyl group of a saccharide derivative is to undergo phosphorylation. An example of this type of procedure is found in the reaction of 2,3,5-tribenzylribose 1-bromide and bibenzyl phosphate. The completely benzylated product formed can subsequently be converted into ribose 1-phosphate in the presence of palladium and hydrogen.

Also, a per-O-acetylglycosyl halide can be allowed to react with trisilver phosphate. In this case, the resulting product is then hydrolyzed under carefully controlled conditions to obtain the desired phosphoryl derivative. Generally, one obtains the anomer in which the phosphoryl group is cis to the hydroxyl group at C(2) of the saccharide. In some instances, however, the other anomer can be obtained by varying the reaction conditions.

## Hydrolysis of Phosphoryl Derivatives of Saccharides

The hydrolysis of the phosphoryl derivatives of saccharides can occur by several different reaction mechanisms. In part, the nature of the reaction depends upon whether it is the phosphoryl derivative of an alcohol hydroxyl group or the phosphoryl derivative of a hemiacetal or hemiketal hydroxyl group that is undergoing hydrolysis. However, even a single compound like α-D-glucopyranosyl 1-phosphate can undergo hydrolytic cleavage by at least three different mechanisms. In this case, in a strongly acid medium the conjugate acid of glucose 1-phosphate undergoes hydrolysis as the result of an A1 mechanism which entails cleavage of the carbon-oxygen bond. On the other hand, at a pH of between 1 and 8, nonionized glucose 1-phosphate undergoes an $S_N1$ reaction which also entails C—O cleavage. However, in this pH range the monoanion of glucose 1-phosphate can undergo an $S_Ni$ reaction† in which the phosphorus-oxygen bond undergoes cleavage. These mechanisms are illustrated in Fig. 3-3. The hydrolysis of α-D-ribofuranosyl 1-phosphate proceeds several hundred times as fast as that of glucose 1-phosphate when the conjugate acid or the nonionized species undergoes cleavage. For the hydrolysis of the pentose phosphate the mechanisms have been designated A1 and $S_N1$, respectively, just as for glucose 1-phosphate. These observations would seem to suggest that formation of the furanosyl carbonium ion is an easier process than that of the pyranosyl carbonium ion. Possibly this is because less ring distortion is required to allow stabilization of the carbonium ion by delocalization in the case of the five-membered ring.

† $S_Ni$ denotes substitution, nucleophilic, internal and refers to a mechanism in which an initial dissociation results in the formation of an intimate ion pair. Subsequently, a nucleophilic atom of the negatively charged member of the ion pair attacks the positively charged member from the front side as the remainder of the negatively charged species departs. The mechanism results in retention of configuration.

A1 mechanism:

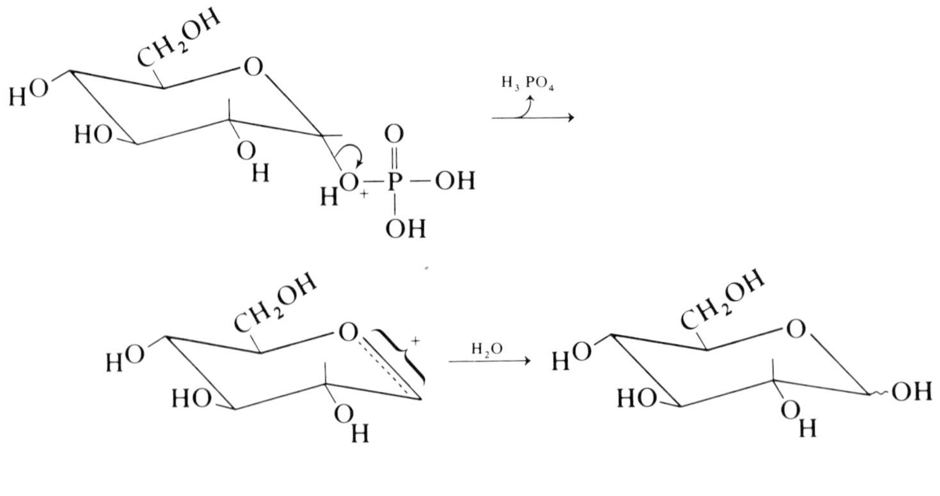

$S_N 1$ mechanism:

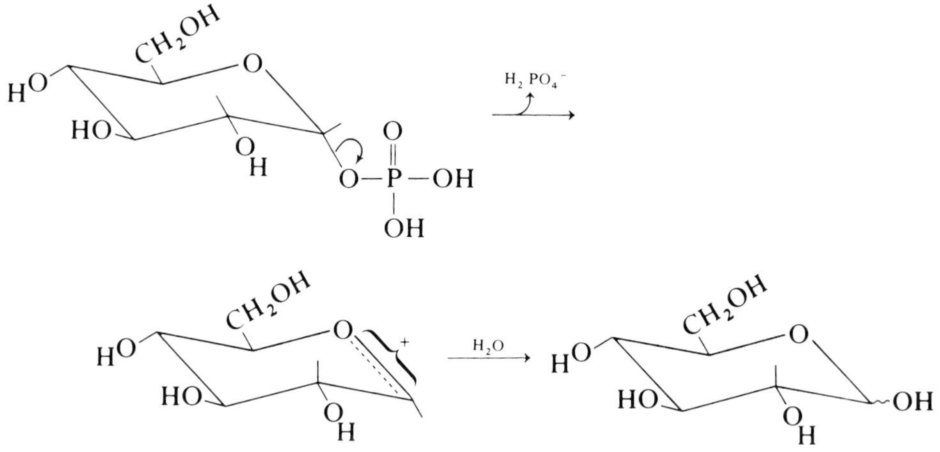

$S_N i$ mechanism:

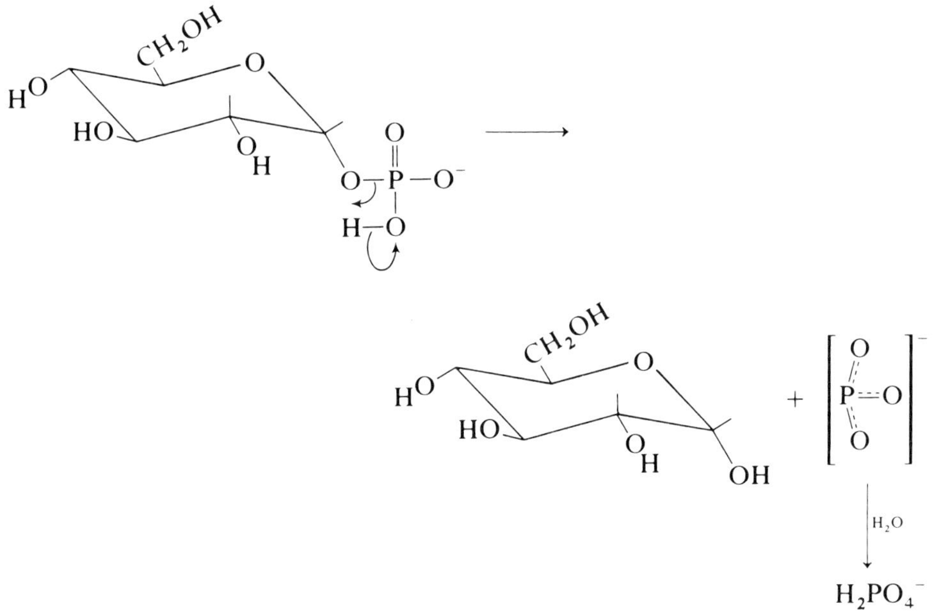

**Fig. 3-3** The hydrolysis of α-D-glucose 1-phosphate as it occurs by an A1 mechanism, an $S_N 1$ mechanism, and an $S_N i$ mechanism. In the latter a metaphosphate monoanion intermediate, which has been compared to the electron-deficient carbonium ion, subsequently reacts with water to yield the orthophosphate monoanion.

The hydrolysis of glucose 6-phosphate in acidic or neutral media parallels that of simple monoalkyl phosphates, e.g., methyl phosphate. At a pH of less than 1 the conjugate acid of a monoalkyl phosphate undergoes hydrolysis by an A2 mechanism in which a water molecule, as the nucleophile, can attack either C(6) or the phosphoryl phosphorus atom of the hexose phosphate. In the former case, hydrolysis occurs with C—O cleavage, while in the latter, it occurs with P—O cleavage. On the other hand, at pH 1 the nonionized monoalkyl phosphate undergoes hydrolysis by means of an $S_N2$ mechanism that entails predominantly C—O cleavage. At a pH of from 3 to 5 the monoalkyl phosphate monoanion undergoes hydrolysis by means of an $S_Ni$ reaction formulated in terms of a metaphosphate monoanion intermediate. In this case, P—O cleavage occurs. These processes are shown below.

A2 mechanism:

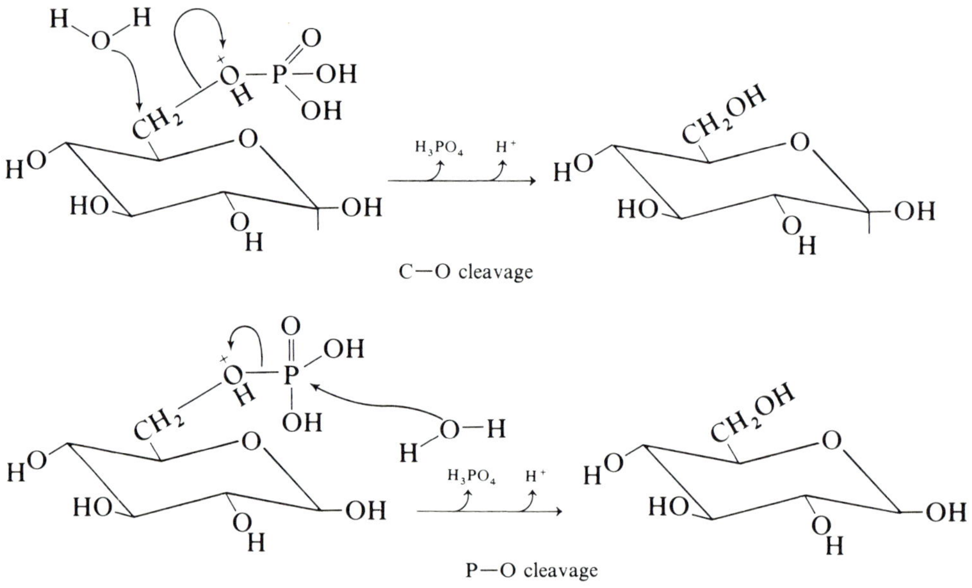

C—O cleavage

P—O cleavage

$S_N2$ mechanism:

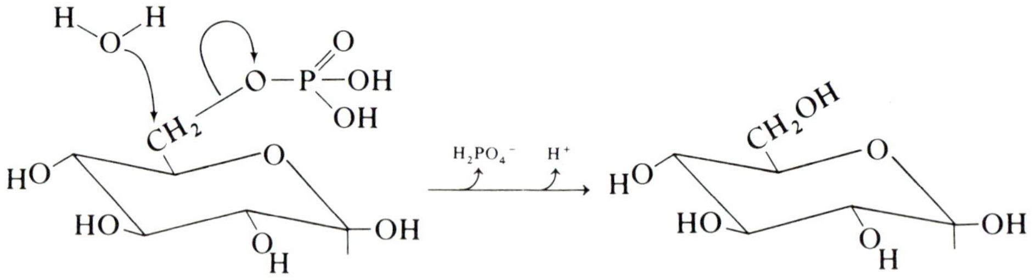

$S_N i$ mechanism:

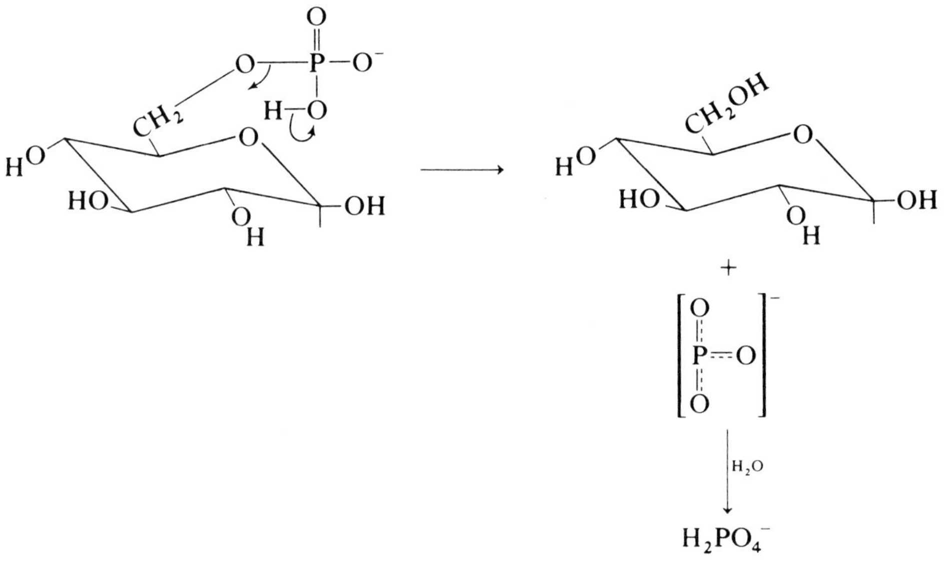

[Reaction scheme showing glucose 6-phosphate undergoing $S_N i$ mechanism to produce glucose and metaphosphate $PO_3^-$, which reacts with $H_2O$ to give $H_2PO_4^-$]

Since the nonionized species is considerably less reactive than either the conjugate acid or the monoanion, a plot of the rate of the hydrolysis of glucose 6-phosphate as a function of pH exhibits a minimum at pH 1. The maximum of this plot is at approximately pH 4.

Glucose 6-phosphate can also undergo reactions which result in its dephosphorylation under alkaline conditions. This characteristic, in fact, distinguishes glucose 6-phosphate from compounds like glucose 1-phosphate or ribose 1-phosphate. Glycosyl phosphates are relatively stable in alkaline media. The dephosphorylation of glucose 6-phosphate is not a simple hydrolytic cleavage, however, but an elimination reaction, as illustrated in Fig. 3-4.

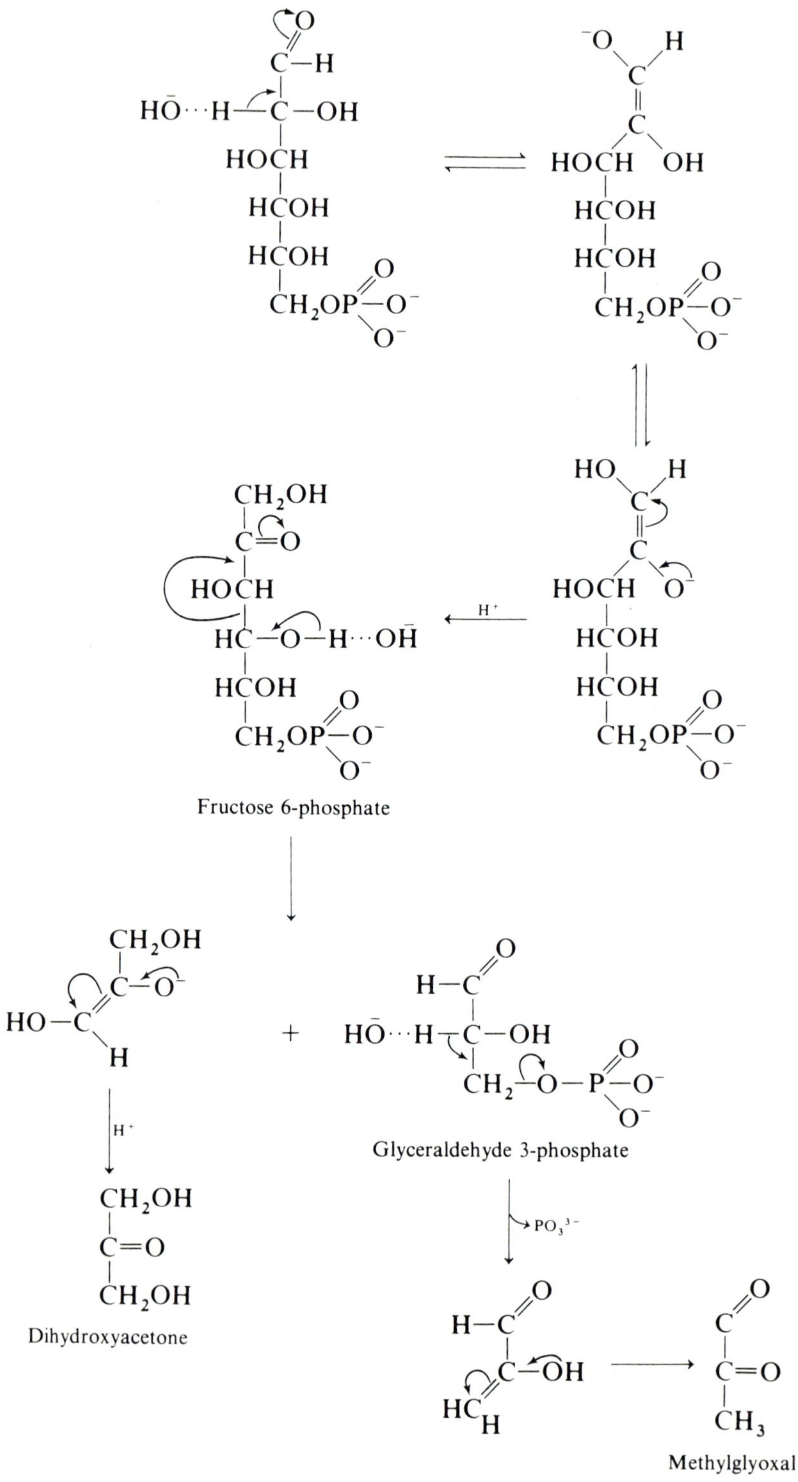

**108** MECHANISMS OF METABOLISM

Fructose 6-phosphate

Dihydroxyacetone

Glyceraldehyde 3-phosphate

Methylglyoxal

## POLYSACCHARIDES

Polysaccharides are polymeric macromolecules comprising monosaccharide units joined by O-glycosidic bonds. Initially, when polysaccharides were synthesized in the laboratory, these processes were carried out in the presence of isolated enzymes since the required stereoregularity was difficult to achieve nonenzymatically. Subsequently, methods were devised whereby high-molecular-weight polymers with the physical characteristics of naturally occurring dextrans can be prepared nonenzymatically in the laboratory.

### Synthesis of Polysaccharides

The laboratory synthesis of polysaccharides can be accomplished by means of a reaction that utilizes an anhydro derivative of a monosaccharide and phosphorus pentafluoride at $-78°C$. The reaction of an appropriately masked 1,6-anhydro-$\beta$-D-glucopyranose and phosphorus pentafluoride is shown in Fig. 3-5. Characterization of the product indicates that the polymerization occurs with a high degree of stereoregularity and that the O-glycosidic bonds thus formed are predominantly $\alpha(1\rightarrow 6)$ linkages.

**Figure 3-4** The dephosphorylation of glucose 6-phosphate in alkaline solution initially entails its conversion to fructose 6-phosphate by formation of enediol intermediates. Fructose 6-phosphate then undergoes a retrograde aldol reaction that yields dihydroxyacetone and glyceraldehyde 3-phosphate. The latter, in turn, undergoes an elimination reaction in which the orthophosphate anion is expelled. Finally a 1,3 prototropic rearrangement yields methylglyoxal.

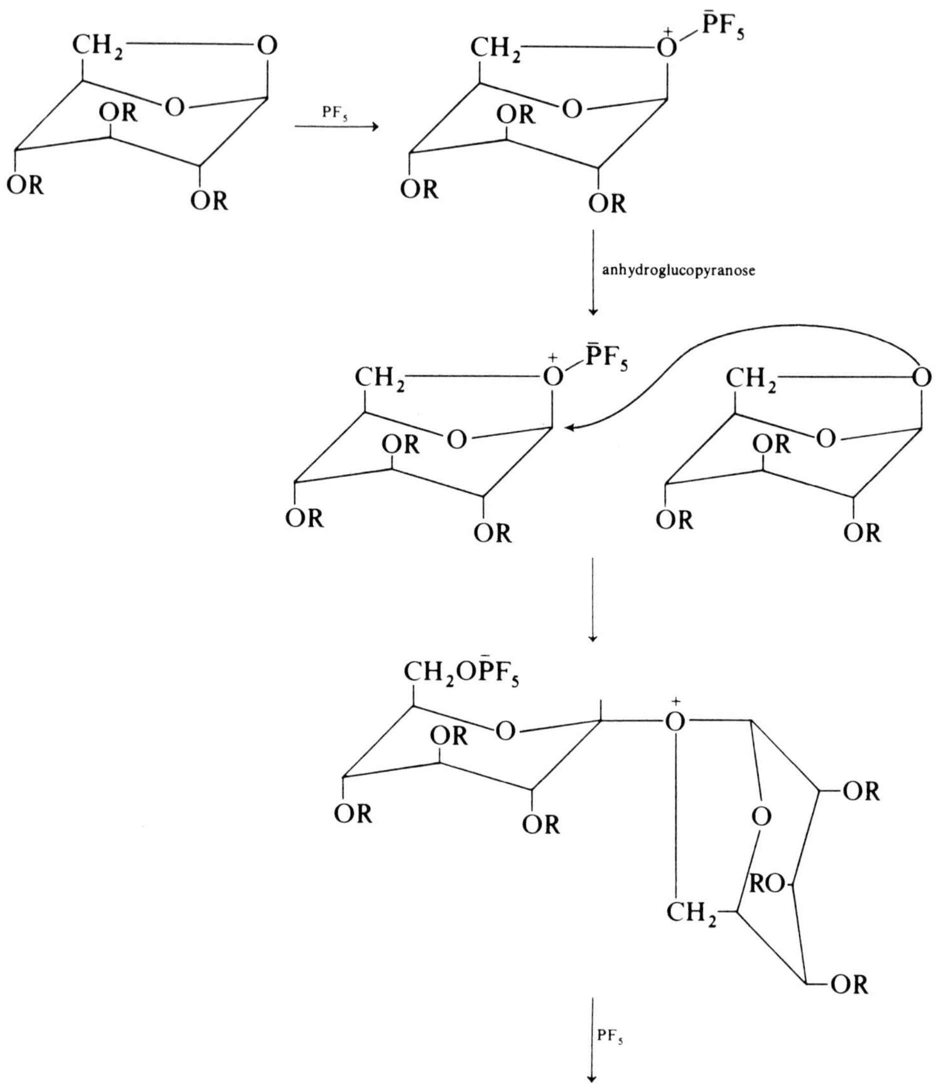

# 110 MECHANISMS OF METABOLISM

anhydroglucopyranose

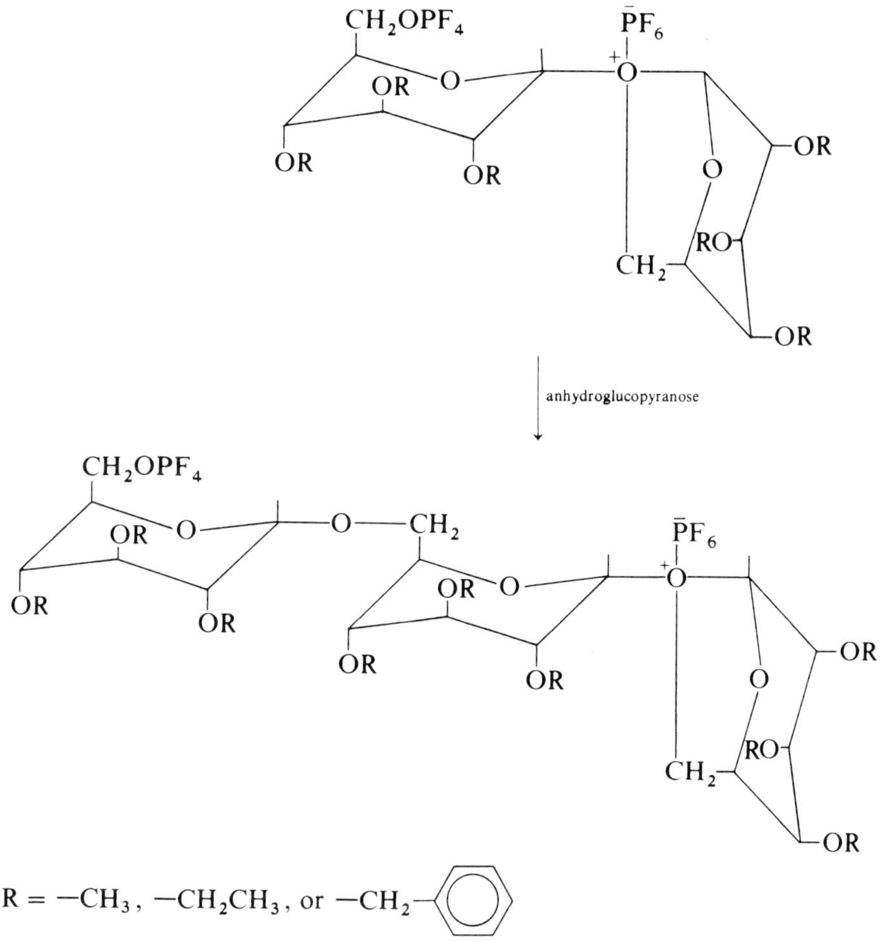

R = —CH$_3$, —CH$_2$CH$_3$, or —CH$_2$—C$_6$H$_5$

**Figure 3-5** Polymerization is initiated as the strongly electrophilic PF$_5$ becomes coordinated with the oxygen atom of the 1,6-anhydro bond. Now a second molecule of the anhydroglucopyranose makes a nucleophilic attack at C(1) of the coordinated species with the result that 1,6-anhydro ring of the first glucopyranose molecule is opened, thus creating a new oxonium ion derived from the second glucopyranose molecule. Coordination with a second molecule of PF$_5$ allows the reaction to be propagated without the necessity for an increasing separation of change which is thermodynamically unfavorable. With a nucleophilic attack by a third molecule of the anhydroglucopyranose, the stage is set for further propagation. [*Modified from Ruckel, E. R., and Schuerch, C. (1966) J. Org. Chem.* **31**, *2233–2239. With permission.*]

CHAPTER
# FOUR

## THE CHEMISTRY OF THE LIPIDS

The term lipid is used to describe a heterogeneous category of compounds that are characteristically hydrophobic, in contrast to the carbohydrates and the proteins. Lipids can be extracted from animal or plant tissue with ether, chloroform, benzene, petroleum ether, and similar solvents. The hydrophobic nature of the lipids is important to their function as components of cellular membranes and causes the lipids to follow a different course from that of carbohydrates and proteins in the processes of digestion and assimilation into the blood. In this chapter some of the chemical properties and chemical characteristics of the lipids will be discussed.

### FATTY ACIDS

Fatty acids, per se, are only minor components in biochemical systems. In most instances, fatty acids occur as components of glycerol esters. In a few cases, amides derived from fatty acids are found as components of biochemical systems. Naturally occurring fatty acids frequently have an even number of carbon atoms and a nonbranched carbon chain. When they are unsaturated, the configuration of the olefinic bond is frequently cis, and when there are multiple olefinic bonds, they are generally nonconjugated. Some of the more commonly occurring fatty acids are shown in Table 4-1 along with their structures, melting points, and boiling points.

### Table 4-1 Some commonly occurring fatty acids

| Name | Formula | mp, °C | bp, °C |
|---|---|---|---|
| **Saturated:** | | | |
| Acetic | $CH_3COOH$ | 16.6 | 118 |
| Propionic | $CH_3CH_2COOH$ | −2.2 | |
| n-Butyric | $CH_3(CH_2)_2COOH$ | −7.9 | 162 |
| Caproic (n-hexanoic) | $CH_3(CH_2)_4COOH$ | −3.4 | 206 |
| Caprylic (n-octanoic) | $CH_3(CH_2)_6COOH$ | 16.7 | 237 |
| Pelargonic (n-nonanoic) | $CH_3(CH_2)_7COOH$ | 12.5 | |
| Capric (n-decanoic) | $CH_3(CH_2)_8COOH$ | 31.2 | 270 |
| Lauric (n-dodecanoic) | $CH_3(CH_2)_{10}COOH$ | 43.9 | 299 |
| Myristic (n-tetradecanoic) | $CH_3(CH_2)_{12}COOH$ | 54.1 | 149† |
| Palmitic (n-hexadecanoic) | $CH_3(CH_2)_{14}COOH$ | 62.7 | 167† |
| Stearic (n-octadecanoic) | $CH_3(CH_2)_{16}COOH$ | 69.9 | 184† |
| Arachidic (n-eicosanoic) | $CH_3(CH_2)_{18}COOH$ | 75.4 | 204† |
| Behenic (n-docosanoic) | $CH_3(CH_2)_{20}COOH$ | 79.9 | 306‡ |
| Lignoceric (n-tetracosanoic) | $CH_3(CH_2)_{22}COOH$ | 84.2 | |
| Cerotic (n-hexacosanoic) | $CH_3(CH_2)_{24}COOH$ | 87.7 | |
| **Unsaturated:** | | | |
| Palmitoleic (cis-9-hexadecenoic) | $CH_3(CH_2)_5\overset{H}{\underset{|}{C}}=\overset{H}{\underset{|}{C}}(CH_2)_7COOH$ | 0.5 | |
| Oleic (cis-9-octadecenoic) | $CH_3(CH_2)_7\overset{H}{\underset{|}{C}}=\overset{H}{\underset{|}{C}}(CH_2)_7COOH$ | 13.4 | 234 |
| Linoleic (cis,cis-9,12-octadecadienoic) | $CH_3(CH_2)_3\left(CH_2\overset{H}{\underset{|}{C}}=\overset{H}{\underset{|}{C}}\right)_2(CH_2)_7COOH$ | −5 | 202§ |
| Linolenic (cis,cis,cis-9,12,15-octadecatrienoic) | $CH_3\left(CH_2\overset{H}{\underset{|}{C}}=\overset{H}{\underset{|}{C}}\right)_3(CH_2)_7COOH$ | −11 | 157¶ |
| Arachidonic (cis,cis,cis,cis-5,8,11,14-eicosatetraenoic) | $CH_3(CH_2)_3\left(CH_2\overset{H}{\underset{|}{C}}=\overset{H}{\underset{|}{C}}\right)_4(CH_2)_3COOH$ | −49.5 | |

† At 1 mmHg.  ‡ At 60 mmHg.  § At 1.4 mmHg.  ¶ At 0.001 mmHg.

## SYNTHESIS OF ACYLGLYCEROLS

The acylglycerols can be synthesized in the laboratory by acylating glycerol. However, such a procedure is useful only for preparing triacylglycerols in which all three acyl groups are the same. In this case, glycerol can be treated with an excess of the acylating agent. On the other hand, preparing a monoacylglycerol, diacylglycerol, or mixed triacylglycerol entails protecting certain glycerol hydroxyl groups during the acylation reactions, as described in the paragraphs that follow.

## Laboratory Synthesis of Monoacylglycerols

A 1-monoacylglycerol can be prepared in the laboratory by a reaction between the isopropylidene derivative of glycerol and the fatty acid in the presence of p-toluenesulfonic acid. Alternatively, the isopropylidene derivative of glycerol can be allowed to react with the acyl chloride derived from the fatty acid, a reaction generally carried out in pyridine. Following acylation, the isopropylidene moiety can be removed by heating the intermediate in the presence of trimethyl borate and boric acid and subsequently hydrolyzing the resulting diborate ester in water. The synthesis when the acyl chloride is used is illustrated below.

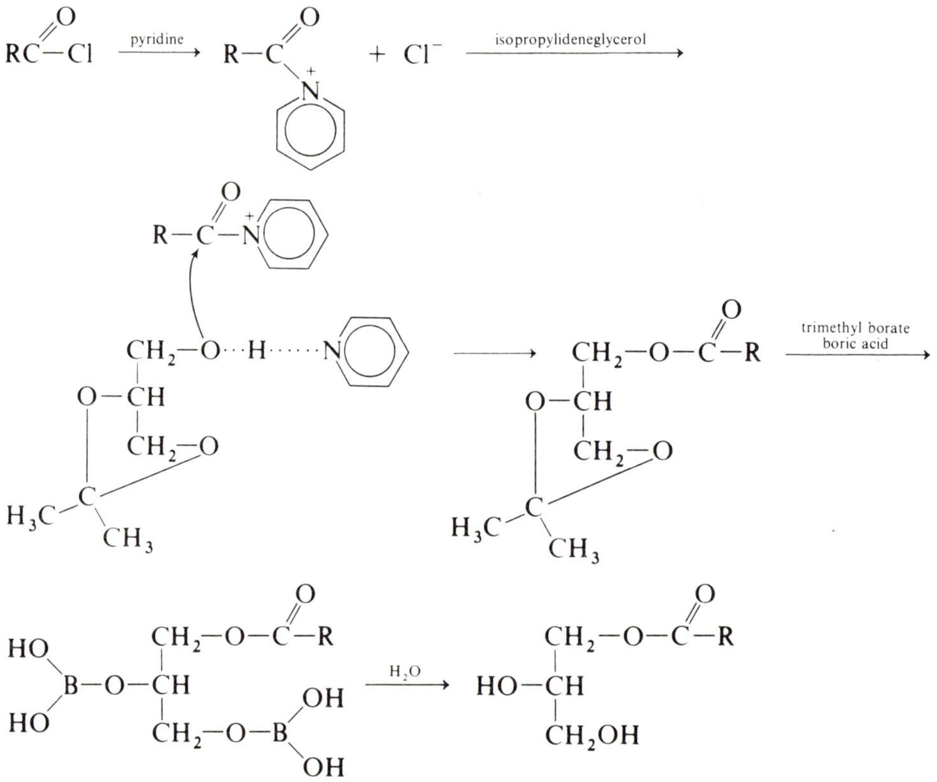

The role of the pyridine is shown as twofold. The acyl chloride can react with pyridine to yield an acyl pyridinium intermediate that is very reactive. In addition, pyridine is thought to increase the nucleophilicity of the oxygen atom at C(1) of isopropylideneglycerol. Furthermore, pyridine neutralizes the hydrochloric acid generated by the reaction. Attempts to remove the isopropylidene moiety by acid hydrolysis result in the migration of the acyl group. An equilibrium mixture of monoacylglycerols generally contains approximately 90 percent of the 1-acylglycerol and 10 percent of the 2-acylglycerol.

When it is wished to prepare a 2-monoacylglycerol, the 1,3-benzylidene derivative of glycerol can be used, again in conjunction with an acyl chloride in a pyridine medium. The masking group can be removed in the same way as the isopropylidene moiety.

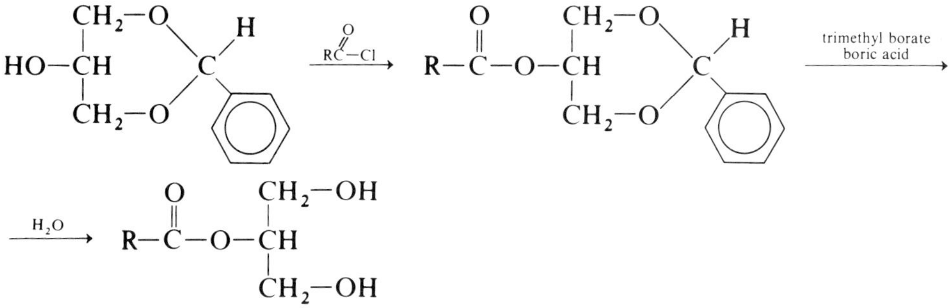

$$\underset{\substack{\text{HO-CH} \\ \text{CH}_2\text{-O}}}{\overset{\text{CH}_2\text{-O}}{|}} \!\!\! \underset{\text{CH}_2\text{-O}}{\overset{H}{\diagdown C \diagup}}\!\!\!\bigcirc \xrightarrow{R\overset{O}{\overset{\|}{C}}-Cl} R-\overset{O}{\overset{\|}{C}}-O-\underset{\substack{\text{CH}_2\text{-O} \\ \text{CH}_2\text{-O}}}{\overset{\text{CH}_2\text{-O}}{|}}\!\!\!\overset{H}{\diagdown C \diagup}\!\!\!\bigcirc \xrightarrow[\text{boric acid}]{\text{trimethyl borate}}$$

$$\xrightarrow{H_2O} R-\overset{O}{\overset{\|}{C}}-O-\underset{\substack{\text{CH}_2\text{-OH} \\ \text{CH}_2\text{-OH}}}{\overset{\text{CH}_2\text{-OH}}{|}}$$

## Laboratory Synthesis of Diacylglycerols

Diacylglycerols can be prepared from a benzylglycerol, as illustrated below.

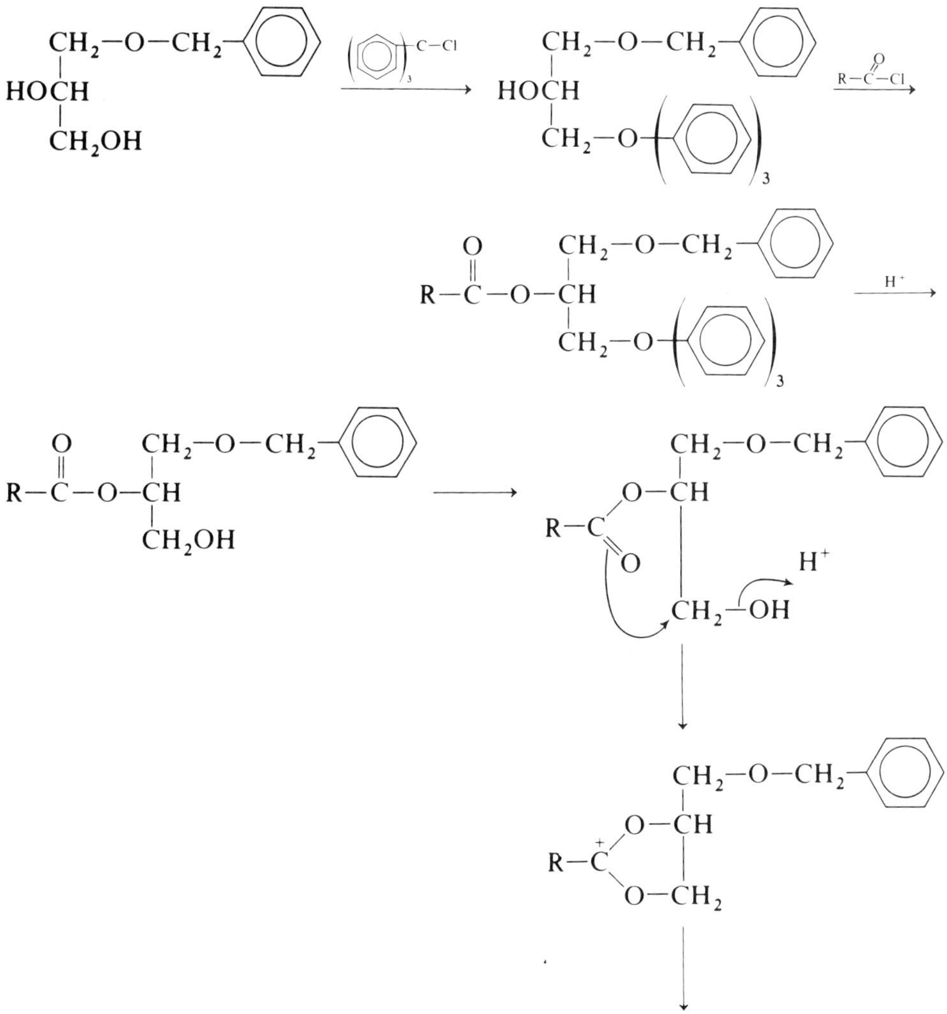

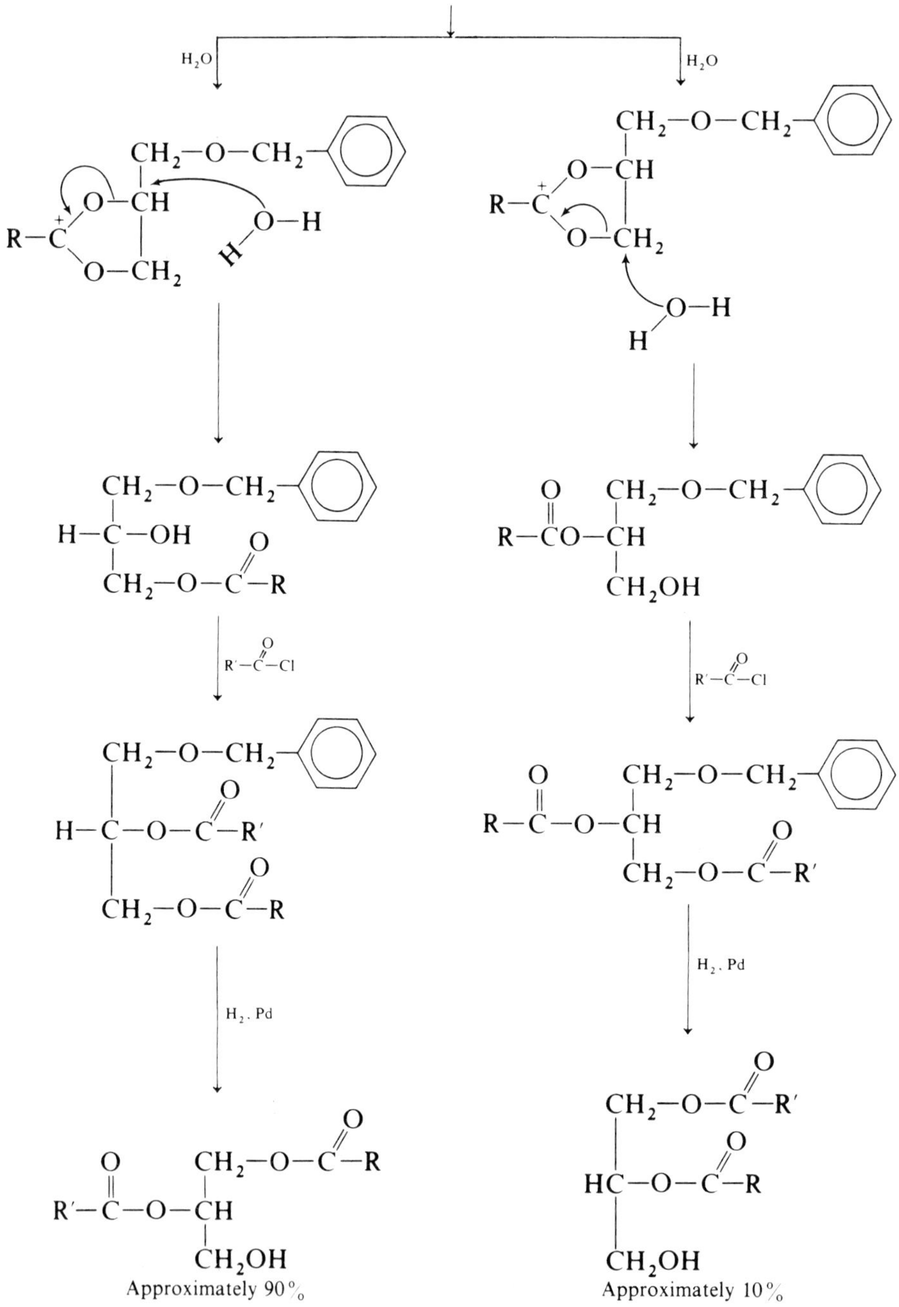

## 116 MECHANISMS OF METABOLISM

[Reaction scheme showing two parallel mechanistic pathways with intermediates leading to products labeled "Approximately 90%" (left) and "Approximately 10%" (right).]

The benzylglycerol is first treated with triphenylmethyl chloride, which reacts preferentially with the less hindered primary alcohol group. Then treatment with an acyl chloride yields the 2-monoacylglycerol derivative. If this is, in turn, placed in an acidic medium to remove the triphenylmethyl moiety, the loss of the masking group is accomplished but with some degree of acyl migration. In practice, if equilibrium is attained, one generally finds approximately 90 percent 1-acylglycerol derivative and 10 percent 2-acylglycerol derivative, even though it was the C(2) hydroxyl group that underwent acylation. Subsequent treatment of the monoacylglycerol derivative with another acyl chloride yields a diacylglycerol derivative. Finally, removal of the benzyl group, in the presence of palladium and hydrogen in acetic acid, yields the 1,2-diacylglycerols shown.

By contrast, 1,3-diacylglycerols can be prepared in the laboratory from isopropylidene or triphenylmethyl derivatives of glycerol. When isopropylidene derivative is used, the synthesis can be conducted as illustrated.

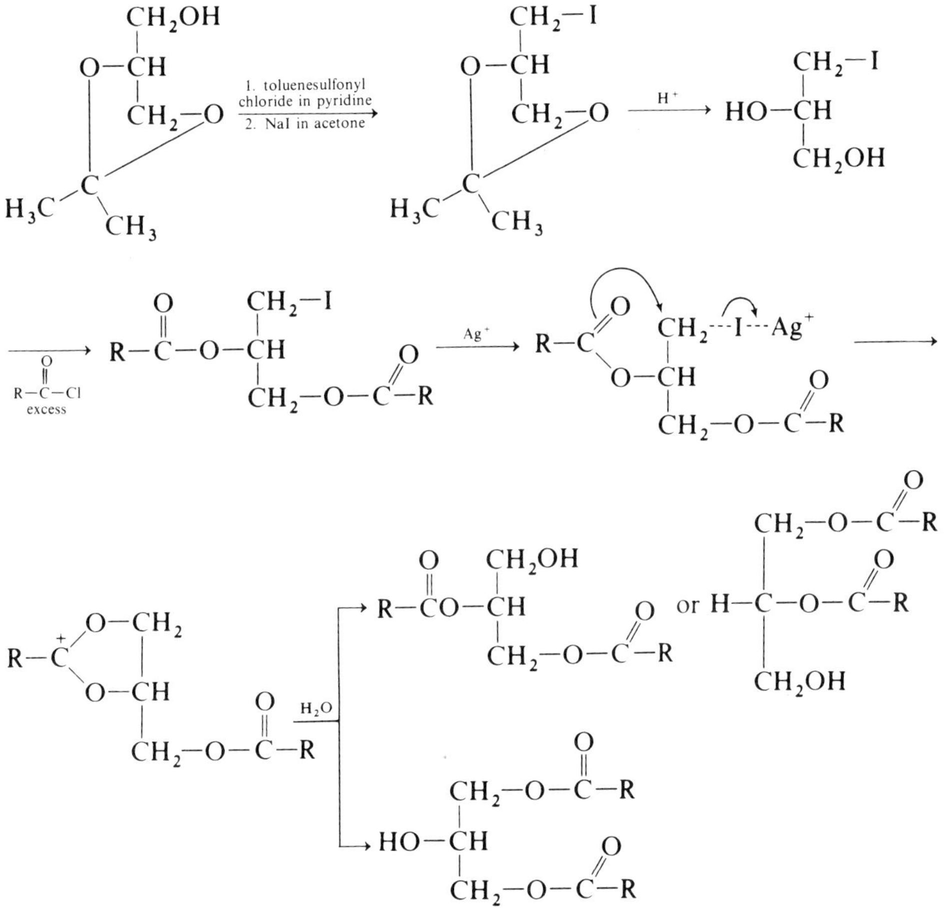

It should be noted that since the opening of the cyclic intermediate is not occurring in an acidic medium, the relative rates of the two reactions will determine the relative amounts of the 1,3-diacylglycerol and the 1,2-diacylglycerol in the reaction product.

The preparation of a 1,3-diacylglycerol in which the two acyl groups are different can be conducted in the following manner. A 1-acylglycerol can be converted into a 1-acyl-3-triphenylmethylglycerol, which in turn can undergo acylation at the C(2) hydroxyl group. If the triphenylmethyl group is removed under acidic conditions, an equilibrium mixture containing predominantly the 1,3-diacylglycerol will be obtained.

## Laboratory Synthesis of Triacylglycerols

Triacylglycerols in which the acyl moieties are different are prepared in the laboratory by a suitable combination of some of the methods discussed above. An example is the preparation of a triacylglycerol in which each of the acyl groups is different.

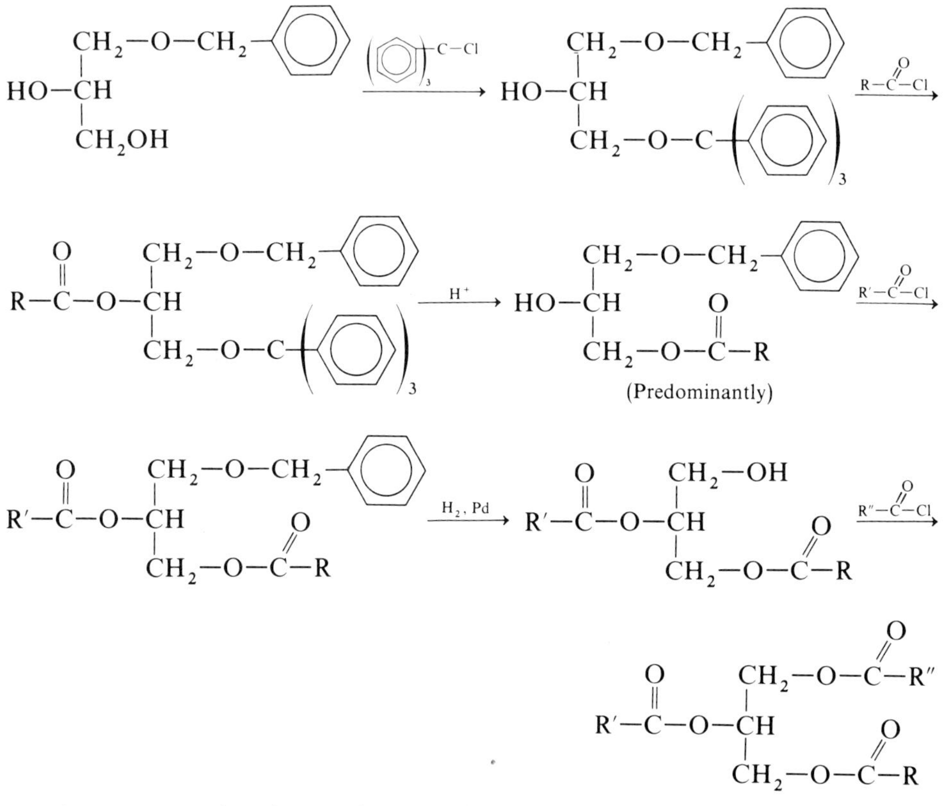

$$\begin{array}{c} CH_2-O-CH_2-C_6H_5 \\ HO-CH \\ CH_2OH \end{array} \xrightarrow{(C_6H_5)_3C-Cl} \begin{array}{c} CH_2-O-CH_2-C_6H_5 \\ HO-CH \\ CH_2-O-C(C_6H_5)_3 \end{array} \xrightarrow{R-\overset{O}{\underset{\|}{C}}-Cl}$$

$$\begin{array}{c} O \\ \| \\ R-C-O-CH \\ \; \; \; \; CH_2-O-CH_2-C_6H_5 \\ CH_2-O-C(C_6H_5)_3 \end{array} \xrightarrow{H^+} \begin{array}{c} CH_2-O-CH_2-C_6H_5 \\ HO-CH \\ CH_2-O-\overset{O}{\underset{\|}{C}}-R \end{array} \xrightarrow{R'-\overset{O}{\underset{\|}{C}}-Cl}$$

(Predominantly)

$$\begin{array}{c} O \\ \| \\ R'-C-O-CH \\ \; \; \; \; CH_2-O-CH_2-C_6H_5 \\ CH_2-O-\overset{O}{\underset{\|}{C}}-R \end{array} \xrightarrow{H_2, Pd} \begin{array}{c} O \\ \| \\ R'-C-O-CH \\ \; \; \; \; CH_2-OH \\ CH_2-O-\overset{O}{\underset{\|}{C}}-R \end{array} \xrightarrow{R''-\overset{O}{\underset{\|}{C}}-Cl}$$

$$\begin{array}{c} O \\ \| \\ R'-C-O-CH \\ \; \; \; \; CH_2-O-\overset{O}{\underset{\|}{C}}-R'' \\ CH_2-O-\overset{O}{\underset{\|}{C}}-R \end{array}$$

An unsaturated acyl group is generally introduced last since olefinic bonds tend to undergo autocatalytic oxidation and other side reactions. (Also, introduction of an unsaturated acyl group must come after the cleavage of the benzyl ether by catalytic hydrogenation.)

## SYNTHESIS OF PHOSPHOLIPIDS

Phospholipids are important components of many biochemical systems, including biological membranes. The laboratory synthesis of phospolipids is similar in several respects to that of the acylglycerols, just described.

## Synthesis of a Phospholipid (Phosphatidylcholine)

The laboratory synthesis of a phosphatidylcholine can be initiated using a 1,2-diacylglycerol, synthesized by one of the procedures described above. Introduction of the substituent at the C(3) hydroxyl group can then be accomplished as follows. Phenylphosphorodichloridate in pyridine is used to obtain the phosphoryl chloride derivative shown. This, in turn, can react with choline to yield the phosphotriester, which in the presence of hydrogen and platinum oxide is converted to the phosphatidylcholine. Variations of this procedure can be used to prepare a phosphatidylethanolamine. It should be noted, however, that the procedure illustrated is inappropriate for the synthesis of compounds in which one or both the acyl moieties are unsaturated. When this is the case, a phosphorodichloridate derived from choline or a suitably masked ethanolamine (the amino group must be masked) is prepared and allowed to react with the 1,2-diacylglycerol containing the unsaturated acyl moiety (or moieties). Subsequent treatment with zinc and acetic acid can yield the phosphatidylcholine or phosphatidylethanolamine which retains the unsaturation.

# HYDROLYSIS OF ACYLGLYCEROL

The reactions of the acylglycerols, or glycerides, are primarily those involving the ester group. In addition, the reactions of the olefinic bonds of unsaturated acyl moieties are often of some interest. Here, the hydrolytic cleavage of the glycerol ester bond is discussed.

## Acid-catalyzed Hydrolysis of Acylglycerols

Three reaction mechanisms for the acid-catalyzed hydrolysis of glycerol (and other) esters can be considered, an $A_{AC}1$, $A_{AC}2$, and $A_{AL}1$ mechanism, illustrated below. The designations $A_{AC}1$, $A_{AC}2$, and $A_{AL}1$, all refer to $S_N1$ or $S_N2$ mechanisms involving the conjugate acid but with acyl-oxygen cleavage in the first two mechanisms and alkyl-oxygen cleavage in the third. In the laboratory, however, it is found that the acid-catalyzed hydrolysis of acylglycerols usually occurs by an $A_{AC}2$ mechanism. The $A_{AC}1$ mechanism requires that the carbonium ion derived from the acyl moiety be relatively stable, while the $A_{AL}1$ mechanism requires that the carbonium ion derived from the alkyl moiety, i.e., the glycerol moiety, be relatively stable. (With respect to the formation of a carbonium ion derived from the alkyl moiety, it should be remembered that primary carbonium ions are the least stabilized.)

$A_{AC}1$ mechanism:

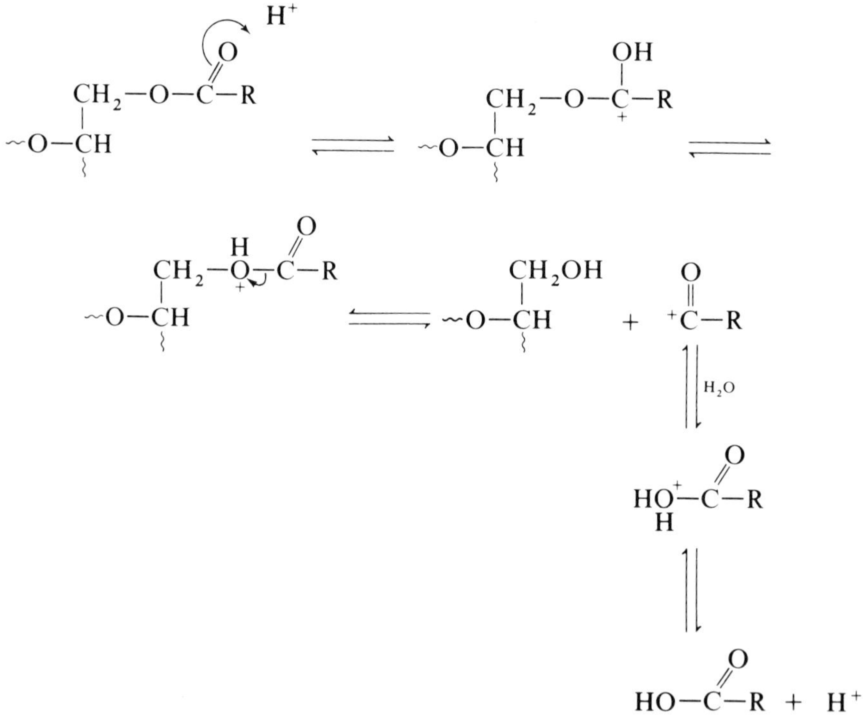

$A_{AC}2$ mechanism:

$A_{AL}1$ mechanism:

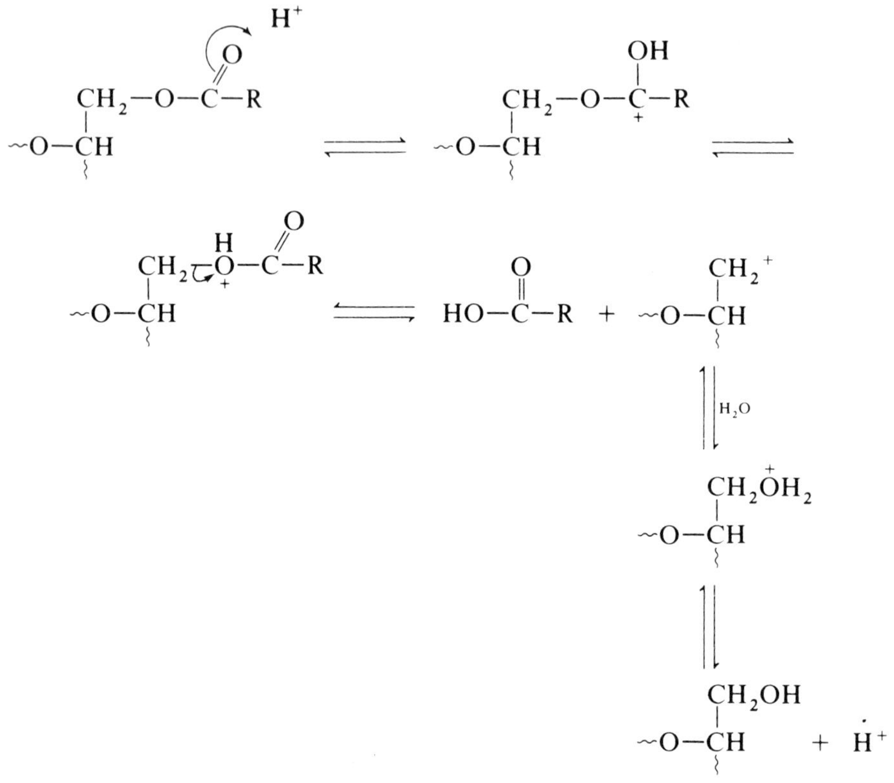

$$\begin{array}{c} CH_2-O-\overset{\overset{\displaystyle H^+}{\curvearrowleft}}{\overset{\displaystyle O}{\underset{\|}{C}}}-R \\ \sim O-CH \\ \} \end{array} \rightleftharpoons \begin{array}{c} CH_2-O-\overset{\overset{\displaystyle OH}{|}}{\underset{+}{C}}-R \\ \sim O-CH \\ \} \end{array} \rightleftharpoons$$

$$\begin{array}{c} CH_2 \overset{H}{\underset{+}{\overset{\frown}{O}}} - \overset{\overset{O}{\|}}{C} - R \\ \sim O-CH \\ \} \end{array} \rightleftharpoons \quad HO-\overset{O}{\underset{\|}{C}}-R \; + \; \begin{array}{c} \overset{+}{CH_2} \\ \sim O-CH \\ \} \end{array}$$

$$\Big\updownarrow H_2O$$

$$\begin{array}{c} \overset{+}{CH_2OH_2} \\ \sim O-CH \\ \} \end{array}$$

$$\Big\updownarrow$$

$$\begin{array}{c} CH_2OH \\ \sim O-CH \\ \} \end{array} + \; H^+$$

It should be mentioned at this point that under acidic conditions and in the presence of a free, i.e., nonacylated, hydroxyl group, acyl migrations can occur. Thus, if one is carrying out the acid-catalyzed hydrolysis of a triacylglycerol, after the first acyl group has been removed, the remaining species can undergo an acyl migration and hence unless all three acyl moieties are removed, a mixture of acyl glycerols is obtained.

## Alkaline Hydrolysis of Acylglycerol

The alkaline hydrolysis of glycerol (and other) esters can occur by one of the following mechanisms. Here the designations $B_{AC}2$, $B_{AL}1$, and $B_{AL}2$ refer to $S_N1$ or $S_N2$ mechanisms all involving the conjugate base but with acyl-oxygen cleavage in the first mechanism and alkyl-oxygen cleavage in the last two. In the laboratory the alkaline hydrolysis of acylglycerols usually proceeds by a $B_{AC}2$ mechanism.

$B_{AC}2$ mechanism:

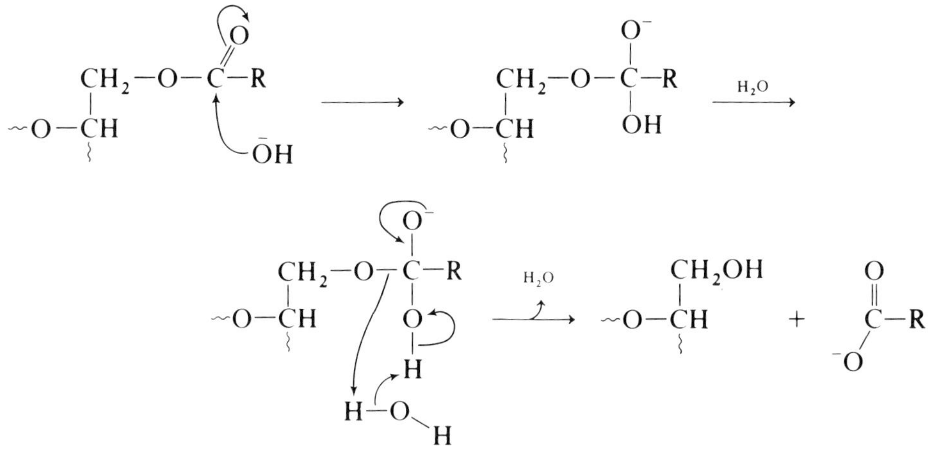

$B_{AL}1$ mechanism:

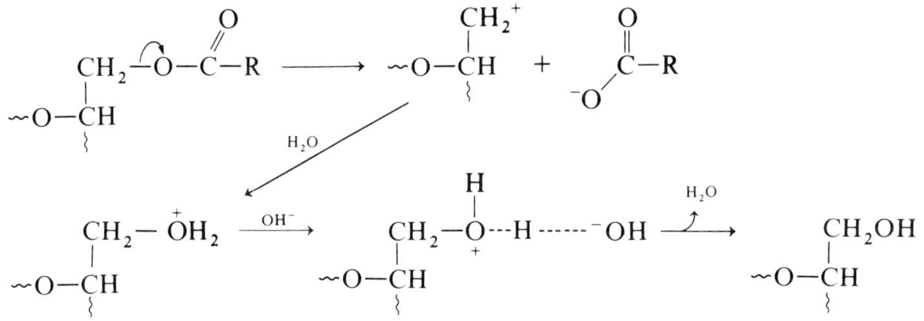

$B_{AL}2$ mechanism:

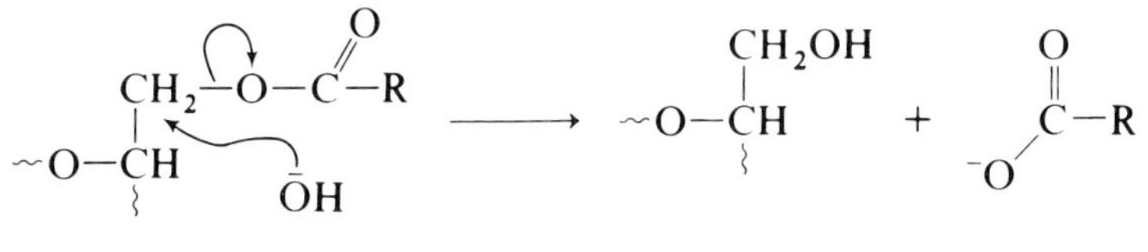

Acyl migrations can also occur in alkaline media when there is a free, i.e., nonacylated, hydroxyl group. In this case the migration is formulated as follows.

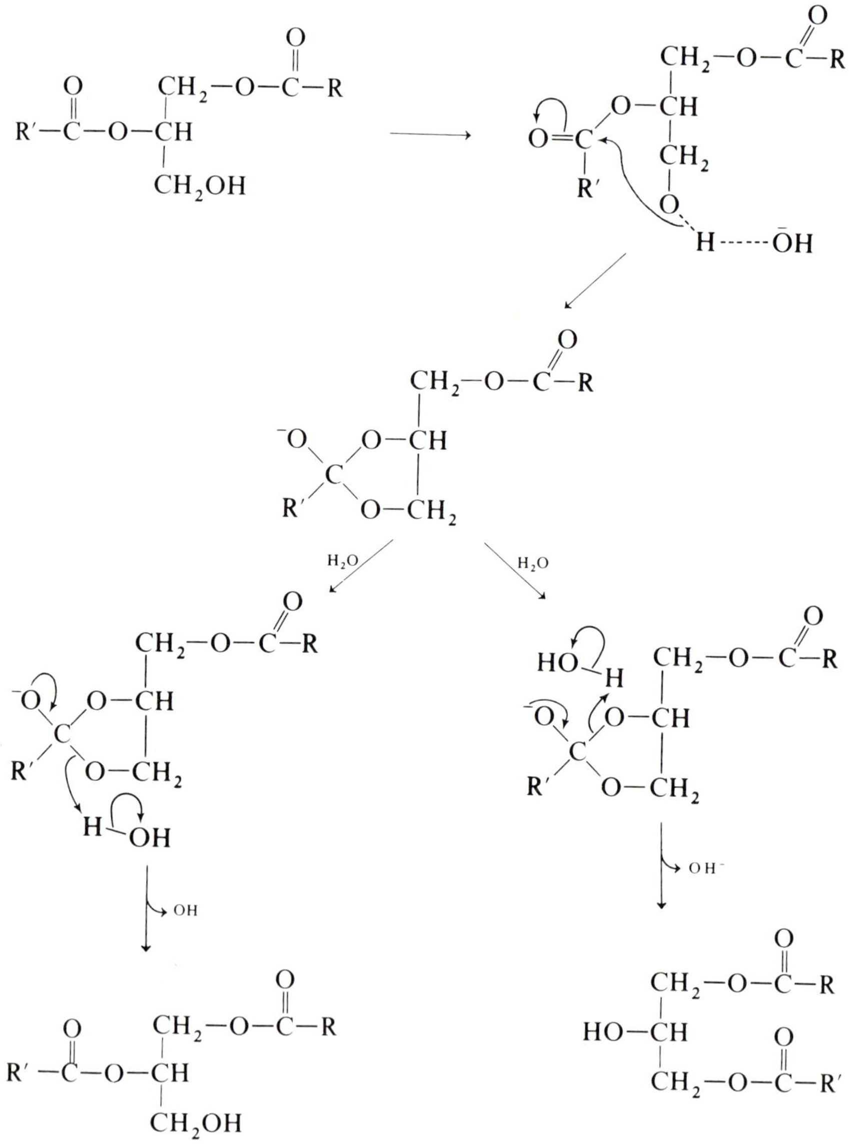

# HYDROLYSIS OF PHOSPHATE ESTER BONDS OF PHOSPHOLIPIDS

In addition to the glycerol ester bonds, phospholipids have phosphomonoester or phosphodiester bonds that can undergo hydrolytic cleavage. These reactions are discussed next.

## Acid-catalyzed Hydrolysis of Phosphomonoesters

Glycerol phosphate has been used as a model compound in studies on the hydrolysis of phosphomonoester bonds. In acidic media, it is the monoanion of monoalkyl phosphates, e.g., glycerol phosphate, that undergoes hydrolysis most readily. Under these conditions, the hydrolysis entails P—O cleavage, and it is thought that a metaphosphate monoanion intermediate is formed.

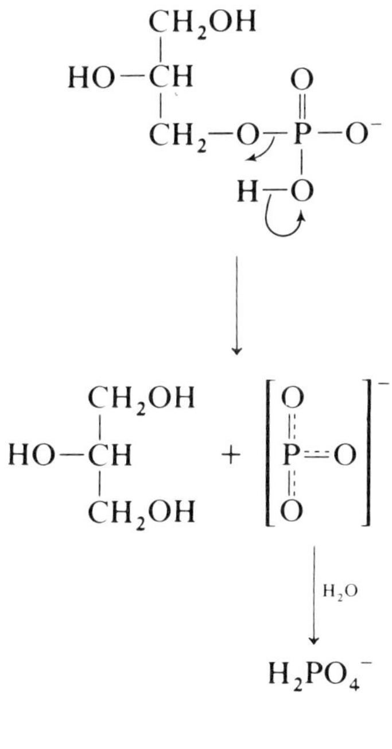

$$\begin{array}{c}
\text{CH}_2\text{OH} \\
\text{HO}-\text{CH} \quad\quad \text{O} \\
\text{CH}_2-\text{O}-\overset{\|}{\text{P}}-\text{O}^- \\
\text{H}-\text{O}
\end{array}$$

$$\downarrow$$

$$\begin{array}{c}
\text{CH}_2\text{OH} \\
\text{HO}-\text{CH} \quad + \quad \left[\overset{\text{O}}{\underset{\text{O}}{\text{P}\!=\!\text{O}}}\right]^- \\
\text{CH}_2\text{OH}
\end{array}$$

$$\downarrow\, H_2O$$

$$H_2PO_4^-$$

As formulated, the hydrolysis exhibits an $S_N i$ mechanism.

In acidic media phosphoryl moieties undergo migration similar to the acyl migrations discussed earlier in this chapter. Acid-catalyzed phosphoryl migration can be formulated as follows:

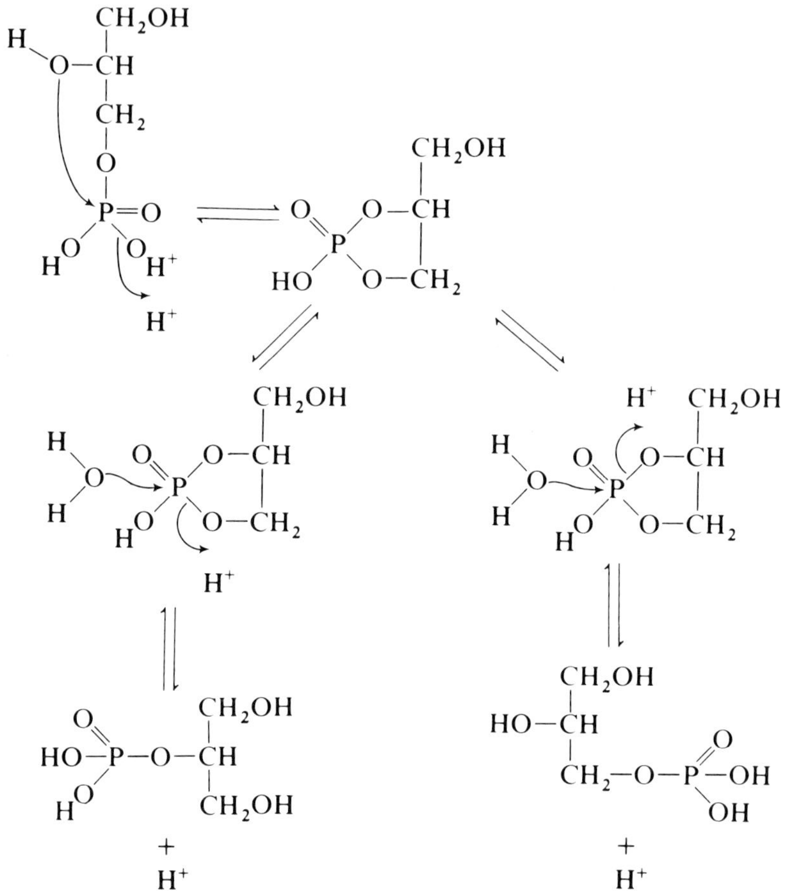

[Scheme showing interconversion of glycerol phosphates via cyclic phosphate intermediate]

An equilibrium mixture of glycerol phosphates contains approximately 85 percent of the glycerol 1-phosphate and 15 percent of the glycerol 2-phosphate.

**Cyclic phosphate esters** The formation of cyclic phosphate esters, like that shown above, is of some interest because these species participate in the reactions not only of certain phospholipids but also of the ribonucleic acids. When a hydrolytic reaction can proceed by the initial formation of a cyclic phosphate that is a five-membered ring, the cleavage is facilitated. This is illustrated by the fact that the acid-catalyzed hydrolysis of ethylene phosphate is $10^8$ times as fast as that of the acyclic dimethyl

---

**Figure 4-1** A water molecule approaches and becomes bonded at the available apical position, thus forming the trigonal bipyramidal transition state I. This, in turn, can undergo ring opening, as shown, to yield a product. Alternatively, transition state I can undergo pseudorotation to yield the trigonal bipyramidal transition state II. If the apical hydroxyl group of II now undergoes protonation and departs as a water molecule, the resulting cyclic ester will have undergone oxygen exchange (but not hydrolysis). The exchange reaction is, in fact, observed. Transition state II, on the other hand, can also undergo the ring opening that leads to product formation.

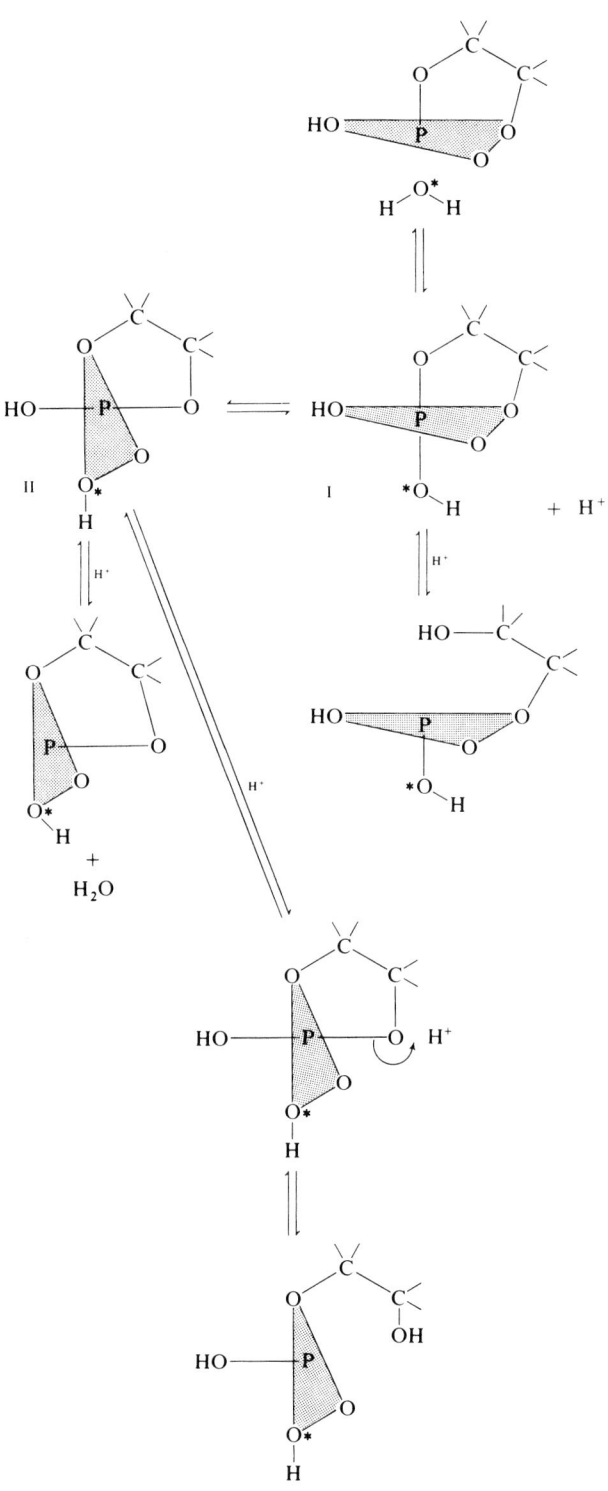

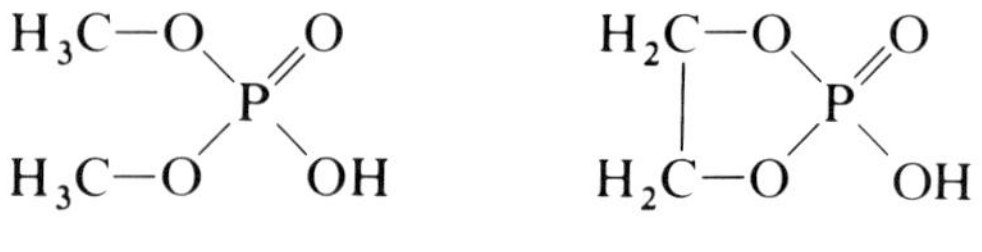

Dimethyl phosphate		Ethylene phosphate

phosphate. In an attempt to rationalize the reactivity of the cyclic phosphate F. H. Westheimer and his colleagues at Harvard University examined the geometrical and thermodynamic aspects of the transition states thought to participate in the hydrolysis. It had been proposed that when phosphate esters undergo hydrolysis, the water molecule approaches the electrophilic phosphoryl phosphorus atom and assumes an apical position in the resulting trigonal bipyramidal transition state. In fact, it had been proposed that any species that is to react at the phosphoryl phosphorus atom will initially assume an apical position as it makes its approach and also that any leaving group will depart from an apical position. In addition, Westheimer and his colleagues proposed that when the ester has a five-membered ring structure, there can be interconversions between transition states such as I and II in Fig. 4-1. This type of interconversion is termed *pseudorotation*.† (Pseudorotation results in two apical substituents becoming basal substituents and two basal substituents becoming apical substituents.) Ultimately, on the basis of the characteristics of these transition states it was concluded that the hydrolysis of five-membered ring phosphate esters is inordinately rapid because the phosphorus-oxygen bond angles are less strained in the transition states than the ground state. The hydrolysis is depicted in terms of these transition states in Fig. 4-1.

## Acid-catalyzed Hydrolysis of Phosphodiesters

Phospholipids such as phosphatidylcholine, phosphatidylethanolamine, or phosphatidylserine contain a phosphodiester bond. In general, dialkyl phosphates are less prone to acid-catalyzed hydrolysis than either monoalkyl phosphates or trialkyl phosphates. The conjugate acid of a dialkyl phosphate can undergo hydrolysis with virtually 100 percent C—O cleavage while the nondissociated species is hydrolyzed with 70 to 80 percent C—O cleavage and the remainder with P—O cleavage. Hydrolysis with P—O cleavage has been formulated in terms of a monoalkyl metaphosphate intermediate, as shown.

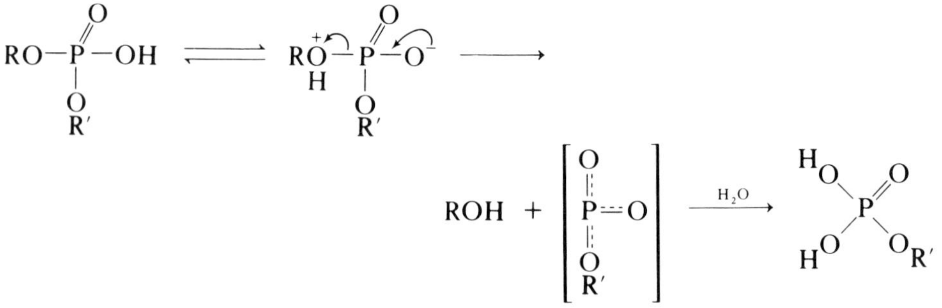

† Dennis, E. A., and Westheimer, F. H. (1966) *J. Am. Chem. Soc.* **88**, 3432–3433; Westheimer, F. H. (1968) *Acc. Chem. Res.* **1**, 70–78.

THE CHEMISTRY OF THE LIPIDS  **129**

In the special case of a neighboring hydroxyl group in proximity to the phosphodiester bond, the acid-catalyzed hydrolysis becomes more complex. Under these circumstances, cyclic esters can be formed, as illustrated by the example below, in which a phospholipid with a free hydroxyl group at C(2) undergoes acid-catalyzed hydrolysis. Initially, either a cyclic diester (I) or cyclic triester (II) is formed. If one assumes that the weaker base is the better leaving group, formation of the cyclic triester would be expected to occur with the greater frequency since water is a weaker base than most alcohols. Each of the cyclic esters subsequently reacts with water to yield the products shown. It might be noted that in one instance the starting compound is regenerated while in another the phosphomonoester moiety has migrated.

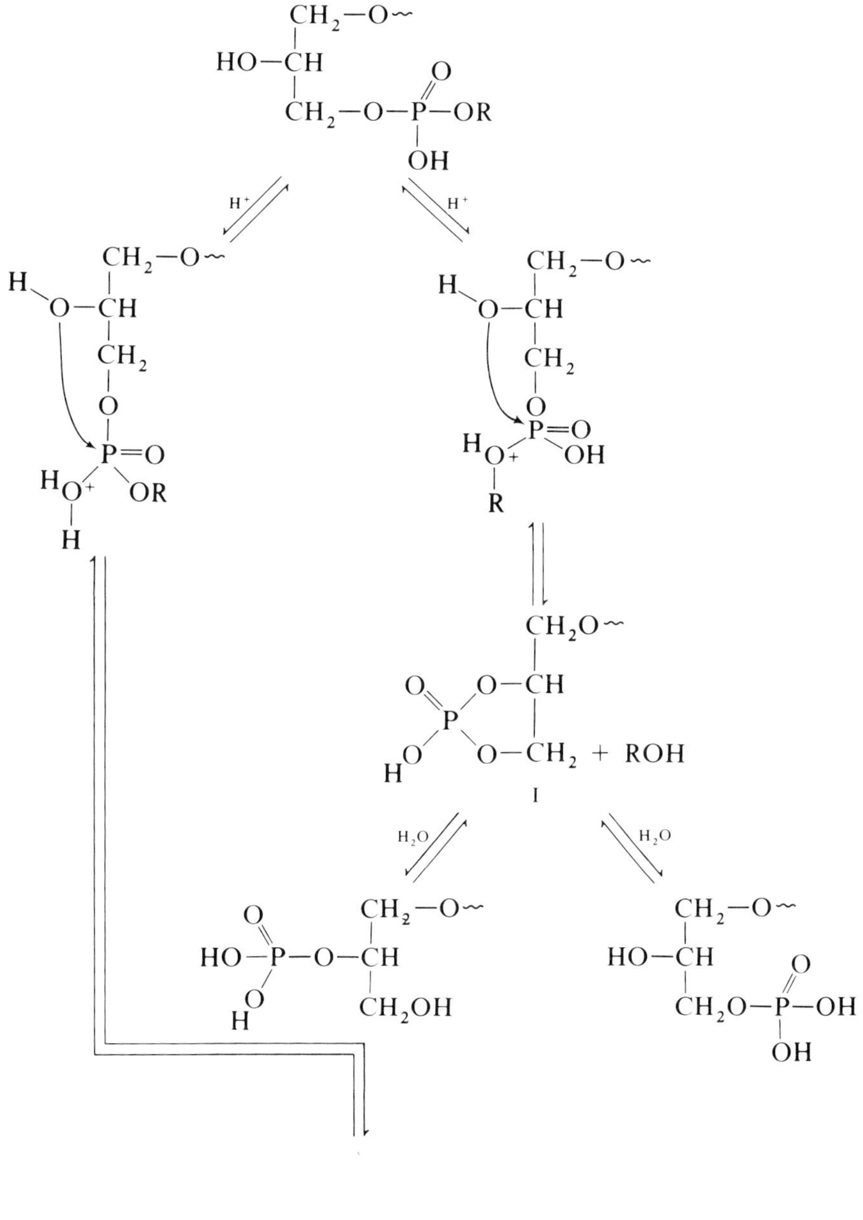

$$\begin{array}{c} CH_2-O\sim \\ | \\ HO-CH \\ | \quad\quad O \\ CH_2-O-\overset{\|}{P}-OR \\ | \\ OH \end{array}$$

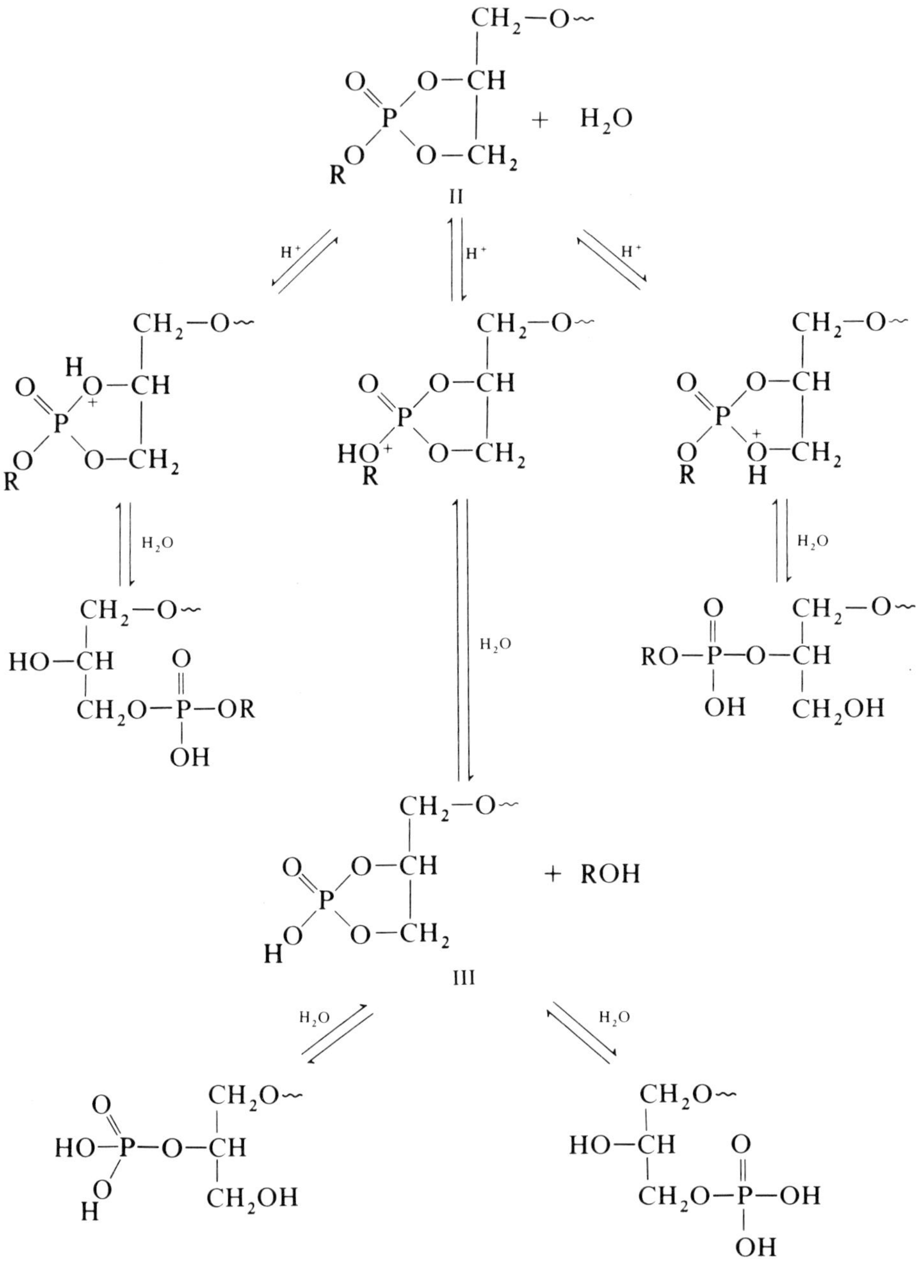

## Alkaline Hydrolysis of Phosphate Esters

Simple monoalkyl phosphates are not readily hydrolyzed in alkaline media. The cause of this lack of reactivity would appear to be the mutual repulsion of the monoalkyl phosphate dianion and the hydroxide ion.

Simple diakyl phosphates are also relatively unreactive in alkaline media. However, when there is a neighboring hydroxyl group, hydrolysis is facilitated by formation of a cyclic ester intermediate. The reader should try to write a mechanism for the hydrolysis under these conditions. A somewhat more complex example of this type of reaction was found when the alkaline hydrolysis of a deacylated phosphatidylinositol was examined. In this case both cyclic ester intermediates and an epoxide intermediate were postulated. The three mechanisms shown differ with respect to the leaving group expelled as a result of the nucleophilic attack by a hydroxyl group. In mechanism A a cyclic ester intermediate is formed as the glycerol anion is expelled. In mechanism B another cyclic ester intermediate is formed as the inositol anion is expelled. In mechanism C an epoxide is formed as the inositol 1-phosphate anion is

Mechanism A:

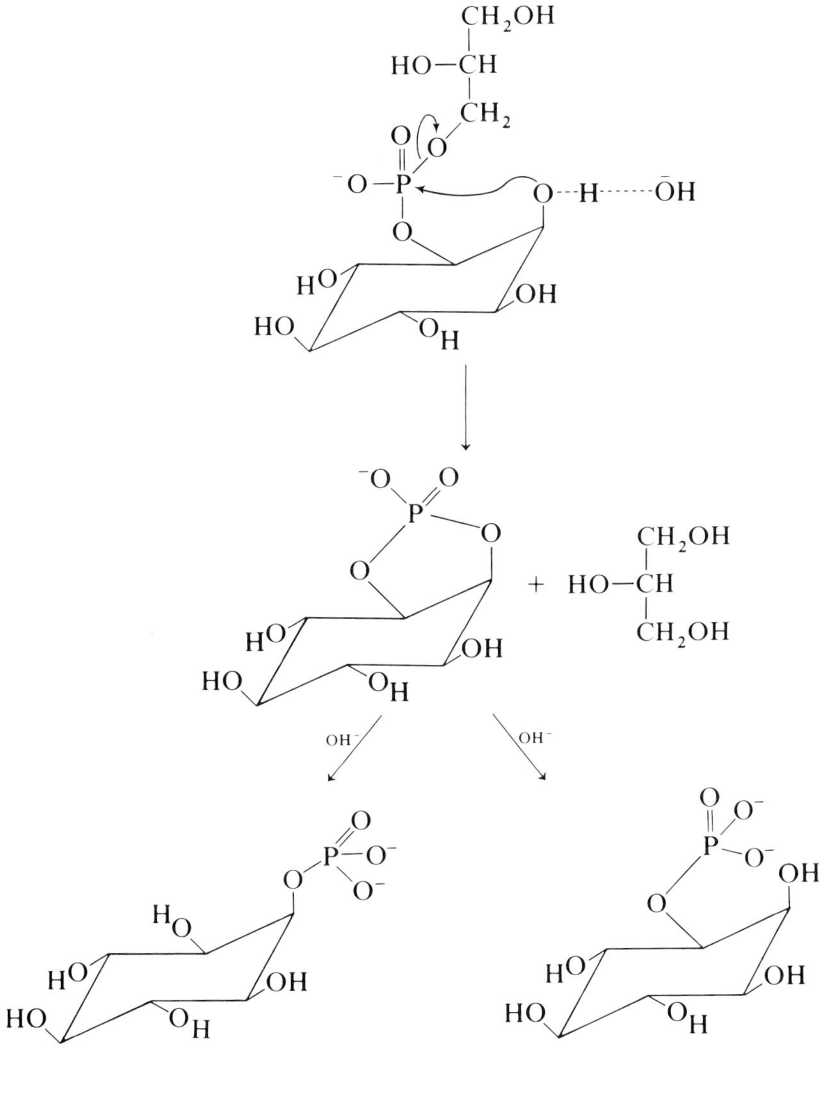

Mechanism B:

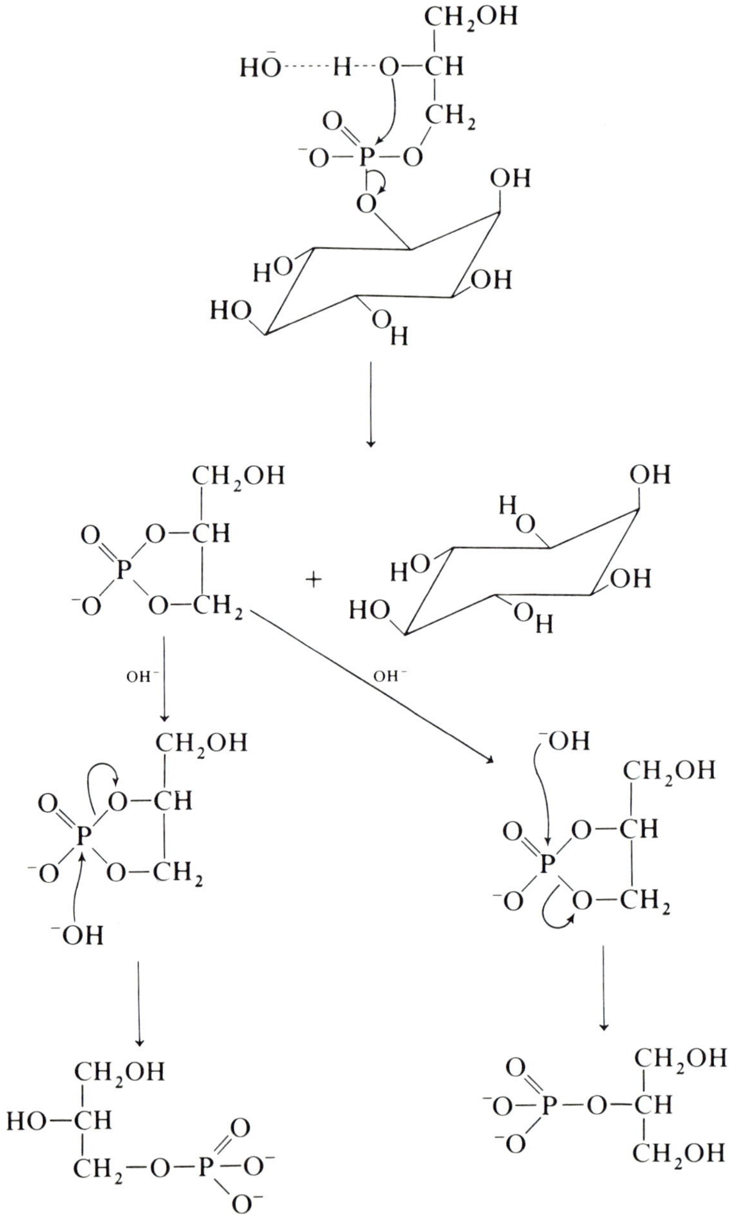

expelled. Generally, formation of a cyclic ester intermediate is favored over formation of an epoxide intermediate. In the expulsion of a glycerol anion or an inositol anion, on the other hand, the former would be expected to be the better leaving group since primary alcohols are usually weaker bases than secondary alcohols.

Mechanism C:

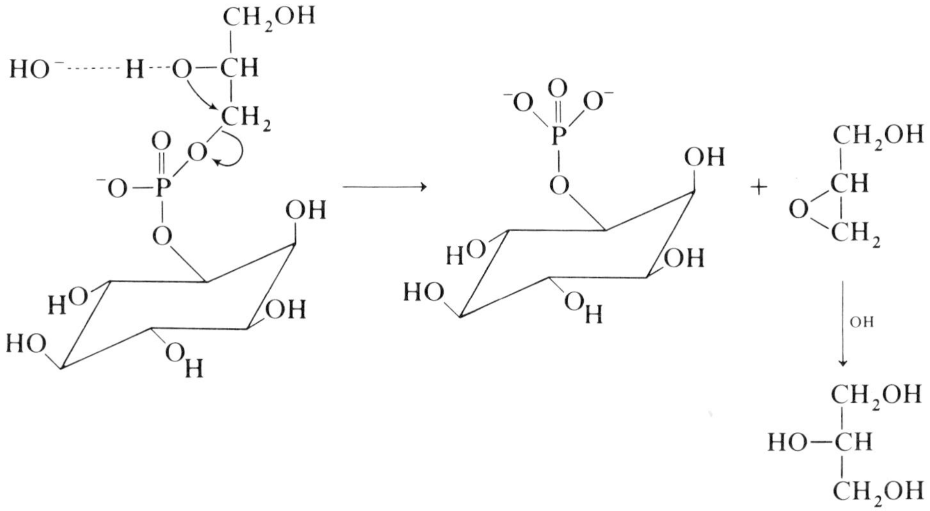

[chemical reaction scheme showing inositol phosphate intermediate forming epoxide and glycerol]

Formation of the epoxide intermediate may offer an alternative to the displacement of the relativity poor leaving groups mentioned above, i.e., the glycerol anion or the inositol anion, in that the inositol 1-phosphate anion is a much better leaving group.

## REACTIONS OF OLEFINIC BONDS OF UNSATURATED FATTY ACIDS

In unsaturated fatty acids or unsaturated acyl moieties of glycerides or phospholipids the reactions of the olefinic bond are often important to the behavior of these species. Three of the principal reactions of the olefinic bonds of these molecules are reduction, oxidation, and hydration, discussed next.

### Reduction of Olefinic Bonds

Olefinic bonds readily undergo reduction in the presence of hydrogen and a suitable catalyst. In the living organism the olefinic bonds of unsaturated acyl moieties undergo reduction in the presence of a cofactor that serves as a vehicle for the hydrogen and the appropriate enzyme. In the laboratory, hydrogen gas may be used in the presence of a metal, such as platinum or palladium, which serves as the catalyst. The reduction reaction as conducted in the laboratory can be virtually quantitative, although if it is stopped before completion, isomers resulting from migrations of double bonds and from cis-trans interconversions can be isolated. On the basis of these observations the reduction of an olefinic bond on the surface of a metal catalyst might be formulated schematically as shown in Fig. 4-2.

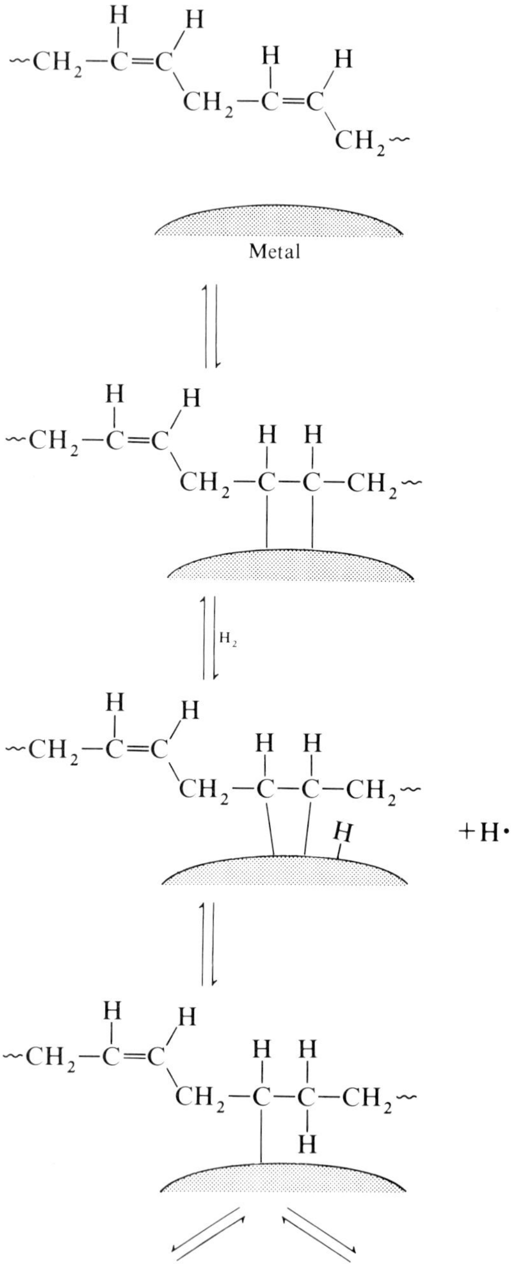

**134** MECHANISMS OF METABOLISM

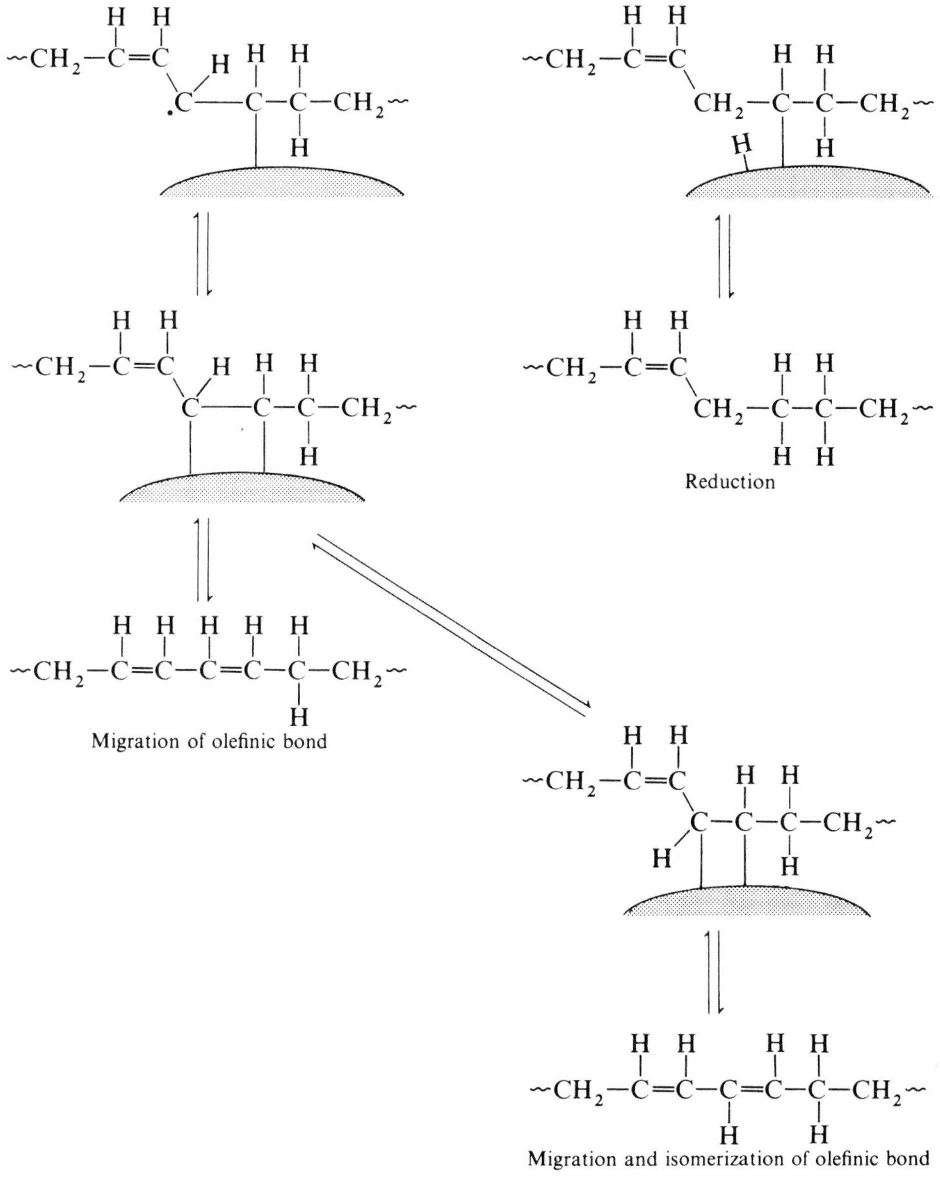

**Figure 4-2** The olefinic moiety becomes bonded at the metal surface at which hydrogen can also become bonded. Under these circumstances reduction can occur, or, alternatively, a hydrogen radical can be abstracted from an allylic carbon atom (presumably by another radical) and migration of the olefinic bond or migration with an accompanying cis-trans isomerization can follow.

## Oxidation of Olefinic Bonds

The olefinic bonds of unsaturated fatty acids and their derivatives can undergo oxidation upon standing in contact with the atmosphere. This process, sometimes referred to as *autocatalytic oxidation*, is in part responsible for the rancidity that develops in oils and certain other food products. The oxidative reactions involve free-radical processes which can, for example, result in fragmentation of the unsaturated hydrocarbon chain. Some of the conversions involved are shown below.

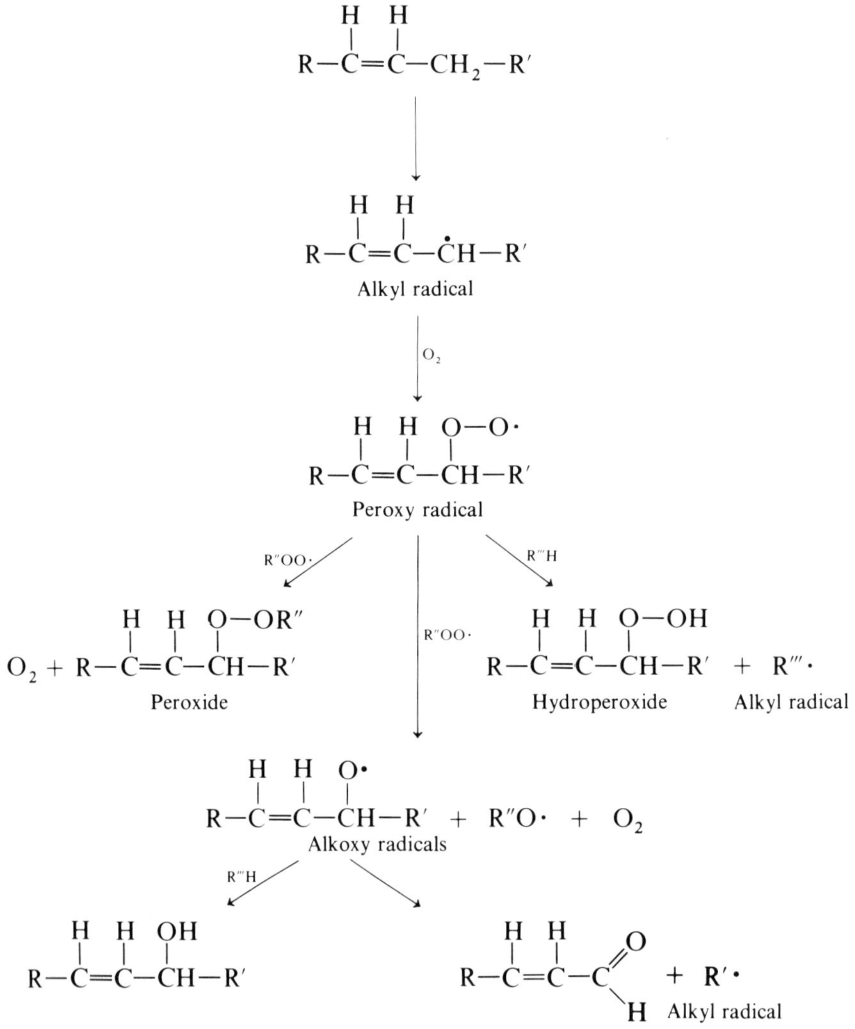

$$R-CH=CH-CH_2-R'$$

$$\downarrow$$

$$R-CH=CH-\overset{\bullet}{C}H-R'$$
Alkyl radical

$$\downarrow O_2$$

$$R-CH=CH-CH(O-O\bullet)-R'$$
Peroxy radical

$R''OO\bullet \swarrow \quad \downarrow R''OO\bullet \quad \searrow R'''H$

$O_2 + R-CH=CH-CH(O-OR'')-R'$ — Peroxide

$R-CH=CH-CH(O-OH)-R' + R'''\bullet$ — Hydroperoxide, Alkyl radical

$$\downarrow$$

$$R-CH=CH-CH(O\bullet)-R' + R''O\bullet + O_2$$
Alkoxy radicals

$R'''H \swarrow \quad \searrow$

$R-CH=CH-CH(OH)-R'$

$R-CH=CH-CHO + R'\bullet$ Alkyl radical

The process is shown as being initiated by the formation of an alkyl radical resulting from the homolytic cleavage of the carbon-hydrogen bond of an allylic carbon atom. This cleavage must be induced by a factor called an *initiator*. Certain metals are thought to function as initiators of radical processes. Also, in alkaline media, alkyl radicals can be generated from a suitable carbanion which undergoes a one-electron oxidation in the presence of molecular oxygen. Once formed, an alkyl radical can undergo several types of reaction. If it reacts with molecular oxygen, a peroxy radical is generated. This, in turn, can react with another peroxy radical, that is, $R''OO\cdot$, to yield either a peroxide plus oxygen or two alkoxy radicals plus oxygen. An alkoxy radical can abstract a hydrogen radical to form an alcohol, or it can undergo homolytic cleavage, with the result that an aldehyde and an alkyl radical are formed. Yet another fate of the peroxy radical is to abstract a hydrogen radical from the solvent or from a hydrocarbon chain, thus generating a hydroperoxide and an alkyl radical. In fact, complex mixtures can be generated particularly when (as is often the case) the acyl moiety contains more than one allylic carbon and initiation can therefore occur at more than one site.

## Hydration of Olefinic Bonds

The hydration of olefinic bonds of unsaturated acyl moieties occurs in several important metabolic pathways, including fatty acid catabolism and anabolism. Although these hydration reactions are catalyzed by the appropriate enzymes, both the enzymatic and the laboratory reactions usually occur by means of an electrophilic mechanism as illustrated here for the case in which multiple olefinic bonds are present, as in the unsaturated fatty acids, e.g., linoleic or linolenic acid.

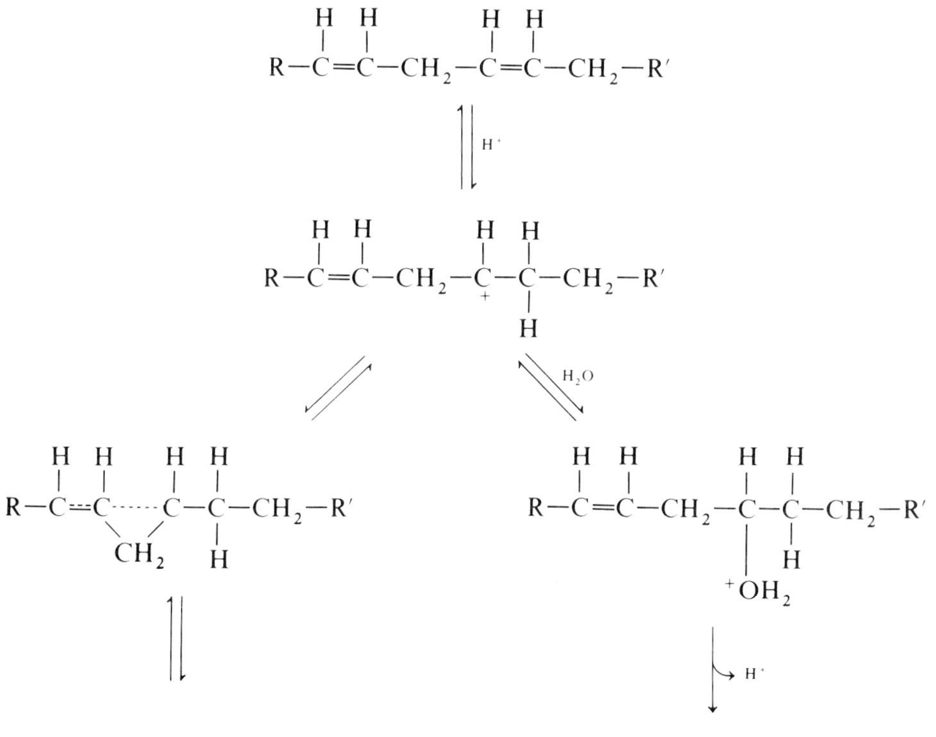

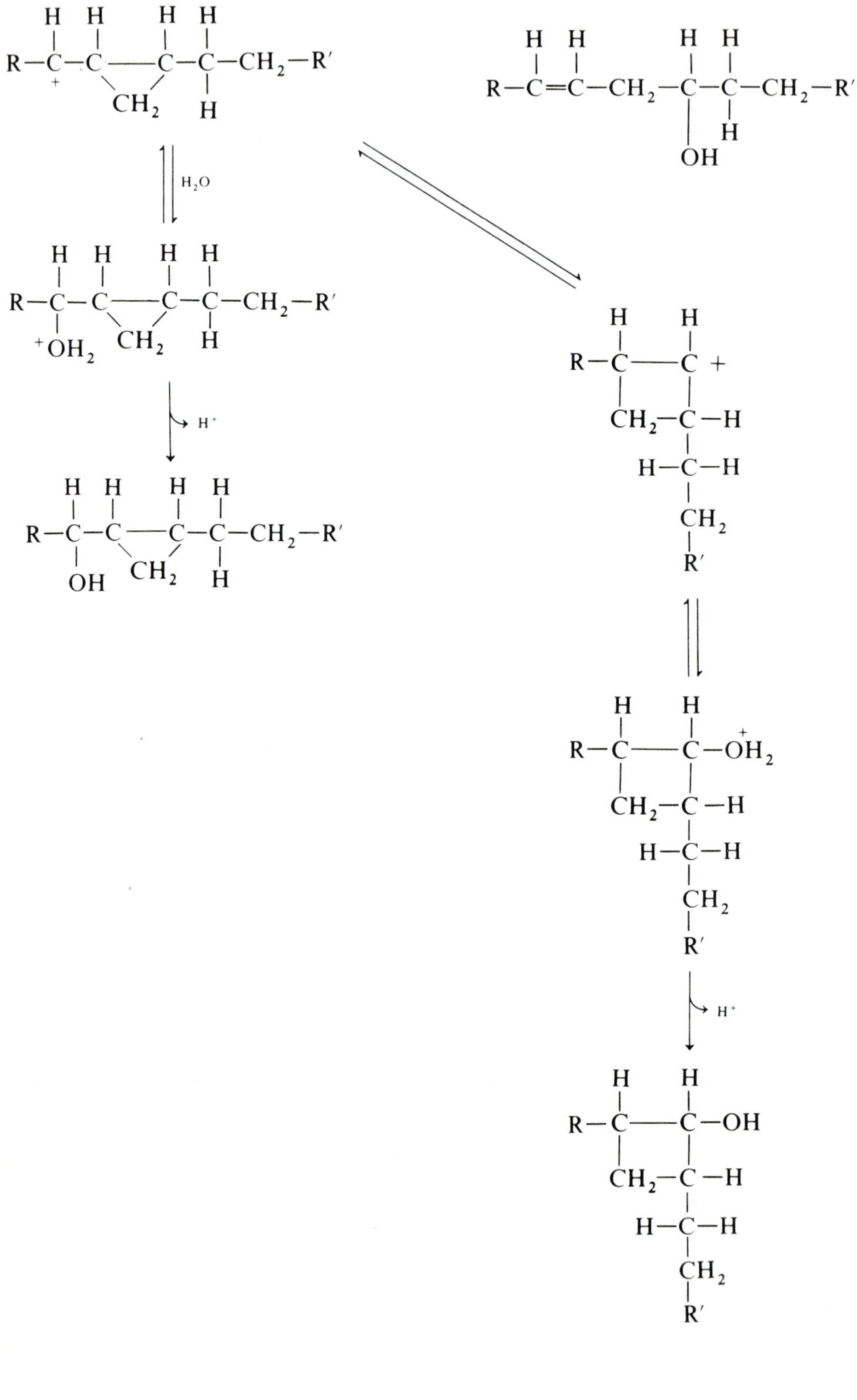

## 138 MECHANISMS OF METABOLISM

$$R-\overset{H}{\underset{+}{C}}-\overset{H}{\underset{CH_2}{C}}\underline{\phantom{-}}\overset{H}{\underset{H}{C}}-\overset{H}{C}-CH_2-R'$$

$$\Updownarrow H_2O$$

$$R-\overset{H}{\underset{+OH_2}{C}}-\overset{H}{\underset{CH_2}{C}}\underline{\phantom{-}}\overset{H}{\underset{H}{C}}-\overset{H}{C}-CH_2-R'$$

$$\downarrow H^+$$

$$R-\overset{H}{\underset{OH}{C}}-\overset{H}{\underset{CH_2}{C}}\underline{\phantom{-}}\overset{H}{\underset{H}{C}}-\overset{H}{C}-CH_2-R'$$

$$R-\overset{H}{C}=\overset{H}{C}-CH_2-\overset{H}{\underset{OH}{C}}-\overset{H}{\underset{H}{C}}-CH_2-R'$$

$$\Longleftarrow$$

$$R-\overset{H}{C}-\overset{H}{C}+\atop{\underset{CH_2-\overset{|}{C}-H}{\phantom{x}}\atop{\underset{H-\overset{|}{C}-H}{\phantom{x}}\atop{\underset{CH_2}{\phantom{x}}\atop{R'}}}}$$

$$\Updownarrow$$

$$R-\overset{H}{C}-\overset{H}{C}-\overset{+}{O}H_2\atop{\underset{CH_2-\overset{|}{C}-H}{\phantom{x}}\atop{\underset{H-\overset{|}{C}-H}{\phantom{x}}\atop{\underset{CH_2}{\phantom{x}}\atop{R'}}}}$$

$$\downarrow H^+$$

$$R-\overset{H}{C}-\overset{H}{C}-OH\atop{\underset{CH_2-\overset{|}{C}-H}{\phantom{x}}\atop{\underset{H-\overset{|}{C}-H}{\phantom{x}}\atop{\underset{CH_2}{\phantom{x}}\atop{R'}}}}$$

Initial protonation of one of the olefinic bonds yields a carbonium ion, which in turn can react with a molecule of water or undergo rearrangement to yield a second carbonium ion. This second carbonium ion can react with a water molecule or again undergo rearrangement before reacting with a water molecule. Thus, the acid-catalyzed hydration process can yield several different alcohols.

## STEROIDS

The steroids are perhydrocyclopentanophenanthrene derivatives with relatively complex structures. When characterizing the steroids structurally one must identify not only the various ring substituents but also the geometry of the ring fusions. In certain instances optical-rotatory-dispersion studies have been used to gain information about the geometric aspects of steroid structure. Optical rotatory dispersion, as mentioned in Chap. 2, is the variation of optical rotation as a function of wavelength. When the absorption spectrum of a molecule does not exhibit a band in the wavelength region under study, the magnitude of the optical rotation simply increases as the wavelength decreases and a plain curve is obtained. A plain curve is designated positive if the rotation becomes more positive as the wavelength decreases and negative if the rotation becomes more negative. By contrast, when the absorption spectrum of a molecule exhibits an absorption band in the wavelength region under study, the magnitude of the optical rotation will generally increase and then decrease sharply in the region of this band (Cotton effect). A Cotton effect is called positive if the maximum of the dispersion curve occurs at a longer wavelength than the minimum and negative if the minimum occurs at the longer wavelength. It has been shown that the sign and the amplitude, i.e., the vertical distance between the maximum, or peak, and the minimum, or trough, of a Cotton effect can be related to the spatial configuration of the absorbing molecule by a semiempirical formation known as the *octant rule*.† The use of the octant rule in determining the geometry of the ring fusion in certain steroid molecules can be illustrated by the following example. The steroids cholestan-3-one and coprostan-3-one were known to differ only in the geometry of the A/B ring fusion. Cholestan-3-one exhibits a positive Cotton effect with a molecular amplitude (difference between molecular rotation at the maximum and the minimum of the Cotton effect) of 6500°. Coprostan-3-one, on the other hand, exhibits a negative Cotton effect with a molecular amplitude of $-2700°$. According to the octant rule, if the molecule under study is assumed to be positioned in a coordinate system defined by three mutually orthogonal planes so that the chromophore is at the intersection of these planes, substituents that lie in the lower right and upper left octants make positive contributions to the Cotton effect while those in upper right and lower left octants make negative contributions. This is illustrated diagrammatically in Fig. 4-3. In steroid molecules, when the structure having a trans fusion of rings A and B is oriented appropriately in the coordinate system, the atoms at the 6 and 7

---

† Moffitt, W., and Moscowitz, A. (1958) *Abstr. Pap. 133d Meet. Am. Chem. Soc.* p. 270; Moffitt, W., and Moscowitz, A. (1959) *J. Chem. Phys.* **30**, 649–660; Moffitt, W., Moscowitz, A., Woodward, R. B., Klyne, W., and Djerassi, C. (1961) *J. Am. Chem. Soc.* **83**, 4013–4018.

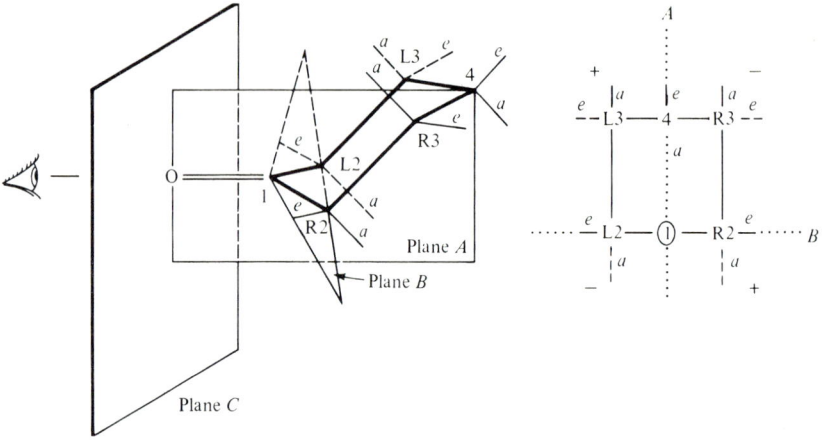

**Figure 4-3** The three mutually orthogonal planes are designated by *A*, *B*, and *C*. The origin of the coordinate system is considered to be the midpoint of the chromophoric group, i.e., the C=O moiety. The contributions to the Cotton effect made by substituents in the four distal octants are indicated, with *e* and *a* as abbreviations for equatorial and axial, respectively. Substituents that lie *in* a plane make no contribution. In the example shown, and in most cases, only the four distal octants are occupied. Should one or more of the four proximal octants be occupied, the contributions of substituents in these octants will be just the opposite of those of substituents in the distal octants. [*From Djerassi, C. (1960) Optical Rotatory Dispersion, p. 181, McGraw-Hill, New York. With permission.*]

positions and those at the 15 and 16 positions are in the upper left (distal) octant. Hence, these atoms should make positive contributions to the Cotton effect. The contributions of atoms like those at the 1 and 2 positions are counterbalanced by the contributions of other atoms like those at the 4 and 5 positions in the example cited. Thus, it was concluded that the steroid that exhibits the positive Cotton effect, i.e., cholestan-3-one, has rings A and B fused trans. On the other hand, when the structure in which rings A and B are fused cis is appropriately oriented in the coordinate system, it can be concluded that such a structure should exhibit a negative Cotton effect. Hence, this structure is assigned to coprostan-3-one.

## Some Reactions of Steroids

Among some of the novel reactions undergone by steroids are the various steroid rearrangements, which occur not only in laboratory reactions but also in the cells of living organisms, e.g., in the anabolism of cholesterol there is a series of methyl-group migrations.

**The dienone-phenol rearrangement** In the laboratory and under acidic conditions certain steroids undergo a rearrangement which can result in the aromatization of the A ring and which can be formulated as shown.

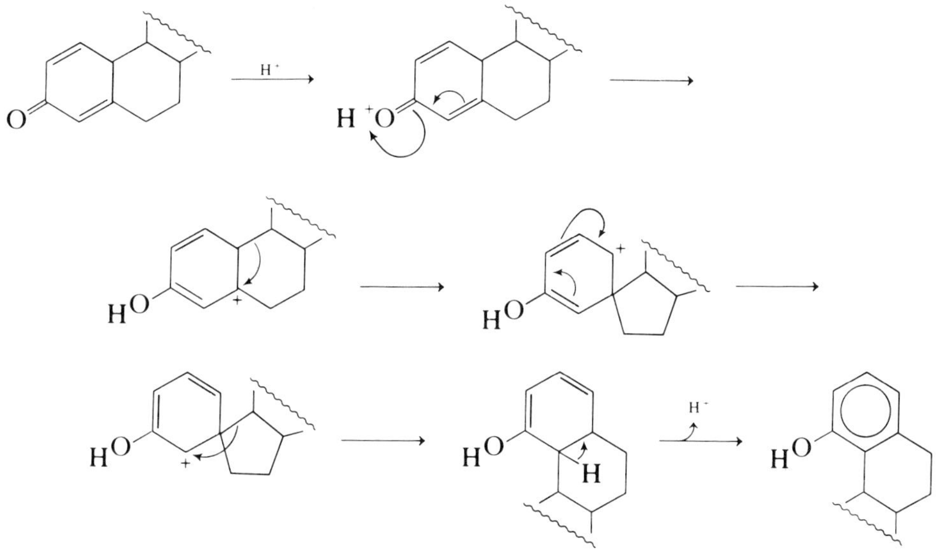

Protonation of the oxygen atom results in generating a carbonium ion and promoting the initial bond migration which results in the formation of the spiro[4.5]decane intermediate. A subsequent bond migration results in the formation of the fused ring system, which then expels a proton and gains aromaticity.

**The Baeyer-Villiger rearrangement** A reaction involving the use of a peracid, e.g., perbenzoic or peroxytrifluoroacetic acid, can bring about the conversion of an oxo compound into an ester. The process has been used to convert progesterone into testosterone in the laboratory. In this reaction, in the presence of the peracid a peroxy derivative is generated. This then expels the carboxylate anion to yield an electron-deficient species that undergoes rearrangement to yield the conjugate acid of testosterone acetate. Hydrolytic cleavage of testosterone acetate produces testosterone.

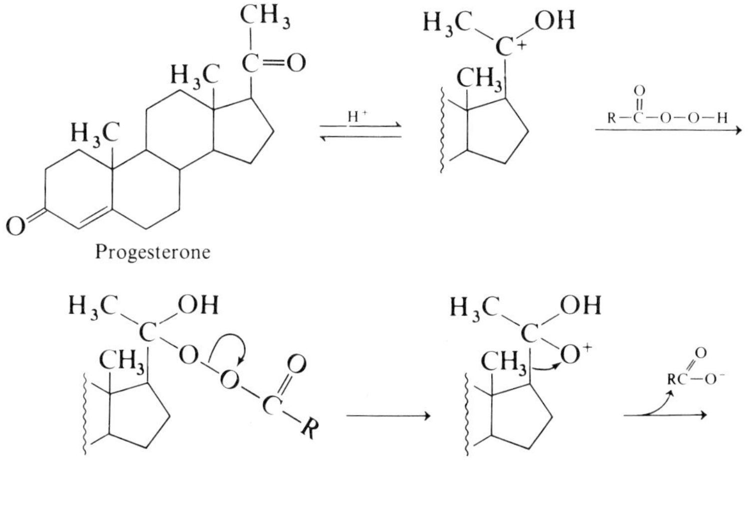

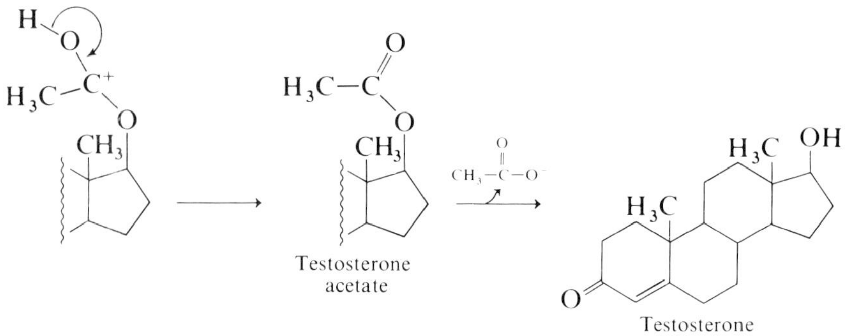

**Pinacol rearrangement of steroids** The pinacol rearrangement converts a vicinal diol into an aldehyde or ketone. The rearrangement is acid-catalyzed and entails the formation of a carbonium ion, as illustrated.

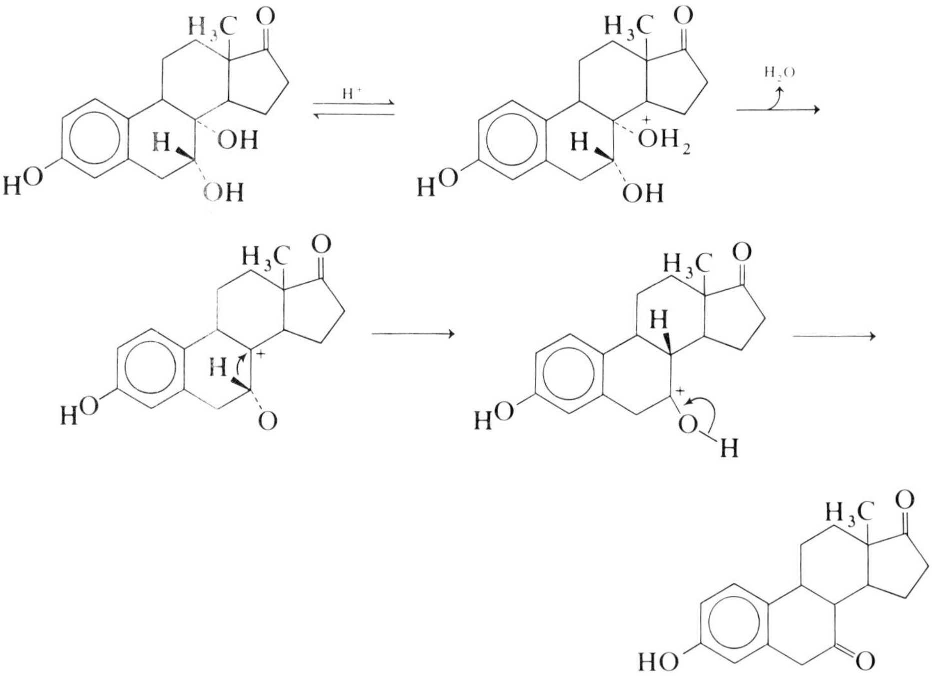

Not only do the appropriate steroids undergo rearrangement, but simple acyclic vicinal diols are readily converted into the corresponding carbonyl compounds and the reaction in fact derives its name from a typical acyclic diol, pinacol, which is converted to pinacolone.

**Isomerization of ergosterol to yield vitamin $D_2$** The plant sterol, or phytosterol, ergosterol can be converted to vitamin $D_2$ by a process that involves both photochemical and ionic reactions.

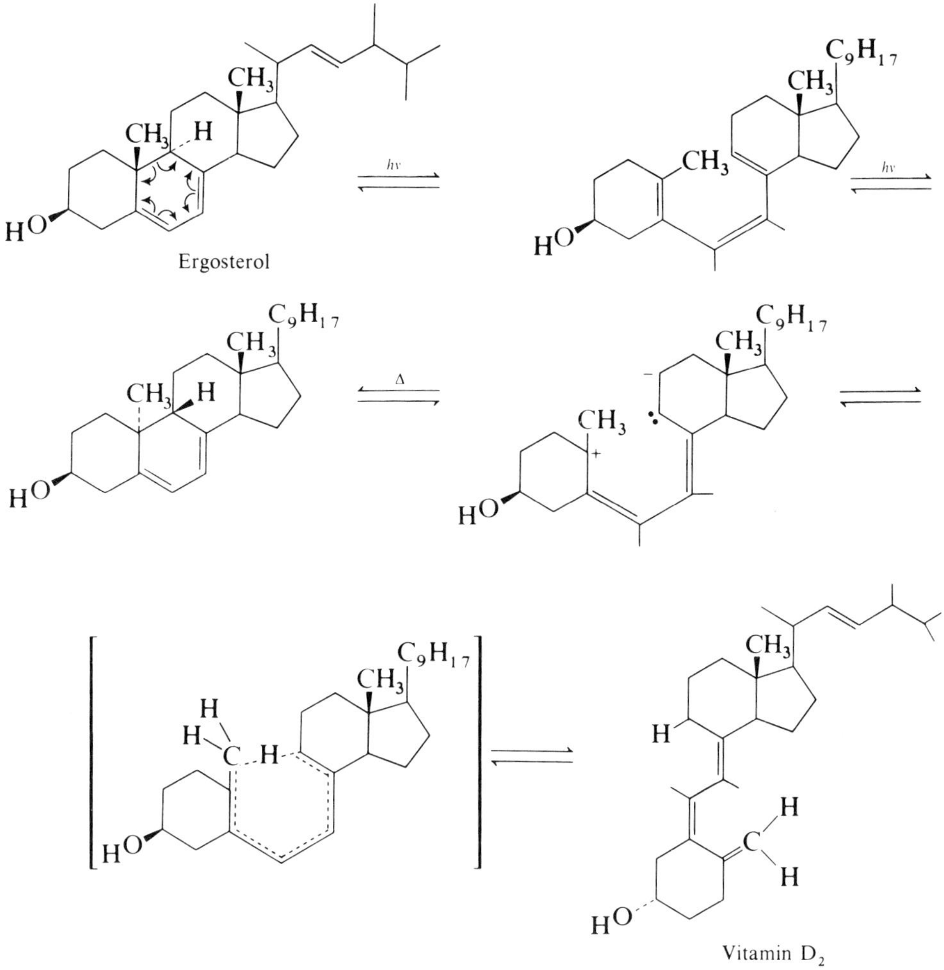

Irradiation of ergosterol with light having a wavelength of approximately 280 nm brings about a homolytic ring cleavage by redistributing the electrons as indicated. The resulting intermediate can then undergo ring closure to yield an isomer of ergosterol which has the opposite configurations at C(9) and C(10). Next, as the result of a thermal process, there is a heterolytic ring cleavage, which is followed by the abstraction of a proton and cis-trans isomerization, with the result that vitamin $D_2$ is formed. The transition state represented by the bracketed structure is thought to participate in the proton-abstraction and isomerization processes.

## LIPIDS AND CELL MEMBRANES

Biological membranes are primarily composed of proteins and lipids while containing small amounts of carbohydrates as well. Besides functioning as the limiting structure of the cell, its organelles, and compartments, biological membranes embody enzymes that catalyze specific reactions, transport systems that translocate ions and molecules, and receptors and other binding sites that interact with such species as hormones, antibodies, ions, and other components.

Generally, biological membranes consist of approximately 60 percent protein and 40 percent lipid. A conceptual model for the interaction of these factors has been suggested by S. J. Singer, of the University of California, San Diego. This model focuses upon the fluidity of the membrane and depicts it as a solution of globular proteins dispersed in a fluid lipid matrix. In fact, the fluidity of the membrane and the lateral mobility of its lipid and protein components are believed to be of importance with respect to its function. The proteins of the membrane have been designated as either integral or peripheral. Integral proteins are intimately interdigitated with the lipids of the membrane, and, generally, even when these proteins removed from the membrane, e.g., through the use of a nonionic detergent, they are obtained in association with a portion of the membrane lipid. (In some cases where the protein is a membrane-associated enzyme, the presence of lipid is absolutely necessary for activity to be expressed.) Peripheral proteins, on the other hand, are less tightly associated with the membrane and are generally isolated without accompanying lipid. The lipids of the membrane are thought to form a bilayer which allows the hydrophobic portions of these molecules, i.e., the hydrocarbon chains, to be internal and not in contact with the aqueous medium while the hydrophilic portions, i.e., the carboxylate groups or the phosphodiester moieties, are external and exposed to the medium. How the proteins are thought to be positioned in the fluid lipid mosaic is represented schematically in Fig. 4-4. Not only are the lipids amphipathic but membrane-associated proteins are usually amphipathic also, and therefore the hydrophobic portions of the

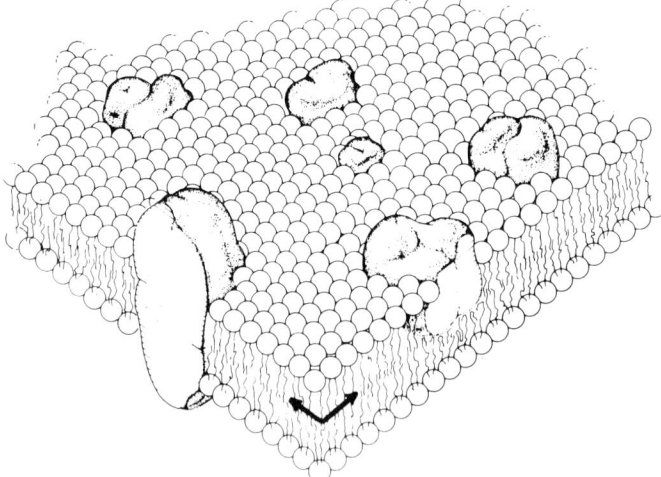

**Figure 4-4** The hydrophobic carbon chains of the lipids are represented by the wavy lines. Their hydrophilic carboxylate or phosphodiester moieties are represented by the spheres. The proteins are represented by the bodies with stippled surfaces. As indicated, some proteins (or protein complexes) span the entire membrane while others do not. [*From Singer, S. J., and Nicolson, G. L. (1972) Science* **175**, *720–731 (see p. 723). With permission.*]

lipids and the hydrophobic portions of the proteins can undergo association in the interior of the membrane. Evidence in support of the schematic representation in Fig. 4-4 can be found in the electron micrographs of biological membranes (Fig. 4-5). When freeze-etching techniques are used, the fracture face of the membrane is interrupted by numerous raised areas that are thought to reflect the presence of the proteins dispersed in the lipid.

The components of biological membranes are known to be distributed asymmetrically across the span from the membrane inner surface to its outer surface. This has been demonstrated with respect to both membrane lipids and membrane proteins. For the former it has been shown that an enzyme that catalyzes the deacylation of phospholipids converts 70 percent of the phosphatidylcholine of the intact human-erythrocyte membrane to its cleavage products although other phospholipids, including phosphatidylserine and phosphatidylethanolamine, remain essentially intact. This observation has been interpreted as indicating that of the various membrane

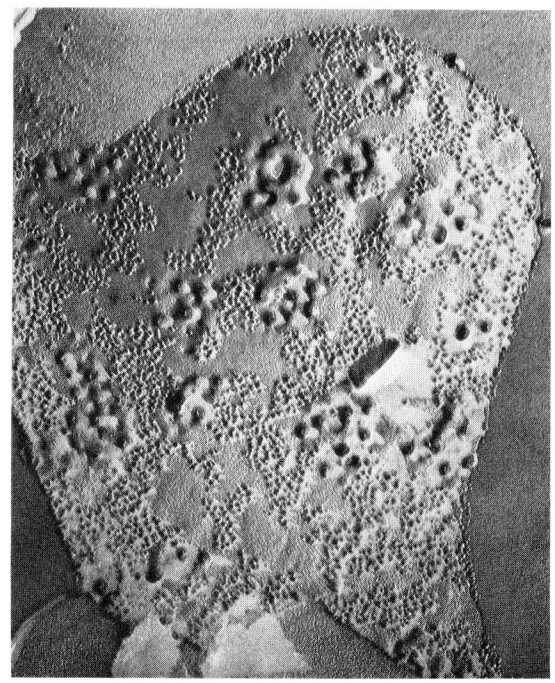

(a)

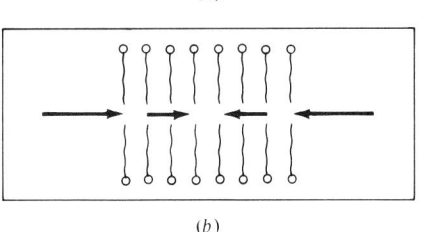

(b)

**Figure 4-5** (a) Electron micrograph of the human erythrocyte membrane obtained using the freeze-fracture technique. Specimen is rapidly frozen and then fractured. The plane of the fracture is indicated in (b). Replicas of the fracture faces are prepared and subsequently examined using the electron microscope. The inner fracture face (shown) exhibits numerous raised areas which are thought to reflect the presence of proteins that are dispersed in the lipid bilayer. [From Deenen, L. L. M. van, Gier, J. de, Demel, R. A., Kruyff, B. de, Blok, M. C., Neut-Kok, E. C. M. van der, Haest, C. W. M., Verveergaert, P. H. J. T., and Verkleij, A. J. (1975) Ann. N.Y. Acad. Sci. **264**, 124–141 (see p. 127). With permission.]

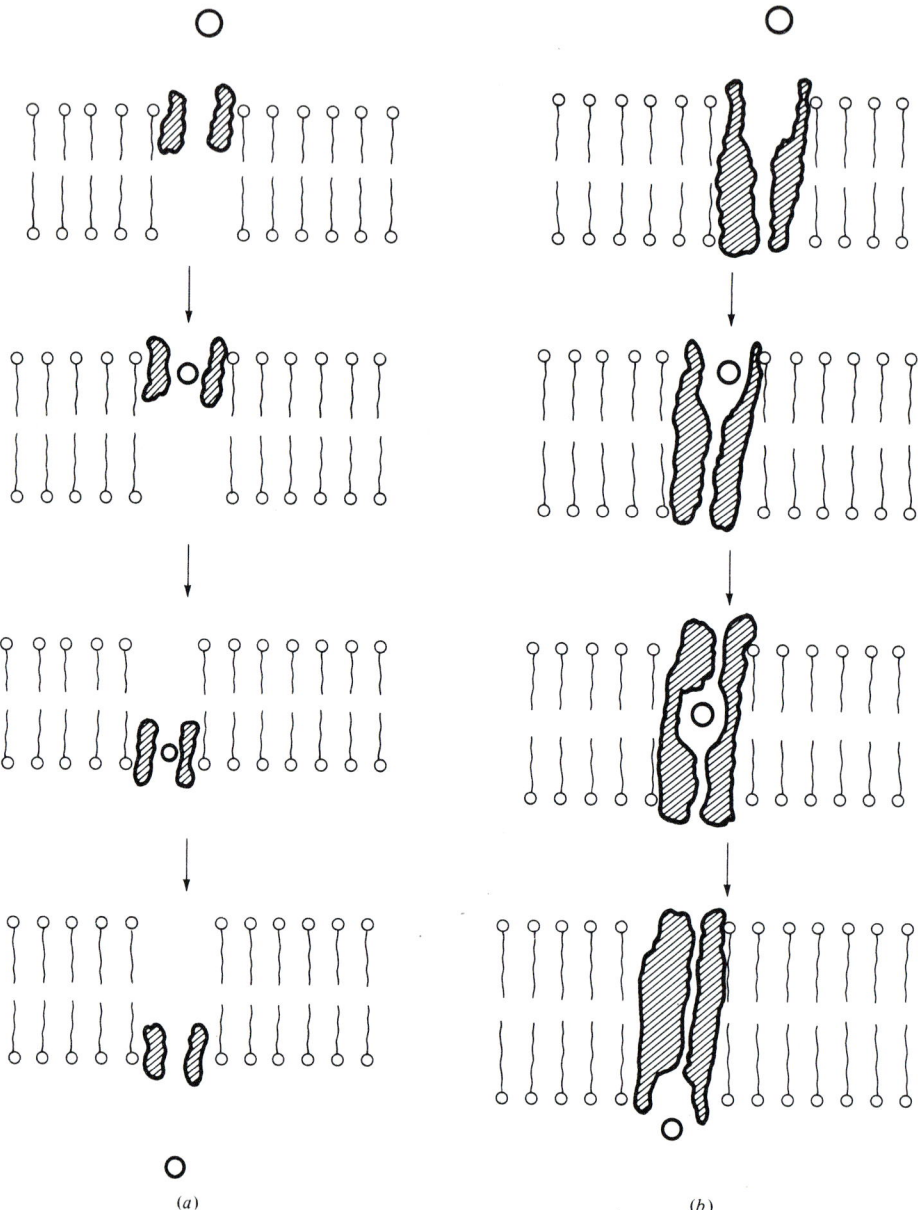

**Figure 4-6** (*a*) The carrier model and (*b*) the channel model of membrane transport.

phospholipids, a greater percentage of the phosphatidylcholine is near the membrane outer surface. For membrane proteins, it has been shown that in certain membrane-associated enzymes and receptors activity is exhibited only when the species with which the enzyme or receptor must react is in the extracellular medium or, alternatively, when this species is present intracellularly. These observations have been taken to indicate that certain types of binding sites or interaction sites are specifically on the outer surface of the membrane while others are specifically on its inner surface.

The question of how various small hydrophilic molecules and ions are translocated across biological membranes remains unanswered. Most models for these processes can be considered to involve either a *carrier* or a *channel*, however. A carrier is usually conceived of as a protein which, while located at one membrane surface, can bind a hydrophilic species and then, in association with this species, pass through the membrane interior and subsequently release the species at the other membrane surface. It is generally agreed, therefore, that the carrier must be able to bind and to release the molecule or ion efficiently and that the carrier in association with the appropriate molecule or ion must be hydrophobic. According to the channel model, on the other hand, conformational changes within a protein-lined pore allow a molecule or ion to be translocated from one membrane surface to the other. Thus, a principal difference between the two models is that the carrier model requires the participation of a mobile component that traverses the distance between the inner and outer membrane surfaces while the channel model requires a passageway that spans the membrane, the translocation of molecules and ions coming about perhaps as the result of a process bearing some degree of resemblance to peristaltic action. (Peristalsis is the periodic contraction and relaxation of a tubular system that allows material in the lumen of the tube to be translocated.) These models for membrane transport are represented schematically in Fig. 4-6.

CHAPTER
# FIVE

## THE CHEMISTRY OF THE AMINO ACIDS AND THE PROTEINS

The word protein is derived from the Greek word *proteios*, meaning "principal" or "prime." The name is quite applicable because the proteins are, in fact, principal components of biochemical systems. Proteins serve a structural function and can be degraded and catabolized to provide a source of energy; furthermore virtually all biochemical reactions are catalyzed by enzymes, and all enzymes are proteins (or protein derivatives).

### AMINO ACIDS

Proteins are polymers comprising aminoacyl units which are joined by the formation of amide, or peptide, bonds. The approximately 20 amino acids that serve as monomeric units in most naturally occurring proteins are listed in Fig. 5-1. At physiological pH in mammalian systems the carboxyl group of an amino acid is ionized and the amino group is protonated. This doubly charged species is called a *zwitterion*.

# THE CHEMISTRY OF THE AMINO ACIDS AND THE PROTEINS

Aliphatic amino acids:

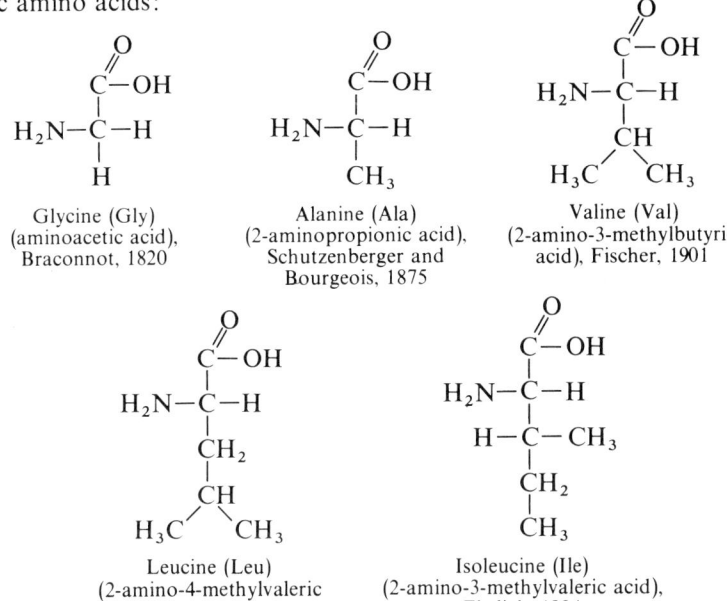

Hydroxyamino acids:

Diamino and guanidinoamino acids:

**Figure 5-1** The trivial name of the amino acid is followed by its abbreviation in parentheses. Next, the systematic name of the amino acid is given, together with its discoverer and the year of the discovery.

Dicarboxylic acids and their amides:

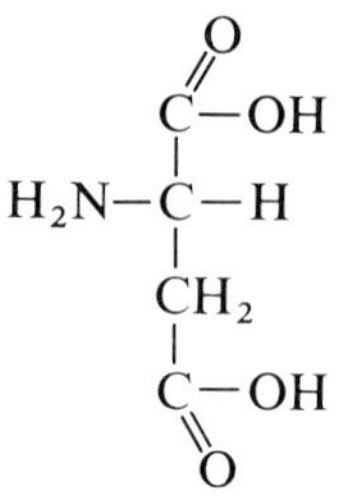

Aspartic acid (Asp)
(2-aminosuccinic acid),
Rittenhausen, 1868

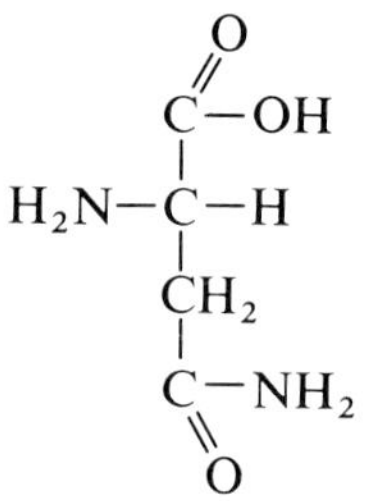

Asparagine (Asn)
(2-amino-succinamic acid),
Damodaran, 1932

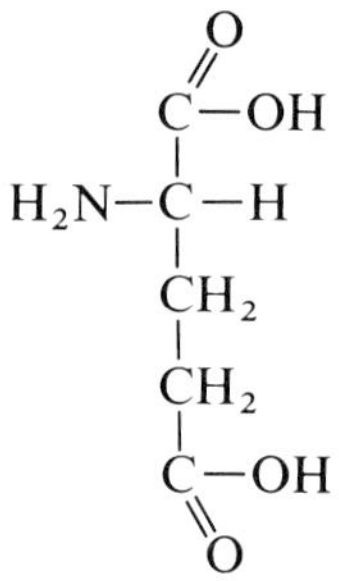

Glutamic acid (Glu)
(2-aminoglutaric acid),
Rittenhausen, 1866

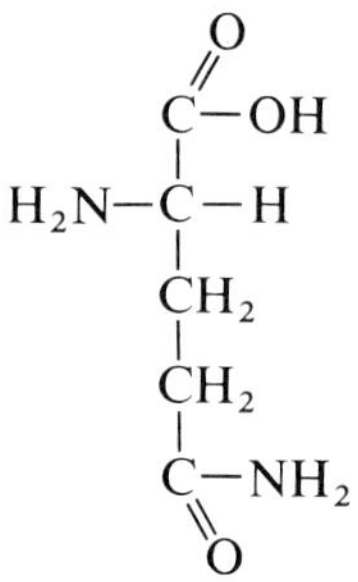

Glutamine (Gln)
(2-aminoglutaramic acid),
Damodaran, 1932

Mercapto- and alkylthioamino acids

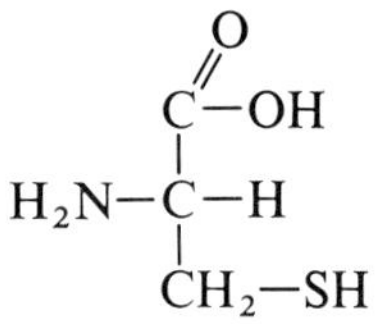

Cysteine (Cys)
(2-amino-3-mercaptoproprionic acid),
Morner, 1899

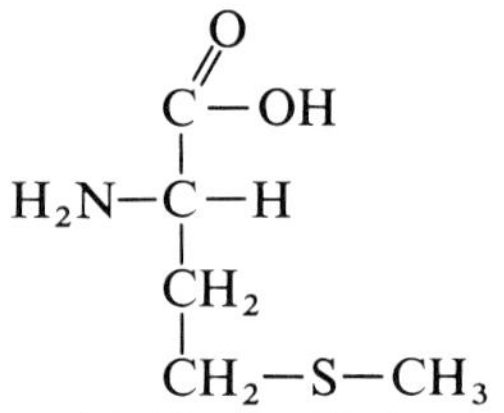

Methionine (Met)
[2-amino-4-(methylthio) butyric acid],
Mueller, 1922

Pyrrolidine derivatives:

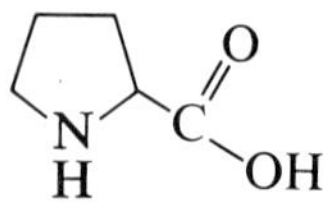

Proline (Pro)
(2-pyrrolidinecarboxylic acid),
Fischer, 1901

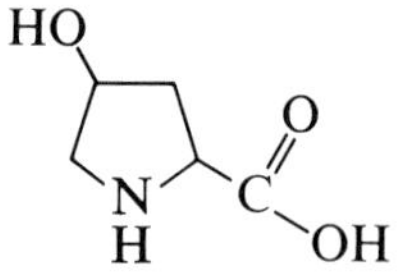

Hydroxyproline
(4-hydroxy-2-pyrrolidinecarboxylic acid),
Fischer, 1902

**Figure 5-1** (*Continued*)

THE CHEMISTRY OF THE AMINO ACIDS AND THE PROTEINS  151

Aromatic amino acids:

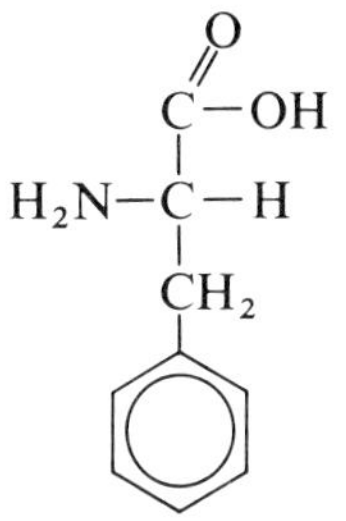

Phenylalanine (Phe)
(2-amino-3-phenylpropionic acid),
Schulze and Barbieri, 1879

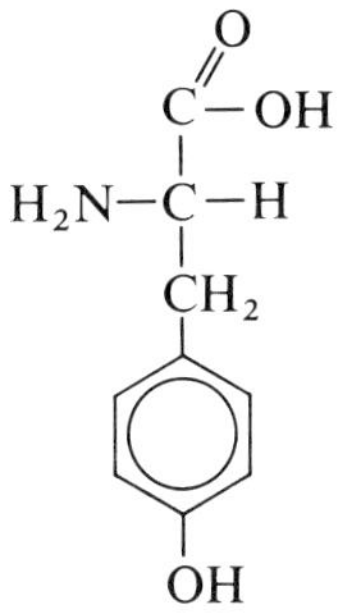

Tyrosine (Tyr)
[2-amino-3-(4-hydroxyphenyl)-propionic acid],
Liebig, 1846

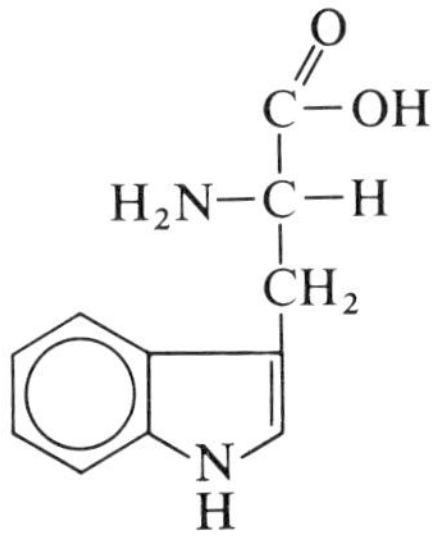

Tryptophan (Trp)
(2-amino-3-(3-indolyl) propionic acid),
Hopkins and Cole, 1901

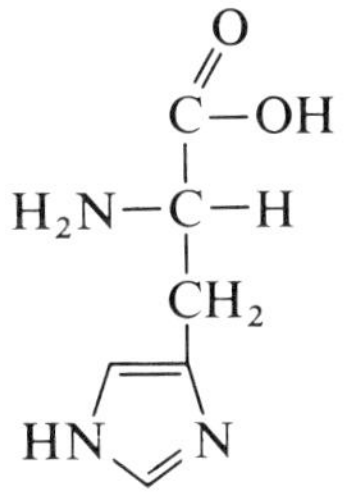

Histidine (His)
(2-amino-3-(4-imidazoyl) propionic acid),
Kossel, Hedin, 1896

**Figure 5-1** (*Continued*)


## Optical Rotation of Amino Acids

All the 2-amino acids, with the exception of glycine, are optically active, and, in fact, threonine, isoleucine, and hydroxyproline have two centers of dissymmetry each. The specific rotations of the optically active 2-amino acids in acidic, neutral, and alkaline media are shown in Table 5-1. Note that the specific rotations of proline and hydroxyproline are greater than those of the 2-amino acids. This has been attributed to the fact that the dissymmetrically substituted carbon atoms of both these amino acids are members of a ring system, and it has been shown that when there is restricted rotation about the bonds that join a dissymmetrically substituted carbon atom and its substituents, the optical rotation due to that center is somewhat larger than expected.†

---

† Kauzmann, W., and Eyring, H. (1941) *J. Chem. Phys.* **9**, 41–53.

## Table 5-1 Specific rotations of optically active amino acids

| Amino acid | Acidic solution | | Neutral solution ($H_2O$), | Alkaline solution | |
|---|---|---|---|---|---|
| | $[\alpha]_D$, deg | Normality (HCl) | $[\alpha]_D$, deg | $[\alpha]_D$, deg | Normality (NaOH) |
| **Aliphatic amino acids:** | | | | | |
| Alanine | +13.70 | 6 N | +2.41 | +3.0 | 3 N |
| Valine | +28.8 | 6 N | +6.42 | | |
| Leucine | +15.2 | 6 N | −10.57 | +7.56 | 3 N |
| Isoleucine | +40.61 | 6.1 N | +11.29 | +11.09 | 0.33 N |
| **Hydroxyamino acids:** | | | | | |
| Serine | +14.95 | 1 N | −6.83 | | |
| Threonine | | | −9.1 | | |
| **Dicarboxylic acids and their amides:** | | | | | |
| Aspartic acid | +24.6 | 6 N | +4.7 | −1.7 | 3 N |
| Asparagine | +34.26 | 3.4 N | −5.3 | −6.35 | 2.5 N |
| Glutamic acid | +31.2 | 6 N | +11.5 | +10.96 | 1 N |
| Glutamine | ...... | ...... | +5.0 | | |
| **Diamino and guanidinoamino acids:** | | | | | |
| Lysine | +25.9 | 6 N | +14.6 | | |
| Arginine | +27.58 | 6 N | +12.5 | +11.8 | 0.5 N |
| **Mercapto- and alkylthioamino acids:** | | | | | |
| Cysteine | +7.6 | 1 N | | | |
| Methionine | +23.4 | 3 N | −8.11 | | |
| **Pyrrolidine derivatives:** | | | | | |
| Proline | ...... | ...... | −85.0 | −93.0 | 0.6 N† |
| Hydroxyproline | ...... | ...... | −75.2 | −70.6 | 0.5 N |
| **Aromatic amino acids:** | | | | | |
| Phenylalanine | ...... | ...... | −35.14 | | |
| Tyrosine | −8.64 | 6.3 N | | −13.2 | 3 N |
| Tryptophan | +2.4 | 0.5 N | −31.5 | +6.17 | 0.5 N |
| Histidine | +13.34 | 6.1 N | −38.95 | −10.9 | 0.5 N |

† KOH.

## Laboratory Synthesis of Amino Acids

The 2-amino acids can be synthesized in the laboratory by several procedures, including a sequence involving the formation of the cyanohydrin of an aldehyde, the replacement of the hydroxyl group of the cyanohydrin by an amino group, and the

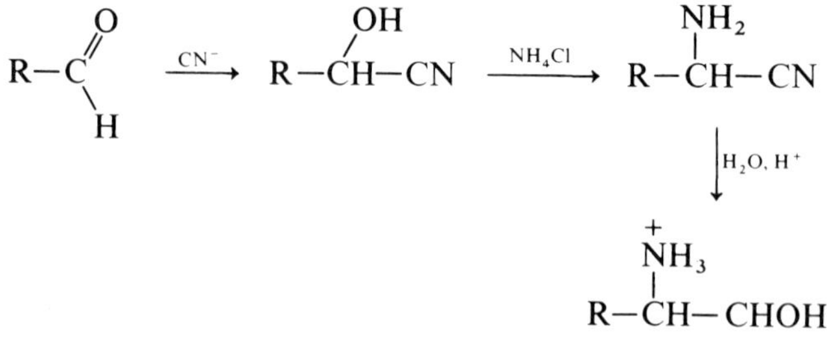

$$R-\underset{H}{\overset{O}{\underset{\|}{C}}} \xrightarrow{CN^-} R-\underset{}{\overset{OH}{\underset{|}{CH}}}-CN \xrightarrow{NH_4Cl} R-\underset{}{\overset{NH_2}{\underset{|}{CH}}}-CN$$

$$\downarrow H_2O, H^+$$

$$R-\underset{}{\overset{\overset{+}{N}H_3}{\underset{|}{CH}}}-CHOH$$

hydrolytic conversion of the nitrile group to a carboxyl group. This sequence is sometimes referred to as the *Strecker synthesis* since Adolph Strecker of the University of Tubingen introduced syntheses of this type.

Another type of sequence is illustrated by the laboratory synthesis of methionine:

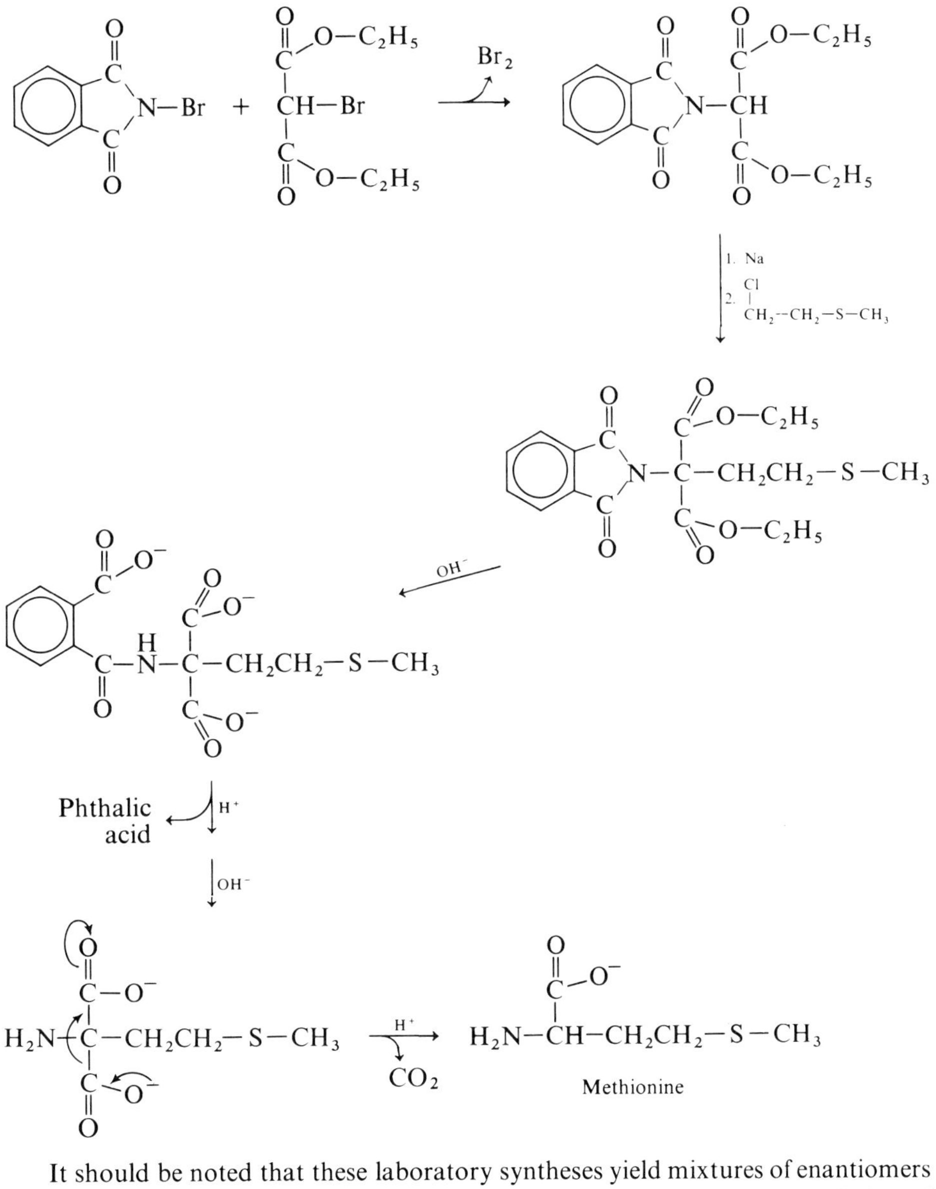

[Reaction scheme: N-bromophthalimide + diethyl bromomalonate (CHBr(COOC$_2$H$_5$)$_2$) with Br$_2$ → N-substituted phthalimide diethyl malonate derivative]

[Next step: 1. Na, 2. Cl–CH$_2$–CH$_2$–S–CH$_3$ → phthalimido diethyl (2-methylthioethyl)malonate]

[Then OH$^-$ → phthalamic diacid intermediate with –CH$_2$CH$_2$–S–CH$_3$ side chain]

[Then H$^+$ → Phthalic acid + substituted aminomalonic acid]

[Then OH$^-$: H$_2$N–C(COO$^-$)$_2$–CH$_2$CH$_2$–S–CH$_3$  $\xrightarrow{H^+, -CO_2}$  H$_2$N–CH(COO$^-$)–CH$_2$CH$_2$–S–CH$_3$   Methionine]

It should be noted that these laboratory syntheses yield mixtures of enantiomers which must be resolved to obtain the optically active amino acids. The resolution of amino acids is frequently carried out with the amino group protected so that in effect the process is that of the resolution of enantiomeric carboxylic acids. This can be accomplished by using an optically active base, e.g., *l*-brucine, *l*-morphine, *l*-strychnine, or *l*-ephedrine. The enantiomeric acids and the optically active base form two salts, which are diastereomeric. The diastereomeric salts can then be separated in most cases, and subsequently each carboxylic acid can be regenerated. Finally, the protecting group is removed, and the optically active amino acid is obtained. In this procedure it is important that it is possible to remove the protecting group under conditions that do not induce the racemization of the amino acid. For this reason protecting groups that can be removed under acidic conditions and at room temperature or below are used in most cases. Among the available protecting groups of this type are the *t*-butyloxycarbonyl group, the triphenylmethyl group, and the 2-nitrophenylsulfenyl group, each of which can be removed with formic acid at room temperature.

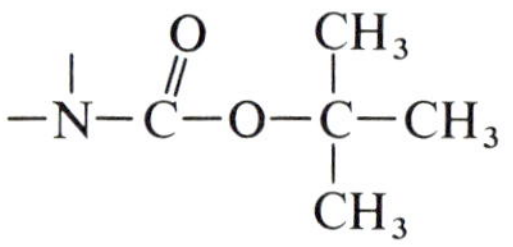

An *N*-(*t*-butyloxycarbonyl) moiety 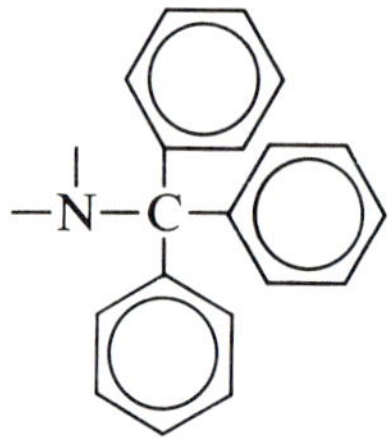     An *N*-triphenylmethyl moiety 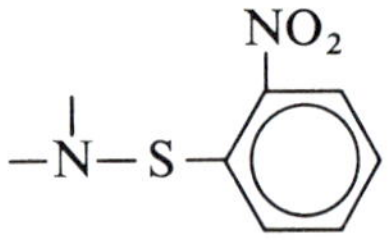     An *N*-(2-nitrophenylsulfenyl) moiety

## Acid-Base Properties of Amino Acids

In the very simplest terms, an acid is a substance that liberates protons in solution. Similarly, a base is a substance that removes protons from solution. Strong acids and strong bases are completely ionized in solution, or nearly so. Weak acids and weak bases are only partially ionized in solution.

The carboxyl group of the amino acids is weakly acidic. The reversible dissociation of such a weak acid HA and the expression for the related dissociation constant are

$$HA + H_2O \rightleftharpoons H_3O^+ + A^- \tag{5-1}$$

$$K = \frac{a_{H_3O^+} a_{A^-}}{a_{HA} a_{H_2O}} \tag{5-2}$$

If it is assumed that the activities $a$ are equivalent to the concentrations, we can write

$$K = \frac{[H_3O^+][A^-]}{[HA][H_2O]} \tag{5-3}$$

If we further assume that the concentration of water in the denominator is a constant, this constant can be incorporated into the dissociation or equilibrium constant $K$, and we can define $K_a$ as

$$K_a = K[H_2O] = \frac{[H_3O^+][A^-]}{[HA]} \tag{5-4}$$

The magnitude of the constant $K_a$ is frequently used as an indication of the strength of an acid.

The amino group of the amino acids is weakly basic. A similar treatment of the reaction of a weak base B in water yields

$$B + H_2O \rightleftharpoons BH^+ + OH^- \tag{5-5}$$

$$K = \frac{a_{BH^+} \, a_{OH^-}}{a_B \, a_{H_2O}} \tag{5-6}$$

If the same types of assumptions are made as for the weak acid, we obtain

$$K = \frac{[B^+][OH^-]}{[B][H_2O]} \tag{5-7}$$

and 

$$K_b = \frac{[B^+][OH^-]}{[B]} \tag{5-8}$$

The constants $K_a$ and $K_b$ express the extent to which an acid releases protons or a base accepts protons, respectively. The constants $K_a$ and $K_b$ are readily converted to $pK_a$ and $pK_b$, respectively, just as hydrogen-ion concentration is converted to pH. The negative logarithm of $X$ is equivalent to $pX$. The constants $pK_a$ and $pK_b$ are interconvertible through the use of the constant $pK_w$, which is the negative logarithm of the dissociation constant for water

$$[H^+][OH^-] = 10^{-14} = K_w \tag{5-9}$$

and, therefore

$$pK_w = 14 \tag{5-10}$$

Since

$$pK_w = pK_a + pK_b \tag{5-11}$$

we have

$$pK_a = pK_w - pK_b \tag{5-12}$$

and

$$pK_b = pK_w - pK_a \tag{5-13}$$

The titration of a simple amino acid, such as glycine or alanine, with a strong acid or a strong base can be represented by a curve like that in Fig. 5-2, in which $pK_{a_1}$ denotes the pH at which the concentration of the completely protonated molecule is equal to that of the zwitterion and $pK_{a_2}$ denotes the pH at which the concentration of the zwitterion is equal to that of the amino acid anion:

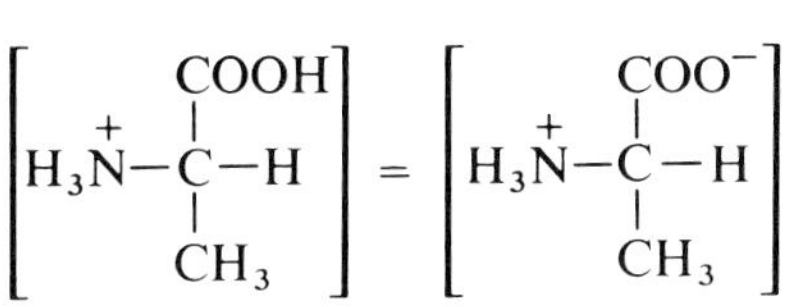

$$\begin{bmatrix} \text{COOH} \\ H_3\overset{+}{N}-\overset{|}{C}-H \\ \text{CH}_3 \end{bmatrix} = \begin{bmatrix} \text{COO}^- \\ H_3\overset{+}{N}-\overset{|}{C}-H \\ \text{CH}_3 \end{bmatrix} \text{ at } pK_{a_1}$$

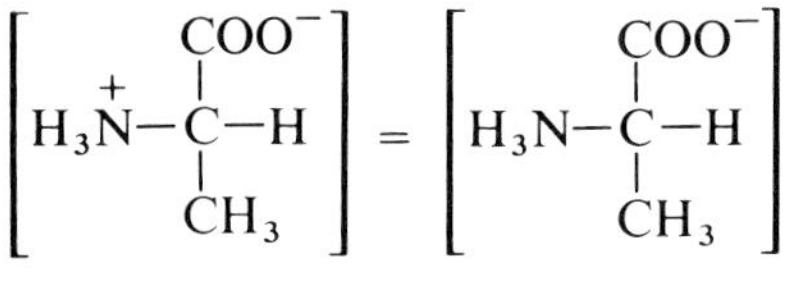

$$\begin{bmatrix} \text{COO}^- \\ H_3\overset{+}{N}-\overset{|}{C}-H \\ \text{CH}_3 \end{bmatrix} = \begin{bmatrix} \text{COO}^- \\ H_3N-\overset{|}{C}-H \\ \text{CH}_3 \end{bmatrix} \text{ at } pK_{a_2}$$

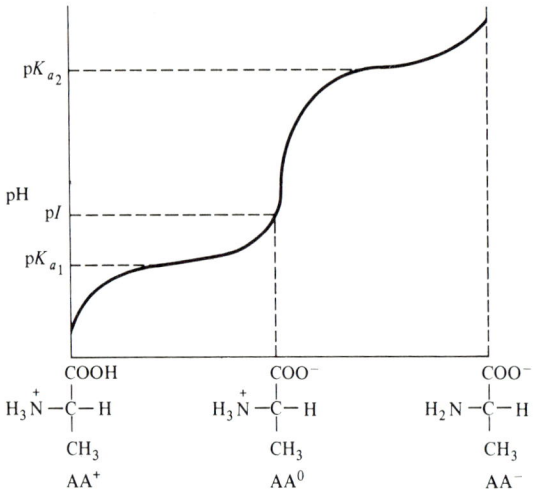

**Figure 5-2** Titration curve for alanine.

The pH at which the amino acid exists as the zwitterion is called the *isoelectric* pH, denoted by p*I*.

The titration of a dicarboxylic amino acid, such as aspartic acid or glutamic acid, with a strong acid or a strong base can be represented by a curve like that in Fig. 5-3.

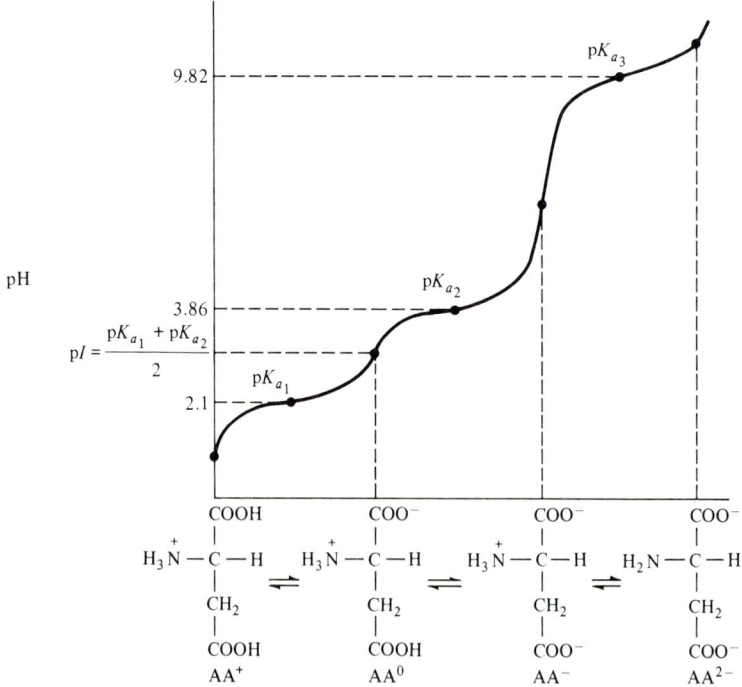

**Figure 5-3** Titration curve for aspartic acid.

In this case, at the pH values indicated by $pK_{a_1}$, $pK_{a_2}$, and $pK_{a_3}$ the following conditions are fulfilled:

$$\begin{bmatrix} \text{COOH} \\ H_3\overset{+}{N}-\underset{|}{\overset{|}{C}}-H \\ CH_2 \\ COOH \end{bmatrix} = \begin{bmatrix} COO^- \\ H_3\overset{+}{N}-\underset{|}{\overset{|}{C}}-H \\ CH_2 \\ COOH \end{bmatrix} \text{ at } pK_{a_1}$$

$$\begin{bmatrix} COO^- \\ H_3\overset{+}{N}-\underset{|}{\overset{|}{C}}-H \\ CH_2 \\ COOH \end{bmatrix} = \begin{bmatrix} COO^- \\ H_3\overset{+}{N}-\underset{|}{\overset{|}{C}}-H \\ CH_2 \\ COO^- \end{bmatrix} \text{ at } pK_{a_2}$$

$$\begin{bmatrix} COO^- \\ H_3\overset{+}{N}-\underset{|}{\overset{|}{C}}-H \\ CH_2 \\ COO^- \end{bmatrix} = \begin{bmatrix} COO^- \\ H_2N-\underset{|}{\overset{|}{C}}-H \\ CH_2 \\ COO^- \end{bmatrix} \text{ at } pK_{a_3}$$

The titration of a diamino acid like lysine is represented by a curve like that in Fig. 5-4. The $pK_a$ values in this case have the following significance:

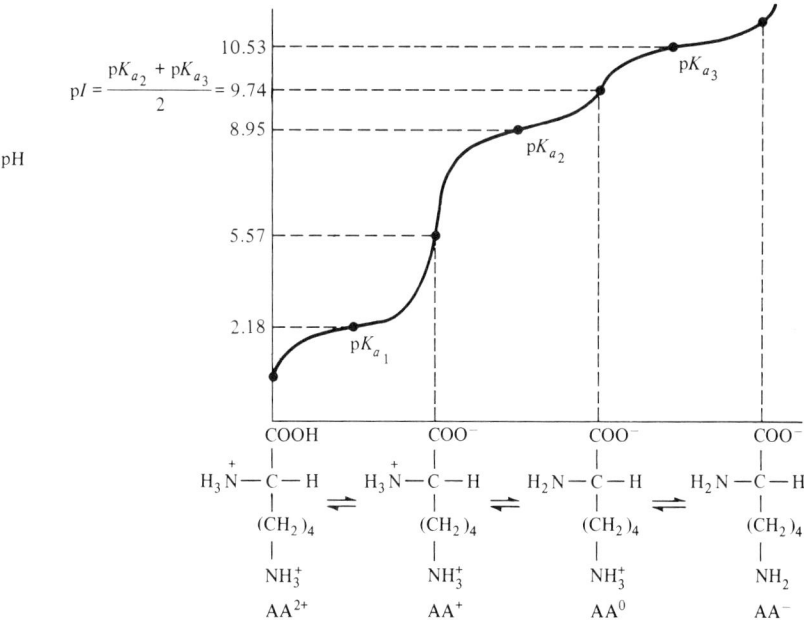

**Figure 5-4** Titration curve for lysine.

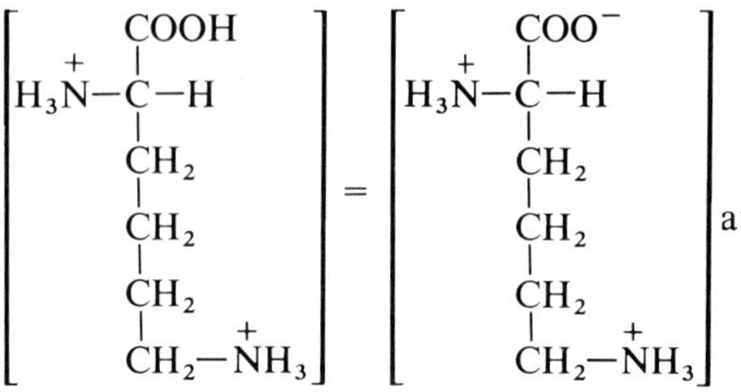

$$\begin{bmatrix} \text{COOH} \\ \overset{+}{\text{H}_3\text{N}}-\text{C}-\text{H} \\ \text{CH}_2 \\ \text{CH}_2 \\ \text{CH}_2 \\ \text{CH}_2-\overset{+}{\text{NH}_3} \end{bmatrix} = \begin{bmatrix} \text{COO}^- \\ \overset{+}{\text{H}_3\text{N}}-\text{C}-\text{H} \\ \text{CH}_2 \\ \text{CH}_2 \\ \text{CH}_2 \\ \text{CH}_2-\overset{+}{\text{NH}_3} \end{bmatrix} \text{ at } pK_{a_1}$$

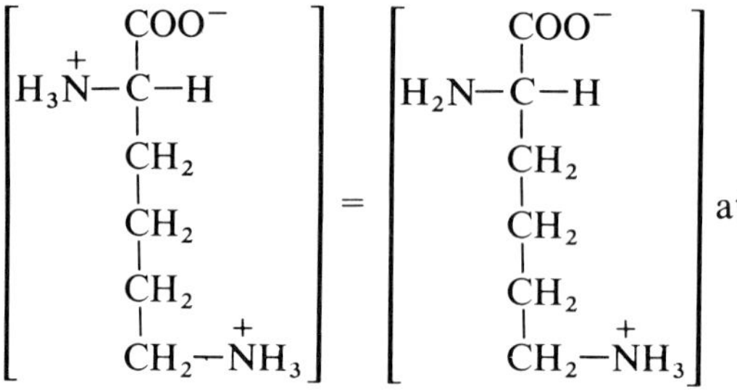

$$\begin{bmatrix} \text{COO}^- \\ \overset{+}{\text{H}_3\text{N}}-\text{C}-\text{H} \\ \text{CH}_2 \\ \text{CH}_2 \\ \text{CH}_2 \\ \text{CH}_2-\overset{+}{\text{NH}_3} \end{bmatrix} = \begin{bmatrix} \text{COO}^- \\ \text{H}_2\text{N}-\text{C}-\text{H} \\ \text{CH}_2 \\ \text{CH}_2 \\ \text{CH}_2 \\ \text{CH}_2-\overset{+}{\text{NH}_3} \end{bmatrix} \text{ at } pK_{a_2}$$

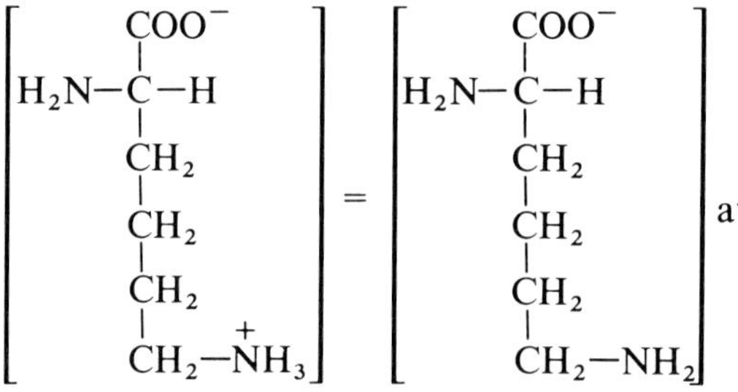

$$\begin{bmatrix} \text{COO}^- \\ \text{H}_2\text{N}-\text{C}-\text{H} \\ \text{CH}_2 \\ \text{CH}_2 \\ \text{CH}_2 \\ \text{CH}_2-\overset{+}{\text{NH}_3} \end{bmatrix} = \begin{bmatrix} \text{COO}^- \\ \text{H}_2\text{N}-\text{C}-\text{H} \\ \text{CH}_2 \\ \text{CH}_2 \\ \text{CH}_2 \\ \text{CH}_2-\text{NH}_2 \end{bmatrix} \text{ at } pK_{a_3}$$

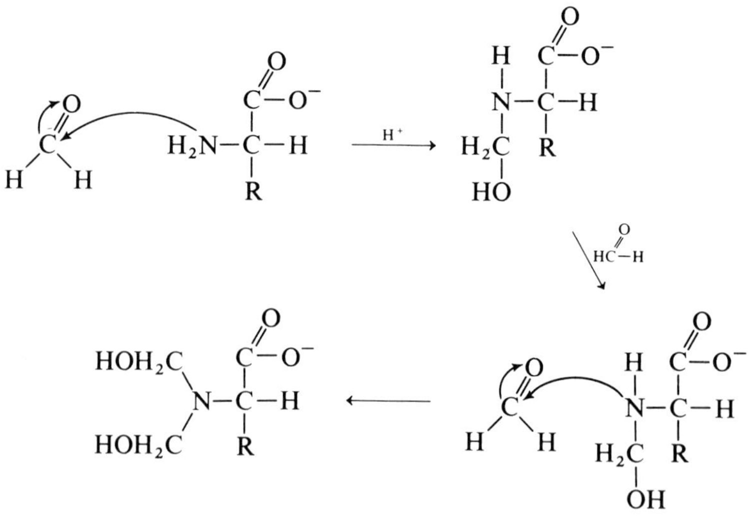

In practice it is frequently difficult to titrate the carboxyl group of an amino acid in aqueous solution because the nitrogen atom of the amino group competes with the added base for protons. To circumvent this situation the titration can be conducted in the presence of formaldehyde, which reacts with amino groups to yield an N-hydroxymethyl derivative or an N,N-bishydroxymethyl derivative. Since these derivatives are less basic than the parent amino group, the competition is diminished.

Table 5-2 Dissociation constants, $pK_a$, $pK_b$, and $pI$ values of some common amino acids

| Compound | Mol. wt. | Conjugate acid | $K_a$ | $pK_a$ | Conjugate base | $K_b$ | $pK_b$ | $pI$ |
|---|---|---|---|---|---|---|---|---|
| α-Alanine | 89.1 | α-COOH | $4.47 \times 10^{-3}$ | 2.35 | α-COO$^-$ | $2.24 \times 10^{-12}$ | 11.65 | 6.02 |
|  |  | α-NH$_3^+$ | $2.04 \times 10^{-10}$ | 9.69 | α-NH$_2$ | $4.90 \times 10^{-5}$ | 4.31 |  |
| β-Alanine | 89.1 | α-COOH | $2.51 \times 10^{-4}$ | 3.60 | α-COO$^-$ | $3.98 \times 10^{-11}$ | 10.40 | 6.90 |
|  |  | β-NH$_3^+$ | $6.46 \times 10^{-11}$ | 10.19 | β-NH$_2$ | $1.55 \times 10^{-4}$ | 3.81 |  |
| Arginine | 174.2 | α-COOH | $6.76 \times 10^{-3}$ | 2.17 | α-COO$^-$ | $1.48 \times 10^{-12}$ | 11.83 | 10.76 |
|  |  | α-NH$_3^+$ | $9.12 \times 10^{-10}$ | 9.04 | α-NH$_2$ | $1.10 \times 10^{-5}$ | 4.96 |  |
|  |  | Guanidinium-NH$_2^+$ | $3.31 \times 10^{-13}$ | 12.48 | Guanidinium-NH | $3.02 \times 10^{-2}$ | 1.52 |  |
| Asparagine | 132.1 | α-COOH | $9.55 \times 10^{-3}$ | 2.02 | α-COO$^-$ | $1.05 \times 10^{-12}$ | 11.98 | 5.41 |
|  |  | α-NH$_3^+$ | $1.58 \times 10^{-9}$ | 8.8 | α-NH$_2$ | $6.31 \times 10^{-6}$ | 5.2 |  |
| Aspartic acid | 133.1 | α-COOH | $8.13 \times 10^{-3}$ | 2.09 | α-COO$^-$ | $1.23 \times 10^{-12}$ | 11.91 | 2.98 |
|  |  | β-COOH | $1.38 \times 10^{-4}$ | 3.86 | β-COO$^-$ | $7.25 \times 10^{-11}$ | 10.14 |  |
|  |  | α-NH$_3^+$ | $1.51 \times 10^{-10}$ | 9.82 | α-NH$_2$ | $6.61 \times 10^{-5}$ | 4.18 |  |
| Citrulline | 175.2 | α-COOH | $3.72 \times 10^{-3}$ | 2.43 | α-COO$^-$ | $2.69 \times 10^{-12}$ | 11.57 | 5.92 |
|  |  | α-NH$_3^+$ | $3.89 \times 10^{-10}$ | 9.41 | α-NH$_2$ | $2.57 \times 10^{-5}$ | 4.59 |  |
| Cysteine | 121.2 | α-COOH | $1.95 \times 10^{-2}$ | 1.71 | α-COO$^-$ | $5.13 \times 10^{-13}$ | 12.29 | 5.02 |
|  |  | α-NH$_3^+$ | $4.68 \times 10^{-9}$ | 8.33 | α-NH$_2$ | $2.14 \times 10^{-6}$ | 5.67 |  |
|  |  | β-SH | $1.66 \times 10^{-11}$ | 10.78 | β-S$^-$ | $6.03 \times 10^{-4}$ | 3.22 |  |
| Cystine | 240.3 | α-COOH | $2.24 \times 10^{-2}$ | 1.65 | α-COO$^-$ | $4.47 \times 10^{-13}$ | 12.35 | 5.06 |
|  |  | α-COOH | $5.50 \times 10^{-3}$ | 2.26 | α-COO$^-$ | $1.82 \times 10^{-12}$ | 11.74 |  |
|  |  | α-NH$_3^+$ | $1.41 \times 10^{-8}$ | 7.85 | α-NH$_2$ | $7.08 \times 10^{-7}$ | 6.15 |  |
|  |  | α-NH$_3^+$ | $1.41 \times 10^{-10}$ | 9.85 | α-NH$_2$ | $7.08 \times 10^{-5}$ | 4.15 |  |
| Glutamic acid | 147.1 | α-COOH | $6.46 \times 10^{-3}$ | 2.19 | α-COO$^-$ | $1.55 \times 10^{-12}$ | 11.81 | 3.22 |
|  |  | γ-COOH | $5.62 \times 10^{-5}$ | 4.25 | γ-COO$^-$ | $1.78 \times 10^{-10}$ | 9.75 |  |
|  |  | α-NH$_3^+$ | $2.14 \times 10^{-10}$ | 9.67 | α-NH$_2$ | $4.68 \times 10^{-5}$ | 4.33 |  |
| Glutamine | 146.1 | α-COOH | $6.76 \times 10^{-3}$ | 2.17 | α-COO$^-$ | $1.48 \times 10^{-12}$ | 11.83 | 5.65 |
|  |  | α-NH$_3^+$ | $7.41 \times 10^{-10}$ | 9.13 | α-NH$_2$ | $1.35 \times 10^{-5}$ | 4.87 |  |
| Glycine | 75.1 | α-COOH | $4.57 \times 10^{-3}$ | 2.34 | α-COO$^-$ | $2.19 \times 10^{-12}$ | 11.66 | 5.97 |
|  |  | α-NH$_3^+$ | $2.51 \times 10^{-10}$ | 9.6 | α-NH$_2$ | $3.98 \times 10^{-5}$ | 4.4 |  |
| Histidine | 155.2 | α-COOH | $1.51 \times 10^{-2}$ | 1.82 | α-COO$^-$ | $6.61 \times 10^{-13}$ | 12.18 | 7.58 |
|  |  | Imidazole-NH$^+$ | $1.0 \times 10^{-7}$ | 6.0 | Imidazole-N | $1.0 \times 10^{-9}$ | 8.0 |  |
|  |  | α-NH$_3^+$ | $6.76 \times 10^{-10}$ | 9.17 | α-NH$_2$ | $1.48 \times 10^{-5}$ | 4.83 |  |
| Homocysteine | 135.2 | α-COOH | $6.03 \times 10^{-3}$ | 2.22 | α-COO$^-$ | $1.66 \times 10^{-12}$ | 11.78 | 5.54 |
|  |  | α-NH$_3^+$ | $1.35 \times 10^{-9}$ | 8.87 | α-NH$_2$ | $7.41 \times 10^{-6}$ | 5.13 |  |
|  |  | γ-SH | $1.38 \times 10^{-11}$ | 10.86 | γ-S$^-$ | $7.25 \times 10^{-4}$ | 3.14 |  |
| Homocystine | 268.3 | α-COOH | $2.57 \times 10^{-2}$ | 1.59 | α-COO$^-$ | $3.89 \times 10^{-13}$ | 12.41 | 5.53 |
|  |  | α-COOH | $2.88 \times 10^{-3}$ | 2.54 | α-COO$^-$ | $3.47 \times 10^{-12}$ | 11.46 |  |
|  |  | α-NH$_3^+$ | $3.02 \times 10^{-9}$ | 8.52 | α-NH$_2$ | $3.31 \times 10^{-6}$ | 5.48 |  |
|  |  | α-NH$_3^+$ | $3.63 \times 10^{-10}$ | 9.44 | α-NH$_2$ | $2.76 \times 10^{-5}$ | 4.56 |  |
| Hydroxylysine | 162.2 | α-COOH | $7.41 \times 10^{-3}$ | 2.13 | α-COO$^-$ | $1.35 \times 10^{-12}$ | 11.87 | 9.15 |
|  |  | α-NH$_3^+$ | $2.40 \times 10^{-9}$ | 8.62 | α-NH$_2$ | $4.17 \times 10^{-6}$ | 5.38 |  |
|  |  | ε-NH$_3^+$ | $2.14 \times 10^{-10}$ | 9.67 | ε-NH$_2$ | $4.68 \times 10^{-5}$ | 4.33 |  |
| Hydroxyproline | 131.1 | α-COOH | $1.20 \times 10^{-2}$ | 1.92 | α-COO$^-$ | $8.32 \times 10^{-13}$ | 12.08 | 5.83 |
|  |  | α-NH$_3^+$ | $1.86 \times 10^{-10}$ | 9.73 | α-NH$_2$ | $5.37 \times 10^{-5}$ | 4.27 |  |

**Table 5-2 Dissociation constants, $pK_a$, $pK_b$, and $pI$ values of some common amino acids** (*Continued*)

| Compound | Mol. wt. | Conjugate acid | $K_a$ | $pK_a$ | Conjugate base | $K_b$ | $pK_b$ | $pI$ |
|---|---|---|---|---|---|---|---|---|
| Isoleucine | 131.2 | α-COOH | $4.37 \times 10^{-3}$ | 2.36 | α-COO$^-$ | $2.29 \times 10^{-12}$ | 11.64 | 6.02 |
| | | α-NH$_3^+$ | $2.09 \times 10^{-10}$ | 9.68 | α-NH$_2$ | $4.78 \times 10^{-5}$ | 4.32 | |
| Leucine | 131.2 | α-COOH | $4.37 \times 10^{-3}$ | 2.36 | α-COO$^-$ | $2.29 \times 10^{-12}$ | 11.64 | 5.98 |
| | | α-NH$_3^+$ | $2.51 \times 10^{-10}$ | 9.60 | α-NH$_2$ | $3.98 \times 10^{-5}$ | 4.40 | |
| Lysine | 146.2 | α-COOH | $6.61 \times 10^{-3}$ | 2.18 | α-COO$^-$ | $1.51 \times 10^{-12}$ | 11.82 | 9.74 |
| | | α-NH$_3^+$ | $1.12 \times 10^{-9}$ | 8.95 | α-NH$_2$ | $8.91 \times 10^{-6}$ | 5.05 | |
| | | ε-NH$_3^+$ | $2.95 \times 10^{-11}$ | 10.53 | ε-NH$_2$ | $3.39 \times 10^{-4}$ | 3.47 | |
| Methionine | 149.2 | α-COOH | $5.25 \times 10^{-3}$ | 2.28 | α-COO$^-$ | $1.91 \times 10^{-12}$ | 11.72 | 5.75 |
| | | α-NH$_3^+$ | $6.17 \times 10^{-10}$ | 9.21 | α-NH$_2$ | $1.62 \times 10^{-5}$ | 4.79 | |
| Ornithine | 132.2 | α-COOH | $1.15 \times 10^{-2}$ | 1.94 | α-COO$^-$ | $8.71 \times 10^{-13}$ | 12.06 | 9.70 |
| | | α-NH$_3^+$ | $2.24 \times 10^{-9}$ | 8.65 | α-NH$_2$ | $4.47 \times 10^{-6}$ | 5.35 | |
| | | δ-NH$_3^+$ | $1.74 \times 10^{-11}$ | 10.76 | δ-NH$_2$ | $5.76 \times 10^{-4}$ | 3.24 | |
| Phenylalanine | 165.2 | α-COOH | $1.48 \times 10^{-2}$ | 1.83 | α-COO$^-$ | $6.76 \times 10^{-13}$ | 12.17 | 5.98 |
| | | α-NH$_3^+$ | $7.41 \times 10^{-10}$ | 9.13 | α-NH$_2$ | $1.35 \times 10^{-5}$ | 4.87 | |
| Proline | 115.1 | α-COOH | $1.02 \times 10^{-2}$ | 1.99 | α-COO$^-$ | $9.77 \times 10^{-13}$ | 12.01 | 6.10 |
| | | α-NH$_3^+$ | $2.51 \times 10^{-11}$ | 10.60 | α-NH$_2$ | $3.98 \times 10^{-4}$ | 3.40 | |
| Serine | 105.1 | α-COOH | $6.17 \times 10^{-3}$ | 2.21 | α-COO$^-$ | $1.62 \times 10^{-12}$ | 11.79 | 5.68 |
| | | α-NH$_3^+$ | $7.08 \times 10^{-10}$ | 9.15 | α-NH$_2$ | $1.41 \times 10^{-5}$ | 4.85 | |
| Taurine | 125.1 | -SO$_3$H | $3.16 \times 10^{-2}$ | 1.5 | -SO$_3^-$ | $3.16 \times 10^{-13}$ | 12.5 | 5.12 |
| | | α-NH$_3^+$ | $1.82 \times 10^{-9}$ | 8.74 | α-NH$_2$ | $5.50 \times 10^{-6}$ | 5.26 | |
| Threonine | 119.1 | α-COOH | $2.35 \times 10^{-3}$ | 2.63 | α-COO$^-$ | $4.27 \times 10^{-12}$ | 11.37 | 6.53 |
| | | α-NH$_3^+$ | $3.72 \times 10^{-11}$ | 10.43 | α-NH$_2$ | $2.69 \times 10^{-4}$ | 3.57 | |
| Tryptophan | 204.2 | α-COOH | $4.17 \times 10^{-3}$ | 2.38 | α-COO$^-$ | $2.40 \times 10^{-12}$ | 11.62 | 5.88 |
| | | α-NH$_3^+$ | $4.07 \times 10^{-10}$ | 9.39 | α-NH$_2$ | $2.46 \times 10^{-5}$ | 4.61 | |
| Tyrosine | 181.2 | α-COOH | $6.31 \times 10^{-3}$ | 2.20 | α-COO$^-$ | $1.59 \times 10^{-11}$ | 11.80 | 5.65 |
| | | α-NH$_3^+$ | $7.76 \times 10^{-10}$ | 9.11 | α-NH$_2$ | $1.29 \times 10^{-5}$ | 4.89 | |
| | | -OH | $8.51 \times 10^{-11}$ | 10.07 | -O$^-$ | $1.18 \times 10^{-4}$ | 3.93 | |
| Valine | 117.1 | α-COOH | $4.79 \times 10^{-3}$ | 2.32 | α-COO$^-$ | $2.09 \times 10^{-12}$ | 11.68 | 5.97 |
| | | α-NH$_3^+$ | $2.40 \times 10^{-10}$ | 9.62 | α-NH$_2$ | $4.17 \times 10^{-5}$ | 4.38 | |

*Source:* Segel, I. H. (1976) *Biochemical Calculations*, pp. 409–411, Wiley, New York, reproduced with the permission of the author and the publishers.

The dissociation constants $pK_a$ and $pK_b$ and the $pI$ values for some of the more common amino acids are given in Table 5-2.

## Buffers and Buffer Capacity

Biochemical systems operate under conditions of controlled pH. Normal human blood plasma has a pH of 7.35 to 7.45, and a variation of a few tenths of a pH unit can cause the malfunction of vital body processes. The pH of the body fluids is controlled by buffer systems which include the bicarbonate–carbonic acid system, the hydrogen phosphate–dihydrogen phosphate system, and the protein-anion–protein system. Each of these buffer systems consists of a weak acid and its salt. The pH that prevails in the presence of a buffer system comprising a weak acid and its salt is approximated by the Henderson-Hasselbalch equation, which is derived from Eq. (5-4) and has the form

$$pH = pK_a + \log \frac{[\text{salt}]}{[\text{acid}]} \qquad (5\text{-}14)$$

As an illustration of the function of a buffer system, consider the following. If 10.00 ml of 1.00 N HCl is added to 990.00 ml of water at pH 7.00, the resulting pH will be 2.00. If, on the other hand, 10.00 ml of 1.00 N HCl is added to 990.00 ml of an aqueous solution containing 0.04 N $HCO_3^-$ and 0.01 N $H_2CO_3$, the influence upon pH will be quite different. The pH of the solution before adding the HCl is given by

$$pH = 6.35 + \log \frac{0.04}{0.01} = 6.95 \qquad (5\text{-}15)$$

If it is assumed that the addition of 0.01 mol of HCl allows the formation of 0.01 mol of $H_2CO_3$ from 0.01 mol of $HCO_3^-$, the pH of the resulting solution is given by

$$pH = 6.35 + \log \frac{0.03}{0.02} = 6.53 \qquad (5\text{-}16)$$

In the absence of a buffer system $\Delta pH$ would be 5.00, while in the presence of the buffer system described $\Delta pH$ would be 0.42.

Different buffer systems have varying capacities to resist a change in hydrogen-ion concentration. Buffer capacity depends not only upon the ratio of the concentrations of the weak acid and its salt but also upon the magnitude of these concentrations. Maximum buffer capacity is exhibited when the hydrogen-ion concentration of the medium is equivalent to the $pK_a$ of the weak acid of the buffer system.

## REACTIONS OF AMINO ACIDS

Among the reactions of the amino acids that are important to biochemical studies are those involving Ninhydrin, carbon dioxide, metal ions, and optically active solvents, discussed in the following paragraphs.

### The Reaction of Amino Acids with Ninhydrin

The reagent trioxohydrindene, or Ninhydrin, is used in both qualitative and quantitative determinations of amino acids. The reaction between an amino acid and Ninhydrin proceeds as follows:

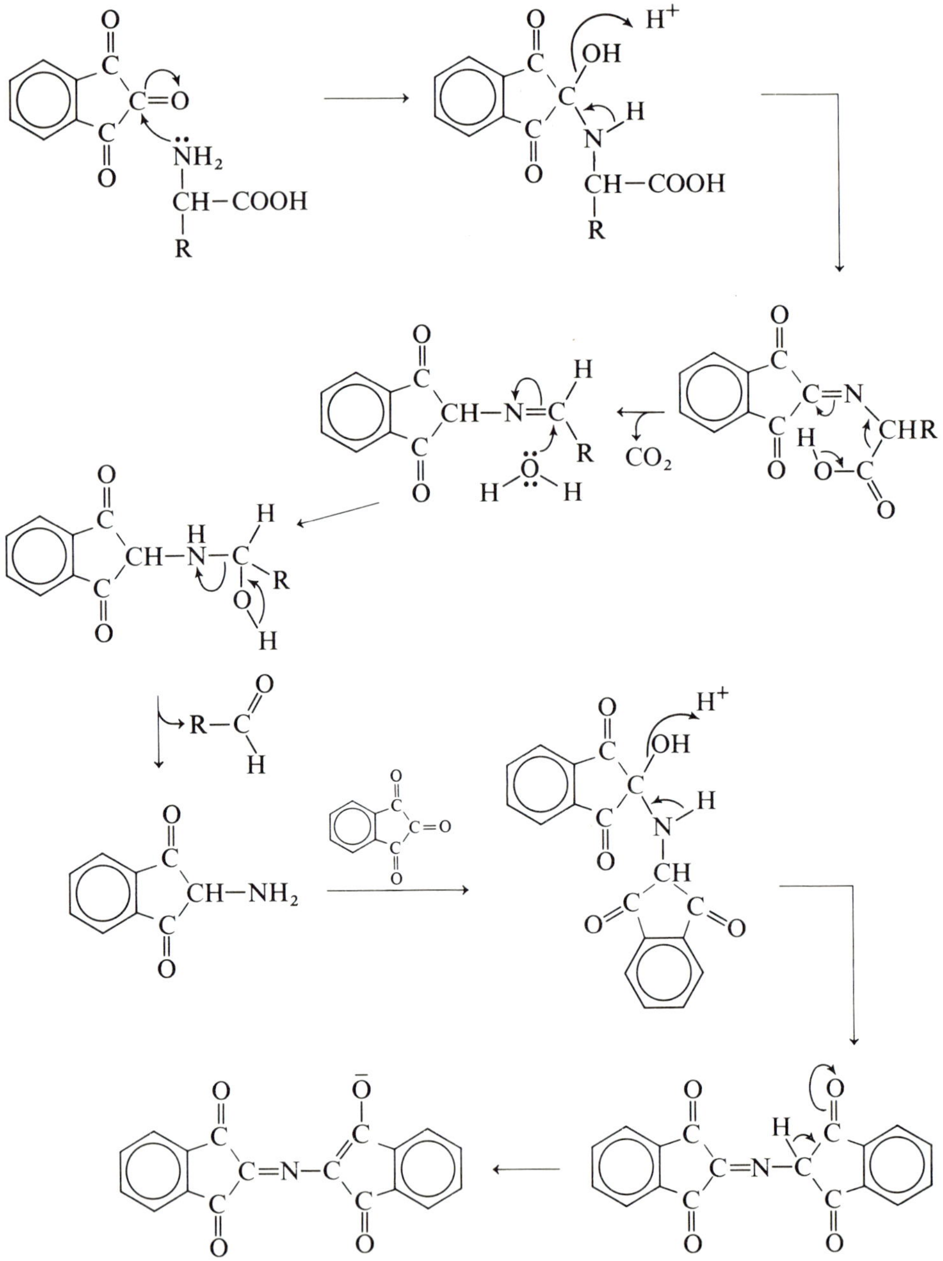

The reaction product shown is a vivid blue or violet, and this color provides the basis for the qualitative and quantitative determinations of the amino acids. Under some conditions, however, the product can also be formed from ammonia or certain peptides, rather than an amino acid, and to establish that a 2-amino acid was involved, the liberation of carbon dioxide must be demonstrated.

The amino acids proline and hydroxyproline give a yellow product instead of the vivid blue one. When a secondary amino group is the source of the nitrogen atom of the product, the dehydration shown in the next to the last step cannot occur and the highly conjugated system is not formed.

## The Reaction of Amino Acids with Carbon Dioxide

Carbon dioxide adds to the amino group of an amino acid. The product is an $N$-carboxyamino derivative.

$$\underset{O}{\overset{O}{\underset{\|}{C}}} + H_2N-\underset{R}{\overset{C-O^-}{\underset{|}{C}}-H} \longrightarrow \underset{O\diagup\diagdown O}{\overset{H}{\underset{C}{N}}-\underset{R}{\overset{C-O^-}{\underset{|}{C}}-H}}$$

The formation of $N$-carboxyamino derivatives of the free amino groups of the protein of hemoglobin provides the means by which approximately 20 percent of the carbon dioxide of the blood is transported.

## Complexation and Chelation Involving the Amino Acids and Their Derivatives

Virtually all amino acids bind metal ions. Among the metal ions that enter into such reactions, particularly in biochemical systems, are those of copper, zinc, nickel, cobalt, iron, manganese, magnesium, and calcium. These metal ions generally interact with two, four, or six ligands. When four ligands are involved, square planar or tetrahedral geometry generally results. The involvement of six ligands usually results in octahedral geometry. If two or more of the ligands are derived from a single molecule, the complex is referred to as a *chelate* (from the Greek *chela*, meaning "claw").

Metal-ion catalysis of reactions involving the carbonyl carbon atom of the amino acids and their derivatives frequently entails complex formation; e.g., the rate of hydrolysis of histidine methyl ester is enhanced by chelation, and the formation of an amide, or peptide, linkage proceeds readily due to chelation. In both cases it has been proposed that chelation increases the electrophilicity of the carbonyl carbon atom involved, making it more prone to nucleophilic attack.

Chelation and complex formation are frequently significant factors in enzymatic reactions in which the aminoacyl units of the protein molecule bind metal ions. Cysteinyl, histidyl, and glycyl units are of particular interest in this respect. For example, it has been suggested that formation of a complex between iron and the sulfhydryl groups of cysteinyl units is important in achieving the appropriate structure for the proper functioning of a group of enzymes that participates in reactions involving electron transfer.

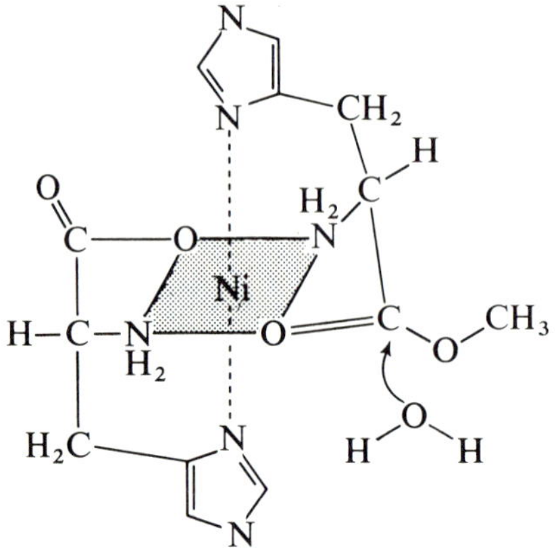

Nickel(II) chelate of
histidinate-histidine
methyl ester
undergoing attack
by water molecule

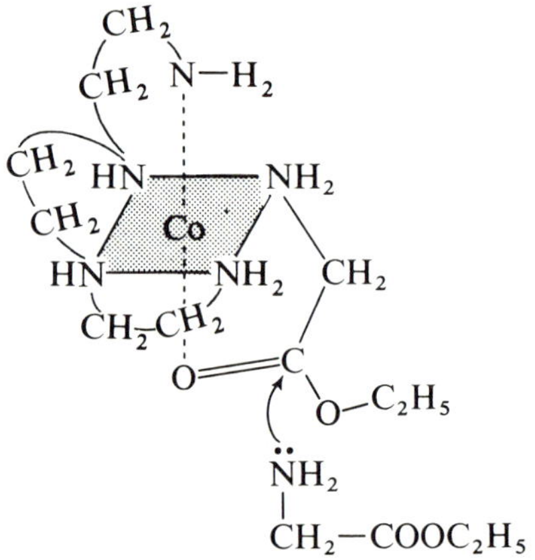

Cobalt(III)
chelate of
triethylenetetramine-
glycine ethyl
ester undergoing
attack by molecule
of glycine ethyl
ester

## PEPTIDES AND PROTEINS AND THEIR SYNTHESES

Peptides consist of from 2 to perhaps 40 or 50 aminoacyl units, although there is no precise line of demarcation between a large peptide and a small protein. To designate the amino acid sequence of a peptide or a protein, the aminoacyl units are listed using the standard abbreviations and starting at the terminus having a free amino group. The aminoacyl unit at this end of the chain is called the *N-terminal* aminoacyl unit. Then the names of the amino acids are written using the suffix *-yl* with each name except the final one, the C-terminal unit. For example, the amino acid sequence of a tripeptide known as glutathione can be designated as shown:

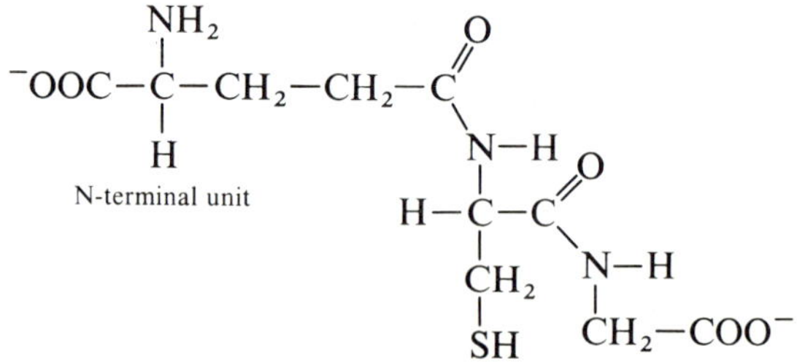

Glutathione
($\gamma$-glutamylcysteinylglycine),
$\gamma$-Glu-Cys-Gly

Peptides and proteins can be synthesized in the laboratory from appropriately modified amino acids. If the synthesis is to proceed from the amino terminus, the amino group of the N-terminal unit is protected and the carboxyl group of this amino acid, in the form of some derivative that permits amide formation, is allowed to react with the amino group of the unit that is to be next in the sequence. The free carboxyl group of the amino acid is not used in the formation of amides since the reaction of a carboxyl group and an amino group generally yields a salt. (Although these salts can be pyrolyzed to yield amides, this procedure is not suitable for the preparation of biochemical compounds.) Among the groups that can be used to protect the amino group during peptide synthesis are the *p*-toluenesulfonyl (tosyl) group, the formyl group, the benzyloxycarbonyl (Bzc) group, the *t*-butyloxycarbonyl (Boc) group, and the triphenylmethyl group.

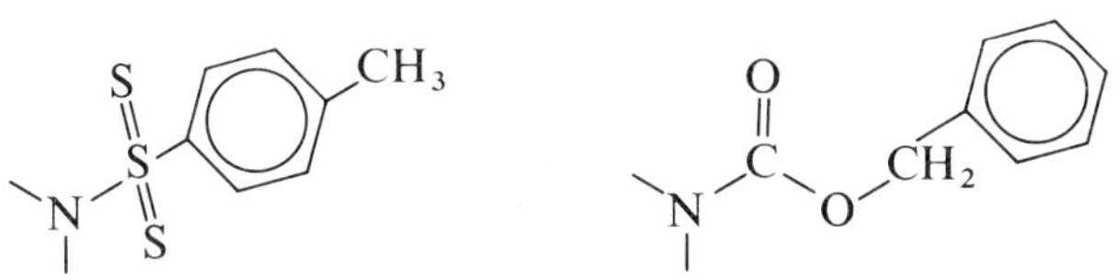

An *N*-(*p*-toluenesulfonyl) group

An *N*-(benzyloxycarbonyl) group

Each of these can be removed under mild nonalkaline conditions that permit the optical activity of the product to be retained. One mode of peptide synthesis can be illustrated by the following reaction between the aspartate derivative and the glycine derivative:

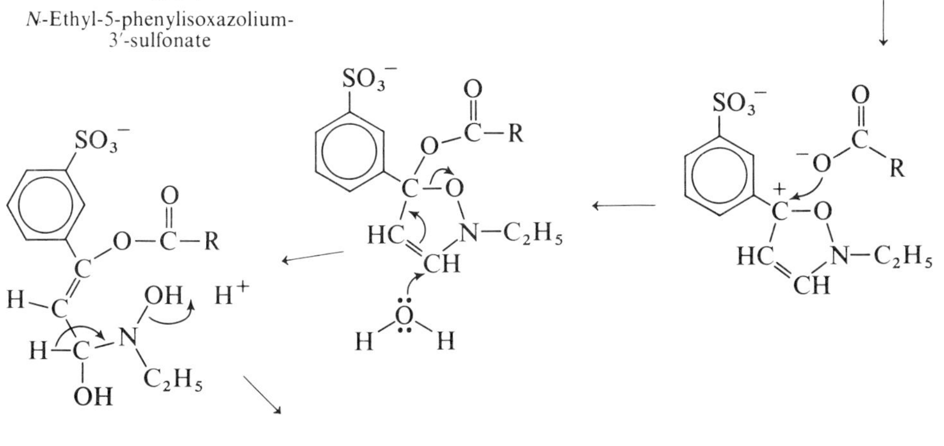

*N*-Ethyl-5-phenylisoxazolium-3'-sulfonate

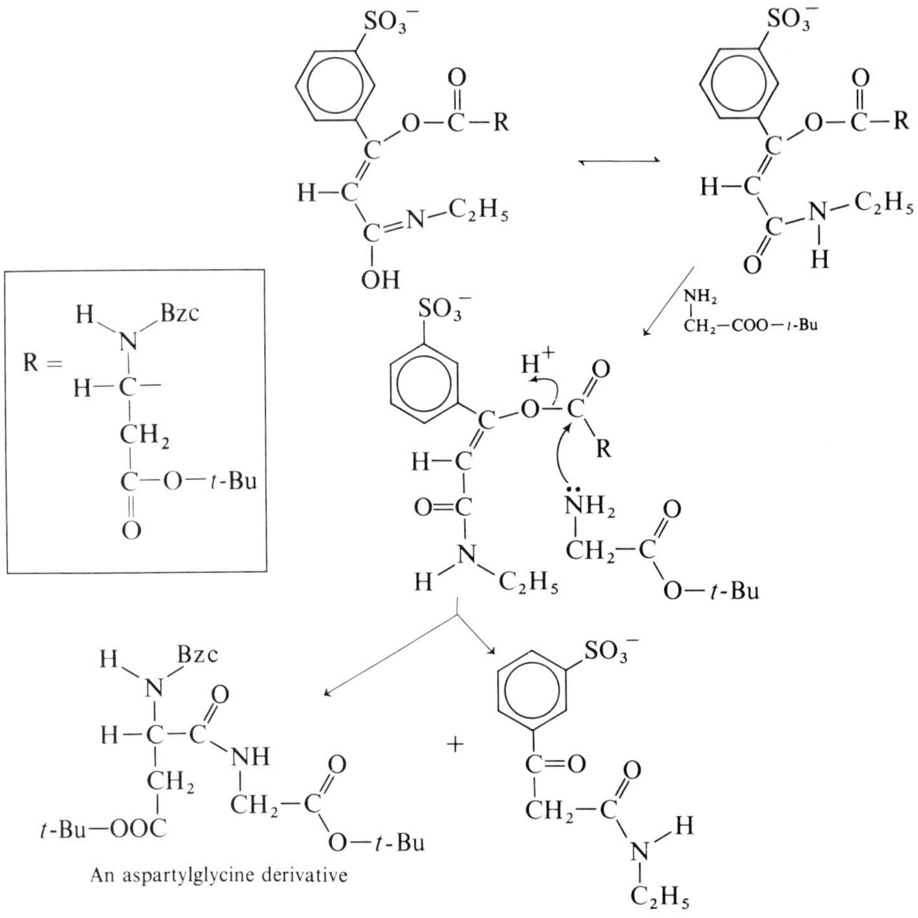

An aspartylglycine derivative

In this synthesis peptide-bond formation is brought about by forming the enol ester of the carboxyl group that is to undergo reaction. The carbonyl groups of enol esters are very reactive, and, in fact, these compounds can function as acylating agents for alcohols. Acyl-oxygen cleavage of enol esters permits the liberation of an enol which isomerizes to yield a very stable product, the ketone. Therefore, acyl-oxygen cleavage of enol esters proceeds readily.

Peptides and proteins can also be synthesized by an elegant automated procedure, developed by R. B. Merrifield and his colleagues at Rockefeller University,[†] which utilizes polystyrene beads of approximately 100 μm diameter as solid supports, upon which peptide-bond formation takes place. The polystyrene is

---

[†] Merrifield, R. B. (1963) *J. Am. Chem. Soc.* **85**, 2149–2154; Merrifield, R. B. (1969) in *Advances in Enzymology* (Nord, F. F., ed.), vol. 32, pp. 221–296, Interscience, New York; Felix, A. M., and Merrifield, R. B. (1970) *J. Am. Chem. Soc.* **92**, 1385–1391.

first modified by the substitution of chloromethyl groups (or methylchloroformyl groups) on the benzene rings of the polystyrene. A suitably protected amino acid that is to be a terminal unit of the chain is then allowed to react with the functional group of the resin. As a result, this amino acid is anchored to the solid support. Its protecting group is then removed, and the amino acid that is to be next in the sequence is introduced into the reaction medium. The second amino acid is again suitably protected so that only the appropriate one of its functional groups can undergo reaction. This functional group reacts with the functional group of the amino acid anchored to the solid support to yield a dipeptide derivative which is still attached to the resin. The protecting group of the second amino acid unit is then removed and the next amino acid is introduced into the medium. When chloromethyl groups are substituted on the benzene rings of the polystyrene, the carboxyl group of the C-terminal amino acid is anchored to the solid support and the chain grows at the amino end.

In order to bring about peptide-bond formation the *p*-nitrophenyl ester of the carboxylic acid component is used. Since the *p*-nitrophenolate anion is an excellent leaving group, the peptide linkage is readily formed.

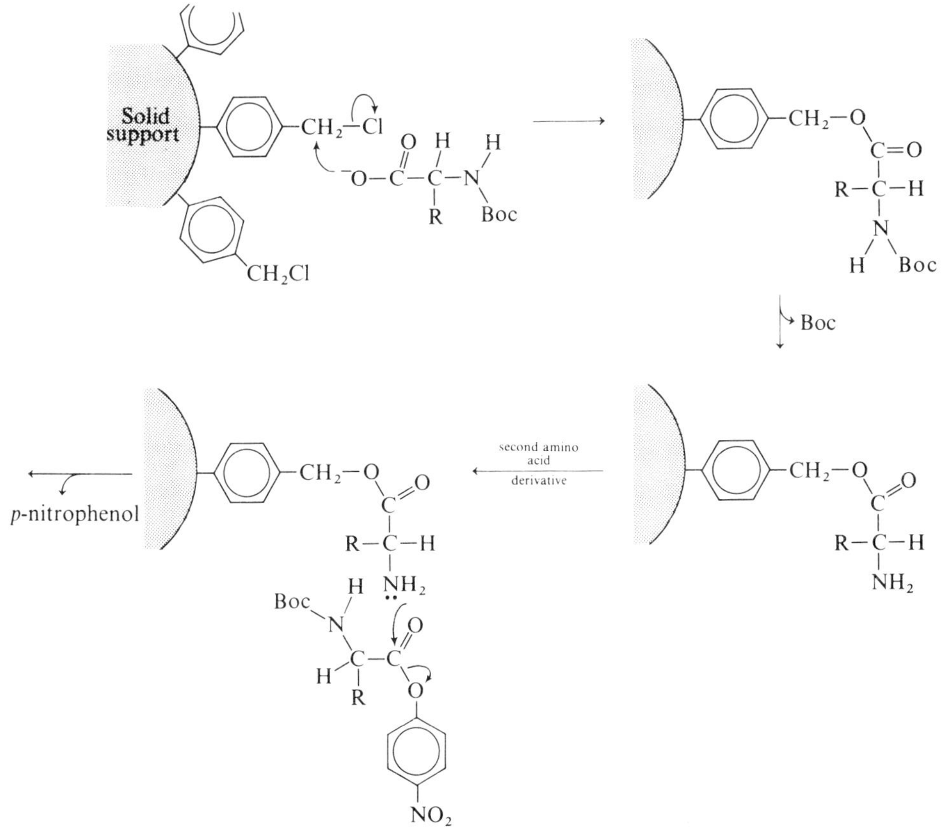

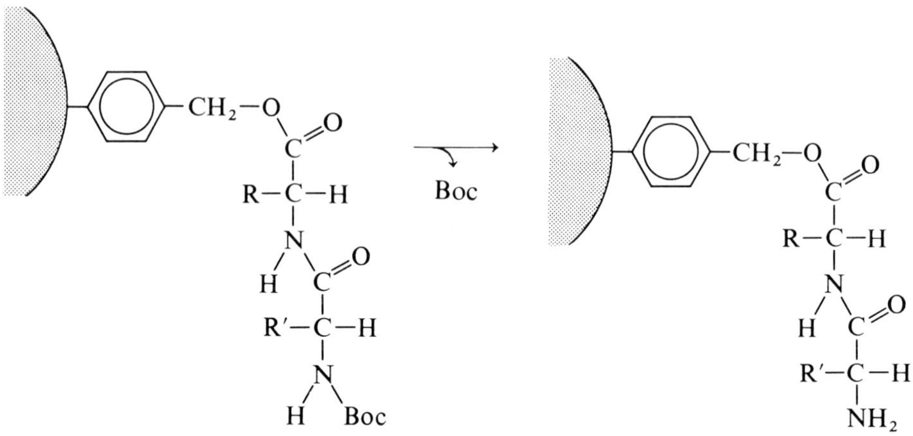

As an alternative to the use of the *p*-nitrophenyl ester of the carboxylic acid component, the carboxylic acid itself can be used in the presence of dicyclohexylcarbodiimide, in which case the course of the reaction is

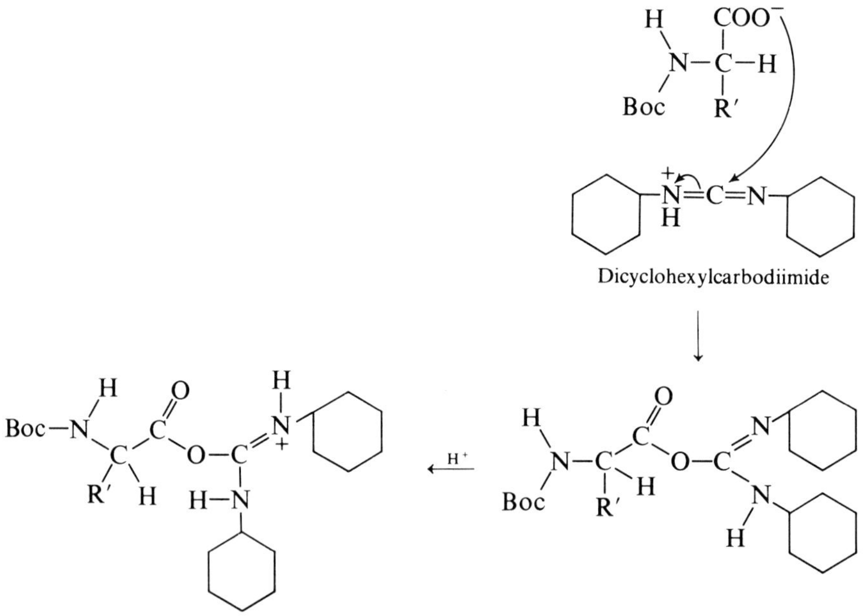

The reaction of this intermediate with the amino group of the resin-bound benzyl ester of the amino acid occurs as shown:

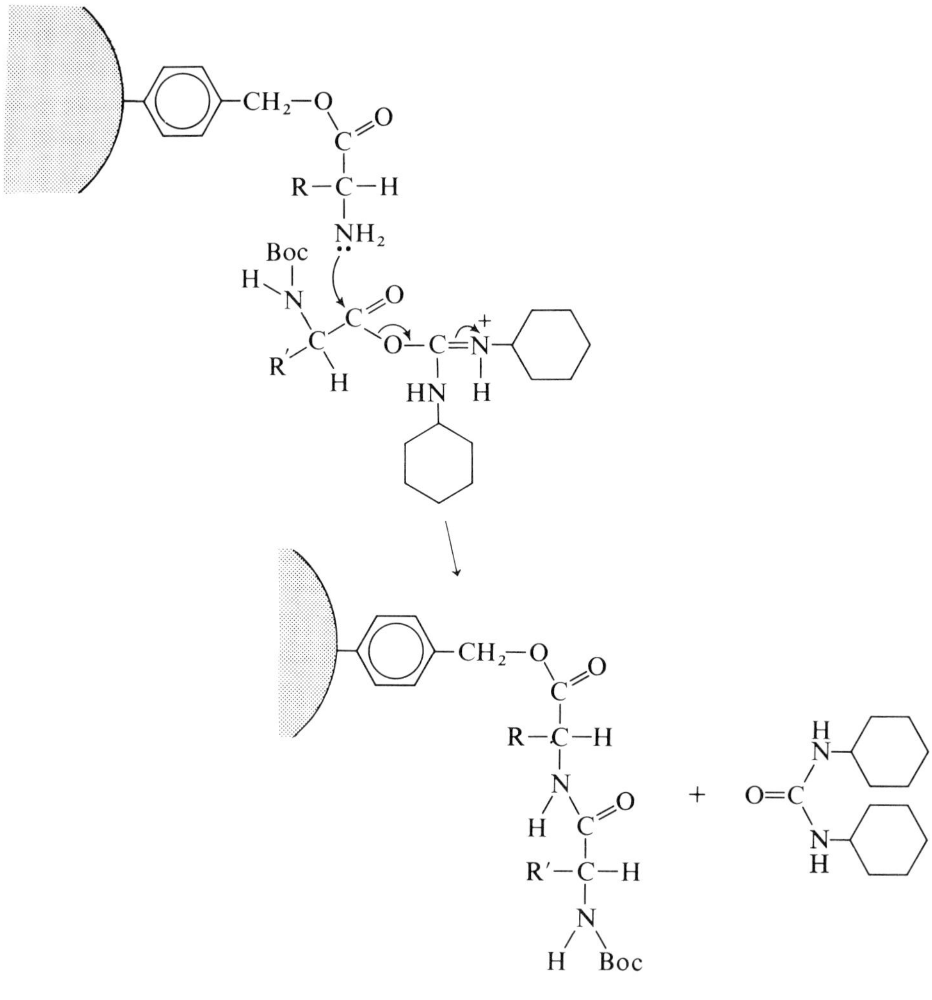

Again, a reactive carboxyl moiety is provided, in effect, by having the carbonyl group bonded to a good leaving group.

When the sequence is completed, the protein or polypeptide chain is liberated from the solid support. With benzyl esters formed as a result of the reaction between the chloromethyl group and the carboxylate group of the C-terminal amino acid this cleavage is brought about in the presence of 30 percent hydrobromic acid in acetic acid or in the presence of trifluoroacetic acid.

When methylchloroformyl groups are substituted on the benzene rings of the polystyrene, the amino group of the N-terminal amino acid is anchored to the resin and the protein or polypeptide chain grows at the carboxyl terminus:

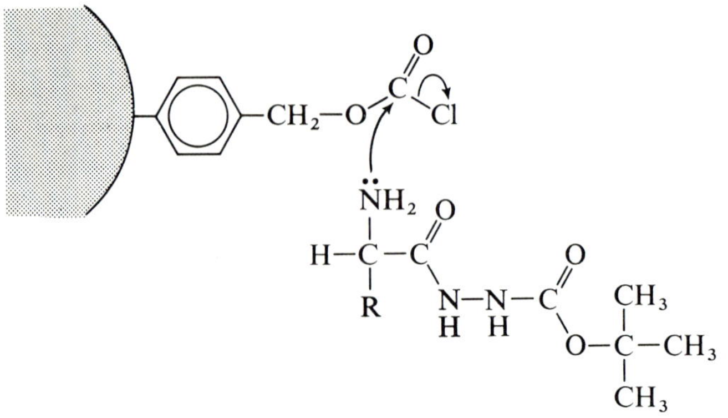

A 1-aminoacyl-2-*t*-butyloxycarbonylhydrazine (Boc-hydrazide)

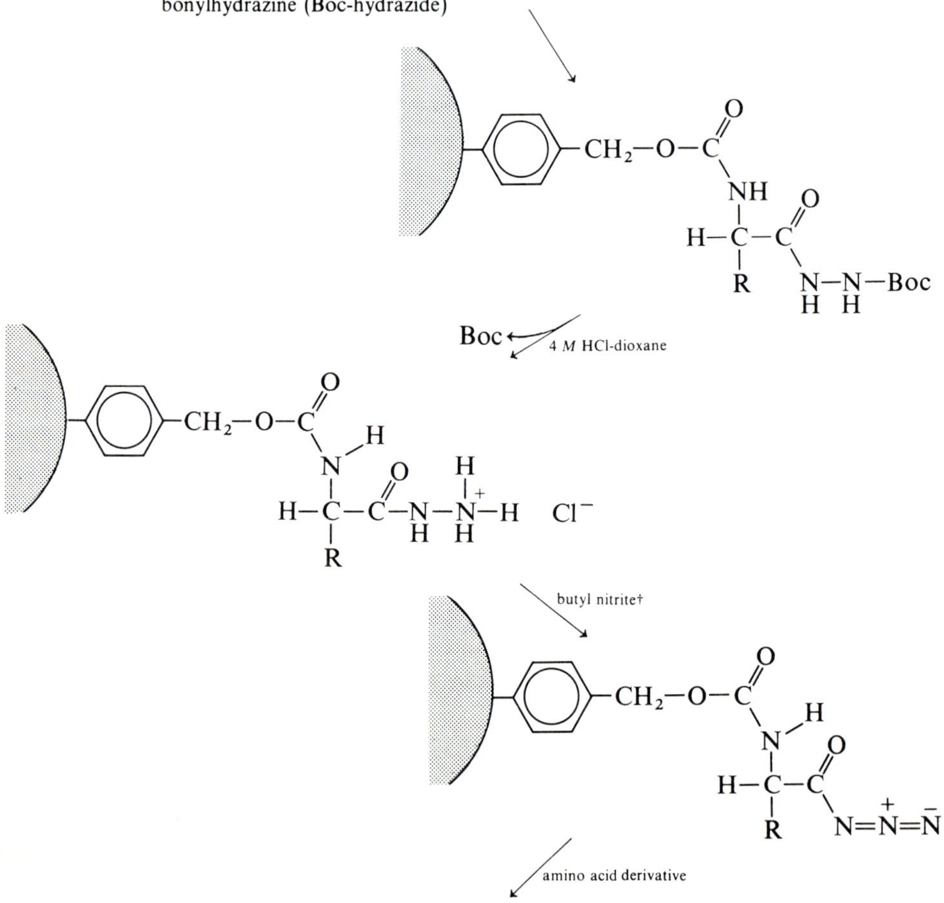
Boc
4 *M* HCl-dioxane
butyl nitrite†
amino acid derivative

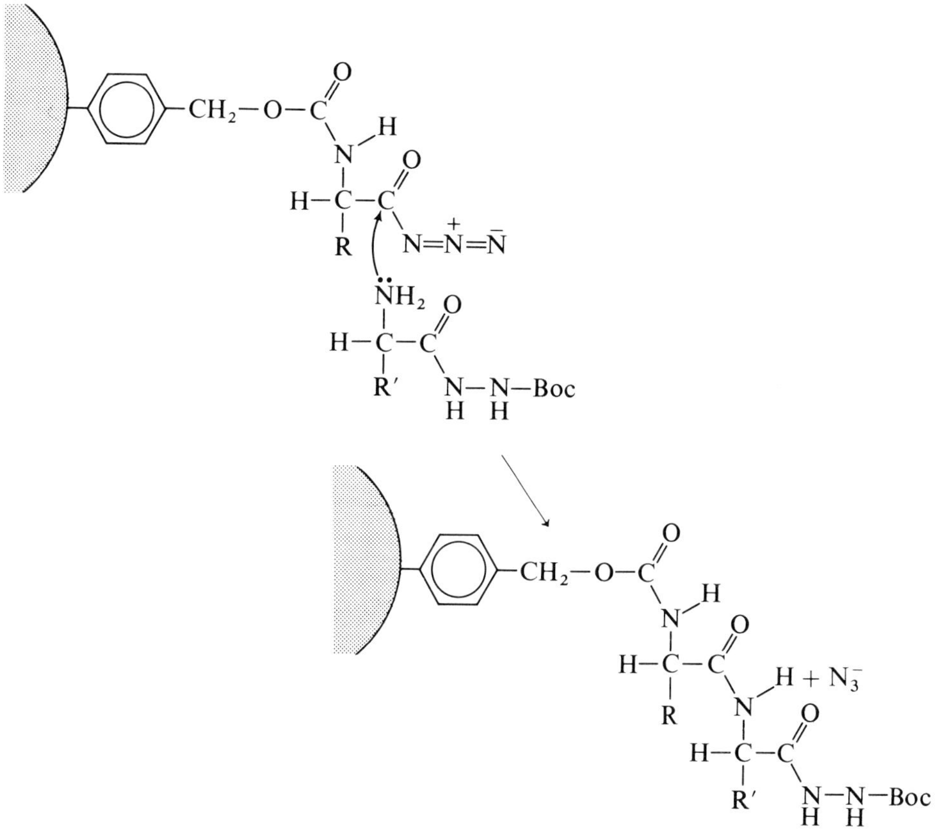

The basic principles of the synthesis are the same as in the previous examples, but this time it is the N-terminal amino acid that is anchored to the solid support and the chain grows as a result of an attack by the amino group of the incoming amino acid at the carbonyl carbon atom of the resin-bound amino acid.

† The conversion of a hydrazide to an azide can be formulated as follows:

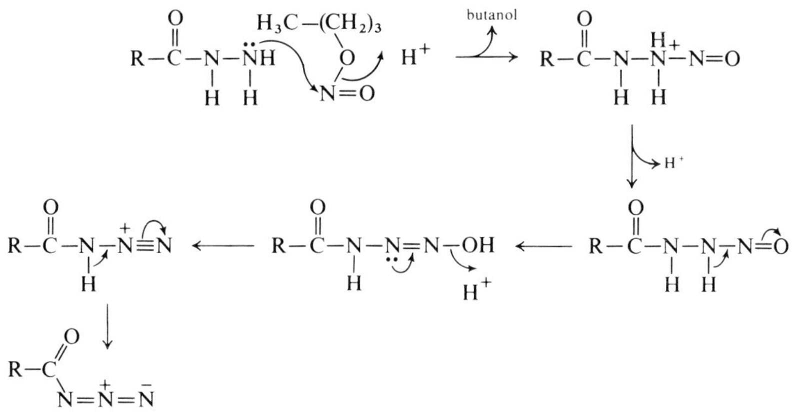

One of the principal advantages of the solid-phase synthesis is that since it allows the use of excess reactants and reagents, the reactions can be forced virtually to completion. After the addition of each aminoacyl unit of the chain the remaining reactants, reagents, and solvents can easily be separated from the product by filtration and washing since the product, the peptide chain, remains anchored to the solid support. The entire process has been automated through the use of a programmer that directs all the operations, including addition of reactants, addition of reagents, the time allotted for reaction, the removal of excess reactants and reagents, and washing the resin-bound product. The solid-phase method has been used in the laboratory synthesis of the enzyme ribonuclease,† the hormones bradykinin,‡ oxytocin,§ vasopressin,¶ and insulin,‖ and the $\beta$ chain of human hemoglobin,†† among other proteins and polypeptides that are of interest to biochemists.

## DETERMINATION OF THE MOLECULAR WEIGHT OF A PROTEIN

Although the molecular weight of smaller molecules is generally determined by methods based upon colligative properties, such methods are not applicable to biopolymers like proteins and nucleic acids. In many cases the molecular weight of these macromolecules is determined by procedures involving ultracentrifugation.

The analytical ultracentrifuge used in molecular-weight determinations provides rotor speeds of up to 70,000 revolutions per minute, and gravitational fields of $500,000g$ can be attained. In addition, both the speed of the rotor and the temperature of the rotor are precisely controlled. The analytical ultracentrifuge is also provided with an optical system that permits observation of the sedimentation behavior of the macromolecules while they are undergoing centrifugation. A schematic diagram of an ultracentrifuge is shown in Fig. 5-5.

There are basically two types of ultracentrifugation procedures used in the determination of molecular weights. Both start with a solution of the sample being studied contained in the ultracentrifuge cell. In one procedure the rate of migration of the boundary between the supernatant and the solution is observed as sedimentation proceeds. These data permit the calculation of a sedimentation coefficient that can be used to derive a value for the molecular weight of the macromolecule. In the other procedure, centrifugation is allowed to proceed to equilibrium. Then, at equilibrium the concentration gradient in the cell is determined and used to calculate the molecular weight of the macromolecule. The first method is called the *sedimentation velocity method* and the second, the *sedimentation equilibrium method*.

---

† Gutte, B., and Merrifield, R. B. (1969) *J. Am. Chem. Soc.* **91**, 501–502. See also Denkewalter, R. G., Veber, D. F., Holly, F. W., and Hirschmann, R. (1969) *J. Am. Chem. Soc.* **91**, 502–503 and following articles for another synthesis of ribonuclease.

‡ Merrifield, R. B. (1964) *J. Am. Chem. Soc.* **86**, 304–305; *Biochemistry* **3**, 1385–1390.

§ Manning, M. (1968) *J. Am. Chem. Soc.* **90**, 1348–1349.

¶ Meinhofer, J., and Sano, Y. (1968) *J. Am. Chem. Soc.* **90**, 2996–2997.

‖ Marglin, A., and Merrifield, R. B. (1966) *J. Am. Chem. Soc.* **88**, 5051–5052.

†† Chillemi, F., and Merrifield, R. B. (1969) *Biochemistry* **8**, 4344–4346.

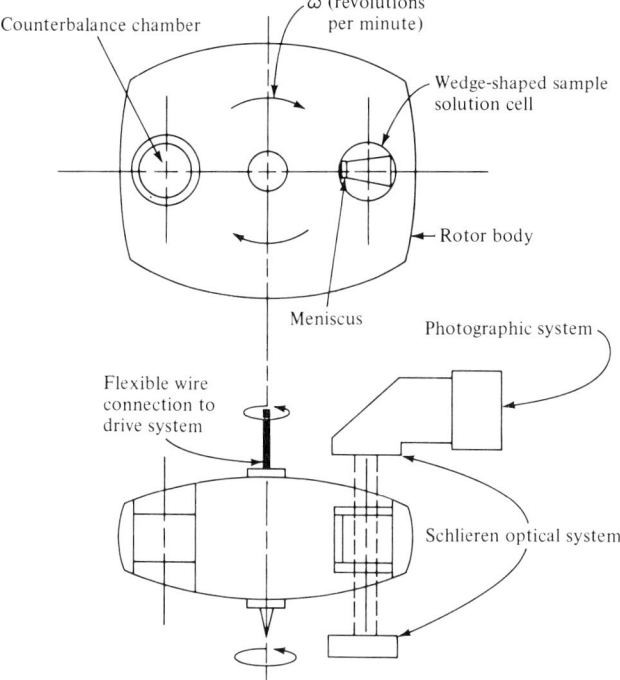

**Figure 5-5** The rotor is suspended from the drive system by a flexible wire. The wedge-shaped ultracentrifuge cell, in which the solution under study is contained, is positioned in the rotor so that it is exposed to the schlieren optical system during each revolution. The photographic system records the images that develop during centrifugation.

## The Sedimentation Velocity Method for Determining Molecular Weights

In the sedimentation velocity procedure the analytical ultracentrifuge is operated at very high rotor speeds, such as 60,000 revolutions per minute. When centrifugation is begun, the macromolecules begin to migrate toward the periphery of the ultracentrifuge cell. As a result of this migration there are soon three regions in the cell, a supernatant region, a region of uniform solute concentration, called the *plateau region*, and a transition region, or boundary, between the supernatant and the plateau region. As centrifugation proceeds, the boundary moves. By monitoring the boundary positions as a function of time, data are obtained that permit the calculation of the *sedimentation coefficient*. The sedimentation coefficient itself is frequently used in the characterization of macromolecules. A value for the molecular weight can be calculated from the sedimentation coefficient when the diffusion coefficient for the macromolecule is also known.

When a molecule is traveling in a circular path at a uniform speed, as in a centrifuge, the force per particle that tends to move a molecule to the outer periphery of the cell is given by

$$F_c = M\omega^2 r(1 - \bar{v}_2 \rho_1) \tag{5-17}$$

where $F_c$ = centrifugal force
$M$ = molecular weight of anhydrous, nonsolvated macromolecule
$\omega$ = velocity of rotation, rad/s
$r$ = distance between macromolecule in cell and axis of rotation
$\bar{v}_2$ = partial specific volume of solute macromolecule†
$\rho_1$ = density of medium

This force $F_c$ is opposed by frictional forces which can be described by

$$F_f = f \frac{dr}{dt} \qquad (5\text{-}18)$$

in which $f$ is the frictional coefficient and $dr/dt$ is the rate of sedimentation. If these frictional forces are expressed in terms of the diffusion coefficient $D$, the equation takes the form‡

$$F_f = \frac{kT}{D} \frac{dr}{dt} \qquad (5\text{-}19)$$

in which $k$ is the Boltzmann constant ($1.3580 \times 10^{-16}$ erg/K·molecule) and $T$ is the absolute temperature. After centrifugation has proceeded for a relatively short time, the centrifugal force and the frictional force exactly balance each other. Under this condition the macromolecules migrate through the cell solution at a constant velocity that depends upon their effective mass, size, and shape. This situation is described by

$$M\omega^2 r(1 - \bar{v}_2 \rho_1) = \frac{kT}{D} \frac{dr}{dt} \qquad (5\text{-}20)$$

---

† The partial specific volume $\bar{v}$ can be looked upon as the increase in volume that would occur if 1 g of solute were added to a sufficiently large amount of solvent so that, in effect, the solvent concentration remained unchanged. The equation that defines partial specific volume is

$$\bar{v} = \frac{dV}{dw}$$

in which $V$ is the total volume of the system and $w$ is the weight of solute. In dilute solutions of proteins the apparent specific volume is sometimes used rather than the partial specific volume since it is easier to determine. The apparent specific volume is given by

$$v_{app} = \frac{1}{\rho_1} - \frac{1}{c_2} \frac{\rho - \rho_1}{\rho_1}$$

in which $\rho$ and $\rho_1$ are the densities of the solution and the solvent, respectively, and $c_2$ is the concentration of protein in grams per milliliter of solution. The partial or apparent specific volume of many proteins is approximately 0.75 ml/g.

‡ Equation (5-19) uses the simple relationship $f = kT/D$. There are several more complicated equations for this relationship, some of which include the activity coefficient of the solute, the partial specific volume of the solvent, and the density of the solution, among other factors. The relationship above is used for simplicity. A person conducting a sedimentation velocity study in the laboratory would want to determine the formulation of the frictional coefficient best suited to the particular investigations planned.

If this equation, which was derived on the basis of the behavior of a single macromolecule, is now converted into an equation which considers the behavior of 1 mol of such macromolecules, one can obtain the rearranged expression

$$M = \frac{RT}{D(1 - \bar{v}_2 \rho_1)} \frac{dr/dt}{\omega^2 r} \tag{5-21}$$

where $R$ is the molar gas constant $(8.3143 \times 10^7 \text{ ergs/K} \cdot \text{mol})$. The quantity $(dr/dt)/\omega^2 r$ in this equation has been designated as the sedimentation coefficient $s$. The sedimentation coefficient is defined as the velocity $dr/dt$ with which a macromolecule moves through a unit centrifugal force field. An expression for the relationship between the molecular weight, the sedimentation coefficient, and the diffusion constant of the given macromolecule is

$$s = \frac{dr/dt}{\omega^2 r} = \frac{M(1 - \bar{v}_2 \rho_1)D}{RT} \tag{5-22}$$

Generally, the value of $s$ is of the order of $10^{-13}$ seconds. For the purposes of convenience a unit called the *svedberg*, in honor of T. Svedberg, who pioneered in studies involving ultracentrifugation, has been defined as equal to $10^{-13}$ seconds. Many of the proteins of interest to biochemists have sedimentation coefficients in the range of from 1 to 50 svedberg units, written 1 to 50 S. In some instances the sedimentation coefficient itself is used as a parameter by which a protein is partially characterized. Also, it is seen that using Eq. (5-22), one could calculate the molecular weight of a protein by determining its sedimentation coefficient and knowing or experimentally determining both the diffusion constant of the macromolecule and its partial specific volume.

The experimental determination of the sedimentation coefficient can be carried out in several ways. One of the simplest is as follows. The boundary positions are photographed during centrifugation (Fig. 5-6). Each photograph is then superimposed on a calibration plate, and the distance $r$ between the boundary and the axis

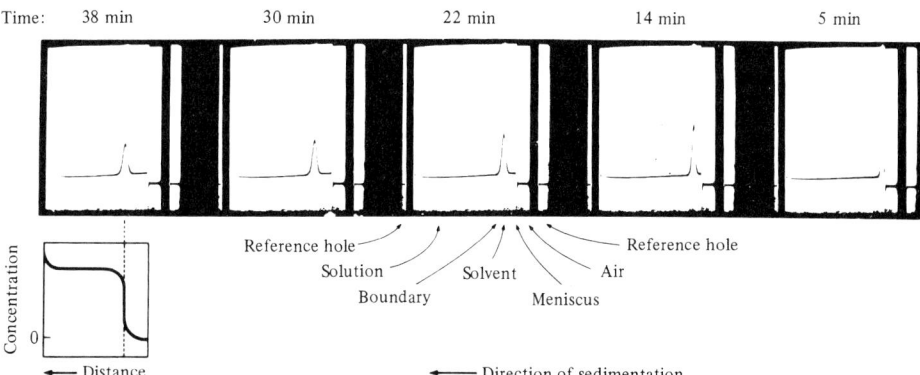

**Figure 5-6** Schlieren photographs depicting the concentration gradient in the ultracentrifuge cell as a function of time. The protein in this case has a molecular weight of approximately 380,000. The inset shows a plot of concentration vs. distance from the meniscus at 38 min. [*From van Holde, K. E. (1971) Physical Biochemistry, p. 101, Prentice-Hall, Englewood Cliffs, N.J. With permission.*]

of rotation (the axis of the rotor) is determined. A graph of ln $r$ as a function of time yields a line of which the slope is directly related to $s$. Specifically, the slope of such a plot is $\omega^2 s$ since

$$s = \frac{d(\ln r)/dt}{\omega^2} \tag{5-23}$$

## Sedimentation Equilibrium Methods for Determining Molecular Weights

In contrast to the sedimentation velocity method, the sedimentation equilibrium method requires slow rotor speeds, such as 6000 to 7000 revolutions per minute, in order to prevent the complete sedimentation of the solute macromolecules. After a relatively long time, sometimes 2 to 3 days, equilibrium can be attained. At equilibrium the migrations of the macromolecules due to the centrifugal force field are exactly balanced by those due to diffusion. This equivalence can be expressed as

$$c_2 \frac{dr}{dt} = D \frac{dc_2}{dr} \tag{5-24}$$

If one now substitutes the expression for $dr/dt$ from Eq. (5-24) into Eq. (5-21), one obtains, after simplifying and rearranging,

$$M = \frac{RT}{\omega^2(1-\bar{v}_2\rho_1)} \frac{dc_2/dr}{c_2 r} \tag{5-25}$$

where $c_2$ is the concentration and $dc_2/dr$ is the concentration gradient of the macromolecule at equilibrium, assuming that there is a single solute in an ideal, two-component system comprising solute and solvent. If $c_2$ is now integrated between the meniscus $m$ and a point $r$, a given distance from the axis of rotation, one can obtain the following equation, which is written in logarithmic form:

$$M = \frac{2RT}{\omega^2(1-\bar{v}_2\rho_1)} \frac{\ln(c_2/c_2{}^m)}{r^2 - m^2} \tag{5-26}$$

where $c_2{}^m$ represents the concentration of the macromolecule at the meniscus. To obtain the molecular weight of the macromolecule with this equation, one must determine values for $c_2$. This is generally accomplished by using a schlieren optical system (*Schlieren* is German for "streaks") or an interferometric optical system. The schlieren optical system is based on the observation that when parallel light rays pass through a medium in which there is a refractive-index gradient, they are deflected, the extent of deflection being directly proportional to the steepness of the gradient. Since a linear relationship exists between the index of refraction of a solution and its solute concentration, this observation can be used to determine solute concentration gradients and, ultimately, solute concentrations in solutions in which there is a refractive-index gradient. In the schlieren optical system represented diagrammatically in Figure 5-7, light rays are shown passing through the ultracentrifuge cell and (because of the existing refractive-index gradient) being deflected. Those passing through regions having the steepest refractive-index gradient are deflected most. Subsequently, the light rays impinge upon a plate which has an oblique slit in it.

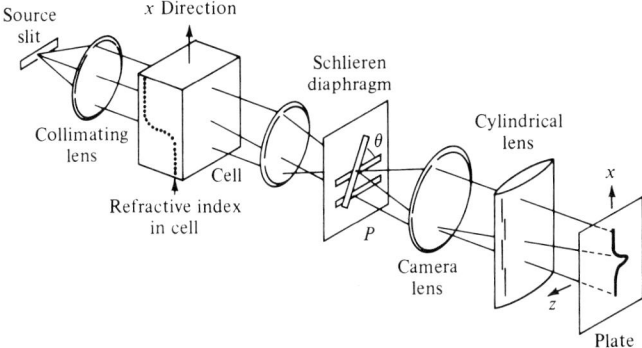

**Figure 5-7** A schematic diagram of a cylindrical-lens schlieren system. There is a diagonal slit at the focal plane $P$. The cylindrical lens focuses images that are at $P$ on the plate at the end of the system. Since light that is off axis passes through only a portion of the diagonal slit, there is a deflection in the $z$ direction proportional to the refractive-index gradient.

Undeflected light rays simply pass through the slit, but deflected rays pass through only a portion of the slit. In fact, rays which have been markedly deflected will pass through the slit only at its lower end, as shown in the diagrammatic representation. After passing through the oblique slit, the light rays pass through a cylindrical lens which focuses light horizontally but not vertically. This causes formation of an image on the photographic or frosted glass plate that is a vertical straight line if none of the light rays was deflected or an image with a horizontal displacement if the light rays were deflected. In the latter case, the magnitude of the horizontal displacement is proportional to the steepness of the refractive-index gradient. Thus, by using a schlieren optical system the refractive-index gradient at a given distance from the axis of rotation can be determined, and from that the solute concentration gradient at this distance can be derived. Having derived values for concentration gradients at a series of distances from the axis of rotation, one can now plot $dc_2/dr$ as a function of $r$ and obtain a curve. Integration of the area under this curve yields the difference in the solute concentration between the two points designated by the $r$ values chosen for the limits of the integration. In practice, one of these $r$ values is frequently that at the meniscus. In this case a value for the solute concentration can be derived by carrying out the ultracentrifugation at a speed such that the solute concentration at the meniscus is negligible. (This procedure is known as the *meniscus depletion method* or the *Yphantis method* since it was introduced by David A. Yphantis.†) Finally, one can compute point-by-point molecular-weight values using Eq. (5-26) with a series of corresponding values for $c_2$, $c_2{}^m$, $r$, and $m$. Ultimately, after the appropriate evaluation of these data, a molecular weight for the macromolecule is obtained.

As mentioned above, an interferometric optical system can also be used in sedimentation equilibrium studies. Such a system, usually derived from the Rayleigh interferometer, can be represented diagrammatically as shown in Fig. 5-8. Certain

† Yphantis, D. A. (1964) *Biochemistry* **3**, 297–317.

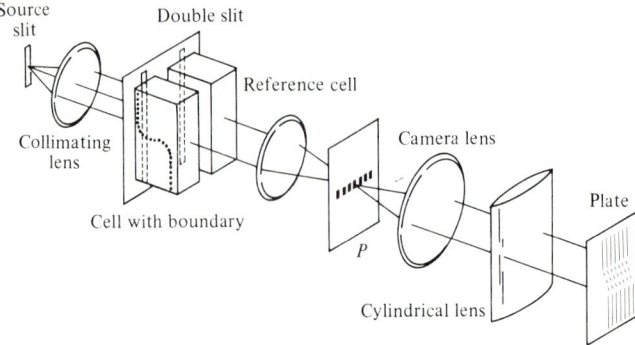

**Figure 5-8** A schematic diagram of a Rayleigh interference system. Again, a cylindrical lens is used. $P$ is the focal plane, where all interference patterns are superimposed. Subsequently, they are sorted by the optical system.

aspects of this optical system bear a degree of similarity to the schlieren optical system, but here the source slit is parallel to the cell axis whereas in the schlieren optical system it is perpendicular to the cell axis (Fig. 5-7). Also in this system a double cell is used. One cell compartment contains only the solvent medium while the other contains solvent plus solute. Behind each cell compartment is a slit parallel to the cell axis. When light rays pass through the double-slit system and then through the solutions contained in the cell compartments, an interference pattern is obtained. This pattern, which is actually quite complex, can be thought of as a composite resulting from the individual interference patterns which would be obtained if each of the compartments were divided into a great number of layers, each perpendicular to the axis of the cell. There would be an interference pattern corresponding to each of these layers, and the fringes of each of these patterns would be shifted in response to the difference in refractive index between the solvent layer in the solvent compartment and the corresponding solution layer in the solution compartment. Therefore, the refractive-index difference between two points on the cell axis in the solution compartment can be determined on the basis of the number of fringes between these two points. Now using the relationship between refractive index and concentration, one can derive the concentration differences between the two points. (Note that when the interferometric optical system is used, concentration differences between two points in the solution compartment can be obtained by counting fringes. Integration of the area under a curve is not required.) Again, the concentration differences derived using the interferometric optical system can be converted into absolute concentrations using the Yphantis technique, as described above. Ultimately, after appropriate treatment of the data, a value for the molecular weight of the macromolecule can be obtained.

One of the disadvantages of the sedimentation equilibrium method for determining molecular weights is that in the time required to achieve equilibrium many proteins (and other biochemical compounds) may undergo degradation. In an attempt to overcome this disadvantage a method referred to as the *approach-to-equilibrium* or *Archibald method* was introduced. It is an outgrowth of the theoretical studies by W. J. Archibald, who pointed out that the equilibrium condition, i.e., an absence of a net migration of solute molecules, is fulfilled throughout the centrifugation at the meniscus of the solution and at the bottom of the cell. On this basis, the determination of the concentration and the concentration gradient just at the meniscus and at the bottom of the cell permits calculation of the molecular weight of the macromolecule. When extremely pure monodisperse samples are used, very accurate values for the molecular weight can be obtained by this method. When polydisperse samples are used, weight-average molecular weights are obtained.

## A Gel-electrophoretic Method for Estimating Molecular Weights

Although the ultracentrifugal methods for determining molecular weights can be quite accurate under appropriate conditions, these procedures require an investment of over $50,000 (the cost of an ultracentrifuge) and each determination requires a considerable investment of time. For these reasons and others the molecular weight of a protein is frequently estimated by a much less complicated and less expensive procedure, which uses polyacrylamide gels. Polyacrylamide gels are produced by the copolymerization of acrylamide and a cross-linking agent, $N,N'$-methylenebisacrylamide. By varying the relative concentrations of these monomers gels with different average pore sizes can be obtained. Such gels, in turn, can be used as a supporting medium in electrophoretic procedures. Electrophoresis is based on the observation that when a charged particle is placed in an electric field, it will migrate. The velocity of his migration is known as the *electrophoretic mobility U*. If the charged particle is spherical, the following equation for its electrophoretic mobility can be derived:

$$U = \frac{ze}{6\pi\eta R} \qquad (5\text{-}27)$$

where $z$ = number of units of charge
$e$ = unit of charge in electrostatic units = $4.8 \times 10^{-10}$ esu
$\eta$ = viscosity of solution containing charged particle
$R$ = radius of particle

In actuality, a much more complex equation is required to express the electrophoretic mobility of a macromolecule since factors which take into account deviations from a spherical shape, the extent to which the macromolecule is hydrated, the ion atmosphere that surrounds the macromolecule, and other parameters must be included.

When conducting a gel-electrophoretic study with polyacrylamide as the supporting medium, one first places the monomers in a small glass tube and causes them to undergo polymerization. Then, an aliquot of the protein or proteins is applied at the top of the polymerized gel column. When a voltage is subsequently applied across the length of the gel column, the macromolecules begin to migrate down the column; the velocity of their migration is a function of both the charge and the size of the migrating species. The charge influences the velocity of migration because of the voltage across the medium. The size influences the velocity of the migration because the polyacrylamide functions as a "molecular sieve," i.e., a porous matrix which separates molecules on the basis of size. When a solution of molecules of varying sizes is applied at the top of a column of a nonreacting, porous matrix, the molecules migrate down the column at varying velocities because molecules which are small enough to diffuse into pores of the matrix will be retarded while those large enough to be excluded from these pores will not be retarded. If one is using a matrix of fairly uniform average pore size, molecules larger than this size will generally be excluded while smaller molecules will generally be retarded, the extent of the retardation reflecting the frequency with which the migrating species diffuses into the pores of the matrix. Thus, larger molecules exhibit a greater velocity than smaller molecules when migrating down a polyacrylamide gel column.

When polyacrylamide gel electrophoresis is to be used for determining molecular weights of proteins, the procedure is frequently conducted in the presence of a denaturing agent such as sodium dodecyl sulfate, which binds proteins with a gram-per-gram binding ratio that is identical for all proteins examined.†

## OPTICAL ACTIVITY OF PROTEINS

All the common amino acids except glycine are optically active, and since the dissymmetry of these molecules is not destroyed by formation of peptide linkages, all proteins are optically active. In view of the fact that the optical rotation of a protein is markedly changed upon its denaturation (which primarily entails alterations in its secondary and tertiary structure) it can be concluded that macromolecular conformation contributes to the optical activity of a protein. How might this come about? An inspection of various macromolecular conformations shows that some of them are themselves dissymmetric. For example, helixes are dissymmetric. A right-handed helix and a similar left-handed helix bear the relationship of enantiomers.

The optical rotation due to the molecular dissymmetry of a helical molecule can be considered to come about in the following way. Again, consider a plane-polarized ray to comprise a right and left circularly polarized component (see Chap. 2 for discussions of plane-polarized light). The electric fields associated with the right circularly polarized component can be represented as in Fig. 5-9a, while those associated with the left circularly polarized component can be represented as in Fig. 5-9b. Magnetic fields accompany each of these electric fields. The relationship between the electric and the magnetic fields in the right circularly polarized component can be represented as in Fig. 5-9c and that in the left circularly polarized component as in Fig. 5-9d.

At the instant when the magnitude of each of the electric fields is increasing, interaction with a conducting medium associated with an induced magnetic moment that is also increasing will reinforce the right circularly polarized component and oppose the left circularly polarized component. Similarly, interaction with a conducting medium associated with an induced magnetic moment that is decreasing will

† Reynolds, J. A., and Tanford, C. (1970) *J. Biol. Chem.* **245**, 5161–5165; Fish, W. W., Reynolds, J. A., and Tanford, C. (1970) *J. Biol. Chem.* **245**, 5166–5168; Fish, W. W. (1975) in *Methods in Membrane Biology* (Korn, E. D., ed.), vol. 4, pp. 189–276, Plenum, New York.

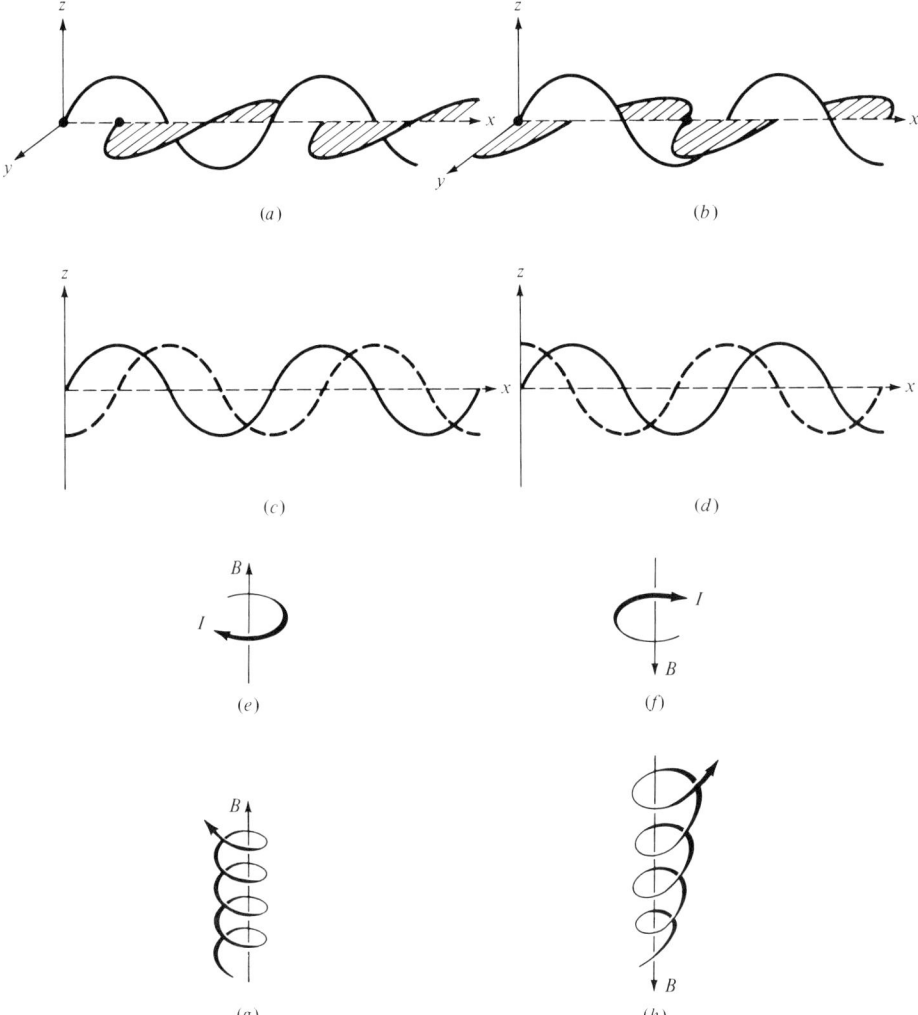

**Figure 5-9** Electric and magnetic fields associated with circularly polarized components of plane-polarized light. In parts (e) to (h), B denotes magnetic induction. The left-hand rule, which relates the direction of the electron current I to that of the magnetic induction in a wire, states that if one grasps the wire with the left hand with the thumb pointing in the direction of the electron current (from − to +), the fingers will point in the direction of the induced magnetic moment.

reinforce the left circularly polarized component and oppose the right circularly polarized component. A wire coil in which current is flowing in the direction shown in Fig. 5-9e will be associated with an induced magnetic moment having the direction indicated. (This can be seen by using the left-hand rule.) Similarly, a wire coil in which current is flowing in the opposite direction, as in Fig. 5-9f will be associated with an induced magnetic moment having the direction indicated. Therefore, the helical structures shown in Fig. 5-9g and h will be associated with the induced magnetic moments indicated. The structure in Fig. 5-9g is a left-handed helix and the structure in Fig. 5-9h is a right-handed helix. The protein macromolecule can be looked upon as a conducting medium, and thus it follows that the interaction between plane-polarized light and a helical conformation of the protein results in a difference between the velocity of the right and the left circularly polarized components of the polarized light. This difference is the basis for optical activity. The magnitude of the optical rotation is given by

$$\alpha = \frac{\pi}{\lambda}(n_L - n_R) \tag{5-28}$$

already presented in Chap. 2.

## Optical-Rotatory-Dispersion and Circular-Dichroism Spectra of Proteins

Proteins, as optically active macromolecules, exhibit characteristic optical-rotatory-dispersion (ORD) and circular-dichroism (CD) spectra. The characteristics of these spectra are determined by the positions of the absorption maxima of the chromophoric moieties of the protein and by the particular environment in which the chromophoric moiety exists. The chromophoric moiety present in all proteins and polypeptides is the amide bond, which exhibits a strong absorption band in the region of 190 nm and a weak band in the region of 210 to 220 nm. Since different macromolecular configurations provide different environments for the amide bond, different ORD and CD spectra are exhibited by proteins which exist predominantly in a helical configuration and those which exist predominantly in one of the pleated-sheet configurations. The characteristics of the ORD spectra and the CD spectra exhibited by proteins having a specific macromolecular configuration are shown in Table 5-3.

**Table 5-3 Characteristics of ORD and CD spectra exhibited by certain polypeptide configurations**

| Configuration | ORD, nm | | | CD, nm | |
|---|---|---|---|---|---|
| | Min | Shoulder | Max | Min | Max |
| α helix | 233 | 215 | 198 | 221<br>209 | 191 |
| β pleated sheet<br>  Antiparallel<br>  Intramolecular | 230<br><br>190 | | <br>205<br> | 219<br><br> | <br><br>196 |
| Poly-L-proline helix (II) | 216 | | 189 | 207 | 226 |
| Random coil | 206 | | | 205 | |

## FLUORESCENCE OF PROTEINS

The characteristic absorptions of several common amino acids result in fluorescent emissions. When a molecule absorbs light energy and consequently assumes a higher energy level, the return to a ground-state level can follow several routes. One is by a process that occurs relatively rapidly and with the emission of light, called *fluorescence*. The lifetime of the high-energy state of a molecule that exhibits fluorescence is of the order of a few nanoseconds (in contrast to a molecule that exhibits phosphorescence; the high-energy state of a phosphorescent molecule may have a lifetime of several seconds). Virtually all naturally occurring proteins exhibit fluorescence, due primarily to the presence of tyrosyl and tryptophanyl moieties. The characteristics of the absorption (excitation) spectra and the fluorescent emission spectra of tryptophan, tyrosine, and phenylalanine are given in Table 5-4.

When the fluorescence of the proteins is determined, rather than that of the monomeric amino acids, the emission spectra of the tryptophanyl and the tyrosyl moieties are influenced by each other. The precise cause of this behavior is unknown. The fluorescent emission of phenylalanine is rarely observed when protein molecules are examined.

The fluorescence of the proteins can be used to study some of the reactions of these macromolecules. For example, experiments involving fluorescence quenching have been carried out in order to study the antigen-antibody reaction between the hemeprotein hemoglobin, which functions as an antigen, and antihemoglobin antibodies. Flourescence quenching occurs when the high-energy state of a molecule that exhibits fluorescence reacts with another species to form a product which no longer emits fluorescence or which has different fluorescence characteristics. The reaction

**Table 5-4 Characteristics of the absorption (excitation) spectra and the fluorescent emission spectra of tryptophan, tyrosine, and phenylalanine**

|  | Absorption maximum, nm | Molar extinction coefficient $\times 10^{-3}$ | Fluorescent emission maximum, nm | Quantum yield of fluorescence,† % |
|---|---|---|---|---|
| Tryptophan | 278 \| in HCl<br>218 / | 5.6<br>33.5 | 350 | 20 |
|  | 280.5 \| in NaOH<br>221.5 / | 5.43<br>34.6 |  |  |
| Tyrosine | 274.4 \| in HCl<br>223 / | 1.34<br>8.2 | 303 | 21 |
|  | 293.5 \| in NaOH<br>240 / | 2.33<br>11.1 |  |  |
| Phenylalanine | 257.5 } in HCl<br>258 } in NaOH | 0.19<br>0.206 | 282 | 3.5 |

† The quantum yield of the fluorescence is the percentage of the absorbed energy that is reemitted as fluorescence.

between hemoglobin and a protein antibody results in the quenching of the tryptophanyl fluorescence of the antibody by the heme moiety of the hemoglobin. By monitoring the progressive decrease in the fluorescent emission at 350 nm the stoichiometry of the antigen-antibody reaction was determined and the rate of the reaction was derived. Data pertaining to the specificity of the association, the number of antigen binding sites on the antibody, the extent of binding, and other reaction characteristics were obtained from experiments involving fluorescence quenching.

Another characteristic of the fluorescent emission of the tryptophanyl moiety is the basis for studies of a different type. The fluorescent emission maximum of the tryptophanyl moiety undergoes a blue shift from 350 to 300 nm when the solvent is changed from water to a hydrocarbon. This behavior suggests that the position of the fluorescent emission maximum could be used to indicate whether this aminoacyl unit is in a hydrophilic or a hydrophobic environment. It is thought that the tertiary structure of the proteins is maintained to a large extent by hydrophobic bonding and that the side chains of the aromatic amino acids participate in this bonding. If the tryptophanyl moiety is involved in hydrophobic bonding and thus buried in the inner regions of the macromolecule, it should behave much as if it were dissolved in a hydrocarbon solvent. On the other hand, if this aminoacyl unit is exposed to the aqueous environment, it should behave much as if it were dissolved in water. Studies on the nature of the tertiary structure of various proteins have been carried out on this basis.

## PROTEIN DENATURATION

Proteins in their native states exist in well-defined three-dimensional structures which are relatively compact and usually essentially globular. (Some native proteins have rodlike shapes.) When a major change in this native structure is induced without an alteration in the primary structure of the macromolecule, the protein is said to have undergone *denaturation*. The stipulation that the structural change be a "major" one is somewhat nebulous, but, in general, it is considered to refer to a change that pervades the entire molecule rather than a localized conformational change like that which sometimes occurs when the catalytic site of an enzyme is altered as a result of substrate or ligand binding. As a result of these pervasive structural changes caused by denaturation, in many cases, the well-defined globular structure is converted into that of a random coil. A randomly coiled protein is one in which there is free rotation about all bonds that would exhibit free rotation in an amino acid or in a small polypeptide. This conversion from a globular protein into a randomly coiled one can often be monitored by observing changes in certain parameters, e.g., light absorption, optical rotation, viscosity, or titratable acidity. Since the change from a globular protein to a random coil entails a change in the spatial arrangement of the peptide bonds of the macromolecule, changes in the amide absorption bands can be used to monitor the extent of protein denaturation. Optical rotation can be used to monitor denaturation since as the macromolecule loses its defined helical or β structure, the magnitude of rotation decreases because helical and β structures contribute to the optical rotation exhibited by a protein. Compact structures like native globular proteins have much lower intrinsic viscosities than denatured proteins, and therefore, as denaturation proceeds, the intrinsic viscosity increases. The titratable acidity undergoes alterations concomitant with denaturation because as the macromolecule unfolds, acidic or basic groups subject to shielding or to other electrostatic interactions involving functional groups forced into close proximity become free from these influences. In the completely denatured protein acidic and basic groups generally exhibit their unperturbed p$K_a$ values. When methods based on changes in such parameters are used to monitor protein denaturation, the transition from the native to the denatured state occurs within a narrow range of temperature or concentration of the denaturing agent. Thus, as the temperature or concentration is increased, little change occurs until some critical condition is attained, and then there is an extensive reorganization of macromolecular structure in response to a small increase in the condition being varied. For example, when the denaturation of the protein lysozyme was monitored by following the optical rotation, the plot shown in Fig. 5-10 was obtained.

## Thermal Denaturation

Reversible thermal denaturation might be considered to reflect the effect of temperature upon the equilibria involving the native state of a protein and its denatured states. When the denatured states are the more stable at higher temperatures, they will prevail under this condition. One factor that may contribute to the stability of the denatured states is that acidic or basic functional groups forced into close proximity in the native state can become more widely separated when the macromolecule unfolds at the higher temperatures. A related consideration is that the less-defined structure attained because of the available thermal energy would be expected to be

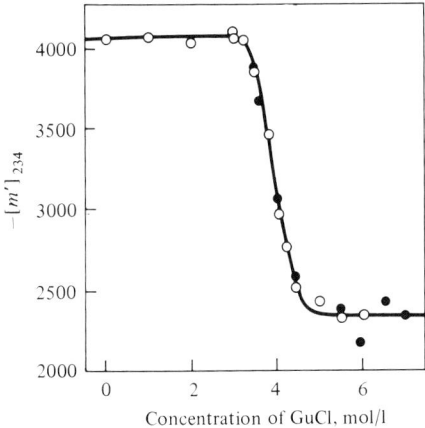

**Figure 5-10** A plot of the optical rotation of the protein lysozyme (an enzyme) at 234 nm as a function of the concentration of guanidinium chloride (GuCl). The decrease in optical rotation, which reflects the unfolding and reorganization of the molecule, is seen to be precipitous. [*From Tanford, C., Pain, R. H., and Otchin, N. S. (1966) J. Mol. Biol.* **15**, 489–504 (*see p. 492*). *With permission.*]

more stable because of a diminution of the constraints imposed upon it. The product of thermal denaturation is not a completely random coil, however, but an incompletely disordered species that retains regions of ordered structure. Generally, a completely thermally denatured protein cannot be obtained as such because as the temperature is increased, other reactions entailing alterations in primary structure take place. In the incompletely disordered structure there is evidence that the degree to which hydrophobic aminoacyl side chains are exposed is minimal.

## Denaturing Agents

Most proteins are at least partially, if not totally, denatured in the presence of 6 to 8 $M$ guanidinium chloride at room temperature. This denaturing agent generally

$$\begin{array}{c} H_2N \\ \phantom{H_2N}\diagdown \\ \phantom{H_2N}C{=}\overset{+}{N}H_2 \\ \phantom{H_2N}\diagup \\ H_2N \phantom{=NH_2} Cl^- \end{array}$$
Guanidinium chloride

destroys all noncovalent bonds, with the result that linear, randomly coiled molecules are obtained except when the protein is cross-linked by disulfide (Cys-Cys) bonds. The effect of this salt has been interpreted on the basis of the following model. The native state and the denatured states of a protein exist in equilibrium. Under physiological conditions the equilibrium strongly favors the native state. Certain changes in the environment of the macromolecule cause this equilibrium to be altered, however. For example, the presence of a salt like guanidinium chloride causes a new equilibrium to be established since not only are the characteristics of the solution per se changed but also the salt binds the protein, thereby creating new macromolecular species. The new equilibria then established involve not only the native and denatured forms but also the various ligated forms of the protein. The new equilibria strongly favor one or more of the denatured forms when an appropriate denaturing agent is being used. Thus, the equilibrium constants for the native to denatured conversion $K_d$ will have higher values in the presence of the denaturing agent than in its absence.

Denaturation by aqueous salt solutions entails the disruption of hydrogen bonds in the interior of the native macromolecule and the exposure of groups that were in the interior, in a relatively nonpolar environment, to the polar environment provided by the solution. The transfer of polar amide groups and polar side chains of the aminoacyl units from a less polar to a more polar solvent is generally accompanied by a liberation of energy. The transfer of nonpolar aminoacyl side chains from a less polar solvent to a more polar one usually requires energy. When a protein is unfolded in a solution of guanidinium chloride, however, the transfer of both the polar and the nonpolar moieties is an energy-yielding process, a characteristic that enhances the effectiveness of guanidinium chloride as a denaturing agent.

A second, widely used denaturing agent is 8 to 9 $M$ urea, although many proteins do not undergo complete denaturation in the presence of even saturated aqueous solutions of this agent. A protein denatured by urea probably exists in the form of a random coil, much like the protein denatured by guanidinium chloride. Again, disulfide bonds are not severed by the denaturing agent. (They can be cleaved by adding a reducing agent to the denaturing solution.)

In addition to guanidinium chloride and urea, various inorganic salts have been used as denaturing agents, among them $CaCl_2$ (2.5 $M$), KSCN (2.5 $M$), LiBr (4 to 10 $M$), NaI (4 $M$), and NaBr (7 $M$). By contrast, NaCl and KCl are not effective as denaturing agents. How inorganic salts induce the denaturation of proteins is thought to entail the binding of both the cation and the anion by the macromolecule. It is proposed that cations associate with the oxygen atom of the amide group and that anions associate with the amide nitrogen atom.

Detergents are also denaturants. In contrast to the salts and urea, detergents are effective at quite low concentrations. For example, 3 m$M$ sodium dodecyl sulfate brings about the complete denaturation of the protein lactoglobulin, and even lower concentrations of this amphiphile stabilize the protein with respect to other denaturants. Once the critical concentration of the amphiphile is attained, extensive denaturation occurs, the transition being quite precipitous. The detergent denaturant also binds the protein as does guanidinium chloride or urea, but it has been proposed that the detergent binding sites are relatively more specific than those of other denaturing agents. Also, as mentioned earlier in this chapter within the framework of molecular-weight determinations, when a protein interacts with sodium dodecyl sulfate, a complex is formed in which there is a stoichiometric relationship between the protein and the detergent.

## DETERMINATION OF THE PRIMARY STRUCTURE OF PROTEINS

The amino acid sequence of a polypeptide of protein can be determined by allowing it to react with a reagent that will attack specifically the N-terminal or C-terminal aminoacyl unit and yield an identifiable derivative of this unit. The repetition of such a procedure leads to the progressive degradation of the polypeptide or protein and the liberation of each of the amino acids in the order of its occurrence in the chain.

### Sequential Degradation Starting at the Amino Terminus

In 1950 P. Edman reported a method for the sequential degradation of proteins in which the amino group of the N-terminal unit is allowed to react with phenyl isothiocyanate. The product is the phenylthiohydantoin derivative of the N-terminal aminoacyl unit plus a protein chain with a new N-terminal unit. The reaction between the amino group and phenyl isothiocyanate is as follows:

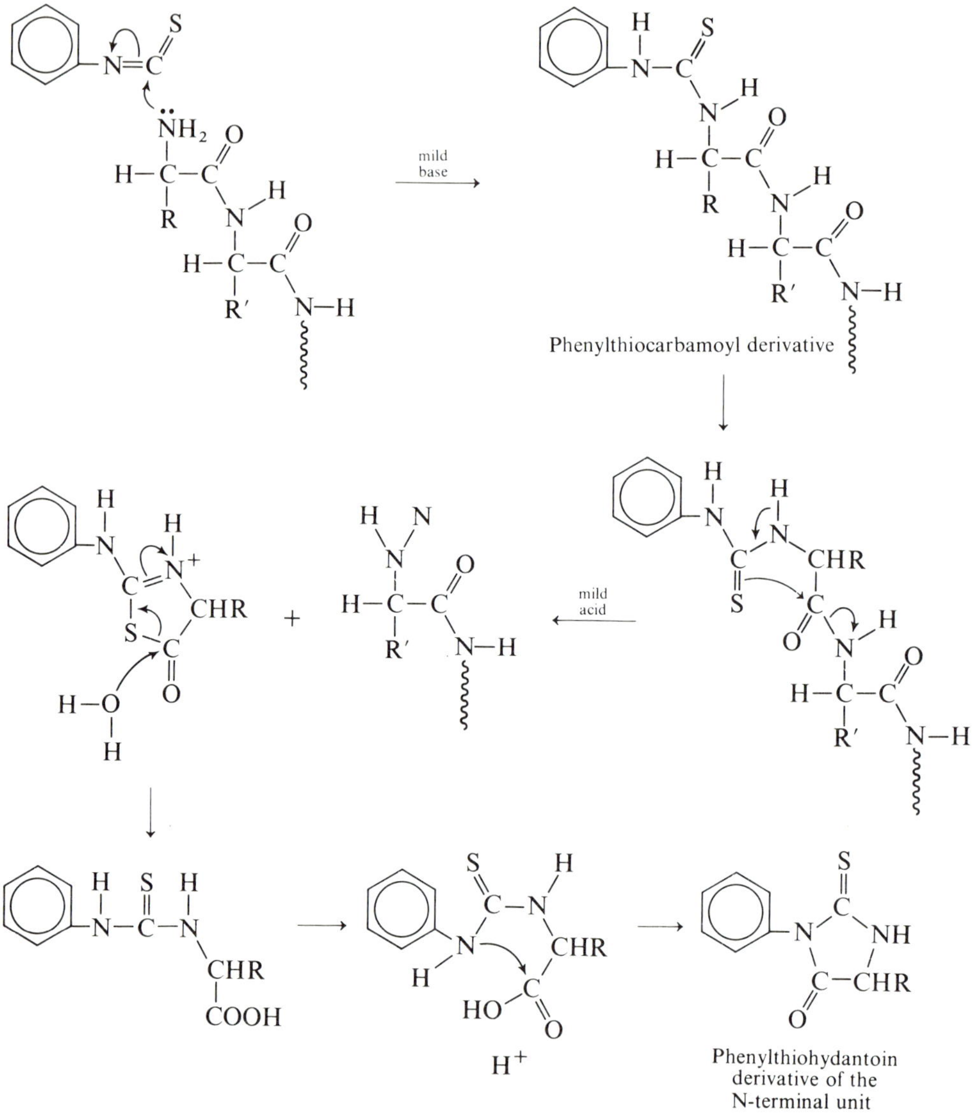

As originally conceived, the Edman degradation involved the formation of the phenylthiocarbamoyl derivative, the cleavage of the protein chain, the isolation of the remaining protein, the conversion of the substituted phenylthiourea derivative to the phenylthiohydantoin derivative, the isolation of this derivative, and then the repetition of the entire procedure for the newly formed N-terminal unit. This was quite tedious. The Edman degradation has now been developed as an automated process using modified polystyrene beads in a manner reminiscent of the automated solid-phase protein synthesis developed by Merrifield. In this automated solid-phase Edman degradation isothiocyanate groups are substituted on the benzene rings of the polystyrene by the following sequence:

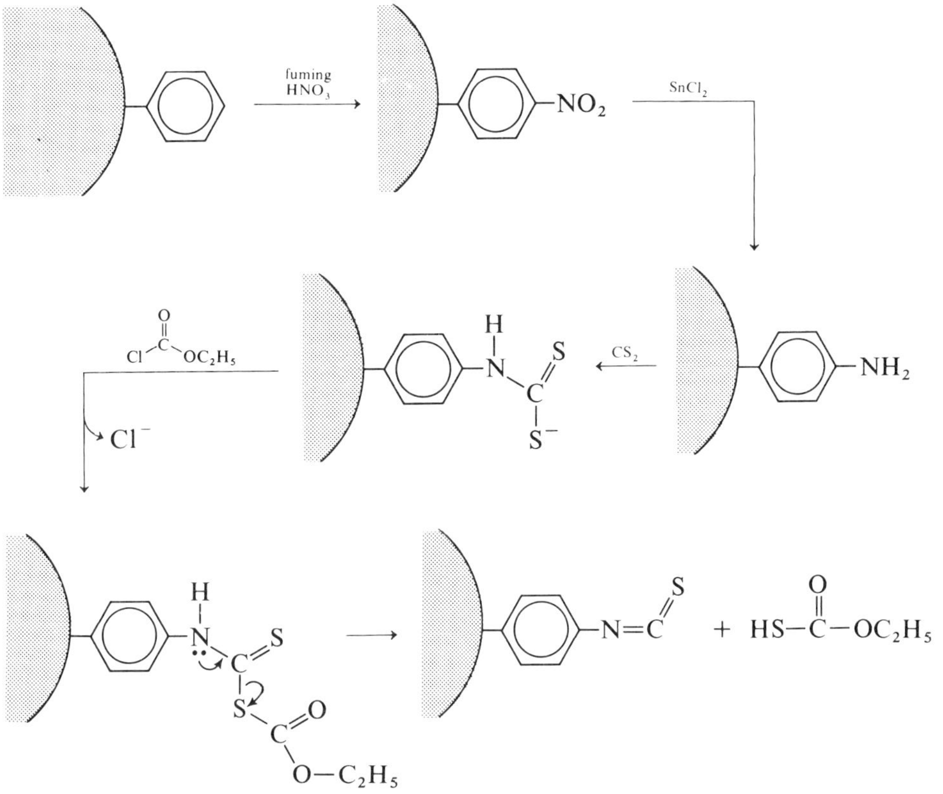

The modified resin is then allowed to react with the protein to give the derivative of the N-terminal unit, anchored to the solid support, and a protein chain with a new N-terminal unit. If a protein containing lysyl units is to be degraded in this manner, the sample can be treated first with a solution of phenyl isothiocyanate, which will react with all free amino groups. Since the phenylthiocarbamoyl derivatives of the $\epsilon$-amino groups of the lysyl units are not converted to substituted phenylthiohydantoins, phenyl isothiocyanate functions as a protecting agent in this case.

Alternatively, the solid-phase Edman degradation can be carried out by procedures that involve the liberation of the substituted phenylthiohydantoin in the reaction medium while the protein or polypeptide chain remains anchored to the solid support. In all cases the goal is the same, i.e., to create a situation in which the derivative and the remaining protein can readily be separated from each other since one is anchored to the resin and the other is in the reaction medium.

In addition to methods involving the use of phenyl isothiocyanate, the amino acid sequence of proteins can be determined using 1-fluoro-2,4-dinitrobenzene, which reacts with free amino groups to yield 2,4-dinitrophenyl derivatives. After a protein has reacted with 1-fluoro-2,4-dinitrobenzene, it is completely hydrolyzed and the amino acid that was N-terminal is obtained as the 2,4-dinitrophenyl derivative. The reaction between 1-fluoro-2,4-dinitrobenzene and an amino group is as follows:

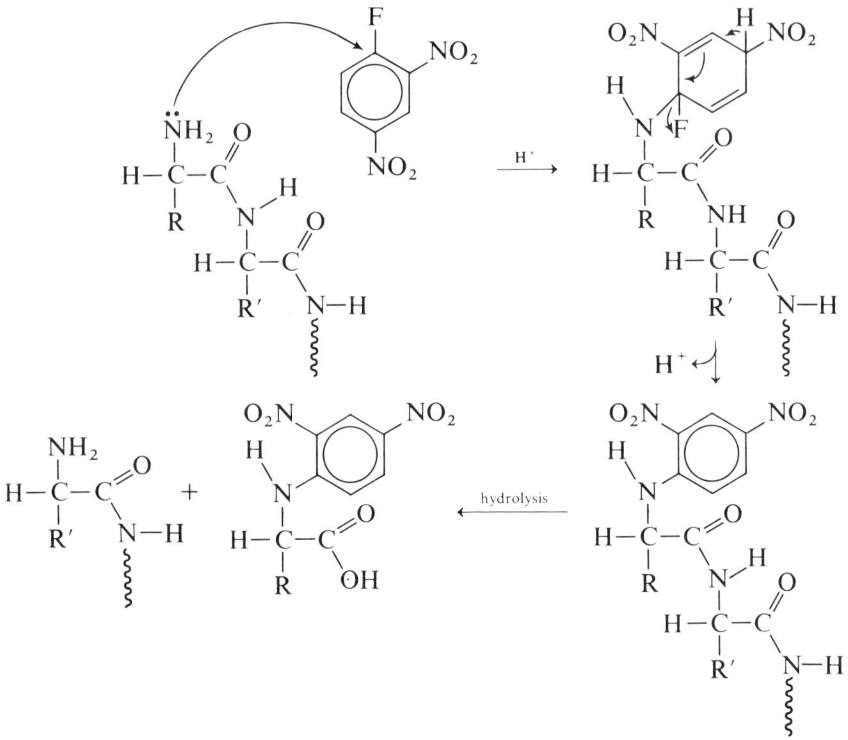

The 2,4-dinitrophenyl derivatives of the amino acids can be identified by chromatographic procedures. The $\epsilon$-amino groups of lysyl units react with 1-fluoro-2,4-dinitrobenzene, but the resulting derivatives are readily separated from those of the N-terminal amino acids.

## Sequential Degradation Starting at the Carboxyl Terminus

A thiohydantoin can be formed from the C-terminal amino acid of a protein by means of a reaction involving a thiocyanate, such as ammonium thiocyanate. This reaction is the basis for another procedure for the determination of the amino acid sequence of proteins:

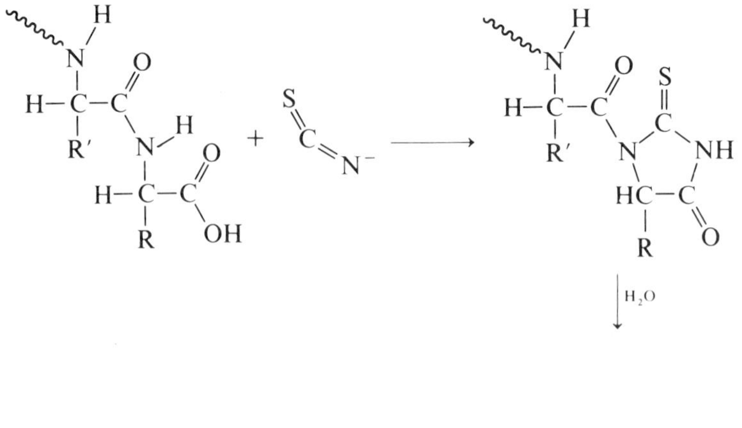

$$\text{HN}\overset{\displaystyle S}{\underset{\displaystyle R}{\overset{\displaystyle \|}{\underset{\displaystyle }{\text{C}}}}}\phantom{...}\text{Thiohydantoin derivative}$$

Thiohydantoin derivative<br>of the<br>C-terminal amino acid

The thiohydantoin derivatives can be isolated and identified, and the process is repeated for the new C-terminal amino acid.

The C-terminal unit of a protein or polypeptide can also be identified by using anhydrous hydrazine. Anhydrous hydrazine produces the acid hydrazides of all amino acids of the protein except the one with a free C(1) carboxyl group. After the reaction with hydrazine, the C-terminal amino acid can be separated from the acid hydrazides and identified.

All the procedures mentioned thus far have involved the use of chemical reagents for the systematic degradation of proteins. Enzymes can also be used for this purpose. Enzymes called *carboxypeptidases* catalyze the hydrolytic cleavage of the peptide bonds of C-terminal amino acid units, and enzymes known as *aminopeptidases* catalyze the cleavage of the peptide bonds of N-terminal aminoacyl units. Since the reactions catalyzed by these enzymes are extremely rapid compared with the nonenzymatic reactions, and since each cleavage produces another protein chain that can react with the enzyme again, the enzymatic reactions are usually carried out for a specific time and then a determination of the relative amounts of the liberated amino acids is made. On this basis, the amino acid obtained in the greatest amount is assumed to have been in a terminal position in the original protein, and the amino acid obtained in the second greatest amount is assumed to have been next in the sequence, and so on. In addition to this use of enzymes, other enzymes that catalyze the cleavage of specific nonterminal peptide linkages are frequently used to cleave large proteins into small peptides, whose primary structures can be determined more conveniently.

## REACTIONS OF PROTEINS

Proteins undergo reactions that involve their functional groups and reactions that involve aspects of their macromolecular structure. With respect to reactions involving functional groups, proteins can be acylated, arylated, and alkylated, their sulfhydryl groups can be oxidized, their carboxyl groups can be reduced, and their aromatic rings can be substituted. Some of these reactions will be discussed in the following paragraphs.

## The Acylation of Proteins

The amino groups, the sulfhydryl groups, and the hydroxyl groups of proteins undergo acylation in the presence of a variety of reagents. Simple anhydrides, e.g., acetic anhydride, and acyl halides, e.g., acetyl chloride, react readily with amino and sulfhydryl groups. Phenolic and aliphatic hydroxyl groups also undergo acylation in the presence of these reagents, but the reactions are slower. Cyclic anhydrides, e.g., succinic anhydride, are milder acylating agents, and reactions using reagents of this type can frequently be carried out with some degree of selectivity. Among other acylating agents that are used by biochemists are cyanates, thiocyanates, isothiocyanates, sulfonyl halides, chloroformates, ethyl thioltrifluoroacetate, $O$-methylisourea, carbon disulfide, and carbon dioxide.

The acylation reactions generally involve a nucleophilic attack by an amino nitrogen atom or a sulfhydryl sulfur atom or a hydroxyl oxygen atom at the electrophilic center of the acylating agent. Selectivity with respect to the various functional groups of the protein can be achieved when the electrophilic center is less than highly reactive. For example, when a protein is allowed to react with $O$-methylisourea, the $\epsilon$-amino groups of the lysyl units undergo acylation although the terminal $\alpha$-amino groups do not:

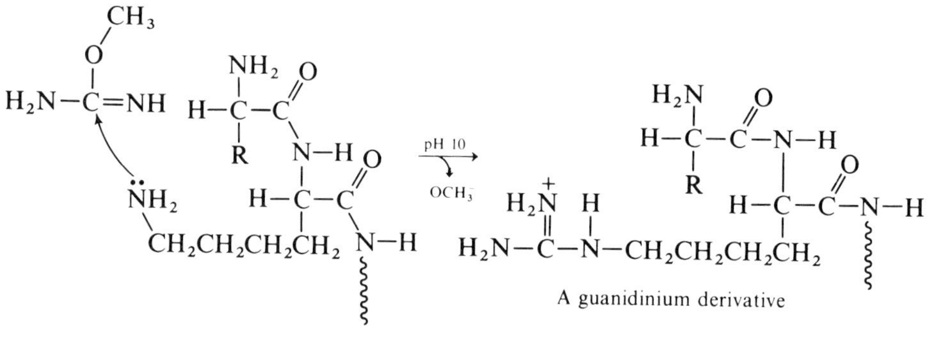

A guanidinium derivative

The similar but more reactive reagent $S$-methylisothiourea reacts with both $\epsilon$-amino groups and terminal $\alpha$-amino groups of proteins.

## The Arylation of Proteins

Reactive aromatic halogen compounds, such as the 1-halo-2,4-dinitrobenzenes, react with the sulfhydryl, amino, and phenolic hydroxyl groups and the imidazole nitrogen atoms of proteins. The products are the corresponding $S$-, $N$-, and $O$-phenyl derivatives. The order of the reactivity of the protein functional groups in the presence of the 1-halo-2,4-dinitrobenzenes is sulfhydryl > amino > phenolic hydroxyl > imidazole nitrogen. This order parallels the general order of the nucleophilicity of these groups. The more reactive 1-fluoro-2,4-dinitrobenzene reacts with each of the functional groups mentioned above under the appropriate conditions, while the less reactive 1-chloro-2,4-dinitrobenzene usually reacts with sulfhydryl groups only.

## The Alkylation of Proteins

Sulfhydryl sulfur atoms, amino nitrogen atoms, imidazole nitrogen atoms, and (in rare cases) carboxyl oxygen atoms of proteins displace the halogen atom of a 2-halo acid or its amide. Because of this, iodoacetic acid and iodoacetamide are frequently used as alkylating agents. Another useful reagent is 2-hydroxy-5-nitrobenzylbromide, which reacts with the cysteine sulfhydryl group and also with the indole moiety of tryptophan, where it is thought that alkylation occurs at C(3) of the indole moiety.

In most cases alkylation proceeds by an $S_N2$ reaction in which the protein functional group is the attacking nucleophile. However, alkylation reactions involving 2-hydroxy-5-nitrobenzylbromide probably proceed by an $S_N1$ reaction involving the formation of a benzyl carbonium ion, which can be stabilized as shown:

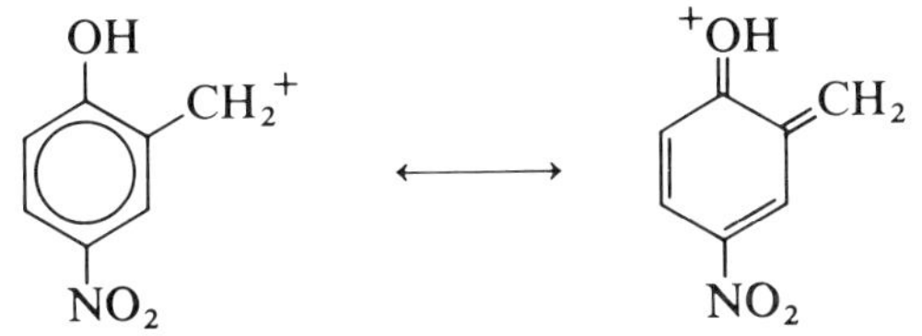

## The Oxidation of Sulfhydryl Groups by Molecular Oxygen

The sulfhydryl groups of the cysteinyl units of proteins undergo oxidation on standing in air. The reaction can yield disulfides as a result of radical coupling:

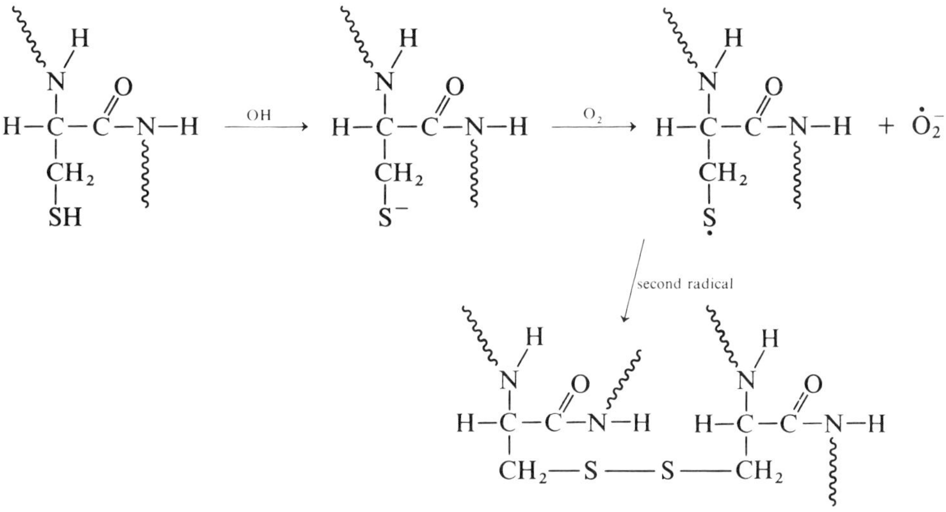

## The Use of Reporter Groups

A functional group with spectral or ionization properties sensitive to the local environment can be introduced into a protein molecule to serve as a probe. The functional group used must become covalently bonded to the protein, and it must bond at known and specific sites. Such a group is called a *reporter group*. One example of the use of a reporter group involves the 2-methoxy-5-nitrobenzyl moiety; it exhibits an ultraviolet absorption maximum at 288 nm in the nonpolar solvent hexane while in the polar solvent dimethyl sulfoxide this maximum is red-shifted to 317 nm.

The 2-methoxy-5-nitrobenzyl moiety can be covalently bonded to cysteinyl or tryptophanyl units of proteins by a reaction not unlike the alkylation reactions discussed above. With the reporter group in place, one can make determinations about the hydrophobicity or hydrophilicity of the immediate environment of the modified aminoacyl unit, based on the position of the absorption maximum of the covalently bonded reporter group.

Another example of a reporter group is the nitroimidazole moiety. The reagent 4-bromo-5-nitroimidazole reacts with cysteinyl sulfhydryl groups to yield *S*-nitroimidazole derivatives. Since the nitroimidazole moiety has a p$K_a$ of 6.5, and since the corresponding anion exhibits a strong characteristic absorption band, information concerning the hydrogen-ion concentration in the immediate vicinity of the reporter group can be obtained by spectrophotometric procedures.

When the enzyme chymotrypsin is allowed to react with 2-bromoacetamido-4-nitrophenol, a methionyl unit very near the catalytic site of the enzyme undergoes alkylation. Since it has been shown that the un-ionized 2-acetamido-4-nitrophenol moiety exhibits an absorption maximum at 318 nm, which is red-shifted to 410 nm upon ionization, determination of the position of the maximum of this reporter group provides information about effective pH in the region of the catalytic site of this enzyme. Studies of this type are frequently conducted to obtain data for use in formulating the mechanism of an enzymatic reaction.

## The Biuret Reaction

When a protein or polypeptide is heated in an alkaline copper sulfate solution, a blue-violet or pink-violet color appears. This reaction, called the *biuret reaction*, is the basis for both qualitative and quantitative procedures for the determination of proteins. Biuret is a diamide derived from urea. When biuret is treated with alkaline copper sulfate, a violet color appears due to the formation of a coordination complex with the structure shown below. A protein or a peptide of three or more aminoacyl units can participate in the formation of a somewhat similar complex:

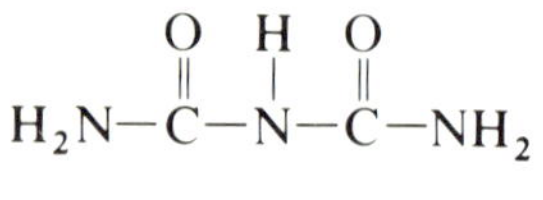

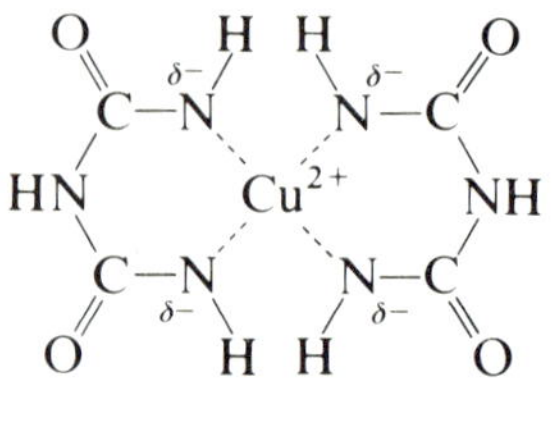

Copper coordination complex derived from biuret

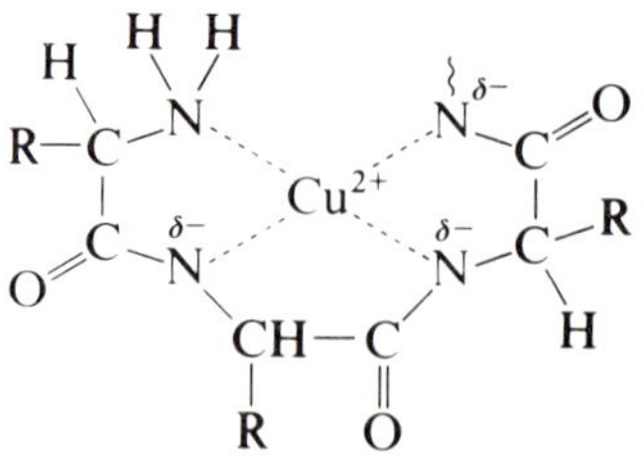

Copper coordination complex derived from a protein

## PLASMA PROTEINS

Blood is a suspension of cells in a colorless solution of salts and proteins, the *plasma*. Plasma makes up 55 to 60 percent of the total blood volume and contains 7 to 8 percent proteins (by weight). Primarily, these proteins are classified as albumins and globulins. Historically, the plasma proteins were separated and isolated using such absorbents as diatomaceous earths. More recently, electrophoretic methods have been used in the separation of these components. These methods include electrophoresis on filter paper, starch gels, agar gels, and polyacrylamide gels. The basis for the separation is essentially the same for all, the electrophoretic mobility being a function of the charge on the protein macromolecule. The various supporting media, i.e., paper or gel, provide a spectrum of conditions under which the separations can be conducted. With electrophoretic techniques,† including immunoelectrophoresis, which utilizes the observation that when a protein migrates into an area in which its antibody is located a precipitate is formed, a multiplicity of distinct plasma proteins have been identified. The principal ones are given in Table 5-5.

Among other important biochemical processes plasma proteins participate in osmotic regulation, the transport of lipids, the transport of certain metal ions, the coagulation, or clotting, of blood, and antigen-antibody reactions. As an adjunct to this brief discussion of the plasma proteins, their participation in two of these processes will be discussed in more detail.

### Blood Coagulation Factors and Blood Coagulation

The coagulation of blood occurs by a rather intricate sequence of reactions involving a series of coagulation factors. These coagulation factors are all proteins except for $Ca^{2+}$, which has also been designated as such a factor. The coagulation of blood can occur by the *intrinsic* or the *extrinsic pathway*. The extrinsic pathway, which is utilized in response to tissue trauma, permits the rapid clotting of blood, i.e., within seconds. On the other hand the clotting of blood as a result of the intrinsic pathway requires minutes (Fig. 5-11).

---

† The classical Tiselius moving-boundary technique entails the use of a U-shaped vessel filled at the bottom with a buffer solution containing the protein to be studied. Buffer solution alone is then carefully layered over the protein solution, and two boundaries are formed, one in each arm of the vessel. A positive electrode is placed in one arm of the vessel and a negative electrode in the other. When a voltage is applied across the system, the two boundaries begin to migrate and the rate of their migration depends upon the charge distribution on the protein molecules. When the protein solution contains more than one component, several moving boundaries are observed.

In other electrophoretic techniques the components migrate on a filter-paper strip or through a starch-gel medium, but the principle is essentially the same; i.e., the components are migrating under the influence of an electric field, and their rates of migration depend upon charge distribution.

The technique of immunoelectrophoresis makes use of the additional principle of antigen-antibody interaction. In immunoelectrophoresis the protein migrates under the influence of an electric field until it comes in contact with its antibody, where upon an antigen-antibody reaction occurs and a precipitate is formed. This procedure is one of the most sensitive of all the electrophoretic techniques.

## Table 5-5 Some of the principal plasma proteins

|  | Mol. wt.† | Isoelectric pH | Concentration in plasma, mg/100 ml | Function |
|---|---|---|---|---|
| **Albumins:** | | | | |
| Prealbumin | 61,000 | 4.7 | 28–35 | |
| Albumin | 69,000 | 4.9 | 3500–4500 | Osmotic regulation |
| **$\alpha_1$ globulins:** | | | | |
| $\alpha_1$ glycoprotein (Schultze) | 50,000 | | | |
| Acidic $\alpha_1$ glycoprotein (orosomucoid) | 44,100 (41% C) | 2.7 | 75–100 | |
| $\alpha_1$ lipoprotein (density 1.093) | 435,000 (67% L) | ... | 37–117 | Transport of lipids |
| $\alpha_1$ lipoprotein (density 1.149) | 195,000 (43% L) | 5.2 | 217–270 | Transport of lipids |
| $\alpha_1$ antitrypsin | 54,000 (12% C) | 4.0 | 210–500 | Inhibition of enzymatic activity of trypsin |
| $\alpha_1$ antichymotrypsin | 68,000 (23% C) | ... | 14–35 | Inhibition of enzymatic activity of chymotrypsin |
| Haptoglobin, type 1-1 | 100,000 (17% C) | 4.1 | 30–190 | Formation of complex with hemoglobin |
| **$\alpha_2$ globulins:** | | | | |
| $\alpha_2$ macroglobulin | 820,000 (10% C) | 5.4 | 220–380 | Inhibition of enzymatic activity of trypsin and plasmin |
| Zn $\alpha_2$ glycoprotein | 41,000 | 3.8 | ......... | |
| Plasminogen | 143,000 | 5.6 | ......... | Precursor of the proteolytic enzyme plasmin |
| Ceruloplasmin | 160,000 | 4.4 | 27–39 | Transport of copper |
| Prothrombin | 68,700 | | | Blood coagulation factor |
| $\alpha_2$ lipoprotein (density < 1.019) | $5–20 \times 10^6$ | ... | 150–230 | Transport of lipids |
| Thrombin | 39,000 | ... | ......... | Blood coagulation factor |
| **$\beta$ globulins:** | | | | |
| $\beta$ lipoprotein (density 0.98–1.002) | 5,000,000 | ... | 130–200 | Transport of lipids |
| $\beta$ lipoprotein (density 1.019–1.063) | 3,200,000 (79% L) | ... | 280–440 | Transport of lipids |
| Transferrin | 89,000 | 5.9 | 200–320 | Transport of iron |
| Fibrinogen | 340,000 | 5.8 | 200–600 | Blood coagulation factor |
| **$\gamma$ globulins:** | | | | |
| Immunoglobulin IgG | 150,000 (2.8% C) | 7.3 | 600–1500 | Antibody to pyrogenic bacteria, viruses |
| Immunoglobulin IgA | $(170,000)_n$ (6.4% C) | ... | 200–300 | Neutralizes viruses of nose, throat, and respiratory and gastrointestinal tracts |
| Immunoglobulin IgM | 900,000 (10.2% C) | ... | 75–150 | Antibodies to new antigens |
| Immunoglobulin IgD | 160,000 | ... | 0–3 | No antibody activity demonstrated |
| Immunoglobulin IgE | 190,000 (11% C) | ... | 0.05 | Reacts with allergens |

† The percentages of carbohydrate (C) or lipid (L) present in the macromolecule are indicated parenthetically.

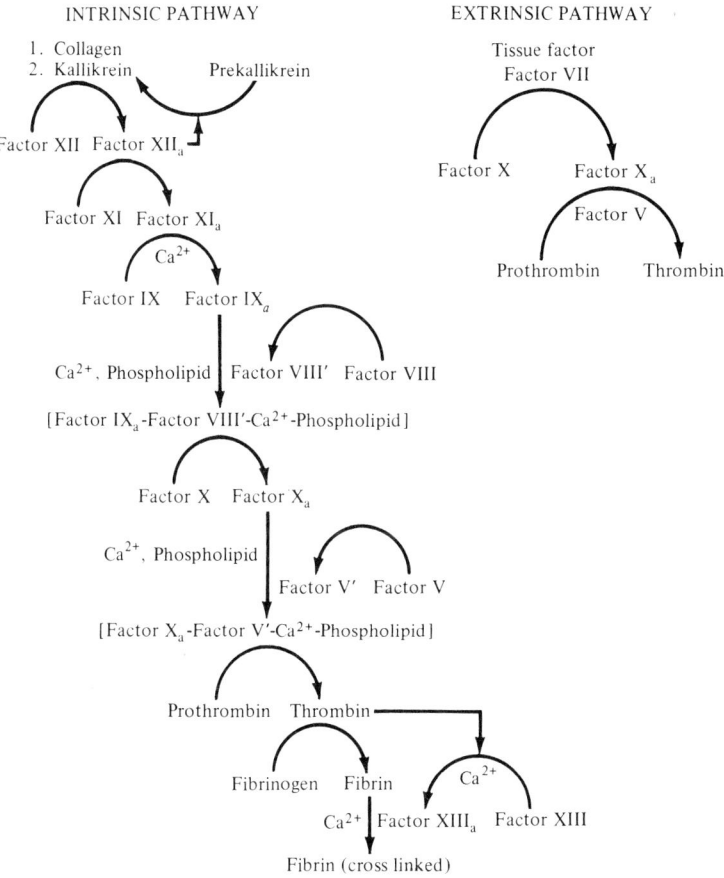

Figure 5-11 Outlines of the intrinsic and extrinsic pathways for blood coagulation.

Blood coagulation entails the sequential conversion of inactive coagulation factors into active ones. In the intrinsic pathway, the process can be considered to begin with the conversion of factor XII (sometimes called the Hageman factor) into its active form, factor XIIa. The mechanism of this activation has not been determined, although it is known that factor XII can bind collagen and basement membranes and that these associations can lead to its conversion into factor XIIa. In the fluid phase factor XII can be activated by kallikrein, a proteolytic enzyme that catalyzes the cleavage of specific plasma proteins. Factor XII and the activated species, factor XIIa, comprise three polypeptide chains, each with a molecular weight of 30,000. (See Table 5-6 for the molecular weights of the coagulation factors.) The active species, XIIa, is an enzyme, and as such it catalyzes the conversion of the inactive factor XI into the active factor XIa. Since this conversion entails the cleavage of certain internal peptide bonds of XI, XIIa is a proteolytic enzyme. Factor XIa now catalyzes the conversion of factor IX to factor IXa. Again a proteolytic reaction occurs, and here

## Table 5-6 Molecular weights of coagulation factors

| Factor | Name | Mol. wt. |
|---|---|---|
| I | Fibrinogen | 340,000 |
| II | Prothrombin | 68,700 |
| III | Tissue factor | 220,000–330,000 |
| IV | Calcium ion | |
| V | Proaccelerin | 300,000–400,000 |
| VII | Proconvertin | 63,000 |
| VIII | Antihemophilic factor | $1.1 \times 10^6$ |
| IX | Christmas factor | 55,400 |
| X | Stuart factor | 55,000 |
| XI | Plasma thromboplastin antecedent | 160,000 |
| XII | Hageman factor | 90,000 |
| XIII | Fibrin stabilizing factor | 320,000 (human plasma) 146,000 (human platelets) |

there is an absolute requirement for a divalent cation such as $Ca^{2+}$. Factor IXa then interacts with factor VIII in the presence of $Ca^{2+}$ and also a phospholipid factor (provided by the platelets) to form a complex that functions as a catalyst in the conversion of factor X to factor Xa. In this reaction, factor VIII is thought to serve as a regulator with the catalysis, per se, being provided by factor IXa. The conversion of X to Xa is also a proteolytic reaction. Factor Xa, once formed, now interacts with factor V, in the presence of $Ca^{2+}$ and a phospholipid, to yield a species that catalyzes the conversion of prothrombin (factor II) into thrombin. The formation of thrombin is thought to entail more than one proteolytic cleavage, each catalyzed by factor Xa. Now all that remains is formation of the blood clot. This results when thrombin, also a proteolytic enzyme, catalyzes the conversion of the soluble protein fibrinogen into the insoluble gel fibrin. The conversion is the result of the cleavage of four peptides from the fibrinogen macromolecule. Fibrin then undergoes polymerization to yield the fibrin clot. The cross-linking that occurs during the formation of this clot is catalyzed by factor XIIIa, an enzyme derived from its precursor in the presence of thrombin.

As indicated in Fig. 5-11, the reactions that occur in the extrinsic pathway are the same as those occurring in the latter stages of the intrinsic pathway except for the way factor X is activated. In the extrinsic pathway the presence of a tissue factor and factor VII are required for the conversion of factor X into factor Xa. The mechanism of this process has not been established, however.

### The Immunoglobulins

The immunoglobulins are plasma proteins that function as antibodies, i.e., proteins produced in response to an antigen which react specifically with that antigen. The immunoglobulins of human plasma have been divided into five classes, IgG, IgA, IgM, IgD, and IgE. The immunoglobulins of each of these classes comprise four

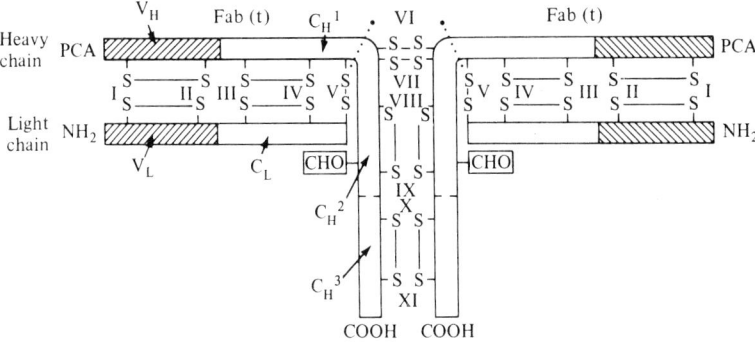

**Figure 5-12** A schematic representation of the human immunoglobulin IgG macromolecule.

PCA = pyrrolidonecarboxylic acid
CHO = carbohydrate
Fab (t) = region cleaved by trypsin to yield characteristic fragment
$C_H$ = constant region, heavy chain
$V_H$ = variable region, heavy chain
$C_L$ = constant region, light chain
$V_L$ = variable region, light chain

polypeptide chains arranged symmetrically about the long axis of the macromolecule. These polypeptide chains are of two types. One, with a molecular weight of approximately 22,000, is referred to as a *light chain*. The other type, with a molecular weight of approximately 53,000, is referred to as a *heavy chain*. An immunoglobulin molecule comprises two dissimilar light chains and two identical heavy chains. The two types of light chains are designed as kappa ($\kappa$) and lambda ($\lambda$). Heavy chains are

**Table 5-7 Properties of human immunoglobulins in class IgG**

| Heavy chain | Number of interchain disulfide bonds | Molecular formula |
| --- | --- | --- |
| $\gamma_1$ | 4 | $(\gamma_1)_2 \kappa_2 (\gamma_1)_2 \lambda_2$ |
| $\gamma_2$ | 6 | $(\gamma_2)_2 \kappa_2 (\gamma_2)_2 \lambda_2$ |
| $\gamma_3$ | 7 | $(\gamma_3)_2 \kappa_2 (\gamma_3)_2 \lambda_2$ |
| $\gamma_4$ | 4 | $(\gamma_4)_2 \kappa_2 (\gamma_4)_2 \lambda_2$ |
| $\alpha_1$ | ... | $[(\alpha_1)_2 \kappa_2]_n [(\alpha_1)_2 \lambda_2]_n$ |
| $\alpha_2$ | ... | $[(\alpha_2)_2 \kappa_2]_n [(\alpha_2)_2 \lambda_2]_n$ |
| $\mu$ | 20 | $(\mu_2 \kappa_2)_5 (\mu_2 \lambda_2)_5$ |
| $\delta$ | ... | $\delta_2 \lambda_2 \delta_2 \kappa_2$ |
| $\epsilon$ | 3 | $\epsilon_2 \lambda_2 \epsilon_2 \kappa_2$ |

*Source:* From Rosen, F. S., and Merler, E. (1972) in *The Metabolic Basis of Inherited Disease* (Stanbury, J. B., Wyngaarden, J. B., and Fredrickson, D. S., eds.), 3d ed., p. 1644, McGraw-Hill, New York.

of five types designed as $\gamma$, $\alpha$, $\mu$, $\delta$, and $\epsilon$. The designation of the immunoglobulin is based upon the type of heavy chain it embodies. IgG contains $\gamma$ heavy chains, IgA contains $\alpha$ heavy chains, IgM contains $\mu$ heavy chains, and so forth. The light and heavy chains of a given macromolecule are bonded covalently by disulfide bonds, as represented diagrammatically in Fig. 5-12. Comparison of the primary structures of various immunoglobulins shows that certain regions of light chains and certain regions of the heavy chains are relatively invariant while certain other regions are quite variable. Variable regions near the amino termini of proximal light and heavy chains constitute the site of the interaction between the immunoglobulin and its antigen. Differences in the variable region near the carboxyl termini of the $\gamma$ chains are the basis for the four subclasses of the immunoglobulins of the IgG class. The molecular formulas and certain other structural parameters of the human immunoglobulins are shown in Table 5-7.

CHAPTER
# SIX

## THE CHEMISTRY OF THE PURINES, PYRIMIDINES, AND NUCLEIC ACIDS

The nucleic acids store and transfer the information necessary for the self-maintenance and the self-reproduction of living organisms. It is because of the information stored by the nucleic acids that as the cells of living organisms are continually replaced, the new cells are replicas of the old cells and that living organisms are able to produce offspring that are replicas of themselves. Since the characteristics of a living organism are a direct consequence of the specific proteins of which it is constituted, it is not surprising that the information stored and transferred by the nucleic acids consists of instructions for synthesizing proteins. By prescribing that the proteins synthesized in the progeny shall be the same as those of the parent(s), the nucleic acids determine that the progeny shall be replicas of the parent(s).

The nucleic acids that store and transfer information for a living organism are referred to as the *genotype* of that organism. The distinguishing characteristics that are manifestations of the genotype are referred to as the *phenotype* of the organism.

Most living organisms begin life as a single cell, as the result of the fusion of two cells, or as a group of nonfusing cells. When the new organism begins life as one cell or as a group of nonfusing cells derived from but one parent, the reproduction process is *asexual*. When two parents contribute cells, the reproduction process is *sexual*. In sexual reproduction two cells called *gametes* fuse during the process of fertilization, and, as a result, one cell, called a *zygote*, is formed. The zygote is the beginning of the new living organism.

The nucleus of the eukaryotic cell (the cell with a nucleus bounded by a nuclear membrane) contains threadlike structures called *chromosomes* (so named because of their staining characteristics in the presence of dyes like crystal violet and basic fuchsin). Chromosomes consist of deoxyribonucleic acid (DNA) and associated proteins (e.g., *histones*). The histones, which contain relatively high concentrations of lysyl and arginyl units, are electrostatically bonded to the negatively charged DNA macromolecules. Chromosomes occur in pairs in the nuclei of somatic cells. Members of a pair are referred to as *homologous chromosomes*. The total number of chromosomes in the nucleus of a cell is a characteristic of the cells of that particular organism; e.g., the somatic cells of a dog contain 78 chromosomes, a horse 64, and a human being 46. The number of paired chromosomes contained in a somatic cell is known as the *diploid number* of chromosomes. Human gametes, as opposed to somatic cells, contain one-half the diploid number of chromosomes. These 23 chromosomes are unpaired. The number of unpaired chromosomes is called the *haploid number*.

The chromosome stores and transfers information. One way this transfer is accomplished is by a process of cell division called *mitosis*. The function of mitosis is to produce two new daughter cells, each with an exact replica of the chromosomes of the parent cell. First, during a period called *interphase*, the DNA content of the chromosomes is doubled. This entails the duplication of the chromosomal DNA, discussed in detail in Chap. 13. Subsequently, the following events take place:

1. *Prophase* Before prophase the nucleus is bounded by its membrane and the chromosomes are not readily visible when viewed under a light microscope. During early prophase the chromosomes begin to shorten and thicken and thus become visible under the microscope. As prophase continues the shortening and thickening process continues and the chromosome can be seen to comprise two *chromatids*, which are joined at a region called the centromere. This species is, in fact, the chromosome that has been duplicated except at the centromere.
2. *Metaphase I* Next, the spindle apparatus appears. (One can get an idea of the shape of the spindle by spreading the fingers on both hands and allowing corresponding fingertips to touch. The hands and fingers now correspond to the spindle while the wrists correspond to the poles of the spindle.) The chromosomes then become aligned along the equatorial plane of the spindle.
3. *Metaphase II* Now the centromere of each chromosome divides and the two chromatids separate.
4. *Anaphase* The two chromatids from a given chromosome migrate to opposite poles of the spindle.
5. *Telophase* The cytoplasm and other cellular components divide, the spindle apparatus disappears, and two daughter cells are formed.

Subsequently, with cell division complete, the chromosomes elongate and become thinner as interphase begins. The process of mitosis is represented schematically in Fig. 6-1.

By mitosis a parent somatic cell with the diploid number of chromosomes produces two daughter cells, each with the diploid number of chromosomes. How,

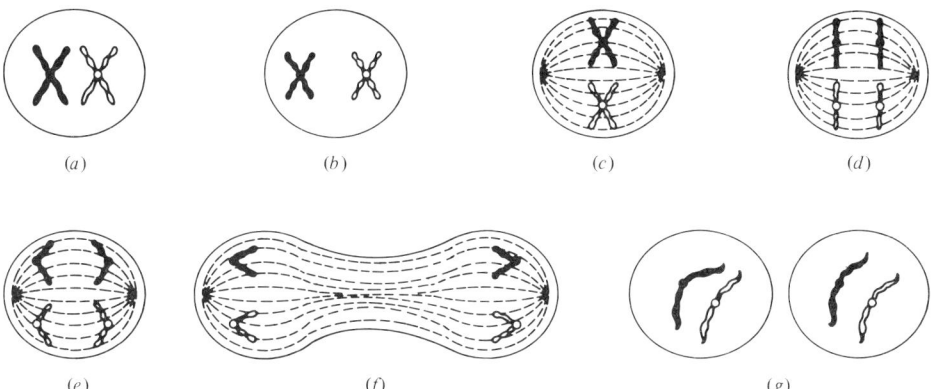

**Figure 6-1** Schematic representation of phases of mitosis: (*a*) early prophase; (*b*) prophase; (*c*) metaphase I; (*d*) metaphase II; (*e*) anaphase; (*f*) telophase; (*g*) daughter cells.

then, are cells with the haploid number of chromosomes produced? By a process called *meiosis* a cell is so divided that the daughter cells receive only one of a pair of homologous chromosomes. Meiosis involves two sequences, each of which results in cell division. The first is a lengthy and somewhat complicated sequence, while the second is reminiscent of mitosis. Before the first meiotic division the chromosomal DNA is duplicated, just as in mitosis. The sequence of events in meiosis then proceeds as follows:

1. *Prophase I* Homologous chromosomes become aligned with each other and closely juxtaposed. At this point, sometimes called *pachynema* (the "thick-thread" stage), it is difficult to distinguish the individual chromosomes of a homologous pair under the light microscope. As prophase I continues, the tight pairing is relaxed and not only are the chromosomes of a homologous pair distinguishable but also the chromatids can be seen. During this stage, referred to as *diplonema* (the "double-thread" stage), the two homologous chromosomes are joined at a point of contact called the *chiasma* (plural, chiasmata). The presence of the chiasma permits the composition of homologous chromosomes to be altered as a result of *crossing-over*, as illustrated in Fig. 6-2. As prophase I continues, the chromosomes become shorter and shorter and thicker and thicker and the stage known as *diakinesis* is attained.

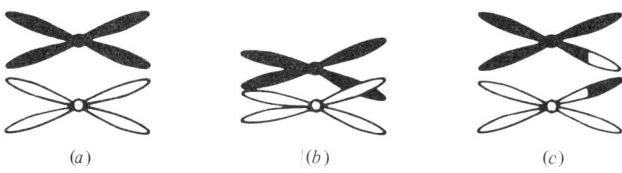

**Figure 6-2** Schematic representation of crossing-over. Two homologous chromosomes (*a*) become aligned with each other, (*b*) become joined at the chiasma, and (*c*) then break at corresponding points and undergo an exchange of fragments.

2. *Metaphase I* The spindle apparatus appears and the paired chromosomes migrate to its equatorial plane where they become aligned in the plane.
3. *Anaphase I* Homologous chromosomes now separate and migrate to opposite poles of the spindle.
4. *Telophase I* Two daughter cells are formed. These daughter cells each contain the haploid number of chromosomes since of each homologous pair one chromosome migrated to one pole of the spindle while the other migrated to the other. Following an interphase, which may be quite brief, prophase II begins.
5. *Prophase II* Chromosomes of daughter cells formed as a result of the first meiotic division shorten and thicken.
6. *Metaphase II* The spindle apparatus appears and the nonpaired chromosomes migrate to its equatorial plane.
7. *Anaphase II* Centromeres divide and homologous chromatids migrate to opposite poles of the spindle.
8. *Telophase II* Two daughter cells are formed from each cell that was generated in telophase I.

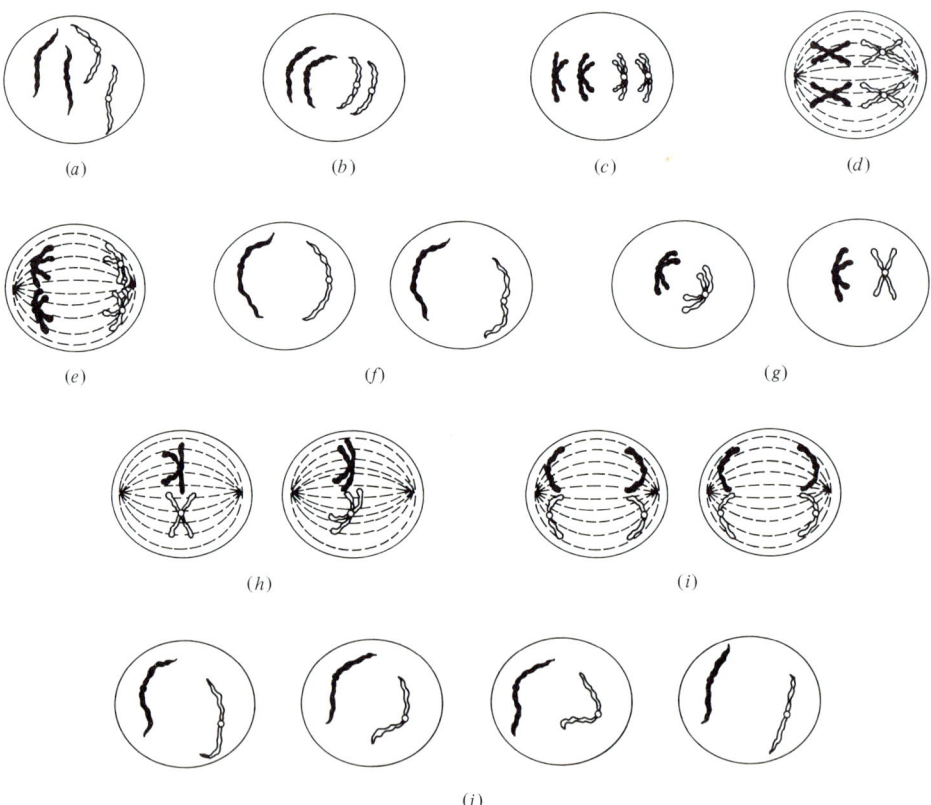

**Figure 6-3** Schematic representation of phases of meiosis: (*a*) to (*c*) prophase I; (*d*) metaphase I; (*e*) anaphase I; (*f*) telophase I, formation of two daughter cells; (*g*) prophase II; (*h*) metaphase II; (*i*) anaphase II; (*j*) telophase II, formation of two daughter cells from each of the two cells formed as a result of the first meiotic division.

THE CHEMISTRY OF THE PURINES, PYRIMIDINES, AND NUCLEIC ACIDS  **205**

As a result of this sequence of events the chromosomes of a cell having the diploid number experience two successive meiotic divisions with the result that the chromosomes of four daughter cells each having the haploid number are generated. This is represented schematically in Fig. 6-3.

A single chromosome comprises many units, each of which provides one or more items of information. These units function independently and remain indivisible during the transfer of information. These units are called *genes*. The location of each gene on its chromosome is a characteristic of that chromosome. In many instances it has been possible to prepare diagrams or maps (Fig. 6-4) that show the relative positions of the genes of a chromosome.

Each gene is capable of existing in two (or more) alternative forms which, in many less complex living organisms, determine alternative characteristics, such as whether a flower is red or white. These alternative forms of a gene are called

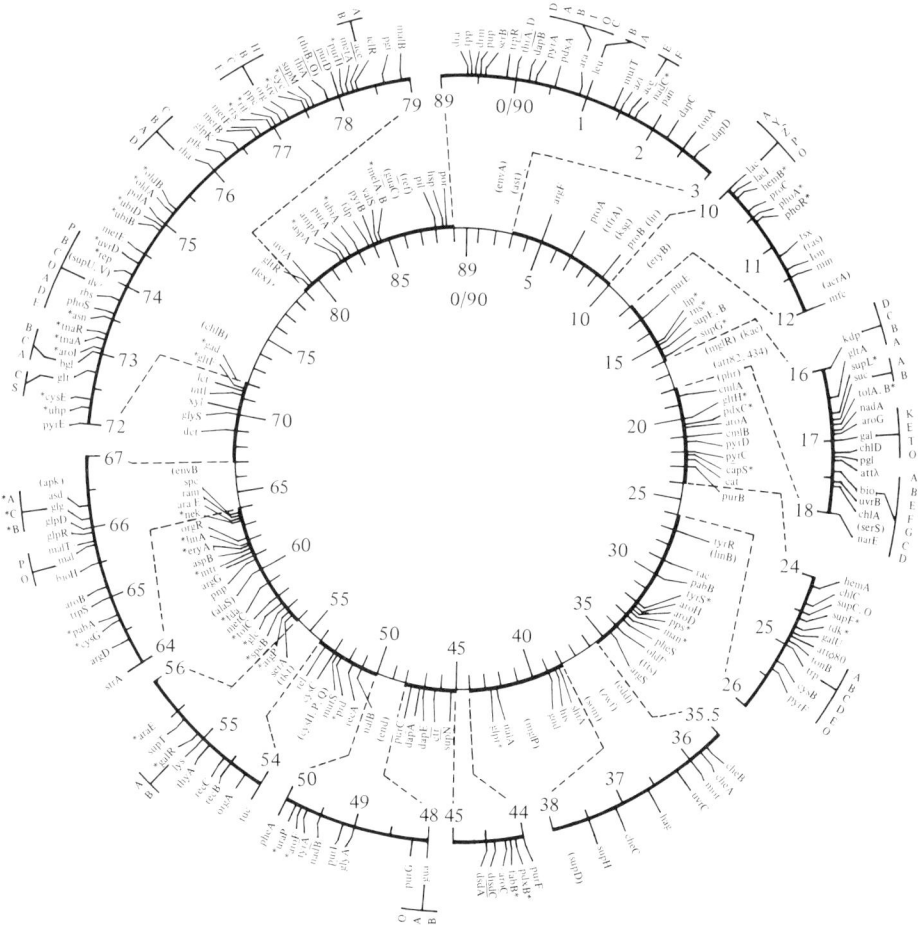

**Figure 6-4** Linkage map of the *E. coli* chromosome. [*From Taylor, A. L. (1970) Bacteriol. Rev.* **34**, *155–175 (see pp. 156–157). With permission.*]

*alleles.* Corresponding segments of two homologous chromosomes can consist of different alleles of the same gene. Let us examine the consequences of this fact. If the cells of an organism that has a genotype denoted by *Aa* undergoes meiosis, 50 percent of the resulting gametes will have a genotype denoted by *A* and the other 50 percent will have a genotype denoted by *a*. If these gametes are then able to combine with gametes derived from another similar organism also having a genotype denoted by *Aa*, zygotes with three different genotypes are possible: *AA*, *Aa*, or *aa*. Zygotes *AA* and *aa* are *homozygotes*, while *Aa* is a *heterozygote*. The relative probabilities of obtaining genotypes *AA*, *Aa*, and *aa* are in the ratio of 1 : 2 : 1. It should be noted, however, that in more complex living organisms, including man, many characteristics are determined by more than one gene.

The information stored and transferred by the genes is contained in the sequence of the purines and pyrimidines that constitute the nucleic acid macromolecule. How this information is utilized will be discussed primarily in Chap. 13. In this chapter we shall be concerned with the physical and chemical characteristics of the nucleic acids and their components.

## THE PURINES AND PYRIMIDINES OF THE NUCLEIC ACIDS

Purines and pyrimidines readily undergo tautomerism. The tautomeric equilibria involved can be illustrated as follows:

Enol tautomer of amine form, or enamine

Oxo tautomer of amine form, or oxamine

Enol tautomer of imine form, or enimine

Oxo tautomer of imine form, or oximine

The positions of these tautomeric equilibria are determined by the relative intrinsic stabilities of the tautomers. In cytosine, for example, the oxo (or keto) tautomer of the amine form is more stable than the enol tautomer to the extent of 13 kcal/mol due to the bond energies involved. However, on the basis of the stabilization due to delocalization, the enol tautomer is favored by 6.5 kcal/mol over the oxo tautomer. Therefore, when both these factors are considered, the oxamine form of cytosine is thermodynamically favored over the enamine form by 6.5 kcal/mol. This means that the oxamine form would constitute over 99.9 percent of an equilibrium mixture of these tautomers at room temperature. Of amine and imine tautomers, the former is more stable than the latter by 2.1 kcal/mol on the basis of stabilization due to delocalization. Since the bond energies of these tautomers are comparable, it can be calculated that an equilibrium mixture of amine and imine tautomers should contain

THE CHEMISTRY OF THE PURINES, PYRIMIDINES, AND NUCLEIC ACIDS  **207**

approximately 97 percent of the former at room temperature. Thus the oxamine form of cytosine can be expected to predominate under most conditions of interest.

The thermodynamically favored forms of the five purines and pyrimidines that are the most common constituents of the nucleic acids are as follows:

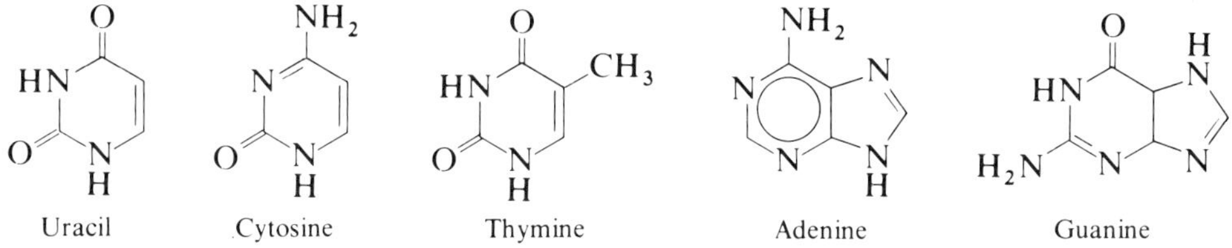

Uracil     Cytosine     Thymine     Adenine     Guanine

Notice that in each instance the oxygen-containing substituent exists as the oxo tautomer and that the nitrogen-containing substituent exists as the amine tautomer. In the purines tautomerism involving the imidazole moiety is also possible. Adenine exists in the 9-H form. Guanine, on the other hand, exists predominantly in the 7-H form

## SYNTHESIS OF PURINES AND PYRIMIDINES

The laboratory synthesis of purines and pyrimidines generally involves cyclization reactions. Some of the classic syntheses of pyrimidines involve the condensation of a 3-oxo acid (in the presence of phosphoryl chloride) or an ester of a 3-oxo acid with urea. Condensations in which thiourea is used instead of urea yield mercaptopyrimidines, which can be converted into the corresponding pyrimidines in the presence of aqueous hydrochloric acid, hydrobromic acid, or chloroacetic acid.

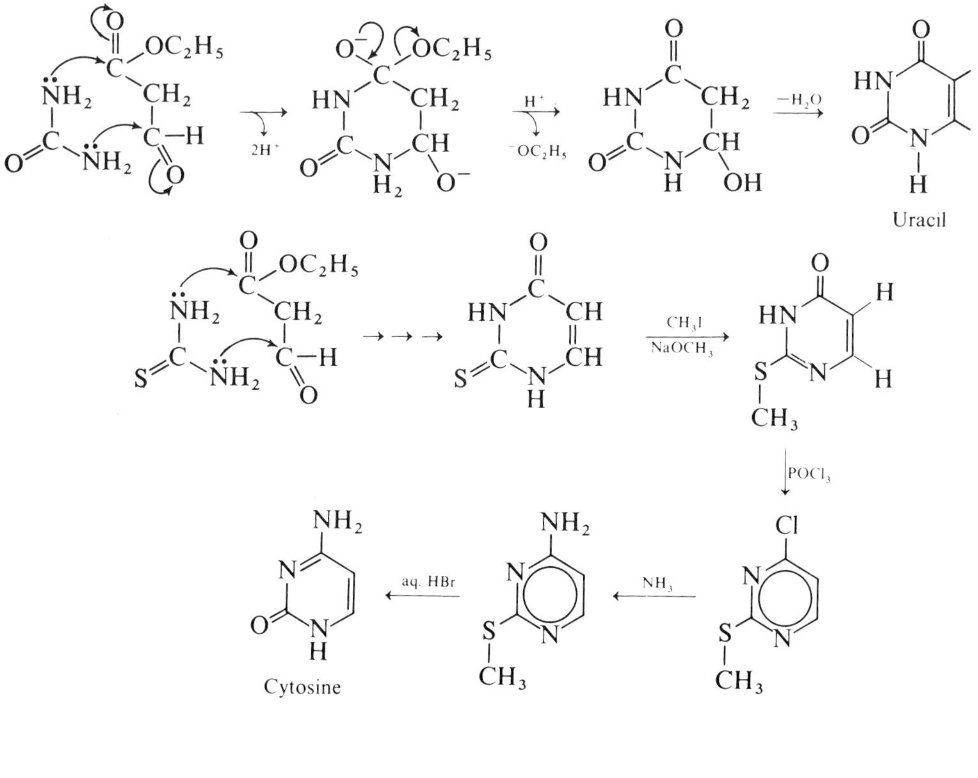

The purines can be prepared in the laboratory by the *Traube synthesis*, in which a 4,5-diaminopyrimidine is formed and subsequently a carbon atom is inserted between the two amino groups, closing the imidazole ring. The use of the Traube synthesis to prepare adenine and guanine is shown below.

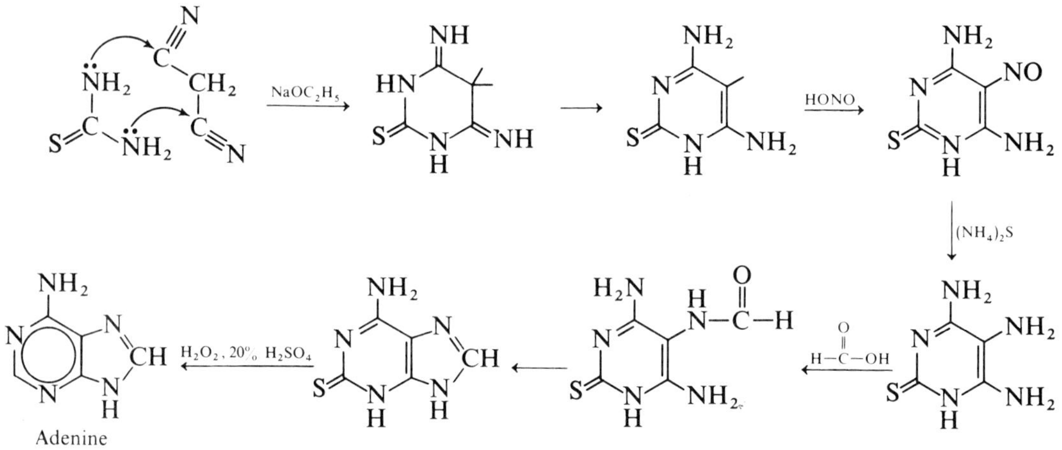

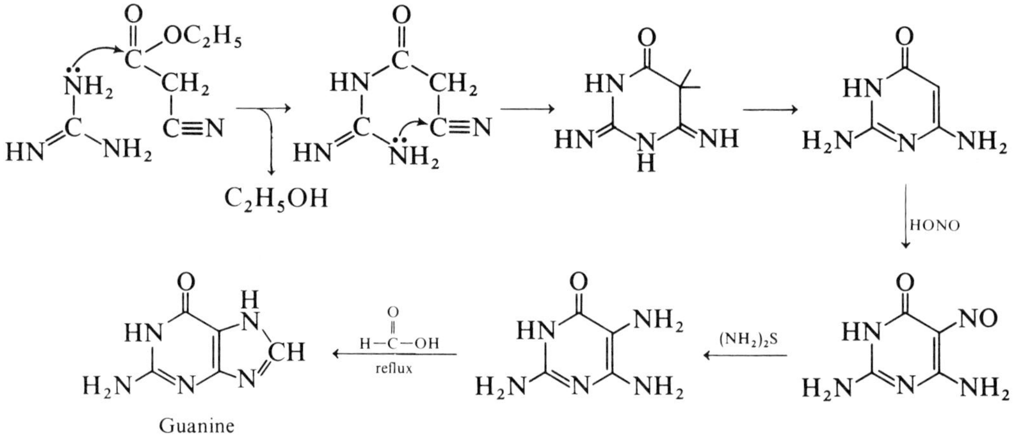

Although there are many variations of this type of synthesis, all utilize the principles shown above. Purines can also be synthesized in the laboratory by preparing a substituted imidazole and then closing the pyrimidine ring.

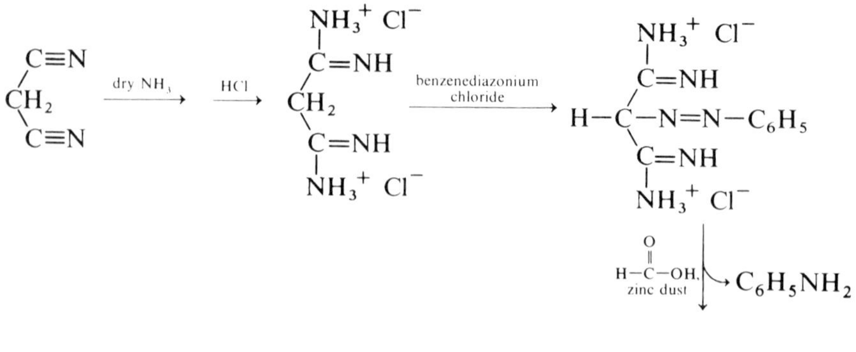

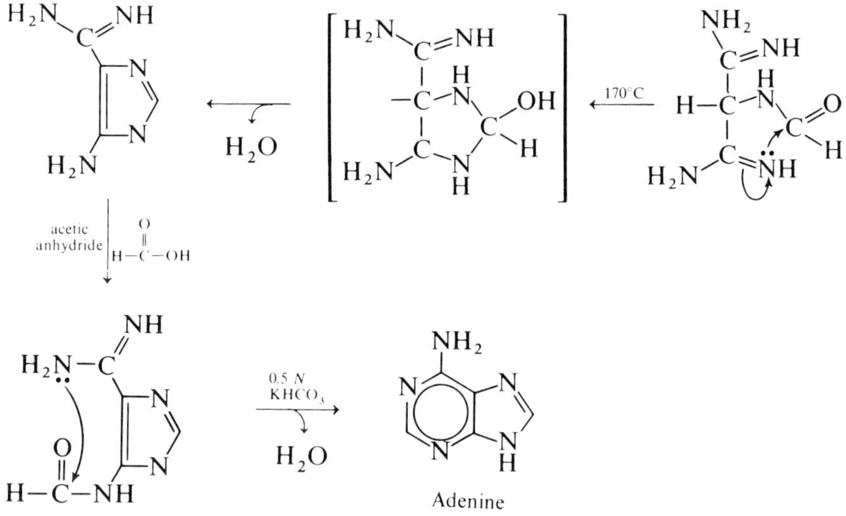

It is interesting to note that the electron irradiation of a mixture of methane, ammonia, hydrogen, and water yields adenine among other products. It has been suggested that reactions involving such simple organic molecules as these may have been responsible for the formation of the purines on earth perhaps $10^9$ years ago.

## SOME REACTIONS OF PURINES AND PYRIMIDINES

Both the ring atoms and the ring substituents of the purines and pyrimidines participate in chemical reactions. Electrophilic reagents like $Br^+$ and $NO^+$ usually attack pyrimidines at C(5) and purines at C(8), but broad generalizations about the chemical reactivity of the purines and pyrimidines are not possible. In guanine, for example, bromination occurs at C(8), alkylation at N(7), cyanoethylation at N(1), and reaction with acetic anhydride at the C(2) amino group.

### Alkylation Reactions

Purines and pyrimidines undergo alkylation in the presence of certain alkyl halides, alkyl sulfates, epoxides, imines, nitrogen mustards [tertiary amines of the general formula $R-N-(CH_2CH_2Cl)_2$], and diazoalkanes, among other reagents. Under most reaction conditions guanine is the most reactive of the five common purines and pyrimidines of the nucleic acids. The alkylation of guanine under neutral conditions yields a 7,9-dialkyl derivative when alkylating agents other than a diazoalkane are used. In aqueous media methylation by diazomethane occurs preferentially at N(7) of the guanine molecule. When 9-substituted guanines, such as guanosine, are treated with diazomethane in ether, methylation occurs at N(1). In addition, the oxygen atom at C(6) can undergo etherification under some conditions. Methylation by diazomethane requires an acidic hydrogen atom, which is provided by the imidazole moiety of the guanine molecule, but in the 9-substituted guanines N(1) of the oxo tautomer the molecule becomes the site of the reaction. *O*-Alkylation appears to result from the reaction of an enol tautomer of the guanine derivative.

## Reactions with Carbonyl Compounds

Purines and pyrimidines with amino substituents react with formaldehyde to yield *N*-hydroxymethyl derivatives. The order of reactivity among the bases is cytosine > guanine > adenine. These reactions are frequently more complicated than might be expected, and reaction of a 9-substituted guanine with formaldehyde yields at least five different products, including products resulting from cross-linking.

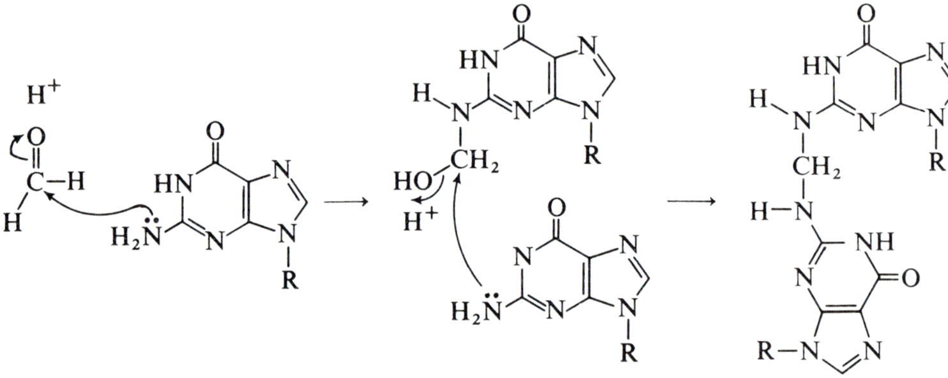

Glyoxal and 2-oxo-3-ethoxybutyraldehyde (a reagent known as kethoxal) react specifically with guanine even in the presence of the other purines and pyrimidines of the nucleic acids. These guanine derivatives are more stable than those formed in the presence of formaldehyde. The reaction of guanine or a 9-substituted guanine with glyoxal is

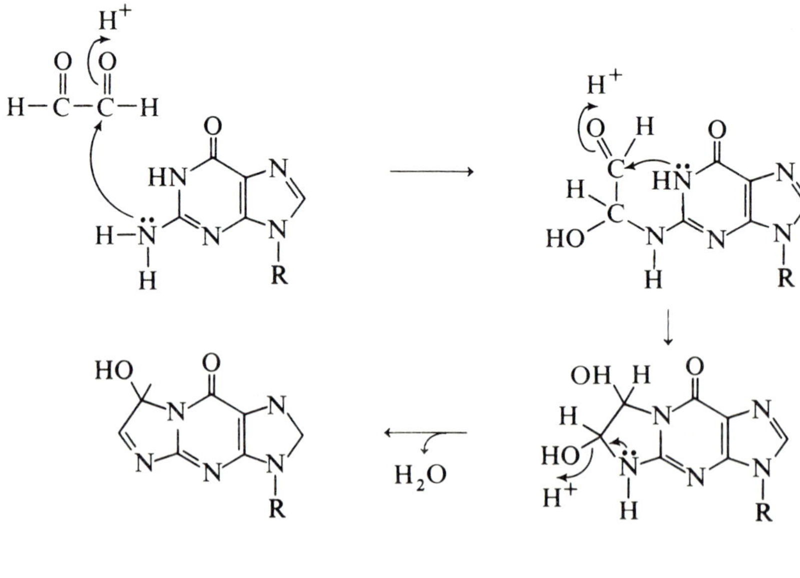

The amino substituents of the purines and pyrimidines also react with acylating agents such as acetic anhydride or benzoyl chloride. These reactions are usually slower than those with aldehydes. Acylation reactions are frequently used to protect the amino group of a purine or pyrimidine during the laboratory synthesis of polynucleotides.

## The Addition of Purines and Pyrimidines at Unsaturated Carbon Atoms

The water-soluble reagent $N$-cyclohexyl-$N'$-2-(4-methylmorpholinium) ethylcarbodiimide, often referred to as CME-carbodiimide, reacts with the heterocyclic nitrogen atoms of purines and pyrimidines.

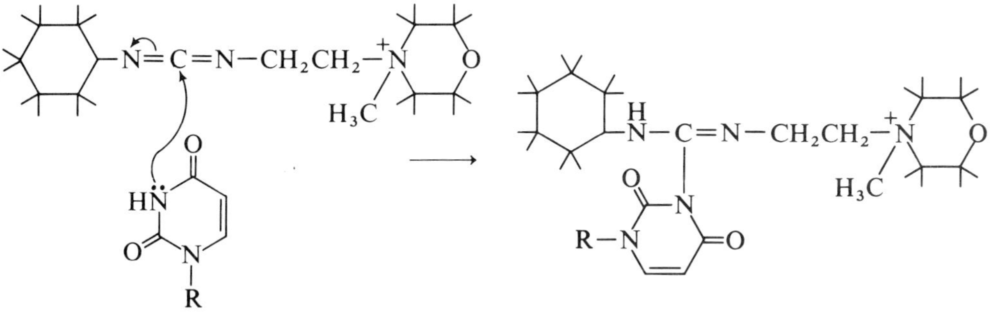

As a result of the reaction between this reagent and N(3) of the uracil moieties or N(2) of the guanine moieties of the nucleic acids, the characteristics of the polynucleotide are significantly altered. The chemical modification of the nucleic acids is discussed later in this chapter.

Acrylonitrile reacts with purines and pyrimidines in somewhat the same manner as the carbodiimide, shown above. A heterocyclic nitrogen atom of the base attacks the terminal carbon atom of acrylonitrile, and an $N$-cyanoethyl derivative is formed. This reaction is also used to effect chemical modification of the nucleic acids.

## Reaction of Hydroxylamine with Purines and Pyrimidines

Hydroxylamine reacts with purines and pyrimidines to yield both addition and substitution products. The Michael addition of hydroxylamine to uracil or a 1-substituted uracil yields urea or an $N$-substituted urea and an isoxazolone.

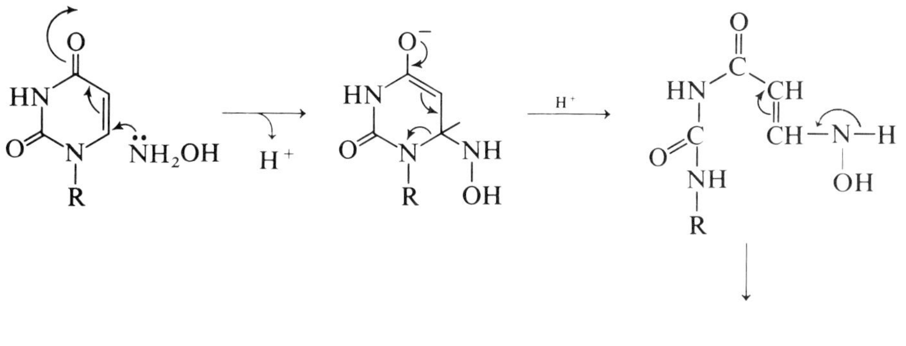

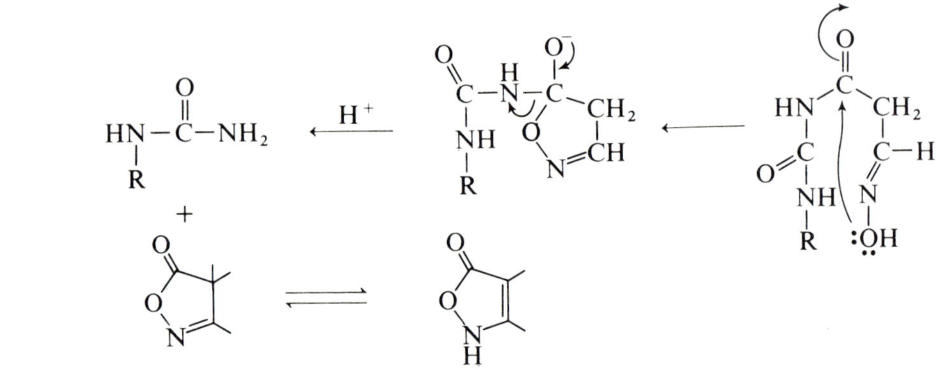

Cytosine and 1-substituted cytosines undergo both addition and substitution in the presence of hydroxylamine.

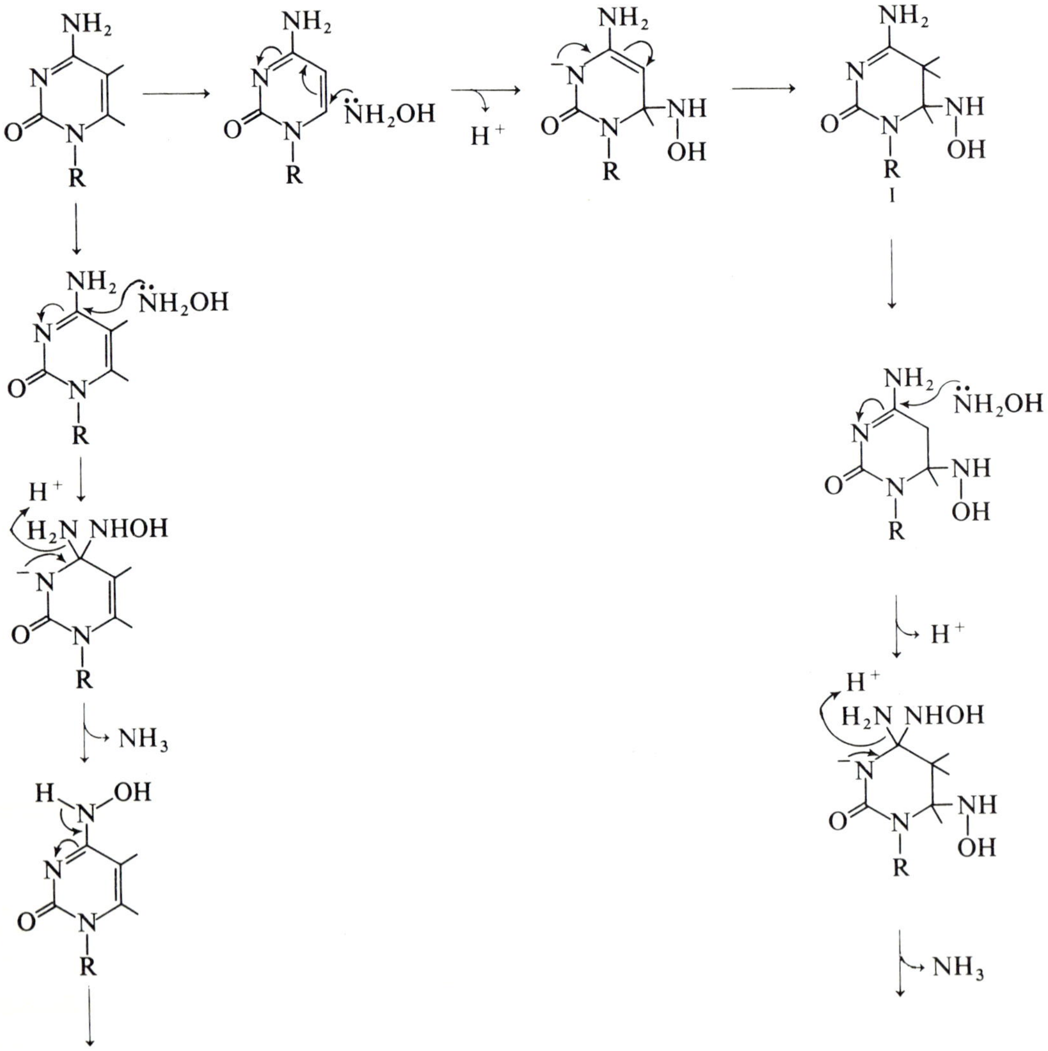

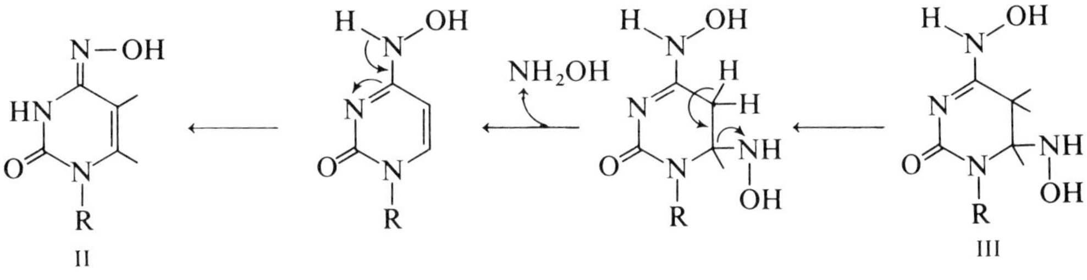

The addition product, I, undergoes rapid substitution at C(4) to yield III, which can subsequently undergo the elimination of hydroxylamine to yield II. This product, II, can also result from the initial reactant directly.

Thymine and the purines are much less readily attacked by hydroxylamine, at least under the conditions used in the reactions involving uracil and cytosine.

## Reaction to Nitrous Acid with the Purines and Pyrimidines

Nitrous acid reacts with purine and pyrimidine bases having amino substituents. Adenine and cytosine undergo deamination to yield hypoxanthine and uracil, respectively. Guanine, on the other hand, yields a small amount of xanthine

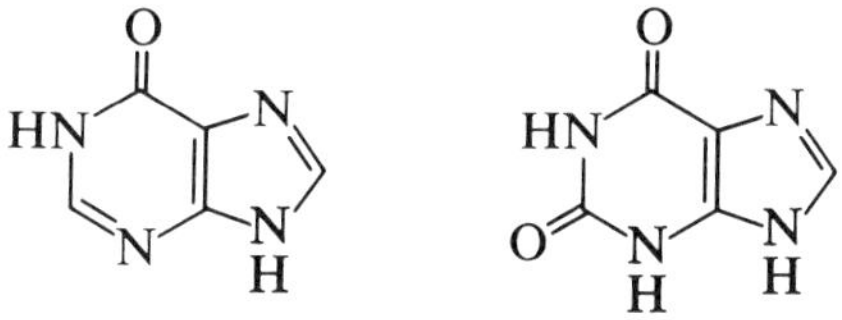

Hypoxanthine
(6-oxopurine)

Xanthine
(2,6-dioxopurine)

and a yellow product, which has been identified as 2-nitrohypoxanthine. The reactions with nitrous acid presumably proceed by formation of a diazonium ion.

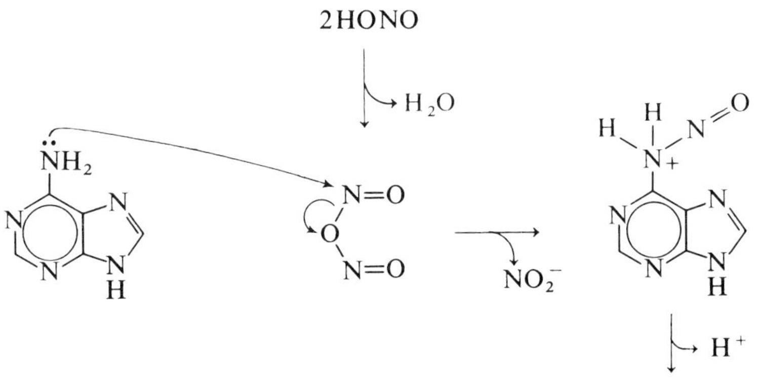

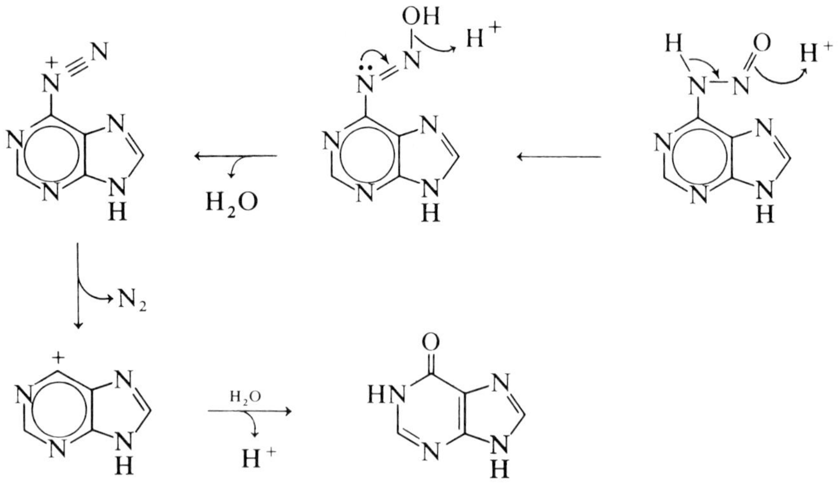

The carbonium ion formed as a result of the elimination of nitrogen from guanine can react either with nitrate ion or with water. The consequences of replacing the amino groups of the purines and pyrimidines of the nucleic acids by hydroxyl groups will be discussed later in this chapter.

## MODIFICATION OF PURINES AND PYRIMIDINES BY RADIATION

The purines and pyrimidines can undergo chemical modification in the presence of nonionizing or ionizing radiation. A type of nonionizing radiation often used is ultraviolet radiation since it is selectively absorbed by purines and pyrimidines with the result that chemical modification occurs. By contrast, x-rays and $\gamma$ rays, which are ionizing radiation, are nonselectively absorbed, and their effects are produced because they generate ionized species in the medium.

Generally, pyrimidines are more susceptible than purines to chemical modification by ultraviolet radiation. The pyrimidines readily undergo two principal reactions in the presence of ultraviolet irradiation, namely, the photohydration of the 5,6 double bond and photodimerization.

It has been proposed that the photohydration of uracil or a 1-substituted uracil proceeds by protonation of the singlet state† of the molecule followed by the reaction

---

† As a result of the absorption of light energy an electron of a bonding or a nonbonding orbital can be promoted to an antibonding orbital. Normally only one electron per molecule undergoes such a transition at a given time, and hence a situation arises in which there is one electron in a half-filled bonding or nonbonding orbital and one electron in an antibonding orbital. The relationship between the spins of these two electrons is no longer prescribed by the Pauli exclusion principle, and they can be either parallel or antiparallel. A quantity referred to as the *multiplicity* is used to indicate whether the spins are paired or not. The multiplicity of a molecule is given by $2S + 1$, where $S$ is the absolute value of the sum of the spin quantum numbers involved. When the spins are antiparallel, the multiplicity is 1 and the molecule is said to exist in the *singlet state*. When the spins are parallel, the multiplicity is 3 and the molecule is said to exist in the *triplet state*.

of the protonated species with a molecule of water to yield the photohydrate plus a proton. Although the pyrimidine photohydrates are relatively unstable, the product obtained from a 1-substituted cytosine has been identified and characterized by formation of the $N$-hydroxyl or $N$-methoxyl derivative of the amino substituent.

Cytosine, uracil, and thymine undergo dimerization when irradiated with ultraviolet light. Four different dimers are possible as the result of the suprafacial, suprafacial† cycloaddition of two cytosine, uracil, or thymine molecules to form a cyclobutane ring from the four carbon atoms of the two 5,6 double bonds. All four of the thymine dimers have been obtained and characterized.

One proposal for the mechanism of cycloaddition of thymine involves the formation of a species called an *excimer*. In concentrated solutions the absorption of a photon by a molecule is sometimes followed by association of that molecule with a second molecule of the same identity. The product of this photoassociation is called

---

† A *suprafacial* process is one in which the bonds that are made or broken lie on the same face of the component undergoing reaction. An *antarafacial* process is one in which the bonds that are made or broken lie on opposite faces of the component undergoing reaction.

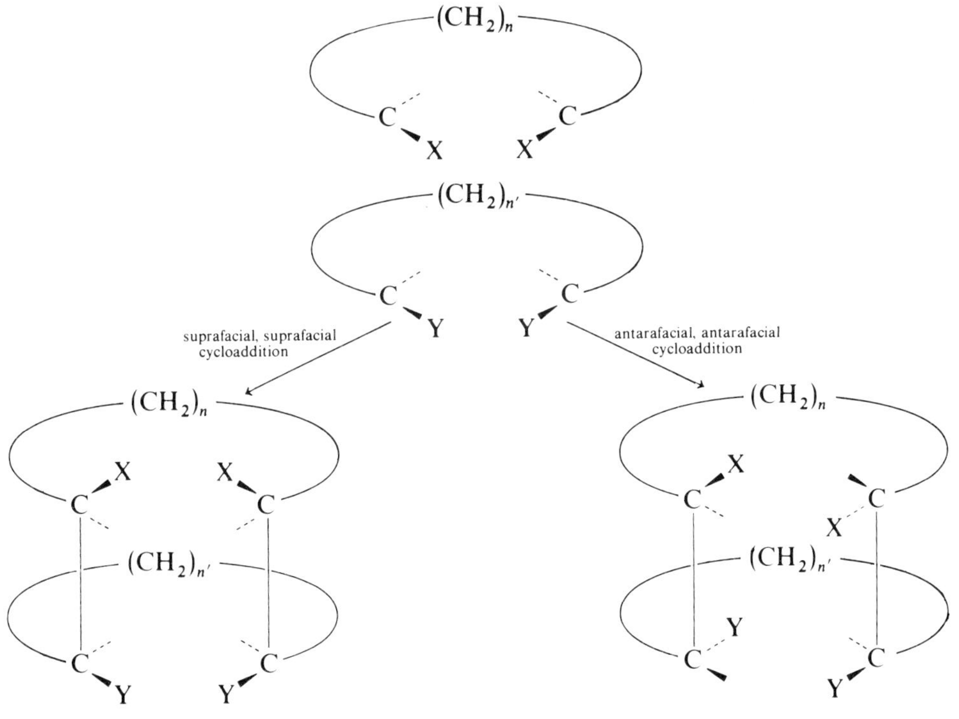

The designation suprafacial, suprafacial or antarafacial, antarafacial indicates the mode of bond formation for each of the two components involved in a cycloaddition reaction. There is also the possibility of bonding in which one component participates by means of a suprafacial process and the other by means of an antarafacial process. Also, in the suprafacial, suprafacial process there are two possibilities which correspond to endo and exo addition.

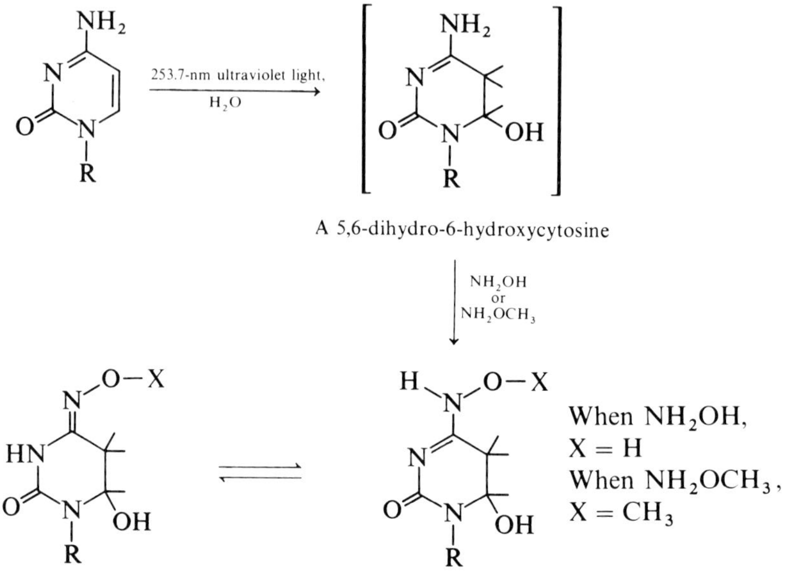

A 5,6-dihydro-6-hydroxycytosine

When NH$_2$OH, X = H
When NH$_2$OCH$_3$, X = CH$_3$

an excimer (to be distinguished from the species obtained when a molecule that is a dimer in the ground state absorbs a photon). According to the suggested mechanism, the excimer derived from the two thymine molecules collapses to the covalently bonded dimer in a time shorter than that required for the absorbed energy to be dissipated by fluorescent emission. Each thymine molecule retains its configuration during the reaction; i.e., rotation about the C(5)—C(6) bond does not occur during

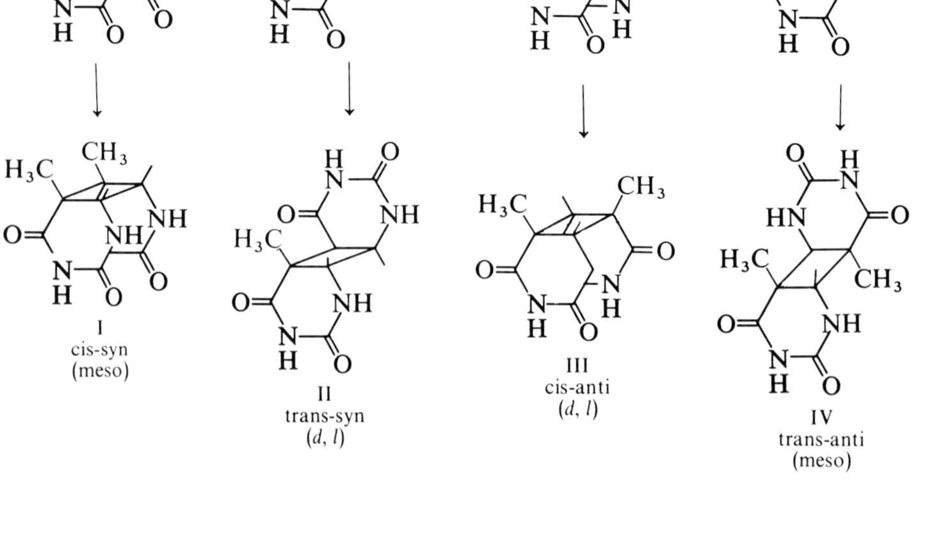

I cis-syn (meso)

II trans-syn (d, l)

III cis-anti (d, l)

IV trans-anti (meso)

the time between the absorption of the photon and the formation of the bonds of the cyclobutane moiety of the dimer.†

Dimers I and II can be converted back to their monomers in the presence of x-rays. Dimers III and IV, on the other hand, are stable in the presence of x-rays. This difference has been attributed to the difference in the steric interactions present in the head-to-head dimers, I and II, compared with that present in the head-to-tail dimers, III and IV. Evidence in support of the presence of significant steric interactions in the head-to-head dimers has been provided by x-ray crystallographic studies on the cis-syn dimer of 1,3-dimethylthymine, which showed that there are distances of 2.08 and 2.24 Å between the hydrogen atoms of the two C(5) methyl groups of the dimer. Each of these distances is less than the sum of the van der Waals radii for two hydrogen atoms, which is 2.40 Å, and the distances between a carbon atom of one methyl group and a hydrogen atom of the other methyl group are again in some cases less than the sum of the van der Waals radii of these atoms.

When aqueous solutions are exposed to ionizing radiation, the principal effects stem from reactions involving the products of the radiolytic decomposition of water:

$$nH_2O \longrightarrow e^-_{aq} + H\cdot + \cdot OH + H_2O_2 + H_2 + H_3O^+ \quad (6\text{-}1)$$

When purines and pyrimidines are present, the hydroxyl radical is responsible for the preponderance of chemical conversions that occur. Purines, which are less susceptible to effects of ionizing radiation that pyrimidines, undergo hydroxylation at C(8) in oxygenated aqueous solutions. When oxygen is excluded from the medium, hydroxylation can occur and also the imidazole moiety of the purine can undergo cleavage, forming an aminoformamidopyrimidine:

2,6-Diamino-5-formamidopyrimidine
(from guanine)

The irradiation of aqueous solutions of pyrimidines with x-rays or $\gamma$ rays induces the addition of a hydroxyl radical to the 5,6 double bond under most conditions:

6-Hydroxy-5,6-dihydrouracil-5-yl radical

5-Hydroxy-5,6-dihydrouracil-6-yl radical

In the presence of oxygen these alkyl radicals can be converted into hydroperoxy radicals, which ultimately yield glycols as the major products. This sequence of

---

† In a somewhat similar case, cis-2-butene is reported to undergo photochemical cyclodimerization with complete retention of its geometric configuration. Yamazaki, H., and Cvetanovic, R. J. (1969) J. Am. Chem. Soc. **91**, 520–522.

events can be illustrated by thymine, which reacts with a hydroxyl radical to yield predominantly the tertiary alkyl radical:

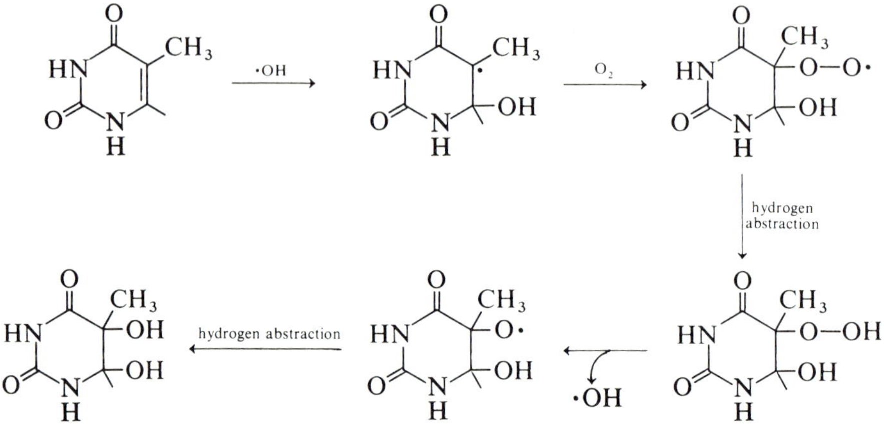

5,6-Dihydroxydihydrothymine

When oxygen is excluded from the medium, the alkyl radical can react with the solvent, water, again to yield glycols as the major products:

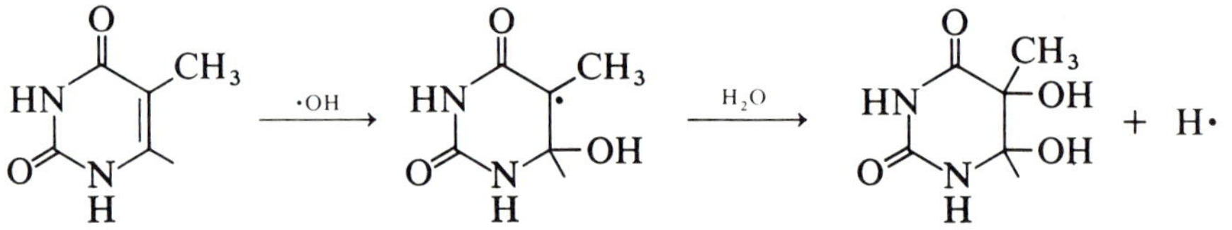

In very strongly acidic solutions the hydrated electron $e_{aq}^-$ is readily converted into a hydrogen radical, and products resulting from attack by a hydrogen radical rather than a hydroxyl radical can be obtained. In very strongly alkaline solutions not only are the pyrimidine bases partially ionized but also the hydroxyl radical can undergo ionization. Under these conditions radical formation and stabilization of the sort shown below can occur.

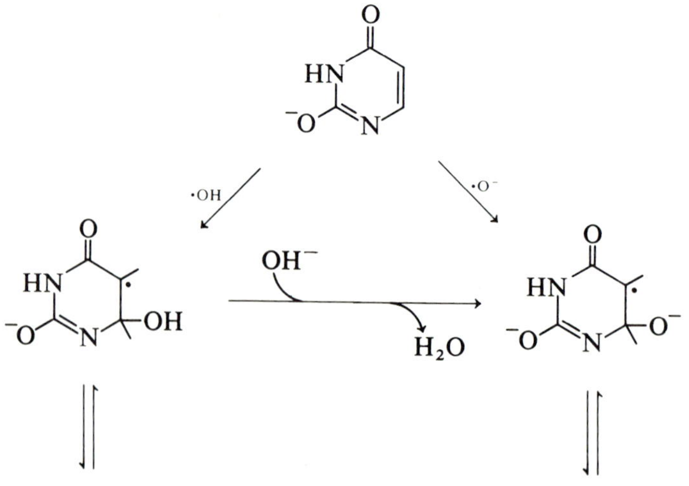

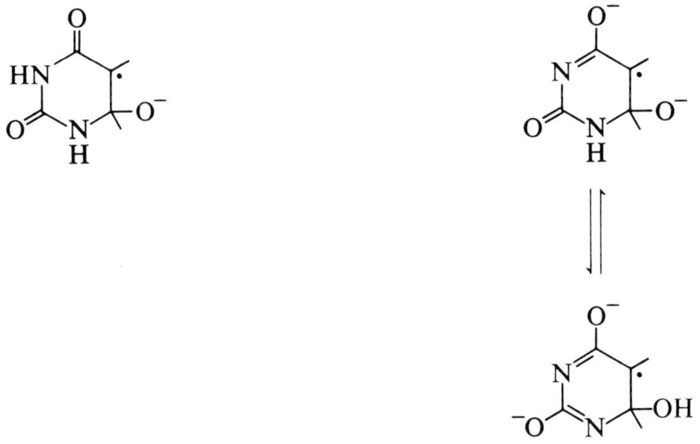

These radical ions can react with the solvent in the absence of oxygen. For thymine the principal reaction between the pyrimidine anion and the ionized hydroxyl radical is hydrogen abstraction.

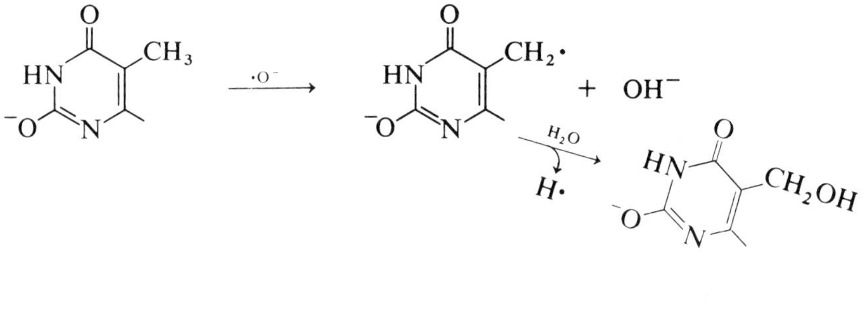

The product under these circumstances is 5-hydroxymethyluracil.

## NUCLEOSIDES AND NUCLEOTIDES

In biochemical systems the purines and pyrimidines are frequently bonded to a pentose by an *N*-glycosidic linkage involving N(9) of the former or N(1) of the latter. In higher organisms the pentose is usually ribose or 2-deoxyribose, although other pentoses are bonded in this manner in certain other species. For example, pyrimidines bonded to an arabinose moiety have been found in some sponges. A purine or pyrimidine bonded to a saccharide is known as a nucleoside. The nucleosides that can be derived from DNA or RNA are shown on page 220.

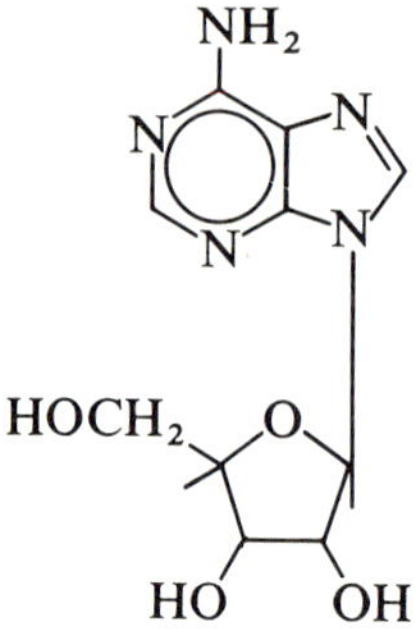

Adenosine

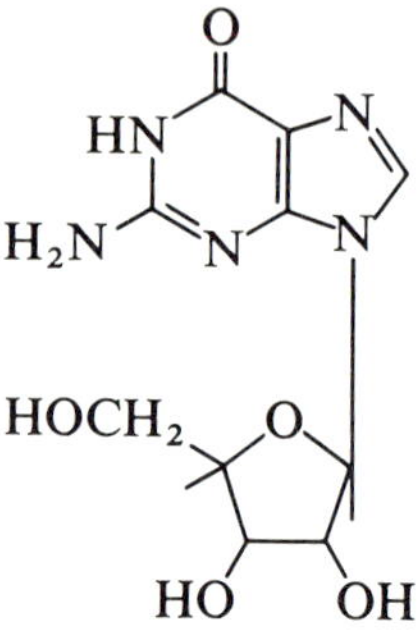

Guanosine

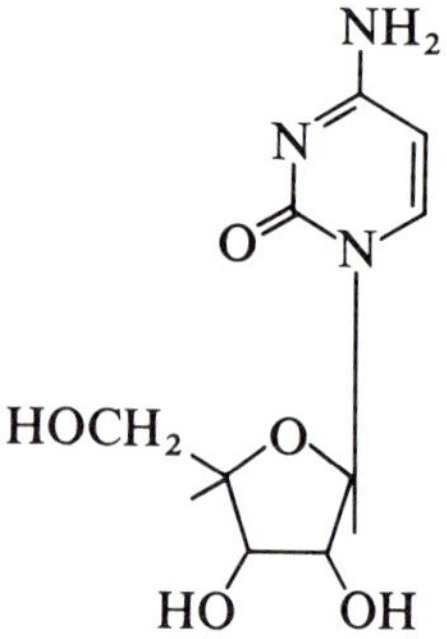

Cytidine

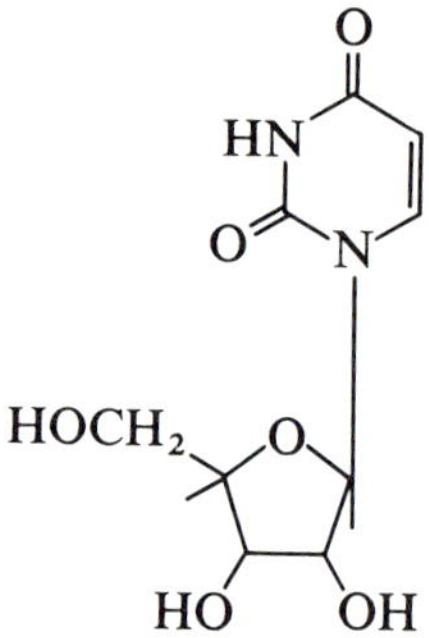

Uridine

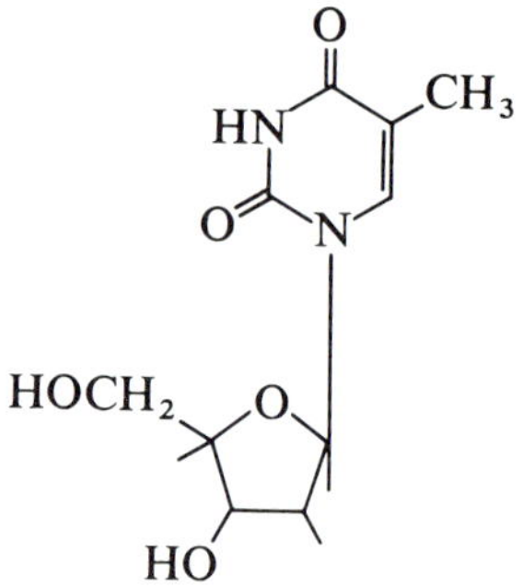

2'-Deoxythymidine

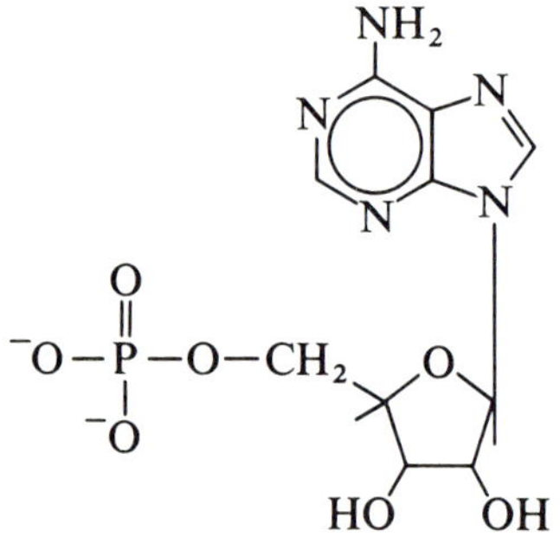

Adenosine 5'-monophosphate, an adenylic acid

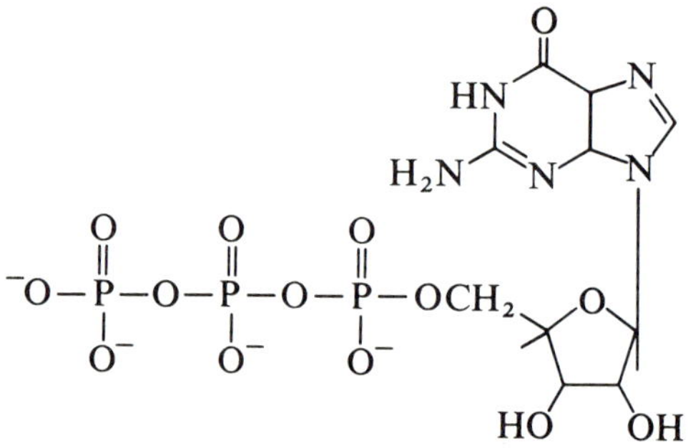

Guanosine 5'-triphosphate, a guanylic acid

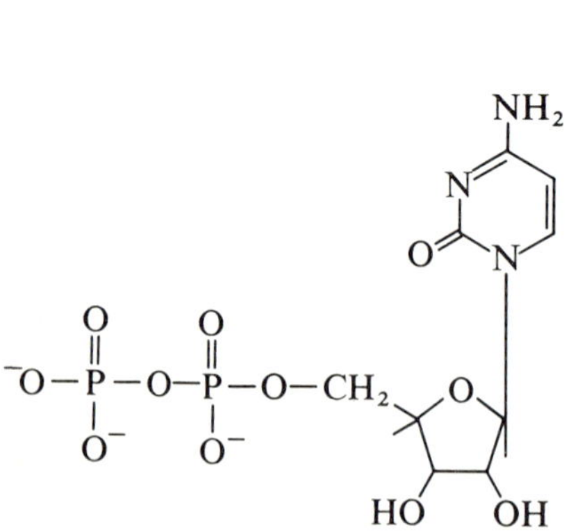

Cytidine 5'-diphosphate, a cytidylic acid

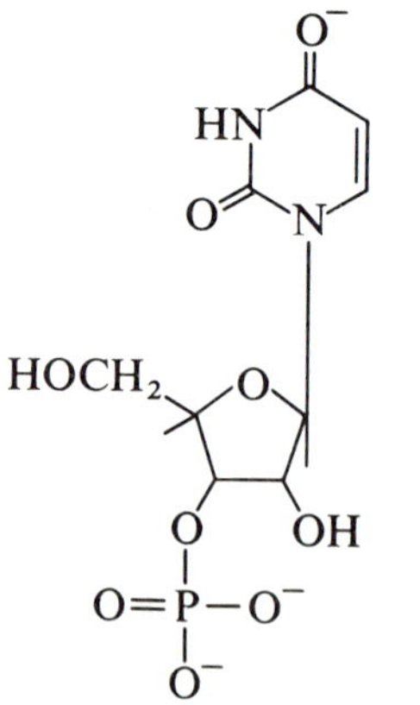

Uridine 3'-monophosphate, a uridylic acid

When one (or more) of the hydroxyl groups of the pentose moiety of a nucleoside is replaced by a phosphoryl group, the molecule is known as a nucleo*t*ide. A nucleotide can be referred to in a somewhat nonspecific manner as an adenhylic acid or a uridylic acid. More specifically, a nucleotide can be designated as adenosine 5′-monophosphate or uridine 3′-monophosphate. The category of nucleotides also includes molecules in which the hydroxyl group of the pentose moiety of the nucleoside is replaced by a diphosphoryl or a polyphosphoryl group.

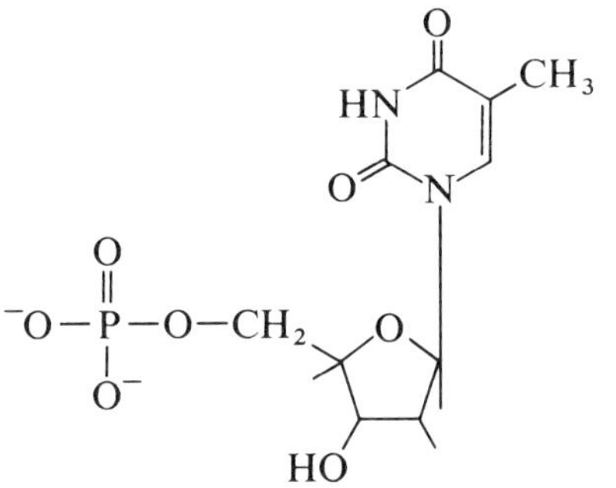
O
HN
CH3
O
N
O
⁻O−P−O−CH2
O
O⁻
HO

2′-Deoxythymidine 5′-monophosphate, a thymidylic acid

## The Laboratory Synthesis of Nucleosides and Nucleotides

Pyrimidine nucleosides have frequently been prepared by the reaction of a suitably protected glycosyl halide and a mercury derivative of the nitrogen heterocycle. Pyrimidine nucleosides are also prepared by various modifications of the reaction of a suitably protected glycosyl halide and an *O*-substituted derivative of the nitrogen heterocycle. An example of this procedure, known as the *Hilbert-Johnson reaction*, follows.

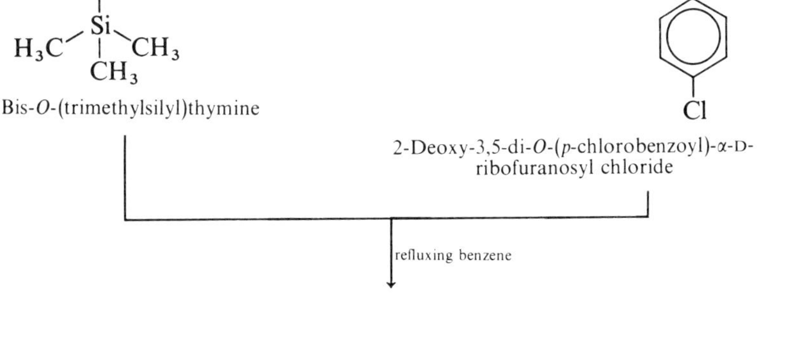
H3C CH3
Si−CH3
O
N
CH3
O
N
Si
H3C CH3
CH3
Bis-O-(trimethylsilyl)thymine
+
O
Cl
C−O−H2C
O
Cl
O
C=O
Cl
2-Deoxy-3,5-di-O-(p-chlorobenzoyl)-α-D-ribofuranosyl chloride
refluxing benzene

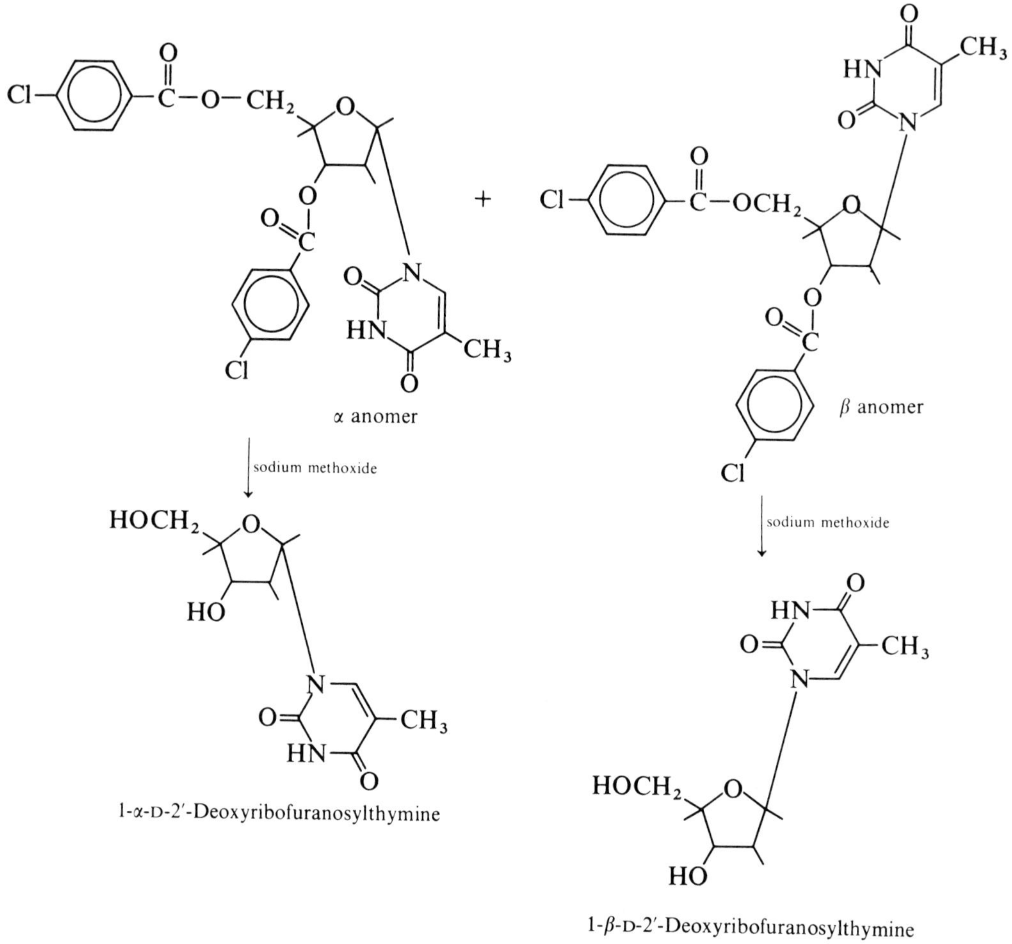

α anomer

sodium methoxide ↓

1-α-D-2′-Deoxyribofuranosylthymine

β anomer

sodium methoxide ↓

1-β-D-2′-Deoxyribofuranosylthymine

The ratio of α and β anomers obtained depends upon the conditions of the reaction.

Purine nucleosides have been prepared by acid-catalyzed fusion of the nitrogen heterocycle and a substituted pentose as shown below.

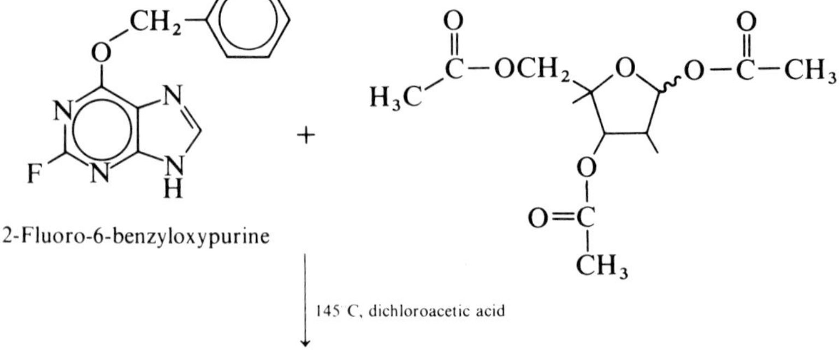

2-Fluoro-6-benzyloxypurine

145 C, dichloroacetic acid ↓

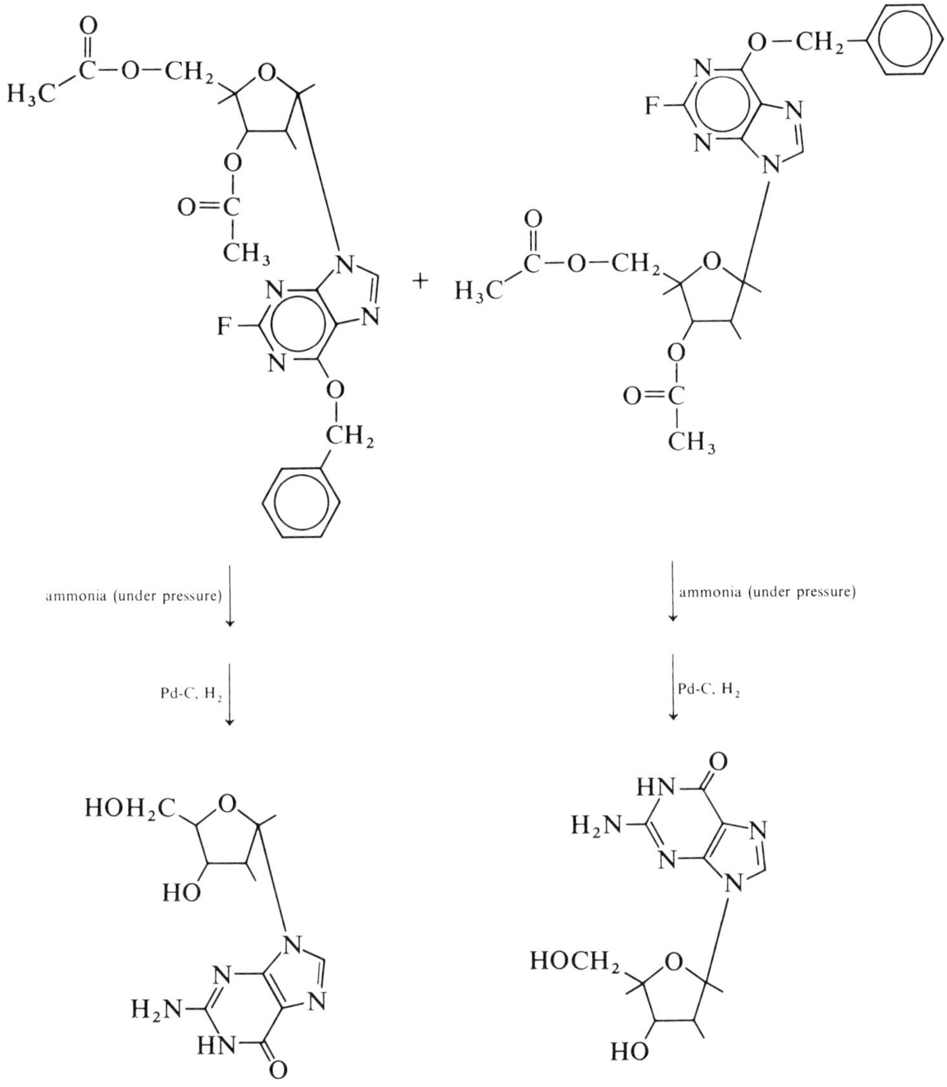

9-α-D-2'-Deoxyribofuranosylguanine        9-β-D-2'-Deoxyribofuranosylguanine

Nucleotides can be prepared from nucleosides by a variety of phosphorylation procedures. Since the pentose moiety of a nucleoside embodies more than one hydroxyl group, it is frequently necessary to protect hydroxyl groups that are not to be phosphorylated. For example, when the primary hydroxyl group is to undergo phosphorylation, the secondary hydroxyl group(s) is protected and the primary group can then be phosphorylated using the reagent 2-cyanoethyl phosphate in the presence of dicyclohexylcarbodiimide.

Guanosine:

## 2'-Deoxythymidine:

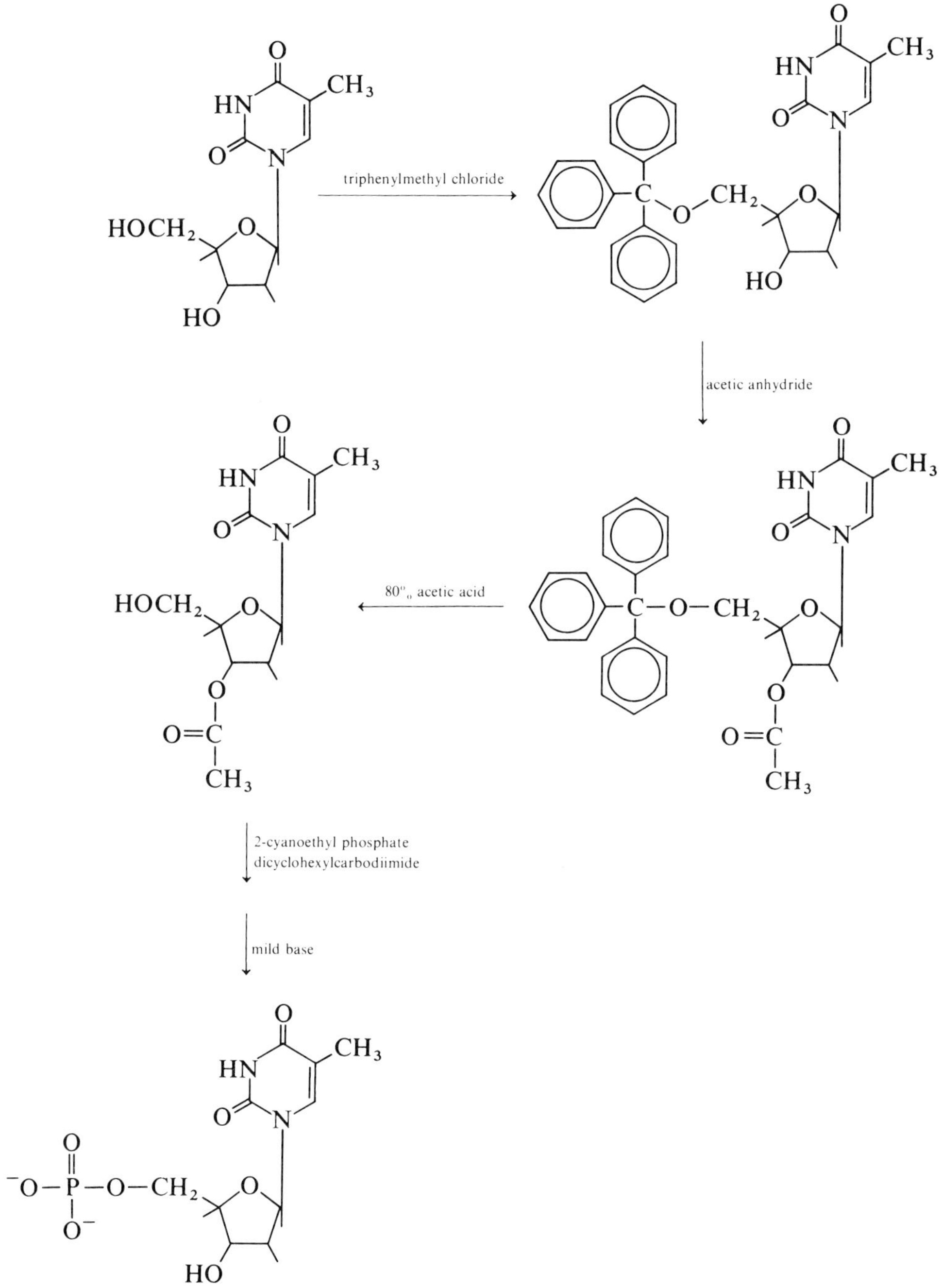

2'-Deoxythymidine 5'-phosphate

In addition, it has been reported that the primary hydroxyl group of a nucleoside can be selectively phosphorylated using an excess of pyrophosphoryl chloride. Adenosine, uridine, and cytidine have been converted into the corresponding 5'-monophosphates in this manner.

When the secondary hydroxyl group of a deoxyribonucleoside is to be phosphorylated, the primary hydroxyl group can be protected by making the 5'-O-triphenylmethyl derivative or the 5'-O-1''-methoxyisopropyl derivative. Both triphenylmethyl chloride and 2,2-dimethoxypropane react exclusively with the primary 5'-hydroxyl group of a nucleoside. When one of the two secondary hydroxyl groups of a ribonucleoside is to be phosphorylated, the other secondary hydroxyl group must also be protected under most circumstances. As an alternative, a mixture of the ribonucleoside 2'- and 3'-phosphates can be obtained and then separated.

The preparation of nucleoside diphosphates has been carried out with the reagent pyrophosphoryl tetrachloride. At low temperatures and without solvent this reagent reacts with the primary hydroxyl group of a 2',3'-O-isopropylidene nucleoside to give the 5'-dichlorophosphoric acid derivative, which is converted into the 5'-monophosphate in the presence of water. However, pyrophosphoryl tetrachloride in triethylamine reacts with the primary hydroxyl group of a suitably protected

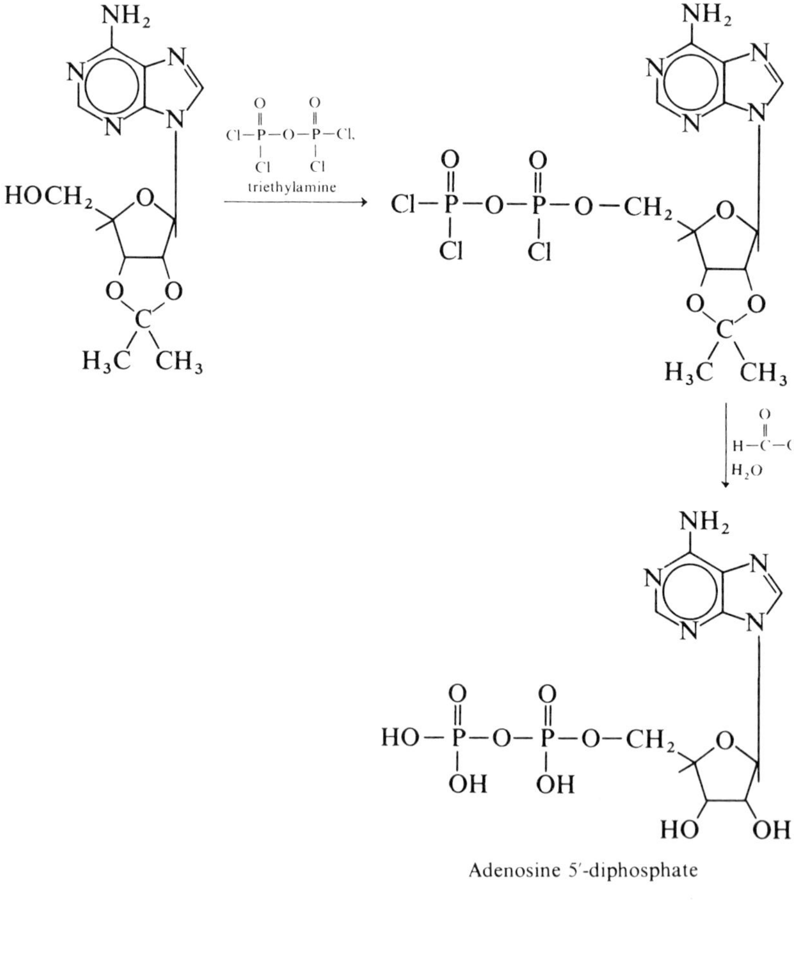

Adenosine 5'-diphosphate

nucleoside to yield a pyrophosphate ester. Adenosine 5′-diphosphate has been prepared in this manner.

Nucleoside triphosphates can be prepared by the reaction of the nucleoside phosphoromorpholidate and a pyrophosphate.

Adenosine 5′-triphosphate

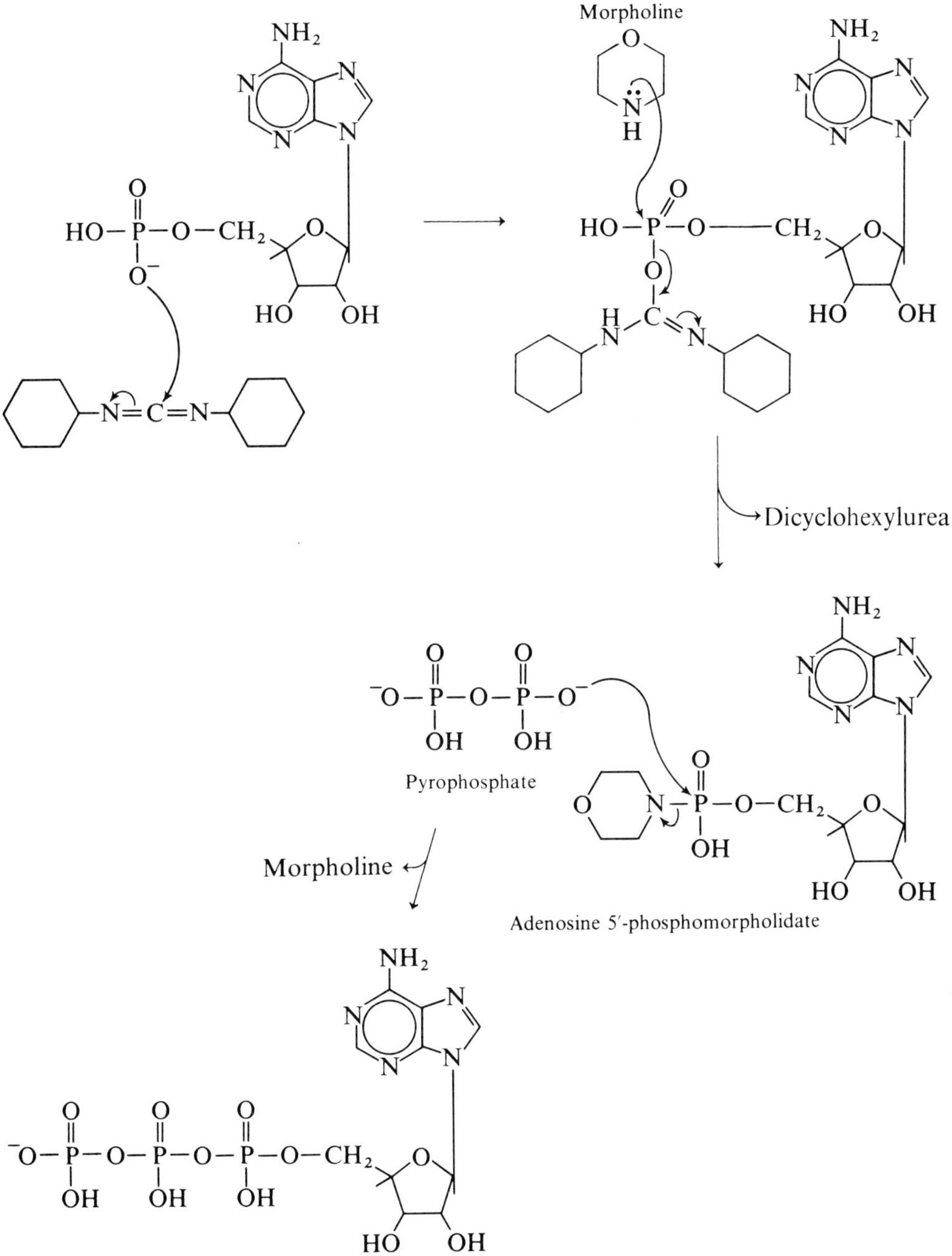

## Hydrolysis of the N-Glycosidic Bonds of Nucleosides

The N-glycosidic bond of a nucleoside is hydrolyzed under acidic conditions. Deoxyribonucleosides are cleaved more rapidly than ribonucleosides, and purine nucleosides are cleaved more rapidly than their pyrimidine counterparts. Studies on the mechanism of the hydrolysis of the N-glycosidic bonds of several guanosines and adenosines have provided evidence in support of a process involving the initial protonation of the purine moiety followed by the cleavage of the carbon-nitrogen bond as the slow, or rate-determining, step.

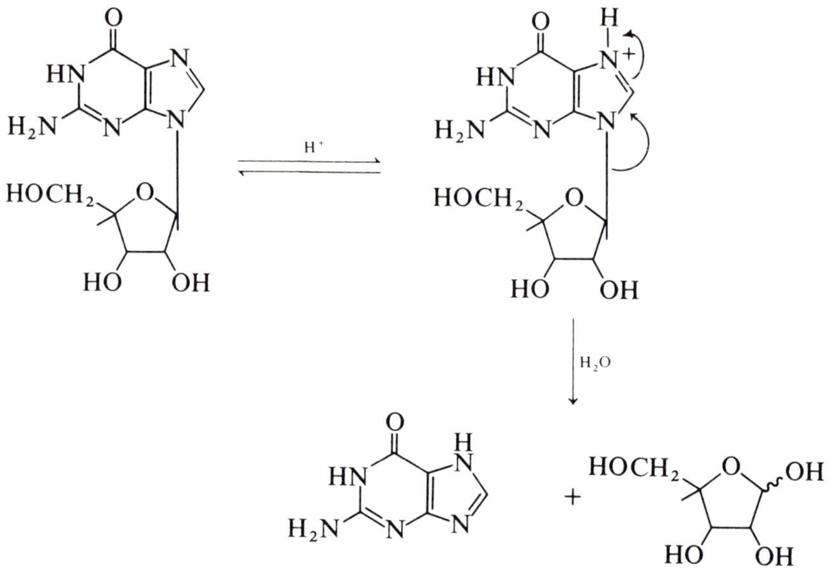

The more rapid hydrolysis of deoxyribonucleosides compared with ribonucleosides can be rationalized on the basis that the hydroxyl group at C(2) of the latter exerts an electron-withdrawing inductive effect (a minus $I$ effect), which opposes the cleavage of the carbon-nitrogen bond.

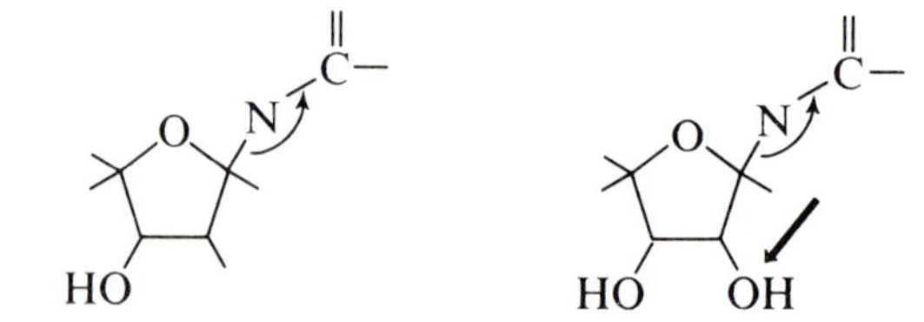

Deoxyribonucleoside        Ribonucleoside

The more rapid hydrolysis of 2-deoxyguanosine and 2′-deoxyadenosine compared with that of 2′-deoxycytidine probably reflects the relative capabilities of the purine and pyrimidine ring systems to accept electrons.

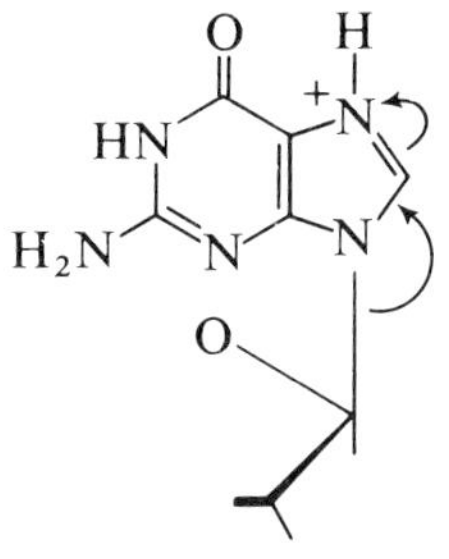

# THE CHEMISTRY OF THE PURINES, PYRIMIDINES, AND NUCLEIC ACIDS

Purine ring system 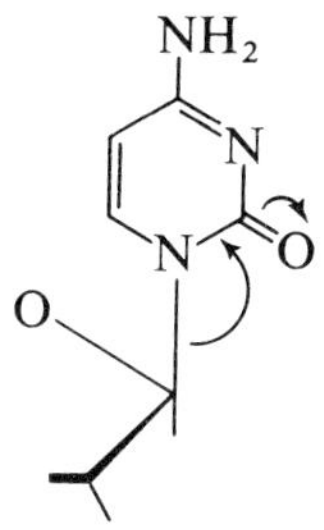         Pyrimidine ring system

## Ribosyluracil and Phosphoribosyluracil

The nucleosides and nucleotides that have been discussed are composed of a purine or a pyrimidine bonded to a pentose or a pentose phosphate by an *N*-glycosidic linkage. There are also naturally occurring pyrimidine derivatives in which the pentose or pentose phosphate is bonded to the nitrogen heterocycle by a carbon-carbon bond. The simplest of these is 5-ribosyluracil, frequently called pseudouridine.

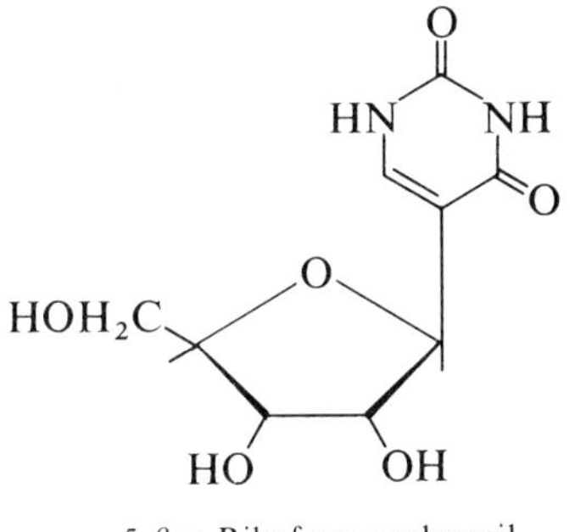

5-β-D-Ribofuranosyluracil
(pseudouridine)

The following sequence has been used to prepare 5-ribosyluracil in the laboratory:

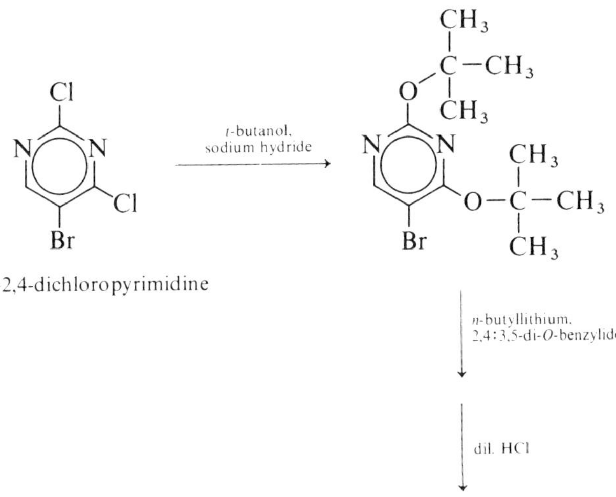

5-Bromo-2,4-dichloropyrimidine

*t*-butanol,
sodium hydride

*n*-butyllithium,
2,4:3,5-di-*O*-benzylideneribose

dil. HCl

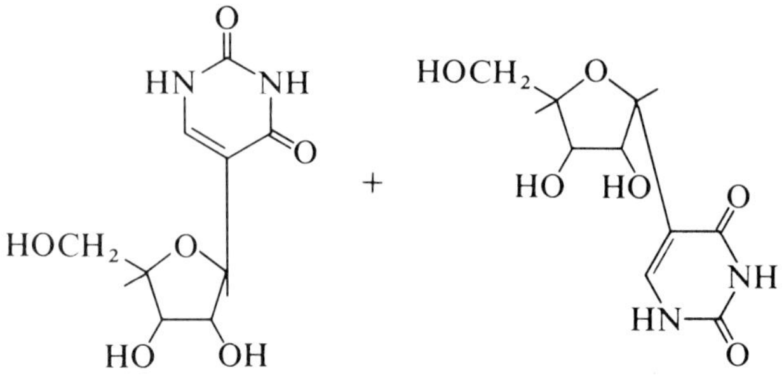

5-β-D-Ribofuranosyluracil     5-α-D-Ribofuranosyluracil

**Some chemical properties of ribosyluracil and phosphoribosyluracil** Ribosyluracil, unlike uridine, possesses two —NH groups. Methylation by diazomethane yields a mixture of the $N(1)$- and $N(3)$-monomethyl derivatives. Cyanoethylation, on the other hand, occurs exclusively at $N(1)$ under controlled conditions, while the reaction with a water-soluble carbodiimide occurs primarily at $N(3)$.

Although the 5,6 double bond of nucleosides such as uridine undergoes catalytic hydrogenation, ribosyluracil undergoes hydrogenolysis under similar conditions. In

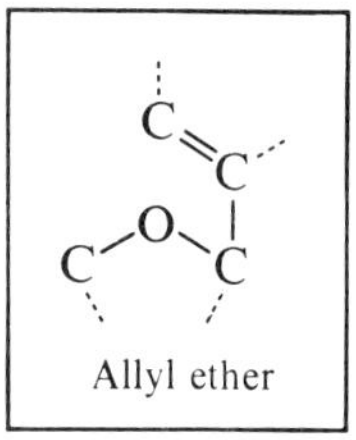

Allyl ether

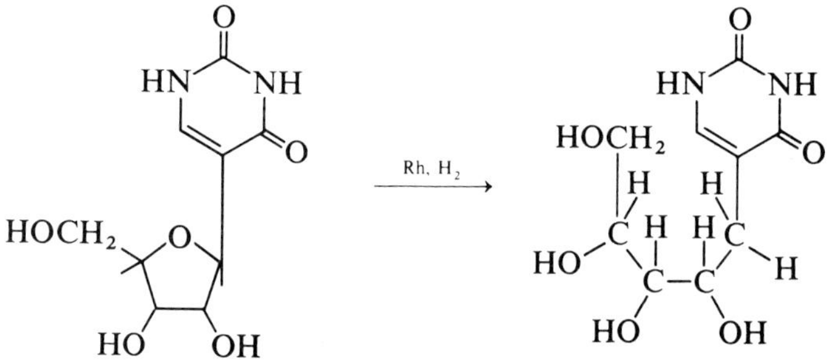

ribosyluracil, carbon atoms 5 and 6 of the pyrimidine moiety plus carbon atom 1', the heterocyclic oxygen atom, and carbon atom 4' of the ribose moiety constitute the elements of an allyl ether. Allyl ethers undergo cleavage in the presence of hydrogen and a catalyst.

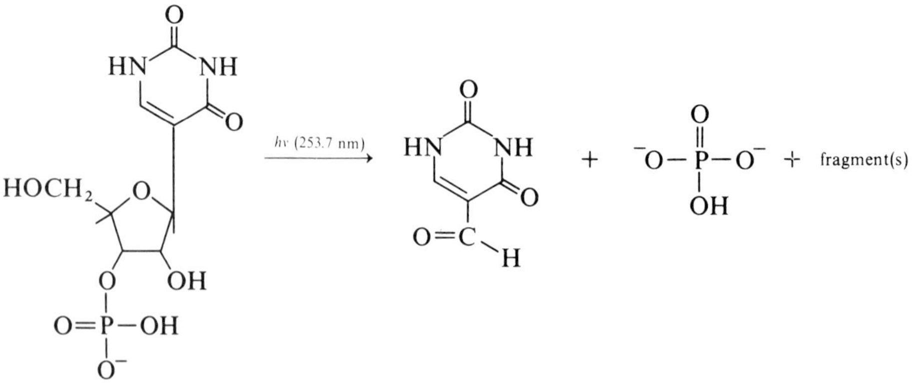

The irradiation of 5-ribosyluracil with ultraviolet light can yield a mixture of as many as seven products while under similar conditions 3'-phospho-5-ribosyluracil yields a somewhat less complex mixture containing 5-formyluracil, orthophosphate, and an unidentified fragment. This behavior is in contrast to the photohydration and photodimerization reactions that the pyrimidines and their N(1) derivatives undergo as a result of ultraviolet irradiation.

When a ribonucleoside 5'-monophosphate is treated with a six- to tenfold excess of periodate in the presence of a primary amine, the purine or pyrimidine is liberated as one of the products of the fragmentation reaction, but treatment of 5'-phospho-5-ribosyluracil under these conditions results in the liberation of 5-carboxyuracil, rather than uracil, among the products of the reaction. Although the precise nature of these reactions is incompletely understood, the fragmentations are represented as shown on the basis of the available information.

A ribonucleoside 5'-monophosphate:

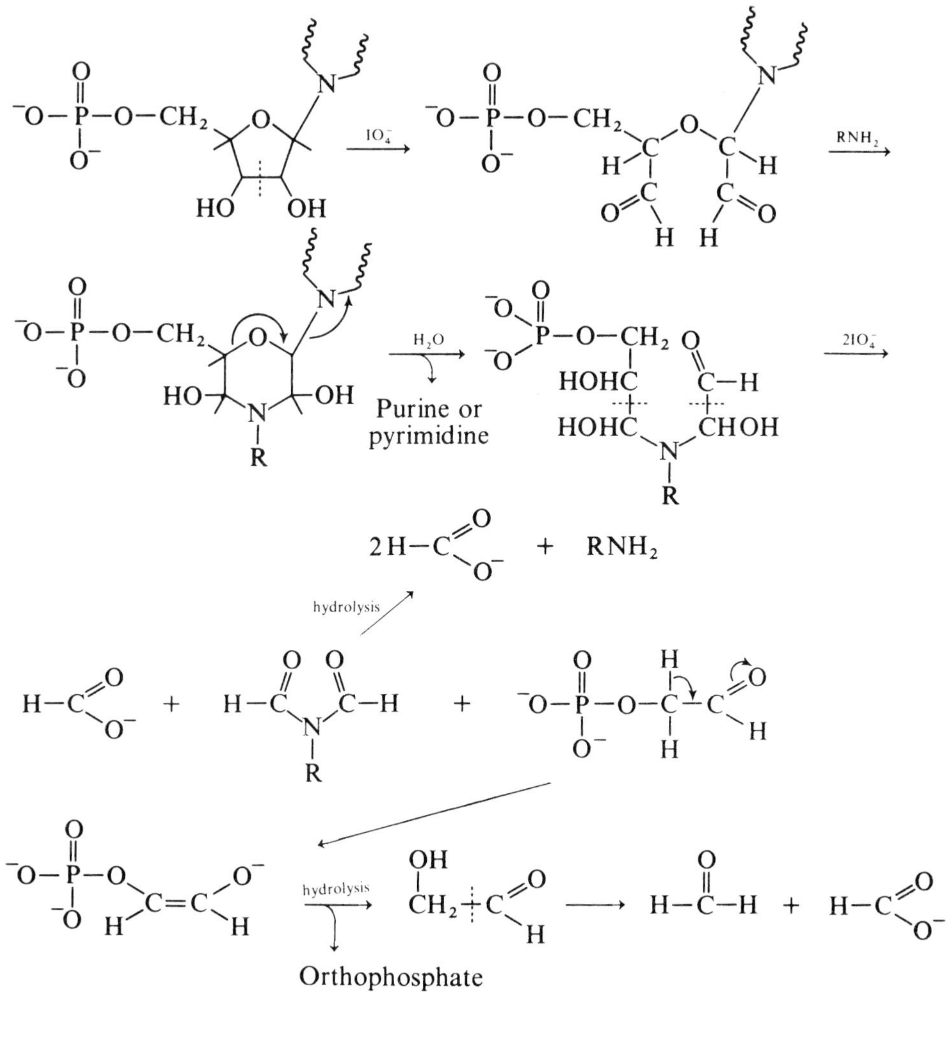

5'-Phospho-5-ribosyluracil:

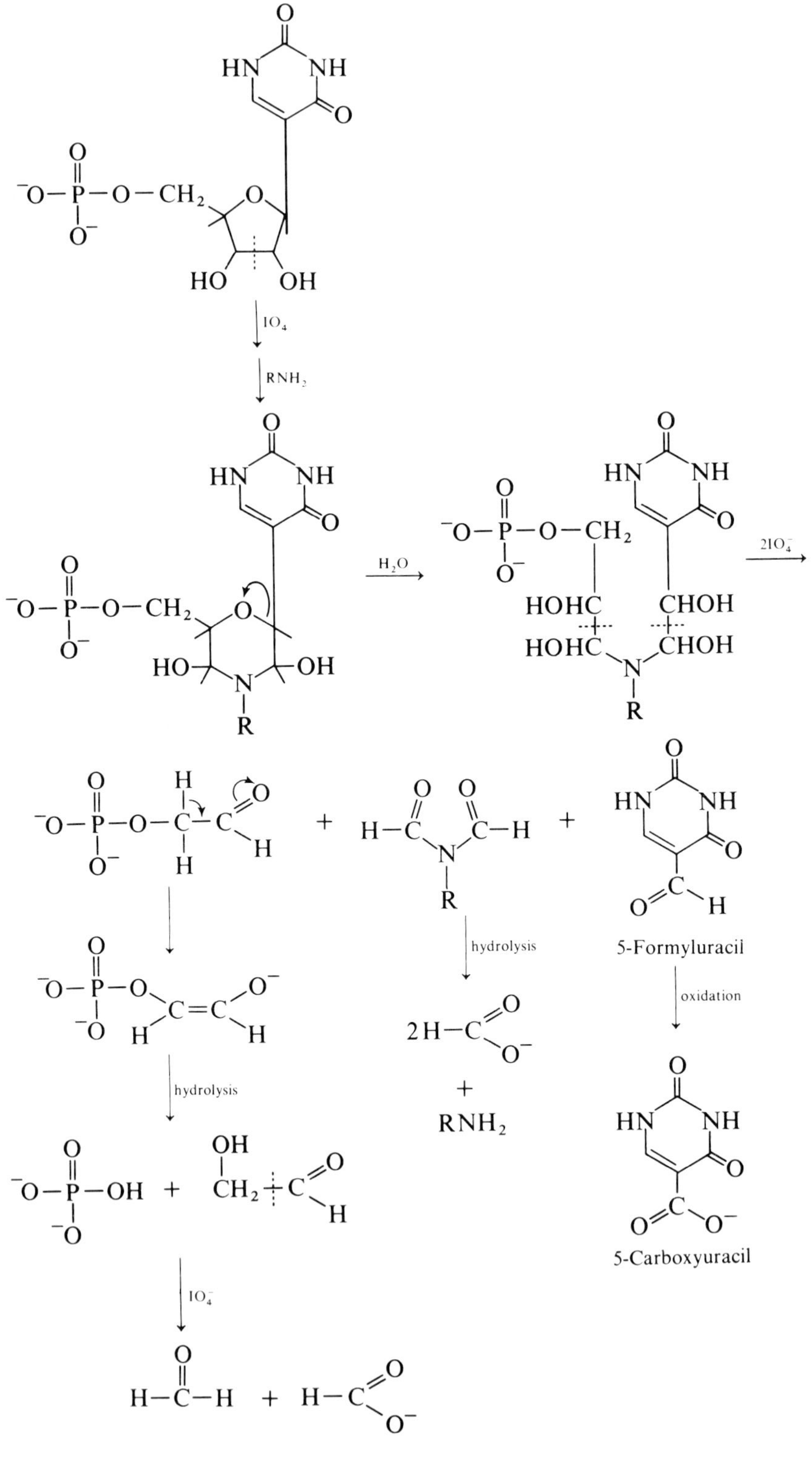

The liberation of the purine or pyrimidine moiety of the ribonucleotide or the phosphoribosyluracil depends upon the ability of the nitrogen heterocycle to accept the electrons of the bond that must be broken. In phosphoribosyluracil, electrons are not readily accepted at C(5).

As might be expected, ribosyluracil fails to undergo an acid-catalyzed cleavage of the bond joining the pyrimidine and ribose moieties. Instead, treatment of ribosyluracil with acid results in isomerization, and a mixture of the $\alpha$ and $\beta$ anomers of both ribofuranosyluracil and ribopyranosyluracil is obtained.

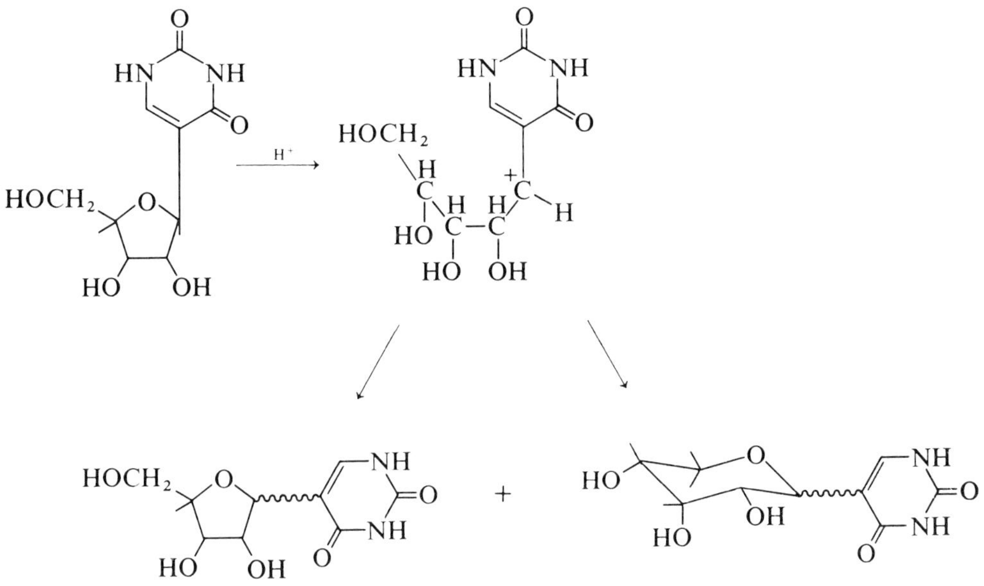

5-α-D-Ribofuranosyluracil and
5-β-D-ribofuranosyluracil

5-α-D-Ribopyranosyluracil and
5-β-D-ribopyranosyluracil

## NUCLEIC ACIDS

The nucleic acids are polymers comprising nucleotides joined by phosphodiester bonds between the 3′ position of one monomeric unit and the 5′ position of the adjacent monomeric unit. The nucleotide units that are the most common components of naturally occurring deoxyribonucleic acid (DNA) are deoxyadenylic acid, deoxyguanylic acid, deoxycytidylic acid, and deoxythymidylic acid. Most naturally occurring ribonucleic acid (RNA) is composed of adenylic acid, guanylic acid, cytidylic acid, and uridylic acid.

### The Laboratory Synthesis of Oligonucleotides and Polynucleotides

There are a variety of methods for the synthesis of oligonucleotides and polynucleotides. Most entail adding suitably protected nucleotides one at a time to a growing polymer chain or joining previously prepared small oligonucleotides to form larger oligonucleotides or polynucleotides. The addition of monomeric units one at a time is illustrated by the preparation shown below and on pages 235 to 237. The substituents used to protect the amino groups can be removed by treatment with an excess of concentrated ammonia at room temperature, and the 4-monomethoxytriphenylmethyl group can be removed with 80% acetic acid, also at room temperature.

When a larger polynucleotide is to be prepared by joining small oligonucleotide units, the procedure is similar to that used in the addition of mononucleotides to the growing polymer chain. Phosphodiester-bond formation between the 5'-phosphomonoester group of the incoming oligonucleotide and the 3'-hydroxyl group of the growing polynucleotide is induced by using a reagent like mesitylenesulfonyl chloride or (in some cases) dicyclohexylcarbodiimide. Chain growth, as in the addition of mononucleotides, occurs at the 3'-hydroxyl terminus. In the addition of oligonucleotides particularly it has been found necessary to use a larger and larger excess of the incoming component as the length of the polynucleotide chain increases.

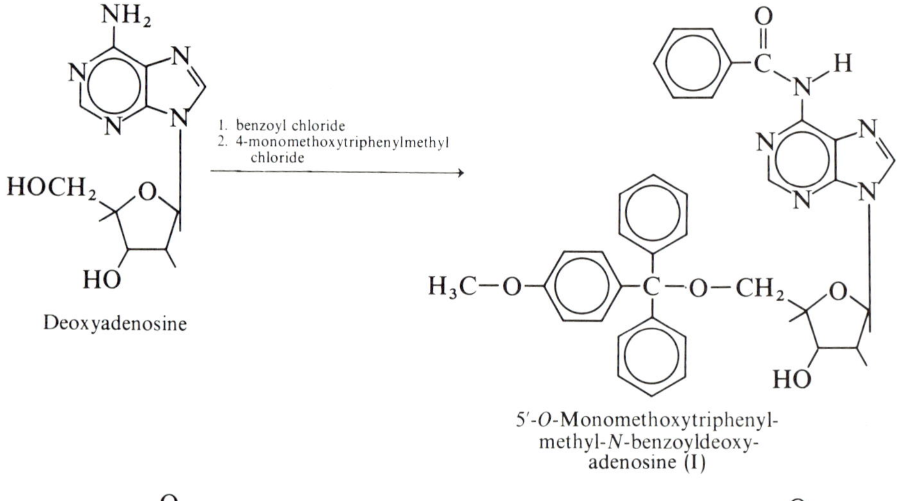

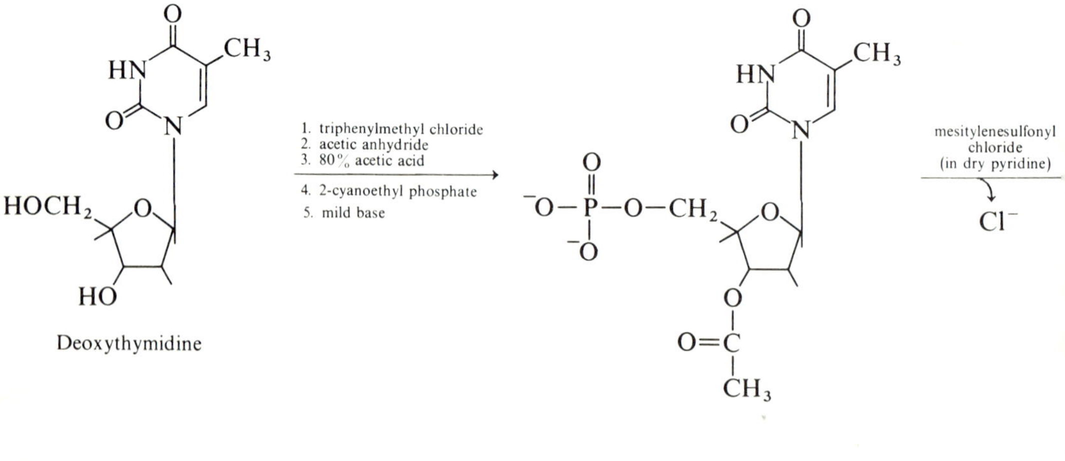

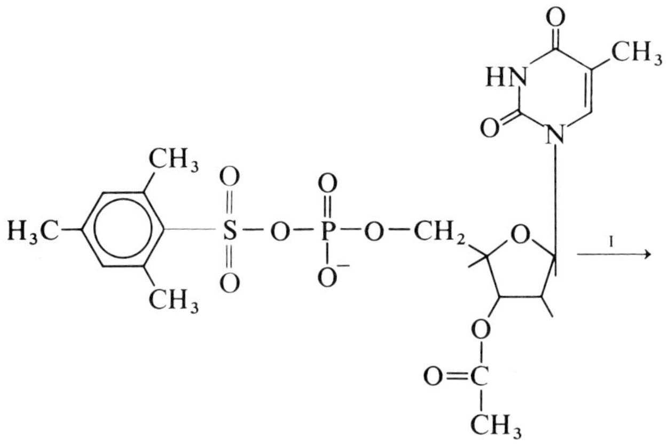

# THE CHEMISTRY OF THE PURINES, PYRIMIDINES, AND NUCLEIC ACIDS 235

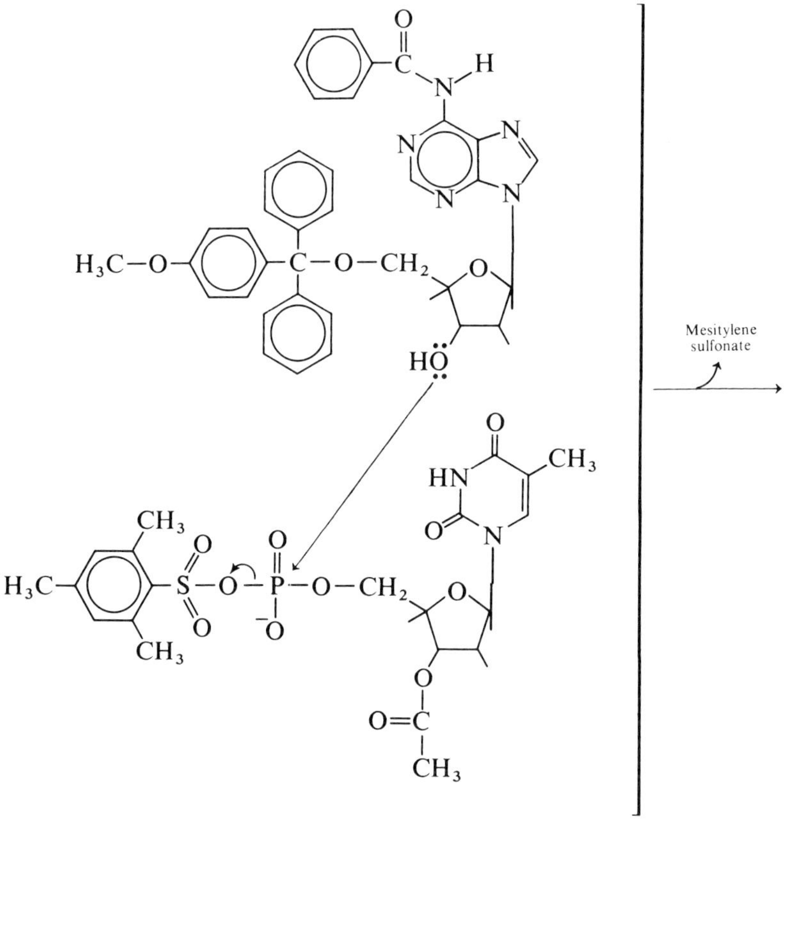

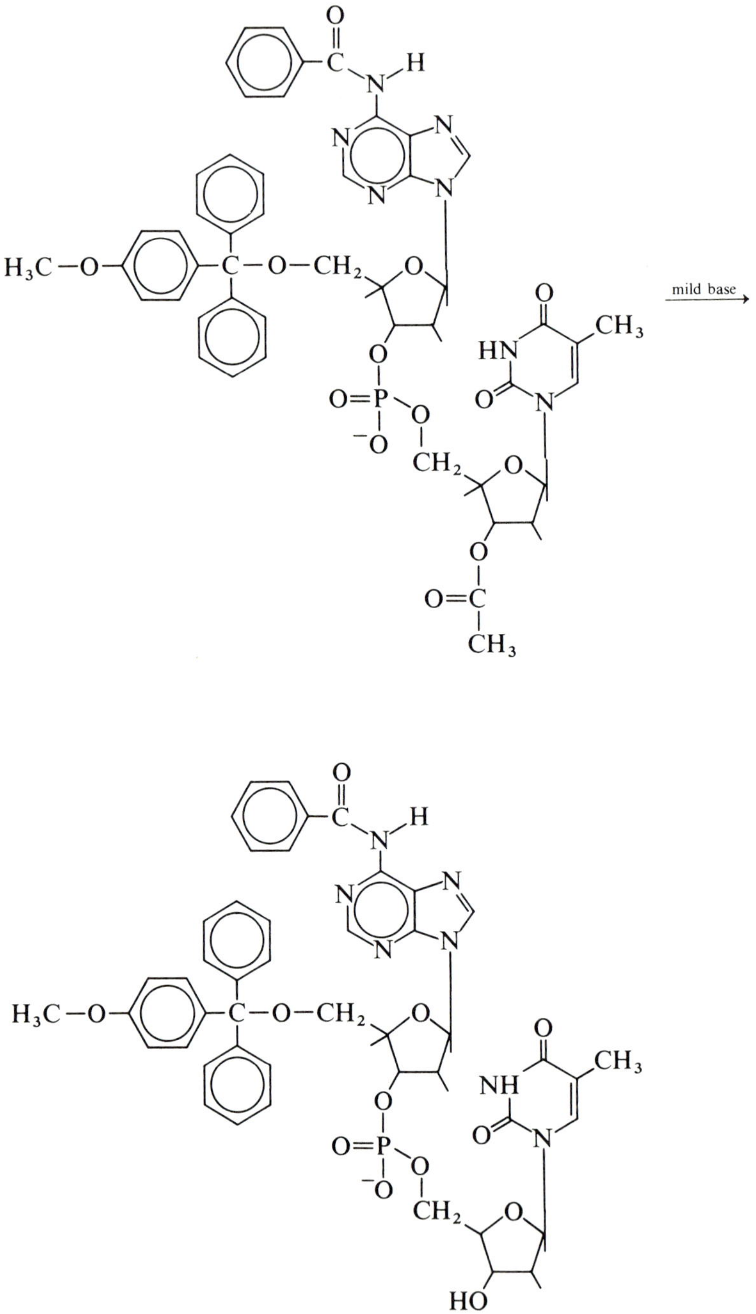

5'-*O*-Monomethoxytriphenylmethyl-*N*-benzoyldeoxyadenylyl-
(3' → 5')-deoxythymidine(II)

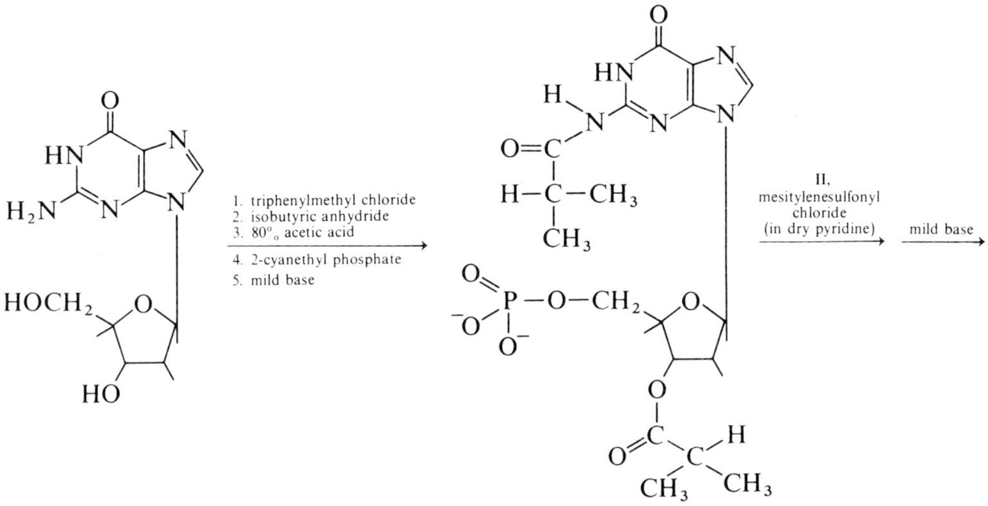

*N*,*O*(3')-Bisisobutyryldeoxyguanosine
5'-phosphate

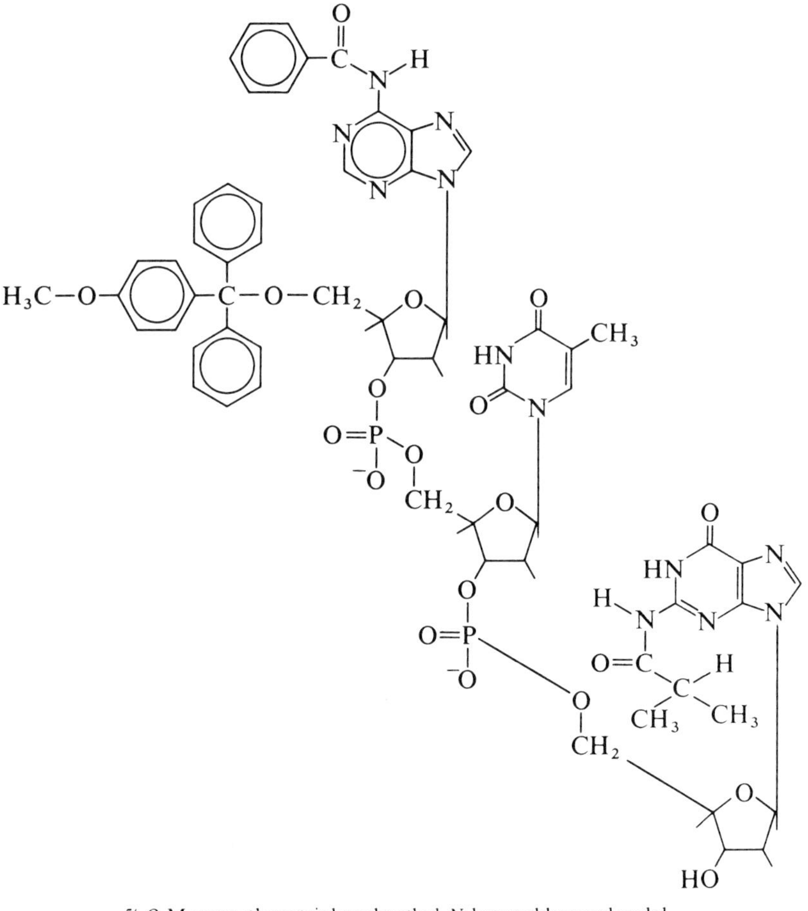

1. triphenylmethyl chloride
2. isobutyric anhydride
3. 80% acetic acid
4. 2-cyanethyl phosphate
5. mild base

II, mesitylenesulfonyl chloride (in dry pyridine)

mild base

5'-*O*-Monomethoxytriphenylmethyl-*N*-benzoyldeoxyadenylyl-
(3' → 5')-deoxythymidylyl-(3' → 5')-*N*-isobutyryldeoxyguanosine

Using methods of the type described above, H. Gobind Khorana and his colleagues synthesized the gene for an alanine transfer RNA from yeast.† In this case, the synthesis was begun from the 5'-hydroxyl end of the DNA molecule, and the initial phosphodiester bond resulted from the condensation of N-isobutyryl-5'-monomethoxytrityldeoxyguanosine and 3'-O-acetyl-N-benzoyldeoxy adenosine 5'-phosphate. Subsequently, the appropriate oligonucleotides, each synthesized as described above, were successively added at the 3'-hydroxyl terminus until the complete sequence of 77 nucleotidyl units was generated.

Oligonucleotides are also synthesized in the laboratory by a procedure based on the same principles as the solid-phase synthesis of proteins (pages 166 to 171). In the oligonucleotide synthesis a polystyrene solid support bearing 4-monomethoxytriphenylmethyl chloride functional groups is used to anchor the 5'-terminal nucleotide by its hydroxyl group. Then a suitably protected nucleotide having a 5'-phosphomonoester group is introduced into the reaction medium, and phosphodiester-bond formation between the 3'-hydroxyl group of the anchored nucleotide and the phosphomonoester group is induced in the presence of mesitylenesulfonyl chloride. After removal of the excess reagents and liberation of the 3'-hydroxyl group of the nucleotide unit most recently added, the process of phosphodiester-bond formation is repeated, using the nucleotide that is to be next in the sequence.

## Chemical Interactions Involved in Maintaining the Helical Conformation of Nucleic Acids

Most DNA molecules consist of two polynucleotide chains coiled about each other to form a right-handed double helix that cannot be separated into its constituent strands without being unwound. The backbone of the helixes is formed by the deoxyribose phosphate chains, which are at the periphery of the structure with the purine and pyrimidine moieties projecting inward. This double-helical structure for the DNA molecule was initially proposed by James D. Watson and Francis H. C. Crick in 1953.‡ Subsequently, the structure was modified by Maurice H. F. Wilkins and his colleagues,¶ and in 1962 Watson, Crick, and Wilkins received the Nobel prize for medicine and physiology in recognition of their important contributions to our understanding of the structure and related functions of DNA. The scale model of the DNA duplex molecule constructed by Watson and Crick is shown in Fig. 6-5.

X-ray crystallographic studies on the alkali-metal salts of DNA have shown that these macromolecules can assume at least three slightly different helical forms in the crystalline state. These forms, designated A, B, and C, differ in the number of nucleotide units per turn of the helix, the pitch of the helix, and the angle at which the purine or pyrimidine moiety is oriented with respect to the axis of the helix (see Table 6-1). The DNA in the cell exists in the B form in most specimens examined thus far.

† Agarwal, K. L., Buchi, H., Caruthers, M. H., Gupta, N., Khorana, H. G., Kleppe, K., Kumar, A., Ohtsuka, E., Rajbhandary, U. L., van de Sande, J. H., Sgaramella, V., Weber, H., and Yamada, T. (1970) *Nature* **227**, 27–34.

‡ Watson, J. D., and Crick, F. H. C. (1953) *Nature* **171**, 737–738.

¶ Feughelman, M., Langridge, R., Seeds, W. E., Stokes, A. R., Wilson, H. R., Hooper, C. W., Wilkins, M. H. F., Barclay, R. K., and Hamilton, L. D. (1955) *Nature* **175**, 834–838.

THE CHEMISTRY OF THE PURINES, PYRIMIDINES, AND NUCLEIC ACIDS **239**

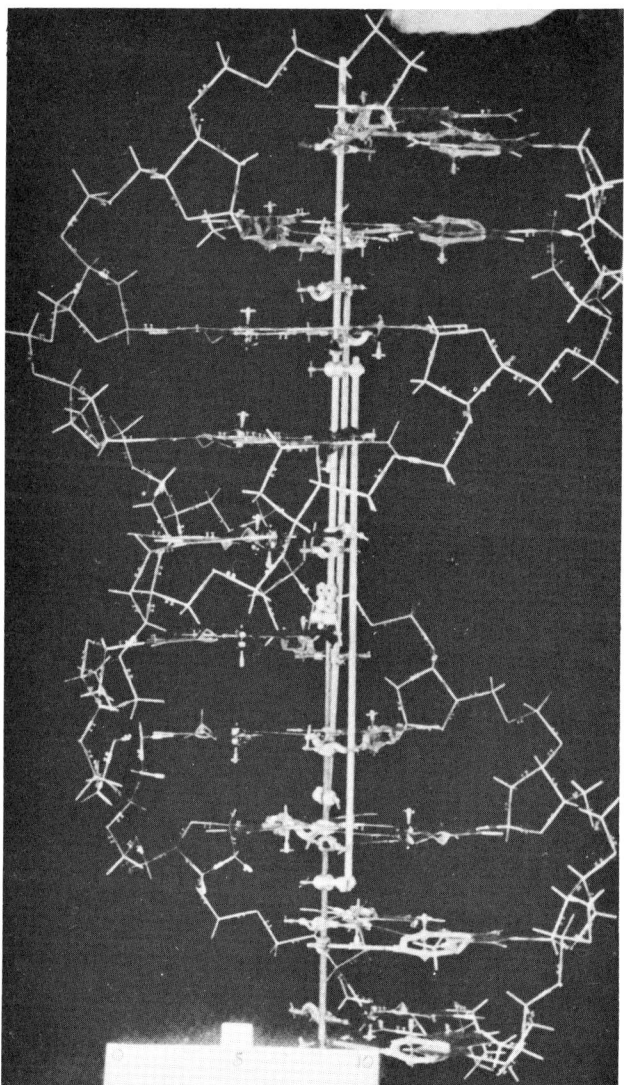

**Figure 6-5** The original demonstration model of the DNA double helix. The scale gives distances in angstroms. [*From Watson, J. D. (1968) The Double Helix, p. 206, Atheneum Press, New York. With permission.*]

In the B form of DNA each complete turn of the helix spans a distance of 34 Å measured along the axis of the helix. Since each nucleotidyl unit corresponds to a height of 3.4 Å, there are 10 nucleotidyl units per turn of the helix. Each of the purine or pyrimidine moieties is oriented at an angle of essentially 90° (88°) with respect to the axis of the double helix. In each case a purine of one strand is opposite to a pyrimidine of the other strand, and in this way the double helix maintains a uniform diameter of approximately 20 Å.

The two strands of the DNA duplex molecule are antiparallel and hydrogen-bonded to each other in the manner shown diagrammatically as follows:

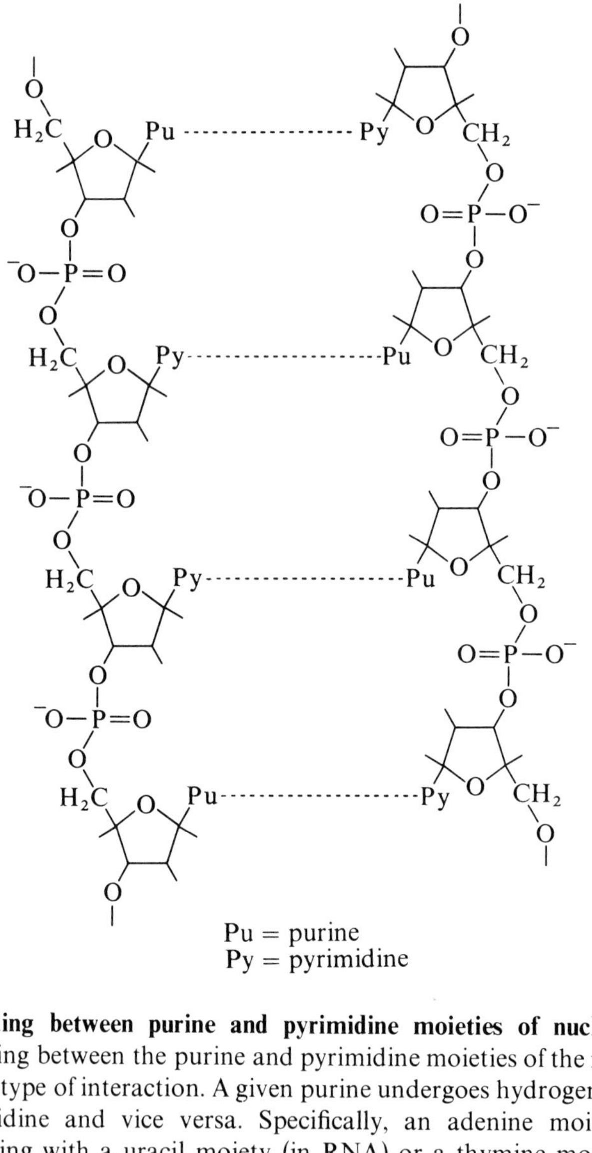

Pu = purine
Py = pyrimidine

**Hydrogen bonding between purine and pyrimidine moieties of nucleic acids** The hydrogen bonding between the purine and pyrimidine moieties of the nucleic acids is a very selective type of interaction. A given purine undergoes hydrogen bonding with a given pyrimidine and vice versa. Specifically, an adenine moiety undergoes hydrogen bonding with a uracil moiety (in RNA) or a thymine moiety (in DNA) while a guanine moiety undergoes hydrogen bonding with a cytosine moiety. This selective hydrogen bonding in nucleic acids is referred to as *base pairing*. Of the various models for base pairing, the two most attractive models are those proposed by K. Hoogsteen and by Watson and Crick. In the Hoogsteen model the hydrogen bonding involves N(7) of the purine and N(1) of the pyrimidine and also the C(6) amino group of the purine and the C(6) oxo group of the pyrimidine. In the Watson and Crick model N(1) of the purine participates in the hydrogen bonding rather than

## Table 6-1 Helix parameters for the A, B, and C forms of DNA

| DNA form† | Base pairs per turn of helix | Height of nucleotide unit along axis of helix, Å | Angle of rotation of successive purine or pyrimidine moieties, deg | Helix diameter, Å | Angle of purine or pyrimidine moiety with respect to axis of helix, deg |
|---|---|---|---|---|---|
| A | 11 | 2.56 | 32.7 | 17.68 | 70 |
| B | 10 | 3.36 | 36 | 18.11 | 88 |
| C | $9\frac{1}{3}$ | 3.32 | 38.6 | 18.11 | 84 |

*Source:* A form: Fuller, W., Wilkins, M. H. F., Wilson, H. R., and Hamilton, L. D. (1965) *J. Mol. Biol.* **12**, 60–80; B form: Langridge, R., Wilson, H. R., Hooper, C. W., Wilkins, M. F. H., and Hamilton, L. D. (1960) *J. Mol. Biol.* **2**, 19–37 and Langridge, R., Marvin, D. A., Seeds, W. E., Wilson, H. R., Hooper, C. W., Wilkins, M. F. H., and Hamilton, L. D. (1960) *J. Mol. Biol.* **2**, 38–64; C form: Marvin, D. A., Spencer, M., Wilkins, M. H. F., and Hamilton, L. D. (1961) *J. Mol. Biol.* **3**, 547–565.

† Conversions among the three forms are brought about by changes in the relative humidity of the environment. At 92 percent relative humidity the B form of the DNA molecule exists. When the relative humidity is lowered to 75 percent, the molecule is converted into the A form. When the relative humidity is lowered to between 66 and 44 percent, the C form of the molecule is obtained.

N(7), and, in addition, in the guanine-cytosine pair a third hydrogen bond involves the C(2) amino group of the purine and the C(2) oxo group of the pyrimidine. X-ray diffraction studies have shown that $N$(9)-methyladenine and $N$(1)-methylthymine and several other purine-pyrimidine pairs undergo hydrogen bonding of the type proposed by Hoogsteen, but on the basis of detailed x-ray diffraction studies in conjunction with molecular model building it appears that the hydrogen bonding that normally occurs between the purines and pyrimidines of the nucleic acids is of the type proposed by Watson and Crick.

Hydrogen bonding is the association between two atoms when one atom bears a hydrogen atom that is somewhat acidic and the other atom is electronegative and somewhat basic. The atom that bears the hydrogen atom is referred to as the *donor* and the electronegative atom is referred to as the *acceptor*. The energy of a hydrogen bond is generally of the order of 2 to 10 kcal/mol. Energy values for the doubly or triply hydrogen-bonded adenine-uracil and guanine-cytosine pairs have been calculated assuming four different modes of interaction in each case. The energy values in Table 6-2 indicate that in the guanine-cytosine pair the Watson-Crick structure is the more stable and in the adenine-uracil pair the Hoogsteen structure is the more stable. It seems possible that in the naturally occurring nucleic acid molecule the guanine and cytosine moieties could interact as proposed by Watson and Crick while the adenine and uracil (or thymine) moieties interact as proposed by Hoogsteen, but this possibility is excluded because the distances between C(1′) of the purine nucleotidyl unit and C(1′) of the pyrimidine nucleotidyl unit are different in these two modes of interaction (i.e. 10.85 Å in the Watson-Crick structure and 8.80 Å in the Hoogsteen structure). However, if both types of pairing were present, the phosphate backbone of the macromolecule would exhibit an irregular profile, dictated by the sequence of bases.

**Table 6-2 Calculated values† for hydrogen-bonding energy of purine-pyrimidine pairs**

| Pair | Mode of interaction | Energy value, kcal/mol |
|---|---|---|
| Adenine-uracil: | | |
| 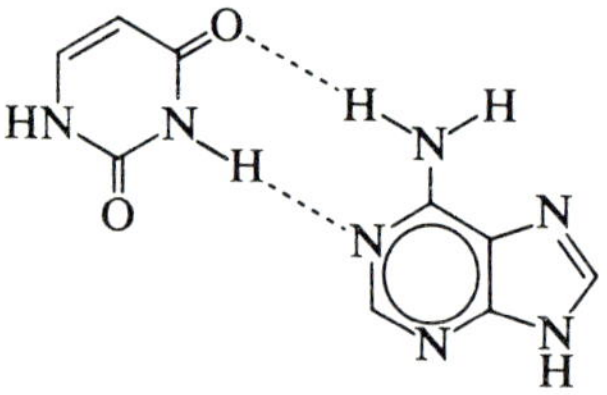 | Watson-Crick | −5.58 |
| 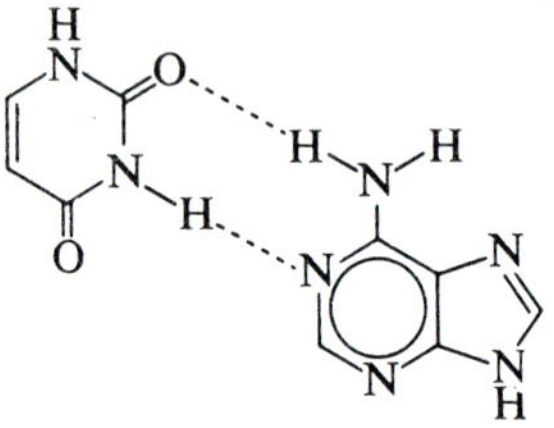 | Reversed Watson-Crick | −4.94 |
| 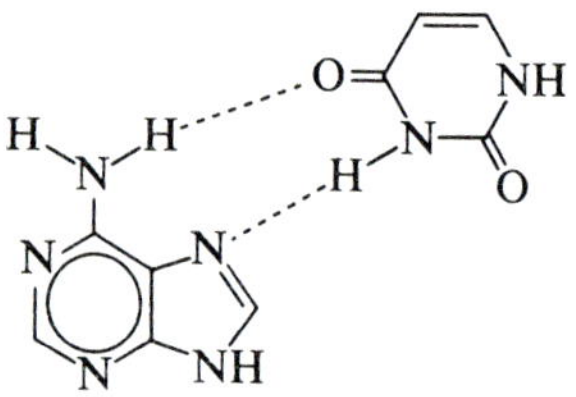 | Hoogsteen | −6.96 |
| 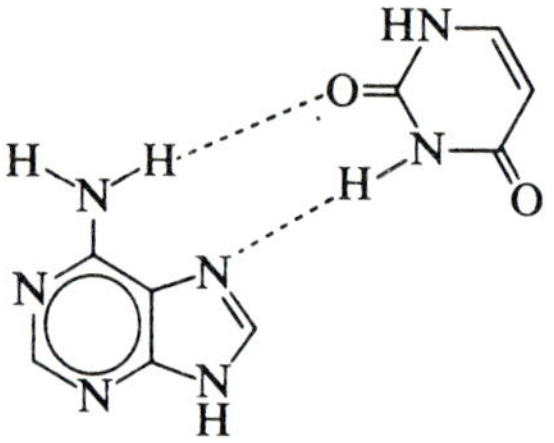 | Reversed Hoogsteen | −6.74 |
| Guanine-cytosine: | | |
| 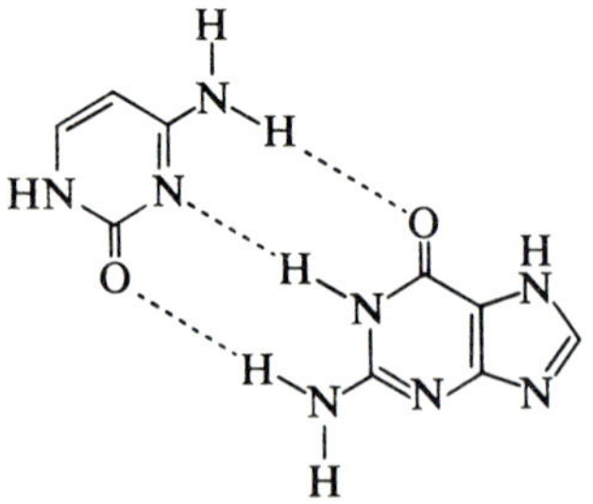 | Watson-Crick | −19.18 |

**Table 6-2 Calculated values† for hydrogen-bonding energy of purine-pyrimidine pairs** (*Continued*)

| Pair | Mode of interaction | Energy value, kcal/mol |
|---|---|---|
| 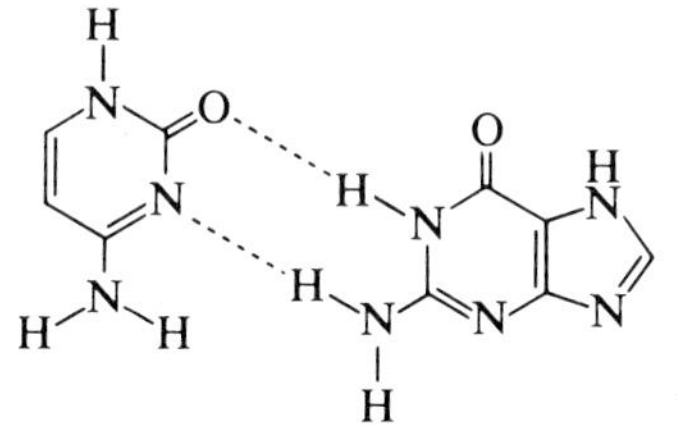 | Reversed Watson-Crick | −12.85 |
| 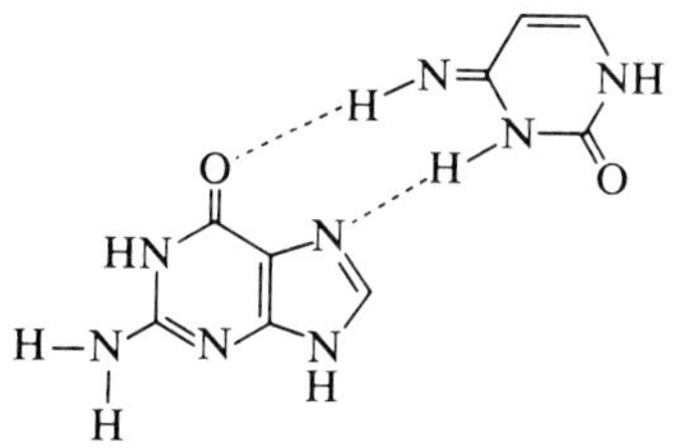 | Hoogsteen | −5.75 |
| 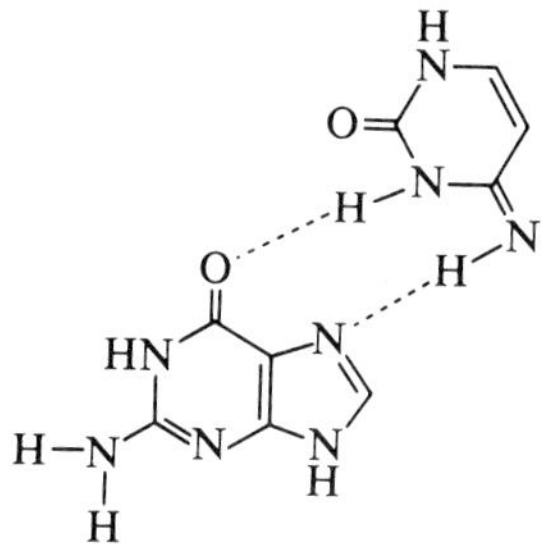 | Reversed Hoogsteen | −3.67 |

*Source:* Data from Pullman, B., and Pullman, A. (1969) in *Progress in Nucleic Acid Research and Molecular Biology* (Davidson, J. N., and Cohn, W. E., eds.), vol. 9, pp. 327–402, Academic, New York.

† The values were derived using a monopole approximation method, in which it is assumed that all the charges in the system interact in a simple coulombic manner. Each of the values shown is the sum of a monopole-monopole term, a monopole-dipole term, and a term representing the dispersion interaction. When these calculations are performed, the value of this sum goes through a minimum which corresponds to the most stable arrangement of that particular mode of interaction. This is the value given. Stability increases, therefore, as the energy values become more negative.

Hydrogen bonding of the reversed Watson-Crick type and of the reversed Hoogsteen type have been observed in some of the polynucleotides and substituted purine-pyrimidine systems prepared in the laboratory.

The selectivity that characterizes base pairing in the nucleic acids results from cooperative factors operating in tandem. Not only do the structural characteristics of the purine and pyrimidine moieties contribute to this selectivity, since the components of a pair must be compatible sterically, but the electronic distributions in the nitrogen heterocycles must also be such that the components of a pair are compatible on the basis of electronic considerations. Atoms and groups brought into juxtaposition in the paired structure must not repel each other. As will be seen, selectivity in biochemical reactions is frequently based upon a combination of steric and electronic factors.

**Hydrophobic bonding between purine and pyrimidine moieties of nucleic acids** Although it was at first assumed that base pairing was solely responsible for the stabilization of the helical conformation of the nucleic acids, it soon became apparent that other factors must contribute to the stability of this structure. Among the indications that led to this conclusion was the observation that the DNA helix remains intact at low pH values although hydrogen bonds are usually severed under these conditions due to the protonation of the acceptor. Also, it was found that when the hydrogen atom that participates in hydrogen bonding is replaced by a methyl group, the methyl derivative of the purine or pyrimidine still undergoes association. In fact, these methyl derivatives associate to a greater extent than the parent compounds. For example, $N(1)$-methylinosine (inosine is the nucleoside derived from hypoxanthine) and $N(6)$-dimethyladenosine associate to a greater extent than inosine and adenosine. Furthermore, the helical structure of DNA is destroyed in dimethyl sulfoxide and other organic solvents although base pairing involving mononucleotides is not destroyed in these solvents. (The extent of base pairing is actually greater in dimethyl sulfoxide and certain other organic solvents than it is in water.) It has now been shown that in addition to base pairing, which is an *in-plane* interaction, there is also a *vertical* interaction between the purine and pyrimidine moieties of the nucleic acids which contributes significantly to the stability of the helical structure of the macromolecule. This vertical interaction has been described as a type of hydrophobic bonding between the planar, parallel purine and pyrimidine moieties of the nucleic acids.† The forces involved in hydrophobic bonding are essentially London–van der Waals, or dispersion, forces. Previously, we mentioned hydrophobic bonding involving the hydrocarbon chains of lipids and proteins, but in the vertical interaction or stacking that occurs in the nucleic acid molecules the association is perhaps more reminiscent of the formation of a pi-pi complex, e.g., that derived from picric acid and an aromatic hydrocarbon or from trinitrobenzene and benzidine.

Studies using various model compounds have been carried out to learn more about the characteristics of this vertical interaction, often referred to as *base stacking*. In one such investigation the preferred conformation of the vertically stacked purine moieties of the dinucleotide adenylyl-(3' → 5')-adenosine was determined.

† Ts'o, P. O. P., Kondo, N. S., Robbins, R. K., and Broom, A. D. (1969) *J. Am. Chem. Soc.* **91**, 5625–5631.

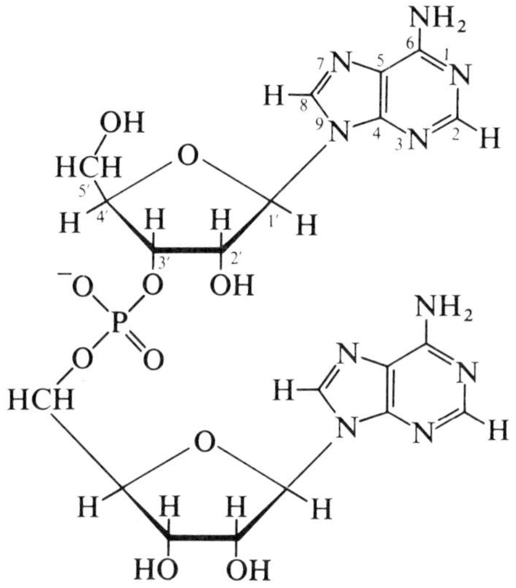

Adenylyl-(3' → 5')-adenosine (ApA)

Four different arrangements are possible.†

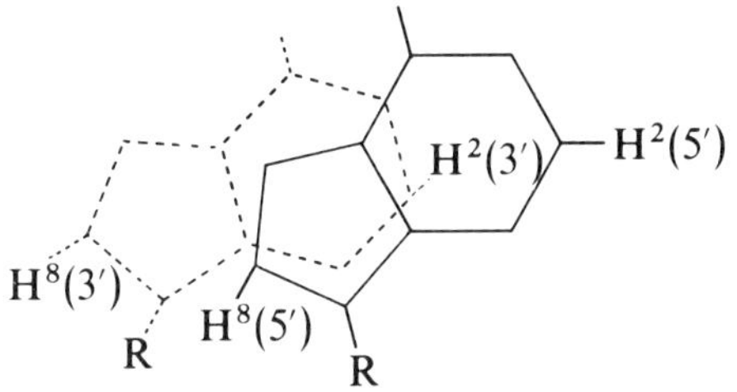

3'-Anti,5'-anti (I)

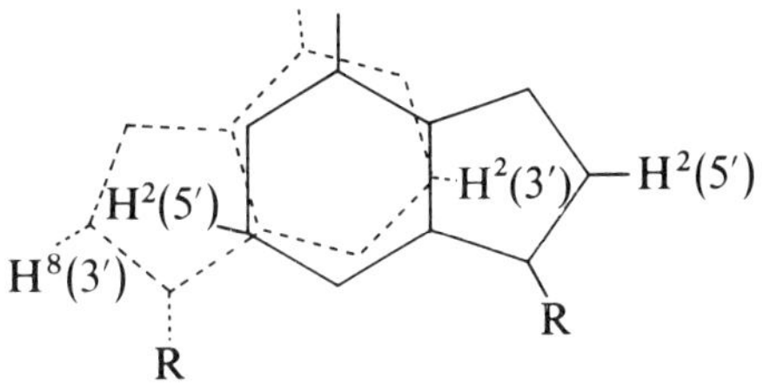

3'-Anti,5'-syn (II)

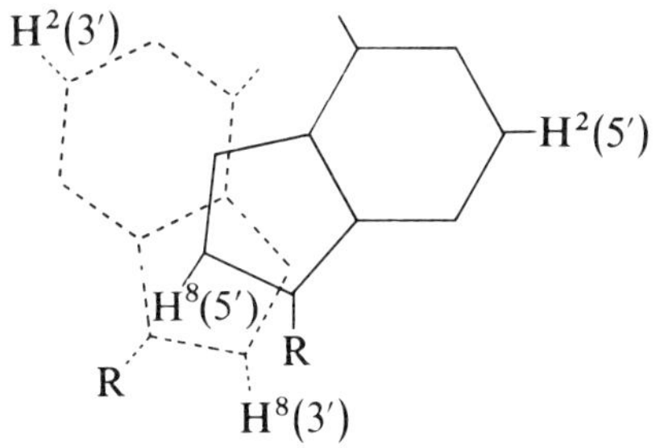

3'-Syn,5'-anti (III)

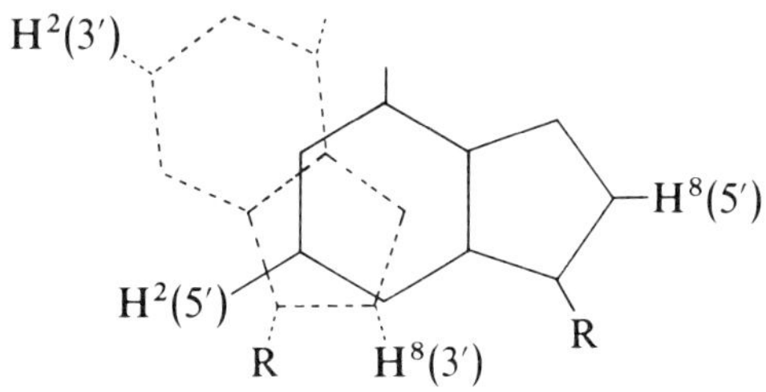

3'-Syn,5'-syn (IV)

NMR spectra of solutions of the stacked dinucleotide obtained at a series of increasing temperatures showed that as the stacking was thermally disrupted, the resonances exhibited by H at C(2) of the nucleotide joined at the 3' position and H at

† Chan, S. I., and Nelson, J. H. (1969) *J. Am. Chem. Soc.* **91**, 168–183.

C(8) of the nucleotide joined at the 5' position were shifted downfield. A shift downfield is associated with a decrease in the electron density of the environment of the atom concerned. In only one of the stacked conformations shown above would the environments of *both* of these hydrogen atoms decrease in electron density as the stacking was disrupted and the planar surfaces of the adenine rings became more widely separated; therefore it was concluded that when the adenine moieties are vertically stacked, the preferred conformation of the adenylyl-(3' → 5')-adenosine molecule is the 3'-*anti*, 5'-*anti* form. Since this is precisely the conformation that exists in the nucleic acid helixes, it appears that base stacking is facilitated by the structural characteristics of these macromolecules.

Purine moieties have a greater tendency to undergo base stacking than pyrimidine moieties. One possible explanation of this observation is that the pi-electron polarizability of the purine ring is greater than that of the pyrimidine ring.

Both quantum-mechanical and semiempirical calculations have been used to determine the magnitude of the influence of base stacking upon the stability of the helical structures of the nucleic acids. The values obtained for the interaction energies involved indicate that the DNA double helix is stabilized to the extent of 5 to 6 kcal/mol as a result of the vertical stacking of two neighboring purine-pyrimidine pairs.†

## Molecular-Weight Determinations on Nucleic Acids

Because of the size and other related characteristics of the larger nucleic acids, molecular-weight determinations on these macromolecules are often carried out by different means than those generally used for smaller macromolecules. For example, one common method for determining the molecular weight of a protein is the sedimentation velocity procedure, in which the sedimentation data are used in conjunction with the diffusion coefficient for the macromolecule. However, in larger DNA macromolecules the diffusion coefficients are extremely small and inordinately difficult to determine with any degree of accuracy; for this reason methods other than this ultracentrifugal procedure are generally used, e.g., autoradiography, light scattering, and procedures involving ultracentrifugal studies carried out in the presence of a density gradient or in conjunction with viscosity measurements.

**Approximation of molecular weight from molecular length** Reasonably accurate values for the molecular weights of nucleic acids can be derived from a knowledge of the contour lengths of the macromolecules. This method requires a value for the linear density of the nucleic acid. In bihelical DNA molecules a linear density of approximately $2 \times 10^6$ daltons/$\mu$m is usually assumed. (The dalton is a unit of mass equivalent to one-twelfth the mass of the carbon atom.) When the contour length is determined by electron microscopy, an enlarged electron micrograph is obtained and the necessary measurements are generally performed using a map ruler.

The lengths of nucleic acid molecules can also be determined by contact autoradiography. When this procedure is to be used, the nucleic acid molecules are uni-

---

† Rein, R., Goel, N. S., Fukuda, N., Pollak, M., and Claverie, P. (1969) *Ann. N.Y. Acad. Sci.* **153**, 805–814.

formly labeled with tritium by extensive incorporation of [³H]thymine during their biosynthesis. The labeled sample of the nucleic acid is then spread upon a microscope slide and overlaid with autoradiographic stripping film. After a suitable period of exposure to the tritium radiation, the film is developed and the lengths of the nucleic acid molecules are determined from the images on the developed film.

**Determination of molecular weight by light scattering** Light scattering can be used to determine molecular weights of macromolecules, a procedure based upon the following principles. When a beam of light impinges upon a solution, the alternating electric fields associated with the beam induce oscillating dipole moments in the molecules of the solution. These oscillating dipole moments become secondary sources of radiation, which are seen as the scattering of the primary, or incident, beam. The amplitude of a scattered beam depends in part upon the polarizability of the molecules of the solution responsible for the scattering. The intensity of the scattered radiation, in turn, is a function of the square of its amplitude. If the molecules of the solution are isotropic, and if their dimensions are less than one-twentieth the wavelength of the incident light, the relationship between the intensity of the scattered beam and that of the incident beam can be expressed by

$$\frac{i}{I_0} = \frac{16\pi^4 \alpha^2 \sin^2 \phi}{r^2 \lambda^4} \quad (6\text{-}2)$$

where $i$ = the intensity of scattered beam
$I_0$ = intensity of incident beam
$\alpha$ = molecular polarizability of scattering species
$\phi$ = angle between direction of polarization of scattering species (direction of electric vector of isotropic molecule) and direction of electric field generated by oscillating dipole
$r$ = distance between dipole of scattering species and induced oscillating dipole
$\lambda$ = wavelength of incident beam

From Eq. (6-2) it is seen that the intensity of the scattered beam is directly dependent upon the polarizability of the scattering species and also dependent upon the angle $\phi$. When $\phi$ is 0, there is no scattered radiation; i.e., there is no scattered radiation in the direction of the electric vector of the scattering species. On the other hand, when $\phi$ is 90°, the intensity of the scattered radiation is maximal. Equation (6-2) also indicates that the intensity of the scattered radiation is inversely proportional to the fourth power of the wavelength of the incident light and inversely proportional to $r^2$. The latter is a characteristic of radiation from any point source. (If the dimensions of a macromolecule are less than one-twentieth the wavelength of the incident light, the species can be considered a point source of radiation.) When the incident light is plane-polarized, the distribution of the intensity of the light scattered by a macromolecule that behaves like a point source is as shown in Fig. 6-6a. When nonpolarized light is used, as is usually the case, this distribution resembles a

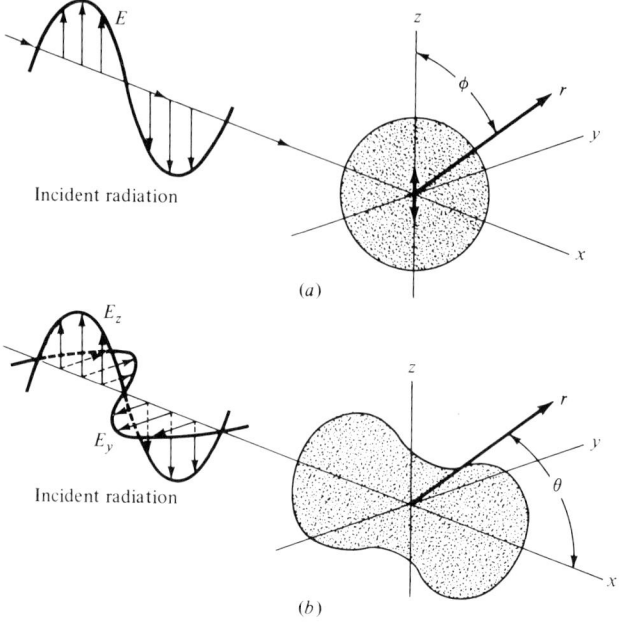

**Figure 6-6** Distribution of intensity of scattering when incident light is polarized in the $z$ direction (a) and when the incident light is nonpolarized (b).

dumbbell (Fig. 6-6b). The equation describing the scattering of nonpolarized radiation as a function of the intensity of the incident beam is

$$\frac{i}{I_0} = \frac{8\pi^4 \alpha^2 (1 + \cos^2 \theta)}{r^2 \lambda^4} \tag{6-3}$$

where $\theta$ is the angle between the incident beam and the direction in which the observation is being made.

Equation (6-3) can be made more useful if the polarizability $\alpha$ is replaced by a function of the refractive index of the solution. The basis for this replacement is the approximation

$$\alpha \approx \frac{(n - n_1)(n + n_1)}{4\pi N'} \tag{6-4}$$

which expresses the relationship between $\alpha$, which in this case is the excess polarizability of a solute molecule compared with a solvent molecule of the solution, and the product of the difference and the sum of the refractive index of the sulution $n$ and the solvent $n_1$. $N'$ is the number of solute particles per cubic centimeter. If the assumption is made that the solution is quite dilute, one can substitute $dn/dc_2$ for $(n - n_1)/c_2$ and $M/N$ for $c_2/N'$, where $M$ is the molecular weight of the scattering species, $N$ is Avogadro's number, and $c_2$ is the concentration of the scattering particle in grams per cubic centimeter. If it is further assumed that the dilute solution $n + n_1 \approx 2n_1$, then Eq. (6-4) can be converted into

$$\alpha \approx \frac{n_1 M \, dn/dc_2}{2\pi N} \tag{6-5}$$

Substituting Eq. (6-5) appropriately in Eq. (6-3) gives

$$\frac{i}{I_0} = \frac{2\pi^2 n_1^2 (dn/dc_2)^2 M^2 (1 + \cos^2 \theta)}{\lambda^4 r^2 N^2} \tag{6-6a}$$

This expression, in fact, relates to the intensity of scattering from a single solute particle. If there are $N'$ such particles per cubic centimeter the equation assumes the form

$$\frac{i_\theta}{I_0} = \frac{2\pi^2 n_1^2 (dn/dc_2)^2 M c_2 (1 + \cos^2 \theta)}{\lambda^4 r^2 N} \tag{6-6b}$$

where $i_\theta$ is the intensity of the scattering when the concentration of the scattering species is given by $c_2$ and the angle between the direction of the incident beam and the direction of observation is given by $\theta$. This rather complex expression can be simplified by using the *Rayleigh ratio* $R_\theta$. The definitive equation in this case is

$$R_\theta = \frac{i_\theta}{I_0} \frac{r^2}{1 + \cos^2 \theta} \tag{6-7}$$

If a factor $K$ is defined as

$$K = \frac{2\pi^2 n_1^2 (dn/dc_2)^2}{\lambda^4 N} \tag{6-8}$$

and both $R_\theta$ and $K$ are substituted in Eq. (6-6b), one obtains the very simple relationship

$$\frac{Kc_2}{R_\theta} = \frac{1}{M} \tag{6-9a}$$

When the solution does not behave like an ideal solution, Eq. (6-9a) is modified to include a second virial coefficient $B$:

$$\frac{Kc_2}{R_\theta} = \frac{1}{M} + 2Bc_2 + \cdots \tag{6-9b}$$

The molecular weight of the scattering species can be obtained in either case by plotting $Kc_2/R_\theta$ as a function of $c_2$. The $y$ intercept is $1/M$. If the solute is heterogeneous, one obtains a weight-average molecular weight.

So far it has been assumed that the dimensions of the scattering species are less than one-twentieth the wavelength of the incident beam, but many nucleic acid macromolecules do not fall in this category. When the incident light beam falls upon a solution of these larger macromolecules, some of the scattered light suffers destructive interference. Light that is scattered in the forward direction, when $\theta = 0$, is not

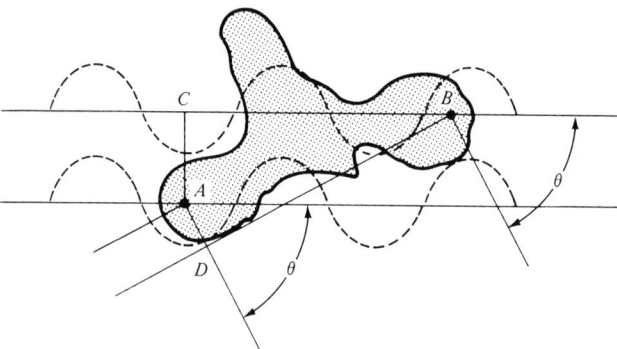

**Figure 6-7** Scattering from a macromolecule with dimensions greater than one-twentieth the wavelength of the incident beam. Scattering considered is that specifically from $A$ and $B$. The path difference $\Delta\lambda$ between two scattered beams is a function of $\theta$. In the 45° forward direction, $\Delta\lambda = CB - AD$ while in the 135° backward direction $\Delta\lambda = CB - BD$.

subject to this destructive interference, but as $\theta$ increases, the destructive interference increases, reaching a maximum when $\theta = 180°$ (see Fig. 6-7).

The fractional decrease in the intensity of the scattered light due to destructive interference is described in terms of the particle scattering function $P(\theta)$. Values for $P(\theta)$ depend upon the observation angle $\theta$, the size of the macromolecule compared with the wavelength of the incident light in solution $\lambda_0$, and the shape of the macromolecule. When the shape of the macromolecule is characterized by one or two major dimensions, relatively simple equations† express the relationship between $P(\theta)$ and $\theta$. These equations have been used to prepare tables of $P(\theta)$ values. The molecu-

† When the shape of the molecule is that of a rigid rod of length $D$,

$$P(\theta) = \frac{1}{x}\int_0^{2x} \frac{\sin u}{u}\, du - \left(\frac{\sin x}{x}\right)^2$$

in which $\int [(\sin u)/u\, du]$ is the integral sine, which can be found in tables of functions, and

$$x = \frac{2\pi D}{\lambda_0} \sin \frac{\theta}{2}$$

When the shape of the macromolecule is that of a linear random coil with the root-mean-square distance between the ends given by $D$,

$$P(\theta) = \frac{2}{\mu^2}[e^{-\mu} - (1 - \mu)]$$

in which

$$\mu = \frac{2x^2}{3} \quad \text{and} \quad x = \frac{2\pi D}{\lambda_0} \sin \frac{\theta}{2}$$

and therefore

$$\mu = \frac{8}{3}\pi^2 \frac{D^2}{(\lambda_0)^2} \sin^2 \frac{\theta}{2}$$

See Beattie, W. H., and Booth, C. (1960) *J. Phys. Chem.* **64**, 696–697.

lar weight of the large macromolecule is then calculated using the following modification of Eq. (6-9a):

$$\frac{Kc_2}{R_\theta} = \frac{1}{P(\theta)}\left(\frac{1}{M} + 2Bc_2\right) \tag{6-9c}$$

The molecular weight of a large macromolecule can also be determined without knowing or assuming its shape. As one approaches the limit of zero solute concentration and also the limit as $\theta$ approaches zero, the equation†

$$\frac{Kc_2}{R_\theta} = \left[1 + \frac{16\pi^2 \sin^2(\theta/2)R_g^2}{3\lambda^2}\right]\left(\frac{1}{M} + 2Bc_2\right) \tag{6-9d}$$

becomes increasingly valid. The factor $R_g$ is the radius of gyration of the macromolecule, defined as the root mean square of the distances of atoms from the center of gravity of the molecule, each distance being modified by a coefficient equal to the atomic number $Z$ of the atom.

Before using Eq. (6-9d) to calculate the molecular weight of a large macromolecule one must extrapolate $Kc_2/R_\theta$ to its value at $c_2 = 0$ and $\theta = 0$. This can be accomplished with a Zimm plot. According to this procedure, introduced by Bruno Zimm at the University of California, Berkeley, a graph of $c_2/R_\theta$ as a function of $\sin^2(\theta/2) + Xc_2$ is prepared ($X$ is a scaling constant). To prepare such a plot one determines $R_\theta$ for a given concentration of the macromolecule for a given value for $\theta$. The point that corresponds to $c_2/R_\theta$ on the ordinate and $\sin^2(\theta/2) + Xc_2$ on the abscissa is then designated. The process is then repeated using the same concentration of the macromolecule but different values for $\theta$. Next, a series of experiments is conducted in which the concentration of the macromolecule is the variable. If the points corresponding to a given concentration are connected and those corresponding to a given value for $\theta$ are connected, a grid like that shown in Fig. 6-8 is generated. Using this grid, or Zimm plot, one can derive extrapolated values $Kc_2/R_\theta$ at $c_2 = 0$ and at $\theta = 0$. Since the equation for the line representing $\theta = 0$ is

$$\frac{Kc_2}{R} = 2Bc_2 + \frac{1}{M} \tag{6-9e}$$

one can evaluate $M$ from the intercept of the line and $B$, the virial coefficient, from the slope of the line. On the other hand, the equation for the line respresenting $c = 0$ is

$$\frac{Kc_2}{R_\theta} = \left[1 + \frac{16\pi^2 \sin^2(\theta/2)R_g^2}{3\lambda^2}\right]\frac{1}{M} \tag{6-9f}$$

Its intercept allows a redetermination of the value for $M$, and the radius of gyration of the macromolecule can be derived from its slope.

---

† For a derivation of Eq. (6-9d) see Zimm, B. H., and Stockmayer, W. H. (1949) *J. Chem. Phys.* **17**, 1301–1314.

**Determination of molecular weights by sedimentation equilibrium in the presence of a density gradient** If a very concentrated salt solution, such as 7 $M$ CsCl or saturated $Cs_2SO_4$, is centrifuged until sedimentation equilibrium is achieved, a continuous, stable, linear gradient of the solute molecules will be established. If this concentrated salt solution contained a relatively small amount of another component, such as a nucleic acid, at sedimentation equilibrium the nucleic acid molecules would be found in a band centered at a point in the density gradient that corresponds to the buoyant density of this macromolecule. The equation that expresses the relationship between the molecular weight of the macromolecule and the parameters involved in the density-gradient sedimentation experiment is

$$M = - \frac{RT \, dc_2/dr}{\omega^2 c_2 r \bar{v}_2 (r - r_0) \, d\rho_1/dr} \qquad (6\text{-}10)$$

where $c_2$ = concentration of the macromolecule
$r$ = distance between center of rotation and a given point in the band
$r_0$ = distance between center of rotation and the midpoint of the band
$\omega$ = angular velocity of the centrifuge rotor
$\bar{v}_2$ = partial specific volume of macromolecule
$\rho_1$ = density of solvent

This equation is similar to that which expresses the relationship between the molecular weight of a macromolecule and the parameters involved in the usual sedimentation equilibrium study [see Eq. (5-25)]. If it is assumed that $r$ is very near

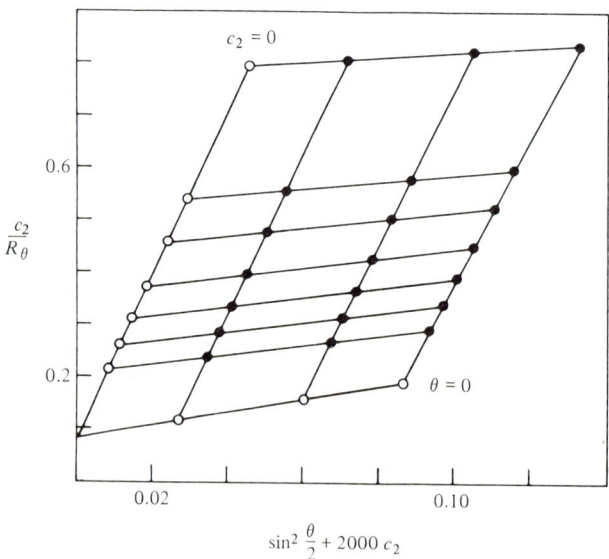

**Figure 6-8** Zimm plot derived from data on DNA from a phage (T7). In calculations a value of $4.61 \times 10^{-7}$ was used for $K$, the optical constant, and a molecular weight of $22.8 \times 10^6$ was obtained. [*From Harpst, J. A., Krasna, A. I., and Zimm, B. H. (1968) Biopolymers* **6**, *595–603. With permission.*]

$r_0$ (and, therefore, $r \approx r_0$) and if one substitutes $\frac{1}{2}d(r - r_0)^2$ for $(r - r_0)\,dr$ then Eq. (6-10) can be approximated as

$$M \approx -\frac{2RT\,d(\ln c_2)}{\omega^2 r_0 \bar{v}_2\,d(r - r_0)^2\,d\rho_1/dr} \qquad (6\text{-}11a)$$

which, following integration, becomes

$$M \approx -\frac{2RT \ln (c_2{}^r/c_2{}^{r_0})}{\omega^2 r_0 \bar{v}_2 (r - r_0)^2 d\rho_1/dr} \qquad (6\text{-}11b)$$

According to this equation, the half-width of the band is inversely proportional to the square root of the molecular weight of the macromolecule, and, in fact, the molecular weight can be calculated using this expression and appropriate values for the constants involved.

It must also be mentioned that density-gradient sedimentation equilibrium is useful as a tool to discriminate among macromolecules that have different densities. In the classic experiments which demonstrated that DNA replication entails each strand of the duplex serving as a template for a complementary strand, Meselson, Stahl, and Vinograd[†] used density-gradient sedimentation equilibrium to distinguish beetween DNA molecules which contained $^{14}N$ and those which contained $^{15}N$.

## Absorption Characteristics of Nucleic Acids

As a result of the presence of the purine and pyrimidine nucleotidyl units the nucleic acids exhibit characteristic absorption spectra in the ultraviolet region. However, if the ultraviolet absorption spectrum of a nucleic acid is obtained and compared with that of its component nucleotides, the absorption due to the macromolecule will be significantly less than that due to the corresponding individual monomeric units (Fig. 6-9). This behavior is known as *hypochromism*.

**Hypochromism** The basis for hypochromism has been formulated as follows.[‡] As a result of the interaction of light with a chromophore, electric-dipole transition moments are induced in the latter. The electric-dipole transition moment of one chromophore can interact with transition moments of higher transitions in other nearby chromophores. These interactions are considered to be essentially coulombic. The total effect of these coulombic interactions is zero when the chromophores are randomly oriented with respect to each other, but when the chromophores are oriented in certain orderly arrangements, e.g., a helical structure, the total effect of the interactions is no longer zero. Instead these coulombic interactions result in a decrease in the electric-dipole transition moments associated with the longer-wavelength absorption band of the molecule (and a corresponding increase in the electric-dipole transition moments associated with absorption bands at shorter wavelengths).

[†] Meselson, M., Stahl, F. W., and Vinograd, J. (1957) *Proc. Natl. Acad. Sci. U.S.A.* **43**, 581–588.
[‡] Tinoco, I., Jr. (1960) *J. Am. Chem. Soc.* **82**, 4785–4790; Rhodes, W. (1961) *J. Am. Chem. Soc.* **83**, 3609–3617; DeVoe, H. (1969) *Ann. N.Y. Acad. Sci.* **158**, 298–307.

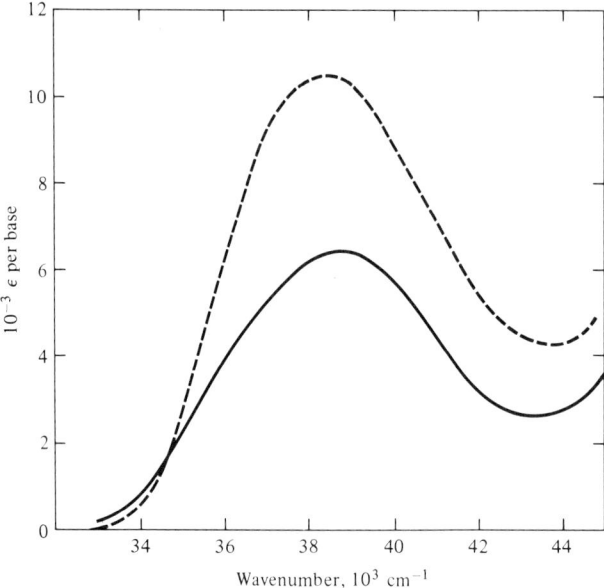

**Figure 6-9** Near ultraviolet absorption band of helical DNA (——) from bovine thymus and its constituent purine and pyrimidine nucleosides (- - -). [*From DeVoe, H. (1969) Ann. N.Y. Acad. Sci.* **158**, *298–307 (see p. 299). With permission.*]

Because the intensity of absorption is directly related to the square of the associated electric-dipole transition moments, the longer-wavelength absorption band exhibits hypochromism. (If the absorption in the region of the shorter-wavelength bands were observed, a *hyperchromic effect* would be seen.)

The absorption spectra of the nucleic acids exhibit pronounced hypochromism in the region of the 260-nm maximum. Because the extent of this hypochromism is directly related to the extent to which ordered, helical structures are present, changes in the absorption at 260 nm (or thereabouts) have been used to monitor the helix-coil transitions of the nucleic acids. The transition from the helix form to the random-coil form is referred to as *melting*, and when this transition is induced by an increase in temperature, the process is called *thermal melting*. If the absorption at 260 nm is plotted as a function of temperature, a characteristic transition curve is obtained. The midpoint of this transition curve is denoted by $T_m$. At $T_m$ the value for $\Delta G_{tr}$ (the difference between the free energy of the helix and that of the coil) is zero.

The value for $T_m$ is a characteristic of a given nucleic acid. Since guanine-cytosine base pairing stabilizes the helical structure of a nucleic acid to a greater extent than adenine-thymine (or uracil) base pairing, the value for $T_m$ is directly related to the proportion of guanine-cytosine base pairs present in the macromolecule. $T_m$ for a polynucleotide composed exclusively of guanylyl and cytidylyl units is approximately 40°C above that for a polynucleotide composed exclusively of adenylyl and thymidylyl units.

The thermal melting of a native nucleic acid macromolecule usually occurs over a range of several degrees rather than at a precise temperature. It has been suggested that this is because the observed melting is actually the resultant of numerous series of helix-coil transitions taking place in various regions of different base composition throughout the macromolecule. The helix-coil transitions of a given series are envisaged as proceeding sequentially, like a zipper. The higher temperature at which the absorption levels off is that at which the macromolecule is completely "unzipped." Following disruption of the helical structure, the strands of the duplex molecules separate. For this reason the curve depicting the helix-coil transition and that depicting the corresponding coil-helix transition are not superimposable, but if the nucleic acid is chemically modified by being cross-linked, the thermal melting is reversible and the curves for helix-coil and coil-helix transitions are superimposable.

## Mutagenesis

The nucleic acids are readily susceptive to modification by both chemical and physical agents. In some instances these modifications prevent the nucleic acid from performing its biochemical function in the transfer of genetic information. As will be discussed in some detail (Chaps. 13 and 14), the performance of this biochemical function involves both the primary structure and the base pairing of the nucleic acids. Altering the primary structure and the base pairing of a nucleic acid, which results in an alteration in the genetic information transferred, is known as *mutagenesis*. The alteration process is referred to as *mutation*, and the resultant progeny, which may be characterized by a visible alteration in phenotype, is called a *mutant*.

The action of chemical agents upon the nucleic acids can result in mutagenic transformations such as the conversion of cytosine moieties into uracil moieties. (Alternatively, the action of chemical agents can result in transformations that render the product unable to participate in base pairing, but in this case the transformations are referred to as inactivating rather than mutagenic.) Ionizing radiation can produce breaks in the strands of the nucleic acid macromolecule, and these breaks, in turn, can result in several types of macrolesions, including deletions, duplications, and rearrangements. Ultraviolet light, on the other hand, induces base-pair substitutions and frameshift mutations. Frameshift mutations result from the addition or deletion of a small number of nucleotide units.

**Chemical mutagens** Nitrous acid was one of the first chemical agents recognized as mutagenic. As a result of deamination by nitrous acid, cytosine moieties are converted into uracil moieties and adenine moieties are converted into hypoxanthine moieties. The cytosine-uracil conversion is designated as a GC → AT transition and the adenine to hypoxanthine conversion is designated as an AT → GC transition, since uracil resembles thymine and hypoxanthine resembles guanine in base-pairing properties. The deamination of guanine moieties is thought to be inactivating rather than mutagenic because xanthine appears unable to enter into base-pairing reactions.

Hydroxylamine is also a chemical mutagen. Although this reagent can react with each of the pyrimidine moieties of the nucleic acids, only the reaction involving cytosine appears to be of significance. The mutagenic action of hydroxylamine is thought to result from the hydroxylation of $N^4$ of cytosine [or that of $N^4$ of 5-hydroxymethylcytosine, in the case of certain bacteriophages in which the DNA contains this moiety rather than cytosine]. The $N^4$-hydroxy compounds exist predominantly in the imino form rather than the amino form and hence resemble uracil or thymine with respect to base-pairing properties. Thus, hydroxylamine induces GC → AT transitions.

Certain alkylating agents are also mutagenic. The principal reaction upon treating a sample of a nucleic acid with an alkylating agent such as dimethyl sulfate or methyl methanesulfonate or the nitrogen mustards is alkylation at N(7) of the guanine moieties. Secondary sites of alkylation include N(1), N(3), and N(7) of the adenine moieties and also N(3) of the cytosine moieties. Although schemes involving transitional mispairings can be formulated, the precise nature of the mutagenic action of alkylating agents is not understood.

A chemical mutagen which acts primarily on replicating DNA is 1-methyl-3-nitro-1-nitrosoguanidine.

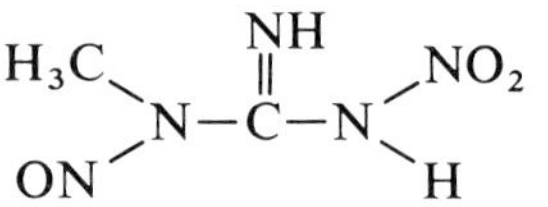

1-Methyl-3-nitro-1-nitrosoguanidine

Although this reagent is an alkylating agent, it does not exhibit the same chemical reactivity as the alkylating agents mentioned above. For example, nitrosoguanidine reacts much more readily with a guanine moiety of a polynucleotide or a nucleic acid than with that of guanylic acid, in contrast to the behavior of the typical alkylating agents. For this reason it has been suggested that the nitrosoguanidine becomes intercalated between the stacked purine and pyrimidine bases before the transfer of the methyl group. However, notwithstanding the fact that polynucleotides and nucleic acids are methylated by 1-methyl-3-nitro-1-nitrosoguanidine, it appears that methylation is not the primary reaction involved in the mutagenesis induced by this reagent.

Proflavin and certain other aminoacridines are mutagenic.

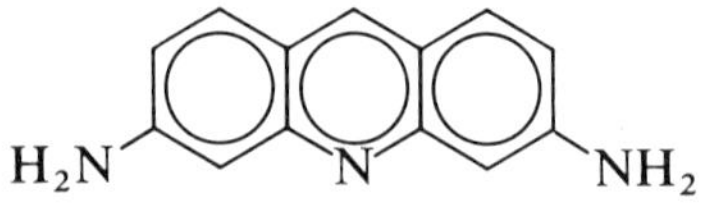

Proflavin

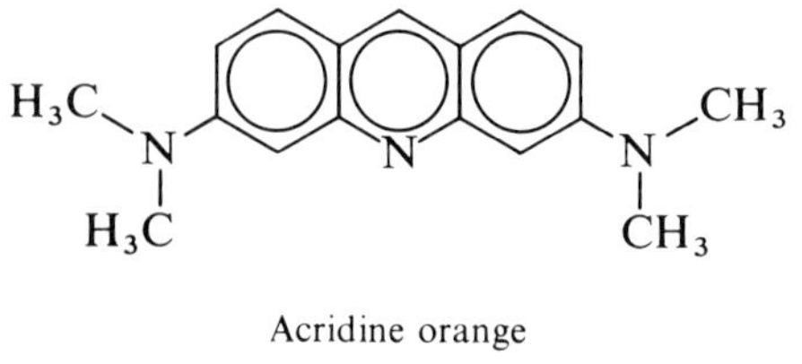

Acridine orange

The basis of the mutagenic effect of these compounds is thought to be their ability to become intercalated between the purine and pyrimidine bases so that it is as if nucleotidyl units have been deleted from the polymeric chain or added to it.

**Radiation-induced mutagenesis** Ionizing radiation can induce two types of mutagenic effects, referred to as *intragenic* mutations and *intergenic* mutations. Intragenic mutations are thought to result from a single encounter, i.e., a single ionization or cluster of ionizations within or near the gene, resulting in a single strand break in the nucleic acid. The yield of intragenic mutations increases linearly with the radiation dose, as would be expected if a single encounter were involved. Intergenic mutations, on the other hand, are thought to result from the cleavage of chromosomes and the subsequent rejoining of the pieces to yield a new arrangement. In this case, more than one encounter and more than one break has occurred. The yield of intergenic mutations is essentially proportional to the square of the radiation dose.

In the living organism when a chromosome is severed or develops a lesion as a result of ionizing radiation, the break or lesion can be enzymatically repaired to yield the original chromosome. This process is known as *restitution*. Alternatively, when there are two or more breaks or lesions, there can be a rejoining to yield a new arrangement. This process is called *exchange*. Exchange and unrepaired lesions or breaks produce detectable chromosomal aberrations. (The enzymatic joining of breaks and lesions in nucleic acid molecules is discussed in conjunction with other aspects of nucleic acid metabolism in Chap. 13.) Observed mutation rates depend upon the rate of the primary event (or events), the probability of restitution, and the probability that in the absence of restitution a recognizably altered phenotype will result.

Ultraviolet radiation can induce both base-pair substitutions (primarily GC → AT transitions) and frameshift mutations. The base-pair substitutions are believed to result from the formation of cytosine photohydrates which undergo base pairing differently from cytosine. The loss of the 5,6 double bond of cytosine is accompanied by an increase in the $pK_a$ of the amino group such that the probability of the reduced cytosine existing as a protonated species is 1 in 20, compared with a probability of 1 in 2000 for the parent compound. It is thought that this increased basicity permits the altered base pairing.

The frameshift mutations induced by ultraviolet irradiation are thought to result from the formation of cis-syn dimers involving adjacent pyrimidine moieties of the nucleic acid strand. The presence of these pyrimidine dimers interferes with the normal mode of replication and information transfer. Under most circumstances as the information is being "read" from the nucleic acid macromolecule, it is as if the dimerized pyrimidines had been deleted from the strand.

As with lesions resulting from ionizing radiation, the damage resulting from ultraviolet radiation can be enzymatically repaired. In *E. coli* three such repair processes have been characterized, *photoreactivation, excision repair,* and *postreplication repair*.

Photoreactivation requires, in addition to an enzyme system, long-wavelength ultraviolet or short-wavelength visible light (having a wavelength in the vicinity of 330 nm). The enzyme system of the photoreactivation process is quite specific for the cis-syn pyrimidine dimers of DNA molecules. The result of the photoreactivation process is the monomerization of the pyrimidine dimers and the regeneration of the native DNA macromolecule.

Excision repair, in contrast to photoreactivation, can occur in the absence of light and is a process whereby the pyrimidine dimers (and other structural defects) are excised from the nucleic acid molecule, presumably by two single-strand breaks which release the defect plus a small number of nucleotide units on either side of it. The missing nucleotide units are then synthesized by an enzymatic process similar to that by which normal nucleic acid biosynthesis occurs, and the new segment is enzymatically joined to the remainder of the macromolecule.

Postreplication repair mends discontinuities that can occur in first-generation daughter strands when the parent DNA molecule has been irradiated with ultraviolet light. The discontinuities in the daughter strands are thought to correspond to sites in the parent molecule where there were pyrimidine dimers which were not excised and replaced.

CHAPTER
# SEVEN

## SOME THERMODYNAMIC ASPECTS OF BIOCHEMICAL SYSTEMS: BIOENERGETICS

Thermodynamics is the study of the observable macroscopic behavior of systems and their interactions with their surroundings. Thermodynamic parameters characterize a system in terms of its macroscopic coordinates. *Intensive* parameters are those which are independent of the size of the system, e.g., pressure or concentration. *Extensive* parameters are those which are dependent upon the size of the system and the amounts of the components present, e.g., volume and mass. A system is in a state of *thermodynamic equilibrium* if its intensive parameters are invariant with respect to time and if no differences in any potentials exist either in its interior or at its boundaries with the surroundings. Thermodynamic equilibrium is characterized by maximum stability.

## FREE-ENERGY CHANGES AND EQUILIBRIUM CONSTANTS

Consider the general reaction

$$a\text{A} + b\text{B} \rightleftharpoons c\text{C} + d\text{D} \tag{7-1}$$

The relative stability of the products with respect to the reactants is indicated by the free-energy change that accompanies the process. When this free-energy change $\Delta G$ is large and negative, the reaction proceeds to the right virtually to completion and useful chemical energy can be derived as a result of the conversion. When the free-energy change is positive, the reaction has less tendency to proceed to the right than to the left, and when the free-energy change is zero, the reaction has no tendency to proceed in either direction since the system is at thermodynamic equilibrium.

The free-energy change that accompanies a reaction can be expressed in terms of the chemical potentials of the components of the system since chemical potential is, in fact, partial molal free energy. Thus, one can write

$$\Delta G = (c\mu_c + d\mu_d) - (a\mu_a + b\mu_b) \tag{7-2}$$

where $\mu$ is the chemical potential of the reaction component denoted by the subscript. Chemical potential, in turn, is defined as

$$\mu = \mu° + RT \ln a \tag{7-3}$$

where $\mu°$ is the standard chemical potential (that of a component in solution at unit activity) and $a$ is the actual activity of the component in the system under study. Combining Eqs. (7-2) and (7-3) gives

$$\Delta G = [(c\mu_c° + RT \ln a_c) + (d\mu_d° + RT \ln a_d)]$$
$$- [(a\mu_a° + RT \ln a_a) + (b\mu_b° + RT \ln a_b)] \tag{7-4a}$$

or

$$\Delta G = (c\mu_c° + d\mu_d°) - (a\mu_a° + b\mu_b°) + RT \ln \frac{a_c a_d}{a_a a_b} \tag{7-4b}$$

Since the difference between the *standard* chemical potentials of the products and that of the reactants is the *standard-free-energy* change $\Delta G°$,

$$\Delta G = \Delta G° + RT \ln \frac{a_c a_d}{a_a a_b} \tag{7-5}$$

This is a general equation for the free-energy change that accompanies a reaction. In the special case where the components of the system are maintained at unit activities at a given temperature (usually 25°C), which means that the reaction is being conducted under standard conditions, the accompanying free-energy change is specifically the standard-free-energy change $\Delta G°$. The magnitude of the standard-free-energy change indicates the amount of chemical energy liberated or required when the reaction is conducted under standard conditions. The value for $\Delta G°$ is negative when the reaction proceeds spontaneously and positive when, under these conditions, the reaction is not spontaneous.

Another special case, with reference to Eq. (7-5), is that in which the reaction is at equilibrium. When a reaction is at equilibrium, $\Delta G = 0$. Therefore, Eq. (7-5) becomes

$$\Delta G° = -RT \ln \frac{a_c a_d}{a_a a_b} \tag{7-6a}$$

In addition, in this special case the quotient $a_c a_d / a_a a_b$ is, in fact, equivalent to the equilibrium constant for the reaction. Therefore, one can write

$$\Delta G° = -RT \ln K_{eq} \tag{7-6b}$$

The experimental determination of the equilibrium constant thus allows $\Delta G°$ to be evaluated.

With all reactants and products at unit activities standard conditions are quite remote from the conditions present in the cells and fluids of living organisms. For this reason, values for $\Delta G°$ are not the most useful as a reference parameter. One principal difference between standard conditions and those which prevail in most biochemical systems is that in the latter, hydrogen-ion activity is not unity. In fact, in a medium having a hydrogen-ion activity of unity the secondary structure of many proteins (including enzymes) and many nucleic acids would be destroyed. For this reason, biochemists frequently use as a reference $\Delta G^{\circ\prime}$, the standard-free-energy change when all components are at unit activity *with the exception of hydrogen ion*. When $\Delta G^{\circ\prime}$ is used, it should be accompanied by a notation of the hydrogen-ion activity (or concentration) used in determining this particular standard-free-energy change. Similarly, as above, $\Delta G^{\circ\prime}$ can be evaluated using

$$\Delta G^{\circ\prime} = -RT \ln \frac{a_c a_d}{a_a a_b} = -RT \ln K'_{eq} \qquad (7\text{-}7)$$

in which the activities are those present when the system is at *equilibrium* at the *specified pH*. The equilibrium constant in this case is denoted by $K'_{eq}$.

Since the evaluation of $\Delta G^{\circ\prime}$ entails determining the concentrations of the reactant species and the product species at the specified pH, when hydrogen ion is a *product* of the reaction, it is generally more convenient to use

$$\Delta G^{\circ\prime} = \Delta G^{\circ} + RT \ln [\text{H}^+]^n \qquad (7\text{-}8a)$$

which can also be written

$$\Delta G^{\circ\prime} = \Delta G^{\circ} - 2.3nRT \log \frac{1}{[\text{H}^+]} \qquad (7\text{-}8b)$$

or
$$\Delta G^{\circ\prime} = \Delta G^{\circ} - n(1364)\text{pH} \qquad (7\text{-}8c)$$

In Eq. (7-8c) the factor $2.3RT$ is evaluated on the basis of a temperature of 25°C (or 298 K) and $R = 1.98$ cal/mol. The factor $n$ is the number of moles of hydrogen ions liberated, as determined by the balanced equation. From these equations it is seen that when hydrogen ions are a product of the reaction, the associated standard-free-energy change becomes more *negative* as the pH of the reaction medium is increased. One could come to this conclusion on an intuitive basis since increasing the pH of the medium provides an increasingly favorable environment for a reaction in which protons are liberated. In effect, as one increases the pH one promotes the extent to which the reaction occurs by removing a product.

Conversely, when hydrogen ion is a *reactant*, the equation

$$\Delta G^{\circ\prime} = \Delta G^{\circ} + n(1364)\text{pH} \qquad (7\text{-}9)$$

pertains. Thus, $\Delta G^{\circ\prime}$ becomes more *positive* as the pH of the medium is increased when the proton is a reactant.

## Free-Energy Changes Involving Some Highly Reactive Biochemical Molecules

Metabolic processes often involve reactions that are unfavorable thermodynamically. This means that the given reaction will not proceed to a very great extent. This has no bearing on how *fast* the reaction occurs. The reaction rate is determined by the particular enzyme that catalyzes the process. When focusing upon thermodynamic considerations, however, one is concerned with whether 90 percent of the reactant molecules are converted into product as a result of the spontaneous process or only 5 percent. In some cases when a biochemical reaction is, of itself, thermodynamically unfavorable, this reaction is in effect combined with another that is quite favorable, with the result that the reactants of the unfavorable reaction are converted into the appropriate products with high efficiency. In these cases the thermodynamically favored process involves a highly reactive biochemical molecule. The most common molecule in this category is adenosine 5'-triphosphate (ATP). Inosine 5'-triphosphate (ITP) and guanosine 5'-triphosphate (GTP) function similarly in certain specific cases. These molecules are able to function as they do because in each instance their cleavage to yield the nucleoside diphosphate and orthophosphate (or in the case of ATP to yield the nucleoside monophosphate and pyrophosphate) is accompanied by the liberation of a large amount of chemical energy. In other words, in each instance the free-energy change associated with the cleavage is large and negative. Hence, if a reaction with a free-energy change of 4.7 kcal/mol were combined with another with a free-energy change of $-9.2$ kcal/mol, the free-energy change for the resulting process would be $-4.5$ kcal/mol. For the thermodynamically unfavorable reaction the ratio of products to reactants would be 0.00036 : 1 at chemical equilibrium, but in the combined system that ratio would be 1950 : 1. As an example of combining thermodynamically unfavorable and favorable reactions, consider the formation of the amide glutamine from the amino acid glutamate and ammonia. In general, one cannot form an amide from a carboxylic acid and ammonia (mixing a carboxylic acid and ammonia usually gives the ammonium salt of the acid), but in the presence of glutamate, ammonia, *and ATP* and with the appropriate enzyme (glutamine synthetase) to provide catalysis, glutamine is formed concomitantly with the cleavage of ATP to yield ADP and orthophosphate. In this case there is evidence which supports the transient formation of an enzyme-bound acyl phosphate involving the glutamate carboxyl group that is to undergo amidation. Such an acyl phosphate would then readily react with ammonia to yield the corresponding amide and orthophosphate, as depicted below.

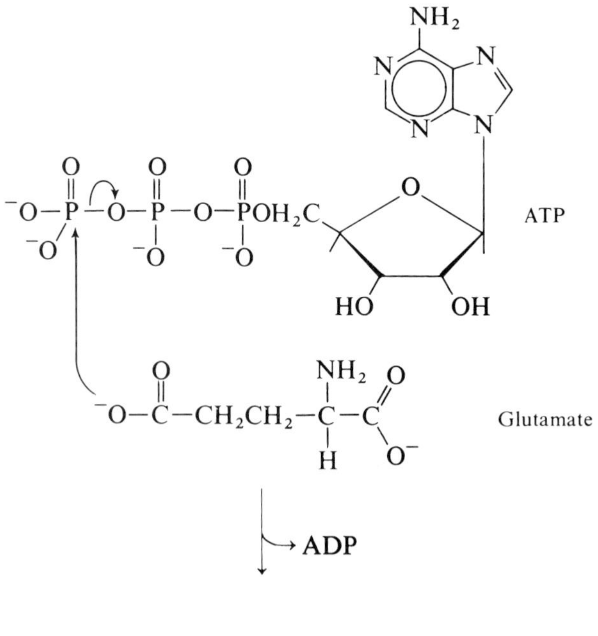

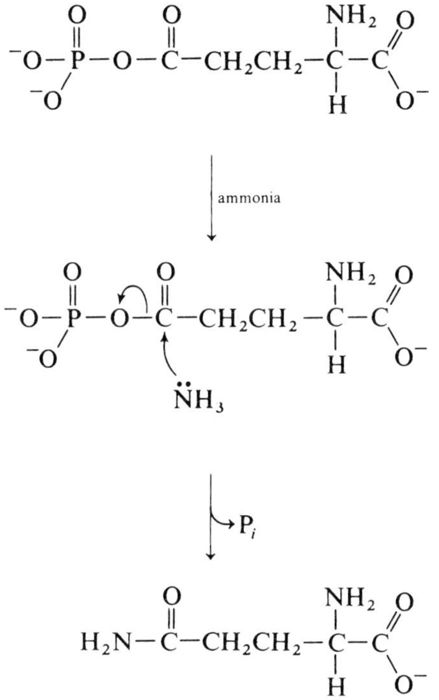

$$\text{}^-\text{O}-\overset{\overset{\text{O}}{\|}}{\underset{\underset{\text{O}^-}{|}}{\text{P}}}-\text{O}-\overset{\overset{\text{O}}{\|}}{\text{C}}-\text{CH}_2\text{CH}_2-\overset{\overset{\text{NH}_2}{|}}{\underset{\underset{\text{H}}{|}}{\text{C}}}-\text{C}\overset{\overset{\text{O}}{\diagup\!\!\!\diagdown}}{\underset{\text{O}^-}{}}$$

↓ ammonia

$$\text{}^-\text{O}-\overset{\overset{\text{O}}{\|}}{\underset{\underset{\text{O}^-}{|}}{\text{P}}}-\text{O}\overset{\frown}{-}\overset{\overset{\text{O}}{\|}}{\text{C}}-\text{CH}_2\text{CH}_2-\overset{\overset{\text{NH}_2}{|}}{\underset{\underset{\text{H}}{|}}{\text{C}}}-\text{C}\overset{\overset{\text{O}}{\diagup\!\!\!\diagdown}}{\underset{\text{O}^-}{}}$$

$$\ddot{\text{N}}\text{H}_3$$

↓ → $P_i$

$$\text{H}_2\text{N}-\overset{\overset{\text{O}}{\|}}{\text{C}}-\text{CH}_2\text{CH}_2-\overset{\overset{\text{NH}_2}{|}}{\underset{\underset{\text{H}}{|}}{\text{C}}}-\text{C}\overset{\overset{\text{O}}{\diagup\!\!\!\diagdown}}{\underset{\text{O}^-}{}} \quad \text{Glutamine}$$

In addition to the nucleoside triphosphates, like ATP, that participate in certain otherwise unfavorable processes, several other types of biochemical molecules are highly reactive and have important functions in metabolic processes, e.g., the thiol esters such as acetyl CoA and other acyl CoA molecules.

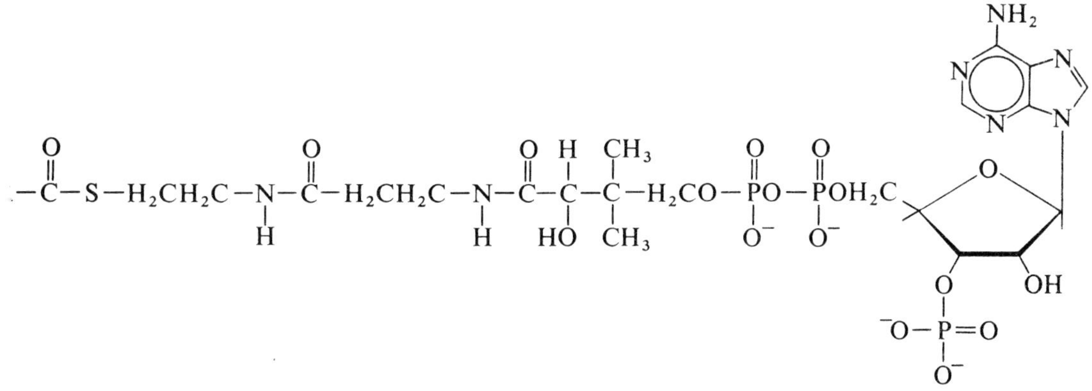

Acetyl CoA when R = $CH_3-$
An acyl-CoA when R = $C_2H_5-$, $C_3H_7-$, $C_4H_9-$, or some other saturated or unsaturated alkyl moiety

Thiol esters are reactive molecules because their cleavage to yield the carboxylic acid plus the thiol is also accompanied by the liberation of chemical energy. The liberation of chemical energy in this case is somewhat similar to the liberation of chemical energy when ATP undergoes cleavage. In each case the *products* that are formed are *more stable* than the reactant. When a thiol ester is cleaved in an aqueous medium at physiological pH, that is 7.5, a carboxylate anion and a mercaptan anion are the principal final products. These charged species are more stable in the aqueous medium than the parent ester; i.e., they exist at lower ground-state levels than the ester. In fact, the contribution made to the total free-energy change as a result of the formation of such anions is designated the *free energy of ionization* $\Delta G_i$ and calculated using

$$\Delta G_i = -2.3RT \log\left(1 + \frac{K_a}{[H^+]}\right) \tag{7-10a}$$

or

$$\Delta G_i = -1364 \log\left(1 + \frac{K_a}{[H^+]}\right) \tag{7-10b}$$

Here, $K_a$ is the dissociation constant for the ionizable functional group. The pH of the medium in which the ionization occurs is reflected by the value for $[H^+]$. It should be mentioned at this point that this formulation is based upon a standard state in which the concentration of the ionized plus the nonionized species is 1 M. When more than one ionization can occur, the effects are summed.

When ATP, which is itself ionizable, undergoes cleavage in an aqueous medium at physiological pH, again ionizable products are formed. In this case the products may be considered to be more stable than the reactant in view of the fact that the extent to which they ionize is greater than that to which the reactant ionizes. This is illustrated below, where the data are for the cleavage of ATP to yield ADP plus orthophosphate.

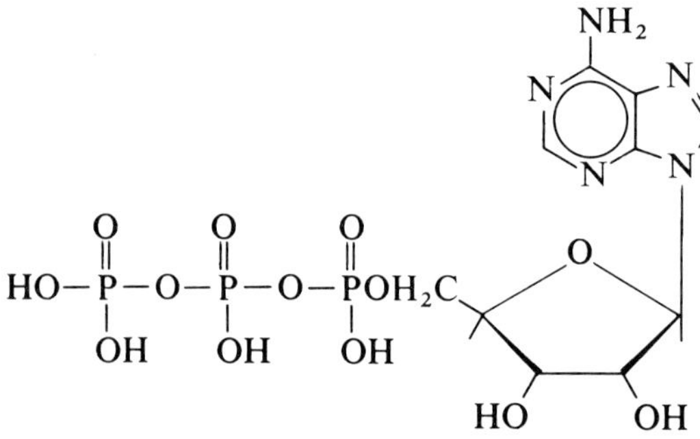

ATP
$pKa_1$ = small
$pKa_2$ = small
$pKa_3$ = 4.06
$pKa_4$ = 6.95

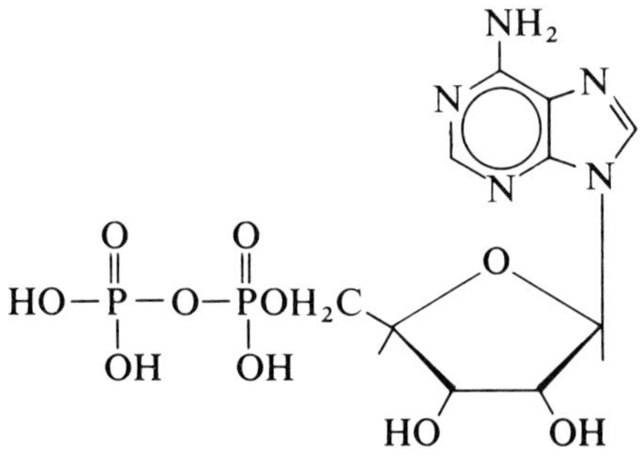

ADP
$pKa_1$ = small
$pKa_2$ = 3.95
$pKa_3$ = 6.88

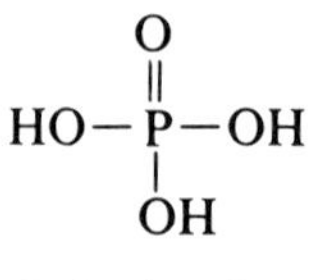

Orthophosphate
$pKa_1$ = 2.12
$pKa_2$ = 7.21
$pKa_3$ = 12.67

A similar situation pertains when ATP is cleaved to yield AMP and pyrophosphate.

Besides the effect of the formation of ionizable products in a polar medium, there is another basis for the inordinate reactivity of certain biochemical molecules. In some cases, the molecule can undergo a reaction yielding products that are stabilized by delocalization to a greater extent than the reactant. ATP falls in this category, as do the acyl phosphates. For ATP, cleavage to yield either ADP and orthophosphate or AMP and pyrophosphate yields products for which a greater number of canonical forms can be written than for ATP. Similarly, cleavage of an acyl phosphate yields a carboxylate anion plus orthophosphate, for which a greater number of canonical forms can be written than for the parent compound.

Yet another rationale offered to explain the ability of certain biochemical compounds to promote otherwise unfavorable reactions focuses upon the diminution of electrostatic repulsion that accompanies the cleavage of a specific bond of such a compound. This reasoning has also been applied to ATP and certain acyl phosphates. For ATP the distribution of charge among the atoms that constitute the triphosphate moiety has been calculated as shown.

One can see that the six atoms making up the backbone of this moiety, that is, P—O—P—O—P—O—, all bear a partial positive charge. These charges tend to repel each other. Furthermore, the three-dimensional structure of the triphosphate moiety shows that the appended oxygen atoms, *each* of which bears almost a full negative charge, are sufficiently close to each other to experience electrostatic repulsion. However, when the triphosphate moiety undergoes cleavage, electrostatic repulsion is diminished to some extent. Hence, the products of the cleavage are more stable than their precursor, the ATP molecule. A similar argument can be made for the acyl phosphate 3-phosphoglyceroyl phosphate, in which case cleavage to 3-phosphoglycerate and orthophosphate relieves the electrostatic repulsion experienced by the two phosphate groups in the parent compound.

In actuality, the large and negative free-energy values associated with the cleavage of nucleoside triphosphates and certain other biochemical molecules reflect a combination of the effects of product ionization, product stabilization due to delocalization, and amelioration of electrostatic repulsion in the products. Table 7-1 shows the free-energy changes which accompany the cleavage of some common highly reactive biochemical compounds that participate in metabolic reactions. Also included, for comparison, are several highly reactive compounds which generally do not participate in metabolic reactions but which will be familiar from organic chemistry.

**Table 7-1 Free-energy changes associated with the cleavage of highly reactive molecules**

|  | Conditions | $\Delta G^{\circ\prime}$, kcal/mol |
|---|---|---|
| Acetic anhydride |  | −21,800 |
| 2-Phosphoenolpyruvate |  | −14,800 |
| Aspartyl 4-phosphate | pH 8.0, 15°C | −13,000 |
| Acetylimidazole |  | −12,970 |
| Carbamoyl phosphate | pH 9.5 | −12,300 |
| 3-Phospho-D-glyceroyl phosphate |  | −11,800 |
| Acetyl phosphate |  | −10,300 |
| ATP (to yield AMP + $PP_i$) | pH 7.5, excess $Mg^{2+}$ | −10,300 |
| Phosphocreatine | 37°C | −10,300 |
| ATP (to yield ADP + $P_i$) | pH 7.4, 1 m$M$ $Mg^+$ | −8,800 |
| Pyrophosphate |  | −8,000 |
| Phosphoarginine | pH 8.0, excess $Mg^{2+}$ | −7,700 |
| Acetyl CoA |  | −7,520 |
| Uridine diphosphoglucose | pH 7.6 | −7,300 |
| Acetylcarnitine | 35°C | −7,200 |
| Acetylcholine |  | −6,000 |
| Glucose 1-phosphate |  | −5,000 |
| Ethyl acetate |  | −4,720 |
| Glucose 6-phosphate |  | −3,300 |
| Glycerol 1-phosphate |  | −2,200 |

*Source:* From Jencks, W. P. (1970) in *Handbook of Biochemistry* (Sober, H. A., ed.), 2d ed., p. J-181, Chemical Rubber Company, Cleveland.

## Calculation of Free-Energy Changes

Values for the free-energy changes that accompany chemical reactions must frequently be calculated indirectly. In fact, values for the free-energy changes that accompany the cleavage of ATP fall in this category because in this case the determination of the equilibrium constant is quite difficult. (Equilibrium is attained only in the presence of vanishingly small concentrations of ATP.) Also, with ATP these calculations are further complicated by the fact that in order to obtain biochemically meaningful values one must take into consideration the ionic equilibria involving the various magnesium complexes of ATP and its products since these are the actual participants in most enzymatic reactions. In the following paragraphs a calculation of the free-energy changes that accompany the hydrolytic cleavage of ATP under specified conditions is detailed as an example of how such determinations can be made.

This calculation of the free-energy change which accompanies the hydrolytic cleavage of ATP utilizes data derived from the ATP-dependent enzymatic formation of glutamine:†

$$\text{Glutamate} + \text{ammonia} + \text{ATP} \rightleftharpoons \text{glutamine} + \text{ADP} + P_i \quad (7\text{-}11)$$

† Rosing, J., and Slater, E. C. (1972) *Biochim. Biophys. Acta* **267**, 275–290.

The observed equilibrium constant is therefore

$$K_{obs,s} = \frac{[\text{Gln}][\text{ADP}][P_i]}{[\text{Glu}][\text{NH}_4^+][\text{ATP}]} \qquad (7\text{-}12)$$

The hydrolysis of glutamine can be represented as follows:

$$\text{Glutamine} + H_2O \rightleftharpoons \text{glutamate} + \text{ammonia} \qquad (7\text{-}13)$$

The observed equilibrium constant in this case is therefore

$$K_{obs,h} = \frac{[\text{Glu}][\text{NH}_4^+]}{[\text{Gln}]} \qquad (7\text{-}14)$$

It then follows that

$$K_{obs,s} K_{obs,h} = \frac{[\text{Gln}][\text{ADP}][P_i][\text{Glu}][\text{NH}_4^+]}{[\text{Glu}][\text{NH}_4^+][\text{ATP}][\text{Gln}]} \qquad (7\text{-}15a)$$

or, simplified,

$$K_{obs,s} K_{obs,h} = \frac{[\text{ADP}][P_i]}{[\text{ATP}]} \qquad (7\text{-}15b)$$

The term on the right in Eq. (7-15b) is, in fact, an expression of the equilibrium constant for the hydrolytic cleavage of ATP to yield ADP and orthophosphate, since this reaction can be written

$$\text{ATP} + H_2O \rightleftharpoons \text{ADP} + P_i \qquad (7\text{-}16)$$

and thus the equilibrium constant is given by

$$K_{\text{ATP}} = \frac{[\text{ADP}][P_i]}{[\text{ATP}][H_2O]} \qquad (7\text{-}17)$$

The observed equilibrium constant (derived using total concentrations of the reacting species but neglecting water) is

$$K_{obs,\text{ATP}} = \frac{[\text{ADP}][P_i]}{[\text{ATP}]} \qquad (7\text{-}18)$$

Since enzymatic reactions involving ATP generally take place in the presence of $Mg^{2+}$ (a magnesium complex of ATP is the actual substrate and magnesium complexes of ADP and of orthophosphate the products), it is usually assumed that [ATP] represents the total concentration of all ionic species, including complexes of ATP, and that [ADP] and $[P_i]$ have similar meanings with respect to ADP and orthophosphate. However, in the presence of $Mg^{2+}$ a portion of the glutamate exists as a $Mg^{2+}$-glutamate complex, as expressed by the following modification of Eq. (7-12):

$$K_{obs,s} = \frac{[\text{Gln}][\text{ADP}][P_i]}{([\text{Glu}] + [\text{MgGlu}])[\text{NH}_4^+][\text{ATP}]} \qquad (7\text{-}19)$$

If one now introduces an expression for [MgGlu] derived from the equation for the formation constant for the $Mg^{2+}$-glutamate complex, i.e.,

$$K_f = \frac{[MgGlu]}{[Mg^{2+}][Glu]} = 7.66 \qquad (7\text{-}20)$$

(determined at 37°C, pH 7.4, and an ionic strength of 0.21),† Eq. (7-19) becomes

$$K_{obs,\,s} = \frac{[Gln][ADP][P_i]}{[NH_4^+][Glu](1 + 7.66[Mg^{2+}])[ATP]} \qquad (7\text{-}21)$$

When the appropriate activities (indicated by parentheses) and activity coefficients (denoted by $\gamma$), that is, $[Gln] = (Gln)/\gamma_{Gln}$ and $[Glu][NH_4^+] = (NH_4Glu)^2/\gamma^2_{NH_4Glu}$, are substituted, Eq. (7-21) becomes

$$K_{obs,\,s} = \frac{\gamma^2_{NH_4Glu}}{\gamma_{Gln}} \frac{(Gln)}{(NH_4Glu)^2(1 + 7.66[Mg^{2+}])} \frac{[ADP][P_i]}{[ATP]} \qquad (7\text{-}22)$$

Using this, rearranged and with the factor $(NH_4Glu)^2/(Gln)K_h$, one obtains

$$K_{obs,\,ATP} = \frac{\gamma_{Gln}}{\gamma^2_{NH_4Glu}} (1 + 7.66[Mg^{2+}]) K_{obs,\,s} K_h \qquad (7\text{-}23)$$

With the required activity coefficients at 37°C, which are available,† and with a value for $K_h$ at 37°C, which is also available,‡ a value for $K_{obs,\,ATP}$ can be calculated. This value is, of course, for equilibrium at 37°C. A value for $K_{obs,\,ATP}$ at 25°C can subsequently be calculated using the van't Hoff isochore, which in the integrated form is

$$\log \frac{K_2}{K_1} = \frac{\Delta H°}{2.3R} \frac{T_2 - T_1}{T_1 T_2} \qquad (7\text{-}24)$$

The value for $\Delta H°$, required to evaluate $K_2$, that is, $K_{obs,\,ATP}$ at 25°C, must either be available or be determined by independent measurement. In the case being discussed here, the value is available.¶ Finally, since a value for the equilibrium constant for the hydrolytic cleavage of ATP has been obtained by this indirect route, a value for $\Delta G°'$ can be calculated. In fact, with this procedure values for $\Delta G°'$ under a variety of conditions can be obtained. For example, the free-energy change $\Delta G°'$ which accompanies the hydrolytic cleavage of ATP (to yield ADP and orthophosphate) is calculated to be $-6.84$ kcal/mol when the process is conducted under the conditions of 25°C, pH 7, an ionic strength $\mu$ of 0.2, and $[Mg^{2+}] = 1$ mM. The variation of $\Delta G°'$ as a function of $[Mg^{2+}]$, expressed as the pMg, that is, $\log(1/[Mg^{2+}])$, and as a function of the pH is shown in Fig. 7-1. One can see that $\Delta G°'$ generally becomes more negative as the pMg increases above 3 and as the pH increases above 7.

It might be mentioned at this point that values for the free-energy change accompanying the hydrolytic cleavage of ATP to yield AMP and pyrophosphate have

† Rosing, J., and Slater, E. C. (1972) *Biochim. Biophys. Acta* **267**, 275–290.
‡ Ibid.
¶ Ibid.

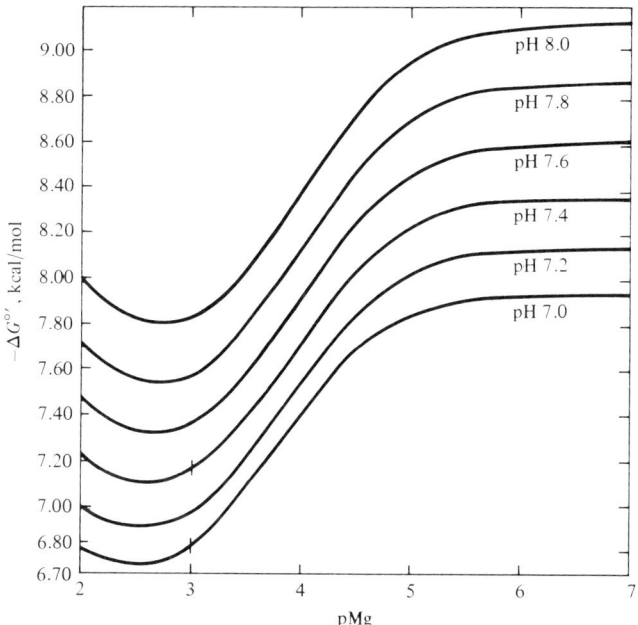

**Figure 7-1** $\Delta G^{\circ\prime}$ for the hydrolysis of ATP. [*From Rosing, J., and Slater, E. C. (1972) Biochim. Biophys. Acta.* **267**, *275*.]

been calculated and found to be generally 1 kcal/mol more negative than when the terminal phosphoryl group is removed under similar conditions. These values are, again, dependent upon both the pH and the pMg of the medium.

## Free-Energy Changes under Nonstandard, Nonequilibrium Conditions

So far the discussion has focused upon the changes in free energy that accompany reactions occurring under (modified) standard conditions or under equilibrium conditions, but in actuality reactions in living organisms frequently occur under conditions that are quite nonstandard and far removed from equilibrium. The free-energy change $\Delta G$ that accompanies these reactions can be calculated using Eq. (7-5). In this case, however, the quotient $a_c a_d / a_a a_b$ is neither unity (as it would be if the reaction were being conducted under standard conditions) nor is it an expression of the equilibrium constant (as it would be if the reaction were being conducted under equilibrium conditions). This quotient is simply the ratio of product activities (or concentrations) and reactant activities (or concentrations). However, it is *this* $\Delta G$ value which in fact indicates the extent to which the reaction actually proceeds under the prevailing conditions. Indeed it is quite possible for a reaction for which $\Delta G^{\circ\prime}$ is positive to proceed to a significant extent under nonstandard, nonequilibrium conditions if under these conditions $\Delta G$ is negative.

# FREE-ENERGY CHANGES ASSOCIATED WITH OXIDATION-REDUCTION REACTIONS

Metabolic pathways frequently include oxidative and reductive reactions. In general, catabolic pathways include reactions in which the carbon atoms of the carbohydrate or lipid or protein derivative undergo oxidation, while anabolic pathways include reactions in which these carbon atoms undergo reduction. The standard-free-energy change that accompanies an oxidation-reduction reaction is determined by the difference between the standard electrode potentials of the two half-reactions involved. This is expressed by

$$\Delta G° = -nF \Delta E_0 \qquad (7\text{-}25)$$

where $n$ is the number of electrons transferred per gram equivalent of the reactants and $F$ is a constant known as the faraday, having a value of 23,063 cal/(V)(equiv). The difference between the standard electrode potentials (those determined when all components are at unit activity) for the two half-reactions is denoted by $\Delta E_0$.

Electrode potentials are compared with that of the normal hydrogen electrode for which the equation

$$H^+ + e^- \longrightarrow \tfrac{1}{2}H_2 \qquad (7\text{-}26)$$

can be written. The normal hydrogen electrode, which has hydrogen ions at unit activity in equilibrium with hydrogen gas at 760 mm, is defined as having zero potential. Half-reactions that have a *greater* tendency to *accept* electrons than the normal hydrogen electrode are assigned *positive reduction potentials*. Half-reactions that have *less* tendency to *accept* electrons than the normal hydrogen electrode are assigned *negative reduction potentials*. Thus, reduction potentials indicate the tendency for the half-reaction to occur as a reduction; i.e., reduction potentials indicate the potential for undergoing reduction.

As with the values for standard-free-energy changes, it is more reasonable for biochemists to use standard electrode potentials that refer to processes as they occur at or near physiological pH. Thus, like the convention used with free-energy changes, $E'_0$ is generally used in biochemistry to denote the electrode potential of a half-reaction when all components are at unit activity with the single exception of hydrogen ion. It then follows that $\Delta E'_0$ is the difference between two such standard potentials. Again, the hydrogen-ion activity or concentration must be designated in conjunction with values for $E'_0$ and $\Delta E'_0$. The relationship between the standard-electrode-potential difference and the standard-free-energy change, both at a given hydrogen-ion activity, is

$$\Delta G°' = -nF \Delta E'_0 \qquad (7\text{-}27)$$

When considering two half-reactions, if the one with the more *positive* reduction potential is written as a *reduction* and the one with the more *negative* reduction potential as an *oxidation* and then these two half-reactions are added, the reaction that proceeds *spontaneously* will be generated. Since

$$\Delta E'_0 = E'_{0,\text{ red}} - E'_{0,\text{ ox}} \qquad (7\text{-}28)$$

## Table 7-2 Standard reduction potentials of some oxidation-reduction half-reactions

| Half-reaction (written as a reduction) | $E'_0$ at pH 7.0, V |
|---|---|
| $\frac{1}{2}O_2 + 2H^+ + 2e^- \rightarrow H_2O$ | 0.816 |
| $Fe^{3+} + e^- \rightarrow Fe^{2+}$ | 0.771 |
| $SO_4^{2-} + 2H^+ + 2e^- \rightarrow SO_3^{2-} + H_2O$ | 0.48 |
| $NO_3^- + 2H^+ + 2e^- \rightarrow NO_2^- + H_2O$ | 0.42 |
| $2I^- + 2e^- \rightarrow I_2$ | 0.536 |
| Cytochrome $a_3$-$Fe^{3+}$ + $e^-$ → cytochrome $a_3$-$Fe^{2+}$ | 0.55 |
| $\frac{1}{2}O_2 + H_2O + 2e^- \rightarrow H_2O_2$ | 0.30 |
| Cytochrome $a$-$Fe^{3+}$ + $e^-$ → cytochrome $a$-$Fe^{2+}$ | 0.29 |
| Cytochrome $c$-$Fe^{3+}$ + $e^-$ → cytochrome $c$-$Fe^{2+}$ | 0.25 |
| 2,6-Dichlorophenolindophenol$_{ox}$ + $2H^+$ + $2e^-$ → 2,6-DCPP$_{red}$ | 0.22 |
| Crotonoyl-CoA + $2H^+$ + $2e^-$ → butyryl-CoA | 0.19 |
| $Cu^{2+} + e^- \rightarrow Cu^+$ | 0.15 |
| Methemoglobin-$Fe^{3+}$ + $e^-$ → hemoglobin-$Fe^{2+}$ | 0.139 |
| Ubiquinone + $2H^+$ + $2e^-$ → ubiquinone-$H_2$ | 0.10 |
| Dehydroascorbate + $2H^+$ + $2e^-$ → ascorbate | 0.06 |
| Metmyoglobin-$Fe^{3+}$ + $e^-$ → myoglobin-$Fe^{2+}$ | 0.046 |
| Fumarate + $2H^+$ + $2e^-$ → succinate | 0.030 |
| Methylene blue$_{ox}$ + $2H^+$ + $2e^-$ → methylene blue$_{red}$ | 0.011 |
| Pyruvate + $NH_3$ + $2H^+$ + $2e^-$ → alanine | −0.13 |
| 2-Oxoglutarate + $NH_3$ + $2H^+$ + $2e^-$ → glutamate + $H_2O$ | −0.14 |
| Acetaldehyde + $2H^+$ + $2e^-$ → ethanol | −0.163 |
| Oxaloacetate + $2H^+$ + $2e^-$ → malate | −0.175 |
| FAD + $2H^+$ + $2e^-$ → FADH$_2$ | −0.18 |
| Pyruvate + $2H^+$ + $2e^-$ → lactate | −0.190 |
| Riboflavin + $2H^+$ + $2e^-$ → riboflavin-$H_2$ | −0.200 |
| Cystine + $2H^+$ + $2e^-$ → 2 cysteine | −0.22 |
| GSSG + $2H^+$ + $2e^-$ → 2 GSH | −0.23 |
| $S^0$ + $2H^+$ + $2e^-$ → $H_2S$ | −0.23 |
| 3-Phospho-D-glyceroyl phosphate + $2H^+$ + $2e^-$ → GAP + $P_i$ | −0.29 |
| Acetoacetate + $2H^+$ + $2e^-$ → 3-hydroxybutyrate | −0.290 |
| Lipoate$_{ox}$ + $2H^+$ + $2e^-$ → lipoate$_{red}$ | −0.29 |
| $NAD^+$ + $2H^+$ + $2e^-$ → NADH + $H^+$ | −0.320 |
| $NADP^+$ + $2H^+$ + $2e^-$ → NADPH + $H^+$ | −0.320 |
| Pyruvate + $CO_2$ + $2H^+$ + $2e^-$ → malate | −0.33 |
| Uric acid + $2H^+$ + $2e^-$ → xanthine | −0.36 |
| Acetyl-CoA + $2H^+$ + $2e^-$ → acetaldehyde + CoA | −0.41 |
| $CO_2$ + $2H^+$ + $2e^-$ → formate | −0.420 |
| $H^+ + e^- \rightarrow \frac{1}{2}H_2$ | −0.420 |
| Ferredoxin-$Fe^{3+}$ + $e^-$ → ferredoxin-$Fe^{2+}$ | −0.432 |
| Gluconate + $2H^+$ + $2e^-$ → glucose + $H_2O$ | −0.45 |
| 3-Phosphoglycerate + $2H^+$ + $2e^-$ → glyceraldehyde-3-phosphate + $H_2O$ | −0.55 |
| Methylviologen$_{ox}$ + $2H^+$ + $2e^-$ → methylviologen$_{red}$ | −0.55 |
| Acetate + $2H^+$ + $2e^-$ → acetaldehyde | −0.60 |
| Succinate + $CO_2$ + $2H^+$ + $2e^-$ → 2-oxoglutarate + $H_2O$ | −0.67 |
| Acetate + $CO_2$ + $2H^+$ + $2e^-$ → pyruvate | −0.70 |

*Source:* From Segel, I. H. (1976) *Biochemical Calculations*, 2d ed., pp. 414–415, Wiley, New York. With permission.

it follows that $\Delta E_0'$ for a spontaneous reaction is positive and, further, that $\Delta G^{\circ\prime}$ for a spontaneous reaction must be negative [see Eq. (7-25)], which is in agreement with the previous discussion.

Table 7-2 shows the modified standard electrode potentials for some common half-reactions.

Under nonstandard, nonequilibrium conditions the electrode potential of a half-reaction is given by

$$E = E_0' + \frac{RT}{nF} \ln \frac{[\text{oxidized component}]}{[\text{reduced component}]} \qquad (7\text{-}29a)$$

which can be rewritten as

$$E = E_0' + \frac{0.059}{n} \log \frac{[\text{oxidized component}]}{[\text{reduced component}]} \qquad (7\text{-}29b)$$

since the factor $2.3RT/F$ has the value 0.059 at 25°C. The electrode-potential difference, for nonstandard, nonequilibrium half-reactions, is given by $\Delta E$.

In the special case where the electrode potentials of the two half-reactions of an oxidation-reduction reaction are equal, the reaction is at *equilibrium*. Under this special circumstance $\Delta E$ is zero. Consequently, the free-energy change which accompanies such a reaction is also zero [see Eq. (7-25)], in agreement with previous discussions.

## Oxidation-Reduction Reactions When Hydrogen Ion Is a Component

When a half-reaction involves the utilization of hydrogen ion, the electrode potential is pH-dependent and can be expressed as

$$\begin{aligned} E &= E_0 + \frac{0.059}{n} \log \frac{[\text{oxidized component}]}{[\text{reduced component}]} + \frac{0.059}{n} \log [\text{H}^+]^{n'} \\ &= E_0 + \frac{0.059}{n} \log \frac{[\text{oxidized component}]}{[\text{reduced component}]} - \frac{0.059}{n} n'\text{pH} \qquad (7\text{-}30) \end{aligned}$$

where $n'$ is the number of hydrogen ions involved in the balanced equation for the half-reaction (generally equivalent to $n$, the number of electrons involved). This equation states that as the pH of the system is increased, the electrode potential of a half-reaction that utilizes hydrogen ion becomes *more negative*.

## Extent of Completion of Oxidation-Reduction Reactions

In oxidation-reduction reactions it is the value of $\Delta E$ that determines the extent to which a given reaction proceeds. Notwithstanding the value for $\Delta E_0'$, if $\Delta E$ for the reaction under the prevailing conditions is large and *positive*, the oxidation-reduction reaction will proceed spontaneously and go virtually to completion because when $\Delta E$ is large and positive, $\Delta G$ for that reaction must be large and *negative*.

## Oxidation-Reduction Cofactors

When oxidation-reduction reactions are carried out in the laboratory, an oxidizing agent, e.g., permanganate, or a reducing agent, e.g., lithium aluminum hydride, is generally used to promote the oxidation or reduction. Alternatively, electrodes can be used to facilitate the electron transfer involved in oxidation-reduction reactions. In living organisms oxidations and reductions are facilitated by specific cofactors that are bound at the catalytic site of the enzyme. Among the common oxidation-reduction cofactors are nicotine adenine dinucleotide, nicotine adenine dinucleotide phosphate, flavin adenine dinucleotide, and flavin mononucleotide. If the metabolic intermediate is to undergo an oxidation, the oxidized form of the appropriate cofactor becomes bound at the catalytic site of the enzyme, as does the intermediate, and reducing equivalents are transferred from the intermediate to the cofactor. As a result, the intermediate is oxidized, and the cofactor is reduced. Similarly, if the intermediate is to undergo a reduction, the reduced form of the appropriate cofactor becomes bound at the catalytic site and reducing equivalents are transferred from the

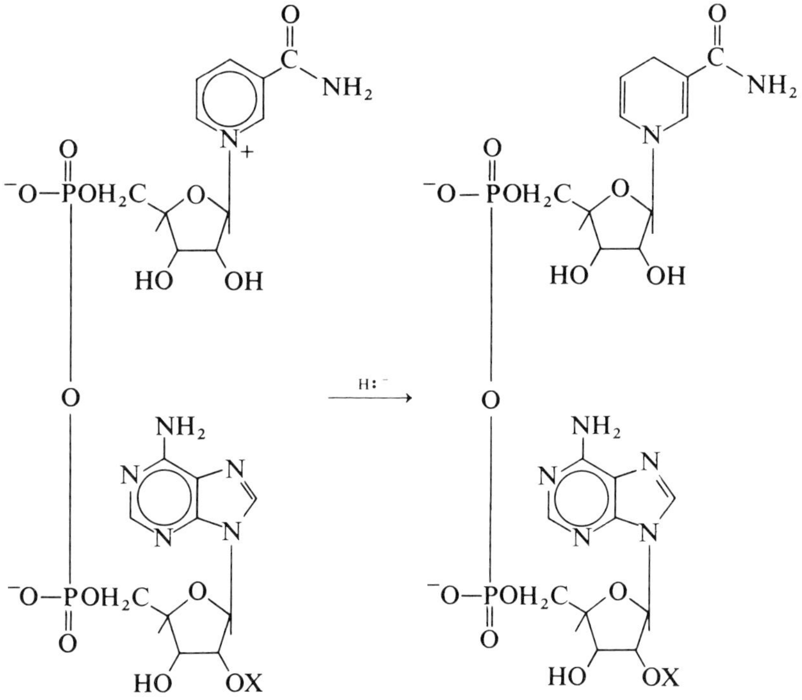

$X = H$: Oxidized nicotine adenine dinucleotide ($NAD^+$)

$X = P(=O)(O^-)(O^-)$ : Oxidized nicotine adenine dinucleotide phosphate ($NADP^+$)

Reduced nicotine adenine dinucleotide (NADH)

Reduced nicotine adenine dinucleotide phosphate (NADPH)

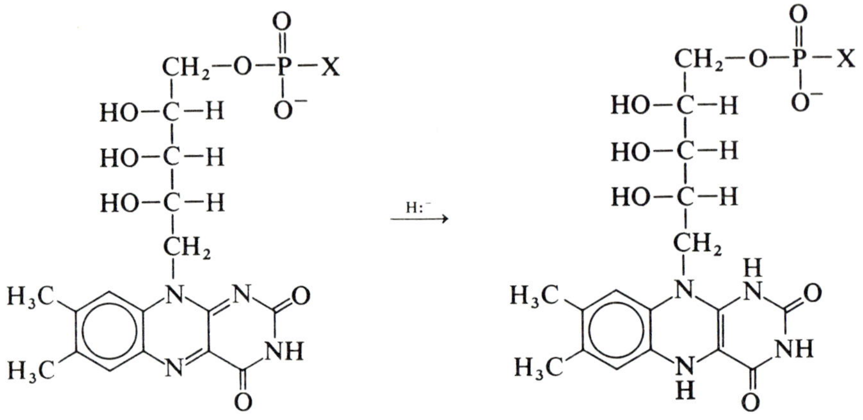

X = O⁻ : Oxidized flavin mononucleotide (FMN)

Fully reduced flavin mononucleotide (FMNH₂)

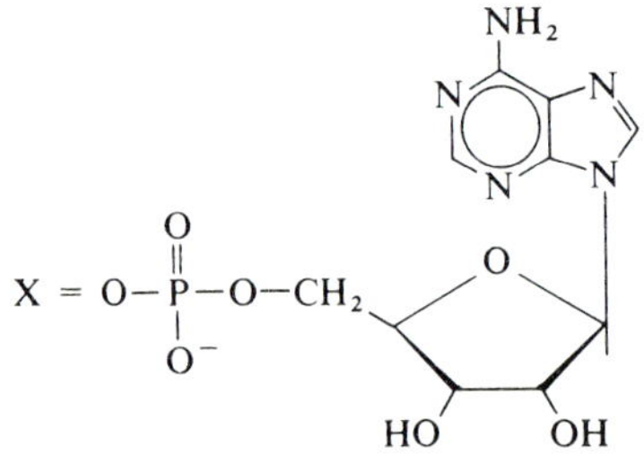

X = O−P(=O)(O⁻)−O−CH₂−[ribose]−adenine : Oxidized flavin adenine dinucleotide (FAD)

Fully reduced flavin adenine dinucleotide (FADH₂)

cofactor to the intermediate. Subsequently, the reduced or the oxidized cofactor dissociates from the enzyme (as does the intermediate which underwent oxidation or reduction), thus providing the opportunity for another molecule of the cofactor to become bound and the oxidation-reduction reaction to occur again.

In nicotine adenine dinucleotide the pyridine moiety is the reaction center of the cofactor. When the metabolic intermediate undergoes oxidation, a hydride ion is transferred from it to C(4) of the pyridinium moiety of $NAD^+$ or $NADP^+$, thus converting this moiety into a 1,4-dihydropyridine moiety. Alternatively, when the intermediate undergoes reduction, a hydride ion is transferred to it from C(4) of the dihydropyridine moiety of NADH or NADPH, thus converting this moiety into a pyridinium moiety. In view of the characteristic absorption of the 1,4-dihydropyridine moiety at 340 nm, enzymatic oxidation-reduction reactions involving the nicotine adenine dinucleotide cofactors can be monitored spectrophotometrically. These reactions can also be monitored fluorometrically since absorption at 340 nm results in fluorescent emission having a maximum at 460 nm.

In some enzymatic reactions in which a flavin cofactor (FAD or FMN) is the participant, reduction of the oxidized cofactor involves the transfer of single unpaired

Flavin semiquinone, neutral form (blue)     Flavin semiquinone, anionic form (red)

electrons to the isoalloxazine moiety. The result is that a flavin semiquinone is formed as a transient.

The existence of this transient can be monitored by a technique known as *electron paramagnetic resonance* (EPR) spectroscopy,† a method used for observing the behavior of species with one or more unpaired electrons. For the flavin semiquinone a characteristic EPR signal is observed at approximately $g = 2.005$. The appearance of this signal (Fig. 7-2) indicates that a one-electron reduction of the oxidized cofactor has taken place.

Semiquinone forms also participate in the mitochondrial electron-transport process, which is, in fact, a series of oxidation-reduction reactions. In this case, besides FAD and FMN, which exhibit semiquinone forms during the electron-transport process, a benzoquinone known as ubiquinone also undergoes one-electron reduction. However, neither the flavins nor ubiquinone is bound at the catalytic site of a specific enzyme, as is the case when a cofactor participates in an oxidation-reduction reaction catalyzed by an enzyme localized in the cell cytoplasm. Instead all components of the mitochondrial electron-transport system are in fact *constituents* of the mitochondrial (inner) membrane, and, as such, they are so positioned within the framework of the membrane that each is in close proximity with

---

† When an atom, an ion, or a molecule which has an unpaired electron is placed in a magnetic field, the magnetic moment of the unpaired electron can become aligned in one of two ways with respect to the direction of the external field. The energy levels of these two states are given by $-\frac{1}{2}g\mu_b H_z$ (corresponding to the ground state) and $+\frac{1}{2}g\mu_b H_z$ (corresponding to the excited state), where $g$ is a proportionality constant which relates the magnetic moment and the angular momentum of the electron, $\mu_b$ is the Bohr magneton (which has a value of $0.92732 \times 10^{-20}$ erg/G), and $H_z$ is the magnitude of the external field. The energy difference between these two states is given by $\Delta E = g\mu_b H_z$. When the energy of the quanta of electromagnetic waves produced by the external field is equal to the energy difference between the two states, that is, $g\mu_b H_z$, energy is absorbed and the orientation of the magnetic moment of the unpaired electron undergoes a transition from the lower (ground-state) energy level to the higher (excited-state) energy level. Only quanta having this specific energy can be absorbed, however. (Think of the parallel between this situation and the absorption of light energy by a compound in spectrophotometric procedures.) This coincidence of the energy of the quanta of electromagnetic waves and the energy difference between the two states of the unpaired electron is referred to as *resonance*.

When an EPR spectrum is to be obtained, the sample is placed in a varying magnetic field and energy absorption is monitored. Absorption produces a signal which is recorded on a chart. (Actually, the display on the chart is in the form of the first derivative of the energy-absorption curve.) The magnitude of the magnetic field that produces resonance is a characteristic of the unpaired electron in the atom, ion, or molecule of which it is a part. An isolated electron is characterized by a $g$ value of 2.002319. An electron that is a part of an atom, ion, or molecule exists in a different environment and will therefore be characterized by a different $g$ value.

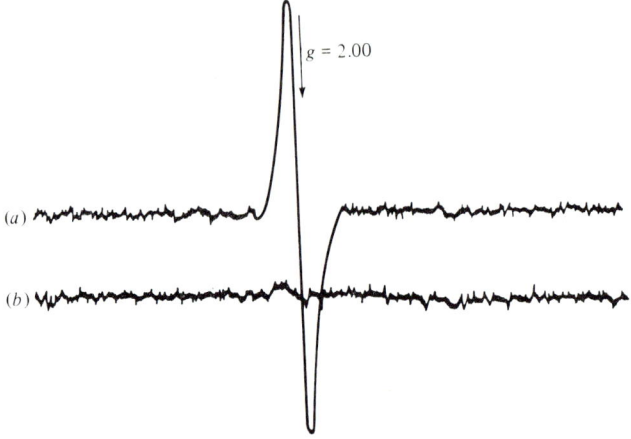

**Figure 7-2** (a) EPR signal obtained as the result of the FAD associated with the enzyme adenylylsulfate reductase accepting an unpaired electron. (The enzyme catalyzes the reduction and cleavage of adenylylsulfate to sulfite and AMP.) (b) Output in the absence of enzymatic activity.

the other components with which it must react. (This will be discussed in some detail in Chapter 11.) Notwithstanding this difference, FAD, FMN, and ubiquinone function in essentially the same manner as described above in that a single unpaired electron is accepted and a transient semiquinone form is generated.† Semiquinone forms of ubiquinone may be represented as shown.

† Backstrom, D., Norling, B., Ehrenberg, A., and Ernester, L. (1970) *Biochim. Biophys. Acta* **197**, 108–111.

As a component of the mitochondrial electron-transport system, this benzosemiquinone passes the electron to the next component in the system, and as a concomitance the benzoquinone form is regenerated.

## ENERGETICS OF PROCESSES INVOLVING BIOLOGICAL MEMBRANES

The cells of living organisms are compartmentalized by membrane systems. A wide variety of processes, including intestinal absorption, maintenance of electrolyte balance, respiration, muscle contraction, and others, involve the translocation of specific molecules or ions across the appropriate biological membrane. Such translocations can occur by diffusion, through the agency of an enzyme that is a constituent of the membrane, or as a result of some combination of these processes. Since diffusion is essentially a process based upon thermodynamic parameters, whereas translocation through the agency of an enzyme reflects kinetic parameters, the former will be discussed at this point.

Diffusion is the movement of molecules or ions in response to a chemical potential gradient. It is a spontaneous process that leads ultimately to thermodynamic equilibrium. Diffusion can be described approximately by Fick's first law, which is

$$\frac{dn}{dt} = -DA\frac{dc}{dx} \qquad (7\text{-}32a)$$

where $dn/dt$ = rate at which molecules or ions pass through cross-sectional area $A$
$dc/dx$ = rate of change of concentration of diffusing species as function of distance, i.e., concentration gradient
$D$ = diffusion coefficient

The diffusion coefficient is a proportionality constant which has the units of area per unit time, but for biological membranes the thickness of the *diffusion barrier dx* (which may or may not be the same as the thickness of the membrane) is usually unknown. For this reason the quantity $D/dx$ is generally replaced by $P_m$, the membrane permeability coefficient, which indicates the number of molecules or ions that cross a unit area of the biological membrane in unit time when a unit concentration gradient is applied. The factor $P_m$ has the dimensions of length per unit time, i.e., velocity. If Fick's first law of diffusion is written in terms of a membrane permeability coefficient, Eq. (7-32a) becomes

$$\frac{dn}{dt} = P_m A\, dc \qquad (7\text{-}32b)$$

Diffusion across a biological membrane is an irreversible process from the standpoint of thermodynamics. According to the principles of classical thermodynamics, a reversible process is not accompanied by an increase in entropy when it is carried out cyclically. In this case the operation occurs infinitely slowly, the forward movement being opposed by a restraint just insufficient to prevent the movement. An irreversible process, by contrast, is accompanied by an increase in the entropy of the system even when the process is carried out cyclically. In fact, the rate of such entropy production is frequently one of the parameters to be determined when an irreversible process is studied. Irreversible processes such as diffusion and the translocation of heat and other forms of energy can be considered as the resultant of forces which produce a flux. (Flux can be defined as the *net* movement of the quantity under consideration.) The force that produces the particular flux is called the *conjugate force* of the flux. The quantity of the flux that is produced is related to the quantity of the conjugate force required to produce it by a phenomenological coefficient. A diffusion coefficient is an example of a phenomenological coefficient. It can be shown that under certain conditions the rate at which entropy is produced in an irreversible process is given by the sum of the product of the fluxes involved and their conjugate forces. This principle serves as the basis for the equation

$$\text{Rate of entropy production} = J_v \, \Delta p + J_D RT \, \Delta c_2 \tag{7-33}$$

where $J_v$ = total volume flow across membrane
$J_D$ = velocity of solute relative to that of solvent (which is similar to *d*iffusion flow and, hence, the subscript)
$\Delta p$ = hydrostatic pressure difference across membrane
$\Delta c_2$ = solute concentration difference across membrane

$R$ and $T$ have their usual meanings. The phenomenological coefficient that relates the flux $J_v$, the total volume flow, to its conjugate force $\Delta p$, the hydrostatic pressure difference, is $L_p$, the pressure-filtration coefficient. Similarly, the phenomenological coefficient that relates the flux $J_D$, the relative velocity of the solute, to its conjugate force, $\Delta c_2$, the solute concentration difference, is $L_D$. The coefficient $L_D$ reflects the permeability of the membrane with respect to solute, just as $L_p$ reflects that with respect to solvent, although the former relationship is more complex. (This will be discussed below.) Under the special conditions noted below the following relationships exist between the appropriate fluxes, forces, and phenomenological coefficients:

$\Delta c_2 = 0$: $\qquad\qquad\qquad\qquad J_v = L_p \, \Delta p \qquad\qquad\qquad\qquad$ (7-34a)

$\Delta p = 0$: $\qquad\qquad\qquad\qquad J_D = L_D RT \, \Delta c_2 \qquad\qquad\qquad\quad$ (7-34b)

In addition, it can be shown that when the membrane is more permeable to the solvent than to the solute (which is often the case), the hydrostatic pressure difference $\Delta p$ influences not only $J_v$ but also the relative velocity of the solute $J_D$. For this reason a phenomenological coefficient known as the *ultrafiltration coefficient* $L_{Dp}$ has been introduced. Its name derives from the fact that the process of changing the composition of fluid that passes across a membrane under an applied pressure is known as ultrafiltration. Furthermore, it can be shown that a solute concentration difference across the membrane $\Delta c_2$ influences not only $J_D$ but also the total volume flow $J_v$. The phenomenological coefficient introduced in this case is known as the *osmotic coefficient* $L_{pD}$. (Remember that the flow of solvent across a membrane in response to a transmembrane solute concentration difference is known as osmosis.) The coefficients $L_{Dp}$ and $L_{pD}$ are referred to as cross coefficients. They reflect certain solute-solvent interactions. When the influences reflected by these cross coefficients are included in the equations that define the fluxes $J_v$ and $J_D$, one obtains

$$J_v = L_p \, \Delta p + L_{pD} RT \, \Delta c_2 \qquad (7\text{-}35a)$$

and
$$J_D = L_{Dp} \, \Delta p + L_D RT \, \Delta c_2 \qquad (7\text{-}35b)$$

These equations permit the permeability characteristics of a biological membrane to be defined in terms of four phenomenological coefficients, $L_p$, $L_{pD}$, $L_D$, and $L_{Dp}$. However, two of these, the two cross coefficients, can be shown to be identical under certain conditions. In a general sense, this is enunciated by the *Onsager reciprocal relationship*, which states that in an irreversible thermodynamic process when appropriate values for the fluxes and forces are used, the cross coefficients will be equal. The values for the fluxes and forces that allow this equivalence of cross coefficients are precisely those which permit the sum of the products of each flux and its conjugate force to equal the rate of entropy production. When these conditions are met in the diffusion of molecules and ions across a membrane, $L_{pD} = L_{Dp}$. Hence, under these conditions the permeability characteristics of the membrane can be defined in terms of three phenomenological coefficients, $L_p$, $L_D$, and $L_{pD} = L_{Dp}$.

When the characteristics of biological membranes are discussed, yet another factor is frequently included, known as *the reflection coefficient* $\sigma$. The reflection coefficient is defined in terms of the pressure-filtration coefficient $L_p$ and the osmotic coefficient $L_{pD}$:

$$\sigma = -\frac{L_{pD}}{L_p} \qquad (7\text{-}36)$$

This coefficient provides an indication of the extent to which the permeability characteristics of the membrane under consideration deviate from those of the *ideal semipermeable membrane*. The ideal semipermeable membrane is one which is totally selective in that it permits solvent to pass through it freely while it prevents the passage of solute completely. The reflection coefficient for an ideal semipermeable membrane is unity because when the membrane is totally impermeable with respect to solute while passing solvent freely, $J_v$, the total volume flow, is simply the flow of solvent alone. However, the value for $J_D$ is also given by this flow but with the opposite sign; therefore, under these conditions,

$$J_v = -J_D \qquad (7\text{-}37a)$$

When the conditions of the Onsager relationship are fulfilled, and since the following relationships must exist [as a consequence of Eq. (7-37a)]

$$L_p = -L_{Dp} \qquad L_D = -L_{pD} \qquad (7\text{-}37b)$$

it follows that

$$L_p = L_D = -L_{Dp} = -L_{pD} \qquad (7\text{-}37c)$$

[The reader should determine to his or her own satisfaction that Eqs. (7-37b) are valid under the stated conditions.] Thus, in view of these equalities, the quotient $-L_{pD}/L_p$ is unity. By contrast, it can be shown that when a membrane is totally

## Table 7-3 Values for the reflection coefficient $\sigma$ for the penetration of the solute into the cell (or tissue) indicated

| Cell or tissue | Solute | $\sigma$ | Calculated value for equivalent pore radius, Å |
|---|---|---|---|
| *Chara australis*, algal cell | Urea | 1.0 | |
| | Ethylene glycol | 1.0 | |
| | Formamide | 1.0 | |
| | Methanol | 0.30 | |
| | Ethanol | 0.27 | |
| | *n*-Propanol | 0.22 | |
| Squid, axon, axolemma | Glycerol | 0.96 | 4.25 |
| | Ethylene glycol | 0.72 | |
| | Urea | 0.70 | |
| | Ethanol | 0.63 | |
| | Formamide | 0.44 | |
| | Methanol | 0.25 | |
| Amphibian (*Necturus maculosus*), kidney cells | Sucrose | 1.0 | 5.6 |
| | Mannitol | 1.0 | |
| | Erythritol | 0.89 | |
| | Glycerol | 0.77 | |
| | Urea | 0.52 | |
| Toad, bladder cells | Thiourea | 0.99 | |
| | Chloride ion | 0.99 | |
| | Urea | 0.79 | |
| Frog, single muscle fibers | Sucrose | 1.0 | 4.0 |
| | Mannitol | 1.0 | |
| | Glycerol | 0.86 | |
| | Urea | 0.82 | |
| | Formamide | 0.65 | |
| Rat, luminal surface of intestinal mucosal cells | Sucrose | 0.99 | 4.0 |
| | Mannitol | 0.99 | |
| | Erythritol | 0.93 | |
| | Urea | 0.81 | |
| | Ethylene glycol | 0.27 | |
| | Formamide | 0.22 | |
| Human erythrocytes | Glycerol | 0.88 | 4.2 |
| | Propylene glycol | 0.85 | |
| | Thiourea | 0.85 | |
| | Methylurea | 0.80 | |
| | Propionamide | 0.80 | |
| | Ethylene glycol | 0.63 | |
| | Urea | 0.62 | |
| | Acetamide | 0.58 | |

*Source:* Modified from Stein, W. D. (1967) *The Movement of Molecules across Cell Membranes*, pp. 56–57, Academic, New York. With permission.

*non*selective and poses no barrier with respect to either solute or solvent, $\sigma$ is zero. This follows because under these conditions $L_{pD}$ is zero. Finally, if a membrane is permeable with respect to the solvent and also somewhat permeable with respect to solute (often referred to as being *leaky*), as is the case for most biological membranes, $\sigma$ has a value less than unity. Table 7-3 lists the reflection coefficients for various solutes as determined in studies on several biological and artificial membranes.

The task of developing a concept for the physical meaning of $L_D$ was deferred above. Let us now consider this point. If the *total* solute flow across the membrane (rather than the relative flow) is denoted by $J_s$, the following expression can be derived using Eqs. (7-35) and (7-36):

$$J_s = J_v(1 - \sigma)c_2 + c_2(L_D - \sigma^2 L_p)RT\,\Delta c_2 \tag{7-38}$$

In the special case where $J_v$ is zero, $J_s$ is proportional to $\Delta c_2$. The proportionality constant in this case is $c_2(L_D - \sigma^2 L_p)RT$. The coefficient of solute permeability at zero volume flow $\omega$ is defined as

$$\omega = c_2(L_D - \sigma^2 L_p) \tag{7-39}$$

Thus, it can be seen that $L_D$ is, in fact, related to solute permeability although in a somewhat complex manner, as stated previously.

CHAPTER
# EIGHT

## THE KINETICS OF BIOCHEMICAL REACTIONS: ENZYMES

Kinetics is the study of the rate at which a chemical reaction proceeds. In contrast to the study of thermodynamics, which aims at characterizing a system in a given state, the study of kinetics aims at characterizing a changing system at each instant in time.

## THE LAWS OF KINETICS

The laws of kinetics are empirical formulations that describe the change in a system as a function of time. The rate or velocity of a reaction is generally stated in terms of a specific rate constant $k$, which is numerically equal to the rate of the conversion when each of the reactants is present at unit concentration. How much the rate of a reaction varies as a function of the concentrations of the reactants is denoted by the *order* of the reaction. A reaction is *first order* with respect to reactant A if its rate is proportional to the *first power* of the concentration of A. It is *second order* with respect to A if its rate is proportional to the *second power* of the concentration of A, and so forth. For the reaction A → P, one can express the disappearance of the reactant A or, alternatively, the appearance of the product P as

$$-\frac{d[A]}{dt} = \frac{d[P]}{dt} = k[A] \qquad (8\text{-}1)$$

As shown, this reaction is first order with respect to A. The differential and integrated

**Table 8-1 Rate equations**

| Reaction | Order | Rate equation | | Units of rate constant |
|---|---|---|---|---|
| | | Differential form | Integrated form | |
| $A \longrightarrow P$ | First | $\dfrac{d[P]}{dt} = k([A]_0 - x)$ | $k = \dfrac{1}{t} \ln\left(\dfrac{[A]_0}{[A]_0 - x}\right)$ | $s^{-1}$ |
| $2A \longrightarrow P$ | Second | $\dfrac{d[P]}{dt} = k([A]_0 - x)^2$ | $k = \dfrac{1}{t}\left(\dfrac{x}{[A]_0([A]_0 - x)}\right)$ | $l\,mol^{-1}s^{-1}$ |
| $A + B \longrightarrow P$ | Second (overall) | $\dfrac{d[P]}{dt} = k([A]_0 - x)([B]_0 - x)$ | $k = \dfrac{1}{t([B]_0 - [A]_0)} \ln\left(\dfrac{[A]_0([B]_0 - x)}{[B]_0([A]_0 - x)}\right)$ | $l\,mol^{-1}s^{-1}$ |
| $3A \longrightarrow P$ | Third | $\dfrac{d[P]}{dt} = k([A]_0 - x)^3$ | $k = \dfrac{1}{2t}\left(\dfrac{2[A]_0 x - x^2}{[A]_0^2([A]_0 - x)^2}\right)$ | $l^2\,mol^{-2}s^{-1}$ |

forms of the rate equations for first-, second-, and third-order reactions are given in Table 8-1. In the table $A_0$ or $B_0$ denote the reactants at time zero and $x$ denotes that amount of reactant which has undergone reaction at time $t$.

## CATALYZED REACTIONS

In 1836, Berzelius recognized that certain reactions are influenced by some factor that remains unchanged at the end of the process. He proposed that such reactions take place under the influence of a catalytic force. (The word catalytic is derived from the Greek *kata-*, meaning "down" or "through," and the Greek word *lyein*, meaning "to loosen.") It is now recognized, however, that catalysis is not a force but is brought about by various chemical substances and physical agents referred to as catalysts. A catalyst is a substance or agent that alters the *velocity* of a reaction but is unchanged at the end of the reaction. A catalyst influences only the rate of the reaction, not its thermodynamic parameters.

Although a catalyst can be isolated unchanged at the end of the reaction, it often undergoes a temporary change during the reaction and frequently an intermediate complex is formed between the catalyst and a reactant. When there is only one reactant this process can be represented as

$$C + A \underset{k_{-1}}{\overset{k_1}{\rightleftharpoons}} CA \xrightarrow{k_2} P + C \qquad (8\text{-}2)$$

where C = catalyst
A = reactant
CA = catalyst-reactant complex
P = product

In reactions of this type the characteristics of the catalyst-reactant complex determine the reaction characteristics. If this complex reverts to the free catalyst plus the reactant at a faster rate than it is converted into the free catalyst plus the product, i.e., if $k_{-1}$ is much greater than $k_2$, the rate of the reaction can be derived by calculating the concentration of CA from the equilibrium equation and multiplying this concentration by the rate constant $k_2$. An intermediate complex that behaves in this manner is called an *Arrhenius complex* since its characteristics are similar to those of the activated complex Arrhenius described. On the other hand, some intermediate complexes are converted into the product plus the free catalyst at a faster rate than they revert to the catalyst plus the reactant. In this case $k_2$ is much greater than $k_{-1}$, and the concentration of CA cannot be calculated from the equilibrium equation. However, the concentration of CA is always small since, once formed, it is very rapidly converted into the product plus the free catalyst. As an approximation this concentration can be considered to be constant throughout the greater part of the reaction time. This approximation is generally called the *steady-state assumption*. A complex that behaves according to this description is known as a *van't Hoff complex* after the Dutch chemist who first described such behavior.

If a catalyzed reaction proceeds by means of an Arrhenius complex and $k_2$ is small enough to permit its contribution with respect to the concentration of the intermediate complex CA to be neglected, the concentration of this complex is determined by

$$K = \frac{k_1}{k_{-1}} = \frac{[CA]}{[C][A]} \tag{8-3}$$

In Eq. (8-3), $K$ is the formation constant for the intermediate complex. Now since $[C] = [C]_0 - [CA]$ and $[A] = [A]_0 - [CA]$, it follows that

$$K = \frac{[CA]}{([C]_0 - [CA])([A]_0 - [CA])} \tag{8-4}$$

which can be solved for [CA] using the formula for the solution of a quadratic equation. However, if the total concentration of A is much greater than that of the catalyst, $[A]_0 - [CA]$ is approximated by $[A]_0$. When this approximation is used,

$$K = \frac{[CA]}{([C]_0 - [CA])[A]_0} \tag{8-5}$$

and therefore

$$[CA] = \frac{K[A]_0[C]_0}{1 + K[A]_0} = \frac{[A]_0[C]_0}{[A]_0 + 1/K} \tag{8-6}$$

Since the reaction velocity $v$ is given by $k_2[CA]$, one can write

$$v = \frac{k_2[A]_0[C]_0}{[A]_0 + 1/K} \tag{8-7}$$

Since this equation is of the form $y = ax/x + b$, a plot of the reaction velocity as a function of $[A]_0$ is a hyperbola (see Fig. 8-1). Reactions catalyzed by solid surfaces can often be formulated in this way, and (more important to this discussion) reactions that occur on the surfaces of enzymes have been so formulated.

In contrast to the formulation above, which is based on the premise that $k_{-1}$ in Eq. (8-2) is much greater than $k_2$, when $k_2$ is much greater than $k_{-1}$, the steady-state assumption can be applied. According to the steady-state assumption, the rate of the change in the concentration of the intermediate complex CA as a function of time is zero, as expressed by

$$\frac{d[CA]}{dt} = k_1[C][A] - k_{-1}[CA] - k_2[CA] = 0 \tag{8-8}$$

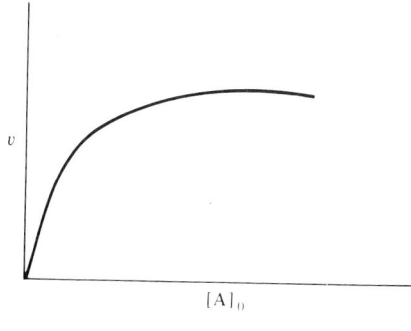

**Figure 8-1** Graph of the equation

$$v = \frac{k_2[A]_0[C]_0}{[A]_0 + 1/K}$$

in which $k_2[C]_0$ corresponds to $a$, $[A]_0$ to $x$, and $1/K$ to $b$ of the equation $y = ax/(b + x)$.

Since $[C] = [C]_0 - [CA]$ and $[A] = [A]_0 - [CA]$, one can write

$$k_1\{([C]_0 - [CA])([A]_0 - [CA])\} - k_{-1}[CA] - k_2[CA] = 0 \quad (8\text{-}9)$$

Solving Eq. (8-9) for [CA] (assuming that [A] is much greater than [C]) gives

$$[CA] = \frac{k_1[A]_0[C]_0}{k_1[A]_0 + k_{-1} + k_2} \quad (8\text{-}10)$$

The reaction velocity is therefore

$$v = \frac{k_1 k_2 [A]_0 [C]_0}{k_1[A]_0 + k_{-1} + k_2} \quad (8\text{-}11a)$$

or

$$v = \frac{k_2 [A]_0 [C]_0}{[A]_0 + (k_{-1} + k_2)/k_1} \quad (8\text{-}11b)$$

The differences between these two types of catalyzed reactions can be shown most graphically by comparing the potential-energy diagrams for a process in which $k_{-1}$ is much greater than $k_2$ and one in which $k_2$ is much greater than $k_{-1}$ (Fig. 8-2). When $k_{-1}$ is much greater than $k_2$, the higher energy barrier is associated with the conversion of the intermediate complex into free catalyst plus product. On the other hand, when $k_2$ is much greater than $k_{-1}$, the higher energy barrier is associated with the formation of the intermediate complex.

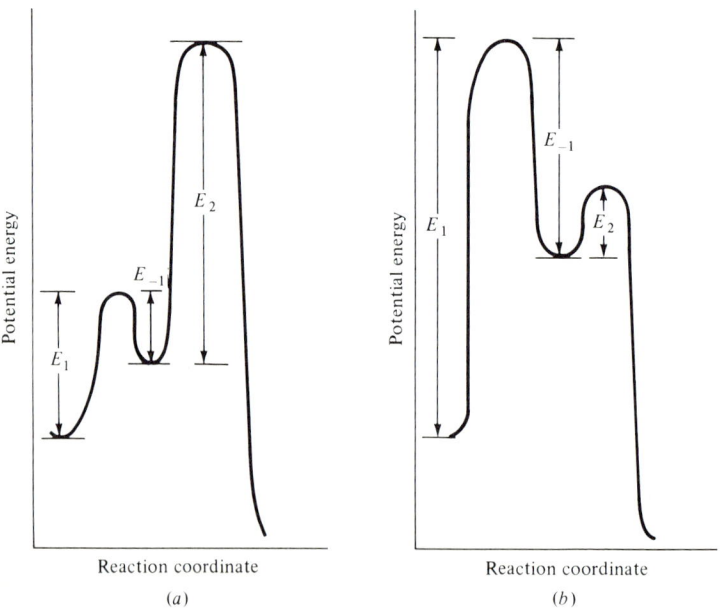

**Figure 8-2** (a) In the formation of an Arrhenius complex, $k_{-1}$ is much *greater* than $k_2$, which reflects the fact that $E_{-1}$ is much *less* than $E_2$. The principal potential-energy barrier in this case is, in fact, the conversion of CA to the product. The magnitude of this barrier is given by $E_2$. (b) On the other hand, when a van't Hoff complex is formed, $k_2$ is much *greater* than $k_{-1}$, reflecting the fact that $E_2$ is much *less* than $E_{-1}$. Now the principal potential-energy barrier is the formation of CA, and once formed, CA is rapidly converted into product.

## ENZYMES AS CATALYSTS

In the laboratory a reaction that proceeds at a very slow rate can in many cases be accelerated by raising the temperature, altering the pH, or adjusting the ionic strength. In the living organism, however, temperature, pH, ionic strength, and various other conditions must be maintained within defined limits. Therefore, the types of influences feasible for reactions conducted in the laboratory cannot be imposed in living organisms. Nevertheless, reactions in living organisms proceed at rates that are faster by several orders of magnitude than comparable laboratory reactions. How is this accomplished? It is due to the effective catalysis of biochemical reactions. The catalysts of biochemical reactions are enzymes. Enzymes are proteins (in some cases lipoproteins or glycoproteins) with the specific function of catalyzing biochemical reactions. Like other catalysts, enzymes alter the rate at which a reaction occurs rather than the thermodynamic parameters of the process. An enzyme catalyzes a biochemical reaction by bonding with the reactants, generally referred to as *substrates*, in such a manner that the reaction between them is highly favored. When two reactants, A and B, are present in solution in a reaction vessel, a molecule of A comes into close proximity with a molecule of B as a result of random motion. In addition, the appropriate functional groups of A and B must achieve the proper mutual orientation if the bond-breaking and bond-making processes are to occur. By contrast, in an enzymatic reaction the substrates A and B become bonded in a precisely defined configuration at a specific location on the enzyme surface. This binding is accomplished by ionic or covalent bonding or hydrophobic interactions between functional groups of the substrate and functional groups of the aminoacyl units of the enzyme. As a result not only are the substrates brought into close proximity but the functional groups that are to undergo reaction are appropriately aligned. In fact, it has been proposed that the binding of an enzyme and its substrates so precisely positions the latter that the electron orbitals to be involved in bond breaking and bond making are directed in a manner that greatly facilitates the reaction.†

Protein molecules are ideally suited to catalyze biochemical reactions for several reasons. The side chains of the aminoacyl units of the protein provide a variety of different functional groups which can participate not only in substrate binding but also in the reaction mechanism. Among these functional groups are the carboxyl or carboxylate group of glutamyl or aspartyl units, the amino group of lysyl units, the hydroxymethyl group of seryl or threonyl units, and the imidazole or imidazolium moiety of histidyl units. Another characteristic of protein molecules that equips them to function as biochemical catalysts is their three-dimensional structure. Each different protein, and hence each different enzyme, has a unique three-dimensional structure which provides a different reaction environment for each biochemical conversion. In addition, as proteins, enzymes can undergo conformational changes, which can alter enzymatic activity. This characteristic will be seen to be important when the regulation of enzyme activity is discussed.

When an enzyme catalyzes a biochemical reaction, the enzyme and the substrate or substrates must first combine to form an enzyme-substrate complex. The location

---

† Storm, D. R., and Koshland, D. E., Jr. (1970) *Proc. Natl. Acad. Sci., U.S.A.* **66**, 445–452.

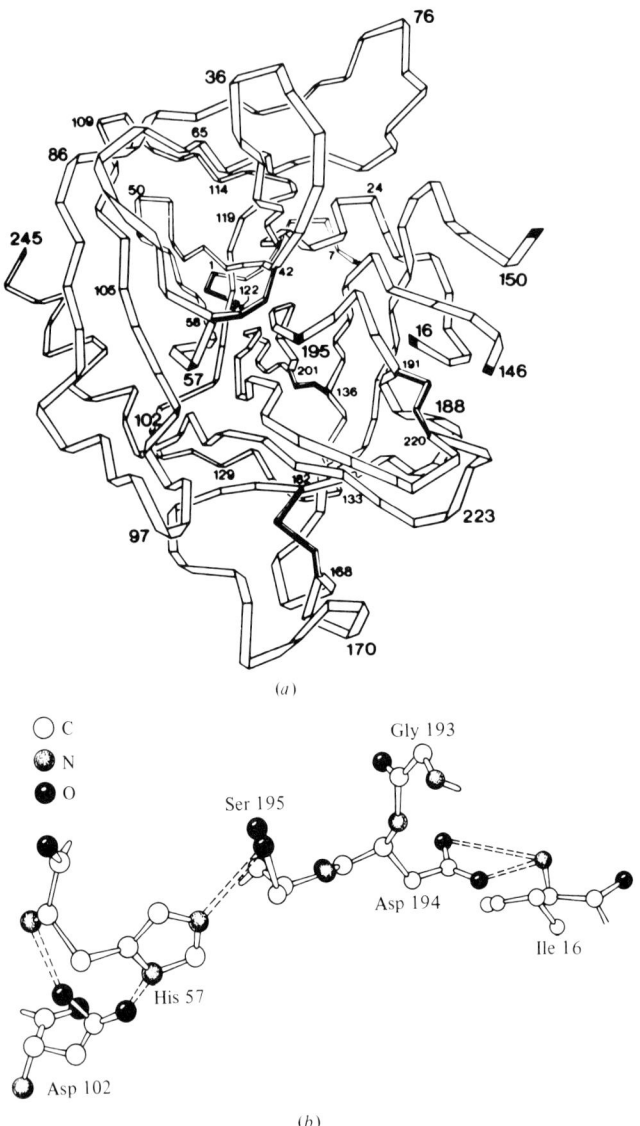

**Figure 8-3** (a) A representation of the three-dimensional structure of α-chymotrypsin, showing the positions of C(2) of the individual aminoacyl units. Notice that a dipeptide (aminoacyl units 147 and 148) is missing. This dipeptide is removed as a result of the action of one molecule of chymotrypsin upon another. This action generates a series of catalytically active species, referred to as δ-chymotrypsin, γ-chymotrypsin, and α-chymotrypsin, the last being the most stable. (b) Also shown is the catalytic site of α-chymotrypsin, where Ser-195, His-57, and Asp-102, which participate in the enzymatic reaction are designated. Also designated are Ile-16 and Asp-194. Conversion of the precursor form of chymotrypsin into the active enzyme entails the cleavage of the peptide bond between Arg-15 and Ile-16, with the result that the C(2) amino group of the isoleucyl unit is liberated. This then forms an ion pair with the C(3) carboxyl group of Asp-194. This ion-pair formation "locks" the enzyme in the conformation required for it to be catalytically active. [*From Blow, D. M. (1971) in The Enzymes (Boyer, P. D., ed.), vol. III, pp. 185–212 (see pp. 194 and 196), Academic Press, New York.*]

where the substrates are bonded is called the *catalytic site* (or the *active site*). The catalytic site of the proteolytic enzyme chymotrypsin is designated in the model shown in Fig. 8-3. As the figure shows, this site is constituted from a group of noncontiguous aminoacyl units which form the environment in which the biochemical reaction occurs. Chymotrypsin is an endopeptidase, i.e., an enzyme that catalyzes the hydrolysis of peptide bonds in the interior of a protein molecule. Chymotrypsin specifically catalyzes the hydrolysis of peptide bonds in which the carboxyl moiety is that of an aromatic aminoacyl unit. The reaction mechanism of the hydrolysis has been shown to entail the formation of a covalently bonded acyl-enzyme intermediate derived from the carboxyl group of the substrate and the hydroxymethyl group of Ser-195. In addition, the imidazole or imidazolium moiety of His-57 and the carboxyl or carboxylate moiety of Asp-102 participate in the reaction mechanism, which has been formulated as follows:

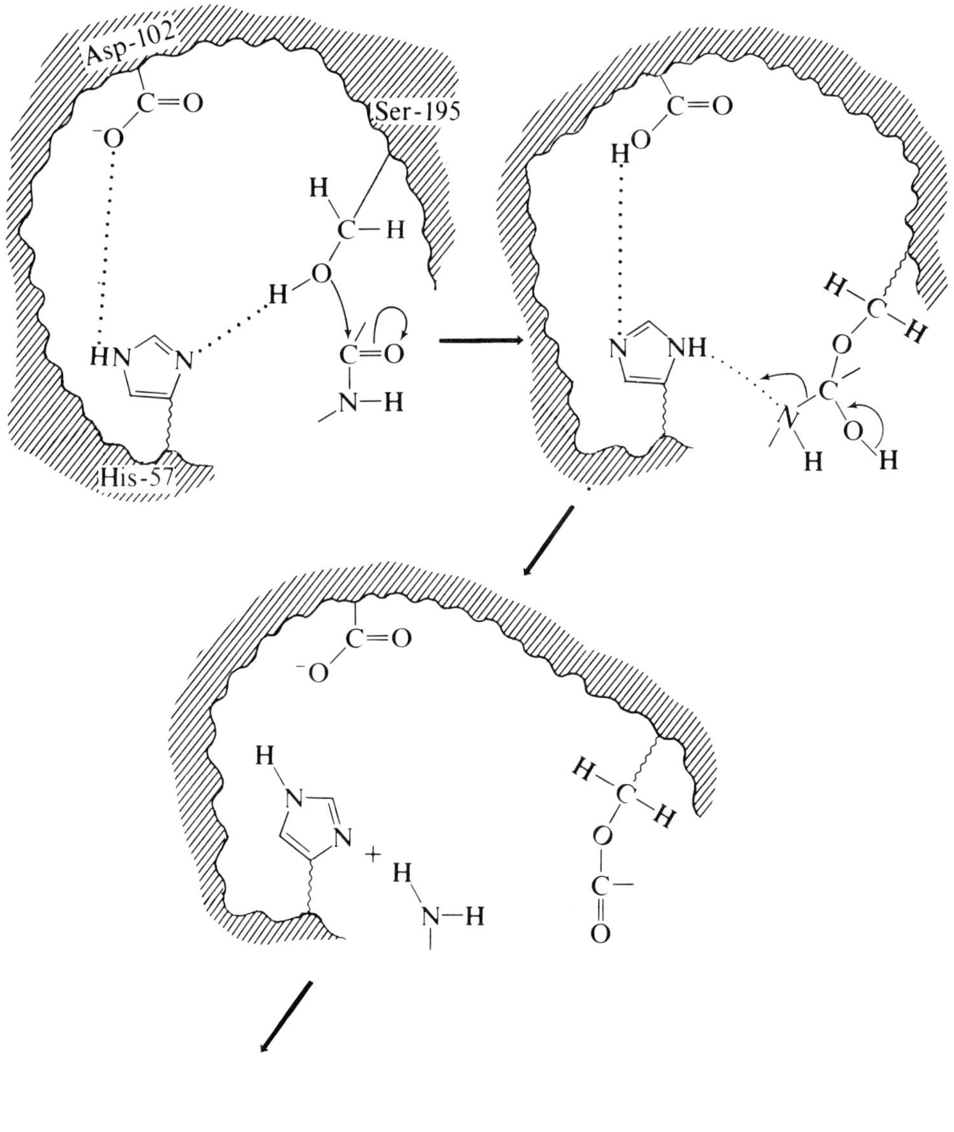

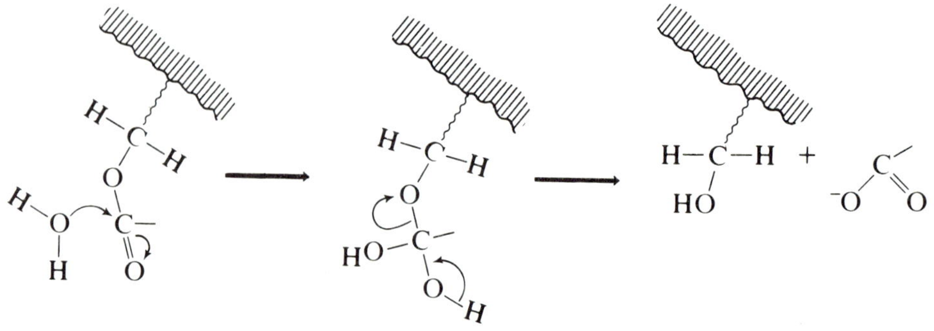

Most reactions that involve a nucleophilic attack at a carbonyl carbon atom proceed through a tetrahedral intermediate, and for this reason the hydrolysis above is shown as involving such an intermediate although its participation has not been rigorously demonstrated.

## Formulation of Equations of Enzymatic Reactions

The reaction between an enzyme and a single substrate to form an enzyme-substrate complex can be written

$$E + A \underset{k_{-1}}{\overset{k_1}{\rightleftharpoons}} EA \qquad (8\text{-}12)$$

If the enzyme-substrate complex EA is then converted irreversibly to the product P with the regeneration of the free enzyme, this can be expressed as

$$E + A \underset{k_{-1}}{\overset{k_1}{\rightleftharpoons}} EA \xrightarrow{k_2} P + E \qquad (8\text{-}13)$$

As in nonenzymatic catalysis, this intermediate complex, the enzyme-substrate complex, can either dissociate more rapidly to yield the products or dissociate more rapidly to regenerate the starting materials. If $k_{-1}$ is much greater than $k_2$, it can be assumed that the process represented by Eq. (8-12) is, in effect, at equilibrium at all times. Since $k_2$ is relatively very small, EA is an Arrhenius complex and [EA] can be calculated from the equilibrium expression

$$K = \frac{k_1}{k_{-1}} = \frac{[EA]}{[E][A]} \qquad (8\text{-}14)$$

Making the substitutions $[E] = [E]_0 - [EA]$ and $[A] = [A]_0 - [EA]$, one obtains

$$K = \frac{[EA]}{([E]_0 - [EA])([A]_0 - [EA])} \qquad (8\text{-}15)$$

When $[A]_0$ is *much greater* than $[E]_0$,

$$K = \frac{[EA]}{([E]_0 - [EA])[A]_0} \qquad (8\text{-}16)$$

and therefore

$$[EA] = \frac{[E]_0[A]_0}{[A]_0 + 1/K} \qquad (8\text{-}17)$$

Since $v = k_2[EA]$,

$$v = \frac{k_2[E]_0[A]_0}{[A]_0 + 1/K} \qquad (8\text{-}18)$$

In an enzymatic reaction the *maximum* velocity is obtained when *all* of the enzyme is complexed with the substrate or substrates. Therefore, since $v = k_2[EA]$, it follows that

$$V_{max} = k_2[E]_0 \qquad (8\text{-}19)$$

Using this relationship, one then obtains

$$v = \frac{V_{max}[A]_0}{[A]_0 + 1/K} \qquad (8\text{-}20)$$

where $K$ is the thermodynamic formation constant for the enzyme-substrate complex. If this constant is replaced by its reciprocal, the thermodynamic dissociation constant, the velocity equation becomes

$$v = \frac{V_{max}[A]_0}{[A]_0 + K_d} \qquad (8\text{-}21)$$

This constant term $K_d$ has historically been referred to as the *Michaelis constant* since Michaelis (and Menten) have been credited with formulating velocity equations for enzymatic reactions in the manner just described.† Their formation led to the concept of the Michaelis constant as a thermodynamic dissociation constant, but, as discussed below, this concept has been revised.

Since the velocity equation (8-21) is of the general form $y = ax/(x + b)$, which is the equation of the rectangular hyperbola, plots of the velocity of an enzymatic reaction as a function of substrate concentration are generally hyperbolic. On the other hand, the corresponding reciprocal equation

$$\frac{1}{v} = \frac{K_d}{V_{max}} \frac{1}{[A]_0} + \frac{1}{V_{max}} \qquad (8\text{-}22)$$

is of the general form $y = ax + b$; hence, with this treatment, data can be plotted to give a straight line. To this end, one plots $1/v$ as a function of $1/[A]$. The resulting linear plot has a slope of $K_d/V_{max}$ and an intercept on the vertical axis that is equal to $1/V_{max}$. Plots of $1/v$ vs. $1/[A]$ are often referred to as *double reciprocal plots* or *Lineweaver-Burk plots* since Lineweaver and Burk are generally credited for having

---

† Michaelis, L., and Menten, M. C. (1913) *Biochem. Z.* **49**, 333–369; see also Henri, V. (1904) *Arch. Fisiol.* **1**, 299–324.

introduced this method of treatment.† Alternatives to this method include one based on the reciprocal velocity equation

$$\frac{[A]_0}{v} = \frac{[A]_0}{V_{max}} + \frac{K}{V_{max}} \qquad (8\text{-}23)$$

and another based on the equation

$$v = V_{max} - K\frac{v}{[A]_0} \qquad (8\text{-}24)$$

For Eq. (8-23) one plots $[A]/v$ as a function of $[A]$, and for Eq. (8-24) one plots $v$ as a function of $v/[A]$. These various means of treating kinetic data are illustrated in Fig. 8-4 for comparison.

In enzymatic reactions there is also the possibility that the conversion of the enzyme-substrate complex into product will be much faster than the dissociation of the complex to regenerate the starting materials. The enzyme-substrate complex is of

---

† Lineweaver, H., and Burk, D. (1934) *J. Am. Chem. Soc.* **56,** 658–666; see also Woolf, B., as quoted by Haldane, J. B. S., and Stern, K. G. (1932) in *Allgemeine Chemie der Enzyme*, p. 119, Steinkopff, Dresden.

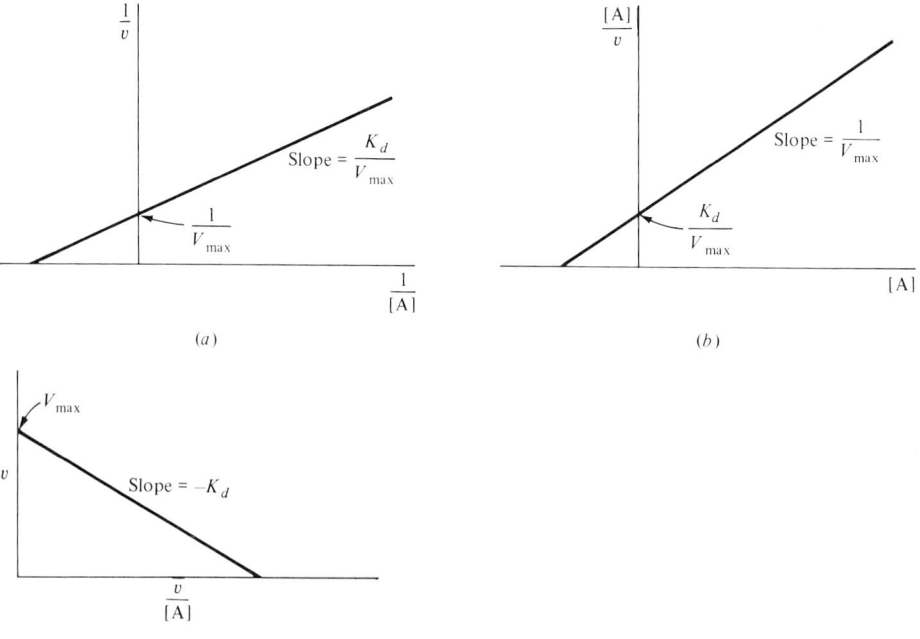

**Figure 8-4** (*a*) Lineweaver-Burk (double reciprocal) plot, (*b*) Eadie plot, and (*c*) Hofstee plot.

the van't Hoff type in this case. Enzymatic reactions of this type can be formulated in terms of the steady-state assumption.† Therefore, one can write

$$\frac{d[EA]}{dt} = k_1[E][A] - k_2[EA] - k_{-1}[EA] = 0 \qquad (8\text{-}25)$$

and since $[E] = [E]_0 - [EA]$ and $[A] = [A]_0 - [EA]$, we have

$$k_1([E]_0 - [EA])([A]_0 - [EA]) - k_2[EA] - k_{-1}[EA] = 0 \qquad (8\text{-}26)$$

When $[A]_0$ is *much greater* than $[E]_0$,

$$k_1([E]_0 - [EA])[A]_0 - k_2[EA] - k_{-1}[EA] = 0 \qquad (8\text{-}27a)$$

and
$$[EA] = \frac{k_1[E]_0[A]_0}{k_1[A]_0 + (k_{-1} + k_2)} \qquad (8\text{-}27b)$$

Now since $v = k_2[EA]$,

$$v = \frac{k_1 k_2 [E]_0 [A]_0}{k_1[A]_0 + k_{-1} + k_2} \qquad (8\text{-}28a)$$

or, substituting $V_{max}$ for $k_2[E]_0$ and rearranging,

$$v = \frac{V_{max}[A]_0}{[A]_0 + (k_{-1} + k_2)/k_1} \qquad (8\text{-}28b)$$

This equation looks quite similar to Eq. (8-21), but instead of the dissociation constant (equal to $k_{-1}/k_1$) that appears in Eq. (8-21) it includes the term $(k_{-1} + k_2)/k_1$. If *this* term is replaced by a $K$, however, Eq. (8-28b) becomes identical in form to Eq. (8-21).

Thus, using either the assumption that the enzyme-substrate complex is an Arrhenius complex or that it is a van't Hoff complex, one can derive similar equations for the reaction velocity. These equations differ, however, in the nature of their constant terms. When the Arrhenius-complex model is used, i.e., the concentration of the enzyme-substrate complex is simply the equilibrium concentration, the constant term is the thermodynamic dissociation constant. On the other hand, when the van't Hoff model is used, i.e., the concentration of the enzyme-substrate complex is the steady-state concentration, this term must also include the rate constant $k_2$ that reflects the collapse of the complex to yield products.

It is now understood that the equilibrium conditions required by the Arrhenius-complex model are rarely met in enzymatic processes and that the steady-state model is much more useful for such reactions. For this reason the constant term, or Michaelis constant, in the velocity equation for a unisubstrate reaction should not be considered a thermodynamic dissociation constant. Instead it can be considered equivalent to the concentration of substrate that allows the reaction to proceed at

---

† Briggs, H. E., and Haldane, J. B. S. (1925) *Biochem. J.* **19,** 338–339.

one-half its maximal velocity. The validity of this concept can be seen if one replaces the constant term, $(k_{-1} + k_2)/k_1$, by $[A]_0$, obtaining

$$v = \frac{V_{max}[A]_0}{[A]_0 + [A]_0} = \frac{V_{max}}{2} \tag{8-29}$$

The enzymatic processes just described are the ultimate with respect to simplicity. Most enzymatic reactions are more complicated, and many enzymatic reactions are much more complicated. As an example, according to Eq. (8-13), the enzyme-substrate complex is irreversibly converted into the product plus the regenerated enzyme. This conversion is frequently reversible, however. Thus,

$$E + A \underset{k_{-1}}{\overset{k_1}{\rightleftarrows}} EA \underset{k_{-2}}{\overset{k_2}{\rightleftarrows}} P + E \tag{8-30a}$$

The velocity of the process represented by Eq. (8-29) is given by

$$v = k_2[EA] - k_{-2}[P][E] \tag{8-30b}$$

Using the steady-state assumption, one can calculate the concentrations of E and EA to be

$$[E] = \frac{(k_{-1} + k_2)[E]_0}{k_1[A] + k_{-2}[P] + k_{-1} + k_2} \tag{8-31a}$$

$$[EA] = \frac{k_1[A][E]_0 + k_{-2}[P][E]_0}{k_1[A] + k_{-2}[P] + k_{-1} + k_2} \tag{8-31b}$$

Then

$$v = \frac{k_1 k_2 [A][E]_0 - k_{-1} k_{-2}[P][E]_0}{k_1[A] + k_{-2}[P] + k_{-1} + k_2} \tag{8-32}$$

which is similar to Eq. (8-28a) but with product terms added.

## More Complex Enzymatic Reactions

More frequently than not, enzymatic reactions involve more than one substrate and more than one product. The descriptions of such processes quickly become cumbersome. To simplify them to some extent a system of nomenclature and diagraming has been introduced by Cleland,† which is, in part, as follows:

1. Substrates are designated by the letters A, B, C, ... in the order in which they combine with the enzyme. Products are designated by the letters P, Q, R, ... in the order in which they are released from the enzyme.
2. The free enzyme is designated by E. Additional *stable* forms of the enzyme are designated by F, G, ...; F is the least complicated of the additional stable forms, G the next least complicated, and so forth.
3. Enzyme-substrate or enzyme-product complexes that are *transitory* can be of two forms, those in which all reacting components are bound at the catalytic site and

† Cleland, W. W. (1963) *Biochim. Biophys. Acta* **67**, 104–137.

those in which not all reacting components are bound at the catalytic site. The former are called *central complexes* and the latter *noncentral transitory complexes*. Central complexes are denoted by the letters which indicate the components that constitute the complex enclosed in parentheses. Noncentral transitory complexes are denoted in the same manner without parentheses.
4. The number of *kinetically significant* reactants or products, with the exception of $H^+$, is indicated by the syllables Uni (one), Bi (two), Ter (three), and Quad (four).
5. Enzymatic reactions in which *all* reacting components *must* combine with the enzyme before the release of any product are designated as *sequential*. Sequential reactions are *ordered* if there is an obligatory order in which the reactants must associate with the enzyme. Sequential reactions in which alternate pathways exist for the associations between the enzyme and the reactants are *random*. Enzymatic reactions in which one or more of the products is released before the association of all the reacting components are said to have a *ping pong* kinetic mechanism.

According to this system, an enzymatic reaction in which the two reactants must both become bound to the enzyme before any of the three products is released has a sequential Bi Ter kinetic mechanism. An enzymatic reaction in which one of the two reactants becomes bound to the enzyme and one of the two products is then released before the other reactant is bound and the second product released has a ping pong Bi Bi kinetic mechanism. These and other examples of enzymatic reactions are named and diagramed in Fig. 8-5.

## Ordered Sequential Reactions

Consider an ordered sequential bireactant process; it can be represented in its simplest form as

$$E + A \underset{k_{-1}}{\overset{k_1}{\rightleftharpoons}} EA \underset{\underset{B}{\overset{k_{-2}}{\longleftarrow}}}{\overset{\overset{B}{\downarrow} \; k_2}{\rightleftharpoons}} EAB \overset{k_3}{\longrightarrow} \text{products} \qquad (8\text{-}33)$$

Under *steady-state conditions* the following relationships can be assumed:

$$\frac{d[EA]}{dt} = k_1[E][A] + k_{-2}[EAB] - k_{-1}[EA] - k_2[EA][B] = 0 \qquad (8\text{-}34a)$$

$$\frac{d[EAB]}{dt} = k_2[EA][B] - k_{-2}[EAB] - k_3[EAB] = 0 \qquad (8\text{-}34b)$$

In addition to these equations, the *conservation equation* for the enzyme is

$$[E]_0 = [E] + [EA] + [EAB] \qquad (8\text{-}34c)$$

Using the relationships above, one can obtain the following expressions for [EA] and [EAB]:

$$[EA] = \frac{k_1[A][E]_0 - (k_1[A] + k_{-2})[EAB]}{k_1[A] + k_2[B] + k_{-1}} \qquad (8\text{-}35)$$

$$[EAB] = \frac{k_1 k_2 [A][B][E]_0}{k_1(k_{-2} + k_3)[A] + k_2 k_3 [B] + k_1 k_2 [A][B] + k_{-1}(k_{-2} + k_3)} \qquad (8\text{-}36)$$

**296** MECHANISMS OF METABOLISM

Ordered sequential Bi Bi:

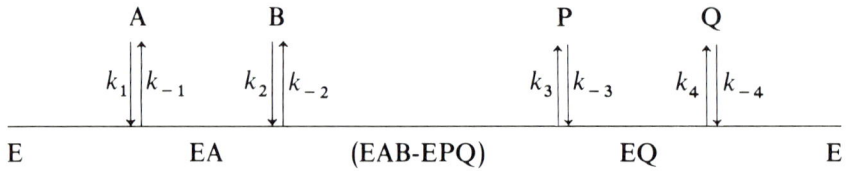

Ping pong Bi Bi:

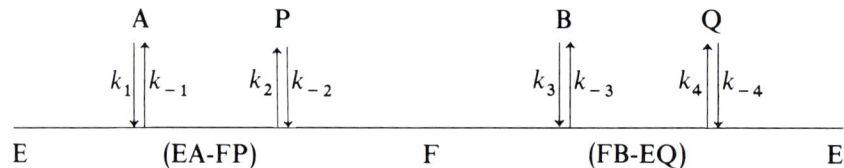

Random sequential Bi Bi:

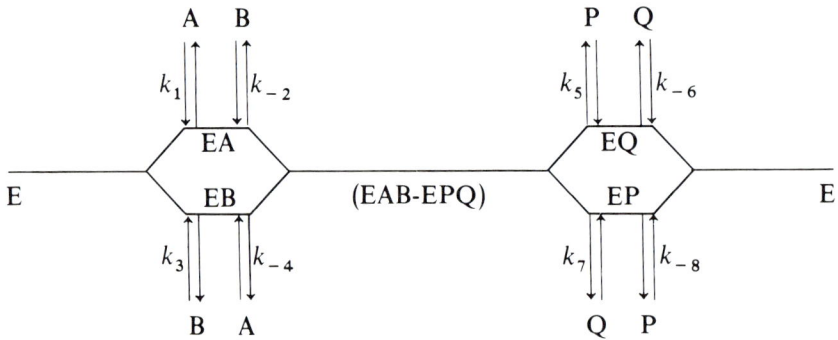

Ping pong Bi Uni Uni Bi:

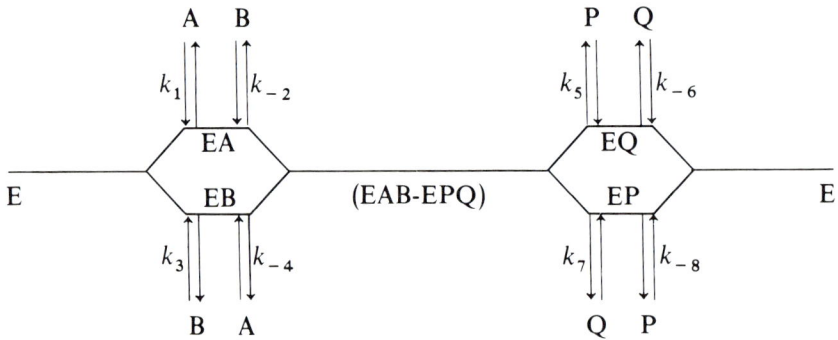

**Figure 8-5** Diagrammatic representation of some of the more common kinetic mechanisms.

Since the velocity of the reaction is given by $v = k_3[\text{EAB}]$, one can write

$$v = \frac{k_1 k_2 k_3 [\text{A}][\text{B}][\text{E}]_0}{k_1(k_{-2} + k_3)[\text{A}] + k_2 k_3 [\text{B}] + k_1 k_2 [\text{A}][\text{B}] + k_{-1}(k_{-2} + k_3)} \qquad (8\text{-}37a)$$

Single constants are frequently substituted for the combinations of rate constants obtained when a velocity equation is developed. Cleland has used the constants $K_a$, $K_b$, ... and $K_{ia}$, $K_{ib}$, ... in the formulation of velocity equations for kinetic mechanisms that do not involve alternate pathways. (An exception is the equations for rapid equilibrium random mechanisms, which are also expressed in terms of these constants.) Constants such as $K_a$ and $K_b$ have been designated as the Michaelis constants for substrates A and B, respectively. When the enzymatic reaction is reversible and the products of the forward reaction become the substrates in the reverse reaction, the constants $K_p$ and $K_q$ are used to designate the Michaelis constants for P and Q, respectively. Remember that earlier, in the discussion of unisubstrate reactions, the constant term was designated as a Michaelis constant, which was stated to have a value equivalent to the concentration of the single substrate permitting the reaction to occur at one-half its maximum velocity. In a similar manner, when bisubstrate or trisubstrate (or polysubstrate) reactions are considered, the Michaelis constant of a given substrate has a value equivalent to the concentration of *that substrate* which permits the reaction to occur at one-half its maximum velocity *when all other substrates are present at saturating concentrations.* This concept of a Michaelis constant is analogous to that for the unisubstrate reaction, since when all other substrates are present at saturating concentrations, the reaction becomes, in effect, a first-order process which depends only upon the concentration of the one substrate under consideration. The constants $K_{ia}$ and $K_{ib}$, on the other hand, have been designated by Cleland as inhibition constants since their value is generally identical to that of the product-inhibition constant if A or B, were functioning as a product inhibitor in the reverse reaction. Considering the denominator of the equation for the ordered sequential Bi Bi reaction above, three such constants are generally introduced in place of the combinations of individual rate constants. These are

$$K_b = \frac{\text{coef A}}{\text{coef AB}} = \frac{k_{-2} + k_3}{k_2} \qquad K_a = \frac{\text{coef B}}{\text{coef AB}} = \frac{k_3}{k_1} \qquad K_{ia} = \frac{\text{const}}{\text{coef A}} = \frac{k_{-1}}{k_1}$$

When these are used, Eq. (8-37$a$) becomes

$$v = \frac{k_1 k_2 k_3 [\text{A}][\text{B}][\text{E}]_0}{K_b [\text{A}] + K_a [\text{B}] + [\text{A}][\text{B}] + K_{ia} K_b} \qquad (8\text{-}37b)$$

If the additional substitution

$$V_{\text{max}} = \frac{k_1 k_2 k_3 [\text{E}]_0}{\text{coef AB}} = k_3 [\text{E}]_0$$

is also made, the velocity equation becomes

$$v = \frac{V_{\text{max}}[\text{A}][\text{B}]}{K_b [\text{A}] + K_a [\text{B}] + [\text{A}][\text{B}] + K_{ia} K_b} \qquad (8\text{-}37c)$$

The reader has probably noted that in Eqs. (8-37$b$) and (8-37$c$) [A] is multiplied by $K_b$ while [B] is multiplied by $K_a$; as shown below, the velocity equation can be written in a form in which $K_b$ modifies [B] and $K_a$ modifies [A], but it is the *reciprocal concentrations* that are so modified:

$$v = \frac{V_{max}}{K_b/[B] + K_a/[A] + 1 + K_{ia}K_b/[A][B]} \tag{8-37d}$$

Generally, equations of the form of Eq. (8-37c) will be used in this text.

In the enzymatic reaction formulated above a single central complex collapses to yield the product and the regenerated enzyme. This is not an accurate representation of most enzymatic reactions, however. Evidence suggests that more often the initial central complex is converted into a second central complex (and perhaps, in some cases, into a third central complex), which then undergoes dissociation to yield the products. A reaction involving the conversion of the initial central complex into a second central complex can be represented as

$$E + A \underset{k_{-1}}{\overset{k_1}{\rightleftarrows}} EA \underset{\underset{B}{\downarrow k_{-2}}}{\overset{\overset{B}{\downarrow k_2}}{\rightleftarrows}} EAB \underset{k_{-3}}{\overset{k_3}{\rightleftarrows}} EPQ \overset{k_4}{\longrightarrow} \text{products} \tag{8-38}$$

Under steady-state conditions,

$$\frac{d[EA]}{dt} = k_1[E][A] + k_{-2}[EAB] - k_{-1}[EA] - k_2[EA][B] = 0 \tag{8-39a}$$

$$\frac{d[EAB]}{dt} = k_2[EA][B] + k_{-3}[EPQ] - k_{-2}[EAB] - k_3[EAB] = 0 \tag{8-39b}$$

$$\frac{d[EPQ]}{dt} = k_3[EAB] - k_{-3}[EPQ] - k_4[EPQ] = 0 \tag{8-39c}$$

Also $\quad [E]_0 = [E] + [EA] + [EAB] + [EPQ] \tag{8-39d}$

These equations can be utilized as above to obtain expressions for [E], [EA], [EAB], and [EPQ]. Then since the velocity of the reaction $v$ is given by $k_4[EPQ]$, one can write

$$v = k_1 k_2 k_3 k_4 [A][B][E]_0 / \{(k_1 k_{-2} k_{-3} + k_1 k_{-2} k_4 + k_1 k_3 k_4)[A]$$
$$+ k_2 k_3 k_4 [B] + (k_1 k_2 k_{-3} + k_1 k_2 k_4 + k_1 k_2 k_3)[A][B]$$
$$+ (k_{-1} k_{-2} k_{-3} + k_{-1} k_3 k_4 + k_{-1} k_{-2} k_4)\} \tag{8-40a}$$

If the substitutions

$$K_b = \frac{\text{coef A}}{\text{coef AB}} = \frac{k_{-2} k_{-3} + k_{-2} k_4 + k_3 k_4}{k_2(k_3 + k_{-3} + k_4)}$$

$$K_a = \frac{\text{coef B}}{\text{coef AB}} = \frac{k_3 k_4}{k_1(k_3 + k_{-3} + k_4)}$$

$$K_{ia} = \frac{\text{const}}{\text{coef A}} = \frac{k_{-1}}{k_1}$$

are made in the denominator, and if the substitution

$$V_{max} = \frac{k_1 k_2 k_3 k_4 [E]_0}{\text{coef AB}}$$

is made in the numerator, one obtains

$$v = \frac{V_{max}[A][B]}{K_b[A] + K_a[B] + [A][B] + K_{ia}K_b} \quad (8\text{-}40b)$$

which is identical in form to Eq. (8-37c) although the terms that were combined to give the various constants, that is, $K_b$, $K_a$, $K_{ia}$, and $V_{max}$, are quite different.

No mention has been made of the possibility of an ordered release of two (or more) products. In actuality, the ordered binding of substrates is frequently accompanied by an ordered release of products, as represented diagrammatically by

$$E + A \underset{k_{-1}}{\overset{k_1}{\rightleftharpoons}} EA \underset{k_{-2}}{\overset{k_2}{\underset{B}{\overset{B}{\rightleftharpoons}}}} EAB \underset{k_{-3}}{\overset{k_3}{\rightleftharpoons}} EPQ \underset{k_{-4}}{\overset{k_4}{\underset{P}{\overset{P}{\rightleftharpoons}}}} EQ \underset{k_{-5}}{\overset{k_5}{\rightleftharpoons}} E + Q$$

(8-41)

The velocity equation for this more complicated reaction can be developed, but the result is cumbersome and of limited usefulness. (The complete equation for an ordered sequential Bi Bi reaction which entails an ordered release of products is developed in Appendix A.) On the other hand, the *initial velocity* of this reaction is a much less complex expression with considerable usefulness. For the purposes of developing an initial-velocity equation it is assumed that the products P and Q are absent or present in only infinitesimal amounts and that the reactions denoted by $k_{-4}$ and $k_{-5}$ can therefore be neglected. Proceeding as previously, one can obtain

$$\frac{d[EA]}{dt} = k_1[E][A] + k_{-2}[EAB] - k_{-1}[EA] - k_2[EA][B] = 0 \quad (8\text{-}42a)$$

$$\frac{d[EAB]}{dt} = k_2[EA][B] + k_{-3}[EPQ] - k_3[EAB] - k_{-2}[EAB] = 0 \quad (8\text{-}42b)$$

$$\frac{d[EPQ]}{dt} = k_3[EAB] - k_4[EPQ] - k_{-3}[EPQ] = 0 \quad (8\text{-}42c)$$

$$\frac{d[EQ]}{dt} = k_4[EPQ] - k_5[EQ] = 0 \quad (8\text{-}42d)$$

$$[E]_0 = [E] + [EA] + [EAB] + [EPQ] + [EQ] \quad (8\text{-}42e)$$

From the equations above, the following initial-velocity equation is obtained:

$$v_i = k_1 k_2 k_3 k_4 k_5 [A][B][E]_0 / \{(k_1 k_{-2} k_{-3} k_5 + k_1 k_{-2} k_4 k_5 + k_1 k_3 k_4 k_5)[A]$$
$$+ k_2 k_3 k_4 k_5 [B] + (k_1 k_2 k_{-3} k_5 + k_1 k_2 k_4 k_5 + k_1 k_2 k_3 k_5 + k_1 k_2 k_3 k_4)[A][B]$$
$$+ (k_{-1} k_{-2} k_{-3} k_5 + k_{-1} k_{-2} k_4 k_5 + k_{-1} k_3 k_4 k_5)\} \quad (8\text{-}43a)$$

If the following substitutions are made as before,

$$K_b = \frac{\text{coef A}}{\text{coef AB}} = \frac{k_5(k_{-2}k_{-3} + k_{-2}k_4 + k_3k_4)}{k_2(k_3k_4 + k_3k_5 + k_{-3}k_5 + k_4k_5)}$$

$$K_a = \frac{\text{coef B}}{\text{coef AB}} = \frac{k_3k_4k_5}{k_1(k_3k_4 + k_3k_5 + k_{-3}k_5 + k_4k_5)}$$

$$K_{ia} = \frac{\text{const}}{\text{coef A}} = \frac{k_{-1}(k_{-2}k_{-3} + k_{-2}k_4 + k_3k_5)}{k_1(k_{-2}k_{-3} + k_{-2}k_4 + k_3k_4)} = \frac{k_{-1}}{k_1}$$

$$V_{max} = \frac{k_1k_2k_3k_4k_5[E]_0}{k_1k_2(k_3k_4 + k_3k_5 + k_{-3}k_5 + k_4k_5)}$$

Eq. (8-43a) becomes

$$v_i = \frac{V_{max}[A][B]}{K_b[A] + K_a[B] + [A][B] + K_{ia}K_b} \tag{8-43b}$$

Thus, the equation can be written in the same form as before [see Eqs. (8-37c) and (8-40b)]. The terms $K_a$, $K_b$, $K_{ia}$, and $V_{max}$ represent *much* more complex collections of rate constants, however.

## Ping Pong Reactions

Remember that in a bisubstrate (or polysubstrate) enzymatic process there is the possibility that a product can be released after the binding of one substrate but before the binding of another. Such processes are referred to as ping pong reactions. A ping pong Bi Bi reaction can be represented as

$$E + A \underset{k_{-1}}{\overset{k_1}{\rightleftharpoons}} (EA\text{-}FP) \underset{k_{-2}}{\overset{k_2}{\underset{P}{\rightleftharpoons}}} F \underset{k_{-3}}{\overset{k_3}{\underset{B}{\rightleftharpoons}}} (FB\text{-}EQ) \underset{k_{-4}}{\overset{k_4}{\rightleftharpoons}} E + Q \tag{8-44}$$

A velocity equation for such a process can be developed, but since it is cumbersome, the initial-velocity equation is generally used instead. The initial-velocity equation for a ping pong Bi Bi reaction can be shown to be as follows (the reader will probably wish to confirm this by developing the equation):

$$v_i = k_1k_2k_3k_4[A][B][E]_0 / \{(k_1k_2k_{-3} + k_1k_2k_4)[A] + (k_{-1}k_3k_4 + k_2k_3k_4)[B]$$
$$+ (k_1k_2k_3 + k_1k_3k_4)[A][B]\} \tag{8-45}$$

If the substitutions

$$K_b = \frac{\text{coef A}}{\text{coef AB}} = \frac{k_2(k_{-3} + k_4)}{k_3(k_2 + k_4)}$$

$$K_a = \frac{\text{coef B}}{\text{coef AB}} = \frac{k_4(k_{-1} + k_2)}{k_1(k_2 + k_4)}$$

$$V_{max} = \frac{k_1k_2k_3k_4[E]_0}{\text{coef AB}} = \frac{k_1k_2k_3k_4[E]_0}{k_1k_3(k_2 + k_4)}$$

are made, Eq. (8-45) becomes

$$v_i = \frac{V_{max}[A][B]}{K_b[A] + K_a[B] + [A][B]} \tag{8-46}$$

which is similar in form to Eq. (8-43b) except that (8-46) lacks the constant term $K_{ia}K_b$ present in the denominator of (8-43b).

## Random Reactions

Yet another possibility in considering enzymatic reactions is that the binding of the substrates by the enzyme occurs in a random manner although all substrates must be bound before the dissociation of the initial product that is released. As an example, consider the random sequential Bi Bi reaction

```
           A B                P Q
           ↕ ↕                ↕ ↕
          /EA\              /EQ\
       E \EB/(EAB · EPQ)\EP/ E
           ↕ ↕                ↕ ↕
           B A                Q P
```

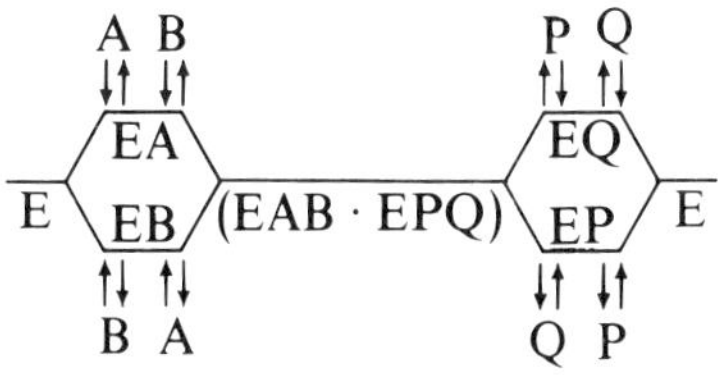

Velocity equations can be developed for such a process, but, as might be expected, they are complex. Even the initial-velocity equation for the random sequential reaction is complex. (It is developed along with certain other velocity equations in Appendix A.) This initial-velocity equation is of the form

$$v_i = V_{max}(K_1[A][B] + K_2[A]^2[B] + [A][B]^2)/\{K_3[A] + K_4[B] + K_5[A]^2 + K_6[B]^2$$
$$+ K_7[A][B] + K_2[A]^2[B] + [A][B]^2 + K_8\} \tag{8-47}$$

The initial-velocity equation for a random sequential Bi Bi reaction includes second-order terms in [A] and [B]. For this reason, even the double reciprocal plots, i.e., plots of $1/v_i$ vs. $1/[A]$ or of $1/v_i$ vs. $1/[B]$, are generally nonlinear.

## Characterization of Enzymatic Reactions

One of the principal goals of enzyme-kinetic studies is to determine the kinetic mechanism of the reaction. This goal is generally approached by attempting to fit experimentally obtained data to a velocity equation. As shown above, a *bisubstrate sequential* reaction will have an initial-velocity equation of the following general form if the process is ordered and also if it is a rapid equilibrium random reaction or of the Theorell-Chance type:

$$v_i = \frac{V_{max}[A][B]}{K_b[A] + K_a[B] + [A][B] + K_{ia}K_b} \tag{8-48}$$

A rapid equilibrium random reaction is a *special case* of a random reaction. It is characterized by the fact that all the substrate binding reactions are *much faster* than the interconversion of the initial central complex to the central complex that dissociates to yield the products. Since this interconversion of the central complexes is the slowest event, it is the *rate-determining* event in a rapid equilibrium random reaction. A Theorell-Chance mechanism, on the other hand, can be considered as a variant of an ordered sequential mechanism in which the steady-state level of the central complex (or complexes) is vanishingly small. Since it is generally easier to fit data to a straight line than to a curve, the reciprocal form of Eq. (8-48) is frequently used in this process of data fitting. Reciprocal forms of Eq. (8-48) are equations of a straight line:

$$\frac{1}{v_i} = \frac{K_a}{V_{max}}\left(1 + \frac{K_{ia}K_b}{K_a[B]}\right)\frac{1}{[A]} + \frac{1}{V_{max}}\left(1 + \frac{K_b}{[B]}\right) \tag{8-49a}$$

$$\frac{1}{v_i} = \frac{K_b}{V_{max}}\left(1 + \frac{K_{ia}}{[A]}\right)\frac{1}{[B]} + \frac{1}{V_{max}}\left(1 + \frac{K_a}{[A]}\right) \tag{8-49b}$$

If one is able to fit the experimentally obtained data to these equations, it is an indication (but not conclusive proof) that the bisubstrate reaction is sequential.

On the other hand, if a bisubstrate reaction has a ping pong mechanism, the data should be fitted best by the reciprocal forms of

$$v_i = \frac{V_{max}[A][B]}{K_b[A] + K_a[B] + [A][B]} \tag{8-50}$$

given by

$$\frac{1}{v_i} = \frac{K_a}{V_{max}}\frac{1}{[A]} + \frac{1}{V_{max}}\left(1 + \frac{K_b}{[B]}\right) \tag{8-51a}$$

and

$$\frac{1}{v_i} = \frac{K_b}{V_{max}}\frac{1}{[B]} + \frac{1}{V_{max}}\left(1 + \frac{K_a}{[A]}\right) \tag{8-51b}$$

Should the bisubstrate reaction have a random kinetic mechanism, this fact will generally have been suggested by the observation that the data cannot be fitted to a straight line using either of the sets of reciprocal equations.

The procedure for fitting experimentally obtained data to an equation, e.g., one of the reciprocal equations above, can be described as follows. This description is specifically applicable to a bisubstrate reaction although data derived from reactions involving more than two substrates can be treated in a generally similar manner. The initial velocity of the reaction is determined (by some convenient means such as spectrophotometry or radiochemical assay) in the presence of a given concentration of one substrate, designated as the *variable substrate*, with a fixed concentration of the other. The velocity is then determined in the presence of another concentration of the variable substrate with the same fixed concentration of the other substrate. The procedure is repeated several times more, and then the reciprocal velocities so obtained are plotted as a function of the appropriate reciprocal concentrations. If the reaction has an ordered sequential (or rapid equilibrium random or Theorell-Chance) or ping pong kinetic mechanism, this plot of $1/v_i$ as a function of $1/[A]$ or $1/[B]$ will be a straight line. The entire process is repeated, again using a series of concentrations of the variable substrate with (in this case) a different fixed concentration of the second substrate. The data so obtained can then be used to generate a second straight line. This is repeated until, generally, data for four or five such lines have been generated. The resulting family of straight lines is then used as described below to provide evidence for the nature of the kinetic mechanism of the reaction.

Double reciprocal initial-velocity plots are perhaps most useful in distinguishing between ordered sequential and ping pong kinetic mechanisms. The family of lines obtained as described above will *intersect* at a point to the left of the vertical axis if the kinetic mechanism of the enzymatic reaction is ordered sequential, rapid equilibrium random, or of the Theorell-Chance type. Because the vertical coordinate of the point of intersection (Fig. 8-6) is given by $(1/V_{max})(1 - K_a/K_{ia})$, these lines will cross *above* the horizontal axis when $K_{ia}$ is greater than $K_a$, *on* the horizontal axis when $K_{ia}$ is equal to $K_a$, and *below* the horizontal axis when $K_{ia}$ is less than $K_a$.

If instead a family of *parallel* lines is obtained, it suggests that the reaction proceeds by means of a ping pong kinetic mechanism. Notice that in contrast to Eqs. (8-49a) and (8-49b), Eqs. (8-51a) and (8-51b) do not contain the concentration of the fixed substrate in the term that defines the slope of the plot. Therefore, the effect of changing the fixed concentration of the nonvariable substrate is simply that of changing the intercept of the line. The slopes of all the lines are the same; therefore, the lines are parallel.

One may ask at this point about the difference between these two types of mechanisms manifested by these two types of double reciprocal plots. The difference is that in the ping pong mechanism there is a product-dissociation step between the

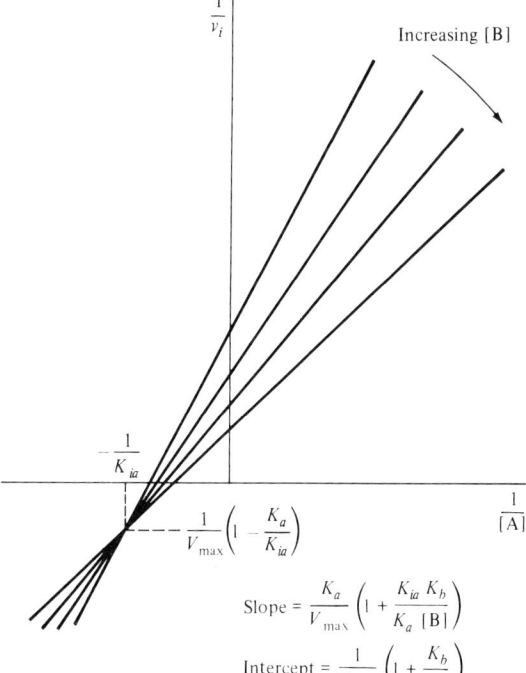

**Figure 8-6** Characteristic double reciprocal plot of data derived from initial-velocity studies on a reaction that has an ordered sequential Bi Bi kinetic mechanism.

point in the reaction at which the first substrate binds and that at which the second substrate binds. The release of a product when there is a vanishingly small ("zero") concentration of that product in the surrounding medium (as would occur under initial-velocity conditions) is referred to as an *irreversible step* in the reaction sequence. If one or more irreversible steps occur between the point in the reaction sequence at which the variable substrate binds and that at which the fixed substrate binds, the double reciprocal plots derived from the initial-velocity data will be parallel. If there are no irreversible steps between the points in the reaction sequence at which the variable and fixed substrates bind the enzyme, the double reciprocal plots will intersect.

The double reciprocal plots described above in conjunction with replots of their slopes and intercepts can also be used to evaluate the constants of the velocity equations. As an example, in an ordered sequential Bi Bi reaction the constants of a velocity equation having the form of Eq. (8-48) can be evaluated as follows. Consider the double reciprocal plots derived when A was the variable substrate. If one plots the vertical-axis intercepts of each of these plots as a function of the corresponding value for 1/[B], a straight line is obtained. The equation for this line is

$$\text{I replot} = \frac{K_b}{V_{\max}} \frac{1}{[B]} + \frac{1}{V_{\max}} \tag{8-52}$$

Its vertical-axis intercept is $1/V_{\max}$. Its slope is $K_b/V_{\max}$. Therefore, $K_b$ can be evaluated. If one now also plots the slopes of each of the double reciprocal plots derived when A was the variable substrate, again as a function of $1/[B]$, another straight line is obtained. Its equation is

$$\text{S replot} = \frac{K_{ia} K_b}{V_{\max}} \frac{1}{[B]} + \frac{K_a}{V_{\max}} \tag{8-53}$$

The value of the intercept term of this replot allows $K_a$ to be evaluated (since $V_{\max}$ has already been evaluated), and the value of the slope term allows $K_{ia}$ to be evaluated (since both $K_b$ and $V_{\max}$ have been evaluated). Thus, values for all four of the constants can be obtained. (See Fig. 8-7.)

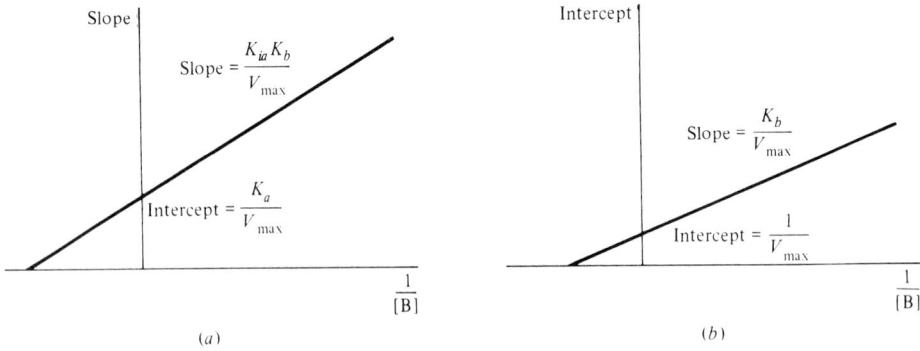

**Figure 8-7** (a) Slope and (b) intercept replots of data from double reciprocal plots derived from initial velocity studies on a reaction that has an ordered sequential Bi Bi kinetic mechanism.

Evaluation of the kinetic constants of an initial-velocity equation is somewhat simpler when the reaction proceeds by a ping pong mechanism. If the data have been fitted to an equation of the form of Eq. (8-50), the kinetic constants can be evaluated as follows. The concentrations of the two substrates are varied together at a constant ratio, and a double reciprocal plot of $1/v_i$ vs. either $1/[A]$ or $1/[B]$ is prepared. The reciprocal-velocity equation when A is the variable substrate and the concentration of B is $[A]/x$ is

$$\frac{1}{v_i} = \frac{K_a + xK_b}{V_{max}} \frac{1}{[A]} + \frac{1}{V_{max}} \tag{8-54}$$

Thus, $V_{max}$ can be evaluated immediately since it is the intercept of the plot of $1/v_i$ as a function of $1/[A]$. The slope of this plot is $(K_a + xK_b)/V_{max}$, and $K_a + xK_b$ can therefore be evaluated. If a second plot is then prepared from data obtained when A and B are again varied together but at a *different* constant ratio, $K_a$ and $K_b$ can be evaluated.

Methods like these for the evaluation of kinetic constants are generally not useful for random sequential reactions, but in the very special case of a rapid equilibrium random reaction, the data can be treated in much the same manner as for an ordered sequential reaction.

**Inhibition studies in the characterization of enzymatic reactions** The rates of enzymatic reactions are subject both to enhancement and inhibition. Inhibition studies are particularly powerful tools in the characterization of kinetic mechanisms. In general, an inhibitor functions as such as a result of its ability to form a complex with one or more of the enzyme forms. Enzyme inhibition has been characterized as being *competitive, uncompetitive,* or *noncompetitive*. These three designations are made on the basis of the effect of the concentration of the inhibitor upon the slopes and intercepts of the double reciprocal plots derived when one substrate of the reaction is varied with each of several fixed concentrations of the inhibitor and with the concentrations of all other substrates constant throughout the entire group of experiments.

If *only* the *slopes* of such plots vary as different fixed concentrations of the inhibitor are used, the inhibition is said to be *competitive* with respect to that variable substrate. Slope effects are seen when an inhibitor causes a diminution in the concentration of the enzyme form with which the variable substrate combines, relative to the concentration of the enzyme-variable-substrate complex. In competitive inhibition, the inhibitor combines with the *same* enzyme form as the variable substrate, and hence there is less of this enzyme form available to this substrate. Thus, if substrate A combines with E, when an inhibitor that also can combine with E is present, there is less E available to A and the ratio [E]/[EA] is diminished. Since competitive inhibition is the result of the inhibitor combining with the same enzyme form as the variable substrate, it follows that the effect of this inhibitor must disappear in the presence of extremely high, i.e., "infinite," concentrations of the variable substrate. The ability of very high concentrations of the variable substrate to obliterate the effect of a competitive inhibitor is characteristic and is, in fact, another expression of the stipulation that competitive inhibition involves only slope effects.

If *only the intercepts* of the double reciprocal plots, described above, vary as different fixed concentrations of the inhibitor are used, the inhibitor is said to be *uncompetitive* with respect to the variable substrate. In this case, the inhibitor combines with a *different* enzyme form than the variable substrate. Its effect with respect to the variable substrate is that of diminishing the total amount of enzyme available for distribution among the various enzyme forms. Infinite concentrations of the variable substrate fail to eliminate the effects of the uncompetitive inhibitor, in contrast to the situation when the inhibitor is a competitive one. When only the intercepts of a family of double reciprocal plots vary, the plots constitute a series of parallel lines.

When several fixed concentrations of some inhibitors are used with a given variable substrate, *both the slopes and the intercepts* of the double reciprocal plots are altered. In these cases the inhibitor is said to be *noncompetitive* with respect to the variable substrate. Noncompetitive inhibition can come about in the following manner. If an inhibitor combines with a different enzyme form than that with which the variable substrate combines, *and* if the point in the reaction sequence at which this inhibitor binds is *before* that at which the variable substrate binds, *and* if there are no irreversible steps between these two points, an intercept effect as well as a slope effect will be seen. The intercept effect occurs because the inhibitor binds a different enzyme form than the variable substrate and therefore "infinite" concentrations of this substrate cannot obliterate the effect of the inhibitor. The slope effect is seen because the inhibitor binds before binding of the variable substrate, and since there are no irreversible steps in between, this binding causes a diminution in the concentration of the enzyme form that the variable substrate binds. Noncompetitive inhibition can also occur when the inhibitor induces an increase in the concentration of the enzyme–variable substrate complex, as will be discussed when the focus is upon product inhibitors. The characteristic double reciprocal plots obtained when competitive, uncompetitive, or noncompetitive inhibition is present are shown in Fig. 8-8.

**Product inhibition** Product-inhibition studies are a routine part of characterizing a kinetic mechanism. All products are inhibitors of the forward reaction since they bind one or more of the enzyme forms that participate in this reaction and thereby diminish their availability. However, different kinetic mechanisms are associated with different product-inhibition patterns.

Suppose that initial-velocity studies have suggested that the kinetic mechanism of the Bi Bi reaction under study is an ordered sequential one and one would like to gain additional evidence in support of this and also to establish the order of substrate binding and product release if possible. To this end, one would carry out four product-inhibition studies, i.e., one with each of the two substrates with each of the two products as the inhibitor. If the kinetic mechanism of the reaction is in fact ordered sequential, in three of the four cases the product inhibition will be of the noncompetitive type while in the fourth it will be competitive. This being the case, the one competitive pattern now provides clues to the order of substrate binding and product release. Specifically, since competitive inhibition is seen when the inhibitor and the variable substrate bind the same enzyme form, the variable substrate that was used when the competitive pattern was obtained must be the first substrate that

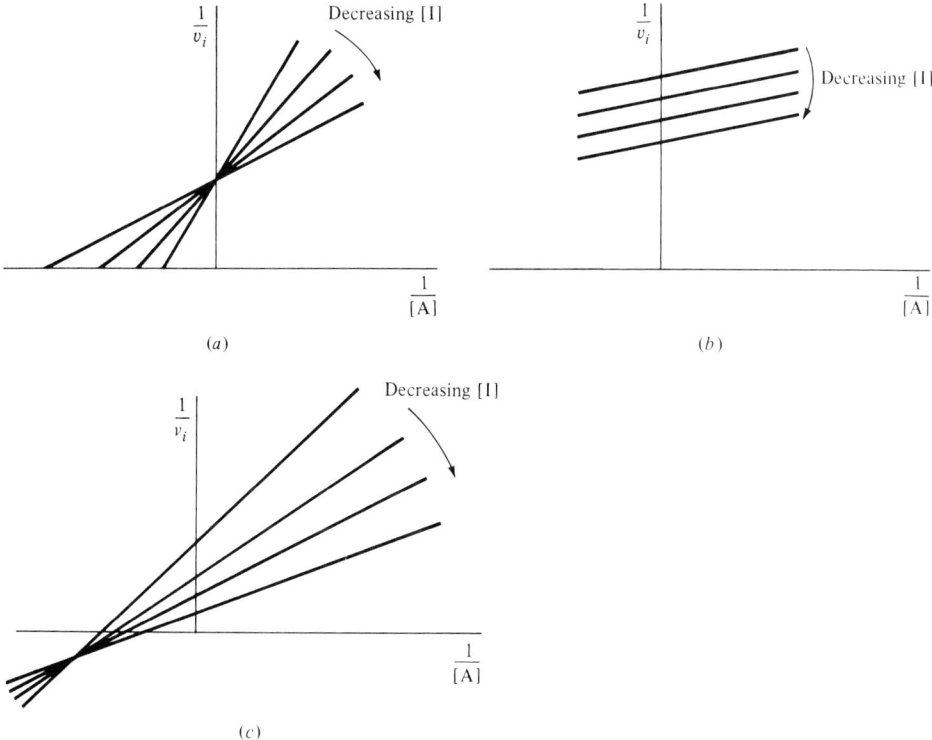

**Figure 8-8** Characteristic double reciprocal plots of data derived from studies in which I (the inhibitor) induces (a) competitive inhibition, (b) uncompetitive inhibition, and (c) noncompetitive inhibition.

binds, while the inhibitor in this instance must be the last product released. This is because *only* the initial substrate and the final product bind the same enzyme form, i.e., the noncomplexed enzyme. Since there are only two substrates and two products, the entire binding and release sequence is thus determined.

Let us now examine the rationale for the three noncompetitive product-inhibition patterns characteristic of an ordered sequential Bi Bi reaction. In each of these three cases, i.e., when A is the variable substrate and P is the inhibitor or when B is the variable substrate and either P or Q is the inhibitor, both an intercept and a slope effect are seen. The intercept effect results because the inhibitor and the variable substrate do not bind the same enzyme form. The slope effect, on the other hand, comes about as follows. In each case the product binds the enzyme at a point in the reaction sequence that is subsequent to that at which the variable substrate binds, *and* there are no irreversible steps between these points of binding (assuming that the concentrations of the nonvaried substrates are not saturating). Under these circumstances the addition of either P or Q produces an increase in the concentration of the enzyme–variable-substrate complex, that is, EA when A is the variable substrate or EAB-EPQ when B is the variable substrate. This is the result of a process which may be viewed as a backing up of the flow of the forward reaction. Thus, when A is the variable substrate and the concentration of EA is increased, causing the ratio

[E]/[EA] to decrease, a slope effect is seen. Similarly, when B is the variable substrate and the concentration of EAB-EPQ is increased, causing the ratio [EA]/[EAB-EPQ] to decrease, a slope effect is seen. Thus, in these cases, the diminution of the concentration of the enzyme form with which the variable substrate combines, relative to the concentration of the enzyme–variable-substrate complex, comes about because the denominator term becomes larger rather than because the numerator term becomes smaller, as when the inhibitor binds at a point in the reaction sequence prior to that at which the variable substrate binds.

If the sequential Bi Bi reaction has a random or a Theorell-Chance mechanism, a different spectrum of product-inhibition patterns will be observed. When substrate binding and product release are random, plots of $1/v_i$ as a function of $1/[A]$ or $1/[B]$ are, under most circumstances, nonlinear as mentioned previously and furthermore all product-inhibition effects are usually noncompetitive because either product can bind the enzyme instead of, and usually in addition to, the substrate that is being varied. The binding of the product inhibitor *instead* of the variable substrate is manifested as a slope effect; the binding of the product inhibitor *in addition to* the variable substrate is manifested as an intercept effect. When both these events occur, four noncompetitive product-inhibition patterns result.

On the other hand, in the special case of the rapid equilibrium random reaction, plots of $1/v_i$ vs. $1/[A]$ are linear, and product-inhibition effects are generally competitive. Again, either product can bind instead of, and in addition to, the substrate that is being varied. It must be remembered, however, that the reaction is *not* occurring under steady-state conditions, and under equilibrium conditions the inhibitory effect of the product can be obliterated if saturating concentrations of either substrate are used. This is because enzyme forms that are components of a system which is in rapid equilibrium can operationally be considered as a single enzyme form. (This actually assumes that all the reaction components bind at a common area on the catalytic site.) It then follows that intercept effects, which result from the binding of an inhibitor by a *different* enzyme form than that bound by the variable substrate, will not be observed. Hence, the product-inhibition patterns will exhibit only slope effects and will be seen as competitive patterns. It might be mentioned at this point, however, that a product may function as a dead-end inhibitor in a rapid equilibrium random reaction. A dead-end inhibitor is one that has no fate other than to dissociate from the enzyme form to which it became bound. When a product functions as a dead-end inhibitor in a rapid equilibrium random reaction, a noncompetitive product-inhibition pattern may be observed. This occurs when saturating concentrations of the variable substrate cannot prevent the binding of the inhibitory product. Generally, it is assumed in these cases that the two components do not bind a totally common area on the catalytic site.

If the sequential Bi Bi reaction has a Theorell-Chance kinetic mechanism, two competitive and two noncompetitive product-inhibition patterns are generally observed. Not only will the final product function as a competitive inhibitor with respect to the initial substrate, but the initial product will also function as a competitive inhibitor with respect to the final substrate. The last situation results because P binds EQ to form EPQ, the central complex which exists at vanishingly small concentrations, and, since EPQ is exceedingly short-lived, the total enzyme concentration is essentially unaltered by the presence of P. Furthermore, the inhibitory effect of P is obliterated in the presence of saturating concentrations of B. Therefore, no intercept effect is seen in this case and P functions as a competitive inhibitor when B is the variable substrate. It should be noted at this point that the order of substrate binding and product release is not determined by the product-inhibition data when a Theorell-Chance mechanism is operative.

If initial-velocity studies suggest that the kinetic mechanism of the Bi Bi reaction under study is ping pong, one would expect to see two competitive and two noncompetitive product-inhibition patterns. Q should appear as a competitive inhibitor when A is the variable substrate, and P should appear as a competitive inhibitor when B is the variable substrate. A and Q can each bind E, while B and P can each bind F. Again, in the ping pong mechanism, the noncompetitive patterns arise as a result of a combination of slope effects, due to backing up of the reaction sequence, and intercept effects, due to the binding of different enzyme forms by the variable substrate and the inhibitor. The product-inhibition patterns associated with the sequential and ping pong mechanisms discussed above are shown in Table 8-2.

**Substrate inhibition** Substrates can also function as inhibitors of enzymatic reactions although frequently it is only supraphysiological concentrations of substrates that are inhibitory. Such inhibition usually occurs when a dead-end complex is formed. Substrate inhibition is often observed in ping pong reactions. For example, if the

**Table 8-2 Product inhibition patterns**

| Kinetic mechanism | Variable substrate | Product | Type of inhibition |
|---|---|---|---|
| Ordered sequential Bi Bi | A | Q | Competitive |
| | B | Q | Noncompetitive |
| | A | P | Noncompetitive |
| | B | P | Noncompetitive |
| Random sequential Bi Bi | A | Q | Noncompetitive |
| | B | Q | Noncompetitive |
| | A | P | Noncompetitive |
| | B | P | Noncompetitive |
| Rapid equilibrium random Bi Bi | A | Q | Competitive |
| | B | Q | Competitive |
| | A | P | Competitive |
| | B | P | Competitive |
| Theorell-Chance Bi Bi | A | Q | Competitive |
| | B | Q | Noncompetitive |
| | A | P | Noncompetitive |
| | B | P | Competitive |
| Ping pong Bi Bi | A | Q | Competitive |
| | B | Q | Noncompetitive |
| | A | P | Noncompetitive |
| | B | P | Competitive |

second substrate that binds, that is, B, is capable of binding the enzyme form E in addition to enyzme form F, which it binds as a step of the normal reaction sequence, an EB dead-end complex is formed. If A is the variable substrate when this EB dead-end complex is formed, B will be seen to be a competitive substrate inhibitor.

On the other hand, uncompetitive substrate inhibition occurs most often when the kinetic mechanism is ordered sequential. Under these circumstances, when B binds EQ and an EQB dead-end complex is formed, one sees only an intercept effect since a dead-end complex *cannot back up the flow* of the reaction sequence. It can only stop it.

*Analogs as inhibitors* Inhibition studies can also be conducted using as the inhibitor a compound that is structurally similar to one of the substrates or products. When such a substrate or product analog binds the enzyme, a dead-end complex is formed. Generally, the analog binds the same enzyme form as the substrate or product of which it is the structural analog. The inhibition patterns observed using these analogs are useful in determining or confirming the order of substrate binding in ordered sequential reactions, for example. Consider, once more, the ordered sequential Bi Bi reaction. When a structural analog of A is used as the inhibitor and A is the variable substrate, competitive inhibition is seen. Noncompetitive inhibition is seen when this analog is used and B is varied. If a structural analog of B is employed, a competitive pattern is seen when B is varied and an uncompetitive pattern is seen when A is varied. In this case, the analog that gives an uncompetitive pattern is structurally analogous to the second substrate that binds, and thus the binding order can be established by a means other than product-inhibition studies.

*Velocity equations of inhibited reactions* The introduction of an inhibitor causes one or more of the terms of the velocity equation for a given reaction to be modified. If, for example, the inhibitor is one which binds EA to form a dead-end complex and the reaction has an ordered sequential Bi Bi kinetic mechanism, the velocity equation of the inhibited reaction is

$$v_i = \frac{V_{\max}[A][B]}{(1 + [I]/K_i)K_b[A] + K_a[B] + [A][B] + K_{ia}K_b} \qquad (8\text{-}55a)$$

It can be seen that the term $K_b[A]$ in the denominator is multiplied by the factor $1 + [I]/K_i$, in which $[I]$ is the concentration of the dead-end inhibitor. Note that when $[I] = 0$, Eq. (8-55a) reverts to the parent equation, (8-48). In Eq. (8-55a), $K_i$ is the dissociation constant for the EAI complex, as it dissociates to regenerate EA and I. It is specifically the term $K_b[A]$ that is multiplied by the factor $1 + [I]/K_i$ since this term determines the concentration of EA available to $I$. If Eq. (8-55a) is written in its reciprocal forms, one obtains

$$\frac{1}{v_i} = \frac{K_a}{V_{\max}}\left(1 + \frac{K_{ia}K_b}{K_a[B]}\right)\frac{1}{[A]} + \frac{1}{V_{\max}}\left\{1 + \frac{K_b}{[B]}\left(1 + \frac{[I]}{K_i}\right)\right\} \qquad (8\text{-}55b)$$

and

$$\frac{1}{v_i} = \frac{K_b}{V_{\max}}\left\{\frac{K_{ia}}{[A]} + \left(1 + \frac{[I]}{K_i}\right)\right\}\frac{1}{[B]} + \frac{1}{V_{\max}}\left(1 + \frac{K_a}{[A]}\right) \qquad (8\text{-}55c)$$

Thus, according to Eq. (8-55b), when A is the variable substrate, I is an uncompetitive inhibitor since [I] appears only in the intercept term. On the other hand, when B· is the variable substrate, Eq. (8-55c) predicts that I will be a competitive inhibitor since now [I] appears only in the slope term. The conclusions derived from these equations are in agreement with those drawn on the basis of the arguments above.

If the inhibitor is a product, the situation is similar but more complex. In an ordered sequential Bi Bi reaction with Q as the inhibitor the velocity equation for the inhibited reaction is

$$v_i = \frac{V_{max}[A][B]}{K_b[A] + K_a[B] + [A][B] + \frac{K_{ia}K_b}{K_{iq}}[Q] + \frac{K_a}{K_{iq}}[B][Q] + K_{ia}K_b} \qquad (8\text{-}56a)$$

The reciprocal form of this equation, assuming that A is the variable substrate, is

$$\frac{1}{v_i} = \frac{K_a}{V_{max}}\left(1 + \frac{K_{ia}K_b}{K_a[B]}\right)\left(1 + \frac{[Q]}{K_{iq}}\right)\frac{1}{[A]} + \frac{1}{V_{max}}\left(1 + \frac{K_b}{[B]}\right) \qquad (8\text{-}56b)$$

which predicts that Q will be a competitive inhibitor when A is the variable substrate. When B is the variable substrate, the reciprocal equation is

$$\frac{1}{v_i} = \frac{K_b}{V_{max}}\left\{1 + \frac{K_{ia}}{[A]}\left(1 + \frac{[Q]}{K_{iq}}\right)\right\}\frac{1}{[B]} + \frac{1}{V_{max}}\left\{1 + \frac{K_a}{[A]}\left(1 + \frac{[Q]}{K_{iq}}\right)\right\} \qquad (8\text{-}56c)$$

Now noncompetitive inhibition is predicted. Again, these predictions are in agreement with the arguments presented above.

In certain cases an alternate reaction occurs in the presence of an inhibitor; then the velocity equation contains [I] in the numerator as well as in the denominator because one has, in effect, a random kinetic mechanism involving the reaction of the appropriate enzyme form with the substrate and also the reaction of this enzyme form with the inhibitor. Under these circumstances the slope term and/or the intercept term of the reciprocal equation is multiplied by a factor having the form $(1 + x[I])/(1 + y[I])$. If it is the slope term that is modified in this way, a replot of the slopes of the appropriate double reciprocal plots as a function of [I] (note that this is not 1/[I]) will be a hyperbola. The effect is therefore referred to as *hyperbolic competitive inhibition*. On the other hand, if it is the intercept term that is modified, the corresponding replot of intercepts vs. [I] will be hyperbolic and the inhibitor will be referred to as a *hyperbolic uncompetitive inhibitor*. Hyperbolic noncompetative inhibition results from a combination of slope and intercept effects, as usual.

It should be mentioned that when there is an alternate pathway, there is the possibility that this pathway will permit the regeneration of the noncomplexed enzyme at a faster rate than the usual pathway. When this occurs, one observes *activation* as a result of the presence of the modifier rather than inhibition. In general, when the modifier is an inhibitor, $x$ is greater than $y$ in the factor $(1 + x[I])/(1 + y[I])$, while the reverse is seen when the modifier is an activator. Also, the hyperbolic replot curve is convex (or concave downward) when the modifier is an inhibitor and concave when it is an activator (Fig. 8-9).

When an inhibitor reacts with more than one enzyme form, the inhibition may

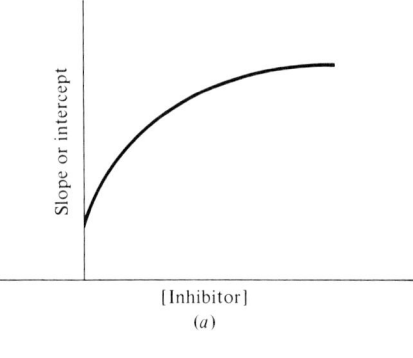

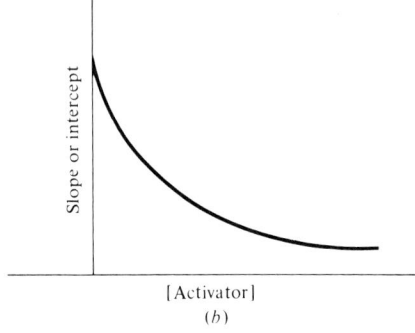

**Figure 8-9** Characteristic forms of slope or intercept replots (a) when $x > y$ and (b) when $x < y$ in the factor $(1 + x[I])/(1 + y[I])$ which modifies a term of the reciprocal velocity equation describing hyperbolic inhibition.

be linear or more complex. A dead-end inhibitor that reacts with more than one enzyme form generally produces linear inhibition since although the factor $1 + [I]/K_i$ modifies more than one term in the denominator, second- (or higher-) order terms in [I] are not generated. On the other hand, if a product inhibitor combines with enzyme forms other than those with which it must combine during the forward or reverse reaction sequence, higher-order terms in [P] or [Q], for example, may be generated. When second-order terms are generated, the result is usually the introduction of a factor having the general form $1 + x[I] + y[I]^2$ into the equation. Because plots of the slopes or intercepts of the appropriate double reciprocal plots, as a function of [I], are in this instance parabolic, the inhibitory effect is referred to as *parabolic*. If the two different enzyme forms with which the inhibitor reacts are at points in the reaction sequence connected by reversible steps including the point at which the variable substrate binds, the slope term of the reciprocal velocity equation is modified by the factor above and the modifier is referred to as a *parabolic competitive inhibitor*. On the other hand, if the two different enzyme forms with which the inhibitor reacts are at points in the reaction sequence that are reversibly connected but this segment of the sequence does not include the point at which the variable substrate binds, the intercept term of the reciprocal equation will be multiplied by the factor $1 + x[I] + y[I]^2$ and the modifier is a *parabolic uncompetitive inhibitor*. When an irreversible step intervenes between the points at which the inhibitor binds, the inhibition is linear (see Fig. 8-10).

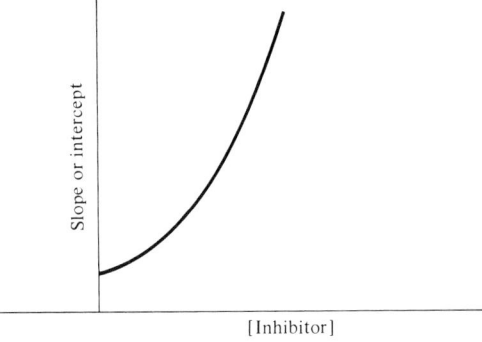

**Figure 8-10** Characteristic form of the slope or intercept replot when the enzymatic process is modified by a parabolic inhibitor.

**Isotope-exchange studies in the characterization of enzymatic reactions** In conjunction with initial-velocity studies and inhibition studies, isotope-exchange studies provide a valuable tool for determining and confirming kinetic mechanisms. To carry out isotope-exchange studies one labels a functional group that is transferred as a result of the enzymatic reaction and then monitors the rate at which this label appears in the appropriate product. Isotope-exchange reactions are often conducted under conditions of chemical equilibrium (to be distinguished from steady-state conditions), where there is no *net* chemical reaction since the forward and reverse processes are proceeding at equal rates. When isotope-exchange studies are conducted under equilibrium conditions, the concentrations of one substrate and one product are varied in tandem while being maintained at a constant ratio with respect to each other in order to maintain the equilibrium conditions. By determining the characteristics of the exchanges, evidence concerning the kinetic mechanism of the reaction can be obtained.

As an example of the usefulness of the procedure, isotope-exchange studies can be used to distinguish between an ordered sequential and a rapid equilibrium random mechanism. The procedure would be to label the appropriate substrates and then monitor the appearance of the label in the appropriate product as the concentrations of a particular substrate-product pair are varied. If the reaction under study has an ordered sequential Bi Bi mechanism and A and Q are varied, plots of $1/v_i^*$ ($v_i^*$ is the initial velocity of the *exchange*) as a function of $1/[A]$ or of $1/[Q]$ will be linear when the A*-to-Q* (or A*-to-P*) exchange is monitored as well as when the B*-to-P* (or B*-to-Q*) exchange is monitored. When B and P are varied, plots of $1/v_i^*$ as a function of $1/[B]$ or of $1/[P]$ will also be linear when the B*-to-P* exchange is monitored. However, when B and P are varied and the A*-to-P* exchange is monitored, one observes total inhibition as saturating concentrations of B are attained. If it is the A*-to-Q* exchange that is being monitored, total inhibition will be observed as saturating concentrations of either B or P are attained. This occurs because when B is saturating the concentration of EA becomes vanishingly small since virtually all EA is converted into EAB. The result is that the dissociation of EA to yield E and A is prevented and A* therefore cannot enter into the reaction sequence. Hence, exchanges involving A* are inhibited. Similarly, saturating P prevents the dissociation of EQ, and as a result Q* cannot enter the reaction sequence. Thus, when the kinetic mechanism is ordered sequential, total inhibition is seen in the presence of saturating concentrations of a component that intervenes between the points in the reaction sequence at which the components undergoing exchange bind.

By contrast, random mechanisms do not exhibit inhibition like that described above. When a reaction is random, one component cannot prevent the entry of another into the reaction sequence. If one pathway is blocked, the alternate pathway is used. The inhibition seen in random mechanisms occurs when a dead-end complex is formed. However, in this event *all* exchanges are inhibited rather than specific ones. In the special case of the rapid equilibrium random mechanism all exchanges proceed at the same velocity because when such a mechanism is operative, the rate-determining step is always the interconversion of the central complexes and all exchanges proceed at the rate at which this interconversion occurs. In fact, to confirm the operation of a rapid equilibrium random mechanism it is generally necessary to demonstrate that all exchanges proceed at the same velocity.

For ping pong mechanisms exchange studies can be conducted on portions of the total reaction sequence. Consequently, one can monitor the exchange between A and P in a ping pong Bi Bi reaction in the absence of the other two reaction components. Since the other reaction components are not present, there can be no net reaction and therefore under steady-state conditions the system is also at chemical equilibrium. If the A*-to-P* exchange is being studied with A as the variable substrate and with fixed concentrations of P, the double reciprocal plots of $1/v_i^*$ vs. $1/[A]$ are parallel. An increase in the concentration of P increases the apparent maximum velocity of the exchange, and therefore an intercept effect is seen. However, an increase in the concentration of P does not induce a slope effect since the concentration of P does not influence the ratio $[E]/[EA]$. This is because under equilibrium conditions there is very little enzyme in the form denoted by F, and hence the addition of P cannot significantly increase the concentration of FP and thereby EA. Similar arguments can be made for the B*-to-Q* exchange, in which case parallel double reciprocal plots are seen. When one is observing the operation of a ping pong kinetic mechanism, the type of inhibition occurring in the ordered sequential mechanism does not take place. However, if one should introduce Q into the reaction medium being used to study the A*-to-P* exchange, one would observe inhibition due to the fact that Q would bind E and thereby diminish its availability to A, although, it should be pointed out that under most circumstances neither Q nor B is present when the A*-to-P* exchange is studied. In fact, the observation that the exchange occurs at the same velocity in the absence of B and Q as in their presence is confirmatory for a ping pong kinetic mechanism.

*Velocity equations for isotope exchange studies* The derivation of velocity equations for isotope exchange is somewhat different from those derivations considered thus far. Consider now the A*-to-Q* exchange in an ordered sequential Bi Bi reaction (shown diagrammatically in Fig. 8-11). The initial velocity of this exchange is given by

$$v_i^* = \frac{dQ^*}{dt} = k_4[EQ^*] \qquad (8\text{-}57)$$

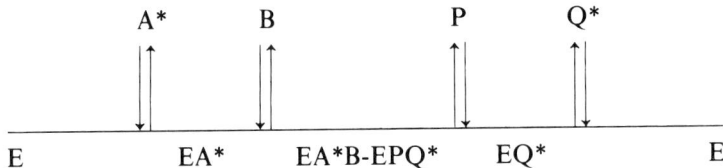

**Figure 8-11** Diagrammatic representation of the A*-to-Q* exchange as it would occur when an ordered sequential Bi Bi mechanism is operative.

where [EQ*] is the steady-state concentration of the *labeled* EQ complex (to be distinguished from the total concentration of the EQ complex). The quantity [EQ*] can be evaluated using a diagrammatic method based on determinants. This method, developed by King and Altman, provides a systematic procedure for obtaining the equations that define the *steady-state concentrations* of the various enzyme forms that participate in a reaction.†

According to the King-Altman technique, the total number of enzyme forms involved in a given reaction is determined, and a polygon having this number $n$ of vertices is constructed. These $n$ vertices are connected by arrows showing the various interconversions that can occur between these enzyme forms. In an ordered sequential Bi Bi reaction involving E, EA, EAB-EPQ, and EQ, $n = 4$, and the King-Altman diagram (Fig. 8-12) has four vertices. For this diagram, $n$ nonspecific patterns can be drawn representing the $n$ possible combinations of $n - 1$ individual steps in the process. These patterns are represented just below the King-Altman diagram. In most cases the King-Altman technique is used to obtain the equations for the concentration of each enzyme form as a function of the total enzyme concentration, that is, $[E]/[E]_0$, $[EA]/[E]_0$, $[EAB]/[E]_0$, and so forth. These equations, which are called *distribution equations*, can then be used in the formulation of velocity equations. This use of the method of King and Altman is illustrated in Appendix A. At present, the method will be used to evaluate the steady-state concentration of a labeled enzyme-product complex EQ*. To this end, one first determines whether there are two or more enzyme forms that *do not* become labeled as the labeled substrate is converted into the labeled product. If such enzyme forms are present, the path (or paths) connecting them is marked in some manner. (Frequently, these paths are denoted by a heavier line.) When one or more such paths are present, only King-Altman patterns that include that path (when there is one) or *all* such paths (when there are more than one) are to be used in this procedure. In the present example there is only one nonlabeled enzyme form, that is, E. Therefore, no path connects two nonlabeled enzyme forms. Hence, all four of the patterns that are possible are to be used, and each term derived from one of these patterns will contain $n - 1 = 3$ rate constants. However, in the case of an A*-to-P* exchange occurring in this same reaction, both E and EQ are nonlabeled. There is therefore one path that connects two nonlabeled enzyme forms. Under this circumstance, only those patterns which include the path between E and EQ are to be used. This allows the use of three of the four patterns,

† King, E. L., and Altman, C. (1956) *J. Phys. Chem.* **60**, 1375-1378.

**316** MECHANISMS OF METABOLISM

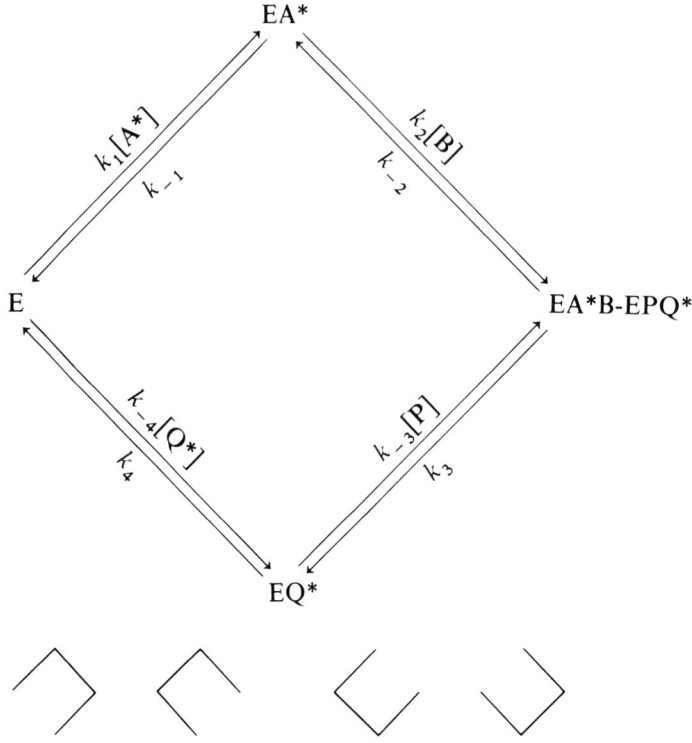

**Figure 8-12** King-Altman diagram to be used in deriving the velocity equation for the A*-to-Q* exchange as it occurs when an ordered sequential Bi Bi mechanism is operative. Below the polygon the four possible nonspecific patterns are shown.

and each of the terms derived from one of these three patterns will contain only two rate constants. The factors $k_4$ and $k_{-4}[Q]$ are never included.

In the present case, one now picks the specific pattern that represents the binding of A* by the free enzyme and the conversion of EA* to the labeled product complex EQ*. This pattern is ⟨⟩, and it is used to derive the numerator of the expression for [EQ*]. This numerator term, which is denoted by $N_{EQ}$, is obtained by writing a rate constant and its concentration term, when applicable, for each line of the King-Altman pattern. The concentration of the unlabeled enzyme form that reacts with the labeled substrate must also be included in this expression. Thus, the numerator term in this instance is

$$N_{EQ} = k_1[A^*][E]k_2[B]k_3 = k_1 k_2 k_3 [A^*][B][E] \qquad (8\text{-}58)$$

Now a term that designates the paths by which the various *labeled* enzyme forms are converted into *nonlabeled* enzyme forms is derived. This term is the denominator of the expression for [EQ*], and, as such, it is denoted by $D$. The denominator term is obtained by using all of the appropriate King-Altman patterns which are now converted into *specific* patterns by writing them as vectors that indicate the conversion of labeled enzyme into nonlabeled enzyme.

Each specific pattern generates a term comprising three rate constants plus the appropriate substrate concentrations. Thus, the denominator term $D$ is:

$$D = k_2 k_3 k_4 [B] + k_{-1} k_{-2} k_{-3} [P] + k_{-1} k_{-2} k_4 + k_{-1} k_3 k_4 \qquad (8\text{-}59)$$

Since $[EQ^*]$ is given by $N_{EQ}/D$, we have

$$EQ^* = \frac{N_{EQ}}{D} = \frac{k_1 k_2 k_3 [A^*][B][E]}{k_2 k_3 k_4 [B] + k_{-1} k_{-2} k_{-3} [P] + k_{-1} k_4 (k_{-2} + k_3)} \qquad (8\text{-}60)$$

Finally, since the initial velocity of the $A^*$-to-$Q^*$ exchange is given by $k_4[EQ^*]$, one can write

$$v_i^* = \frac{k_1 k_2 k_3 k_4 [A^*][B][E]}{k_2 k_3 k_4 [B] + k_{-1} k_{-2} k_{-3} [P] + k_{-1} k_4 (k_{-2} + k_3)} \qquad (8\text{-}61a)$$

or

$$v_i^* = \frac{k_1 k_2 k_3 k_4 [E]_0 [A^*][B][E]/[E]_0}{k_2 k_3 k_4 [B] + k_{-1} k_{-2} k_{-3} [P] + k_{-1} k_4 (k_{-2} + k_3)} \qquad (8\text{-}61b)$$

As shown earlier in this chapter, certain constants can now be substituted for collections of individual rate constants. In this case it is convenient to use the constants that are used in developing the (complete) velocity equation for an ordered sequential Bi Bi reaction under steady-state conditions. This equation is developed in Appendix A. The constants used in simplifying Eq. (8-61b) are

$$K_b = \frac{\text{coef A}}{\text{coef AB}} = \frac{k_4}{k_2} \frac{k_{-2} + k_3}{k_3 + k_4} \qquad K_a = \frac{\text{coef B}}{\text{coef AB}} = \frac{k_4}{k_1} \frac{k_3}{k_3 + k_4}$$

$$K_{ia} = \frac{\text{const}}{\text{coef A}} = \frac{k_{-1}}{k_1} \qquad K_p = \frac{\text{coef Q}}{\text{coef PQ}} = \frac{k_{-1}}{k_{-3}} \frac{k_{-2} + k_3}{k_{-1} + k_{-2}}$$

$$K_q = \frac{\text{coef P}}{\text{coef PQ}} = \frac{k_{-1}}{k_{-4}} \frac{k_{-2}}{k_{-1} + k_{-2}} \qquad K_{iq} = \frac{\text{coef B}}{\text{coef BQ}} = \frac{k_4}{k_{-4}}$$

When these constants and

$$V_{max} = \frac{k_1 k_2 k_3 k_4 [E]_0}{\text{coef AB}}$$

are used, Eq. (8-61b) becomes

$$v_i^* = \frac{V_{max}[A^*][B][E]/[E]_0}{K_a[B] + (K_{ia} K_b K_q / K_p K_{iq})[P] + K_{ia} K_b} \qquad (8\text{-}61c)$$

It now remains to evaluate $[E]/[E]_0$. If the isotope-exchange study is conducted under equilibrium conditions, as is frequently the case, $[E]/[E]_0$ under *equilibrium* conditions must be evaluated. This can be done using the equations that define the equilibrium concentration of each of the enzyme forms in conjunction with the conservation equation

$$[E]_0 = [E] + [EA] + [EAB\text{-}EPQ] + [EQ] \tag{8-62}$$

Under *equilibrium* conditions the concentration of each of these enzyme forms is simply the quotient of the individual rate constants and concentrations involved in its formation divided by those involved in its dissociation. Hence, one can write

$$[E]_0 = [E] + \frac{k_1}{k_{-1}}[A][E] + \frac{k_1 k_2}{k_{-1} k_{-2}}[A][B][E] + \frac{k_1 k_2 k_3}{k_{-1} k_{-2} k_{-3}} \frac{[A][B][E]}{[P]} \tag{8-63a}$$

and therefore

$$\frac{[E]}{[E]_0} = \frac{[P]}{\frac{k_1}{k_{-1}} \frac{k_2}{k_{-2}} \frac{k_3}{k_{-3}}[A][B] + \frac{k_1}{k_{-1}}[A][P] + \frac{k_1}{k_{-1}} \frac{k_2}{k_{-2}}[A][B][P] + [P]} \tag{8-63b}$$

When the constants

$$K_{ia} = \frac{k_{-1}}{k_1} \qquad K_{ib} = \frac{k_{-2}}{k_2} \qquad K_{ip} = \frac{k_3}{k_{-3}}$$

are used, Eq. (8-63b) becomes

$$\frac{[E]}{[E]_0} = \frac{[P]}{\frac{K_{ip}}{K_{ia} K_{ib}}[A][B] + \frac{1}{K_{ia}}[A][P] + \frac{1}{K_{ia} K_{ib}}[A][B][P] + [P]} \tag{8-63c}$$

Substituting this expression for $[E]/[E]_0$ in Eq. (8-61c) gives the velocity equation for the A*-to-Q* exchange:

$$v_i^* = V_{\max}[A^*][B][P] \Big/ \Bigg\{ \frac{K_b K_{ip}}{K_{ib}}[A][B] + K_b[A][P] + K_a[B][P] + \frac{K_a K_{ip}}{K_{ia} K_{ib}}[A][B]^2$$

$$+ \frac{K_b K_q}{K_p K_{iq}}[A][P]^2 + \left(\frac{K_a}{K_{ia}} + \frac{K_b}{K_{ib}} + \frac{K_b K_{ip} K_q}{K_{ib} K_p K_{iq}}\right)[A][B][P] + \frac{K_a}{K_{ia} K_{ib}}[A][B]^2[P]$$

$$+ \frac{K_b K_q}{K_{ib} K_p K_{iq}}[A][B][P]^2 + K_{ia} K_b[P] + \frac{K_{ia} K_b K_q}{K_p K_{iq}}[P]^2 \Bigg\} \tag{8-64a}$$

When B and P are being varied together and B is the variable substrate, the reciprocal equation is

$$\frac{1}{v_i^*} = \frac{K_b}{V_{\max}} \frac{1}{[B]} + \frac{(K_b K_q/K_p K_{iq})[P]}{V_{\max}} \frac{1}{[B]} + \frac{K_{ia} K_b}{V_{\max}[A^*]} \frac{1}{[B]} + \frac{(K_{ia} K_b K_q/K_p K_{iq})[P]}{V_{\max}[A^*]} \frac{1}{[B]}$$

$$+ \frac{(K_a K_{ip}/K_{ia} K_{ib})[B]}{V_{\max}[P]} + \frac{(K_a/K_{ia} K_{ip})[B]}{V_{\max}} + \frac{(K_b K_{ip}/K_{ib})}{V_{\max}[P]} + \frac{K_a}{V_{\max}[A^*]}$$

$$+ \frac{(K_b K_q/K_{ib} K_p K_{iq})[P]}{V_{\max}} + \left(\frac{K_a}{K_{ia}} + \frac{K_b}{K_{ib}} + \frac{K_b K_{ip} K_q}{K_{ib} K_p K_{iq}}\right) \tag{8-64b}$$

This reciprocal equation is nonlinear since [B] appears in both the numerator and denominator. The equation predicts that as [B] becomes very large, $1/v_i^*$ will approach infinity and $v_i^*$ will therefore approach zero. This is consistent with the conclusions derived on the basis of the arguments presented previously.

Consider now, by contrast, the A*-to-P* exchange as it occurs in a ping pong Bi Bi mechanism.

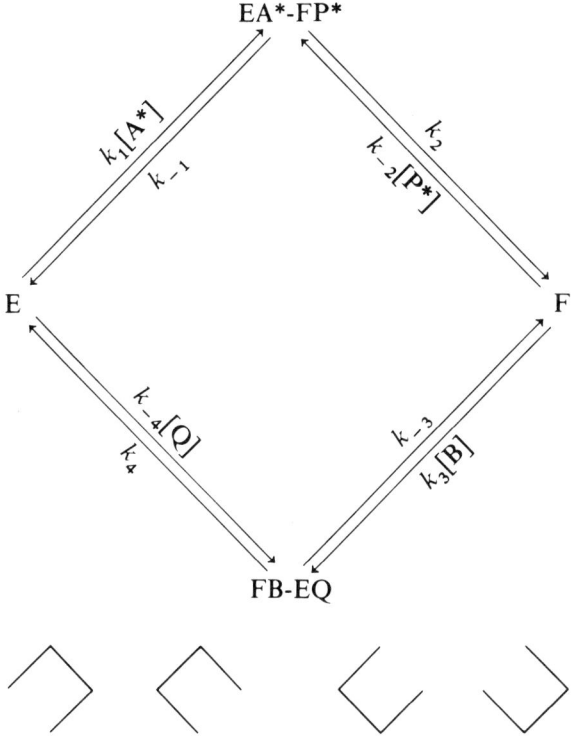

The initial velocity of the A*-to-P* exchange is given by

$$v_i^* = \frac{dP^*}{dt} = k_2[\text{EA*-FP*}] \tag{8-65}$$

As above, in order to obtain [EA*-FP*], the steady-state concentration of the labeled enzyme form, the expression

$$[\text{EA*-FP*}] = \frac{N_{\text{EA-FP}}}{D} \tag{8-66a}$$

is used, where $N_{\text{EA-FP}}$ is given by $k_1[\text{A*}][\text{E}]$. The denominator term can, again, be derived using the method of King and Altman. In this case, there are two enzyme forms, in addition to E, that do not become labeled during the exchange and, thus, the path connecting F and FB-EQ and that connecting FB-EQ and E are to be designated as connecting nonlabeled enzyme forms. Only patterns containing *both* these paths are to be used in the derivation. Specifically, these patterns are

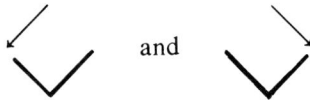

Therefore, one can write

$$[EA^*\text{-}FP^*] = \frac{N_{EA\text{-}FP}}{D} = \frac{k_1[A^*][E]}{k_{-1} + k_2} \quad (8\text{-}66b)$$

Hence, one rather easily obtains the velocity equation

$$v_i^* = \frac{k_1 k_2 [A^*][E]}{k_{-1} + k_2} \quad (8\text{-}67a)$$

which can be written

$$v_i^* = \frac{k_1 k_2 [E]_0 [A^*][E]/[E]_0}{k_{-1} + k_2} \quad (8\text{-}67b)$$

Now, in the usual manner, substitutions can be made to simplify the form of the equation. In the present case, we use

$$K_a = \frac{k_{-1} + k_2}{k_1} \quad \text{and} \quad V_{\max} = k_2[E]_0$$

Therefore
$$v_i^* = \frac{V_{\max}[A^*][E]/[E]_0}{K_a} \quad (8\text{-}67c)$$

Now $[E]/[E]_0$ must be evaluated. This can be done using the King-Altman method. For this purpose the entire King-Altman polygon is used, as follows:

E =

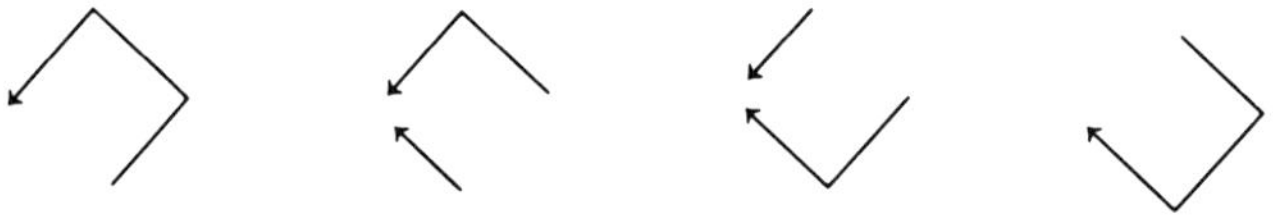

$$E = k_{-1}k_{-2}k_{-3}[P] + k_{-1}k_{-2}k_4[P] + k_{-1}k_3k_4[B] + k_2k_3k_4[B] \quad (8\text{-}68a)$$

EA-FP =

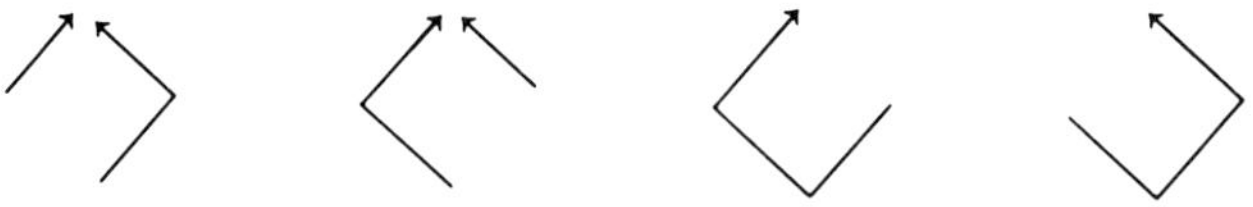

$$EA\text{-}FP = k_1 k_{-2} k_{-3}[A][P] + k_1 k_{-2} k_4[A][P] + k_1 k_3 k_4[A][B] + k_{-2} k_{-3} k_{-4}[P][Q] \quad (8\text{-}68b)$$

F =

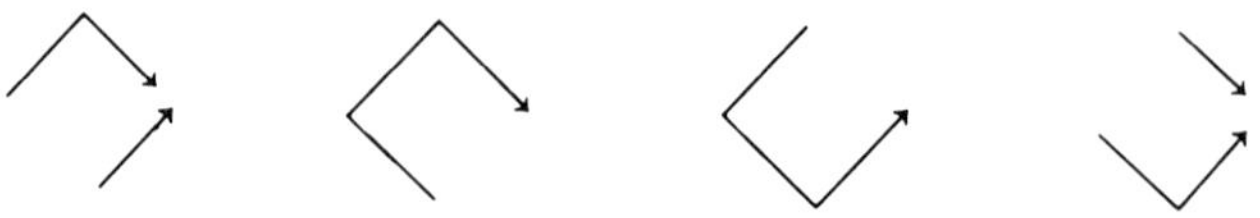

$$F = k_1 k_2 k_{-3}[A] + k_1 k_2 k_4[A] + k_{-1} k_{-3} k_{-4}[Q] + k_2 k_{-3} k_{-4}[Q] \quad (8\text{-}68c)$$

FB-EQ =

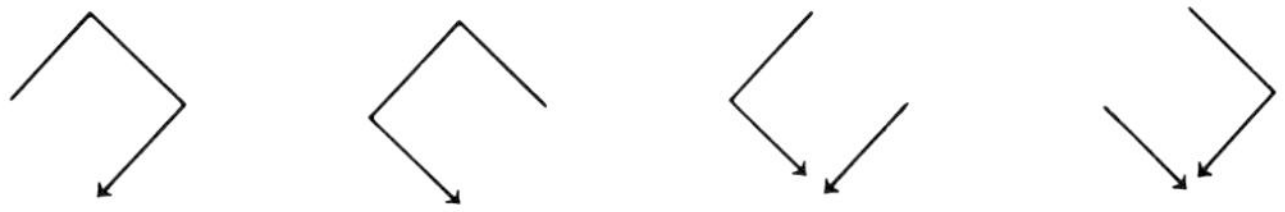

$$\text{FB-EQ} = k_1 k_2 k_3 [A][B] + k_{-1} k_{-2} k_{-4} [P][Q] + k_{-1} k_3 k_{-4} [B][Q] + k_2 k_3 k_{-4} [B][Q] \tag{8-68d}$$

Therefore, after collecting terms appropriately, one claims

$$\frac{[E]}{[E]_0} = (k_{-1} k_3 k_4 + k_2 k_3 k_4)[B] + (k_{-1} k_{-2} k_{-3} + k_{-1} k_{-2} k_4)[P]/$$

$$\{(k_1 k_2 k_{-3} + k_1 k_2 k_4)[A] + (k_{-1} k_3 k_4 + k_2 k_3 k_4)[B]$$
$$+ (k_1 k_2 k_3 + k_1 k_3 k_4)[A][B] + (k_1 k_{-2} k_{-3} + k_1 k_{-2} k_4)[A][P]$$
$$+ (k_2 k_3 k_{-4} + k_{-1} k_3 k_{-4})[B][Q] + (k_{-1} k_{-2} k_{-4} + k_{-2} k_{-3} k_{-4})[P][Q]$$
$$+ (k_{-1} k_{-2} k_{-3} + k_{-1} k_{-2} k_4)[P] + (k_{-1} k_{-3} k_{-4} + k_2 k_{-3} k_{-4})[Q]\} \tag{8-68e}$$

Using the substitutions

$$K_b = \frac{\text{coef A}}{\text{coef AB}} = \frac{k_2}{k_3} \frac{k_{-3} + k_4}{k_2 + k_4} \qquad K_a = \frac{\text{coef B}}{\text{coef AB}} = \frac{k_4}{k_1} \frac{k_{-1} + k_2}{k_2 + k_4}$$

$$K_{ia} = \frac{\text{coef P}}{\text{coef AP}} = \frac{k_{-1}}{k_1} \qquad K_{ib} = \frac{\text{coef Q}}{\text{coef BQ}} = \frac{k_{-3}}{k_3}$$

$$K_p = \frac{\text{coef Q}}{\text{coef PQ}} = \frac{k_{-3}}{k_{-2}} \frac{k_{-1} + k_2}{k_{-1} + k_{-3}} \qquad K_{ip} = \frac{\text{coef A}}{\text{coef AP}} = \frac{k_2}{k_{-2}}$$

$$K_{iq} = \frac{\text{coef B}}{\text{coef BQ}} = \frac{k_4}{k_{-4}}$$

and rearranging, one obtains

$$\frac{[E]}{[E]_0} = K_a[B] + \frac{K_{ia} K_b}{K_{ip}}[P] \bigg/ \bigg\{ K_b[A] + K_a[B] + [A][B] + \frac{K_b}{K_{ip}}[A][P] + \frac{K_a}{K_{iq}}[B][Q]$$

$$+ \frac{K_{ia} K_b}{K_{ip}}[P] + \frac{K_a K_{ib}}{K_{iq}}[Q] + \frac{K_a K_{ib}}{K_p K_{iq}}[P][Q] \bigg\}$$

Finally, substituting for $[E]/[E]_0$ in Eq. (8-67c) gives the velocity equation for the A*-to-P* exchange in a ping pong Bi Bi reaction:

$$v_i^* = V_{\max} \bigg( [B] + \frac{K_{ia} K_b}{K_a K_{ip}}[P] \bigg) [A^*] \bigg/ \bigg\{ K_b[A] + K_a[B] + [A][B] + \frac{K_b}{K_{ip}}[A][P]$$

$$+ \frac{K_a}{K_{iq}}[B][Q] + \frac{K_{ia} K_b}{K_{ip}}[P] + \frac{K_a K_{ib}}{K_{iq}}[Q] + \frac{K_a K_{ib}}{K_p K_{iq}}[P][Q] \bigg\} \tag{8-69a}$$

The reciprocal form of this velocity equation for the A*-to-P* exchange when B and Q are absent is given by

$$\frac{1}{v_i^*} = \frac{K_a}{V_{\max}}\frac{1}{[\text{A}]} + \frac{K_a}{V_{\max}K_{ia}}\left(1 + \frac{K_{ip}}{[\text{P}]}\right) \qquad (8\text{-}69b)$$

The reciprocal equation thus predicts that when the A*-to-P* exchange is conducted with A as the variable substrate and with fixed concentrations of P, B and Q being absent, a family of parallel plots will be obtained, in agreement with previous arguments.

## THE MODIFICATION OF ENZYMATIC ACTIVITY

Since the catalysis provided by an enzyme involves its secondary, tertiary, and quaternary protein structure, it is not surprising that enzymatic activity can be modified by altering one or more of these structural characteristics. Several models have been proposed for the means by which enzymatic activity is modified in living organisms as a result of changes in the secondary, tertiary, or quaternary structure of the enzyme protein. One of the proposals which has been extensively examined is that of Monod, Wyman, and Changeux.[†] According to their proposal, certain enzymes undergo changes in their quaternary structure, with the result that their catalytic capability is modified. These changes in quaternary structure are induced by conformational changes that are in turn induced as a result of the enzyme's binding specific ligands. These ligands do not bind at the catalytic site of the enzyme but rather at a separate binding site referred to as the *allosteric site*. Since these ligands bind at a site other than the catalytic site, it was inferred that they did not necessarily have the same shape as a substrate. Hence, rather than being *iso*steric with respect to the substrate they were assumed to be *allo*steric. (The Greek *iso-* means "same" and *allo-* means "other.") The changes in quaternary structure that occur in response to the binding of an allosteric ligand are referred to as *allosteric transitions*.

Enzymes that undergo allosteric transitions are generally composed of subunits, the smallest of which is called a *monomer*. All the monomers of a given allosteric enzyme are not necessarily identical; e.g., such enzymes may comprise two or four different monomers. A specific number of these monomers associate to yield what is referred to as a *protomer*. All the protomers of a given enzyme are identical. The protomers of an allosteric enzyme can in turn associate to yield even larger aggregates. An association of identical protomers yields an *oligomer*. A given allosteric enzyme may have several oligomeric forms.

The proposal of Monod, Wyman, and Changeux states that the oligomeric enzyme must exist in at least two different states, which differ in the arrangement of the protomers and therefore in the energy of the interprotomer bonds. One of these states (assuming only two) is denoted as the R state and the other as the T state. In the R state the protomers are less constrained or in a more *r*elaxed arrangement. In

[†] Monod, J., Wyman, J., Changeux, J.-P. (1965) *J. Mol. Biol.* **12**, 88–118.

the T state the protomers are in a more constrained or a more *taut* arrangement. The R and T states exist in equilibrium with each other, i.e.,

$$R_0 \underset{r}{\overset{f}{\rightleftharpoons}} T_0 \qquad (8\text{-}70a)$$

where $R_0$ and $T_0$ are the oligomeric enzyme forms in the absence of bound allosteric ligands. The constant for the equilibrium above is therefore given by

$$K_{eq} = \frac{[T_0]}{[R_0]} = \frac{k_f}{k_r} \qquad (8\text{-}70b)$$

This equilibrium can be shifted, however, by the binding of an allosteric ligand by one or both of the oligomeric forms. Consider, for example, the allosteric ligand L, which binds both $R_0$ and $T_0$. Thus, one could write

$$L + R_0 \rightleftharpoons LR_1 \quad \text{and} \quad L + T_0 \rightleftharpoons LT_1 \qquad (8\text{-}71)$$

The dissociation constant for $LR_1$ will be designated by $K_R$ and that for $LT_1$ will be designated by $K_T$. Also, a constant called the *saturation function* $\bar{Y}$ denotes the fraction of the sites that is occupied by molecules of the ligand. When considering both the R and T states of the enzyme, one can write

$$\bar{Y} = \frac{K_{eq}([L]/K_T)(1 + [L]/K_T)^{n-1} + ([L]/K_R)(1 + [L]/K_R)^{n-1}}{K_{eq}(1 + [L]/K_T)^n + (1 + [L]/K_R)^n} \qquad (8\text{-}72a)$$

where $n$ is the total number of ligand binding sites on the oligomeric enzyme. The equation predicts that when $K_{eq}$ is very small, i.e., when the equilibrium strongly favors the R form, a plot of $\bar{Y}$ as a function of the concentration of L will be a hyperbolic curve. This is because when $K_{eq}$ is negligible, Eq. (8-72a) approaches

$$\bar{Y} = \frac{[L]/K_R}{1 + [L]/K_R} = \frac{[L]}{K_R + [L]} \qquad (8\text{-}72b)$$

It can be seen that Eq. (8-72b) is of the form $y = x/(b + x)$, which is the equation of a rectangular hyperbola. A plot of $\bar{Y}$ as a function of [L] is also hyperbolic when $K_T$ and $K_R$ are equal, i.e., when L does not discriminate between the R and T forms. In this case, $K_T = K_R$ and, thus

$$\bar{Y} = \frac{\{([L]/K_R)(1 + [L]/K_R)^{n-1}\}(K_{eq} + 1)}{(1 + [L]/K_R)^n(K_{eq} + 1)} = \frac{L/K_R}{1 + ([L]/K_R)} = \frac{[L]}{K_R + [L]} \qquad (8\text{-}72c)$$

However, when the equilibrium favors the T form, i.e., when $K_{eq}$ is very large, and when under these circumstances $K_T$ is much greater than $K_R$, which means that L binds the R form preferentially, Eq. (8-72a) becomes

$$\bar{Y} = \frac{([L]/K_R)(1 + [L]/K_R)^{n-1}}{K_{eq} + (1 + [L]/K_R)^n} \qquad (8\text{-}72d)$$

Since $[L]^n$ appears in both the numerator and the denominator of the equation, intuitively one might reason as follows. When [L] is very small, the large value for $K_{eq}$ is the dominant factor. Changes in small values for [L] have little effect upon $\bar{Y}$.

Then as larger and larger concentrations of L are introduced, the influence of $K_{eq}$ becomes less and less and the precipitousness with which [L] becomes the dominant factor depends directly upon the value for $n$. Finally, further increases in [L] have no further effect since at this point $\bar{Y}$ is essentially $[L]^n/[L]^n$, or unity. This qualitative description suggests that a plot of $\bar{Y}$ as a function of [L] might be a sigmoidal curve (Fig. 8-13) as, in fact, it generally is.

The model of Monod, Wyman, and Changeux also includes considerations of the influence of ligand molecules upon the binding of additional ligand molecules. For the purpose of these considerations, they have introduced the terms *homotropic effect* and *heterotropic effect*. A homotropic effect is in operation when the binding of one ligand molecule promotes the binding of additional molecules of the same ligand. On the other hand, a heterotropic effect is in operation when the binding of one ligand molecule promotes either the binding or release of a different ligand molecule. Homotropic effects result from interactions between molecules of the same ligand. Heterotropic effects result from interactions between different ligand molecules. In the homotropic effect, the binding of one ligand molecule facilitates binding of a second, presumably because the binding of the initial molecule induces a conformational change in the protein that makes the binding sites for additional ligand molecules more exposed or more available. The heterotropic effect, by contrast, is attributed to the displacement of the equilibria involving the R and T states as a result of the binding of the different ligand L'. When L' binds the T forms preferentially, its effect will be that of shifting the R $\rightleftharpoons$ T equilibria to the right. Thus, increases in the concentration of L' when the equilibria favor the T state and when L binds the R forms preferentially will cause the plot of $\bar{Y}$ vs. [L] to become an even more slowly ascending sigmoidal curve. This is because L', in effect, diminishes the concentration of the species with which L reacts preferentially. On the other hand, when L' binds the R forms preferentially, its effect is that of shifting the R $\rightleftharpoons$ T equilibria to the left. Now a plot of $\bar{Y}$ as a function of [L] under the conditions stated above will become less and less sigmoidal as the concentration of L' is increased. Ultimately, this plot will become hyperbolic.

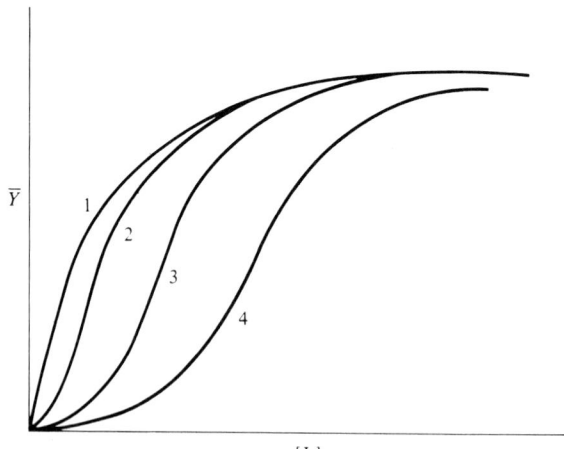

**Figure 8-13** Plots of $\bar{Y}$ as a function of [L] when $K_{eq}$ is approximately 10 (curve 2), 100 (curve 3), and 1000 (curve 4). When $K_{eq}$ is equal to 1 (curve 1), the plot is hyperbolic, but as the value for $K_{eq}$ increases, the sigmoidicity of the plot also increases.

When the protein that undergoes allosteric transitions is also an enzyme, Monod, Wyman, and Changeux have predicted that the binding of the allosteric ligand will alter the enzyme's activity. One way in which this might occur is the following. If the allosteric ligand and the substrate exhibit different binding capabilities with respect to the R and T forms, the allosteric ligand will be able to influence the extent of substrate binding by shifting the equilibria involving these forms. If substrate binding is the rate-determining event in the enzyme reaction sequence, influences upon this parameter will be reflected by the enzyme reaction velocity. It should be noted at this point, however, that the influence of an allosteric ligand is upon thermodynamic parameters, and therefore if these ligands can influence the velocity of a reaction, it must be that certain *thermodynamic* parameters determine the *kinetic* parameters of the process.

A second way in which an allosteric ligand might alter the velocity of an enzymatic reaction can be seen if the T and R states of the enzyme differ markedly in their ability to catalyze the reaction. Under these circumstances if the allosteric ligand shifted the $T \rightleftharpoons R$ equilibria (while failing to exert any influence upon substrate binding), its effect would be to enhance or inhibit the apparent reaction velocity as a result of increasing or decreasing the availability of the more active enzyme species.

When the allosteric ligand influences the extent of substrate binding, Monod and his colleagues refer to the enzyme and its ligands as a *K system* since the effect of the allosteric ligand is upon the apparent Michaelis constant $K$ for the substrate involved. On the other hand, when the allosteric ligand influences the relative concentrations of R forms and T forms which have different catalytic capabilities, Monod, Wyman, and Changeux refer to the enzyme and its ligands as a *V* system since now it is the maximum velocity $V_{max}$ of the reaction that is altered.

Several alternatives to the model of Monod, Wyman, and Changeux have been offered. One is that of Atkinson, Hathaway, and Smith.† Whereas the Monod model depicts concerted ligand-induced conformational changes, i.e., changes in which all the protomers of an oligomer undergo a synchronous rearrangement, Atkinson and his colleagues have proposed that in at least some instances the rearrangements that take place do so sequentially. According to this model, the association of one ligand alters the conformation of the protomer to which it becomes bound, and this conformational change in turn induces conformational changes in one or more neighboring protomers, with the ultimate result that the quaternary structure of the oligomeric enzyme is altered.

Koshland and his colleagues have developed several detailed models for allosteric transitions based upon the premise that the binding of ligands induces sequential conformational changes in the enzyme protomers and that the energy involved in the interactions between these protomers is altered as a result of these ligand-induced conformational changes.‡ If ligand-induced conformational changes result in greater stabilization of this enzyme form, a second ligand molecule will be bound more

---

† Atkinson, D. E., Hathaway, J. A., and Smith, E. C. (1965) *J. Biol. Chem.* **240**, 2682–2690.

‡ Koshland, D. E., Jr., Nemethy, G., and Filmer, D. (1966) *Biochemistry* **5**, 365–385; Koshland, D. E., Jr. (1970) in *The Enzymes* (Boyer, P. D., ed.), vol. 2, 3d ed., pp. 341–396, Academic, New York; Cornish-Bowden, A., and Koshland, D. E., Jr. (1970) *J. Biol. Chem.* **245**, 6241–6250.

readily than the first. Koshland calls this behavior *positive cooperativity*. It is comparable to the homotropic effect described by Monod, Wyman, and Changeux. If the ligand-induced conformational changes result in decreased stabilization of the enzyme form, the binding of the initial ligand molecule will result in relatively fewer additional ligand molecules being bound. Koshland calls this behavior *negative cooperativity*. Plots of $\bar{Y}$ as a function of [L] for a ligand-binding process showing positive cooperativity are generally sigmoidal while the corresponding plots of $1/\bar{Y}$ vs. $1/[L]$ are nonlinear and in fact concave. On the other hand, plots of $\bar{Y}$ as a function of [L] for a ligand-binding process that exhibits negative cooperativity are generally hyperbolic although the curve will rise more rapidly in the region of low ligand concentration and the hyperbola will approach the limiting value more slowly than if the cooperativity were absent. Plots of $1/\bar{Y}$ vs. $1/[L]$ are also nonlinear, but in this case they are convex (or "concave downward").

## Use of the Hill Coefficient in Categorizing Cooperative Effects

A useful procedure for determining the absence or presence of cooperative effects as well as for identifying the type of cooperativity when it is present makes use of a *Hill plot*. A Hill plot is based on the equation below,† which was formulated some 50 years before the proposals of Monod et al., Atkinson, or Koshland:

$$\log \frac{\bar{Y}}{1 - \bar{Y}} = n_H \log [L] - \log K \qquad (8\text{-}73)$$

where $K$ is the constant for the equilibria involving the protein and its ligand. The factor $n_H$ is the Hill coefficient, an empirical constant that reflects both the number of ligand binding sites present on the protein and the degree of interaction between these sites. If one plots $\log [\bar{Y}/(1 - \bar{Y})]$ as a function of $\log [L]$, a straight line is usually obtained and its slope gives the value for the Hill coefficient $n_H$. When this value is unity, it indicates that the binding of the ligand is noncooperative; when it is greater than unity, it indicates that the ligand binding involves positive cooperativity; when it is less than unity, it indicates negative cooperativity. More recently the Hill plot has been used for determining whether or not substrate binding by an enzyme is cooperative. To do this one must make the assumption that the rate-determining event in the reaction sequence is the binding of the substrate molecule by the enzyme and that the maximum velocity of the enzymatic reaction occurs when all the substrate binding sites are occupied. Under these conditions, Eq. (8-73) can be written

$$\log \frac{v}{V_{\max} - v} = n_H \log [A] - \log K \qquad (8\text{-}74)$$

where [A] is the substrate concentration. Similarly, as before, the slope of a plot of $\log [v/(V_{\max} - v)]$ vs. $\log [A]$ gives a value for $n_H$, and depending upon whether this

---

† Hill, A. V. (1910) *J. Physiol. Lond.* **40**, iv–viii; see also *Biochem. J.*, **7**, 471–480 (1913).

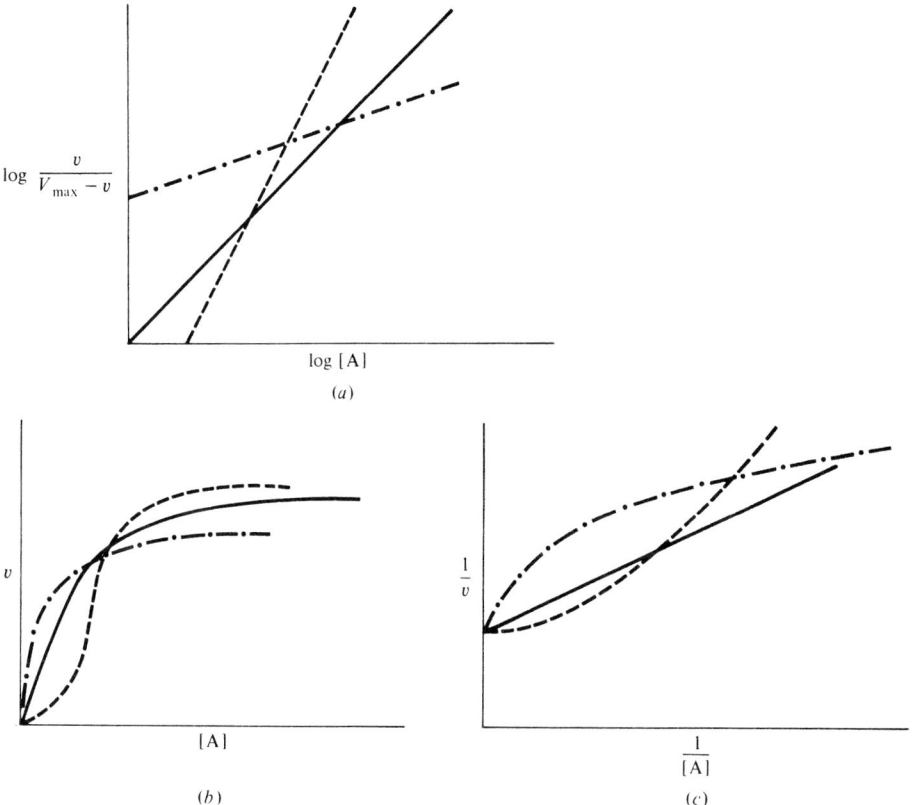

**Figure 8-14** Plots that would be obtained when the binding of A is noncooperative (———) or when it exhibits positive (- - - -) or negative (-·-·-) cooperativity. Data in (a) are displayed in terms of a Hill plot, data in (b) are displayed in terms of a velocity versus substrate-concentration ("direct") plot, and data in (c) are displayed in terms of a double reciprocal plot.

value is 1; > 1, or < 1, the substrate binding is exhibiting noncooperativity, positive cooperativity, or negative cooperativity, respectively.

In Fig. 8-14 the effects of cooperative binding upon direct (velocity-vs.-substrate-concentration) plots, double reciprocal plots, and Hill plots are shown.

## CLASSIFICATION OF ENZYMES

Each of the biochemical reactions occurring in living organisms is catalyzed by a specific enzyme. Thus there are hundreds of different enzymes participating in metabolic pathways, and it is not surprising that an effort has been made to classify them. In 1955 an International Commission on Enzymes was established by the General Assembly of the International Union of Biochemistry during the meeting of the Third International Congress of Biochemistry in Brussels. This commission comprised biochemists from the United Kingdom, Russia, Denmark, France, Austria, Germany, and the United States. The members of the commission appointed additional biochemists to various subcommissions, and the monumental task of classifying the currently known enzymes was begun. Six years later, in 1961, the final version of this commission's report was formulated and presented to the General Assembly of the International Union of Biochemistry during the meeting of the Fifth International Congress of Biochemistry in Moscow. The proposed nomenclature and classification system was adopted. Following the acceptance of its final report, the commission was disbanded, but a Standing Committee on Enzymes was established to consider criticisms and add new enzymes as they were isolated and characterized. To date, nearly 1800 enzymes have been classified by the commission and its successor, the Standing Committee on Enzymes. The classification system is as follows.

Each enzyme is given an identifying number which consists of four parts. The first is a number that stipulates the main category to which the enzyme belongs, of which there are six:

Group 1: oxidoreductases
Group 2: transferases
Group 3: hydrolases
Group 4: lyases
Group 5: isomerases
Group 6: ligases

Oxidoreductases catalyze oxidation-reduction reactions, e.g., the conversion of a secondary alcohol into a ketone or that of an aldehyde into a carboxylic acid with the concomitant reduction of the appropriate cofactor. The other kinds of oxidation-reduction reactions that occur in biochemical systems, e.g., the oxidative cleavage of aromatic rings, the oxidation of a dithiol to a disulfide, and the oxidation and reduction of iron-heme complexes, are also catalyzed by enzymes that are categorized as oxidoreductases.

Transferases are enzymes that catalyze the transfer of various functional groups from one molecule to another or from one position in a molecule to another. For example, aminotransferases catalyze the transfer of an amino group from an amino acid to an oxo acid.

Hydrolases catalyze the hydrolytic cleavage of esters, thiol esters, peptides, glycosides, anhydrides, and similar compounds.

A lyase is an enzyme that catalyzes an addition reaction resulting in the saturation of a double bond or an elimination reaction resulting in a double bond. For example, the enzyme that catalyzes the conversion of serine into pyruvate is a lyase since a carbon-carbon double bond is created upon the elimination of the C(3) hydroxyl group of serine. (The resulting enamine then undergoes tautomerism to yield the ketimine, which is, in turn, hydrolyzed to yield pyruvate.) Another example of a lyase is provided by the enzyme that catalyzes the conversion of fructose 1,6-bisphosphate into glyceraldehyde 3-phosphate and dihydroxyacetone phosphate. In this case the double bond formed is that of the carbonyl group of the glyceraldehyde 3-phosphate formed as dihydroxyacetone phosphate is eliminated. Enzymes that catalyze the removal of hydrogen from an alkane moiety to yield an alkene moiety are not considered lyases but classified as oxidoreductases.

Isomerases, as the name implies, catalyze reactions involving an isomerization. As examples, there are isomerases that catalyze the conversion of one enantiomer into another, those which catalyze the conversion of one diastereomer into another, and those which catalyze cis-trans interconversions.

Ligases catalyze reactions that involve the formation of a new carbon-oxygen, carbon-nitrogen, carbon-sulfur, or carbon-carbon bond concomitantly with the cleavage of ATP or a similar nucleoside triphosphate. Examples of reactions catalyzed by ligases include the formation of an acyl-CoA from a carboxylic acid and CoA and the formation of glutamine from glutamate and ammonia. In each case the cleavage of ATP is required for the thiol ester or the amide to be formed. Ligases are sometimes called synthetases.

The second number of the enzyme classification system designates the subclass to which the enzyme belongs. In general, the subclass stipulates the type of functional group that undergoes the reaction catalyzed by the enzymes of the particular category. For example, for the oxidoreductases, the subclass stipulates the type of functional group that undergoes oxidation, and for the transferases the subclass stipulates the type of functional group that is transferred; the functional group that is hydrolyzed is specified by this subclassification of the hydrolases.

The third number of the enzyme classification system, which designates the sub-subclass, allows yet further distinctions to be made. For enzymes of category 1, the oxidoreductases, the sub-subclassification indicates the electron acceptor involved in the oxidation-reduction reaction. On the other hand, in the case of the hydrolases the third of the four numbers is used to stipulate more explicitly the type of ester or glycosyl or ether or peptide bond that is acted upon. Thus, the esterases, designated by 3.1._._, are sub-subclassified as those acting upon carboxylic acid esters, thiol esters, phosphoric acid monoesters, phosphoric acid diesters, triphosphoric acid monoesters, and diphosphoric acid monoesters.

Finally, the fourth number of the system is used simply to identify the members of a given sub-subclass.

CHAPTER
# NINE
## CARBOHYDRATE METABOLISM

## INTRODUCTION

In living organisms specific sequences of interrelated reactions convert the ingested food into the biochemical compounds required for growth and maintenance. These sequences are generally referred to as metabolic pathways. The word metabolism is derived from the Greek *metabolos* which means "changeable." Metabolic pathways *change* ingested food into compounds that the organism must have in order to sustain life. A given sequence of biochemical reactions may bring about the degradation of ingested foods, or it may carry out the synthesis of required compounds. Sequences which bring about degradation are referred to as *catabolic pathways*, while those which carry out biosynthesis are referred to as *anabolic pathways*. The words catabolism and anabolism were formulated from the Greek *kata*, "down," and *ana*, "up."

Catabolic pathways are effectively oxidative pathways. The catabolism of carbohydrates, lipids, and proteins involves the oxidation of the carbon atoms that constitute these molecules. Anabolic pathways are effectively reductive pathways. The biosynthesis of carbohydrates, lipids, and amino acids generally entails carbon reduction. As a result of the oxidation of carbon atoms, useful chemical energy is made available. Another way of expressing this is to say that these oxidative pathways are associated with negative $\Delta G$ values. By contrast, the biosynthesis of the compounds required for the growth and maintenance of living organisms is an energy-requiring process. This chemical energy is supplied from that which is made available by catabolism.

How is this energy exchange accomplished? When the carbon atoms of carbohydrate, lipid, and protein derivatives are oxidized, the resulting reducing equivalents are concomitantly transferred to specific oxidation-reduction cofactors such as $NAD^+$, FAD, or $NADP^+$. The appropriate one of these cofactors is bound at the catalytic site of the enzyme that catalyzes the oxidation-reduction reaction. The reduced cofactor in turn transfers these reducing equivalents to a component of a pathway known as the mitochondrial electron-transport system, and as a result of this transfer, the oxidized form of the cofactor is regenerated. The function of the mitochondrial electron-transport system, in this case, is that of transferring the reducing equivalents to the ultimate acceptor, which is molecular oxygen. This is accomplished by passing the reducing equivalents along a sequence of components which in general have progressively more positive reduction potentials. This process is accompanied by a free-energy change which is large and negative and which corresponds to the electrode potential difference between the initial and final electron-transfer processes that occur in the system. The energy that is thus made available is utilized initially to synthesize the compound that, in effect, functions as a "medium of exchange" between catabolic and anabolic pathways. This compound is the nucleotide adenosine 5'-triphosphate (ATP), which is produced as a result of catabolic processes and is used in anabolic processes.

At this point, one might ask how ATP is used in anabolic processes. In general terms, the answer is as follows. In most instances anabolic pathways entail at least one reaction that is thermodynamically unfavorable. The participation of ATP in such a process can cause the overall conversion to be much more thermodynamically favorable. Consider, for example, the thermodynamically unfavorable reaction $A + B \rightarrow C + D$. This conversion proceeds only to a very limited extent; however, A can react with ATP. (In most cases this reaction entails an attack by A at the terminal phosphoryl phosphorus atom and the formation of a phosphoryl derivative of A and ADP. In some cases, however, attack is at the internal phosphoryl phosphorus atom, and the products are an adenylyl derivative of A and pyrophosphate.)

Attack at the terminal phosphorus atom:

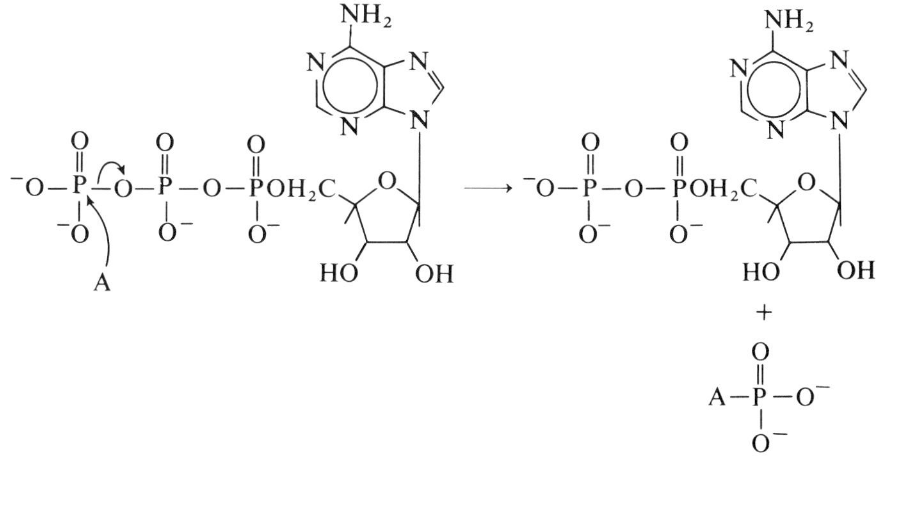

**332** MECHANISMS OF METABOLISM

Attack at the internal phosphorus atom:

$$\text{}^-\text{O}-\overset{\overset{\text{O}}{\|}}{\underset{\text{O}^-}{\text{P}}}-\text{O}-\overset{\overset{\text{O}}{\|}}{\underset{\text{O}^-}{\text{P}}}-\text{O}-\overset{\overset{\text{O}}{\|}}{\underset{\text{O}^-}{\text{P}}}\text{OH}_2\text{C}-\text{Adenosine} \longrightarrow \text{A}-\overset{\overset{\text{O}}{\|}}{\underset{\text{O}^-}{\text{P}}}-\text{O}-\text{H}_2\text{C}-\text{Adenosine} + \text{}^-\text{O}-\overset{\overset{\text{O}}{\|}}{\underset{\text{O}^-}{\text{P}}}-\text{O}-\overset{\overset{\text{O}}{\|}}{\underset{\text{O}^-}{\text{P}}}-\text{O}^-$$

The reaction between A and ATP would be expected to be thermodynamically favored since hydrolytic cleavage of ATP at the terminal phosphoryl group or the internal phosphoryl group is very favorable thermodynamically. However, when ATP reacts with A (which frequently is a molecule containing a nucleophilic oxygen atom, just as the water molecule contains such an atom), a portion of the available chemical energy is utilized in the synthesis of a highly reactive derivative of A rather than being liberated, as in the hydrolytic reaction. This highly reactive derivative of A embodies sufficient chemical energy to allow the reaction between itself and B to be thermodynamically favorable. This is shown diagrammatically in Fig. 9-1b. In certain specific instances it is the cleavage of GTP or ITP, rather than ATP, that facilitates the unfavorable reaction.

Characteristically, metabolic pathways are sequences of biochemical reactions whereby a significant chemical change is accomplished as the result of a multiplicity of small steps. For example, glycolysis, a pathway by which carbohydrates are catabolized, effects the conversion of one molecule of glucose into two molecules of pyruvate. This conversion is accomplished by 10 individual reactions, each carrying out a small part of the total conversion. During the process of glycolysis, as a molecule of glucose undergoes catabolism, two molecules of $NAD^+$ are reduced to molecules of NADH (as a concomitance of the oxidation of two of the carbon atoms of the hexose). Subsequently, the reducing equivalents embodied by the NADH molecules are introduced into the mitochondrial electron-transport system, wherein after a sequence of at least seven electron-transfer reactions these reducing equivalents are utilized for the reduction of molecular oxygen. From a teleological standpoint, the fact that chemical changes are accomplished in living organisms as a result of a series of small chemical changes means that the liberation (or the utilization) of chemical energy occurs in small increments rather than as a huge surge. Certainly such small changes in energy are much more readily tolerated by living organisms than large changes would be.

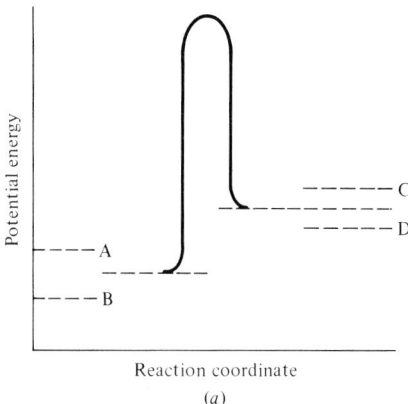
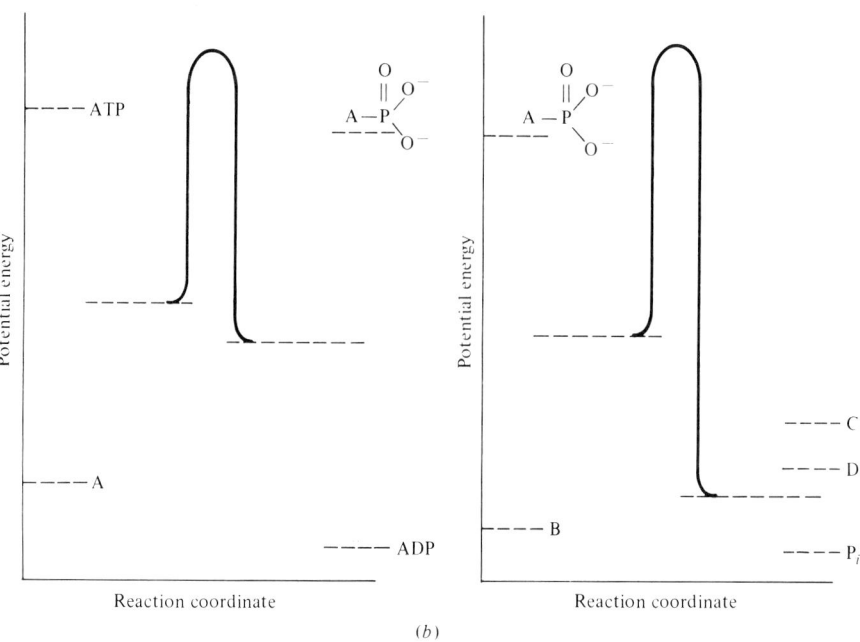

**Figure 9-1** Schematic representation of potential energy versus reaction coordinate for the thermodynamically unfavorable reaction $A + B \rightarrow C + D$. In (a) without the participation of ATP, the reactants are simply converted into the products which exist at a higher potential-energy level than their precursors. In (b), through the agency of ATP, a highly reactive derivative of A is formed and this then reacts with B to yield C and D and to liberate orthophosphate. Again, C and D exist at a higher potential-energy level than A and B but because of the participation of ATP, the mean of the potential energies of the products is lower than that of their immediate precursors.

## THE GLYCOLYTIC PATHWAY

When a polysaccharide is to undergo catabolism, it is first degraded to its component monosaccharides in the process of digestion. The resulting monosaccharides can then enter an appropriate catabolic pathway and undergo further degradation. If the monosaccharide is a hexose, it can undergo a sequence of catabolic processes which results in its complete catabolism to carbon dioxide and water. The overall process can be written

$$C_6H_{12}O_6 + 6O_2 \longrightarrow 6CO_2 + 6H_2O \quad \begin{array}{l} \Delta G^{\circ\prime} = -686 \text{ kcal/mol} \\ \Delta H = 673 \text{ kcal/mol} \end{array} \quad (9\text{-}1)$$

In actuality, this conversion is accomplished as a result of over 20 different individual reactions. First, if the hexose is not glucose, it is converted into glucose by the appropriate interconverting reactions (discussed subsequently in this chapter; see Hexose Interconversions). The glucose can then undergo glycolysis; the product of glycolysis in turn can undergo the reactions of the tricarboxylic acid cycle; and the reducing equivalents resulting from the processes of glycolysis and the tricarboxylic acid cycle can finally be utilized by the mitochondrial electron-transport system. The resultant is that glucose is oxidized through the agency of molecular oxygen to yield carbon dioxide and water, as expressed by Eq. (9-1). The manner in which this is accomplished is the subject of this chapter and Chaps. 10 and 11.

Glycolysis, as the name implies, is the "cleavage of a sugar." Specifically, glycolysis is the oxidation and cleavage of a molecule of glucose to yield two molecules of pyruvate. The sequence of reactions by which this is accomplished is as follows.

### Step 1: Phosphorylation of Glucose

The reactions of glycolysis utilize phosphoryl derivatives as substrates, and thus the initial reaction of the sequence is the phosphorylation of glucose. This reaction is catalyzed by the enzyme glucokinase (ATP: D-glucose 6-phosphotransferase, EC 2.7.1.2)[†] or by the somewhat less specific enzyme hexokinase (ATP: D-hexose 6-phosphotransferase, EC 2.7.1.1). The reaction in either case is

$$\text{Glucose} + \text{ATP} \rightleftharpoons \text{glucose 6-phosphate} + \text{ADP} \quad (9\text{-}2)$$

Reactions of this type, which are encountered many times in metabolic pathways, are generally assumed to proceed by a reaction mechanism similar to that demonstrated in the case of the comparable nonenzymatic reaction. This mechanism entails the attack by a nucleophile at an electrophilic phosphoryl phosphorus atom of the phosphoryl donor. In the enzymatic reaction as catalyzed by glucokinase or hexokinase the oxygen atom of the primary alcohol group of glucose

---

[†] The trivial name of each enzyme mentioned for the first time is followed in parentheses by its systematic name and its classification number.

is the nucleophile, and the terminal phosphoryl phosphorus atom of ATP is the electrophilic center that is attacked. The product is glucose 6-phosphate. The enzymatic (like the nonenzymatic) phosphorylation utilizes a divalent cation such as $Mg^{2+}$. The function of this cation is that of forming a complex with the ionized oxygen atoms of the phosphoryl groups of ATP and thereby shielding their negative charges, which, in turn, facilitates the approach of the nucleophilic hydroxyl group. In addition, the formation of such a complex with the oxygen atoms of the terminal phosphoryl group increases the electrophilicity of the phosphorus atom of this group, thus further promoting the reaction.

Mammalian hexokinase exists in several forms, referred to as *isoenzymes*.[†] One of these, which is found predominantly in brain, has been designated as the type I isoenzyme, while the form that predominates in skeletal muscle is referred to as the type II isoenzyme. Kinetic studies on each of these types of hexokinase have indicated that the phosphorylation reaction they catalyze proceeds by a random sequential Bi Bi mechanism.[‡] As with other kinases, the actual substrate in the reaction catalyzed by a hexokinase is MgATP, i.e., the magnesium-ATP complex. In fact, noncomplexed ATP is a potent inhibitor of the reaction. When product-inhibition studies were conducted on hexokinase I from bovine brain[§] and from rat brain,[¶] both glucose 6-phosphate and ADP were found to be inhibitory. However, in the case of the nucleotide product it was found that plots of $1/v_i$ as a function of [ADP] were parabolic (Fig. 9-2). Since the equation of a parabola has the general form $y = ax^2$, it was concluded that the concentration of ADP appears as a second-order term in the velocity equation and hence that ADP binds the enzyme at two different sites.

In addition to the observations concerning the products of the reaction, it has also been found that the activities of the type I and type II hexokinases are both modulated by orthophosphate, but the effects of this modulator upon the type I and type II enzyme are quite different. In the case of the type I enzyme from (bovine) brain, orthophosphate reverses the inhibitory effect of the product, glucose 6-phosphate. Hence, orthophosphate can be viewed as an activator with respect to the activity of this enzyme. On the other hand, the activity of the type II enzyme, from (rat) skeletal muscle is inhibited by orthophosphate. More specifically, orthophosphate appears to be a competitive inhibitor when MgATP is the variable substrate and a noncompetitive inhibitor when glucose is the variable substrate. These observations can be rationalized within the framework of a random

---

[†] The term isoenzymes is ideally restricted to describing enzyme species arising from genetically determined differences in primary structure. However, it is sometimes used, operationally, to designate proteins having the same catalytic activity but distinct physical properties (such as electrophoretic mobility or chromatographic behavior). See *Eur. J. Biochem.* **24**, 1-3 (1971).

[‡] Ning, J., Purich, D. L., and Fromm, H. J. (1969) *J. Biol. Chem.* **244**, 3840–3846; Purich, D. L., and Fromm, H. J. (1971) *J. Biol. Chem.* **246**, 3456–3463; Lueck, J. D., and Fromm, H. J. (1974) *J. Biol. Chem.* **249**, 1341–1347; Ellison, W. R., Lueck, J. D., and Fromm, H. J. (1975) *J. Biol. Chem.* **250**, 1864–1871.

[§] Ning, Purich, and Fromm, loc. cit.

[¶] Purich and Fromm, loc. cit.

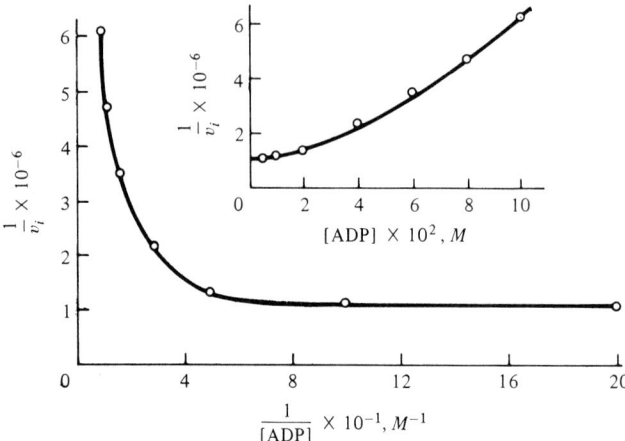

**Figure 9-2** Plot of $1/v_i$ as a function of $1/[ADP]$ for the phosphorylation reaction catalyzed by hexokinase from bovine brain. Note that the double reciprocal plot is concave, suggesting that the equation describing the inhibited reaction contains second- (or higher-) order terms in [ADP]. Additional evidence in support of this is provided by the plot of $1/v_i$ as a function of [ADP] (inset) which is parabolic. [*From Ning, J., Purich, D. I., and Fromm, H. J. (1969) J. Biol. Chem.* **244**, *3840–3846 (see p. 3843). With permission.*]

sequential kinetic mechanism if an enzyme-glucose-$P_i$ dead-end complex can be formed but an enzyme-MgATP-$P_i$ dead-end complex cannot.

Hexokinase has also been isolated from yeast cells; however, the properties of the yeast enzyme are, in some cases, distinct from those of the mammalian enzymes. This is frequently true for enzymes obtained from sources belonging to different kingdoms and sometimes true for enzymes obtained from sources belonging to different genera or species. Often it is the response to modulators that is seen to differ when one compares enzymes from different sources. Thus, although yeast hexokinase also exhibits a random kinetic mechanism,† neither of the two forms of the enzyme that have been isolated and purified is so strongly inhibited by the product glucose 6-phosphate as the mammalian enzymes are. On the other hand, orthophosphate and, to a greater degree, 3-phosphoglycerate (an intermediate in the glycolytic pathway) enhance the activity of yeast hexokinase when studies‡ are conducted at pH 6.6. It is appropriate that these studies were conducted at the lower pH since the intracellular pH of yeast cells lies between 5.8 and 6.2.

## Step 2: Isomerization of Glucose 6-Phosphate

Glucose 6-phosphate, formed in the initial reaction of glycolysis, next undergoes isomerization to yield fructose 6-phosphate. This isomerization is catalyzed by the

---

† Danenberg, K. D., and Cleland, W. W. (1975) *Biochemistry* **14**, 28–39.
‡ Kosow, D. P., and Rose, I. A. (1971) *J. Biol. Chem.* **246**, 2618–2625.

enzyme glucosephosphate isomerase (D-glucose-6-phosphate ketol-isomerase, EC 5.3.1.9). Studies on glucosephosphate isomerase from rabbit skeletal muscle have indicated that the maximum velocity of the reaction is dependent upon pH.† Specifically, a plot of $V_{max}$ as a function of pH was found to be a bell-shaped curve. Bell-shaped rate-vs.-pH curves are frequently obtained when the reaction concerned proceeds in two steps, one involving a protonated species and the other a nonprotonated species. (For example, rate-vs.-pH curves for the formation of phenylhydrazones and oximes are bell-shaped. The phenylhydrazine or hydroxylamine molecule that attacks the carbonyl group must be nonprotonated, while the subsequent elimination of the elements of water involves the protonated carbinolamine intermediate.) In the enzymatic isomerization of glucose 6-phosphate to fructose 6-phosphate the relationship between the maximum velocity of the reaction at a given pH and that pH can be formulated as

$$V'_{max} = \frac{V_{max}^{opt}}{1 + [H^+]/K_1 + K_2/[H^+]} \qquad (9\text{-}3)$$

where $V'_{max}$ = maximum velocity at pH defined by $[H^+]$
$V_{max}^{opt}$ = maximum velocity at pH optimum for reaction
$K_1, K_2$ = dissociation constants for the nonprotonated and protonated species, respectively, that participate in reaction

The dissociation constants $K_1$ and $K_2$ were computed to be 6.7 and 9.3, respectively. On the basis of the values for these dissociation constants plus other corroborating data it was proposed that these two groups are an imidazole moiety of a histidyl unit, with a $pK_a$ of 6.7, and an $\epsilon$-amino group of a lysyl unit, with a $pK_a$ of 9.3.‡·§ The enzymatic mechanism has, therefore, been formulated as shown on page 338. The protonated $\epsilon$-amino group donates a proton to the heterocyclic oxygen atom, thus facilitating ring opening. The resulting positively charged species then loses a proton, and an enediol is formed. A prototropic rearrangement, in which an imidazolium moiety may participate, leads to the formation of fructose 6-phosphate.

The enzymatic reaction catalyzed by glucosephosphate isomerase is reversible. For the enzyme from rabbit muscle, the equilibrium constant (at 38°C) has been determined to be

$$K_{eq} = \frac{[\text{D-fructose 6-phosphate}]}{[\text{D-glucose 6-phosphate}]} = 0.306 \qquad (9\text{-}4)$$

The enzymatic activity of glucosephosphate isomerase from mammalian sources, e.g., rabbit muscle or rabbit brain, is inhibited by ATP, orthophosphate, phosphoenolpyruvate (a compound formed in a subsequent step of glycolysis), and 6-phosphogluconate (a compound formed in an alternate pathway for the catabolism of hexoses).

---

† Dyson, J. E. D., and Noltmann, E. A. (1968) *J. Biol. Chem.* **243**, 1401–1414.
‡ Ibid.
§ Schnackerz, K. D., and Noltmann, E. A. (1970) *J. Biol. Chem.* **245**, 6417–6423.

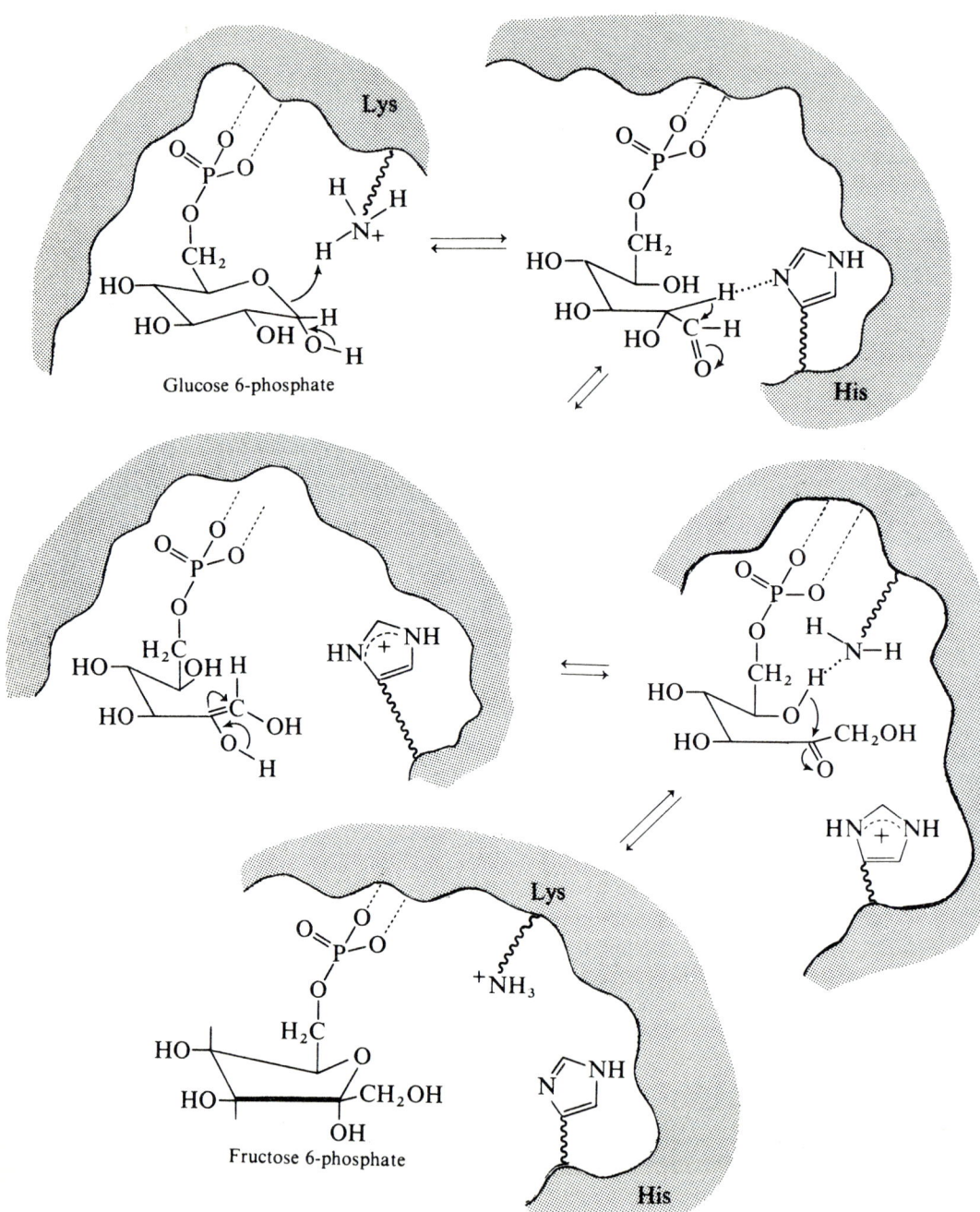

## Step 3: Phosphorylation of Fructose 6-Phosphate

In a reaction catalyzed by phosphofructokinase (ATP:D-fructose-6-phosphate 1-phosphotransferase, EC 2.7.1.11), fructose 6-phosphate is converted into the diphosphoryl compound fructose 1,6-bisphosphate. When kinetic studies on the enzyme from rabbit skeletal muscle were conducted, it was found that plots of $1/v_i$ as a function of either $1/[\text{MgATP}]$ or $1/[\text{fructose 6-phosphate}]$ with fixed concentrations of the other substrate were usually intersecting although when fructose 6-phosphate was the variable substrate and the fixed concentrations of MgATP were relatively high, the plots became virtually parallel.† With respect to product inhibition, fructose 1,6-bisphosphate was found to be a competitive inhibitor when fructose 6-phosphate was the variable substrate and a noncompetitive inhibitor when MgATP was varied. On the other hand, MgADP functioned as a competitive inhibitor with respect to MgATP and a noncompetitive inhibitor with respect to fructose 6-phosphate. When 1-deoxyfructose 6-phosphate was used as a dead-end inhibitor, the inhibition exhibited a slope effect when fructose 6-phosphate was the variable substrate and both a slope and an intercept effect when MgATP was varied. On the other hand, when a chromium complex of ATP (shown to be inert in this reaction and therefore also a dead-end inhibitor) was used, a slope effect was observed when MgATP was the variable substrate while both a slope and an intercept effect were observed when fructose 6-phosphate was the variable substrate. These data were interpreted as indicating that the kinetic mechanism of the reaction catalyzed by phosphofructokinase is, in fact, random sequential. The product-inhibition data are compatible with a random sequential mechanism in which the dead-end complexes involving a substrate and the structurally similar product, i.e., MgATP and MgADP or fructose 6-phosphate and fructose 1,6-bisphosphate, are not formed. Recall that generally *all* product-inhibition patterns are noncompetitive when a random sequential Bi Bi mechanism is operative. It would also appear that dead-end complexes involving a substrate and its analog are not formed, since 1-deoxyfructose 6-phosphate produced only a slope effect when fructose 6-phosphate was varied and CrATP produced only a slope effect when MgATP was varied. However, it should be noted that if the reaction had been ordered, one of these dead-end inhibitors should have produced only an intercept effect when the dissimilar substrate was varied. With respect to the apparently parallel initial-velocity plots, simulation studies showed that when a random mechanism is operative, as the inhibition constant for a given substrate, for example, $K_{ia}$, becomes very small compared with the Michaelis constant for the same substrate, that is, $K_a$, plots of $1/v_i$ vs. $1/[A]$, where A is the substrate, can in fact become parallel. It might be remembered at this point that in ordered sequential Bi Bi reactions or rapid equilibrium random Bi Bi reactions the vertical coordinate of the point at which plots of $1/v_i$ as a function of $1/[A]$ intersect is given by $1/V_{\max}(1 - K_a/K_{ia})$. Therefore, in these cases, as $K_{ia}$ becomes negligible

---

† Hanson, R. L., Rudolph, F. B., and Lardy, H. A. (1973) *J. Biol. Chem.* **248**, 7852–7859; Bar-Tana, J., and Cleland, W. W. (1974) *J. Biol. Chem.* **249**, 1271–1276.

compared with $K_a$, the vertical coordinate of the point at which the plots intersect approaches negative infinity.

Metabolic pathways can be regulated by several different means: the availability of the required substrates and cofactors; the modification of the activity of an enzyme that catalyzes a slow or rate-determining step by an ultimate product of the pathway; by a product (or substrate) of a pathway that follows this pathway; or by some other modulator. In the glycolytic pathway in many living organisms regulation is achieved by modifying the activity of phosphofructokinase by certain modulators (including 3′,5′-AMP and AMP), which enhance the activity of the enzyme, and ATP and citrate, which function as inhibitors.[†] The reaction catalyzed by phosphofructokinase is the first reaction of the glycolytic pathway that is unique to this pathway, since the phosphorylation of glucose to yield glucose 6-phosphate can be considered the initial step of other pathways that can utilize this phosphorylated intermediate. Thus, it is perhaps not surprising that flow through the glycolytic pathway is regulated, at least in part, by the activity of phosphofructokinase. The means by which this comes about has been shown in certain cases to be the result of a modulator functioning as an allosteric ligand. For example, it has been indicated that ATP becomes bound at a site other than the catalytic site and that as a result of this binding the enzyme assumes a different form. In most mammalian systems studied the transition that attends this ATP binding is also accompanied by a change with respect to the binding of the substrate fructose 6-phosphate. Thus, for the enzyme from ovine heart, as the concentration of ATP was increased, the curve depicting the relationship between reaction velocity and the fructose 6-phosphate concentration shifted from hyperbolic to sigmoidal.[‡] When one compares a hyperbolic velocity-vs.-substrate plot with a sigmoidal one, the reaction velocity in the presence of a given substrate concentration (particularly at low substrate concentration) is inhibited when the plot is sigmoidal rather than hyperbolic. It has also been shown that when the reaction velocity is a sigmoidal function of the concentration of a given substrate, small changes in that concentration result in relatively large changes in the reaction velocity. More specifically, Koshland has demonstrated that when the velocity-vs.-substrate plot is hyperbolic, an 81-fold increase in substrate concentration is required to increase the velocity from 10 percent of the maximum to 90 percent of the maximum. On the other hand, when this curve is sigmoidal a three- to sixfold change in the substrate concentration will increase the reaction velocity from 10 to 90 percent.[§] Hence, when the velocity of an enzymatic reaction is a sigmoidal function of the concentration of a substrate, this reaction can be inordinately sensitive to regulatory controls imposed by changes in that substrate concentration.

---

[†] Mansour, T. E. (1963) *J. Biol. Chem.* **238**, 2285–2292; Lowry, O. H., and Passonneau, J. V. (1966) *J. Biol. Chem.* **241**, 2268–2279; Lindell, T. J., and Stellwagen, E. (1968) *J. Biol. Chem.* **243**, 907–912; Mansour, T. E., and Ahlfors, C. E. (1968) *J. Biol. Chem.* **243**, 2523–2533; Kemp, R. G. (1969) *Biochemistry* **8**, 4490–4496; Kemp, R. G. (1971) *J. Biol. Chem.* **246**, 245–252.

[‡] Mansour and Ahlfors, ibid.

[§] Koshland, D. E., Jr., Nementhy, G., and Filmer, D. (1966) *Biochemistry* **5**, 365–385.

Citrate, the other principal inhibitor of phosphofructokinase activity, also causes the curve depicting reaction velocity vs. [fructose 6-phosphate] to change from hyperbolic to sigmoidal. However, although citrate is also thought to bind at a site other than the catalytic site, this site is apparently distinct from that bound by ATP since the effects of these two inhibitors are essentially synergistic.

The modulators 3',5'-AMP and 5'-AMP, which bring about an increase in the activity of phosphofructokinase, are also thought to function as allosteric ligands. In effect, these modulators reverse the inhibitory effects of ATP or citrate by causing the curve depicting velocity vs. [fructose 6-phosphate] to revert from sigmoidal to hyperbolic.

The regulation of phosphofructokinase in microorganisms exhibits some differences compared with the regulatory mechanisms operative in the mammalian systems just discussed. In general, regulatory mechanisms in lower organisms are less complex than those in higher organisms. For example, in yeasts ATP appears to be the principal inhibitor, and 5'-AMP is believed to be the only modulator that brings about an increase in activity. The modulator 3',5'-AMP is without effect in yeasts. However, ATP and 5'-AMP modify the characteristics of fructose 6-phosphate binding in yeasts much as they do in mammalian systems. In *E. coli* phosphofructokinase activity is, again, most sensitive to ATP and 5'-AMP, and, again, 3',5'-AMP is without effect.

In part because it is a regulatory enzyme, the physical characteristics of phosphofructokinase have been of interest to biochemists. Enzymes which catalyze reactions that are subject to metabolic regulation are frequently composed of multiple subunits. Certainly this is the case for phosphofructokinase. For example, the catalytically active form of this enzyme from rabbit skeletal muscle or from ovine heart has a molecular weight of $3.8 \times 10^5$, and in each case this species can be dissociated to yield a subactive form which has a molecular weight of 93,000. The latter is thought to be a protomeric form of the enzyme. Since the protomer of the heart enzyme can bind two molecules of fructose 6-phosphate and four of ATP, it is thought that the protomer possesses two catalytic sites and two allosteric sites which bind ATP.[†] In addition, both the rabbit-muscle phosphofructokinase and that from ovine heart can undergo even more extensive dissociation to yield yet smaller proteins, thought to be the monomeric forms that constitute the protomers. Although catalytically active, oligomeric phosphofructokinase from yeast has a greater molecular weight than the mammalian enzymes ($5.8 \times 10^5$), the enzymes from *E. coli* or *Clostridium pasteurianum* have molecular weights of only $1.4 \times 10^5$. Each of these oligomers can be dissociated to yield a species having a molecular weight of approximately 36,000, which is thought to be the protomer.

The reaction mechanism of the phosphorylation of fructose 6-phosphate parallels that which is operative in the phosphorylation of glucose, discussed previously. Again, a primary alcohol group is the nucleophile, and attack is at the terminal phosphoryl phosphorus atom of MgATP.

---

† Lorenson, M. Y., and Mansour, T. E. (1969) *J. Biol. Chem.* **244**, 6420–6431.

## Step 4: Conversion of Fructose 1,6-Bisphosphate into Glyceraldehyde 3-Phosphate and Dihydroxyacetone Phosphate

As a result of glycolysis a six-carbon molecule is converted into two three-carbon molecules, with the cleavage of the carbon-carbon bond occurring as a result of a retrograde aldol reaction. The enzyme that catalyzes this reaction is fructose-bisphosphate aldolase (D-fructose-1,6-bisphosphate D-glyceraldehyde-3-phosphate-lyase, EC 4.1.2.13). The reaction is

$$\text{D-Fructose 1,6-bisphosphate} \rightleftharpoons \text{dihydroxyacetone phosphate} + \text{D-glyceraldehyde 3-phosphate} \quad (9\text{-}5)$$

Fructose-bisphosphate aldolases have been divided into two classes. Class I aldolases, found in animals and higher plants, catalyze the reversible conversion of fructose 1,6-bisphosphate into glyceraldehyde 3-phosphate and dihydroxyacetone phosphate through the agency of a Schiff base formed from the $\epsilon$-amino group of a lysyl unit at the enzyme catalytic site and the oxo group of the substrate. Class II enzymes, found in yeasts, fungi, and certain bacteria and algae, catalyze the same reaction without the participation of a Schiff base. These aldolases are metalloproteins which bind $Zn^{2+}$ or some other divalent cation.

Mammalian aldolases have been further categorized on the basis of organ specificity, and three types have been designated. Type A aldolase, generally most prevalent, is the only form found in liver, while Type B aldolase is the predominant form in liver and kidney. Brain, on the other hand, contains a third type of aldolase, referred to as C. Type A aldolase from rabbit skeletal muscle is a tetramer which has a molecular weight of 160,000 and is composed of non-identical subunits. Types B and C appear to have similar structures.

Kinetic studies on fructose-bisphosphate aldolase from rabbit skeletal muscle indicate that the reaction proceeds by an ordered sequential Uni Bi mechanism. Evidence in support of this mechanism was obtained when it was found that the aldolase could be modified (in the presence of a proteolytic enzyme) in such a manner that the isotope exchange between glyceraldehyde 3-phosphate and fructose 1,6-bisphosphate is not impeded while that between dihydroxyacetone phosphate and fructose 1,6-bisphosphate is diminished a hundredfold.[†] These observations are interpreted to mean that there is an obligatory order of product release in the forward direction and an obligatory order of substrate binding in the reverse reaction, namely dihydroxyacetone phosphate followed by glyceraldehyde 3-phosphate. The last conclusion is based on the fact that when an ordered sequential mechanism is operative, isotope exchange between two components is inhibited if there is an irreversible step between the points in the reaction sequence at which these components bind the enzyme. An irreversible step is introduced when a component is present at saturating concentrations. An irreversible step is also

---

[†] Rose, I. A., O'Connell, E. L., and Mehler, A. H. (1965) *J. Biol. Chem.* **240**, 1758–1765.

introduced when a component is released from the enzyme at "zero concentration," i.e., in the absence, of that component in the medium. Therefore, the observations above concerning fructose-bisphosphate aldolase can be rationalized as follows. In the presence of unlabeled fructose 1,6-bisphosphate and labeled glyceraldehyde 3-phosphate, the fructose bisphosphate binds the enzyme and is converted into glyceraldehyde 3-phosphate and dihydroxyacetone phosphate. The former can then dissociate from the enzyme, and a labeled molecule of this compound can subsequently become bound in its place. Now if the condensation reaction occurs, labeled fructose 1,6-bisphosphate will be obtained, and thus the isotope exchange will have been accomplished. On the other hand, when it is the dihydroxyacetone phosphate that is labeled and when glyceraldehyde 3-phosphate is absent, following the binding of unlabeled fructose 1,6-bisphosphate and its conversion into the two triose phosphates, both can then dissociate from the enzyme, but now the binding of labeled dihydroxyacetone phosphate cannot result in the formation of labeled fructose 1,6-bisphosphate in the absence of glyceraldehyde 3-phosphate. Thus, the exchange is not accomplished. In order to explain the very small amount of dihydroxyacetone phosphate-fructosebisphosphate exchange that occurs it is suggested that the reaction can take place to a very small extent by an alternate pathway, involving the opposite order of triose phosphate binding and release. This would mean that in actuality the mechanism is random sequential but with one of the two pathways so strongly preferred that for all practical purposes an ordered sequential mechanism prevails.

The reaction mechanism of the conversion of fructose 1,6-bisphosphate into glyceraldehyde 3-phosphate and dihydroxyacetone phosphate has been formulated as shown.

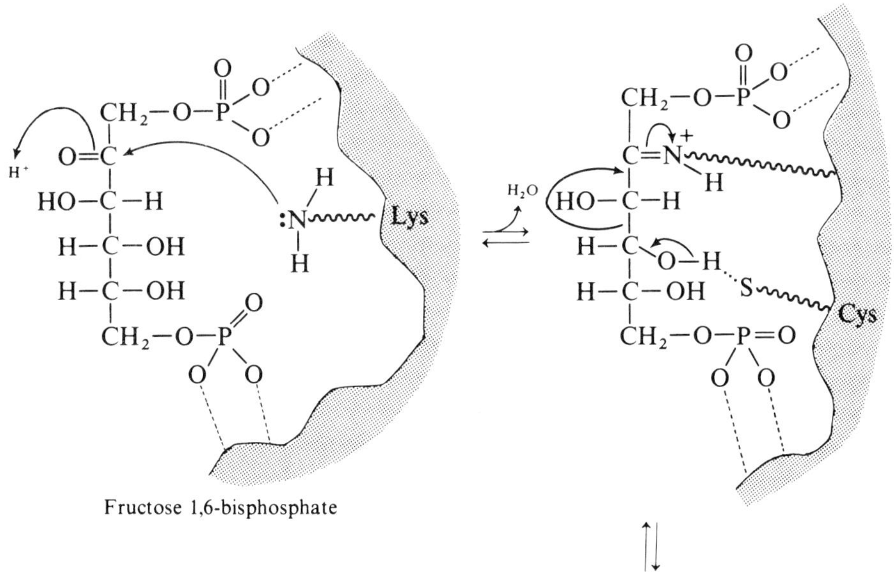

Fructose 1,6-bisphosphate

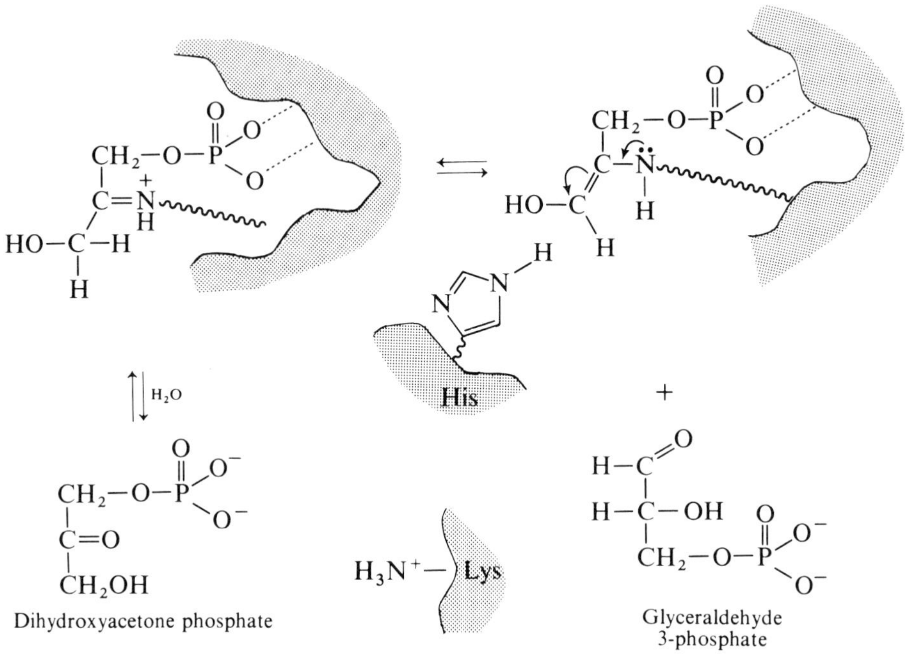

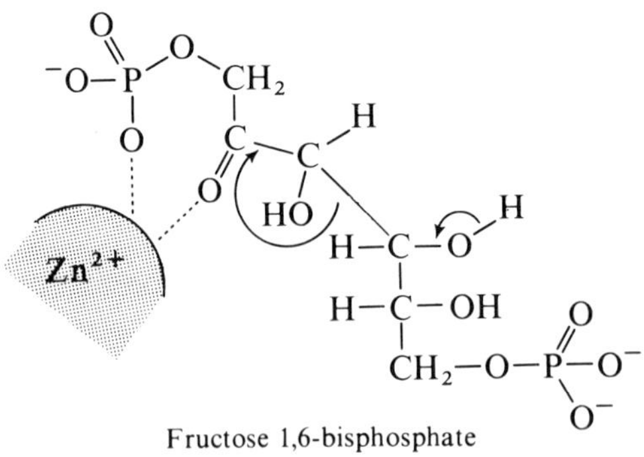

Dihydroxyacetone phosphate

Glyceraldehyde 3-phosphate

Fructose 1,6-bisphosphate binds the catalytic site, and a Schiff base is formed. The protonated imine moiety of the Schiff base provides an electron-deficient center, which can accept an electron pair following removal of the proton from the hydroxyl group at C(4). Glyceraldehyde 3-phosphate is thus eliminated while the dihydroxyacetone phosphate enamine remains bound. Following acceptance of a proton, the second product is then released.

As mentioned earlier, the reaction as catalyzed by fructose-bisphosphate aldolase from yeasts and certain other microorganisms does not entail the formation of a Schiff base. Rather, the reaction is facilitated by divalent cations. The reaction mechanism of the cleavage in yeasts, which utilizes $Zn^{2+}$, has been formulated as follows. Here, the metal cation provides the electron-deficient center rather than the protonated-imine moiety of a Schiff base.†

Fructose 1,6-bisphosphate

† Mildvan, A. S., Kobes, R. D., and Rutter, W. J. (1971) *Biochemistry* **10,** 1191–1204.

## Step 5: Isomerization of Dihydroxyacetone Phosphate

The hexose has now been converted into two three-carbon carbonyl compounds, but only glyceraldehyde 3-phosphate is utilized by the glycolytic pathway. In order for all six of the carbon atoms of the hexose to be utilized by this pathway dihydroxyacetone phosphate must undergo isomerization to glyceraldehyde 3-phosphate. This is accomplished by a reaction catalyzed by triosephosphate isomerase (D-glyceraldehyde-3-phosphate ketol-isomerase, EC 5.3.1.1). The reaction mechanism of this isomerization involves the formation of an enediol intermediate similar to that formed in the conversion of glucose 6-phosphate into fructose 6-phosphate. Studies on the variation of the maximum reaction velocity as a function of pH have provided evidence that two functional groups, one having a $pK_a$ of 6.5 and the other having a $pK_a$ of 9.5, participate in the enzymatic reaction. Although the functional group having a $pK_a$ of 6.5 was thought to be an imidazole moiety of a histidyl unit, there is some evidence that this functional group is, in fact, the carboxylate group of a glutamyl unit.[†] The role of this functional group is to abstract a proton from C(3) of dihydroxyacetone phosphate, thus inducing the formation of a *cis* enediol. Since the basic reaction mechanism is the same as that shown for the reaction catalyzed by glucosephosphate isomerase (only proceeding in the opposite direction), it will be left to the reader to write the mechanism.

## Step 6: Oxidation and Phosphorylation of Glyceraldehyde 3-Phosphate

In the next step of the glycolytic pathway the aldehyde group of glyceraldehyde 3-phosphate initially undergoes oxidation to the level of a carboxylate group and is then converted to an acyl phosphate group. The product is 3-phospho-D-glyceroyl phosphate (which has been commonly called 1,3-diphosphoglycerate). Glyceraldehyde-phosphate dehydrogenase [D-glyceraldehyde-3-phosphate: $NAD^+$ oxidoreductase (phosphorylating), EC 1.2.1.12] catalyzes the reaction, which can be written

$$\text{D-Glyceraldehyde 3-phosphate} + NAD^+ + P_i \rightleftharpoons \text{3-phospho-D-glyceroyl phosphate} + NADH \quad (9\text{-}6)$$

Glyceraldehyde-phosphate dehydrogenases as isolated from a wide variety of sources are generally quite similar with respect to their physical properties. The dehydrogenase from rabbit liver, which has been studied rather extensively, has a molecular weight of 144,000 and consists of four apparently identical subunits which have molecular weights of 36,000. The enzyme has been crystallized as an $NAD^+$ complex.

The reaction catalyzed by glyceraldehyde-phosphate dehydrogenase involves three substrates, glyceraldehyde 3-phosphate, $NAD^+$, and orthophosphate, and two products, 3-phosphoglyceroylphosphate and NADH. It is, thus, a Ter Bi reaction. In interpreting kinetic studies the conclusions that can be drawn from the data when one is dealing with a tersubstrate process are different from those which can be

[†] Hartman, F. C. (1971) *Biochemistry* **10**, 146–154.

drawn when the reaction is a bisubstrate process. For example, plots of $1/v_i$ as a function of 1/[substrate] can be *parallel* when the reaction is *sequential* if an irreversible step intervenes between the point in the reaction sequence at which the variable substrate adds and that at which the fixed substrate adds. Hence, plots of $1/v_i$ vs. 1/[A] will be parallel when the mechanism is sequential and fixed concentrations of C and a (constant) saturating concentration of B are used. On the basis of kinetic studies on glyceraldehyde-phosphate dehydrogenase from rabbit muscle it was concluded that the reaction proceeds by means of an ordered sequential mechanism, since plots of $1/v_i$ as a function of the reciprocal concentration of any one of the three substrates with fixed concentrations of a second and a constant concentration of the third were intersecting.† Product-inhibition studies have been conducted only when the nucleotide is the inhibitor, since 3-phospho-D-glyceroyl phosphate is relatively unstable, and in these studies NADH was found to be a competitive inhibitor when $NAD^+$ is the variable substrate. On the other hand, the dead-end inhibitor 3-phosphoglycerate functioned as an uncompetitive inhibitor when each of the substrates was the variable one. Thus, 3-phosphoglycerate must bind at a point in the reaction sequence that is subsequent to that at which the substrates bind. Since 3-phosphoglycerate is structurally similar to the product 3-phospho-D-glyceroyl phosphate, it was reasoned that 3-phosphoglycerate binds at the binding site for 3-phospho-D-glyceroyl phosphate and that 3-phospho-D-glyceroyl phosphate is the first product that is released. After it was observed that the substrate analog nitrate functions as an uncompetitive inhibitor when either $NAD^+$ or glyceraldehyde 3-phosphate is varied and as a competitive inhibitor when orthophosphate is varied, the order of substrate binding and product release was formulated as shown.‡

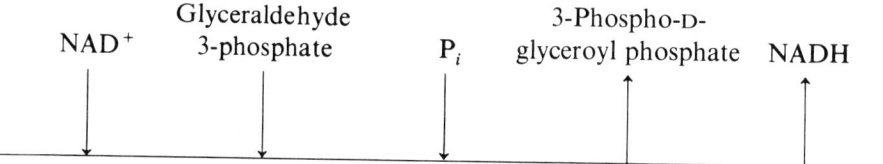

An alternative formulation, involving the random addition of $NAD^+$ and glyceraldehyde 3-phosphate followed by the addition of orthophosphate, has been proposed;§ however, as mentioned in discussing fructosebisphosphate aldolase, there are instances when a reaction can occur by more than one pathway although one is so strongly favored that under most experimental conditions it appears to be the only pathway.

Although the reaction catalyzed by glyceraldehyde-phosphate dehydrogenase is reversible, in the mammalian liver the prevailing concentrations of $NAD^+$ and orthophosphate promote the oxidation and phosphorylation of the aldehyde rather than the dephosphorylation and reduction of 3-phospho-D-glyceroyl phosphate. When it is

---

† Smith, C. M., and Velick, S. F. (1972) *J. Biol. Chem.* **247**, 273–284.
‡ Orsi, B. A., and Cleland, W. W. (1972) *Biochemistry* **11**, 102–109.
§ Keleti, T. (1970) in *Pyridine Nucleotide-Dependent Dehydrogenases* (Sund H., ed.), pp. 103–120, Springer-Verlag, Berlin.

required that the latter reaction takes place, specific regulatory mechanisms can be imposed, as discussed later in this chapter when gluconeogenesis is considered.

The reaction mechanism of the conversion of glyceraldehyde 3-phosphate into 3-phospho-D-glyceroyl phosphate involves the initial formation of a hemithioacetal. This results from an attack by a sulfhydryl group of a cysteinyl unit upon the aldehyde group of glyceraldehyde 3-phosphate. In the dehydrogenase from rabbit muscle the sulfhydryl group has been identified as that of Cys-149. It should perhaps be pointed out that as a result of the formation of the hemithioacetal, the substrate becomes covalently bonded at the catalytic site. Now a molecule of the oxidation-reduction cofactor, $NAD^+$, which is thought to be bound in part by an electrostatic interaction involving the protonated $\epsilon$-amino group of a lysyl unit,† accepts a hydride ion from the hemithioacetal. Thus, the pyridinium moiety of $NAD^+$ is reduced to a 1,4-dihydropyridine moiety, and concomitantly, C(1) of the hemithioacetal is oxidized to the carboxylate level. There is at this point a thioacyl moiety covalently bound at the catalytic site and this can, in fact, be isolated in the absence of orthophosphate.‡ When orthophosphate is present, however, it readily attacks the carboxylate carbon atom, and thus an acyl phosphate is formed and released from the enzyme.

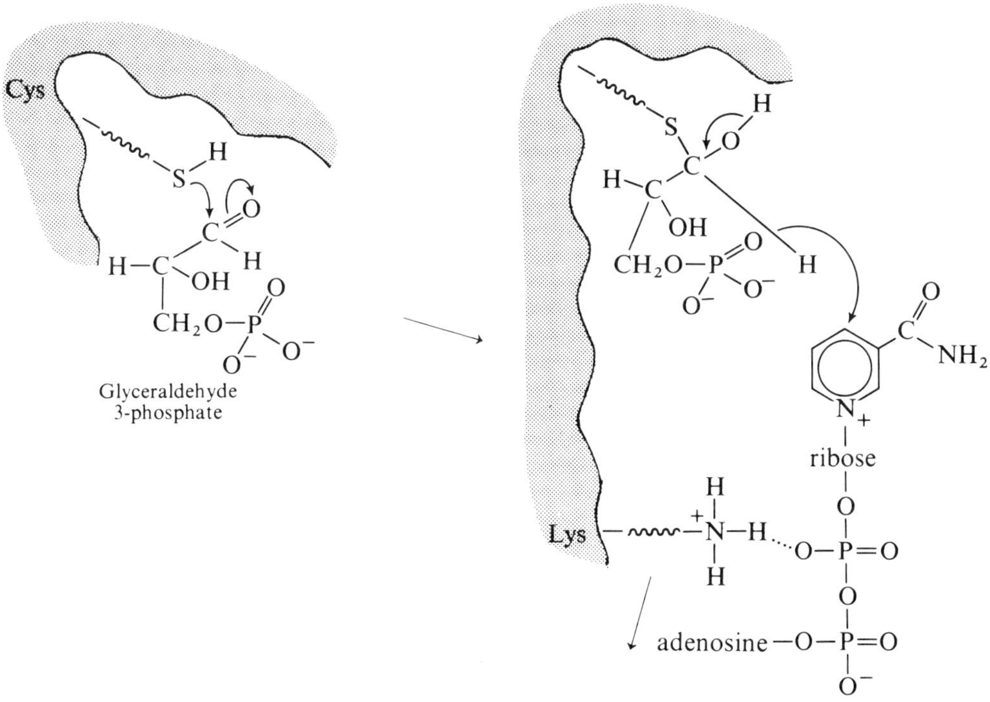

† Fenselau, A. (1970) *J. Biol. Chem.* **245**, 1239–1246.
‡ Bloch, W., MacQuarrie, R. A., and Bernhard, S. A. (1971) *J. Biol. Chem.* **246**, 780–790.

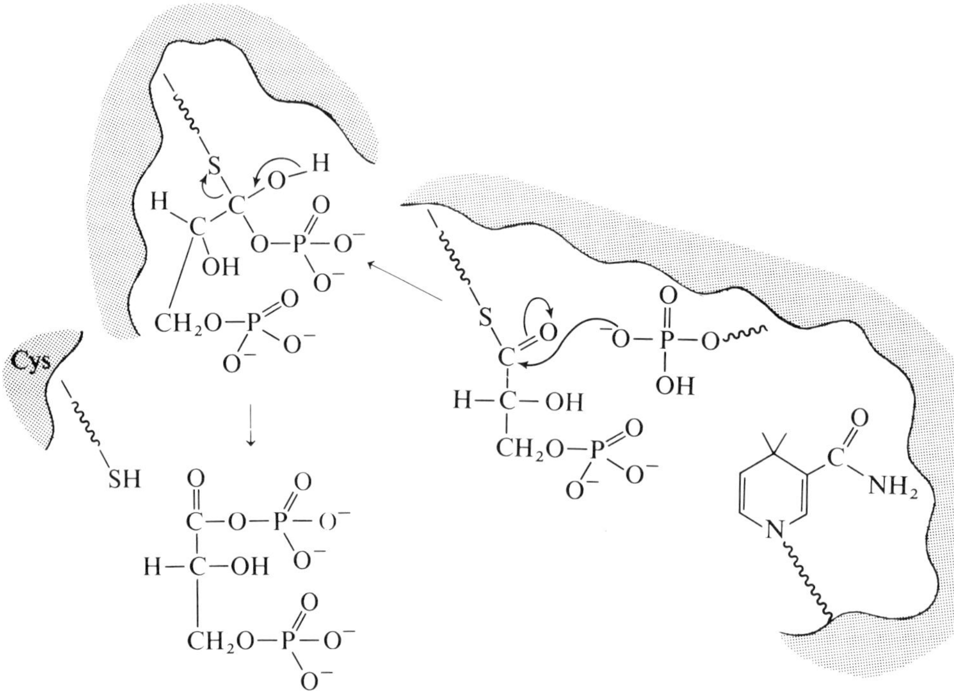

3-Phospho-D-glyceroyl phosphate

The reaction catalyzed by glyceraldehyde-phosphate dehydrogenase entails the formation of an acyl phosphate which is a very reactive molecule, and in this case the phosphoryl donor is not ATP but orthophosphate. It should be noted, however, that orthophosphate reacts with an enzyme-bound thiol ester and thiol esters are reactive molecules. More specifically, the carboxylate carbon-sulfur bond is very reactive, and it is this bond, as shown above, that is broken when the acyl phosphate is formed. Hence, the energy of the carbon-sulfur bond is available for the formation of the acyl phosphate bond.

When $NAD^+$ (or $NADP^+$) functions as an oxidizing agent in reactions catalyzed by dehydrogenases, the transfer of the hydride ion from the substrate to C(4) of the pyridinium moiety of the cofactor is stereoselective, addition being specifically to one of the two faces of the planar heterocyclic ring. Some dehydrogenases catalyze hydride transfer specifically to the *re* face of the pyridinium ring, while others catalyze a transfer specifically to the *si* face. Addition to the *re* face at C(4) generates a tetrahedral carbon atom having the pro-*R* configuration, while addition to the *si* face generates a tetrahedral carbon atom having the pro-*S* configuration. The terms pro-*R* and pro-*S* are used to designate configurations of tetrahedral carbon atoms which are not dissymmetric but would become so if one of the two identical substituents were replaced by a different substituent. (*R* and *S* have their usual meanings.) It follows, therefore, that if one prepares a substrate in which the hydrogen atom that is transferred (as a hydride ion) has been replaced by a deuterium or tritium atom, and if this substrate is allowed to undergo oxidation in the presence of the appropriate $NAD^+$- or $NADP^+$-dependent dehydrogenase, a reduced cofactor in which C(4) is now dissymmetrically substituted would be generated.

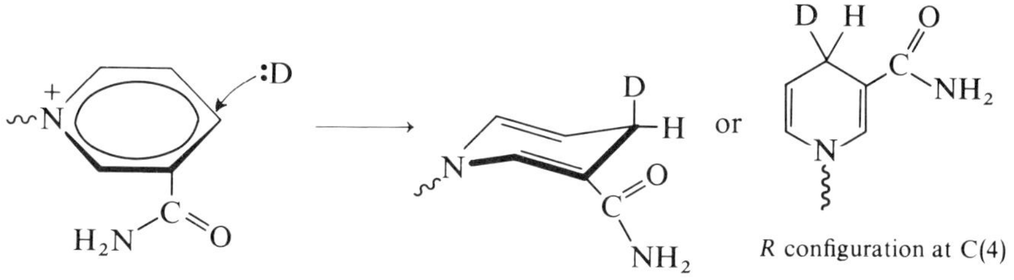

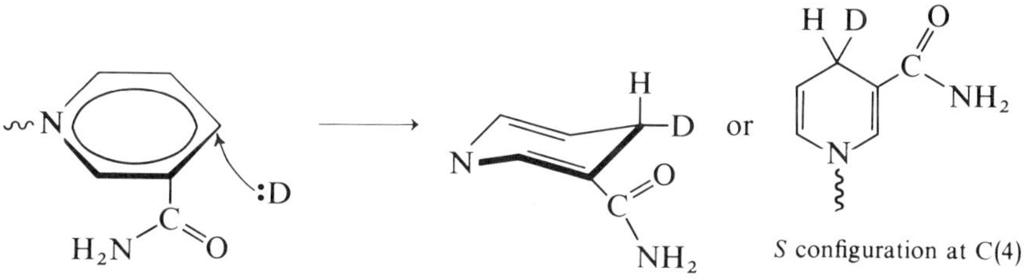

*R* configuration at C(4)

*S* configuration at C(4)

Glyceraldehyde-phosphate dehydrogenase has been shown to catalyze the transfer of a hydride ion from C(1) of the enzyme-bound thioacyl moiety to the *si* face of the pyridinium moiety of $NAD^+$.

Glyceraldehyde-phosphate dehydrogenase from yeast exhibits properties somewhat different from those of the mammalian enzymes; e.g., the activity of the yeast enzyme is inhibited in the presence of 3',5'-AMP. Because this modifier functions as a noncompetitive inhibitor with respect to both $NAD^+$ and glyceraldehyde 3-phosphate, it is suggested that the cyclic nucleotide binds at an allosteric site.† As an apparent consequence of the binding of 3',5'-AMP, the ability of the enzyme to bind $NAD^+$ is diminished. Hence, when one compares reaction velocities in the absence of and in the presence of 3',5'-AMP and with a given concentration of $NAD^+$, the velocity is diminished when the cyclic nucleotide is present.

Kinetic studies on another nonmammalian dehydrogenase, that from pea (*Pisum sativum*) seeds, have been interpreted in terms of a mechanism similar to that formulated for the enzyme from rabbit skeletal muscle except that the free enzyme is not a participant in each catalytic event. Rather, it is suggested that most reactions begin with the binding of glyceraldehyde 3-phosphate by an enzyme-$NAD^+$ complex, which, after a second molecule of $NAD^+$ is bound, is regenerated as a concomitance of the release of 3-phospho-D-glyceroyl phosphate.‡ Possibly the differences observed are a reflection of the different experimental conditions employed in the studies on the two enzymes, such as the relatively higher concentrations of

---

† Rock, M. G., and Cook, R. A. (1974) *Biochemistry* **13**, 4200–4204.
‡ Duggleby, R. G., and Dennis, D. T. (1974) *J. Biol. Chem.* **249**, 167–174.

NAD$^+$ that were used in the study on the enzyme from pea seeds. It is also possible that the kinetic mechanism of the reaction as catalyzed by the plant enzyme is a modification of that exhibited by the mammalian enzyme.

### Step 7: Transfer of a Phosphoryl Group from 3-Phospho-D-glyceroyl Phosphate

In this step of the glycolytic pathway ADP undergoes phosphorylation to yield ATP. The phosphoryl donor is 3-phospho-D-glyceroyl phosphate. The reaction is catalyzed by phosphoglycerate kinase (ATP: 3-phospho-D-glycerate 1-phosphotransferase, EC 2.7.2.3). It can be expressed as

3-Phospho-D-glyceroyl phosphate + ADP $\rightleftharpoons$

$$\text{3-phospho-D-glycerate} + \text{ATP} \quad (9\text{-}7)$$

This reaction is one of two in the glycolytic pathway in which ATP is formed as a result of the transfer of a phosphoryl group from a highly reactive donor to ADP. Although most of the ATP derived as a result of the catabolism of hexoses is formed through the agency of the mitochondrial electron-transport system, there are three reactions (two in the glycolytic pathway and a third in the tricarboxylic acid cycle) in which ADP undergoes phosphorylation in the presence of a highly reactive phosphorylated substrate.

Phosphoglycerate kinase has been isolated from a variety of sources and purified. Its molecular weight, determined by several different methods, is approximately 47,000 in all cases, and the enzyme is apparently not composed of subunits.

Kinetic studies on phosphoglycerate kinase have been carried out in most instances on the crystalline enzyme from yeast. Initial-velocity studies on this enzyme have suggested that the kinetic mechanism is sequential since plots of $1/v_i$ as a function of 1/[3-phosphoglycerate] are intersecting.† (It is difficult to carry out studies on the reaction in the direction of 3-phosphoglycerate formation because the substrate 3-phospho-D-glyceroyl phosphate is very reactive and hence very unstable.) When inhibition studies on the reverse reaction were conducted in the presence of CrATP, which can only form a dead-end complex, the substrate analog functioned as a competitive inhibitor with respect to both MgATP and 3-phosphoglycerate. When product-inhibition studies were also conducted on the reaction in the direction of 3-phospho-D-glyceroyl phosphate formation, MgADP functioned as a noncompetitive product inhibitor when MgATP was varied at lower concentrations but as a competitive product inhibitor when MgATP was varied at higher concentrations. MgADP also functioned as a competitive product inhibitor when 3-phosphoglycerate was the variable substrate.‡ The observation that the chromium complex of ATP functions as a competitive inhibitor with respect to *each* of the two substrates indicates that the mechanism is random rather than ordered. If it were ordered, the substrate analog would have been an uncompetitive inhibitor with respect to the substrate

---

† Janson, C. A., and Cleland, W. W. (1974) *J. Biol. Chem.* **249**, 2567–2571.
‡ Larsson-Raznikiewicz, M., and Arvidsson, L. (1971) *Eur. J. Biochem.* **22**, 506–512.

that binds second. The product-inhibition studies also indicate that the kinetic mechanism is random. In this case, the observation that MgADP is a noncompetitive inhibitor when MgATP is varied in the lower concentration range (between 0.1 and 0.5 m$M$) suggests a random sequential mechanism. The competitive patterns observed when MgATP is varied in the higher concentration range (between 0.5 and 5.0 m$M$) and when 3-phosphoglycerate is varied while using a constant and high concentration (1.0 m$M$) of MgATP are probably due to the presence of the high concentrations of the nucleotide substrate. It might well be expected that in view of the structural similarities between MgADP and MgATP the binding of the product, MgADP, by the enzyme–3-phosphoglycerate complex or the enzyme-MgATP complex would be greatly diminished in the presence of very high concentrations of MgATP. On this basis, the intercept effects usually seen when a random sequential mechanism is operative would be obliterated.

A minimal reaction mechanism of the reaction catalyzed by phosphoglycerate kinase follows:

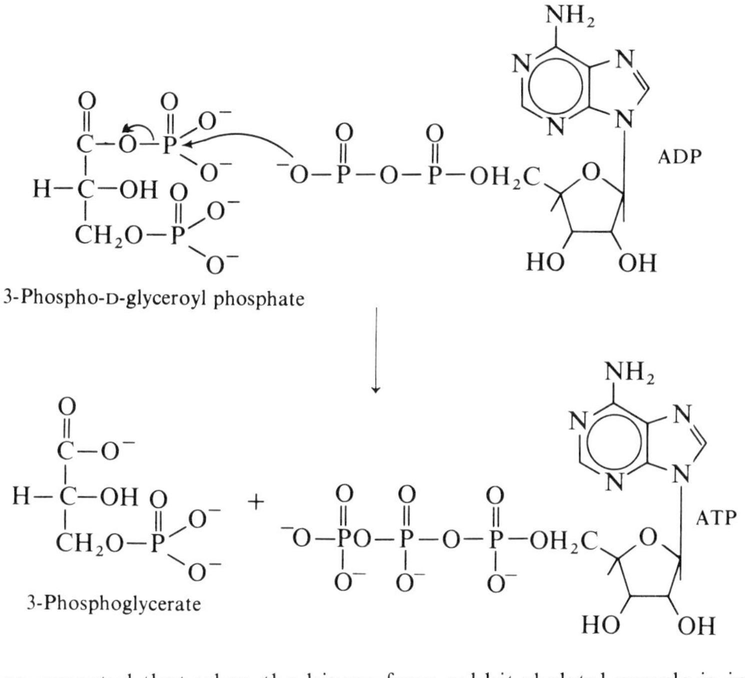

It has been reported that when the kinase from rabbit skeletal muscle is incubated in the presence of MgATP, a phosphoryl-enzyme intermediate can be isolated.† However, the velocity of the ADP-ATP isotope exchange as catalyzed by this enzyme in the absence of the three-carbon components is much slower than when all substrates are present. Therefore, this phosphoryl enzyme is not an obligatory intermediate in the reaction.

---

† Walsh, C. T., and Spector, L. B. (1971) *J. Biol. Chem.* **246**, 1255–1261.

## Step 8: Conversion of 3-Phosphoglycerate into 2-Phosphoglycerate

The 3-phosphoglycerate resulting from the previous step is next converted into 2-phosphoglycerate as the result of a reaction catalyzed by phosphoglyceromutase (2,3-bisphospho-D-glycerate:2-phospho-D-glycerate phosphotransferase, EC 2.7.5.3). This can be written

$$\text{3-Phospho-D-glycerate} \rightleftharpoons \text{2-phospho-D-glycerate} \tag{9-8}$$

Note that this enzyme is called a mutase. In general, a mutase catalyzes a reaction that involves the transfer of a substituent from one location to another within a given molecule. Isomerases, by contrast, generally catalyze reactions that involve a change in the identity of the parent compound as a result of epimerization, cis-trans interconversion, tautomerism, or some other means.

The reversible reaction catalyzed by phosphoglyceromutase from muscle and yeast, among other sources, requires 2,3-bisphosphoglycerate as a cofactor. This cofactor becomes bound at the catalytic site of the enzyme, but it does not dissociate from the enzyme each time a conversion of 3-phosphoglycerate to 2-phosphoglycerate, or the reverse, occurs. One model which has been presented for this enzymatic conversion is as follows:†

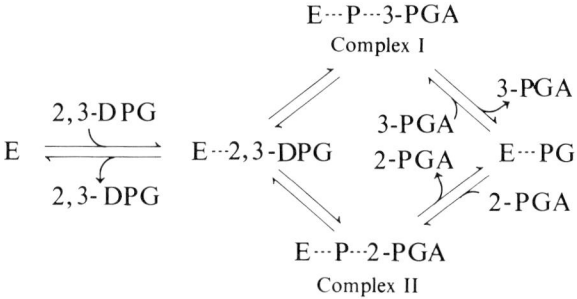

The cofactor, 2,3-bisphosphoglycerate, binds the enzyme and transfers one of its two phosphoryl groups to it. In this manner, either a species which can be considered to be 3-phosphoglycerate plus the phosphoryl enzyme (complex I) or one which can be considered to be 2-phosphoglycerate plus the phosphoryl enzyme (complex II) is generated. The monophosphoglycerate then dissociates from the phosphoryl enzyme. If the substrate 3-phosphoglycerate binds at the catalytic site of the phosphoryl enzyme, a sequence of conversions resulting in the formation of 2-phosphoglycerate plus the phosphoryl enzyme (complex II) occurs. The dissociation of 2-phosphoglycerate then regenerates the phosphoryl enzyme, which in turn can accept another substrate molecule. Thus, the function of the cofactor, 2,3-bisphosphoglycerate, is to initiate the reaction by promoting the formation of the phosphoryl enzyme.

Data from the kinetic studies on phosphoglyceromutase from chicken-breast

---

† Grisolia, S., and Cleland, W. W. (1968) *Biochemistry* **7**, 1115–1121.

muscle are compatible with the model shown above in that when initial-velocity studies were conducted using 3-phosphoglycerate and the cofactor 2,3-bisphosphoglycerate as the substrates parallel double reciprocal plots were obtained.† The reaction was also very sensitive to substrate inhibition, which is again indicative of a ping pong kinetic mechanism.

## Step 9: Conversion of 2-Phosphoglycerate into 2-Phosphoenolpyruvate

In this, the next to last step of the glycolytic pathway, 2-phosphoglycerate undergoes a dehydration reaction, which results in the formation of 2-phosphoenolpyruvate. The elimination of the elements of water from 2-phosphoglycerate is catalyzed by an enzyme frequently called enolase (2-phospho-D-glycerate hydro-lyase, EC 4.2.1.11). The enzyme also has the trivial name phosphopyruvate hydratase. The reaction catalyzed by this enzyme is

$$\text{2-Phospho-D-glycerate} \rightleftharpoons \text{2-phosphoenolpyruvate} + H_2O \quad (9\text{-}9)$$

Enolase has been isolated from a wide variety of sources, including rabbit skeletal muscle, salmon muscle, yeast, E. coli, and potato tubers. In all cases these enzymes exhibit molecular weights of between 82,000 (rabbit skeletal muscle) and 100,000 (coho salmon muscle), and the active enzymes are dimers which are composed of two identical (or very similar) subunits. Also, in all cases enolase has been shown to bind $Mg^{2+}$, which not only participates in the enzymatic reaction but also stabilizes the dimeric structure.

The reaction mechanism of the conversion of 2-phosphoglycerate to 2-phosphoenolpyruvate, as catalyzed by enolase from rabbit skeletal muscle, has been examined by using studies on kinetic isotope effects.‡ These studies showed that when $(R) - [2\text{-}^2H]$2-phosphoglycerate was used rather than the nonlabeled substrate, the reaction velocity remained unchanged. There was no kinetic isotope effect. However, if the proton exchange with water was monitored rather than the reaction velocity, a kinetic isotope effect was observed. It was also shown in these studies that the rate of the $^{18}O$ exchange between water and the C(3) hydroxyl group of 2-phosphoglycerate is slightly faster than the reaction velocity. Furthermore, when the reverse reaction, the conversion of 2-phosphoenolpyruvate to 2-phosphoglycerate, was conducted using $[3\text{-}^3H]$2-phosphoenolpyruvate, the reaction velocity was faster than when the nonlabeled substrate was used. These observations were interpreted as follows. When 2-phosphoglycerate is converted into 2-phosphoenolpyruvate, the substrate binds the enzyme and a proton is released from C(2) as a result of a rapid equilibrium process. The resulting enzyme-bound carbanion then expels the hydroxide ion at C(3), and C(2) and C(3) undergo a change from $sp^3$ to $sp^2$ hybridization. This change in hybridization is believed to be

---

† Ibid.
‡ Dinovo, E. C., and Boyer, P. D. (1971) J. Biol. Chem. **246**, 4586–4593.

a rate-determining event in view of the secondary kinetic isotope effect† seen when [3-$^3$H]2-phosphoenolpyruvate is used as a substrate in the reverse reaction. The absence of a primary kinetic isotope effect when $(R) - $[2-$^2$H]2-phosphoglycerate is used as a substrate indicates that the loss of the proton is not rate-determining with respect to the formation of 2-phosphoenolpyruvate, and the $^{18}$O exchange indicates that the expulsion of the hydroxide ion is not rate-determining. The reaction mechanism might therefore be formulated as

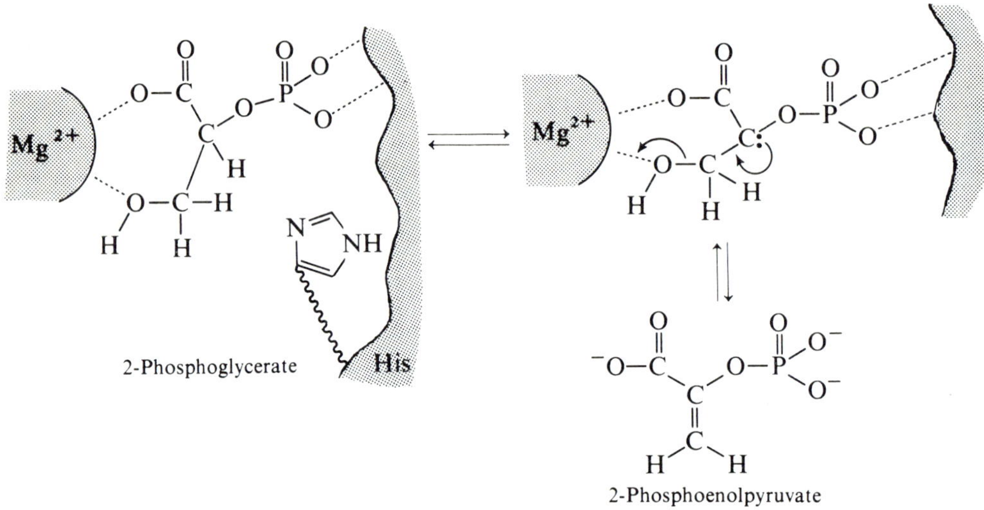

2-Phosphoglycerate

2-Phosphoenolpyruvate

The elimination of the elements of water from 2-phosphoglycerate generates a highly reactive molecule. Enol phosphates are highly reactive because they readily undergo hydrolysis to yield two very stable molecules, a ketone and orthophosphate. In the present case, the ketone formed is pyruvate. The conversion of 2-phosphoglycerate into 2-phosphoenolpyruvate is the second instance of the formation of a highly reactive molecule as the result of a reaction of the glycolytic pathway. The other instance, already discussed, is the formation of 3-phospho-D-glyceroyl phosphate. In both cases the highly reactive molecule has a phosphoryl group that can be transferred to ADP to form ATP. The transfer of the phosphoryl group of 2-phosphoenolpyruvate to ADP is the final reaction of the glycolytic pathway and is discussed next.

## Step 10: Conversion of Phosphoenolpyruvate into Pyruvate

The initial step of the glycolytic pathway is the phosphorylation of the six-carbon compound glucose, and in the final step of this pathway the three-carbon compound

---

† A secondary kinetic isotope effect is one that is seen when the bond involving the isotope is not broken during the course of the reaction although the presence of the isotope is able to influence the reaction velocity. In the present case as a result of the substitution of a tritium atom for a hydrogen atom at C(3) of 2-phosphoenolpyruvate, the difference between the ground-state and transition-state energy levels is less than it is when a substitution has not been made. Thus, the reaction is faster when the labeled substrate is used.

2-phosphoenolpyruvate undergoes dephosphorylation. The phosphorylation of glucose utilizes ATP as the phosphoryl donor. As a concomitance of the dephosphorylation of 2-phosphoenolpyruvate in the final step, ATP is formed. The enzyme that catalyzes the conversion of 2-phosphoenolpyruvate and ADP into pyruvate and ATP is pyruvate kinase (ATP: pyruvate 2-$O$-phosphoryltransferase, EC 2.7.1.40). The reaction is

$$\text{2-Phosphoenolpyruvate} + \text{ADP} \rightleftharpoons \text{pyruvate} + \text{ATP} \quad (9\text{-}10)$$

Pyruvate kinase has been isolated and purified from rabbit skeletal muscle, human skeletal muscle, porcine liver, rat liver, yeast, and *E. coli*, among other sources. In each instance the active enzyme is a tetramer which is composed of apparently identical subunits. Molecular weights of these enzymes are between 265,000 (for the porcine liver enzyme) and 100,000 (for the enzyme from *E. coli*). The mammalian enzymes exhibit an absolute requirement for a monovalent cation such as $K^+$, in addition to the requirement for the divalent cation $Mg^{2+}$ characteristic of kinases.

In at least some mammalian systems there appear to be three types of pyruvate kinase. One, found in liver, erythrocytes, and kidney, has been termed the L type; a second, found in muscle and brain, is called the $M_1$ type; and a third, found in adipose tissue, kidney, leukocytes, and also in the liver, is called the $M_2$ type. These different species are noninterconvertible, and, in general terms, the L type is subject to the most extensive regulation, the $M_1$ type is least subject to regulation, and the $M_2$ type is regulated to an intermediate extent.

When initial-velocity studies were conducted on pyruvate kinase from rabbit muscle (presumably the $M_1$ enzyme), linear intersecting double reciprocal plots were obtained, indicating that the kinetic mechanism of the reaction is sequential. Product-inhibition studies showed that when 2-phosphoenolpyruvate was the variable substrate, both MgATP and pyruvate were competitive product inhibitors. However, when ADP was varied, MgATP functioned as a competitive product inhibitor while pyruvate functioned as a noncompetitive one. These data were interpreted as indicating that the reaction proceeds by means of a rapid equilibrium random mechanism and that an enzyme-ADP-pyruvate dead-end complex is formed.†

Kinetic studies on the $M_2$ type enzyme (from rat liver) indicated that the reaction in this case is more complex. Although plots of $1/v_i$ as a function of $1/[\text{MgADP}]$ are linear and intersecting, the double reciprocal plots are concave when phosphoenolpyruvate is the variable substrate and the corresponding "direct plots," i.e., plots of the reaction velocity as a function of phosphoenolpyruvate concentration, are sigmoidal; however, the nonlinearity of the double reciprocal plots and the sigmoidicity of the direct plots can be abolished by fructose 1,6-bisphosphate. This product of the third step of the glycolytic pathway is thought to enhance the velocity of the reaction catalyzed by pyruvate kinase by binding the enzyme at an allosteric site.‡ As a result of this binding, plots of $1/v_i$ vs. $1/[\text{phosphoenolpyruvate}]$ become

---

† Ainsworth, S., and Macfarlane, N. (1973) *Biochem. J.* **131**, 223–236.
‡ Van Berkel, T. J. C. (1974) *Biochim. Biophys. Acta* **370**, 140–152.

linear, and plots of the reaction velocity vs. [phosphoenolpyruvate] become hyperbolic.

Kinetic studies conducted on L-type pyruvate kinase (in this instance from rabbit liver), again indicated that the enzyme activity is subject to modulation. The plots of $1/v_i$ as a function of 1/[phosphoenolpyruvate] or $1/[K^+]$ are concave, and the corresponding direct plots are sigmoidal. Again these relationships are altered by fructose 1,6-bisphosphate, and the nonlinear double reciprocal plots become linear while the sigmoidal direct plots become hyperbolic under the influence of this intermediate.†

It has also been reported that type-L pyruvate kinase (from rat liver) can undergo phosphorylation in the presence of MgATP and a 3′,5′-AMP–dependent protein kinase.‡ As will be discussed in some detail later in this chapter (when the focus is upon glycogen metabolism), protein kinases catalyze the phosphorylation of certain proteins, including certain enzymes, and as a result of this phosphorylation the biochemical characteristics of the protein are altered. In those instances in which the protein is an enzyme, phosphorylation alters enzymatic activity. Phosphorylation sometimes results in an enhancement of the enzymatic activity and sometimes in inhibition. The activity of the type-L pyruvate kinase is inhibited as a result of the enzyme phosphorylation. Generally, protein kinase activities that are sensitive to 3′,5′-AMP are, in fact, sensitive to specific hormonal influences. This is because the biosynthesis of 3′,5′-AMP is usually under hormonal control. Therefore, it may be that the activity of the L-type pyruvate kinase is, at least in part, under hormonal control.

In yeasts the activity of pyruvate kinase is modulated in a manner that is similar in some respects to that seen in the case of the L-type enzyme from mammalian sources. Specifically, the reaction velocity of the yeast enzyme was found to be a sigmoidal function of the concentrations of phosphoenolpyruvate, $K^+$, and $Mg^{2+}$. Again fructose 1,6-bisphosphate functions as an activator by causing the sigmoidal relationship to be converted into a hyperbolic one.

The activity of pyruvate kinase from the spore-forming bacterium *Bacillus licheniformis* is also subject to modulation, but in this case plots of the velocity as a function of substrate concentration are sigmoidal when either phosphoenolpyruvate or MgADP is varied. Furthermore, it is 5′-AMP that converts this sigmoidal relationship into a hyperbolic one, rather than fructose 1,6-bisphosphate.§ AMP also functions in this capacity with respect to pyruvate kinases from certain other bacteria, including *E. coli* and *Brevibacterium flavum*. Thus, again, a difference in the mode of regulation is observed when enzymes from higher and lower organisms are compared.

The reaction mechanism of the phosphorylation of ADP by 2-phosphoenolpyruvate would be expected to entail a nucleophilic attack by an oxygen atom of the $\beta$-phosphoryl group of ADP at the phosphoryl phosphorus atom of the enol phosphate. This results in the formation of the ketone group and the shift of an

---

† Irving, M. G., and Williams, J. F. (1973) *Biochem. J.* **131**, 287–301.
‡ Ljungstrom, O., Hjelmquist, G., and Engstrom, L. (1974) *Biochim. Biophys. Acta* **358**, 289–298.
§ Tuominen, F. W., and Bernlohr, R. W. (1971) *J. Biol. Chem.* **246**, 1746–1755.

electron pair to C(3). Addition of a proton at C(3) then completes the conversion of 2-phosphoenolpyruvate into pyruvate. The proton addition at C(3) has been shown to occur with stereoselectivity in that this transfer is specifically at the *si* face of the three-carbon substrate.† Hence, the reaction might be formulated as shown.

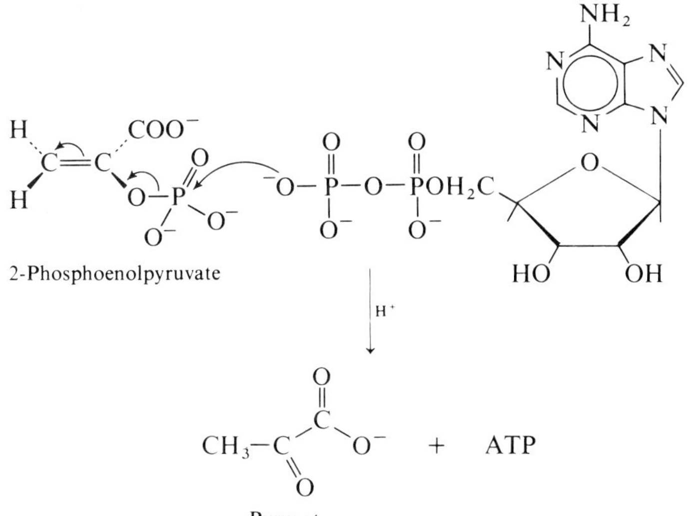

2-Phosphoenolpyruvate

Pyruvate + ATP

## Interconversion of Pyruvate and Lactate

In higher organisms and under aerobic conditions, i.e., in the presence of molecular oxygen, pyruvate can undergo an oxidative decarboxylation, and the resulting acetyl moiety of acetyl CoA can then enter the tricarboxylic acid cycle. There the carbon atoms of the acetyl moiety are further oxidized to yield carbon dioxide. Subsequently, the reducing equivalents that were transferred to oxidation-reduction cofactors as a concomitance of the oxidation of the carbon atoms are introduced into the mitochondrial electron-transport system and ultimately accepted by molecular oxygen. An important event in this sequence is the oxidation of the reduced cofactors, which occurs as a result of the introduction of their reducing equivalents into the mitochondrial electron-transport system. This event results in the regeneration of the oxidized forms of the cofactors, which are required in the glycolytic pathway (for the conversion of pyruvate into the acetyl moiety of acetyl-CoA) and in the tricarboxylic acid cycle. However, there is a reaction that permits the conversion of NADH into $NAD^+$ in the absence of molecular oxygen, namely the reduction of pyruvate to L- (or S-) lactate. The enzyme which catalyzes this reaction is lactate dehydrogenase (L-lactate:$NAD^+$ oxidoreductase, EC 1.1.127), and the interconversion is

$$\text{Pyruvate} + \text{NADH} \rightleftharpoons \text{L-lactate} + NAD^+ \qquad (9\text{-}11)$$

The reaction catalyzed by lactate dehydrogenase is of particular importance in white skeletal muscle, which derives almost all the energy required for contraction

† Rose, I. A. (1970) *J. Biol. Chem.* **245**, 6052–6056.

from anaerobic glycolysis. The reaction is also very important in red muscle when there is an unusually great demand for energy, e.g., during physical exertion. The reduction of pyruvate is also of prime importance in lower organisms that do not carry out the reactions of the tricarboxylic acid cycle and the mitochondrial electron-transport system and therefore depend upon this reaction to a great extent to sustain glycolysis.

In higher vertebrates five different forms of lactate dehydrogenase have been identified. Each form is a tetramer which is composed of subunits that each have a molecular weight of 35,000. There are two types of subunits. One, the H subunit, predominates in tetramers from heart muscle; the second type, the M subunit, predominates in tetramers from white skeletal muscle. The five forms of lactate dehydrogenase are constituted from four H subunits, four M subunits, or a combination of H and M subunits. These species are denoted $H_4$, $M_4$, $H_3M$, $H_2M_2$, and $HM_3$.

Kinetic studies on lactate dehydrogenase $H_4$ from bovine heart have indicated that the kinetic mechanism is ordered sequential with NADH binding first and $NAD^+$ being released last.† This mechanism has been confirmed by studies on enzymes from various other sources, including bovine heart, porcine heart, dogfish muscle, and porcine skeletal muscle. Studies on the enzyme from bovine heart have also suggested that under steady-state conditions the dissociation of $NAD^+$ from the enzyme (when pyruvate is undergoing reduction) is the slow, or rate-determining, event in the reaction.‡

The activity of lactate dehydrogenase is notably inhibited in the presence of high concentrations of the substrate pyruvate. In this case inhibition is due, at least in part, to the formation of a covalently bonded $NAD^+$-pyruvate adduct. This adduct, which has the structure shown,§ may be formed as follows

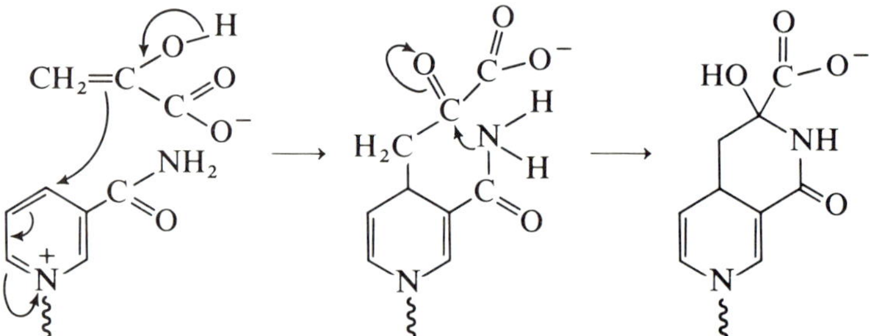

X-ray diffraction studies on type $M_4$ lactate dehydrogenase from dogfish muscle have shown that there is one catalytic site on each of the four subunits of the tetrameric enzyme. Each catalytic site has a crevice in which the cofactor (NADH

---

† Schwert, G. W. (1970) in *Pyridine Nucleotide–Dependent Dehydrogenases* (Sund, H., ed.), pp. 135–143, Springer-Verlag, Berlin.
‡ Borgmann, U., Moon, T. W., and Laidler, K. J. (1974) *Biochemistry* **13**, 5152–5158.
§ Arnold, L. J., and Kaplan, N. O. (1974) *J. Biol. Chem.* **249**, 652–655.

or $NAD^+$) becomes bound in such a manner that C(4) of the pyridine moiety is most deeply buried.†

The reduction of pyruvate by NADH occurs with stereospecificity, as is generally the case when a reaction utilizes a nicotine–adenine diphosphate cofactor. In the reaction being discussed it is the pro-R hydrogen at C(4) of the dihydropyridine moiety that is transferred to the re face of C(2) of the pyruvate molecule. As a result, L- (or S-) lactate is formed. The reaction is

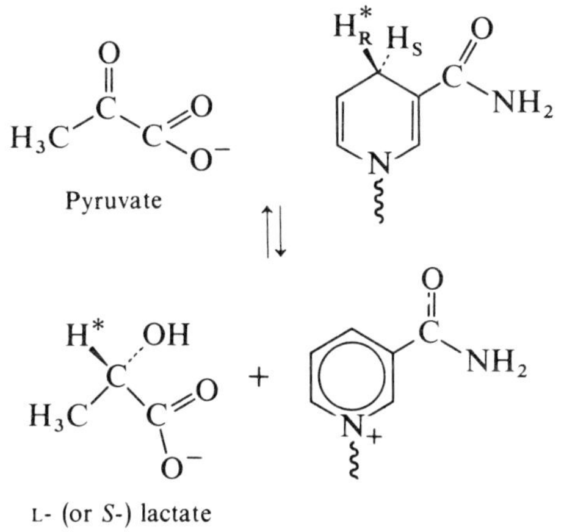

Certain microorganisms, including *Aerobacter aerogenes*, and some fungi belonging to the subclasses Oomycetes, Hypochytridiomycetes, and Chytridiomycetes contain a D-lactate dehydrogenase (D-lactate:$NAD^+$ oxidoreductase, EC 1.1.1.28), which catalyzes the formation of D- (or R-) lactate. D-Lactate dehydrogenase has been isolated from a fungus of the Oomycetes subclass and purified and found to have a molecular weight of 100,000. Thus, this species is smaller than the tetrameric mammalian enzyme. The kinetic properties of this enzyme were found to be essentially the same as those of the mammalian lactate dehydrogenases; i.e., the reaction proceeds by an ordered sequential Bi Bi mechanism, in which NADH binds first and $NAD^+$ is released last. The enzyme from the fungus catalyzes the formation of D-lactate, however, and only D-lactate can serve as a substrate in the reverse reaction. Plots of $1/v_i$ vs. 1/[NADH] and $1/v_i$ vs. 1/[D-lactate], in the case of the reverse reaction, are both concave, and the extent of this concavity is enhanced in the presence of GTP, which is thought to function as an allosteric inhibitor.‡ High concentrations of pyruvate again result in substrate inhibition.

In some microorganisms, including *E. coli*, there is a membrane-bound D-lactate dehydrogenase which functions in the energy-dependent transport of amino acids and other metabolic intermediates across the cell membrane. This enzyme catalyzes

---

† Adams, M. J., McPherson, M. G., Jr., Rossman, M. G., Shevitz, R. W., Smiley, I. E., and Wonacott, A. J. (1970) in *Pyridine Nucleotide-Dependent Dehydrogenases* (Sund, H., ed.), pp. 157–174, Springer-Verlag, Berlin.

‡ LeJohn, H. B. (1971) *J. Biol. Chem.* **246**, 2116–2126.

primarily the oxidation of D-lactate to pyruvate, but in this case the oxidation-reduction cofactor is not $NAD^+$. Instead, the membrane-bound enzyme is a flavoprotein which has a molecular weight of 75,000 and which binds one molecule of FAD.†  The FAD accepts the reducing equivalents from D-lactate and subsequently transfers them to specific electron-transport components. Ultimately, as a result of the electron-transport process, the energy required for the translocation of metabolic intermediates across the cell membrane is made available.

## Glycolysis in Erythrocytes

Erythrocytes are unusual among mammalian cells in that virtually all their energy requirements are fulfilled by the functioning of the glycolytic pathway. Mammalian erythrocytes do not carry out the reactions of the tricarboxylic acid cycle or those of the mitochondrial electron-transport system. The enzymes that catalyze the reactions of these pathways are contained in the mitochondria of mammalian cells, and mammalian erythrocytes lack mitochondria. The glycolytic pathway as it occurs in mammalian erythrocytes is as described but with an important difference. In the erythrocyte not only can 3-phospho-D-glyceroyl phosphate serve as a phosphoryl donor with respect to ADP, but, in addition, this compound can undergo isomerization to yield 2,3-bisphosphoglycerate, a reaction catalyzed by bisphosphoglyceromutase (3-phospho-D-glyceroyl-phosphate:3-phospho-D-glycerate phosphotransferase, EC 2.7.5.4). The 2,3-bisphosphoglycerate can subsequently undergo hydrolysis to yield 3-phosphoglycerate, which then serves as a substrate for phosphoglyceromutase. Thus, in the erythrocyte there is the possibility of circumventing one of the two steps in which ATP is generated. The result of this circumvention is that there is no net production of ATP as a result of the catabolism of a molecule of glucose by means of glycolysis since two molecules of ATP are utilized (one by the reaction catalyzed by hexokinase and the other by that catalyzed by phosphofructokinase) and two are generated (as a result of the reaction catalyzed by pyruvate kinase occurring, in effect, twice). The extent to which this alternate pathway is used varies and is quite probably subject to regulation, as discussed below. It should also be mentioned that since the tricarboxylic acid cycle and the mitochondrial electron-transport system do not operate in the mammalian erythrocyte, pyruvate is converted into lactate in order to regenerate the $NAD^+$ required for glycolysis.

## Summary

A summary of the glycolytic pathway is presented in Fig. 9-3.

† Kohn, L. D., and Kaback, H. R. (1973) *J. Biol. Chem.* **248**, 7012–7017.

---

**Figure 9-3** Summary of the glycolytic pathway with values for $\Delta G^{\circ\prime}$ at pH 7.0 (and also values for $\Delta G^{\circ}$ for comparison) for each of the 10 reactions. The summation equation takes into consideration the fact that two molecules of glyceraldehyde 3-phosphate must pass through the latter stages of the glycolytic process for all six carbon atoms of glucose to be utilized.

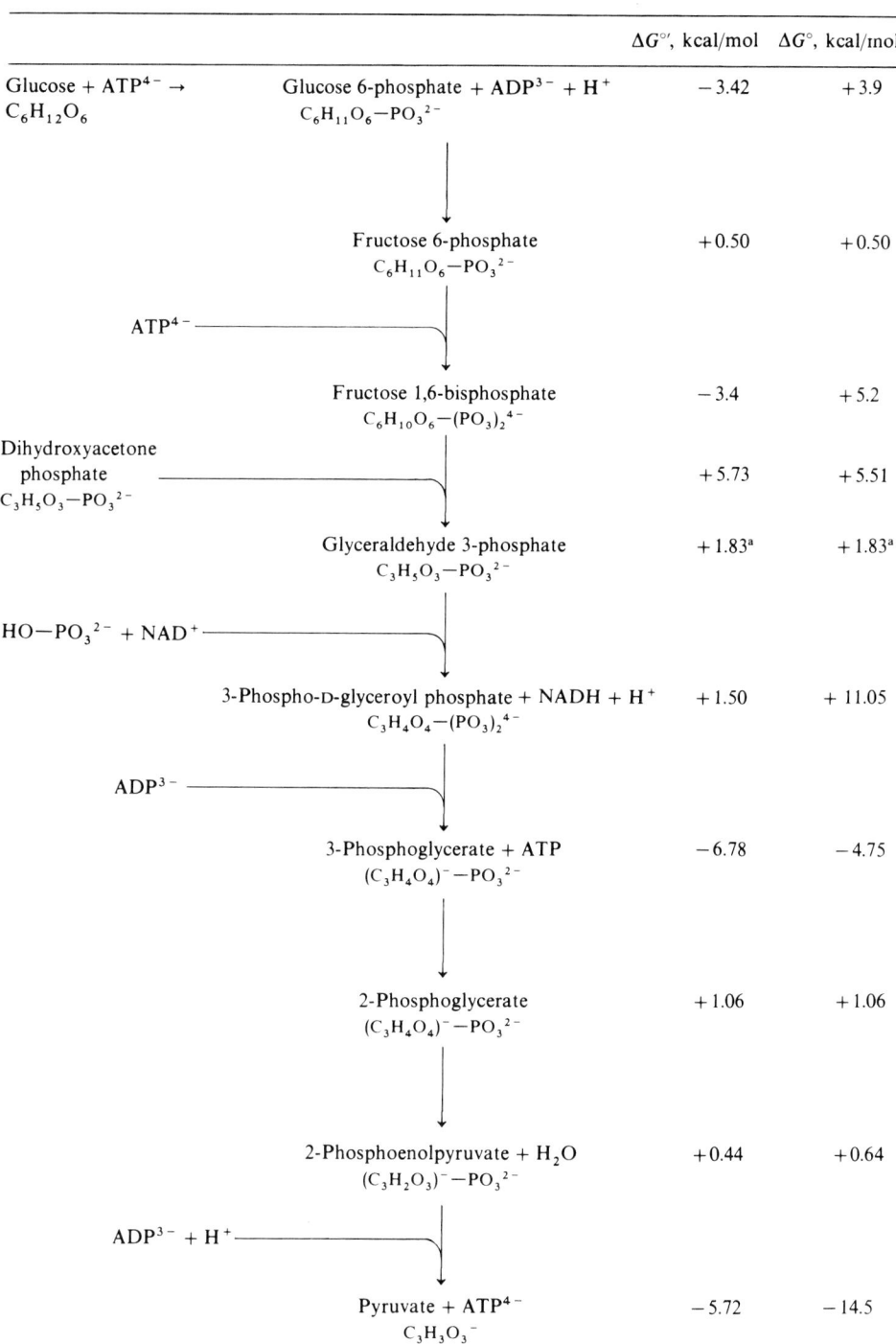

[a] Values for the conversion of dihydroxyacetone phosphate to glyceraldehyde 3-phosphate.

*Summation Equation*

$C_6H_{12}O_6 + 2ATP^{4-} + 2HO-PO_3^{2-} + 2NAD^+ + 4ADP^{3-} + 2H^+ \rightarrow 2C_3H_3O_3^- + 2ADP^{3-} + 4ATP^{4-} + 2NADH + 2H_3O) + 4H^+$

## Regulation of Glycolysis

In general terms, metabolic pathways are regulated by an interplay of factors, including the concentrations of the enzymes that catalyze the reactions of the pathway, the activities of these enzymes, and the concentrations of the substrates and cofactors required by these enzymes. The concentration of an enzyme in a given cell is essentially under genetic control, with modulation by hormones in certain cases. In a metabolic pathway, under given conditions the rate of one of the reactions of the pathway is the slowest, and the activity of the enzyme catalyzing this reaction then determines the rate at which the appropriate intermediates flow through the pathway. In mammalian tissues glycolysis is usually regulated by the activity of phosphofructokinase or (in some cases and under certain conditions) hexokinase or pyruvate kinase. Since the regulatory processes involved may differ in different tissues, the regulation of glycolysis as it occurs in specific tissues will be discussed.

**In muscle** Since glycolysis provides virtually all the energy required for contraction in white skeletal muscle in vertebrates, this pathway is exceedingly important in this tissue. It has been shown that in skeletal muscle the regulation of glycolysis is accomplished primarily by modulating the activity of phosphofructokinase. In muscle the activity of hexokinase is apparently far from rate-limiting since even in the presence of the hormone insulin, which promotes the entry of glucose into the muscle cell, the presence of intracellular glucose cannot be demonstrated. Thus, as rapidly as glucose enters into the muscle cell, it is phosphorylated. The activity of phosphofructokinase, as noted previously, is inhibited by concentrations of ATP above a specific level, and this inhibitory effect is potentiated by citrate. However, a point that must be considered if citrate does, in fact, participate in the regulation of glycolysis is the means by which the tricarboxylic acid is translocated from the mitochondrion, where it is formed, to the cytoplasm of the cell, where the enzymes of glycolysis are located. The membranes of the various cell organelles, such as the mitochondria, are not universally permeable with respect to metabolic intermediates. In this case it has been demonstrated, e.g., in cardiac muscle, that there is a specific transport system that functions to translocate citrate from the inside to the outside of the mitochondrion. Thus, the intramitochondrial concentration of citrate can be reflected in the cytoplasm. The observation that ATP inhibits phosphofructokinase activity and that this inhibitory effect can be potentiated by citrate can be rationalized quite readily when one considers that the primary goal of hexose catabolism in muscle is the formation of ATP from ADP and orthophosphate. Under anaerobic conditions this occurs primarily as a result of glycolysis alone, which theoretically yields two molecules of ATP for each molecule of glucose converted into two molecules of pyruvate. Under aerobic conditions in cells with mitochondria this formation of ATP occurs in part as a result of glycolysis and in part as a result of a sequence that entails glycolysis followed by the reactions of the tricarboxylic acid cycle and, in turn, the reactions of the mitochondrial electron-transport system. When concentrations of ATP are high, the need to produce more is diminished, and therefore it is reasonable that ATP should impede glycolysis. Also, in view of the fact that citrate is the product of the initial (and usually rate-determining) step of the tricarboxylic acid cycle it is reasonable that high concentrations of citrate should impede glycolysis. In this case the need to produce more pyruvate would also be diminished. Pyruvate, it should be remembered, can be converted into the acetyl moiety of acetyl CoA, which in turn undergoes a condensation reaction with oxaloacetate to yield citrate.

In muscle the inhibition of phosphofructokinase activity that is imposed by ATP can be relieved by several metabolic intermediates, including orthophosphate and AMP. It should be remembered that in vertebrates muscular activity is accompanied by the cleavage of ATP as a result of the activity of the actomyosin adenosine triphosphatase (ATPase). This cleavage results in the conversion of ATP into ADP and orthophosphate. Thus, before muscular activity, when concentrations of ATP are relatively high, glycolysis proceeds at less than its maximal rate due to the inhibitory effect of the ATP. However, as a concomitance of muscular activity the concentration of ATP is diminished while that of orthophosphate is increased. As a result, the rate of glycolysis is enhanced due to each of these changes, which is precisely the action that is necessary in order to generate more ATP. The observed effect of AMP, on the other hand, has been rationalized as follows. Concentrations of ATP, ADP, and AMP in muscle are adjusted by a reaction catalyzed by adenylate kinase (ATP: AMP phosphotransferase, EC 2.7.4.3), sometimes referred to as myokinase. Adenylate kinase catalyzes the reaction

$$2ADP \rightleftharpoons ATP + AMP$$

The concentration of adenylate kinase is particularly high in white skeletal muscle, and the reaction is always near equilibrium. It has also been shown that concentrations of ATP are generally maintained at approximately 50 times the concentration of AMP in muscle. Therefore, when there is a relatively small decrease in the concentration of ATP, which causes adenylate kinase to catalyze the formation of ATP and AMP, the *percentage* increase in the concentration of ATP will be relatively small but the *percentage* increase in the concentration of AMP will be relatively large. (Under specified conditions a 10 percent increase in ATP concentration is accompanied by a 400 percent increase in AMP concentration.) This permits the effect of a small diminution in ATP concentration to be amplified since the large percentage increase in AMP concentration results in a large *de*inhibitory effect with respect to phosphofructokinase activity. It has been presumed that this deinhibition comes about as a result of the binding of AMP at an allosteric site on the enzyme. In addition to AMP, 3',5'-AMP has also been shown to bind muscle phosphofructokinase again, presumably, at an allosteric site. However, since the concentrations required for this binding are considerably greater than those present in muscle, it would appear that 3',5'-AMP does not serve in a regulatory capacity in this tissue. On the other hand, 3',5'-AMP has been shown to function in a regulatory capacity with respect to phosphofructokinase activity in a lower organism, i.e., the liver fluke, *Fasciola hepatica*. In this instance, phosphofructokinase exists in both active and subactive forms, and 3',5'-AMP, in conjunction with ATP, $Mg^{2+}$, and presumably at least one additional enzyme, converts the subactive form into the active form; however, this type of regulatory mechanism has not been demonstrated for phosphofructokinase from mammalian sources.

**In liver** In the liver the metabolism of carbohydrates, lipids, and amino acids is closely integrated, and the principal role of glycolysis in this tissue may well be to provide certain precursors for anabolic pathways rather than to provide a precursor for the tricarboxylic acid cycle. In liver, it can be shown that events pertaining to lipid metabolism can influence the rate at which glycolysis occurs. For example, the degradation of fatty acids results in the formation of the acetyl moiety of acetyl-CoA, and when this acetyl moiety undergoes condensation with oxaloacetate, citrate is formed. Therefore, glycolysis can be impeded as a result of fatty acid oxidation since the activity of phosphofructokinase is the principal determining factor with respect to the rate of glycolysis in the liver.

In addition, in the liver (and also in renal cortex) gluconeogenesis, the synthesis of glucose from precursors not derived from carbohydrates, is an important metabolic pathway. Gluconeogenesis is regulated, in part, by the modulation of the activity of the enzyme hexosediphosphatase, which catalyzes the hydrolysis of fructose 1,6-bisphosphate to yield fructose 6-phosphate and orthophosphate. Accumulated evidence now suggests that the modulation of activities of hexosediphosphatase and phosphofructokinase may be interrelated.† More specifically, it has been demonstrated that AMP not only relieves the inhibitory effect imposed by ATP upon phosphofructokinase but also inhibits the activity of hexosediphosphatase. Thus, in the presence of high concentrations of AMP glycolysis is promoted while gluconeogenesis is impeded; low concentrations of AMP favor gluconeogenesis. Furthermore, additional studies have indicated that the hormone glucagon can, in part, determine whether glucose will undergo catabolism (glycolysis) or whether it will be synthesized (gluconeogenesis).‡

**In brain** It has been determined that in (murine) brain glycolysis can be regulated by the modulation of the activities of both phosphofructokinase and hexokinase. Phosphofructokinase activity in brain, as in muscle and in liver, is inhibited by ATP, and this inhibitory effect is relieved by AMP and orthophosphate. Hexokinase activity in brain, as noted earlier, is markedly inhibited by the product glucose 6-phosphate; this inhibitory effect can be relieved by orthophosphate. However, the rate of glycolysis in the brain is generally less sensitive to the effects of modulators than it is in muscle or liver. In fact, the brain maintains a relatively constant rate of glycolysis. (The rate of glycolysis in muscle is the most sensitive to modulators, and by far the greatest changes in this rate occur in this tissue.) It should be noted at this point, however, that although the rate of glycolysis is relatively constant in brain, this tissue is particularly intolerant with respect to hypoxic conditions. Hypoxia brings about a marked increase in the rate of glycolysis in the brain, and this change reflects changes in the concentrations of ATP, AMP, and orthophosphate that are produced as a result of the diminished oxygen supply.

† Clark, M. G., Bloxham, D. P., Holland, P. C., and Lardy, H. A. (1974) *J. Biol. Chem.* **249**, 279–290.
‡ Clark, M. G., Kneer, N. M., Bosch, A. L., and Lardy, H. A. (1974) *J. Biol. Chem.* **249**, 5695–5703.

**In erythrocytes** In general the activities of the enzymes that determine the rate of glycolysis can be modulated by certain biochemical intermediates that embody one or more phosphoryl groups. Included in this category are ATP, AMP, 3′,5′-AMP, orthophosphate, and glucose 6-phosphate. In addition, certain other phosphoryl compounds, including 3-phosphoglycerate and 2,3-bisphosphoglycerate, can function as modulators of phosphofructokinase and hexokinase activities in vitro although in the cell the concentrations of these biochemical intermediates are generally not high enough to warrant their consideration as regulators of glycolysis. An exception occurs in the erythrocyte. In this cell concentrations of 2,3-bisphosphoglycerate are of the same order of magnitude as those which are inhibitory with respect to the activities of phosphofructokinase and hexokinase, and in fact it appears that the rate of glycolysis is regulated by the bisphosphoryl compound. The compound 2,3-bisphosphoglycerate is known to bind the deoxyhemoglobin of the erythrocyte to a far greater extent that it binds the oxyhemoglobin. Therefore, under hypoxic conditions, when the concentrations of deoxyhemoglobin are relatively high, more 2,3-bisphosphoglycerate will be bound by this protein and less will be bound by the enzymes of the glycolytic pathway. Hence, glycolysis will proceed at an increased rate as a result of the deinhibition of the activities of phosphofructokinase and hexokinase.

## SYNTHESIS OF GLUCOSE FROM PYRUVATE: GLUCONEOGENESIS

Pyruvate, which occupies a pivotal position in metabolic pathways, is a product of the degradation of certain amino acids. It can undergo decarboxylation and oxidation to yield the acetyl moiety of acetyl CoA, which in turn can be utilized by the tricarboxylic acid cycle or in the anabolism of fatty acids. In addition, the carbon atoms of pyruvate can be utilized in the synthesis of glucose by a pathway that is, in effect, a reversal of the glycolytic pathway. Since pyruvate can be derived from noncarbohydrate compounds, such as amino acids, this process, which is known as *gluconeogenesis*, provides a means of incorporating the carbon atoms of such compounds into carbohydrates. The word gluconeogenesis expresses precisely this; i.e. *neo* means "new," and *genesis* means "formation of." Hence, the word gluconeogenesis means the formation of glucose (or carbohydrates) from new, or noncarbohydrate, precursors. The reactions involved in gluconeogenesis bring about the condensation of two three-carbon molecules to yield one six-carbon molecule, which is just the opposite result of the reactions of glycolysis. In fact, the processes of glycolysis and gluconeogenesis utilize seven of the same enzymes. Each of these enzymes catalyzes a reaction that is demonstrably reversible; in glycolysis the reaction occurs in one direction, while in gluconeogenesis it occurs in the opposite direction. The three enzymes of the glycolytic pathway that are not utilized by the process of gluconeogenesis are hexokinase, phosphofructokinase, and pyruvate kinase. Note that each of these enzymes catalyzes a reaction which can determine the rate at which glycolysis proceeds. As a general rule, reactions which can be rate-determining proceed unidirectionally. In the process of gluconeogenesis an enzyme that does not participate in glycolysis catalyzes the conversion of glucose

6-phosphate into glucose, another enzyme that does not participate in glycolysis catalyzes the conversion of fructose 1,6-bisphosphate into fructose 6-phosphate, and two enzymes that do not participate in glycolysis catalyze the two reactions that allow the conversion of pyruvate into 2-phosphoenolpyruvate.

The process of gluconeogenesis begins with the conversion of pyruvate into 2-phosphoenolpyruvate, although, as mentioned above, this conversion requires two distinct reactions. The first entails the carboxylation of pyruvate to yield oxaloacetate. The second entails the phosphorylation and decarboxylation of oxaloacetate to yield 2-phosphoenolpyruvate.

## Step 1: Carboxylation of Pyruvate

The carboxylation of pyruvate is catalyzed by pyruvate carboxylase [pyruvate: carbon-dioxide ligase (ADP-forming), EC 6.4.1.1], an enzyme that requires acetyl-CoA as an activator and covalently bound biotin as a cofactor.

$$\text{Biotin structure}$$

The formation of oxaloacetate from pyruvate as catalyzed by this enzyme can be written

$$\text{Pyruvate} + \text{ATP} + \text{HCO}_3^- \rightleftharpoons \text{oxaloacetate} + \text{ADP} + P_i \quad (9\text{-}12)$$

Highly purified pyruvate carboxylase has been obtained from a variety of sources including mammalian liver and renal cortex, avian liver, and several microorganisms. The mammalian and avian enzymes are tetramers. Each monomeric unit binds a divalent cation ($Mn^{2+}$ or $Mg^{2+}$) and embodies a catalytic site where a biotin molecule is bound by the formation of an amide derived from the carboxyl group of the cofactor and an $\epsilon$-amino group of a lysyl unit. Pyruvate carboxylase from the yeast *Saccharomyces cerevisiae* is also a tetrameric protein containing four molecules of biotin, although here each monomeric unit binds one $Zn^{2+}$. On the other hand, pyruvate carboxylase from *Pseudomonas citronellolis* appears to be a dimer. The molecular weight of a mammalian enzyme (from rat liver) is 500,000, approximately the same as that of the enzymes from chicken liver or yeast, but the enzyme from *P. citronellolis* has a molecular weight of only 270,000.

The reaction catalyzed by pyruvate carboxylase occurs as two partial reactions which take place at distinct sites on the enzyme surface. The first entails the formation of an enzyme–biotin–carbon dioxide intermediate by a process that requires the cleavage of ATP to yield ADP and orthophosphate. The second partial reaction entails the transfer of the carboxyl moiety from this enzyme–biotin–carbon dioxide intermediate to C(3) of pyruvate. When kinetic studies were conducted on pyruvate carboxylase from rat liver, the following observations were made. Plots of $1/v_i$ as a function of $1/[\text{HCO}_3^-]$, with fixed concentrations of MgATP and a near saturating concentration of pyruvate, were intersecting. However, plots of $1/v_i$ as a function of $1/[\text{MgATP}]$ with fixed concentrations of pyruvate and a constant concentration of $\text{HCO}_3^-$ or plots of $1/v_i$ vs. $1/[\text{HCO}_3^-]$ with fixed concentrations of pyruvate and a constant concentration of MgATP were parallel at low pyruvate concentrations although as the concentration of pyruvate was increased, these plots became more nonparallel.† These observations are compatible with the formulation of the reaction in terms of a ping pong Bi Bi Uni Uni mechanism, in which MgATP and $\text{HCO}_3^-$ bind and MgADP and orthophosphate are released prior to the binding of pyruvate. The finding that the use of high concentrations of pyruvate results in the plots becoming nonparallel might be rationalized on the basis that saturation of the binding sites for pyruvate in effect induces a change in the mechanism of the reaction by impeding the release of MgADP and orthophosphate prior to the binding of pyruvate. Parallel initial-velocity plots indicate that an irreversible step (such as the release of a product into a medium that is devoid of product or the presence of a saturating concentration of an intervening substrate) occurs between the points in the reaction sequence at which the variable and the fixed substrates bind the enzyme. Inhibition studies on pyruvate carboxylase showed that MgADP and certain other purine nucleotides function as competitive inhibitors when MgATP is the variable substrate. Orthophosphate is also a competitive inhibitor with respect to MgATP. The observation that each of the products released as a result of the first partial reaction functions as a competitive inhibitor when MgATP is the variable substrate suggests that the kinetic mechanism of the first partial reaction may be rapid equilibrium random. Therefore, isotope-exchange studies were conducted, and it was found that the [8-$^{14}$C]ADP-ATP exchange and the [$^{32}$P$_i$]ATP exchange occurred at the same velocity.‡ Since this is consistent with the rapid equilibrium random postulation, the kinetic mechanism of the complete reaction was formulated as follows:

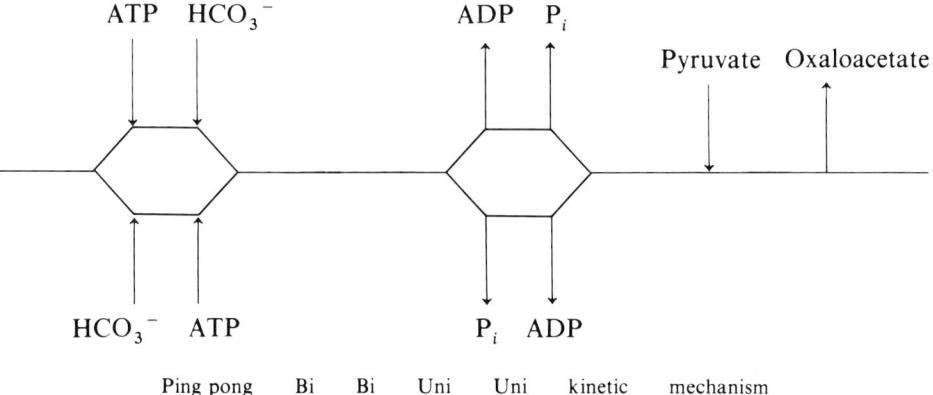

Ping pong Bi Bi Uni Uni kinetic mechanism

† McClure, W. R., Lardy, H. A., Wagner, M., and Cleland, W. W. (1971) *J. Biol. Chem.* **246**, 3579–3583.
‡ McClure, W. R., Lardy, H. A., and Cleland, W. W. (1971) *J. Biol. Chem.* **246**, 3584–3590.

The reaction catalyzed by pyruvate carboxylase involves a nonclassical ping pong mechanism, however. In this reaction MgATP and $HCO_3^-$ bind the enzyme, an enzyme–biotin–carbon dioxide intermediate is formed, MgADP and orthophosphate are released, and then the biotin with its covalently bound carbon dioxide moves to the second site, where the second partial reaction takes place. This has been represented schematically in Fig. 9.4. At the second site the carboxyl moiety is transferred to C(3) of pyruvate, and oxaloacetate is formed. In support of this nonclassical two-site mechanism, it was found that when the products MgADP and orthophosphate were introduced (together) and the concentration of pyruvate was varied, uncompetitive inhibition was observed. It should be remembered that when a reaction proceeds by means of the classical ping pong mechanism a product that binds a different enzyme form than that bound by the variable substrate functions as a noncompetitive inhibitor. However, in the present case because the two partial reactions occur at distinct sites, the binding of products at site I does not produce a slope effect when the variable substrate binds at site II. Thus, only an intercept effect, uncompetitive inhibition, is seen. Similar patterns were obtained when kinetic studies were conducted on pyruvate carboxylase from ovine kidney.† MgADP and orthophosphate (individually in this case) were each competitive product inhibitors when MgATP was varied and uncompetitive inhibitors when pyruvate was varied. When bicarbonate was varied, on the other hand, MgADP, orthophosphate, and oxaloacetate each functioned as a noncompetitive inhibitor. Presumably this is because the carboxyl moiety, derived from bicarbonate and

† Ashman, L. K., and Keech, D. B. (1975) *J. Biol. Chem.* **250**, 14–21.

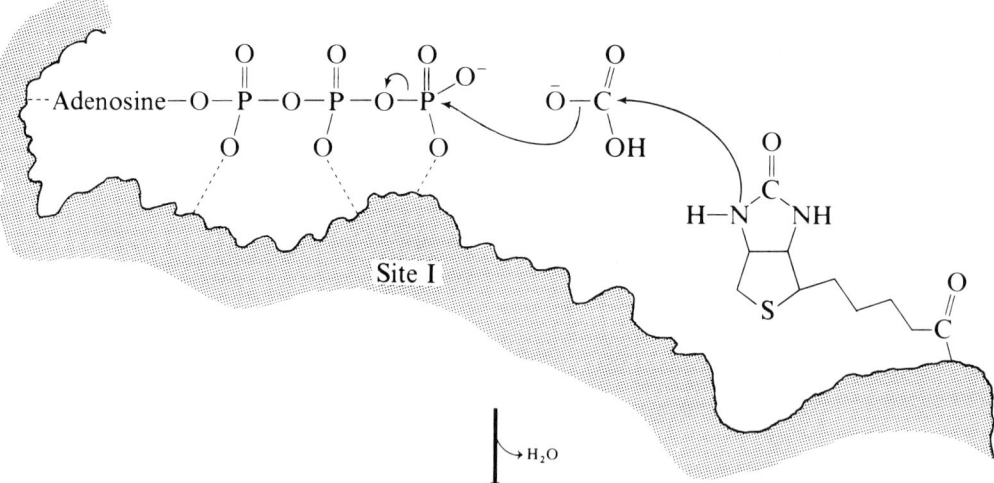

**Figure 9-4** Schematic representation of the reaction mechanism for the carboxylation of pyruvate as catalyzed by pyruvate carboxylase. The reaction proceeds by a nonclassical ping pong Bi Bi Uni Uni kinetic mechanism involving two catalytic sites. The formation of the enzyme–biotin–carbon dioxide intermediate, occurring at site I, is depicted as a concerted process for which there is considerable evidence.

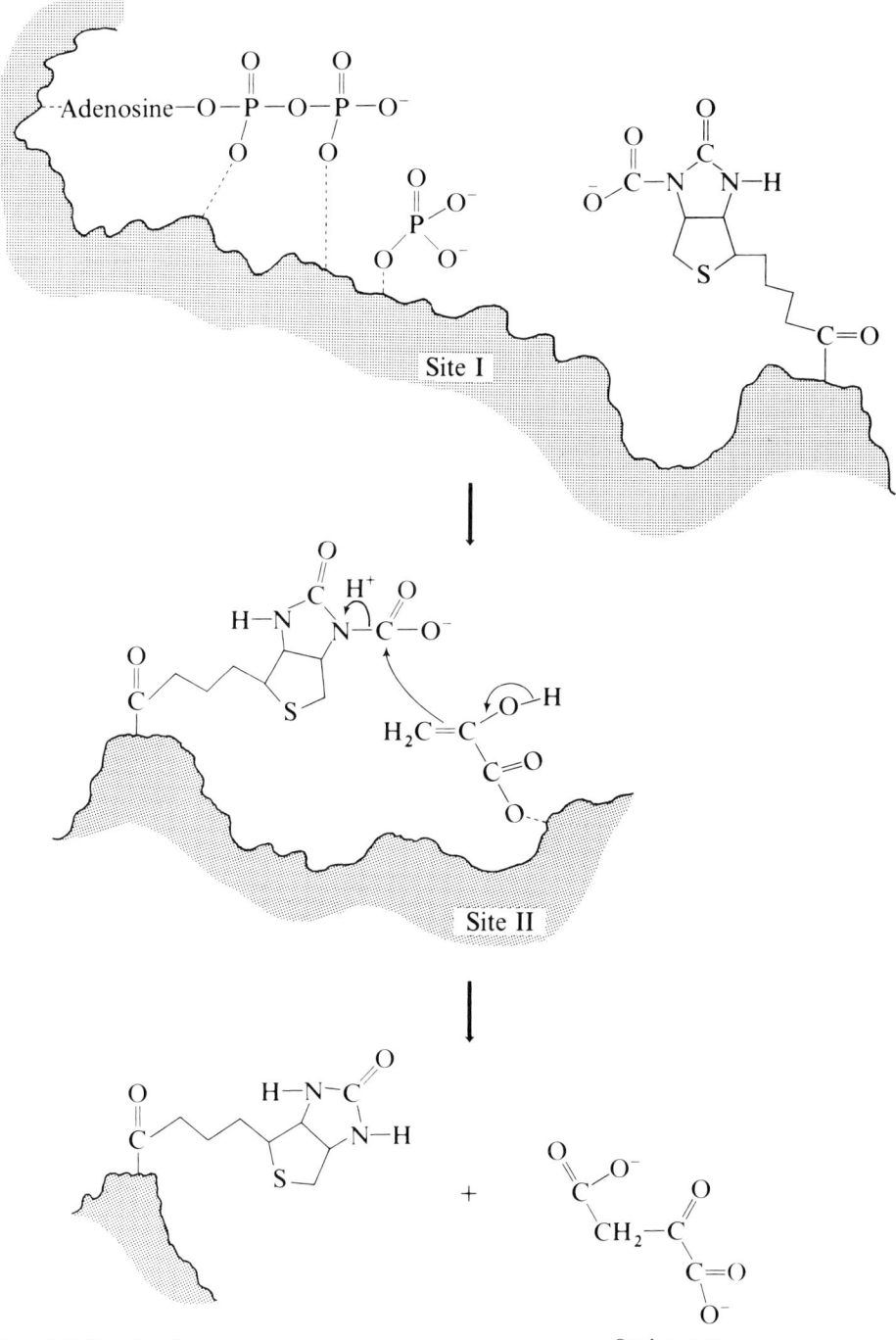

**Figure 9-4** (*Continued*).  Oxaloacetate

bound to biotin, can move back and forth between site I and site II and, therefore, a slope effect is seen when products that bind either site are present.

The reaction catalyzed by pyruvate carboxylase is one which can be rate-determining with respect to gluconeogenesis. Thus, as might be expected, the activity of pyruvate carboxylase is modulated by certain biochemical intermediates. One of these is acetyl CoA, which is, in fact, required by the enzymes from mammalian liver, mammalian renal cortex, avian liver, and *Bacillus stearothermophilus*. The function of the acetyl CoA molecule was established for the pyruvate carboxylase from chicken liver; in this case it was determined that acetyl CoA, the modulator, prevents the dissociation of the enzyme tetramer. This dissociation is accompanied by a loss of enzymatic activity. When the velocity of the reaction is plotted as a function of the concentration of acetyl CoA, a sigmoidal curve is obtained, and thus it is suggested that the binding of this modulator is cooperative. Corroborative evidence was provided when Hill plots, i.e., plots of $\log[v/(V_{max} - v)]$ vs. log [acetyl CoA], were prepared and it was found that the Hill coefficient, $n_H$, is approximately 3 for the avian enzyme. A Hill coefficient greater than unity implies that the binding of the component being varied occurs with positive cooperativity.

Although pyruvate carboxylases from yeasts, such as *Saccharomyces cerevisiae*, do not have an absolute requirement for acetyl CoA, the activities of such enzymes are enhanced in the presence of this intermediate. Acyl derivatives other than the acetyl derivative of CoA are effective, and in fact palmitoyl-CoA is frequently more effective than acetyl CoA as a modulator. The activity of pyruvate carboxylase from *S. cerevisiae* can also be modulated by the amino acid L-aspartate; however, in this case the modulator functions as an inhibitor. By contrast, the activities of carboxylases from mammalian sources appear to be insensitive to aspartate.

The activities of pyruvate carboxylases from certain microorganisms, such as *Aspergillus niger*, are unaffected by acetyl-CoA (or an acyl-CoA). However, aspartate functions as a potent noncompetitive inhibitor of the activity of these enzymes when pyruvate is the variable substrate.

When considering the reaction mechanism of the carboxylation of pyruvate as catalyzed by pyruvate carboxylase, the question has been raised whether the participation of ATP (in the first partial reaction) entails the formation of a phosphoryl intermediate or whether ATP is cleaved by means of a concerted process. When the reaction catalyzed by pyruvate carboxylase from ovine kidney was examined, this enzyme failed to catalyze isotope exchange between [$\beta$-$^{32}$P]ADP and ATP in the absence of added orthophosphate. This observation provides evidence against a reaction mechanism in which a phosphoryl group of ATP binds to a functional group (such as a glutamyl carboxyl group or a histidyl imidazole moiety) of the enzyme. If such a phosphoryl enzyme intermediate were formed, it should be capable of phosphorylating ADP to yield ATP and the isotope exchange would be observed. This is one item of evidence which has been used in support of a concerted mechanism at site I.

The carboxylation of pyruvate occurs in a stereoselective manner which entails the removal of a specific hydrogen at C(3) of the substrate. This was demonstrated by using pyruvate with a specific hydrogen atom replaced by tritium. This labeled pyruvate was then used as a substrate in the reaction catalyzed by pyruvate carboxylase, the resulting oxaloacetate was subsequently converted to malate [in which the hydrogen atoms at C(3) are not labile], and the radioactivity of the malate was determined. When (S)-[3-$^3$H]pyruvate was the substrate, the tritium atom was retained, but when (R)-[3-$^3$H]pyruvate was used, the tritium was lost,† indicating that the carboxylation reaction entails the stereoselective replacement of the 3R hydrogen of pyruvate by a carboxyl group.

**Pyruvate carboxylase as an anaplerotic enzyme** Catabolic pathways result in the oxidative degradation of many of the intermediates of metabolism, while anabolic pathways continually incorporate many intermediates into various macromolecules. Thus, both types of pathways can bring about a diminution in the available concentrations of biochemical intermediates. In order that the concentrations of certain important intermediates might be maintained at the required levels certain biochemical reactions have an auxiliary function of providing for their synthesis. The reaction catalyzed by pyruvate carboxylase is one such reaction. These reactions are referred to as *anaplerotic reactions*, and the enzymes that catalyze them are called *anaplerotic enzymes*. Anaplerotic is derived from the Greek *ana*, meaning "up" or "in," and the Greek *pleroein*, "to fill." Thus, an anaplerotic reaction is one that fills up or fills in the supply of an important biochemical intermediate. Oxaloacetate, the intermediate synthesized as a result of the reaction catalyzed by pyruvate carboxylase, not only is the product of the initial reaction of gluconeogenesis but also is a substrate in the initial reaction of the tricarboxylic acid cycle. In addition, oxaloacetate is a participant in a mechanism for transporting reducing equivalents across the mitochondrial membrane (see the discussion of the malate-aspartate shuttle in Chap. 10).

## Step 2: Phosphorylation and Decarboxylation of Oxaloacetate

The second part of the conversion of pyruvate into phosphoenolpyruvate entails the phosphorylation and concomitant decarboxylation of oxaloacetate. This reaction is catalyzed by phosphoenolpyruvate carboxykinase [GTP:oxaloacetate carboxy-lyase (transphosphorylating), EC 4.1.1.32]. The reaction can be written

$$\text{GTP} + \text{oxaloacetate} \rightleftharpoons \text{GDP} + \text{phosphoenolpyruvate} + \text{CO}_2 \quad (9\text{-}13)$$

Relatively high concentrations of the carboxykinase are found in liver and kidney, the principal sites of gluconeogenesis, while lower concentrations are found in mammary tissue, adipose tissue, and muscle. Phosphoenolpyruvate carboxykinase has been isolated from several sources, including porcine, rat, and chicken liver and ovine kidney. Each of these enzymes has a molecular weight of approximately 70,000. A carboxykinase from *Bacillus stearothermophilus* appears to be almost twice as large (130,000), however, while a carboxykinase from yeast is reported to have a molecular weight of 252,000. Phosphoenolpyruvate carboxykinase has an absolute requirement for a divalent metal ion which appears to be $Mn^{2+}$, and many of the enzymes from higher organisms can utilize either ITP or GTP as the phosphoryl donor. On the other hand, the yeast enzyme and also the

---

† Rose, I. A. (1970) *J. Biol. Chem.* **245**, 6052–6056.

carboxykinases from certain other microorganisms, including *E. coli*, utilize ATP as the phosphoryl donor. In this case, the enzyme has a separate classification, i.e., it is called phosphoenolpyruvate carboxykinase (ATP) [ATP:oxaloacetate carboxy-lyase (transphosphorylating), EC 4.1.1.49].

Kinetic studies conducted on phosphoenolpyruvate carboxykinase from chicken liver have indicated that the mechanism of the reaction is a sequential one since plots of $1/v_i$ vs. 1/[oxaloacetate] with fixed concentrations of ITP or those of $1/v_i$ vs. 1/[ITP] with fixed concentrations of oxaloacetate are intersecting. In addition, a product-inhibition study showed that IDP is a competitive inhibitor with respect to ITP. Also, when the oxaloacetate-$CO_2$ isotope exchange was monitored while the concentration of oxaloacetate was varied with fixed concentrations of ITP, the product IDP functioned as an uncompetitive inhibitor. These observations suggest that the kinetic mechanism is ordered sequential with IDP as the final and $CO_2$ as the initial products that are released.† Additional studies are needed in order to confirm this proposal.

The reaction mechanism of the conversion of oxaloacetate into 2-phosphoenolpyruvate and $CO_2$ has been formulated in terms of a concerted process since it was found that the labeled oxygen of $[^{18}O]H_2O$ in the medium is not incorporated into the products.

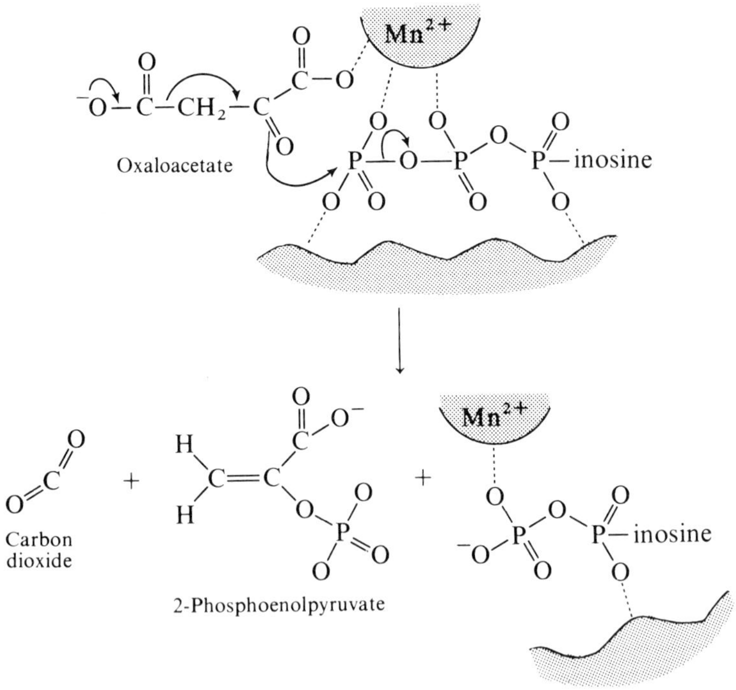

† Felicioli, R. A., Barsacchi, R., and Ipata, P. L. (1970) *Eur. J. Biochem.* **13**, 403–409.

According to this formulation, the loss of the carboxyl group is facilitated by the cleavage of the nucleoside triphosphate since the $\beta$-phosphoryl group serves as the acceptor of electrons released as a concomitance of the bond-breaking process. The divalent cation, $Mn^{2+}$, participates by coordinating with the substrates and presumably causing each to be positioned appropriately to facilitate the reaction.

The reaction catalyzed by phosphoenolpyruvate carboxykinase is the first of the gluconeogenic pathway that is unique to this pathway. Thus, it might be expected that gluconeogenesis would be regulated, at least in part, as a result of influences upon the decarboxylation and phosphorylation reaction. In fact, it appears that both the concentration of the carboxykinase in the cell and its activity are subject to modulation. It has been suggested that in mammalian systems the activity of the enzyme may be modulated by the prevailing ATP/ADP ratio in the cell. Since higher concentrations of ATP are generally reflected by higher concentrations of the other nucleoside triphosphates, including GTP and ITP, it may be that substrate availability is in fact the critical factor. On the other hand, the activity of phosphoenolpyruvate carboxykinase (ATP) from *E. coli* is inhibited in the presence of NADH. Increasing concentrations of NADH cause plots of the reaction velocity vs. the concentration of oxaloacetate to change from hyperbolic to increasingly sigmoidal. These and other aspects of the modulation of the second step of gluconeogenesis will be discussed later in this chapter within the framework of the regulation of the pathway.

## Steps 3 to 8: Reactions Culminating in the Formation of Fructose 1,6-Bisphosphate

With the formation of phosphoenolpyruvate, the gluconeogenic pathway proceeds by reactions that are catalyzed by enzymes shared with the glycolytic pathway. Phosphoenolpyruvate is converted into 2-phosphoglycerate, in the presence of enolase; phosphoglyceromutase then catalyzes the conversion of 2-phosphoglycerate into 3-phosphoglycerate; and phosphoglycerate kinase subsequently catalyzes the conversion of 3-phosphoglycerate and ATP into 3-phospho-D-glyceroyl phosphate and ADP. Next, 3-phospho-D-glyceroyl phosphate undergoes dephosphorylation and reduction in the presence of glyceraldehyde 3-phosphate dehydrogenase, and glyceraldehyde 3-phosphate is formed. Isomerization of glyceraldehyde 3-phosphate, as catalyzed by triosephosphate isomerase, provides dihydroxyacetone phosphate, which can then undergo condensation with glyceraldehyde 3-phosphate in the presence of fructosebisphosphate aldolase, to yield fructose 1,6-bisphosphate. If gluconeogenesis is, in effect, the reverse of glycolysis, the next step in the gluconeogenic pathway should be the conversion of fructose 1,6-bisphosphate into fructose 6-phosphate. However, the conversion of fructose 6-phosphate into fructose 1,6-bisphosphate in the glycolytic pathway is the principal rate-determining step of this pathway under many circumstances, and, in general, rate-determining reactions are unidirectional, as mentioned. Thus, in the gluconeogenic pathway the conversion of fructose 1,6-bisphosphate into fructose 6-phosphate is not catalyzed by phosphofructokinase but rather by a distinctly different enzyme.

## Step 9: Conversion of Fructose 1,6-Bisphosphate into Fructose 6-Phosphate

Fructose 1,6-bisphosphate is converted into fructose 6-phosphate and orthophosphate by the enzyme hexosediphosphatase (D-fructose 1,6-bisphosphate 1-phosphohydrolase, EC 3.1.3.11). The reaction, which is a hydrolysis, can be written

$$\text{D-Fructose 1,6-bisphosphate} + H_2O \rightleftharpoons \text{D-fructose 6-phosphate} + P_i$$
(9-14)

A hexosediphosphatase has been isolated from rabbit liver and crystallized. This enzyme, which has been extensively studied, is composed of four subunits, two of one type and two of another. It has now been determined that this species is a proteolytically modified form of native hexosediphosphatase which is composed of four identical subunits. Each of these subunits has a molecular weight of 34,000.† Thus, the tetramer has a molecular weight of approximately 135,000. The proteolytic modification (which presumably takes place during the isolation procedure) is accompanied by certain changes in the characteristics of the hexosediphosphatase. For example, while the activity of the modified enzyme is maximal at a pH greater than 9, that of the native enzyme is maximal at pH 7. Also, with respect to the absolute requirement for a divalent cation exhibited by all hexosediphosphatases, the modified species utilizes $Mn^{2+}$ as well as $Mg^{2+}$, the activity of the native enzyme being maximal when $Mg^{2+}$ is present.

When initial-velocity studies were conducted on a homogeneous preparation of hexosediphosphatase from bovine liver, plots of $1/v_i$ as a function of $1/[Mg^{2+}]$ with fixed concentrations of fructose 1,6-bisphosphate were intersecting, indicating that both $Mg^{2+}$ and fructose 1,6-bisphosphate must bind the enzyme prior to the release of either of the products. In addition, a replot of the slopes of the plots described above vs. 1/[fructose 1,6-bisphosphate] does not pass through the origin as it would if there were an ordered addition of the two components, with the addition of the $Mg^{2+}$ occurring first and under conditions of thermodynamic equilibrium.‡ Although this type of mechanism is known to occur when a cation binds an enzyme, it is apparently not operative here. When such a mechanism is operative, the slope replot passes through the origin because very high concentrations of the second component that binds the enzyme in effect eliminate the dependence of the reaction velocity upon the concentration of the initial component that binds. (High concentrations of B allow all E to be converted into EAB regardless of the concentration of A.)

Studies on the native hexosediphosphatase from rabbit liver have indicated that the tetrameric enzyme binds four molecules of fructose 1,6-bisphosphate and that the binding is cooperative. In this case, the binding exhibits negative cooperativity; i.e., the binding of the initial substrate molecule by one subunit makes binding of a second substrate molecule by a second subunit more difficult. In fact, the association constant for the binding of the first substrate molecule is 20 times that

---

† Nakashima, K., and Horecker, B. L. (1971) *Arch. Biochem. Biophys.* **146**, 153–160; Traniello, S., Pontremoli, S., Tashima, Y., and Horecker, B. L. (1971) *Arch. Biochem. Biophys.* **146**, 161–166.
‡ Marcus, C. J., Geller, A. M., and Byrne, W. L. (1973) *J. Biol. Chem.* **248**, 8567–8573.

for the binding of the second. Association constants for the binding of the third and fourth molecules of fructose 1,6-bisphosphate are only slightly less than that for the binding of the second, however.†

The activity of hexosediphosphatases can be modulated by its substrate, fructose 1,6-bisphosphate. Since this inhibitory effect exhibits both a slope and an intercept effect when the concentration of $Mg^{2+}$ is varied, it is referred to as noncompetitive substrate inhibition. This observation is not that which would be expected if the kinetic mechanism of the reaction were a purely ordered sequential one with $Mg^{2+}$ as the initial component that binds the enzyme. If this were the case, fructose 1,6-bisphosphate would function as an uncompetitive substrate inhibitor.

Hexosediphosphatases from all sources examined thus far, with the exception of two slime molds, are strongly inhibited in the presence of AMP. This inhibition is thought to result from the binding of AMP at an allosteric site. A total of four molecules of AMP can bind the tetrameric enzyme (one binds each subunit), and the binding exhibits positive cooperativity. When the value for the Hill coefficient was determined, it was found to be 2.5 (values greater than unity imply positive cooperativity).

## Step 10: Conversion of Fructose 6-Phosphate into Glucose 6-Phosphate

In the next step of the gluconeogenic pathway, fructose 6-phosphate is converted into glucose 6-phosphate through the agency of the enzyme glucosephosphate isomerase. This enzyme catalyzes the second step of the glycolytic pathway. As mentioned previously, the reaction catalyzed by this enzyme has an equilibrium constant not far from unity, and thus the reaction is readily reversible.

## Step 11: Formation of Glucose from Glucose 6-Phosphate

The final step in the gluconeogenic pathway is the dephosphorylation (or hydrolysis) of glucose 6-phosphate to yield glucose and orthophosphate. This reaction, catalyzed by glucose-6-phosphatase (D-glucose-6-phosphate phosphohydrolase, EC 3.1.3.9), is

$$\text{Glucose 6-phosphate} + H_2O \rightleftharpoons \text{glucose} + P_i \quad (9\text{-}15)$$

Glucose-6-phosphatase is unique compared with the enzymes of the glycolytic pathway or most of those of the gluconeogenic pathway in that it is not localized in the cytoplasm of the cell but rather in association with the endoplasmic reticulum. Primarily, the enzyme is found in the liver and in the kidney although it has also been identified in the small intestine and in the pancreas.

Homogeneous preparations of glucose-6-phosphatase have yet to be obtained although several purified preparations have been reported. These have been obtained by treatment of an endoplasmic-reticulum fraction with a detergent that solubilizes the enzyme; as is usually the case, such preparations contain portions of the

---

† Libby, C. B., Frey, W. A., Villafranca, J. J., and Benkovic, S. J. (1975) *J. Biol. Chem.* **250**, 7564–7573.

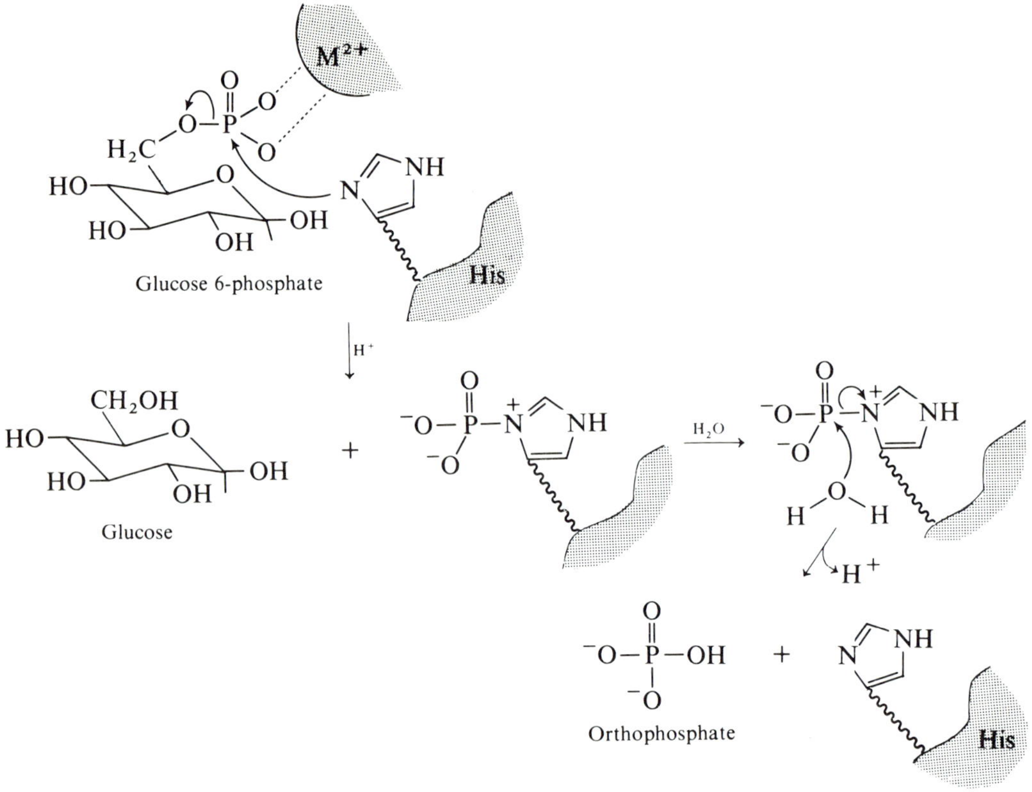

membrane lipid. Some of these preparations were found to catalyze the transfer of the phosphoryl group from glucose 6-phosphate to a hydroxyl group of other sugars (or polyols) or to a hydroxyl group of other phosphoryl compounds in addition to the transfer of this phosphoryl group to the hydroxyl group of a water molecule. The former activities are referred to as the *phosphotransferase activities* of the enzyme, while the transfer to the hydroxyl group of a water molecule (which results in the formation of orthophosphate) is referred to as the *phosphohydrolase activity*. There is now evidence, however, that the phosphotransferase activities may be artifacts resulting from the extraction of the enzyme from the endoplasmic reticulum.† There are other instances in which the solubilization of a membrane-bound enzyme alters the nature of the activity that is, subsequently exhibited.

The reaction catalyzed by glucose-6-phosphatase has been formulated in terms of a phosphoryl-enzyme intermediate since when [$^{32}$P]glucose 6-phosphate is used

---

† Arion, W. J., and Wallin, B. K. (1973) *J. Biol. Chem.* **248**, 2372–2379.

as the substrate, the radioactive phosphorus atom is incorporated into an $N(3)$-phosphorylhistidyl moiety. A reaction mechanism for the hydrolysis of glucose 6-phosphate is shown on page 376.

## Summary

A summary of the gluconeogenic pathway is presented in Fig. 9-5.

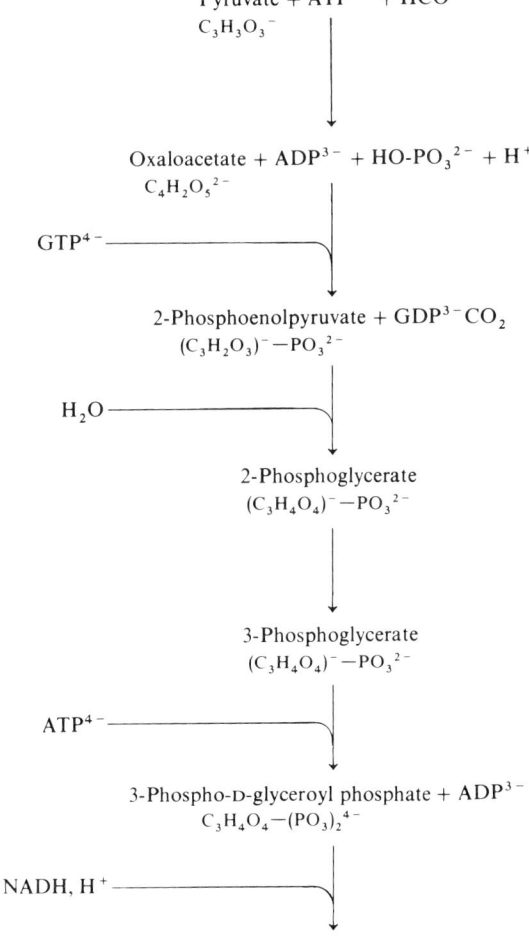

Figure 9-5 Summary of the gluconeogenic pathway, which allows pyruvate to be utilized for the synthesis of glucose. This figure is continued on page 378.

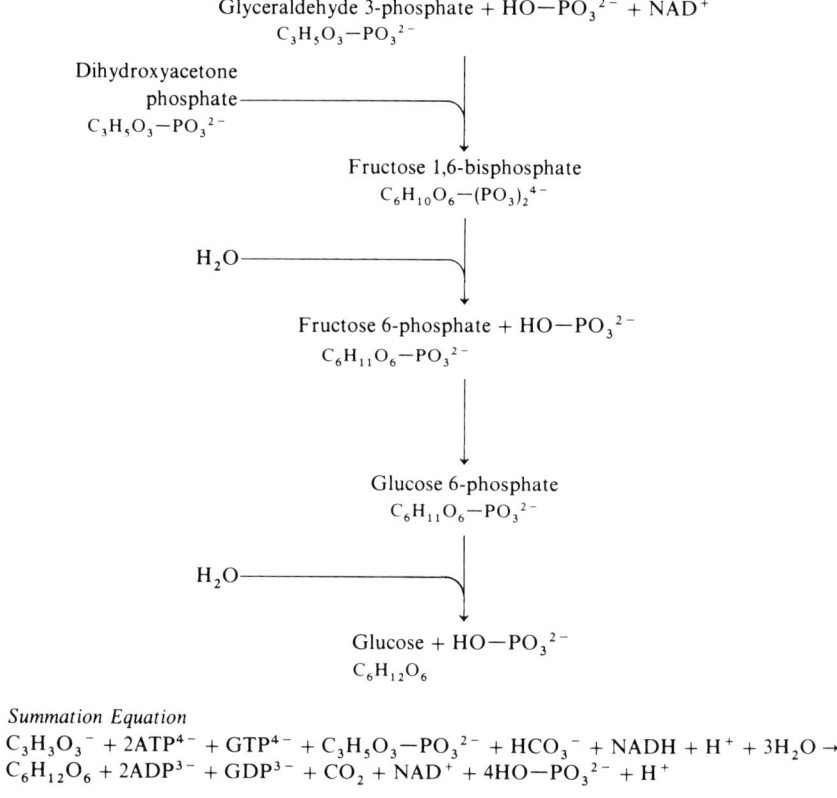

**Figure 9-5** (*Continued*)

## Regulation of Gluconeogenesis

Certain tissues in higher animals, including the brain, nerves, erythrocytes, the renal medulla, and the testes, have a continuous need for glucose. The brain is particularly sensitive to glucose deprivation since reversible deterioration occurs within 1 min and irreversible changes occur within several minutes when glucose is unavailable. It has been determined that glucose utilization in the brain is approximately 120 g/day while the renal medulla, erythrocytes, and the testes utilize approximately 40 g/day. Notwithstanding the fact that glucose requirements diminish to some extent during deprivation, the carbohydrate reserves of the body (primarily in the form of glycogen) can satisfy its need for only about 12 h. Beyond this, glucose must be synthesized if the requirements of the body are to be met. In the absence of carbohydrate precursors this synthesis is accomplished by gluconeogenesis.

The principal sites of gluconeogenesis are the liver and the renal cortex. In these tissues the reactions that are concerned with the regulation of gluconeogenesis are those catalyzed by pyruvate carboxylase, phosphoenolpyruvate carboxykinase, hexosediphosphatase, and glucose-6-phosphatase. Note that these are the enzymes not shared with the glycolytic pathway.

As mentioned above, the activity of pyruvate carboxylase is enhanced in the presence of acetyl-CoA. Therefore, since fatty acid oxidation in the liver or renal cortex and utilization of ketone bodies in the renal cortex cause an increased availability of acetyl-CoA, these processes which are associated with fatty acid catabolism can increase the rate of gluconeogenesis. Recall that fatty acid oxidation was also mentioned when the regulation of glycolysis was discussed. There the production of acetyl-CoA followed by the condensation of the acetyl moiety with oxaloacetate to produce citrate resulted in the inhibition of glycolysis since citrate inhibits the activity of phosphofructokinase. Thus, the catabolism of fatty acids induces opposing effects upon gluconeogenesis and glycolysis. The wisdom of this becomes apparent when one remembers that gluconeogenesis and glycolysis are, in effect, opposing processes. Gluconeogenesis is an anabolic process that results in the synthesis of glucose, while glycolysis is a catabolic process that results in the degradation of glucose.

There has also been a report that the hormones glucagon and epinephrine can each induce an enhancement in the rate of hepatic gluconeogenesis by influencing the activity of pyruvate carboxylase,† although the precise manner in which this is accomplished is unknown. However, it should be realized that pyruvate carboxylase does not function only in the gluconeogenic pathway. In fact, pyruvate carboxylase is one of the anaplerotic enzymes. Furthermore, pyruvate carboxylase is not a cytoplasmic enzyme, as most of the enzymes of the gluconeogenic pathway are. (Pyruvate carboxylase is localized in the mitochondria.) Therefore, the regulation of the activity of this enzyme might be expected to be more or less complex.

Considering once again the reciprocal relationships between the regulation of gluconeogenesis and that of glycolysis, a further example is to be found in the regulatory influences upon hexosediphosphatase and phosphofructokinase. As mentioned earlier, AMP enhances the activity of phosphofructokinase by relieving the inhibition imposed by ATP or citrate. On the other hand, AMP is an inhibitor with respect to the activity of hexosediphosphatase. Hence, the presence of high concentrations of AMP (and relatively low concentrations of ATP) causes the rate at which glycolysis proceeds to be increased and that at which gluconeogenesis occurs to be impeded. This is precisely the desired action.

Studies on isolated (rat) liver cells have shown that the hormone glucagon promotes gluconeogenesis while impeding glycolysis. The specific reactions involved are those catalyzed by hexosediphosphatase and phosphofructokinase. Flux through

---

† Garrison, J. C., and Haynes, R. C., Jr. (1975) *J. Biol. Chem.* **250**, 2769–2777.

the reaction catalyzed by hexosediphosphatase was increased while that through the reaction catalyzed by phosphofructokinase was decreased in response to glucagon.† These effects are duplicated if 3',5'-AMP is added rather than the hormone. This observation, coupled with the observation that the effects of glucagon and 3',5'-AMP are not additive, leads to speculation that these effects by glucagon are mediated by 3',5'-AMP.

In addition to the regulatory mechanisms mentioned above, which operate under essentially normal conditions, the rate of renal gluconeogenesis is increased in the presence of metabolic acidosis. More specifically, it has been shown that this increase is the result of an increase in the synthesis of the enzyme phosphoenolpyruvate carboxykinase.‡ It was then hypothesized that the increased synthesis of phosphoenolpyruvate carboxykinase and the resulting increase in the rate at which gluconeogenesis proceeds is a response to the acidosis. The reasoning was as follows. In metabolic acidosis there is an increased requirement for ammonia. Ammonia reacts with protons and allows them to be excreted by the kidneys in the form of ammonium ions. Ammonia can be derived from glutamine by deamidation. The resulting glutamate can then be converted into 2-oxoglutarate, the carbon atoms of which can in turn be utilized in the synthesis of glucose. Thus, the increased renal gluconeogenesis is a part of an adaptive mechanism that is utilized in the presence of acidosis. This hypothesis has yet to be proved, however.

# GLYCOGEN METABOLISM

Glucose, including that derived from gluconeogenesis, can be incorporated into glycogen as a result of undergoing phosphorylation and subsequently being incorporated into the uridine diphosphoglucose from which the glucosyl moiety is utilized. The phosphorylation of glucose is catalyzed by hexokinase or glucokinase, enzymes discussed earlier in this chapter. Next the glucose 6-phosphate must be converted into glucose 1-phosphate by a reaction catalyzed by a phosphomutase. This reaction, discussed now, bears considerable similarity to that catalyzed by another phosphomutase, namely phosphoglyceromutase.

## Conversion of Glucose 6-Phosphate into Glucose 1-Phosphate

Glucose 6-phosphate is transformed into glucose 1-phosphate in the presence of phosphoglucomutase ($\alpha$-D-glucose-1,6-bisphosphate:$\alpha$-D-glucose-1-phosphate phosphotransferase, EC 2.7.5.1) and the cofactor glucose 1,6-bisphosphate. A divalent cation such as $Mg^{2+}$ is also required.

---

† Clark, M. G., Kneer, M. N., Bosch, A. L., and Lardy, H. A. (1974) *J. Biol. Chem.* **249**, 5695–5703.
‡ Iynedjian, P. B., Ballard, F. J., and Hanson, R. W. (1975) *J. Biol. Chem.* **250**, 5596–5603.

Phosphoglucomutases have been isolated from a wide variety of sources and purified. Most of these enzymes have molecular weights of approximately 65,000; e.g., the enzyme from rabbit skeletal muscle, which has been rather thoroughly studied, has a molecular weight of 66,000, that from human muscle has a molecular weight of 60,000, and that from *E. coli* has a molecular weight of 64,000. Other phosphoglucomutases which have been characterized include the enzyme from flounder, with a molecular weight of 63,000, and the enzyme from the potato tuber, with a molecular weight of 63,000. In all cases phosphoglucomutase is apparently a single polypeptide chain with a single catalytic site.

Initial-velocity studies on the reaction catalyzed by phosphoglucomutase suggest that a ping pong mechanism is operative, just as in the case of the reaction catalyzed by phosphoglyceromutase. Also, as in the case of phosphoglyceromutase and many ping pong reactions, the reaction catalyzed by phosphoglucomutase is subject to substrate inhibition. Furthermore, parallel with observations concerning phosphoglyceromutase, it has been demonstrated that the function of the cofactor, glucose 1,6-bisphosphate, is that of phosphorylating the enzyme, although the nonphosphorylated enzyme and glucose 1,6-bisphosphate are not obligatory intermediates during each reaction sequence.† Thus, the reaction catalyzed by phosphoglucomutase has been formulated as paralleling that catalyzed by phosphoglycerimutase with the cofactor (in this case glucose 1,6-bisphosphate) combining with the enzyme and transferring one of its phosphoryl groups to the catalytic site and thus forming glucose 1-phosphate plus a phosphoryl enzyme or glucose 6-phosphate plus a phosphoryl enzyme. Following the dissociation of the hexose-monophosphate, the substrate glucose 6-phosphate can bind at the catalytic site and be converted into glucose 1-phosphate, as in the interconversion of the triosephosphates.

## Incorporation of Glucose 1-Phosphate into Uridine Diphosphoglucose

The next step in the synthesis of glycogen is the incorporation of glucose 1-phosphate into uridine diphosphoglucose abbreviated as UDP-glucose.‡ The reaction is

$$\text{Glucose 1-phosphate} + \text{UTP} \rightleftharpoons \text{UDP-glucose} + \text{PP}_i \qquad (9\text{-}16)$$

The reaction is catalyzed by glucose-1-phosphate uridylyltransferase (UDP:α-D-glucose-1-phosphate uridylyltransferase, EC 2.7.7.9). The enzyme is also referred to as UDPglucose pyrophosphorylase.

The glucose-1-phosphate uridylyltransferase from bovine liver exists as an octomer which is composed of eight apparently identical subunits, each with a

---

† Ray, W. J., Jr., and Peck, E. J., Jr. (1972) in *The Enzymes* (Boyer, P. D., ed.), vol. 6, 3d ed., pp. 407–477. Academic, New York.

‡ The abbreviations UDP-glucose, UDP-galactose, and ADP-glucose are used for uridine diphosphoglucose, uridine diphosphogalactose, and adenosine diphosphoglucose, respectively.

molecular weight of 60,000. It has also been found that octomers, with molecular weights of 480,000, can undergo aggregation to yield species having molecular weights of 1 million and more. Uridylyltransferases from a variety of other sources, including the human liver and erythrocyte, are similar to the bovine liver enzyme. However, in some microorganisms multiple forms of the enzyme are found, and it has been speculated that, in some cases at least, the different forms may provide UDP-glucose for different metabolic pathways. UDP-glucose is required for the synthesis not only of glycogen in mammals but also of cellulose, callose (in certain plants), the polysaccharide component of some antigens, teichoic acids, and glucuronates.

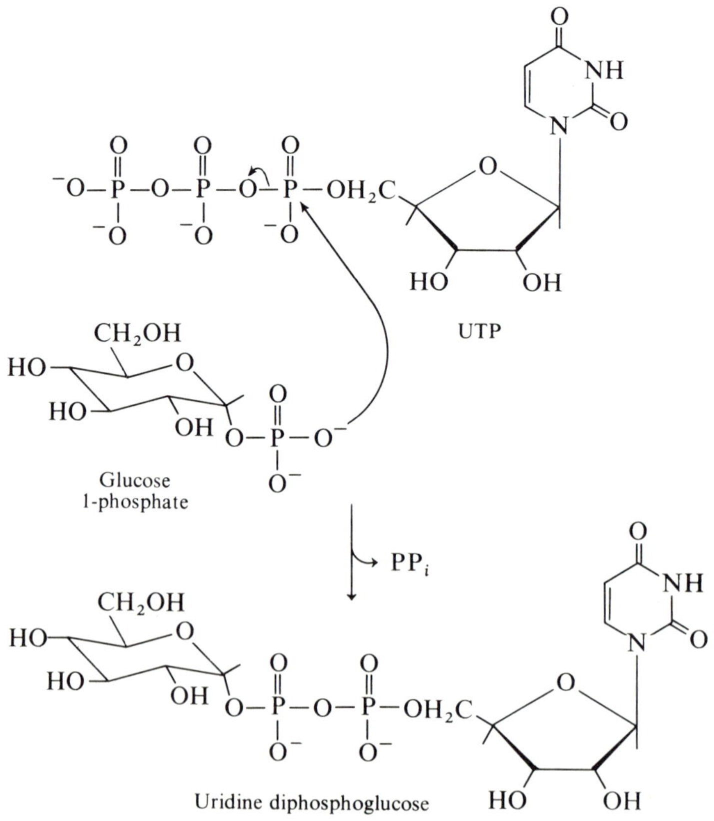

Kinetic studies on the uridylyltransferase from the human erythrocyte have indicated that the reaction occurs by means of an ordered sequential Bi Bi mechanism. Plots of $1/v_i$ vs. reciprocal substrate concentrations are linear and intersecting. Product-inhibition studies showed UDP-glucose to be a competitive inhibitor when UTP was varied and a noncompetitive inhibitor when glucose 1-phosphate was varied. Pyrophosphate functioned as a noncompetitive inhibitor when either substrate was varied. Therefore, UTP is the initial substrate that binds and UDP-glucose is the final product released. This kinetic mechanism characterizes the reactions catalyzed by uridylyltransferases from a variety of sources, including bovine liver, canine heart, yeast, sorghum seedlings, and the protozoa *Acanthamoeba castellanii*.

The reaction mechanism for the formation of UDP-glucose is assumed to involve a nucleophilic attack by the oxygen atom of the phosphoryl group of glucose 1-phosphate upon the phosphorus atom of the α-phosphoryl group of UTP. The pyrophosphate anion is thus displaced, and the UDP-glucose is formed. A minimal mechanism is shown on page 382.

## Incorporation of Glucosyl Moieties into Glycogen

In mammals and certain other higher organisms glycogen synthesis takes place as a result of the sequential addition of glucosyl moieties from UDP-glucose to the C(4) hydroxyl group of the terminal unit of a glycogen molecule. An oligosaccharide of at least three or four α-D-glucosyl units may substitute for the glycogen molecule. However, a primer is required, and synthesis cannot begin with a single glucose unit. This glucosylation reaction is catalyzed by glycogen synthase (UDPglucose: glycogen 4-α-glucosyltransferase, EC 2.4.1.11). The reaction is

$$\text{UDP-glucose} + (1,4\text{-}\alpha\text{-D-glucosyl})_n \rightleftharpoons \text{UDP} + (1,4\text{-}\alpha\text{-D-glucosyl})_{n+1} \quad (9\text{-}17)$$

Molecular weights of purified glycogen synthase are difficult to determine because the enzyme readily undergoes aggregation. However, molecular weights of 250,000 to 350,000 have been estimated, and it is known that the enzyme is composed of subunits which each have a molecular weight of 90,000 (the enzyme from rabbit skeletal muscle) or 80,000 (the enzyme from rat liver). Hence, the active synthase is probably a trimer or a tetramer. The complexity of the situation is increased by the fact that glycogen synthase exists in two forms, glycogen synthase *a*, the active form of the enzyme, and glycogen synthase *b*, which is subactive or inactive under physiological conditions. Glycogen synthase *a* is converted into glycogen synthase *b* by undergoing a phosphorylation reaction in which specific seryl hydroxyl groups of the protein are the phosphoryl acceptors. The phosphoryl donor is ATP. Studies on the synthase from rabbit skeletal muscle have shown that two seryl hydroxyl groups per subunit undergo phosphorylation. The phosphoryl transfer is catalyzed by a protein kinase (ATP:protein phosphotransferase, EC 2.7.1.37). The reaction can be expressed as

$$\text{ATP} + \text{protein} \rightleftharpoons \text{ADP} + \text{phosphoprotein} \quad (9\text{-}18)$$

This enzyme phosphorylation and other similar protein phosphorylations are of some interest since they are a part of regulatory sequences that function in a variety of different metabolic processes. In these sequences, the modulation of the protein is only the final step in a sequence. First, the activity of the protein kinase is subject to modulation with the modulator being 3′,5′-AMP. Protein kinases are composed of two different types of subunits. One exhibits no catalytic activity although it can bind 3',5'-AMP. This subunit is called the *binding protein*. The other subunit exhibits, phosphotransferase activity, and is called the *catalytic protein*. In the absence of 3',5'-AMP the associated binding protein and catalytic protein is subactive or inactive, but in the presence of 3',5'-AMP the binding protein can interact with the cyclic nucleotide, with the result that the two subunits dissociate. Since the liberated catalytic protein is active, 3',5'-AMP functions as an activator, or deinhibitor, with respect to phosphotransferase activity. Furthermore, the chain of regulatory processes extends even farther since the available concentration of 3',5'-AMP is usually under hormonal control. Hence, the activities of enzymes (and the functions of noncatalytic proteins) that can be modulated as a result of this type of protein phosphorylation are, in effect, under hormonal control. This will be discussed again within the framework of the regulation of glycogen metabolism.

Kinetic studies on glycogen synthase $b$ from human polymorphonuclear leukocytes have been carried out in the presence of a constant concentration of glucose 6-phosphate, which is known to function as an activator of the subactive or inactive synthase. Such studies on glycogen synthase are attended by an unusual problem, however, since glycogen is both a substrate and a product of the reaction. Thus, the usual initial-velocity studies are not possible since one product, glycogen, is always present. In the studies being described this problem was circumvented by monitoring the transfer of $^{14}C$ from [*glucosyl*-U-$^{14}$C] UDP-glucose to glycogen. Using this technique, it was found that plots of $1/v_i$ as a function of 1/[UDP-glucose] with fixed concentrations of glycogen or those of $1/v_i$ vs. 1/[glycogen] with fixed concentrations of UDP-glucose were (apparently) linear and intersecting. The product-inhibition studies showed UDP to be a competitive inhibitor when UDP-glucose was varied and a noncompetitive inhibitor when glycogen was varied. In interpreting these studies it must be noted that the equation expressing the initial velocity of the reaction and also the equations for the product-inhibited reactions differ from those generally derived because glycogen is both a substrate and a product. The difference is that since either A and Q or A and P or B and P or B and Q represent glycogen, the initial-velocity equation will not have the usual simple form because its denominator will contain some of the more complex terms that appear in the denominator of the full rate equation for a sequential process (see Appendix A). However, when A and Q represent glycogen, the equation predicts that the initial-velocity plots will be linear. This is because although the denominator of the full rate equation for a sequential reaction contains AP, BQ, ABP, and BPQ terms, it does not contain AQ terms and, therefore, when A = Q = glycogen, there will be no second-order terms representing glycogen concentration. Hence, it was concluded that the kinetic mechanism is sequential and that glycogen can bind before UDP-glucose, and that it can be released after UDP. The product-inhibition data, however, are incompatible with an ordered sequential Bi Bi reaction with A = Q = glycogen because the equations for the reaction under these circumstances predict that UDP will be a noncompetitive product inhibitor when either glycogen or UDP-glucose is varied and this was not observed. Therefore, on the basis of these and additional experiments it was proposed that the reaction catalyzed by glycogen synthase *b* has a random kinetic mechanism.† A similar conclusion was drawn when comparable kinetic studies were conducted on glycogen synthase *b* from rat liver.‡ Studies on glycogen synthase *a* from rabbit skeletal muscle§ and on glycogen synthase *b* from yeast (*Saccharomyces cerevisiae*)¶ have confirmed the sequential nature of the kinetic mechanism.

A minimal mechanism for the glucosylation reaction as catalyzed by glycogen synthase is shown below.

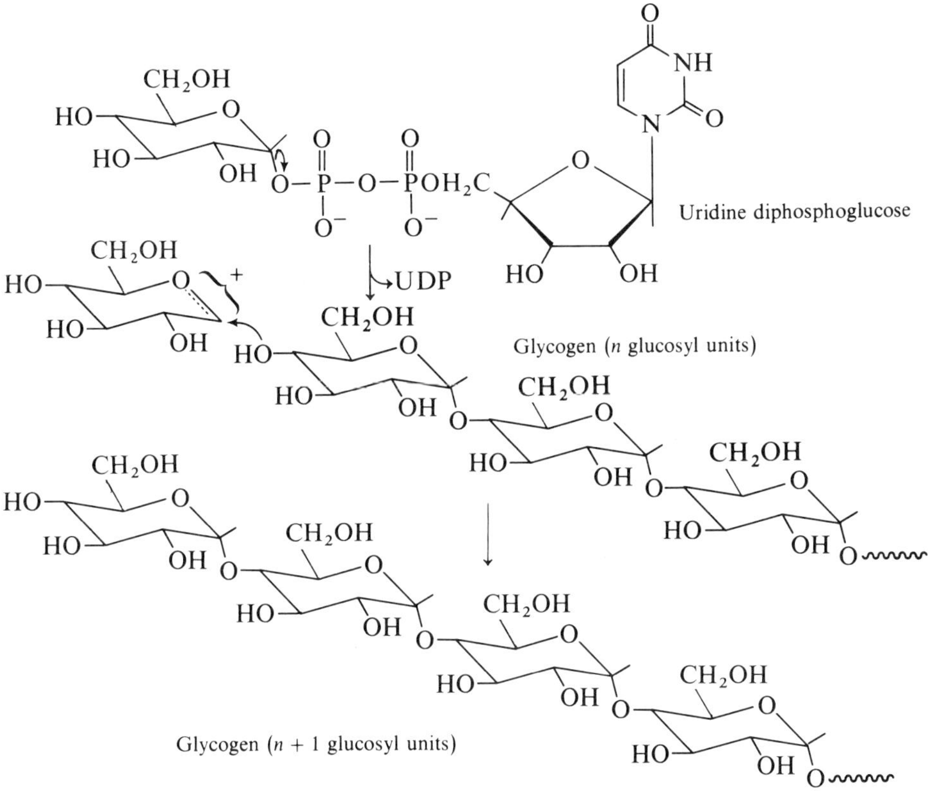

Here, the formation of an oxonium-ion transition-state intermediate and the UDP anion is followed by a reaction between the former and the C(4) hydroxyl moiety of the terminal unit of the primer. Some support for the participation of an oxonium-ion transition-state intermediate has been provided by studies in which 1,5-gluconolactone, known to exist in the half-chair conformation, was found to be a potent inhibitor of glycogen synthase activity. This suggests that 1,5-gluconolactone can bind the enzyme at the catalytic site, and it is thus implied that a transition-state intermediate having the half-chair conformation could be formed at the catalytic

† Plesner, L., Plesner, I. W., and Esmann, V. (1974) *J. Biol. Chem.* **249**, 1119–1125.
‡ McVerry, P. H., and Kim, K. -H. (1974) *Biochemistry* **13**, 3505–3511.
§ Salsas, E., and Larner, J. (1975) *J. Biol. Chem.* **250**, 3471–3475.
¶ Huang, K. -P., and Cabib, E. (1974) *J. Biol. Chem.* **249**, 3851–3857.

site. An oxonium-ion intermediate usually exists in the half-chair conformation since it allows the positive charge that is developed at C(1) to be delocalized.

**Branching of glycogen** Glycogen is a highly branched polymer composed of D-glucosyl units linked by glycosidic bonds. Most of these glycosidic bonds are between C(1) of one unit and C(4) of its neighboring unit. However, branch points occur following a linear sequence of approximately 12 to 18 glucosyl units, and at these points glycosidic bonds between C(1) of one unit and C(6) of the adjoining unit occur. The formation of these 1→6-glycosidic bonds is catalyzed by 1,4-α-glucan branching enzyme [1,4-α-D-glucan:1,4-α-D-glucan 6-α-(1,4-α-glucano)-transferase, EC 2.4.1.18]. The enzyme catalyzes a reaction in which a 1→4-glycosidic bond is broken and a 1→6-glycosidic bond formed instead.

## Synthesis of Bacterial Glycogen

Glycogen synthesis in certain microorganisms differs from the process just described, which pertains primarily to mammalian systems. In these microorganisms instead of activation of the glucosyl moiety by formation of UDP-glucose, glucose 1-phosphate reacts with ATP to form ADP-glucose and pyrophosphate. Subsequently, this glycosyl moiety is incorporated into bacterial glycogen by a reaction catalyzed by a different synthase than that described above. (Glucosyl moieties of ADP-glucose are also incorporated into starch in plants.)

The formation of ADP-glucose is catalyzed by glucose-1-phosphate adenylyltransferase (ATP:α-D-glucose-1-phosphate adenylyltransferase, EC 2.7.7.27). The reaction is

$$\text{ATP} + \text{glucose 1-phosphate} \rightleftharpoons \text{ADP-glucose} + \text{PP}_i \qquad (9\text{-}19)$$

Several adenylyltransferases have been purified to apparent homogeneity. One, from *Rhodospirillum rubrum*, has a molecular weight of 225,000. Another, from a mutant of *E. coli B* has a molecular weight of 211,000; in this case it has also been determined that the enzyme is composed of four subunits which each have a molecular weight of 53,000. Adenylyltransferases from other sources, including plants, appear to be similar. Kinetic studies have indicated that the kinetic mechanism of the reaction by which ADP-glucose is formed is ordered sequential, just as in the formation of UDP-glucose. In the present case, ATP is the initial substrate that binds, and ADP-glucose is the final product released.

The activity of glucose-1-phosphate adenylyltransferase is subject to modulation; however, enzymes from different sources are sensitive to different modulators. Enterobacteria which accumulate glycogen, e.g., *E. coli*, *Aerobacter aerogenes*, *Salmonella typhimurium*, and *Citrobacter freundii*, contain adenylyltransferase activities which are enhanced in the presence of fructose 1,6-bisphosphate, NADPH, and pyridoxal 5-phosphate while being inhibited by AMP. On the other hand, certain microorganisms which degrade glucose via the Entner-Doudoroff pathway contain adenylyltransferases that exhibit enhanced activities in the presence of fructose 6-phosphate or pyruvate. By contrast, the activity of the adenylyltransferase from *Serratia marcescens* is not enhanced by any of the modulators mentioned above or by any of the common metabolic intermediates.

The glucosylation reaction in microorganisms in which ADP-glucose is the donor is catalyzed by starch (bacterial glycogen) synthase (ADPglucose:1,4-α-D-glucan 4-α-glucosyltransferase, EC 2.4.1.21). The reaction is presumed to proceed much in the same manner as that catalyzed by the mammalian glycogen syntheses.

## Phosphorylytic Cleavage of Glycogen

Glycogen is a storage form of carbohydrate. When carbohydrate (glucose) is required, glycogen can undergo a phosphorylytic cleavage which results in the formation of glucose 1-phosphate molecules. These in turn can be converted into glucose molecules. The phosphorylytic cleavage is catalyzed by the enzyme phosphorylase (1,4-α-D-glucan:orthophosphate α-glucosyltransferase, EC 2.4.1.1). The reaction is

$$(1,4\text{-}\alpha\text{-}D\text{-Glucosyl})_n + P_i \rightleftharpoons (1,4\text{-}\alpha\text{-}D\text{-glucosyl})_{n-1} + \alpha\text{-}D\text{-glucose 1-phosphate} \quad (9\text{-}20)$$

Like glycogen synthase, phosphorylase exists in two forms. One, phosphorylase *a*, is the active form, while the other, phosphorylase *b*, is subactive or inactive. Both forms can be isolated from rabbit skeletal muscle and other sources. Again as in the case of glycogen synthase, the phosphorylases undergo aggregation. However, when the molecular weights of these enzymes were determined, it was found that the form of phosphorylase *a* that is usually obtained in dilute solutions has a molecular weight of 3.6 to $3.8 \times 10^5$ while the species of phosphorylase *b* most frequently encountered has a molecular weight of 1.8 to $1.9 \times 10^5$, or half that of the phosphorylase *a*. It has also been shown that phosphorylase *b* is a dimer which is composed of two monomeric units, each with a molecular weight of $0.95 \times 10^5$. Each of the monomeric units binds one molecule of pyridoxal 5-phosphate, which is apparently required in order for the enzyme to be functional, although its precise role is unknown. Subactive or inactive phosphorylase *b* is converted into the active phosphorylase when the former undergoes a phosphorylation reaction that is similar to that which occurs when glycogen synthase *a* is converted to glycogen synthase *b*. There is one significant difference, however: phosphorylation converts active glycogen synthase into a subactive or inactive form, while phosphorylation converts a subactive or inactive phosphorylase into an active form. The phosphorylation of phosphorylase *b* is catalyzed by the enzyme phosphorylase kinase (ATP:phosphorylase *b* phosphotransferase, EC 2.7.1.38). The reaction can be written

$$2\text{ATP} + \text{phosphorylase } b \rightleftharpoons 2\text{ADP} + \text{phosphorylase } a \quad (9\text{-}21)$$

Initially, it was believed that in rabbit skeletal muscle in order for an active enzyme to be formed the phosphorylation of phosphorylase *b* must be accompanied by the dimerization of the phosphorylated species to yield a tetrameric species, but it is now known that the dimeric phosphorylated enzyme is more active catalytically than the tetrameric form.† Usually the two species are distinguished by referring to

---

† Huang, C. Y., and Graves, D. J. (1970) *Biochemistry* **9**, 660–671.

one as dimeric phosphorylase *a* and the other as tetrameric phosphorylase *a*. The conversion of subactive or inactive hepatic phosphorylase into the active form shows no evidence of being accompanied by formation of a tetramer, by contrast.

The regulatory mechanism involving the phosphorylases extends even beyond phosphorylase kinase in that this enzyme itself exists in two forms, one subactive or inactive and the other active. Conversion of the subactive or inactive form into the active form again entails the phosphorylation of the former, which in this instance is catalyzed by a protein kinase. This protein kinase can catalyze not only the phosphorylation of the phosphorylase kinase from skeletal muscle, but also the glycogen synthase from that tissue. Thus, the regulation of glycogen synthesis and of glycogen degradation are interrelated. More will be said about this interrelationship when the regulation of glycogen metabolism is discussed.

Kinetic studies on the phosphorylases present the same problem as those on glycogen synthase; i.e., glycogen is both a substrate and a product. Therefore, velocities have again been determined by using isotopes. When this was done and initial-velocity studies on phosphorylase *a* from rabbit skeletal muscle were carried out, the data suggested that the degradation of glycogen occurs by a sequential kinetic mechanism. Since other data suggested that this sequential mechanism might be rapid equilibrium random, isotope-exchange studies were then conducted. In these experiments, the velocities of the [$^{32}$P]orthophosphate–to–glucose 1-phosphate exchange and the [U-$^{14}$C]glucose 1-phosphate–to–glycogen exchange were monitored. The observation that the initial velocities of these two exchanges are equal under a variety of conditions provided strong support for the proposal of a rapid equilibrium random mechanism.†

In addition to the regulatory effect imposed by the conversion of phosphorylase *b* into phosphorylase *a* (and vice versa), there are certain metabolic intermediates that function as modulators of the activity of the phosphorylases. A principal one of these is AMP, which functions as an activator with respect to the activity of phosphorylase *b*. AMP is believed to bind the enzyme at an allosteric site, and as a result the nature of the binding of the substrate orthophosphate is converted from cooperative to noncooperative. Thus, in the absence of AMP a plot of the reaction velocity as a function of orthophosphate concentration is sigmoidal, while in the presence of AMP the plot is hyperbolic. As mentioned earlier, the conversion of substrate binding which exhibits positive cooperativity into that which is noncooperative is, in effect, an enhancement of enzymatic activity. There is some evidence that ATP can also bind, but the binding of ATP appears to negate the effect of AMP. Hence, ATP functions as a deactivator or an inhibitor of phosphorylase activity. Another deactivator or inhibitor of phosphorylase activity is glucose 6-phosphate. This hexose phosphate is also thought to bind at an allosteric site, but this site is apparently different from that at which the nucleotides bind. Again, the binding of this modulator is accompanied by a lessening of the enhancement brought about by AMP.

The reaction catalyzed by phosphorylase entails the C—O cleavage of the

---

† Gold, A. M., Johnson, R. M., and Tseng, J. K. (1970) *J. Biol. Chem.* **245**, 2564–2572.

glucosyl bond of the terminal unit at the nonreducing end of the glycogen macromolecule. The resulting species then interacts with the orthophosphate anion, and glucose 1-phosphate is formed. The process occurs with absolute stereospecificity in that the product is α-D-glucose 1-phosphate. The reaction can be depicted as shown.

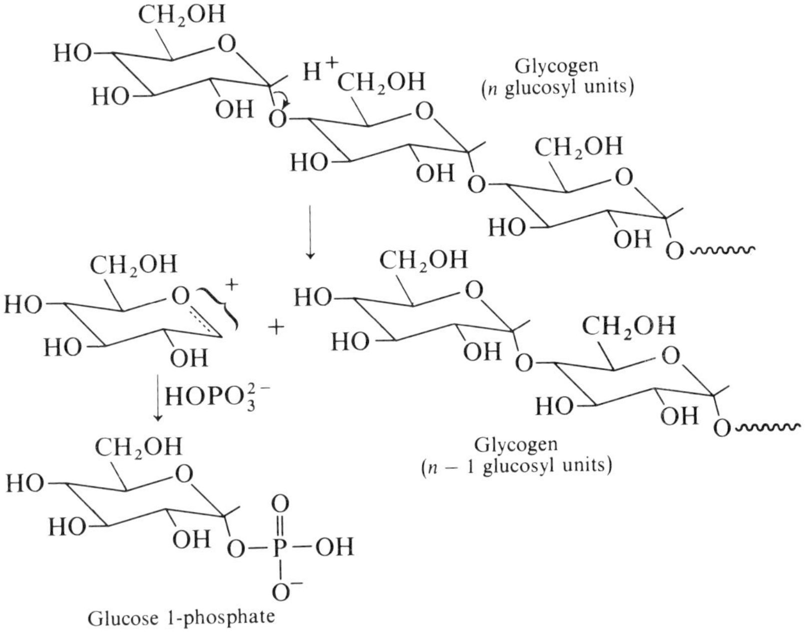

[Reaction scheme showing glycogen (n glucosyl units) + $HOPO_3^{2-}$ → glucose 1-phosphate + glycogen (n − 1 glucosyl units)]

## Regulation of Glycogen Metabolism

Glycogen metabolism in mammals is regulated in part by the phosphorylation and dephosphorylation of certain enzymes. Specific kinases catalyze the phosphorylation reactions, and specific phosphatases catalyze the dephosphorylation reactions. The presence of a phosphoprotein phosphatase (phosphoprotein phosphohydrolase, EC 3.1.3.16) has been demonstrated in most of the mammalian tissues that carry out glycogen metabolism. For example, a phosphatase that catalyzes the dephosphorylation of glycogen synthase b has been isolated from rabbit skeletal muscle and purified,[†] while one that catalyzes the dephosphorylation of phosphorylase a has been isolated from rabbit liver and purified.[‡] In fact, the latter has been extensively purified and found to be a single polypeptide chain which has a molecular weight of 34,000. There is now considerable speculation that when the phosphatase which catalyzes the dephosphorylation of glycogen synthase b and that which catalyzes the dephosphorylation of the active form of phosphorylase kinase are purified and characterized, it will be found that a single enzyme catalyzes

---

[†] Kato, K., and Bishop, J. S. (1972) *J. Biol. Chem.* **247**, 7420–7429.
[‡] Brandt, H., Capulong, Z. L., and Lee, E. Y. C. (1975) *J. Biol. Chem.* **250**, 8038–8044.

all three dephosphorylation reactions involved in glycogen metabolism. The interrelated reactions in mammalian glycogen metabolism are summarized diagrammatically in the figure below:

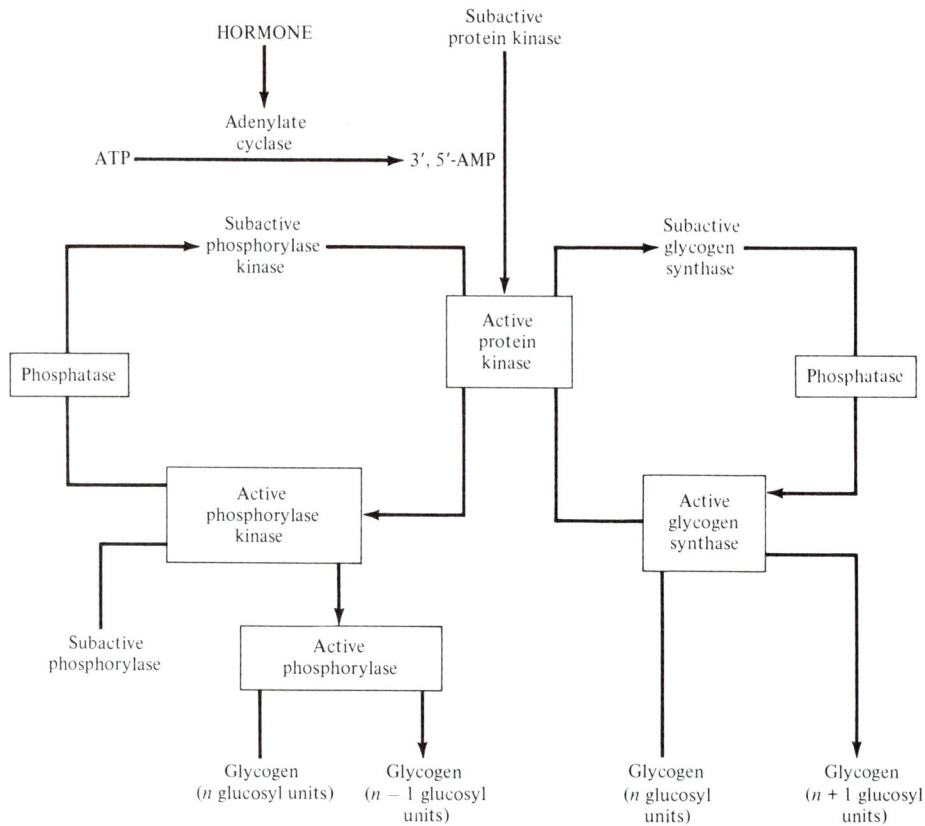

The reaction catalyzed by glycogen synthase is rate-determining with respect to glycogen formation, while glycogen degradation is carried out by the single reaction catalyzed by phosphorylase. As mentioned earlier, the available concentrations of 3′,5′-AMP are under hormonal control. Specifically, both epinephrine and glucagon in the liver and epinephrine in skeletal muscle increase the activity of the enzyme adenylate cyclase [ATP pyrophosphate-lyase (cyclizing), EC 4.6.1.1], which catalyzes the synthesis of 3′,5′-AMP. The synthesis is

$$\text{ATP} \rightleftharpoons 3',5'\text{-AMP} + \text{PP}_i \qquad (9\text{-}22)$$

Adenylate cyclase is a component of the surface membrane of the liver and the skeletal muscle (and other) cells. Epinephrine or glucagon that is being transported by the blood interacts with specific receptors on the outer surface of the membrane, and as a result the activity of the membrane-bound adenylate cyclase is enhanced.

Thus, an increase in the circulating level of the appropriate hormone brings about an increase in the concentration of 3′,5′-AMP in the appropriate tissue. In the present case, the cyclic nucleotide can be introduced into the cytoplasm, where it interacts with the protein kinase. As an ultimate result of this interaction, glycogen synthesis is impeded while glycogen degradation is promoted. When one considers that epinephrine and glucagon are hormones that are elaborated in response to certain types of stress, the appropriateness of this system of controls becomes apparent. As a result of the stress, energy is required, and this is precisely the resultant of the regulatory system just described. Glycogen is degraded so that ADP can undergo phosphorylation to ATP, and lest this process be thwarted, the synthesis of glycogen is impeded.

In addition to this rather complex cascading system, mammalian glycogen metabolism can be regulated as a result of the prevailing levels of certain metabolic intermediates, including AMP, ATP, and glucose 6-phosphate. The effect of these modulators is similar to that of some of the modulators of the rate of glycolysis. Thus, in the present case, during periods of carbohydrate deprivation concentrations of ATP and glucose 6-phosphate are diminished while that of AMP is increased. Under these circumstances glycogen degradation by phosphorylase will be promoted, since phosphorylase *b* will be able to function catalytically (without having to be converted into phosphorylase *a*). When the opposite situation prevails, the inhibitory effects of ATP and glucose 6-phosphate upon the activity of phosphorylase *b* will diminish the extent to which glycogen is degraded.

In organisms that synthesize glycogen from glucosyl moieties derived from ADP-glucose, the reaction in which ADP-glucose is formed is rate-determining and not the reaction catalyzed by the synthase. Thus, as might be expected, the activity of bacterial glycogen synthase is not subject to the elaborate phosphorylation-dephosphorylation system of controls; instead the control mechanisms are focused upon the activity of glucose-1-phosphate adenylyltransferase. As mentioned above, various metabolic intermediates function as modulators of the activities of the various adenylyltransferases. In *E. coli* it has been proposed that there is coordinate control of glycogen synthesis and glycolysis by means of the following mechanism, which becomes operative when the intracellular concentration of ATP falls below a critical level. Upon this signal, the activity of phosphofructokinase is enhanced, as described earlier, and this results in a decrease in the intracellular concentration of glucose 6-phosphate. (More glucose 6-phosphate is converted into fructose 6-phosphate, which is a substrate for phosphofructokinase.) This lowered concentration of glucose 6-phosphate results in less of this intermediate being converted into glucose 1-phosphate, which is a substrate in the rate-determining reaction of glycogen synthesis. Hence, in response to diminished ATP concentrations the rate of glycolysis is enhanced while the rate of glycogen synthesis is impeded.† This is precisely the needed response.

---

† Dietzler, D. N., Leckie, M. P., Magnani, J. L., Sughrue, M. J., and Bergstein, P. E. (1975) *J. Biol. Chem.* **250**, 7194–7203.

# ANOTHER PATHWAY OF CARBOHYDRATE CATABOLISM: THE PENTOSE PHOSPHATE PATHWAY

In addition to the glycolytic pathway, which converts a molecule of glucose into two molecules of pyruvate, there are other pathways by which carbohydrates can be degraded. One of these is the pentose phosphate pathway, which allows C(1) of glucose to be oxidized to $CO_2$. The reactions of the pentose phosphate pathway, like those of the glycolytic pathway, utilize the phosphoryl derivatives of the various intermediates involved. These intermediates include hexoses, pentoses, tetroses, and trioses, each of which is present as its phosphoryl derivative. The pentose phosphate pathway also includes a series of rearrangements of the carbon skeletons of these intermediates, as will be seen.

## Oxidation of C(1) of Glucose 6-Phosphate

Initially, glucose is converted into glucose 6-phosphate, as described when the glycolytic pathway was discussed. Glucose 6-phosphate then undergoes oxidation of C(1) by means of a reaction catalyzed by glucose-6-phosphate dehydrogenase (D-glucose-6-phosphate:$NADP^+$ 1-oxidoreductase, EC1.1.1.49). The oxidation-reduction reaction is

$$\text{D-Glucose 6-phosphate} + NADP^+ \rightleftharpoons \text{D-glucono-}\delta\text{-lactone-6-phosphate} + NADPH \quad (9\text{-}23)$$

Since the discovery of glucose-6-phosphate dehydrogenase by Warburg and Christian in 1931, the enzyme has been isolated from a variety of sources including the human erythrocyte; bovine mammary glands, ovaries, and adrenals; and rat liver. The dehydrogenase from bovine adrenals has been extensively purified and, in fact, crystallized. This enzyme has been found to be a tetramer which is composed of four apparently identical subunits, each with a molecular weight of 64,000.[†]

Kinetic studies on glucose-6-phosphate dehydrogenase have been attended by some problems due to the instability of the product, gluconolactone 6-phosphate, which has a half-life of 1.5 min at pH 7.4. However, the available data support an ordered sequential mechanism, and studies on a dehydrogenase from the microorganism *Leuconostoc mesenteroides* have provided evidence that $NADP^+$ is the initial substrate that binds while NADPH is the final product that is released.[‡]

In view of the fact that glucose-6-phosphate dehydrogenase catalyzes the rate-determining step of the pentose phosphate pathway, it is not surprising that the activity of this enzyme is subject to modulation. To a large extent, this modulation involves alterations in the rates of enzyme synthesis and enzyme degradation, which will be discussed later. In addition, there is evidence that in the human erythrocyte, at least, the activity of the dehydrogenase can be modulated as a result of one of the products, NADPH, functioning as an allosteric ligand. Specifically, it has been

---

[†] Singh, D., and Squire, P. G. (1974) *Biochemistry* **13**, 1819–1825.
[‡] Olive, C., Geroch, M. E., and Levy, H. R. (1971) *J. Biol. Chem.* **246**, 2047–2057.

proposed that when concentrations of the substrate $NADP^+$ are low, NADPH can bind at an allosteric site and thereby cause the binding of $NADP^+$ to change from a cooperative mode to a noncooperative mode. Within this framework NADPH is thus functioning as an activator or deinhibitor.

In the microorganism *E. coli*, on the other hand, it is NADH that functions as an allosteric ligand. Again, the binding of the modulator is associated with a change in the nature of the binding of the substrate, $NADP^+$, although in this case the change is from noncooperative to cooperative. Hence, NADH is seen as an inhibitor. In yeast, on the other hand, ATP is an inhibitor of the activity of glucose-6-phosphate dehydrogenase, and the inhibition has been shown to be noncompetitive with respect to glucose 6-phosphate.

The reaction catalyzed by glucose-6-phosphate dehydrogenase entails the oxidation of C(1) of the hexose phosphate, with the formation of a lactone. The transfer of the hydride ion is specifically to the *si* face of the pyridinium moiety of $NADP^+$.

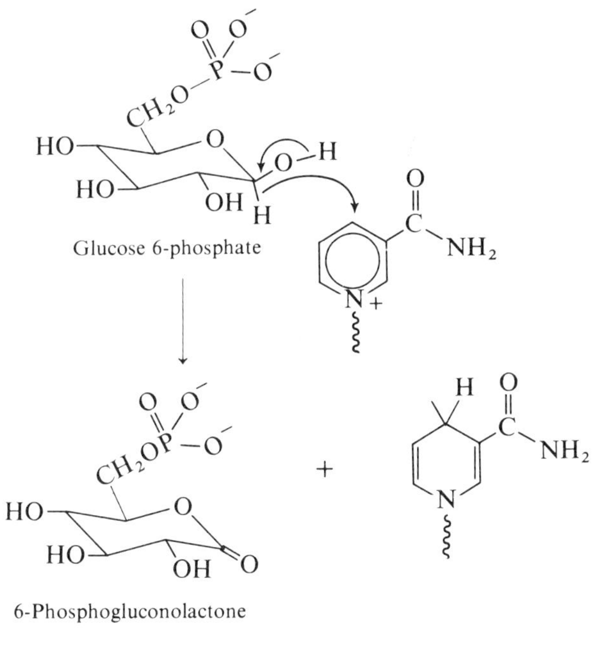

Glucose 6-phosphate

6-Phosphogluconolactone

## Decarboxylation of 6-Phosphogluconate

The lactone formed as a result of the reaction catalyzed by glucose-6-phosphate dehydrogenase is first hydrolyzed to yield the corresponding hydroxy acid, which then undergoes oxidation and decarboxylation. The hydrolysis is catalyzed by gluconolactonase (D-glucono-δ-lactone hydrolase, EC 3.1.1.17). Oxidation and decarboxylation are catalyzed by phosphogluconate dehydrogenase (decarboxylating) [6-phospho-D-gluconate:$NADP^+$ 2-oxidoreductase (decarboxylating), EC

1.1.1.44]. The reaction is

6-Phospho-D-gluconate + NADP$^+$ $\rightleftharpoons$ D-ribulose 5-phosphate
    + $CO_2$ + NADPH   (9-24)

Again, NADP$^+$ is the substrate, and NADPH is formed.

Phosphogluconate dehydrogenase was first isolated from the yeast *Candida utilis*. Since then, dehydrogenases have been isolated from other sources, including ovine liver, rat liver, human erythrocytes, *Neurospora*, and *Streptococcus faecalis*. Each of these enzymes, including that from *C. utilis*, has a molecular weight of approximately $1 \times 10^5$ and is composed of two apparently identical subunits, which in the enzyme from *Streptococcus* have a molecular weight of 57,000.

Kinetic studies conducted on phosphogluconate dehydrogenase from ovine liver indicated that the mechanism of the reaction is a sequential one since the initial-velocity plots intersect. Subsequently, a choice between an ordered and a random mechanism was made in the following manner. The reverse reaction, a terreactant process, was studied because the initial-velocity equations for a terreactant ordered sequential reaction and a terreactant random sequential reaction can be distinguished: the equation for the ordered process lacks the interaction term for A and C since an enzyme-A-C complex is not formed. Since the initial-velocity data for the reductive carboxylation of ribulose 5-phosphate were best fitted by the appropriate equation lacking an interaction term for A and C, one was able to imply that the reaction catalyzed by phosphogluconate dehydrogenase occurred by an ordered sequential process. In addition, it was determined that NADPH and NADP$^+$ can each bind the free enzyme. Also, it has previously been suggested that when the reductive carboxylation is being conducted, ribulose 5-phosphate and NADPH can bind the enzyme in the absence of $CO_2$. Therefore, on the basis of the accumulated data the following kinetic mechanism was formulated.†

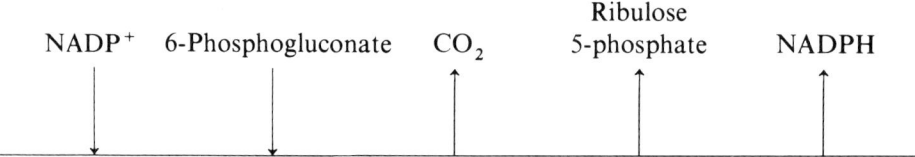

The activity of phosphogluconate dehydrogenase from ovine liver is inhibited in the presence of fructose 1,6-bisphosphate and since the inhibition appears to be competitive when 6-phosphogluconate is varied, it is implied that the modulator binds the same site as this substrate.

The reaction mechanism of the formation of ribulose 5-phosphate has been formulated in terms of an initial oxidation of the secondary alcohol group at C(3) of 6-phosphogluconate followed by the decarboxylation of the resulting 3-oxo acid, but it has been impossible to demonstrate the existence of the proposed intermediate, 3-oxo-6-phosphogluconate. It must be assumed that if such an intermediate is in fact

---

† Villet, R. H., and Dalziel, K. (1972) *Eur. J. Biochem.* **27**, 244–250.

formed, its lifetime is relatively short and it can never dissociate from the enzyme. The reaction might be depicted as shown.

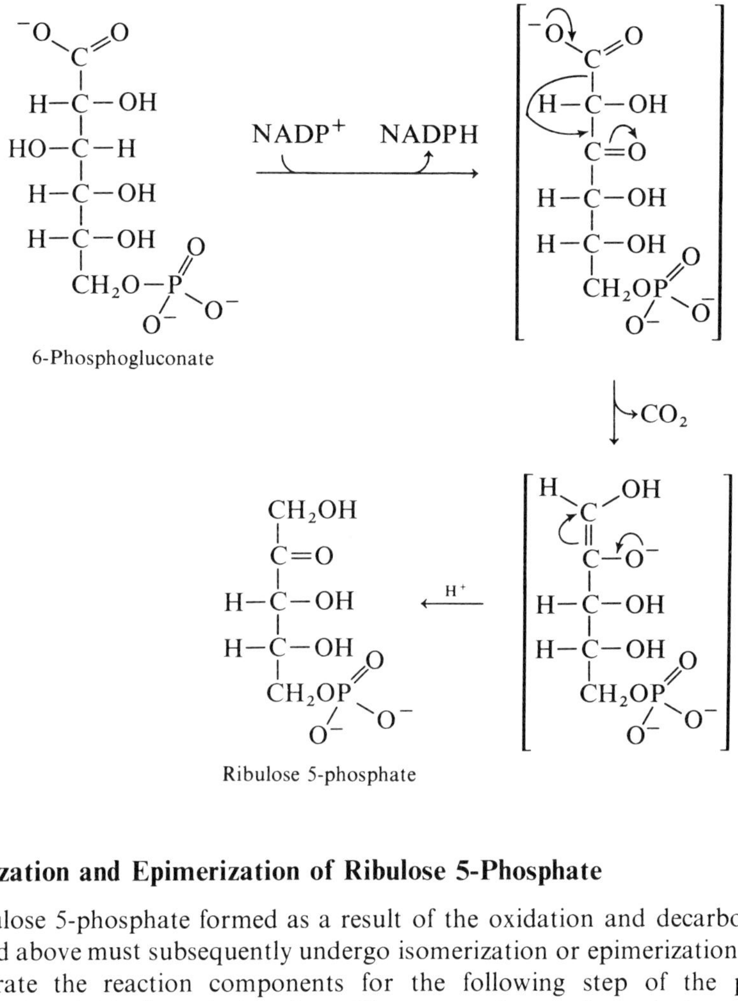

$$
\begin{array}{c}
^-O\diagdown C \diagup ^O \\
| \\
H-C-OH \\
| \\
HO-C-H \\
| \\
H-C-OH \\
| \\
H-C-OH \\
| \\
CH_2O-PO_3^{2-}
\end{array}
\quad \xrightarrow{NADP^+ \quad NADPH} \quad
\left[\begin{array}{c}
^-O\diagdown C \diagup ^O \\
| \\
H-C-OH \\
| \\
C=O \\
| \\
H-C-OH \\
| \\
H-C-OH \\
| \\
CH_2OPO_3^{2-}
\end{array}\right]
$$

6-Phosphogluconate

$$\downarrow CO_2$$

$$
\begin{array}{c}
CH_2OH \\
| \\
C=O \\
| \\
H-C-OH \\
| \\
H-C-OH \\
| \\
CH_2OPO_3^{2-}
\end{array}
\quad \xleftarrow{H^+} \quad
\left[\begin{array}{c}
H\diagdown C\diagup OH \\
\| \\
C-O^- \\
| \\
H-C-OH \\
| \\
H-C-OH \\
| \\
CH_2OPO_3^{2-}
\end{array}\right]
$$

Ribulose 5-phosphate

## Isomerization and Epimerization of Ribulose 5-Phosphate

The ribulose 5-phosphate formed as a result of the oxidation and decarboxylation described above must subsequently undergo isomerization or epimerization in order to generate the reaction components for the following step of the pathway. Isomerization yields ribose 5-phosphate. The enzyme that catalyzes the isomerization is ribosephosphate isomerase (D-ribose-5-phosphate ketol-isomerase, EC 5.3.1.6). The reaction can be written

$$\text{D-Ribulose 5-phosphate} \rightleftharpoons \text{D-ribose 5-phosphate} \qquad (9\text{-}25)$$

Epimerization, on the other hand, yields xylulose 5-phosphate as the result of a reaction catalyzed by ribulosephosphate 3-epimerase (D-ribulose-5-phosphate 3-epimerase, EC 5.1.3.1). The epimerization reaction is

$$\text{D-Ribulose 5-phosphate} \rightleftharpoons \text{D-xylulose 5-phosphate} \qquad (9\text{-}26)$$

The reaction catalyzed by the isomerase has been assumed to be another example of an aldose-ketose isomerization involving an enediol intermediate, although this has not been firmly established since the enzyme has yet to be extensively purified. The 3-epimerase has been purified in a few cases, on the other hand, and an enzyme from yeast has been reported to have a molecular weight of 46,000. The reaction mechanism of the epimerization has likewise been formulated in terms of an enediol intermediate.

## Formation of Sedoheptulose 7-Phosphate

As mentioned before, the pentose pathway entails several rearrangements of carbon skeletons. The first to be discussed is one which results in the formation of sedoheptulose 7-phosphate. This rearrangement is catalyzed by an enzyme referred to as transketolase (sedoheptulose-7-phosphate:D-glyceraldehyde-3-phosphate glycolaldehydetransferase, EC 2.2.1.1.). Transketolase catalyzes the reaction

D-Ribose 5-phosphate + D-xylulose 5-phosphate $\rightleftharpoons$
$$\text{sedoheptulose 7-phosphate + D-glyceraldehyde 3-phosphate} \quad (9\text{-}27)$$

The enzyme transketolase requires thiamine diphosphate as a cofactor, and in fact the thiazolium ring of this cofactor is a participant in the reaction. The proton at C(2) of this ring is readily ionizable, and therefore the ring exists as an ylide, which can function as a nucleophile. In fact, this nucleophilic species participates in several biochemical reactions, and in each instance its participation entails an attack upon a carbonyl carbon atom. In the present case it is the carbon atom of the oxo group of xylulose 5-phosphate that is attacked by the nucleophilic C(2) of the thiazolium moiety. This results in the elimination of glyceraldehyde 3-phosphate and the formation of a 2-(1,2-dihydroxyethyl)-thiamine diphosphate. Now since this intermediate can also function as a nucleophile, it can attack the carbonyl carbon atom of ribose 5-phosphate; in this manner the carbon atoms that were C(1) and C(2) of xylulose 5-phosphate are donated to ribose 5-phosphate, with the result that sedoheptulose 7-phosphate is formed. Thus, this rearrangement utilizes two five-carbon molecules for the synthesis of a seven-carbon molecule and a three-carbon molecule. A minimal reaction mechanism is shown on page 397.

## Cleavage of Sedoheptulose 7-Phosphate

The following step of the pentose phosphate pathway is a dealdolization reaction which results in the cleavage of sedoheptulose 7-phosphate. This reaction, which is also a rearrangement of the carbon skeleton, is catalyzed by transaldolase (sedoheptulose-7-phosphate:D-glyceraldehyde-3-phosphate dihydroxyacetonetransferase, EC 2.2.1.2). The reaction is

Sedoheptulose 7-phosphate + D-glyceraldehyde 3-phosphate $\rightleftharpoons$
$$\text{D-erythrose 4-phosphate + D-fructose 6-phosphate} \quad (9\text{-}28)$$

The reaction entails the transfer of C(1), C(2), and C(3) from sedoheptulose 7-phosphate to glyceraldehyde 3-phosphate. Transaldolase can also utilize donor substrates other than sedoheptulose 7-phosphate and acceptor substrates other than glyceraldehyde 3-phosphate, although with less efficiency in all cases.

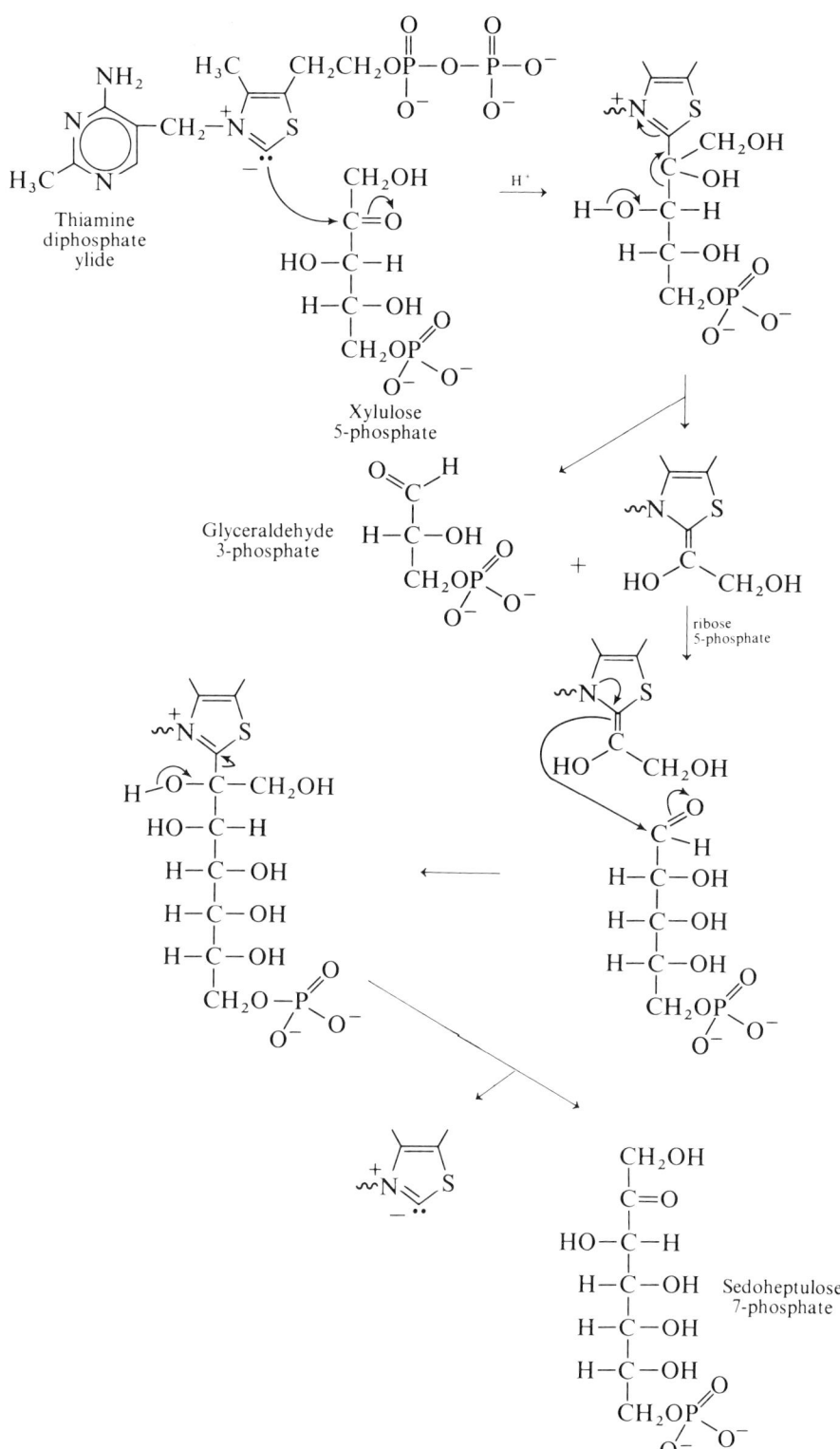

Two forms of transaldolase have been isolated from the yeast *Candida utilis*. One has a molecular weight of 76,000 and the other a molecular weight of 65,000. Each form is composed of two subunits.

The reaction mechanism of the cleavage of sedoheptulose 7-phosphate entails the initial formation of a Schiff base derived from the C(2) oxo group of the seven-carbon substrate and an $\epsilon$-amino group of a specific lysyl unit at the catalytic site of the enzyme. This is reminiscent of the reaction catalyzed by fructose-bisphosphate aldolase. Following the covalent bonding, and just as in the reaction catalyzed by the aldolase, a fragment comprising the carbon atoms beyond C(3) is eliminated while the first three carbon atoms of the substrate remain bound at the catalytic site. In the present case the species eliminated is erythrose 4-phosphate and the three-carbon moiety bound at the catalytic site has the characteristics of a nucleophile, which then attacks the carbonyl carbon atom of glyceraldehyde 3-phosphate. With the transfer of this three-carbon moiety to glyceraldehyde 3-phosphate, fructose 6-phosphate is formed.

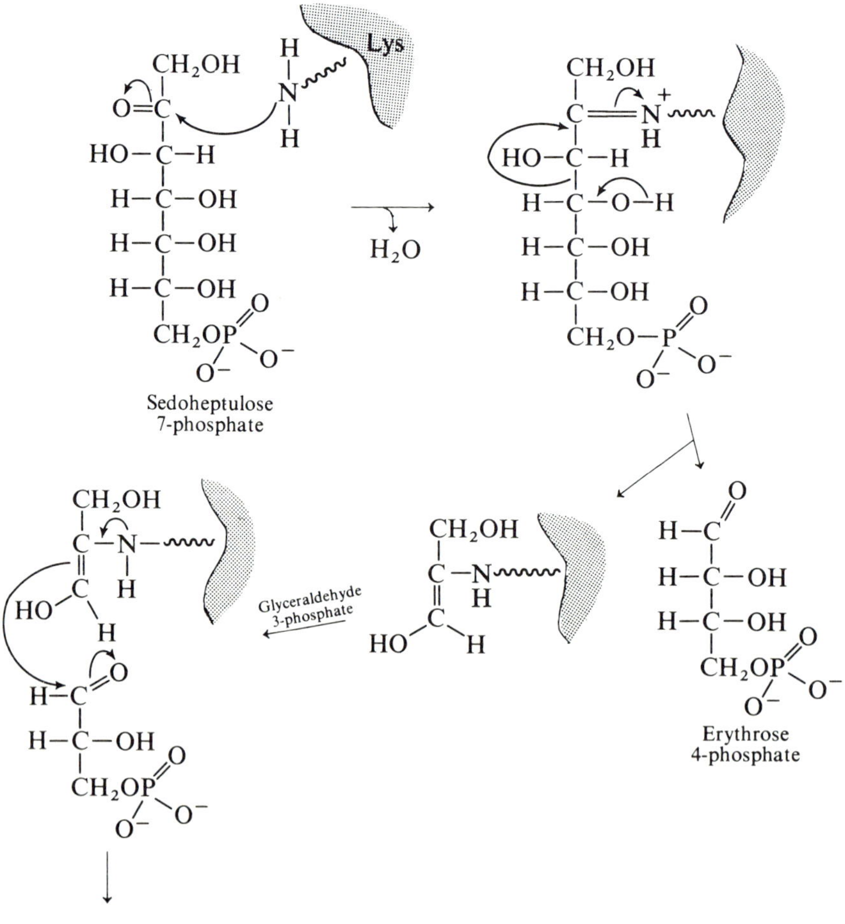

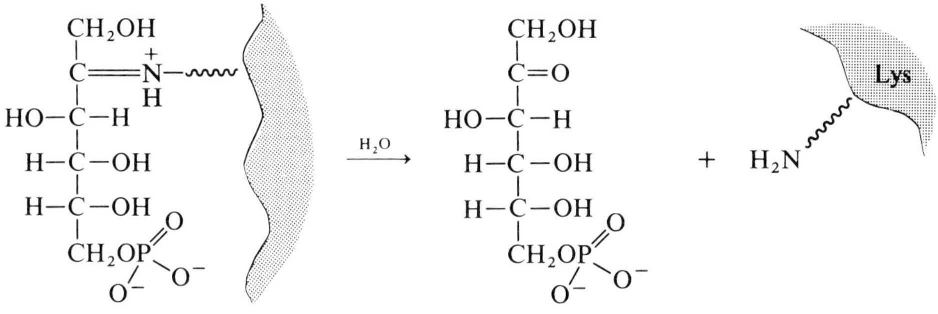

$$\begin{array}{c} CH_2OH \\ | \\ C=\overset{+}{\underset{H}{N}}-\text{\large\textasciitilde} \\ | \\ HO-C-H \\ | \\ H-C-OH \\ | \\ H-C-OH \\ | \\ CH_2OP(=O)(O^-)(O^-) \end{array} \xrightarrow{H_2O} \begin{array}{c} CH_2OH \\ | \\ C=O \\ | \\ HO-C-H \\ | \\ H-C-OH \\ | \\ H-C-OH \\ | \\ CH_2OP(=O)(O^-)(O^-) \end{array} + H_2N-\text{Lys}$$

Fructose 6-phosphate

## Additional Reactions Resulting in the Formation of Fructose 6-Phosphate

The erythrose 4-phosphate that results from the cleavage of sedoheptulose 7-phosphate can subsequently be utilized in the synthesis of fructose 6-phosphate. To this end and in the presence of a molecule of xylulose 5-phosphate and the enzyme transketolase, glyceraldehyde 3-phosphate and an enzyme-bound two-carbon moiety are generated. This two-carbon moiety can then be transferred to erythrose 4-phosphate, and fructose 6-phosphate is formed. Recall that fructose 6-phosphate can also be formed from two molecules of glyceraldehyde 3-phosphate. The required reactions have already been discussed within the framework of the gluconeogenic pathway.

## Summary of the Pentose Phosphate Pathway

As a result of the oxidation-reduction reactions and the rearrangements of the carbon atoms, certain carbon atoms of glucose are oxidized to $CO_2$ while the remaining ones are incorporated into fructose 6-phosphate. The latter can, of course, be converted into glucose 6-phosphate, which can then reenter the pentose phosphate pathway. Because of the numerous rearrangements of the carbon skeletons of the intermediates of this pathway the stoichiometry of its net reaction is somewhat difficult to formulate. One way in which this is frequently done is as follows:

6 Glucose 6-phosphate + 12 NADP$^+$ $\longrightarrow$
$\quad$ 6 $CO_2$ + 5 fructose 6-phosphate + 6 P$_i$ + 12 NADPH + 12 H$^+$ $\quad$ (9-29)

The pathway is summarized in Fig. 9-6.

## Regulation of the Pentose Phosphate Pathway

In most organisms the principal function of the pentose phosphate pathway is thought to be that of supplying the NADPH that is required by many anabolic pathways. Perhaps, then, it is not surprising that the rate-determining reaction of the pentose phosphate pathway is the one which is catalyzed by glucose-6-phosphate dehydrogenase. This reaction is not only the first that is unique to this pathway but also the first of the two that produce NADPH.

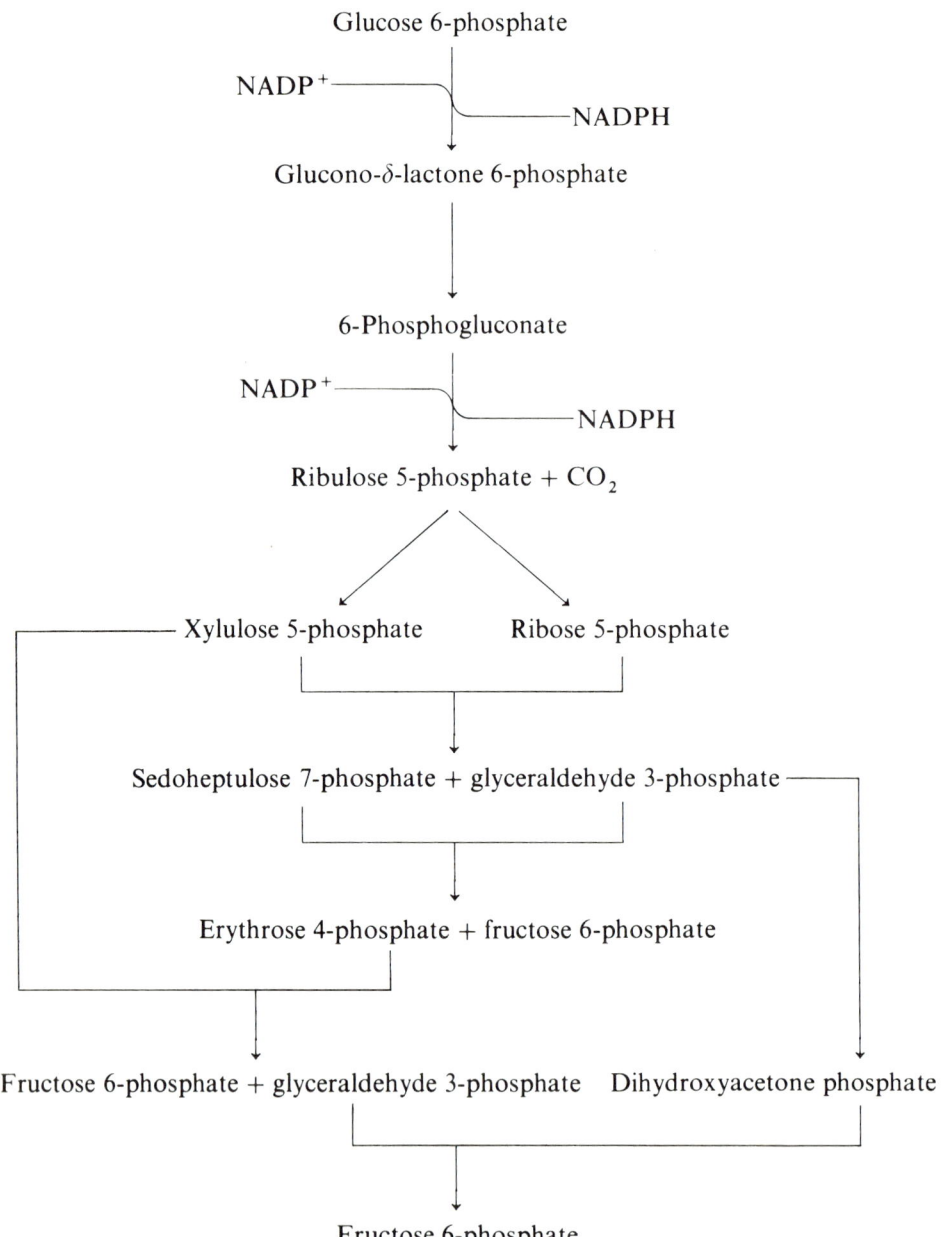

**Figure 9-6** Summary of the pentose phosphate pathway.

In mammals, activities of glucose-6-phosphate dehydrogenases are sensitive to hormonal state, nutritional state, and genetic modification. More than 50 genetic variants of this enzyme have been identified in human erythrocytes alone. Each of these variants is believed to result from a mutation which causes the synthesis of an enzyme which has an abnormal primary structure. In some instances it is known that this is a single point mutation which results in the substitution of one amino acid for another. Such a substitution can, however, induce significant changes in the apparent level of glucose-6-phosphate dehydrogenase activity. For example, one genetic variant in which a tyrosyl unit is substituted for a histidyl unit is associated with a fourfold increase in enzyme activity. On the other hand, the genetic variant present in the erythrocytes of those who exhibit "glucose-6-phosphate dehydrogenase deficiency" (a pathological condition characterized by an abnormal sensitivity to certain drugs) is associated with diminished levels of dehydrogenase activity. In the former case it has been shown that the increased activity is the result of an increased rate of enzyme synthesis. In the latter, the "deficiency" is the result of an increased rate of enzyme degradation. More specifically, it has been shown that while the corresponding normal enzyme has a half-life of 62 days, the variant has a half-life of only 13 days.

Certain hormones influence the rate at which glucose-6-phosphate dehydrogenase is synthesized. Estradiol, for example, induces increased enzyme synthesis in rat uteri and this effect can be blocked by prior administration of cycloheximide or actinomycin D.[†] Since cycloheximide blocks protein synthesis at the level of translation while actinomycin blocks protein synthesis at the level of transcription, it appears that the hormone can modulate enzyme synthesis at both the translational and transcriptional levels. (Protein synthesis is discussed in detail in Chap. 14.)

It has also been reported that glucagon inhibits the induction of glucose-6-phosphate dehydrogenase, which can occur in rat liver in response to an increased intake of carbohydrate.[‡] This effect is duplicated if $3',5'$-AMP is administered rather than the hormone. Thus, it is indicated that this is another example of a hormone-initiated regulatory mechanism that is mediated by $3',5'$-AMP. In the present case it has been proposed that this action of glucagon is coordinated with that which modulates the activity of the enzymes of glycogen metabolism. In both instances the hormone would cause glucose 6-phosphate to be diverted from other pathways, i.e., from glycogen synthesis and the pentose phosphate pathway, in order to be utilized by the glycolytic pathway.

Finally, it may be mentioned that although glucose-6-phosphate dehydrogenase from mammalian sources and from certain microorganisms (including yeasts and *E. coli*) exhibit absolute or nearly absolute specificity with respect to the cofactor $NADP^+$ (or NADPH), there are organisms in which glucose-6-phosphate dehydrogenase activity that utilizes or requires $NAD^+$ can be demonstrated. It has been shown in at least some of these cases that the principal function of the

---

[†] Smith, E. R., and Barker, K. L. (1974) *J. Biol. Chem.* **249**, 6541–6547.
[‡] Garcia, D. R., and Holten, D. (1975) *J. Biol. Chem.* **250**, 3960–3965.

pentose phosphate pathway is that of providing an energy source rather than reducing equivalents for anabolic reactions. It is therefore not surprising that in these cases the activity of the $NAD^+$-dependent glucose-6-phosphate dehydrogenase is inhibited by ATP.

## HEXOSE INTERCONVERSIONS

The glycolytic pathway, the pathway of glycogen synthesis, and the pentose phosphate pathway all utilize glucose. This does not mean, however, that the carbon atoms of other hexoses cannot be used by these pathways. Rather, the carbon atoms of other hexoses can be converted to those of glucose, as described below.

### Formation of Glucose 6-Phosphate from Galactose

When carbon atoms of galactose are to be used by one of the pathways mentioned above, the hexose initially undergoes phosphorylation at C(1). This is catalyzed by galactokinase (ATP:D-galactose 1-phosphotransferase, EC 2.7.1.6). This reaction is

$$\text{D-Galactose} + \text{ATP} \rightleftharpoons \alpha\text{-D-galactose 1-phosphate} + \text{ADP} \quad (9\text{-}30)$$

Next, the galactose 1-phosphate is converted to uridine diphosphogalactose by a reaction catalyzed by hexose-1-phosphate uridylyltransferase (UDPglucose:α-D-galactose-1-phosphate uridylyltransferase, EC 2.7.7.12). This reaction can be written

$$\alpha\text{-D-Galactose 1-phosphate} + \text{UDP-glucose} \rightleftharpoons \text{UDP-galactose} + \alpha\text{-D-glucose 1-phosphate} \quad (9\text{-}31)$$

Studies on a uridylyltransferase from *E. coli* have shown that during the reaction a uridylyl-enzyme intermediate can be formed. This suggests that the reaction may proceed by a ping pong kinetic mechanism. Further support for this proposal was subsequently provided when it was observed that the [*uracil*-5,6-$^3$H]UDP-glucose–UDP-galactose exchange occurs in the absence of added hexose phosphates and also that the [*glucose*-U-$^{14}$C]UDP-glucose–glucose 1-phosphate exchange occurs in the absence of added galactose 1-phosphate.†

Next, UDP-galactose can be converted into UDP-glucose by a reaction catalyzed by UDPglucose 4-epimerase (UDPglucose 4-epimerase, EC 5.1.3.2). The epimerization requires $NAD^+$ and has been shown to proceed by formation of a 4-oxo hexose intermediate. The secondary alcohol group at C(4) of the galactose moiety is oxidized and then subsequently reduced to yield the secondary alcohol group having the epimeric configuration. The glucosyl moiety of UDP-glucose can subsequently be converted into that of glucose 1-phosphate and then into that of glucose 6-phosphate by reactions discussed previously.

---

† Wong, L.-J., and Frey, P. A. (1974) *J. Biol. Chem.* **249**, 2322–2324.

## Formation of Glucose 6-Phosphate from Mannose

Mannose undergoes phosphorylation at C(6) as the result of a reaction catalyzed by either hexokinase or mannokinase (ATP:D-mannose 6-phosphotransferase, EC 2.7.1.7). The resulting mannose 6-phosphate can then be converted into fructose 6-phosphate in the presence of the enzyme mannosephosphate isomerase (D-mannose-6-phosphate ketol-isomerase, EC 5.3.1.8); this zinc metalloenzyme catalyzes a reaction which entails an enediol intermediate and is similar to that catalyzed by glucosephosphate isomerase. Fructose 6-phosphate can then enter into the glycolytic pathway, as such, or undergo isomerization to yield glucose 6-phosphate.

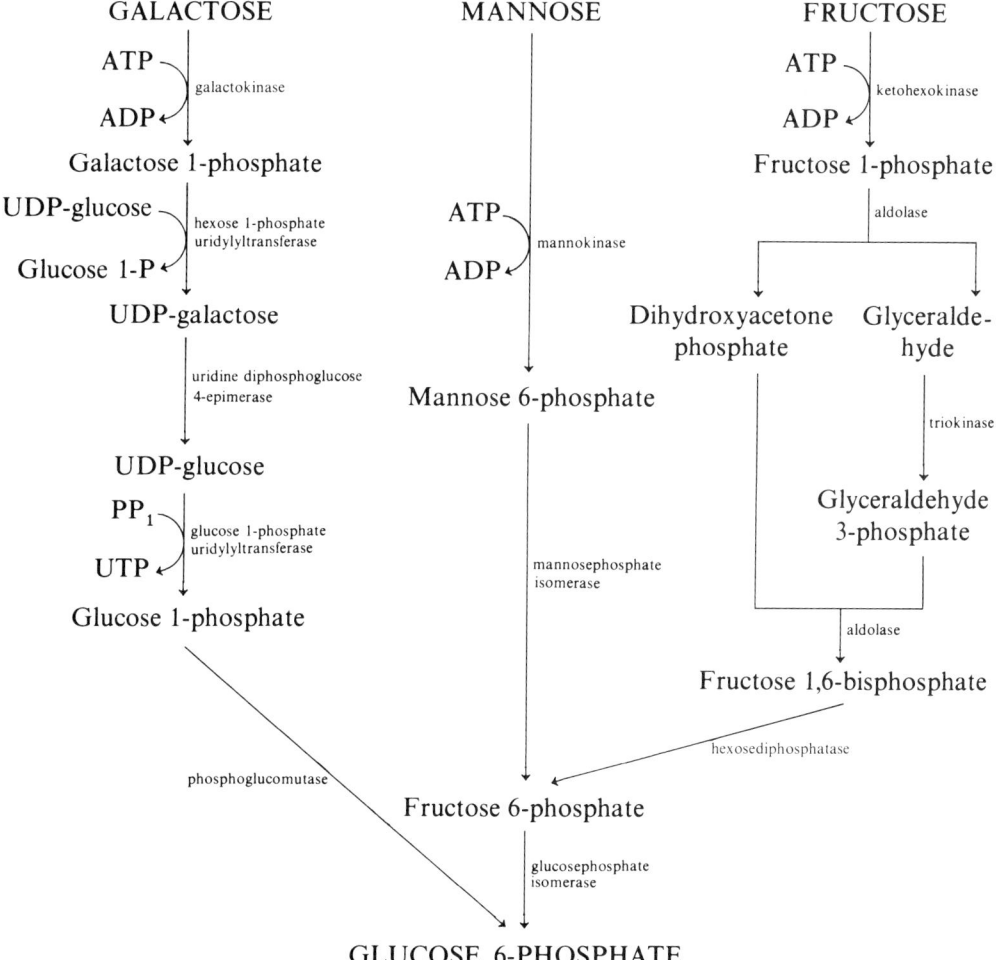

**Figure 9-7** Hexose interconversions.

## Formation of Glucose 6-Phosphate from Fructose

The pathway from fructose to glucose 6-phosphate begins with the phosphorylation of fructose at C(1), a reaction catalyzed by ketohexokinase (ATP:D-fructose 1-phosphotransferase, EC 2.7.1.3). The resulting fructose 1-phosphate then undergoes a dealdolization reaction catalyzed by fructose-bisphosphate aldolase (which also utilizes fructose 1,6-bisphosphate as a substrate). The dealdolization of fructose 1-phosphate can be written

$$\text{D-Fructose 1-phosphate} \rightleftharpoons \text{dihydroxyacetone phosphate} + \text{D-glyceraldehyde} \tag{9-32}$$

The glyceraldehyde then undergoes a phosphorylation reaction catalyzed by triokinase (ATP:D:glyceraldehyde 3-phosphotransferase, EC 2.7.1.28). The resulting glyceraldehyde 3-phosphate and dihydroxyacetone phosphate then undergo a condensation reaction (catalyzed by fructose-bisphosphate aldolase), and fructose 1,6-bisphosphate aldolase is formed. Hydrolysis of the C(1) phosphoryl group followed by isomerization of the fructose 6-phosphate yields glucose 6-phosphate.

## Summary of Hexose Interconversions

The conversion of the carbon atoms of galactose, mannose, and fructose into those of glucose 6-phosphate is summarized in Fig. 9-7.

# UTILIZATION OF PYRUVATE IN CERTAIN MICROORGANISMS

As mentioned at the beginning of this chapter, glucose is converted into two molecules of pyruvate by reactions of the glycolytic pathway, and subsequently pyruvate can be converted into the acetyl moiety of acetyl-CoA, which in turn can enter the tricarboxylic acid cycle. However, in the less complex organisms and under anaerobic conditions there are less complex fates for pyruvate. Pyruvate can be converted into acetaldehyde, which can, in turn, be converted into ethanol or acetate.

## Decarboxylation of Pyruvate

The conversion of pyruvate into acetaldehyde is catalyzed by pyruvate decarboxylase (2-oxo acid carboxy-lyase, EC 4.1.1.1), an enzyme that requires thiamine diphosphate. The reaction is

$$\text{Pyruvate} \rightleftharpoons \text{acetaldehyde} + CO_2 \tag{9-33}$$

A purified decarboxylase from yeast has a molecular weight of 208,000 and the enzyme comprises two subunits. Thiamine diphosphate participates in the reaction, much as in the reaction catalyzed by transketolase. In the present case, the strongly nucleophilic C(2) of the thiazolium ring attacks the carbonyl carbon atom of pyruvate, and as a result carbon dioxide is eliminated. The resulting two-carbon species then accepts a proton and dissociates from the enzyme as acetaldehyde.

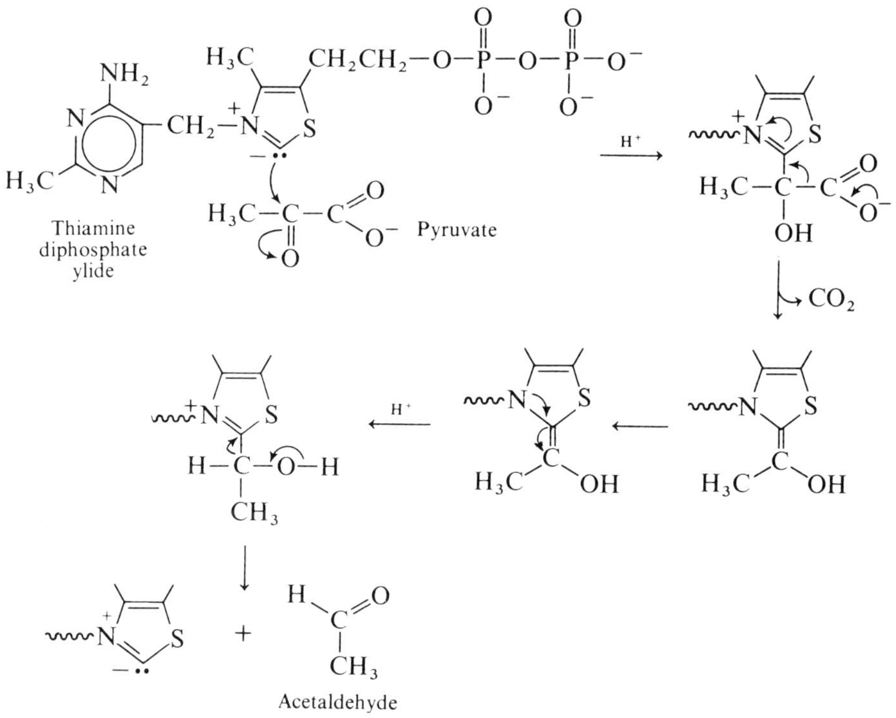

## Reduction of Acetaldehyde

Acetaldehyde can be reduced to ethanol in the presence of the enzyme alcohol dehydrogenase (alcohol:$NAD^+$ oxidoreductase EC 1.1.1.1). The reaction is

$$\text{Acetaldehyde} + \text{NADH} \rightleftharpoons \text{ethanol} + NAD^+ \tag{9-34}$$

As isolated from yeast alcohol dehydrogenase is a tetramer which has a molecular weight of 190,000. The active enzyme binds a single atom of $Zn^{2+}$. When kinetic studies were conducted on the yeast enzyme, the data indicated that the mechanism is probably random sequential although the formation of an enzyme-NADH complex is more facile than the formation of the other binary complex.

## Oxidation of Acetaldehyde

Acetaldehyde can also be oxidized to acetate by a reaction catalyzed by aldehyde dehydrogenase (aldehyde:$NAD^+$ oxidoreductase, EC 1.2.1.3). The reaction can be expressed as

$$\text{Acetaldehyde} + NAD^+ + H_2O \longrightarrow \text{acetate} + \text{NADH} \tag{9-35}$$

The reduction of acetate to acetaldehyde has not been demonstrated under any of the conditions used thus far.

An aldehyde dehydrogenase from yeast has been purified and found to have a molecular weight of $2 \times 10^5$. The oxidation proceeds by a sequential mechanism which again is thought to be random but with a preferred binding sequence.

## THE REDUCTIVE PENTOSE PHOSPHATE CYCLE OF PHOTOSYNTHESIS

Photosynthesis is the process by which carbon dioxide is assimilated and molecular oxygen is liberated through the agency of light energy. The light energy is utilized in processes which produce molecular oxygen (derived from water), ATP, and reducing equivalents. These processes will be discussed in Chap. 11, which focuses upon bioenergetics. The ATP and the reducing equivalents, in the form of NADPH, can subsequently be utilized in reactions required for the growth and maintenance of the organism. Here, the pathway by which carbon dioxide is incorporated into carbohydrates will be discussed.

The details of the pathway which allows carbon dioxide to be utilized for the synthesis of carbohydrate intermediates in green plants, algae, and photosynthetic bacteria were formulated by Melvin Calvin and James Bassham and their colleagues during the years from 1948 to 1960. Since the process is cyclic, it is sometimes referred to as the Calvin-Bassham cycle. It is also called the reductive pentose phosphate cycle. This cycle in fact shares part of the sequence of the gluconeogenic pathway, and it also includes reactions of the pentose phosphate pathway.

### Formation of Ribulose 1,5-Bisphosphate

In what might be called the initial reaction of the cycle, ribulose 5-phosphate undergoes phosphorylation. The reaction, shown below, is catalyzed by phosphoribulokinase (ATP:D-ribulose-5-phosphate 1-phosphotransferase, EC 2.7.1.19):

$$\text{D-Ribulose 5-phosphate} + \text{ATP} \rightleftharpoons \text{D-ribulose 1,5-bisphosphate} + \text{ADP} \quad (9\text{-}36)$$

### Carboxylation of Ribulose 1,5-Bisphosphate

The next reaction is that in which carbon dioxide is incorporated. It is catalyzed by ribulosebisphosphate carboxylase [3-phospho-D-glycerate carboxy-lyase (dimerizing), EC 4.1.1.39]. The reaction is

D-Ribulose 1,5-bisphosphate + $CO_2$ ⟶

(2-carboxy-3-dehydroribitol 1,5-bisphosphate) ⟶ 2 3-phosphoglycerate  (9-37)

The compound shown in parentheses is the postulated transient intermediate which would then undergo cleavage to yield two molecules of 3-phosphoglycerate.

Ribulosebisphosphate carboxylase has been isolated from a wide variety of plants, algae, and photosynthetic bacteria. The enzyme generally has a molecular weight of approximately $5 \times 10^5$. For example, the carboxylase from spinach leaves, which has been extensively studied, has a molecular weight of 560,000; those from chinese cabbage and *Chromatium* have a molecular weight of 511,000; and that from *Rhodopseudomonas speroides* has a molecular weight of 550,000. However, the carboxylase from *Rhodospirillum rubrum* has a molecular weight of only 112,000. Further examination of the carboxylase from spinach leaves has indicated that the enzyme is composed of two different types of subunits with the larger having a molecular weight of 56,000 and the smaller having a molecular weight of 14,000. The simplest structure compatible with the existing data is one in which the oligomeric enzyme is composed of eight large subunits and eight small ones, arranged so that there is a catalytic portion of the enzyme composed of the eight large subunits, while the eight small subunits have a regulatory function.† The enzyme has also been shown to bind one $Cu^{2+}$ per oligomer and to require $Mg^{2+}$. Other carboxylases from higher plants and algae are generally similar to the enzyme from spinach, although the smaller carboxylase from *Rhodospirillum rubrum* is composed of only two subunits which each have a molecular weight of 56,000.

Kinetic studies on ribulosephosphate carboxylase from *R. rubrum* have indicated that the reaction has a sequential mechanism,‡ and similar interpretations have been made on the basis of studies on carboxylases from other sources. It has also been observed that although plots of the reaction velocity as a function of the concentration of ribulose 1,5-bisphosphate are hyperbolic, comparable plots when carbon dioxide is the varied substrate are sigmoidal. Both the smaller carboxylase from *R. rubrum* and the larger enzyme from spinach exhibit this behavior. In the case of the spinach enzyme fructose 6-phosphate can cause the sigmoidal relationship between velocity and carbon dioxide concentration to become hyperbolic.§ Thus, fructose 6-phosphate functions as an activator. However, it was also shown that the effect of fructose 6-phosphate can be obliterated by fructose 1,6-bisphosphate, and therefore the activity of the carboxylase is in fact modulated by the relative concentrations of these two intermediates.

Ribulosebisphosphate carboxylase from spinach and other sources has now been found to catalyze not only the carboxylation of ribulose 1,5-bisphosphate but also the incorporation of molecular oxygen into this pentose phosphate. The incorporation of oxygen results in the formation of one molecule of phosphoglycolate and one of 3-phosphoglycerate.¶ This is called the *oxygenase activity* of the enzyme.

The reaction mechanism of the carboxylation of ribulose 1,5-bisphosphate has been examined with some interest since C(2) of the pentose phosphate and the carbon atom of carbon dioxide become bonded to each other and each is initially electrophilic. The proposed mechanism, however, involves the formation of a transient enediol:

Ribulose 1,5-bisphosphate

† Takabe, T., and Akazawa, T. (1975) *Biochemistry* **14**, 46–50.
‡ Tabita, F. R., and McFadden, B. A. (1974) *J. Biol. Chem.* **249**, 3459–3464.
§ Buchanan, B. B., and Schurmann, P. (1973) *J. Biol. Chem.* **248**, 4956–4964.
¶ Lorimer, G. H., Andrews, T. J., and Tolbert, N. E. (1973) *Biochemistry* **12**, 18–23.

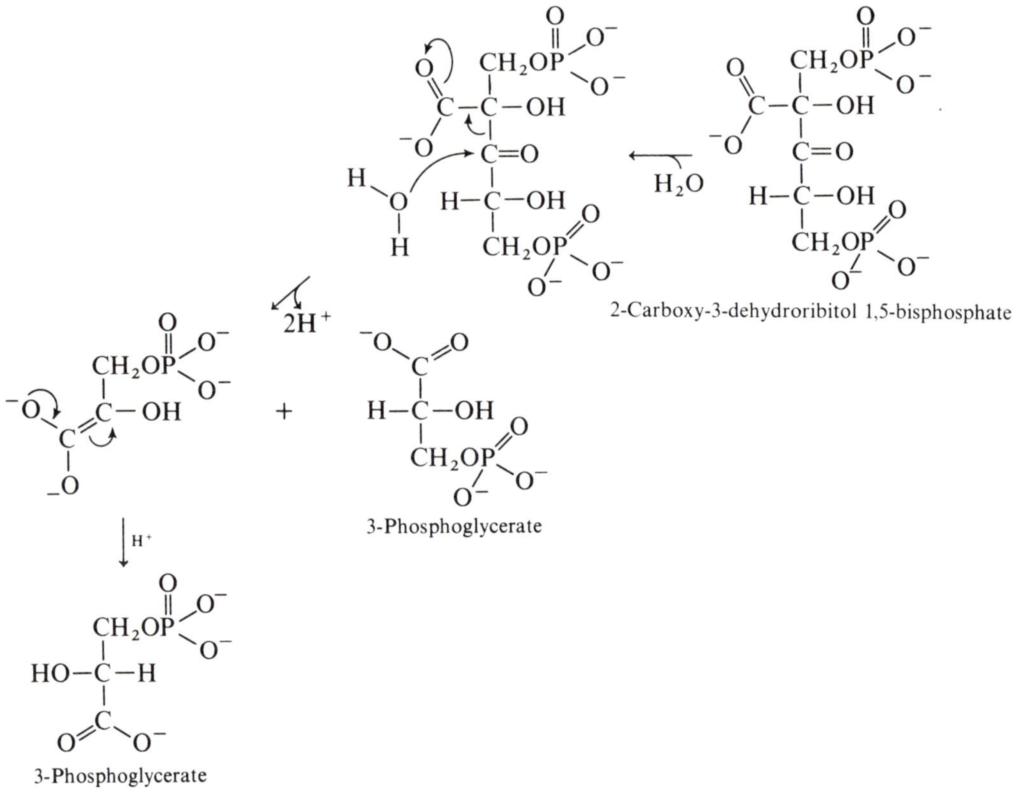

## Formation of Tetrose-, Pentose-, Hexose-, and Heptosephosphates

The remainder of the reductive pentose phosphate cycle entails reactions that with a few exceptions have been discussed within the framework of the gluconeogenic pathway or the pentose phosphate pathway. One of these exceptions involves the conversion of 3-phospho-D-glyceroyl phosphate into glyceraldehyde 3-phosphate through the agency of glyceraldehyde 3-phosphate dehydrogenase. As a part of the reductive pentose phosphate cycle this reaction is catalyzed by an $NADP^+$-dependent enzyme rather than an $NAD^+$-dependent enzyme. Another exception involves the aldol-type condensation of erythrose 4-phosphate and dihydroxyacetone phosphate to yield sedoheptulose 1,7-bisphosphate, which subsequently undergoes hydrolysis to yield sedoheptulose 7-phosphate.

## Summary of the Reductive Pentose Phosphate Cycle

The reactions of this pathway are summarized in Fig. 9-8.

## Regulation of the Reductive Pentose Phosphate Cycle

The rate-determining step in the reductive pentose phosphate cycle in green plants, algae, and photosynthetic bacteria is that in which the molecule of carbon dioxide is actually incorporated, i.e., the reaction catalyzed by ribulosebisphosphate

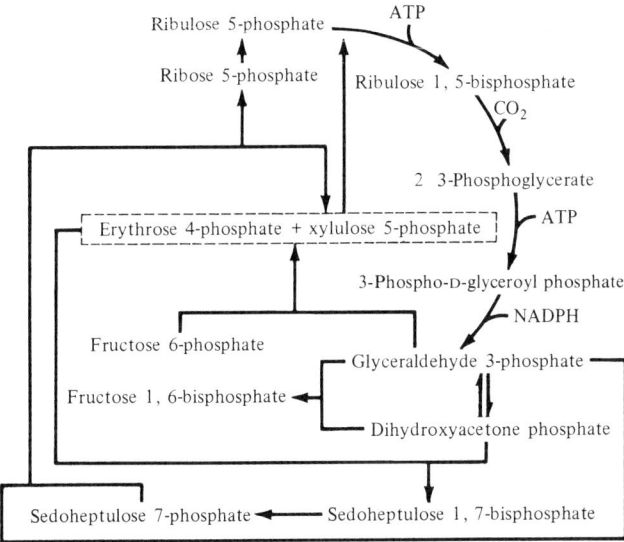

**Figure 9-8** Summary of the reductive pentose phosphate cycle of photosynthesis. Following the incorporation of carbon dioxide and the reductive step, glyceraldehyde 3-phosphate and dihydroxyacetone phosphate can undergo the reaction catalyzed by fructose-bisphosphate aldolase, which yields fructose 1,6-bisphosphate. The aldolase also catalyzes the conversion of dihydroxyacetone phosphate and erythrose 4-phosphate into sedoheptulose 1,7-bisphosphate. On the other hand, the conversion of glyceraldehyde 3-phosphate and fructose 6-phosphate into erythrose 4-phosphate plus xylulose 5-phosphate and the conversion of glyceraldehyde 3-phosphate and sedoheptulose 7-phosphate into ribose 5-phosphate plus xylulose 5-phosphate are catalyzed by transketolase.

carboxylase. The activity of the carboxylase is modulated primarily by the relative concentrations of fructose 6-phosphate and fructose 1,6-bisphosphate, which, in turn, can be modulated by light energy. This process has been formulated as follows. In organisms carrying out photosynthesis fructose 1,6-bisphosphate can be converted into fructose 6-phosphate by a reaction catalyzed by a hydratase which is subactive in the dark but active in the presence of light (of the appropriate wavelength). Light interacts with the chlorophyll of the cell, and, as a result, electrons pass along a series of components that constitute an electron-transport system. This will be discussed in some detail in Chap. 11. One of the components of this transport system is ferredoxin, a small metalloprotein which accepts an electron and is thus reduced. The reduced ferredoxin in conjunction with a protein (which has not been fully characterized) causes the subactive hydratase to be converted into its active form. This, then, catalyzes the hydrolysis of fructose 1,6-bisphosphate into fructose 6-phosphate. The increased concentration of fructose 6-phosphate and the decreased concentration of the bisphosphate then enhance the activity of ribulosebisphosphate carboxylase. Thus, the incorporation of carbon dioxide is promoted. Furthermore, the 3-phosphoglycerate that is formed not only participates in the subsequent steps of the reductive pentose phosphate cycle but also can function as an activator with respect to the activity of glucose-1-phosphate adenylyltransferase, the enzyme that catalyzes the rate-determining step of the synthesis of starch in these organisms. Thus, light energy initiates a sequence of events that results in an increased assimilation of carbon dioxide into carbohydrate intermediates and, ultimately, in an increased utilization of the appropriate carbohydrate intermediates in the synthesis of starch.

As mentioned earlier, ribulosebisphosphate carboxylase also catalyzes the incorporation of molecular oxygen into ribulose 1,5-bisphosphate, and there is substantial evidence that this is a part of the process of photorespiration, i.e., the utilization of molecular oxygen and the liberation of carbon dioxide through the agency of light energy. Thus photorespiration is, in effect, the converse of photosynthesis. It is therefore of some interest that a single enzyme can catalyze both the incorporation of carbon dioxide as it occurs in photosynthesis and the incorporation of molecular oxygen as it occurs in photorespiration. Furthermore, it has been found that while fructose 6-phosphate enhances and fructose 1,6-bisphosphate impedes the carboxylase activity of the enzyme, these intermediates have just the opposite effects upon the oxygenase activity of the enzyme. Fructose 1,6-bisphosphate enhances oxygenase activity, which is impeded by fructose 6-phosphate.†
Thus, it appears that there is coordinate regulation of photosynthesis and photorespiration and that a principal focal point of this regulation is the activity of ribulosebisphosphate carboxylase.

† Ryan, F. J., and Tolbert, N. E. (1975) *J. Biol. Chem.* **250**, 4234–4238.

CHAPTER
# TEN
## THE TRICARBOXYLIC ACID CYCLE

The complete catabolism of a molecule of glucose to carbon dioxide and water begins with the entry of the hexose into the glycolytic pathway. As a result of the reactions of the glycolytic pathway, glucose is both oxidized and cleaved, and two molecules of pyruvate are formed. Overall, this is a four-electron oxidation and as a concomitance two molecules of $NAD^+$ are reduced to NADH. The pyruvate can subsequently be converted into three molecules of carbon dioxide after first being oxidatively decarboxylated to yield the acetyl moiety of acetyl CoA, which then enters the tricarboxylic acid cycle. The reactions of the tricarboxylic acid cycle generate the remaining two molecules of carbon dioxide. The reactions of the tricarboxylic acid cycle also reduce three molecules of $NAD^+$ to NADH, and, in addition, two more reducing equivalents are transferred to an enzyme of the mitochondrial electron-transport system. Ultimately, the reducing equivalents resulting from all the oxidative reactions of both glycolysis and the tricarboxylic acid cycle can be channeled into the mitochondrial electron-transport system, where molecular oxygen is reduced to form water while the chemical energy derived from this process is utilized in the phosphorylation of ADP to yield ATP. In this chapter the tricarboxylic acid cycle is discussed.

Unlike glycolysis, which occurs in the cytoplasm of the cell, the enzymes of the tricarboxylic acid cycle are located in the mitochondria of the cells that carry out this metabolic process. Mitchondria are organelles found in eukaryotic cells. They were first observed as "threadlike granules within the cell"—hence, their name. The word mitochondrion is derived from the Greek *mitos*, meaning "thread," and *chondrion*, meaning "granule." The number of mitochondria in a given cell varies from generally less than 20 in yeast cells to several hundred in animal cells.

**Table 10-1 Some morphological, physical, and chemical characteristics of the inner and outer membranes of liver mitochondria**

|  | Inner membrane | Outer membrane |
|---|---|---|
| *Morphological:* | | |
| Thickness | 50–70 Å | 50–70 Å |
| Shape | Folded | Distended |
| Surfaces | Outer surface smooth, inner surface covered with regularly spaced projecting subunits | Inner surface smooth, occasional projections on outer surface |
| Effect of phospholipid extraction | Double-layered structure retained | Double-layered structure destroyed |
| *Physical:* | | |
| Density | 1.192–1.230 | 1.094–1.122 |
| Permeability | Only uncharged molecules of 100–150 mol wt | Most substances up to ~10,000 mol wt |
| Osmotic behavior | Reversible unfolding and refolding, contraction | Irreversible stretching, rupture |
| X-ray diffraction pattern | Fundamentally similar | |
| *Chemical:* | | |
| Phospholipid/protein (w/w) | 0.27 | 0.82 |
| Cardiolipin | High | Low |
| Phosphatidylinositol | Low | High |
| Cholesterol | Low | High |
| Ubiquinone | Present | Absent |

*Source:* Data from Ernster, L., and Kuylenstierna, B. (1969) in *Mitochondria, Structure and Function* (Ernster, L., and Drahota, Z., eds.), pp. 5–31 (see p. 7), Academic, New York. With permission.

Under the microscope, mitochondria appear to be constantly changing shape. However, regardless of their shape, electron micrographs have shown that all mitochondria have both an outer (or "limiting") membrane and an inner membrane. These two membranes are distinct with respect to morphological, physical, and chemical characteristics, as shown in Table 10-1. The inner membrane of the mitochondrion is characterized by having many invaginations, called *cristae* (see Fig. 10-1). The word *crista* (the singular form) is Latin for "crest."

Operationally, the mitochondrion can be considered to have four compartments, namely, the outer membrane, the inner membrane, the intermembrane space, and the matrix (Fig. 10-2). A given enzyme or metabolic intermediate is usually localized in a specific one (or two) of these compartments, and in many cases these components do not pass freely from one compartment to another. The locations of some of the mitochondrial enzymes are shown in Table 10-2. With a single exception, all the enzymes that participate in the tricarboxylic acid cycle are localized in the matrix of the mitochondrion.

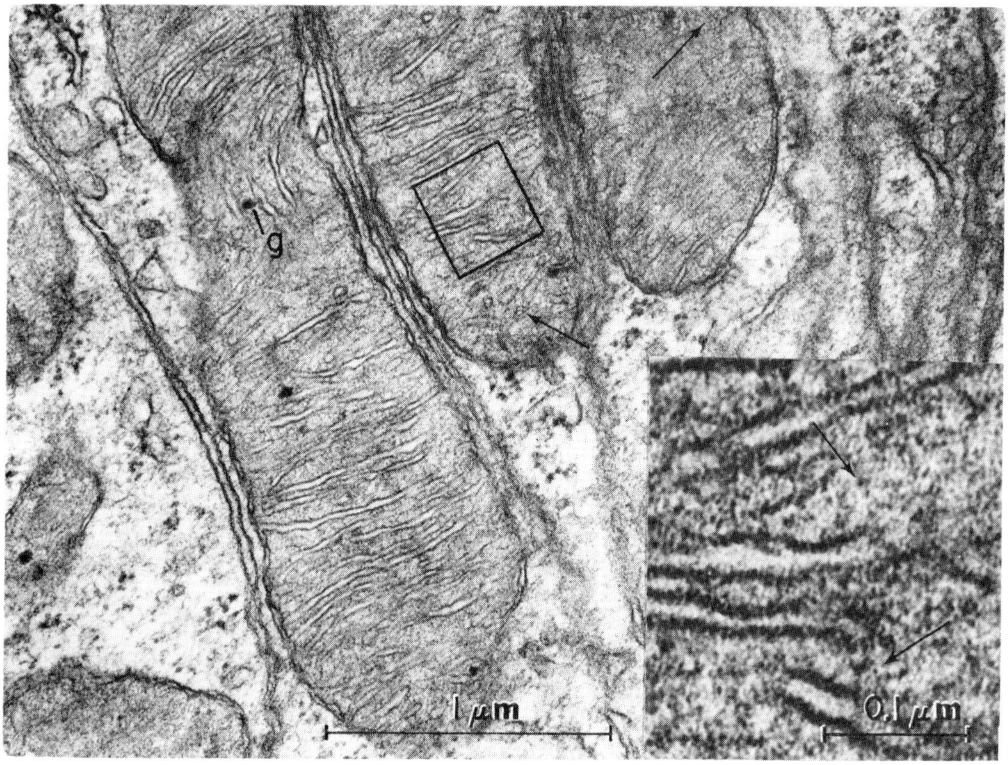

**Figure 10-1** An electron micrograph of mitochondria from the proximal convoluted tubule of the rat kidney. The mitochondria are elongated with cristae that virtually traverse the organelle. Inset: A higher magnification. [*From Burgos, M. H., Aoki, A., and Sacerdote, F. L.* (1964) *J. Cell Biology* **23**, 207–215 (*see p. 209*). *With permission.*]

Discussion of the tricarboxylic acid cycle can begin with a consideration of the conversion of pyruvate to the acetyl moiety of acetyl CoA. This reaction provides a link between the glycolytic pathway, which leads to the production of pyruvate, and the tricarboxylic acid cycle, which begins with the condensation of acetyl

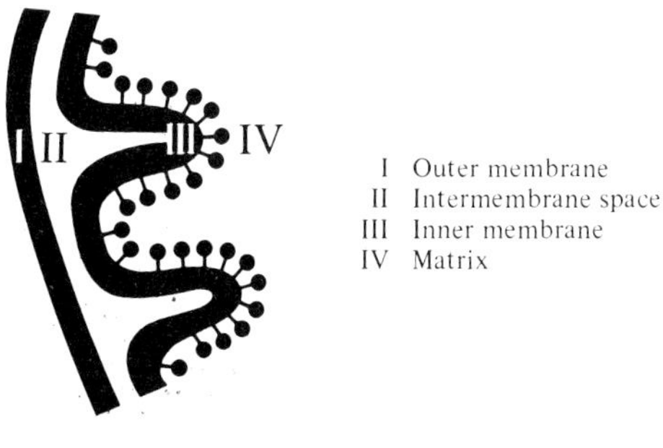

MITOCHONDRIAL COMPARTMENTS

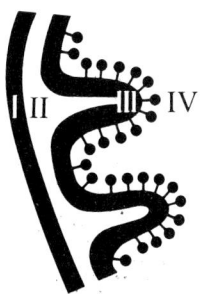

I  Outer membrane
II  Intermembrane space
III  Inner membrane
IV  Matrix

**Figure 10-2** Compartmentalization of the mitochondrion.

## Table 10-2 Localization of some enzymes in the rat-liver mitochondrion

| Enzyme | Metabolic pathway† |
|---|---|
| Outer membrane: | |
|   Acyl-CoA synthetase | L |
|   Glycerophosphate acyltransferase | L |
|   Lysophosphatidylcholine acyltransferase | L |
|   Phospholipase $A_2$ | L |
|   Phosphatidate phosphatase | L |
|   Kynurenine 3-monooxygenase | P |
|   Amine oxidase (flavin-containing) | P |
|   Nucleosidediphosphate kinase | N |
| Intermembrane space: | |
|   Adenylate kinase | N |
|   Nucleosidediphosphate kinase | N |
| Inner membrane: | |
|   NADH dehydrogenase | MET |
|   Succinate dehydrogenase | TCA, MET |
|   Cytochromes $b, c_1, c, a, a_3$ | MET |
|   3-Hydroxybutyrate dehydrogenase | L |
|   Acyl-CoA dehydrogenase | L |
|   5-Aminolevulinate synthase | H |
| Matrix: | |
|   Citrate synthase | TCA |
|   Aconitate hydratase | TCA |
|   Fumarate hydratase | TCA |
|   Succinyl-CoA synthetase | TCA |
|   Nucleosidemonophosphate kinase | N |
|   Aminotransferases | P |

† H = heme anabolism, L = lipid metabolism, MET = mitochondrial electron transport, N = nucleic metabolism, P = protein metabolism, TCA = tricarboxylic acid cycle.

*Source:* Data from Ernster, L., and Kuylenstierna, B. (1969) in *Mitochondria, Structure and Function* (Ernster, L., and Drahota, Z., eds.), pp. 5–31 (see pp. 12 and 13), Academic, New York. With permission.

CoA and oxaloacetate. The conversion of pyruvate to the acetyl moiety of acetyl CoA is an oxidative decarboxylation catalyzed by the enzymes of the pyruvate dehydrogenase complex.

## PYRUVATE DEHYDROGENASE COMPLEX

The pyruvate dehydrogenase multienzyme complex consists of three components that participate in the conversion of pyruvate into the acetyl moiety of acetyl CoA: the thiamine diphosphate–dependent pyruvate dehydrogenase component (to be distinguished from the pyruvate dehydrogenase complex), a lipoate acetyltransferase, and a lipoamide dehydrogenase, which is a flavoprotein. Mammalian pyruvate dehydrogenase complexes also include a kinase and a phosphatase that function in a regulatory capacity with respect to the activity of the pyruvate dehydrogenase component. Complexes that are isolated from porcine heart or bovine kidney exhibit particle weights of approximately 6.5 to 7.5 $\times$ $10^6$. The architecture of these complexes has been described as follows. The core of the complex is the lipoamide acetyltransferase, to which the pyruvate dehydrogenase component, the lipoamide dehydrogenase, and the kinase and phosphatase are bound. The pyruvate dehydrogenase component has a molecular weight of 154,000 and is composed of two subunits which have molecular weights of 41,000 and two which have molecular weights of 36,000. The lipoamide dehydrogenase has a molecular weight of 110,000 and is apparently a dimer which binds two molecules of FAD. The kinase, which is tightly bound to the acetyltransferase, has a molecular weight of 50,000, while the more loosely bound phosphatase has a molecular weight of 10,000. Finally, the acetyltransferase itself has a molecular weight of $3 \times 10^6$ and is composed of 60 subunits, arranged to form a pentagonal dodecahedron. Each of these subunits binds a molecule of lipoate covalently.

$$\underset{^-O}{\overset{O}{\underset{\|}{C}}}-H_2CH_2CH_2CH_2C-\underset{}{\overset{S-S}{\underset{CH_2}{CH}}} \underset{}{\overset{}{CH_2}}$$

Lipoate

The multienzyme complex is thought to comprise 20 to 30 pyruvate dehydrogenase components, 5 to 6 lipoamide dehydrogenase molecules, and no more than 5 or 6 molecules of the kinase with a similar number of molecules of the phosphatase.[†] Electron micrographs of the pyruvate dehydrogenase complex as isolated from porcine heart are shown in Fig. 10-3.

A pyruvate dehydrogenase complex from *E. coli* is similar to the mammalian enzyme although smaller and considerably less intricate.

## Decarboxylation and Oxidation of Pyruvate

Pyruvate undergoes decarboxylation and oxidation as a result of a reaction catalyzed by the pyruvate dehydrogenase component [pyruvate:lipoate oxidoreductase (decarboxylating and acceptor-acetylating), EC 1.2.4.1]. The reaction, which can be written

$$\text{Pyruvate} + \text{oxidized lipoamide} \rightleftharpoons S^6\text{-acetyldihydrolipoamide} + CO_2 \quad (10\text{-}1)$$

requires the participation of two cofactors, thiamine diphosphate and lipoate. The lipoate molecule is covalently bonded to the acetyltransferase by the formation of

---

[†] Reed, L. J., Petit, F. H., Roche, T. E., Butterworth, P. J., Barrera, C. R., and Tsai, C. S. (1974) in *Metabolic Interconversion of Enzymes, 1973* (Fischer, E. H., Krebs, E. G., Neurath, H., and Stadtman, E. R., eds.), pp. 99–106, Springer-Verlag, New York.

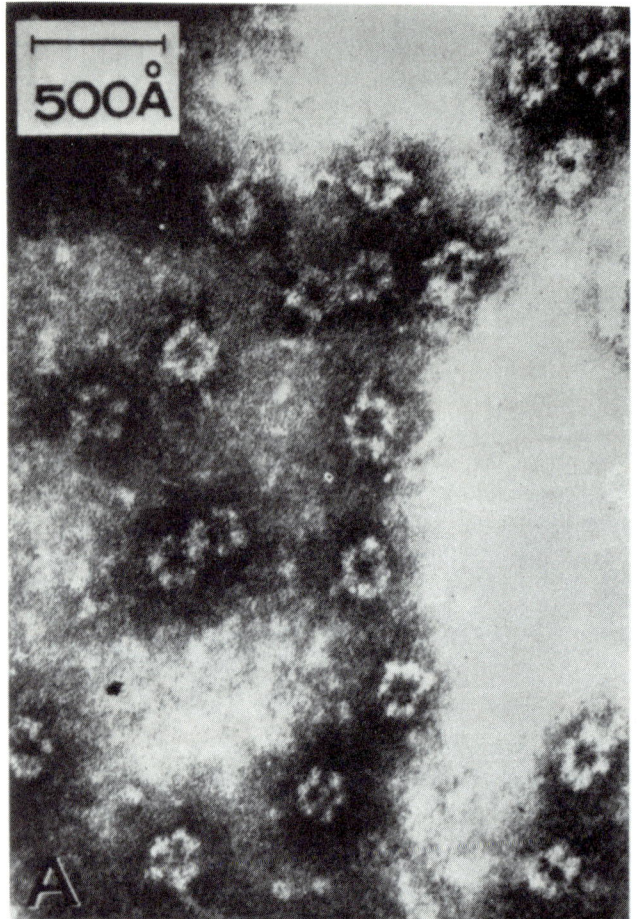

**Figure 10-3** An electron micrograph of the native pyruvate dehydrogenase complex as isolated from porcine-heart mitochondria (X 300,000). [*From Hayakawa, T., Kanzaki, T., Kitamura, T., Fukuyoshi, Y., Sakurai, Y., Koike, K., Suematsu, T., and Koike, M.* (1969) *J. Biol. Chem.* **244**, 3660–3670 (*see p.* 3667). *With permission.*]

an amide bond involving the $\epsilon$-amino group of a lysyl unit of this component. The lysyl unit, in fact, provides a flexible arm (approximately 14 Å in length) which allows the dithiolane ring of lipoamide to be appropriately positioned at the dehydrogenase component.

The reaction begins as the ylide derived from thiamine diphosphate attacks the oxo carbon atom of pyruvate in a manner reminiscent of the participation of this cofactor in the reaction catalyzed by transketolase. In the present case, however, the eliminated species is carbon dioxide, and the decarboxylation is facilitated by the ability of the thiazolium nitrogen atom to accept an electron pair, as shown. Following the decarboxylation, the resulting 1-hydroxyethyl moiety now functions as a nucleophile and attacks the disulfide bond of the lipoamide, with the result that

$S^6$-acetyldihydrolipoamide is formed. This is an oxidation-reduction reaction in that the carbon atom that was C(2) of pyruvate is oxidized (from the level of an oxo group to that of a carboxylate group) while a sulfur atom of the lipoamide is reduced (from the level of a disulfide to that of a sulfhydryl group). A minimal reaction mechanism is shown below.

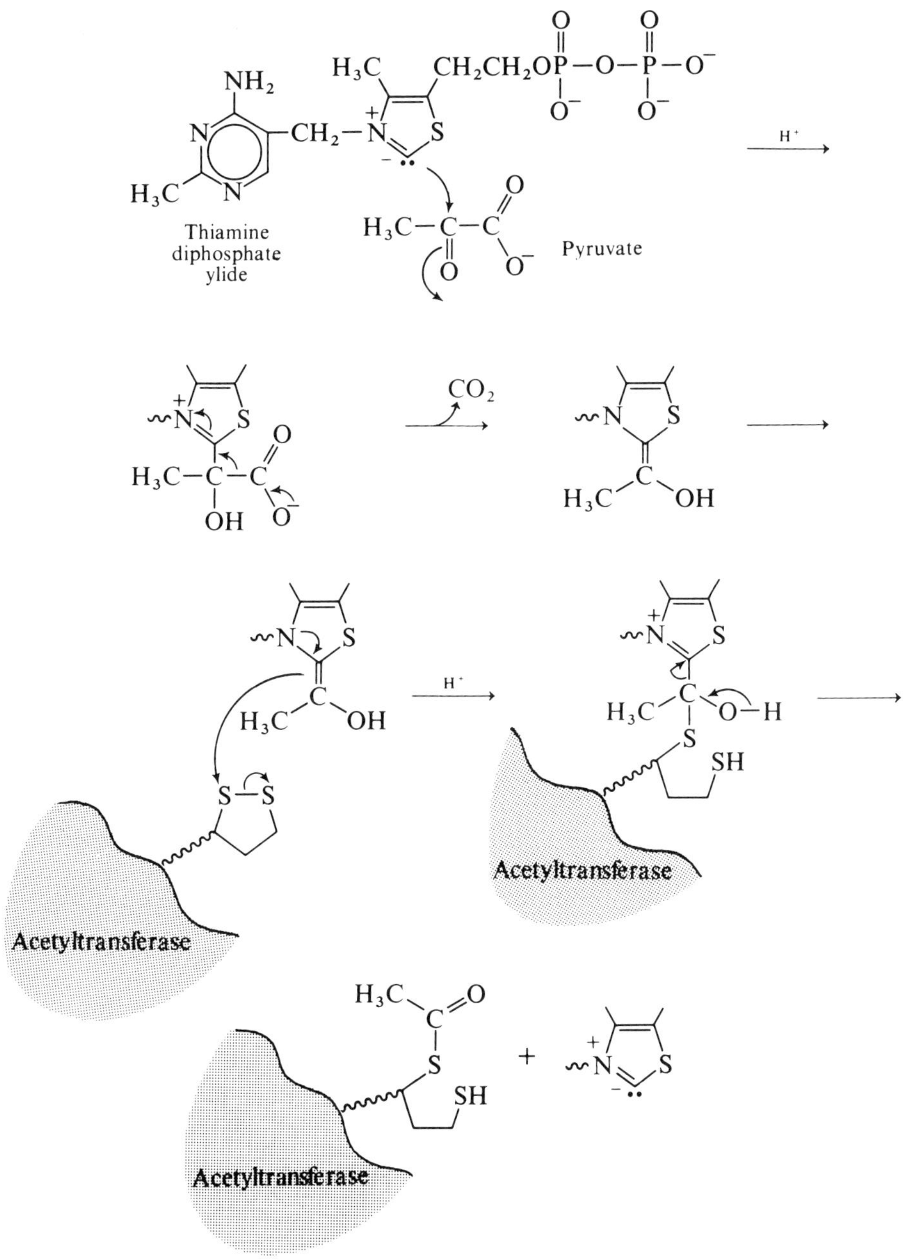

## Acetylation of CoA

The next event in the process catalyzed by the pyruvate dehydrogenase complex is the transfer of the acetyl moiety of $S^6$-acetyldihydrolipoamide to CoA, catalyzed by the lipoate acetyltransferase (acetyl-CoA:dihydrolipoate $S$-acetyltransferase, EC 2.3.1.12). As a result of this reaction an acetyl moiety derived from C(2) and C(3) of pyruvate is transferred from the sulfhydryl group of the enzyme-bound dihydrolipoamide to the sulfhydryl group of CoA. The reaction can be written

$$S^6\text{-Acetyldihydrolipoamide} + \text{CoA} \rightleftharpoons \text{acetyl CoA} + \text{dihydrolipoamide} \quad (10\text{-}2)$$

Now the enzyme-bound lipoamide has been reduced to a bissulfhydryl derivative, as shown.

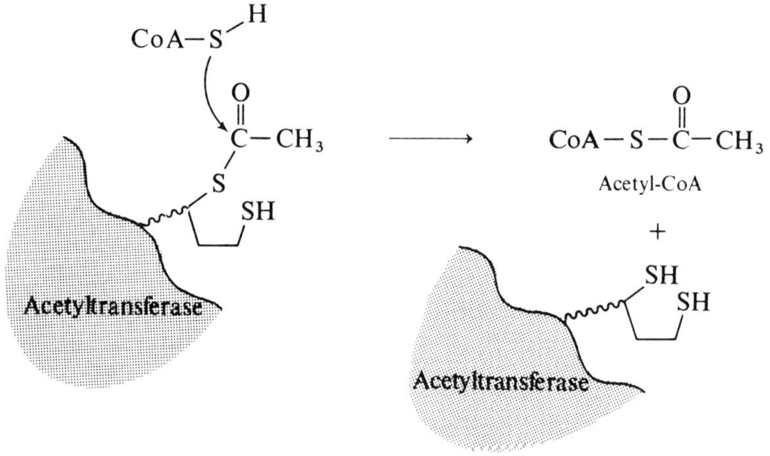

## Oxidation of Dihydrolipoamide

The function of the flavoprotein enzyme of the pyruvate dehydrogenase complex is that of oxidizing the dihydrolipoamide moiety back to lipoamide. This process, which is catalyzed by lipoamide dehydrogenase (NADH:lipoamide oxidoreductase, EC 1.6.4.3), utilizes both FAD and $NAD^+$. The reactions can be written

$$\text{Dihydrolipoamide} + \text{oxidized FAD} \rightleftharpoons \text{lipoamide} + \text{reduced FAD} \quad (10\text{-}3a)$$

and

$$\text{Reduced FAD} + NAD^+ \rightleftharpoons \text{oxidized FAD} + \text{NADH} \quad (10\text{-}3b)$$

Initially, electrons are transferred from the dihydrolipoamide to the FAD and a disulfide group derived from two cysteinyl units at the catalytic site of the lipoamide dehydrogenase. The removal of electrons from dihydrolipoamide constitutes the oxidation of this cofactor. Their acceptance by the FAD and the disulfide group constitutes their reduction. Two electrons are removed from dihydrolipoamide, and it has been proposed that the FAD and the disulfide group act in concert to accept them. During this process, the transient formation of the anionic (red) form of a flavin semiquinone can be demonstrated, and thus it is indicated that FAD undergoes a one-electron reduction. Subsequently, $NAD^+$ acts as the ultimate acceptors of the two electrons. The reaction catalyzed by lipoamide dehydrogenase might therefore be depicted as follows.

NADH +

## Kinetic Studies on the Pyruvate Dehydrogenase Complex

Kinetic studies on the reactions catalyzed by the pyruvate dehydrogenase complex indicate that a three-site ping pong mechanism is operative.† When initial-velocity studies were conducted, it was found that the double reciprocal plots were parallel when pyruvate was the variable substrate with fixed concentrations of CoA (and a constant concentration of $NAD^+$) or when CoA was varied with fixed concentrations of $NAD^+$ (and a constant concentration of pyruvate) or when $NAD^+$ was varied with fixed concentrations of pyruvate (and a constant concentration of CoA). With respect to product inhibition, acetyl CoA was found to be a competitive inhibitor when CoA was varied, while NADH was a competitive inhibitor when $NAD^+$ was varied. These data are in agreement with the predictions that would be made on the basis of the appropriate kinetic equations. Specifically, such equations predict that the double reciprocal plots based upon the initial-velocity studies will be parallel regardless of whether pyruvate, CoA, or $NAD^+$ is varied with the other two as either the fixed substrate or the substrate that is maintained at one constant concentration. The equations also predict that, unlike the product-inhibition patterns seen when a classical ping pong mechanism is operative, a product will be a competitive inhibitor with respect to a variable substrate that binds at the same site.‡ (Remember that this pattern was also observed when studies were conducted on the reaction catalyzed by pyruvate carboxylase.)

In addition to studies on the overall reaction, kinetic studies have been conducted on the partial reaction catalyzed by the acetyltransferase and the partial reaction catalyzed by the lipoamide dehydrogenase. The former, which involves transfer of an acetyl group from the sulfhydryl group of lipoamide to the sulfhydryl group of CoA, was found to proceed by a sequential mechanism which is random. Since the products were found to be competitive inhibitors with respect to the structurally similar substrate and noncompetitive inhibitors with respect to the structurally dissimilar substrate, it was proposed that there are two distinct but adjacent binding sites on acetyltransferase and that one binds CoA and acetyl CoA while the other binds S-acetyldihydrolipoamide and dihydrolipoamide.§

Studies on lipoamide dehydrogenase from rat-liver mitochondria have suggested that this partial reaction proceeds by a ping pong mechanism. In addition to the expected parallel initial-velocity plots, it was found that NADH is a noncompetitive product inhibitor when dihydrolipoamide is the variable substrate although this inhibitory effect becomes competitive in the presence of high fixed concentrations of the other substrate, $NAD^+$. Similarly, NADH is a noncompetitive inhibitor when $NAD^+$ is the variable substrate at low fixed concentrations of dihydrolipoamide, but this changes to a competitive pattern in the presence of high concentrations of dihydrolipoamide. Product-inhibition studies with lipoamide paralleled those described above, and noncompetitive inhibition was observed except in the presence

---

† Tsai, C. S., Burgett, M. W., and Reed, L. J. (1973) *J. Biol. Chem.* **248**, 8348–8352.

‡ Cleland, W. W. (1973) *J. Biol. Chem.* **248**, 8353–8355.

§ Butterworth, P. J., Tsai, C. S., Eley, M. H., Roche, T. E., and Reed, L. J. (1975) *J. Biol. Chem.* **250**, 1921–1925.

of a high concentration of the fixed substrate. Under those circumstances, the inhibition was competitive. These data were interpreted to reflect the presence of a ping pong mechanism in which NADH can also bind the same enzyme form as $NAD^+$ and lipoamide can also bind the same enzyme form as dihydrolipoamide.†  This can be represented diagrammatically as shown.

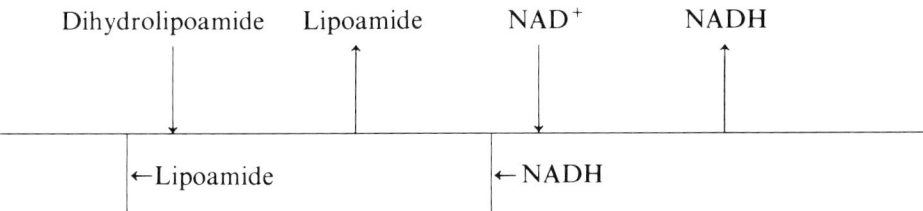

Accordingly, when dihydrolipoamide is the variable substrate and NADH is the inhibitor, both a slope and an intercept effect are observed since NADH binds both E, the same enzyme form as the variable substrate, and also F, a different enzyme form. However, in the presence of high concentrations of $NAD^+$ the different enzyme form F becomes unavailable to NADH. Similarly, when $NAD^+$ is the variable substrate, NADH binds both E and F unless high concentrations of dihydrolipoamide cause E to be unavailable to NADH. In such an event, the inhibitory effect of NADH must be the result of its binding only the same enzyme form as the variable substrate. Similar arguments can be made to rationalize the inhibition patterns observed when lipoamide is the inhibitor.

A very convincing piece of evidence in support of a ping pong mechanism is found in the isotope-exchange studies on the reaction catalyzed by lipoamide dehydrogenase. These studies demonstrated that the [*carboxamide*-$^{14}C$]$NAD^+$-to-NADH exchange proceeds at the same velocity both in the absence of and in the presence of dihydrolipoamide and lipoamide. This is as would be expected if a ping pong mechanism is operative.

The overall reaction catalyzed by the pyruvate dehydrogenase complex has been depicted as follows. Pyruvate binds the pyruvate dehydrogenase complex, reacts with thiamine diphosphate, and undergoes decarboxylation. Then the lipoamide, which is covalently bound to acetyltransferase, is positioned at the catalytic site of the dehydrogenase component by the flexible arm provided by the lysyl moiety. There the *S*-acetyldihydrolipoamide is formed, and the thiamine diphosphate ylide is regenerated. Now the *S*-acetyldihydrolipoamide is positioned at the catalytic site of acetyltransferase, again by means of the flexible arm, where the acetyl group is transferred to CoA. This results in the formation of dihydrolipoamide, which is now positioned at the catalytic site of the third enzyme, i.e., the lipoamide dehydrogenase. As a result of the reactions that occur at this site, the oxidized form of the lipoamide is regenerated and can now be positioned at the first catalytic site as the process begins again. The overall reaction as catalyzed by the pyruvate dehydrogenase complex can be written

$$\text{Pyruvate} + \text{CoA} + NAD^+ \longrightarrow CO_2 + \text{acetyl CoA} + NADH \quad (10\text{-}4)$$

† Reed, J. K. (1973) *J. Biol. Chem.* **248**, 4834–4839.

### Regulation of the Activity of the Pyruvate Dehydrogenase Complex

The rate-determining step in the reaction catalyzed by this multienzyme complex is the decarboxylation and oxidation of pyruvate. This step is catalyzed by the pyruvate dehydrogenase component. In mammalian systems the activity of this enzyme is modulated by the phosphorylation and dephosphorylation of the enzyme. Phosphorylation, which requires ATP, $Mg^{2+}$, and the kinase, converts the active enzyme into an inactive form. Dephosphorylation of the phosphorylated form, which requires $Mg^{2+}$ and $Ca^{2+}$ and the phosphatase, regenerates the active enzyme. Furthermore, it has been found that the phosphorylation-dephosphorylation mechanism is itself influenced by the ATP/ADP ratio in the mitochondria. The percentage of the dehydrogenase component that exists in the (active) nonphosphorylated form varies directly with the concentration of ADP or inversely with the ATP/ADP ratio.† This effect apparently stems from the fact that ADP functions as an inhibitor with respect to the activity of the kinase. (ADP is a product of the phosphorylation reaction catalyzed by the kinase.) Thus, when ADP concentrations are high and ATP concentrations are low, the conversion of pyruvate into the acetyl moiety of acetyl CoA is promoted. Since formation of acetyl CoA and its utilization by the tricarboxylic acid cycle can ultimately result in the production of ATP, this mode of regulation is readily rationalized.

By contrast, the activity of the pyruvate dehydrogenase component of the multienzyme complex from *E. coli* is modulated as a result of the inhibitory effect of acetyl CoA. This inhibitory effect can be relieved by nucleoside monophosphates, including AMP and GMP. There is also some evidence that GTP is an inhibitor of the activity of this pyruvate dehydrogenase component and that the inhibition can be relieved by GDP. There is, however, no evidence that the bacterial system is modulated as a result of enzyme phosphorylation and/or dephosphorylation.

## REACTIONS OF THE TRICARBOXYLIC ACID CYCLE

The tricarboxylic acid cycle is a catabolic pathway by which carbon atoms are oxidized to the level of carbon dioxide. As a concomitance of this oxidation on carbon $NAD^+$ and FAD, two oxidation-reduction cofactors, are reduced. The reducing equivalents that are accepted by these cofactors are subsequently transferred to the mitochondrial electron-transport system, where they are ultimately utilized for the reduction of molecular oxygen. The energy derived from the reactions of the mitochondrial electron-transport system is then used in the phosphorylation of ADP, and thus ATP is formed. All of these processes take place as the result of many individual steps, and it is these individual steps of the tricarboxylic acid cycle that will be discussed here.

---

† Walajtys, E. I., Gottesman, D. P., and Williamson, J. R. (1974) *J. Biol. Chem.* **249**, 1857–1865.

## Step 1: Formation of Citrate

The first and rate-determining step of the tricarboxylic acid cycle is catalyzed by citrate (*si*)-synthase [citrate oxaloacetate-lyase (*pro*-3*S*-$CH_2COO^-$ → acetyl-CoA), EC 4.1.3.7]. The reaction,

$$\text{Acetyl CoA} + \text{oxaloacetate} + H_2O \rightleftharpoons \text{citrate} + \text{CoA} \qquad (10\text{-}5)$$

is in fact, an aldol condensation involving the acetyl moiety of acetyl CoA and oxaloacetate. The condensation is stereospecific in that (in mammalian systems) the enolate anion derived from the acetyl moiety of acetyl CoA attacks the *si* face of the oxo group of oxaloacetate. As a result, a citrate molecule is formed in which the pro-*S* carboxymethyl group is derived *specifically* from the acetyl moiety of the acetyl CoA.

Citrate synthase has been isolated from a wide variety of sources. Most enzymes from eukaryotic cells and from the cells of gram-positive bacteria have a molecular weight of approximately $1 \times 10^5$, while synthases from gram-negative bacteria are larger. For example, the enzyme citrate synthase from *E. coli* has a molecular weight of 280,000. Synthases from all sources are apparently composed of subunits; in the enzymes from porcine heart, rat heart, and rat liver there are two identical subunits.

Kinetic studies on citrate synthase from rat kidney and rat brain have shown that the kinetic mechanism of the reaction is a sequential one, since the double reciprocal plots of the initial-velocity data are intersecting. With respect to product inhibition, CoA was found to be a competitive inhibitor when acetyl CoA was varied and a noncompetitive inhibitor when oxaloacetate was varied. Citrate was found to be a competitive inhibitor vs. oxaloacetate and a noncompetitive inhibitor vs. acetyl CoA.† These data may be interpreted as indicating that the kinetic mechanism is random sequential and that the enzyme has a CoA site and a di- or tricarboxylic acid site. Hence, a product functions as a competitive inhibitor with respect to the structurally similar substrate and as a noncompetitive inhibitor with respect to the structurally dissimilar substrate.

Since the reaction catalyzed by citrate synthase is the rate-determining step of the tricarboxylic acid cycle, it is to be expected that the activity of the synthase would be subject to modulation. In mammalian systems this modulation comes about as a result of influences imposed by certain metabolic intermediates including short-chain acyl-CoA derivatives. The most important of these in the living organism is thought to be succinyl CoA. Also, there are data which suggest that substrate availability may be a factor in determining the level of citrate synthase activity.

As already mentioned, the reaction mechanism of the formation of citrate entails an aldol-type condensation which may be depicted as shown on page 424. The acyl moiety reacts in the form of the enolate anion, and, in fact, the formation of this anion is the rate-determining step in the formation of citrate.

---

† Matsuoka, Y., and Srere, P. A. (1973) *J. Biol. Chem.* **248**, 8022–8030.

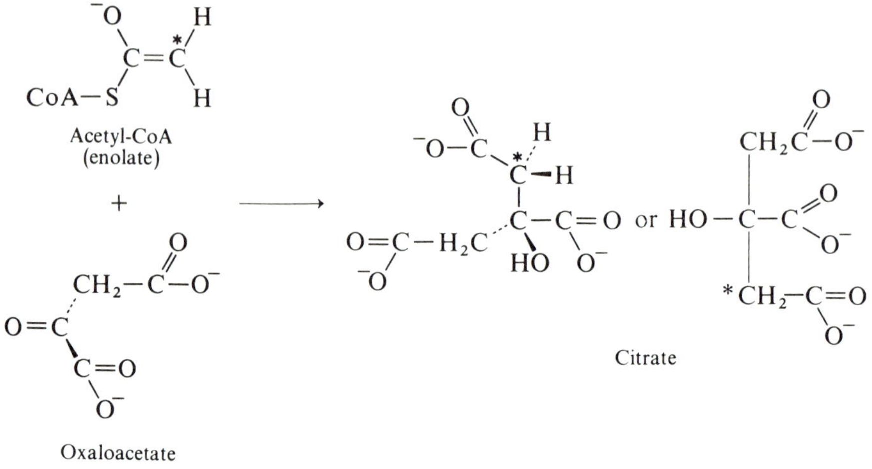

## Step 2: Conversion of Citrate into Isocitrate

In the next step of the tricarboxylic acid cycle citrate is converted into isocitrate as a result of a dehydration reaction followed by a hydration reaction. Aconitate hydratase [citrate(isocitrate) hydro-lyase, EC 4.2.1.3] catalyzes the conversion, which can be expressed as

$$\text{Citrate} \rightleftharpoons \textit{cis}\text{-aconitate} + H_2O \rightleftharpoons \text{isocitrate} \quad (10\text{-}6)$$

Aconitate hydratase isolated from porcine-heart mitochondria has a molecular weight of 89,000 and contains one atom of (high-spin) $Fe^{3+}$, which is thought to have a structural role. Hydratases have also been isolated from bovine liver and from various microorganisms. The enzymes from microorganisms are generally larger than the mammalian hydratases.

The dehydration-hydration sequence as catalyzed by aconitate hydratase is readily reversible, and, in fact, the interconversions involving citrate, *cis*-aconitate, and isocitrate can be initiated by the introduction of any one of these three components into an appropriate medium containing the enzyme. Only (2R), (3S)-isocitrate participates in the interconversions, however. Both the dehydration and the hydration catalyzed by aconitate hydratase are stereoselective. Of the two carboxymethyl groups of citrate, only the pro-R group is involved in the reactions catalyzed by this enzyme. The pro-R carboxymethyl group of citrate is that derived specifically from oxaloacetate. It has also been shown that a specific one of the two hydrogen atoms of the pro-R carboxymethyl group is involved in the reaction, as shown in Fig. 10-4. As one can see, the dehydration reaction entails the trans elimination of water with the removal of a proton from one face of the molecule while the hydration reaction entails the addition of the elements of water, the proton being added at the opposite face of the molecule. Furthermore, it has been shown that the proton removed is the same one that is subsequently added. On the basis of these data, coupled with data which implicate $Fe^{2+}$ in the reaction mechanism (this $Fe^{2+}$ is to be distinguished from the $Fe^{3+}$ which is thought to have a structural role), the dehydration of citrate and the subsequent hydration of

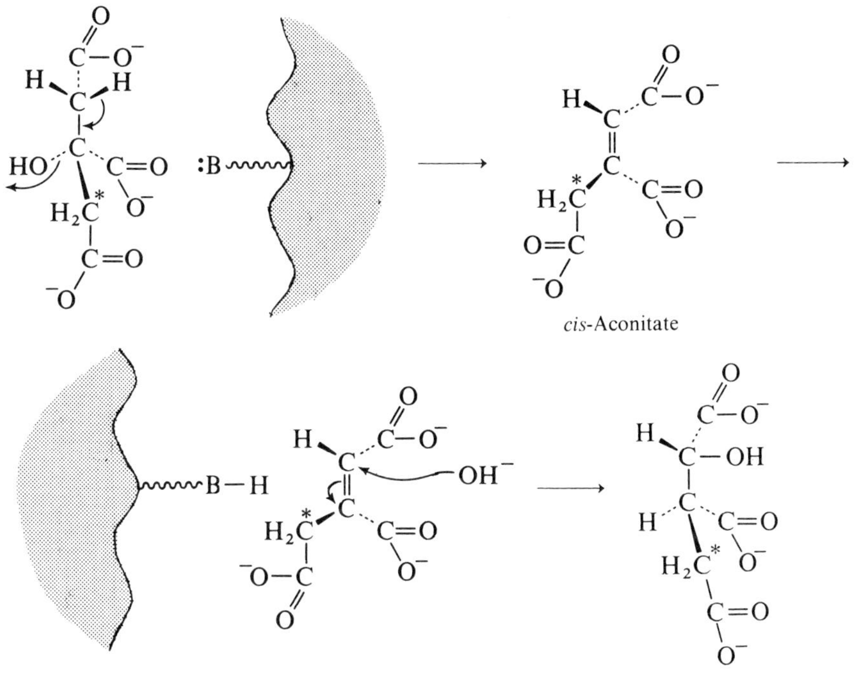

**Figure 10-4** A minimal reaction mechanism for the conversion of citrate into isocitrate. B represents a basic functional group that accepts a proton during the course of the dehydration. The protonated form of this basic group subsequently returns the same proton to the substrate during the course of the hydration. The carbon atom that was C(2) of the acetyl moiety of acetyl-CoA is designated by an asterisk.

cis-aconitate have been depicted as shown in Fig. 10-5.† According to this formulation, which has been called the *ferrous wheel mechanism*, the role of the $Fe^{2+}$ is that of coordinating with the substrate. Following the formation of this coordination complex, the dehydration occurs, and an aconitate intermediate complex is generated. This particular complex is, in turn, converted into a second which then undergoes hydration to yield the isomeric tricarboxylic acid. The product is specifically (2R), (3S)-isocitrate.

### Step 3: Oxidation of Isocitrate

Isocitrate is now oxidized to yield 2-oxoglutarate as the result of a reaction catalyzed by isocitrate dehydrogenase [*threo*-$D_S$-isocitrate: $NAD^+$ oxidoreductase (decarboxylating), EC 1.1.1.41]. The reaction is

$$(2R), (3S)\text{-Isocitrate} + NAD^+ \longrightarrow 2\text{-oxoglutarate} + CO_2 + NADH \quad (10\text{-}7)$$

† Glusker, J. P. (1971) in *The Enzymes* (Boyer, P. D., ed.), 3d ed., vol. 5, pp. 413–439, Academic, New York.

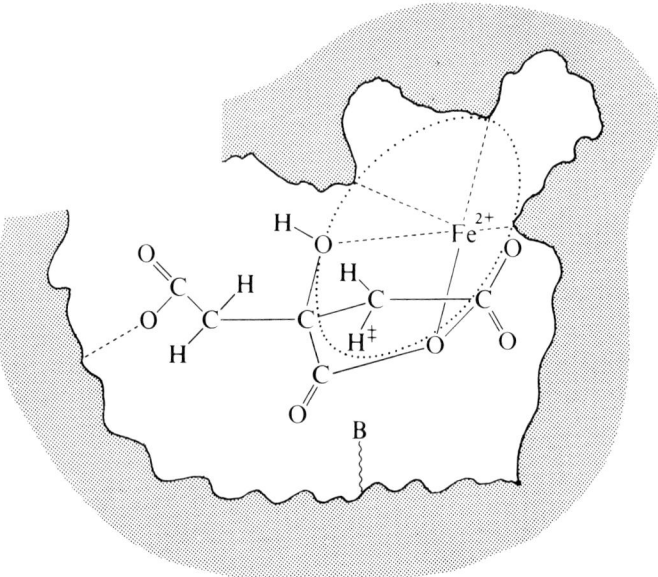

Citrate

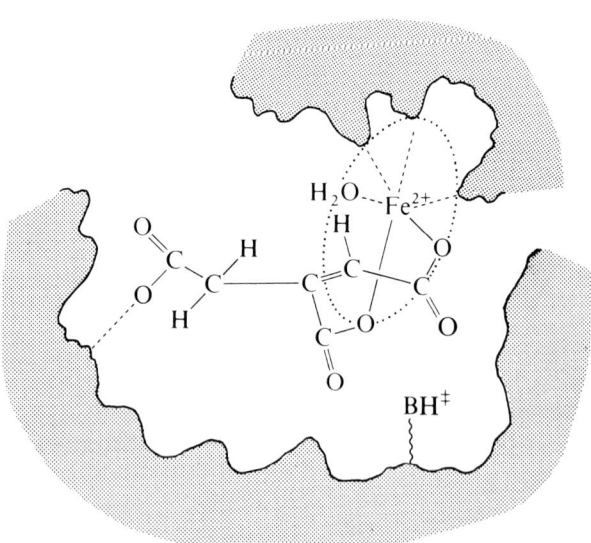

cis-Aconitate complex configuration I

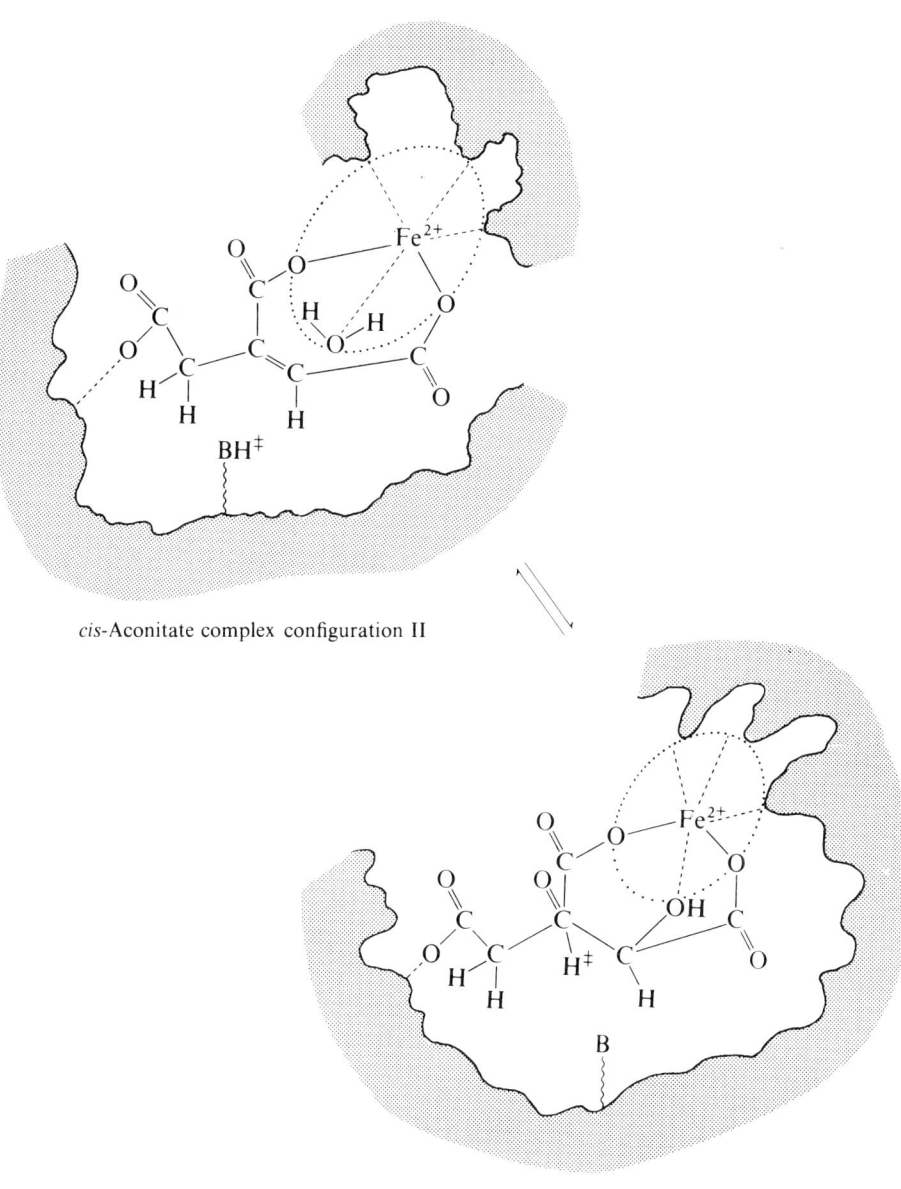

**Figure 10-5** *Ferrous wheel mechanism* for the conversion of citrate into isocitrate. Citrate becomes coordinated with the ferrous ion and the elements of water are eliminated through the agency of a basic functional group, B, at the catalytic site. This generates the aconitate complex, configuration I. This configuration is then converted into a second configuration, II, which allows the proton that was removed ($H^{\ddagger}$) to be introduced at the carbon atom to which the hydroxyl group was bonded initially. [Modified from Glusker, J. P. (1968) J. Mol. Biol. **38**, 149–162 (see p. 158).]

Two distinct isocitrate dehydrogenases exist in most mammalian tissues. One of these utilizes $NAD^+$ as the oxidation-reduction cofactor, while the other utilizes $NADP^+$ (or NADPH in the reverse reaction). The former is localized in the matrix of the mitochondria, where it functions as one of the enzymes of the tricarboxylic acid cycle. The $NADP^+$-dependent enzyme, on the other hand, is found in both the mitochondria and in the cytoplasm. In general, the $NADP^+$-dependent dehydrogenase is a relatively small protein with a molecular weight of less than 90,000 while the $NAD^+$-dependent enzyme is several times this size. For example, the $NAD^+$-dependent isocitrate dehydrogenase from porcine-heart mitochondria has been purified and found to have a molecular weight of 340,000. This species is composed of apparently identical subunits which each have a molecular weight of 40,000. Presumably, the oligomeric enzyme is an octomer.

Kinetic studies on the $NAD^+$-dependent isocitrate dehydrogenase have shown that the reaction has a sequential mechanism. However, the usual sequence of kinetic experiments has not been carried out since it has not been possible to demonstrate the reverse reaction. (Studies on the reaction catalyzed by the $NADP^+$-dependent enzyme, which can be conducted in the reverse direction, have shown that in this case a random sequential mechanism is operative.)

The oxidation and decarboxylation of isocitrate, as catalyzed by the $NAD^+$-dependent isocitrate dehydrogenase, entail the transfer of a hydride ion from C(2) of isocitrate to the *re* face of the pyridinium moiety of $NAD^+$. The hydride ion that is removed in this reaction is *specifically* from the same carboxymethyl group from which a proton was abstracted during the dehydration of citrate. In both instances the hydrogen that is removed is bonded to the carbon atom that was the C(3) of oxaloacetate. The removal of the hydride ion results in an oxidation at C(2) of isocitrate. However, the predicted oxidation product cannot be demonstrated; instead decarboxylation occurs and 2-oxoglutarate is obtained. It might be mentioned, however, that the predicted oxidation product, oxalosuccinate, would be expected to undergo the observed decarboxylation reaction very readily since the carboxylate group that is eliminated is bonded to the carbon atom adjacent to the oxo carbon atom. Under these conditions the negative charge that remains behind after the elimination reaction can be delocalized as illustrated below.

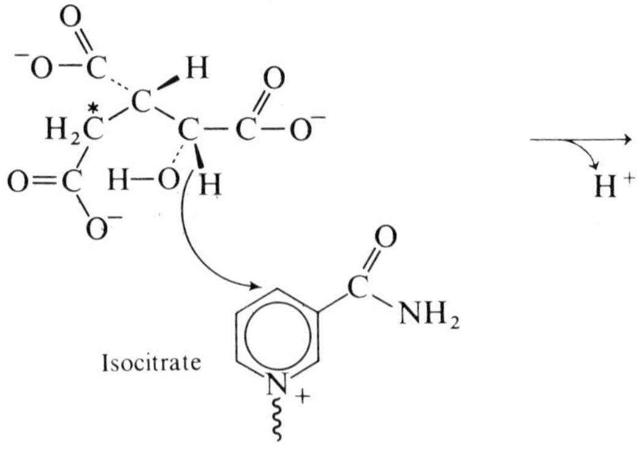

† Shen, W.-C., Mauck, L., and Colman, R. F. (1974) *J. Biol. Chem.* **249**, 7942–7949.

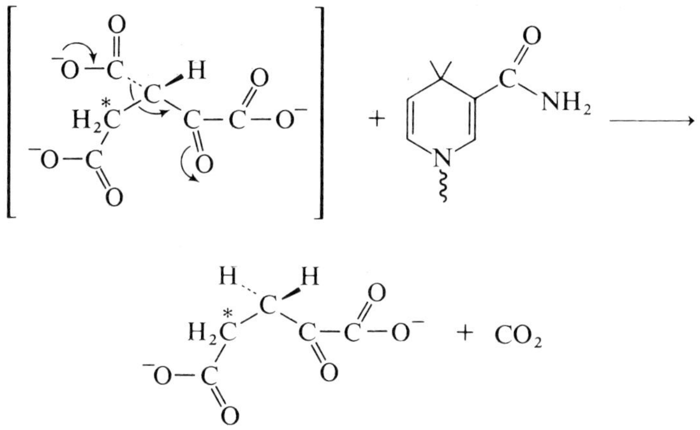

[chemical structures shown, with 2-Oxoglutarate labeled and $CO_2$ released]

Activities of $NAD^+$-dependent isocitrate dehydrogenases from mammalian sources are enhanced in the presence of ADP, and it has been suggested that this modulator promotes the binding of the substrates and also that of $Mg^{2+}$. The dehydrogenases have an absolute requirement for a divalent metal ion, such as $Mg^{2+}$. In addition, the activities of the mammalian enzymes are severely inhibited in the presence of NADH, and this inhibitory effect is potentiated by NADPH. The activities of yeast dehydrogenases are also enhanced by ADP, although the reduced nucleotides, NADH and NADPH, have little effect in these cases.

## Step 4: Conversion of 2-Oxoglutarate into the Succinyl Moiety of Succinyl CoA

Next 2-oxoglutarate is converted into the succinyl moiety of succinyl CoA as the result of a sequence of reactions that parallels the conversion of pyruvate into the acetyl moiety. The conversion is catalyzed by a 2-oxoglutarate dehydrogenase complex, which, as isolated from porcine-heart mitochondria, exhibits a particle weight of $2.7 \times 10^6$. When viewed by the electron microscope, the complex appears as a polyhedron with a diameter of approximately 260 Å. The core of the complex is the lipoate succinyltransferase, which has a molecular weight of $1 \times 10^6$ and is composed of 24 similar subunits, each of which has a molecular weight of 41,000. Eight molecules of lipoate are bound covalently to the succinyltransferase. In addition, six molecules of the 2-oxoglutarate dehydrogenase component (molecular weight, 216,000) and six of lipoamide dehydrogenase are noncovalently bound to the succinyltransferase.†

Just as in the conversion of pyruvate to the acetyl moiety of acetyl CoA, the four-carbon oxo acid, oxaloacetate, initially undergoes decarboxylation and oxidation

---

† Tanaka, N., Koike, K., Hamada, M., Otsuka, K.-I., Suematsu, T., and Koike, M. (1972) *J. Biol. Chem.* **247**, 4043–4049; Tanaka, N., Koike, K., Otsuka, K.-I., Hamada, M., Ogasahara, K., and Koike, M. (1974) *J. Biol. Chem.* **249**, 191–198; Koike, K., Hamada, M., Tanaka, N., Otsuka, K.-I., Ogasahara, K., and Koike, M. (1974) *J. Biol. Chem.* **249**, 3836–3842.

as the result of a reaction that is catalyzed by the thiamine diphosphate-dependent 2-oxoglutarate dehydrogenase component [2-oxoglutarate:lipoate oxidoreductase (decarboxylating and acceptor-succinylating) EC 1.2.4.2]. The reaction can be written

2-Oxoglutarate + oxidized lipoamide $\rightleftharpoons$
$$S^6\text{-succinyldihydrolipoamide} + CO_2 \quad (10\text{-}8a)$$

The succinyl moiety is then transferred from the sulfhydryl group of the reduced lipoamide to the sulfhydryl group of CoA. This is catalyzed by lipoate succinyltransferase. Finally, the resulting dihydrolipoamide is oxidized back to lipoamide, as in the reaction catalyzed by the pyruvate dehydrogenase complex. The lipoamide dehydrogenase that participates in the formation of succinyl CoA is thought to be the same as that which participates in the formation of acetyl CoA.

A 2-oxoglutarate dehydrogenase complex has also been isolated from *E. coli* and found to be similar to that described above although there appear to be some differences in the numbers of the dehydrogenase molecules that are noncovalently bonded to the succinyltransferase.†

## Step 5: Formation of Succinate

Succinyl CoA can be converted into succinate by at least three different reactions. One involves simple hydrolysis, as catalyzed by succinyl-CoA hydrolase. Another entails the reaction of succinyl CoA and a 3-oxo acid (such as acetoacetate) with the result that a 3-oxoacyl-CoA and succinate are formed. (Since the principal function of this reaction is that of forming acetoacetyl CoA, it will be discussed in Chap. 12, on lipid metabolism.) The third reaction, which is generally considered to be a step of the tricarboxylic acid cycle, entails the cleavage of succinyl CoA in the presence of a nucleoside diphosphate and orthophosphate. The products are succinate and the nucleoside triphosphate. In mammalian systems the nucleoside diphosphate is GDP, and the reaction, which is

$$\text{Succinyl CoA} + \text{GDP} + P_i \rightleftharpoons \text{succinate} + \text{CoA} + \text{GTP} \quad (10\text{-}8b)$$

is catalyzed by a GDP-dependent succinyl-CoA synthetase [succinate:CoA ligase (GDP-forming), EC 6.2.1.4].

Succinyl-CoA synthetase has been isolated from porcine heart and purified to homogeneity. This enzyme has a molecular weight of 76,000 and is composed of two nonidentical subunits. The larger has a molecular weight of 42,000, while the smaller has a molecular weight of 34,000.

In microorganisms such as *E. coli*, the nucleoside diphosphate that functions as a substrate in the reaction is ADP rather than GDP, and an ADP-dependent succinyl-CoA synthetase [succinate:CoA ligase (ADP-forming), EC 6.2.1.5] catalyzes the reaction. The ADP-dependent succinyl-CoA synthetase from *E. coli* has a molecular weight of 136,000 and is, again, composed of two types of subunits. The

---

† Petit, F. H., Hamilton, L., Munk, P., Namihira, G., Eley, M. H., Willms, C. R. and Reed, L. J. (1973) *J. Biol. Chem.* **248**, 5282–5290.

larger has a molecular weight of 39,000; the smaller has a molecular weight of 29,000. In this case the active enzyme is composed of two subunits of each type.

Kinetic studies on the synthetase from *E. coli* have indicated that the Ter Ter reaction proceeds by means of a sequential mechanism which involves the initial binding of ADP followed by a random-order binding of succinyl CoA and orthophosphate. According to this formulation, succinate and CoA are then randomly released, followed by the release of ATP.†

The cleavage of succinyl CoA as catalyzed by either the mammalian or the bacterial enzyme has been shown to entail the formation of a phosphoryl enzyme, which, in fact, can be isolated. The phosphoryl group is bonded to N(3) of an imidazolium moiety of a histidyl unit of a smaller subunit. An imidazolium moiety was identified as the phosphoryl acceptor on the basis of the conditions under which dephosphorylation occurs. Phosphorylhistidyl units undergo dephosphorylation in the presence of 1 $N$ sulfuric acid at 100°C for 2 min. Acyl phosphates, such as phosphorylglutamyl units, undergo dephosphorylation upon exposure to 0.03 $M$ sodium hydroxide for 10 min, while phosphorylseryl or phosphorylthreonyl units require 1 $N$ potassium hydroxide at 100°C for 15 min.

It has also been shown that as a consequence of the reaction an oxygen atom is transferred from orthophosphate to succinate. On the basis of these and other data, the following reaction mechanism has been proposed.

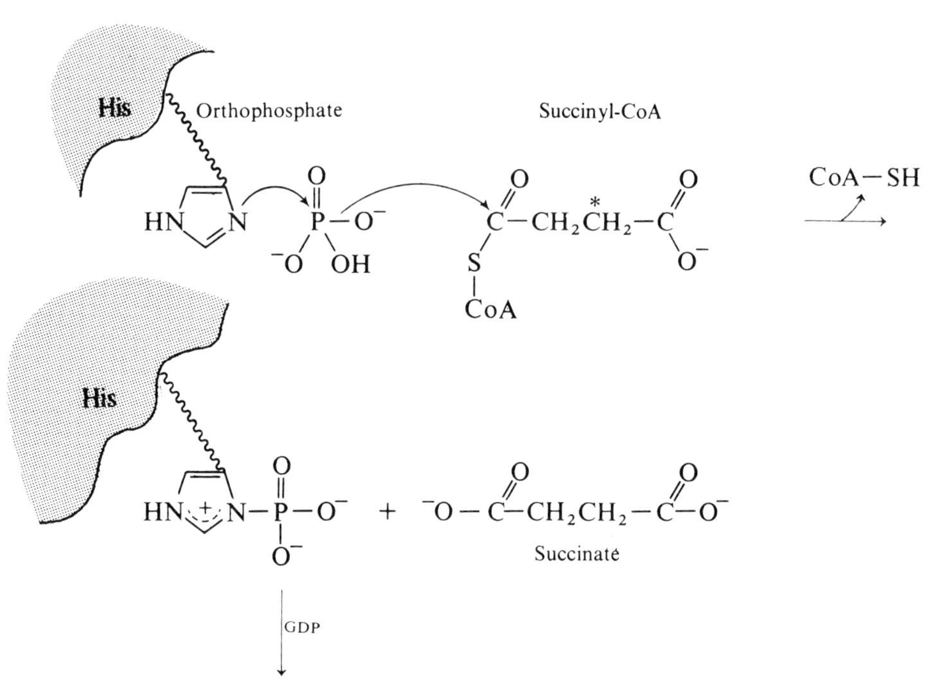

† Bridger, W. A. (1974) in *The Enzymes* (Boyer, P. D., ed.), 3d ed., vol. 10, pp. 581–606, Academic, New York.

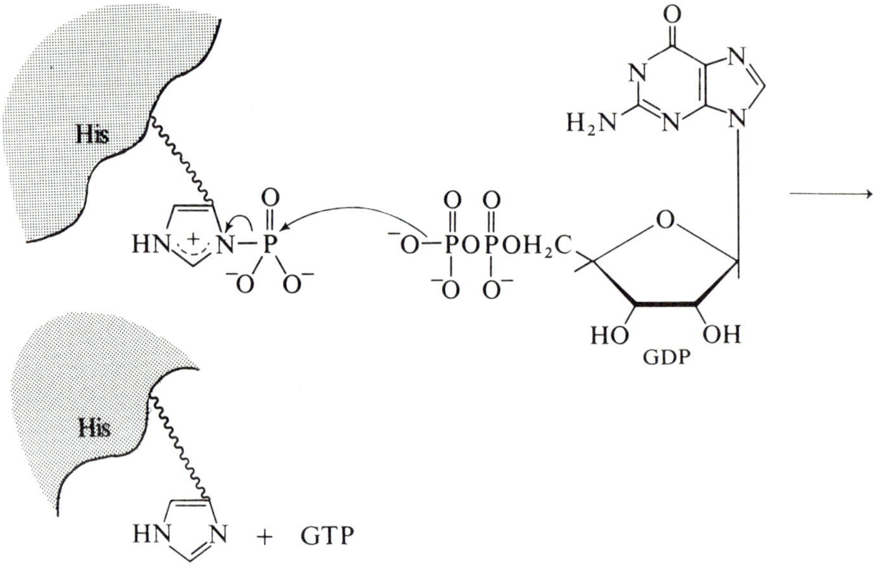

**Formation of ATP from GTP in mammalian systems** As noted above, the succinyl-CoA synthetase of mammalian cells uses GDP as the nucleoside dephosphate, and therefore GTP is formed. However, this GTP can be readily converted into ATP through the agency of a nucleosidediphosphate kinase (ATP:nucleosidediphosphate phosphotransferase, EC 2.7.4.6). The reaction entails the transfer of a phosphoryl group from GTP to ADP, i.e.,

$$\text{GTP} + \text{ADP} \rightleftharpoons \text{ATP} + \text{GDP} \qquad (10\text{-}9)$$

Nucleosidediphosphate kinase isolated from bovine-heart mitochondria has a molecular weight of 103,000. Other mitochondrial kinases have similar molecular weights. The reaction catalyzed by these enzymes proceeds by a ping pong kinetic mechanism. The double reciprocal plots derived from the initial-velocity data are parallel, and isotope exchange occurs between a given nucleoside triphosphate-nucleoside diphosphate pair in the absence of the other reaction components. Also, a phosphoryl enzyme can be isolated (although as was seen in the case of the reaction catalyzed by succinyl-CoA synthetase, this can sometimes be accomplished when the reaction has a sequential kinetic mechanism). The phosphoryl enzyme derived from nucleosidediphosphate kinase again contains an $N$-phosphorylhistidyl unit.

## Step 6: Oxidation of Succinate to Fumarate

The next reaction of the tricarboxylic acid cycle is, once more, an oxidation-reduction reaction. In this case the oxidation-reduction cofactor is FAD, and the enzyme that catalyzes the reaction is the one enzyme that participates in the tricarboxylic acid cycle although it is not localized in the matrix of the mitochondria.

Instead, this enzyme is localized in the mitochondrial inner membrane, where it also functions as a component of the mitochondrial electron-transport system. The enzyme is succinate dehydrogenase [succinate:(acceptor) oxidoreductase, EC 1.3.99.1]. Note that the third figure of the classification number is 99. In the case of oxidoreductases the sub-subclass designates the type of acceptor (of the reducing equivalents) involved. Sub-subclass 99 is used for cases in which the acceptor cannot be described simply. The reaction catalyzed by succinate dehydrogenase can be expressed as

$$\text{Succinate} + \text{acceptor} \rightleftharpoons \text{fumarate} + \text{reduced acceptor} \quad (10\text{-}10)$$

Actually, the oxidation of succinate entails the removal of two hydrogen atoms and two electrons. Their fate can best be described within the framework of the discussion of the mitochondrial electron-transport system, and therefore the present discussion will simply focus upon the oxidation of succinate and not the reduction of the acceptor.

Succinate dehydrogenase is a membrane-bound enzyme that can be solubilized to yield a species which has a molecular weight of 99,000. This species, as obtained from bovine-heart mitochondria, is composed of two unlike subunits. The first has a molecular weight of 69,000 and contains one covalently bonded FAD and also a coordination complex comprising four iron atoms and four sulfur atoms. Complexes of this type are generally referred to as *nonheme iron–sulfur complexes*. The iron is referred to as nonheme iron to distinguish it from the iron atoms of hemoglobin or the cytochromes. The sulfur atoms are derived from cysteinyl units at the catalytic site of the enzyme. The FAD is covalently bonded at C(8) of the isoalloxazine moiety of the cofactor as shown.

The other subunit of the dehydrogenase has a molecular weight of 30,000 and also contains a coordination complex of nonheme iron and sulfur.

The oxidation (or dehydrogenation) of succinate results from the trans elimination of two hydrogen atoms from the antiperiplanar configuration of succinate (see below). The reaction occurs with stereospecificity in that two nonequivalent hydrogen atoms are removed. However, there are two sets of two nonequivalent hydrogen atoms in succinate, and either set can be lost. More specifically, one methylene group of succinate can be considered to have a pro-R hydrogen and a pro-S hydrogen while the other has a pro-R' hydrogen and a pro-S' hydrogen. The dehydrogenation involves the loss of either a pro-S hydrogen and a pro-R' hydrogen or a pro-S' hydrogen and a pro-R hydrogen.

| Succinate | Antiperiplanar configuration | | Fumarate |

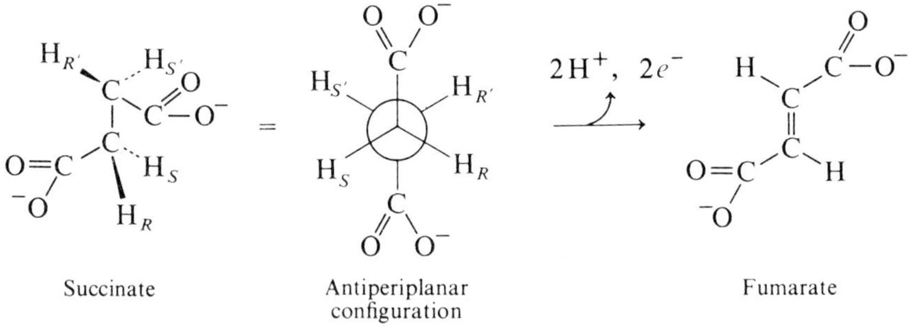

It should also be noted that since C(2) and C(3) are equivalent in the reaction catalyzed by succinate dehydrogenase, the carbon atoms derived from the acetyl moiety of acetyl CoA can no longer be distinguished from those derived from the oxaloacetate with which it underwent condensation (in step 1).

## Step 7: Hydration of Fumarate

Fumarate now undergoes a stereospecific hydration reaction which yields L- (or S-) malate. Fumarate hydratase (L-malate hydro-lyase, EC 4.2.1.2) catalyzes the reaction, which can be written

$$\text{Fumarate} + H_2O \rightleftharpoons \text{L-malate} \quad (10\text{-}11)$$

As isolated from porcine-heart mitochondria, fumarate hydratase has a molecular weight of 194,000 and is composed of four subunits which each have a molecular weight of 48,500.

The reaction catalyzed by fumarate hydratase exhibits standard kinetics, i.e., a hyperbolic velocity-vs.-substrate-concentration plot in the presence of low concentrations of fumarate. However, in the presence of high fumarate concentrations substrate activation is observed. This has been rationalized in terms of negative cooperativity; i.e., the binding of the initial substrate molecule by the oligomeric (in the present case, tetrameric) enzyme makes binding a second substrate molecule by that oligomer more difficult. In such cases, the *direct* plots (plots of velocity vs. substrate concentration) are more rapidly ascending hyperbolas and the double reciprocal plots are convex (or concave downward). Thus, at lower substrate concentrations the reaction velocity is faster than would be expected on the basis of the velocity observed in the presence of higher substrate concentrations.

The hydration of fumate entails the trans addition of the elements of water. A proton is initially added at the *re* face of one of the trigonal carbon atoms, and then a hydroxyl group is added at the *si* face of the other.

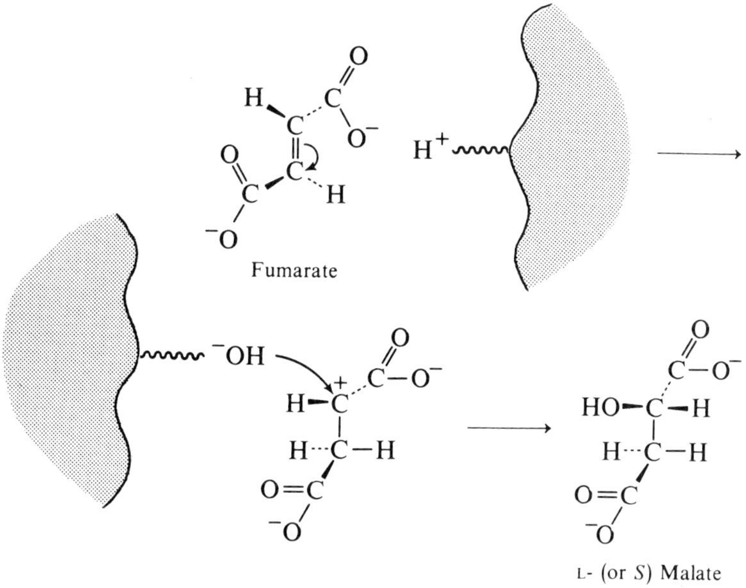

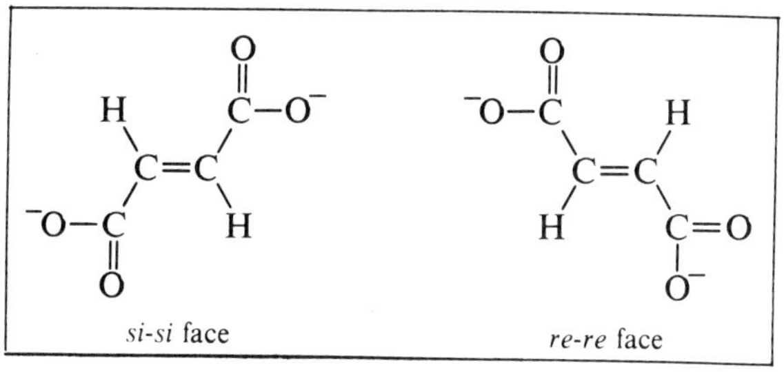

## Step 8: Oxidation of Malate to Oxaloacetate

The tricarboxylic acid cycle is completed as malate is oxidized to regenerate oxaloacetate. This, the fourth oxidation-reduction reaction of the cycle, is catalyzed by malate dehydrogenase (L-malate:NAD$^+$ oxidoreductase, EC 1.1.1.37) and is

$$\text{L-Malate} + \text{NAD}^+ \rightleftharpoons \text{oxaloacetate} + \text{NADH} \qquad (10\text{-}12)$$

Malate dehydrogenase isolated from porcine-heart mitochondria is a dimer which has a molecular weight of 65,000. The reaction catalyzed by this enzyme has an ordered sequential kinetic mechanism as indicated by the observations that the double reciprocal plots prepared from the initial-velocity data are linear and intersecting and that saturating concentrations of malate or oxaloacetate inhibit the [*carboxamide*-$^{14}$C]NAD$^+$-to-NADH exchange totally. Hence, NAD$^+$ must be the initial substrate that binds, and NADH must be the final product released.

The reaction, which involves the transfer of a hydride ion from C(2) of L-malate to the *re* face of the pyridinium moiety of NAD$^+$, can be depicted as shown.

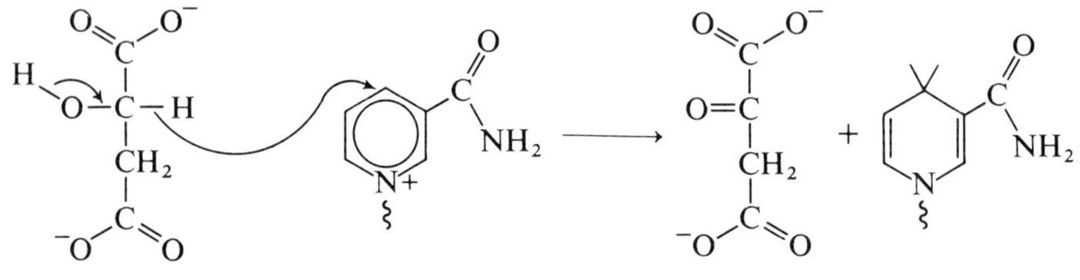

[Chemical structure diagram: Malate → Oxaloacetate with NAD+/NADH]

Malate                    Oxaloacetate

## Summary of the Reactions of the Tricarboxylic Acid Cycle

The reactions of the tricarboxylic acid cycle are summarized in Fig. 10-6.

## Regulation of the Tricarboxylic Acid Cycle

The regulation of the tricarboxylic acid cycle has been studied rather extensively in rat-heart mitochondria.[†] These studies showed that the activity of the pyruvate dehydrogenase complex is not rate-determining with respect to the reactions of the cycle. Rather, under many conditions flow through the tricarboxylic acid cycle is limited by the activity of citrate synthase. The principal factors that determine the activity of the synthase are the available concentration of the substrate oxaloacetate and the extent to which certain acyl derivatives of CoA function as competitive inhibitors with respect to acetyl CoA. One such derivative is succinyl CoA, which functions as a competitive inhibitor with respect to acetyl CoA when the available concentration of acetyl CoA is low while that of oxaloacetate is high.

Succinyl CoA is also a potent inhibitor of the activity of the lipoate succinyltransferase of the 2-oxoglutarate dehydrogenase complex. This is of particular importance since it provides a means by which the utilization of 2-oxoglutarate from sources other than the earlier steps of the tricarboxylic acid cycle can be regulated.

Finally, the available concentration of succinyl CoA itself is inversely related to the intramitochondrial GTP/GDP ratio. Since nucleosidediphosphate kinase activity is generally more than adequate in the mitochondria, a GTP/GDP ratio is readily translated into an ATP/ADP ratio. Therefore, in the presence of a high intramitochondrial ATP/ADP ratio, flux through the tricarboxylic acid cycle is impeded. Again, this would seem to be the desired effect.

[†] La Noue, K. F., Bryla, J., and Williamson, J. R. (1972) *J. Biol. Chem.* **247**, 667–679.

---

**Figure 10-6** Summary of the conversion of pyruvate into the acetyl moiety of acetyl-CoA and the utilization of the latter by the tricarboxylic acid cycle. Values for $\Delta G^{\circ\prime}$ at pH 7.0 are given for each reaction. (Values for $\Delta G^{\circ}$ are also given when available.)

|  | $\Delta G^{o\prime}$, kcal/mol | $\Delta G^{o}$, kcal/mol |
|---|---|---|

Pyruvate + CoA—SH + NAD$^+$ → Acetyl-CoA + CO$_2$ + NADH      −9.38
$C_3H_3O_3^-$                                    $C_2H_3O$—CoA

Oxaloacetate + H$_2$O ──┐
$C_4H_2O_5^{2-}$         │
                         ↓
                 Citrate + CoA—SH + H$^+$                     −9.08
                 $C_6H_5O_7^{3-}$
                         │
                         ↓
                 Isocitrate                                   +1.59      +1.59
                 $C_6H_5O_7^{3-}$

NAD$^+$ ──┐
          ↓
          2-Oxoglutarate + CO$_2$ + NADH                      −1.70
          $C_5H_4O_5$

CoA—SH + NAD$^+$ ──┐
                   ↓
                   Succinyl-CoA + CO$_2$ + NADH               −8.82
                   $C_4H_4O_3^-$—CoA

HO—PO$_3^{2-}$ + GDP$^{3-}$ ──┐
                              ↓
                              Succinate + CoA—SH + GTP$^{4-}$   −0.8
                              $C_4H_4O_4^{2-}$

FAD ──┐
      ↓
      Fumarate + 2H$^+$ + FAD·2$e^-$                          −0.0
      $C_4H_4O_4^{2-}$

H2O ──┐
      ↓
      L-Malate                                                −0.88      −0.88
      $C_4H_4O_5^{2-}$

NAD$^+$ ──┐
          ↓
          Oxaloacetate + NADH + H$^+$                         +6.69
          $C_4H_2O_5^{2-}$

*Summary Equation*
$C_3H_3O_3^-$ + 4NAD$^+$ + FAD + GDP$^{3-}$ + 2CoA—SH + HO—PO$_3^{2-}$ + 2H$_2$O → 3CO$_2$ + 4NADH
FAD·2$e^-$ + GTP$^{4-}$ + 2CoA—SH + 4H$^+$

# PASSAGE OF TRICARBOXYLIC ACID INTERMEDIATES ACROSS MITOCHONDRIAL MEMBRANES

Biological membranes generally define cellular compartments and impose a barrier to the passage of biochemical intermediates from one compartment to another. The inner membrane of the mitochondrion presents a barrier to the translocation of many biochemical intermediates, including adenine nucleotides and other compounds that are involved in the tricarboxylic acid cycle. One important adenine nucleotide that does not pass across the mitochondrial inner membrane is acetyl CoA. CoA undergoes acetylation in the mitochondria, but a portion of this acetyl CoA must be made available in the cytoplasm of the cell, where it is required for processes including the *de novo* synthesis of fatty acids. This is accomplished as follows.

The mitochondrial inner membrane embodies a component which binds citrate and facilitates its translocation across the membrane. As is frequently the case, the translocation of one molecule from within the membrane-bound compartment to the outside is accompanied by the translocation of another molecule from the outside of the compartment to the inside. In the present case, another dicarboxylic or tricarboxylic acid intermediate is exchanged for the citrate molecule. In rat liver, malate frequently enters the mitochondrion as a concomitance of the exit of a molecule of citrate. Once citrate is outside of the mitochondrion and in the cytoplasm it can undergo a cleavage reaction, catalyzed by ATP citrate-lyase [ATP:citrate oxaloacetate-lyase (*pro*-3S-$CH_2COO^-$ → acetyl-CoA; ATP-dephosphorylating), EC 4.1.3.8], as follows:

$$ATP + citrate + CoA \rightleftharpoons ADP + P_i + oxaloacetate + acetyl\ CoA \quad (10\text{-}13)$$

ATP citrate-lyase isolated from rat liver (molecular weight, 500,000) has been examined with respect to its kinetic mechanism, and the following observations were made.† Plots of $1/v_i$ vs. $1/[MgATP]$ with fixed concentrations of CoA and one constant concentration of citrate were intersecting at subsaturating concentrations of citrate while they were parallel in the presence of saturating concentrations of

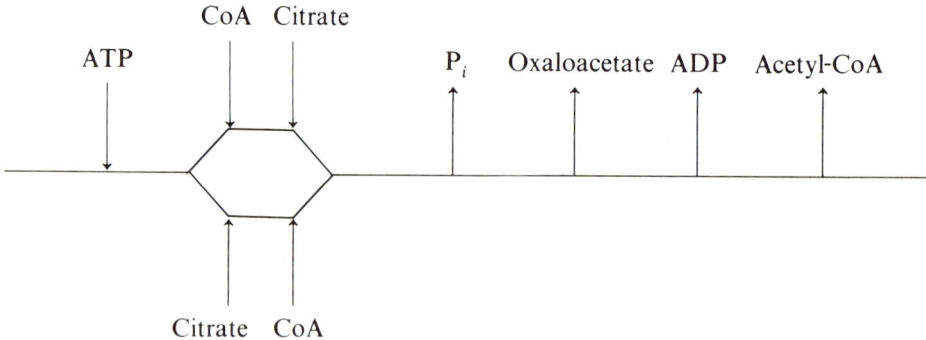

† Farrar, Y. J. K., and Plowman, K. M. (1971) *J. Biol. Chem.* **246**, 3777–3782, 3783–3788.

citrate. Plots of $1/v_i$ vs. $1/[\text{MgATP}]$ with fixed concentrations of citrate and one constant concentration of CoA were intersecting when the concentration of CoA was subsaturating and parallel when it was saturating. Plots of $1/v_i$ vs. $1/[\text{CoA}]$, with fixed concentrations of MgATP and one constant concentration of citrate exhibited similar behavior. However, when either CoA or citrate was the variable substrate with fixed concentrations of the other, plots were intersecting even in the presence of saturating concentrations of MgATP. These data, combined with additional data derived from studies on the reverse reaction and isotope-exchange studies, may be interpreted as indicating the kinetic mechanism shown diagrammatically on page 438. It should be pointed out, however, that the kinetic mechanism depicted above is somewhat simpler than may be the case. The data, in fact, indicate that ADP can be released at more than one point in the reaction sequence. A minimal reaction mechanism for the cleavage of citrate is shown below.

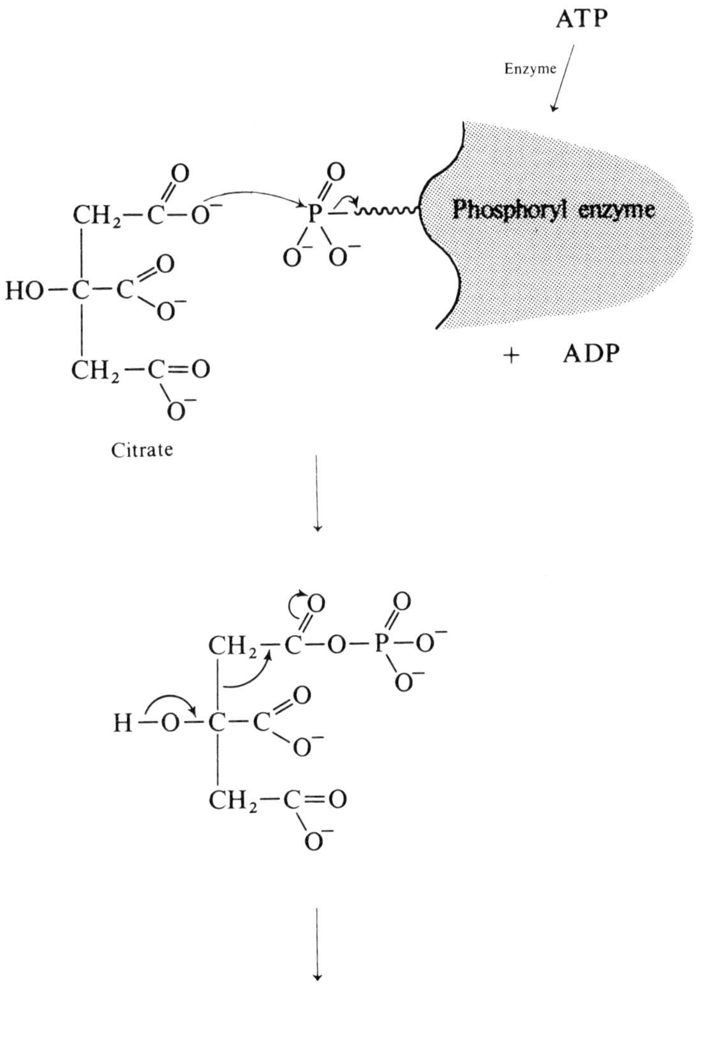

$$\text{O}=\text{C}-\text{C}\begin{array}{c}\text{O}\\\parallel\\\text{O}^-\end{array} \quad + \quad \text{CH}_2=\text{C}\begin{array}{c}\text{O}^-\\\\\text{O}-\text{P}-\text{O}^-\\|\\\text{O}^-\end{array}$$
$$\underset{\text{Oxaloacetate}}{\overset{|}{\text{CH}_2-\text{C}=\text{O}}\atop\overset{|}{\text{O}^-}}$$

$$\text{CH}_3-\overset{\text{O}}{\overset{\parallel}{\text{C}}}\overset{\text{O}}{\overset{\parallel}{\text{O}-\text{P}-\text{O}^-}}\quad\xleftarrow{\text{CoA}}\quad\text{CH}_3-\overset{\text{O}}{\overset{\parallel}{\text{C}}}\overset{\text{O}}{\overset{\parallel}{\text{O}-\text{P}-\text{O}^-}}$$
$$\text{CoA}-\text{S}-\text{H}$$

$$\downarrow$$

$$\underset{\text{Acetyl-CoA}}{\text{CoA}-\text{S}-\overset{\text{O}}{\overset{\parallel}{\text{C}}}-\text{CH}_3\ ,\ +\ \text{P}_i}$$

The mechanism includes the formation of a phosphoryl enzyme, which has been isolated, and the formation of citroylphosphate, which has not been demonstrated. The cleavage is a retrograde aldol reaction.

As a result of the process just described not only acetyl CoA but also oxaloacetate is, in effect, translocated across the mitochondrial inner membrane and into the cytoplasm. However, oxaloacetate is unable to diffuse back across the inner membrane and into the mitochondrial matrix (where it participates in the tricarboxylic acid cycle); thus, in order that this intermediate is not irreversibly exported from the matrix, the following sequence of events can occur. In the cytoplasm, oxaloacetate undergoes reduction to yield malate as the result of a reaction catalyzed by a cytoplasmic malate dehydrogenase:

$$\text{Oxaloacetate} + \text{NADH} \rightleftharpoons \text{L-malate} + \text{NAD}^+ \qquad (10\text{-}14)$$

This is the reverse of the reaction which occurs as the final step of the tricarboxylic acid cycle. Both the mitochondrial and the cytoplasmic dehydrogenases are dimers which each have a molecular weight of approximately 65,000. The malate that is thus formed can then undergo oxidation and decarboxylation as the result of a reaction catalyzed by an $\text{NADP}^+$-dependent malate dehydrogenase (decarboxylating) [L-malate:$\text{NADP}^+$ oxidoreductase (oxaloacetate-decarboxylating), EC 1.1.1.40], also localized in the cytoplasm. This enzyme as obtained from pigeon liver is a tetramer having a molecular weight of 260,000 and it catalyzes the reaction

$$\text{L-Malate} + \text{NADP}^+ \rightleftharpoons \text{pyruvate} + \text{CO}_2 + \text{NADPH} \qquad (10\text{-}15)$$

which has been shown to proceed by the ordered sequential Bi Ter mechanism shown.

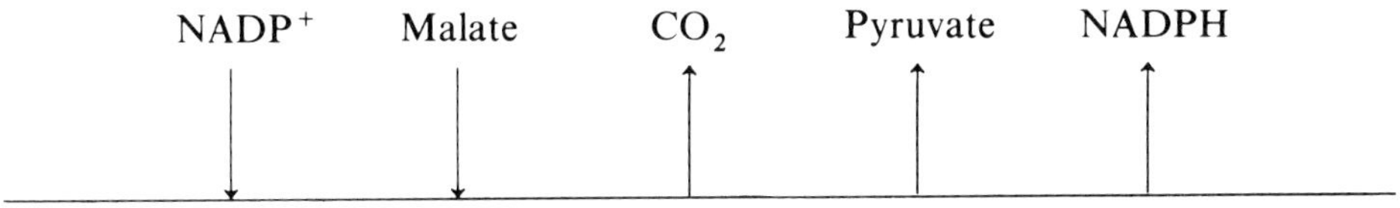

```
     NADP⁺     Malate      CO₂      Pyruvate    NADPH
       │         │          ↑          ↑          ↑
       ↓         ↓          │          │          │
───────────────────────────────────────────────────────
```

The resulting pyruvate can then pass across the mitochondrial inner membrane into the matrix, where in the presence of ATP, bicarbonate, and the enzyme pyruvate carboxylase, oxaloacetate can be formed. Thus, the oxaloacetate that, in effect, moved out of the mitochondrial matrix and across the inner membrane with acetyl CoA can subsequently be regenerated in the matrix.

CHAPTER
# ELEVEN
## ELECTRON TRANSPORT AND ENERGY PRODUCTION

### PART I IN MITOCHONDRIA

In 1884 a British pathologist and biochemist, Charles Alexander MacMunn, detected and described the species known today as the *cytochromes*, the heme proteins that function as electron carriers in the mitochondrial electron-transport system. By 1912, it was possible to make cell preparations that could catalyze the enzymatic dehydrogenation of a variety of substrates, and in 1922 Heinrich Wieland proposed that biological oxidations and reductions entail the transfer of hydrogen to molecular oxygen. Five years later, David Keilin described the function of the cytochromes as mediation of the transport of electrons from the dehydrogenases to molecular oxygen. Thus, the concept of the mitochondrial electron-transport system began to take form. At this stage considerable information concerning the characteristics of the mitochondrial electron-transport system was available. For example, the electrode potentials of the cytochromes could be determined, and these data could be used in determining the order of cytochromes *a*, *b*, and *c* in the electron-transport system. Subsequently it was learned at which points reducing equivalents are introduced into the transport system, and still later the roles of ubiquinone (also called coenzyme Q) and other nonheme components were proposed. However, there are still many unanswered questions concerning the mitochondrial electron-transport system and the manner in which it functions to provide usable chemical energy.

The mitochondrial electron-transport system is a process by which reducing equivalents derived from the oxidation of the carbon atoms of saccharides, fatty

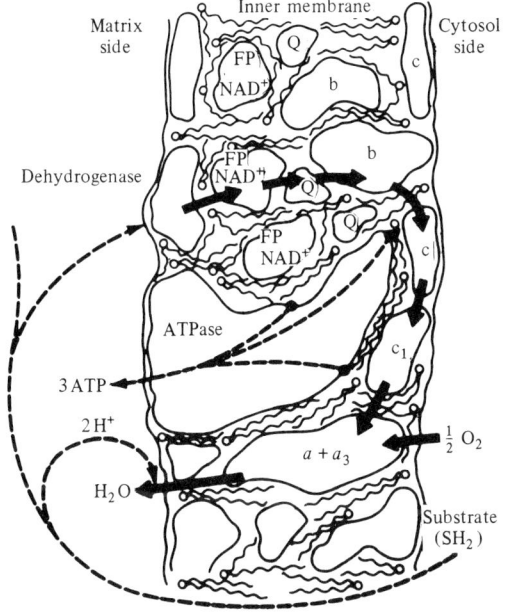

**Figure 11-1** Schematic representation of the organization of some of the components of the mitochondrial electron-transport system in the inner membrane. Components localized at the membrane surface are thought to be associated by electrostatic bonds while those in the interior interact by hydrophobic bonds.

FP = flavoprotein
Q = ubiquinone
$a, a_3, b, c, c_1$ = cytochromes designated as a, $a_3$, b, c, and $c_1$, respectively
ATPase = adenosinetriphosphatase, an enzyme thought to be involved in the conversion of ADP and $P_i$ into ATP

[*From* Packer, L. (1972) *Bioenergetics* 3, 115-127 (see p. 116).]

acids, and amino acids are utilized for the reduction of molecular oxygen. As a concomitance of this process usable chemical energy is made available in the form of the ATP molecule. The components of the mitochondrial electron-transport system are associated with its inner membrane, which has been shown to be assymmetrical. Certain components of the electron-transport system are localized primarily on the cytoplasmic side (the C side), facing the outer membrane, while other components are localized primarily on the matrix side (the M side). There is also considerable evidence that there is a vectorial organization of the components of the electron-transport system within the inner membrane and that this organization is essential to the functioning of the system. One concept of the structural organization of the mitochondrial inner membrane is shown in Fig. 11-1.

When the carbon atoms of a saccharide are oxidized as a result of glycolysis or the tricarboxylic acid cycle, the reducing equivalents are transferred to $NAD^+$ or (in the reaction catalyzed by succinate dehydrogenase) to the flavin cofactor of the enzyme. When the carbon atoms of a fatty acid are oxidized as a result of the $\beta$-oxidation pathway, the reducing equivalents are transferred to FAD or to $NAD^+$. The same occurs when carbon atoms derived from an amino acid are oxidized by the tricarboxylic acid cycle or the $\beta$-oxidation pathway. These reducing equivalents, in the form of NADH or a reduced flavin cofactor, can then be introduced into the mitochondrial electron-transport system, where as a concomitance of their use for the reduction of molecular oxygen, the chemical energy required for the phosphorylation of ADP, to yield ATP, is generated.

When reducing equivalents from NADH are introduced into the system, they are initially transferred to a lipoprotein complex known as NADH-ubiquinone reductase, also referred to as complex I.

## INTRODUCTION OF REDUCING EQUIVALENTS FROM NADH

NADH-ubiquinone reductase can be isolated in particulate form from the inner membrane of bovine-heart mitochondria through the use of the detergent cholate. This species has a minimum particle weight of 700,000 and contains FMN, coordination complexes of nonheme iron and sulfur, phospholipids, and ubiquinone-10.† The flavin, nonheme iron, and sulfur are present in a ratio of 1 : 23 : 22. Ubiquinone-10 is a benzoquinone that participates in the electron-transfer process.

$$\text{H}_3\text{CO} \underset{\underset{O}{\|}}{\overset{\overset{O}{\|}}{\bigcirc}} \begin{matrix} \text{CH}_3 \\ \\ (\text{CH}_2\text{CH}=\overset{\overset{\text{CH}_3}{|}}{\text{C}}-\text{CH}_2)_{10}-\text{H} \end{matrix}$$

Ubiquinone-10

Treatment of NADH-ubiquinone reductase again with cholate or alternatively with enzymes that catalyze the cleavage of phospholipids yields a soluble preparation that can also accept reducing equivalents from NADH and introduce them into the mitochondrial electron-transport system (although this species does not have all the characteristics of NADH-ubiquinone reductase). This soluble preparation is referred to as NADH dehydrogenase [NADH:(acceptor) oxidoreductase, EC 1.6.99.3]. Dehydrogenases have somewhat lower molecular weights than the reductase, which reflects, in part, the loss of phospholipid. This loss is accompanied by the loss or alteration of some of the properties of the reductase. If either the reductase or the dehydrogenase is treated with certain other reagents, including thiocyanate, perchlorate, or iodide, a much smaller species having a molecular weight of approximately 70,000 can be obtained. The properties of this species, however, are quite different from those of the particulate reductase or the (larger) soluble dehydrogenase.

Digressing for the moment, the isolation of the components of biological membranes can be accomplished in a variety of ways, including the use of detergents and salts and other low-molecular-weight reagents. However, one is always concerned whether the species extracted from the membrane retains the characteristics which it had as a component of the membrane. Many of the procedures for the isolation of membrane components entail the disruption of the interactions between the proteins and the phospholipids of the membrane. Many of these procedures result in the isolation of species which have been separated from much of the phospholipid that was a part of their environment in the membrane, and this change in environment often results in a change in the characteristics of the isolated component. Therefore, although one generally undertakes the isolation of a membrane component in order to learn more about its behavior and mechanism of action, it is always necessary to determine whether

---

† In most mammalian systems the side chain of this molecule comprises ten isoprenoid units, and therefore it is designated as ubiquinone-10.

or not the observed behavior of the isolated component is the same as that exhibited prior to isolation.

The NADH-ubiquinone reductase carries out that portion of the electron-transport process from NADH to ubiquinone, as the name implies. This portion of the process requires the participation of FMN and four distinct nonheme iron–sulfur centers,† which have reduction potentials ranging from approximately $-400$ to $0\,\mathrm{mV}$. Iron-sulfur coordination complexes such as these exhibit characteristic EPR spectra when participating in electron-transfer processes, i.e., when accepting single, unpaired electrons and thereby undergoing reduction. When this occurs, a characteristic resonance centered at approximately $g = 1.94$ is observed. Also, the EPR spectra of flavins that are undergoing one-electron reduction (to the semiquinone level) exhibit a characteristic resonance which is centered at $g = 2.00$. As reducing equivalents are transferred from NADH along the sequence of components present in NADH-ubiquinone reductase, EPR spectra suggest that these electrons are initially accepted by the flavin and then by each of the iron-sulfur centers in sequence, and finally by the ubiquinone. The process might be represented as follows:

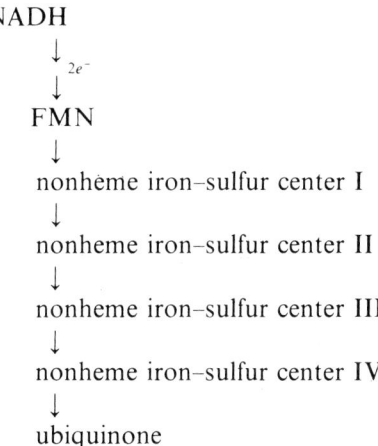

## INTRODUCTION OF REDUCING EQUIVALENTS FROM SUCCINATE

As mentioned in Chap. 10, succinate dehydrogenase, which participates in the tricarboxylic acid cycle, is in fact a component of the mitochondrial electron-transport system. The dehydrogenase can be isolated as a part of a lipoprotein complex known as succinate-ubiquinone reductase. This particulate species is also called complex II. Succinate-ubiquinone reductase carries out that portion of the electron-transport process from succinate to ubiquinone. This complex has been isolated, again from bovine-heart mitochondria, as a particle which has a weight of 240,000 and which contains FAD, nonheme iron–sulfur coordination complexes, ubiquinone, a cytochrome of the $b$ family, and phospholipids.

---

† Ohnishi, T. (1975) *Biochim. Biophys. Acta* **387,** 475–490.

Like complex I, the particulate complex II can be treated with reagents which allow its enzyme component to be isolated in a soluble form. Soluble succinate dehydrogenase can thus be obtained from succinate-ubiquinone reductase through the use of several reagents, including 0.8 $N$ sodium perchlorate.† The solubilized succinate dehydrogenase has a molecular weight of 97,000 and comprises two subunits. The larger (70,000) contains iron-sulfur coordination complexes and FAD, while the smaller (27,000) contains iron-sulfur complexes but lacks flavin.

The electron transfer that is carried out by succinate-ubiquinone reductase involves the participation of three nonheme iron–sulfur centers, in addition to that of FAD. The process is, perhaps, similar to that which occurs in the case of NADH-ubiquinone reductase. Thus, the introduction of reducing equivalents from succinate into the mitochondrial electron-transport system may be represented diagrammatically as shown.

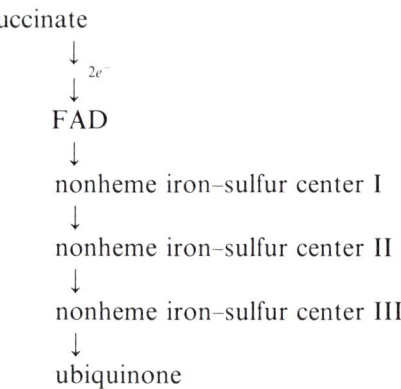

## UBIQUINONE

Both NADH-ubiquinone reductase and succinate-ubiquinone reductase accept reducing equivalents and transfer them ultimately to ubiquinone. Thus this factor occupies a position at the confluence of two portions of the mitochondrial electron-transport system. From this point forward in the sequence electrons donated by NADH or by succinate are transferred along the same series of carriers. When ubiquinone accepts an electron, it undergoes reduction to the level of a semiquinone. When this electron is subsequently passed on to the next carrier in the transfer sequence, ubiquinone is regenerated.

In most mammalian systems, the hydrocarbon side chain of ubiquinone consists of 10 isoprenoid units, although in the rat this side chain consists of 9 isoprenoid units and the compound is, accordingly, referred to as ubiquinone-9. The biosynthesis of ubiquinone in mammalian systems utilizes $p$-hydroxybenzoate and isopentenyl diphosphate as the principal intermediates.‡

---

† Coles, C. J., Tisdale, H. D., Kenney, W. C., and Singer, T. P. (1974) *J. Biol. Chem.* **249**, 381–385.
‡ Trumpower, B. L., Houser, R. M., and Olson, R. E. (1974) *J. Biol. Chem.* **249**, 3041–3048.

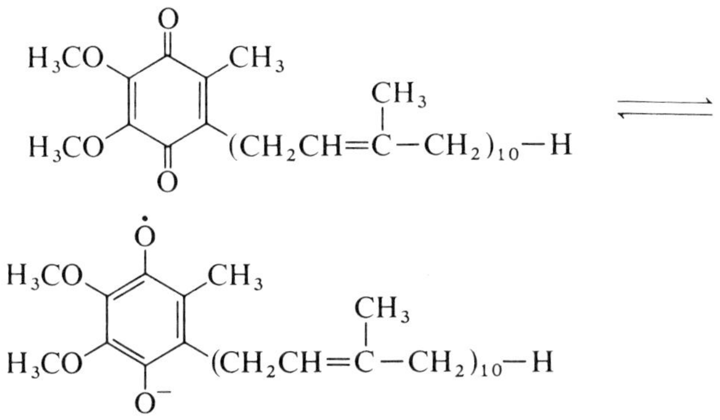

[Structure of ubiquinone-10 oxidized form shown equilibrating]

Semiquinone form of ubiquinone-10

## REDUCED UBIQUINONECYTOCHROME $c$ REDUCTASE

Reducing equivalents accepted by ubiquinone from either complex I or complex II are subsequently passed along a sequence of carriers and, ultimately, to molecular oxygen. A lipoprotein complex known as reduced ubiquinone–cytochrome $c$ reductase, or complex III, can carry out the first part of this process. Complex III contains cytochromes of the $b$ family, cytochrome $c_1$, and nonheme iron-sulfur coordination complexes. The function of complex III is that of accepting reducing electrons from ubiquinone, as stated, and passing them to cytochrome $c$.

Cytochromes are heme-protein complexes. They are classified on the basis of

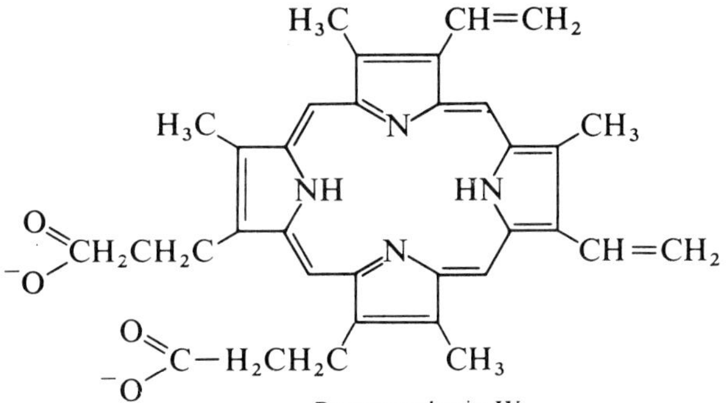

Protoporphyrin IX

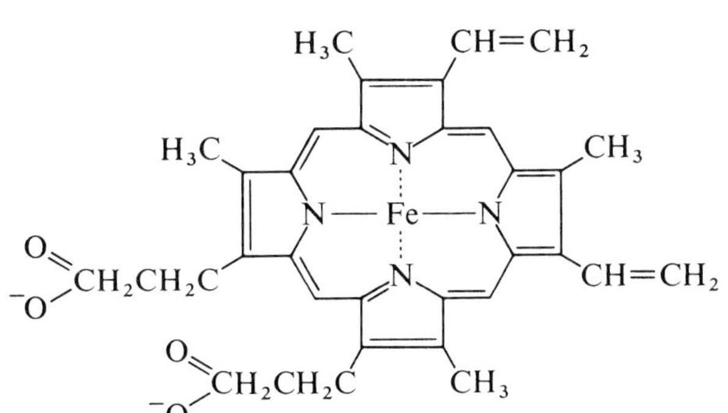

Heme b

the porphyrin moiety of the heme which they embody. Cytochromes of the $b$ family embody the same porphyrin moiety as hemoglobin or myoglobin. However, while the central iron atom of the heme is in the ferrous state (specifically, low-spin $d^6$ iron) in hemoglobin and myoglobin, it is in the ferric state (low-spin, $d^5$ iron) in the cytochromes as they are isolated. During electron transport it is the iron center that accepts an electron and is thereby momentarily reduced. The porphyrin moiety of the $b$-type cytochromes is shown on page 447, along with its iron coordination complex, heme b.

In cytochromes of the $b$ family the heme coordination complex and protein are not covalently bonded but rather are joined by electrostatic bonds. The protein moieties of these cytochromes are relatively small. For example, one such protein has a molecular weight of 28,000.

The cytochromes exhibit characteristic ultraviolet absorption spectra. They also exhibit characteristic EPR spectra when they have undergone a one-electron reduction, as occurs when they participate in the mitochondrial electron-transport system. Since the absorption spectra of the oxidized and reduced cytochromes are different, both types of spectroscopy can be used to monitor the electron-transfer process that is carried out by these components. Using such techniques it has been determined that complex III contains two different $b$-type cytochromes. One has a midpoint reduction potential (or half-reduction potential) of approximately 100 mV and a characteristic ultraviolet absorption band at 561 nm in the reduced form. This species is known as cytochrome $b$-561. The other has a midpoint potential of approximately 0 mV and a characteristic absorption band at 566 nm when reduced. It is called cytochrome $b$-566.

Complex III also contains cytochrome $c_1$, a cytochrome of the $c$ family. The heme of this hemeprotein has the following structure.

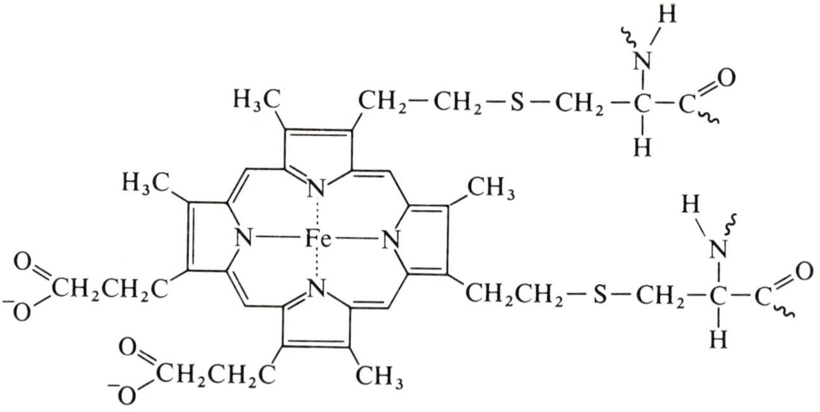

Heme c

As indicated, two of the bonds between the heme and the protein are covalent. The ligand binding between heme and protein is thought to involve the nitrogen atom of His-18 (at the fifth ligand position) and the sulfur atom of Met-80 (at the sixth ligand position). Cytochrome $c_1$ has a characteristic absorption band at 554 nm when reduced and a midpoint potential of approximately 280 mV.

In addition, complex III contains at least one nonheme iron–sulfur center, which has a midpoint potential of 280 mV.

Electron transport through complex III is as follows:

$$\begin{array}{c}
\text{Reduced ubiquinone} \\
\downarrow e^- \\
\text{cytochrome } b\text{-566} \\
\downarrow \\
\text{cytochrome } b\text{-561} \\
\downarrow \\
\text{cytochrome } c_1 \\
\downarrow \\
\text{nonheme iron–sulfur center} \\
\downarrow \\
\text{cytochrome } c
\end{array}$$

## CYTOCHROME c OXIDASE AND THE REDUCTION OF MOLECULAR OXYGEN

The fourth lipoprotein complex derived from the mitochondrial electron-transport system carries out the terminal segment of the process, which culminates in the reduction of molecular oxygen. This complex is known as cytochrome c oxidase (ferrocytochrome c:oxygen oxidoreductase, EC 1.9.3.1). Cytochrome c oxidase specifically accepts electrons from reduced cytochrome c and transfers them ultimately to molecular oxygen.

This component of the mitochondrial electron-transport system has been isolated from both mammalian sources (including bovine-heart mitochondria) and nonmammalian sources (including *Saccharomyces cerevesiae* and *Neurospora crassa*). These species have been extensively purified in some cases, and they are known to contain two cytochromes of the *a* family and also two copper atoms. Heme a has the structure shown.

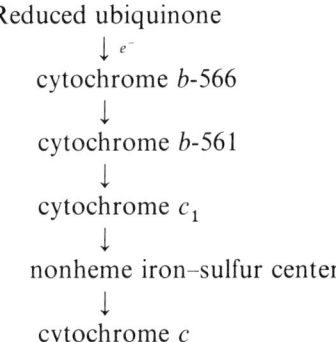

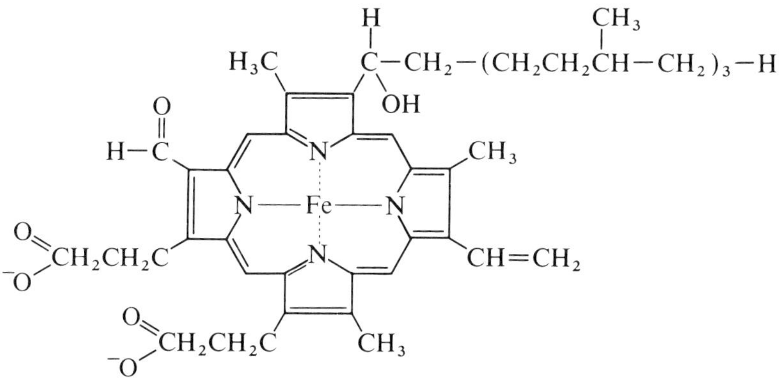

Heme a

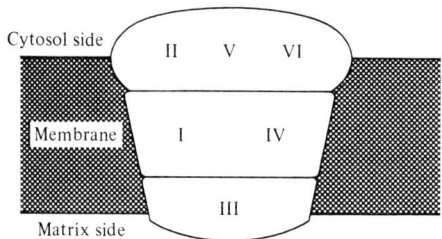

**Figure 11-2** Highly schematic representation of the asymmetric arrangement of the six polypeptides of cytochrome c oxidase. [*From Eytan, G. D., Carroll, R. C., Schatz, G., and Racker, E. (1975) J. Biol. Chem.* **250**, *8598–8603 (see p. 8601).*]

Cytochrome $c$ oxidase can be isolated as a deep-green lipoprotein complex. The color is due to the presence of the metal ions, i.e., the copper and the iron. This lipoprotein complex contains approximately 20 percent lipid. If this is removed, the resulting species loses its ability to carry out the electron-transport process, although this capability can be restored by the addition of phospholipids.

The protein components of cytochrome $c$ oxidase can be fractionated to yield six polypeptides. They are arranged in a specific manner in the mitochondrial inner membrane, certain ones being located on the M (matrix) side, certain others on the outer, or C (cytoplasmic), side, and still others located internally (see Fig. 11-2).

EPR studies on the electron-transfer process that is conducted by cytochrome $c$ oxidase indicate that the two cytochromes designated $a$ and $a_3$ and one of the two copper atoms participate in the electron-transfer process. The midpoint potentials of cytochrome $a$ and cytochrome $a_3$ are 210 and 395 mV, respectively. The midpoint potential of the copper, which is thought to exist as $Cu^{2+}$ prior to accepting an electron, is 250 mV.

As stated above, cytochrome $c$ oxidase transfers electrons to molecular oxygen, and as a concomitance of this the oxygen atoms are reduced to the level of the oxygen atoms of water. The reduction reaction can be written

$$O_2 + 4e^- + 4H^+ \longrightarrow 2H_2O \tag{11-1}$$

Four electrons are required for this reaction, and, in fact, there has been considerable interest in the mechanism by which four electrons are supplied as the terminal step of a process which involves the transfer of single, unpaired electrons. Most of the models for the reaction propose that electrons are transferred according to the sequence shown below which is repeated four times in order to bring about the complete reduction. However, the process is by no means as simple as stated, and it is also known to be subject to regulatory influences.

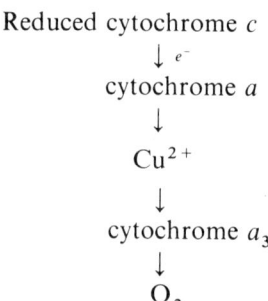

## SUMMARY AND BIOENERGETICS OF THE MITOCHONDRIAL ELECTRON-TRANSPORT SYSTEM

The mitochondrial electron-transport system is a group of membrane-bound enzymes and electron carriers which have the function of accepting reducing equivalents from NADH, succinate, and certain other factors, and transferring them to molecular oxygen. The transfer process entails the passage of electrons along a sequence of carriers arranged in the order of increasing reduction potential; i.e., components which function at the beginning of the sequence have low reduction potentials and those which function near the end of the sequence have high reduction potentials. Since the passage of an electron from an environment of lower reduction potential to an environment of higher reduction potential is a thermodynamically favorable process, mitochondrial electron transport is accompanied by the liberation of chemical energy. (Remember that reduction potential is the tendency to accept electrons and thereby be reduced. An environment having a higher reduction potential has a greater tendency to accept electrons than one having a lower reduction potential.) The chemical energy generated as a result of the mitochondrial electron-transport system is utilized for the phosphorylation of ADP to yield ATP, i.e.,

$$ADP + P_i \longrightarrow ATP \tag{11-2}$$

The total transport process as conducted in the mitochondrial inner membrane can be summarized as shown in Fig. 11-3. Again, a process (this time, the transfer of electrons from NADH or succinate to molecular oxygen) is accomplished by many small steps rather than one large one. At specific points in the sequence the chemical energy that has been generated by a preceding segment of the transport process is channeled into the system that carries out the synthesis of ATP. This latter system is also a part of the mitochondrial inner membrane. The utilization of chemical energy derived from the oxidation of NADH or succinate for the phosphorylation of ADP to ATP is referred to as *oxidative phosphorylation*. There are three points, or sites, in the mitochondrial electron-transport system at which oxidative phosphorylation occurs.

When electrons pass from an environment having a lower reduction potential to one having a higher reduction potential, the maximum theoretical energy yield can be calculated using

$$\Delta G = -nF \Delta E \tag{11-3}$$

If one considers, for example, the overall process from the oxidation of NADH to the reduction of molecular oxygen, the maximum theoretical energy yield can be calculated as shown. First, the two half-reactions are

$$NAD^+ + 2H^+ + 2e^- \longrightarrow NADH + H^+$$
$$E_0' = -320 \text{ mV} = -0.320 \text{ V} \tag{11-4a}$$

and $\quad \frac{1}{2}O_2 + 2H^+ + 2e^- \longrightarrow H_2O \quad E_0' = 816 \text{ mV} = 0.816 \text{ V} \tag{11-4b}$

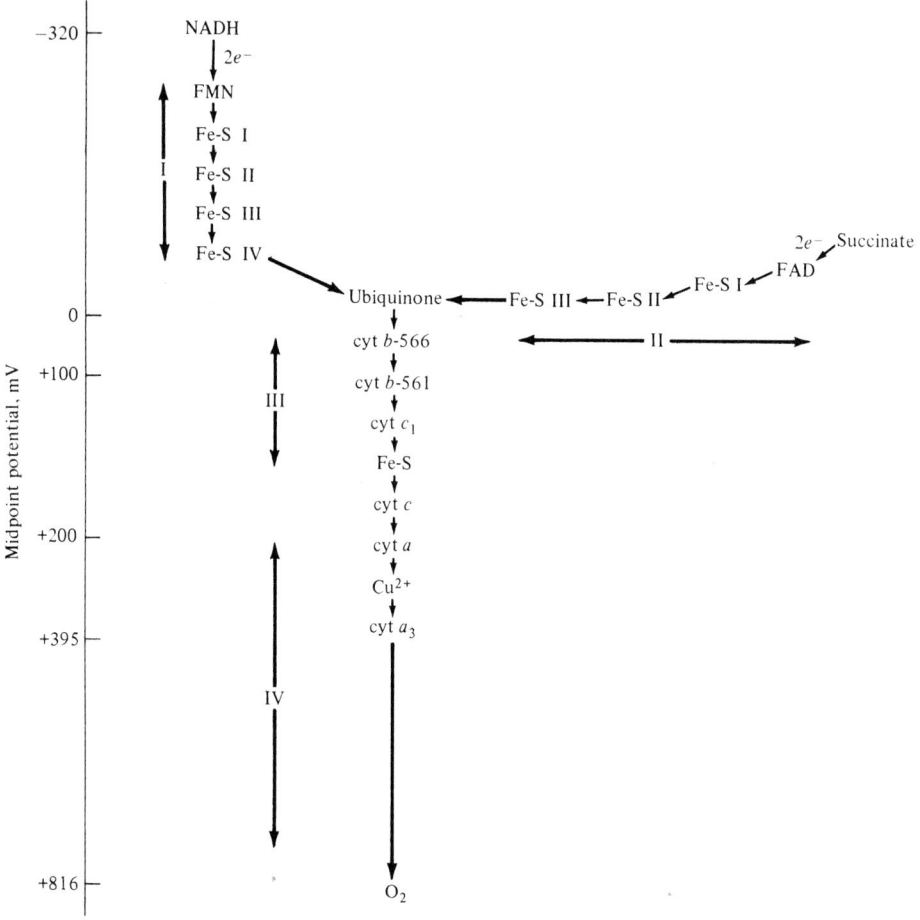

**Figure 11-3** Passage of electrons down the potential gradient as it occurs in the mitochondrial electron-transport system. The portion of the transport process that is carried out by a given one of the four lipoprotein complexes is indicated by the numerals I, II, III, and IV with arrows denoting the appropriate potential span. Nonheme iron-sulfur centers are represented by Fe-S followed by a numeral that allows those centers of a given complex to be distinguished.

The reaction which occurs in the mitochondrion, which is the spontaneous reaction, is therefore

$$NADH + H^+ + \tfrac{1}{2}O_2 \longrightarrow NAD^+ + H_2O \qquad (11\text{-}4c)$$

The associated maximum theoretical free-energy change is thus given by

$$\Delta G^{\circ\prime} = -2 \times 23{,}063 \times 1.136 \text{ cal/mol} \qquad (11\text{-}4d)$$

From this, it can be calculated that $\Delta G^{\circ\prime} = -52{,}399$ cal/mol, or $-52.4$ kcal/mol. This is the maximum amount of chemical energy that would be liberated if NADH and molecular oxygen were allowed to react under conditions that are all standard except for the hydrogen-ion concentration. (Values for $E_0'$ are for processes at pH 7.) If the energy requirement for the phosphorylation of ADP is assumed to be approximately 7.5 kcal/mol,† the quantity of chemical energy generated is more than sufficient to allow the formation of 3 mol of ATP.

The first of the three sites at which the phosphorylation of ADP occurs is associated with the NADH-ubiquinone reductase, or complex I. The second lies between ubiquinone and cytochrome $a_3$, and the third lies between cytochrome $a_3$ and molecular oxygen.‡ The electron-transfer process carried out by the succinate-ubiquinone reductase, or complex II, does not provide energy utilized for the synthesis of ATP. Thus, the passage of electrons derived from 1 mol of succinate through the mitochondrial electron-transport system can lead to the production of only 2 mol of ATP, rather than 3.

## SEARCH FOR THE MECHANISM OF OXIDATIVE PHOSPHORYLATION

The mechanism by which chemical energy derived from the oxidation of NADH or succinate is utilized to phosphorylate ADP remains unknown, although several hypotheses have been formulated and explored, among them the chemical-intermediate hypothesis, the chemiosmotic hypothesis, and a hypothesis which focuses upon a protein conformational change.

The chemical-intermediate hypothesis was introduced by Britton Chance and G. R. Williams (of the Johnson Research Foundation of the University of Pennsylvania Medical School) in 1956. It was subsequently restated and expanded by E. C. Slater (of the Jansen Institute of the University of Amsterdam) in 1958. According to this hypothesis, electron transport results in the formation of a series of very reactive chemical intermediates, including one which reacts with orthophosphate to yield a very reactive phosphoryl intermediate. This phosphoryl intermediate then transfers its phosphoryl group to ADP, with the result that ATP is formed. Such a mechanism would be analogous to the sequence of events which converts glyceraldehyde 3-phosphate into 3-phospho-D-glyceroyl phosphate, which in turn phosphorylates ADP. As formulated, the chemical-intermediate hypothesis proposes the transient existence of an acid anhydride; this then reacts with orthophosphate to yield an acyl phosphate which subsequently phosphorylates ADP. (In the reaction that is catalyzed by the glycolytic enzymes the acid anhydride is the 3-phospho-glyceroyl derivative of the enzyme glyceraldehyde-3-phosphate dehydrogenase. Thiol esters can be regarded as acid anhydrides derived from a carboxylic acid and a mercaptan, which is also an acid.) One of the principal objections to the chemical-intermediate hypothesis, however, is that none of the proposed chemical intermediates can be isolated or demonstrated.

Another hypothesis concerning the mechanism of oxidative phosphorylation

---

† Rosing, J., and Slater, E. C. (1972) *Biochim. Biophys. Acta* **267**, 275–290.
‡ Slater, E. C., Rosing J., and Mol, A. (1973) *Biochim. Biophys. Acta* **292**, 534–553.

has been put forth by Peter Mitchell, of the Glynn Research Laboratories in Bodmin, England. This proposal, originally presented in 1961, is known as the *chemiosmotic hypothesis*. Basically, it states that the energy required for the phosphorylation of ADP is derived as a result of the potential difference that is established across the mitochondrial inner membrane as a result of the electron-transport process. During these oxidation-reduction reactions hydrogen ions are transported from inside the mitochondrion to the outside in exchange for certain other cations. Since the mitochondrial inner membrane is impermeable with respect to hydrogen ions, a chemical as well as an electrical transmembrane potential difference is created. According to the Mitchell hypothesis, the facilitated entry of hydrogen ions into the mitochondrion, which *is* a thermodynamically favorable process (since hydrogen ions are moving "down" the potential gradients), can be coupled with the phosphorylation of ADP, which *is not* a thermodynamically favored process. Proof of this hypothesis is also lacking, however.

Yet another hypothesis concerning the mechanism of oxidative phosphorylation was proposed in 1973 by Paul D. Boyer of the Molecular Biology Institute of the University of California, Los Angeles. He suggested that the phosphorylation of ADP per se requires little energy input under the conditions that exist in the mitochondrial inner membrane although an energy-dependent protein conformational change is required in order for the ATP that is synthesized to be released from the enzyme. This hypothesis is being explored.†

## ISOLATION AND CHARACTERIZATION OF INNER-MEMBRANE COMPONENTS PARTICIPATING IN OXIDATIVE PHOSPHORYLATION

Although the energy-transduction mechanism that takes place in the mitochondrial inner membrane is unknown, a component that is thought to catalyze the phosphoryl transfer to ADP has been isolated. When isolated and therefore separated from the mitochondrial inner membrane, this component catalyzes the hydrolytic cleavage of ATP, i.e.,

$$ATP + H_2O \rightleftharpoons ADP + P_i \qquad (11\text{-}5)$$

This component is also presumed to be responsible for the hydrolytic cleavage of ATP which is observed when mitochondrial oxidation and phosphorylation are uncoupled. Hence, the component is referred to as an adenosinetriphosphatase or an ATPase (ATP phosphohydrolase, EC 3.6.1.3), although it is speculated that when it is a part of the inner membrane and oxidation and phosphorylation are coupled, it can catalyze the phosphorylation of ADP. Many of the studies on the isolation and characterization of this ATPase and other membrane components thought to participate in the phosphorylation of ADP have been carried out in the laboratories of Efraim Racker at Cornell University.

† Cross, R. L., and Boyer, P. D. (1975) *Biochemistry* 14, 392–398.

As isolated from bovine-heart mitochondria, the ATPase has a molecular weight of 347,000 and is composed of multiple subunits. In fact, five different polypeptides, having molecular weights of 54,000, 50,000, 33,000, 17,000, and 5700, can be isolated from this species. It has been proposed that the species having a molecular weight of 347,000 comprises three subunits each with a molecular weight of 54,000, three each with a molecular weight of 50,000 and one with a molecular weight of 33,000. The role of the two small peptides has not been defined. When this ATPase is removed from the inner membrane (to which it is somewhat loosely bound), the mitochondrion is no longer able to carry out the phosphorylation of ADP in conjunction with the electron-transport process. However, if the ATPase is added back, the capability for phosphorylation is restored. For this reason the ATPase and certain other membrane components which appear to have supporting roles are referred to as *coupling factors*. The ATPase, which is the catalytic component, is known as coupling factor 1, or $F_1$. The properties of the solubilized ATPase, or $F_1$, differ in several respects from those which can be demonstrated using particulate preparations exhibiting ATPase activity, e.g., submitochondrial particles. This is often the case when a membrane-associated enzyme is separated from its membrane. However, in the present case, three additional membrane-associated components have been isolated, which, when added to $F_1$, confer certain of the characteristics of the particulate preparations upon the soluble enzyme. These factors are known as *conferring factors*. One of these, $FC_1$, confers sensitivity to the antibiotic oligomycin. Oligomycin inhibits oxidative phosphorylation and it also inhibits the ATPase activity that is exhibited by particulate preparations such as submitochondrial particles. The second conferring factor, $FC_2$, acts in conjunction with the third, a lipoprotein, to confer sensitivity to $N,N'$-dicyclohexylcarbodiimide upon $F_1$. The activity of particulate preparations of the ATPase is inhibited by $N,N'$-dicyclohexylcarbodiimide. (The actions of uncouplers and inhibitors will be discussed in some detail later in this chapter.) It is assumed that in the inner membrane $F_1$ is in close proximity to $FC_1$, $FC_2$, the lipoprotein component, and other components which modulate the behavior of the catalytic component.

## ENERGY-DEPENDENT PROCESSES ASSOCIATED WITH THE MITOCHONDRIAL INNER MEMBRANE

The mitochondrial inner membrane is the site of certain processes that require ATP. Hence, these processes occur only when oxidation and phosphorylation are coupled. Among these processes are the transport of ions, the transport of adenine nucleotides, and transhydrogenation.

### Ion Transport

The cation that is present in the highest concentration in coupled mitochondria is $K^+$. Coupled mitochondria accumulate $K^+$ against a concentration gradient as the result of an energy-dependent process. This influx of $K^+$ is accompanied by an efflux of hydrogen ions. The cation present in the next highest concentration is $Mg^{2+}$, which is also accumulated as the result of an energy-dependent process. Orthophosphate accompanies $Mg^{2+}$ into the mitochondrion, and, again, there is a concomitant efflux of hydrogen ions.

Calcium ions are also accumulated by the mitochondrion. There are two processes by which this occurs. Along with electron transport there is an uptake of $Ca^{2+}$ that is stoichiometric with respect to oxygen consumption; i.e., two $Ca^{2+}$ enter the mitochondrion for each two electrons that pass a site at which oxidative phosphorylation can occur. This influx of $Ca^{2+}$ is balanced by the efflux of approximately four hydrogen ions. In addition an energy-dependent uptake of $Ca^{2+}$ is observed as mitochondria which have been in a resting state are transformed to an active state. This influx of $Ca^{2+}$ is very rapid and occurs with an accompanying rapid efflux of hydrogen ions. In this case, there is no stoichiometric relationship between $Ca^{2+}$ influx, electron transport, and oxygen utilization.†

## Transport of Adenine Nucleotides

The mitochondrial inner membrane is impermeable with respect to adenine nucleotides. However, the synthesis of ATP which occurs as a result of oxidative phosphorylation takes place at the matrix side of the inner membrane and, thus ADP must be present at this site. Furthermore, ATP that is synthesized at this site must be made available in the cytoplasm. Thus, adenine nucleotides must be able to cross the inner membrane. This is accomplished through the agency of a transport system that is a part of the inner membrane. This transport system transports ADP from outside to inside the mitochondrial matrix in opposition to a concentration gradient, one molecule of ATP being exported for each ADP which enters. This process leads to an extramitochondrial ATP/ADP ratio that is higher than the intramitochondrial ATP/ADP ratio. However, when oxidation and phosphorylation are uncoupled, the intramitochondrial and extramitochondrial ATP/ADP ratios become identical.

## Transhydrogenation

Since the mitochondrial inner membrane is impermeable with respect to adenine nucleotides, $NAD^+$, NADH, $NADP^+$, and NADPH cannot diffuse into (or out of) the mitochondrial matrix. There are several mechanisms for the entry of reducing equivalents into the mitochondrial matrix (some of which are discussed below); however, in most of these instances these reducing equivalents can be transferred to $NAD^+$ to form NADH but not to $NADP^+$ to form NADPH. However, as a result of the reaction that is catalyzed by the membrane-bound $NAD(P)^+$ transhydrogenase (NADPH:$NAD^+$ oxidoreductase, EC 1.6.1.1), NADH can transfer

---

† Reynafarje, B., and Lehninger, A. L. (1974) *J. Biol. Chem.* **249**, 6067–6073.

its reducing equivalents to $NADP^+$, thus generating NADPH. The reaction can be written

$$NADH + NADP^+ \rightleftharpoons NAD^+ + NADPH \tag{11-6}$$

Transhydrogenation can be either an energy-dependent or an energy-independent process, and these two processes can be distinguished on the basis of their characteristics. For example, in the energy-dependent process, the reverse reaction, i.e., the transfer of reducing equivalents from NADPH to $NAD^+$, occurs to a lesser extent than in the energy-independent process.

The mitochondrial transhydrogenation reactions occur with absolute stereospecificity. The enzyme removes the pro-$R$ hydrogen atom from NADH and transfers it to the $si$ face of $NADP^+$.

## OTHER TRANSPORT PROCESSES INVOLVING THE MITOCHONDRIAL INNER MEMBRANE

As stated, the mitochondrial inner membrane is impermeable with respect to adenine nucleotides. It is also impermeable with respect to certain other biochemical intermediates. In certain cases specific intermediates are translocated across the mitochondrial inner membrane as a result of energy-dependent transport processes, as described above. There are, in addition, other processes by which intermediates are translocated across the inner membrane. Some of these are discussed here.

### Transport of Reducing Equivalents by Glycerol 3-Phosphate

Although neither NADH nor NADPH can diffuse across the mitochondrial inner membrane, their reducing equivalents can be translocated across this barrier. One way in which reducing equivalents from NADH can be translocated from outside to inside the mitochondrial matrix is through the agency of the glycerolphosphate dehydrogenases. The cytoplasm of many cells contains an $NAD^+$-dependent glycerol-3-phosphate dehydrogenase ($sn$-glycerol-3-phosphate:$NAD^+$ 2-oxidoreductase, EC 1.1.1.8), which catalyzes the reaction

Dihydroxyacetone phosphate + NADH $\rightleftharpoons$

$$sn\text{-glycerol 3-phosphate} + NAD^+ \tag{11-7}$$

(The denotation $sn$ indicates that the stereochemically numbered convention is being used.) Glycerol 3-phosphate then enters the matrix of the mitochondrion, where it can function as the substrate for a glycerol-3-phosphate dehydrogenase that is a component of the inner membrane. This glycerol-3-phosphate dehydrogenase [$sn$-glycerol-3-phosphate:(acceptor) oxidoreductase, EC 1.1.99.5] is a flavoprotein which catalyzes the reaction

$sn$-Glycerol 3-phosphate + oxidized acceptor $\longrightarrow$

$$\text{dihydroxyacetone phosphate} + \text{reduced acceptor} \tag{11-8}$$

This reaction is essentially irreversible. The dihydroxyacetone phosphate formed can then return to the cytoplasm, while the two reducing equivalents that have been donated to the acceptor of the membrane-bound dehydrogenase are introduced into the mitochondrial electron-transport system as a result of being passed to ubiquinone. This process thus provides a means by which the reducing equivalents from extramitochondrial NADH (such as the NADH produced as a result of glycolysis) can enter the mitochondrial electron-transport system. It should be noted, however, that when this means is utilized, the two reducing equivalents enter at a point in the electron-transport system which allows only two molecules of ATP to be generated by coupled oxidation and phosphorylation. This process involving the two glycerol-3-phosphate dehydrogenases is of less importance quantitatively in mammalian systems than the process to be discussed next, however.

## Transport of Reducing Equivalents by the Malate-Aspartate Shuttle

In mammalian systems the principal route by which reducing equivalents from extramitochondrial NADH are introduced into the mitochondrial electron-transport system is the series of reactions and transport processes known as the malate-aspartate shuttle. This process entails the influx of malate and glutamate and the efflux of aspartate and 2-oxoglutarate. Initially, oxaloacetate is reduced to L-malate in the cytoplasm. This reaction is catalyzed by an $NAD^+$-dependent malate dehydrogenase in the cytoplasm, and results in transfer of two reducing equivalents from NADH to oxaloacetate, forming L-malate. Malate then enters the matrix of the mitochondria by means of a transport system which facilitates the transfer of dicarboxylic acids. As is generally the case, the entry of malate is balanced by the exit of some other intermediate. In this case, a molecule of 2-oxoglutarate is lost from the matrix for each molecule of malate that enters. In the matrix, L-malate is oxidized back to oxaloacetate as the result of a reaction catalyzed by the $NAD^+$-dependent malate dehydrogenase of the mitochondrion. Thus, the two reducing equivalents of the extramitochondrial NADH molecule have been transported across the inner membrane and into the matrix, where they are now the two reducing equivalents of an intramitochondrial NADH molecule. Now, the mitochondrial inner membrane is also impermeable with respect to oxaloacetate, and thus oxaloacetate cannot simply diffuse out of the matrix and back into the cytoplasm. Instead oxaloacetate undergoes a reaction known as transamination in which an oxo acid and an amino acid in effect exchange functional groups so that the oxo acid becomes an amino acid and the amino acid becomes an oxo acid. In the present case, glutamate participates in the transamination reaction with oxaloacetate, and as a result 2-oxoglutarate and aspartate are formed. Each of these can be transported across the inner membrane by the transport system for dicarboxylic acids. The efflux of 2-oxoglutarate occurs in tandem with the influx of malate, and the efflux of aspartate occurs in tandem with the influx of glutamate. In the cytoplasm, aspartate and 2-oxoglutarate undergo transamination, and oxaloacetate and glutamate are regenerated. The shuttle process can now begin again. The system is represented diagrammatically in Fig. 11-4.

In cyclic transport processes like this at least one step must be energy-dependent

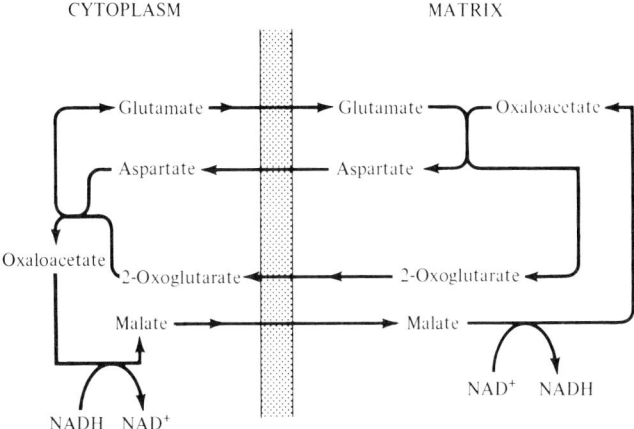

**Figure 11-4** Diagrammatic representation of the malate-aspartate shuttle, a mechanism by which reducing equivalents from extramitochondrial NADH are introduced into the mitochondrial electron-transport system.

or irreversible. Otherwise, the system would attain chemical equilibrium and remain at equilibrium. In the case of the malate-aspartate shuttle it has been demonstrated that the efflux of aspartate is energy-dependent. A transmembrane potential generated as a result of the electron-transport process is thought to be the source of the required energy.†

## INFLUENCE OF ATP UPON THE OXIDATION-REDUCTION POTENTIALS OF COMPONENTS OF THE MITOCHONDRIAL ELECTRON-TRANSPORT SYSTEM

The midpoint reduction potentials of specific components of the mitochondrial electron-transport system change in value when the mitochondrion changes from an uncoupled to a coupled state (or vice versa). A reason for this may be that this change in the state of the mitochondrion is associated with conformational (or other) changes in the inner membrane that cause the environments of certain components to be altered. Changes in the environment of a reaction center can be reflected by changes in certain thermodynamic parameters associated with the reaction. It has been suggested that such changes in midpoint reduction potential are involved in the energy-transduction mechanism since the potential of at least one component at each of the three sites at which oxidative phosphorylation occurs is responsive to changes in the state of the mitochondrion. The reduction potential of a nonheme iron–sulfur center of NADH-ubiquinone reductase, complex I, undergoes a change from a higher value to a lower one as the mitochondrion is

---

† La Noue, K. F., Bryla, J., and Bassett, D. J. P. (1974) *J. Biol. Chem.* **249**, 7514–7521.

transformed from the uncoupled to the coupled, or energized, state. On the other hand, the potential of cytochrome $b$-566, of complex III, changes from a lower to a higher value as the mitochondrion becomes energized. The responsive component of cytochrome $c$ oxidase, which is cytochrome $a_3$, exhibits a higher potential value in the uncoupled mitochondrion, which shifts to a lower potential value as the mitochondrion becomes energized. Among other possibilities, these observations suggest that the potential difference between two consecutive components of the mitochondrial electron-transport system may become great enough so that the passage of electrons from one to the other provides the energy required for the phosphorylation of a molecule of ADP.

# INHIBITORS OF MITOCHONDRIAL ELECTRON TRANSPORT

The use of reagents that inhibit mitochondrial electron transport at specific points has proved to be a valuable tool for studying this process. Here some of the more widely used inhibitors are discussed.

## Through NADH-Ubiquinone Reductase

The passage of electrons through complex I is inhibited by certain barbiturates, including Amytal, by an antibiotic known as piericidin A, and by a compound known as rotenone, which is derived from the roots of certain plants.

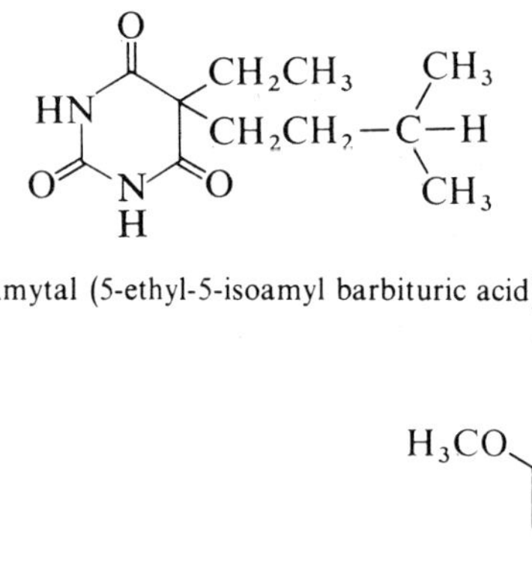

Amytal (5-ethyl-5-isoamyl barbituric acid)

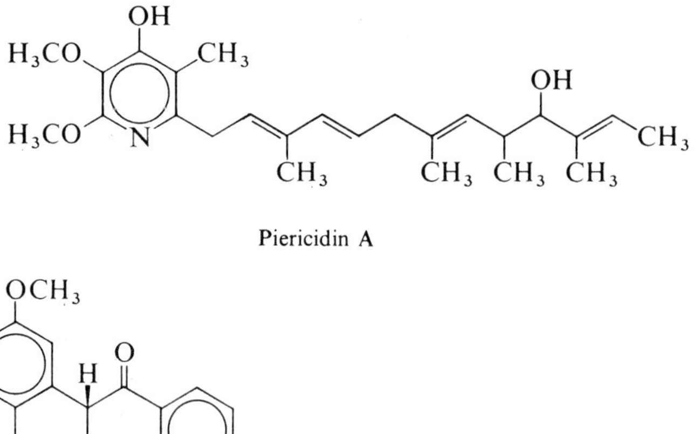

Piericidin A

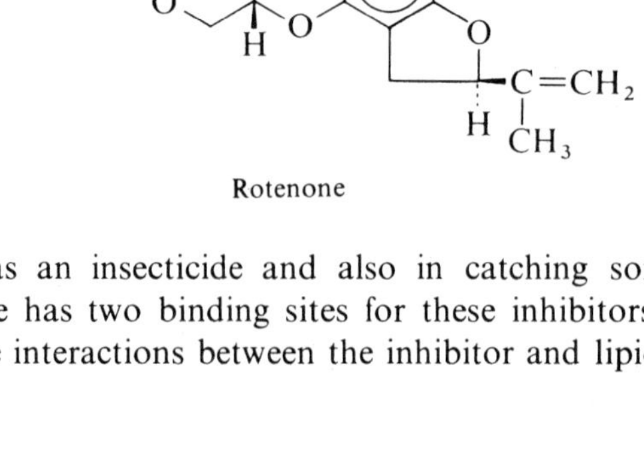

Rotenone

(Rotenone is used as an insecticide and also in catching some fish.) NADH-ubiquinone reductase has two binding sites for these inhibitors and this binding is believed to involve interactions between the inhibitor and lipids of the complex.

The point at which these inhibitors function in the electron-transport sequence is after that at which at least some of the nonheme iron–sulfur centers participate. It has not been established that each of these inhibitors functions at precisely the same point in the sequence, however.

## Through Succinate-Ubiquinone Reductase

Perhaps the most widely used inhibitor of electron transport by complex II is the compound 2-thenoyltrifluoroacetone, which is sometimes referred to as TTFA.

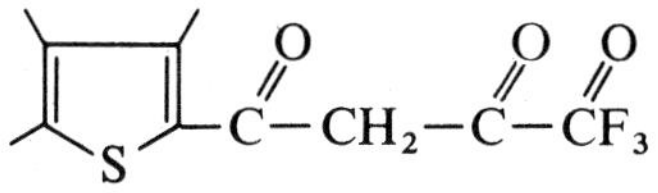

2-Thenoyltrifluoroacetone (TTFA)
[4,4,4-trifluoro(2-thienyl)-1,3-butanedione]

Thenoyltrifluoroacetone exists in an enolate form, which is a metal chelating agent. This characteristic is believed responsible for the inhibitory effect of the agent since it impedes electron transfer by a nonheme iron–sulfur center of complex II. In the presence of 10 $\mu M$ thenoyltrifluoroacetone electron transport is inhibited by 50 percent. Oxaloacetate is also an inhibitor of electron transport by succinate-ubiquinone reductase. Again, the effective concentration is approximately 10 $\mu M$.

## Through Complex III

The transfer of electrons by this segment of the mitochondrial electron-transport system is inhibited by antimycin A, which is, in fact, a mixture of at least four structurally similar antibiotics.

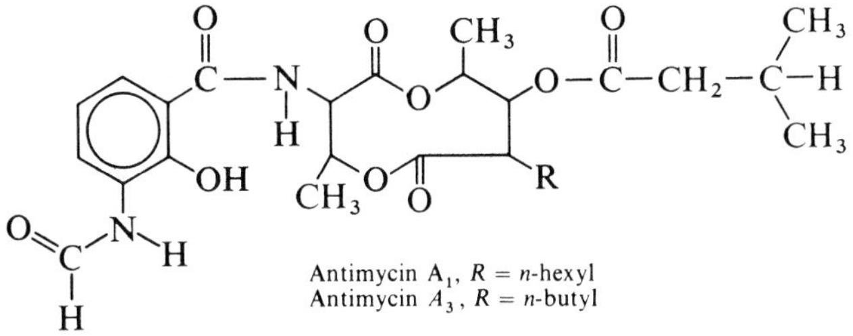

Antimycin $A_1$, R = n-hexyl
Antimycin $A_3$, R = n-butyl

Antimycin

The site at which antimycin functions is between cytochromes $b$ and $c_1$. This is a very potent inhibitor since concentrations of 0.05 $\mu M$ are effective.

Electron transport in this segment of the mitochondrial electron-transport system is also impeded by 2-heptyl-4-hydroxyquinoline N-oxide

[Structure of 2-Heptyl-4-hydroxyquinoline N-oxide]

2-Heptyl-4-hydroxyquinoline N-oxide

although as an inhibitor this compound is only one-tenth as effective as antimycin A. The site at which this component binds is thought to be the same as or very near the site bound by antimycin A.

## Through Cytochrome c Oxidase

Agents which inhibit transport by complex IV can be categorized as (1) those which compete for the oxygen binding site, (2) those which bind the heme moiety, and (3) those which interfere with the interaction between cytochrome c and cytochrome c oxidase. Inhibitors of the first type include carbon monoxide, which at a concentration of 40 $\mu M$, inhibits electron transport by 50 percent. Carbon monoxide binds specifically to ferrocytochrome $a_3$. The association constant for the cytochrome $a_3^{2+}$–CO complex is 0.8 to $1.2 \times 10^5$ $(M \cdot s)^{-1}$ while the dissociation constant is $0.02$ s$^{-1}$ (at pH 7, 25°C).

Inhibitors that bind the heme moiety of cytochrome c oxidase include hydrogen cyanide, azide, and hydrogen sulfide. Hydrogen cyanide can bind either ferrocytochrome $a_3$ or ferricytochrome $a_3$, although the reactions (and their products) are different. These reactions are shown diagrammatically in Fig. 11-5. It can be seen

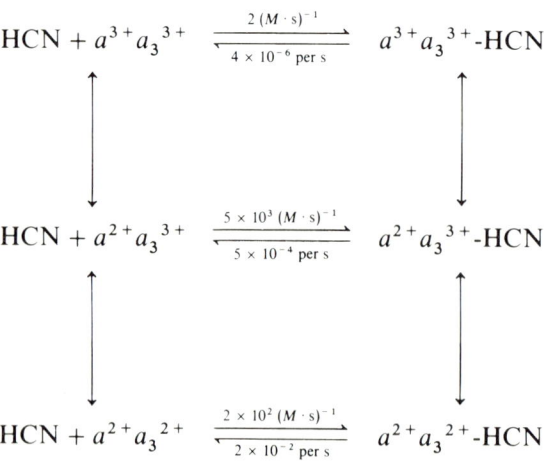

**Figure 11-5** In this figure, $a^{3+}a_3^{3+}$ represents cytochrome c oxidase containing ferricytochrome a and ferricytochrome $a_3$; $a^{2+}a_3^{3+}$ represents that containing ferrocytochrome a and ferricytochrome $a_3$; $a^{2+}a_3^{2+}$ represents that containing ferrocytochrome a and ferrocytochrome $a_3$. Modified from Nicholls, P. and Chance, B. (1974) in Molecular Mechanisms of Oxygen Activation, (Hayaishi, O., ed), pp. 479–534 (see p. 506), Academic, New York.]

that the ferrocytochrome $a$–ferricytochrome $a_3$–HCN complex is the most stable; it is the formation of this complex that is most probably responsible for the inhibitory effect of hydrogen cyanide.

Azide binds ferricytochrome $a_3$, thereby preventing this component from accepting electrons. The formation constant for the ferricytochrome $a$–ferricytochrome $a_3$–HN$_3$ complex is approximately $1 \times 10^4$ $(M \cdot s)^{-1}$ while the dissociation constant for the complex is $0.5\ s^{-1}$. Hydrogen sulfide also binds ferricytochrome $a_3$. In this case, the binding process is much more rapid, and the complex formed is more stable (by approximately fiftyfold) than with azide.

The inhibitors that interfere with the interaction between cytochrome $c$ and cytochrome $c$ oxidase include cations and polycations. They are thought to compete with cytochrome $c$ for its binding site on cytochrome $c$ oxidase.

## UNCOUPLERS OF OXIDATIVE PHOSPHORYLATION

An uncoupler is an agent that prevents the chemical energy that is derived from electron transport from being utilized for the phosphorylation of ADP. Thus, it uncouples oxidation and phosphorylation. In general, the classical uncoupling agent (1) stimulates electron transport and oxygen utilization, (2) enhances the ATPase activity exhibited by mitochondrial and submitochondrial preparations, (3) relieves the inhibitory effect upon oxygen utilization induced by the antibiotic oligomycin, and (4) at *high* concentrations, inhibits both oxygen utilization and the ATPase activity.

The compound 2,4-dinitrophenol is a classical uncoupling agent. At a concentration of 10 $\mu M$ it causes the ratio of ADP phosphorylated to oxygen utilized, i.e., the P/O ratio, to be diminished by 50 percent. (A P/O ratio of 3 is observed when NADH is oxidized by a tightly coupled mitochondrial electron-transport system.) Dinitrophenol also inhibits the influx of orthophosphate into the mitochondrion. Orthophosphate is transported across the inner membrane by either of two transport systems. One allows orthophosphate to enter the mitochondrion in exchange for hydroxide ion, and the other allows orthophosphate to enter in exchange for certain dicarboxylic acid anions, including malate and succinate. The precise mechanism by which 2,4-dinitrophenol induces these effects is unknown, although it has been shown that the mitochondrial inner membrane possesses specific sites at which several uncoupling agents bind, and it has been suggested that this binding causes an energized conformation of the inner membrane to undergo a change which blocks the energy-transduction pathway.

Other uncoupling agents which function similarly to 2,4-dinitrophenol include certain hydrazones, such as carbonylcyanide *p*-trifluoromethoxyphenylhydrazone (FCCP) and carbonylcyanide *m*-chlorophenylhydrazone (CCCP), and also certain isothiocyanates, including *p*-bromophenylisothiocyanate.

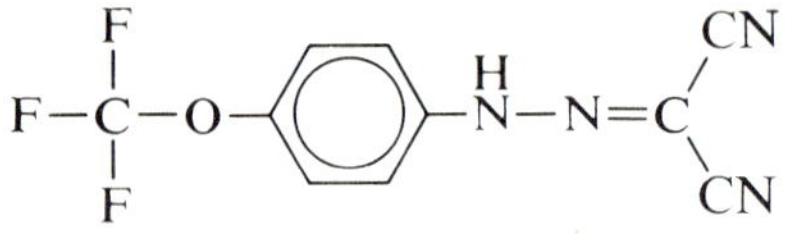

Carbonylcyanide *p*-trifluoromethoxyphenylhydrazone (FCCP)

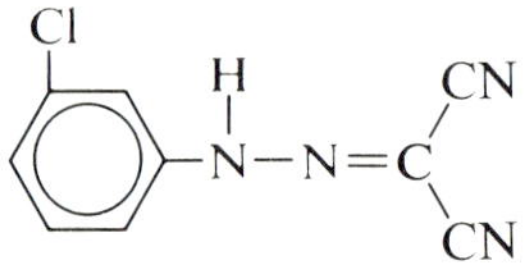

Carbonylcyanide *m*-chlorophenylhydrazone (CCCP)

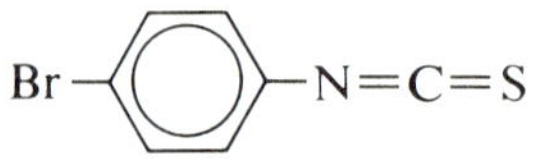

*p*-Bromophenylisothiocyante

## INHIBITORS OF OXIDATIVE PHOSPHORYLATION AND RELATED PROCESSES

The antibiotic oligomycin is one of the more widely used inhibitors of oxidative phosphorylation. Oligomycin is, in fact, a mixture of three components designated A, B, and C. In addition to inhibiting oxygen utilization by the mitochondrial electron-transport system, micromolar concentrations of oligomycin inhibit the ATPase activity that is induced in the presence of uncoupling agents such as 2,4-dinitrophenol. The mechanism by which these inhibitory effects occurs has not been established, although it has been shown that the mitochondrial inner membrane contains specific sites at which oligomycin binds. One hypothesis is that these membrane components which function as binding sites are actually participants in the energy-transduction process and that as a result of interacting with oligomycin they can no longer function in that capacity.†

The antibiotic aurovertin (which is isolated from the mold *Calcarisporium arbuscula*) is also an inhibitor of oxidative phosphorylation. Aurovertin inhibits 2,4-dinitrophenol-induced ATPase activity, as does oligomycin, although total inhibition is not achieved with the former and the inhibitory effect is complex. Studies using submitochondrial particles as the source of the ATPase activity have shown that when MgATP was the variable substrate with fixed concentrations of aurovertin, the slopes of the double reciprocal plots decreased while the intercepts increased with increasing concentrations of the antibiotic. This pattern represents I-hyperbolic inhibition with S-hyperbolic activation. It was interpreted as reflecting that of the two alternate pathways, i.e., one involving aurovertin and one not, the

---

† Bertina, R. M., Steenstra, J. A., and Slater, E. C. (1974) *Biochim. Biophys. Acta* **368**, 279–297.

pathway involving the antibiotic is the slower although the binding of the antibiotic causes the Michaelis constant for MgATP (the concentration of MgATP which produces half-maximal velocity) to be decreased.†

The translocation of adenine nucleotides across the mitochondrial inner membrane is inhibited in the presence of either of two closely related compounds that are obtained from the thistle *Atractylis gummifera*, atractyloside and gummiferin.

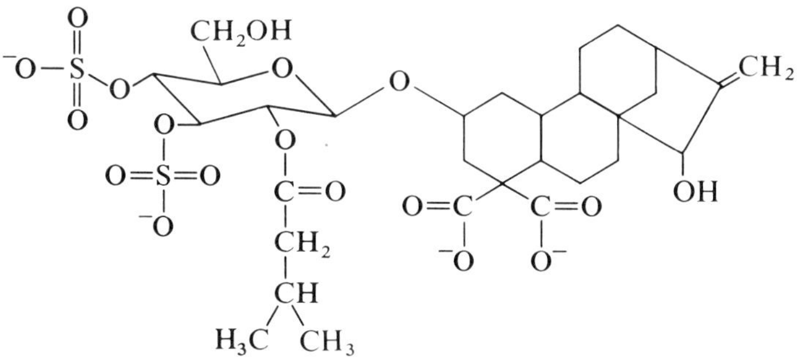

Gummiferin
(atractyloside lacks one of the geminal carboxylate groups)

These compounds have been shown to bind the mitochondrial inner membrane and thereby interfere with the binding of ADP by the appropriate component of the translocation system. Atractyloside functions as a competitive inhibitor whereas gummiferin functions as a noncompetitive inhibitor with respect to the velocity at which ADP is translocated across the membrane.

Another inhibitor of adenine nucleotide translocation is a toxic compound that is produced by the microorganism *Pseudomonas cocovenenans*. This compound is bongkrekic acid.

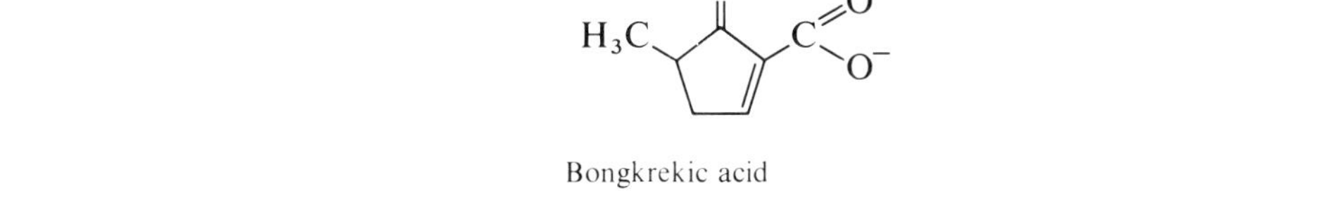

Bongkrekic acid

(The presence of *Pseudomonas cocovenenans* in a food product called bongkrek, derived from the coconut, resulted in widespread, fatal food poisoning in Indonesia.) In the presence of bongkrekic acid the adenine nucleotides are much more tightly

† Ebel, R. E., and Lardy, H. A. (1975) *J. Biol. Chem.* **250**, 4992–4995.

bound by the mitochondrial inner membrane. This causes the observed velocity of the translocation process to be diminished because now the dissociation of the translocated adenine nucleotides becomes rate-determining.

# PART II ELECTRON TRANSPORT AND ENERGY PRODUCTION IN PLANTS AND CERTAIN PHOTOSYNTHETIC BACTERIA

In this book we focus primarily upon the biochemical reactions which occur in man or in other mammals. These reactions include the oxygen-requiring degradation of carbohydrates, lipids, and proteins, which results in the production of carbon dioxide and water, and the utilization of the energy that is produced as a result of this degradation for the phosphorylation of ADP. If these processes occurred continuously in the absence of compensatory processes, it is conceivable that the $CO_2/O_2$ ratio in our atmosphere would be altered. However, there are compensatory processes, the principal one being photosynthesis. By this process carbon dioxide is assimilated and molecular oxygen is liberated through the agency of light energy. Thus, while mammalian systems degrade biochemical intermediates to carbon dioxide by an oxygen-requiring process, photosynthetic systems assimilate carbon dioxide into biochemical intermediates by a process that liberates oxygen. The assimilation of carbon dioxide into biochemical intermediates was discussed in Chap. 9 since this process bears some relationship to the reactions of carbohydrate metabolism in mammalian systems. The light-dependent process which results in the cleavage of water to yield molecular oxygen (plus hydrogen ions and a reduced oxidizing agent) is discussed here since it bears some relationship to the mammalian mitochondrial electron-transport system.

## PHOTOSYNTHESIS IN PLANTS

Photosynthesis takes place in organelles known as *plastids*. In green plants and in green unicellular organisms, such as algae, these plastids contain chlorophyll and hence are known as *chloroplasts*. The chloroplasts of higher plants contain stacks of membrane-limited sacs, called *grana* (singular, *granum*), and the sacs themselves are called *thylakoids*. The thylakoid membrane contains, among other factors, the components of the system which allows molecular oxygen to be generated during photosynthesis. In addition, this membrane contains the components of an electron-transport system that is associated with the production of molecular oxygen. The electron-transport system also provides energy that is utilized for the phosphorylation of ADP in photosynthetic organisms. The various components that are a part of the thylakoid membrane are arranged asymmetrically within the membrane, just as in the case of the components of the mitochondrial electron-transport system, which are arranged asymmetrically within the inner membrane. It is known that the counterpart of the uncoupler-induced ATPase, which in plants is known as $CF_1$, is localized on the outer surface of the thylakoid membrane (which is in contact with the stromal matrix). Also, ribulosebisphosphate carboxylase, which catalyzes the assimilation of carbon dioxide, is localized (at least in part) on the outer surface of the thylakoid membrane. The components which catalyze the production of molecular oxygen, on the other hand, are localized on the inner surface of the thylakoid membrane (which is in contact with the intrathylakoid space). Other components of the electron-transport system of photosynthesis are arranged appropriately within the membrane. One model of the arrangement of the components of the electron-transport system is shown in Fig. 11-6.

The production of molecular oxygen in higher plants results from a photochemical reaction which also initiates the transfer of electrons along a sequence of carriers. The ultimate acceptor of the electrons is the oxidized pyridine nucleotide cofactor, $NADP^+$. This is, in effect, the reverse of the process that occurs in the mammalian mitochondrion, in which electrons are accepted from a reduced pyridine

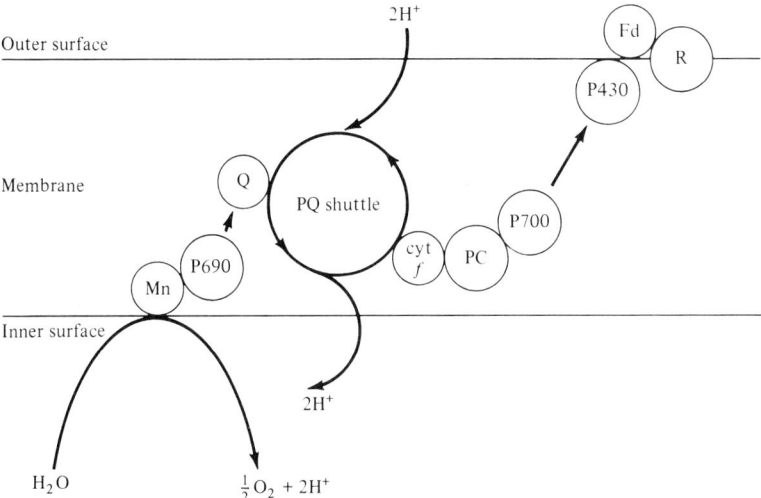

**Figure 11-6** Schematic representation of the asymmetrical arrangement of the components of the thylakoid electron-transport system within its membrane.

      Mn = manganese ion
   P690 = pigment 690, a photochemically reactive pigment
       Q = an electron acceptor
PQ shuttle = plastiquinone shuttle
   cyt $f$ = cytochrome $f$
     PC = plastocyanin
   P700 = pigment 700, a photochemically reactive pigment
   P430 = electron acceptor
     Fd = ferredoxin
      R = ferredoxin-$NADP^+$ reductase

[*Modified from Trebst, A. (1974) Ann. Rev. Plant Physiol.* **25**, *423–458 (see p. 447).*]

nucleotide cofactor, NADH, and transferred ultimately to molecular oxygen. The production of molecular oxygen and the associated electron-transport process will now be discussed in some detail.

## The Light Reaction at Photocenter II and Associated Reactions

Two photochemical reactions occur in photosynthetic organisms. The first occurs at a photochemical reaction center designated as photocenter II. The light reaction at photocenter II results in the production of a strong oxidant and a weak reductant. The strong oxidant in effect oxidizes water; i.e., it accepts electrons from a water molecule, thus allowing one-half of a molecule of oxygen to be formed along with two hydrogen ions. The weak reductant is ultimately oxidized back to its initial form when it donates its reducing equivalents to the electron-transport system.

Photocenter II as isolated from spinach, for example, contains $\beta$-carotene, xanthophylls, and both chlorophyll $a$ and chlorophyll $b$.

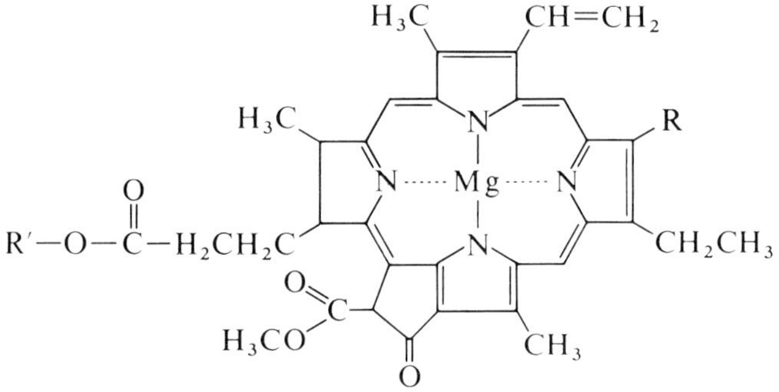

$R = CH_3$ in chlorophyll $a$

$R = C\begin{smallmatrix}O\\H\end{smallmatrix}$ in chlorophyll $b$

$$R' = -CH_2CH=\underset{\underset{CH_3}{|}}{C}-CH_2-(CH_2CH_2\underset{\underset{CH_3}{|}}{C}HCH_2)_2-CH_2CH_2-\underset{\underset{CH_3}{\backslash}}{\overset{\overset{CH_3}{/}}{C}}-H$$

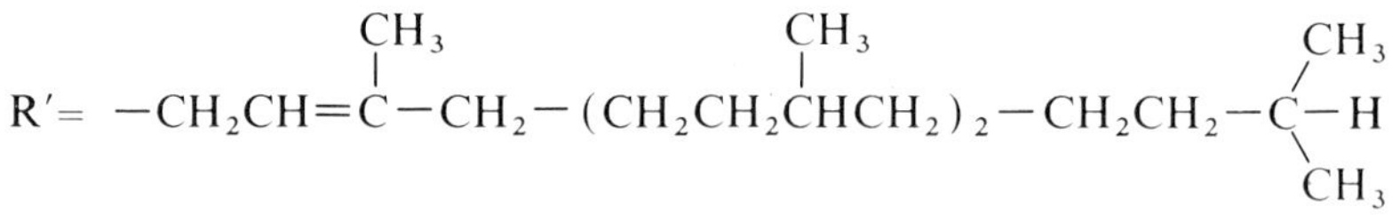

A species of chlorophyll a which exhibits an absorption maximum near 690 nm has been identified as the principal photochemically reactive pigment at photocenter II. This species is referred to as P690 (or pigment 690). The photochemical reaction is depicted as involving the chlorophyll, a primary electron donor, and a primary electron acceptor. When light having a wavelength of less than 680 nm falls upon this center, an excited state of the chlorophyll is generated. This then transfers an electron to the primary acceptor, thus leaving the chlorophyll electron-deficient. This electron deficiency is subsequently relieved by the primary electron donor. The identity of the primary electron donor is unknown; however, having donated an electron to the chlorophyll it is now electron-deficient and thus able to function as an oxidizing agent in the cleavage of water. The cleavage of water can be written

$$2H_2O \longrightarrow O_2 + 4H^+ + 4e^- \tag{11-9}$$

The oxidation of the oxygen atoms of two water molecules to yield molecular oxygen requires the removal of four electrons. Since these are accepted by an oxidant that is generated as a result of a photochemical event, and since this oxidant accepts but one electron, four photochemical events are required for one molecule of oxygen to be formed. The manner in which the resultants of these four photochemical events are combined and coordinated to allow the formation of the oxygen molecule is unknown, although manganese ions are known to have a role in this process.

It is generally agreed that the primary electron acceptor at photocenter II is a species which has been designated as Q (because it quenches the fluorescent emission that accompanies the photoreaction). Following the photochemical event at center II, the reduced form of Q then transfers an electron to plastoquinone, which can be considered to be the initial carrier in an electron-transport system.

Plastoquinone (PQ – 9)

Plastoquinone is present in much greater amounts than most of the other components in the membrane system, and in fact the plastoquinone pool spans the thylakoid membrane. This allows plastoquinone to function in an additional capacity, i.e., participating in the establishment of an electrochemical gradient across the membrane. Plastoquinone accepts protons at the outer side of the thylakoid membrane as a concomitance of accepting electrons, while it releases protons at the inner side of the membrane in conjunction with transferring electrons to the next component in the transport system.

Plastoquinone transfers electrons to a cytochrome of the $c$ family,[†] which is, however, referred to as cytochrome $f$. (The $f$ stands for the Latin *folium*, "leaf.") Cytochrome $f$ has been isolated from parsley as a species which has a molecular weight of 250,000 and which contains four heme $c$ moieties. Since ferrocytochrome $f$ exhibits a characteristic absorption band at 550 nm, it would seem that this component might be called cytochrome $c$-550.

The next component in the transport system is an acidic deep blue copper-containing protein having a molecular weight of 21,000 and known as plastocyanin.

---

[†] Wood, P. M., and Bendall, D. S. (1975) *Biochim. Biophys. Acta* **387**, 115–128.

On the basis of EPR studies, it has been concluded that the copper of plastocyanin undergoes reduction and then oxidation as the component accepts and then transfers an electron.

## The Light Reaction at Photocenter I and Associated Reactions

Plastocyanin functions as the primary electron donor in the photochemical reaction that occurs at photocenter I. A complex which embodies the components involved in the light reaction at photocenter I has been isolated from the leaves of swiss chard, and five different polypeptides have been identified as components of this species. These polypeptides have molecular weights of 70,000, 25,000, 20,000, 18,000, and 16,000. The polypeptide with a molecular weight of 70,000 is associated with both the primary oxidation and the primary reduction that take place at photocenter I.[†] The principal photochemically reactive pigment at photocenter I is a species of chlorophyll a which exhibits an absorption maximum at 700 nm and is thus called P700. When light having a wavelength of less than 700 nm falls upon photocenter I, a (singlet) excited form of P700 is generated, and this then transfers an electron to the primary electron acceptor. The result is the formation of a strong reductant. Plastocyanin, as the primary donor, then transfers an electron to the electron-deficient P700, and oxidized plastocyanin, which is a weak oxidant, is formed. (Note that the reaction at photocenter II generated a strong oxidant and a weak reductant, while in the present case a weak oxidant and a strong reductant are formed.)

It has been proposed that the primary electron acceptor at photocenter I is a component which has an absorption maximum at 430 nm and is, therefore, designated as P430.[‡] On the basis of its spectral characteristics and its reduction potential it is suspected that P430 is an iron-sulfur protein that is similar to ferredoxin which is discussed next.

Electrons are transferred from the primary acceptor to a small red nonheme iron protein called ferredoxin. In higher plants ferredoxins contain two iron and two acid-labile sulfur atoms. (Acid-labile sulfur atoms become the sulfide of hydrogen sulfide in the presence of strong mineral acids.) The iron atoms of these ferredoxins are coordinated both with the acid-labile sulfur atoms and with cysteinyl sulfhydryl groups, as shown diagrammatically.

$$\begin{array}{c} \text{Cys-S} \quad\quad\quad \text{S-Cys} \\ \diagdown \quad \text{S} \quad \diagup \\ \text{Fe} \quad\quad \text{Fe} \\ \diagup \quad \text{S} \quad \diagdown \\ \text{Cys-S} \quad\quad\quad \text{S-Cys} \end{array}$$

The polypeptide moiety of spinach ferredoxin consists of 97 amino acyl units and has a molecular weight of 10,700.

---

[†] Bengis, C., and Nelson, N. (1975) *J. Biol. Chem.* **250**, 2783–2788.
[‡] Ke, B. (1973) *Biochim. Biophys. Acta* **301**, 1–33.

As the final event in the electron-transport sequence, electrons are transferred from ferredoxin to $NADP^+$. This reaction is mediated by ferredoxin–$NADP^+$ reductase (NADPH:ferredoxin oxidoreductase, EC 1.6.7.1), which is a flavoprotein. Thus, electron transfer which was initiated by the light reaction at photocenter II has resulted in the reduction of $NADP^+$. This process and the associated cleavage of a water molecule are summarized schematically in Fig. 11-7.

## Cyclic Electron Flow

An alternative pathway of electron flow has been demonstrated for electron-transport in the region near photocenter I. Instead of being transferred from the primary acceptor to ferredoxin and ultimately to $NADP^+$, electrons from the reduced P430

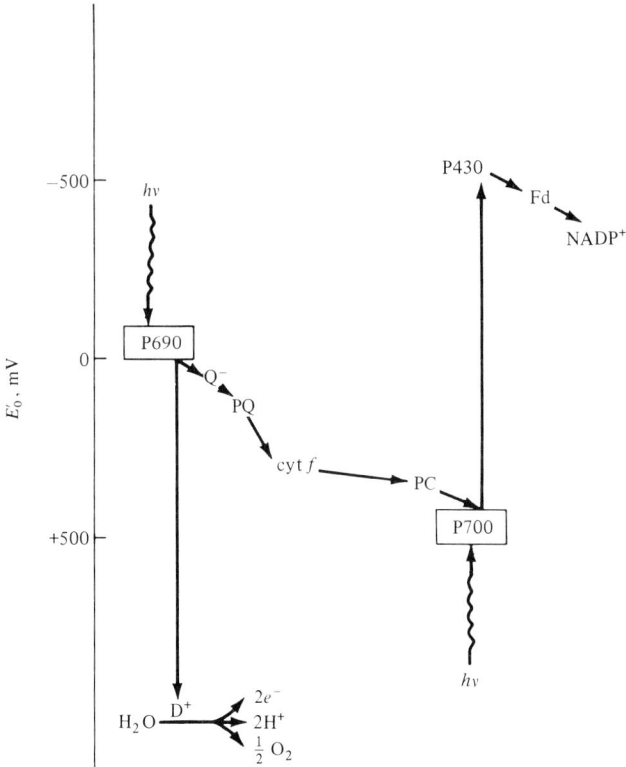

**Figure 11-7** Schematic representation of the electron-transport system associated with photosynthesis in higher plants. Light ($hv$) of the appropriate wavelength interacts with the pigment P690 and an electron is transferred from the pigment to Q, the primary acceptor. D, the primary donor, then transfers an electron to the electron-deficient pigment. As a result, D becomes electron deficient and, in fact, a strong oxidant which oxidizes the oxygen of water. On the other hand, Q is regenerated in its original form as it introduces an electron into the transport system. During passage through this transport system another photochemical reaction, involving P700, takes place. Ultimately, electrons are donated to $NADP^+$. As a concomitance of the electron-transport process energy is made available for the phosphorylation of ADP to yield ATP.

can be introduced into an alternate pathway which results in their being donated to P700 once more. Hence, the pathway is cyclic. Components thought to be included in this alternate pathway are a cytochrome of the $b$ family (cytochrome $b$-563), plastoquinone, and cytochrome $f$. Cytochrome $b$-563 has been isolated from spinach chloroplasts as a species composed of approximately one-third lipid and two-thirds protein. The protein moiety is, in turn, composed of one polypeptide having a molecular weight of 20,000, one polypeptide having a molecular weight of 9600, and two polypeptides each having a molecular weight of 6600. These four polypeptide chains are associated with one heme b moiety. A suggested function for cyclic electron flow will be discussed in the following section.

## Oxidative Photophosphorylation

Electron transport as carried out by the thylakoid system can provide the energy for the phosphorylation of ADP, just as that which is carried out by the mitochondrial system. The reduction potentials of the various components of the system in higher plants are indicated approximately in Fig. 11-7, and it can be calculated that the potential span is more than that required for one molecule of ADP to be converted to ATP. However, there is not a clear consensus as to the maximum yield of ATP which accompanies the electron transport from water to $NADP^+$. Some of the data are interpreted to indicate that one molecule of ADP undergoes phosphorylation as two electrons pass through the system, while other data indicate that two molecules of ATP can be formed for every two electrons that are donated to $NADP^+$. The stoichiometry of the reactions involved in the assimilation of a molecule of carbon dioxide into a molecule of hexose, by means of the reductive pentose phosphate cycle, is such that three molecules of ATP are required for every two molecules of NADPH that are utilized. If only one molecule of ATP can be generated for each molecule of NADPH that is formed, it might be argued that an additional source of ATP is needed. In response to such arguments it has been suggested that the cyclic flow of electrons, mentioned above, can provide the additional ATP since it has been shown that electron transport through the loop at photocenter I can provide energy for the phosphorylation of ADP.

Finally, it might be reiterated that the mechanism of oxidative photophosphorylation, as well as that of oxidative phosphorylation, is unknown. Presumably the mechanism which is operative in the mitochondrial inner membrane and that which is operative in the thylakoid membrane bear some degree of similarity.

## Isolation of a Component Having ATPase Activity from the Thylakoid Membrane

As in the mitochondrial system, attempts have been made to resolve and isolate thylakoid-membrane components thought to participate in oxidative photophosphorylation. Much of this work also has been conducted in the laboratories of E. Racker at Cornell University. One of the components isolated as a part of studies in these laboratories is the counterpart of the mitochondrial membrane factor, $F_1$. The component from the thylakoid membrane is designated $CF_1$. As in

the mitochondrial system, $CF_1$ has been shown to restore the capability for ADP phosphorylation to chloroplast particles from which it has been removed. Also, as in the mitochondrial system, the isolated $CF_1$ exhibits ATPase activity. As isolated from spinach chloroplasts, $CF_1$ has a molecular weight of 325,000 and yields five different polypeptides upon denaturation and dissociation. These have molecular weights of 59,000, 56,000, 37,000, 17,000, and 13,000. The catalytic site involved in the expression of the ATPase activity is formed from areas of the two largest polypeptides. The polypeptide having a molecular weight of 13,000 functions as an inhibitor of the ATPase activity that is exhibited by the two larger polypeptides although the polypeptide having a molecular weight of 33,000 must also be present.†
The function of the polypeptide having a molecular weight of 17,000 remains obscure.

† Deters, D. W., and Racker, E. (1975) *J. Biol. Chem.* **250**, 1041–1047.

CHAPTER
# TWELVE
## LIPID METABOLISM

### PART I ACYLGLYCEROLS

Catabolism of the acylglycerols provides one of the most efficient means by which living organisms derive energy for growth and maintenance. However, in order for exogenous acylglycerols to be utilized they must first be digested and assimilated, by means of a series of processes that is somewhat more complex than that involved when exogenous carbohydrates or proteins are utilized. For this reason, the digestion and assimilation of acylglycerols and other lipids will be discussed briefly prior to the consideration of their catabolism.

### DIGESTION AND ASSIMILATION

The digestion of acylglycerols (and other exogenous lipids) begins in the stomach, where the size of ingested lipid particles is decreased. The resulting lipid material, contained in the chyme, is then slowly introduced into the duodenum. The acylglycerols that enter the duodenum are pimarily unhydrolyzed, although there is evidence suggesting the presence of a gastric lipase which catalyzes the limited hydrolysis of acylglycerols containing short- or medium-chain acyl groups. In the duodenum the lipid-containing chyme is mixed with bile salts, which promote the formation of micelles, and pancreatic secretions, which contain enzymes that catalyze the hydrolysis of acylglycerols. Micelles are supramolecular aggregates formed on the basis of thermodynamic considerations. In aqueous media the structure of micelles is such that hydrophobic components or functional groups are localized in the interior of the aggregate (shielded from the medium) while hydrophilic components or functional groups are localized on the surface of the aggregate (in contact with the medium). In the present case the formation of micelles serves an additional purpose, namely, that of permitting the necessary contact between hydrophilic enzymes and their hydrophobic substrates. Hydrolysis of the acylglycerols occurs primarily in the jejunum, in which the prevailing pH is approximately that at which the pancreatic lipases operate most effectively. As a result of the action of the pancreatic lipases exogenous triacylglycerols are converted primarily into fatty acids and monoacylglycerols. Aggregates of hydrolysis products then pass into the epithelial cells of the jejunal mucosa, although the bile salts do not cross the epithelial cell membrane. Rather, the bile salts pass into the lower intestine, from which they are absorbed and ultimately returned to the gall bladder. The entry of fatty acids and acylglycerols into the epithelial cells of the jejunum is the rate-determining event in the assimilation of exogenous acylglycerols.

Within the epithelial cell fatty acids having 10 or more carbon atoms undergo reesterification by mono- or diacylglycerols; triacylglycerols are formed. Fatty acids having less than 10 carbon atoms generally pass out of the cell at this point and enter the portal circulation. The newly formed triacylglycerols and also small amounts of other lipids and proteins, then form aggregates known as *chylomicrons*. The chylomicrons are subsequently ejected from the cell into the intestinal lymphatics. From the lymphatics they enter the blood, by way of the thoracic duct. The lifetime of a chylomicron in the blood is only a matter of minutes since they are rapidly removed by the tissues. At the tissue site triacylglycerol components of the chylomicrons can undergo catabolism, or they can be incorporated into the circulating form of the lipids, known as the lipoproteins, or they can be stored.

Lipoproteins are supramolecular aggregates which serve as vehicles for the transport of lipids in the blood. Lipoproteins have been categorized as very-low-density lipoproteins (VLDL), low-density lipoproteins (LDL), and high-density lipoproteins (HDL) on the basis of their behavior when density-gradient ultracentrifugation studies are carried out. The properties of the lipoproteins in each of these classes are listed in Table 12-1.

Each class of lipoproteins can be characterized on the basis of the proteins with which it is associated. Very-low-density lipoproteins contain a protein component which has been designated apoprotein B (apoB) and another designated apoprotein C (apoC). The ratio of apoC to apoB increases with the size of the lipoprotein aggregate. Both apoB and apoC can be resolved to yield additional polypeptides. For example, three polypeptides can be obtained from apoC. These are apoC-I, which consists of 57 aminoacyl units, apoC-II, which consists of approximately 95 aminoacyl units, and apoC-III, which consists of 79 aminoacyl units. ApoC-II is an activator of a heparin-induced lipoprotein lipase present in human plasma. By contrast, low-density lipoproteins, which are believed to be derived in some cases from the very-low-density lipoproteins, contain apoB as the principal protein component. ApoC and apoprotein A (apoA) are only minor components of the low-density lipoproteins. ApoA comprises two polypeptides, which have been designated apoA-I and apoA-II. The former consists of 245 aminoacyl units while the latter is, in effect, a dimer which comprises two identical polypeptide chains of 77 aminoacyl units each joined by a disulfide bond derived from the sulfhydryl groups of the Cys-6 units of each chain. High-density lipoproteins, on the other

## Table 12-1 Some properties of chylomicrons and lipoproteins

| Species | Density range, g/ml | Diameter range, Å | Triacylglycerols, % | Cholesterol, % | Cholesterol esters, % | Phospholipids, % | Proteins, % | Principal apoprotein(s) |
|---|---|---|---|---|---|---|---|---|
| Chylomicrons | <0.93 | 750-10,000 | 80-95 | 1-3 | 2-4 | 3-6 | 1-2 | |
| Very-low-density lipoproteins | 0.93-1.006 | 250-550 | 50-60 | 10-12 | 4-6 | 18-20 | 8-12 | B, C |
| Low-density lipoproteins | 1.006-1.063 | 200-220 | 8-10 | 10-11 | 47-55 | 28-30 | 20-22 | B |
| High-density lipoproteins | 1.063-1.21 | 70-100 | 8 | 3 | 14 | 22 | 50 | A |

hand, contain two types of polypeptide chains. One has a molecular weight of 28,000 while the other has a molecular weight of 8700. These exist in a stoichiometric ratio of 1:1 in high-density lipoproteins.

## CATABOLISM OF FATTY ACIDS

At the tissue site triacylglycerols of the lipoproteins can undergo hydrolysis to yield the component fatty acids (and the resulting triacylglycerol or glycerol), which can, in turn, undergo catabolism. The hydrolyses are catalyzed by lipases. The catabolism of the fatty acids occurs by means of processes to be discussed next.

### $\beta$ Oxidation

A saturated, nonbranched fatty acid which has $n$ carbon atoms can undergo a stepwise catabolic process known as $\beta$ oxidation with the result that $n/2$ acetyl moieties are produced. In mammals all the enzymes that participate in $\beta$ oxidation are localized in the matrix of the mitochondrion, with the exception of an $NAD^+$-dependent dehydrogenase that is a component of the inner membrane.

A fatty acid undergoing $\beta$ oxidation must first be converted into the corresponding CoA ester. This esterification requires the participation of a nucleoside triphosphate, which is cleaved as a concomitance of the reaction. The enzymes that catalyze the esterification of fatty acids are called acyl-CoA synthetases. Several different synthetases have been characterized on the basis of the chain lengths of the fatty acids that they utilize as substrates.

Fatty acids having up to 10 or 11 carbon atoms can be converted into the corresponding CoA derivative by the reaction catalyzed by butyryl-CoA synthetase [butyrate:CoA ligase (AMP-forming), EC 6.2.1.2]. The reaction is

$$\text{Fatty acid} + \text{CoA} + \text{ATP} \rightleftharpoons \text{acyl-CoA} + \text{AMP} + PP_i \quad (12\text{-}1)$$

This synthetase, referred to as a medium-chain fatty-acid synthetase, is localized in the mitochondria. Fatty acids of medium chain length can also undergo esterification by CoA as the result of a reaction catalyzed by a GTP-dependent synthetase. This enzyme is acyl-CoA synthetase (GDP-forming) [acid:CoA ligase (GDP-forming), EC 6.2.1.10]. The reaction is

$$\text{Fatty acid} + \text{CoA} + \text{GTP} \rightleftharpoons \text{acyl-CoA} + \text{GDP} + P_i \quad (12\text{-}2)$$

The GTP-dependent synthetase is also localized in the mitochondrion. Long-chain fatty acids (those having from 8 to 20 carbon atoms) on the other hand, serve as substrates for yet another acyl-CoA synthetase [acid:CoA ligase (AMP-forming), EC 6.2.1.3]. This synthetase utilizes ATP as the nucleoside triphosphate and the reaction is the same as that given by Eq. (12-1). The synthetase which utilizes long-chain fatty acids is predominantly associated with the microsomal fraction of the cell.

A long-chain acyl-CoA synthetase has been isolated from a rat-liver microsomal fraction and has been purified. This enzyme species has a particle weight of 168,000 and contains phospholipid. This enzyme is presumably composed of subunits which each have a molecular weight of 27,000. When kinetic studies were conducted on this enzyme it was found that plots of $1/v_i$ vs. $1/[\text{palmitate}]$ with fixed concentrations of CoA and a single concentration of ATP were parallel. Similarly, plots of $1/v_i$ vs. $1/[\text{ATP}]$ with fixed concentrations of CoA and a single concentration of palmitate were parallel. Intersecting double reciprocal plots were obtained, however, when ATP was the variable substrate with palmitate as the fixed substrate and the concentration of CoA was constant.† Certainly, this initial-velocity pattern suggests a kinetic mechanism in which both ATP and palmitate bind the enzyme and then a product (presumably pyrophosphate) dissociates prior to the binding of CoA. Additional data are required to establish the kinetic mechanism, however.

With respect to the reaction mechanism, when [$^{18}$O]palmitate is employed as the substrate, the labeled oxygen is incorporated into both AMP and palmitoyl CoA. A minimal mechanism such as that shown below can therefore be formulated.

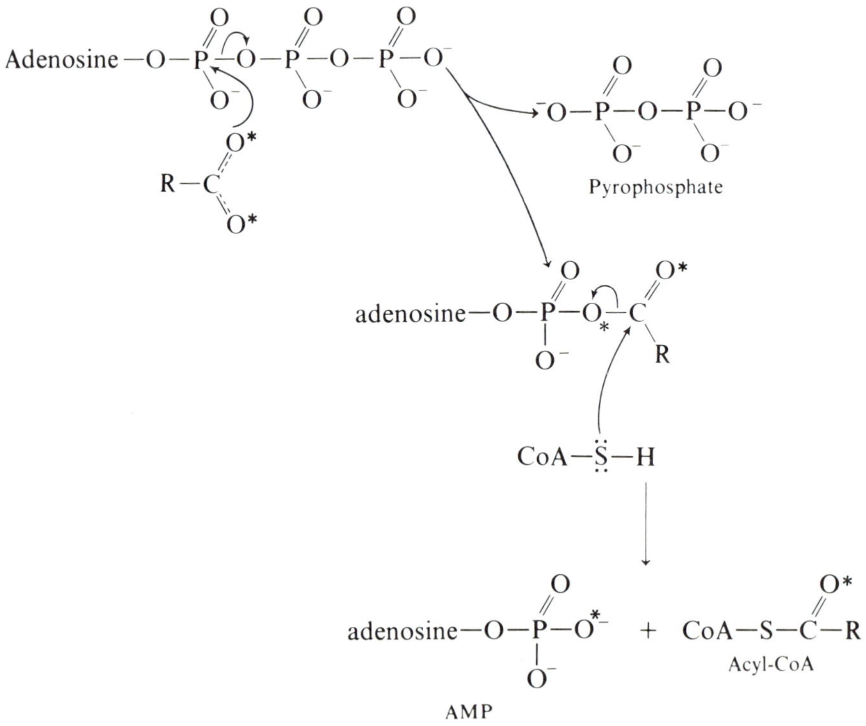

A similar minimal mechanism can be formulated for the reaction catalyzed by the GTP-dependent synthetase, but in this case the nucleophilic attack by the oxygen atom of the fatty acid would be upon the terminal phosphoryl phosphorus atom of the nucleoside triphosphate. There is little experimental evidence either to support or refute such a reaction mechanism at present, however.

† Bar-Tana, J., Rose, G., Brandes, R., and Shapiro, B. (1973) *Biochem. J.* **131**, 199–209.

**Role of carnitine in β oxidation** The formation of the CoA esters of long-chain fatty acids occurs primarily outside the mitochondrion. However, as mentioned previously, adenine nucleotides (and their derivatives) do not diffuse across the mitochondrial inner membrane. Hence, these CoA esters cannot diffuse into the mitochondrial matrix, where the enzymes of β oxidation are localized. Rather, the acyl moiety is transferred from CoA to another component, the resulting acylated component is translocated across the inner membrane, and then the acyl moiety is transferred back to a CoA molecule within the mitochondrial matrix. The component which functions as a vehicle for the transport of the acyl moiety is L-carnitine.

$$H_3C-\underset{\underset{CH_2-\underset{\underset{OH}{|}}{\overset{\overset{H}{|}}{C}}-CH_2-C\underset{O^-}{\overset{O}{\diagup\diagdown}}}{\overset{|}{C}H_3}}{\overset{\overset{CH_3}{|}}{\overset{+}{N}}}-CH_3$$

L-Carnitine (3-hydroxy-4-trimethylammonium butyrate)

The acyl moiety is transferred from CoA to the hydroxyl group of carnitine by a transesterification reaction catalyzed by carnitine palmitoyltransferase (palmitoyl-CoA:L-carnitine O-palmitoyltransferase, EC 2.3.1.21). Once across the inner membrane, another transesterification reaction allows the acyl-CoA to be regenerated. The reactions catalyzed by carnitine palmitoyltransferase are

Palmitoyl CoA + L-carnitine $\rightleftharpoons$ palmitoyl-L-carnitine + CoA     (12-3)

**Step 1: Dehydrogenation** Within the mitochondrial matrix the acyl moiety of an acyl-CoA molecule can undergo a repetitive sequence of reactions which results in the cleavage of C(1) and C(2) from the moiety, in the form of an acetyl group, and the formation of another acyl-CoA molecule having two fewer carbon atoms. The first step of this sequence is the dehydrogenation of the acyl moiety, as catalyzed by an acyl-CoA dehydrogenase. (It should be remembered that dehydrogenation reactions are oxidation reactions.) Acyl moieties of medium chain length are oxidized by butyryl-CoA dehydrogenase [butyryl-CoA:(acceptor) oxidoreductase, EC 1.3.99.2], while long-chain acyl moieties are oxidized by acyl-CoA dehydrogenase [acyl-CoA:(acceptor) oxidoreductase, EC 1.3.99.3]. The dehydrogenation reactions are

Acyl-CoA + oxidized acceptor $\rightleftharpoons$ 2,3-dehydroacyl-CoA + reduced acceptor

(12-4)

The acyl-CoA dehydrogenases are flavoproteins. They are associated with, and function in conjunction with, another flavoprotein, known as the electron-transferring flavoprotein (ETF). As isolated from bovine or porcine liver, the acyl-CoA dehydrogenase which utilizes acyl moieties of medium chain length is a tetramer which comprises subunits each having a molecular weight of approximately 40,000. Each of the subunits binds one molecule of FAD. The electron-transferring flavoprotein from porcine liver is a dimer and the ETF has a molecular weight of

58,000.† One molecule of FAD is bound by each of these subunits, also. The dehydrogenation reaction involves the removal of two hydrogens, each with an electron, from the acyl moiety, with the result that an olefinic bond is formed between C(2) and C(3). The two reducing equivalents are transferred to the flavin cofactor of the dehydrogenase and then to the flavin cofactor of the electron-transferring flavoprotein, which subsequently introduces the electrons into the mitochondrial electron-transport system at the level of complex III. When an acyl moiety is undergoing oxidation in the presence of the acyl-CoA dehydrogenase and the electron-transferring flavoprotein, the transient appearance of the blue (neutral) semiquinone form of the FAD of the dehydrogenase as well as the red (anionic) semiquinone form of the FAD of electron-transferring flavoprotein can be demonstrated, thus indicating that unpaired electrons are being transferred by these cofactors.

The dehydrogenation of the acyl moiety of the acyl-CoA, as catalyzed by an acyl-CoA dehydrogenase, yields specifically a *trans*-$\Delta^2$-acyl moiety.

**Step 2: Hydration of the $\Delta^2$-acyl moiety** The next reaction of $\beta$ oxidation is the hydration of the olefinic bond produced in the previous step. The hydration reaction is catalyzed by an enzyme known as enoyl-CoA hydratase (L-3-hydroxyacyl-CoA hydro-lyase, EC 4.2.1.17). As isolated from bovine-liver mitochondria, the enzyme enoyl-CoA hydratase has a molecular weight of 164,000 and is a hexamer. The hydration of the olefinic bond catalyzed by enoyl-CoA hydratase is stereospecific, and with *trans*-$\Delta^2$-acyl-CoA as the substrate L(+)-3-hydroxyacyl-CoA is formed, i.e.,

$$\text{*trans*-}\Delta^2\text{-Acyl-CoA} + H_2O \rightleftharpoons \text{L(+)-3-hydroxyacyl-CoA} \qquad (12\text{-}5)$$

The activity of the enoyl-CoA hydratase which catalyzes the hydration of long-chain $\Delta^2$-acyl moieties is inhibited by its substrates.

**Step 3: Oxidation of the 3-hydroxyacyl moiety** The third step of this pathway entails the oxidation of the secondary alcohol group at C(3) of the acyl moiety. The enzyme 3-hydroxyacyl-CoA dehydrogenase (L-3-hydroxyacyl-CoA:$NAD^+$ oxidoreductase, EC 1.1.1.35) catalyzes the reaction, which can be written

$$\text{L-3-Hydroxyacyl-CoA} + NAD^+ \rightleftharpoons \text{3-oxoacyl-CoA} + NADH \qquad (12\text{-}6)$$

This enzyme, in contrast to the others of this pathway, is a component of the mitochondrial inner membrane rather than being localized in the matrix.

3-Hydroxyacyl-CoA dehydrogenase has been isolated from porcine-heart mitochondria and it is found to have a molecular weight of 65,000. The native enzyme comprises two identical or similar subunits. The enzyme specifically utilizes L-3-hydroxyacyl-CoA as its substrate and transfers the hydride ion that it removes from C(3) of the acyl moiety specifically to the *si* face of C(4) of the pyridinium ring of $NAD^+$.

† Hall, C. L., and Kamin, H. (1975) *J. Biol. Chem.* **250**, 3476–3486.

**Step 4: Cleavage of the 3-oxoacyl moiety** The fourth and last step of $\beta$ oxidation is the cleavage of the 3-oxoacyl moiety in the presence of CoA to yield acetyl CoA plus another acyl-CoA molecule in which the acyl moiety has two fewer carbon atoms. The cleavage is catalyzed by acetyl-CoA acyltransferase (acyl-CoA:acetyl-CoA C-acyltransferase, EC 2.3.1.16). The cleavage can be written

$$3\text{-Oxoacyl-CoA} + \text{CoA} \rightleftharpoons \text{acetyl CoA} + \text{acyl-CoA} \qquad (12\text{-}7)$$

The reaction mechanism of the cleavage as catalyzed by acetyl-CoA acyltransferase has been formulated as the reverse of a Claisen condensation.† After an initial formation of a Schiff base derived from an amino group at the catalytic site and the C(3) oxo group of the acyl moiety, a sulfhydryl group, also at the catalytic site, attacks the methenyl carbon atom of the Schiff base. The resulting species then expels acetyl CoA. Subsequently, as the result of a process which is essentially a transesterification followed by a reversal of the Schiff base formation, the new acyl-CoA is generated.

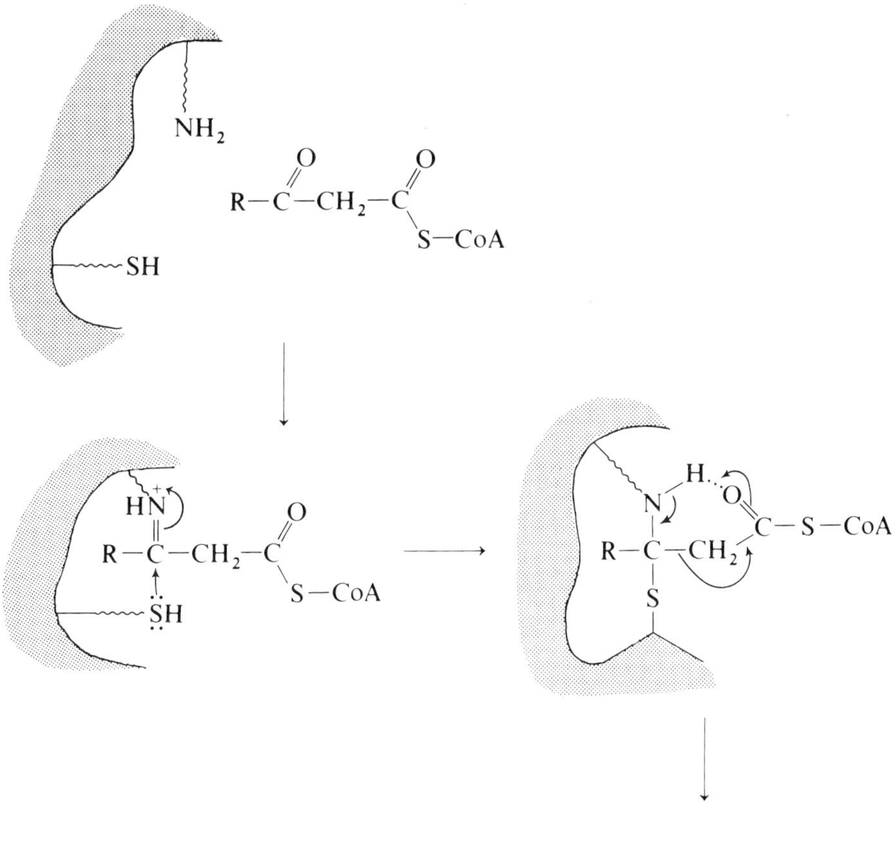

† Holland, P. C., Clark, M. G., and Bloxham, D. P. (1973) *Biochemistry* **12**, 3309–3315.

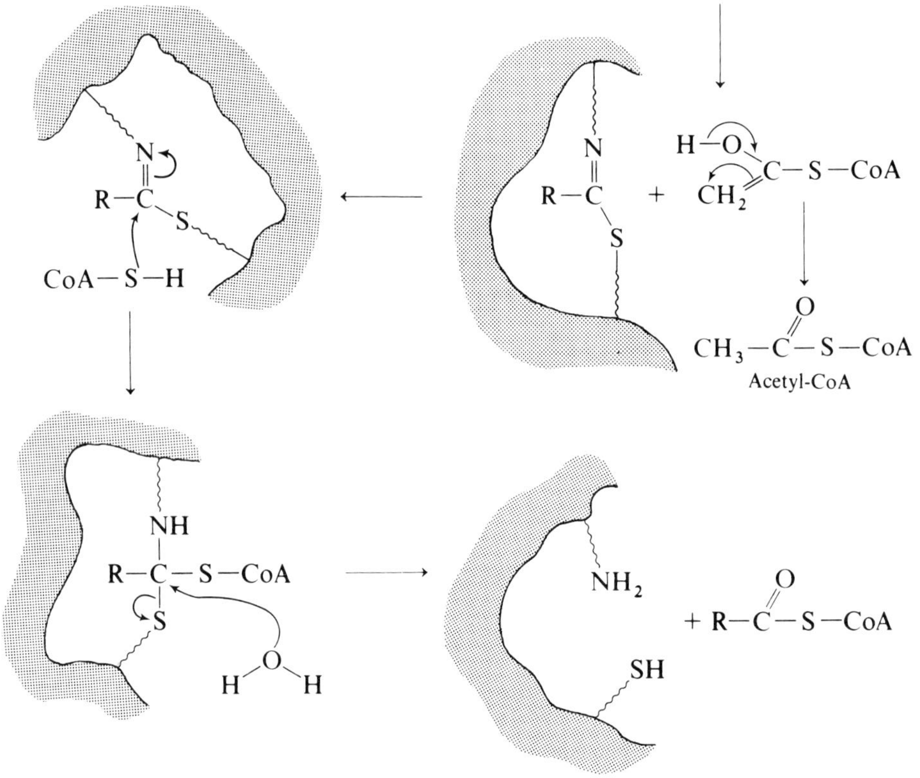

The process of β oxidation can now begin again. Thus, the complete degradation of a 16-carbon fatty acid would entail seven $(n/2 - 1)$ revolutions of the β-oxidation cycle, and as a result eight molecules of acetyl CoA would be generated.

## Summary of β Oxidation

The process of β oxidation can be summarized as shown in Fig. 12-1. As mentioned at the beginning of this chapter, the catabolism of acylglycerols is one of the most efficient means by which living organisms derive energy. Consider now the maximum theoretical energy yield that can result from the degradation of a fatty acid by β oxidation and the introduction of the acetyl CoA thus formed into the tricarboxylic acid cycle. For this purpose, the six-carbon acid, caproate, can be used. The complete degradation of caproate by β oxidation would require two revolutions of the cycle and would generate three acetyl moieties. As a concomitance of the two revolutions of the β-oxidation cycle, two molecules of $NAD^+$ would be reduced and four electrons would enter the mitochondrial electron-transport system at the level of complex III. In addition, three acetyl moieties (of acetyl CoA) could enter the tricarboxylic acid cycle. Each revolution of the tricarboxylic acid cycle allows three molecules of $NAD^+$ to be reduced and 2 electrons to enter the mitochondrial electron-transport system at the level of complex II. In addition, each revolution of the tricarboxylic acid cycle yields one molecule of ATP as a result

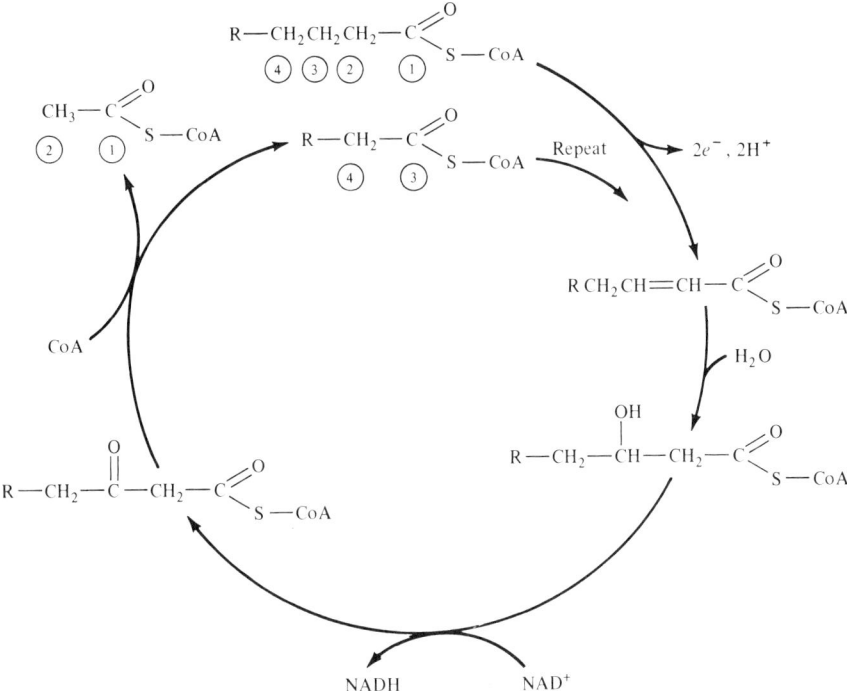

**Figure 12-1** Summary of β oxidation. As a result of one revolution of the cycle, C(1) and C(2) of the acyl moiety that entered the cycle are converted into the acetyl moiety of acetyl-CoA while C(3) and C(4) of that acyl moiety become the carbonyl carbon atom and the adjacent methylene carbon atom, respectively, of the new acyl moiety that is generated. With the formation of the new acyl moiety, which comprises two less carbon atoms, the cycle can begin again.

of the conversion of succinyl CoA into succinate. Thus, the maximum theoretical energy yield from the complete catabolism of caproate can be calculated as shown in Table 12-2. The maximum theoretical energy yield from the complete catabolism of the hexose glucose is also calculated for comparison.

## Catabolism of Fatty Acids That Have an Odd Number of Carbon Atoms

A saturated, nonbranched fatty acid having an odd number of carbon atoms can also be degraded by the β-oxidation cycle but only to the point at which the acyl moiety has three carbon atoms. Propionyl CoA then undergoes a sequence of reactions which results in the formation of succinyl CoA, which in turn can enter the tricarboxylic acid cycle.

**Conversion of propionyl CoA into methylmalonyl CoA** When propionyl CoA is to be converted into succinyl CoA, the former initially undergoes a carboxylation reaction which results in the formation of methylmalonyl CoA. The carboxylation reaction is catalyzed by propionyl-CoA carboxylase [propionyl-CoA:carbon-dioxide

## Table 12-2

| Catabolism of 1 mol of caproate | | Catabolism of 1 mol of glucose | |
| --- | --- | --- | --- |
| Process | Moles of ATP produced | Process | Moles of ATP produced |
| β oxidation: | | Glycolysis: | |
| 2 NADH | 6 | 2 NADH | 6 |
| 4$e^-$, complex III | 4 | 3-PG-P to 3-PGA | 2 |
| Tricarboxylic acid cycle: | | PEP to Pyr | 2 |
| 9 NADH | 27 | Pyr to Ac-CoA: | |
| 6$e^-$, complex II | 6 | 2 NADH | 6 |
| Suc CoA to Suc | 3 | Tricarboxylic acid cycle: | |
| | — | 6 NADH | 18 |
| | 46 | 4$e^-$, complex II | 4 |
| | | Suc CoA to Suc | 2 |
| | | | — |
| | | | 40 |
| | | ATP utilized, glycolysis | 2 |
| | | | — |
| | | | 38 |

ligase (ADP-forming), EC 6.4.1.3]. The formation of methylmalonyl CoA can be written

Propionyl CoA + $HCO_3^-$ + ATP + $H_2O$

$$\rightleftharpoons \text{methylmalonyl CoA} + ADP + P_i \quad (12\text{-}8)$$

The reaction catalyzed by propionyl-CoA carboxylase parallels that catalyzed by pyruvate carboxylase. The formation of methylmalonyl CoA requires biotin and ATP, and a carbon dioxide–biotin intermediate is formed.

Propionyl-CoA carboxylase has been isolated from porcine-heart mitochondria and purified. The crystalline enzyme has a molecular weight of 700,000 and comprises four subunits, each having a molecular weight of 175,000 and binding a molecule of biotin.

The kinetic mechanism of the formation of methylmalonyl CoA is presumed to be the same as that of the formation of oxaloacetate from pyruvate. The isotope-exchange studies which have been carried out are in fact compatible with a two-site ping pong Bi Bi Uni Uni mechanism. The reaction mechanism of the carboxylation of propionyl CoA is also analogous to that of the carboxylation of pyruvate and can thus be depicted as shown on pages 485 and 486. The methylmalonyl CoA formed has the S configuration at C(2) of the acyl moiety.

**Rearrangement of methylmalonyl CoA to succinyl CoA** Succinyl CoA is formed from methylmalonyl CoA by means of a rearrangement catalyzed by methylmalonyl-CoA mutase (methylmalonyl-CoA CoA-carbonylmutase, EC 5.4.99.2). However, methylmalonyl-CoA mutase utilizes only methylmalonyl CoA, which has the $R$ configuration at C(2) of the acyl moiety; therefore, the product of the reaction catalyzed by propionyl-CoA carboxylase must undergo a change in configuration at C(2) of the acyl moiety prior to the rearrangement. This is catalyzed by a specific

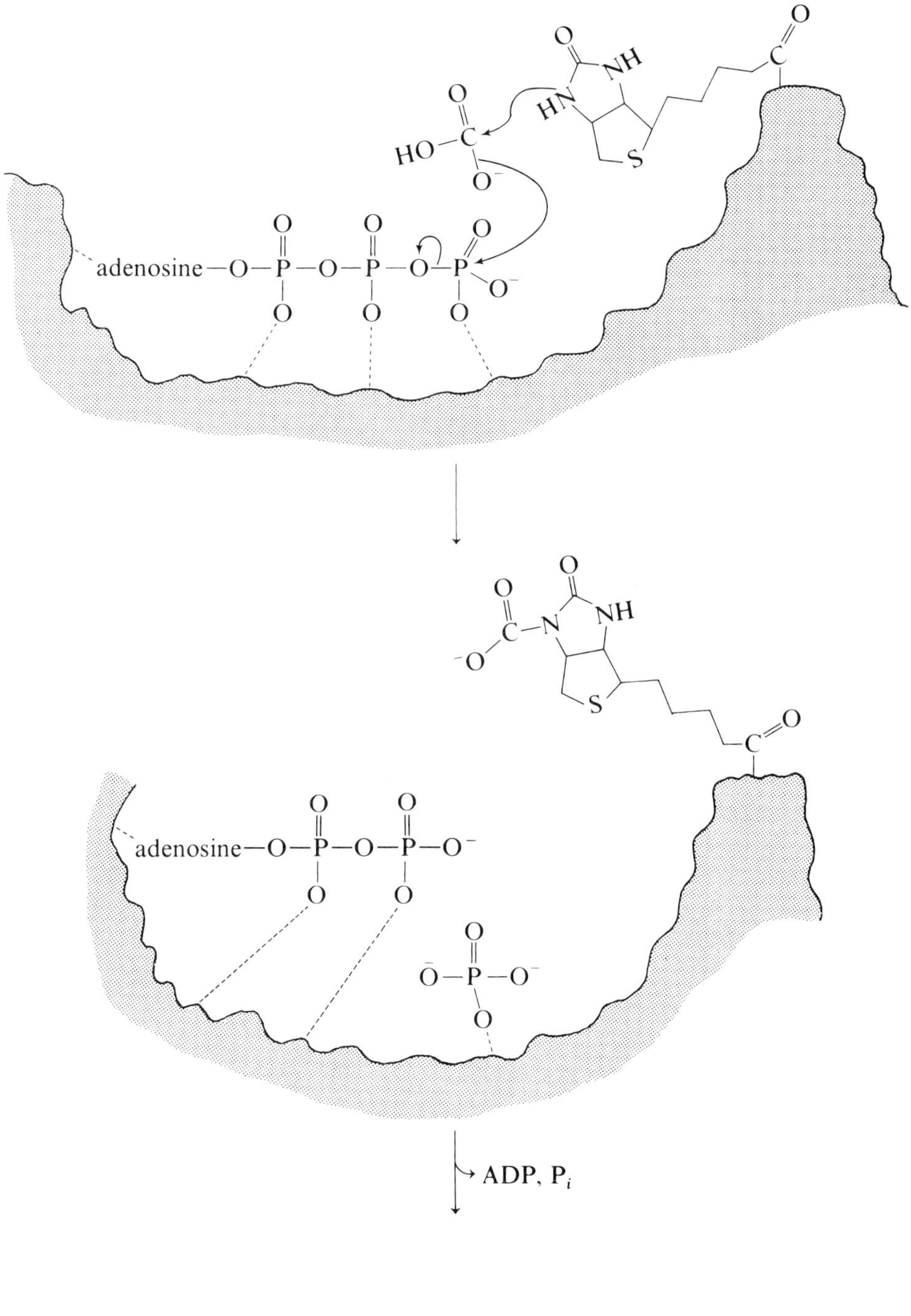

→ ADP, P$_i$

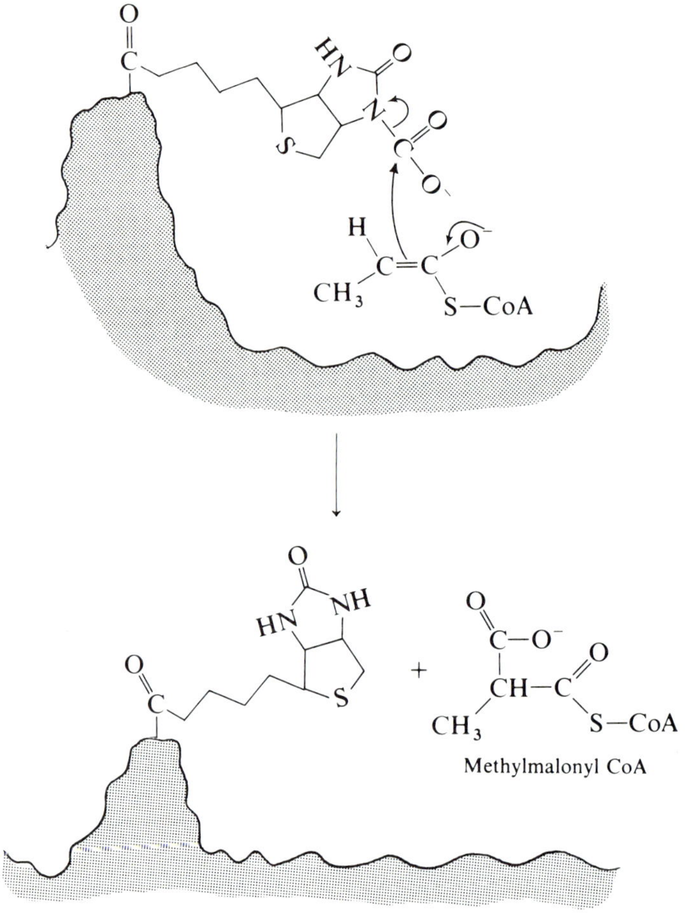

racemase, methylmalonyl-CoA racemase (methylmalonyl-CoA racemase, EC 5.1.99.1), which is apparently present in all tissues containing the mutase. The racemization involves the formation of an enolate, as shown.

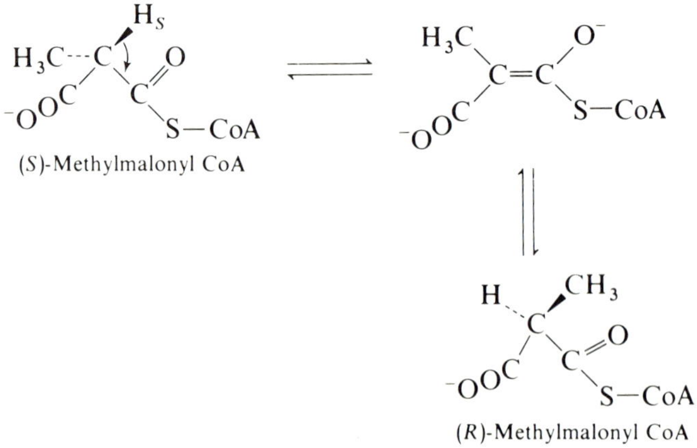

The rearrangement of (R)-methylmalonyl CoA requires the participation of a cofactor derived from vitamin $B_{12}$. The structure of vitamin $B_{12}$ was established in 1955 on the basis of x-ray crystallographic studies conducted in the laboratory of Dorothy Hodgkin at Oxford University. Nine years later, she received the Nobel prize in chemistry for these and relates studies. The vitamin $B_{12}$ molecule embodies a corrin ring, which bears some resemblance to the porphyrin ring. However, it should be noted that one of the methene bridges present in the porphyrin system is absent from the corrin ring. Also, the corrin ring is less unsaturated than the porphyrin ring system. The nitrogen atoms of the corrin ring provide four of the ligands that bind the central atom, which is cobalt. The fifth ligand is provided by an imidazolium nitrogen atom of the 5,6-dimethylbenzimidazolyl nucleotide. Cofactors derived from vitamin $B_{12}$ have a component at the sixth ligand position which participates in the formation of a carbon-cobalt bond. In the present case, this component is a 5'-deoxyadenosyl moiety.

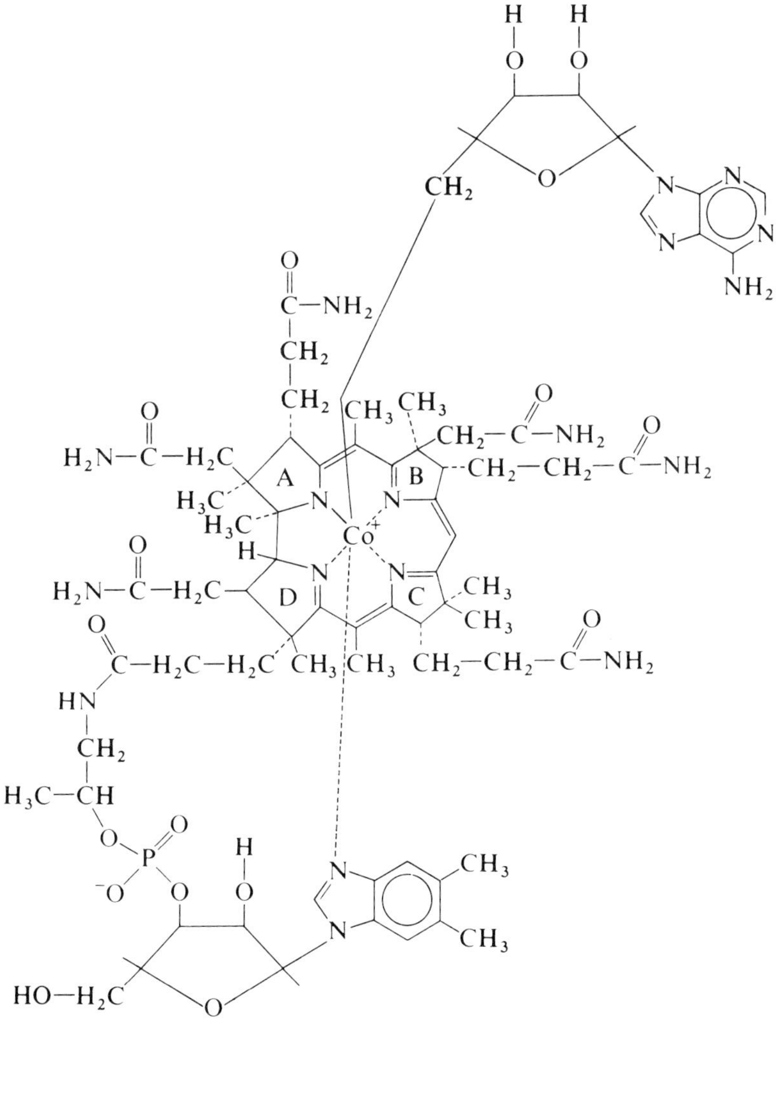

**488** MECHANISMS OF METABOLISM

Methylmalonyl-CoA mutase has been isolated from ovine liver as a pink metalloprotein which has a molecular weight of 165,000. This species contains two cobalt atoms.

The rearrangement is thought to be initiated by a homolytic cleavage of the carbon-cobalt bond, thus forming cobalamin [containing Co(II)] and a 5′-deoxyadenos-5′-yl radical. The latter can, in turn, abstract a hydrogen atom from the methylmalonyl CoA, generating a substrate radical. It has been proposed that this radical becomes bonded to the cobalt prior to the rearrangement, which entails the migration of the thiol ester group, although the details of this migration are unknown. It is known, however, that subsequently one of the three hydrogen atoms of the methyl group of the 5′-deoxyadenosine moiety is returned to the substrate as the original form of the cofactor is regenerated.

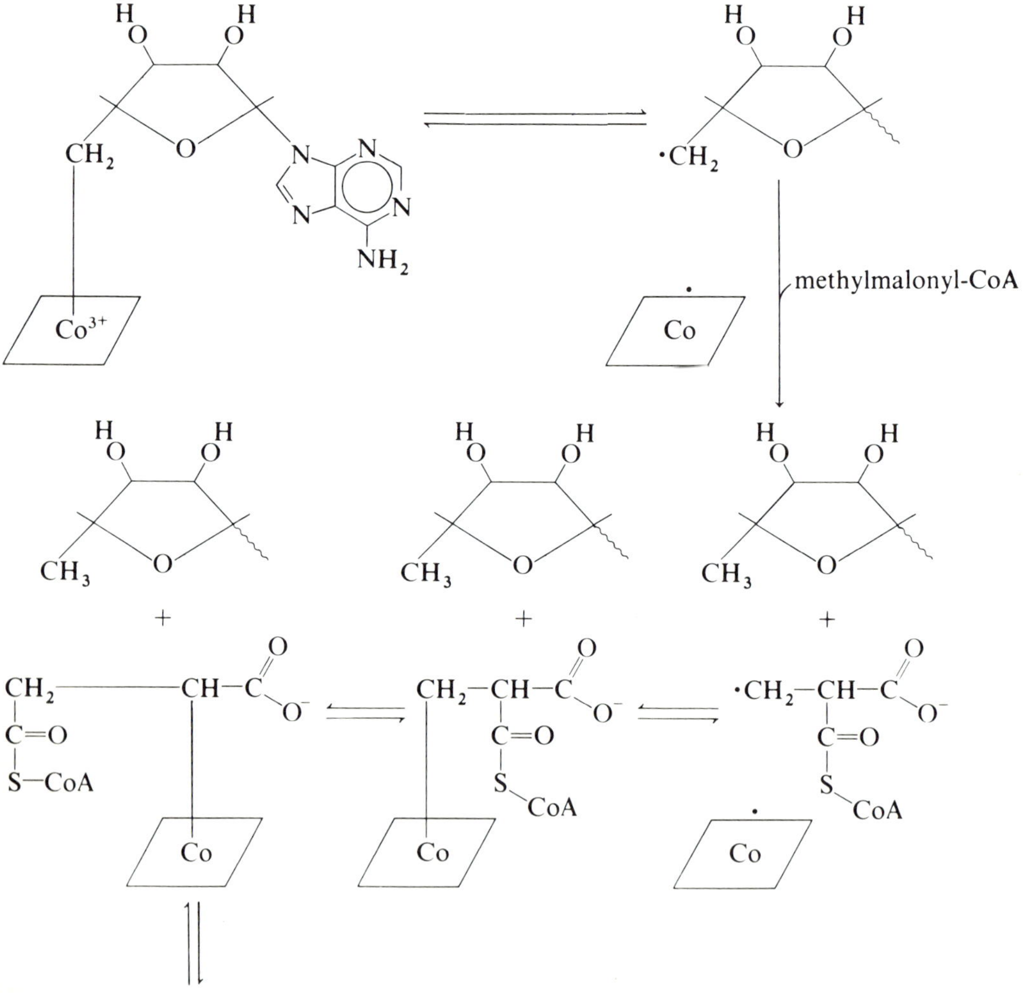

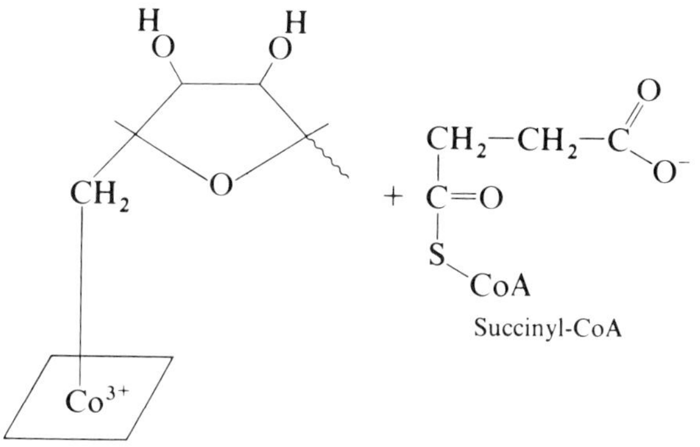

[Structure diagram showing a cobalt complex with CH₂ group and two OH groups, plus Succinyl-CoA structure: CH₂—CH₂—C(=O)O⁻ with C=O bonded to S-CoA]

Succinyl-CoA

## Catabolism of Branched-Chain Fatty Acids

Branched-chain fatty acids can also be partially degraded by $\beta$ oxidation. In this case, $\beta$ oxidation proceeds until there is a branch point at either C(2) or C(3) of the newly formed acyl moiety. When this occurs, alternate pathways are used.

An example of an acyl moiety with a branch point at C(2) is found in 2-methylbutyryl CoA. Here the acyl moiety can be degraded just as if the chain were nonbranched, but the cleavage of the 3-oxoacyl moiety yields an acetyl moiety and a propionyl moiety rather than two acetyl moieties. The utilization of the propionyl moiety of propionyl CoA has just been described.

An example of an acyl moiety having a branch point at C(3) can be found in isovaleryl CoA. Here the initial step of $\beta$ oxidation, the dehydrogenation, occurs in the usual manner, and 3-methylcrotonoyl CoA is formed. However, rather than undergoing a hydration reaction, the acyl moiety of 3-methylcrotonoyl CoA undergoes a carboxylation reaction, catalyzed by a biotin-dependent carboxylase. The reaction parallels those catalyzed by pyruvate carboxylase and propionyl-CoA carboxylase. In the present case, the enzyme is methylcrotonoyl-CoA carboxylase [3-methylcrotonoyl-CoA:carbon-dioxide ligase (ADP-forming), EC 6.4.1.4], and the reaction is

3-Methylcrotonoyl CoA + $HCO_3^-$ + ATP + $H_2O$

$$\rightleftharpoons \text{3-methylglutaconyl CoA} + \text{ADP} + P_i \quad (12\text{-}9)$$

The resulting 3-methylglutaconyl CoA now undergoes a hydration reaction and 3-hydroxy-3-methylglutaryl CoA is formed. This, in turn, can undergo a retrograde aldol reaction which yields acetyl CoA and acetoacetate. The cleavage is catalyzed by hydroxymethylglutaryl-CoA lyase (3-hydroxy-3-methylglutaryl-CoA acetoacetate-lyase, EC 4.1.3.4). As isolated from bovine-liver mitochondria, the lyase is a single polypeptide chain which has a molecular weight of 50,000. The cleavage of hydroxymethylglutaryl CoA appears to be irreversible. (A different enzyme is known to catalyze the formation of hydroxymethylglutaryl CoA.) A minimal reaction mechanism for the cleavage of 3-hydroxy-3-methylglutaryl CoA is

$$\text{}^-\text{OOC}-\text{CH}_2-\underset{\underset{\text{CH}_3}{|}}{\overset{\overset{\text{H}}{\overset{|}{\text{O}}}}{\text{C}}}-\text{CH}_2-\overset{\overset{\text{O}}{\parallel}}{\text{C}}-\text{S}-\text{CoA} \longrightarrow$$

$$\text{}^-\text{OOC}-\text{CH}_2-\underset{\underset{\text{CH}_3}{|}}{\overset{\overset{\text{O}}{\parallel}}{\text{C}}} + \text{CH}_2=\text{C}\overset{\text{O}^-}{\underset{\text{S}-\text{CoA}}{}}$$

Acetoacetate

$$\Updownarrow \text{H}^+$$

$$\text{CH}_3-\text{C}\overset{\text{O}}{\underset{\text{S}-\text{CoA}}{}}$$

Acetyl-CoA

The degradation of isovaleryl CoA is summarized below.

$$\underset{\text{CH}_3}{\overset{\text{CH}_3}{\diagdown}}\!\!\!\overset{\text{H}}{\underset{|}{\text{C}}}-\text{CH}_2-\overset{\overset{\text{O}}{\parallel}}{\text{C}}-\text{S}-\text{CoA} \longrightarrow \underset{\text{CH}_3}{\overset{\text{CH}_3}{\diagdown}}\!\!\!\text{C}=\text{CH}-\overset{\overset{\text{O}}{\parallel}}{\text{C}}-\text{S}-\text{CoA} \longrightarrow$$

Isovaleryl-CoA　　　　　3-Methylcrotonoyl-CoA

$$\underset{\text{}^-\text{O}-\overset{\overset{\text{O}}{\parallel}}{\text{C}}-\text{H}_2\text{C}}{\diagdown}\!\!\!\overset{\text{CH}_3}{\diagup}\!\!\!\text{C}=\text{CH}-\overset{\overset{\text{O}}{\parallel}}{\text{C}}-\text{S}-\text{CoA} \longrightarrow \underset{\text{}^-\text{O}-\overset{\overset{\text{O}}{\parallel}}{\text{C}}-\text{H}_2\text{C}}{\diagdown}\!\!\!\overset{\overset{\text{CH}_3\ \text{HO}}{|\ \ \ |}}{\text{C}}-\text{CH}_2-\overset{\overset{\text{O}}{\parallel}}{\text{C}}-\text{S}-\text{CoA} \longrightarrow$$

3-Methylglutaconyl-CoA　　　　　3-Hydroxy-3-methylglutaryl-CoA

$$\text{}^-\text{O}-\overset{\overset{\text{O}}{\parallel}}{\text{C}}-\text{CH}_2-\overset{\overset{\text{O}}{\parallel}}{\text{C}}-\text{CH}_3 + \text{CH}_3-\text{C}\overset{\text{O}}{\underset{\text{S}-\text{CoA}}{}}$$

Acetoacetate　　　　　Acetyl-CoA

**Acetoacetate metabolism and the formation of "ketone bodies"** In many tissues acetoacetate can be converted into acetoacetyl CoA by a reaction catalyzed by 3-oxo-acid CoA-transferase (succinyl CoA:3-oxo-acid CoA-transferase, EC 2.8.3.5). This reaction permits succinyl CoA to be converted into succinate as a concomitance of the esterification of a 3-oxo acid such as acetoacetate. Thus, in the case of acetoacetate the reaction is

$$\text{Acetoacetate} + \text{succinyl CoA} \rightleftharpoons \text{succinate} + \text{acetoacetyl CoA} \qquad (12\text{-}10)$$

As isolated from porcine-heart mitochondria, the 3-oxo-acid CoA-transferase has a molecular weight of 78,000. The reaction proceeds by a ping pong Bi Bi mechanism which is thought to entail the formation of a thioacyl intermediate derived from the carboxylate group of a glutamyl unit at the catalytic site and CoA.

The acetoacetyl CoA thus formed can subsequently undergo $\beta$ oxidation, with the result that two acetyl moieties of acetyl CoA are formed. These, in turn, can enter the tricarboxylic acid cycle.

In the liver, however, acetoacetate cannot be utilized in this manner since the 3-oxo-acid CoA-transferase is not present. Rather, acetoacetate can undergo reduction to yield 3-hydroxybutyrate. This reduction is catalyzed by 3-hydroxybutyrate dehydrogenase (D-3-hydroxybutyrate:$NAD^+$ oxidoreductase, EC 1.1.1.30), a component of the mitochondrial inner membrane. The reaction

$$\text{Acetoacetate} + \text{NADH} \rightleftharpoons \text{D-3-hydroxybutyrate} + NAD^+ \quad (12\text{-}11)$$

proceeds by an ordered Bi Bi kinetic mechanism. Acetoacetate can also undergo decarboxylation in the liver. This is catalyzed by acetoacetate decarboxylase (acetoacetate carboxy-lyase, EC 4.1.1.4). The products of the reaction are acetone and carbon dioxide. Acetoacetate and its two derivatives, 3-hydroxybutyrate and acetone, are sometimes referred to collectively as the *ketone bodies*.

Under certain conditions, e.g., starvation or uncontrolled diabetes mellitus (mellitus is derived from the Latin word for "honey"), the production of ketone bodies increases because the activity of the tricarboxylic acid cycle in the liver is diminished while the degradation of fatty acids is accelerated. Thus, concentrations of acetyl CoA are increased. In the presence of high concentrations of acetyl CoA acetoacetyl CoA can be formed as the result of the reaction catalyzed by acetyl-CoA acetyltransferase (acetyl-CoA:acetyl-CoA C-acetyltransferase, EC 2.3.1.9), i.e.,

$$2 \text{ Acetyl CoA} \rightleftharpoons \text{acetoacetyl CoA} + \text{CoA} \quad (12\text{-}12)$$

Acetoacetyl CoA can then undergo a condensation reaction with a third molecule of acetyl CoA to yield 3-hydroxy-3-methylglutaryl CoA. The condensation is catalyzed by hydroxymethylglutaryl-CoA synthase [3-hydroxy-3-methylglutaryl-CoA acetoacetyl-CoA-lyase (coenzyme A-acetylating), EC 4.1.3.5]. The condensation reaction is

$$\text{Acetoacetyl CoA} + \text{acetyl CoA} + H_2O \rightleftharpoons$$
$$\text{3-hydroxy-3-methylglutaryl CoA} + \text{CoA} \quad (12\text{-}13)$$

Now 3-hydroxy-3-methylglutaryl CoA can undergo the reaction catalyzed by hydroxymethylglutaryl-CoA lyase, and acetoacetate is formed while one molecule of acetyl CoA is regenerated. This process has a cyclic nature, as shown on page 492. In effect, acetyl CoA is channeled into the production of 3-hydroxybutyrate and acetone.

It might be mentioned that although the liver, which produces ketone bodies, cannot utilize them, certain other tissues, including the brain, can and do utilize them under such circumstances as prolonged starvation.

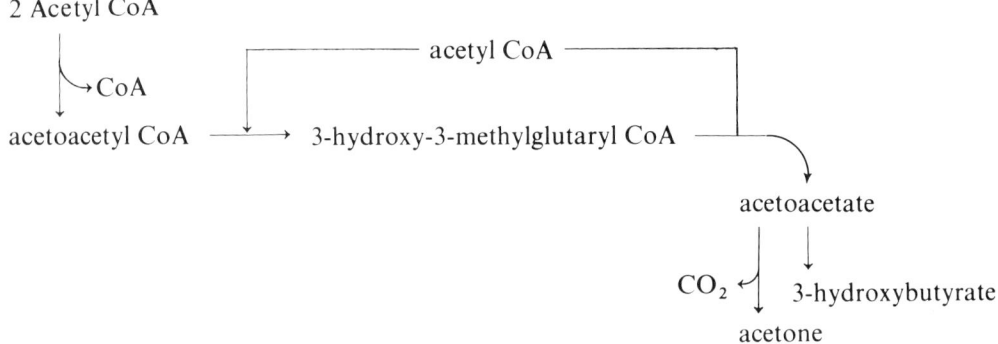

## Oxidation of Unsaturated Fatty Acids

The degradation of an unsaturated fatty acid initially parallels that of a saturated one, with $\beta$ oxidation proceeding until a $\Delta^3$- or a $\Delta^2$-acyl moiety is produced. For example, palmitoleyl CoA (cis-$\Delta^9$-hexadecenoyl CoA) can undergo $\beta$ oxidation until cis-$\Delta^3$-decenoyl CoA is produced. At this point, the acyl moiety undergoes an isomerization which results in the cis double bond between C(3) and C(4) being converted into a trans double bond between C(2) and C(3). The trans-$\Delta^2$-decenoyl CoA can then serve as a substrate in the reaction catalyzed by enoyl-CoA hydratase, and the acyl moiety can now be completely degraded by $\beta$ oxidation in the usual manner.

The degradation of linoleate (cis, cis-$\Delta^{9,12}$-octadecadienoate), on the other hand, leads to the formation of cis-$\Delta^2$-octenoyl CoA following production of the fifth molecule of acetyl CoA. The cis-$\Delta^2$-acyl moiety can undergo the hydration reaction catalyzed by enoyl-CoA hydratase; however, the resulting hydroxyacyl moiety is of the D configuration (in the case being discussed, it is specifically a D-3-hydroxyoctanyl moiety). As such, the acyl moiety cannot undergo the oxidation reaction catalyzed by 3-hydroxyacyl-CoA dehydrogenase since this enzyme utilizes only hydroxyacyl moieties that have the L configuration. Therefore, the D-3-hydroxyacyl moiety must undergo racemization, which it does in the presence of a racemase. Subsequently, the acyl moiety can be completely degraded by $\beta$ oxidation in the usual manner.

## $\omega$ Hydroxylation of Fatty Acids

Medium- and long-chain fatty acids can undergo hydroxylation at the terminal, or omega ($\omega$), carbon atom. This hydroxylation is catalyzed by enzymes associated with the endoplasmic reticulum of the cell. Enzyme systems which catalyze the $\omega$ hydroxylation of fatty acids have been isolated from hepatic endoplasmic-reticulum fractions and resolved into three components, a cytochrome called cytochrome P-450, an NADPH-dependent cytochrome P-450 reductase, and phosphatidylcholine. Cytochrome P-450 is, in fact, a cytochrome of the $b$ family; it was so named because it was initially identified on the basis of the absorption maximum at

450 nm exhibited by the carbon monoxide complex of its reduced form. The central atom of the heme moiety of isolated cytochrome P-450 is (low-spin) ferric iron. The hydroxylation requires molecular oxygen, one atom of which is incorporated into the product. The hydroxylation per se can be written

$$CH_3-(CH_2)_n-COO^- + NADPH + O_2 \longrightarrow$$

$$\underset{|}{\overset{OH}{C}}H_2-(CH_2)_n-COO^- + NADP^+ + H_2O \quad (12\text{-}14)$$

The cytochrome functions as an electron carrier during the process, which has been formulated as follows. The fatty acid initially binds ferricytochrome P-450. Then the reductase catalyzes the transfer of reducing equivalents from NADPH to the cytochrome. This step is facilitated by phosphatidylcholine. Next, molecular oxygen binds the ferrocytochrome P-450, and the $\omega$ carbon atom of the fatty acid undergoes hydroxylation, which is an oxidation reaction, while molecular oxygen undergoes reduction.† The reduction of molecular oxygen requires four electrons. Two are provided by the $\omega$ carbon atom of the substrate, and two are provided by the NADPH.

Hydroxylation of the terminal carbon atom of a fatty acid has also been observed in the case of certain microorganisms, including *Pseudomonas oleovorans*. As isolated from the *Pseudomonas*, the hydroxylation system comprises an NADH-dependent reductase, a hydroxylase, and a small red nonheme iron–sulfur protein known as rubredoxin. The reductase catalyzes the transfer of reducing equivalents from NADH to rubredoxin in this case. Rubredoxin has a molecular weight of approximately 20,000 and embodies a coordination complex in which cysteinyl sulfhydryl groups ligate iron.

Fatty acids which have undergone $\omega$ hydroxylation can be further oxidized to yield the corresponding dicarboxylic acids. These reactions utilize $NAD^+$ as the oxidation-reduction cofactor.

## $\alpha$ Hydroxylation of Fatty Acids

In certain mammalian tissues, including the brain, certain nerves, and the liver, fatty acids can undergo hydroxylation at C(2), the $\alpha$ carbon atom. This process also utilizes molecular oxygen. The hydroxylation system as isolated from hepatic mitochondria utilizes a variety of fatty acid substrates, including an isoprenoid fatty acid known as phytanic acid. In fact, it has been found that the principal pathway for the degradation of phytanic acid is by its initial hydroxylation at C(2). The resulting 2-hydroxyphytanate then undergoes an oxidative decarboxylation which yields the 19-carbon acid pristanate. Pristanate is subsequently degraded by $\beta$ oxidation.

In man there can be a pathological accumulation of phytanate in the liver and the kidneys, known as *Refsum's syndrome*. This abnormality results from the absence (or diminution) of the activity of the mitochondrial hydroxylating system. The

---

† Guengerich, F. P., Ballou, D. P., and Coon, M. J. (1975) *J. Biol. Chem.* **250,** 7405–7414.

syndrome is transmitted as an autosomal recessive trait. The condition can be managed by omitting foods which contain chlorophyll (and thus phytanate) from the diet.

## Regulation of Fatty Acid Catabolism

The liver is capable of carrying out virtually all of the major reactions of fatty acid metabolism in mammals. For this reason the discussion here focuses upon the role of the liver in the regulation of fatty acid catabolism.

The rate at which fatty acids undergo catabolism at the various tissue sites is determined by the rate at which the liver introduces triacylglycerols, in the form of very-low-density lipoproteins, into the blood and also by the activity of the lipoprotein lipase at the particular tissue site. At the tissue site, following the hydrolysis of the triacylglycerols of lipoproteins, $\beta$ oxidation can occur at a rate which is thought to depend upon the intramitochondrial carnitine palmitoyltransferase activity.

The concentrations of ketone bodies that reach the various peripheral tissues are also determined by the liver, which synthesizes these compounds but does not utilize them. Ketone bodies are a water-soluble energy source (in contrast to medium- and long-chain fatty acids) which can be utilized during carbohydrate, i.e., glucose, deprivation. Under such conditions the following events may occur. Fatty acids are released from their storage form (i.e., triacylglycerols) in adipose tissue as the result of the action of the appropriate lipases and introduced into the blood. At the various tissue sites these fatty acids are degraded to yield acetyl moieties of acetyl CoA. Concentrations of acetyl CoA are thus increased. However, the utilization of acetyl CoA by the tricarboxylic acid cycle is at the same time impeded, presumably because of a decrease in the concentration of oxaloacetate available to citrate synthase. (It has been suggested that the decrease in oxaloacetate concentration reflects the increased utilization of oxaloacetate by the gluconeogenic pathway.) Therefore, in the presence of increased synthesis of acetyl CoA and decreased utilization, acetyl CoA is channeled into the production of ketone bodies in the liver. These ketone bodies are then introduced into the blood and transported to tissue sites at which they can be utilized. Meanwhile, the increased concentration of ketone bodies in the blood induces the secretion of the hormone insulin. Insulin inhibits the hydrolysis of triacylglycerols in adipose tissue (among other actions); therefore the continued release of fatty acids into the blood is prevented. This regulatory mechanism thus operates as a closed loop in that the initial stimulus, glucose deprivation, induces a response which runs its course and then subsides.

## ANABOLISM OF FATTY ACIDS

Unlike $\beta$ oxidation, which takes place in the mitochondria of eukaryotic cells, the *de novo* synthesis of fatty acids takes place in the cytoplasm. There are, however, some parallels between fatty acid anabolism and fatty acid catabolism. Each entails four reactions, which are carried out repetitively. In the case of the anabolic pathway these include a condensation reaction, the reduction of an oxo group to a secondary alcohol group, a dehydration reaction, and the saturation of an olefinic bond. In the case of the catabolic pathway the four repetitive reactions are a desaturation reaction which yields an olefinic bond, a hydration reaction, the oxidation of a secondary alcohol group to an oxo group, and a retrograde condensation reaction. Hence, with respect to the chemical conversion that is carried out, fatty acid anabolism and fatty acid catabolism are essentially the converse of each other. Another similarity is that the reactions of both pathways utilize thiol esters of carboxylic acids as substrates. CoA derivatives of fatty acids are substrates for the reactions of the $\beta$-oxidation cycle, while the reactions involved in the *de novo* synthesis of fatty acids utilize derivatives of a thiol known as the *carrier protein*.

Before the repetitive steps of fatty acid anabolism can be carried out, a preliminary activation process must take place. This begins with the ATP-dependent carboxylation of the acetyl moiety of acetyl CoA. The carboxylation reaction is catalyzed by acetyl-CoA carboxylase [acetyl-CoA:carbon-dioxide ligase (ADP-forming), EC 6.4.1.2]. This carboxylation reaction is similar to those catalyzed by pyruvate carboxylase, propionyl-CoA carboxylase, and methylcrotonoyl-CoA carboxylase. Biotin is required, and an enzyme–biotin–carbon dioxide intermediate is formed. In the present case the product of the carboxylation reaction is malonyl CoA, and thus the reaction can be written

$$\text{Acetyl CoA} + \text{HCO}_3^- + \text{ATP} \rightleftharpoons \text{malonyl CoA} + \text{ADP} + P_i \quad (12\text{-}15)$$

Acetyl-CoA carboxylase has been isolated from a variety of sources, including rat epididimal adipose tissue, rat mammary gland, rat liver, avian liver, bovine adipose tissue, and numerous microorganisms. The carboxylase from bovine adipose tissue exists as an inactive or subactive protomer which has a molecular weight of 560,000 and an active oligomer which has a molecular weight of several million. The oligomeric enzyme exists as long filaments, which can be observed as such when viewed under the electron microscope. The formation of the active oligomeric form of the enzyme is promoted by citrate. Acetyl-CoA carboxylase from chicken liver is similar to the bovine enzyme. The active species is a filamentous oligomer which has a molecular weight of from 4 to 10 million. The protomer derived from the oligomeric enzyme has a molecular weight of 500,000 and can, in turn, be resolved to yield four subunits, two with molecular weights of approximately 117,000, one with a molecular weight of 129,000, and another with a molecular weight of 139,000. Biotin is covalently bound to one of the subunits with a molecular weight of 117,000.† Protomers derived from the acetyl CoA carboxylase of *E. coli* are much more readily resolved into subunits than those derived from the animal or the avian enzymes. In the microorganism, the protomer comprises three subunits, a small one (molecular weight of 22,000) to which the biotin is bound, a second one which comprises two polypeptides (51,000 each) and a third that is a tetramer comprising two polypeptides of one type (30,000 each) and two of another (35,000 each). The dimeric subunit

---

† Guchhait, R. B., Zwergel, E. E., and Lane, M. D. (1974) *J. Biol. Chem.* **249**, 4776–4780.

catalyzes the ATP-dependent carboxylation of biotin, while the tetrameric subunit catalyzes the formation of malonyl CoA.

Kinetic studies on acetyl-CoA carboxylase are compatible with the formulation of the reaction in terms of a two-site ping pong Bi Bi Uni Uni mechanism, in parallel with the conclusions concerning the reactions catalyzed by pyruvate carboxylase, propionyl-CoA carboxylase, and methylcrotonoyl-CoA carboxylase.

## The Fatty Acid Synthase Complex

In mammalian, avian, and yeast systems the *de novo* synthesis of fatty acids is catalyzed by a multienzyme complex that embodies seven enzymes. This complex is called the fatty acid synthase. Fatty acid synthases have been isolated from chicken liver, rat liver, rat mammary gland, and pigeon liver, and in each case the complex exhibits a particle weight of approximately 500,000.

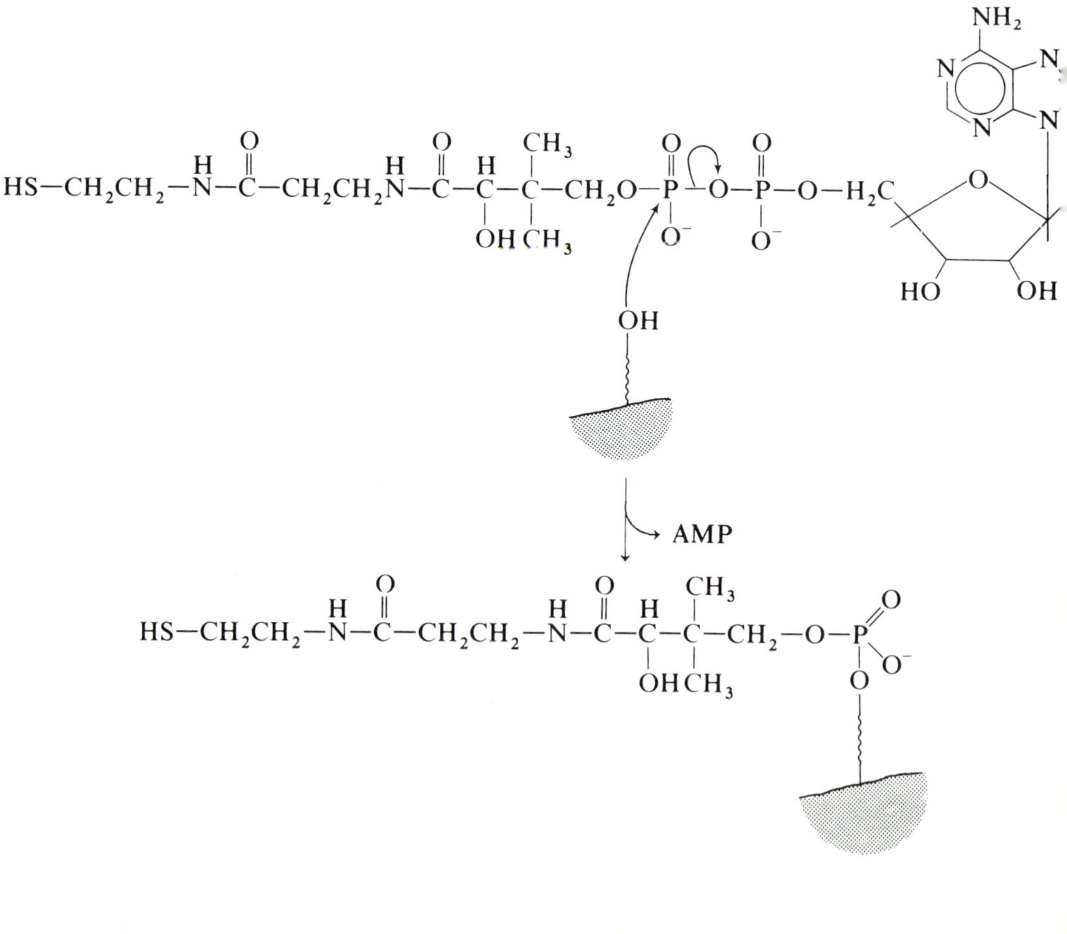

The fatty acid synthase contains a 4′-phosphopantetheinyl moiety which participates in the reaction as described below. 4′-Phosphopantetheine is, in fact, a part of the CoA molecule, and it is presumed that the presence of this group at the catalytic site of the synthase results from the reaction of a molecule of CoA and the hydroxyl group of a seryl or threonyl unit of the enzyme. The polypeptide of the synthase complex to which the 4'-phosphopantetheinyl moiety is bonded is referred to as the *carrier protein.*

When fatty acid synthesis is to occur, acetyl CoA first binds the synthase at a specific site, and the acetyl moiety becomes covalently bound as CoA is released. Now the sulfhydryl group of the 4'-phosphopantetheinyl moiety binds the catalytic site and the acetyl moiety is transferred to this substituent. The transfer is catalyzed by [acyl-carrier-protein]acetyltransferase (acetyl-CoA:[acyl-carrier-protein] S-acetyltransferase, EC 2.3.1.38). The acetyl moiety is next transferred to a cysteinyl sulfhydryl group at the catalytic site, and thus the sulfhydryl group of the 4'-phosphopantetheinyl moiety becomes available, as such, to participate in the next stage of the process. The next stage begins as malonyl CoA binds the synthase, also at a specific site, and by means of a reaction which parallels that described above the malonyl moiety is transferred to the 4'-phosphopantetheinyl moiety. The enzyme which catalyzes this is [acyl-carrier-protein]malonyltransferase (malonyl CoA:[acyl-carrier-protein] S-malonyltransferase, EC 2.3.1.39). Finally with the acetyl moiety having acylated the cysteinyl sulfhydryl group and the malonyl moiety having acylated the sulfhydryl group of the 4'-phosphopantetheinyl moiety, the sequence of repetitive reactions can begin.

**Step 1: Decarboxylation and condensation** In the first of the repetitive reactions the acetyl moiety, covalently bonded to a cysteinyl sulfhydryl group (Cys-E), and the malonyl moiety, covalently bonded to the 4'-phosphopantetheinyl sulfhydryl group (pp-E), undergo a condensation reaction which forms an acetoacetyl moiety and carbon dioxide. This reaction

Acetyl (or acyl)-Cys-E + malonyl-pp-E $\longrightarrow$

$$\text{acetoacetyl (or 3-oxoacyl)-pp-E} + CO_2 + \text{Cys-E} \quad (12\text{-}16)$$

is catalyzed by 3-oxoacyl-[acyl-carrier-protein] synthase {acyl-[acyl-carrier-protein]: malonyl-[acyl-carrier-protein] C-acyltransferase (decarboxylating), EC 2.3.1.41}. A minimal reaction mechanism is given below.

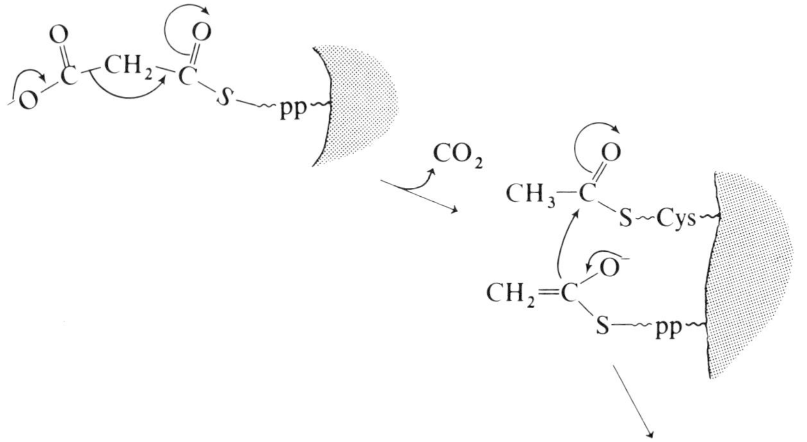

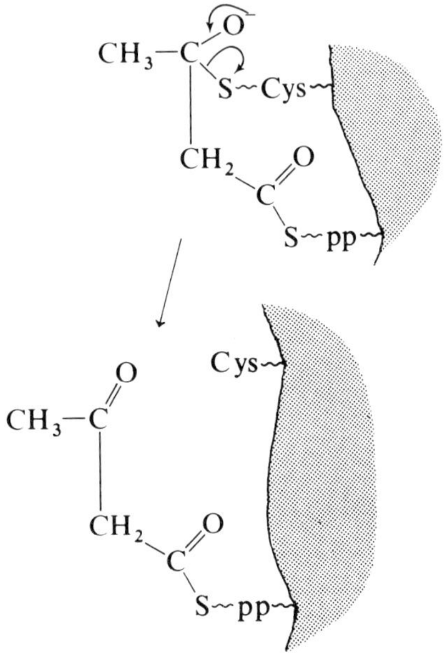

**Step 2: Reduction of the 3-oxo group of the acyl moiety** The oxo group of the 3-oxoacyl moiety is now reduced to yield a secondary alcohol group. The reduction is catalyzed by the NADPH-dependent 3-oxo-[acyl-carrier-protein] reductase (D-3-hydroxyacyl-[acyl-carrier-protein]:NADP$^+$ oxidoreductase, EC 1.1.1.100). The reaction can be written

Acetoacetyl (or 3-oxoacyl)-pp-E + NADPH $\longrightarrow$

$\qquad$ D-3-hydroxybutyryl (or D-3-hydroxyacyl)-pp-E + NADP$^+$ (12-17)

Note that the 3-hydroxyacyl moiety which is formed has the opposite configuration from that formed in the second step of the $\beta$-oxidation cycle.

**Step 3: Dehydration of the 3-hydroxyacyl moiety** The elements of water are now removed from the 3-hydroxyacyl moiety, and an unsaturated acyl moiety results. When the acyl moiety has four to eight carbon atoms a crotonoyl-[acyl-carrier-protein] dehydratase (D-3-hydroxybutyryl-[acyl-carrier-protein] hydro-lyase, EC 4.2.1.58) catalyzes the dehydration. The product is specifically the *trans-$\Delta^2$*-acyl moiety. The reaction is

D-3-hydroxybutyryl (or D-3-hydroxyacyl)-pp-E $\longrightarrow$

$\qquad$ crotonoyl (or *trans-$\Delta^2$-acyl*)-pp-E + H$_2$O (12-18)

**Step 4: Saturation of the olefinic bond of the $\Delta^2$-acyl moiety** The final one of the four repetitive steps is the formation of the saturated acyl moiety. This is a reduction reaction, and it is catalyzed by enoyl-[acyl-carrier-protein]reductase (acyl-[acyl-carrier-protein]:NADP$^+$ oxidoreductase, EC 1.3.1.10). With the reduction of the olefinic bond of the $\Delta^2$-acyl moiety, one revolution of the cyclic pathway is completed. The saturated acyl moiety is now transferred to the cysteinyl sulfhydryl group to which the acetyl moiety was initially bonded, the sulfhydryl group of the 4'-phosphopantetheinyl moiety is acylated by another malonyl moiety, and the four repetitive steps can occur once more.

Each revolution of this cyclic anabolic pathway allows two carbon atoms to be added to the chain. The carbon atoms that are added are C(1) and C(2) of the malonyl moiety. The carboxylate group that was introduced as a result of the reaction catalyzed by acetyl-CoA carboxylase is lost as a concomitance of the condensation reaction that is catalyzed by the 3-oxoacyl synthase. Thus, the carboxylation reaction is in effect an activation process since the loss of the carboxylate group that was introduced results in the generation of a very reactive nucleophile, which, in turn, initiates the condensation reaction. The carbon atoms that are added become C(1) and C(2) of the new acyl moiety.

The process described above can continue until the carbon chain of the acyl moiety reaches a specified length. In many instances this is 16 carbon atoms. At this point the acyl moiety rather than being transferred to the cysteinyl sulfhydryl group is released as the result of a hydrolytic reaction which is catalyzed by a thiolester hydrolase.

**Kinetic studies on the fatty acid synthase** Kinetic studies have been conducted on the reactions of fatty acid synthesis as they are catalyzed by the fatty acid synthase from pigeon liver. The results of these studies support the formulation of the process in terms of a seven-site ping pong mechanism. The fatty acid synthase is considered to have seven enzymatic sites, namely, (1) the acetyltransferase site, (2) the malonyltransferase site, (3) the 3-oxoacyl synthase site, (4) the 3-oxoacyl reductase site, (5) the 3-hydroxyacyl dehydratase site, (6) the enoyl reductase site, and (7) the thiolester hydrolase site. The data derived from the kinetic studies indicate that the reactions at sites 1 to 3 have ping pong mechanisms. At sites 1 and 2, acetyl CoA or malonyl CoA, respectively, binds the enzyme, CoA dissociates (leaving behind an acyl-enzyme intermediate), and then the 4'-phosphopantetheinyl moiety binds the site. At site 3, the acetyl- or acyl-4'-phosphopantetheinyl moiety binds the enzyme, the acyl moiety is transferred to the cysteinyl sulfhydryl group, and the 4'-phosphopantetheinyl moiety dissociates (leaving behind an acyl-enzyme intermediate). Subsequently, the malonyl-4'-phosphopantetheinyl moiety binds the enzyme, the condensation reaction occurs, and carbon dioxide and the oxoacyl-4'-phosphopantetheinyl moiety then dissociate. The latter subsequently binds at site 4. The oxidation-reduction reactions at sites 4 and 6 exhibit sequential mechanisms, on the other hand.† The catalytic site of the synthase has been depicted diagrammatically as shown in Fig. 12-2. It is thus proposed that the 4'-phosphopantetheinyl moiety functions as an arm which allows the acyl moiety to move from one site to another. Remember that when the reaction catalyzed by pyruvate carboxylase was discussed, it was proposed that the side chain of the lysyl unit to which the biotin is bonded functions as an arm which allows the cofactor to move from one site to another.

† Katiyar, S. S., Cleland, W. W., and Porter, J. W. (1975) *J. Biol. Chem.* **250**, 2709–2717.

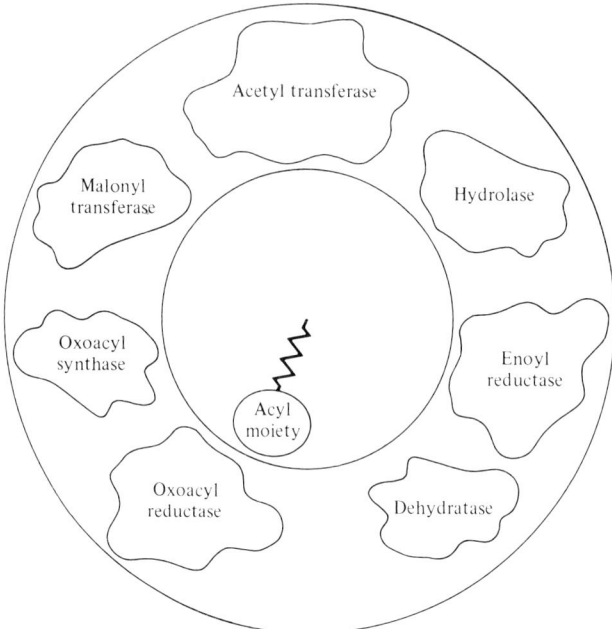

**Figure 12-2** Schematic representation of the fatty acid synthase with the 4′-phosphopantetheinyl moiety functioning as an arm which allows an acyl moiety that is bonded to it to be positioned at the sites of the individual reactions.

**Fatty acid synthesis in bacteria** In bacteria and plants the enzymes that catalyze the *de novo* synthesis of fatty acids are not components of a tightly associated multienzyme complex. Rather, upon disruption of the bacterial cell the individual enzymes can readily be isolated, and they exhibit no tendency to associate.

A carrier protein was first isolated from *Clostridium kluyveri*, although most of the structural determinations which have been carried out have focused upon the carrier protein from *E. coli*. The carrier protein from *E. coli* is a polypeptide which comprises 77 aminoacyl units. The protein has a molecular weight of 8847, as determined on the basis of its primary structure. The 4′-phosphopantetheinyl moiety of this component is bonded to Ser-36.

A 3-oxoacyl synthase has been isolated from *E. coli* and purified. This enzyme species has a molecular weight of 66,000 and can be converted into a relatively stable acyl enzyme in the presence of an acyl-CoA and the appropriate supporting system.

**Synthesis of unsaturated fatty acids** One of the major products of fatty acid synthesis in *E. coli* is *cis*-vaccenate (*cis*-$\Delta^{11}$-octadecenoate). Unsaturated fatty acids are synthesized by a variation of the process described above. When an unsaturated fatty acid is to be synthesized, a 3-hydroxyacyl moiety is converted into a *cis*-$\Delta^3$-acyl moiety rather than a *trans*-$\Delta^2$-acyl moiety. This dehydration is catalyzed by D-3-hydroxydecanoyl-[acyl-carrier-protein] dehydratase (D-3-hydroxydecanoyl-

[acyl-carrier-protein] hydro-lyase, EC 4.2.1.60), an enzyme that in fact catalyzes the formation of both the *trans*-$\Delta^2$-acyl moiety and the *cis*-$\Delta^3$-acyl moiety. The *cis*-$\Delta^3$-acyl moiety can subsequently undergo the condensation reaction catalyzed by 3-oxoacyl synthase, followed by the remaining three reactions of the anabolic cycle, as shown below.

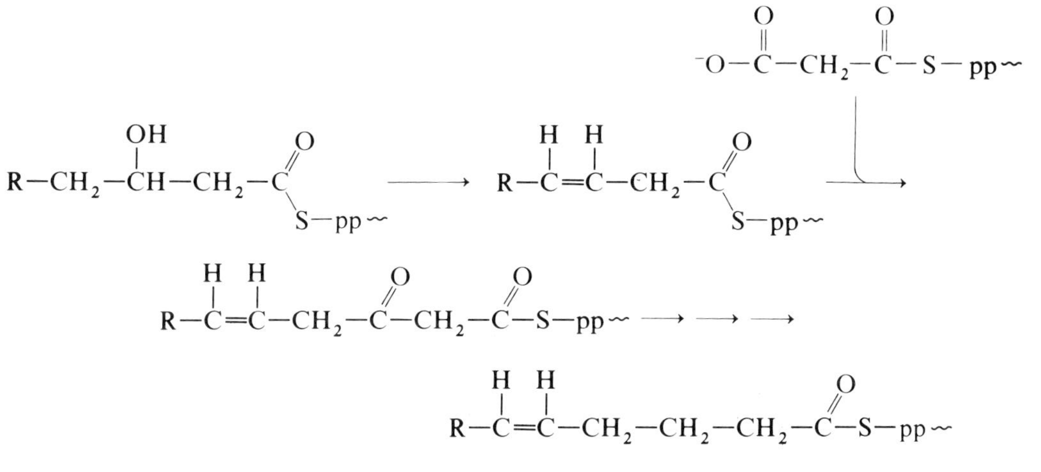

$$\text{R-CH}_2\text{-CH(OH)-CH}_2\text{-C(=O)-S-pp}\sim \longrightarrow \text{R-CH=CH-CH}_2\text{-C(=O)-S-pp}\sim \longrightarrow$$

$$^-\text{O-C(=O)-CH}_2\text{-C(=O)-S-pp}\sim$$

$$\text{R-CH=CH-CH}_2\text{-C(=O)-CH}_2\text{-C(=O)-S-pp}\sim \longrightarrow \longrightarrow \longrightarrow$$

$$\text{R-CH=CH-CH}_2\text{-CH}_2\text{-CH}_2\text{-C(=O)-S-pp}\sim$$

### Summary of the *de Novo* Synthesis of Fatty Acids and Its Regulation

The reactions involved in the *de novo* synthesis of fatty acids are summarized in Fig. 12-3. Since the activity of acetyl-CoA carboxylase is lower than the activities of the enzymes of the fatty acid synthase complex, it is presumed that the formation of malonyl CoA is the rate-determining step of the *de novo* synthesis of fatty acids. The activity of acetyl-CoA carboxylase is enhanced in the presence of citrate and inhibited by palmitoyl CoA. It has been suggested, therefore, that impaired fatty acid synthesis as a response to prolonged starvation or as a concomitance of diabetes mellitus may reflect the increased concentrations of long-chain fatty acids present in the blood under these conditions. The question has also been raised as to whether the level at which acetyl CoA carboxylase functions is influenced by the cytoplasmic concentration of acetyl CoA.

**Elongation and desaturation of fatty acids** The principal product of the *de novo* synthesis of fatty acids is palmitate. Fatty acids having more than 16 carbon atoms are synthesized by reactions that lengthen the carbon chain of existing fatty acids. Enzyme systems which catalyze the elongation of fatty acids are associated with the mitochondria and with endoplasmic reticulum fractions of the cell.

The mitochondrial system that catalyzes the elongation of fatty acids utilizes the acetyl moiety of acetyl CoA as the source of the carbon atoms that are added. The reactions parallel those of the *de novo* synthesis in general, although the initial condensation reactions occurs without the benefit of the decarboxylation of a malonyl moiety. Another difference is that the reduction of the 3-oxoacyl moiety involves the cofactor NADH rather than NADPH.

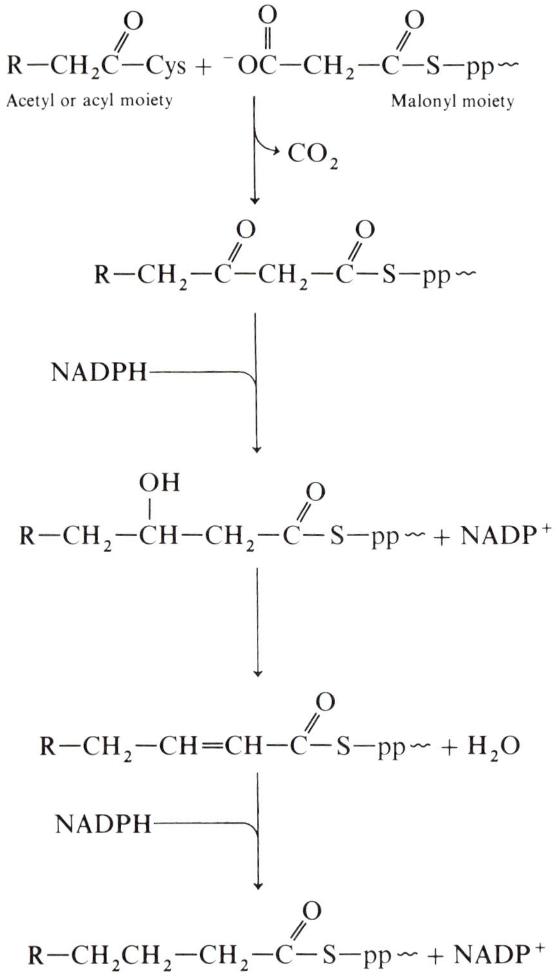

$$\underset{\text{Acetyl or acyl moiety}}{R-CH_2\overset{O}{\overset{\|}{C}}-Cys} + \underset{\text{Malonyl moiety}}{^-O\overset{O}{\overset{\|}{C}}-CH_2-\overset{O}{\overset{\|}{C}}-S-pp\sim}$$

$$\downarrow CO_2$$

$$R-CH_2-\overset{O}{\overset{\|}{C}}-CH_2-\overset{O}{\overset{\|}{C}}-S-pp\sim$$

$$NADPH \longrightarrow \downarrow$$

$$R-CH_2-\overset{OH}{\overset{|}{CH}}-CH_2-\overset{O}{\overset{\|}{C}}-S-pp\sim \; + \; NADP^+$$

$$\downarrow$$

$$R-CH_2-CH=CH-\overset{O}{\overset{\|}{C}}-S-pp\sim \; + \; H_2O$$

$$NADPH \longrightarrow \downarrow$$

$$R-CH_2CH_2-CH_2-\overset{O}{\overset{\|}{C}}-S-pp\sim \; + \; NADP^+$$

**Figure 12-3** Summary of the *de novo* anabolism of saturated fatty acids. Comparison with $\beta$ oxidation indicates that although the biochemical conversions involved in the anabolic and catabolic pathways are similar, the pathways differ with respect to (1) the thiol moiety of the thiol ester involved, (2) the oxidation-reduction cofactors, and (3) the reaction mechanism by which the carbon-carbon bond making or bond breaking occurs.

In contrast to the mitochondrial elongation system, the elongation system associated with the endoplasmic reticulum involves the condensation of a malonyl moiety and an acetyl moiety, although in this case these are CoA derivatives. Another difference between the mitochondrial system and that from the endoplasmic reticulum is that the reduction of the 3-oxoacyl moiety requires NADPH. Thus, the reactions of the *de novo* synthesis, which occurs in the cytoplasm, and the elongation, which occurs in association with the endoplasmic reticulum, are essentially the same. It is the substrates that are different.

A system that catalyzes the desaturation of fatty acids is also associated with the endoplasmic reticulum of animal cells. This multienzyme system, which is known as the acyl-CoA desaturase (acyl-CoA, hydrogen-donor:oxygen oxidoreductase, EC 1.14.99.5) utilizes molecular oxygen and NADH. It includes a small (molecular weight, 53,000) protein that binds catalytically-active iron and catalyzes the desaturation per se in addition to cytochrome $b_5$ and cytochrome $b_5$ reductase (NADH:ferricytochrome $b_5$ oxidoreductase, EC 1.6.2.2). The cytochrome and the reductase, which is a flavoprotein, participate in an electron-transport process that allows the reducing equivalents that are removed from a saturated acyl moiety of a CoA derivative to be transferred to the ultimate acceptor. The system is known to convert stearoyl CoA into oleoyl CoA.

## SYNTHESIS OF ACYLGLYCEROLS

The synthesis of acylglycerols in animals entails acylation of sn-glycerol 3-phosphate or that of dihydroxyacetone phosphate. Glycerol 3-phosphate is formed primarily by the reduction of dihydroxyacetone phosphate and to a lesser extent by the phosphorylation of glycerol. The former reaction allows the carbon atoms of glucose to become carbon atoms of the glycerol moiety of acylglycerols (and also phospholipids), and the reduction is catalyzed by the $NAD^+$-dependent glycerol-3-phosphate dehydrogenase. The phosphorylation of glycerol, on the other hand, is catalyzed by glycerol kinase (ATP:glycerol 3-phosphotransferase, EC 2.7.1.30). The phosphorylation reaction is

$$\text{Glycerol} + \text{ATP} \rightleftharpoons \textit{sn}\text{-glycerol 3-phosphate} + \text{ADP} \qquad (12\text{-}19)$$

When dihydroxyacetone phosphate undergoes acylation, the resulting 1-acyldihydroxyacetone phosphate is then reduced to yield 1-acyl-sn-glycerol 3-phosphate. The reduction is catalyzed by an NADPH-dependent oxidoreductase.

The acylation of glycerol 3-phosphate is catalyzed by glycerophosphate acyltransferase (acyl-CoA:sn-glycerol-3-phosphate O-acyltransferase, EC 2.3.1.15), an enzyme found in association with both the mitochondrial outer membrane and the endoplasmic reticulum in tissues such as the mammalian liver. The enzyme catalyzes the transfer of an acyl moiety from an acyl-CoA molecule to either the C(1) or the C(2) hydroxyl group of the glycerol 3-phosphate. The reaction can be written

Acyl-CoA + sn-glycerol 3-phosphate

$$\rightleftharpoons \text{1-(or 2-) acylglycerol 3-phosphate} + \text{CoA} \qquad (12\text{-}20)$$

In most instances it is the nature of the acyl moiety that determines whether a 1-acylglycerol 3-phosphate or a 2-acylglycerol 3-phosphate is formed. Generally, saturated acyl moieties are preferentially transferred to the C(1) hydroxyl group while unsaturated acyl moieties are preferentially transferred to the C(2) hydroxyl group of the glycerol phosphate.

The acylation of dihydroxyacetone phosphate is catalyzed by dihydroxyacetone-

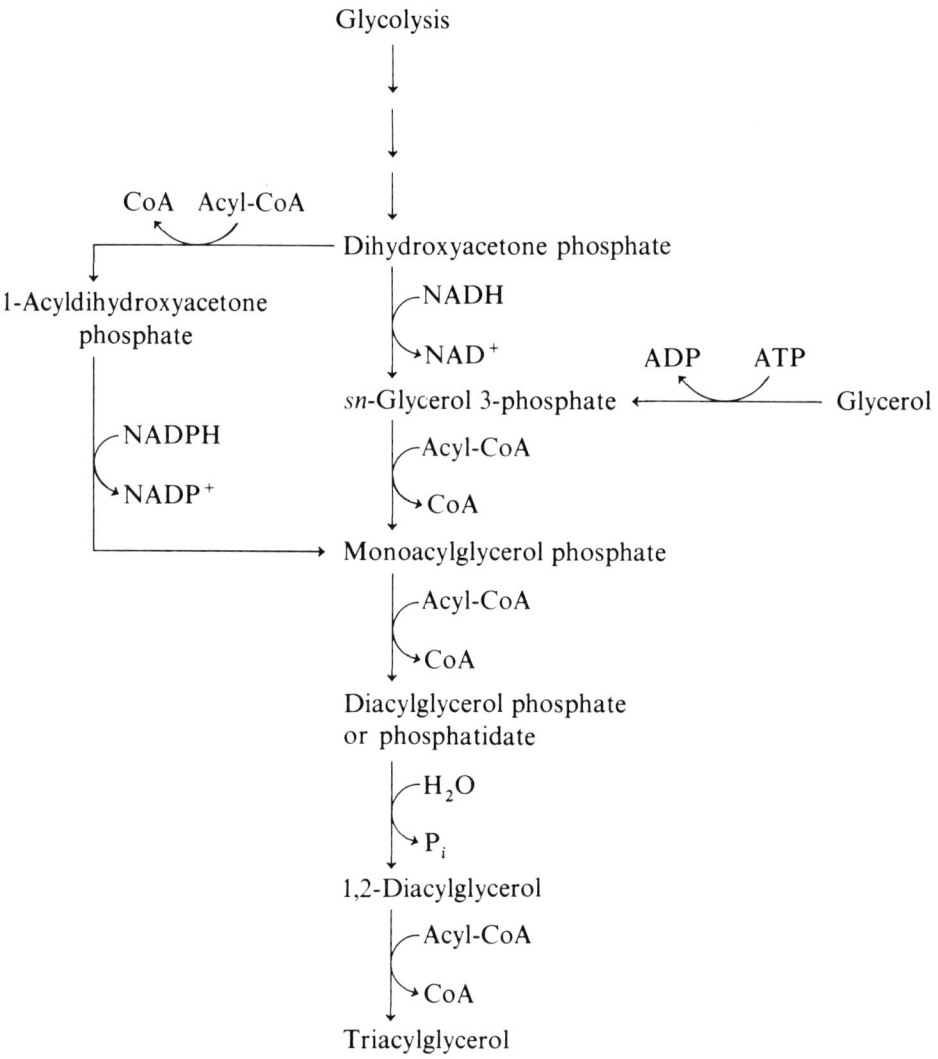

**Figure 12-4** Anabolism of acylglycerols.

phosphate acyltransferase (acyl-CoA:dihydroxyacetone-phosphate O-acyltransferase, EC 2.3.1.42). This enzyme utilizes primarily palmitoyl CoA as its acyl-CoA substrate. The reduction of the resulting 1-palmitoyldihydroxyacetone phosphate is catalyzed by palmitoyldihydroxyacetone-phosphate reductase (1-palmitoylglycerol-3-phosphate:$NADP^+$ oxidoreductase, EC 1.1.1.101). Generally, the acylation of sn-glycerol 3-phosphate is the pathway more frequently utilized in synthesizing monoacylglycerol phosphates.

Monoacylglycerol phosphates can undergo a second acylation reaction, which results in the formation of diacylglycerol phosphates. This acylation is catalyzed by a different enzyme than that which catalyzes the formation of monoacylglycerol phosphates, at least in some tissues. Diacylglycerol phosphates are known as phosphatidic acids or phosphatides. The phosphatidate formed as a result of the second acylation reaction must then undergo a hydrolysis reaction that removes the phosphoryl group in order for a diacylglycerol (or diglyceride) or, subsequently, a triacylglycerol (or triglyceride) to be formed. This hydrolysis is catalyzed by phosphatidate phosphatase (L-3-phosphatidate phosphohydrolase, EC 3.1.3.4). The product is a 1,2-diacylglycerol, which in turn can undergo yet another acylation reaction to form a triacylglycerol. The acylation of a diacylglycerol is catalyzed by diacylglycerol acyltransferase (acyl-CoA:1,2-diacylglycerol $O$-acyltransferase, EC 2.3.1.20).

The anabolism of the acylglycerols is summarized in Fig. 12-4.

# PART II PHOSPHOLIPIDS

Phospholipids can undergo hydrolytic cleavage reactions which liberate the component fatty acids. In addition, the phosphodiester moiety of the phospholipid can undergo hydrolytic cleavage reactions. These reactions are catalyzed by enzymes known as phospholipases.

Hydrolytic cleavage reactions which result in the liberation of a fatty acid from a phosphatidylcholine or a phosphatidylethanolamine, for example, are catalyzed by phospholipase $A_1$ or phospholipase $A_2$. Phospholipase $A_1$ (phosphatidate 1-acylhydrolase, EC 3.1.1.32) catalyzes the hydrolytic cleavage of the ester bond involving the C(1) hydroxyl group of the glycerol moiety of the phospholipid. The reaction can be written

$$\text{Phosphatidylcholine} + H_2O \rightleftharpoons$$
$$\text{2-acylglycerophosphocholine} + \text{fatty acid anion} \quad (12\text{-}21)$$

Phospholipase $A_1$ is generally associated with the endoplasmic reticulum in animal cells.

Phospholipase $A_2$ (phosphatidate 2-acylhydrolase, EC 3.1.1.4), on the other hand, is primarily associated with the outer membrane of the mitochondrion in animal cells. This enzyme catalyzes the hydrolytic cleavage of the ester bond involving the C(2) hydroxyl group of the glycerol moiety of a phospholipid. Either saturated or unsaturated acyl groups can be removed from phosphatidylcholine or phosphatidylethanolamine as a result of the reaction catalyzed by this enzyme.

Phospholipase $A_2$ is a principal component of snake venoms that induce the lysis of erythrocytes. As isolated from cobra (*Naja naja*) venom, phospholipase $A_2$ is a small polypeptide which has a molecular weight of 11,000. Both phospholipase $A_1$ from mammalian endoplasmic reticulum and phospholipase $A_2$ from mammalian mitochondria or snake venom require $Ca^{2+}$ to be catalytically active.

Enzymes that catalyze the deacylation of 1-acylglycerophosphocholine or

2-acylglycerophosphocholine, as well as that of the corresponding phosphoethanolamine derivatives, have also been isolated. These enzymes are known as lysophospholipases (lysophosphatidylcholine acylhydrolase, EC 3.1.1.5). They are referred to as lysophospholipases since the partially deacylated phospholipids are known as lysophospholipids or, more specifically, as lysophosphatidylcholine or lysophosphatidylethanolamine. The reaction catalyzed by a lysophospholipase is

1-(or 2-) Acylglycerophosphocholine + $H_2O$ ⇌

glycerophosphocholine + fatty acid anion    (12-22)

A phospholipid such as phosphatidylcholine can be converted into a 1,2-diacylglycerol as the result of the reaction catalyzed by phospholipase C (phosphatidylcholine cholinephosphohydrolase, EC 3.1.4.3). In this case, the reaction is

Phosphatidylcholine + $H_2O$ ⇌ 1,2-diacyglycerol + phosphocholine

(12-23)

Phospholipase C is also reported to catalyze the hydrolytic cleavage of sphingomyelin to yield the corresponding $N$-acylsphingosine (or ceramide) plus phosphocholine.

A phospholipase which catalyzes the conversion of phosphatidylcholine into a phosphatidate and choline has also been isolated and characterized. It is known as phospholipase D (phosphatidylcholine phosphatidohydrolase, EC 3.1.4.4).

The points at which a phospholipid such as phosphatidylcholine is attacked by the various phospholipases are shown diagrammatically.

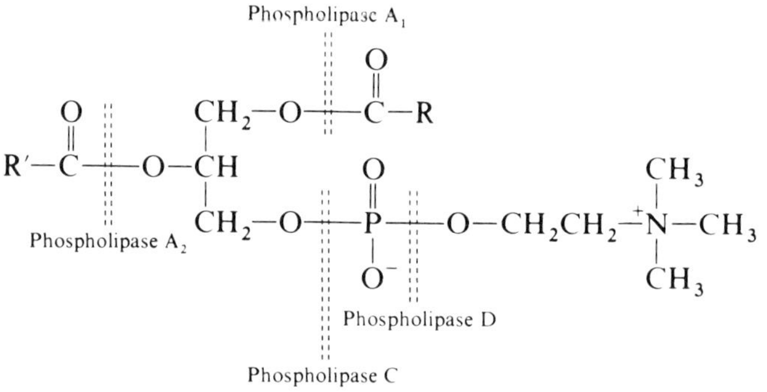

## SYNTHESIS OF PHOSPHOLIPIDS

The synthesis of phosphatidylcholine or phosphatidylethanolamine in mammalian systems utilizes a 1,2-diacylglycerol, CTP, and phosphocholine or phosphoethanolamine. The reactions involved are the subject of the following discussion.

## Synthesis of Phosphatidylcholine and Phosphatidylethanolamine

As is frequently the case, this anabolic sequence requires the participation of a nucleoside triphosphate, in this instance CTP. Its function is, in effect, that of activating phosphocholine or phosphoethanolamine. In a reaction catalyzed by phosphocholine cytidylyltransferase (CTP:phosphocholine cytidylyltransferase, EC 2.7.7.15) CDP-choline is formed, according to the equation

$$\text{CTP} + \text{phosphocholine} \longrightarrow \text{CDP-choline} + \text{PP}_i \qquad (12\text{-}24)$$

A similar reaction allows the formation of CDP-ethanolamine. The enzyme is phosphoethanolamine cytidylyltransferase (CTP:phosphoethanolamine cytidylyltransferase, EC 2.7.7.14) in this case. A phosphoethanolamine cytidylyltransferase which has been isolated from the cytoplasm of rat hepatocytes has a molecular weight of approximately 100,000 and comprises two subunits, each with a molecular weight of 50,000. Kinetic studies indicate that the reaction that is catalyzed by this enzyme proceeds by an ordered sequential Bi Bi reaction in which CTP is the initial substrate that binds and CDP-ethanolamine is the final product that is released.

The transfer of a phosphocholine moiety to a 1,2-diacylglycerol is catalyzed by cholinephosphotransferase (cytidine diphosphocholine:1,2-diacylglycerol cholinephosphotransferase, EC 2.7.8.2). The reaction is

$$\text{CDP-choline} + 1{,}2\text{-diacylglycerol} \rightleftharpoons \text{CMP} + \text{phosphatidylcholine} \qquad (12\text{-}25)$$

A minimal reaction mechanism for the formation of phosphatidylcholine is shown below.

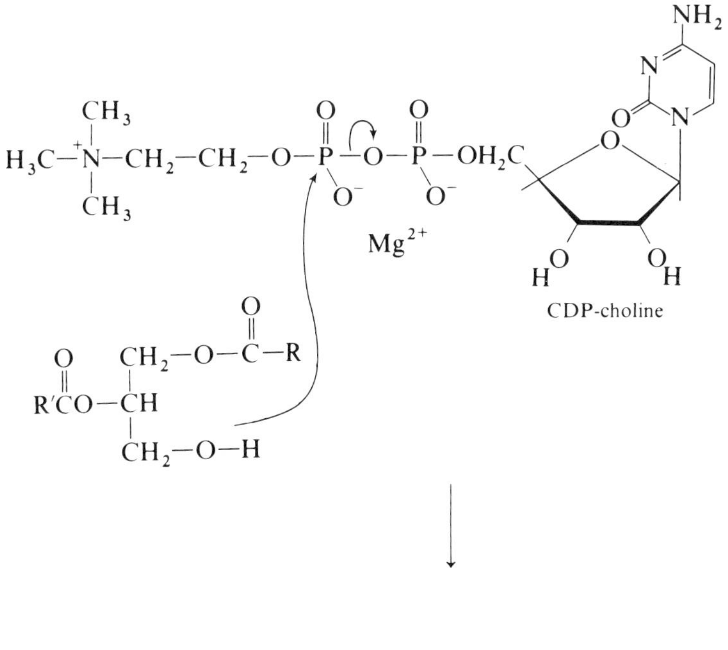

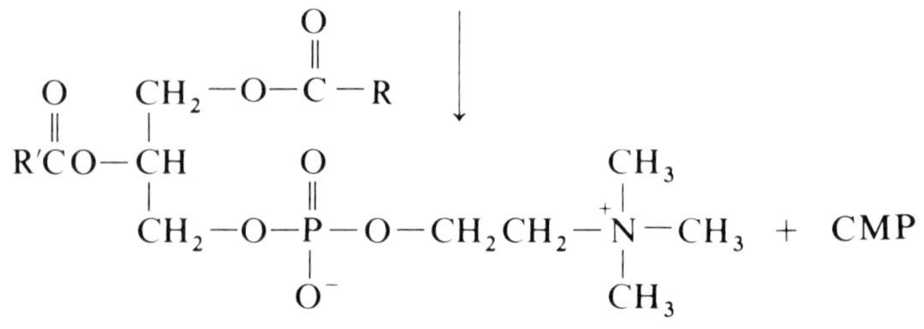

$$\begin{array}{c} \text{O} \quad \text{CH}_2-\text{O}-\overset{\text{O}}{\underset{\|}{\text{C}}}-\text{R} \\ \underset{\|}{\text{R'CO}}-\text{CH} \\ \text{CH}_2-\text{O}-\overset{\text{O}}{\underset{\|}{\text{P}}}-\text{O}-\text{CH}_2\text{CH}_2-\overset{+}{\underset{\text{CH}_3}{\text{N}}}-\text{CH}_3 \quad + \quad \text{CMP} \\ \text{O}^- \end{array}$$

Phosphatidylcholine

As the result of a similar reaction, catalyzed by ethanolaminephosphotransferase (cytidine diphosphoethanolamine:1,2-diacylglycerol ethanolaminephosphotransferase, EC 2.7.8.1), phosphatidylethanolamine is formed.

It has also been demonstrated that phosphatidylethanolamine can be converted into phosphatidylcholine in animals. The conversion entails the methylation of the amino group of phosphatidylethanolamine. The methyl groups are transferred from S-adenosylmethionine to the phospholipid.

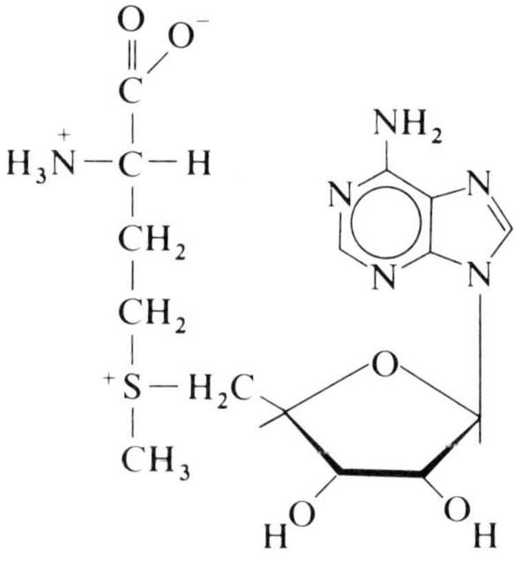

S-Adenosylmethionine

## Synthesis of Phosphatidylserine

In mammals, phosphatidylserine is apparently formed as the result of an exchange reaction involving phosphatidylethanolamine and serine. Microorganisms such as *E. coli*, on the other hand, can carry out the synthesis of phosphatidylserine from cytidine diphosphodiacylglycerol and serine. Cytidine diacyldiphosphoglycerol also participates in the synthesis of phosphatidylinositols in mammalian systems, as discussed in the following paragraphs.

## Synthesis of Phosphatidylinositols and Phosphatidylglycerophosphates

The nucleoside triphosphate CTP participates in a second activation process, which in this case involves the formation of cytidine diphosphodiacylglycerol. This intermediate is involved in the synthesis of phosphatidylinositols and phosphatidylglycerophosphates in mammalian systems. Cytidine diacyldiphosphoglycerol is formed as a result of the reaction between CTP and phosphatidate in the presence of the enzyme phosphatidate cytidylyltransferase (CTP:phosphatidate cytidylyltransferase, EC 2.7.7.41). A minimal mechanism for the reaction, which can be expressed by

CTP + phosphatidate $\rightleftharpoons$ cytidine diphosphodiacylglycerol + $PP_i$    (12-26)

is shown below.

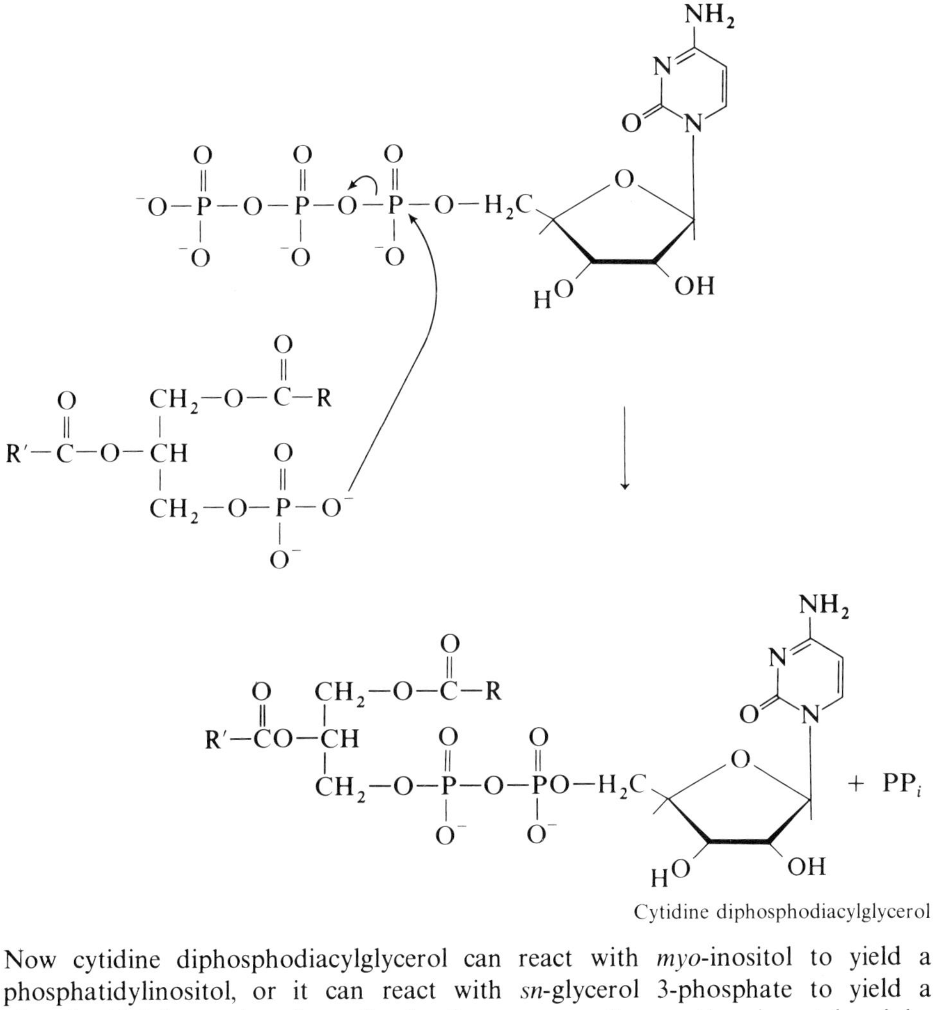

Cytidine diphosphodiacylglycerol

Now cytidine diphosphodiacylglycerol can react with *myo*-inositol to yield a phosphatidylinositol, or it can react with *sn*-glycerol 3-phosphate to yield a phosphatidylglycerophosphate. In the former case, the reaction is catalyzed by cytidine diphosphodiacylglycerol–inositol phosphatidyltransferase (cytidine diphosphodiacylglycerol:*myo*-inositol phosphatidyltransferase, EC 2.7.8.11). In the latter, it is catalyzed by glycerophosphate phosphatidyltransferase (cytidine diphosphodiacylglycerol:*sn*-glycerol-3-glycerol-3-phosphate phosphatidyltransferase, EC 2.7.8.5).

The C(4) hydroxyl group of the inositol moiety of a phosphatidylinositol undergoes phosphorylation in the presence of ATP and the enzyme phosphatidylinositol kinase (ATP:phosphatidylinositol 4-phosphotransferase, EC 2.7.1.67). The product, which is phosphatidylinositol 4-phosphate, can in turn undergo a second phosphorylation reaction, this time at the C(5) hydroxyl group of the inositol moiety. In this instance, the reaction is catalyzed by phosphatidylinositol phosphate kinase (ATP:phosphatidylinositol 4-phosphate 5-phosphotransferase, EC 2.7.1.68)

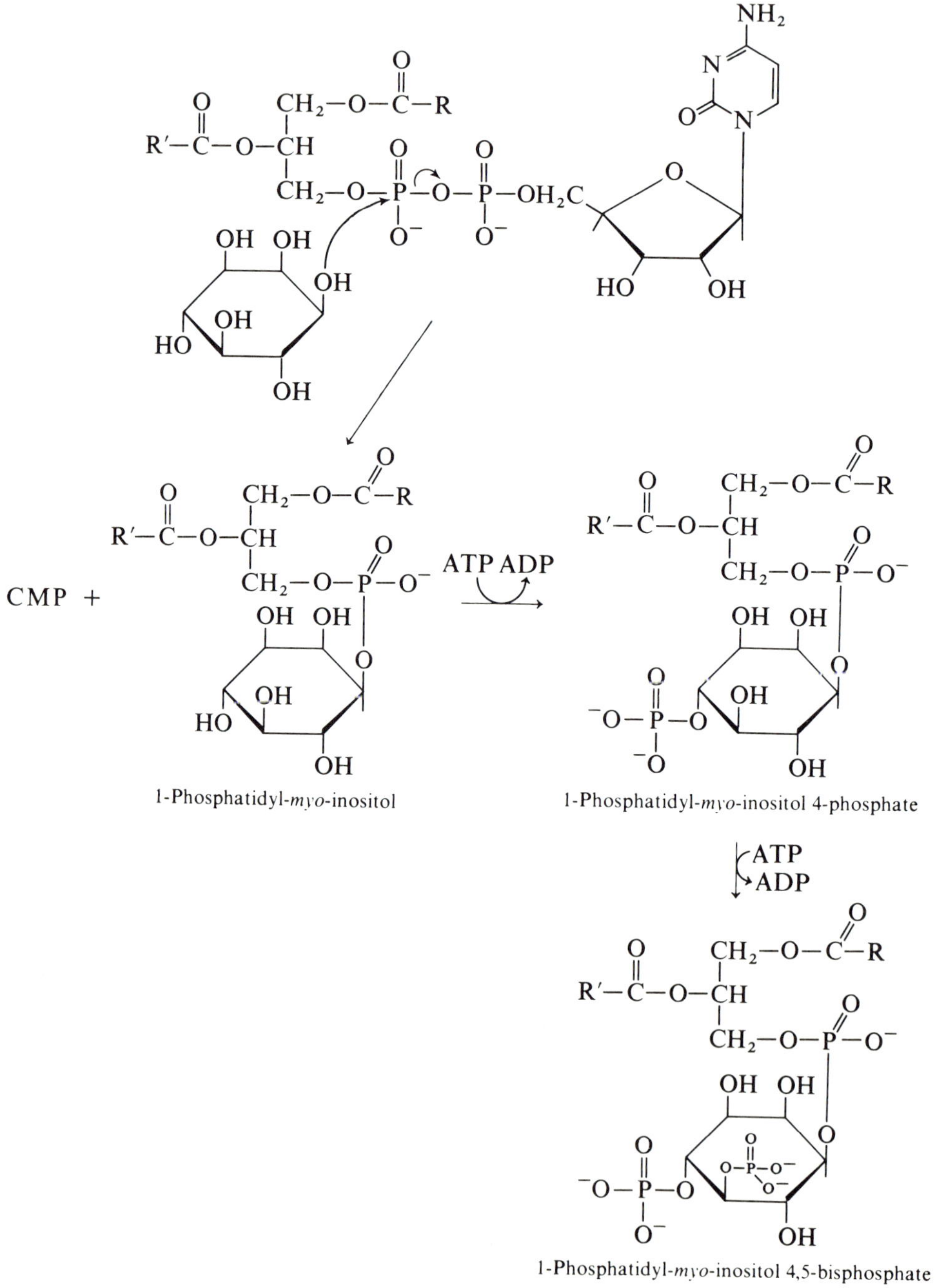

1-Phosphatidyl-*myo*-inositol

1-Phosphatidyl-*myo*-inositol 4-phosphate

1-Phosphatidyl-*myo*-inositol 4,5-bisphosphate

and the product is phosphatidylinositol 4,5-bisphosphate. These reactions and the formation of phosphatidylinositol are depicted on page 510.

The phosphorylation of phosphatidylinositols that are membrane components and the dephosphorylation of phosphatidylinositol phosphates that are membrane components are believed by some to be involved in changes in the permeability characteristics of certain biological membranes. [The dephosphorylation of phosphatidylinositol 4,5-bisphosphate is catalyzed by phosphatidylinositol-bisphosphate phosphatase (phosphatidyl-*myo*-inositol-4,5-bisphosphate phosphohydrolase, EC 3.1.3.36). There is some evidence that this enzyme can also catalyze the dephosphorylation of phosphatidylinositol 4-phosphate.]

Phosphatidylglycerophosphates also function in reactions involving biological membranes. Phosphatidylglycerophosphate can undergo dephosphorylation in the presence of phosphatidylglycerophosphatase (phosphatidylglycerophosphate phosphohydrolase, EC 3.1.3.27). The product, phosphatidylglycerol, can then be converted into bis(phosphatidyl)glycerol, sometimes called cardiolipin. Bis(phosphatidyl)glycerol is one of the principal phospholipid components of the mitochondrial inner membrane. The reactions involved in the formation of bis(phosphatidyl)glycerol are depicted below.

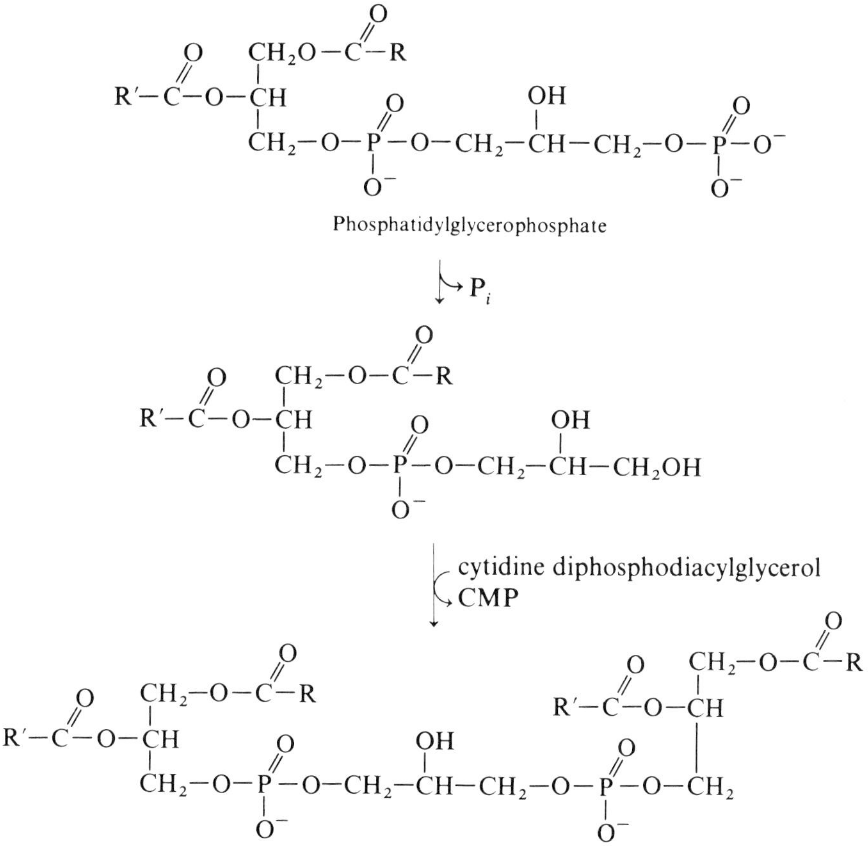

Phosphatidylglycerophosphate

Bis(phosphatidyl)glycerol

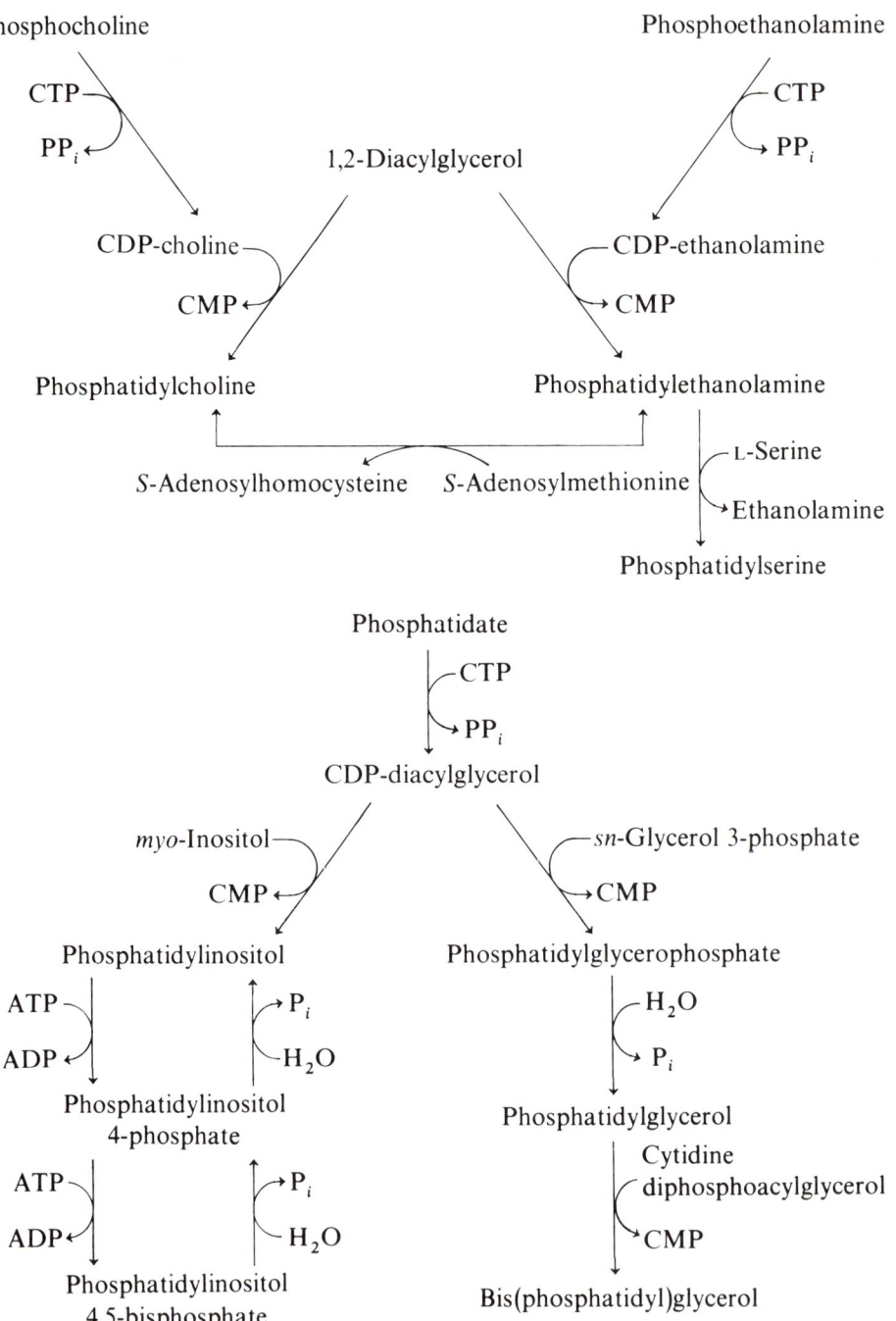

Figure 12-5 Anabolism of some of the more common phospholipids.

## ANABOLISM OF SPHINGOLIPIDS

The anabolic pathways involved in the formation of some of the more widely distributed phospholipids are summarized in Fig. 12-5.

The sphingomyelin molecule contains an alcohol moiety, an acyl moiety, and phosphocholine. The alcohol moiety is an amino diol, rather than glycerol, and the acyl moiety is bonded by the amino group of the amino diol, rather than by a hydroxyl group of glycerol.

Most frequently the amino diol of the sphingolipids has 18 carbon atoms and is known as sphingenine. In certain sphingolipids an amino diol having 20 carbon atoms and known as eicosasphingenine is found, however.

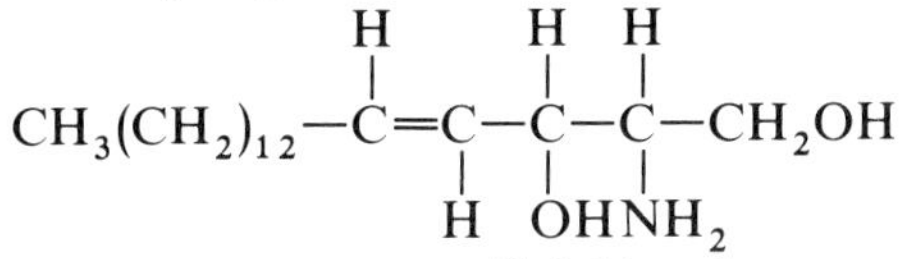

$$CH_3(CH_2)_{12}-\overset{H}{\underset{H}{C}}=\overset{H}{\underset{OH}{C}}-\overset{H}{\underset{NH_2}{C}}-CH_2OH$$

*trans*-$\Delta^4$-Sphingenine

The synthesis of sphingenine or eicosasphingenine entails an initial condensation

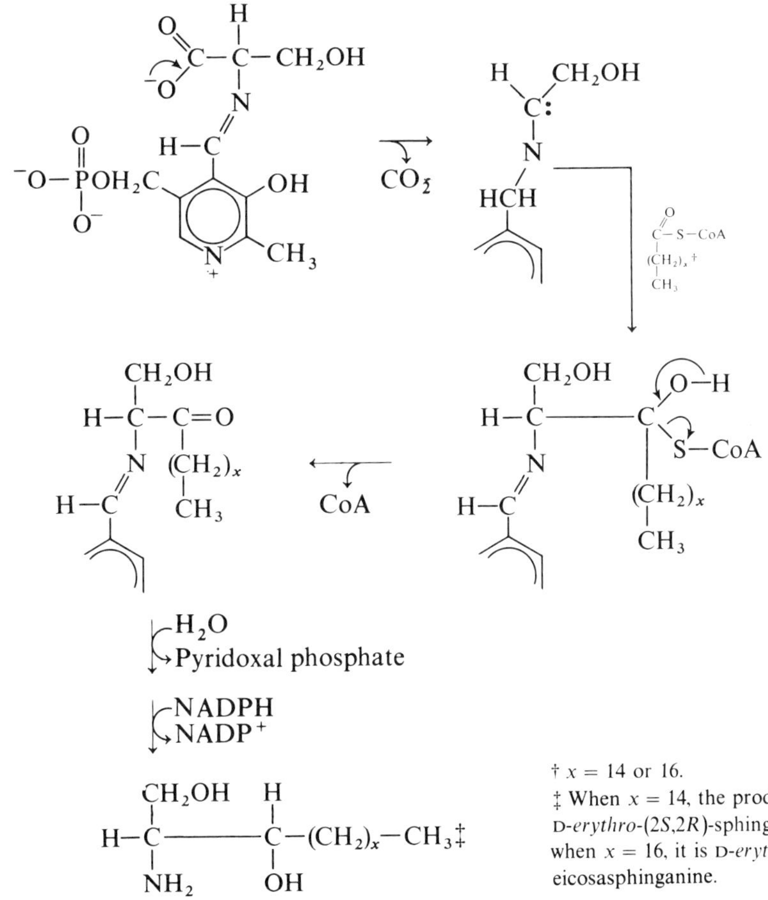

† $x = 14$ or 16.
‡ When $x = 14$, the product is D-*erythro*-(2S,2R)-sphinganine and when $x = 16$, it is D-*erythro*-eicosasphinganine.

reaction between serine and palmitoyl CoA or stearoyl CoA. A Schiff base derived from serine and pyridoxal phosphate participates in the reaction, which can be formulated as shown on page 513.

Formation of the Schiff base facilitates the initial decarboxylation of serine, as discussed in some detail in Chap. 14. The decarboxylation generates a nucleophile, which then attacks the carbonyl carbon atom of palmitoyl or stearoyl CoA. The resulting 3-dehydrosphinganine subsequently undergoes reduction at C(3) to yield sphinganine. The reduction—more specifically the conversion of the oxo group into a secondary alcohol—is catalyzed by D-dehydrosphinganine reductase (D-*erythro*-dehydrosphinganine:$NADP^+$ 3-oxidoreductase, EC 1.1.1.102). The reaction is stereo-specific, and the resulting amino diol has the $R$ configuration at C(3). Presumably

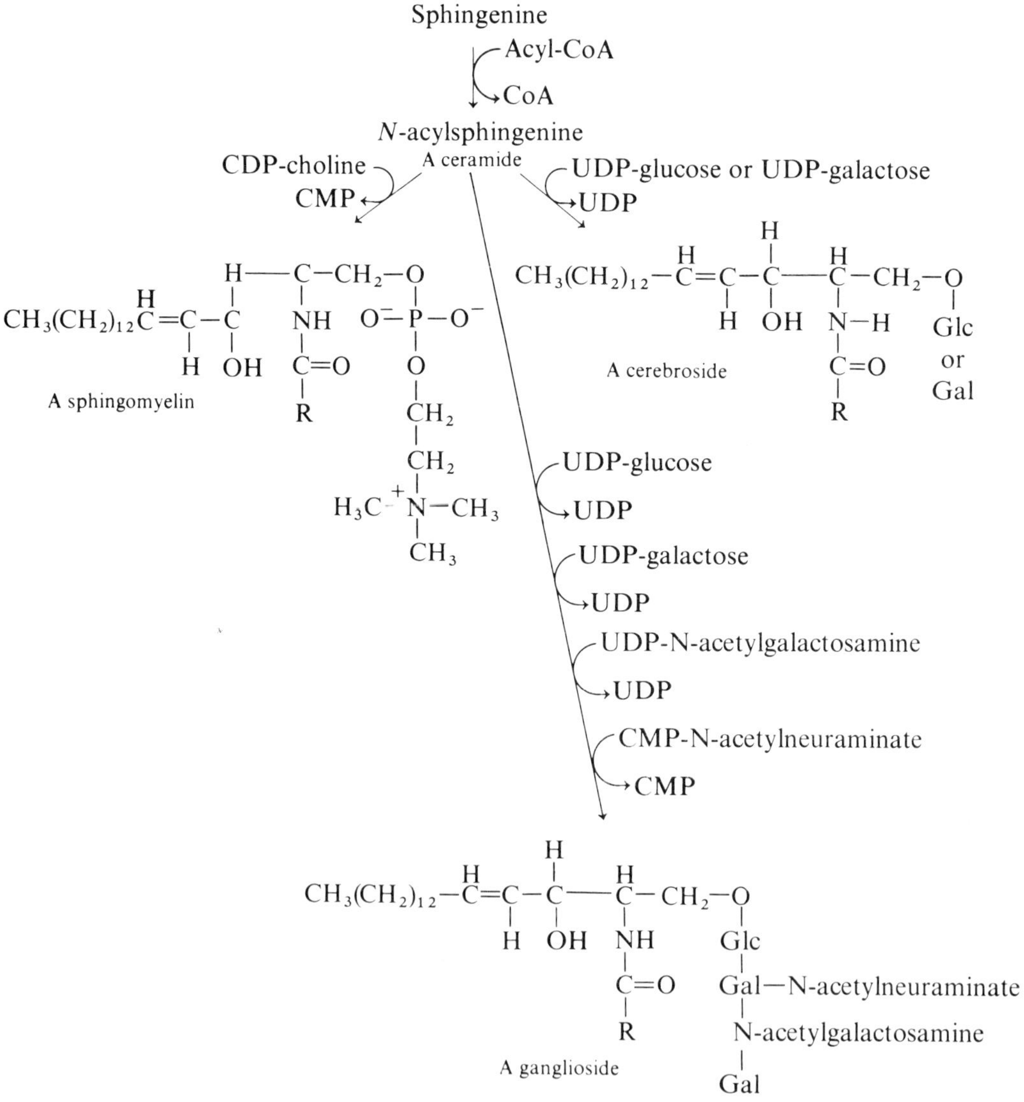

Sphingenine
  ⌐Acyl-CoA
  ⌐CoA
N-acylsphingenine
A ceramide

CDP-choline ⌐    ⌐UDP-glucose or UDP-galactose
CMP ⌐       ⌐UDP

$$CH_3(CH_2)_{12}\overset{H}{C}=C-\overset{H}{\underset{NH}{C}}-CH_2-O\;\;\;\;\;\;\;\;\;CH_3(CH_2)_{12}-\overset{H}{C}=\overset{}{C}-\overset{H}{\underset{N-H}{C}}-\overset{H}{C}-CH_2-O$$

A sphingomyelin           A cerebroside         Glc or Gal

(with phosphocholine head group: $O^-\!-\!P\!=\!O$, $O$, $CH_2$, $CH_2$, $H_3C\!-\!\overset{+}{N}\!-\!CH_3$, $CH_3$)

⌐UDP-glucose
⌐UDP

⌐UDP-galactose
⌐UDP

⌐UDP-N-acetylgalactosamine
⌐UDP

⌐CMP-N-acetylneuraminate
⌐CMP

$$CH_3(CH_2)_{12}-\overset{H}{\underset{H}{C}}=C-\overset{H}{\underset{OH}{C}}-\overset{H}{\underset{NH}{C}}-CH_2-O$$

                       C=O    Glc
                       R       Gal—N-acetylneuraminate
                               N-acetylgalactosamine
A ganglioside      Gal

3-dehydroeicosasphinganine undergoes a similar reaction, which results in the formation of eicosasphinganine. Now the saturated carbon chain is converted into an unsaturated one as the result of the introduction of an olefinic bond at C(4). The enzyme which catalyzes the desaturation reaction is a flavoprotein, and specifically *trans*-D-sphingenine or *trans*-D-eicosasphingenine is formed.

Sphingenine can undergo a reaction with an acyl-CoA and one with CDP-choline to form sphingomyelin. Sphingenine can also react with an acyl-CoA and with UDP-glucose or UDP-galactose. In this case, a cerebroside is formed. The enzymes which catalyze the formation of sphingomyelin and the cerebrosides are associated with the endoplasmic reticulum of brain cells and those of other neural tissues. The gangliosides are formed as a result of the reaction of an *N*-acylsphingenine, which is known as a ceramide, with successive molecules of a UDP sugar and with CMP-*N*-acetylneuraminic acid. These processes are summarized on page 514.

# PART III PROSTAGLANDINS

The prostaglandins are 20-carbon fatty acid derivatives which embody a five-membered ring. These compounds were initially identified in human seminal plasma, from which they were isolated and were found to function as vasodepressors and stimulators of smooth muscle. They were named prostaglandins by U. S. von Euler, who carried out many of the early studies on these compounds as obtained from ovine prostate glands.

The prostaglandins are involved in a variety of physiological and pathological processes. For example, the prostaglandin $PGE_1$ (see structures below) is a bronchial dilator, while $PGF_{2\alpha}$ is a bronchial constrictor. Also, $PGF_{2\alpha}$ is released during anaphylaxis and has also been implicated in the etiology of broncial asthma.

## ANABOLISM OF THE PROSTAGLANDINS

The prostaglandins are derived from 20-carbon unsaturated fatty acids. Arachidonate (5,8,11,14-eicosatetraenoate), 8,11,14-eicosatrienoate, and 5,8,11,14,17-eicosapentenoate can be converted into primary prostaglandins, as indicated.

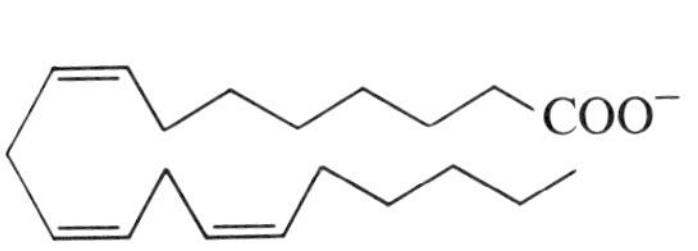

8,11,14-Eicosatrienoate

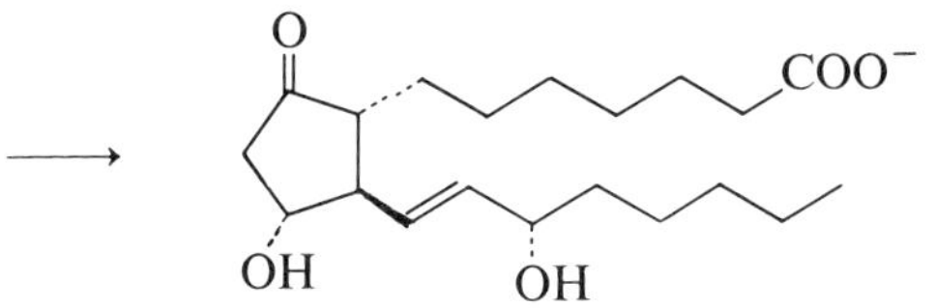

$PGE_1$(11α,15-Dihydroxy-9-oxoprost-13-*trans*-enoate)

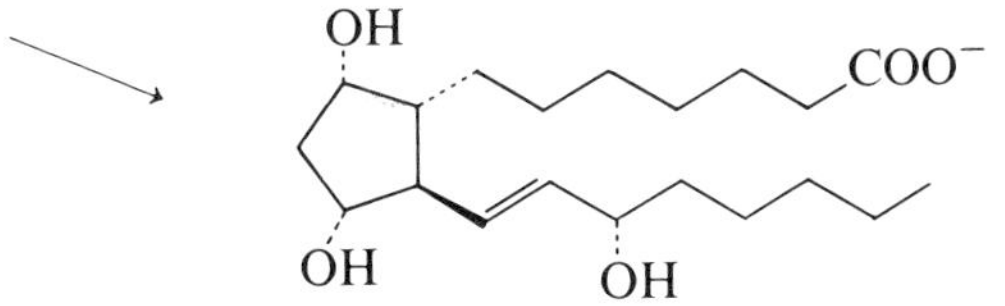

$PGF_{1\alpha}$(9α,11α,15-Trihydroxyprost-13-*trans*-enoate)

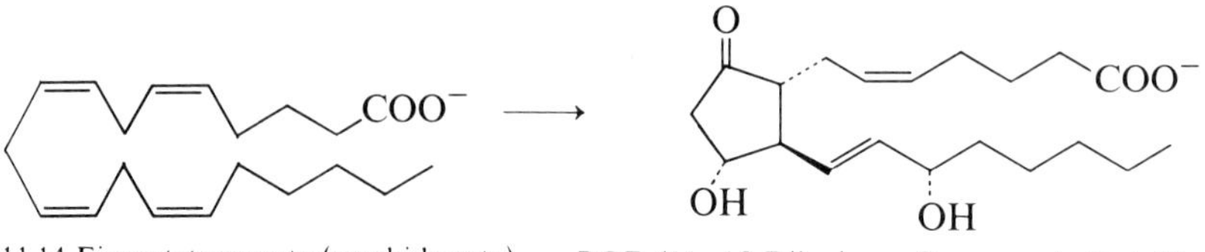

5,8,11,14-Eicosatetraenoate (arachidonate)

$PGE_2$(11α,15-Dihydroxy-9-oxoprosta-5-*cis*,13-*trans*-dienoate)

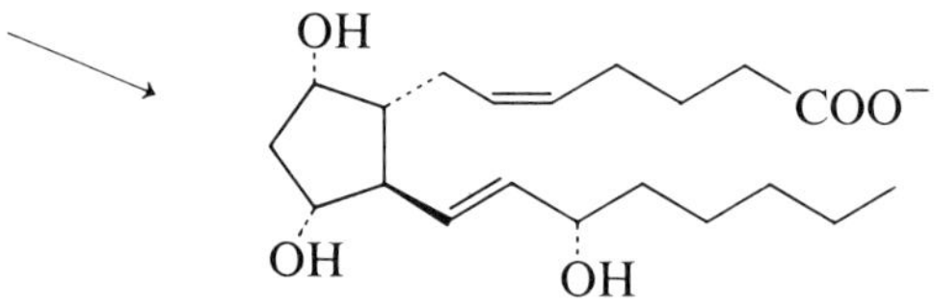

$PGF_{2\alpha}$(9α,11α,15-Trihydroxyprosta-5-*cis*,13-*trans*-dienoate)

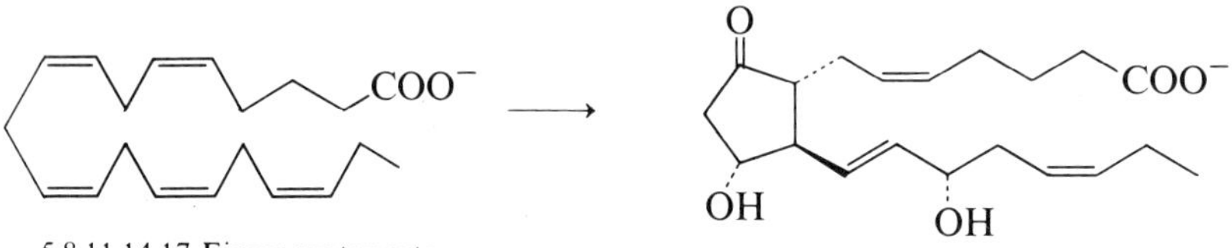

5,8,11,14,17-Eicosapentenoate

$PGE_3$(11α,15-Dihydroxy-9-oxoprosta-5-*cis*,13-*trans*,17-*cis*-trienoate)

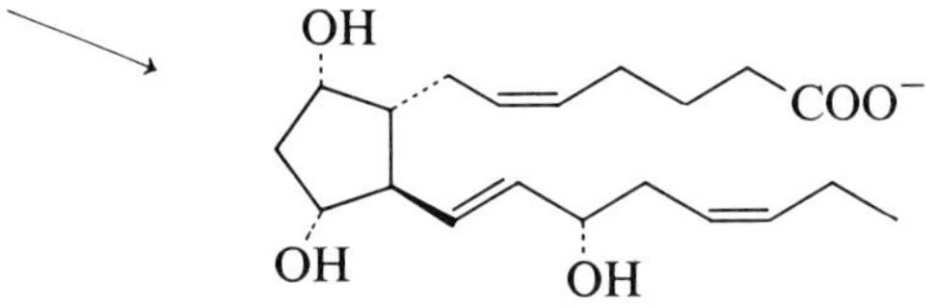

$PGF_{3\alpha}$(9α,11α,15-Trihydroxyprosta-5-*cis*,13-trans,17-*cis*-trienoate)

The synthesis of these prostaglandins is catalyzed by a prostaglandin synthase complex which although it has not been completely characterized has been classified (as 8,11,14-eicosatrienoate, hydrogen-donor:oxygen oxidoreductase, EC 1.14.99.1). The prostaglandin synthase complex is associated with the endoplasmic reticulum

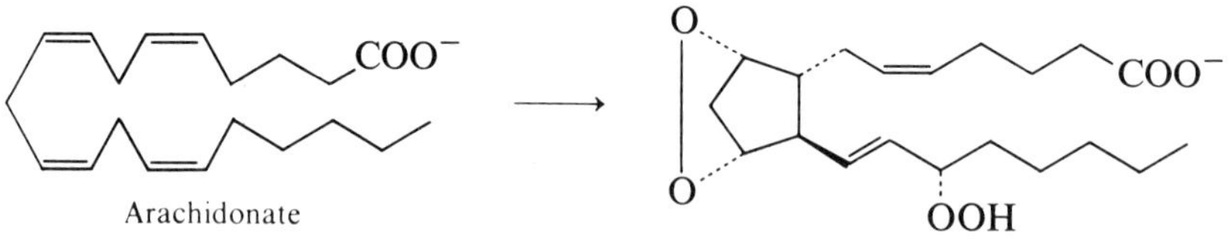

Arachidonate

$PGG_2$

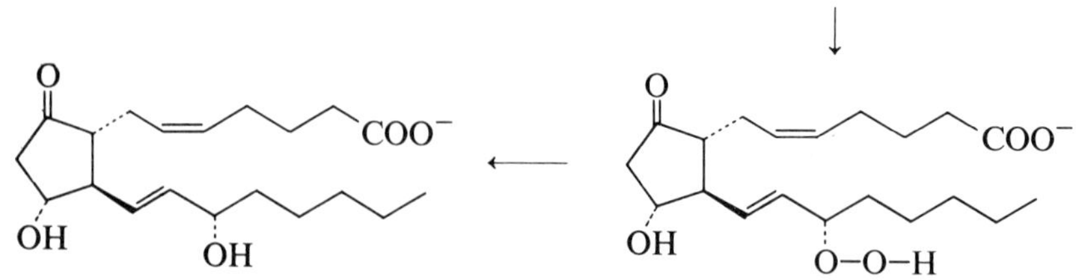

$PGE_2$

15-HydroperoxyPGE$_2$

of the cell and consists of (at least) a cyclooxygenase which catalyzes the formation of a cyclic *endo*-peroxide and an enzyme which catalyzes the conversion of this peroxide into an oxo group plus a hydroxyl group. These reactions are shown at the bottom of page 516 along with the reaction which converts a hydroperoxy group into a hydroxyl group. At least in some systems an enzyme that catalyzes the conversion of the hydroperoxy group into a hydroxyl group is found in the cytoplasm of the cell.

The reactions catalyzed by prostaglandin synthase entail the introduction of three oxygen atoms, all derived from molecular oxygen. A single molecule of oxygen provides the oxygen atoms introduced at C(9) and C(11), while a second molecule of oxygen provides the oxygen atom that becomes a part of the C(15) hydroxyl group. A minimal reaction mechanism for these transformations is given below.

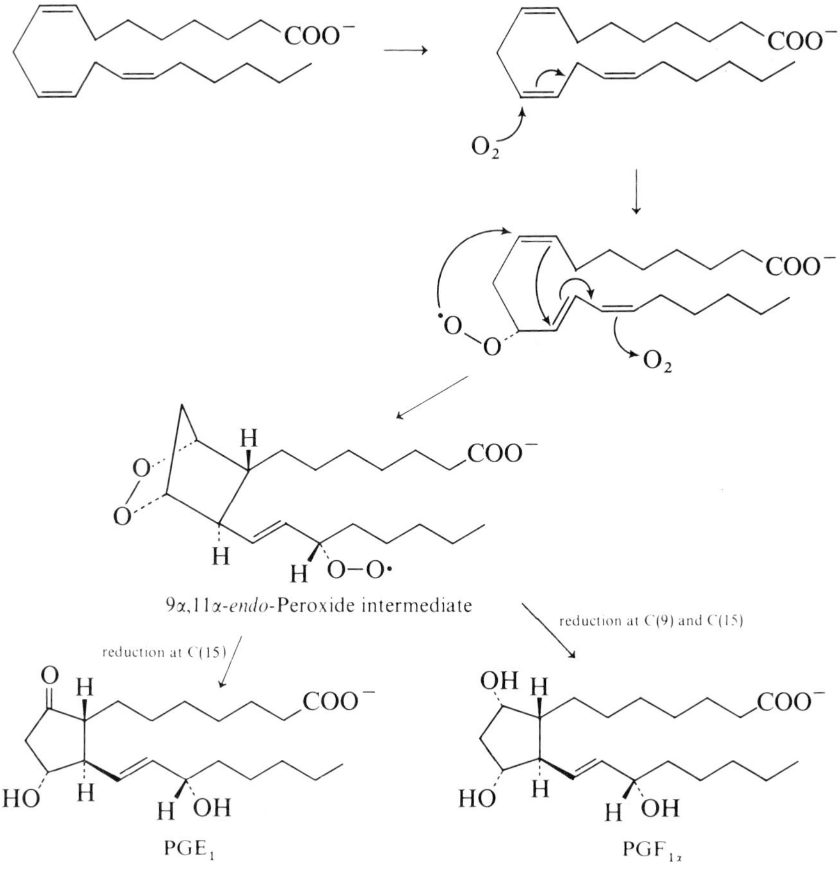

9α,11α-*endo*-Peroxide intermediate

reduction at C(15)

reduction at C(9) and C(15)

PGE$_1$

PGF$_{1\alpha}$

## CATABOLISM OF THE PROSTAGLANDINS

The biological inactivation and catabolism of the prostaglandins generally begins with the oxidation of the C(15) hydroxyl group to an oxo group. This is catalyzed by 15-hydroxyprostaglandin dehydrogenase (11α,15-dihydroxy-9-oxoprost-13-

enoate:NAD⁺ 15-oxidoreductase, EC 1.1.1.141). This enzyme is present in the lung, among other tissues, where during pulmonary circulation it oxidizes prostaglandins present in the blood. A second hydroxyprostaglandin dehydrogenase, which utilizes NADP⁺ preferentially, has been identified in human erythrocytes and brain. Having undergone oxidation at C(15), the prostaglandin derivative can subsequently undergo a reduction reaction which results in the saturation of the olefinic bond at C(13). Also, the C(9) oxo group of prostaglandins of the E series can undergo reduction, thus converting the prostaglandin to a member of the F series. In addition, human serum converts a prostaglandin of the E series into one of the A series as the result of a dehydration reaction involving the C(11) hydroxyl group. The prostaglandin of the A series can then undergo isomerization to yield a member of the C series.

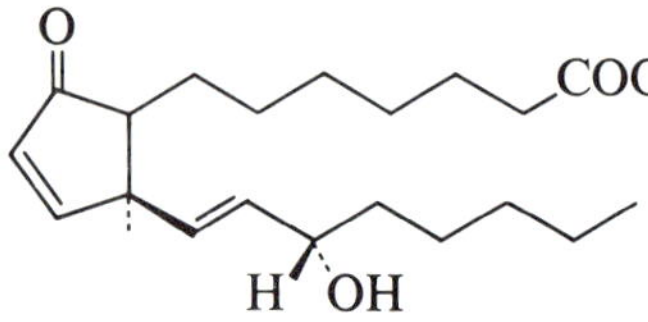

PGA₁        PGC₁

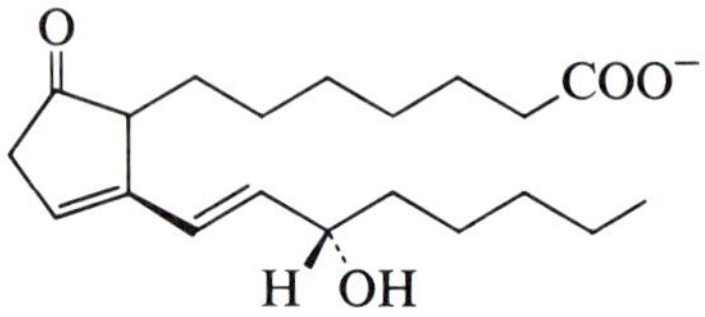

Finally, prior to excretion in the urine, prostaglandin derivatives resulting from oxidation at C(15), reduction at C(13) and C(14), and other modifications undergo one or two cycles of β oxidation. Alternatively, these derivatives can undergo ω hydroxylation followed by oxidation to yield a dicarboxylic acid. The latter can also undergo β oxidation, with the result that six carbon atoms are removed from that which was the ω end of the prostaglandin. These 16- and 14-carbon degradation products are ultimately excreted.

# PART IV STEROIDS

As early as 1937 it was recognized that acetate is utilized (by yeasts) in the *de novo* synthesis of cholesterol. Five years later Konrad Bloch and David Rittenberg demonstrated that both carbon atoms of acetate are incorporated when cholesterol is synthesized in animals. Subsequently, the distribution pattern of the acetate carbon atoms in the cholesterol molecule was determined by R. B. Woodward (at Harvard

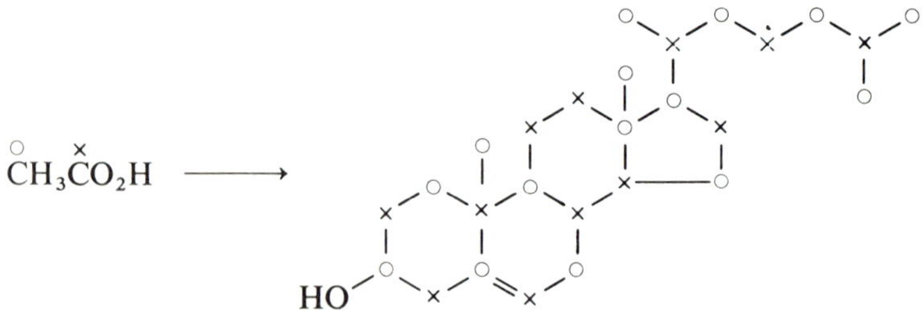

$CH_3\overset{×}{C}O_2H \longrightarrow$

Carbon skeleton of cholesterol

University) and Konrad Bloch (at the University of Chicago) and also by W. G. Dauben and his colleagues (at the University of California).

Finally, the complete degradation of cholesterol and determination of the origin of each of its carbon atoms was carried out in the laboratories of John W. Cornforth and George Popjak. These studies confirmed the formulations of Woodward, Bloch, and Dauben. At this point, it was also known that squalene, a 30-carbon, unsaturated intermediate, is a precursor of cholesterol and that squalene is an isoprenoid compound. When it was subsequently shown that squalene is derived from a six-carbon dihydroxy acid known as mevalonate, the manner in which acetate is incorporated into cholesterol was established.

## ANABOLISM OF CHOLESTEROL

As implied above, an important intermediate in the *de novo* synthesis of cholesterol is mevalonate. Its formation is discussed in the following paragraphs.

### Synthesis of Mevalonate

The initial step of the *de novo* synthesis of cholesterol can be considered to be the condensation of two acetyl moieties of acetyl CoA molecules. The condensation is catalyzed by acetyl-CoA acetyltransferase and the product is acetoacetyl CoA. Acetyl-CoA acetyltransferase was mentioned earlier in this chapter, when the formation of the ketone bodies was discussed. The enzyme involved in ketogenesis is localized in the mitochondrion, however, while that involved in cholesterol anabolism is localized in the cytoplasm. (The mitochondrial and cytoplasmic enzymes have distinct primary structures and are readily separated on the basis of their physical properties.) The acetoacetyl moiety can now undergo a condensation reaction with yet another acetyl moiety of acetyl CoA with the result that 3-hydroxy-3-methylglutaryl CoA is formed. This condensation is catalyzed by a cytoplasmic hydroxymethylglutaryl CoA synthase (to be distinguished from the mitochondrial enzyme that is involved in ketogenesis). The cytoplasmic synthase from avian liver has been isolated and purified and it was found to be a dimer which has a molecular weight of 100,000.[†] Next, the 3-hydroxy-3-methylglutaryl moiety undergoes a reduction reaction which results in its release from CoA and the conversion of the thiol ester carbonyl carbon atom into that of a primary alcohol. This reaction is catalyzed by an NADPH-dependent hydroxymethylglutaryl-CoA reductase [mevalonate:NADP$^+$ oxidoreductase (CoA-acylating), EC 1.1.1.34]. It can be written

$$\text{3-Hydroxy-3-methylglutaryl CoA} + 2\text{NADPH} \rightleftharpoons \text{mevalonate} + \text{NADP}^+ + \text{CoA} \quad (12\text{-}27)$$

---

[†] Clinkenbeard, K. D., Sugiyama, T., Reed, W. D., and Lane, M. D. (1975) *J. Biol. Chem.* **250**, 3124–3135.

Hydroxymethylglutaryl CoA reductase, which is associated with the endoplasmic reticulum of the cell, has been isolated as a species has a molecular weight of 200,000. The reduction reaction catalyzed by the reductase involves two direct, sequential transfers of pro-$R$ hydrogen atoms (as hydride ions) from the two NADPH molecules. The product is ($R$)-mevalonate. This reaction is the rate-determining step of cholesterol anabolism under most circumstances. A minimal reaction mechanism for the formation of mevalonate is shown below.

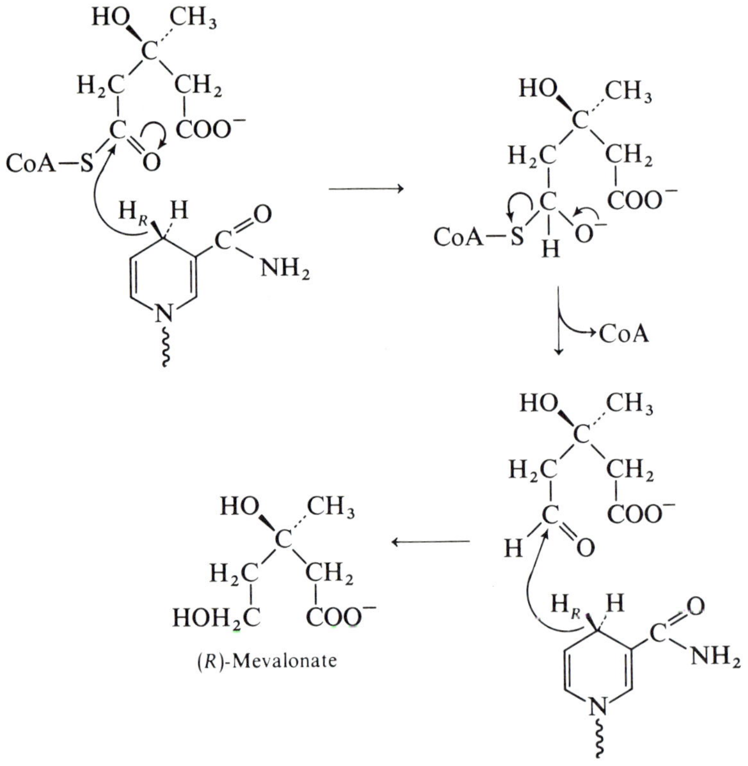

## Formation of Squalene

The next step in the *de novo* synthesis of cholesterol is the phosphorylation of mevalonate, which is catalyzed by mevalonate kinase (ATP:mevalonate 5-phosphotransferase, EC 2.7.1.36). The product is mevalonate 5-phosphate. Mevalonate kinase utilizes only ($R$)-mevalonate as its substrate. As isolated from porcine liver, mevalonate kinase has a molecular weight of 98,000. The phosphorylation proceeds by an ordered sequential Bi Bi reaction in which mevalonate is the initial substrate that binds and ADP is the final product that is released.†

Mevalonate 5-phosphate subsequently undergoes another phosphorylation reaction, which results in the formation of mevalonate 5-diphosphate. The enzyme

---

† Beytia, E., Dorsey, J. K., Marr, J., Cleland, W. W., and Porter, J. W. (1970) *J. Biol. Chem.* **245**, 5450–5458.

catalyzing this phosphorylation reaction is phosphomevalonate kinase (ATP:5-phosphomevalonate phosphotransferase, EC 2.7.4.2). Mevalonate 5-diphosphate now undergoes an ATP-dependent decarboxylation and desaturation reaction, which results in the formation of the isoprenoid intermediate $\Delta^3$-isopentenyl diphosphate. The reaction, which is catalyzed by diphosphomevalonate decarboxylase [ATP:5-diphosphomevalonate carboxy-lyase (dehydrating), EC 4.1.1.33], can be written

ATP + mevalonate 5-diphosphate $\rightleftharpoons$

$$\text{isopentenyl diphosphate} + CO_2 + ADP + P_i \quad (12\text{-}28)$$

Since it has been observed that $^{18}O$ is transferred from the C(3) hydroxyl group of mevalonate diphosphate to orthophosphate during the reaction, a minimal reaction mechanism such as that shown can be formulated.

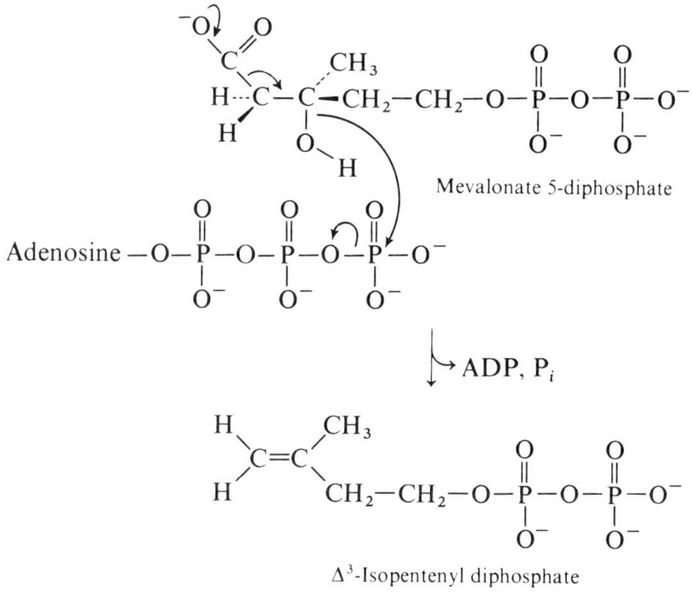

A series of condensation reactions now occurs. Initially, two 5-carbon isoprenoid compounds undergo condensation to yield a 10-carbon isoprenoid compound. Then another 5-carbon isoprenoid compound undergoes a condensation reaction with the 10-carbon isoprenoid compound, and a 15-carbon isoprenoid compound is generated. Finally, two of the 15-carbon isoprenoid compounds undergo a condensation reaction, and the 30-carbon intermediate, squalene, is formed.

In order for the two 5-carbon isoprenoid compounds to react a molecule of $\Delta^3$-isopentenyl diphosphate must undergo isomerization. This isomerization, which is in effect an allylic rearrangement, is catalyzed by isopentenyldiphosphate $\Delta$-isomerase (isopentenyldiphosphate $\Delta^3$-$\Delta^2$-isomerase, EC 5.3.3.2). The product, which is dimethylallyl diphosphate, then reacts with a molecule of $\Delta^3$-isopentenyl diphosphate and the 10-carbon isoprenoid compound *trans*-geranyl diphosphate is formed. The condensation is catalyzed by dimethylallyltransferase (dimethylallyl-diphosphate:isopentenyldiphosphate dimethylallyltransferase, EC 2.5.1.1). The formation of geranyl diphosphate can be depicted as follows.

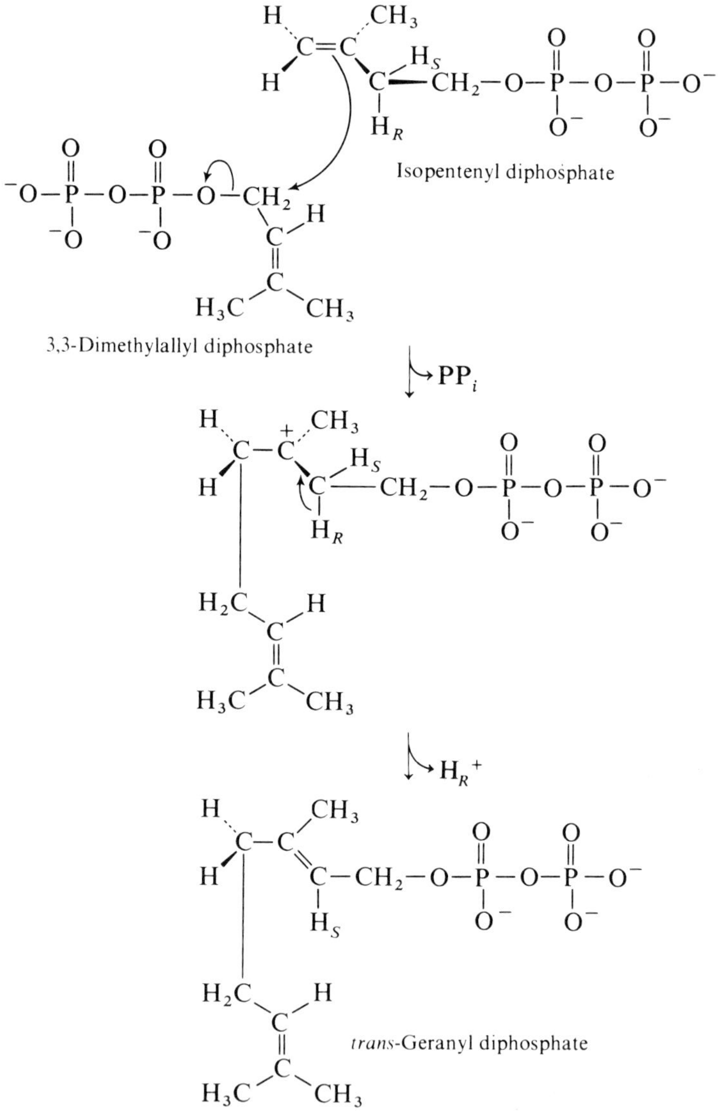

3,3-Dimethylallyl diphosphate

Isopentenyl diphosphate

trans-Geranyl diphosphate

The making of the new carbon-carbon bond is facilitated by the displacement of the allylic diphosphate group of dimethylallyl diphosphate. Subsequently, the pro-$R$ hydrogen atom, shown, is eliminated as a proton, and an olefinic bond is formed between C(2) and C(3) of the 10-carbon intermediate. Since this intermediate, geranyl diphosphate, also has an allylic diphosphate group, another condensation reaction involving another molecule of isopentenyl diphosphate can occur. Geranyltransferase (geranyldiphosphate:isopentenyldiphosphate geranyltransferase, EC EC 2.5.1.10) catalyzes the formation of the 15-carbon intermediate, farnesyl diphosphate.

Two molecules of farnesyl diphosphate now undergo a condensation reaction, which ultimately results in the formation of squalene. Actually, two consecutive reactions are involved. First the two molecules of farnesyl diphosphate undergo a condensation reaction catalyzed by farnesyltransferase (farnesyl-diphosphate: farnesyl-diphosphate farnesyltransferase, EC 2.5.1.21) which yields presqualene diphosphate plus pyrophosphate. Then presqualene diphosphate undergoes an NADPH-dependent reduction which yields squalene. The overall reaction can be written

$$2 \text{ Farnesyl diphosphate} + \text{NADPH} \rightleftharpoons \text{squalene} + \text{NADP}^+ + 2 \text{ pyrophosphate} \quad (12\text{-}29)$$

Enzyme systems which catalyze the overall reaction have been isolated from several sources, including porcine-liver endoplasmic reticulum and the yeast *Saccharomyces cerevisiae*. The yeast-enzyme system has a molecular weight of approximately 425,000.

Kinetic studies on both the mammalian enzyme and the yeast enzyme have indicated that the mechanism of the overall reaction includes a ping pong sequence since plots of $1/v_i$ vs. 1/[farnesyl diphosphate] with fixed concentrations of NADPH are linear and parallel. The apparent linearity of these plots is taken as an indication that the binding of the first molecule of farnesyl diphosphate and that of the second are separated by an irreversible step, such as the release of a product under initial-velocity conditions. When two molecules of a variable substrate bind the enzyme and there is a reversible connection between the points at which they bind in the reaction sequence, plots of $1/v_i$ vs. the reciprocal of the concentration of that substrate are parabolic. This is because under these circumstances the reciprocal-velocity equation contains second-order concentration terms. Therefore, on the basis of the data obtained, the formation of presqualene diphosphate was formulated in terms of a ping pong mechanism in which the first molecule of farnesyl diphosphate binds the enzyme and the pyrophosphate anion is then released prior to the binding of the second molecule of farnesyl diphosphate. When the conversion of presqualene diphosphate to squalene was examined, a sequential mechanism was indicated since plots of $1/v_i$ vs. 1/[NADPH] with fixed concentrations of presqualene diphosphate were intersecting. In addition, $NADP^+$ was found to be a competitive product inhibitor when NADPH was the variable substrate, thus suggesting an ordered sequential mechanism in which NADPH is the initial substrate that binds and $NADP^+$ is the final product that is released.†

The reaction mechanism of the overall process has been formulated as illustrated on pages 524 and 525.†

---

† Beytia, E., Qureshi, A. A., and Porter, J. W. (1973) *J. Biol. Chem.* **248**, 1856–1867.

**524** MECHANISMS OF METABOLISM

Initially, a nucleophilic group at the catalytic site displaces the allylic pyrophosphate group of the first molecule of farnesyl diphosphate that binds the enzyme. Then, the second molecule of farnesyl diphosphate attacks C(1) of the enzyme-bound farnesyl moiety. This may also be promoted by a nucleophilic group at the catalytic

Presqualene diphosphate

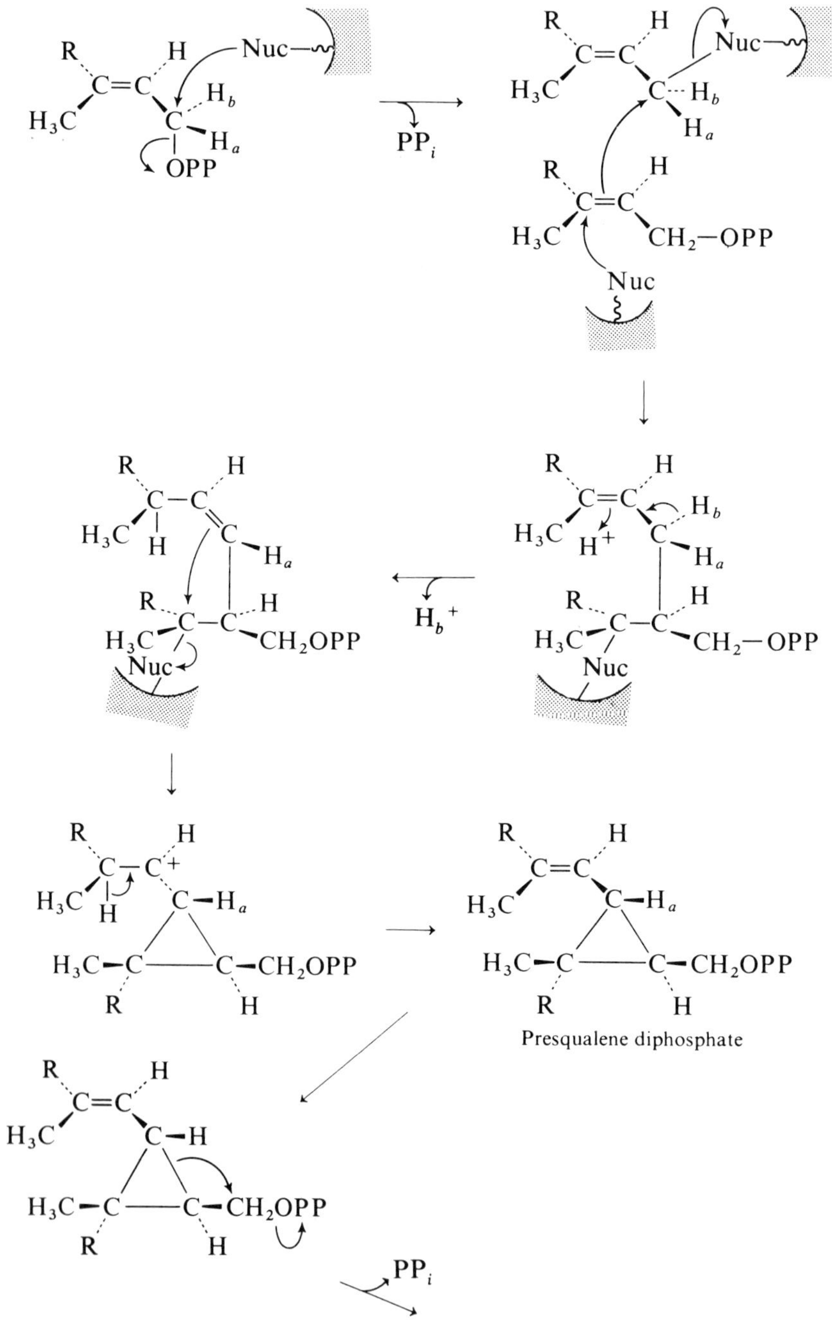

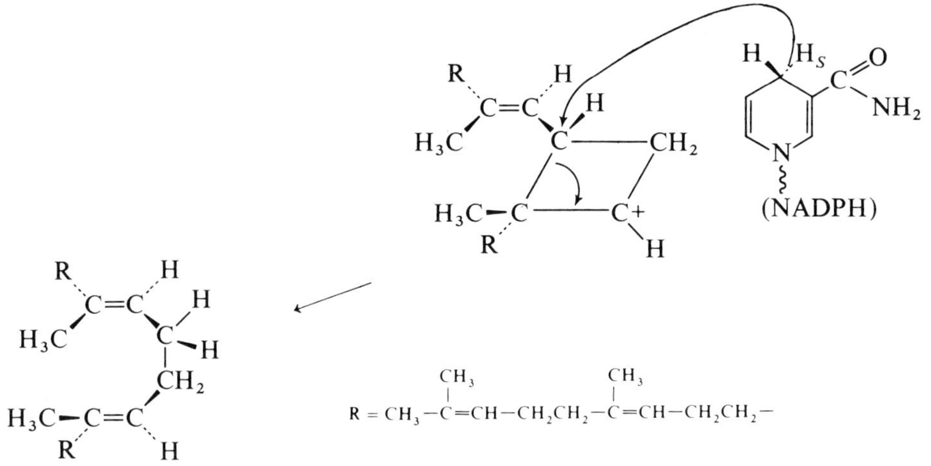

site. The two consecutive $S_N2$ reactions at C(1) of the first farnesyl moiety that binds result in the retention of the configuration of this carbon atom, as has been observed. Now there is an isomerization of the double bond resulting from a 1,3-prototropic rearrangement. Following this, a cyclopropyl ring is formed, and the resulting electron deficiency is satisfied by the elimination of a proton. This generates the intermediate presqualene diphosphate. The ring expansion which follows promotes the elimination of the second pyrophosphate anion. Finally, the addition of a hydride ion from NADPH completes the reaction and squalene is formed.

From an overview, the formation of squalene entails the head-to-head condensation of two farnesyl moieties with the elimination of the two diphosphate groups as pyrophosphate anions. The condensation occurs with the retention of three of the four hydrogen atoms that were originally bonded at C(1) of a farnesyl diphosphate molecule. In place of the hydrogen atom that is eliminated (as a proton) a hydride ion from NADPH is introduced.

## Cyclization of Squalene

Squalene undergoes epoxidation and cyclization to yield the perhydrocyclopentanophenanthrene ring system which is characteristic of cholesterol and its derivatives. The epoxidation, which is in effect an activation process, is catalyzed by squalene monooxygenase (2,3-epoxidizing) [squalene, hydrogen-donor:oxygen oxidoreductase (2,3-epoxidizing), EC 1.14.99.7]. The reaction can be expressed as follows:

$$\text{Squalene} + AH_2 + O_2 \rightleftharpoons \text{2,3-oxidosqualene} + A + H_2O \quad (12\text{-}30)$$

Squalene monooxygenase is associated with the endoplasmic-reticulum fraction of the cell. As isolated from the endoplasmic reticulum of the rat hepatocyte, the monooxygenase consists of two components.† Both appear to be flavoproteins, which presumably participate in the activation of the molecular oxygen.

Following the formation of the 2,3-epoxide, the cyclization reaction takes place. The product is lanosterol, and its formation is catalyzed by 2,3-oxidosqualene lanosterol-cyclase [2,3-oxidosqualene mutase(cyclizing, lanosterol-forming), EC 5.4.99.7]. The reaction mechanism of the cyclization was proposed as early as 1955 by Albert Eschenmoser and Leopold Ruzicka and their colleagues, in Zurich, and also by Gilbert Stork and Albert Burgstahler at Harvard University and Columbia University, respectively. Since then there have been other studies aimed at establishing the detailed mechanism of this rather complex process. A minimal reaction mechanism compatible with the accumulated data is shown below.

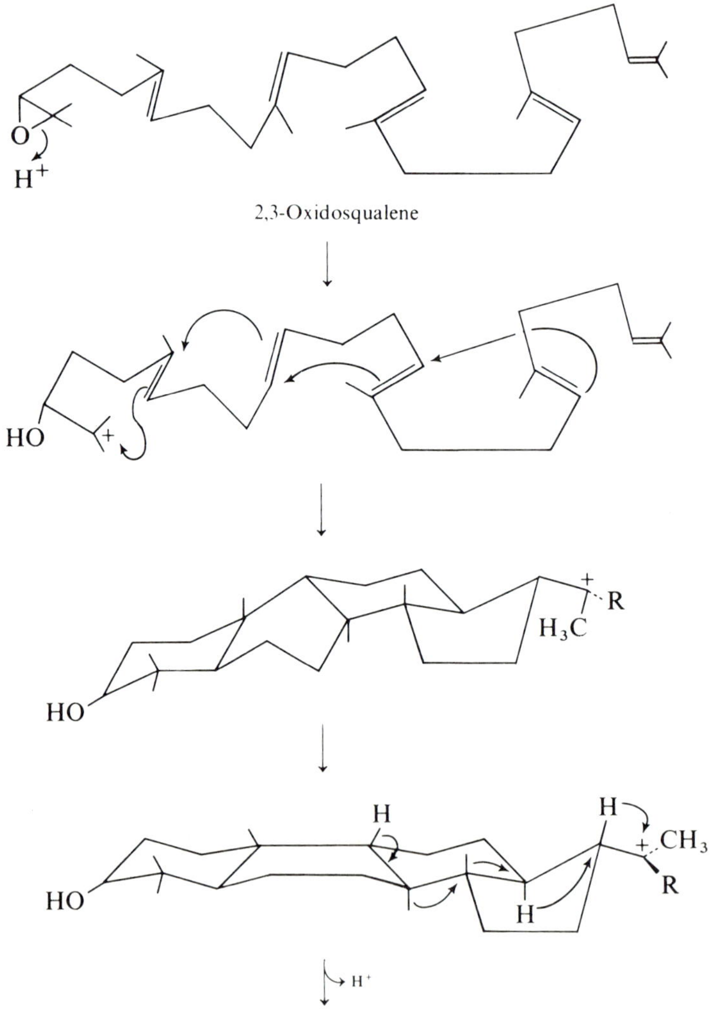

2,3-Oxidosqualene

† Ono, T. and Bloch, K. (1975) *J. Biol. Chem.* **250**, 1571–1579.

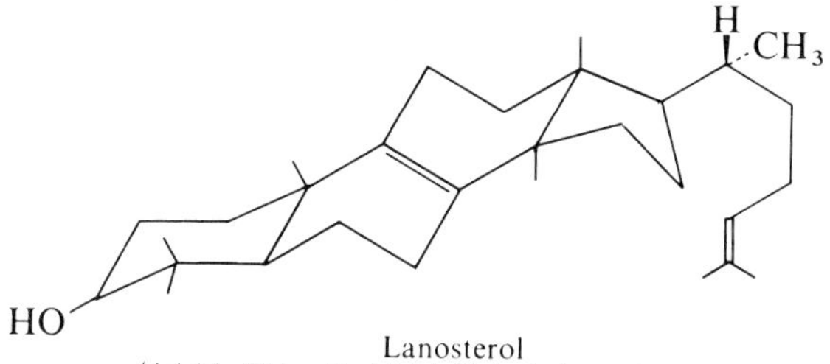

Lanosterol
(4,4,14α-Trimethyl-8,24-(5α)-cholestadien-3β-ol)

According to this formulation, the epoxide ring opens, thus generating an electron-deficient carbon atom, as shown. This provides the driving force for the series of ring closures which follows. With the closure of the fourth (five-membered) ring, a carbon atom of the side chain becomes electron-deficient. This, in turn, is the driving force for the sequence of hydride-ion and methyl-group migrations which culminate in the formation of the olefinic bond between C(8) and C(9).

The cyclization of squalene occurs not only in animals but also in plants, fungi, protozoa, and other organisms. The cyclization does not always yield lanosterol, however. Plants, which generally synthesize phytosterols rather than cholesterol, carry out the cyclization of squalene to yield cycloartenol. Certain fungi carry out the cyclization of squalene to yield an intermediate known as fusidic acid. On the other hand, the protozoon *Tetrahymena pyriformis* carries out the cyclization of squalene to yield an intermediate called tetrahymanol.

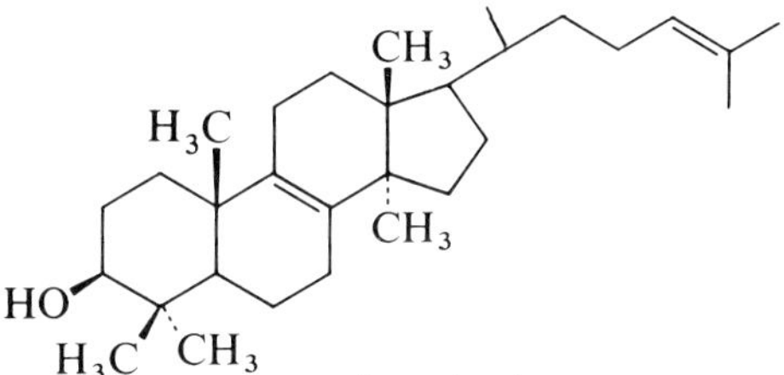

Lanosterol

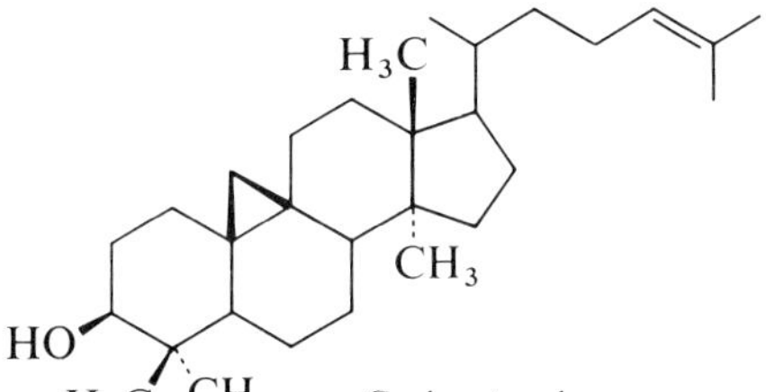

Cycloartenol

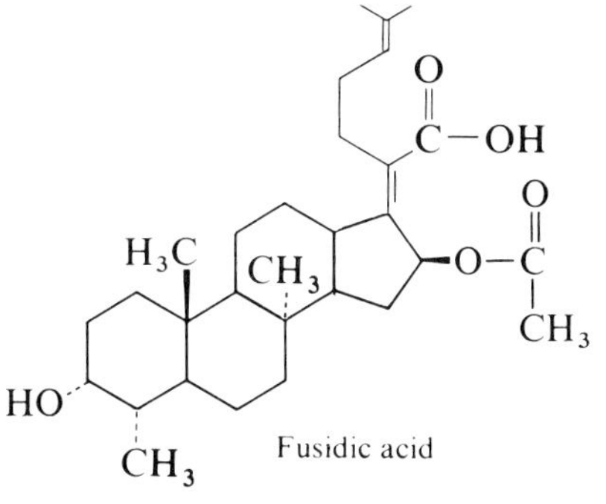

Fusidic acid

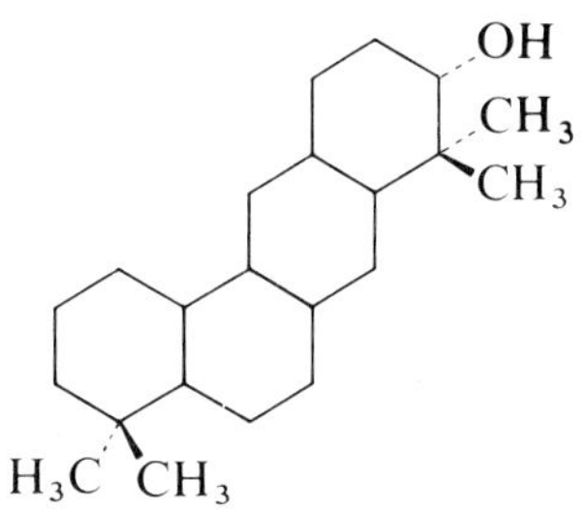

Tetrahymanol

In each instance the cyclization takes place as the result of a mechanism that is similar (if not identical) to that shown above.

## Conversion of Lanosterol to Cholesterol

From an overview, the conversion of lanosterol to cholesterol entails the loss of the geminal methyl groups at C(4) and the methyl group at C(14), isomerization of the C(8)—C(9) olefinic bond, introduction of the C(5)—C(6) olefinic bond, and saturation of the C(7)—C(8) and C(24)—C(25) olefinic bonds. There are several alternatives with respect to the order in which these reactions occur, however, as shown diagrammatically below.

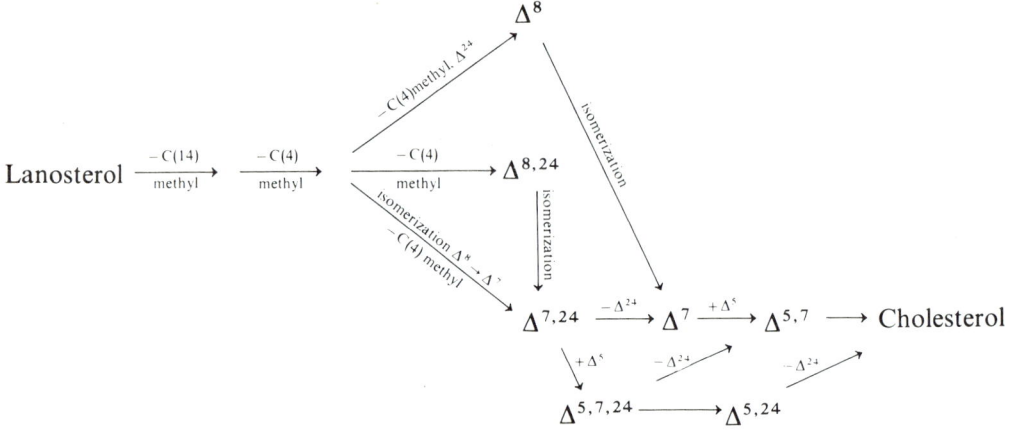

**Demethylation reactions** The removal of the methyl groups at C(4) and C(14) of lanosterol entails the oxidation of the methyl carbon atom to the level of a carboxylate carbon atom followed by decarboxylation. An enzyme system which can catalyze the overall reaction has been isolated from the endoplasmic reticulum of the rat hepatocyte. This enzyme system is known as the methylsterol monooxygenase (4,4-dimethyl-5α-cholest-7-en-3β-ol, hydrogen-donor:oxygen oxidoreductase, EC 1.14.99.16), and the overall reaction can be written

4,4-Dimethyl-5α-cholest-7-en-3β-ol + 3AH$_2$ + 3O$_2$ $\rightleftharpoons$

4α-methyl-5α-cholest-7-en-3β-ol + 3A + 4H$_2$O + CO$_2$   (12-31)

The methylsterol monooxygenase specifically acts upon a methyl group that is occupying an α position. Such a substituent undergoes a stepwise oxidation from methyl to hydroxymethyl to aldehyde to carboxylate group. The carboxylate group is then eliminated. If the initial substrate was the geminal dimethyl derivative, the remainging methyl group, which is occupying the 4β position, can become a 4α methyl group. Then, as such, it can also be removed. The change in configuration at C(4) is thought to result from the oxidation of the 3β hydroxyl group to an oxo group, formation of the corresponding enolate ion, conversion back to an oxo form having the opposite configuration at C(4), and reduction of the oxo group back to a 3β hydroxyl group.

**Isomerization, formation, and saturation of olefinic bonds** The isomerization of the C(8)—C(9) olefinic bond to a C(7)—C(8) olefinic bond is catalyzed by cholestenol

Δ-isomerase (Δ$^7$-cholestenol Δ$^7$-Δ$^8$-isomerase, EC 5.3.3.5). The reaction mechanism is formulated in terms of a 1,3 prototropic rearrangement.

Introduction of the C(5)—C(6) olefinic bond is catalyzed by lathosterol oxidase (5α-cholest-7-en-3β-ol:oxygen Δ$^5$-oxidoreductase, EC 1.3.3.2). As indicated, the reaction requires molecular oxygen. It is also known that during the reaction the (axial) 5α hydrogen atom and the (equatorial) 6α hydrogen atom are removed. The mechanism of the desaturation process is unknown.

Finally, formation of cholesterol requires saturation of both the C(7)—C(8) olefinic bond and the C(24)—C(25) olefinic bond. The former reaction is catalyzed by 7-dehydrocholesterol reductase (cholesterol:NADP$^+$ Δ$^7$-oxidoreductase, EC 1.3.1.21).

## Regulatory Mechanisms of Cholesterol Anabolism

The principal regulatory site in the anabolism of cholesterol, summarized in Fig. 12-6, is generally agreed to be the reaction catalyzed by hydroxymethylglutaryl-CoA reductase, i.e., the formation of mevalonate. The activity of the reductase exhibits a circadian rhythm, as does the synthesis of cholesterol. The

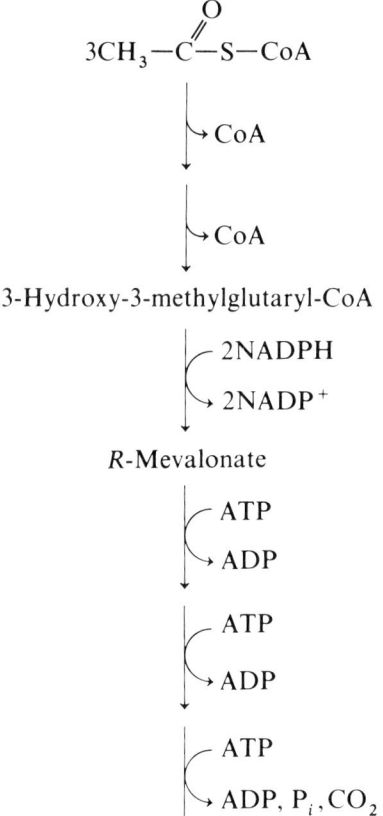

**Figure 12-6** Anabolism of cholesterol. (Figure continued on next page.)

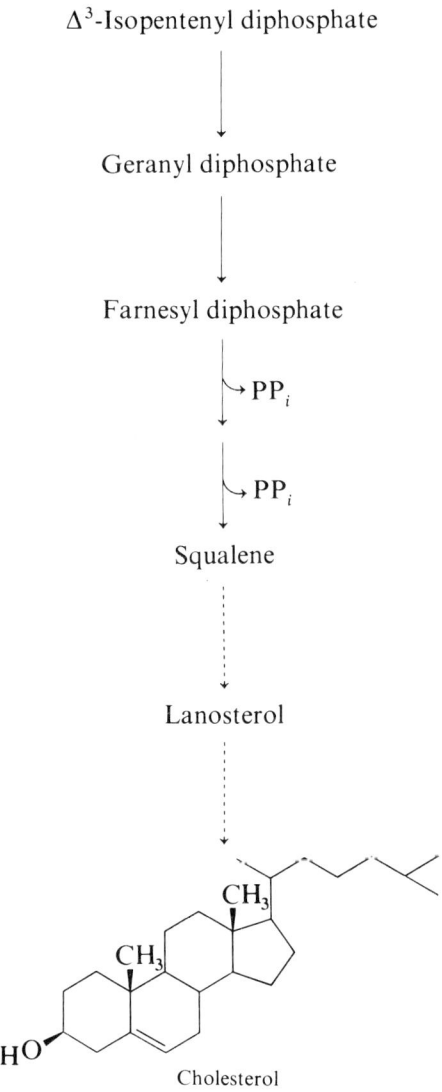

**Figure 12-6** (*Continued*)

factors which control this rhythm are unknown, although it has been shown that if an agent that inhibits protein synthesis is injected into an animal, the circadian rhythm is abolished.

It is recognized, however, that factors other than the activity of hydroxymethylglutaryl-CoA reductase influence the rate at which cholesterol is synthesized. More specifically, it has been shown that a small protein (with a molecular weight of 16,000) is required in order for the water-insoluble precursors of cholesterol to be converted into their appropriate products. This small protein is known as the sterol carrier protein (SCP) and it binds sterols and certain other water-insoluble components. With respect to the intermediates in the synthesis of cholesterol it has been shown that when the water-insoluble intermediate is bound to an aggregated form of the sterol carrier protein, the resulting complex is more readily utilized as a substrate by the appropriate enzyme than the noncomplexed intermediate.

## CONVERSION OF CHOLESTEROL INTO STEROID HORMONES

Cholesterol is the precursor of the progestins, the androgens, the estrogens, and the corticoids in most mammalian systems. The formation of these steroid hormones from cholesterol entails the cleavage of a six-carbon fragment from the side chain at C(17) followed by the conversion of the resulting intermediate, pregnenolone, into the various products.

### Formation of Pregnenolone

Cholesterol is converted into pregnenolone and isocapraldehyde in the presence of molecular oxygen, NADPH, and an electron-transport system that includes a flavoprotein known as ferredoxin-NADP$^+$ reductase (NADPH:ferredoxin oxidoreductase, EC 1.6.7.1), a nonheme iron–sulfur protein, called adrenodoxin, and a cytochrome. The nonheme iron–sulfur complex of adrenodoxin consists of two iron atoms and two acid-labile sulfur atoms. The protein moiety has a molecular weight of 15,000. The cytochrome is a species of cytochrome P-450, which has a molecular weight of 850,000 and comprises 16 subunits. These subunits bind 8 heme b moieties. The cleavage of the side chain of cholesterol entails the initial formation of 20(R), 22(R)-dihydroxycholesterol. The formation of this glycol requires molecular oxygen, NADPH, and the electron-transport system mentioned above. Two sequential hydroxylation reactions, involving two distinct oxygen

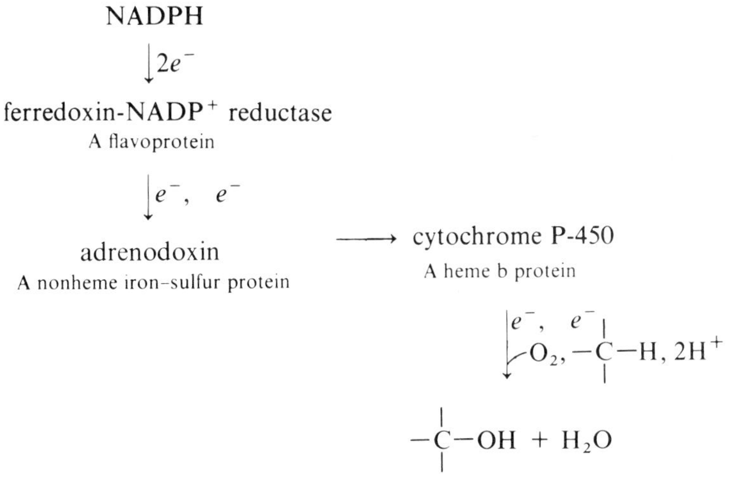

$$\begin{array}{c} \text{NADPH} \\ \downarrow 2e^- \\ \text{ferredoxin-NADP}^+ \text{ reductase} \\ \text{A flavoprotein} \\ \downarrow e^-, \ e^- \\ \text{adrenodoxin} \longrightarrow \text{cytochrome P-450} \\ \text{A nonheme iron–sulfur protein} \quad \text{A heme b protein} \\ \downarrow \begin{matrix} e^-, \ e^- \\ O_2, -\overset{|}{\underset{|}{C}}-H, 2H^+ \end{matrix} \\ -\overset{|}{\underset{|}{C}}-OH + H_2O \end{array}$$

molecules, are involved.† These hydroxylation reactions are typical of those catalyzed by monooxygenases; i.e., one of the atoms of the oxygen molecule is introduced into the substrate while the second becomes the oxygen atom of a water molecule. The function of the associated electron-transport system is that of transferring electrons from NADPH to oxygen, as shown diagrammatically on page 531. The glycol $20(R),22(R)$-dihydroxycholesterol is then cleaved to yield pregnenolone ($3\beta$-hydroxypregn-5-ene-20-one) and isocapraldehyde. The conversion of cholesterol into pregnenolone occurs in the mitochondria in mammalian systems. In adrenal steroidogenesis this conversion is the rate-determining process.

## Conversion of Pregnenolene into Corticosteroids

The principal pathways leading to the corticosteroids entail the initial conversion of pregnenolone into progesterone as a result of the oxidation of the C(3) hydroxyl group and the isomerization of the C(5)—C(6) olefinic bond to a C(4)—C(5) olefinic bond. The latter is in conjugation with the oxo group at C(3).

Oxidation of the C(3) hydroxyl group of pregnenolone is catalyzed by $\beta$-hydroxysteroid dehydrogenase [3 (or 17) $\beta$-hydroxysteroid:NAD(P)$^+$ oxidoreductase, EC 1.1.1.51]. The isomerization is catalyzed by steroid $\Delta$-isomerase (3-oxosteroid $\Delta^4$-$\Delta^5$-isomerase, EC 5.3.3.1). These enzymes are primarily associated with the endoplasmic reticulum of mammalian adrenal-cortical cells. The reactions that are catalyzed by these enzymes are as shown.

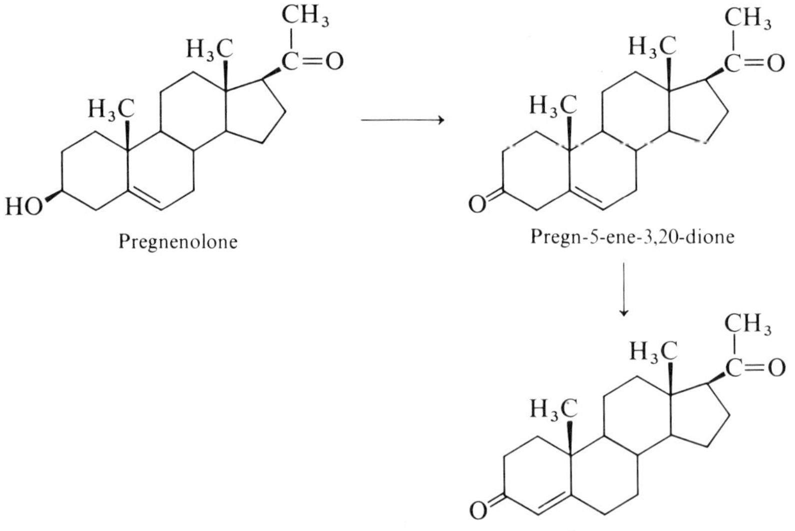

Pregnenolone → Pregn-5-ene-3,20-dione → Progesterone

In addition to serving as an intermediate in steroidogenesis, progesterone is itself a hormone. One of its principal target organs is the uterine endometrium. Progesterone, in conjunction with certain estrogens, causes an increase in the

---

† Burstein, S., Middleditch, B. S., and Gut, M. (1975) *J. Biol. Chem.* **250**, 9028–9037.

vascularity and the secretory activity of the uterine endometrium, responses that are necessary for the survival of the fertilized ovum during early pregnancy.

The conversion of progesterone into corticosteroids generally entails hydroxylation reactions. These may occur at C(11), C(17), C(18), or C(21), and they are catalyzed by specific monooxygenases. Hydroxylation reactions involved in the conversion of progesterone into corticosterone, cortisol, cortisone, or aldosterone are designated below.

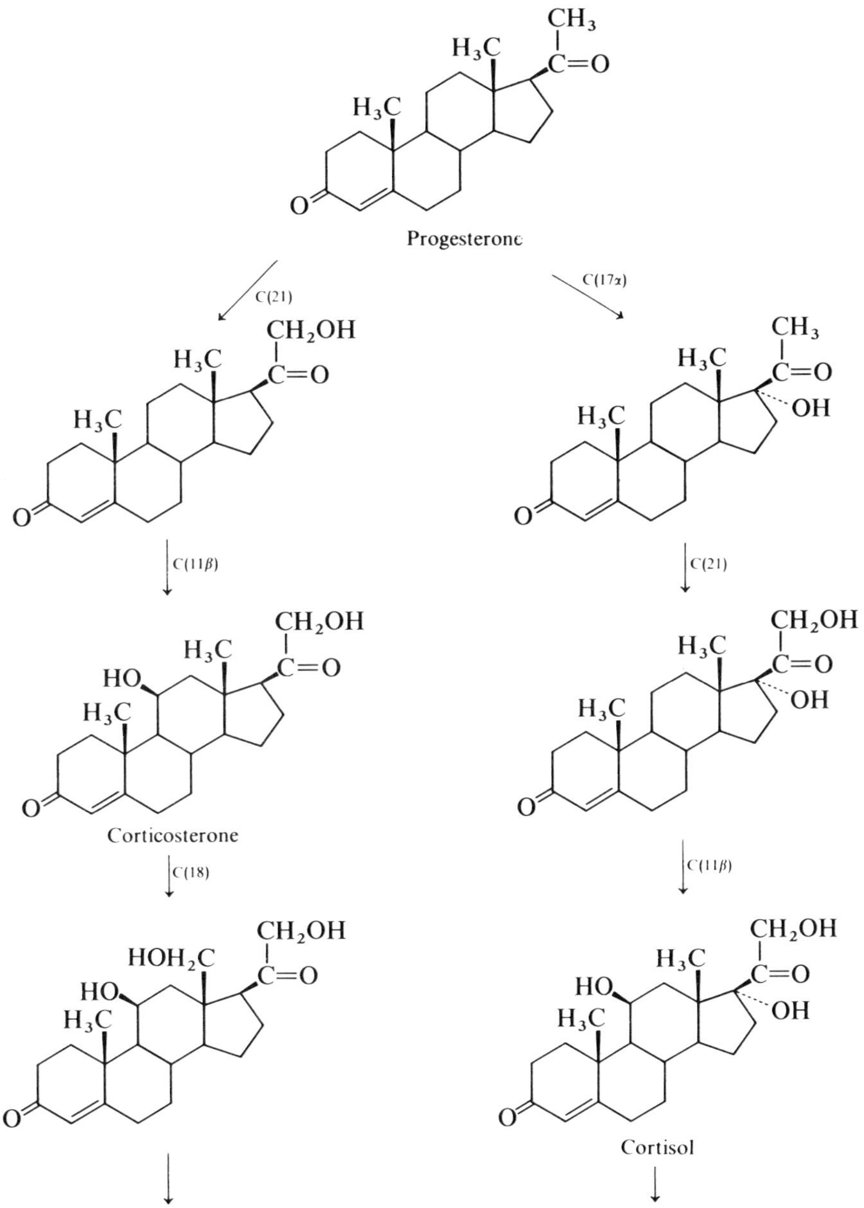

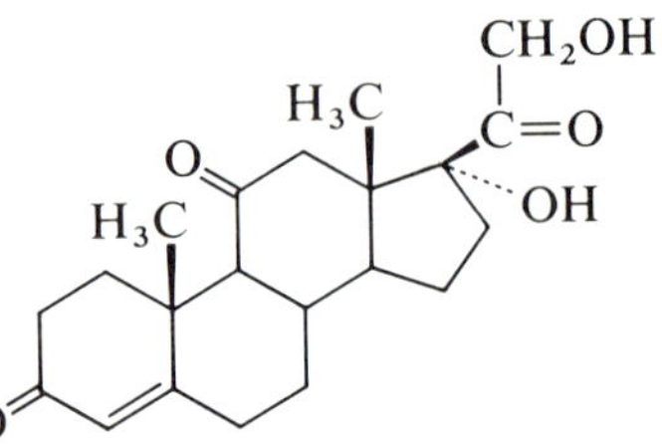

Hydroxylation at the 11β position is catalyzed by steroid 11β-monooxygenase [steroid, reduced-adrenal-ferredoxin:oxygen oxidoreductase (11β-hydroxylating), EC 1.14.15.4], an enzyme system that is localized in the mitochondrial inner membrane. The 11β-monooxygenase requires molecular oxygen and NADPH and utilizes an electron-transport system in a manner similar to that described when discussing other monooxygenases. The electron-transport system in the present case consists of ferredoxin–NADP$^+$ reductase, adrenodoxin, and a cytochrome P-450. It appears that the reductase and the nonheme iron–sulfur protein, adrenodoxin, are the same as those that participate in the side-chain cleavage. The cytochrome P-450 is different, however.

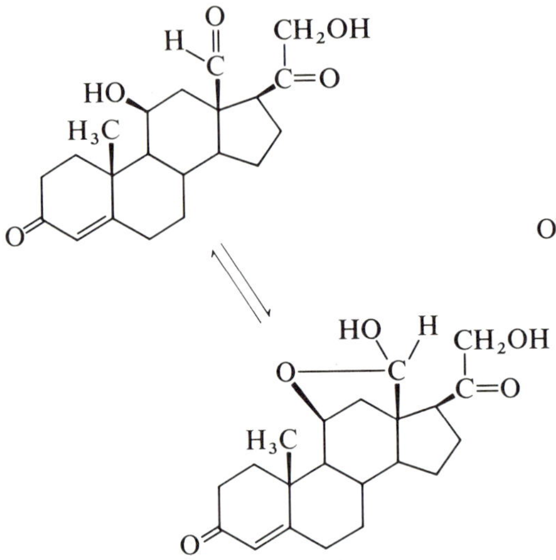

Hydroxylation at the 17α position is catalyzed by steroid 17α-monooxygenase [steroid, hydrogen-donor:oxygen oxidoreductase (17α-hydroxylating), EC 1.14.99.9], an enzyme system found in the adrenals and the testes. Certain 17α-hydroxylated steroid intermediates are precursors of the androgens.

Hydroxylation at C(18), which is involved in the synthesis of aldosterone, is catalyzed by corticosterone 18-monooxygenase [corticosterone, reduced-adrenal-ferredoxin:oxygen oxidoreductase (18-hydroxylating), EC 1.14.15.5]. This hydroxylation reaction parallels that catalyzed by the 11β-monooxygenase.

Finally, an enzyme system that catalyzes hydroxylation at C(21) has been isolated from the endoplasmic reticulum of adrenal-cortical cells. This system, steroid 21-monooxygenase [steroid, hydrogen-donor:oxygen oxidoreductase (21-hydroxylating), EC 1.14.99.10], also utilizes a cytochrome P-450, although a different one than those mentioned above is involved.

## Biosynthesis of the Androgens

The earlier steps in the conversion of pregnenolone into the androgens include 17α-hydroxylation, elimination of the substituent at the 17β position and oxidation of the 17α-hydroxyl group, and oxidation of the 3β-hydroxyl group followed by

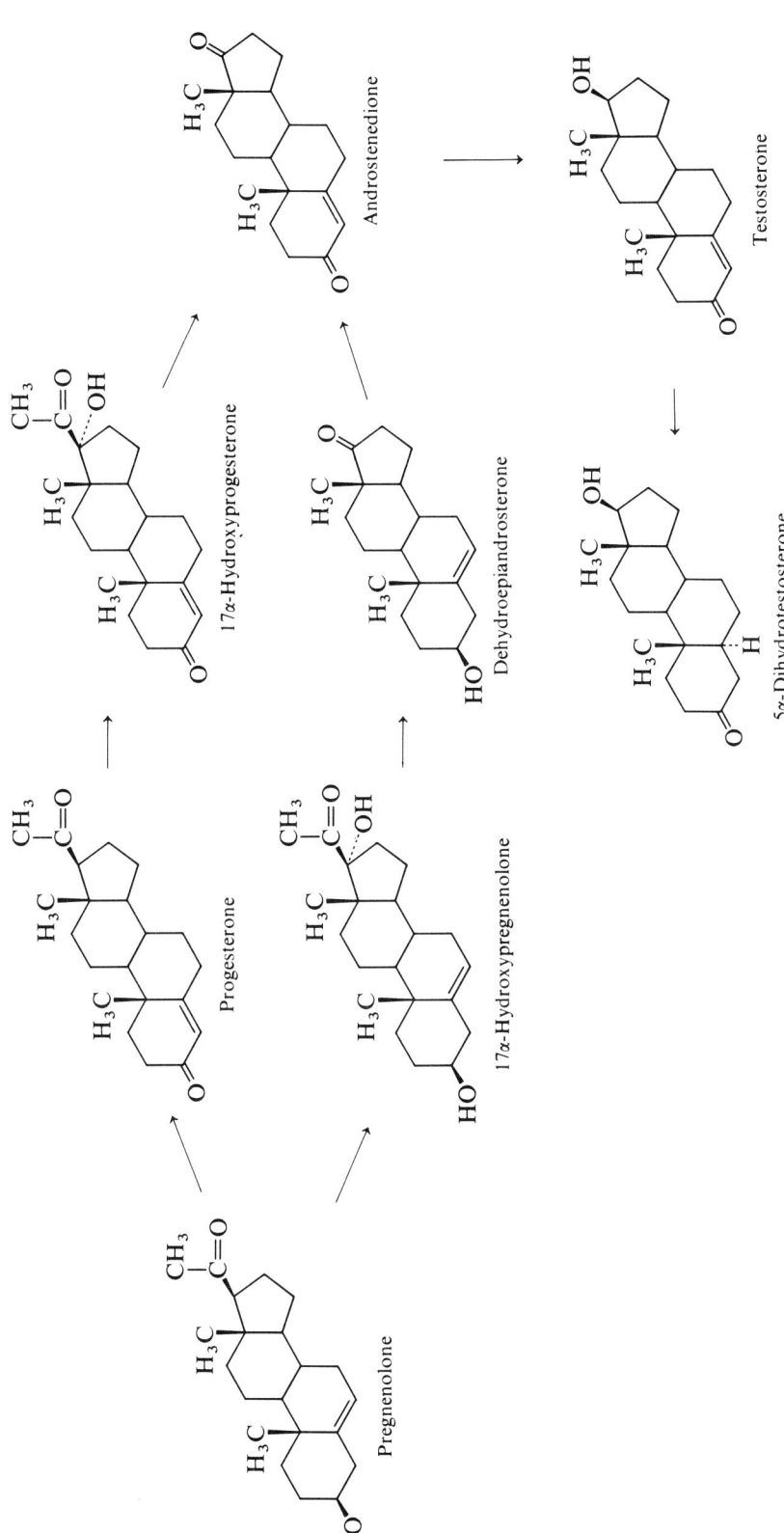

isomerization of the C(5)—C(6) double bond. The order of the occurrence of these steps may vary, however, as shown by studies on androgen synthesis in the adrenal glands, the testes, the theca and granulosa cells of the ovarian follicle, and the ovarian stroma.

Studies that employed 17α-hydroxypregnenolone in which the C(17) hydroxyl group was labeled with $^{18}O$ showed that the oxygen of the hydroxyl group at C(17) becomes the oxo group at C(17). The mechanism of the elimination of the 17β substituent and the formation of the oxo group is thought to resemble that of the cleavage of the cholesterol side chain. In the present case, the reaction utilizes molecular oxygen and NADPH, and a two-carbon fragment is eliminated as acetaldehyde.

As a result of the 17α-hydroxylation, elimination of the two-carbon fragment and formation of the C(17) oxo group, oxidation of the 3β-hydroxyl group, and isomerization of the C(5)—C(6) olefinic bond, pregnenolone is converted into androstenedione. This intermediate is, in turn, converted into testosterone as the result of a reaction that is catalyzed by testosterone 17β-dehydrogenase (17β-hydroxysteroid: $NAD^+$ 17-oxidoreductase, EC 1.1.1.63).

Although testosterone functions as a hormone with respect to certain tissues, e.g., bone and muscle, it is converted into 5α-dihydrotestosterone by others, e.g., the prostate, and it is the latter which induces the hormonal effect.

## Biosynthesis of Estrogens

The principal estrogens are derived from the androgen androstenedione. As a result of desaturation and demethylation reactions, which culminate in the aromatization of the A ring of the steroid, estrone is formed. The reaction mechanism of the aromatization has been formulated as shown.

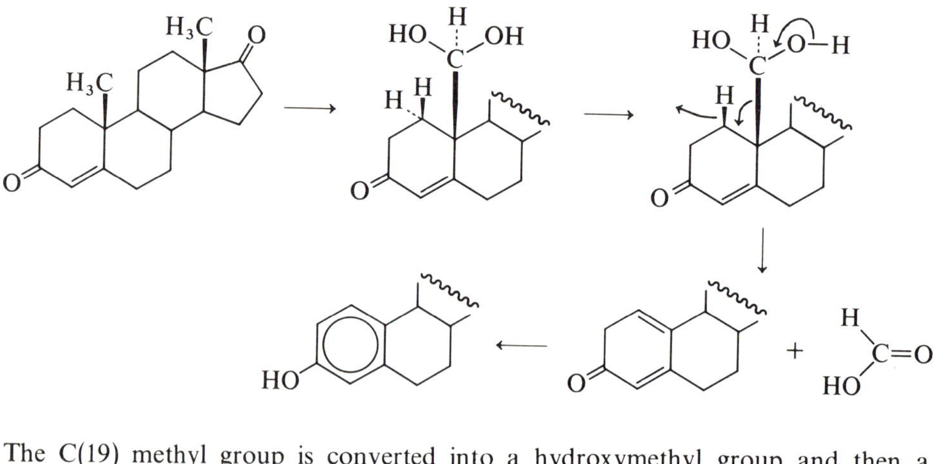

The C(19) methyl group is converted into a hydroxymethyl group and then a dihydroxymethyl group. Formate is then eliminated, and as a concomitance of the loss of a hydrogen and two electrons an olefinic bond is formed. Now tautomerization allows the aromatic ring to be generated. With the aromatization of the A ring of the steroid, estrone is formed. Estrone can be converted into 17$\beta$-estradiol in the presence of estradiol 17$\beta$-dehydrogenase (estradiol-17$\beta$:NAD$^+$ 17-oxidoreductase EC 1.1.1.62).

## Functions of Steroid Hormones

A hormone is an agent that is synthesized by an endocrine gland and, subsequently introduced into the circulation, which, in turn, transports it to a target organ. There the hormone exerts its influence upon a metabolic pathway or some other biochemical process. Included among the hormones that are derived from cholesterol, i.e., the steroid hormones, are cortisol and cortisone, which are referred to as the glucocorticoids; aldosterone, which is referred to as a mineralocorticoid; testosterone and dihydrotestosterone, which are androgens; and estradiol, which is an estrogen.

Cortisol and cortisone are called glucocorticoids because they exert influences upon carbohydrate metabolism. Specifically, cortisol and cortisone promote gluconeogenesis and hepatic glycogen deposition. They can also bring about an increase in the blood-glucose concentration. In addition, glucocorticoids can accelerate the catabolism of proteins, the hepatic uptake of amino acids, and the deamination of amino acids. The glucocorticoids also induce an anti-inflammatory response. They can inhibit the passage of leukocytes through capillary walls (diapedesis), they can inhibit granuloma formation, they can interfere with the host responses to bacterial infection, and they can suppress the delayed-sensitivity response. At supraphysiological concentrations, glucocorticoids can inhibit the inflammatory response and allergic reactions. Glucocorticoids also function as immunosuppressive agents in that they are lympholytic, i.e. they can induce a decrease in the number of circulating lymphocytes and a decrease in the size of lymph nodes, the thymus, and the spleen. In addition, glucocorticoids cause the production of antibodies to be decreased.

The cells of the liver and the thymus, which are the principal target organs for the glucocorticoids, contain cytoplasmic proteins which specifically bind these steroid hormones. These proteins are referred to as glucocorticoid receptor proteins. Many of the steroid hormones enter the cell and bind specific receptor proteins, the resulting receptor-hormone complex undergoes modification, and subsequently the modified complex is translocated across the nuclear membrane. In the nucleus, these hormone complexes promote the induction of specific enzymes or other proteins. In the case of the glucocorticoids it has been shown that the receptor-hormone complex that is present in the nucleus of (rat) hepatocytes can bind the nuclear DNA.†  Thus, it is suggested that the observed induction of protein synthesis may be the result of an interaction between the DNA that codes for that protein and the nuclear receptor-hormone complex.

Aldosterone is referred to as a mineralocorticoid because it exerts its influence upon ion transport by epithelial cells. As a result of the action of this hormone, Na$^+$

---

† Rousseau, G. G., Higgins, S. J., Baxter, J. D., Gelfand, D., and Tomkins, G. M. (1975) *J. Biol. Chem.* **250**, 6015-6021.

is conserved by the body and $K^+$ is excreted. Aldosterone is the most potent mineralocorticoid, while 11-deoxycorticosterone, which has only one-twentieth the potency of aldosterone, is the second most potent. The surface membranes of the epithelial cells of the renal tubules, sweat glands, and glands of the alimentary system have ion-transport systems which respond to the mineralocorticoids. For example, the distal convoluted tubule of the mammalian nephron embodies a transport system that promotes the reabsorption of $Na^+$ from the fluid in the lumen while promoting the introduction of $K^+$ and $H^+$ into the lumen. The activity of this transport system is enhanced by the mineralocorticoids.

The androgens are the biochemical compounds that produce and maintain the secondary sex characteristics in the adult male. The principal androgens are 5α-dihydrotestosterone and testosterone. Androgens promote the growth of the male genitalia, the development of the prostate and the seminal vesicles, the activity of the sebaceous glands, and the development of the characteristic male hair patterns. They can also induce a generalized increase in protein anabolism and in muscle mass.

Androgen receptor proteins have been isolated from the prostate and this with other data have been interpreted as indicating that a mechanism similar to that which operates in the case of the glucocorticoids also operates to facilitate the entry of dihydrotestosterone into the nucleus of the prostate cell.

Estrogens are responsible for the development and maintenance of the secondary sex characteristics of the female. These hormones promote the deposition of fat on the hips and breasts, soft skin texture, vocal-cord development that produces a higher pitch and a lighter timbre than in the male, and the characteristic female hair patterns.

In mammals the principal target organs of the estrogens are the uterus and the vagina, the cells of which contain estrogen receptor proteins. Studies on uterine cells have shown that estradiol enters the cell and initially binds a cytoplasmic protein which has a molecular weight of 80,000. The receptor-estradiol complex then associates with another protein component which has a molecular weight of 50,000 and the resulting complex, which now has a protein component with a molecular weight of 130,000, is translocated into the nucleus.† Other studies have suggested that once within the nucleus, the complex binds the chromatin and induces conformational changes which expose additional initiation sites and RNA nucleotidyltransferase binding sites. This allows an increased synthesis of specific messenger RNA molecules and, in turn, an increased synthesis of the specific proteins which correspond to the RNA messages.‡

## Regulation of the Anabolism of Steroid Hormones

Synthesis of the steroid hormones in the adrenal cortex is regulated by adrenocorticotropic hormone (ACTH), a polypeptide of 39 aminoacyl units. This poly-

---

† Notides, A. C., and Nielsen, S. (1974) *J. Biol. Chem.* **249**, 1866–1873.
‡ Schwartz, R. J., Tsai, M.-J., Tsai, S. Y., and O'Malley, B. W. (1975) *J. Biol. Chem.* **250**, 5175–5182.

peptide hormone is produced in the adenohypophysis and its target organ is the adrenal cortex. Circulating ACTH is bound by specific receptors on the surface of adrenal-cortical cells. Since the association constant for this binding process is approximately $1 \times 10^{12}$, ACTH can be very efficiently concentrated at the surface of the adrenal-cortical cell. When ACTH is bound by these cell surface receptors, and when $Ca^{2+}$ is also present, the activity of the enzyme adenylate cyclase, a component of the adrenal cell membrane, is enhanced. This enzyme catalyzes the formation of 3',5'-AMP. As a result of the enhanced activity of the membrane-associated adenylate cyclase, the intracellular concentration of 3',5'-AMP is increased. This in turn initiates a sequence of events culminating in the increased production of adrenocortical steroids. The mechanism by which this is brought about is not completely understood, but it is known that the effect of 3',5'-AMP is upon the reaction in which cholesterol is converted into pregnenolone. It is also known that the response to ACTH is rapid since both the synthesis of 3',5'-AMP and the increased synthesis of the adrenocortical steroid hormones can be demonstrated a few minutes after the tropic hormone is administered.

## CATABOLISM OF CHOLESTEROL: THE BILE ACIDS

In 1943 Bloch, Berg, and Rittenberg, then at the College of Physicians and Surgeons of Columbia University, demonstrated that in the dog the intravenous infusion of deuterium-labeled cholesterol results in the presence of deuterium-labeled cholate in the urine. Later, the work of Sune Bergstrom and his colleagues, including Bengt Samuelsson, Arne Norman, Jan Sjovall, and Henry Danielsson, at the University of Lund and at the Karolinska Institutet in Sweden, provided most of the details of the pathways by which cholesterol is converted into bile acids.

In man between 25 and 75 percent of the cholesterol that undergoes catabolism is converted into bile acids. While the remaining part is converted into neutral 27-carbon sterols such as coprostanol (5$\beta$-cholestan-3$\beta$-ol). Both the bile acids and the neutral sterols are excreted in the feces. The conversion of cholesterol into neutral sterols is usually carried out by the microorganisms of the intestinal tract. The conversion of cholesterol into cholate and chenodeoxycholate, two of the principal bile acids, occurs in the liver while the third of the principal bile acids, deoxycholate, is a product of intestinal microorganisms.

### Formation of Cholate and Chenodeoxycholate

The conversion of cholesterol into cholate and to chenodeoxycholate entails hydroxylation, saturation of an olefinic bond, epimerization at C(3), and the partial degradation of the side chain at C(17). The major pathways for the formation of these components are illustrated on pages 540 and 541.

The hydroxylation reactions at C(7) and C(12) are catalyzed by monooxygenases associated with the endoplasmic reticulum of the hepatocyte. As in cases previously discussed, these monooxygenases require molecular oxygen and NADPH

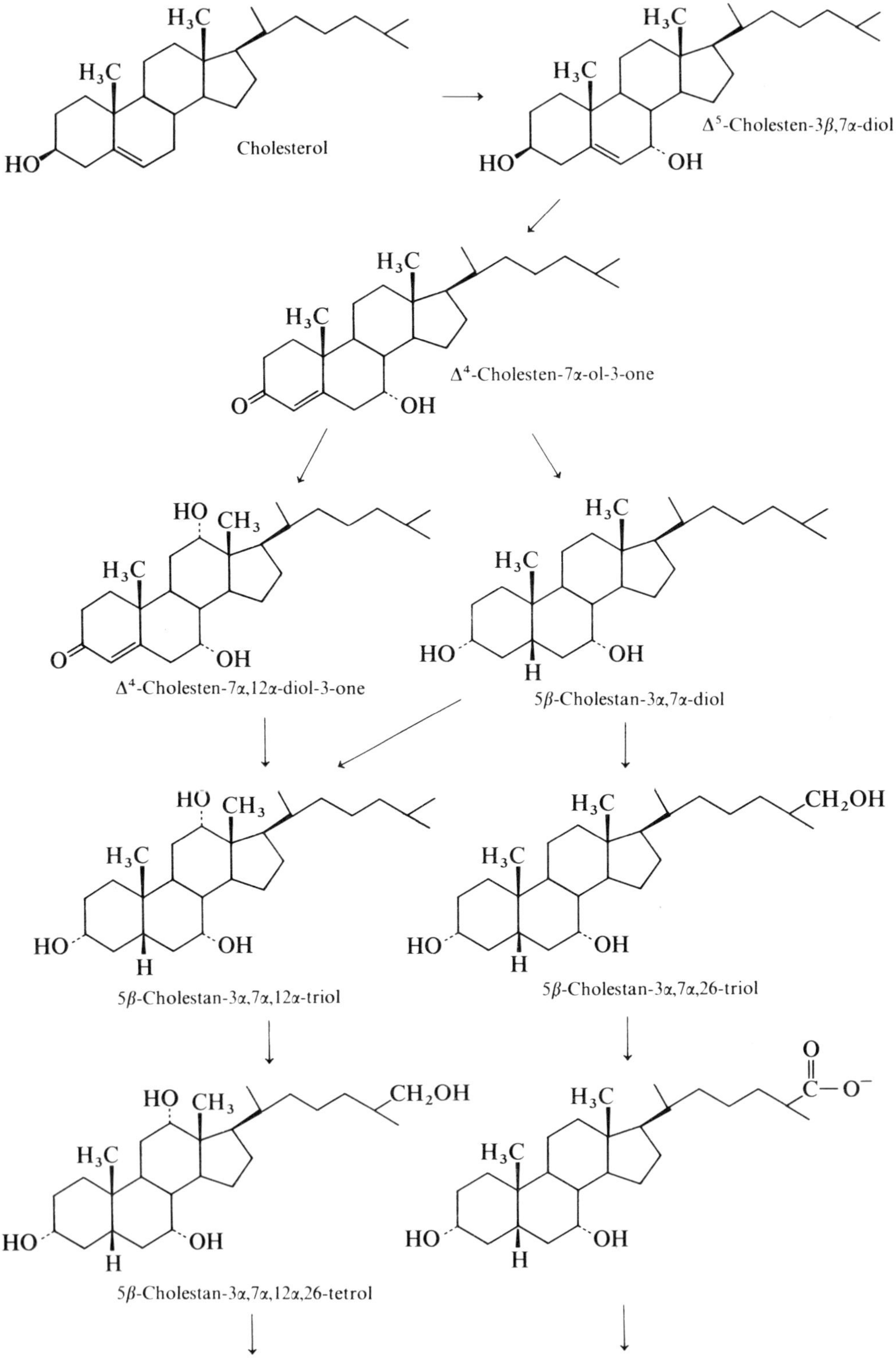

**540** MECHANISMS OF METABOLISM

Cholesterol

$\Delta^5$-Cholesten-3$\beta$,7$\alpha$-diol

$\Delta^4$-Cholesten-7$\alpha$-ol-3-one

$\Delta^4$-Cholesten-7$\alpha$,12$\alpha$-diol-3-one

5$\beta$-Cholestan-3$\alpha$,7$\alpha$-diol

5$\beta$-Cholestan-3$\alpha$,7$\alpha$,12$\alpha$-triol

5$\beta$-Cholestan-3$\alpha$,7$\alpha$,26-triol

5$\beta$-Cholestan-3$\alpha$,7$\alpha$,12$\alpha$,26-tetrol

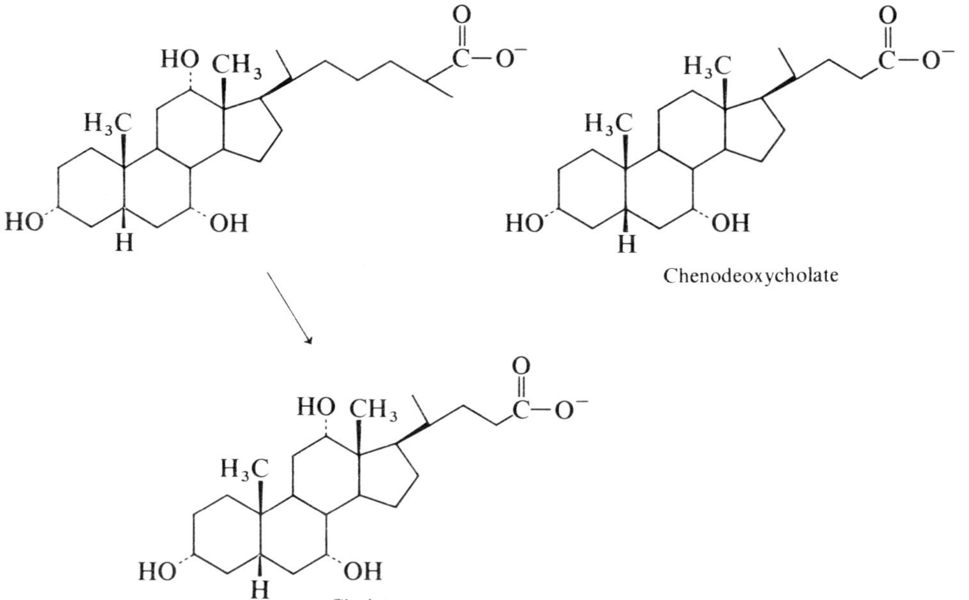

and an electron-transport system which includes a flavoprotein capable of accepting electrons from NADPH, a nonheme iron–sulfur protein, and cytochrome P-450. The introduction of the 7α-hydroxyl group is the rate-determining step in the conversion of cholesterol into cholate or chenodeoxycholate.

Hydroxylation at C(26) can be catalyzed by a mitochondrial monooxygenase or by a monooxygenase associated with the endoplasmic reticulum. In man, this hydroxylation reaction occurs primarily in the mitochondria. The reaction catalyzed by the mitochondrial monooxygenase appears to parallel other hydroxylation reactions catalyzed by monooxygenases. One atom of molecular oxygen is inserted into the substate, and the other becomes the oxygen atom of a water molecule. NADPH is required as the oxidation-reduction cofactor. The components of the supporting electron-transport system have not yet been identified. Conversion of the C(26) hydroxymethyl group into a carboxylate group entails successive oxidation reactions catalyzed by an alcohol dehydrogenase and an aldehyde dehydrogenase, respectively.

The elimination of C(25), C(26), and C(27) also involves a hydroxylation reaction, but in this instance a monooxygenase is not involved. The cleavage has been formulated in terms of a desaturation reaction followed by a hydration reaction that introduces a hydroxyl group at C(24).† Presumably, this secondary alcohol group is oxidized to yield an oxo group, and subsequently C(25), C(26), and C(27) are eliminated as propionate.

---

† Gustafsson, J. (1975) *J. Biol. Chem.* **250**, 8243–8247.

## Formation of Deoxycholate and Lithocholate

The microorganisms of the intestine can modify the structures of the bile acids. One of the principal modifications is the removal of the 7α-hydroxyl group. When the 7α-hydroxyl group is eliminated from cholate, deoxycholate is formed. When the 7α-hydroxyl group is eliminated from chenodeoxycholate, lithocholate is formed. Deoxycholate and lithocholate can subsequently be returned to the liver by the enterohepatic circulation.

## Conjugation of Bile Acids

Following their synthesis, the bile acids are converted into the corresponding glycine or taurine amides. It is, in fact, these conjugates that are excreted in the bile.

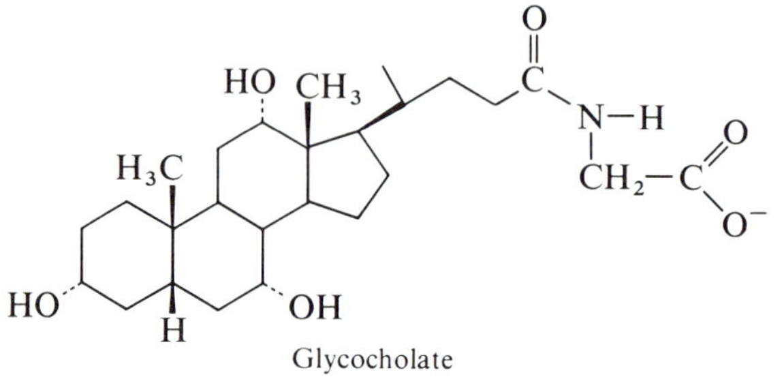

Glycocholate

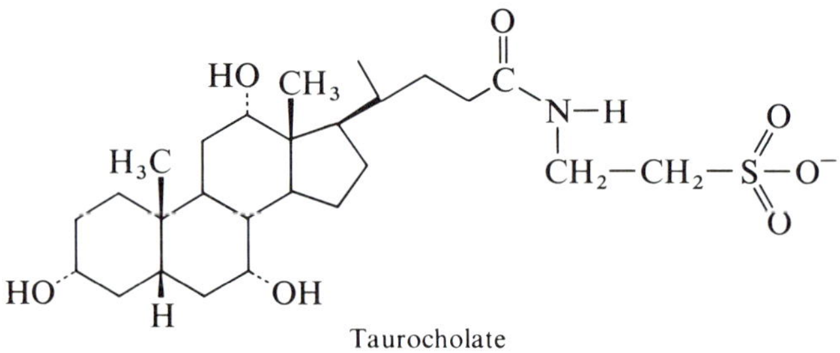

Taurocholate

CHAPTER
# THIRTEEN

## METABOLISM OF PURINES, PYRIMIDINES, AND NUCLEIC ACIDS

Unlike the carbohydrates, lipids, and proteins, the nucleic acids are not catabolized to obtain usable chemical energy. Rather, the prime function of the nucleic acids is that of retaining and transferring genetic information. This chapter focuses upon the metabolism of the components of the nucleic acids, i.e., the purines and pyrimidines, the metabolism of the nucleic acids themselves, and some aspects of the manner in which nucleic acids participate in the transfer of genetic information.

## PURINE ANABOLISM

The *de novo* synthesis of the purine nucleus requires a sequence of 11 reactions which allow carbon atoms from glycine, formate, and carbon dioxide and nitrogen atoms from glutamine, glycine, and aspartate to be utilized for the construction of the bicyclic nitrogen heterocycle.

### Step 1: Formation of 5-Phospho-α-D-Ribose 1-Diphosphate

The initial reaction of the *de novo* synthesis of the purine nucleus can be considered to be the formation of phosphoribose diphosphate although the reaction is not unique to this pathway. The reaction requires a nucleoside triphosphate, as do the initial reactions of glycogen synthesis, fatty acid synthesis, and protein synthesis, and it is catalyzed by ribosephosphate diphosphotransferase (ATP:D-ribose-5-phosphate diphosphotransferase, EC 2.7.6.1). The formation of phosphoribose diphosphate can be written

ATP + D-ribose 5-phosphate $\rightleftharpoons$

AMP + 5-phospho-$\alpha$-D-ribose 1-diphosphate     (13-1)

Ribosephosphate diphosphotransferase has been isolated from a wide variety of sources, including human erythrocytes, avian liver, and *Salmonella typhimurium;* the enzyme is obtained in multiple states of aggregation in all cases. Generally, enzyme subunits which have molecular weights of 30,000 to 35,000 can be isolated under denaturing conditions, but the size of the smallest catalytically active diphosphotransferase is unknown. Enzyme species known to be catalytically active have molecular weights of 700,000 to 1.2 million.

Kinetic studies on ribosephosphate diphosphotransferase have demonstrated that the reaction proceeds by means of a sequential mechanism. When product-inhibition studies were conducted on the erythrocyte enzyme, AMP was found to be a noncompetitive inhibitor with either ATP or ribose 5-phosphate as the variable substrate (in the presence of a single concentration of the other substrate). Phosphoribose diphosphate, on the other hand, was found to be a noncompetitive inhibitor when ATP was varied and a competitive inhibitor when ribose 5-phosphate was varied. These data are compatible with an ordered sequential mechanism in which ribose 5-phosphate is the initial substrate that binds the enzyme and phosphoribose diphosphate is the final product released. Data derived from studies using ADP as a dead-end inhibitor are at variance with this formulation, however, since ADP is a competitive inhibitor with respect to ATP and a noncompetitive inhibitor with respect to ribose 5-phosphate.† If ADP binds the enzyme form that is usually bound by ATP (or that usually bound by AMP), it would be expected to be an *uncompetitive* inhibitor when ribose 5-phosphate is varied since it binds at a point in the reaction sequence that is subsequent to that at which the variable substrate binds. In an ordered sequential Bi Bi mechanism a dead-end inhibitor that binds the enzyme subsequent to the binding of the variable substrate does not produce a slope effect. It produces only an intercept effect. Thus, uncompetitive inhibition is observed.

Kinetic studies were also conducted on ribosephosphate diphosphotransferase from the microorganism *Salmonella typhimurium;* here AMP was found to be a noncompetitive inhibitor when either ATP or ribose 5-phosphate was the variable substrate, and phosphoribose diphosphate functioned as a competitive inhibitor vs. ATP and a noncompetitive inhibitor vs. ribose 5-phosphate. When the influence of the dead-end inhibitor, ADP, was determined, it was found that with ATP as the variable substrate and with a single sub-saturating concentration of ribose 5-phosphate, the inhibition pattern was noncompetitive. Subsequently, in an effort to gain additional insight into the kinetic mechanism of the reaction, the reverse reaction was examined. In the reverse reaction, it should be remembered, phosphoribose diphosphate and AMP are the substrates, and ribose 5-phosphate

---

† Fox, I. H., and Kelley, W. N. (1972) *J. Biol. Chem.* **247**, 2126-2131.

and ATP are the products. With ADP as the inhibitor of the reverse reaction and phosphoribose diphosphate as the variable substrate and with a single low concentration of the second substrate, AMP, noncompetitive inhibition was observed. However, when phosphoribose diphosphate was varied and a single high concentration of AMP was employed, ADP functioned as a competitive inhibitor.† These data derived from the studies on ribosephosphate diphosphotransferase from the microorganism can be interpreted in terms of an ordered sequential Bi Bi mechanism in which ATP is the initial substrate that binds the enzyme and phosphoribose diphosphate is the final product released. The observation that ADP functions as a noncompetitive inhibitor when ATP is the variable substrate can be rationalized if it is assumed that ADP can bind both the enzyme form that is bound by ATP and another enzyme form. The data derived from the study on the reverse reaction show that ADP not only binds the noncomplexed enzyme but also the enzyme–phosphoribose diphosphate complex when a low concentration of the second substrate, AMP, is used. However, when a high concentration of AMP is used, the inhibitor can bind only the noncomplexed enzyme. The reaction might therefore be represented diagrammatically as shown.

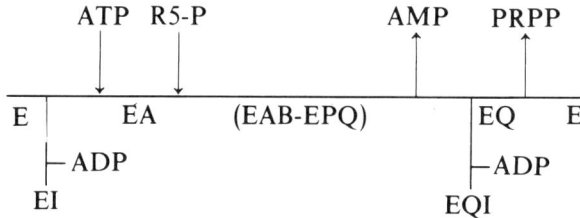

The data obtained from the product-inhibition studies on the erythrocyte enzyme could reflect the operation of a different kinetic mechanism or the ability of phosphoribose diphosphate to bind both the noncomplexed enzyme and another enzyme form when ATP is varied but only the enzyme–ATP complex when ribose 5-phosphate is varied under the conditions of these studies. In addition to this, the data on the inhibitory effect of ADP might be rationalized if the inhibitor bound only the noncomplexed enzyme. Such variability in the behavior of the components of this reaction might be due to the fact that all are structurally similar, i.e., each is a ribose phosphate or a ribose phosphate derivative.

The formation of phosphoribose diphosphate as the result of the transfer of a diphosphoryl moiety from ATP to the other substrate is one of the three reactions known to proceed in this manner. Generally, in reactions in which the triphosphate moiety of a nucleoside triphosphate is cleaved, a nucleophilic species attacks either the $\alpha$- or the $\gamma$-phosphoryl phosphorus atom, and either the pyrophosphate anion or ADP becomes the leaving group. However, in order to transfer the diphosphoryl moiety to a substrate, the nucleophilic attack must be upon the $\beta$-phosphoryl phosphorus atom, as shown in the minimal reaction mechanism on page 546.

† Switzer, R. L. (1971) *J. Biol. Chem.* **246,** 2447–2458; Switzer, R. L., and Sogin, D. C. (1973) *J. Biol. Chem.* **248,** 1063–1073.

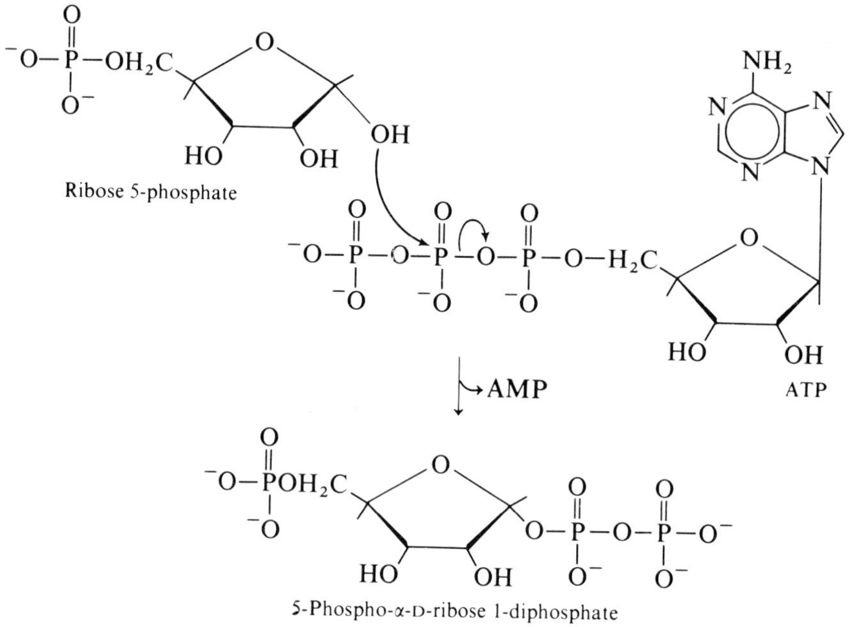

[Structural diagram: Ribose 5-phosphate + ATP → 5-Phospho-α-D-ribose 1-diphosphate + AMP]

## Step 2: Conversion of 5-Phospho-α-D-Ribose 1-Diphosphate into 5-Phospho-β-D-Ribosylamine

The first reaction unique to purine anabolism is the formation of phosphoribosylamine. The amino group is derived from the amide nitrogen of glutamine. The reaction is catalyzed by amidophosphoribosyltransferase [5-phosphoribosylamine:pyrophosphate phosphoribosyltransferase (glutamate-amidating), EC 2.4.2.14] and can be written

5-Phospho-α-D-ribose 1-diphosphate + L-glutamine + $H_2O$ ⇌

$\qquad$ 5-phospho-β-D-ribosylamine + L-glutamate + $PP_i$ $\qquad$ (13-2)

Amidophosphoribosyltransferases have been isolated from such widely divergent sources as human placental tissue, human lymphoblasts, murine spleen, an adenocarcinoma, the yeast *Schizosaccharomyces pombe*, and *Aerobacter aerogenes*. The enzyme activity has been shown to be localized in the cytoplasm of the mammalian cells. The enzyme amidophosphoribosyltransferase from the human placenta exists in two interconvertible forms. The larger form has a molecular weight of 270,000, while the smaller has a molecular weight of 135,000. In the absence of the substrate phosphoribose diphosphate and the ultimate products of this anabolic pathway, the purine ribonucleotides, the smaller and the larger species, can coexist. Purine ribonucleotides promote the conversion of the smaller species into the larger one, while phosphoribose diphosphate promotes the conversion of the larger species into the smaller one. The smaller protein is, in fact, the catalytically active enzyme, while the larger protein is subactive or inactive.

On the basis of incomplete kinetic studies, it appears that the formation of phosphoribosylamine occurs by a sequential mechanism. With respect to the reaction mechanism, it might be speculated that the diphosphate group at C(1) is eliminated as the pyrophosphate anion and then the resulting electron-deficient species accepts an amino group from glutamine while the latter is converted into glutamate. The overall process results in a change in configuration at C(1) of the ribose moiety.

### Step 3: Formation of 5-Phosphoribosylglycinamide

Phosphoribosylamine is now converted into 5-phosphoribosylglycinamide. The reaction, which can be written

ATP + 5-phosphoribosylamine + glycine $\rightleftharpoons$
$$5\text{-phosphoribosylglycinamide} + \text{ADP} + P_i \quad (13\text{-}3)$$

is catalyzed by phosphoribosylglycinamide synthetase [5-phosphoribosylamine: glycine ligase (ADP-forming), EC 6.3.4.13]. In general, carboxylic acids (or carboxylate groups) and amines do not form amides unless energy is provided. In the present case, this energy is derived as a result of the cleavage of ATP to yield ADP and orthophosphate. A concerted reaction mechanism is suggested.

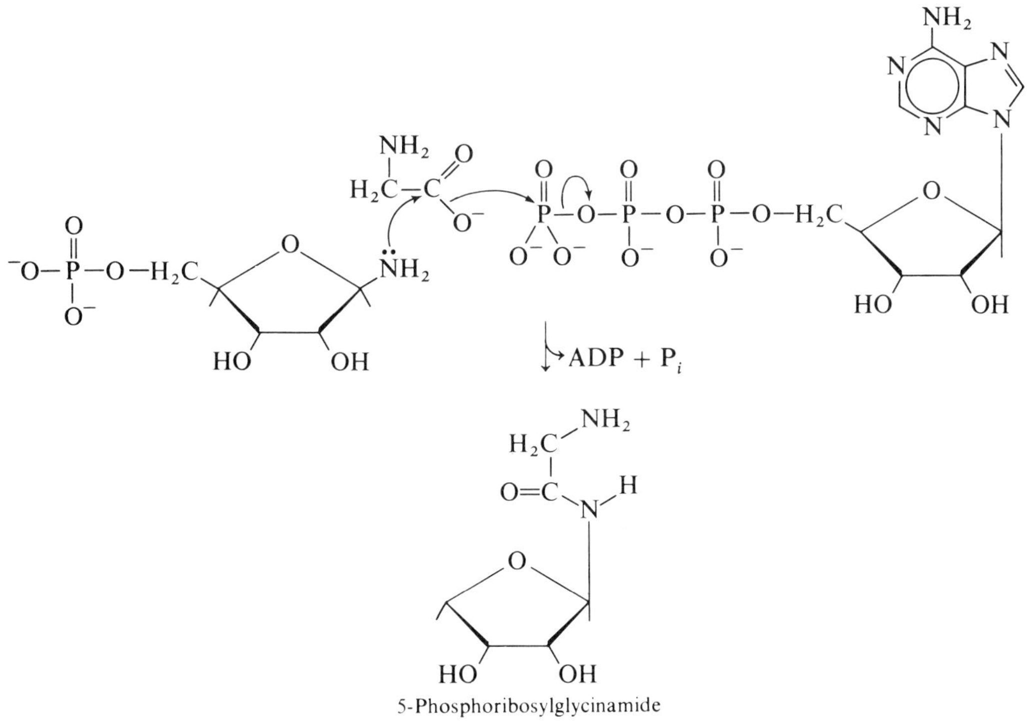

5-Phosphoribosylglycinamide

## Step 4: Conversion of 5-Phosphoribosylglycinamide into 5-Phosphoribosyl-N-Formylglycinamide

In this step of the anabolic pathway, the amino group of the glycinamide moiety undergoes a formylation reaction catalyzed by phosphoribosylglycinamide formyltransferase (5,10-methenyltetrahydrofolate:5′-phosphoribosylglycinamide formyltransferase, EC 2.1.2.2). The formyl donor is 5,10-methenyltetrahydrofolate, a substituted form of the cofactor tetrahydrolate. Tetrahydrofolate is derived from the vitamin folate.

The cofactor can be substituted at N(5), N(10), or both positions (by means of cyclic structures) with a carbon atom that is at the oxidation level of that of formate, or formaldehyde, or a hydroxymethyl group. (Remember that a nitrogen atom is essentially equivalent to an oxygen atom when one is considering the oxidation level of a carbon atom covalently bonded to either or both.) Tetrahydrofolate cofactors and their one-carbon substituents will be discussed in greater detail in Chap. 14. In the present case, a carbon atom at the oxidation level of that

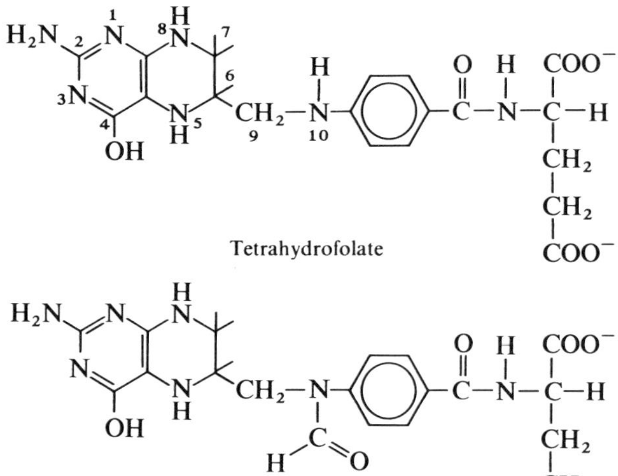

Tetrahydrofolate

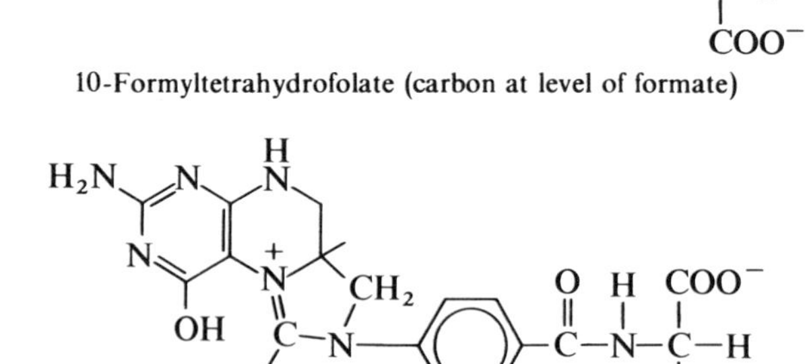

10-Formyltetrahydrofolate (carbon at level of formate)

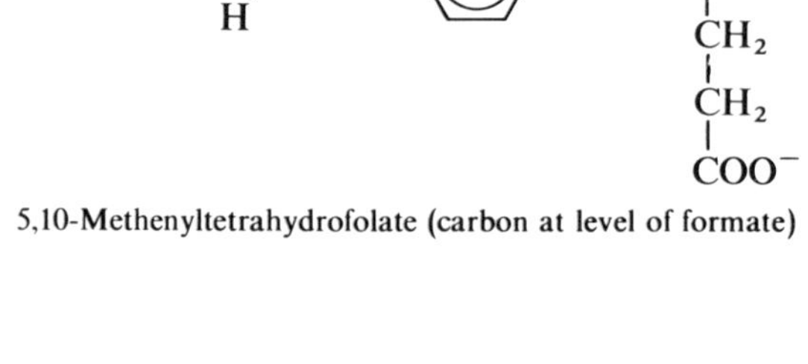

5,10-Methenyltetrahydrofolate (carbon at level of formate)

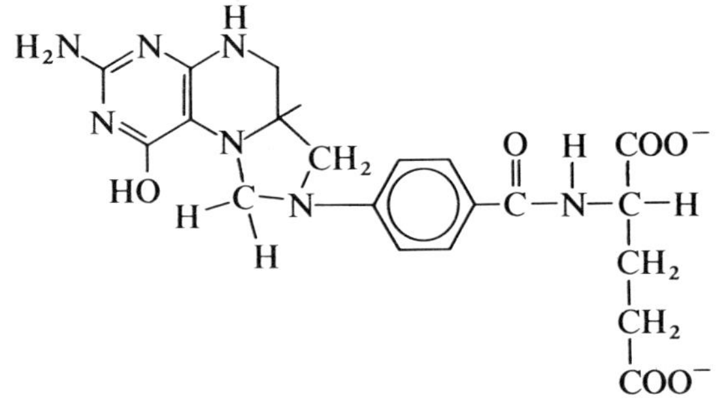

5,10-Methylenetetrahydrofolate (carbon at level of formaldehyde)

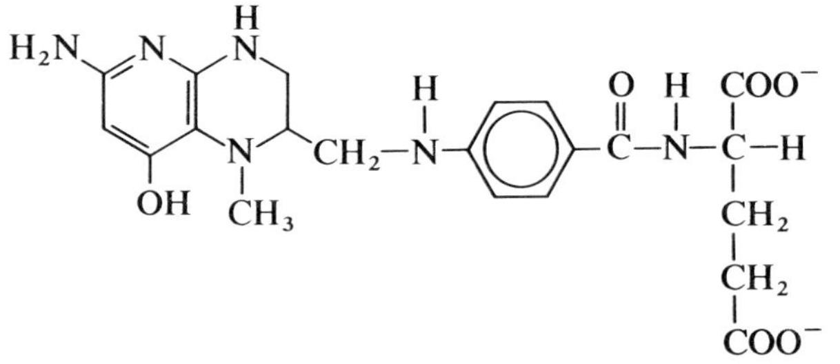

5-Methyltetrahydrofolate (carbon at level of hydroxymethyl group)

of formate is transferred to the amino nitrogen atom of the glycinamide moiety. The reaction can be written

5,10-Methenyltetrahydrofolate + 5-phosphoribosylglycinamide $\rightleftharpoons$
5-phosphoribosyl-$N$-formylglycinamide + tetrahydrofolate  (13-4)

Mechanistically, it might be formulated as shown.

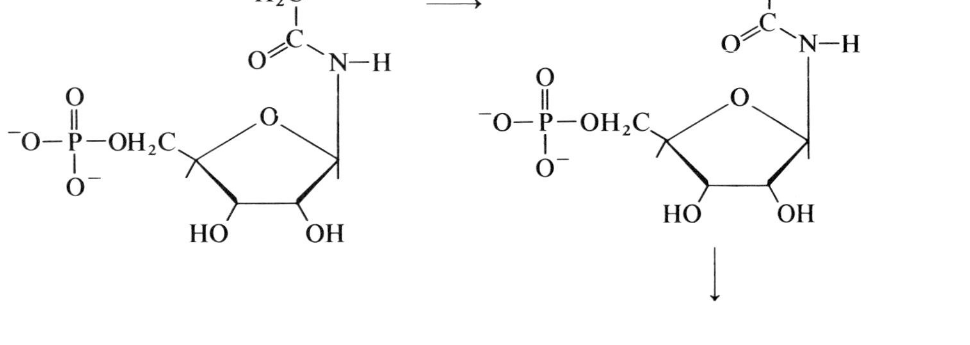

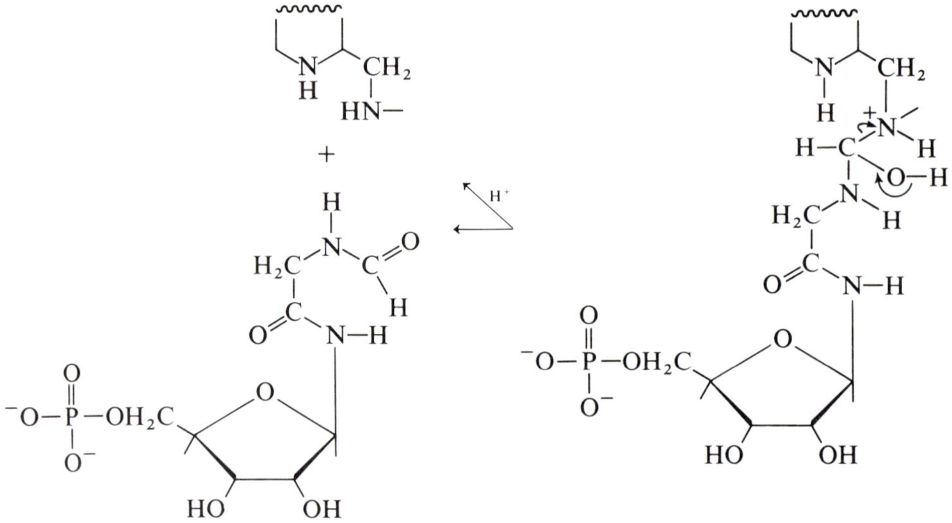

5-Phosphoribosyl-$N$-formylglycinamide

## Step 5: Formation of 5-Phosphoribosylformylglycinamidine

Now the glycinamide moiety is converted into a glycinamidine moiety. The nitrogen atom required is again derived from the amide moiety of glutamine. Phosphoribosylformylglycinamidine synthetase [5-phosphoribosylformylglycinamide:L-glutamine amido-ligase (ADP-forming), EC 6.3.5.3] catalyzes the reaction, which is

ATP + 5-phosphoribosylformylglycinamide + L-glutamine + $H_2O$ ⇌
5-phosphoribosylformylglycinamidine + L-glutamate + ADP + $P_i$   (13-5)

This synthetase enzyme has been isolated from chicken liver as a protein having a molecular weight of 133,000. Initial-velocity studies on this enzyme indicate that the reaction proceeds by a sequential mechanism. In an attempt to learn more about the substrate binding, studies were conducted in which one substrate was varied, a second was used at several fixed concentrations, and the third was used at a single saturating concentration. In the case of a Ter-reactant sequential mechanism, if one varies the concentration of the initial substrate that binds and uses fixed concentrations of the third substrate that binds, with a single saturating concentration of the second substrate that binds, the double reciprocal plots of $1/v_i$ vs. $1/[A]$ will be parallel. This is because a saturating concentration of a substrate that binds at a point in the reaction sequence that is between that at which the variable substrate binds and that at which the fixed substrate binds interposes an irreversible step. Thus, just as in a ping pong mechanism when a product is released (under initial-velocity conditions) prior to the binding of the second substrate, parallel double reciprocal plots are obtained. In the present case, when phosphoribosylformylglycinamide was the variable substrate with fixed concentrations of ATP and a saturating concentration of glutamine, the double reciprocal plots were intersecting. However, when glutamine was varied with fixed concentrations of phosphoribosylglycinamide and a saturating concentration of ATP, parallel double reciprocal plots were obtained. Also, when ATP was the variable substrate with fixed concentrations of glutamine and a single saturating concentration of phosphoribosylformylglycinamide, parallel double reciprocal plots were again obtained. These observations were interpreted as indicating a partially ordered, partially random binding of the substrates. Since ATP can bind the enzyme at a point in the reaction sequence that is between those at which glutamine and phosphoribosylformylglycinamide bind, and since phosphoribosylformylglycinamide can bind at a point in the reaction sequence that is between those at which ATP and glutamine bind, the binding of the substrates was formulated as shown.†

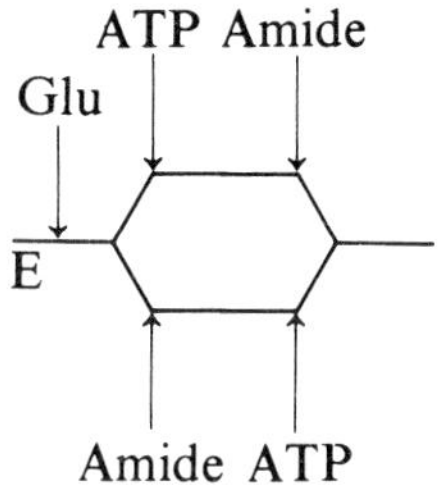

$$\begin{array}{c} \text{ATP Amide} \\ \text{Glu} \downarrow \downarrow \\ \text{E} \longrightarrow \bigcirc \\ \uparrow \uparrow \\ \text{Amide ATP} \end{array}$$

This formulation was supported by product-inhibition studies and by studies using substrate analogs. As an example of the latter, when the glutamine analog albizzin was used as an inhibitor with either ATP or phosphoribosylformylglycinamide as the variable substrate, a noncompetitive pattern was obtained.

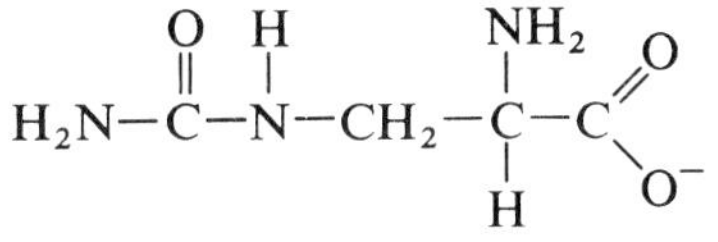

$$H_2N-\overset{O}{\underset{\|}{C}}-\overset{H}{\underset{|}{N}}-CH_2-\overset{NH_2}{\underset{|}{\underset{H}{C}}}-C\overset{O}{\underset{O^-}{\diagdown}}$$

L-Albizzin

Thus it is indicated that glutamine binds the enzyme prior to either ATP or phosphoribosylformylglycinamide. (A slope effect is seen in the presence of a dead-end inhibitor that binds a different enzyme form than the variable substrate only when it binds prior to the binding of the variable substrate.) Albizzin is one of several structural analogs of glutamine which have been tested as antitumor agents.

A suggested reaction mechanism for the formation of phosphoribosylformylglycinamidine is shown on page 552. There is some evidence that a sulfhydryl group at the catalytic site participates in the reaction.

† Li, H.-C., and Buchanan, J. M. (1971) *J. Biol. Chem.* **246**, 4720–4726.

5-Phosphoribosylformylglycinamidine

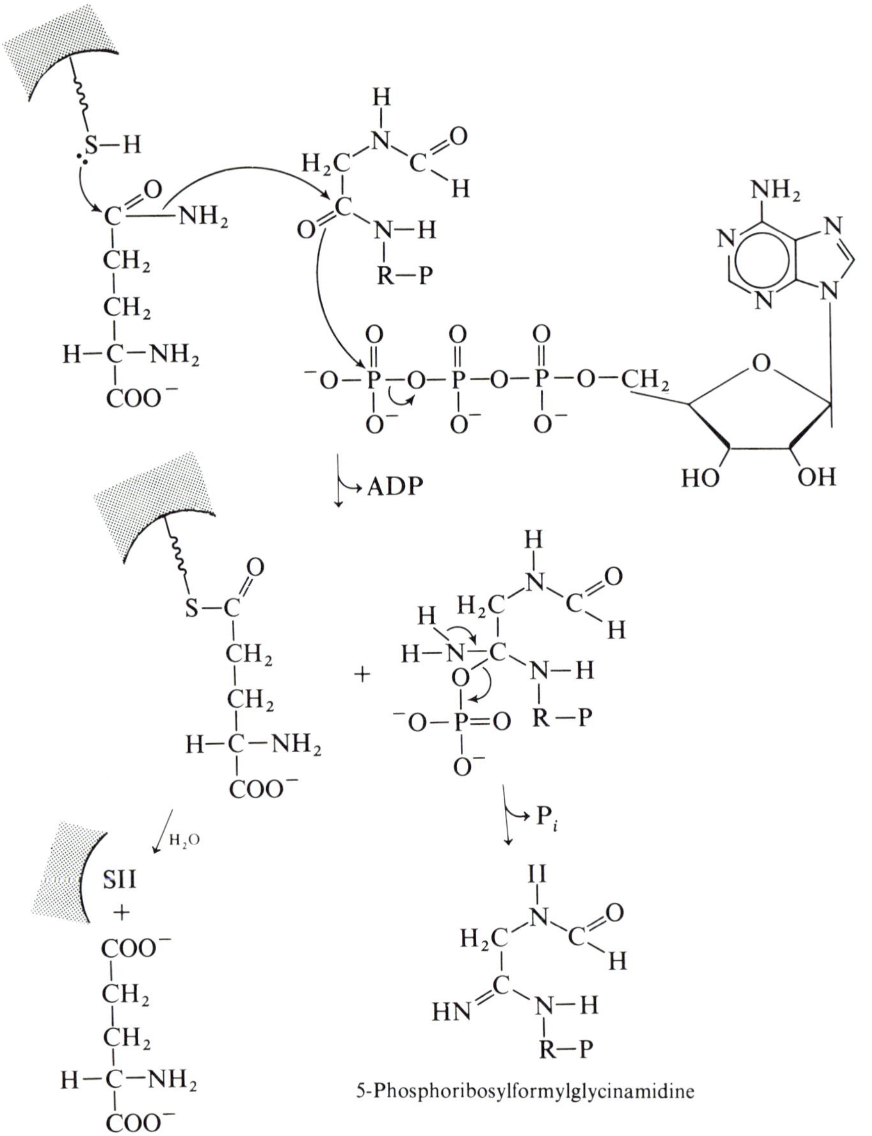

### Step 6: Formation of Phosphoribosylaminoimidazole

The imidazole ring of the purine nucleus is now formed by a reaction which also involves the cleavage of ATP. This reaction is catalyzed by phosphoribosylaminoimidazole synthetase [5-phosphoribosylformylglycinamidine cyclo-ligase (ADP-forming), EC 6.3.3.1]. The reaction is

$$\text{ATP} + \text{5-phosphoribosylformylglycinamidine} \rightleftharpoons \text{5}'\text{-phosphoribosyl-5-aminoimidazole} + \text{ADP} + P_i \quad (13\text{-}6)$$

This cyclization might be considered to be the reaction of an amidine nitrogen atom and a carbonyl group. The reader should be able to write a minimal reaction mechanism for the formation of phosphoribosylaminoimidazole on this basis. The precise role of the cleavage of ATP is unknown in this case. (One might speculate that it is involved in making the carbonyl group more reactive, however.)

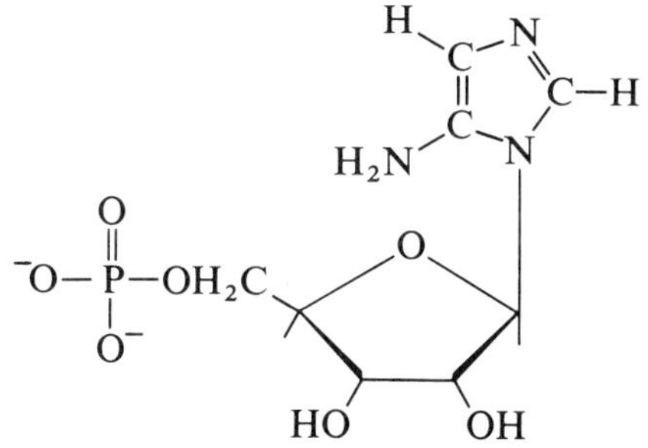

5'-Phosphoribosyl-5-aminoimidazole

## Step 7: Carboxylation of Phosphoribosylaminoimidazole

The pyrimidine moiety of the purine nucleus is now developed. In this step of the anabolic pathway, the carbon atom that will become C(6) of the purine ring is introduced by a carboxylation reaction. The reaction is

5'-Phosphoribosyl-5-aminoimidazole + $CO_2$ ⇌

$\qquad$ 5'-phosphoribosyl-5-amino-4-imidazolecarboxylate   (13-7)

and it is catalyzed by phosphoribosylaminoimidazole carboxylase (5'-phosphoribosyl-5-amino-4-imidazolecarboxylate carboxy-lyase, EC 4.1.1.21). The carboxylation does not utilize either ATP or biotin. A suggested minimal reaction mechanism is shown below.

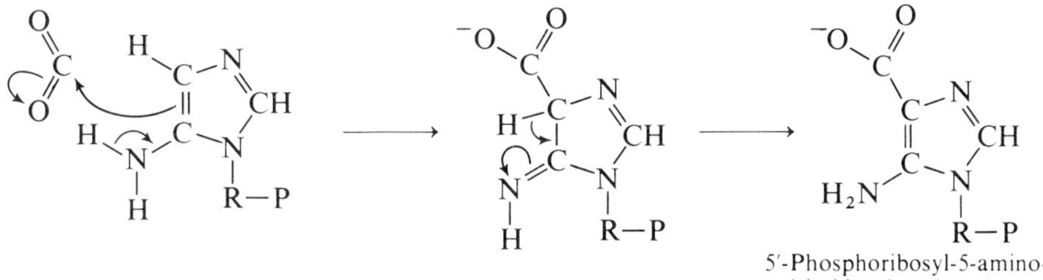

5'-Phosphoribosyl-5-amino-4-imidazolecarboxylate

## Step 8: Formation of 5'-Phosphoribosyl-4-(N-Succinocarboxamide)-5-Aminoimidazole

The fourth and final nitrogen atom of the purine nucleus is derived from aspartate. The amino group of aspartate and the carboxyl group of the imidazolecarboxylate moiety react, in the presence of ATP, to form an amide bond. Subsequently, fumarate is eliminated from the resulting intermediate and the carboxylate group of the imidazolecarboxylate moiety is concomitantly converted into a carboxamide group. The reaction between 5′-phosphoribosyl-5-amino-4-imidazolecarboxylate and aspartate is catalyzed by phosphoribosylaminoimidazole-succinocarboxamide synthetase [5′-phosphoribosyl-4-carboxy-5-aminoimidazole:L-aspartate ligase (ADP-forming), EC 6.3.2.6]. The reaction is

ATP + 5′-phosphoribosyl-5-amino-4-imidazolecarboxylate

$+$ L-aspartate $\rightleftharpoons$ 5′-phosphoribosyl-4-(N-succinocarboxamide)-

5-aminoimidazole + ADP + $P_i$ (13-8)

The reaction mechanism is thought to be similar to that of the reaction catalyzed by phosphoribosylglycinamide synthetase.

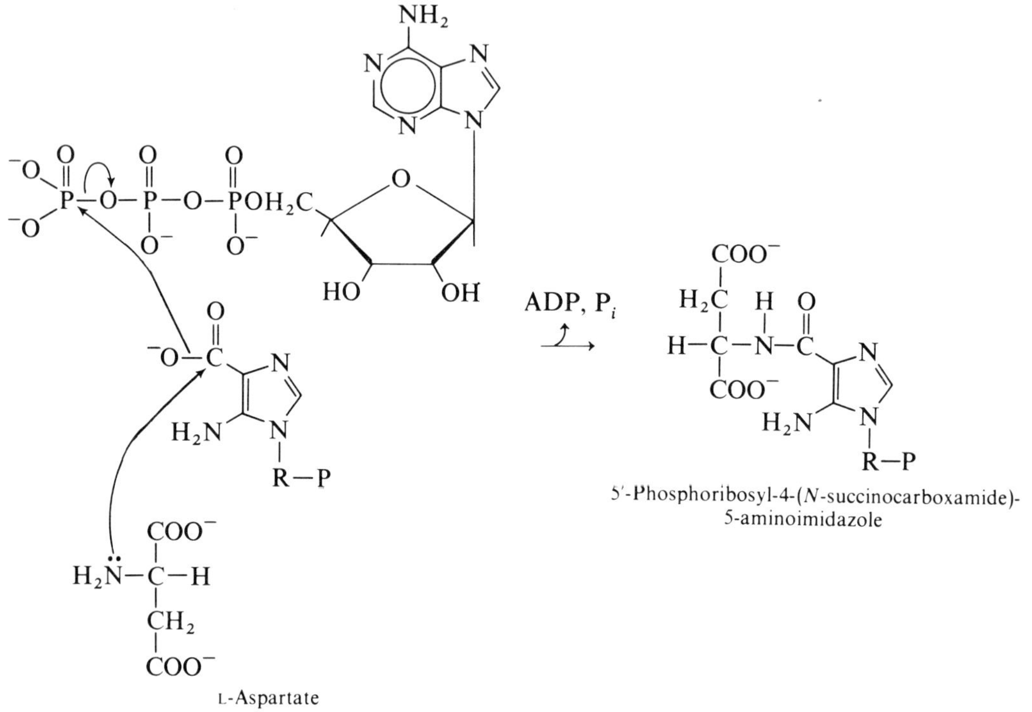

### Step 9: Elimination of Fumarate

The elimination of fumarate from 5′-phosphoribosyl-4-(N-succinocarboxamide)-5-aminoimidazole is catalyzed by adenylosuccinate lyase (adenylosuccinate AMP-lyase, EC 4.3.2.2), an enzyme that also catalyzes a similar reaction which converts adenylosuccinate into AMP and fumarate. In the present case, the reaction is

5′-Phosphoribosyl-4-(N-succinocarboxamide)-5-aminoimidazole $\rightleftharpoons$

5′-phosphoribosyl-5-amino-4-imidazolecarboxamide + fumarate (13-9)

It might be formulated mechanistically as shown.

Fumarate

5′-Phosphoribosyl-5-amino-4-imidazolecarboxamide

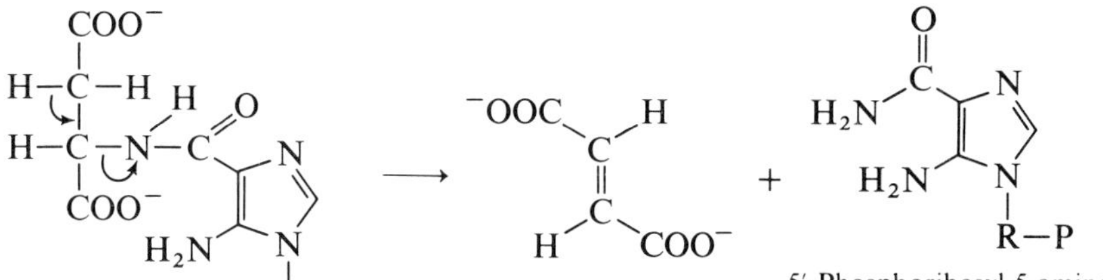

### Step 10: Formylation of 5′-Phosphoribosyl-5-Amino-4-Imidazolecarboxamide

The only atom lacking at this point in the anabolic pathway is the one that will become C(2) of the purine nucleus. This carbon atom is derived from the one-carbon substituent of 10-formyltetrahydrofolate as the result of a reaction catalyzed by phosphoribosylaminoimidazolecarboxamide formyltransferase (10-formyltetrahydrofolate:5′-phosphoribosyl-5-amino-4-imidazolecarboxamide formyltransferase, EC 2.1.2.3). The reaction is

$$\text{10-Formyltetrahydrofolate} + \text{5′-phosphoribosyl-5-amino-4-imidazolecarboxamide} \rightleftharpoons \text{5′-phosphoribosyl-5-formamido-4-imidazolecarboxamide} + \text{tetrahydrofolate} \quad (13\text{-}10)$$

Once all the atoms of the purine nucleus are present, a very facile cyclization reaction takes place, and inosine 5′-monophosphate, the product of the *de novo* synthesis, is formed.

### Step 11: Cyclization to Form IMP

The ring closure is catalyzed by IMP cyclohydrolase [IMP 1,2-hydrolase (decyclizing), EC 3.5.4.10]. The reaction entails the elimination of the elements of water:

$$\text{5′-Phosphoribosyl-5-formamido-4-imidazolecarboxamide} \rightleftharpoons \text{IMP} + H_2O \quad (13\text{-}11)$$

A suggested reaction mechanism for the introduction of the final atom of the purine nucleus and the subsequent ring closure follows.

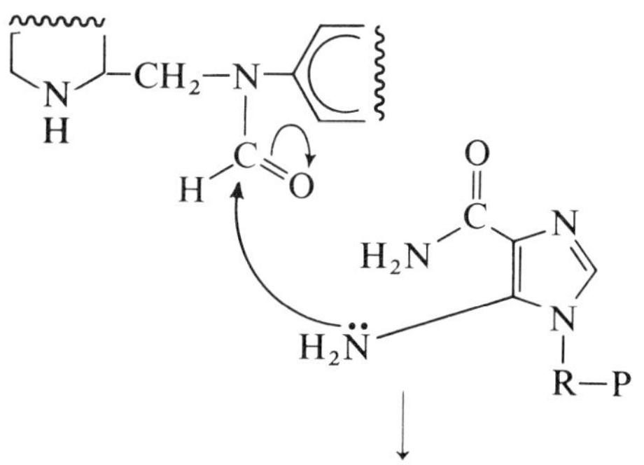

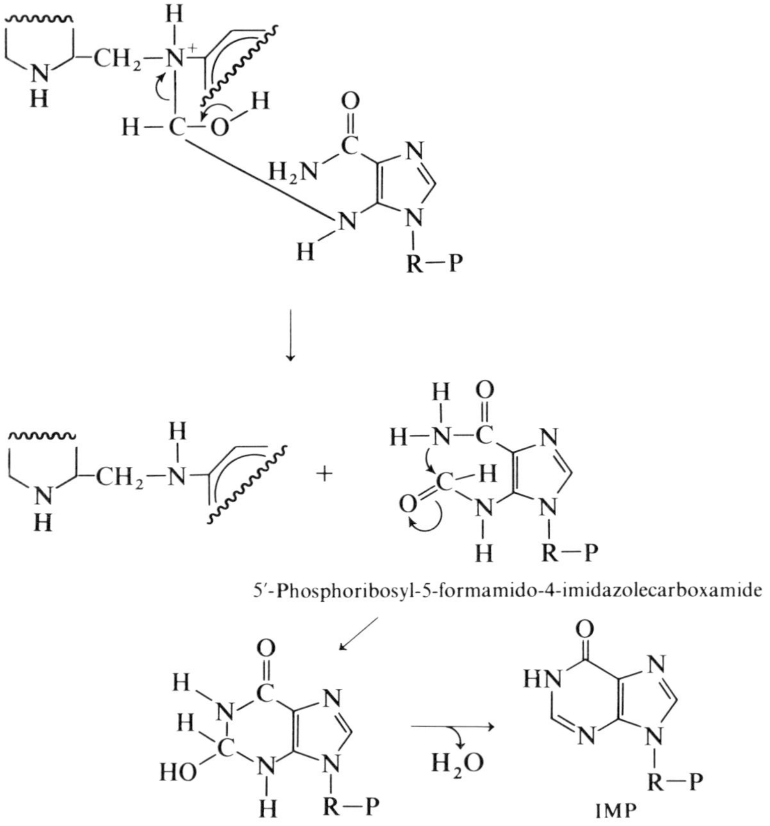

[Reaction scheme showing formation of 5′-Phosphoribosyl-5-formamido-4-imidazolecarboxamide and its cyclization to IMP with loss of H₂O]

5′-Phosphoribosyl-5-formamido-4-imidazolecarboxamide

IMP

## Summary of the *de Novo* Synthesis of the Purine Ring System

The *de novo* synthesis of the purine nucleus entails the incorporation of carbon atoms from glycine, the one-carbon substituents of tetrahydrofolate, and carbon dioxide, while the nitrogen atoms are derived from glutamine, glycine, and aspartate. The results of these incorporations can be represented diagrammatically as shown.

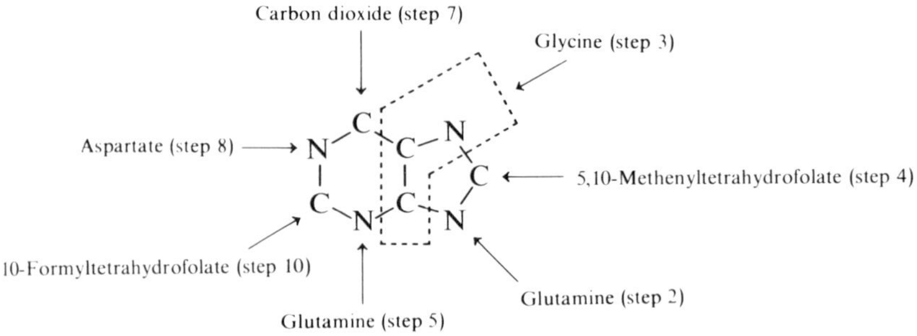

- Carbon dioxide (step 7)
- Glycine (step 3)
- Aspartate (step 8)
- 5,10-Methenyltetrahydrofolate (step 4)
- 10-Formyltetrahydrofolate (step 10)
- Glutamine (step 2)
- Glutamine (step 5)

# INTERCONVERSIONS INVOLVING PURINE NUCLEOSIDES AND NUCLEOTIDES

Inosine 5'-monophosphate (IMP), which is the product of the *de novo* synthesis of the purine nucleus, is readily converted into AMP or to GMP, as described below. It is also converted into hypoxanthine, xanthine, and urate. Urate is the catabolic product of the purines in man, and it is excreted in the urine. These and other conversions and interconversions involving the purines are discussed in the following paragraphs.

## Conversion of IMP into AMP

The conversion of IMP into AMP requires the introduction of an amino substituent at C(6). The nitrogen atom of this amino substituent is derived from aspartate, and the reaction by which this nitrogen atom is introduced is catalyzed by adenylosuccinate synthetase [IMP:L-aspartate ligase (GDP-forming), EC 6.3.4.4]. As indicated by the name of the enzyme, i.e., synthetase, the introduction of this nitrogen atom is an energy-requiring process. The energy in the present case, is provided by the cleavage of GTP. The reaction is

$$\text{GTP} + \text{IMP} + \text{L-aspartate} \rightleftharpoons \text{adenylosuccinate} + \text{GDP} + P_i \quad (13\text{-}12)$$

It is reminiscent of the reaction in which 5'-phosphoribosyl-4-(N-succinocarboxamide)-5-aminoimidazole is formed. Since when [oxo-$^{18}$C]IMP is utilized as a substrate, labeled orthophosphate is formed, the minimal mechanism shown below is suggested.

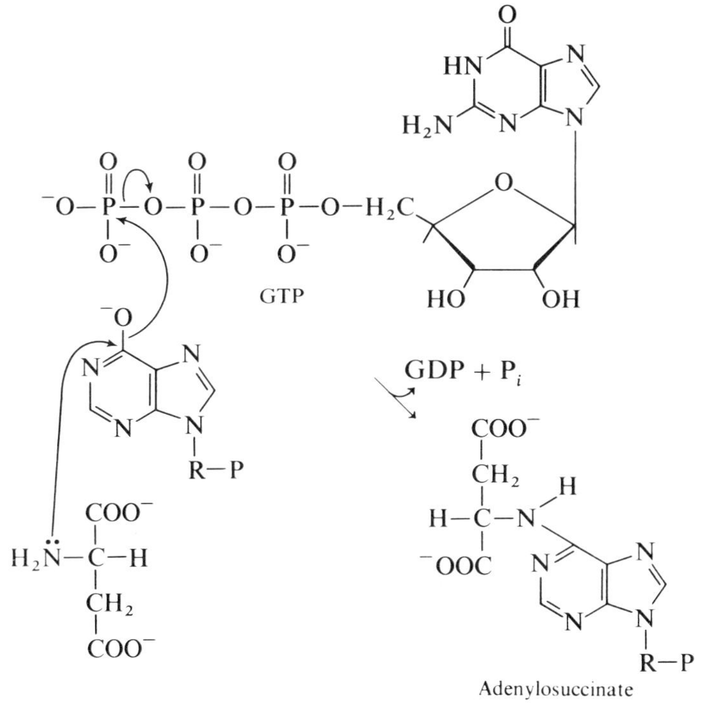

Adenylosuccinate

Adenylosuccinate synthetase has been purified from several sources, including rabbit skeletal muscle. This synthetase exhibits a molecular weight of 54,000 and is apparently a single polypeptide chain. A partially purified synthetase from human placenta has been used in a series of kinetic studies. Initial-velocity studies on this enzyme indicated that the formation of adenylosuccinate occurs by a sequential mechanism since the appropriate double reciprocal plots were intersecting. When product-inhibition studies were conducted, adenylosuccinate was found to function as a competitive product inhibitor when IMP was the variable substrate while it functioned as a noncompetitive product inhibitor when either GTP or aspartate was varied. Similarly, the product GDP was a competitive inhibitor when GTP was the variable substrate, while it was a noncompetitive inhibitor when either IMP or aspartate was varied.† These data are incompatible with the operation of a completely ordered sequential mechanism since in this case there would be only one product that would function as a competitive inhibitor and it would do so only when the initial substrate that binds was varied. On the other hand, all product-inhibition patterns are frequently competitive in the event that the kinetic mechanism is rapid equilibrium random. Therefore, it was suggested that although the reaction proceeds by a rapid equilibrium random mechanism, certain varied substrates and products cannot occupy the same location on the catalytic site and, hence, form kinetically significant dead-end complexes. Under such circumstances, one will observe a noncompetitive product-inhibition pattern because saturating concentrations of the variable substrate fail to prevent the formation of the dead-end complex.

Once formed, adenylosuccinate can undergo the elimination of fumarate with the result that AMP is formed. This elimination reaction is catalyzed by adenylosuccinate lyase, the enzyme that catalyzes the elimination of fumarate from 5'-phosphoribosyl-4-(N-succinocarboxamide)-5-aminoimidazole.

## Conversion of IMP into GMP

The formation of guanosine 5'-monophosphate (GMP) from IMP entails the oxidation of IMP to xanthosine 5'-monophosphate (XMP) followed by an energy-dependent introduction of a nitrogen atom to yield the guanosine derivative.

The oxidation of IMP to XMP is catalyzed by IMP dehydrogenase (IMP:$NAD^+$ oxidoreductase, EC 1.2.1.14). The reaction is

Inosine 5'-monophosphate + $NAD^+$ + $H_2O$ $\rightleftharpoons$

xanthosine 5'-monophosphate + NADH   (13-13)

The reaction mechanism of the formation of XMP must entail the removal of a hydride ion from C(2) of the purine substrate and the substitution of a hydroxyl ion, presumably from a water molecule. Few details of this reaction are known, however.

The conversion of XMP into GMP is catalyzed by GMP synthetase (glutamine-

---

† Weyden, M. B. van der, and Kelly, W. N. (1974) *J. Biol. Chem.* **249**, 7282–7289.

hydrolyzing) [xanthosine-5′-monophosphate:L-glutamine amido-ligase (AMP-forming), EC 6.3.5.2]. This reaction utilizes energy derived from the cleavage of ATP to yield AMP and pyrophosphate:

ATP + xanthosine 5′-monophosphate + L-glutamine + H$_2$O $\rightleftharpoons$

GMP + L-glutamate + AMP + PP$_i$   (13-14)

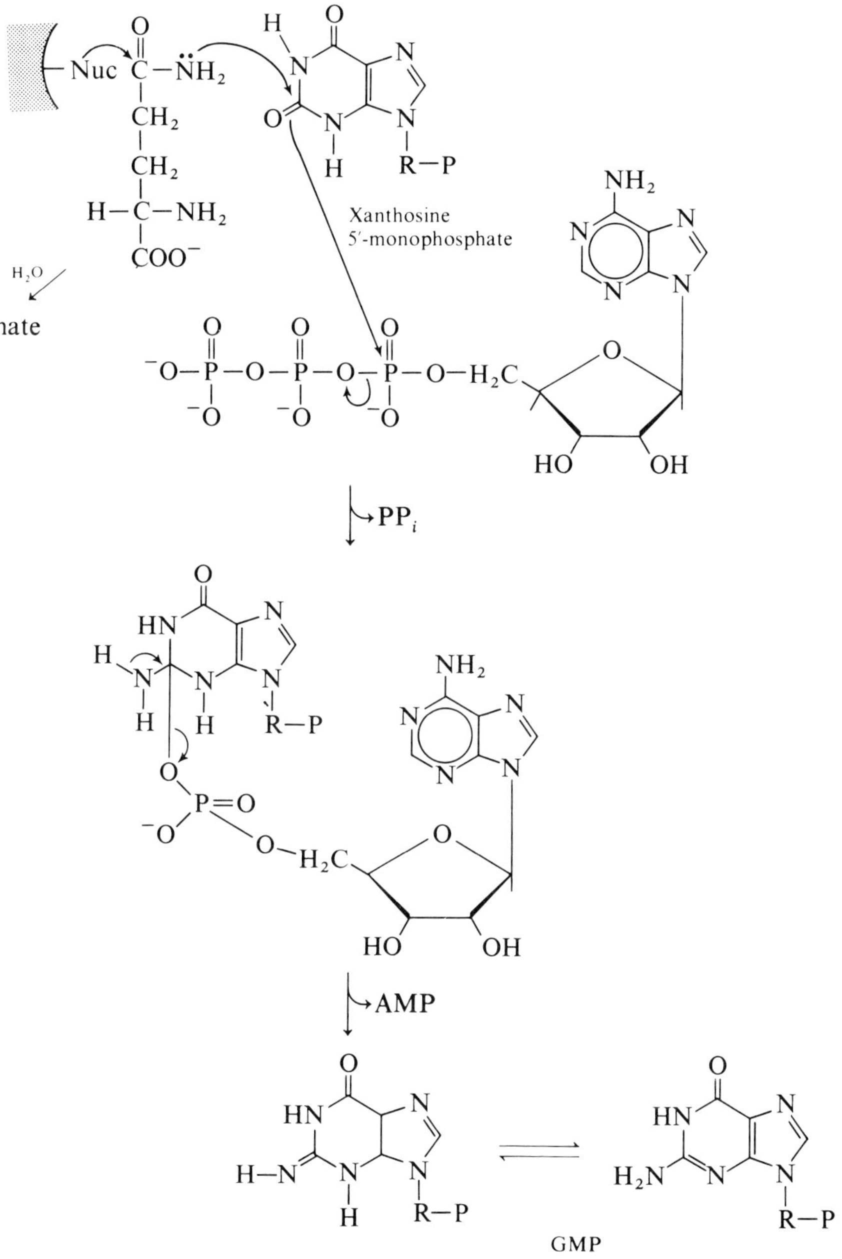

In some microorganisms, the enzyme that catalyzes the conversion of XMP into GMP utilizes ammonia rather than the amido nitrogen atom of glutamine as the source of the nitrogen atom introduced.

The reaction mechanism for the formation of GMP is similar to that of the reaction in which phosphoribosylformylglycinamidine is formed, but in the present case the nucleophilic attack upon ATP is at the α-phosphoryl phosphorus atom, rather than at the γ-phosphoryl phosphorus atom.

## Conversion of AMP and GMP into IMP

AMP and GMP can be converted back into IMP, but (as is often the case) this is not accomplished by reversal of the reactions by which they were formed. AMP is converted into IMP and ammonia in the presence of the enzyme AMP deaminase (AMP aminohydrolase, EC 3.5.4.6). The reaction is

$$AMP + H_2O \rightleftharpoons IMP + NH_3 \qquad (13\text{-}15)$$

This reaction in conjunction with those by which AMP is formed from IMP constitute the *purine nucleotide cycle*. This cycle is thought to be involved in the regulation of the glycolytic pathway, as discussed later in this chapter.

The conversion of GMP into IMP is catalyzed by GMP reductase [NADPH·GMP oxidoreductase (deaminating), EC 1.6.6.8]. The nitrogen atom that is removed is, again, eliminated in the form of ammonia. In this case, the reaction is

$$NADPH + GMP \rightleftharpoons IMP + NH_3 + NADP^+ \qquad (13\text{-}16)$$

## Formation of Purine Nucleoside Diphosphates and Triphosphates

Purine (and pyrimidine) nucleotides are incorporated into the nucleic acids, but in order for this incorporation to occur the appropriate monophosphates must be converted into the corresponding triphosphates. These conversions are catalyzed by nucleosidemonophosphate kinase (ATP:nucleosidemonophosphate phosphotransferase, EC 2.7.4.4) and nucleosidediphosphate kinase (ATP:nucleosidediphosphate phosphotransferase, EC 2.7.4.6) in many instances. These enzymes are relatively nonspecific with respect to both the phosphoryl donor (designated above as ATP) and the phosphoryl acceptor. The reactions that are catalyzed by these enzymes are

$$ATP + \text{nucleoside monophosphate} \rightleftharpoons ADP + \text{nucleoside diphosphate} \qquad (13\text{-}17a)$$

$$ATP + \text{nucleoside diphosphate} \rightleftharpoons ADP + \text{nucleoside triphosphate} \qquad (13\text{-}17b)$$

A nucleosidemonophosphate kinase from bovine liver can utilize ITP, UTP, or CTP, in addition to ATP, as the phosphoryl donor. Similarly, a nucleosidediphosphate kinase from human erythrocytes can utilize GTP and dGTP, in addition to ATP, as the phosphoryl donor.

These reactions generally proceed by ping pong kinetic mechanisms. Hence, it is not surprising that in the case of the reaction catalyzed by a nucleosidediphosphate kinase which has been extensively studied, a labeled phosphoryl-enzyme intermediate was isolated when the enzyme was incubated in the presence of $[\gamma\text{-}^{32}P]$ATP. Since this intermediate was stable when heated at pH 9.2, although orthophosphate was released when it was heated at pH 0.5, it is suggested that the intermediate may embody an $N$-phosphorylhistidyl moiety.

## CATABOLISM OF THE PURINE: FORMATION OF URATE

In man the purine nucleus is catabolized to yield uric acid or urate. AMP is initially converted into adenosine, and then inosine, and subsequently hypoxanthine. Hypoxanthine in turn is converted into xanthine and finally urate. GMP, on the other hand, is converted into guanosine and then guanine, which is then converted into xanthine. As will be seen in the following paragraphs, these conversions frequently entail the oxidation of the purine ring system, which is in keeping with the general statement that catabolic processes are oxidative in nature.

### Catabolism of AMP

Initially, the nucleotide AMP is converted to the nucleoside adenosine in the presence of a nonspecific 5′-nucleotidase (5′-ribonucleotide phosphohydrolase, EC 3.1.3.5). The reaction is a hydrolytic cleavage, which can be written

$$\text{5′-Ribonucleotide} + H_2O \rightleftharpoons \text{nucleoside} + P_i \qquad (13\text{-}18)$$

Next, adenosine undergoes deamination. The nitrogen atom at C(6) is released as ammonia, just as in the deamination of AMP; however, a different enzyme than that mentioned above catalyzes this reaction. Here, the enzyme is adenosine deaminase (adenosine aminohydrolase, EC 3.5.4.4). Studies on the adenosine deaminase from bovine duodenum have provided data which suggest that an ordered sequential Uni Bi mechanism is operative with ammonia as the initial product released. A reaction mechanism which involves the participation of an imidazole moiety (of a histidyl unit) and a sulfhydryl group (of a cysteinyl unit), as suggested by studies on this enzyme, is shown on page 562.

With respect to the attack of a water molecule at C(6) of the adenine moiety, it should be remembered that C(6) is analogous to the carbonyl carbon of an amide. The reaction might therefore be considered similar to the hydrolysis of an amide.

Once formed, inosine is readily converted into hypoxanthine as a result of the elimination of the ribose moiety. This is catalyzed by a nucleosidase ($N$-ribosylpurine ribohydrolase, EC 3.2.2.1). The reaction can be written

$$N\text{-Ribosylpurine} + H_2O \rightleftharpoons \text{purine} + \text{D-ribose} \qquad (13\text{-}19)$$

The oxidation of hypoxanthine to xanthine and that of xanthine to urate are catalyzed by xanthine oxidase (xanthine:oxygen oxidoreductase, EC 1.2.3.2). As

Inosine

isolated from rat liver, the xanthine oxidase has a molecular weight of 300,000 and it comprises two presumably identical subunits. Each subunit binds one molecule of FAD and one molybdenum ion and contains four nonheme iron–sulfur moieties. These components constitute an electron-transport system that conveys electrons from the substrate to the ultimate acceptor, molecular oxygen. The reaction catalyzed by xanthine oxidase with xanthine as the purine substrate can be stated as

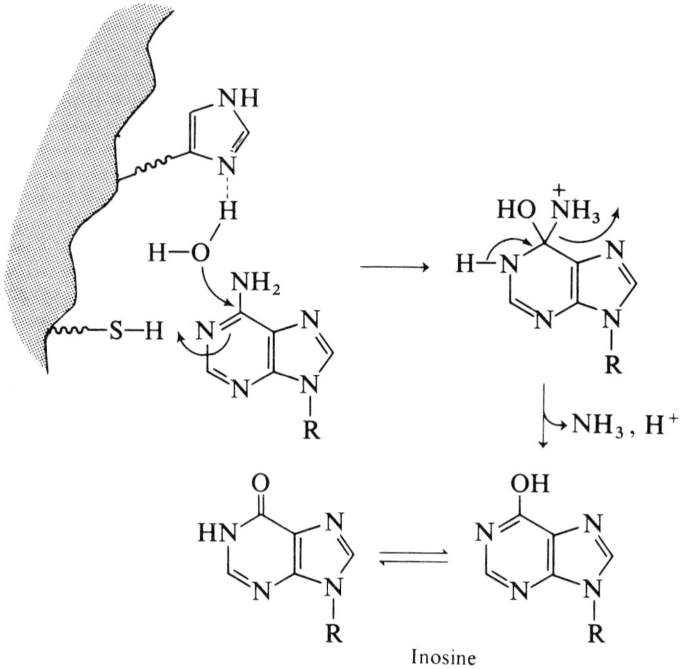

$$\text{Xanthine} + H_2O + O_2 \rightleftharpoons \text{urate} + O_2{\cdot}^- \qquad (13\text{-}20)$$

The species $O_2^-$ is the superoxide anion, which is formed when an oxygen molecule accepts one electron.

Molecular oxygen ($O_2$) Superoxide anion ($O_2^-$)

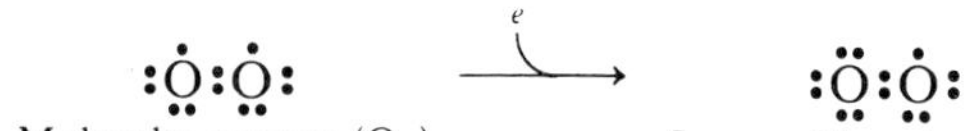

The conversion of hypoxanthine into xanthine or that of xanthine into urate entails the removal of a proton and two electrons from C(2) of hypoxanthine or from C(8) of xanthine and the substitution of a hydroxyl ion in each instance. The hydroxyl ion is derived from a molecule of water. The molybdenum ion (which exists as $Mo^{6+}$ in the fully oxidized enzyme) is thought to be the initial acceptor of electrons from the purine substrate while the flavin passes the electrons to the oxygen molecules. The superoxide anion that is generated is a reactive species which readily undergoes the reaction

$$O_2{\cdot}^- + O_2{\cdot}^- + 2H^+ \longrightarrow H_2O_2 + O_2 \qquad (13\text{-}21)$$

This reaction is catalyzed by superoxide dismutase (superoxide:superoxide oxido-

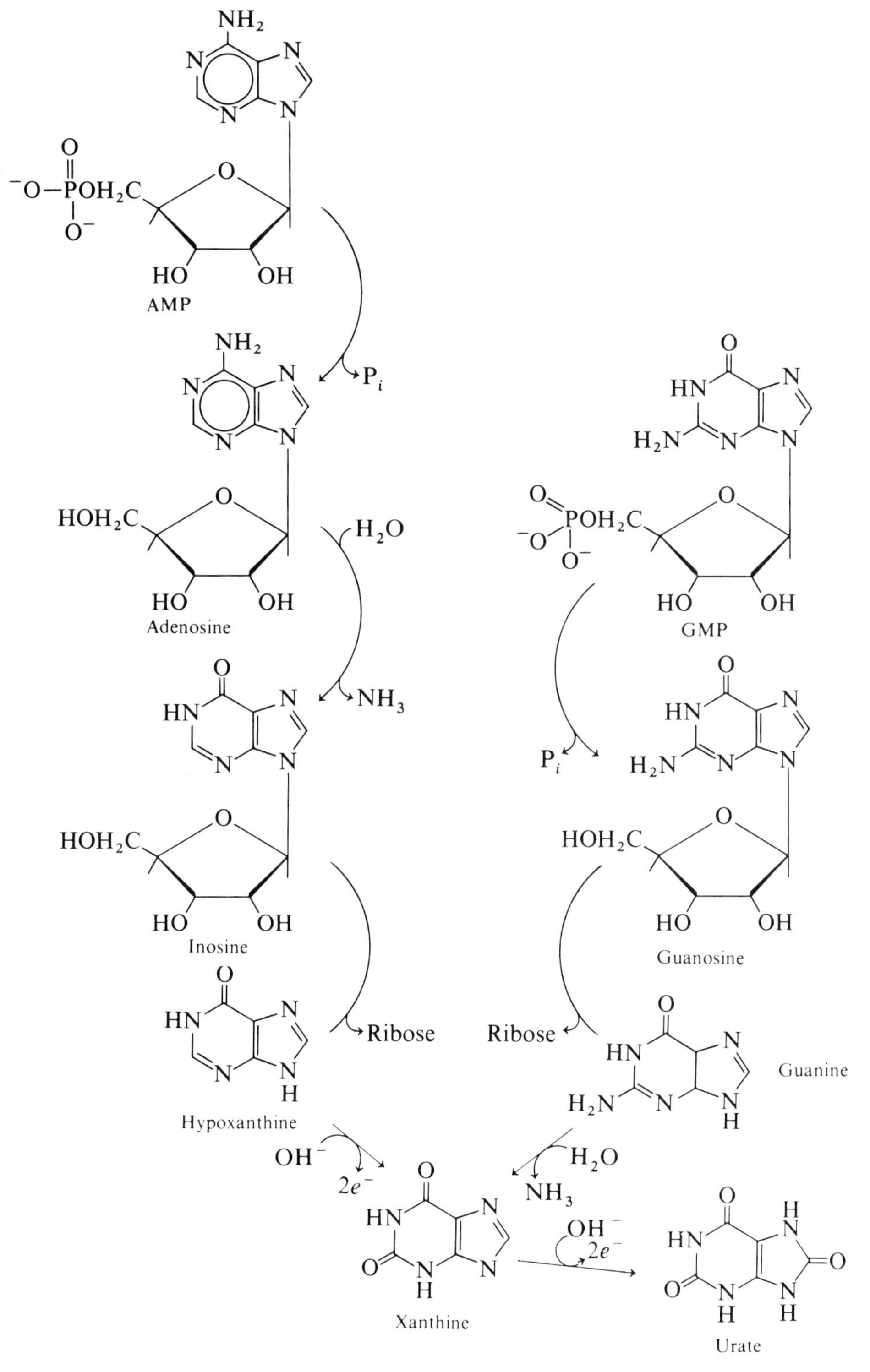

# METABOLISM OF PURINES, PYRIMIDINES, AND NUCLEIC ACIDS

reductase, EC 1.15.1.1). Hydrogen peroxide in turn is converted into water and molecular oxygen in the presence of the enzyme catalase (hydrogen-peroxide: hydrogen-peroxide oxidoreductase, EC 1.11.1.6).

## Catabolism of GMP

The conversion of GMP into urate begins with the conversion of the former into guanosine, as catalyzed by 5'-nucleotidase. Guanosine in turn is converted into guanine in the presence of nucleosidase. Then guanine undergoes deamination to yield xanthine. This reaction, catalyzed by guanine deaminase (guanine aminohydrolase, EC 3.5.4.3), is

$$\text{Guanine} + H_2O \rightleftharpoons \text{xanthine} + NH_3 \tag{13-22}$$

The deamination of guanine to form xanthine parallels that of adenosine to yield inosine. Xanthine is subsequently converted into urate, as described above. The catabolism of GMP and AMP is illustrated on page 563.

## Summary of Interconversions Involving Purines and Their Nucleosides and Nucleotides

The principal interconversions involving the purines adenine, guanine, and hypoxanthine, and their derivatives are as follows:

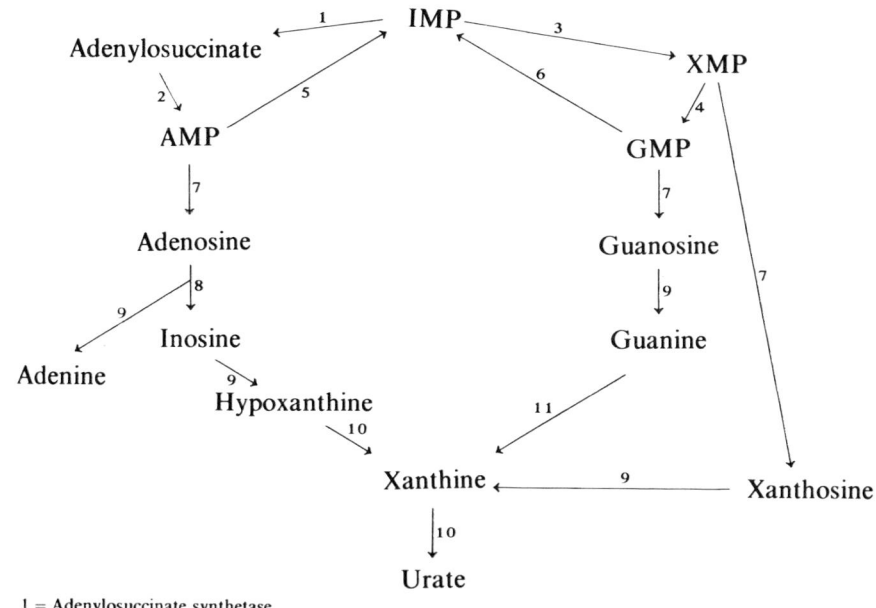

1 = Adenylosuccinate synthetase
2 = Adenylosuccinate lyase
3 = IMP dehydrogenase
4 = GMP synthetase
5 = AMP deaminase
6 = GMP reductase
7 = 5'-Nucleotidase
8 = Adenosine deaminase
9 = Nucleosidase
10 = Xanthine oxidase
11 = Guanine deaminase

# PURINE SALVAGE PATHWAYS

In addition to the pathway for the *de novo* synthesis of the purine nucleotides, purine nucleotides can be formed from existing purines or purine nucleosides by means of *purine salvage pathways*. These pathways allow the utilization of purines or purine nucleosides from ingested foods and also the reutilization of purines and purine nucleosides resulting from the degradation of nucleic acids. In general terms, there are two routes for salvaging purines. One involves the reaction of a purine and ribose 1-phosphate, followed by the phosphorylation of the resulting nucleoside. The second involves the reaction of a purine and phosphoribose diphosphate, which results in the direct formation of a purine nucleotide.

The reaction between a purine and ribose 1-phosphate is catalyzed by purine-nucleoside phosphorylase (purine-nucleoside:orthophosphate ribosyltransferase, EC 2.4.2.1). The reaction can be written

$$\text{Purine} + \alpha\text{-D-ribose 1-phosphate} \rightleftharpoons \text{purine nucleoside} + P_i \quad (13\text{-}23)$$

The phosphorylation of the resulting nucleoside is catalyzed by an appropriate kinase. For example, when the nucleoside is adenosine, adenosine kinase (ATP:adenosine 5'-phosphotransferase, EC 2.7.1.20) catalyzes the reaction.

The formation of a purine nucleotide from the purine and phosphoribose diphosphate is catalyzed by a phosphoribosyltransferase, such as adenine phosphoribosyltransferase or hypoxanthine phosphoribosyltransferase. Adenine phosphoribosyltransferase (AMP:pyrophosphate phosphoribosyltransferase, EC 2.4.2.7) catalyzes the reaction

$$\text{Adenine} + 5\text{-phospho-}\alpha\text{-D-ribose 1-diphosphate} \rightleftharpoons \text{AMP} + PP_i \quad (13\text{-}24)$$

The enzyme has been isolated from human erythrocytes as a protein which has a molecular weight of 34,000. There is particular interest in this enzyme since the erythrocytes of persons who exhibit the Lesch-Nyhan syndrome contain a concentration of adenine phosphoribosyltransferase two or three times that found in normal persons. The Lesch-Nyhan syndrome is an inherited disorder associated with a virtual absence of hypoxanthine phosphoribosyltransferase activity. The disorder is found only in males, and it is characterized by hyperuricemia and certain neurological characteristics including spasticity, mental retardation, and a propensity for self-mutilation. The elevated concentrations of adenine phosphoribosyltransferase in the erythrocytes of those exhibiting the Lesch-Nyhan syndrome result from the increased stability and resistance to degradation of this enzyme in the presence of high concentrations of its substrate, phosphoribose diphosphate.

Hypoxanthine phosphoribosyltransferase (IMP:pyrophosphate phosphoribosyltransferase, EC 2.4.2.8) catalyzes a reaction which parallels that catalyzed by adenine phosphoribosyltransferase but with hypoxanthine (or guanine, in the case of mammalian enzymes) as the purine substrate. Hypoxanthine phosphoribosyltransferase has been isolated from human erythrocytes as a dimeric protein which has a molecular weight of 68,000. Again, there is particular interest in the enzyme because of its involvement in certain pathological conditions, one of which is gout.

## Gout

The term *gout* refers to a heterogeneous group of disorders of diverse etiology, all of which involve an aberration in purine metabolism. In general, gout is a condition of hyperuricemia which is manifested by recurrent attacks of arthritis or renal lithiasis, or both. Ultimately, the arthritis may become chronic as a result of the destructive effects of deposited urate crystals in and around the joints. The hyperuricemia of gout may be due to a decreased ability of the kidney to excrete urate or to an increased production of urate, or both. Primary gout results from the presence of an abnormal ribosephosphate diphosphotransferase or (possibly) an abnormal amidophosphoribosyltransferase or diminished hypoxanthine phosphoribosyltransferase activity. When an abnormal ribosephosphate diphosphotransferase is present, increased amounts of its product, phosphoribose diphosphate, are produced. This ultimately leads to an overproduction of urate since phosphoribose diphosphate is a substrate in the reaction catalyzed by amidophosphoribosyltransferase, the rate-determining step of the *de novo* synthesis of the purines. The presence of the abnormal amidophosphoribosyltransferase also leads to the overproduction of urate since in this case the activity of the enzyme is not responsive to increased concentrations of the ultimate products of the pathway, the purine ribonucleotides. The activity of the normal amidophosphoribosyltransferase is subject to inhibition by ultimate products. Diminished hypoxanthine phosphoribosyltransferase activity, the most common enzyme defect associated with gout, also results in an overproduction of urate. In this instance, the diminished activity of an enzyme involved in the salvage operation results in decreased recycling of purines and hence their increased catabolism to form urate.

## PURINE CATABOLISM IN OTHER SPECIES

Although in man and certain other primates the ultimate product of purine catabolism is urate, this is not true in all species. The cells of many species contain the enzyme urate oxidase (urate:oxygen oxidoreductase, EC 1.7.3.3), which catalyzes the conversion of urate into the more polar allantoin. Most mammals other than man and certain monkeys excrete allantoin, but allantoin is further degraded by amphibia, marine animals, and certain microorganisms. In the presence of the enzyme allantoinase (allantoin amidohydrolase, EC 3.5.2.5) allantoin is converted into the even more polar allantoate. Teleost fish excrete allantoate. Other fish and amphibians can carry the degradative process still farther. In the presence of allantoicase (allantoate amidinohydrolase, EC 3.5.3.4) allantoate can be converted into ureidoglycollate and urea. Allantoicase can also convert ureidoglycollate into a second molecule of urea and glyoxylate. Finally, some invertebrates convert urea into ammonium ions and carbon dioxide in the presence of urease (urea amidohydrolase, EC 3.5.1.5). These degradative reactions are illustrated on page 567. The reaction catalyzed by urate oxidase entails the removal of two electrons from urate and the transfer of these electrons to molecular oxygen by a process not

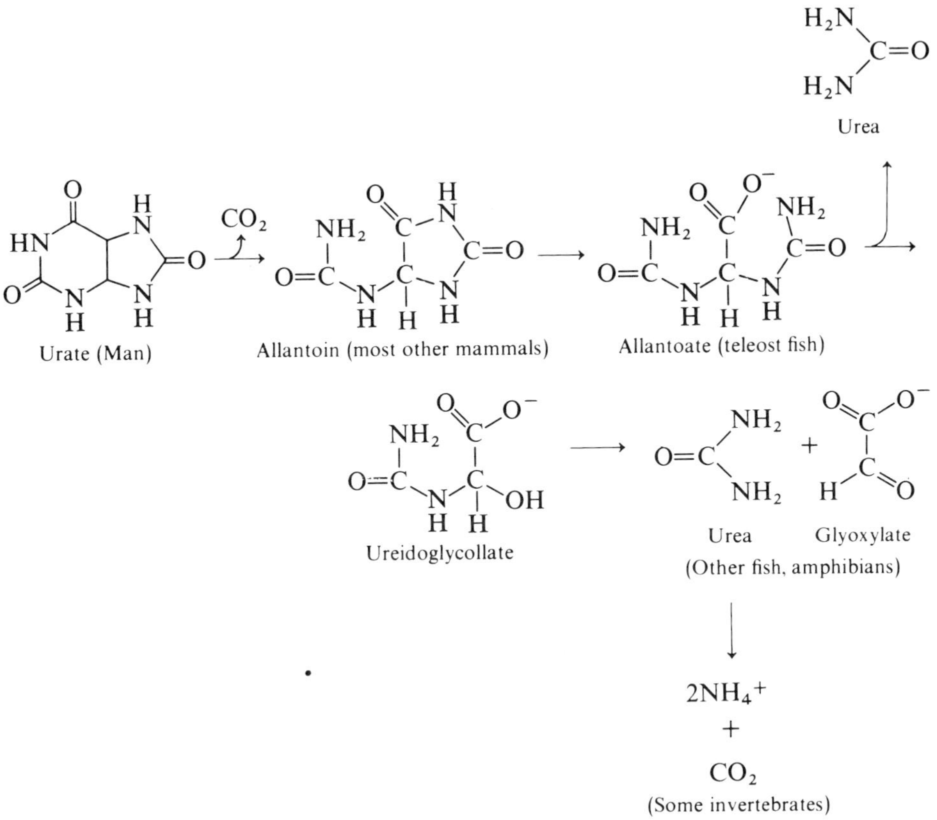

Urate (Man) → (CO₂) Allantoin (most other mammals) → Allantoate (teleost fish) → Ureidoglycollate → Urea + Glyoxylate (Other fish, amphibians) → 2NH₄⁺ + CO₂ (Some invertebrates); Urea (H₂N-CO-NH₂)

completely understood. The carbon atom that was C(6) of the purine is eliminated as carbon dioxide during the reaction. The remainder of the degradative reactions are essentially hydrolytic in nature.

## REGULATION OF PURINE METABOLISM

The *de novo* synthesis of the purine nucleus is regulated primarily by the concentrations of the ultimate products of the pathway, the purine ribonucleotides. The reaction catalyzed by amidophosphoribosyltransferase is the rate-determining step of the *de novo* pathway, and the activity of the transferase is inhibited by AMP and by GMP, which can function synergistically. IMP, ADP, and GDP can also function as ultimate product inhibitors. Neither purine deoxyribonucleotides nor purine nucleosides are inhibitors, however. The effect of the purine ribonucleotides can be seen if one plots the velocity of the formation of phosphoribosylamine as a function of the concentration of the substrate, phosphoribose diphosphate, in the absence and the presence of the ultimate product. When this is done, increasing concentrations of the purine ribonucleotide cause the direct plot to change from hyperbolic to increasingly sigmoidal.

## Purine Nucleotide Cycle

It has been proposed that certain reactions involved in the metabolism of purine nucleotides are also involved in the regulation of glycolysis. These reactions are the deamination of AMP as catalyzed by AMP deaminase, the formation of adenylosuccinate as catalyzed by adenylosuccinate synthetase, and the conversion of adenylosuccinate to AMP as catalyzed by adenylosuccinate lyase; and they are considered to constitute a purine nucleotide cycle. This cycle is thought to operate to prevent the [ATP]/[ADP] ratio from declining precipitously during periods of high energy demand. It is known that the deamination of AMP is promoted in the presence of a low [ATP]/[ADP] ratio while formation of AMP is promoted in the presence of a high [ATP]/[ADP] ratio. It then follows that during a period of rapid energy consumption, e.g., repeated muscle contraction, AMP is converted into IMP and ammonia more rapidly. Ammonia, however, induces increased phosphofructokinase activity. Hence, the rate of glycolysis increases not only because of diminished ATP concentrations but also because of increased concentrations of ammonia. It is believed that these circumstances allow the glycolytic pathway to respond appropriately to a much smaller diminution in ATP concentration; as a result, ATP concentrations can be maintained within a relatively narrow range even during periods of greatly increased energy demand.†

## PYRIMIDINE ANABOLISM

In mammals the *de novo* synthesis of the pyrimidine ring entails the incorporation of the amide nitrogen atom of glutamine, bicarbonate, and aspartate. The initial and rate-determining step, of the six steps involved in this anabolic pathway, is the energy-dependent synthesis of the very reactive intermediate carbamoyl phosphate.

### Step 1: Formation of Carbamoyl Phosphate

The formation of carbamoyl phosphate is the first step, not only of the *de novo* synthesis of the pyrimidine ring but also of the synthesis of arginine and urea. When the pyrimidine ring is to be synthesized in mammalian cells, carbamoyl phosphate is formed from the amide nitrogen atom of glutamine, bicarbonate, and the phosphoryl group of ATP. This reaction is catalyzed by the glutamine-dependent carbamoyl-phosphate synthase [ATP:carbamate phosphotransferase (dephosphorylating, amido-transferring), EC 2.7.2.9], which is localized in the cytoplasm of the cell. The reaction

$$2\text{ATP} + \text{L-glutamine} + \text{HCO}_3^- \rightleftharpoons \text{carbamoyl phosphate} + \text{L-glutamate} + 2\text{ADP} + \text{P}_i \quad (13\text{-}25)$$

utilizes two molecules of ATP. One provides the phosphoryl group of carbamoyl phosphate while the other provides the energy that is required to incorporate the

---

† Tornheim, K., and Lowenstein, J. M. (1975) *J. Biol. Chem.* **250**, 6304–6314.

amido nitrogen atom from glutamine into the product. In mammalian cells this glutamine-dependent carbamoyl-phosphate synthase appears to exist as a component of a complex that also includes the enzymes that catalyze the second and third steps of the anabolic pathway. The activity of the carbamoyl-phosphate synthase component is inhibited in the presence of an ultimate product of the pathway, UTP, and is enhanced in the presence of phosphoribose diphosphate, a substrate in the fifth reaction of the pathway.

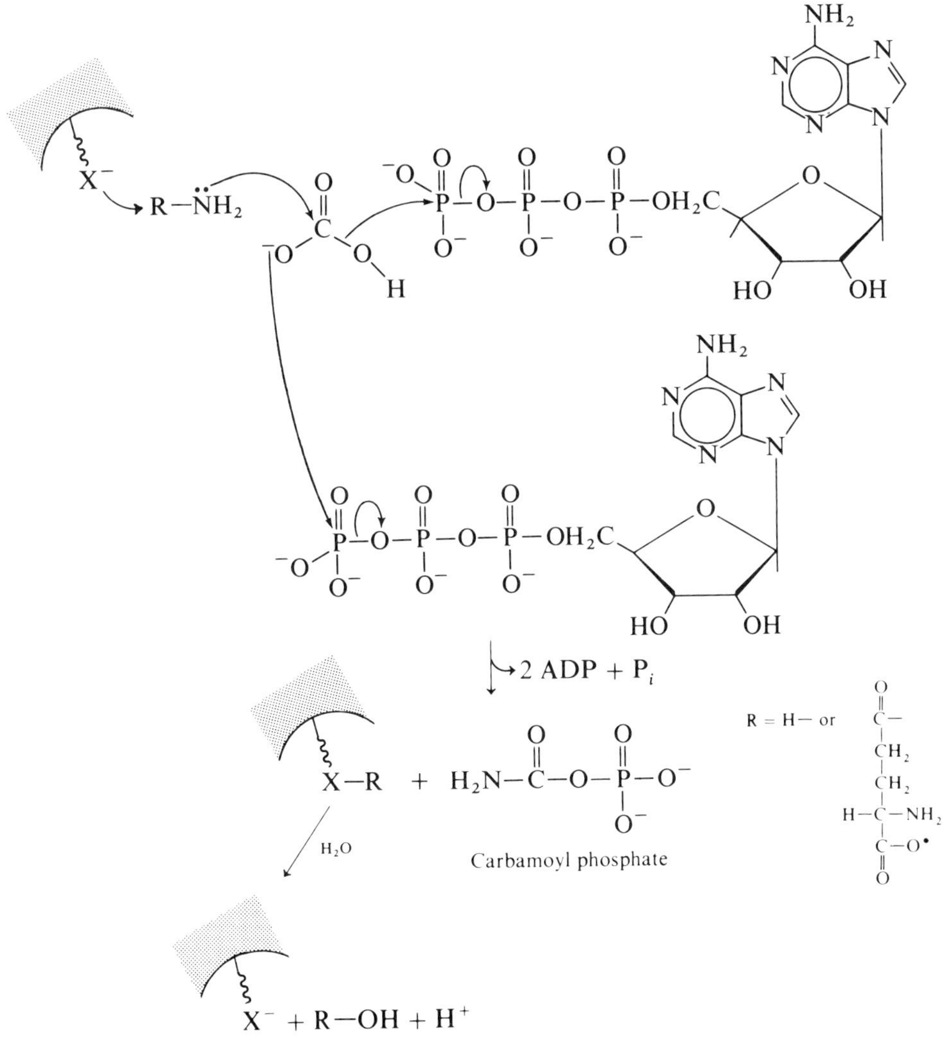

In microorganisms such as *E. coli* or *Salmonella typhimurium* carbamoyl-phosphate synthase can utilize either glutamine or ammonia as the nitrogen donor, and the resulting carbamoyl phosphate can be utilized either in the synthesis of the pyrimidine ring or in the synthesis of arginine. This is in contrast to the situation in mammalian cells, in which carbamoyl phosphate that is utilized for pyrimidine anabolism is formed in the cytoplasm while carbamoyl phosphate utilized for arginine and urea synthesis is formed in the mitochondrion. As isolated from *E. coli*, carbamoyl-phosphate synthase has a molecular weight of approximately 170,000 and this synthase comprises two subunits which have molecular weights of 130,000 and 40,000. The larger subunit can catalyze the formation of carbamoyl phosphate only when ammonia is the nitrogen donor. The ability to utilize glutamine as the nitrogen donor is conferred by the smaller subunit. In addition to the catalytic site at which carbamoyl phosphate is formed, the larger subunit also contains the binding sites for the ultimate product inhibitor UMP and the activators ornithine and ammonia.† The activators ornithine and ammonia function with respect to the participation of carbamoyl phosphate in the synthesis of arginine. Carbamoyl-phosphate synthase from *S. typhimurium* is similar to the synthase from *E. coli*. The enzyme has a molecular weight of 150,000, and comprises two subunits which have molecular weights of 110,000 and 40,000. Its properties are similar to those described above.

A minimal mechanism for the reaction catalyzed by carbamoyl-phosphate synthase is shown on page 569. The incorporation of the amide nitrogen atom of glutamine or the nitrogen atom of ammonia is similar to the incorporation of the amide nitrogen atom of glutamine in the reaction catalyzed by phosphoribosyl-formylglycinamidine synthase.

## Step 2: Conversion of Carbamoyl Phosphate into *N*-Carbamoyl-L-Aspartate

In the second step of this pathway carbamoyl phosphate reacts with L-aspartate to form *N*-carbamoyl-L-aspartate. The enzyme aspartate carbamoyltransferase (carbamoylphosphate:L-aspartate carbamoyltransferase, EC 2.1.3.2) catalyzes the reaction:

Carbamoyl phosphate + L-aspartate $\rightleftharpoons$

$$N\text{-carbamoyl-L-aspartate} + P_i \quad (13\text{-}26)$$

In mammalian cells aspartate carbamoyltransferase is associated with the cytoplasmic carbamoyl-phosphate synthase and the enzyme that catalyzes the third reaction of this pathway, as mentioned previously. When a partially purified transferase from rat liver was used in preliminary kinetic studies, plots of the reaction velocity as a function of the concentration of either substrate were hyperbolic. Also, the activity of the transferase was not inhibited by ultimate products, e.g., pyrimidine nucleotides. Thus, it appears that this enzyme does not exhibit the characteristics frequently associated with a regulatory enzyme.

Aspartate carbamoyltransferase from microorganisms exhibits characteristics that contrast sharply with those of the mammalian enzymes, however. In microorganisms carbamoyl phosphate synthesis is not compartmentalized, as it is

---

† Trotta, P. P., Pinkus, L. M., Haschemeyer, R. H., and Meister, A. (1974) *J. Biol. Chem.* **249**, 492–499.

in mammals, and aspartate carbamoyltransferase catalyzes the first of the anabolic reactions that is unique to pyrimidine synthesis. Under these circumstances it is not surprising that aspartate carbamoyltransferase functions as a regulatory enzyme in microorganisms.

As isolated from *E. coli*, aspartate carbamoyltransferase exhibits a molecular weight of 300,000 and comprises 12 polypeptide chains of two different types. One polypeptide chain has a molecular weight of 33,000 while the other chain has a molecular weight of 17,000. The native transferase comprises six of the larger and six of the smaller polypeptides. The larger polypeptides contain the catalytic site and in fact catalyze the formation of *N*-carbamoylaspartate. The smaller polypeptides exhibit no catalytic activity, on the other hand, although they do possess the binding sites for the ultimate product inhibitor, CTP, and the ultimate product activator (or deinhibitor), ATP. In native aspartate carbamoyltransferase the catalytic polypeptides are arranged to form two trimeric catalytic subunits, while the binding polypeptides exist as three dimeric subunits. A model for the arrangement of the polypeptide chains of the native enzyme is shown in Fig. 13-1.

Kinetic studies on the isolated catalytic subunit of aspartate carbamoyltransferase indicate that the reaction proceeds by a sequential mechanism since the double reciprocal plots derived from the initial-velocity data are intersecting. Product-inhibition studies showed orthophosphate to function as a competitive inhibitor when carbamoyl phosphate was the variable substrate and as a noncompetitive inhibitor when aspartate was varied. The other product, *N*-carbamoylaspartate, functioned as a noncompetitive inhibitor vs. either substrate. Thus, at this point the data suggested an ordered sequential mechanism although a random mechanism

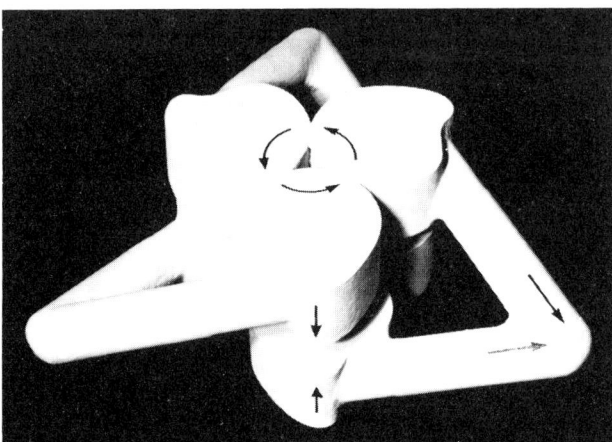

**Figure 13-1** A model for the arrangement of the polypeptide chains of aspartate carbamoyltransferase. Each of the two catalytic subunits comprises three polypeptide chains triangularly arranged. The binding polypeptides exist as three dimeric subunits, depicted as the angular moieties surrounding the catalytic polypeptides. [*From Cohlberg, J. A., Pigiet, V. P., Jr., and Schachman, H. K. (1972) Biochemistry* **11**, *3396–3411 (see p. 3407). With permission.*]

was also a possibility. Next, studies using substrate analogs as dead-end inhibitors were conducted. Succinate, an analog of aspartate, was a competitive inhibitor when aspartate was varied and a noncompetitive inhibitor when carbamoyl phosphate was varied. Monomethyl phosphate, an analog of carbamoyl phosphate, on the other hand, functioned as a competitive inhibitor vs. carbamoyl phosphate and a noncompetitive inhibitor when aspartate was varied. These data are incompatible with an ordered sequential mechanism. If such a mechanism were operative, the dead-end-inhibitor that is an analog of the second substrate that binds would function as an *uncompetitive* inhibitor vs. the first substrate that binds. Therefore, a mechanism that involves the random binding of the substrates is implied. Further evidence in support of a random mechanism was obtained when it was found that either carbamoyl phosphate or aspartate can bind the noncomplexed enzyme in the absence of the other substrate. Hence, it appears that the reaction proceeds by a rapid equilibrium random mechanism and that the formation of three dead-end complexes, the enzyme-aspartate-orthophosphate complex, the enzyme–carbamoyl phosphate–$N$-carbamoylaspartate complex, and the enzyme–aspartate–$N$-carbamoylaspartate complex can occur. This is supported by the fact that the rates at moylaspartate complex can occur. This is supported by the fact that rates at which the from carbamoyl [$^{32}$P]phosphate to orthophosphate, and from [$^{14}$C]carbamoyl phosphate to $N$-carbamoylaspartate are the same.† Thus, it is indicated that the conversion of the substrate central complex to the product central complex is rate-determining, with all other events much faster, as must be the case when a reaction proceeds by a rapid equilibrium random mechanism.

Kinetic studies conducted on the native aspartate carbamoyltransferase from *E. coli* demonstrated that the association of the binding polypeptides with the catalytic polypeptides alters the relationship between the observed reaction velocity and the substrate concentration. When the isolated catalytic subunit is used as the enzyme, plots of the reaction velocity vs. the concentration of aspartate or carbamoyl phosphate are hyperbolic, although when the native enzyme is used, these plots are sigmoidal. If the ultimate product inhibitor, CTP, is introduced, the plots of the reaction velocity vs. aspartate concentration become even more sigmoidal. This effect of CTP can be countered by ATP.

A minimal mechanism for the formation of $N$-carbamoylaspartate is shown below.

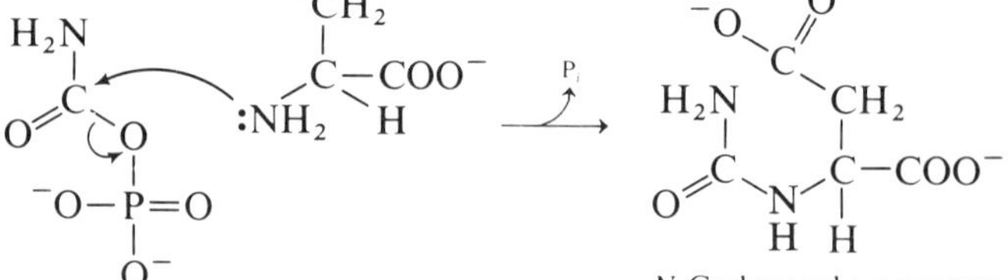

$N$-Carbamoyl-L-aspartate

† Heyde, E., Nagabhushanam, A., and Morrison, J. F. (1973) *Biochemistry* **12**, 4718–4726.

## Step 3: Cyclization to Form Dihydroorotate

$N$-Carbamoylaspartate now undergoes a cyclization reaction which results in the formation of a 5,6-dihydropyrimidine ring. The cyclization is catalyzed by dihydroorotase (L-5,6-dihydroorotate amidohydrolase, EC 3.5.2.3). The reaction is, in effect, an elimination of the elements of water:

$$N\text{-Carbamoyl-L-aspartate} \rightleftharpoons \text{L-5,6-dihydroorotate} + H_2O \quad (13\text{-}27)$$

Few details of this reaction are known.

## Step 4: Dehydrogenation and the Formation of the Pyrimidine Ring

The initial pyrimidine formed as a result of the *de novo* synthesis is orotate. Its formation is a consequence of the dehydrogenation of dihydroorotate catalyzed by dihydroorotate oxidase (L-5,6-dihydroorotate:oxygen oxidoreductase, EC 1.3.3.1). In mammalian cells dihydroorotate oxidase is localized in the mitochondria, and it has been shown that electrons that are removed from dihydroorotate as a concomitance of its oxidation can be introduced into the mitochondrial electron-transport system. However, since it has also been shown that the superoxide anion can be produced as an early event in the course of the reaction,† the reaction might be written similar to the reaction catalyzed by xanthine oxidase:

$$\text{L-5,6-Dihydroorotate} + O_2 \rightleftharpoons \text{orotate} + O_2\cdot^- \quad (13\text{-}28)$$

Few other details of this reaction are known at present.

## Step 5: Conversion of Orotate into Orotidine 5'-Monophosphate

Unlike the *de novo* synthesis of the purines, the *de novo* synthesis of the pyrimidines proceeds through the step in which the ring is formed before the ribosephosphate moiety is introduced. This is accomplished in the fifth step of the pathway, and the reaction, which is catalyzed by orotate phosphoribosyltransferase (orotidine 5'-monophosphate:pyrophosphate phosphoribosyltransferase, EC 2.4.2.10), is as follows:

Orotate + 5-phospho-α-D-ribose 1-diphosphate $\rightleftharpoons$ orotidine

$$5'\text{-monophosphate} + PP_i \quad (13\text{-}29)$$

## Step 6: Formation of UMP

The final step of the *de novo* synthesis of the pyrimidine ring is the decarboxylation of orotidine 5'-monophosphate to yield uridine 5'-monophosphate, or UMP. This reaction,

$$\text{Orotidine 5'-monophosphate} \rightleftharpoons \text{UMP} + CO_2 \quad (13\text{-}30)$$

is catalyzed by orotidine-5'-phosphate decarboxylase (orotidine-5'-phosphate carboxy-lyase, EC 4.1.1.23).

---

† Forman, H. J., and Kennedy, J. (1975) *J. Biol. Chem.* **250**, 4322–4326.

## Summary of the *de Novo* Synthesis of the Pyrimidine Ring

The formation of the pyrimidine ring from the amide nitrogen atom of glutamine (or ammonia), bicarbonate, and aspartate is summarized below.

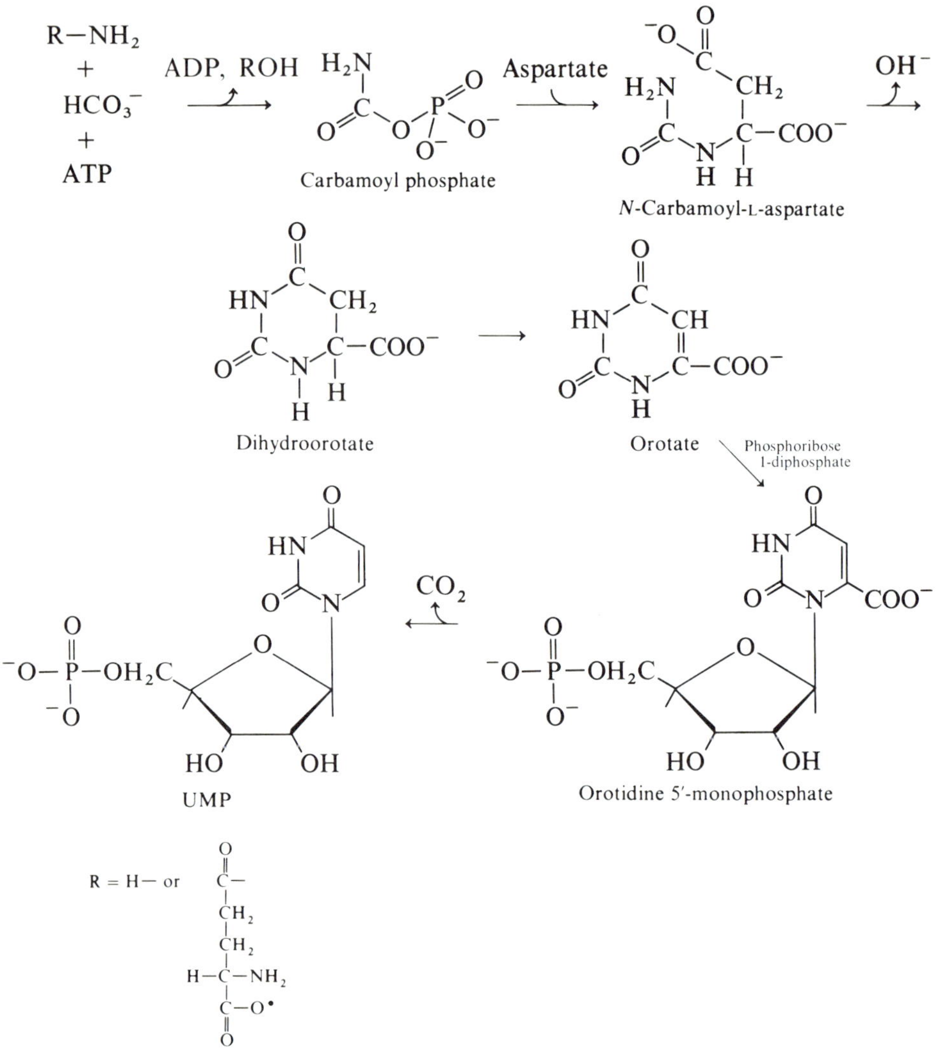

[Reaction scheme: R—NH$_2$ + HCO$_3^-$ + ATP → (ADP, ROH) → Carbamoyl phosphate → (Aspartate) → N-Carbamoyl-L-aspartate → (OH$^-$) → Dihydroorotate → Orotate → (Phosphoribose 1-diphosphate) → Orotidine 5'-monophosphate → (CO$_2$) → UMP]

$$R = H- \text{ or } \underset{\substack{\text{CH}_2\\\text{CH}_2\\\text{H}-\text{C}-\text{NH}_2\\\text{C}=\text{O}\cdot\\\text{O}}}{\overset{\text{O}}{\text{C}-}}$$

## INTERCONVERSIONS INVOLVING PYRIMIDINE NUCLEOTIDES

As in the synthesis of purine nucleotides, the *de novo* synthesis of the pyrimidine ring results in the synthesis of one of the pyrimidine nucleotides, and the others are derived from it. Thus, UMP can be converted into CTP, and also into deoxyribonucleotides, including dCTP and dTTP. These and other conversions involving pyrimidine nucleotides are discussed in the paragraphs that follow.

## Conversion of UMP into CTP

Initially, UMP must be converted into UDP and then into UTP by reactions that are catalyzed by nucleosidemonophosphate kinase and nucleosidediphosphate kinase, respectively. UTP can then undergo an energy-dependent amination reaction which results in the formation of CTP. This amination reaction is catalyzed by CTP synthetase [UTP:ammonia ligase (ADP-forming), EC 6.3.4.2]. However, since glutamine, rather than ammonia, is the preferred nitrogen source in the case of the enzyme from *E. coli* (which is perhaps the most extensively studied) and since mammalian synthetases are thought to utilize only glutamine as the nitrogen source, the reaction might best be expressed as follows:

$$\text{UTP} + \text{L-glutamine} + \text{ATP} \rightleftharpoons \text{CTP} + \text{L-glutamate} + \text{ADP} + P_i \quad (13\text{-}31)$$

CTP synthetase has been isolated from rat and bovine liver and partially purified. The activities of these enzymes are markedly dependent upon the presence of a sulfhydryl compound, e.g., 2-mercaptoethanol. When preliminary kinetic studies were conducted on these enzymes it was found that all plots of the reaction velocity as a function of the concentration of UTP, ATP, or glutamine were hyperbolic.

As isolated from *E. coli*, CTP synthetase is a tetramer which has a molecular weight of 210,000. By way of contrast, when kinetic studies were conducted on this enzyme it was found that plots of the reaction velocity as a function of the concentration of UTP or ATP were sigmoidal, rather than hyperbolic. Plots of the reaction velocity as a function of the concentration of glutamine also deviated from the usual hyperbolic form. In this case the plots were the very rapidly ascending hyperbolic curves that are frequently seen when the binding of the varied substrate occurs with negative cooperativity. When plots of $1/v_i$ as a function of $1/[\text{glutamine}]$ were prepared from these same data, they were found to be convex (or concave downward), also characteristic of a situation in which the binding of the varied substrate occurs with negative cooperativity. Thus, it is suggested that the binding of UTP and ATP by CTP synthetase can occur with positive cooperativity while that of glutamine can occur with negative cooperatively.† Daniel E. Koshland, Jr. has pointed out that when the binding of a substrate occurs with positive cooperativity, small changes in the concentration of that substrate can have a major effect upon the reaction velocity while when the binding of a substrate occurs with negative cooperativity, large changes in substrate concentration can have a relatively minor effect upon the reaction velocity.

The activities of CTP synthetases from mammalian sources or from microorganisms such as *E. coli* are enhanced in the presence of GTP. This enhancement is due to the fact that GTP promotes the formation of the enzyme-glutamyl intermediate, which in turn allows the amide nitrogen atom of glutamine to be utilized. This enzyme-glutamyl intermediate is specifically the thiol ester that is

---

† Koshland, D. E., Jr., and Levitzki, A. (1974) in *The Enzymes* (Boyer, P. D., ed.), 3d ed., vol. 10, pp. 539–559, Academic, New York.

derived from a cysteinyl sulfhydryl group at the catalytic site and the glutamyl moiety of glutamine, as is indicated below.

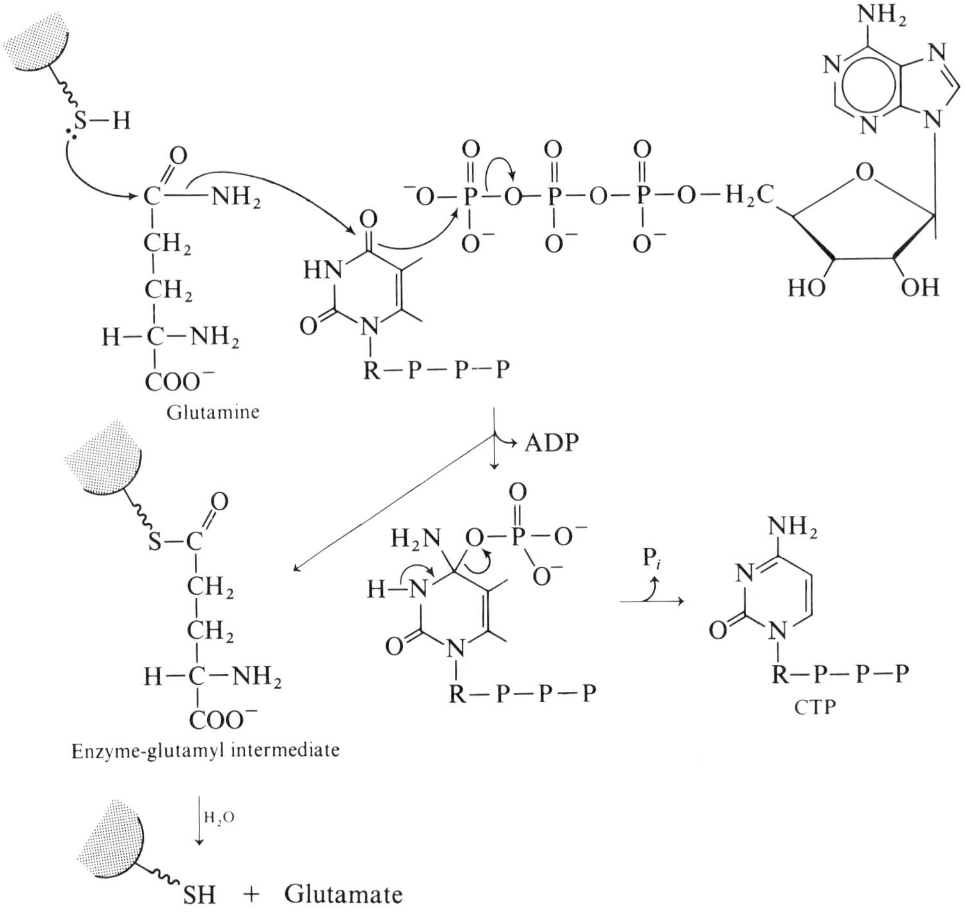

The mechanism is similar to that of the formation of phosphoribosylformylglycinamidine.

## Conversion of UMP into dTMP

UMP can be converted into dTMP, but this requires that the ribose moiety first be reduced to a deoxyribose moiety. In mammalian cells and in those of many microorganisms it is the ribose moiety of a ribonucleoside diphosphate that undergoes reduction. However, there are species in which the ribonucleoside triphosphate undergoes this reduction.

**Formation of deoxyribonucleotides** In mammalian cells and in those of microorganisms such as *E. coli*, UMP or any ribonucleoside mono- or triphosphate that is to be transformed into a deoxyribonucleotide is first converted into the ribonucleoside diphosphate. Then in the presence of ribonucleoside-diphosphate reductase (2′-deoxyribonucleoside diphosphate:oxidized thioredoxin 2′-oxidoreductase, EC 1.17.4.1), the following reaction can occur:

Ribonucleoside diphosphate + reduced thioredoxin $\rightleftharpoons$

2′-deoxyribonucleoside diphosphate + oxidized thioredoxin + $H_2O$   (13-32)

The reduction of UDP, CDP, ADP, or GDP is catalyzed by the same enzyme. As isolated from *E. coli* ribonucleoside-diphosphate reductase has a molecular weight of 238,000 and comprises two nonidentical subunits, the larger subunit has a molecular weight of 160,000 and the smaller subunit a molecular weight of 78,000. Each subunit is, itself, a dimer, and neither of the two subunits alone exhibits catalytic activity. The larger subunit contains the substrate binding sites and the binding sites for the modulators, which are nucleoside triphosphates. The smaller subunit contains nonheme iron and an unidentified organic free radical that participates in the electron-transport process associated with the reaction. The conversion of the ribose moiety of a ribonucleoside diphosphate into a deoxyribose moiety requires the removal of the $C(2')$ hydroxyl group and its replacement with a hydrogen. This constitutes a reduction of $C(2')$. The initial event in this process is the reaction between the larger subunit of the reductase and reduced thioredoxin, which results in the transfer of reducing equivalents from the thioredoxin to the subunit. Thioredoxin is a small polypeptide (of approximately 100 aminoacyl units) which functions as a carrier of reducing equivalents. Specifically, it contains a bissulfhydryl-disulfide system that can accept reducing equivalents from a donor and subsequently donate them to an appropriate acceptor. The reducing equivalents that are donated to the larger subunit of ribonucleoside-diphosphate reductase are accepted by specific disulfide groups of that protein. The resulting sulfhydryl groups then transfer these reducing equivalents to $C(2')$ of the nucleotide substrate. Finally, in order to regenerate the reduced form of thioredoxin the enzyme thioredoxin reductase (NADPH:oxidized-thioredoxin oxidoreductase, EC 1.6.4.5) catalyzes the transfer of reducing equivalents from NADPH to the small polypeptide. These reactions can be expressed diagrammatically as shown on page 578.

Preliminary kinetic studies on the reaction catalyzed by the ribonucleoside-diphosphate reductase from *E. coli* suggest that a ping pong sequence occurs since plots of $1/v_i$ as a function of $1/[CDP]$ with fixed concentrations of reduced thioredoxin and constant concentrations of all other components are parallel. An initial-velocity pattern such as this would be obtained if thioredoxin bound the enzyme, converted it to its reduced form, and then dissociated from the enzyme prior to the binding of the ribonucleoside diphosphate.†

The activity of ribonucleoside-diphosphate reductase from *E. coli* is inhibited by dATP while it is enhanced by ATP, GTP, or dTTP. The influences of these modulators help ensure that adequate concentrations of the appropriate deoxyribonucleotides are available for the synthesis of DNA.

† Thelander, L. (1974) *J. Biol. Chem.* **249**, 4858–4862.

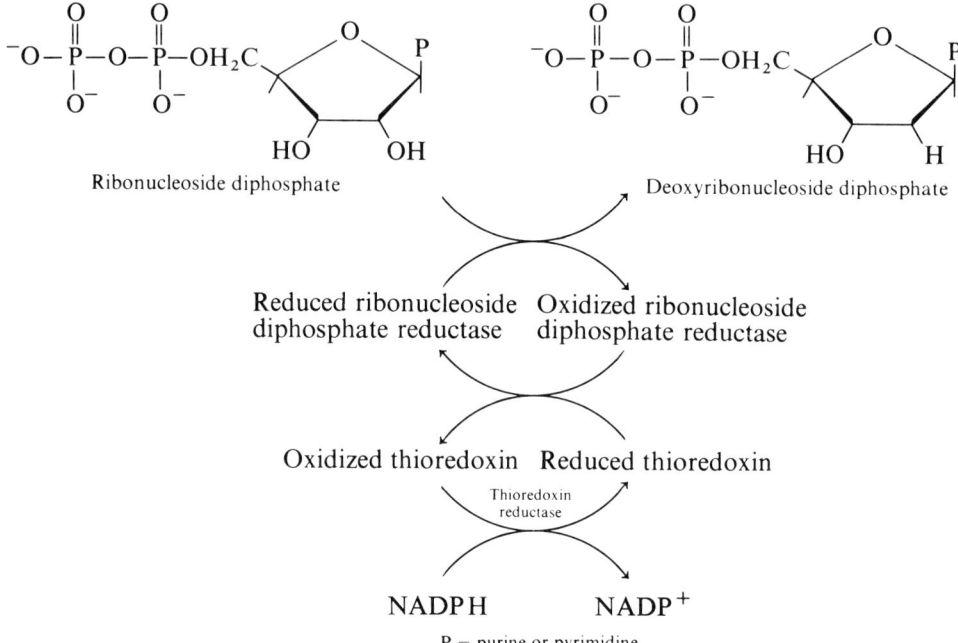

P = purine or pyrimidine

The formation of deoxyribonucleotides in certain microorganisms (including *Lactobacillus leichmannii*) and in the alga *Euglena gracilis* is catalyzed by a ribonucleoside-triphosphate reductase (2'-deoxyribonucleoside triphosphate:oxidized-thioredoxin 2'-oxidoreductase, EC 1.17.4.2). The preferred substrate in this case is a ribonucleoside triphosphate. In addition, this enzyme requires the participation of the vitamin $B_{12}$ cofactor, deoxyadenosylcobalamin.

Ribonucleoside-triphosphate reductase from *L. leichmannii* has been isolated as a single polypeptide chain which has a molecular weight of 76,000. In this case, the smaller subunit (which contains the nonheme iron and an organic free radical in the case of the *E. coli* reductase) is absent. The reaction catalyzed by this enzyme parallels that which is catalyzed by the reductase from *E. coli* except that ribonucleoside triphosphates are the preferred substrates. The deoxyadenosylcobalamin of the ribonucleoside-triphosphate reductase, which functions at the catalytic site, perhaps assumes the same role as the unidentified free radical of the enzyme from *E. coli*. Thioredoxin, thioredoxin reductase, and NADPH are required for the reaction in *L. leichmannii*, as in *E. coli*.

**Formation of dTMP** Having converted UMP into UDP and then into dUDP (in most cells), this intermediate can then be converted into dUMP and subsequently into dTMP. The conversion of dUMP into dTMP requires the introduction of a methyl group at C(5) of the pyrimidine ring. This methyl group is derived from 5,10-methylenetetrahydrofolate. The introduction of the methyl group is catalyzed by thymidylate synthase (which is not completely characterized). The reaction is

dUMP + 5,10-methylenetetrahydrofolate $\rightleftharpoons$ dTMP + dihydrofolate

(13-33)

Thymidylate synthases have been isolated from several sources, including Ehrlich ascites carcinoma cells, chick embryo, and *Lactobacillus casei*. These enzymes are all moderately small proteins; the molecular weight of the synthase from the carcinoma cells is 67,000, that from chick embryo is 58,000, and that from the *Lactobacillus* is 70,000. (The last comprises two subunits.)

The formation of dTMP entails the transfer of the methylene group of the tetrahydrofolate derivative plus the hydrogen and its electrons from C(6) of the tetrahydropteridine moiety of the cofactor to dUMP. Since electrons are lost from the tetrahydropteridine moiety, it undergoes oxidation (to a dihydropteridine moiety), and, as a concomitance, the methylene group is reduced to a methyl group. This may occur as follows:

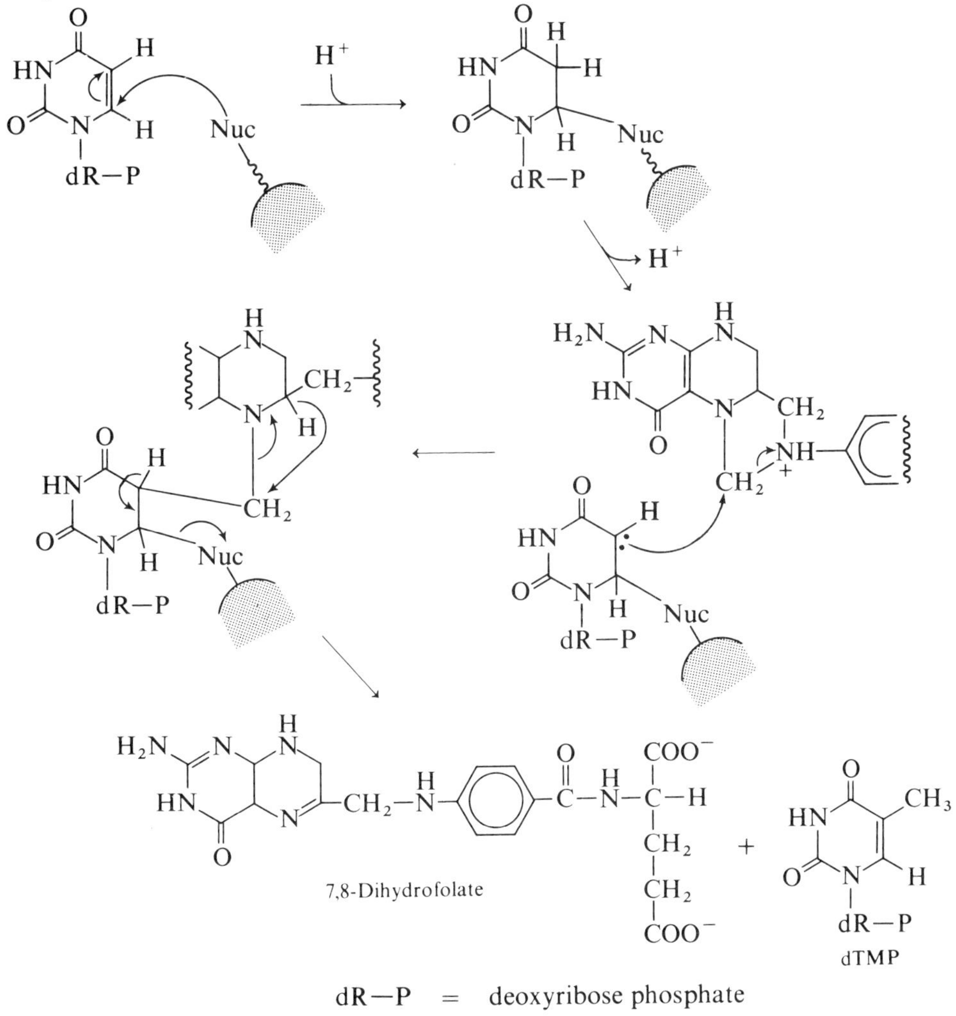

dR—P = deoxyribose phosphate

Following a nucleophilic attack at C(6) of the uracil moiety, which eliminates the olefinic bond, a proton is abstracted from C(5). Now the nucleophilic C(5) attacks the carbon atom of the one-carbon unit. A hydride ion is then transferred from C(6) of the tetrahydropteridine moiety of the cofactor, and the methylene group is converted into a methyl group. Reestablishment of the C(5)—C(6) olefinic bond of the pyrimidine moiety completes the reaction.

The formation of dTMP results in the conversion of a tetrahydrofolate derivative into dihydrofolate. In order to regenerate tetrahydrofolate the dihydrofolate must be reduced in the presence of NADPH and the enzyme tetrahydrofolate dehydrogenase (5,6,7,8-tetrahydrofolate:$NADP^+$ oxidoreductase, EC 1.5.1.3). The reaction is

7,8-Dihydrofolate + NADPH $\rightleftharpoons$ 5,6,7,8-tetrahydrofolate + $NADP^+$ (13-34)

As isolated from bovine liver, tetrahydrofolate dehydrogenase is a single polypeptide chain which has a molecular weight of 20,000.

The reaction catalyzed by thymidylate synthase provides the only means for the *de novo* synthesis of thymine and its nucleosides and nucleotides. Since deoxythymidine phosphates are required for the synthesis of all DNA, considerable attention has been focused upon the conversion of dUMP into dTMP and upon the reduction of dihydrofolate to tetrahydrofolate, with the thought that the modulation of these reactions might be of value in arresting or curing cancer. Compounds found to inhibit the activity of thymidylate synthase or tetrahydrofolate dehydrogenase have therefore been tested as cancer chemotherapeutic agents. Among these compounds is 5-fluorouracil, which appears to inhibit the activity of thymidylate synthase. Actually, its effect is due largely to the fact that it is readily converted into 5-fluoro-dUMP, which is thought to participate in the reaction in the same manner as dUMP except that the C(5)—C(6) olefinic bond cannot be reestablished at the end of the reaction.

Another component used as a cancer chemotherapeutic agent is the folate analog amethopterin.

Amethopterin (methotrexate)

Amethopterin binds tetrahydrofolate dehydrogenase, and since the dissociation constant for the resulting complex is less than 0.1 n$M$, the dehydrogenase is, in effect, rendered inactive.

## Conversion of dCMP into dUMP

The activity of the enzyme dCMP deaminase (dCMP aminohydrolase, EC 3.5.4.12) has been reported to be a factor in maintaining sufficient concentrations of dTTP for DNA synthesis since the dUMP formed as a result of this deamination can in turn be converted into dTMP. In support of this proposal is the observation that the activity of the deaminase is subject to modulation. More specifically, the activity of dCMP deaminase is enhanced by dCTP while it is inhibited by dTTP. These effects can be seen if one examines the relationship between the reaction velocity and the concentration of the substrate, dCMP. Plots of $v_i$ vs. [dCMP] are sigmoidal in the absence of modifiers, but upon the addition of sufficient concentrations of dCTP these plots are converted into hyperbolic ones. On the other hand, as increasing concentrations of dTTP are introduced, plots of the reaction velocity vs. the concentration of dCMP become progressively more sigmoidal. Thus, it seems that when concentrations of dCTP are high, more dUMP and, in turn, more dTMP will be produced, whereas when there is sufficient dTTP for DNA synthesis, the formation of dUMP, a precursor of dTTP, is curtailed.

## Conversion of dCMP into 5-Hydroxymethyldeoxycytidylate in Bacteriophages

The DNA of the T-even bacteriophages contains 5-hydroxymethyldeoxycytidylyl units rather than deoxycytidylyl units. Synthesis of the substituted cytidylyl moiety occurs upon introduction of a hydroxymethyl group by a reaction similar to that catalyzed by thymidylate synthase. In the present case, the enzyme is deoxycytidylate hydroxymethyltransferase (5,10-methylenetetrahydrofolate:deoxycytidylate 5-hydroxymethyltransferase, EC 2.1.2.8), and the reaction is

dCMP + 5,10-methylenetetrafolate $\rightleftharpoons$

5-hydroxymethyl-dCMP + tetrahydrofolate    (13-35)

The reaction may be considered to proceed by a reaction mechanism similar to that proposed for the synthesis of dTMP but with the introduction of a hydroxyl group rather than a hydride ion at the end, as shown.

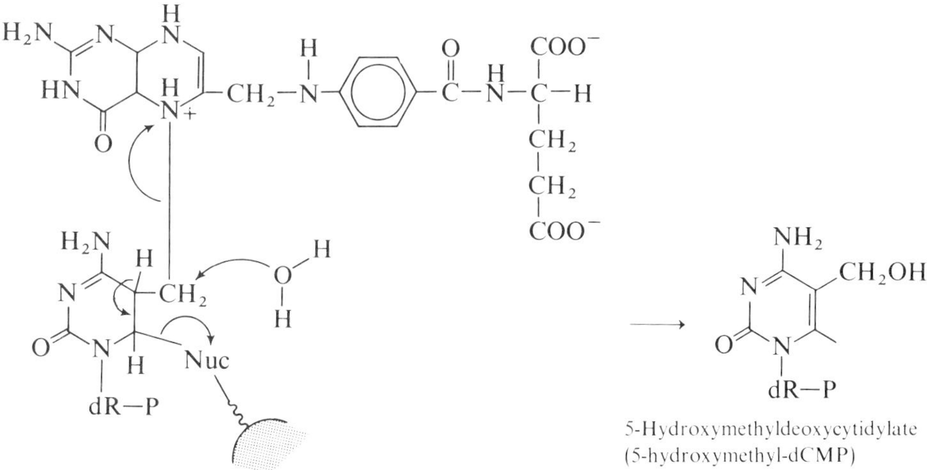

5-Hydroxymethyldeoxycytidylate
(5-hydroxymethyl-dCMP)

+

Tetrahydrofolate

## PYRIMIDINE SALVAGE PATHWAYS

Existing pyrimidines and pyrimidine nucleosides can be utilized or reutilized in a manner similar to that of the purines and their derivatives. In mammalian cells, these salvage pathways generally entail the conversion of the pyrimidine into the corresponding nucleoside and the conversion of pyrimidine nucleosides into the corresponding nucleoside triphosphates.

The conversion of a pyrimidine into the pyrimidine nucleoside is catalyzed by an enzyme such as uridine phosphorylase (uridine:orthophosphate ribosyltransferase, EC 2.4.2.3) or thymidine phosphorylase (thymidine:orthophosphate deoxyribosyltransferase, EC 2.4.2.4). The reactions catalyzed by these enzymes can be written

$$\text{Uracil} + \alpha\text{-D-ribose 1-phosphate} \rightleftharpoons \text{uridine} + P_i \quad (13\text{-}36)$$

$$\text{Thymine} + 2\text{-deoxy-D-ribose 1-phosphate} \rightleftharpoons \text{deoxythymidine} + P_i \quad (13\text{-}37)$$

Uridine formed as a result of the reaction catalyzed by uridine phosphorylase or existing uridine can undergo phosphorylation to yield UMP in the presence of uridine kinase (ATP:uridine 5'-phosphotransferase, EC 2.7.1.48). There has been particular interest in this enzyme since its activity can be correlated with the extent to which cell proliferation is occurring. For example, in tumor tissue in which cells are proliferating rapidly the activity of uridine kinase is relatively high compared with normal tissue. This observation lends support to the hypothesis that the pyrimidine salvage pathway becomes even more important when cells are proliferating rapidly.

Activity of the enzyme that catalyzes the phosphorylation of deoxythymidine is also increased as a concomitance of the rapid proliferation of cells. This enzyme, deoxythymidine kinase (ATP:deoxythymidine 5'-phosphotransferase, EC 2.7.1.75), has been isolated from the bovine thymus as a protein which has a molecular weight of 55,000. Kinetic studies on this bovine kinase suggest that the conversion of deoxythymidine to dTMP occurs by a sequential mechanism. It is also known that the activity of this enzyme is inhibited by the ultimate product dTTP, which functions as a competitive inhibitor vs. deoxythymidine. A deoxythymidine kinase from *E. coli* has been shown to differ from the mammalian enzyme in that plots of the reaction velocity as a function of the concentration of ATP are sigmoidal although they become hyperbolic upon the addition of the modulator dCDP.

The conversion of deoxycytidine into dCMP is catalyzed by deoxycytidine kinase (NTP:deoxycytidine 5'-phosphotransferase, EC 2.7.1.74). In this case ATP, GTP, or dTTP can function as the phosphoryl donor. The kinase has been isolated from the bovine thymus as a small protein having a molecular weight of 56,000. When initial-velocity studies were conducted on this bovine kinase it was determined that plots of $1/v_i$ as a function of $1/[\text{deoxycytidine}]$ or as a function of $1/[\text{MgATP}]$ are convex. These data were then used to construct Hill plots; i.e., $\log \{v/(V_{max} - v)\}$ was plotted as a function of $\log [\text{deoxycytidine}]$ or $\log [\text{MgATP}]$. In each case Hill coefficients less than unity were obtained. These observations imply that the binding of each substrate occurs with negative cooperativity. The kinetic studies also demonstrated that the activity of the enzyme is inhibited by the ultimate product dCTP and that this inhibitory effect is countered by dTTP. These characteristics would appear to be designed to ensure constant and adequate concentrations of the deoxyribonucleotide precursors of DNA. Thus, the substrate binding with negative cooperativity would prevent fluctuations in those concentrations from being reflected by the reaction velocity, and the effects of dCTP and dTTP would allow comparable concentrations of dCTP and dTTP to be maintained.†

## CATABOLISM OF PYRIMIDINES

The catabolism of the pyrimidine nucleosides and nucleotides initially involves their conversion into the pyrimidine base. In turn, the pyrimidine base can undergo reduction and subsequently hydrolytic cleavage, as shall be described.

Cytidylates are converted into cytidine as a result of the appropriate dephosphorylation reactions, catalyzed by nucleotidases. Cytidine is then converted into uridine in the presence of cytidine deaminase (cytidine aminohydrolase, EC 3.5.4.5). The uridine can then be converted into uracil by uridine phosphorylase. Deoxythymidylates can be converted into deoxythymidine and then into thymine by similar reactions. Either uracil or thymine can now serve as a substrate for the enzyme dihydrouracil dehydrogenase (5,6-dihydrouracil:$NADP^+$ oxidoreductase, EC 1.3.1.2). The reaction that is catalyzed by this dehydrogenase is

$$\text{Uracil (thymine)} + \text{NAD(P)H} \rightleftharpoons \text{5,6-dihydrouracil (5,6-dihydrothymine)} + \text{NAD(P)}^+ \quad (13\text{-}38)$$

The reduction of the pyrimidine ring to a dihydropyrimidine ring is rate-determining with respect to the catabolic pathway. In rat liver, enzymes that catalyze the virtually irreversible reduction of uracil or thymine are found in association with the mitochondria and (to a lesser extent) the plasma membranes and the endoplasmic reticulum. The mitochondrial enzyme utilizes NADH as the oxidation-reduction cofactor while the enzymes associated with the plasma membrane or the endoplasmic reticulum utilize NADPH.

Dihydropyrimidines undergo hydrolytic cleavage to yield acyclic derivatives. The enzyme dihydropyrimidinase (5,6-dihydropyrimidine amidohydrolase, EC 3.5.2.2), which catalyzes the cleavage, can use either 5,6-dihydrouracil or 5,6-dihydrothymine as a substrate. The product of the reaction is $N$-carbamoyl-3-aminopropionate (sometimes called 3-ureidopropionate) when dihydrouracil undergoes cleavage, while it is $N$-carbamoyl-3-aminoisobutyrate when dihydrothymine undergoes cleavage. Finally, in the presence of 3-ureidopropionase ($N$-carbamoyl-3-aminopropionate amidohydrolase, EC 3.5.1.6), $N$-carbamoyl-3-aminopropionate undergoes further hydrolysis to yield 3-aminopropionate (sometimes called $\beta$-alanine) plus carbon dioxide and ammonia. This enzyme also converts $N$-carbamoyl-3-

---

† Ives, D. H., and Durham, J. P. (1970) *J. Biol. Chem.* **245**, 2285-2294.

aminoisobutyrate to 3-aminoisobutyrate plus carbon dioxide and ammonia. The catabolism of the pyrimidine ring is summarized below.

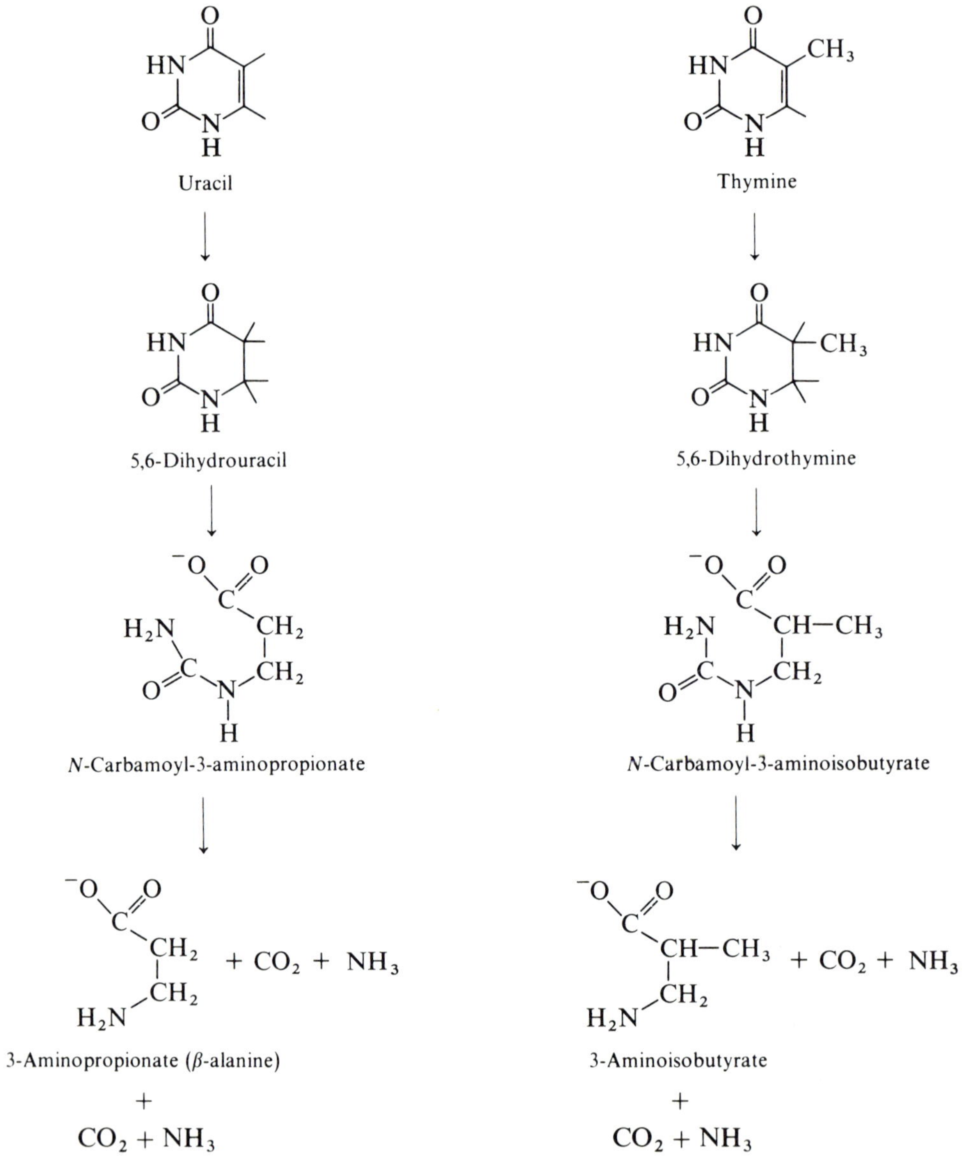

Uracil → 5,6-Dihydrouracil → N-Carbamoyl-3-aminopropionate → 3-Aminopropionate ($\beta$-alanine) + $CO_2$ + $NH_3$

Thymine → 5,6-Dihydrothymine → N-Carbamoyl-3-aminoisobutyrate → 3-Aminoisobutyrate + $CO_2$ + $NH_3$

## REGULATION OF PYRIMIDINE METABOLISM

In mammals the rate-determining step in the *de novo* synthesis of the pyrimidine ring is that which is catalyzed by one of the two carbamoyl-phosphate synthases present in mammalian cells. This synthase is localized in the cytoplasm, probably as a component of a complex that includes other enzymes of the anabolic pathway. The major regulatory influences upon the activity of this carbamoyl-phosphate synthase are those imposed by the ultimate products of the pathway, such as UTP. The activity of aspartate carbamoyltransferase, the enzyme that catalyzes the second reaction of the pathway, is neither rate-limiting nor subject to modulation by ultimate products. By contrast, the prokaryotic organism E. coli has only one carbamoyl-phosphate synthase, which catalyzes the formation of the carbamoyl phosphate used in the synthesis of both arginine and the pyrimidine ring. In this case, the activity of aspartate carbamoyltransferase is rate-determining and subject to modulation by the ultimate products CTP (an inhibitor) and ATP (an activator).

Quantitatively, the most important pyrimidine salvage pathway in the mammals appears to be the conversion of uracil into uridine (as catalyzed by uridine phosphorylase) and then the phosphorylation of uridine to yield UMP. However, uracil can also be converted directly into UMP by a reaction catalyzed by uracil phosphoribosyltransferase (UMP:pyrophosphate phosphoribosyltransferase, EC 2.4.2.9). The reaction is similar to that catalyzed by orotate phosphoribosyltransferase.

## ANABOLISM OF DEOXYRIBONUCLEIC ACIDS

The biosynthesis of DNA is a complex process by which the appropriate deoxyribonucleotidyl units are bonded by phosphodiester bonds to yield linear polymers. The phosphodiester bonds involve the $C(3')$ hydroxyl group of one deoxyribonucleotidyl unit and the $C(5')$ phosphoryl group of the neighboring unit. The formation of these phosphodiester bonds is catalyzed by a DNA nucleotidyltransferase (deoxyribonucleosidetriphosphate:DNA deoxyribonucleotidyltransferase, EC 2.7.7.7). These enzymes are generally called DNA polymerases. The reaction which they catalyze can be stated in general terms as

$n$ Deoxyribonucleoside triphosphate $\rightleftharpoons$ $DNA_n$ + $n$ pyrophosphate  (13-39)

This reaction requires

1. $Mg^{2+}$
2. The presence of all four deoxyribonucleoside triphosphate substrates (dATP, dGTP, dCTP, and dTTP) for maximal efficiency
3. A template, which is a polynucleotide macromolecule (either DNA or RNA) that dictates the nucleotide sequence of the DNA being formed
4. An initiator, which is an oligo- or polynucleotide having a free $C(3')$ hydroxyl group at its terminus

A minimal reaction mechanism for the formation of the phosphodiester bond is shown on page 586.

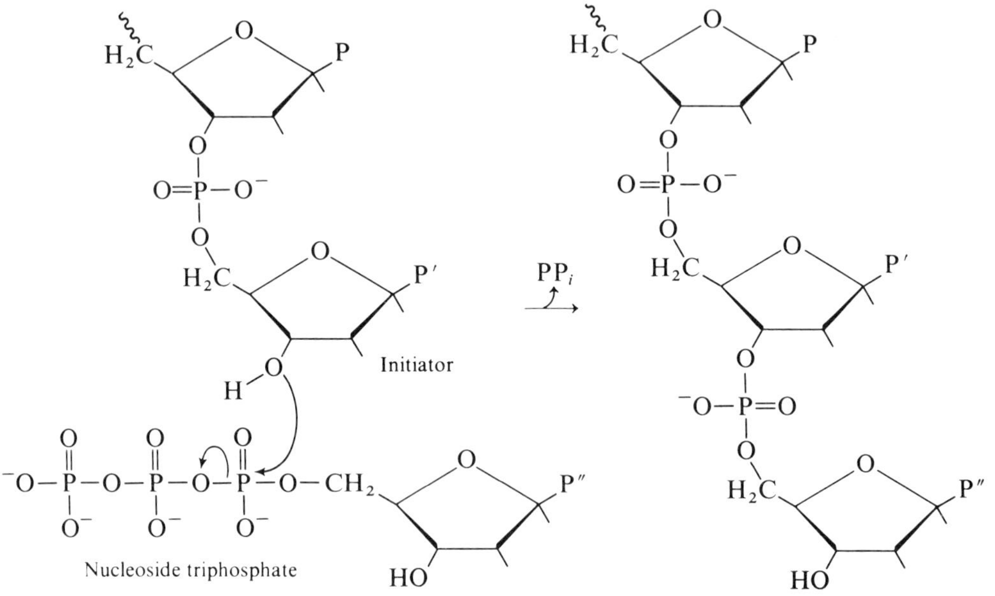

## DNA Polymerases

Both eukaryotic and prokaryotic cells contain more than one enzyme that exhibits DNA nucleotidyltransferase activity. In eukaryotic cells four DNA polymerases have been described. One, DNA polymerase $\alpha$,[†] has a molecular weight greater than 100,000 and is probably an enzyme complex. This polymerase is localized in the nucleus,[‡] and its enzymatic activity correlates positively with the rate of cell proliferation. Since the increase in polymerase $\alpha$ activity usually accompanying increased cell proliferation can be abolished by drugs that inhibit protein synthesis, it is suggested that during periods of growth and regeneration, polymerase molecules are synthesized. A second polymerase, DNA polymerase $\beta$, is a much smaller protein. As isolated from bovine thymus chromatin, this polymerase has a molecular weight of 44,000; however, its activity does not respond to an increased rate of cell proliferation. A third polymerase, DNA polymerase $\gamma$, also has a molecular weight greater than 100,000. This polymerase utilizes an RNA template with greater efficiency than a DNA template, in contrast to the other two polymerases. Finally, the fourth polymerase in eukaryotic cells is the mitochondrial DNA polymerase which catalyzes the synthesis of DNA in this cell organelle.

Much more is known concerning the DNA polymerases of prokaryotic cells and, more specifically, the DNA polymerases of *E. coli*. Three DNA polymerases have been isolated from this microorganism.

---

[†] Weissback, A., Baltimore, D., Bollum, F., Gallo, R., and Korn, D. (1975) *Science*, **190**, 401–402.
[‡] Lynch, W. E., Surrey, S., and Lieberman, I. (1975) *J. Biol. Chem.* **250**, 8179–8183.

DNA polymerase I, as isolated in the laboratory of Arthur Kornberg at the Stanford University School of Medicine, is a single polypeptide chain which has a molecular weight of 109,000. The enzyme binds one atom of zinc. There are approximately 400 molecules of DNA polymerase I per *E. coli* cell.

The incorporation of deoxyribonucleotidyl units as catalyzed by any one of the DNA polymerases entails chain elongation in the $5' \rightarrow 3'$ direction; i.e., the C(5') phosphoryl group of the incoming deoxyribonucleotidyl unit becomes bonded to the C(3') hydroxyl group of the initiator or of the growing polynucleotide chain. The various polymerases can be distinguished on the basis of the type of polynucleotide substrate they use most efficiently and the type of hydrolytic (nuclease) activity they exhibit in addition to their polymerase activity. DNA polymerase I binds single-stranded DNA. It also binds double-stranded DNA which has a scission (nick) or a gap. A scission is a point at which a phosphodiester bond of the polynucleotide chain has been cleaved. If as a result of a scission nucleotidyl units are removed from the chain, a hiatus, or gap, is created. DNA polymerase I does not bind an intact DNA duplex macromolecule. In addition to its nucleotidyl-transferase activity, polymerase I exhibits $3' \rightarrow 5'$ exonuclease activity, with single-stranded DNA as the substrate, and $5' \rightarrow 3'$ exonuclease activity, with double-stranded DNA as the substrate. An exonuclease is an enzyme that catalyzes the hydrolytic cleavage of a phosphodiester bond by which a terminal nucleotidyl unit is bonded. A $3' \rightarrow 5'$ exonuclease catalyzes the removal of nucleotidyl units from the 3' terminus of the polynucleotide chain, while a $5' \rightarrow 3'$ exonuclease catalyzes the removal of nucleotidyl units from the 5' terminus of the chain. The reactions catalyzed by such exonucleases are represented diagrammatically below.

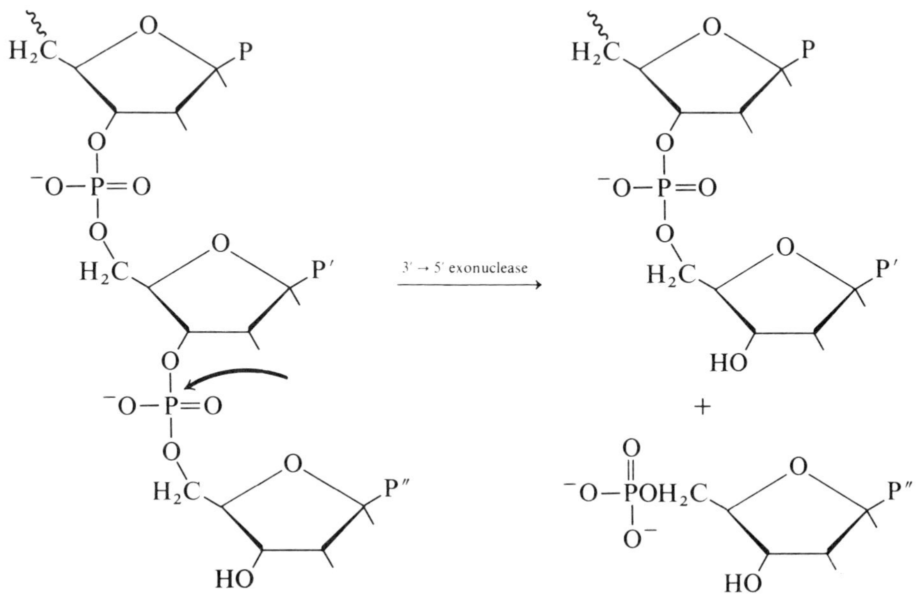

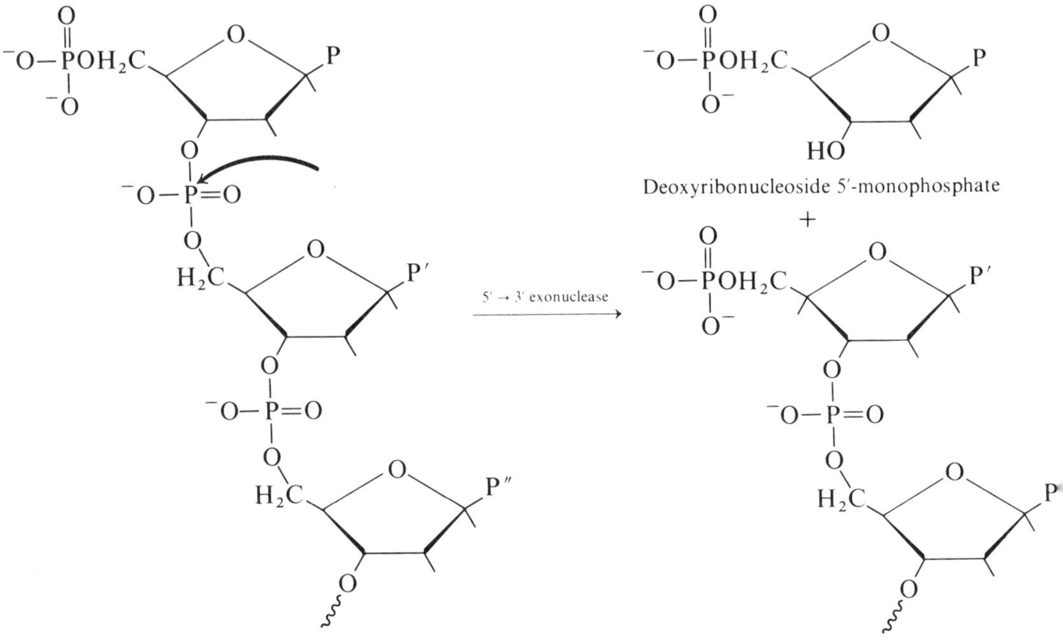

It has been proposed that one function of DNA polymerase I is that of removing an RNA oligonucleotide (thought to serve as an initiator) from the 5' terminus of the nascent DNA strand. The possible role of an RNA oligonucleotide in DNA synthesis will be discussed below. This excision would utilize the 5' → 3' exonuclease activity of polymerase I. It has also been suggested that polymerase I then catalyzes the filling in of the gap created as a result of the excision of the initiator. Thus, the nucleotidyltransferase activity of the enzyme would be utilized. In addition, it has been shown that the 3' → 5' nuclease activity of the polymerase may allow it to serve as a "proofreader" in that the enzyme can catalyze the removal of a mispaired purine or pyrimidine base that has been incorporated at the end of the growing chain.

DNA polymerase II from *E. coli*, as isolated in the laboratory of Jerard Hurwitz at Albert Einstein College of Medicine, Yeshiva University, is a single polypeptide which has a molecular weight of 120,000. An *E. coli* cell contains approximately 40 molecules of polymerase II. The enzyme DNA polymerase II binds neither single-stranded DNA nor intact double-stranded DNA. It also fails to bind double-stranded DNA which has a scission, although it does bind DNA which has a gap. In addition to its nucleotidyltransferase activity, polymerase II also exhibits 3' → 5' exonuclease activity. It has been suggested that this enzyme may participate in DNA synthesis by catalyzing the elongation of short oligonucleotides (called *Okazaki fragments*, discussed below) that are formed during the polymerization process.

The third polymerase in prokaryotic cells, DNA polymerase III, is present to the extent of only about 10 molecules per cell in *E. coli*, but it is the only one of the three polymerases that catalyzes the incorporation of deoxyribonucleotidyl units at a rate of the same order of magnitude as that seen during chromosomal replication. For this reason and others it is generally agreed that DNA polymerase III is the enzyme that catalyzes the principal elongation step in the synthesis of DNA. Polymerase III, initially isolated by Thomas Kornberg and Malcolm L. Gefter at Columbia University, has nucleotide binding characteristics similar to those of polymerase II. Polymerase III exhibits both $3' \rightarrow 5'$ and $5' \rightarrow 3'$ nuclease activity, however, in addition to its nucleotidyltransferase activity. Although DNA polymerase III catalyzes a rapid incorporation of deoxyribonucleotidyl units, the extent of this incorporation is only 10 to 100 units, even when the template is a very long polynucleotide strand. Two protein factors have been isolated, however, which if added to polymerase III along with ATP promote the synthesis of long polynucleotide strands in the presence of an appropriate template. Also, a species of polymerase III designated polymerase III* can catalyze the synthesis of long polynucleotide strands in the presence of an appropriate template. Polymerase III*, which is thought to be a dimer of polymerase III, is composed of subunits which each have a molecular weight of 90,000. The factor copolymerase III*, on the other hand, has a molecular weight of 76,000 and exhibits no nucleotidyltransferase or other enzymatic activity. In support of the concept that polymerase III* and copolymerase III* can interact to generate a species which has properties much like those of the polymerase that functions in vivo, a complex comprising two of the polymerase III* subunits and two molecules of copolymerase III* has been isolated. This complex, which has a molecular weight of 330,000, catalyzes the formation of long polynucleotide strands in the absence of added copolymerase III*.

## Replication of DNA

Replication is the production of a copy of the original. Thus, the replication of DNA is the production, or synthesis, of a copy of the originial, or template, DNA. Since most studies on DNA replication have been carried out on *E. coli*, in general, the observations that have been made with respect to this prokaryotic system serve as the basis for the discussion which follows.

From an overview, DNA replication entails the interaction of the DNA template, the enzyme that catalyzes the formation of the phosphodiester bonds, the four deoxyribonucleoside triphosphates (dATP, dGTP, dCTP, and dTTP), and supporting factors. The template dictates the order in which the nucleotidyl units are introduced into the polynucleotide strand and this is accomplished in the following manner. In order for a deoxyribonucleotidyl unit to be incorporated it must undergo very specific hydrogen bonding, or base pairing, with the deoxyribonucleotidyl unit of the template which at that time must be appropriately positioned at the catalytic site. If a deoxyadenylyl unit of the template is at the catalytic site, only a deoxythymidylyl moiety can hydrogen-bond appropriately with it. Therefore, only a deoxythymidylyl unit will be incorporated at that point in the nascent strand. Deoxycytidylyl units, on the other hand, can undergo base pairing only with deoxyguanylyl moieties. It then follows that if a template has at some point the sequence deoxyadenylyl-deoxycytidylyl-deoxyguanylyl, the nascent strand will have

**590** MECHANISMS OF METABOLISM

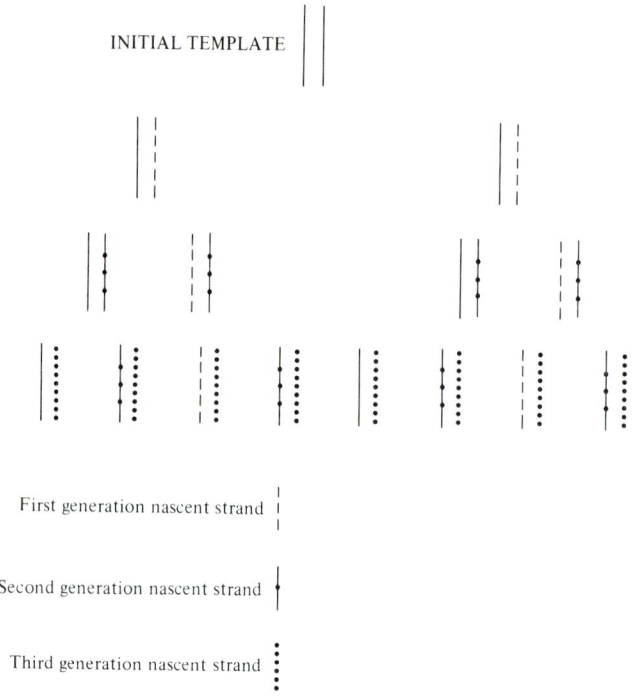

**Figure 13-2** Diagrammatic representation of the replication of DNA. In each instance replication entails the formation of a strand that is complementary to an existing strand.

a deoxythymidylyl unit paired with the first, a deoxyguanylyl unit paired with the second, and a deoxycytidylyl unit paired with the third of the template units.† Thus, a given template strand, in fact, dictates the sequence of the complementary strand. Furthermore, when the other template strand has similarly dictated the synthesis of *its* complementary strand, one has two identical DNA molecules, each containing one template strand and one nascent strand, as represented diagrammatically in Fig. 13-2.

Consider now the events that occur when DNA is replicated. First, replication of a chromosome begins at a specific locus on that chromosome. For example, the *E. coli* chromosome is circular. The origin of replication is at 74 min on the chromosome linkage map. Since replication then proceeds bidirectionally and at approximately the same velocity, the termination point is at 25 min on the linkage map (Fig. 13-3). Not all the factors and steps that are involved in DNA replication are known; some that are known and some that have been proposed are discussed in the following paragraphs.

**Initiation** DNA replication requires as an initiator an oligo- or polynucleotide which has a C(3′) hydroxyl group at its terminus. In some cases short ribonucleotide

---

† Since sequences are read from the 5′→3′ direction by convention, the corresponding sequence of the nascent (antiparallel) strand is stated as deoxycytidylyl-deoxyguanylyl-deoxythymidylyl.

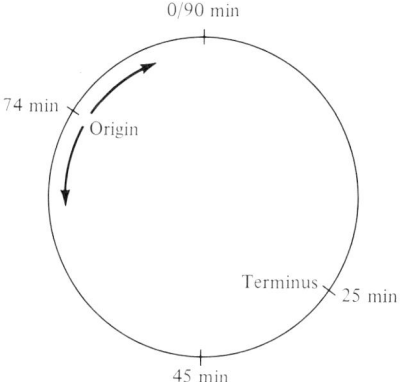

**Figure 13-3** Representation of the bidirectional replication of the *E. coli* chromosome, which begins at 74 min and terminates at 25 min on the linkage map.

strands (of approximately 10 nucleotidyl units) can function in this capacity, and it has been suggested that such oligoribonucleotides may serve as initiators in chromosome replication. RNA synthesis, unlike DNA synthesis, does not require an initiator, and therefore all that is necessary to generate oligoribonucleotides is the appropriate enzyme (RNA nucleotidyltransferase discussed subsequently) and the appropriate ribonucleotide substrates. In fact, it has been shown that DNA replication can be initiated in the presence of the DNA template and six proteins, i.e., an RNA nucleotidyltransferase, DNA polymerase III*, copolymerase III*, DNA polymerase I, DNA unwinding protein, and a ligase, as the only macromolecules.†

The DNA unwinding protein, mentioned above, facilitates and maintains the disengagement of the two strands of the DNA template. The protein, in fact, masks the separated template strands except at the points at which the strand is bound by enzymes and other factors involved in the replication process. This protects the strands from being cleaved by nucleases during replication. The DNA unwinding protein of *E. coli* has been isolated, purified, and found to be a tetramer which has a molecular weight of 76,000. The rapidly dividing cell contains approximately 300 copies of the unwinding protein. It has been calculated that each protein molecule can bind and mask a span of 32 nucleotidyl units on a template strand.

Prior to DNA synthesis the strands of a segment of the template at the origin are disengaged and masked by the unwinding protein. Since only a segment of the chromosome is unwound, a forked structure is created. The bifurcation is called the *replication fork*. As DNA synthesis, i.e., elongation, proceeds, more and more of the template is unwound since the unwinding protein is released and made available to an additional portion of the double-stranded structure as a concomitance of the growth of the nascent strand. Thus, as elongation proceeds, the position of the replication fork moves at the same rate at which the nascent strand grows.

A complex that can catalyze the incorporation of the initial deoxyribonucleotidyl units can be formed in the presence of polymerase III*, copolymerase III*, a template, an initiator, the DNA unwinding protein, and ATP. Upon addition of the

---

† Weiner, J. H., Bertsch, L. L., and Kornberg, A. (1975) *J. Biol. Chem.* **250**, 1972–1980.

appropriate deoxyribonucleoside triphosphates DNA synthesis begins concomitantly with the release of ADP and orthophosphate.

**Elongation** The elongation process in DNA replication entails the synthesis of at least one, and possibly both, of the nascent strands by a discontinuous process. The utilization of a discontinuous process is required in the case of at least one of the strands since elongation proceeds only in the $5' \to 3'$ direction and yet synthesis is observed to progress in a parallel manner beside the two *antiparallel* template strands. In view of the antiparallel relationship between the two template strands, a continuous process can occur only if synthesis proceeds in the $5' \to 3'$ direction with one of the strands as the template and in the $3' \to 5'$ direction with the other strand as the template.

If it is assumed that both nascent strands are synthesized by a discontinuous process, each template strand must be associated with several sites at which synthesis can be begun (once replication has been initiated). As synthesis occurs in conjunction with one of the template strands, the growth of the nascent strand will be in the same direction as the movement of the replication fork. However, as synthesis occurs in conjunction with the other template strand, the growth of the nascent strand will be in the direction opposite to that of the movement of the replication fork. This is illustrated in Fig. 13-4. Note that in both cases synthesis is proceeding in the $5' \to 3'$ direction. The oligodeoxyribonucleotides thus formed are called Okazaki fragments since this pattern of discontinuous synthesis was formulated by Reiji Okazaki at Nagoya University in Japan. Okazaki fragments generally consist of approximately 1000 deoxyribonucleotidyl units. As synthesis of an Okazaki fragment proceeds, the polymerase and its supporting components are thought to move toward the point on the template at which the synthesis of the neighboring fragment was begun. When this point is reached, the polymerase system dissociates from the template and synthesis stops. Meanwhile, the initiator is cleaved from the nascent fragment and the resulting hiatus is filled in through the agency of DNA polymerase I. Finally, the fragment must be joined to the neighboring fragment in order to complete this segment of the nascent strand.

The joining of the Okazaki fragments is catalyzed by enzymes frequently called DNA ligases although because they utilize energy derived from the cleavage of ATP or $NAD^+$, they have been classified as synthetases.

In *E. coli* the joining of polydeoxyribonucleotide fragments is catalyzed by an $NAD^+$-dependent polynucleotide synthetase [poly(deoxyribonucleotide):poly-(deoxyribonucleotide) ligase (AMP-forming, NMN-forming), EC 6.5.1.2]. This enzyme has a molecular weight of 77,000. Approximately 300 copies of the synthetase are contained in an *E. coli* cell.

Joining of the two polydeoxyribonucleotide fragments entails the formation of a phosphodiester bond derived from the terminal $C(5')$ phosphoryl group of one polynucleotide and the $C(3')$ hydroxyl group of the other. Two intermediates are formed during the course of the reaction, and both have been isolated. Initially, the nucleophilic $\epsilon$-amino group of a lysyl unit at the enzyme catalytic site attacks the adenylyl phosphoryl phosphorus atom of $NAD^+$, with the result that an adenylyl-enzyme intermediate is formed as nicotinamide mononucleotide (NMN) is eliminated.

# METABOLISM OF PURINES, PYRIMIDINES, AND NUCLEIC ACIDS

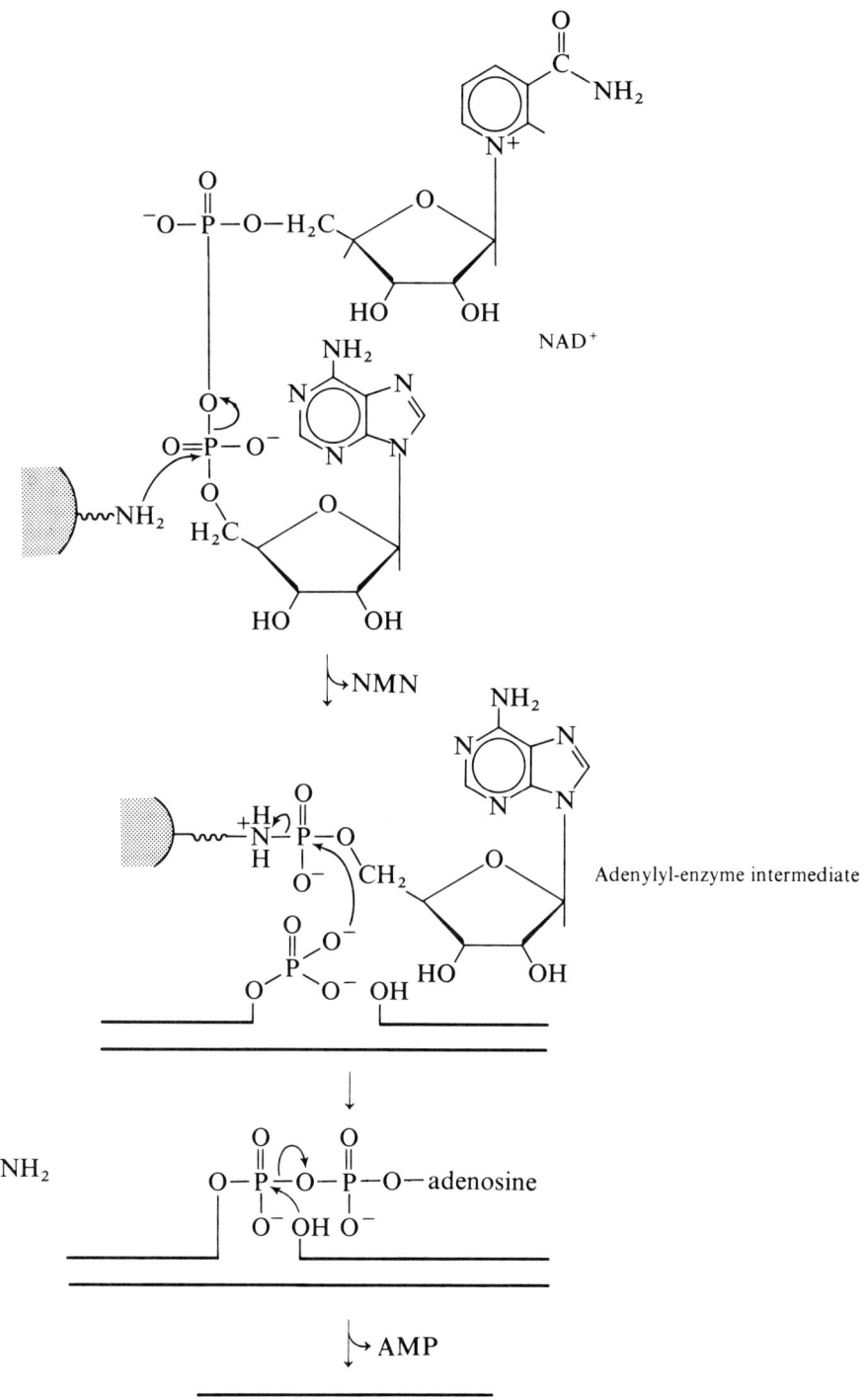

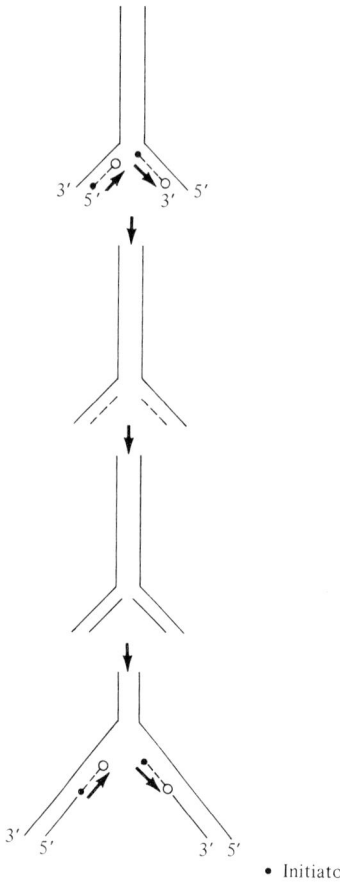

**Figure 13-4** Diagrammatic representation of the replication of DNA by a discontinuous process. Synthesis occurs in the $5' \to 3'$ direction with each of the two existing strands as a template. In the top diagram synthesis has progressed from the site of the initiator to the site at which the polymerase is, at that time, positioned. Subsequently, completed fragments are joined and elongation continues as the replication fork moves up the DNA double-stranded template.

• Initiator
○ Polymerase

Next an oxygen atom of the terminal C(5') phosphoryl group attacks the phosphoramidate bond of the adenylyl-enzyme intermediate, and an adenylyl derivative is formed at the 5'-terminus. This second intermediate is finally attacked by the C(3') hydroxyl group at the other terminus, and the phosphodiester bond is formed as AMP is eliminated. Thus the energy of the diphosphate bond of NAD$^+$ is utilized to form a phosphodiester bond joining two polydeoxyribonucleotide fragments.

Kinetic studies on the reaction catalyzed by polynucleotide synthetase have suggested that a ping pong mechanism is operative. When initial-velocity studies were conducted, plots of $1/v_i$ vs. either $1/[\text{NAD}^+]$ or $1/[\text{poly}[d(A-T)]]$ with fixed concentrations of the other substrate were parallel, indicating that there is an irreversible step between the points in the reaction sequence at which NAD$^+$ and the polydeoxyribonucleotide (the polydeoxyadenylate-polydeoxythymidylate copolymer) bind. Presumably, this reflects the release of nicotinamide mononucleotide (under initial-velocity conditions) prior to the binding of the polydeoxyribonucleotide.

**Termination** The mechanism by which replication is terminated is essentially unknown. It has been suggested, however, that the observed terminal redundancy in the nucleotide sequence is involved in the separation of the two completed DNA molecules.

## Replication in Mammalian Systems

Many of the characteristics of the replication process as it occurs in the prokaryotic E. coli cell have also been observed in eukaryotic cells. For example, replication in mammalian cells appears to be initiated at specific orgination sites although there are multiple origination sites. Also, replication in mammalian cells occurs bidirectionally. Furthermore, the formation of Okazaki fragments has been demonstrated in mammalian cells and also in the cells of mammalian viruses; however, the joining of Okazaki fragments is catalyzed by an ATP-dependent polynucleotide synthetase [poly(deoxyribonucleotide):poly(deoxyribonucleotide) ligase (AMP-forming), EC 6.5.1.1]. An ATP-dependent polynucleotide synthetase, isolated from rat liver and having a molecular weight of 100,000, has been shown to catalyze a reaction which parallels the reaction catalyzed by the $NAD^+$-dependent enzyme except that initially a pyrophosphate anion is eliminated in order to form the adenylyl-enzyme intermediate (see scheme above).

## Mitochondrial DNA

Mitochondrial DNA (mtDNA) from a variety of animals is circular, has a contour length of 5 $\mu$m, and comprises approximately 15,000 base pairs. The macromolecule has a molecular weight of approximately $1 \times 10^7$. Several types of animal cells have been shown to contain approximately $1 \times 10^3$ molecules of this DNA per cell. Mitochondrial DNA has long been known to be sensitive to alkali, and this characteristic reflects the presence of a few ribonucleotidyl units interspersed throughout the macromolecule.

The replication of DNA in the mitochondria is in some respects similar to that occurring in E. coli. Thus, replication begins at a specific origination site, and synthesis is discontinuous. However, there are notable differences. For example, in the mitochondrion elongation is unidirectional, and the initial synthesis results in the formation of a short, triple-stranded region in the template, called the *displacement loop* or D loop. The D loop appears to be formed without the introduction of a scission in the template. Rather, it appears that one of the template strands is displaced while the other serves as a template for the synthesis of a short deoxyribonucleotide strand which may subsequently function as an initiator. This short deoxyribonucleotide strand comprises approximately 450 nucleotidyl units. Its participation in the replication process has been formulated as shown in Fig. 13-5.

As mentioned above, mitochondrial DNA comprises approximately 15,000 base pairs. This number of base pairs can dictate the synthesis of polypeptides or proteins containing a total of 5000 aminoacyl units. Included among the proteins thought to be coded for by mitochondrial DNA are one of the components involved in conferring oligomycin sensitivity upon the mitochondrial ATPase and

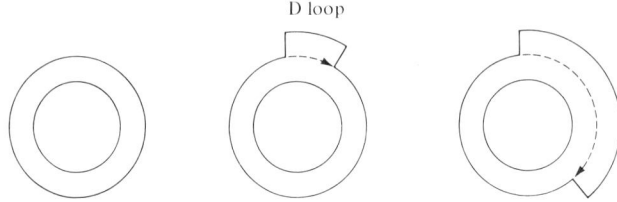

**Figure 13-5** Diagrammatic representation of the formation of a D loop during the replication of mitochondrial DNA. As synthesis progresses the loop is expanded. When approximately two-thirds of one template strand has been displaced, synthesis using the other template strand begins. Ultimately, two complete nascent strands are synthesized, and each with its template becomes a new double-stranded DNA molecule. [*From Kasamatsu, H., Grossman, L. I., Robberson, D. L., Watson, R., and Vinograd, J. (1974) Cold Spring Harbor Symp. Quant. Biol.* **38**, *281–288 (see p. 282). With permission.*]

also a polypeptide that is a part of the cytochrome oxidase complex. Clearly, however, in view of the size of the mitochondrial genome most of the mitochondrial proteins are coded for by nuclear DNA. Included in this latter category is the polymerase that catalyzes the synthesis of mitochondrial DNA. Such a polymerase has been isolated from rat liver and found to have a molecular weight of 140,000.

## RNA-dependent DNA Synthesis

Usually the flow of genetic information is from DNA to RNA, but in certain animal tumor viruses the flow of genetic information is from RNA to DNA. These animal tumor viruses have virions of approximately 100 nm diameter which contain single-stranded RNA and DNA polymerases capable of utilizing this RNA as a template. These enzymes are usually called RNA-dependent DNA polymerases (although they can utilize either RNA or DNA as a template). Such an enzyme has also been called a *reverse transcriptase*. These animal tumor virus are noncytopathic; i.e., they do not kill the cell they infect. They do, however, introduce their RNA genome and the RNA-dependent DNA polymerase into the host cell, and although the virion does not contain DNA, the synthesis of DNA must occur in order for infection to take place. This concept was initially proposed in 1964 by Howard M. Temin of the McArdle Laboratory for Cancer Research at the University of Wisconsin. According to his proposal, which has now been substantiated, the RNA and RNA-dependent DNA polymerase enters the host cell, and there DNA is synthesized using a portion of the viral genome as a template. The initial product is a single strand of DNA that is complementary to and hydrogen-bonded to the RNA template. Subsequently, a DNA strand that is complementary to the initial DNA strand is synthesized, and double-stranded DNA is formed. This DNA, which was synthesized through the use of the viral genome as a template, is referred to as the *viral DNA provirus intermediate*, and it in turn becomes a part of the host DNA. As such, it is transmitted to progeny cells. There is increasing evidence that this process is involved in cell transformation by RNA tumor viruses.

RNA-dependent DNA polymerases have been isolated from the avian myeloblastosis virus, the Rous sarcoma virus, and the Rauscher murine leukemia virus. The polymerases from the myeloblastosis virus and the sarcoma virus have both been isolated in two forms. In each instance, the enzyme can be isolated as a protein having a molecular weight of 65,000 or 70,000 and also as a protein having a molecular weight of approximately 175,000. The latter comprises the protein having a molecular weight of 65,000 or 70,000 plus a subunit that has a molecular weight of 105,000. The velocity of DNA synthesis as catalyzed by the species having a molecular weight of 175,000 (from the myeloblastosis virus) is 7 times that catalyzed by the one having a molecular weight of 65,000.

The RNA-dependent DNA polymerase from the leukemia virus has only been isolated as a protein having a molecular weight of 70,000.

The nucleotidyltransferase activities of these RNA-dependent DNA polymerases are not unlike those of other DNA polymerases. Deoxyribonucleoside triphosphates and an initiator which has an available C(3') hydroxyl group are required, and synthesis occurs in the $5' \rightarrow 3'$ direction. The initial product of this synthesis is an RNA-DNA hybrid, however. The RNA-dependent DNA polymerase also exhibits nuclease activity. In this case, hybrid nuclease activity is exhibited; i.e., the enzyme can degrade the RNA strand of an RNA-DNA hybrid. (Hybrid nuclease activity has also been demonstrated in mammalian, avian, and bacterial systems and is briefly discussed later in this chapter.) The hybrid nuclease activity of the polymerase from the myeloblastosis virus is considered to be exonucleolytic since free termini must be present in order for the activity to be expressed. Covalently closed circular RNA-DNA hybrids cannot serve as a substrate. Degradation can proceed in either the $3' \rightarrow 5'$ or the $5' \rightarrow 3'$ direction, and when catalyzed by the 175,000-dalton polymerase, the process is processive, with a given strand being initially degraded to yield large oligonucleotides which are further degraded to yield small oligonucleotides (of approximately 10 units).† Since it is known that synthesis of the second, i.e., complementary, DNA strand does not begin until a portion of the RNA strand has been degraded, it is speculated that the function of the hybrid nuclease activity of the polymerase is that of degrading (and thus removing) the RNA template while also providing an initiator to be used in the synthesis of the second DNA strand.

## ANABOLISM OF RIBONUCLEIC ACIDS

Synthesis of most, if not all, of the cellular RNA is catalyzed by RNA nucleotidyltransferases (ribonucleosidetriphosphate:RNA ribonucleotidyltransferase, EC 2.7.7.6), generally called RNA polymerases. As has been stated previously, the function of the genetic information that is transferred from parent to progeny as a result of chromosomal replication is ultimately that of directing the synthesis of the cellular proteins of the progeny. The genome directs the synthesis of cellular proteins by transferring its genetic information initially to a form of RNA known as messenger RNA. Subsequently, messenger RNA, in conjunction with certain other (noninformational) species of RNA, e.g., transfer RNA and ribosomal RNA, utilizes this genetic information in directing the synthesis of the specific proteins of the cell.

† Grandgenett, D. P., and Green, M. (1974) *J. Biol. Chem.* **249**, 5148–5152.

A DNA genome transfers its genetic information to messenger RNA through the agency of DNA-dependent RNA polymerases. The use of a DNA template in the synthesis of RNA is called *transcription*. The following discussion focuses upon the DNA-dependent RNA polymerases and their role in transcription.

## RNA Polymerases

Eukaryotic cells contain more than one RNA polymerase, just as they contain more than one DNA polymerase. In an effort to arrive at a system of nomenclature for the eukaryotic nuclear RNA polymerases, a classification has been based upon the response of the RNA polymerase activity to the toxin α-amanitin (a factor derived from the toadstool *Amanita phalloides*). According to this system, polymerases that have activities which are not inhibited by this toxin belong to class A, those that have activities which are inhibited by low (10-n$M$) concentrations of the toxin belong to class B, and those that have activities which are inhibited only by higher (0.1-m$M$) concentrations belong to class C. Of the eukaryotic RNA polymerases that have been isolated and purified, most have molecular weights in the range of 400,000 to 600,000. In general, polymerases of the A class are slightly smaller than those of the B class.

RNA polymerase AI, which is localized in the nucleolus, catalyzes the synthesis of (predominantly) ribosomal RNA. This enzyme has been isolated from several sources including a plasmacytoma (murine myeloma MOPC 315) which is actively involved in protein synthesis. This enzyme, which has a molecular weight of 466,000, comprises six subunits which have molecular weights of 195,000, 117,000, 60,500, 50,500, 27,000, and 16,500. An RNA polymerase having a comparable structure has been isolated from a mammalian source (bovine thymus).

RNA polymerases of the B family are localized in the nucleoplasm. These enzymes provide catalysis for the synthesis of certain specific RNA species, including messenger RNA. Three different forms of RNA polymerase B have been isolated from the cells of the murine plasmacytoma and from rat liver. These are designated as BI, BIIa, and BIIb. Each comprises multiple subunits and is distinguished on the basis of its largest subunit which has a molecular weight of 240,000 in the case of BI, 205,000 in the case of BIIa, and 170,000 in the case of BIIb. Total molecular weights of BI, BIIa, and BIIb have been determined to be 554,000, 519,000, and 484,000, respectively.

RNA polymerases of class C catalyze the synthesis of 5-S RNA and also the pre-4-S RNA species. The latter are precursors of cytoplasmic transfer RNA molecules. RNA polymerases of this class are also localized in the nucleoplasm. Two polymerases of class C have been identified in the murine myeloma although neither has been purified to the extent that its subunit structure can be determined. The RNA polymerases of this class are present at lower concentrations than the those of the A or B class. For example, the activity of class C polymerases is somewhat less than 15 percent of the total polymerase activity of the bovine thymus cell.

In general, it appears that the mammalian nuclear RNA polymerases comprise two relatively large subunits and several smaller ones. As discussed below, a similar situation is observed in the case of the bacterial RNA polymerases.

Prokaryotic cells contain only one DNA-dependent RNA polymerase, which is responsible for the synthesis of all the various types of RNA present in the cell. The bacterial RNA polymerases generally have molecular weights between 400,000 and 500,000, and are composed of multiple subunits. The core enzyme, thought to be the catalytically functional unit of the polymerase, comprises three different subunits, designated $\beta'$, $\beta$, and $\alpha$. As isolated from the polymerase from *E. coli* these subunits have molecular weights of 160,000, 150,000, and 40,000, respectively. The core enzyme, which can be represented as $\alpha_2 \beta\beta'$, has a molecular weight of 390,000. A species known as the holoenzyme can also be isolated. The holoenzyme includes a fourth subunit, known as the $\sigma$ subunit, which has a molecular weight of 90,000 and participates in the initiation phase of RNA synthesis. The core enzyme binds one $\sigma$ subunit to yield the holoenzyme.

**Initiation of RNA synthesis** RNA synthesis as catalyzed by either an eukaryotic or prokaryotic DNA-dependent RNA polymerase requires a suitable template and the presence of all four ribonucleoside triphosphates (ATP, GTP, CTP, and UTP) for maximal velocity. An initiator is not required, however. Since most of the studies on the catalytic process have been conducted on the polymerase from *E. coli*, this process will be discussed.

When RNA synthesis is to take place, the RNA polymerase must first bind the DNA template. This template can be double-stranded DNA, which remains unaltered following its use, or single-stranded DNA. Core RNA polymerase binds its template readily but without selectivity; i.e., the core enzyme will bind at any locus on the template. However, when the $\sigma$ subunit is present, template binding is selective and only specific loci on the genome are bound. These loci are those at which transcription can be initiated, and they are known as the *promoter loci* of the genome.

As mentioned above, RNA synthesis is initiated without the participation of an initiator. Rather, when synthesis is to begin, two nucleoside triphosphates interact to yield a dinucleoside tetraphosphate. A minimal mechanism for this reaction is shown.

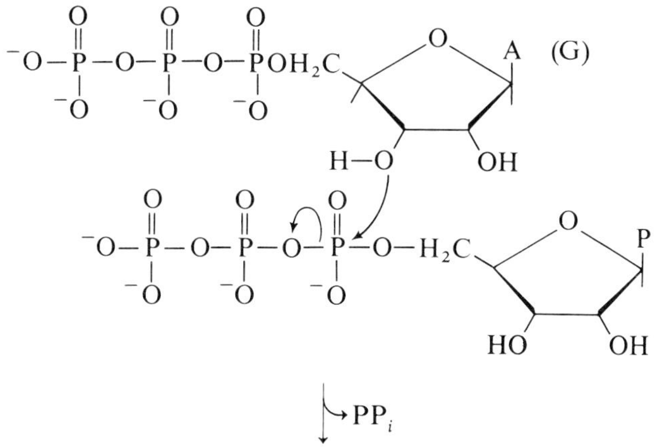

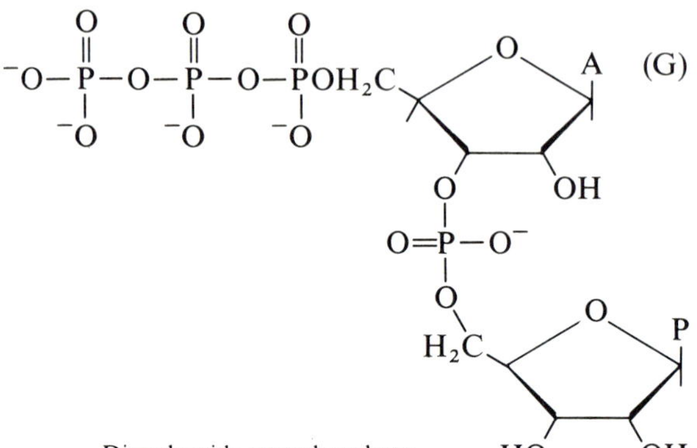

Dinucleoside tetraphosphate

This initiation reaction requires that either ATP or GTP be the nucleoside triphosphate that attacks the second nucleoside triphosphate and that either ATP or GTP is at the C(5′) triphosphate terminus. The binding of ATP or GTP at the appropriate initiation site is the rate-determining event with respect to the initiation process. A widely used inhibitor of RNA synthesis, rifampicin, functions as such because it can bind at the binding site for ATP or GTP and thereby prevent formation of the initial phosphodiester bond.

**Elongation** The ternary complex formed as a result of the initiation process, i.e., the polymerase–DNA–nascent RNA complex, does not undergo dissociation during the elongation process. Elongation entails (1) binding of the nucleoside triphosphate as dictated by the template, (2) formation of the phosphodiester bond between the terminal C(3′) hydroxyl group and the C(5′) phosphoryl group of the incoming nucleotidyl unit with the concomitant elimination of the pyrophosphate anion, and (3) the isomerization and translocation of the polymerase in order to align its catalytic site with the next template base.

The sequence of nucleotides that is incorporated into the RNA molecule is dictated by the template molecule just as in the case of DNA synthesis. There is also evidence that the enzyme plays a role in the selection process, however, since when the RNA polymerase is damaged by x-rays, the fidelity of the selection process is decreased.

Elongation with double-stranded DNA as the template probably entails the disengagement of the strands in the region being used, and, in fact, the transient formation of DNA-RNA hybrid structures had been reported. However, such structures are difficult to isolate because they are less stable than the double-stranded DNA structure; i.e., the DNA-RNA interaction is less favorable than the DNA-DNA interaction.

**Termination** When transcription of a specific portion of a genome has been completed, the process must be terminated and the newly formed RNA and the RNA polymerase released from the template. In some instances there appears to be a template sequence which signals the end of the segment of the genome that codes for a given protein or polypeptide. In several cases this is believed to be a polypyrimidine sequence, and termination under these circumstances appears to occur without accessory factors or components. In addition to this type of termination, there can be a cessation of elongation without the release of the RNA product or the polymerase. This, too, may be a manifestation of a signal given by the template.

A protein factor that promotes the termination of transcription has been isolated from *E. coli*. This factor, designated $\rho$, is thought to bind the RNA polymerase, with the result that elongation ceases and the newly synthesized RNA is released from the template. The polymerase remains bound to the template, however.

As in the case of DNA synthesis, termination is the least understood phase of the transcription process. One of the technical problems that is met in carrying out studies on the termination of transcription arises because termination occurs very soon after initiation; i.e., a transcript having a molecular weight of $2.5 \times 10^6$ is produced in less than 3 min.

## A Mechanism for the Regulation of Transcription in *E. Coli*: The Operon

As noted in 1961 by Francois Jacob and Jacques Monod, of the Institut Pasteur in Paris, genes that specify functionally related proteins are in certain cases located contiguously on the bacterial genome and they are expressed coordinately. This coordinate expression is regulated through the agency of additional genes which constitute a controlling element. This controlling element consists of the promoter locus, the operator locus, and the regulator gene. The genes that specify the functionally related proteins are known as structural genes, and they with their controlling element constitute an operon.

An example of such a system is found in the *E. coli lac* operon, which includes the genes that code for proteins involved in lactose utilization in that microorganism. These proteins are the enzymes $\beta$-galactosidase ($\beta$-D-galactoside galactohydrolase, EC 3.2.1.23) and galactoside acetyltransferase (acetyl-CoA: galactoside 6-*O*-acetyltransferase, EC 2.3.1.18) and a factor that facilitates the entry of galactosides into the *E. coli* cell. The *lac* operon can be represented as shown in Fig. 13-6. The promoter is the site on the genome at which transcription is initiated. The operator is the site on the genome at which a regulatory protein, known as a repressor, can bind. The regulator gene codes for that regulatory protein. Regulation of the coordinate expression of the structural genes of the *lac* operon results from influences upon

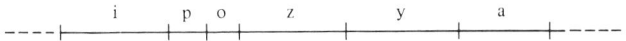

**Figure 13-6** Schematic representation of the *lac* operon, where

i = regulator gene
p = promoter locus
o = operator locus
z = structural gene for the $\beta$-galactosidase
y = structural gene for the factor that facilitates the entry of galactosides into the cell
a = structural gene for the galactoside acetyltransferase

the initiation phase of transcription. Since this transcription process results in the formation of messenger RNA, and since messenger RNA is synthesized, utilized in protein synthesis, and then rapidly degraded, the frequency with which transcription is initiated to a great extent determines the prevailing concentrations of the proteins that are specified by the structural genes of the operon. In other words, when proteins are specified by genes that are constituents of an operon, determination of whether or not they are synthesized takes place at the level of transcription.

Considering the regulatory mechanism, per se, the expression of the structural genes of the operon depends upon whether or not the repressor protein is bound at the operator locus. When the repressor is not bound, transcription will occur. The repressor protein, in this case, is a tetrameric protein having a molecular weight of 150,000, and it is specifically this tetrameric form of the repressor that interacts at the operator locus. At this point, the question may be raised: What factors determine whether or not the repressor binds at the operator locus? One factor is the presence of a corepressor. A corepressor promotes the binding of the repressor at the operator locus. Another factor is the presence of an inducer. An inducer impedes the binding of the corepressor. Allolactose, an isomer of lactose, functions as an inducer with respect to the *lac* operon. Binding of the RNA polymerase at the promoter locus of the *lac* operon requires the presence of a small protein (mol wt, 45,000) and also 3',5'-AMP. Presumably, it is a protein-3',5'-AMP complex that, in fact, functions in this capacity. The protein is known as the *catabolite gene-activator protein* (CAP protein). This name reflects the fact that early studies on the functioning of the *lac* operon showed that expression of the structural genes was inhibited when the bacterium was grown on glucose, and the phenomenon was known as catabolite repression. Catabolite repression is now understood to reflect the fact that growth on glucose is accompanied by diminished concentrations of 3',5'-AMP, and thus it was the diminished cyclic nucleotide concentration (rather than the availability of the protein factor) that was responsible for the observations.

## Inhibitors of Transcription

In general terms, transcription can be inhibited by factors that interact with the RNA polymerase or by factors that interact with the DNA template. Included in the first category are several members of the ansamycin antibiotics, including the rifamycins, the streptovaricins, and streptolydigin. Rifampicin, a rifamycin derivative, has been widely used as an inhibitor of bacterial RNA polymerases both in vitro and in vivo. This drug binds the $\beta$ subunit of the polymerase and prevents the binding of the initial ribonucleoside triphosphate during the initiation process. The elongation phase of bacterial RNA synthesis is not affected by rifampicin. Eukaryotic nuclear RNA polymerases are not affected by this drug.

The drug streptolydigin also binds the $\beta$ subunit of bacterial RNA polymerases, but in this case both initiation and the velocity of the elongation process are impeded.

Compounds that react with DNA and prevent it from functioning as a template for RNA synthesis include actinomycin D (the most widely used and studied), ethidium bromide, proflavine, neomycin, and chloroquine. Actinomycin D impedes the elongation process by binding guanylyl moieties of double-stranded DNA templates and thereby preventing the translocation of the RNA polymerase along the template strand. (Transcription of a double-stranded DNA template that does not contain guanylyl units is unaffected by actinomycin D.)

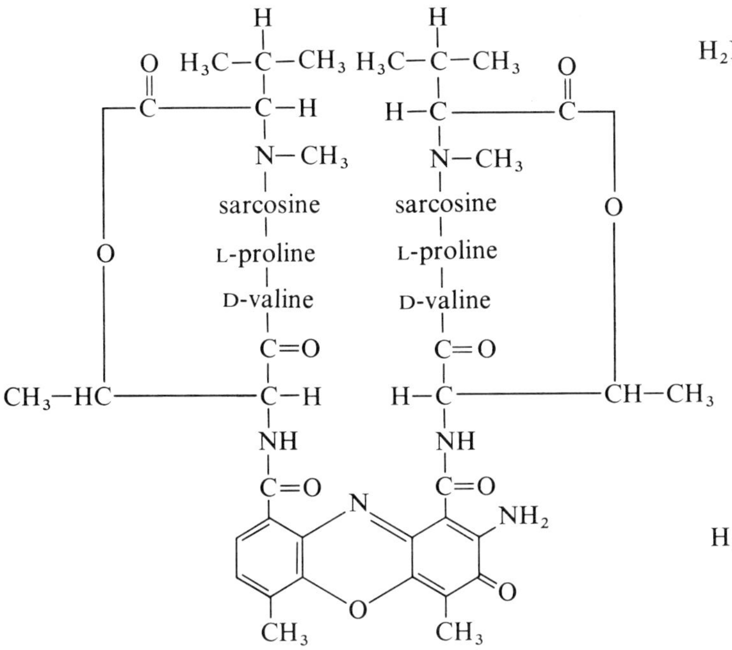

Actinomycin D

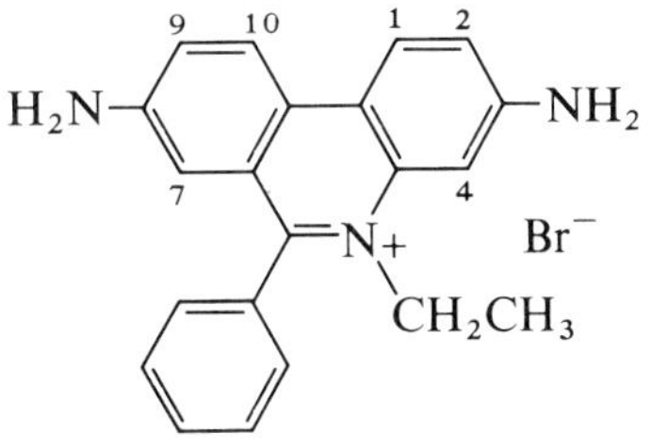

Ethidium bromide

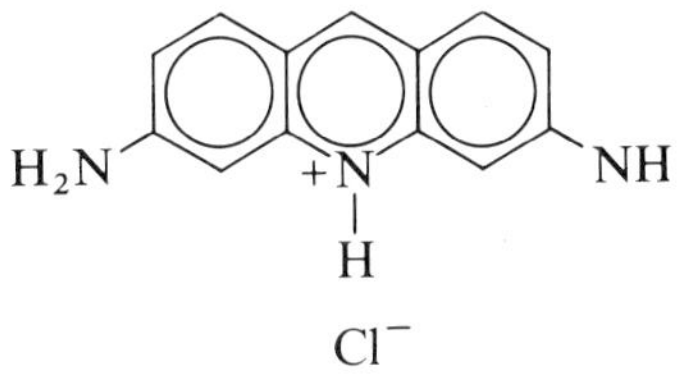

Proflavine hydrochloride

## ENZYMES THAT DEGRADE NUCLEIC ACIDS

Nucleic acids are degraded by undergoing hydrolytic cleavages of their phosphodiester bonds. These hydrolytic cleavages are catalyzed by nucleases, of which the principal ones will be discussed.

### Pancreatic Deoxyribonucleases

Deoxyribonuclease I (deoxyribonucleate 5'-oligonucleotidohydrolase, EC 3.1.4.5), which has been isolated from bovine pancreas and crystallized, comprises four components, designated deoxyribonuclease A, B, C, and D. Each of these species is a glycoprotein. Deoxyribonuclease A, the major component, is a single polypeptide chain of 257 aminoacyl units which has a carbohydrate moiety bonded to an asparaginyl unit. The carbohydrate moiety is composed, on the average, of six mannose units and two $N$-acetylglucosamine units with C(1) of one of the $N$-acetylglucosamine units bonded to the amide nitrogen atom of Asn-18.

Bonding between $N$-acetylglucosamine unit and asparagine

The second $N$-acetylglucosamine unit is next in the oligosaccharide chain, followed by the mannose units. The protein moiety of deoxyribonuclease B is the same as that of deoxyribonuclease A, although the carbohydrate moieties of the two macromolecules are different. The carbohydrate moiety of deoxyribonuclease B consists of three $N$-acetylglucosamine units, five mannose units, one galactose unit, and one sialic acid (or sialate) unit. Deoxyribonuclease C, on the other hand, has the same carbohydrate moiety as deoxyribonuclease A, but its protein moiety differs in that His-118 of deoxyribonuclease A is substituted by a prolyl unit. Finally, deoxyribonuclease D, the component present in the least amount, has the same protein moiety as C and the same carbohydrate moiety as B. Thus, these deoxyribonucleases have two kinds of protein moieties and two kinds of carbohydrate moieties, and all combinations are found to occur. The relative proportions of deoxyribonuclease A, deoxyribonuclease B, deoxyribonuclease C, and deoxyribonuclease D in a typical preparation are 1 : 0.2 : 0.5 : 0.1.

With respect to the specificity of deoxyribonuclease I, it has been shown that when presented with a double-stranded DNA substrate, the enzyme(s) functions as an endonuclease which introduces single-strand scissions. An endonuclease is an enzyme that catalyzes the hydrolytic cleavage of a phosphodiester bond involving nonterminal nucleotidyl units. The precise specificity of the deoxyribonuclease appears to depend upon whether the degradation is in the early or late stages and also upon the prevailing concentrations of certain cations, including $Mg^{2+}$ and $Ca^{2+}$. Studies on deoxyribonuclease I have shown that in the early stages of the degradation the enzyme introduces single-strand scissions in a more or less random manner, with many being introduced before a double-strand scission is introduced. In fact, one such study indicated that an average of 200 single-strand scissions were introduced before the average molecular weight of the substrate decreased by a factor of 2.

A minimal reaction mechanism for the hydrolytic cleavage of a phosphodiester bond, as catalyzed by deoxyribonuclease I, is shown following.

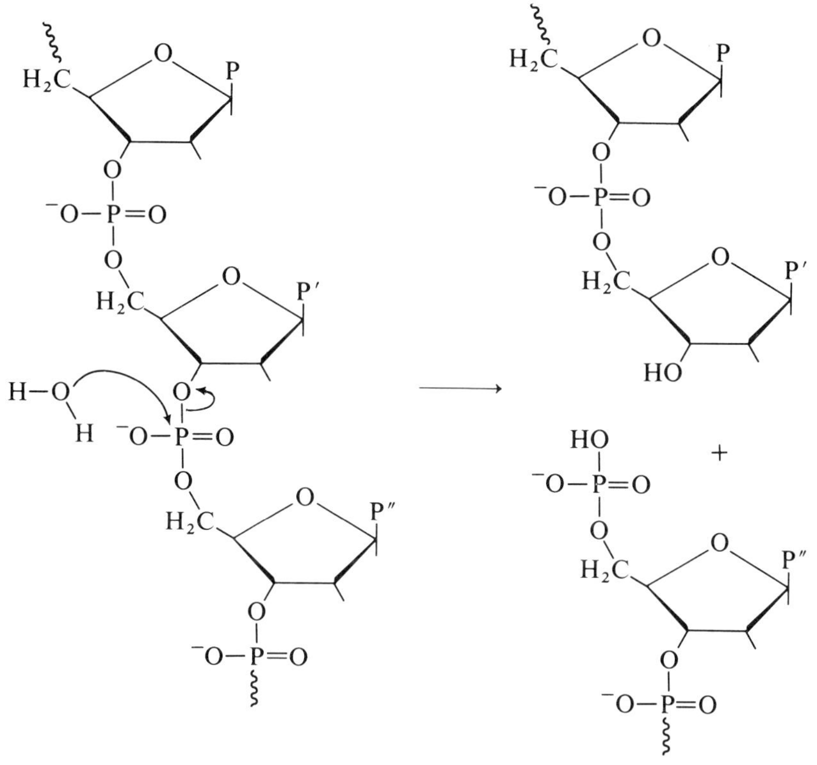

At the point of scission one nucleotidyl unit has a C(3′) hydroxyl group and the other has a C(5′) phosphoryl group.

## Spleen Deoxyribonucleases

Deoxyribonuclease II (deoxribonucleate 3′-oligonucleotidohydrolase, EC 3.1.4.6) is generally isolated from porcine spleen and as with deoxyribonuclease I the preparation has been resolved to yield more than one component. In the present case, these components have been designated as deoxyribonuclease II A and B. Each is a glycoprotein with possibly the same protein moiety, although there are recognized differences between the carbohydrate moieties. Glucosamine and mannose are components of these carbohydrate moieties, as in deoxyribonuclease I.

Deoxyribonuclease II is an endonuclease which catalyzes the hydrolytic cleavages of double-stranded DNA by both a diplotomic and a haplotomic process. A diplotomic process is one which results in the scission of both strands of the DNA at the same level. A haplotomic process is one which results in a single-strand scission. The word *diplotomic* is derived from the Greek *diplos*, meaning "double," and the Greek *temnein* to "sever" or "break." Haplotomic is similarly derived from the Greek *haplos*, meaning "single." Both the diplotomic and haplotomic processes are in operation from the onset of the reaction catalyzed by deoxyribonuclease II.

The products of the hydrolytic cleavage catalyzed by deoxyribonuclease II are a nucleotidyl unit with a C(5') hydroxyl terminus and one with a C(3') phosphoryl group at the point of the scission. This contrasts with the products of the reaction catalyzed by deoxyribonuclease I. A minimal reaction mechanism for the cleavage of a phosphodiester bond in the presence of deoxyribonuclease II is given below.

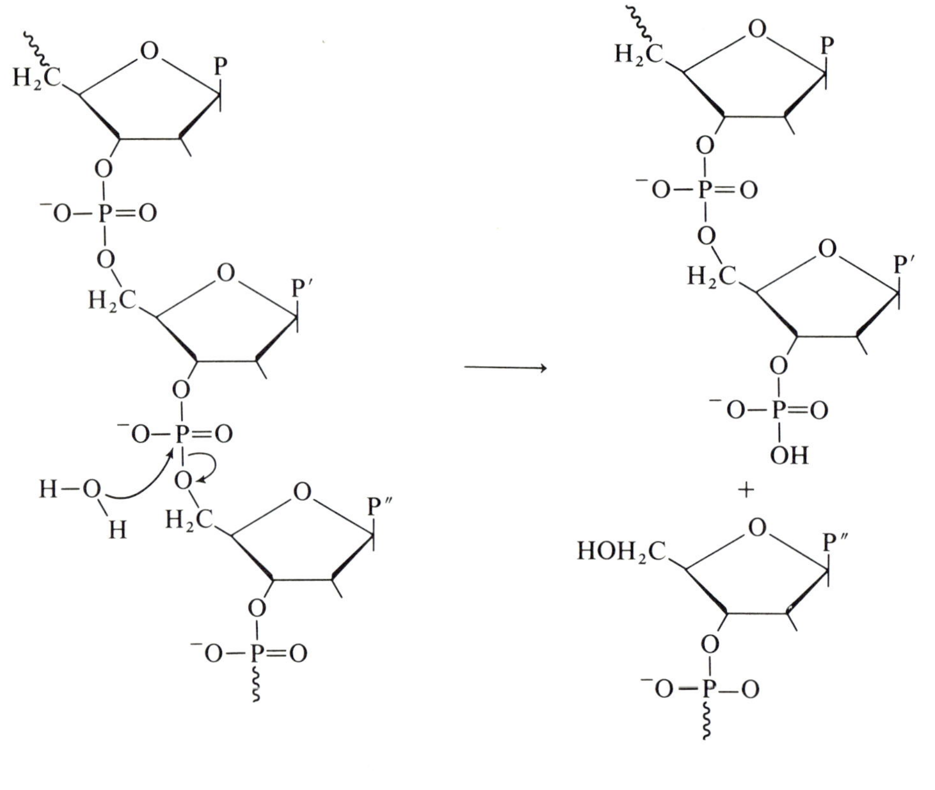

## Bacterial Deoxyribonucleases

The bacterial deoxyribonucleases have been classified as exonucleases and endonucleases. In *E. coli*, seven exonuclease activities have been identified. These are shown in Table 13-1, along with the type of substrate used, the positional specificity of the exonucleolytic activity, and the types of nonpolymeric products generated. Exodeoxyribonuclease I [deoxyribonucleate (single-stranded) 5'-oligonucleotidohydrolase, EC 3.1.4.25] does not catalyze the cleavage of dinucleotides, and therefore the terminal and penultimate nucleotidyl units at the 5' terminus remain as dinucleotides. Exodeoxyribonuclease activities II and VI are, in fact, the activities that are exhibited by DNA polymerase I. The activity of exodeoxyribonuclease IV (double-stranded-deoxyribonucleate 5'-oligonucleotidohydrolase, EC 3.1.4.28) is distinguished from the rest in that it is preferentially directed toward oligodeoxyribonucleotides. Native DNA is degraded by this enzyme at a rate one-twentieth that at which double-stranded oligodeoxyribonucleotides are degraded. The exode-

## Table 13-1 Exodeoxyribonuclease activities present in *E. coli*

| Exodeoxyribo-nuclease | DNA substrate | Positional specificity | Nonpolymeric products |
|---|---|---|---|
| I | Single-stranded | $3' \to 5'$ | Deoxyribonucleotide 5'-monophosphates, 5'-terminal dinucleotides |
| II | Single-stranded | $3' \to 5'$ | Deoxyribonucleotide 5'-monophosphates |
| III | Double-stranded | $3' \to 5'$ | Deoxyribonucleotide 5'-monophosphates |
| IV | Oligonucleotide | $5' \to 3'$ | Deoxyribonucleotide 5'-monophosphates |
| V | Single- and double-stranded | $3' \to 5'$ and $5' \to 3'$ | Oligonucleotides |
| VI | Double-stranded | $5' \to 3'$ | Deoxyribonucleotide 5'-monophosphates, oligonucleotides |
| VII | Single-stranded | $3' \to 5'$ and $5' \to 3'$ | Oligonucleotides |

*Source:* Data modified from Chase, J. W., and Richardson, C. C. (1974) *J. Biol. Chem.* **249**, 4545–4552.

oxyribonuclease IV is also heterogeneous. The enzyme exodeoxyribonuclease VII has been isolated, purified, and found to have a molecular weight of 88,000.† As isolated, the enzyme degrades single-stranded DNA or double-stranded DNA which has single-stranded termini, from either the 3' or the 5' terminus. Initially, the enzyme releases large oligonucleotides, which it can subsequently act upon in a processive manner to generate smaller and smaller oligonucleotides. Although the limit products of this reaction are oligonucleotides, a DNA terminus is required for activity, and therefore the enzyme is classified as an exonuclease.

Endodeoxyribonucleases have also been isolated from *E. coli* and other bacteria. One endodeoxyribonuclease from *E. coli* catalyzes a diplotomic process which results in the cleavage of both strands of a DNA duplex molecule at approximately the same level. This enzyme appears to exhibit exonuclease activity too, however, since following the endonucleolytic cleavage, several hundred deoxyribonucleotidyl units are released from the vicinity of the scission.

### Restriction Endonucleases

*E. coli* also contains restriction endonucleases, or enzymes that participate in the destruction, i.e., restriction, of DNA that is recognized by a given cell as being "foreign." Under several circumstances, DNA is transferred from one bacterium to another. Once within the recipient cell, this DNA may survive and even undergo replication, or it may be degraded as a result of the process known as restriction. The survival or restriction of the alien DNA depends upon the restriction specificity of the recipient cell and upon the specific *noninheritable* characteristics

† Chase, J. W., and Richardson, C. C. (1974) *J. Biol. Chem.* **249** 4545–4552.

imparted to that DNA by the cell from which it came. Such characteristics are referred to as *host-controlled modifications*. There is some evidence that resistance to a given restriction endonuclease is conferred as a result of specific methylation reactions that modify the DNA in such a manner that it cannot serve as a substrate for the restriction enzyme. A restriction endonuclease from *E. coli* strain K has been isolated, purified, and classified as an ATP- and *S*-adenosylmethionine–dependent endodeoxyribonuclease [deoxyribonucleate polynucleotidohydrolase (ATP- and *S*-adenosyl-L-methionine–dependent), EC 3.1.4.32]. This enzyme catalyzes the cleavage of double-stranded DNA that is synthesized by other strains of *E. coli* but not that synthesized by *E. coli* strain K. Initially, the endonuclease introduces a single-strand scission into the double-stranded DNA molecule. Subsequently, a scission in the other strand at or near the same level is introduced, and as a result, the limit products are short double-stranded fragments. The process requires *S*-adenosylmethionine and ATP. The latter is cleaved to ADP and orthophosphate as a concomitance of the reaction. The function of the *S*-adenosylmethionine and ATP is unknown, although other restriction endonucleases also require these components.

## Bovine Pancreatic Ribonuclease

Bovine pancreatic ribonuclease, or ribonuclease I (ribonucleate 3′-pyrimidinooligonucleotidohydrolase, EC 3.1.4.22), is an endoribonuclease that catalyzes cleavage of a phosphodiester bond to yield one nucleotidyl unit with a C(3′) phosphoryl group and the other with a C(5′) hydroxyl group at the point of scission. Generally, the base of the nucleotidyl unit with the C(3′) phosphoryl group is a pyrimidine. Ribonuclease I can be isolated as a glycoprotein (sometimes referred to as ribonuclease B) which has two *N*-acetylglycosamine units and six mannose units. One of the *N*-acetylglucosamine units is bonded to Asn-34 by an aspartamido-[2-acetamido]-1,2-dideoxy-β-D-glucose linkage, as in the mammalian deoxyribonucleases. Ribonuclease I has also been obtained as a protein, i.e., without the carbohydrate moiety. This species is called ribonuclease A. It is a single polypeptide chain of 124 aminoacyl units and a molecular weight of 13,680 (as calculated from its primary structure).

Several reaction mechanisms have been proposed for the hydrolytic cleavage of RNA as catalyzed by ribonuclease I. In general, they differ in the mode of participation by various functional groups at the catalytic site of the enzyme. The scheme below presents a simplistic mechanism that takes into account some of the aspects of the reaction upon which there is general agreement. It is agreed that the nucleophilicity of the oxygen atom of the C(2′) hydroxyl group that attacks the phosphoryl phosphorus atom is enhanced as a result of coordination with a hydrogen atom. This coordination is thought to involve an imidazole moiety of a histidyl unit. In fact, two histidyl units, His-12 and His-119, are thought to participate in the reaction, as is the $\epsilon$-amino group of a lysyl unit (Lys-41). It is also agreed that a 2′,3′-cyclic phosphate intermediate is formed. This, in turn, undergoes hydrolysis to complete the reaction.

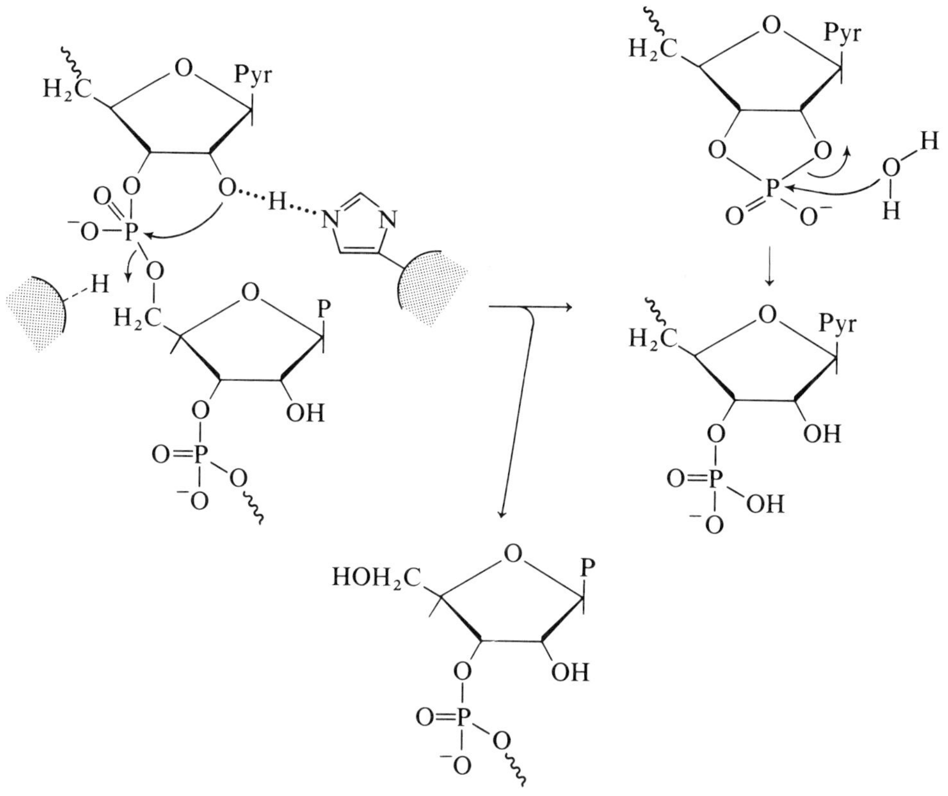

## Hybrid Nuclease

Hybrid nuclease (RNA-DNA-hybrid ribonucleotidohydrolase, EC 3.1.4.34) was initially demonstrated in and isolated from bovine thymus. (This enzyme is sometimes referred to as ribonuclease H.) The nuclease catalyzes the endonucleolytic cleavage of the RNA strand of an RNA-DNA hybrid. Circular RNA-DNA hybrids (that are covalently closed) can serve as a substrate for this nuclease, as well as linear hybrids. Hybrid nuclease has been isolated from human and avian cells in addition to the bovine thymus. Hybrid nuclease activity has also been found in E. coli.

## BACTERIAL RIBONUCLEASES

Several ribonuclease activities have been demonstrated in E. coli and other microorganisms. Ribonuclease II (ribonucleate 3'-oligonucleotidohydrolase, EC 3.1.4.23) from E. coli is an endonuclease which produces nucleotidyl units that have C(3') phosphoryl groups and nucleotidyl units that have C(5') hydroxyl groups. The specificity of this enzyme is relatively broad. The enzyme has been referred to as ribonuclease I of *E. coli*. A second ribonuclease from *E. coli* (called ribonuclease II of *E. coli*) is an exonuclease that is specific for single-stranded polyribonucleotides. This enzyme attacks the phosphodiester bond linking a terminal ribonucleotidyl unit which has a C(3') hydroxyl group. The cleavage yields a ribonucleoside 5'-monophosphate. A third ribonuclease from *E. coli* (referred to as ribonuclease III from *E. coli*) is associated with the ribosomes of the cell. This enzyme, which is an endonuclease, is thought to participate in the processing of polycistronic messenger RNA.

CHAPTER
# FOURTEEN
## METABOLISM OF AMINO ACIDS AND PROTEINS

The catabolism of proteins initially entails their hydrolytic cleavage, as catalyzed by proteolytic enzymes, to yield the constituent amino acids. Subsequently, these amino acids undergo degradation and catabolism by means that ultimately produce chemical energy. This degradation and catabolism differ from that of hexoses or fatty acids however, in that there is not a specific catabolic pathway, such as the glycolytic pathway or the $\beta$-oxidation cycle, into which amino acids enter. Rather, the degradation and catabolism of amino acids generally begin with the removal of the nitrogen atom, followed by the entry of the remaining carbon skeleton into one of the pathways utilized in the catabolism of hexoses or fatty acids.

## REMOVAL OF THE NITROGEN ATOM FROM AN AMINO ACID

The degradation of an amino acid begins with the removal of its nitrogen atom, which can be reutilized or ultimately excreted as a nitrogen atom of urea, as discussed subsequently in this chapter. In this section nitrogen removal will be discussed.

### Catalyzed by Amino-Acid Oxidases

L-Amino-acid oxidases [L-amino-acid:oxygen oxidoreductase (deaminating), EC 1.4.3.2] have been isolated from avian liver, bacteria, molds, and rattlesnake venom, among other sources. D-Amino-acid oxidases [D-amino-acid:oxygen oxidoreductase (deaminating), EC 1.4.3.3] have been isolated from porcine kidney, the kidney and liver of other mammals, and also bacteria, molds, amphibians, and even insects. The physiological function of the D-amino-acid oxidases is somewhat obscure, however, because most naturally occurring amino acids are of the L configuration. On the other hand, the presence of enzymes that catalyze the interconversion of L- and D-amino acids has been described in several instances.

The reaction catalyzed by an amino acid oxidase can be written

$$\text{L- or D-amino acid} + O_2 + H_2O \rightleftharpoons \text{2-oxo acid} + NH_3 + H_2O_2 \quad (14\text{-}1)$$

Both L-amino-acid oxidase and D-amino-acid oxidase are flavoproteins. L-Amino-acid oxidase has been isolated from rattlesnake (*Crotalus adamanteus*) venom as a protein which has a molecular weight of 130,000. There are, in fact, three electrophoretically distinct forms of this enzyme, although each form exhibits virtually the same catalytic activity. Since each form of the enzyme comprises two subunits, it has been speculated that the three forms are an $\alpha_2$ form, a $\beta_2$ form, and an $\alpha\beta$ form. Each form binds two molecules of FAD. D-Amino-acid oxidase, which has been isolated from porcine kidney and purified, has a molecular weight of 38,000 and binds one molecule of FAD.

The amino-acid oxidases catalyze the removal of a hydrogen atom and two electrons from an amino group, thus oxidizing it to an imine group, and the transfer of these two reducing equivalents ultimately to molecular oxygen, which is thereby reduced to the level of peroxide. The flavin cofactor is the initial acceptor of the reducing equivalents. A simplified reaction mechanism for this process is shown below.

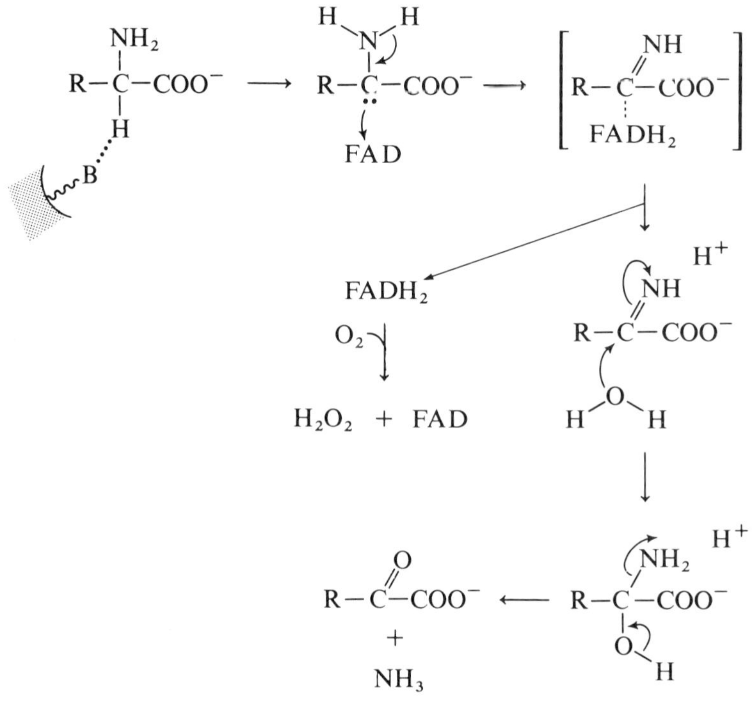

A proton is abstracted from C(2) of the amino acid substrate in what has been shown, by its kinetic isotope effect, to be the rate-determining step of the reaction. Now two electrons are transferred from the amino acid substrate to the FAD cofactor of the enzyme, forming an enzyme–$FADH_2$–imino acid complex. The precise structure of this complex has not been established. Subsequently, the 2-imino acid dissociates from the enzyme and is readily hydrolyzed, nonenzymatically, to yield the 2-oxo acid. Meanwhile, molecular oxygen binds the reduced flavoprotein enzyme, accepts two reducing equivalents, and is reduced to the level of a peroxide, concomitantly with the regeneration of the oxidized flavoprotein enzyme.

A single kinetic mechanism has been proposed for the reactions catalyzed by each of the two amino-acid oxidases (and also other flavoprotein oxidases).† This mechanism entails alternate pathways and can be represented diagrammatically as follows:

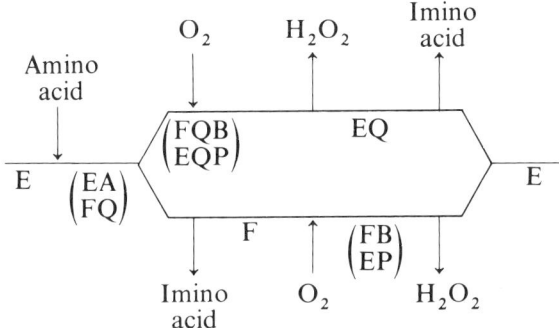

The amino acid substrate A binds the oxidized flavoprotein enzyme E and subsequently donates two electrons to the flavin moiety (which is considered to be a part of the enzyme), thus generating the imino acid product Q and the reduced flavoprotein enzyme F. According to the top pathway in the diagram, the molecular oxygen B now binds and accepts two electrons from the reduced flavoprotein enzyme. Hydrogen peroxide P is released, and the oxidized flavoprotein enzyme with the imino acid still bound EQ remains. Finally, the imino acid dissociates. According to the alternate pathway, the imino acid Q dissociates from the reduced flavoprotein enzyme F, which then binds molecular oxygen B and is oxidized back to its original form E as hydrogen peroxide P dissociates. The data from which these conclusions were drawn were obtained primarily from stopped-flow spectrophotometric studies. The reaction catalyzed by the L-amino-acid oxidase can proceed by either pathway, and the initial-velocity plots derived on the basis of this reaction were frequently both nonintersecting and nonlinear, as might be expected. In the presence of low or moderate concentrations of molecular oxygen, the pathway involving the release of the imino acid prior to the binding of molecular

---

† Bright, H. J., and Porter, D. J. T. (1975) in *The Enzymes* (Boyer, P. D., ed.), 3d ed., vol. 12, pp. 421–505, Academic, New York.

oxygen is favored. High concentrations of molecular oxygen favor its binding prior to the release of the imino acid. The reaction that is catalyzed by the D-amino-acid oxidase proceeds by the pathway in which the imino acid is the final product released in most instances. The exception appears to be those instances in which a basic amino acid is the substrate. When arginine is the substrate, for example, the imino acid is the initial product that is released.

## Catalyzed by Amine Oxidases

There are two types of amine oxidases. The pyridoxal phosphate–dependent amine oxidases [amine:oxygen oxidoreductase (deaminating)(pyridoxal-containing), EC 1.4.3.6] contain both the pyridoxal phosphate cofactor and copper. An enzyme of this type catalyzes the deamination of histamine, e.g., in the reaction

$$\text{Histamine} + O_2 + H_2O \rightleftharpoons \text{imidazoleacetaldehyde} + NH_3 + H_2O_2$$

(14-2)

These amine oxidases are found in a wide variety of organisms. In animals, they may be localized in the plasma. The FAD-dependent amine oxidases [amine: oxygen oxidoreductase (deaminating) (flavin-containing), EC 1.4.3.4], on the other hand, are localized in the outer membrane of the mitochondria in animals. One of the primary functions of these enzymes is to inactivate norepinephrine and other biogenic monoamines. (This enzyme has been referred to as monoamine oxidase.) The reaction catalyzed by the FAD-dependent amine oxidases is, in effect, the same as that catalyzed by the pyridoxal phosphate enzymes. With norepinephrine as the substrate, the flavin-dependent oxidase catalyzes the reaction

$$\text{Norepinephrine} + O_2 + H_2O \rightleftharpoons$$
$$\text{3,4-dihydroxymandelic aldehyde} + NH_3 + H_2O_2 \quad (14\text{-}3)$$

The amine oxidase from bovine-kidney mitochondria has a molecular weight of 115,000, while the amine oxidase from porcine-liver mitochondria has a molecular weight of approximately 112,000. These enzymes appear to be prone to polymerization or aggregation, however, since species having molecular weights 2, 3, 4, or even 10 times the values cited are readily isolated. (It should be remembered, however, that these enzymes are actually components of the mitochondrial outer membrane, and it has been observed that membrane-associated enzymes which have been solubilized are often prone to aggregation.) The oxidation-reduction

Covalent bonding of FAD to amine oxidase

cofactor, FAD, is covalently bonded to the mitochondrial amine oxidase and in the cases of the oxidases from bovine kidney and liver and porcine liver, this bonding entails the formation of a thiol ether between the sulfhydryl group of a cysteinyl unit of the enzyme and the C(8α) carbon atom of the isoalloxazine moiety of the cofactor.

The mechanism of the reaction catalyzed by the amine oxidases parallels that catalyzed by the amino-acid oxidases. Since the amino group in the present case is bonded to a carbon atom which has *two* hydrogens attached, the hydrolysis product of the imine is an aldehyde rather than an oxo acid, however.

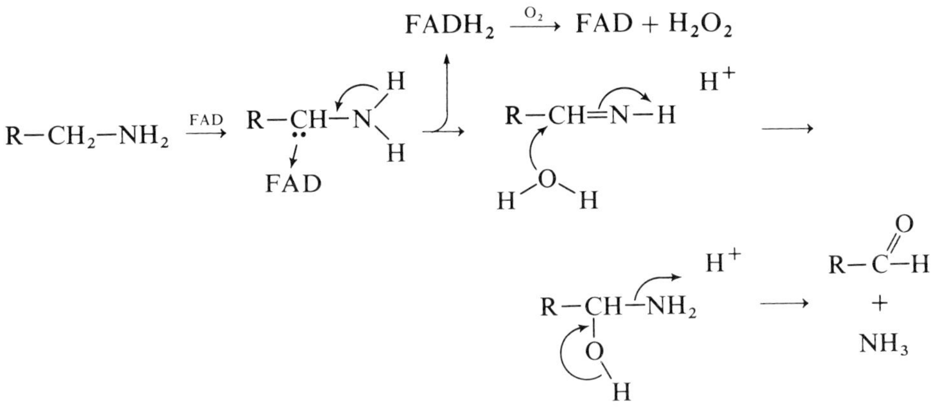

$$FADH_2 \xrightarrow{O_2} FAD + H_2O_2$$

$$R-CH_2-NH_2 \xrightarrow{FAD} R-CH-N\begin{matrix}H\\H\end{matrix} \longrightarrow R-CH=N-H \longrightarrow$$

$$\xrightarrow{H^+} R-CH-NH_2 \longrightarrow R-C-H + NH_3$$

The FAD-dependent amine oxidase is primarily responsible for the rapid inactivation of norepinephrine at the nerve endings. Hence, inhibition of the activity of the amine oxidase can alter the response to sympathetic stimulation. For this reason, inhibitors of amine oxidase activity have been used in the treatment of hypertension and also certain types of depression. One such inhibitor is pargyline, which reacts stoichiometrically and irreversibily with the amine oxidase. The reaction between enzyme and inhibitor entails the formation of a covalent adduct with the FAD.

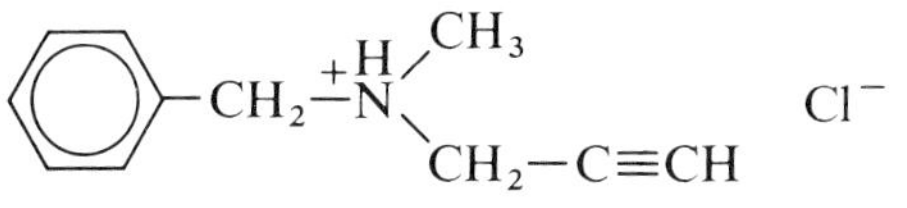

Pargyline (*N*-methyl,*N*′-2-propynylbenzylamine hydrochloride)

## Catalyzed by Glutamate Dehydrogenases

Glutamate dehydrogenases catalyze reactions that occupy pivotal positions in metabolism since the reactions that are catalyzed by these enzymes provide the principal route by which the nitrogen atoms of amino acids are incorporated into the urea molecule and, thus, excreted. These reactions are a primary link between amino acid and carbohydrate metabolism, and they also provide a route by which the nitrogen atom of ammonia can be incorporated into biochemical compounds.

Three glutamate dehydrogenases have been classified and distinguished on the basis of their cofactor specificity. Glutamate dehydrogenases from animals can utilize either NAD$^+$ and NADH or NADP$^+$ and NADPH as the oxidation-reduction cofactors. This enzyme is classified as glutamate dehydrogenase [NAD(P)$^+$] [L-glutamate:NAD(P)$^+$ oxidoreductase (deaminating), EC 1.4.1.3]. Dehydrogenases from most other species specifically utilize either one or the other of the cofactor pairs. Bacteria such as *E. coli* or *Salmonella typhimurium* have only the NADP$^+$-dependent enzyme [L-glutamate:NADP$^+$ oxidoreductase (deaminating), EC 1.4.1.4], while certain *Clostridia* and *Rhodospirillum rubrum* contain the NAD$^+$-dependent dehydrogenase [L-glutamate:NAD$^+$ oxidoreductase (deaminating), EC 1.4.1.2]. Yeasts, *Neurospora crassa*, and certain bacteria contain two distinct dehydrogenases, with one being NAD$^+$-dependent and the other NADP$^+$-dependent. The reaction catalyzed by these enzymes can be written

$$\text{L-Glutamate} + \text{NAD(P)}^+ + \text{H}_2\text{O} \rightleftharpoons \text{2-oxoglutarate} + \text{NH}_3 + \text{NAD(P)H}$$

(14-4)

In mammals the highest concentrations of glutamate dehydrogenase are generally in the liver. The enzyme is localized in the mitochondrion, and in view of the relative ease with which it is isolated, it is presumed to be specifically in the mitochondrial matrix. The purified dehydrogenase from bovine-liver mitochondria has a molecular weight of 332,000 and is a hexamer. The hexamer, which is thought to be the smallest unit that is catalytically active, readily undergoes aggregation to form linear polymers which are also catalytically active. These have molecular weights of several million. The subunits of glutamate dehydrogenase are polypeptides of 500 aminoacyl units in the bovine-liver and rat-liver enzymes. The molecular weight of a subunit is 55,390, as calculated from the primary structure. The arrangement of the subunits to form the hexameric enzyme is shown diagrammatically in Fig. 14-1.

The reaction mechanism of the oxidative deamination catalyzed by glutamate dehydrogenase is similar to that of the reaction catalyzed by the amino acid oxidases; i.e., an imino acid is generated as the result of the removal of electrons from the substrate. Since a lysyl unit (Lys-126) participates in the reaction, the

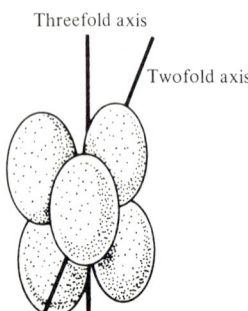

**Figure 14-1** Model for the arrangement of the subunits of glutamate dehydrogenase. The vertical axis is the threefold axis. There are three two-fold axes, one of which is indicated. [*From Josephs, R. (1971) J. Mol. Biol.* **55**, *147–153 (see p. 150). With permission.*]

mechanism has been formulated in terms of a Schiff base intermediate, as shown below.

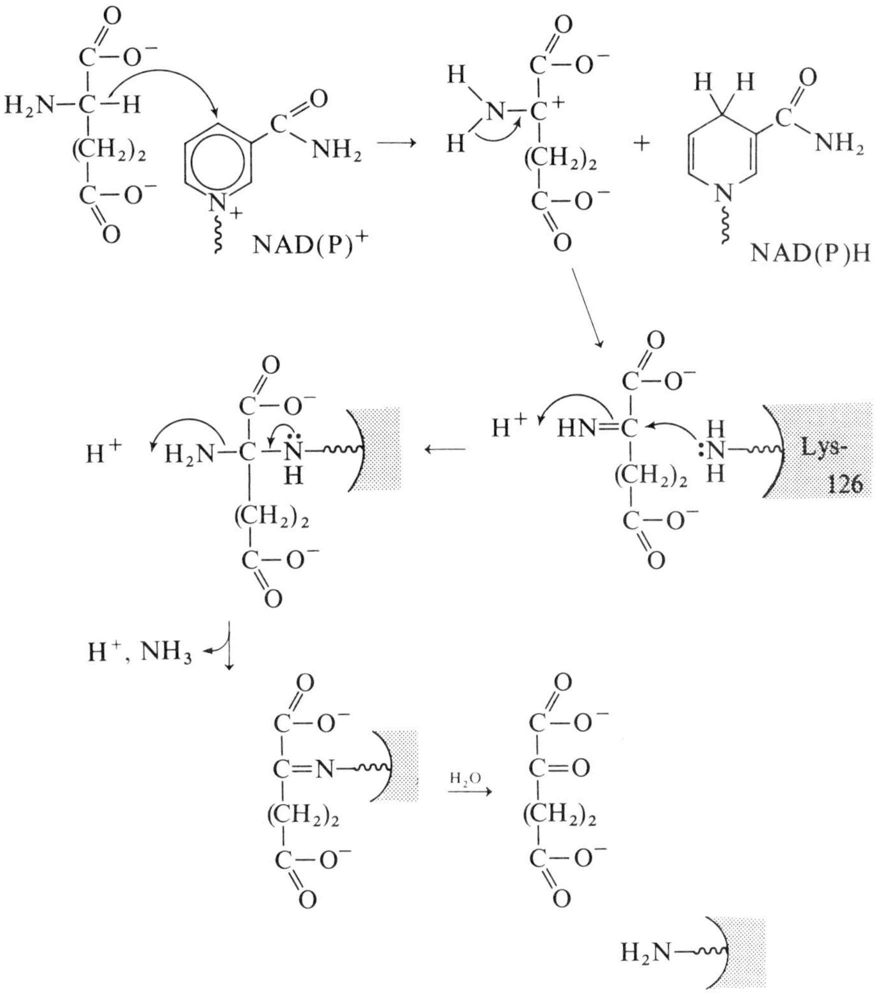

[Scheme showing Schiff base mechanism of glutamate dehydrogenase with NAD(P)+ → NAD(P)H, involving Lys-126]

Kinetic studies on glutamate dehydrogenase from bovine liver have indicated that the reaction proceeds by sequential mechanism since when initial-velocity studies were conducted plots of $1/v_i$ as a function of 1/[glutamate] with fixed concentrations of NADP$^+$ were intersecting. However, plots of $1/v_i$ as a function of 1/[NADP$^+$] or 1/[NAD$^+$] with fixed glutamate concentrations were notably non-linear. More specifically, these plots were convex and exhibited several abrupt discontinuities.

When equilibrium isotope-exchange studies were conducted on this reaction, increasing concentrations of glutamate and 2-oxoglutarate (raised in tandem) failed to inhibit the [carboxamide-$^{14}$C]NAD$^+$-NADH exchange although under these circumstances the [carboxamide-$^{14}$C]NADP$^+$-NADPH exchange was partially inhibited. Increasing concentrations of $NAD^+$ and NADH (raised in tandem) caused the partial inhibition of the $[^{14}C]$2-oxoglutarate-glutamate exchange, while increasing concentrations of glutamate and ammonia (raised in tandem) caused the partial inhibition of both the [*carboximide*-$^{14}C$]$NAD^+$-NADH and the $[^{14}C]$2-oxoglutarate-glutamate exchanges. Also, increasing concentrations of glutamate and NADH (raised in tandem) partially inhibited both the [*carboximide*-$^{14}C$]$NAD^+$-NADH and the $[^{14}C]$2-oxoglutarate-glutamate exchanges. Since when a sequential mechanism is *totally* ordered, *total* inhibition is observed in the presence of saturating concentrations of a reactant that intervenes in the binding sequence between components undergoing exchange, it is concluded that the reaction is not totally ordered. On the other hand, since partial inhibition was observed, the reaction does not appear to be totally random. Rather, it is implied that the reactants bind the enzyme in a random manner although they dissociate from their binary complexes more readily than from their ternary complexes.†

With respect to the discontinuities observed when the initial-velocity data were plotted, it was noted that this behavior was most pronounced in the presence of the higher concentrations of glutamate. Hence, it was speculated that the binding of the oxidation-reduction cofactor by the binary (enzyme-glutamate) complex was somehow responsible. This speculation was supported by studies which showed that the binding of $NAD(P)^+$ to form a ternary complex at one subunit site can induce a conformational change in the oligomeric enzyme, which in turn caused substrate binding at other nonligated sites to become more difficult. Thus, substrate binding by the subunits of a given oligomer is believed to exhibit negative cooperativity.‡ The presence of partially random substrate binding which exhibits negative cooperativity may well account for the behavior of the plots of the initial-velocity data.

The activity of glutamate dehydrogenase can be modulated by purine nucleoside diphosphates and triphosphates, certain hormones, and the cofactor pyridoxal phosphate, among other agents. The first category of modulators includes GTP, which functions as an inhibitor, and ADP, which functions as an activator. The dehydrogenase from bovine liver is thought to have one binding site for either GTP or ADP on each subunit. The effect of these modulators is upon the binding of $NAD(P)^+$. The roles of GTP and ADP are those that would be expected if a principal function of glutamate dehydrogenase is that of providing 2-oxoglutarate for the tricarboxylic acid cycle.

In addition to GTP and ADP, which are the most important modulators in the cell under most circumstances, certain hormones, including norepinephrine, can induce an inhibition of glutamate dehydrogenase activity, while other hormones, including epinephrine, can induce an activation. It has also been shown that the cofactor pyridoxal phosphate can inhibit glutamate dehydrogenase activity. In view of the participation of this cofactor in transamination and other reactions involving

---

† Silversterin, E., and Sulebele, G. (1973) *Biochemistry* **12**, 2164–2172.
‡ Dalziel, K. (1975) in *The Enzymes* (Boyer, P. D., ed), 3d ed., vol. 11, pp. 1–60, Academic, New York.

amino acids, it is tempting to speculate that pyridoxal phosphate has a role in determining whether an amino acid will undergo oxidative deamination or transamination.

## Catalyzed by Aminotransferases

Reactions catalyzed by aminotransferases are known as transamination reactions. Virtually all amino acids undergo transamination. Transamination reactions involve an amino acid and an oxo acid. As the result of the reaction the amino acid is converted into an oxo acid and the initial oxo acid is converted into an amino acid:

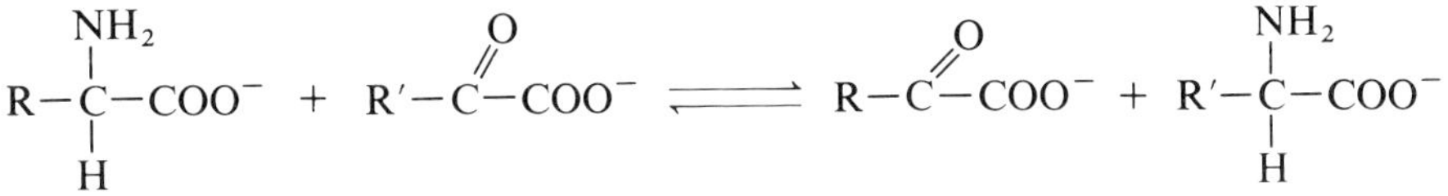

$$\underset{H}{\underset{|}{R-\overset{NH_2}{\underset{|}{C}}-COO^-}} + R'-\overset{O}{\overset{\|}{C}}-COO^- \rightleftharpoons R-\overset{O}{\overset{\|}{C}}-COO^- + \underset{H}{\underset{|}{R'-\overset{NH_2}{\underset{|}{C}}-COO^-}}$$

Aminotransferases require pyridoxal 5-phosphate as a cofactor.

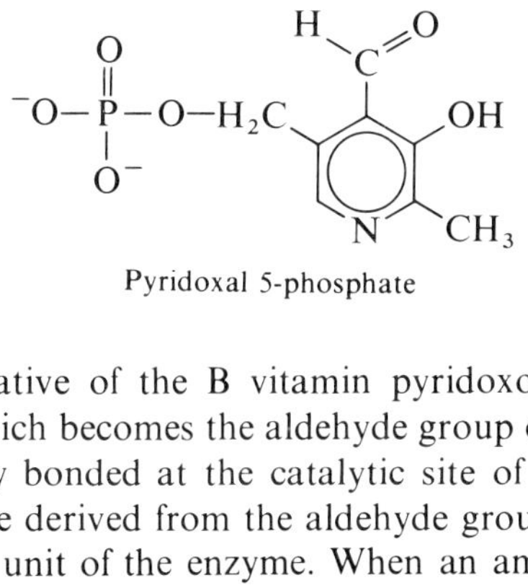

Pyridoxal 5-phosphate

This cofactor is a derivative of the B vitamin pyridoxol. Pyridoxol has a C(4) hydroxymethyl group which becomes the aldehyde group of the cofactor. Pyridoxal 5-phosphate is covalently bonded at the catalytic site of the aminotransferase by formation of a Schiff base derived from the aldehyde group of the cofactor and an $\epsilon$-amino group of a lysyl unit of the enzyme. When an amino acid substrate binds at the catalytic site of an aminotransferase, a transaldimination reaction occurs, thus forming a Schiff base derived from the amino group of the substrate and the aldehyde group of the cofactor.

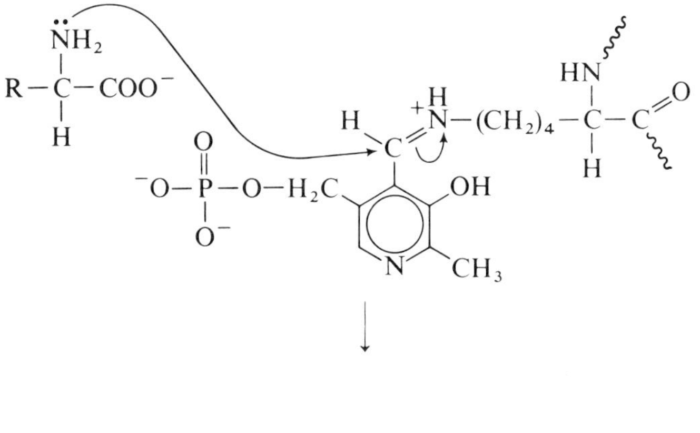

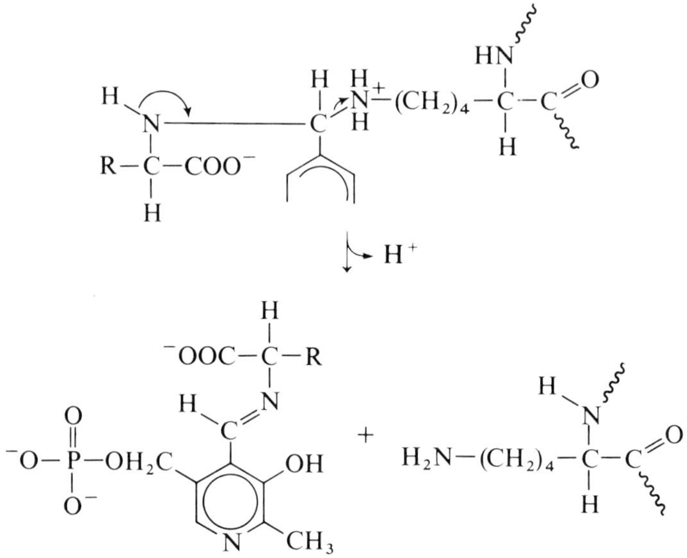

The generalized mechanism of a transamination reaction is shown below.

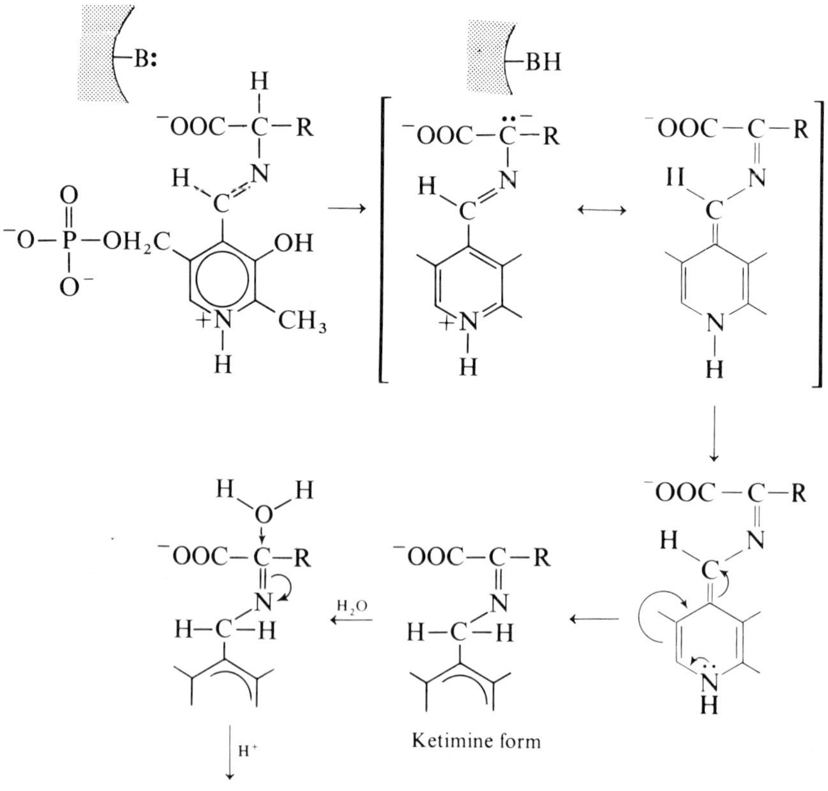

Ketimine form

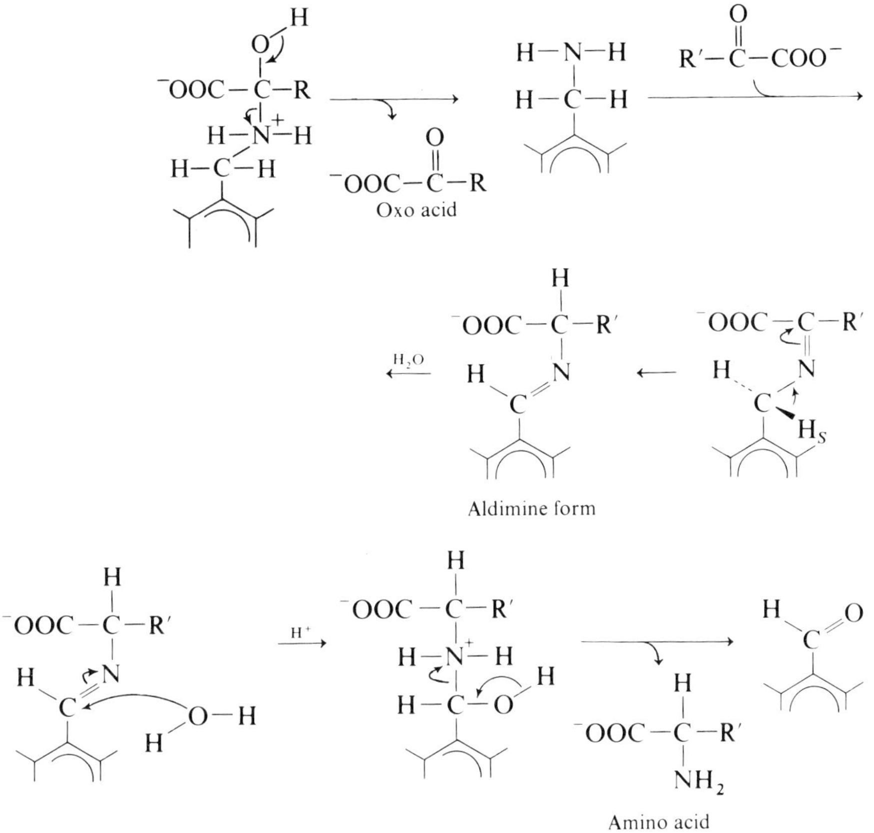

The first event is the removal of a proton from C(2) of the amino acid moiety, thus generating a carbanion, which is stabilized as a result of the delocalization of the negative charge, as indicated by the bracketed structures. Thus, a primary function of the pyridoxal phosphate cofactor is that of facilitating the formation of this carbanion. The amino acid carbanion is then converted into a ketimine form, and, thus, an aldimine-to-ketimine rearrangement has taken place. This is the rate-determining step of the reaction. Hydrolysis of the ketimine generates the new oxo acid and the pyridoxamine form of the cofactor. The second substrate, the original oxo acid, now reacts with the pyridoxamine moiety to form a ketimine, which in turn undergoes a ketimine-to-aldimine rearrangement. As a concomitance of the hydrolysis of this aldimine the new amino acid if formed, and the pyridoxal form of the cofactor is regenerated.

The reaction catalyzed by the aminotransferase exhibits stereoselectivity with respect to the proton transfer to and from the C(4α) carbon atom of the pyridoxal phosphate moiety. Proton transfer as a part of the aldimine-to-ketimine conversion occurs specifically at the *si* face of the methenyl carbon atom. In the latter part of the process, it is specifically the pro-*S* hydrogen atom that is removed from the methylene carbon atom as a part of the ketimine-to-aldimine conversion.

Kinetic studies on the reactions catalyzed by aminotransferases show these reactions to proceed by a ping pong mechanism. A generalized kinetic mechanism can be represented diagrammatically as follows:

$$\begin{array}{ccccc}
\text{NH}_2 & & \text{O} & \text{O} & \text{NH}_2 \\
| & & \| & \| & | \\
\text{R—CH—COO}^- & \text{R—C—COO}^- & & \text{R}'\text{—C—COO}^- & \text{R}'\text{—CH—COO}^- \\
\downarrow & \uparrow & & \downarrow & \uparrow \\
\end{array}$$

| E | $\begin{pmatrix}EA\\FP\end{pmatrix}$ | F | $\begin{pmatrix}FB\\EQ\end{pmatrix}$ | E |
(Pyridoxal form)      (Pyridoxamine form)

In the discussions that follow the characteristics of individual aminotransferases will be noted as individual amino acids and their metabolism are considered. In these discussions the amino acids have been grouped, insofar as possible, on the basis of structural relationships and/or relationships among their metabolic pathways.

## METABOLISM OF GLYCINE, SERINE, AND THREONINE

Glycine, serine, and threonine are three relatively small amino acids which participate in a wide variety of catabolic and anabolic pathways, of which the principal ones are discussed now.

### Glycine Metabolism

Included among the principal reactions of glycine metabolism are its transamination, oxidation, incorporation into heme, incorporation into phosphocreatine, and conversion into serine.

The enzyme glycine aminotransferase (glycine:2-oxoglutarate aminotransferase, EC 2.6.1.4) catalyzes the transamination of glycine with 2-oxoglutarate as the oxo acid, i.e.,

$$\text{Glycine} + \text{2-oxoglutarate} \rightleftharpoons \text{glyoxalate} + \text{L-glutamate} \qquad (14\text{-}6)$$

Glycine can also undergo transamination with oxaloacetate as the oxo acid. In this case, the enzyme is glycine–oxaloacetate aminotransferase (glycine:oxaloacetate aminotransferase, EC 2.6.1.35), and the reaction parallels that given by Eq. (14-6) but with oxaloacetate and L-aspartate as the oxo acid substrate and the amino acid product, respectively. Both these aminotransferases have been isolated and purified, the former from rat and human liver and the latter from *Micrococcus denitrificans*.

In mammals, glyoxalate can undergo a variety of reactions. Among these are its reaction with 2-oxoglutarate to form 2-hydroxy-3-oxoadipate plus carbon dioxide, as catalyzed by 2-hydroxy-3-oxoadipate carboxylase [2-hydroxy-3-oxoadipate glyoxalate-lyase (carboxylating), EC 4.1.3.15]. Glyoxalate also undergoes a dismutation reaction, thought to be catalyzed by lactate dehydrogenase. This reaction results in the formation of the reduction product of glyoxalate, which is glycolate, plus the oxidation product of glyoxalate, which is oxalate. Oxalate is a metabolic end product in man. It is excreted in the urine.

In the microorganism *Micrococcus denitrificans* glycine–oxaloacetate aminotransferase is a component of an enzyme system that converts glycine plus glyoxalate ultimately into oxaloacetate. This pathway entails the formation of *erythro*-3-hydroxy-L-aspartate, as catalyzed by 3-hydroxyaspartate aldolase (*erythro*- -3-hydroxy-L$_S$-aspartate glyoxalate-lyase, EC 4.1.3.14), and its conversion into oxaloacetate and ammonia in the presence of the pyridoxal phosphate–dependent enzyme *erythro*-3-hydroxyaspartate dehydratase [*erythro*-3-hydroxy-L$_S$-aspartate hydro-lyase (deaminating), EC 4.2.1.38].

In other microorganisms, e.g., *Mycobacterium tuberculosis*, a glycine dehydrogenase [glycine:NAD$^+$ oxidoreductase (deaminating), EC 1.4.1.10] catalyzes the following reaction, in which glyoxalate is again a product:

$$\text{Glycine} + \text{NAD}^+ + \text{H}_2\text{O} \rightleftharpoons \text{glyoxalate} + \text{NH}_3 + \text{NADH} \quad (14\text{-}7)$$

Glycine undergoes oxidation in the microorganism *Peptococcus glycinophilus* to yield carbon dioxide, ammonia, and a one-carbon unit. This reaction, which has also been demonstrated in avian liver, is catalyzed by glycine synthase [5,10-methylenetetrahydrofolate:ammonia hydroxymethyltransferase (carboxylating, reducing), EC 2.1.2.10], which utilizes pyridoxal phosphate, tetrahydrofolate, and NAD$^+$. The enzyme system consists of four proteins which function coordinately to catalyze the reaction

Glycine + tetrahydrofolate + oxidized hydrogen-carrier protein $\rightleftharpoons$

$\text{CO}_2 + \text{NH}_3$ + 5,10-methylenetetrahydrofolate

+ reduced hydrogen-carrier protein   (14-8)

A suggested minimal mechanism for this process is shown below and on page 634.

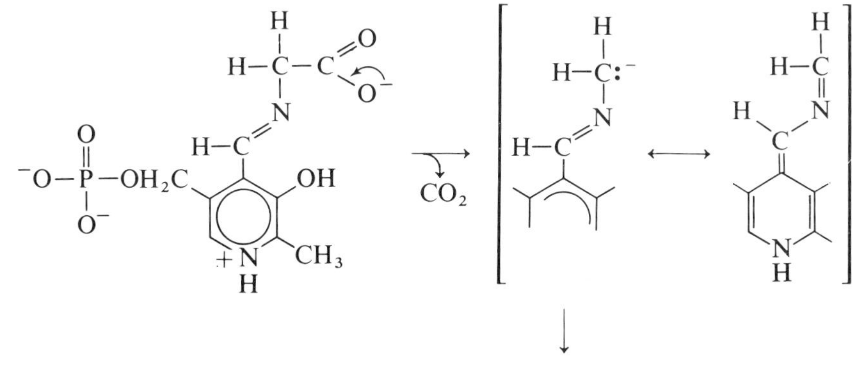

First glycine becomes covalently bonded by the pyridoxal phosphate–dependent component (molecular weight of 125,000 as isolated from the microorganism). The glycine moiety of the resulting Schiff base then undergoes decarboxylation and a small protein (molecular weight of 12,500) which contains a reactive disulfide group accepts an electron pair from the carbanion that is generated as a concomitance of the decarboxylation. These electrons are transferred to a third component, a flavoprotein which has a molecular weight of 100,000, and subsequently to $NAD^+$. Meanwhile, tetrahydrofolate reacts with the carbonium ion derived from C(2) of glycine, and a methylene group is transferred to this cofactor as ammonia is liberated and pyridoxal phosphate is regenerated. In this reaction the function of the pyridoxal phosphate is that of facilitating the decarboxylation reaction. Decarboxylation, like the ionization of a proton, results in the formation of a carbanion, the negative charge of which can be delocalized by the pyridinium ring of the cofactor. There are several other instances in which pyridoxal phosphate facilitates a decarboxylation reaction.

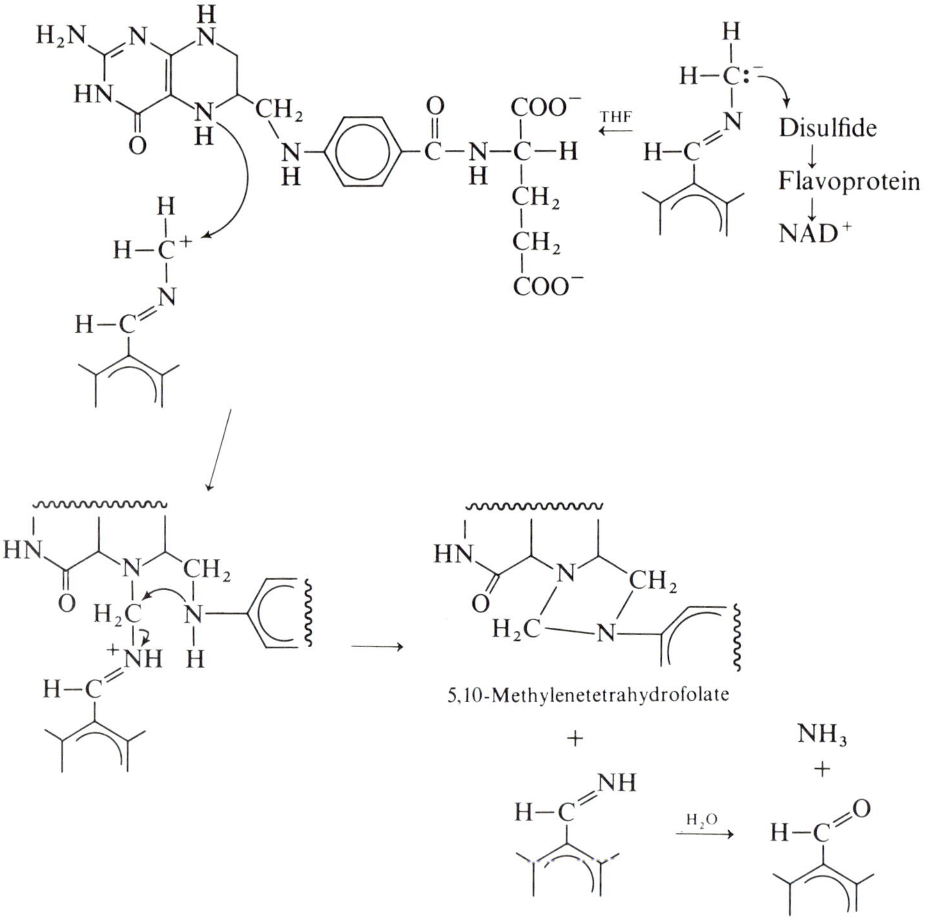

**Incorporation of glycine into heme** The four nitrogen atoms and eight of the carbon atoms of the porphyrin moiety of heme are derived from the glycine molecule. Glycine is incorporated into the porphyrin moiety as a result of the initial (and generally rate-determining) reaction in the synthesis of heme. This pathway also provides intermediates which can be converted into the corrin moiety of vitamin $B_{12}$ or into the chlorophylls.

The anabolism of heme begins with the reaction of glycine and succinyl-CoA to yield 5-aminolevulinate. The reaction is catalyzed by 5-aminolevulinate synthase [succinyl-CoA:glycine C-succinyltransferase (decarboxylating), EC 2.3.1.37], and it can be written

$$\text{Succinyl CoA} + \text{glycine} \rightleftharpoons \text{5-aminolevulinate} + CO_2 + \text{CoA} \quad (14\text{-}9)$$

In mammalian cells 5-aminolevulinate synthase is localized in the mitochondria (although it is synthesized in the cytoplasm). The synthase from rat-liver mitochondria has been isolated, purified, and found to have a molecular weight of 113,000. A synthase from rabbit reticulocytes has also been purified and has a molecular weight of 200,000.

The reaction catalyzed by 5-aminolevulinate synthase has been formulated as shown.

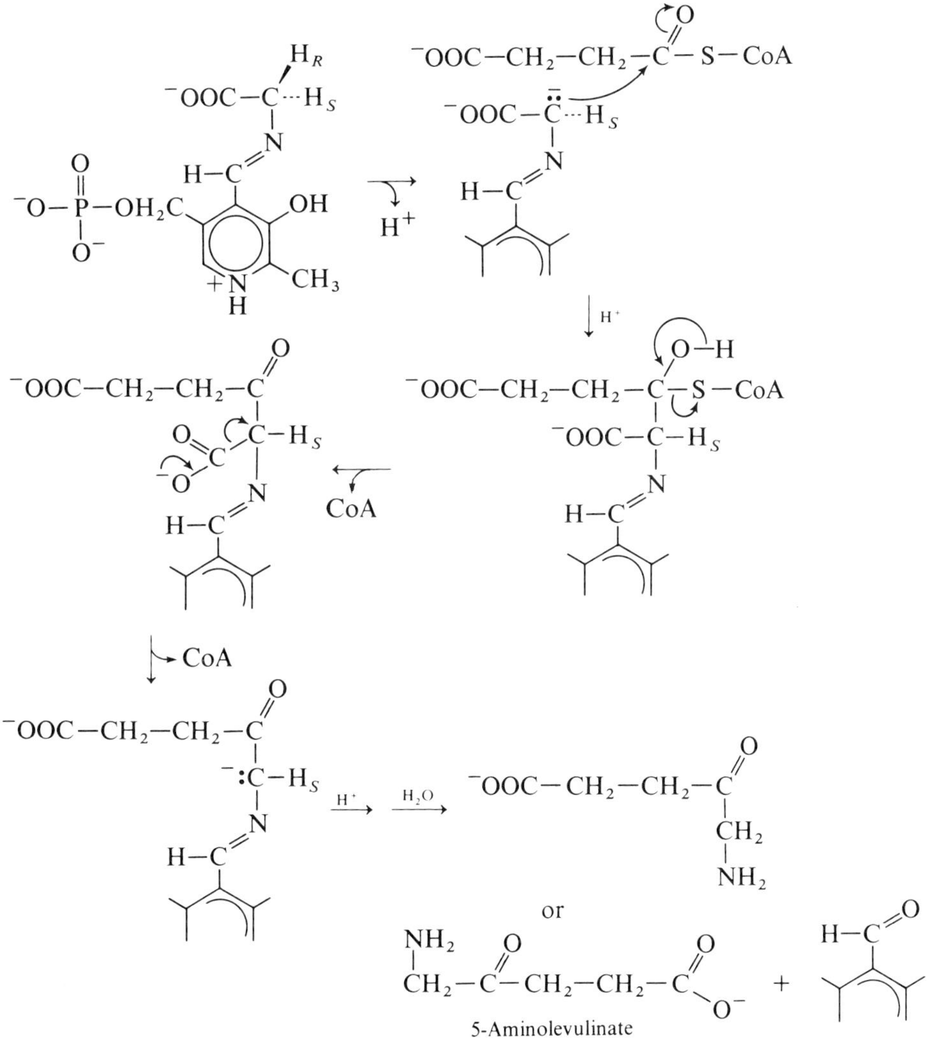

Porphobilinogen

Again, a Schiff base of glycine is formed, and the carbanion resulting from the loss of the pro-$R$ hydrogen atom of the glycine moiety is stabilized as a result of charge delocalization, as described previously. The carbanion then attacks the carbonyl carbon atom of the thiol ester moiety of succinyl CoA. Following the elimination of CoA, C(1) of the glycine moiety is eliminated as carbon dioxide. This decarboxylation is facilitated by the pyridoxal phosphate. Finally, the product, 5-aminolevulinate, is released as a result of a hydrolytic reaction that also allows the pyridoxal phosphate to be regenerated.

In the next step of the synthesis of heme, two molecules of 5-aminolevulinate undergo condensation to yield a molecule of porphobilinogen. The condensation is catalyzed by porphobilinogen synthase [5-aminolevulinate hydro-lyase (adding 5-aminolevulinate and cyclizing), EC 4.2.1.24], a cytoplasmic enzyme. Porphobilinogen synthase has been isolated from plants, yeasts, bacteria, animals, and human erythrocytes. As obtained from human erythrocytes, the synthase has a molecular weight of 283,000. Generally, these enzymes have molecular weights of 200,000 or more, and they are hexamers.

The formation of prophobilinogen is formulated as shown on page 626. An $\epsilon$-amino group of a lysyl unit at the catalytic site of the enzyme reacts with the oxo group of one molecule of 5-aminolevulinate, and a Schiff base is formed. Now a basic functional group, also at the catalytic site, abstracts a proton from C(3) of the covalently bonded substrate molecule, thus generating a carbanion. This then attacks the oxo group of the second substrate molecule. Meanwhile, the amino group of the second substrate molecule attacks the methenyl carbon atom of the Schiff base, thus closing the ring structure. A subsequent loss of the elements of water and cleavage of the Schiff base generates porphobilinogen.

The synthesis of the porphyrins from porphobilinogen requires that the pyrrole moieties of four porphobilinogen molecules become linked initially by methylene carbon atoms which, in turn, become methenyl carbon atoms. Following the dehydrogenation of the pyrrole moieties, the characteristic conjugated structure is generated. Although the precise mechanism by which these changes occur is not completely understood, the formation of the principal porphyrins, including that from which heme is derived, is outlined in the schematic diagram presented on page 628. Uroporphyrinogen I and III differ structurally in that the four pyrrole moieties have the same orientation in the ring structure of uroporphyrinogen I while in uropor-

Uroporphyrinogen I  Uroporphyrinogen III

$A = -CH_2COO^-$    $P = -CH_2CH_2COO^-$

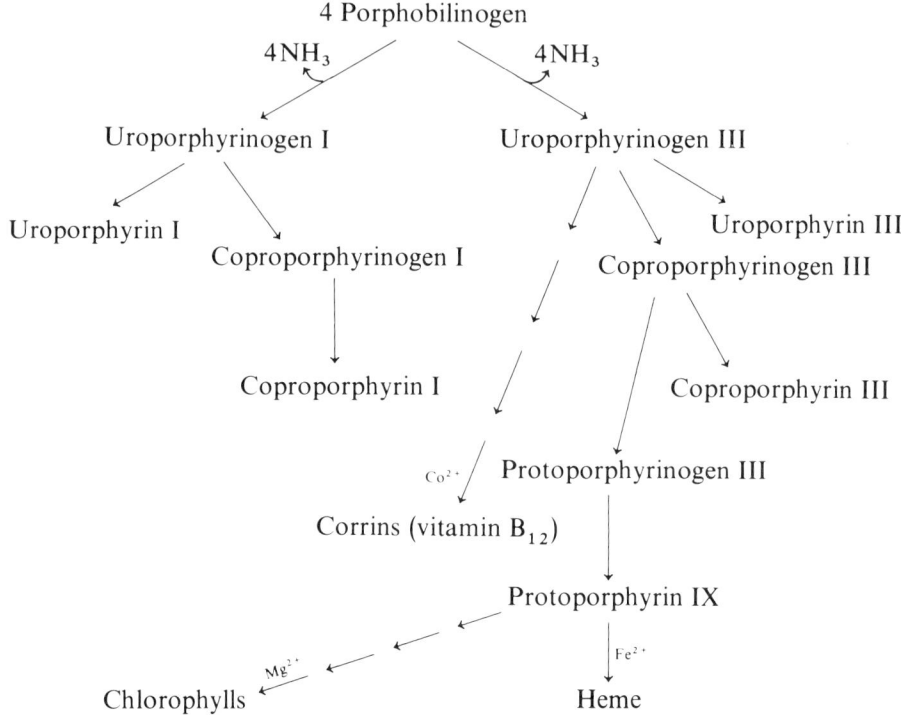

phyrinogen III one of the pyrrole moieties is oriented in the sense opposite to the other three. The formation of uroporphyrinogen I is catalyzed by uroporphyrinogen I synthase [porphobilinogen:ammonia-lyase (polymerizing), EC 4.3.1.8]. The synthesis of uroporphyrinogen III is catalyzed by uroporphyrinogen I synthase plus a second protein, which is thought to participate in the incorporation of the pyrrole moiety having the opposite orientation. The conversion of uroporphyrinogens into coproporphyrinogens entails the decarboxylation of the carboxymethyl substituents and their conversion into methyl substituents. This transformation is catalyzed by uroporphyrinogen decarboxylase (uroporphyrinogen-III carboxy-lyase, EC 4.1.1.37). The conversion of coproporphyrinogen III into protoporphyrinogen III is catalyzed by coproporphyrinogen oxidase [coproporphyrinogen:oxygen oxidoreductase (decarboxylating), EC 1.3.3.3]. The reaction entails the conversion of two of the carboxyethyl substituents into vinyl substituents. Hence, both decarboxylation and oxidation, i.e., dehydrogenation, occur, as indicated by the equation

$$\text{Coproporphyrinogen III} + O_2 \rightleftharpoons \text{protoporphyrinogen III} + 2CO_2 + 2H_2O \quad (14\text{-}10)$$

A reaction mechanism involving the hydroxylation of the carboxyethyl substituent followed by dehydration and decarboxylation has been proposed.

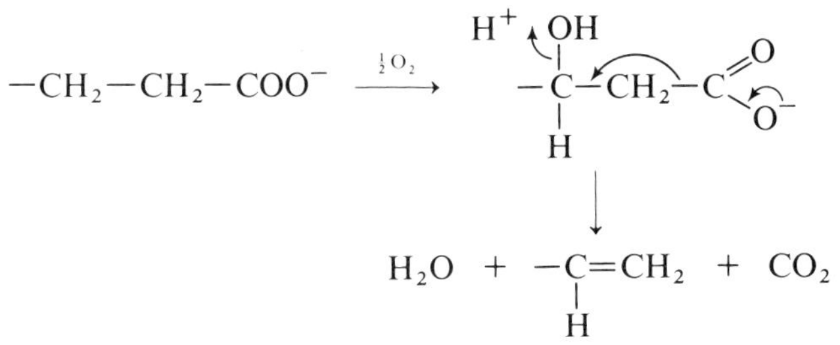

$$-CH_2-CH_2-COO^- \xrightarrow{\frac{1}{2}O_2} \overset{H^+ \ OH}{\underset{H}{-C-}}CH_2-C\overset{O}{\underset{O^-}{\diagdown}}$$

$$H_2O + \underset{H}{-C}=CH_2 + CO_2$$

The coproporphyrinogen oxidase as isolated from yeast (*Saccharomyces cerevisiae*) mitochondria and from rat-liver mitochondria has a molecular weight of approximately 75,000. The formation of protoporphyrin IX from protoporphyrinogen III entails the removal of six hydrogen atoms and six electrons and the introduction of three new olefinic bonds. (The porphyrin is referred to as protoporphyrin IX because it was the ninth of the 15 possible isomers of the protoporphyrins which Hans Fischer synthesized. In fact, protoporphyrin IX is a type III porphyrin.) An enzyme which has a molecular weight of 180,000 and which catalyzes this reaction has been isolated from the yeast mitochondrial membrane. Finally, in the presence of $Fe^{2+}$ and the enzyme ferrochelatase (protoheme ferrolyase, EC 4.99.1.1) the heme moiety is generated.

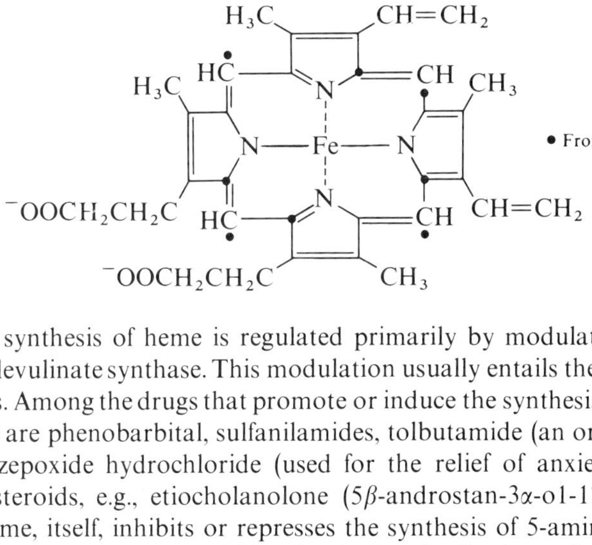

• From C(2) of glycine

The synthesis of heme is regulated primarily by modulation of the activity of 5-aminolevulinate synthase. This modulation usually entails the regulation of enzyme synthesis. Among the drugs that promote or induce the synthesis of 5-aminolevulinate synthase are phenobarbital, sulfanilamides, tolbutamide (an oral antidiabetes drug), chlordiazepoxide hydrochloride (used for the relief of anxiety and tension), and certain steroids, e.g., etiocholanolone (5β-androstan-3α-ol-17-one). On the other hand, heme, itself, inhibits or represses the synthesis of 5-aminolevulinate synthase. Since the synthase has a half-life of only 68 min (in the rat), regulation of enzyme synthesis is an effective means of regulating the expressed activity of the enzyme.

**The porphyrias** The porphyrias are pathological conditions characterized by the excretion of abnormally high concentrations of porphyrins and/or intermediates in porphyrin synthesis in the urine or feces. The condition is also associated with certain neurological and/or cutaneous manifestations. Most of the porphyrias are hereditary. In some cases a specific metabolic aberration has been identified as the cause of the manifestations of the disease. For example, acute intermittent porphyria results from an overproduction of 5-aminolevulinate in the liver, and it is manifested by the urinary excretion of greatly increased concentrations of 5-aminolevulinate and porphobilinogen. Congenital erythropoietic porphyria, on the other hand, results from an overproduction of porphyrins in the maturing erythroid cells of the bone marrow. Under these circumstances there may be a fifteen- to twentyfold increase in the concentration of uroporphyrin I in the urine. Congenital erythropoietic porphyria is also associated with chronic cutaneous photosensitivity and a hemolytic anemia.

**Incorporation of glycine into phosphocreatine** Glycine is also a substrate in the first reaction of the synthesis of phosphocreatine. This initial reaction, which is catalyzed by glycine amidinotransferase (L-arginine:glycine amidinotransferase, EC 2.1.4.1), is

$$\text{L-Arginine} + \text{glycine} \rightleftharpoons \text{L-ornithine} + \text{guanidinoacetate} \quad (14\text{-}11)$$

The reaction involves the formation of a covalent amidino-enzyme intermediate, which has, in fact, been isolated when the transferase from porcine kidney was studied. The amidino group becomes bonded to the sulfhydryl group of a cysteinyl unit at the catalytic site.

$$\underset{\text{S-Amidinocysteinyl unit}}{\overset{HN}{\underset{H_2N}{\diagdown}}\!\!\!\!C\!-\!S\!-\!CH_2\!-\!\underset{H}{\overset{NH}{\underset{|}{C}}}\!-\!\overset{O}{\underset{}{C}}}$$

The formation of guanidinoacetate is rate-determining with respect to the synthesis of creatine.

Guanidinoacetate undergoes *N*-methylation in the presence of *S*-adenosyl-L-methionine to yield creatine. The methylation is catalyzed by guanidinoacetate methyltransferase (*S*-adenosyl-L-methionine:guanidinoacetate *N*-methyltransferase, EC 2.1.1.2).

Creatine can accept the terminal phosphoryl group from ATP to yield phosphocreatine. In vertebrates phosphocreatine serves as an energy reservoir, particularly in the muscles and also in the brain, liver, and kidney. The phosphoryl transfer is catalyzed by creatine kinase (ATP:creatine *N*-phosphotransferase, EC 2.7.3.2). The reaction is

$$\text{Creatine} + \text{ATP} \rightleftharpoons \text{phosphocreatine} + \text{ADP} \quad (14\text{-}12)$$

Three forms of creatine kinase are found in mammalian systems. One of these predominates in mammalian smooth muscle although it is generally referred to as the brain-type enzyme since it is present in most tissues during development and it persists in the brain. A second form of creatine kinase predominates in mammalian heart tissue and in red and white striated muscle fibers. This is referred to as the muscle-type enzyme. Each of these forms consists of two identical subunits. The third type of kinase is a hybrid, comprising one subunit of the brain-type enzyme and one of the muscle-type enzyme. Each of these three forms has a molecular weight of approximately 82,000.

The reaction catalyzed by creatine kinase has a sequential kinetic mechanism, as shown by the initial-velocity data. Since each of the four reactants can bind the noncomplexed enzyme in the absence of the others, it is implied that the mechanism is a random one. Studies on creatine kinase from rabbit skeletal muscle† and from bovine brain and muscle‡ have suggested the presence of a rapid equilibrium random mechanism since the interconversion of the central complexes, i.e., the enzyme-ATP-creatine complex and the enzyme-ADP-phosphocreatine complex, appears to be the rate-determining event in the reaction. However, in the case of the enzyme from bovine brain the dissociation of each of the substrates from its binary complex (the enzyme-ATP complex in the case of ATP) is much faster than that from its ternary complex (the enzyme-ATP-creatine complex in the case of ATP), thus indicating that the substrate binding is not *totally* random and independent.

Phosphocreatine serves as a reservoir for chemical energy (in the vertebrates) because of the facility with which it can return its phosphoryl group to ADP, thus generating ATP. This occurs in muscle, for example, during periods of muscular activity when the demand for ATP is increased due to its utilization in the process of muscle contraction. The reactions involved in the synthesis of phosphocreatine are shown below.

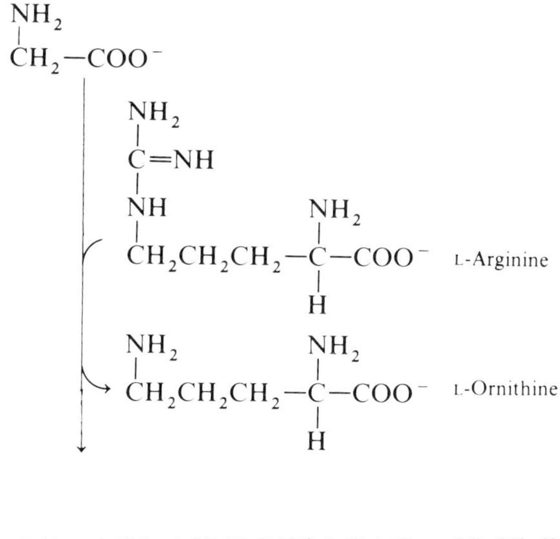

$$\begin{array}{l} NH_2 \\ | \\ CH_2-COO^- \\ \quad \Big| \\ \quad \quad NH_2 \\ \quad \quad | \\ \quad \quad C=NH \\ \quad \quad | \\ \quad \quad NH \quad\quad\quad NH_2 \\ \quad \quad | \quad\quad\quad\quad | \\ \quad \nearrow CH_2CH_2CH_2-C-COO^- \quad \text{L-Arginine} \\ \quad \Big| \quad\quad\quad\quad\quad | \\ \quad \Big| \quad\quad\quad\quad\quad H \\ \quad \Big| \quad NH_2 \quad\quad NH_2 \\ \quad \Big| \quad | \quad\quad\quad\quad | \\ \quad \searrow CH_2CH_2CH_2-C-COO^- \quad \text{L-Ornithine} \\ \quad \downarrow \quad\quad\quad\quad\quad | \\ \quad\quad\quad\quad\quad\quad\quad H \end{array}$$

† Morrison, J. F., and Cleland, W. W. (1966) *J. Biol. Chem.* **241**, 673–683.
‡ Jacobs, H. K., and Kuby, S. A. (1970) *J. Biol. Chem.* **245**, 3305–3314.

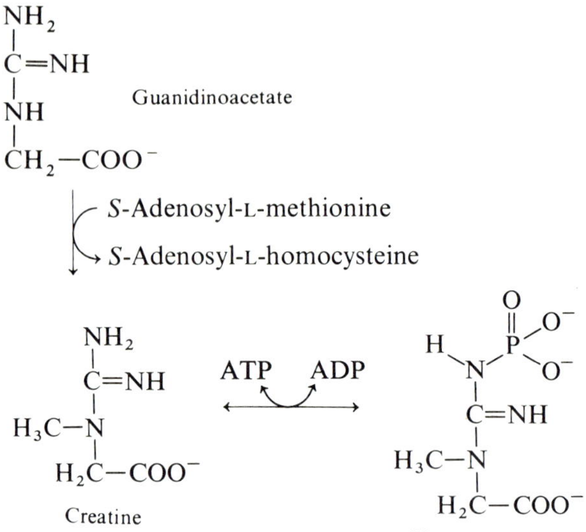

$$\underset{\text{Guanidinoacetate}}{\begin{array}{c} NH_2 \\ | \\ C=NH \\ | \\ NH \\ | \\ CH_2-COO^- \end{array}}$$

↓ S-Adenosyl-L-methionine
↓ S-Adenosyl-L-homocysteine

$$\underset{\text{Creatine}}{\begin{array}{c} NH_2 \\ | \\ C=NH \\ | \\ H_3C-N \\ | \\ H_2C-COO^- \end{array}} \xrightleftharpoons[ADP]{ATP} \underset{\text{Phosphocreatine}}{\begin{array}{c} O \\ \| \\ H\diagdown N\diagup P\diagdown O^- \\ \phantom{xx}\diagup\phantom{xx}O^- \\ | \\ C=NH \\ | \\ H_3C-N \\ | \\ H_2C-COO^- \end{array}}$$

In the invertebrate muscle, phosphoarginine serves a similar function.

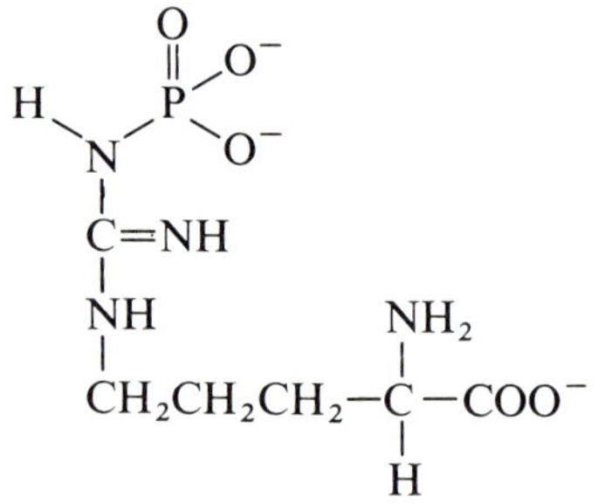

$$\underset{\text{Phospho-L-arginine}}{\begin{array}{c} O \\ \| \\ H\diagdown N\diagup P\diagdown O^- \\ \phantom{xxx}O^- \\ | \\ C=NH \\ | \\ NH \phantom{xxxx} NH_2 \\ | \phantom{xxxxxx} | \\ CH_2CH_2CH_2-C-COO^- \\ | \\ H \end{array}}$$

In human muscle creatine is converted at an essentially constant rate (approximately 2 percent per day) into creatinine, an end product which is excreted in the urine.

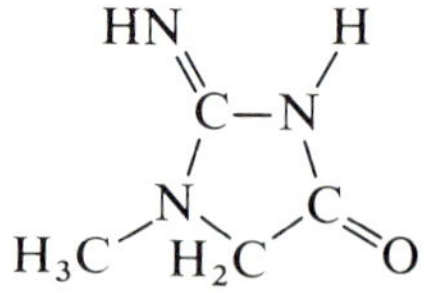

$$\underset{\text{Creatinine}}{\begin{array}{c} HN \phantom{xxx} H \\ \diagdown\phantom{x}\diagup \\ C-N \\ \diagup\phantom{xx}\diagdown \\ N \phantom{xxx} C=O \\ H_3C\phantom{x} H_2C \end{array}}$$

Since this rate of excretion is relatively constant, the creatinine content of a pooled urine specimen is sometimes used as an indication of the time span over which the specimen was collected. A decrease in the average daily excretion of creatinine accompanies certain of the muscular dystrophies, reflecting the decrease in muscle mass due to these diseases.

**The glycine-serine interconversion** Glycine is converted into serine in the presence of 5,10-methylenetetrahydrofolate and the pyridoxal phosphate–dependent enzyme serine hydroxymethyltransferase (5,10-methylenetetrahydrofolate:glycine hydroxymethyltransferase, EC 2.1.2.1). The reaction is

5,10-Methylenetetrahydrofolate + glycine $\rightleftharpoons$

$$\text{tetrahydrofolate} + \text{L-serine} \quad (14\text{-}13)$$

The reaction is demonstrably reversible and exhibits the following equilibrium constant:

$$\frac{[\text{Tetrahydrofolate}][\text{L-serine}]}{[5,10\text{-Methylenetetrahydrofolate}][\text{glycine}]} \approx 0.1 \quad \text{at } 25°C, \text{pH } 7.4$$

Serine hydroxymethyltransferase has been isolated from the cytoplasm and from the mitochondria of rat and rabbit liver, among other sources. A purified enzyme from the cytoplasm of rabbit hepatocytes has a molecular weight of 331,000 and is a tetramer. The tetrameric enzyme binds four molecules of pyridoxal phosphate. The mechanism of the reaction catalyzed by serine hydroxymethyltransferase can be formulated as shown.

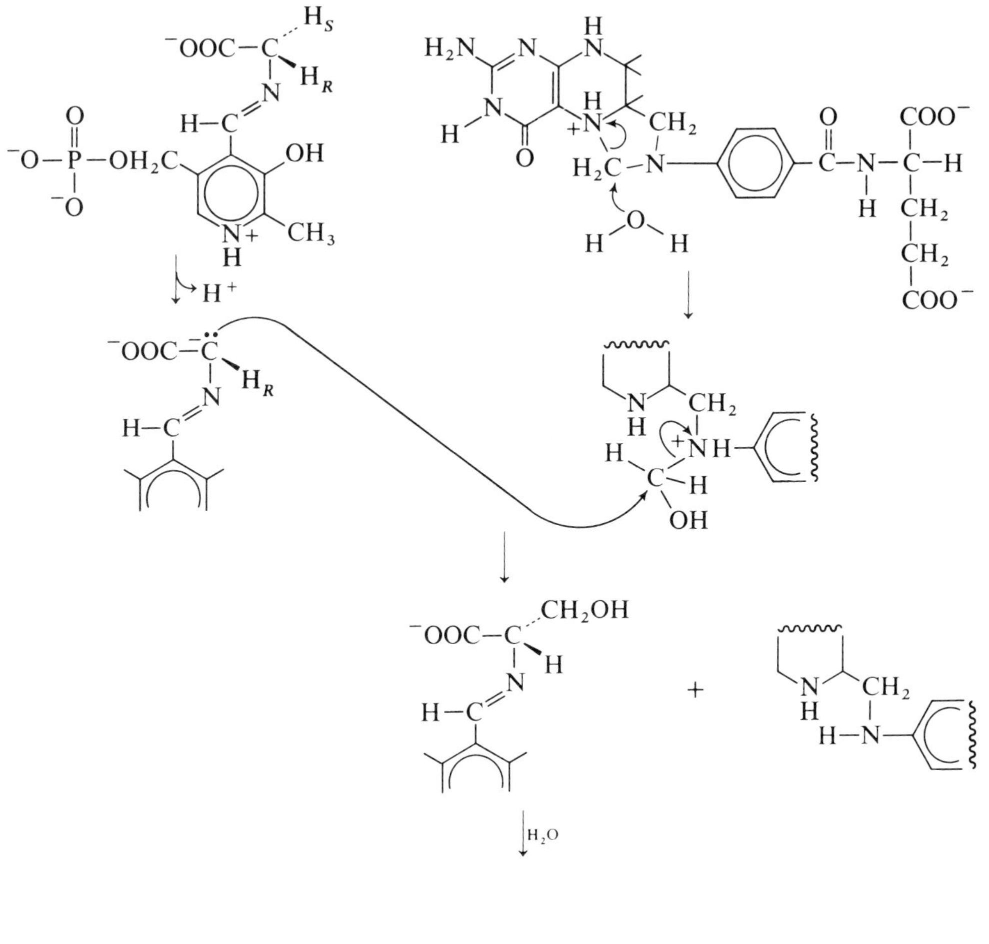

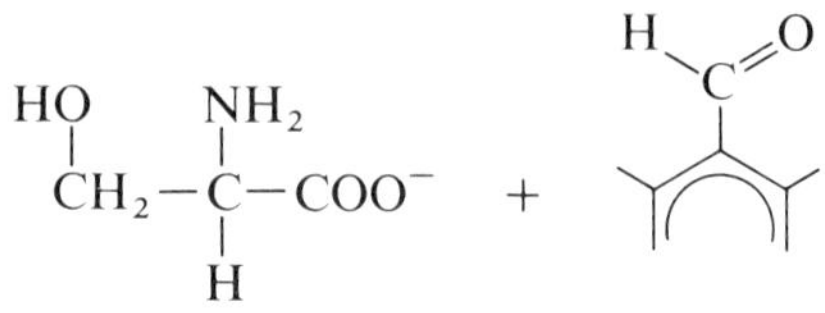

$$\underset{\text{L-Serine}}{\overset{\text{HO} \quad \text{NH}_2}{\underset{\text{H}}{\text{CH}_2-\text{C}-\text{COO}^-}}} \quad + \quad \text{(pyridoxal phosphate)}$$

The glycine Schiff base is formed, and specifically the pro-$S$ hydrogen atom of the glycine moiety is then abstracted, as a proton. The resulting carbanion is stabilized in the manner described previously. Meanwhile, a water molecule reacts with the methylene group of the tetrahydrofolate cofactor, with the result that an $N$-hydroxymethyl intermediate is formed. This in turn is attacked by the carbanion, and the hydroxymethyl group is transferred to C(2) of the glycine moiety. Hydrolysis of the Schiff base releases L-serine and generates tetrahydrofolate.

In addition to catalyzing the glycine-serine interconversion, serine hydroxymethyltransferase can also catalyze the formation of L-serine from glycine and formaldehyde in the absence of a tetrahydrofolate cofactor. The enzyme also catalyzes the formation of L-threonine from glycine and acetaldehyde, again in the absence of a tetrahydrofolate cofactor. The reader should be able to formulate minimal mechanisms for these reactions.

## Serine Metabolism

The catabolism of serine may entail its conversion into glycine, in the presence of serine hydroxymethyltransferase, or its conversion into pyruvate or into 3-hydroxypyruvate. In addition, serine or its carbon atoms can be incorporated into phosphatidylserine, cysteine (in mammals), and tryptophan.

The conversion of L-serine into pyruvate is catalyzed by L-serine dehydratase [L-serine hydro-lyase (deaminating), EC 4.2.1.13], a pyridoxal phosphate–dependent enzyme, which can also utilize L-threonine as its substrate. The reaction with L-serine as the substrate is

$$\text{L-Serine} + \text{H}_2\text{O} \rightleftharpoons \text{pyruvate} + \text{NH}_3 + \text{H}_2\text{O} \qquad (14\text{-}14)$$

When L-threonine is the substrate, the oxo acid product is 2-oxobutyrate.

Two forms of L-serine dehydratase have been isolated from rat liver. Each form has a molecular weight of 68,000 and comprises two subunits which have approximately equal molecular weights. The two forms are distinguished on the basis of their electrophoretic mobilities, their amino acid compositions, and the fact that they respond to different modulators. One form of the enzyme can be induced (in the rat liver) by the steroid hormone cortisone, while the other can be induced by the hormone glucagon.

The reaction catalyzed by serine dehydratase is an elimination reaction that is facilitated by the pyridoxal phosphate cofactor. The mechanism is shown below.

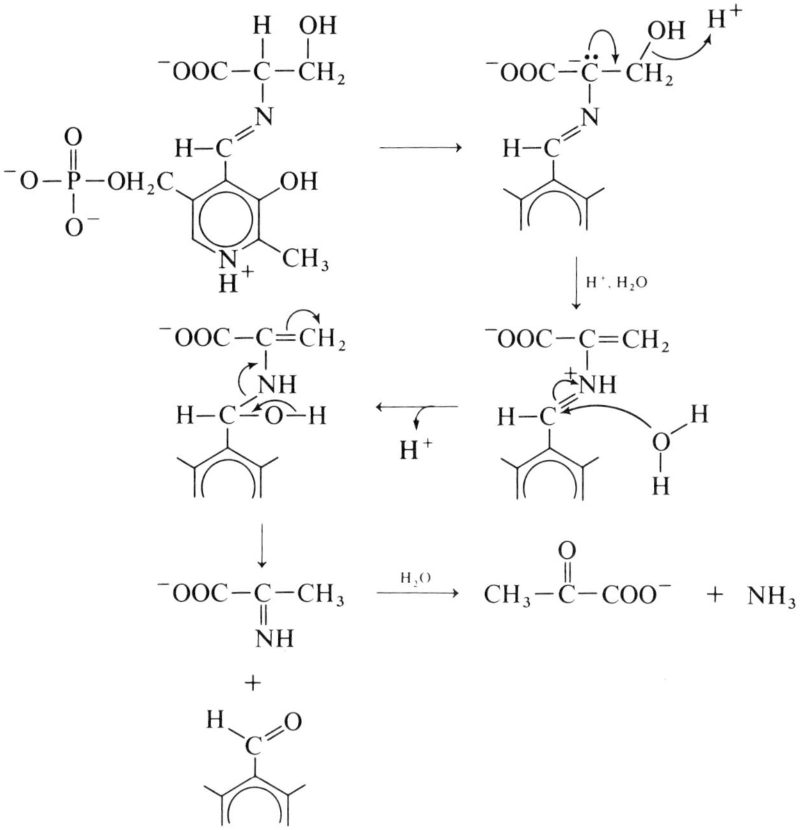

Following formation of the serine Schiff base, a proton is abstracted from C(2) of the serine moiety, and the resulting (stabilized) carbanion in this instance expels a hydroxyl ion from C(3). Hydrolytic cleavage of the Schiff base liberates 2-iminopropionate, which then undergoes nonenzymatic hydrolysis to yield pyruvate and ammonia.

Certain microorganisms, including *E. coli*, contain a D-serine dehydratase [D-serine hydro-lyase (deaminating), EC 4.2.1.14]. In this case, D-threonine is also a substrate, albeit a poor one.

In the presence of pyruvate and the enzyme serine–pyruvate aminotransferase (L-serine:pyruvate aminotransferase, EC 2.6.1.51) serine is converted into 3-hydroxypyruvate. The amino acid product is L-alanine. The presence of this aminotransferase has been demonstrated in human, bovine, and rat liver. In mammals, 3-hydroxypyruvate can undergo reduction to yield either L- or D-glycerate. The formation of L-glycerate is catalyzed by lactate dehydrogenase. The formation of D-glycerate is catalyzed by hydroxypyruvate reductase [D-glycerate:NAD(P)$^+$ 2-oxidoreductase, EC 1.1.1.81]. D-Glycerate can, in turn, be converted into 3-phosphoglycerate in the presence of glycerate kinase (ATP:D-glycerate 3-phosphotransferase, EC 2.7.1.31) and the 3-phosphoglycerate can then enter the gluconeogenic pathway.

**Anabolism of serine** Besides being formed from glycine and a methylene group, serine can be derived from the carbon atoms of glucose. In mammals this entails the oxidation of the glycolytic intermediate 3-phosphoglycerate to yield 3-phosphohydroxypyruvate and then the transamination of the latter to yield phosphoserine. Hydrolysis of phosphoserine yields serine. The conversion of 3-phosphoglycerate into 3-phosphohydroxypyruvate is catalyzed by phosphoglycerate dehydrogenase (3-phosphoglycerate:$NAD^+$ 2-oxidoreductase, EC 1.1.1.95). Phosphoserine aminotransferase (O-phospho-L-serine:2-oxoglutarate aminotransferase, EC 2.6.1.52) catalyzes the transamination reaction, and phosphoserine phosphatase (O-phosphoserine phosphohydrolase, EC 3.1.3.3) converts phosphoserine into serine. These reactions are summarized below.

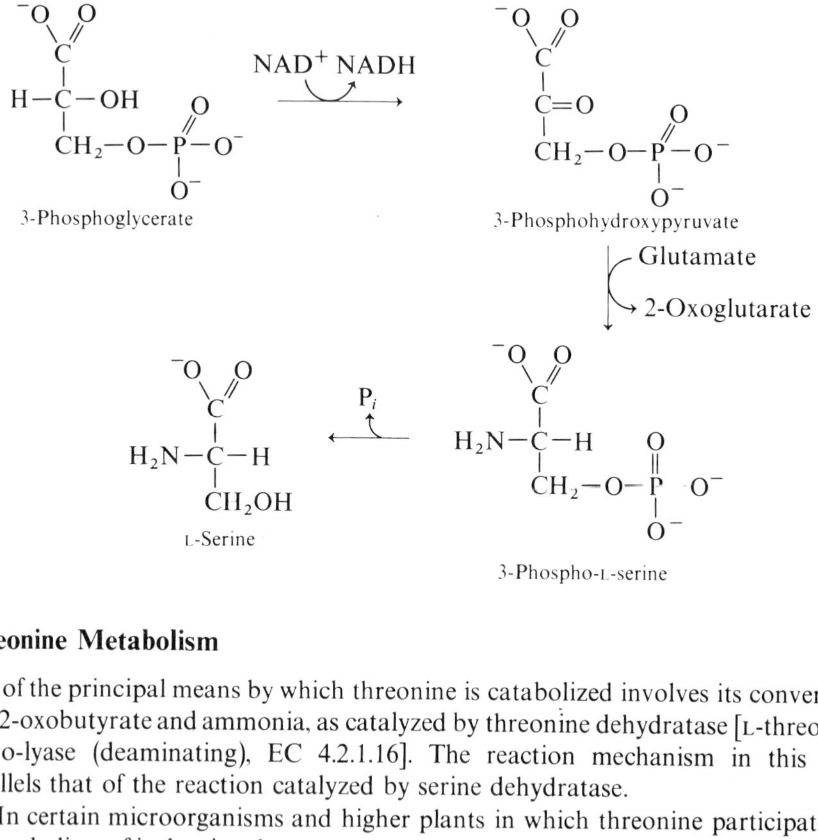

## Threonine Metabolism

One of the principal means by which threonine is catabolized involves its conversion into 2-oxobutyrate and ammonia, as catalyzed by threonine dehydratase [L-threonine hydro-lyase (deaminating), EC 4.2.1.16]. The reaction mechanism in this case parallels that of the reaction catalyzed by serine dehydratase.

In certain microorganisms and higher plants in which threonine participates in the anabolism of isoleucine there are two enzymes that can catalyze the conversion of threonine into 2-oxobutyrate and ammonia. One of these, sometimes referred to as the *biodegradative enzyme*, exhibits an activity that is enhanced in the presence of AMP. The other, sometimes referred to as the *biosynthetic enzyme*, exhibits an activity that is inhibited by the ultimate product, isoleucine. The biodegradative enzyme threonine dehydratase from *E. coli* has a molecular weight of 147,000. This enzyme is a tetramer. Each subunit binds one pyridoxal phosphate molecule and has one binding site for AMP. The activity of this dehydratase is insensitive to isoleucine. However, the reaction product, 2-oxobutyrate, is reported to bind at an allosteric site on the enzyme and thus promote the dissociation of the tetramer. Dissociation is accompanied by a decrease in enzymatic activity. Thus, 2-oxobutyrate functions as an allosteric inhibitor. AMP, on the other hand, is a deinhibitor in that it prevents the dissociation induced by 2-oxobutyrate.

In animals, L-threonine can be converted into glycine and acetaldehyde by a reaction catalyzed by serine hydroxymethyltransferase. This reaction, as mentioned above, does not require a tetrahydrofolate cofactor.

In certain microorganisms, threonine can also undergo oxidation in the presence of $NAD^+$ and the enzyme L-threonine 3-dehydrogenase (L-threonine:$NAD^+$ oxidoreductase, EC 1.1.1.103). The reaction is

$$\text{L-Threonine} + NAD^+ \rightleftharpoons \text{L-2-amino-3-oxobutyrate} + NADH \quad (14\text{-}15)$$

The product, L-2-amino-3-oxobutyrate, undergoes spontaneous decarboxylation to yield aminoacetone.

**Anabolism of threonine** In certain microorganisms and higher plants the synthesis of three different amino acids, threonine, methionine, and lysine, entails the incorporation of carbon atoms derived from aspartate, and in each case the initial reaction of the anabolic pathway is the formation of aspartyl 4-phosphate. In *E. coli*, three distinct enzymes that catalyze the formation of aspartyl 4-phosphate have been identified. One participates in the synthesis of threonine, the second participates in the synthesis of methionine, and the third participates in the synthesis of lysine.

When threonine is to be synthesized, the formation of aspartyl 4-phosphate is catalyzed by aspartate kinase I–homoserine dehydrogenase I, a bifunctional enzyme. As isolated from *E. coli* K-12, this enzyme has a molecular weight of 340,000 and it is a tetramer. Each 85,000-dalton subunit has a catalytic site near its amino terminus at which aspartyl 4-phosphate is formed and a site near its carboxyl terminus at which homoserine (a product of the third reaction of the pathway) is formed. The aspartate kinase (ATP:L-aspartate 4-phosphotransferase, EC 2.7.2.4) activity of the enzyme catalyzes the reaction

$$\text{L-Aspartate} + ATP \rightleftharpoons \text{aspartyl 4-phosphate} + ADP \quad (14\text{-}16)$$

This activity, as well as the homoserine dehydrogenase activity of the enzyme, is inhibited by the ultimate product of the pathway, L-threonine, which binds the enzyme in a cooperative manner. In addition, the synthesis of this bifunctional enzyme is repressed in the presence of high concentrations of threonine or isoleucine. (Threonine undergoes catabolism to yield 2-oxobutyrate which is, in turn, required for the synthesis of isoleucine.)

In the next step of the anabolism of threonine aspartyl 4-phosphate undergoes reduction and dephosphorylation to yield L-aspartate semialdehyde. The enzyme aspartate-semialdehyde dehydrogenase [L-aspartate-4-semialdehyde:$NADP^+$ oxidoreductase (phosphorylating), EC 1.2.1.11] catalyzes the reaction

$$\text{Aspartyl 4-phosphate} + NADPH \rightleftharpoons \text{L-aspartate-4-semialdehyde} + NADP^+ + P_i \quad (14\text{-}17)$$

This reaction is reminiscent of that catalyzed by glyceraldehyde 3-phosphate dehydrogenase in which glyceraldehyde 3-phosphate is formed from 3-phospho-D-glyceroyl phosphate. Here too a cysteinyl sulfhydryl group participates in the reaction, as shown below.

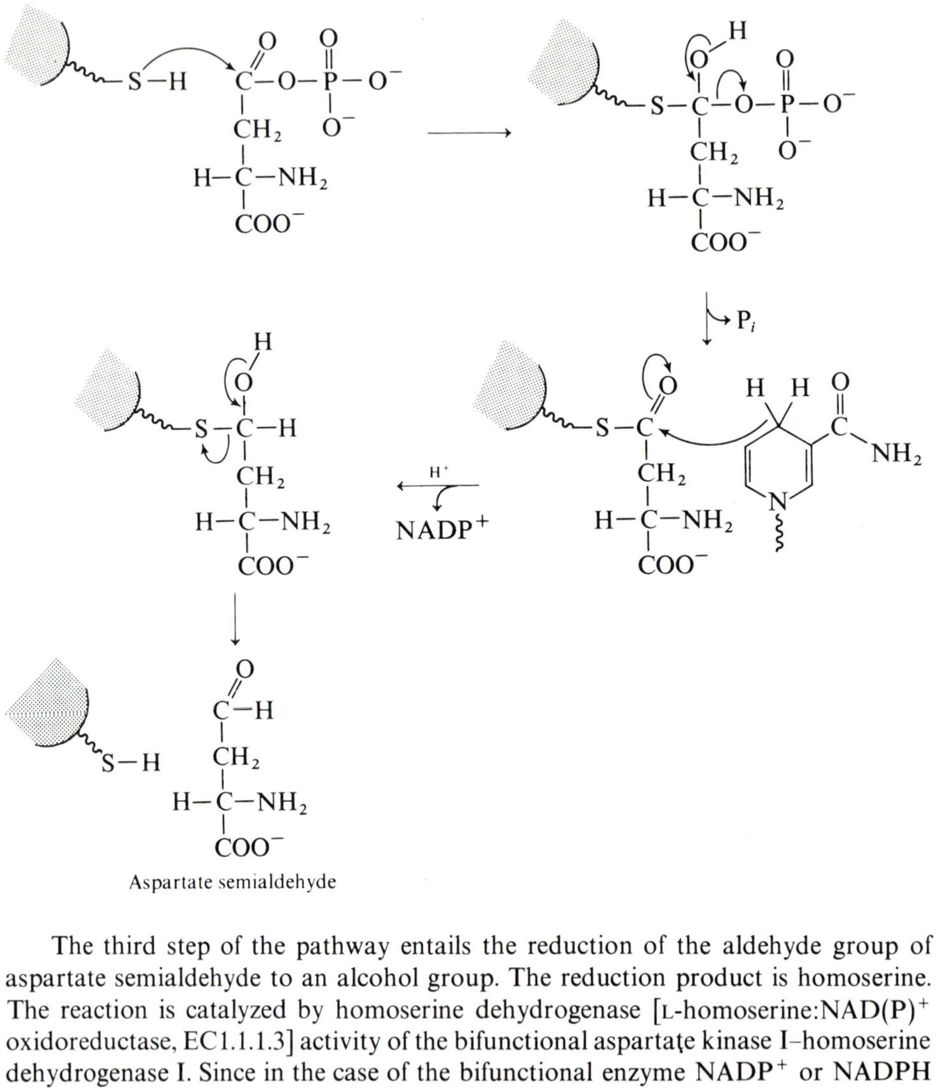

[Reaction scheme showing aspartate semialdehyde formation via cysteinyl sulfhydryl intermediate with NADP+/NADPH]

Aspartate semialdehyde

The third step of the pathway entails the reduction of the aldehyde group of aspartate semialdehyde to an alcohol group. The reduction product is homoserine. The reaction is catalyzed by homoserine dehydrogenase [L-homoserine:NAD(P)$^+$ oxidoreductase, EC1.1.1.3] activity of the bifunctional aspartate kinase I–homoserine dehydrogenase I. Since in the case of the bifunctional enzyme NADP$^+$ or NADPH appears to be the preferred cofactor, the reaction can be stated as

L-Aspartate semialdehyde + NADPH $\rightleftharpoons$ L-homoserine + NADP$^+$ (14-18)

Homoserine then undergoes a phosphorylation reaction catalyzed by homoserine kinase (ATP:L-homoserine O-phosphotransferase, EC 2.7.1.39), and the resulting O-phospho-L-homoserine is in turn converted into threonine as the result of the reaction catalyzed by threonine synthase [O-phospho-L-homoserine phospho-lyase (adding water), EC 4.2.99.2]. Threonine synthase is a pyridoxal phosphate–dependent enzyme that catalyzes an elimination reaction followed by a hydration reaction:

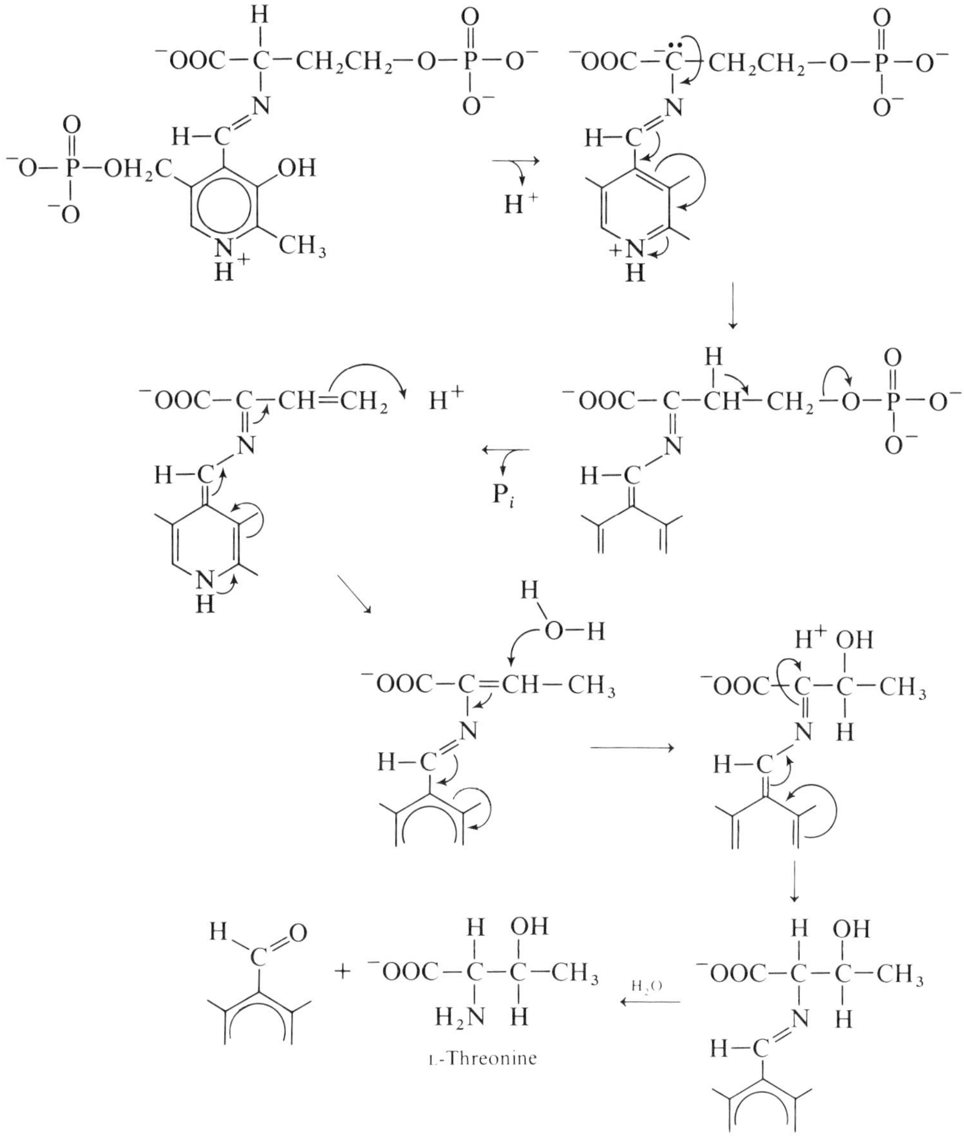

Following formation of the phosphohomoserine Schiff base, a proton is abstracted from C(2), and the carbanion is generated. In this instance the aldimine undergoes isomerization to yield the ketimine, and since C(2) of the phosphohomoserine moiety is now a ketimine carbon atom, which is analogous to an oxo carbon atom, a hydrogen atom at C(3) is readily removed as a proton. The ionization of this proton provides the impetus for the elimination of orthophosphate. (When this

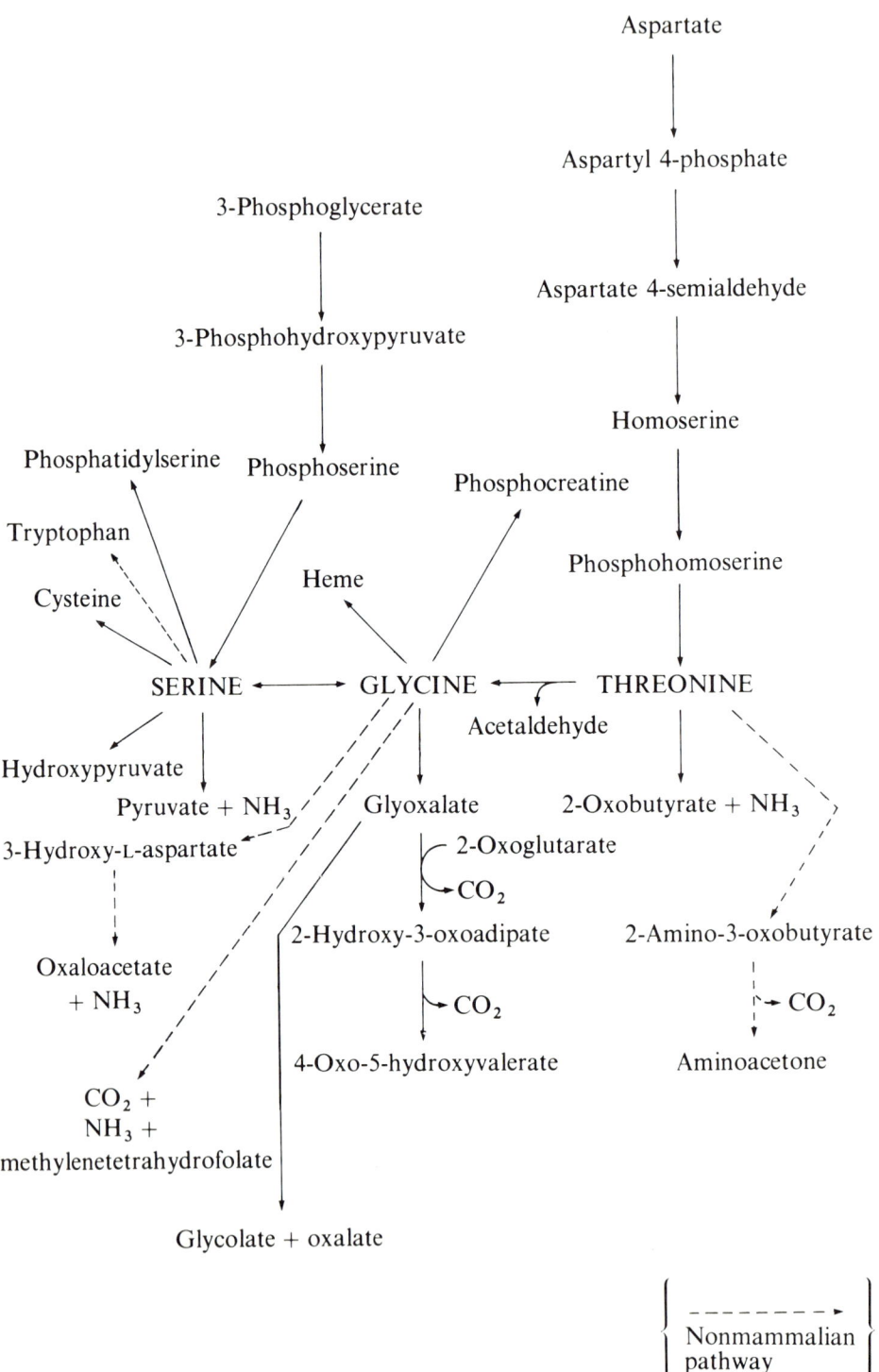

Figure 14-2 A summary of reactions involved in the metabolism of glycine, serine, and threonine.

reaction is conducted in the presence of $[^{18}O]H_2O$, the orthophosphate that is produced is unlabeled, indicating a direct elimination rather than a hydrolytic cleavage.) A proton is subsequently added at C(4), and then the elements of water are, in effect, added across the C(2)—C(3) olefinic bond. This creates the threonine Schiff base. Hydrolysis releases the threonine and regenerates the pyridoxal phosphate.

## A Summary of the Metabolism of Glycine, Serine, and Threonine

The principal reactions involved in the metabolism of these three amino acids are summarized in Fig. 14-2.

# METABOLISM OF METHIONINE AND CYSTEINE

The principal pathway for the utilization and degradation of methionine in mammals entails its conversion into 2-oxobutyrate and ammonia, the sulfur atom being incorporated into cysteine. This pathway begins with the conversion of methionine into S-adenosyl-L-methionine, which is catalyzed by methionine adenosyltransferase (ATP:L-methionine S-adenosyltransferase, EC 2.5.1.6). The reaction can be written

$$ATP + \text{L-methionine} + H_2O \rightleftharpoons S\text{-adenosyl-L-methionine} + P_i + PP_i$$

(14-19)

This reaction is unique in that all three of the phosphoryl groups are removed from ATP as the very reactive sulfonium compound is formed. It has been suggested that a tripolyphosphate moiety is initially eliminated from ATP and that this is subsequently cleaved to yield a pyrophosphate anion derived from the two nonterminal phosphoryl groups of ATP plus an orthophosphate anion derived from the terminal phosphoryl group. S-Adenosyl-L-methionine can transfer its methyl group to a variety of acceptors, including guanidoacetate, as mentioned above. As the result of such a transfer, S-adenosylhomocysteine is formed. This intermediate can in turn undergo a hydrolytic cleavage catalyzed by adenosylhomocysteinase (S-adenosyl-L-homocysteine hydrolase, EC 3.3.1.1), which results in the formation of homocysteine and adenosine. Now the homocysteine can react with L-serine to form cystathionine:

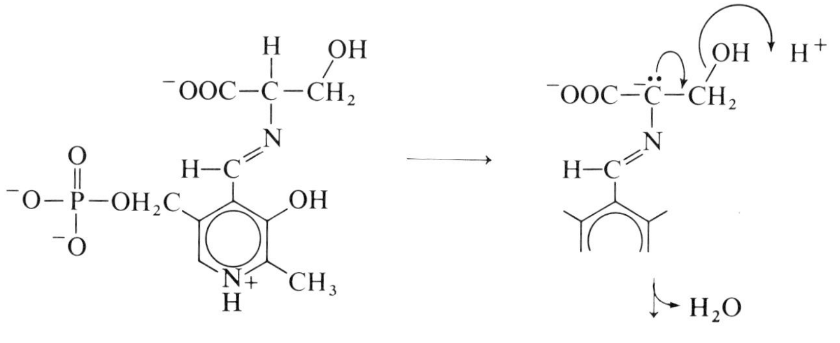

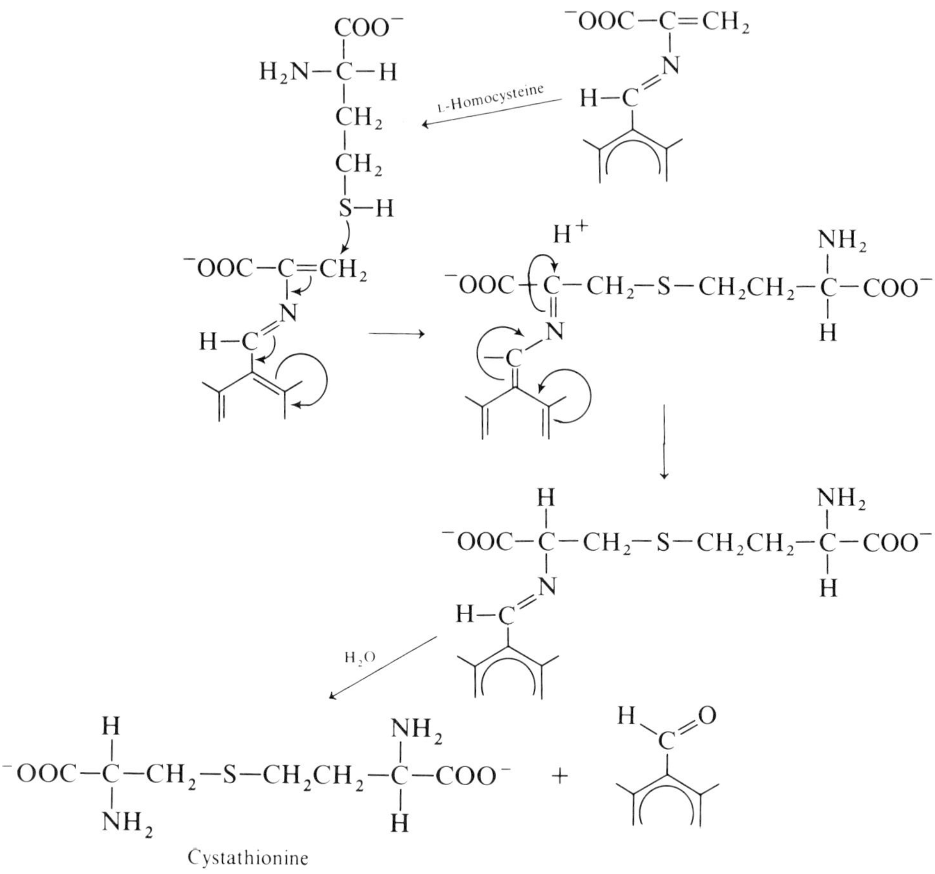

The reaction is catalyzed by cystathionine β-synthase [L-serine hydro-lyase (adding homocysteine), EC 4.2.1.22], which is a pyridoxal phosphate–dependent enzyme that catalyzes several mechanistically related reactions. As isolated from rat liver, cystathionine β-synthase is a tetramer which has a molecular weight of 250,000. Cystathionine can then undergo cleavage to yield L-cysteine plus 2-oxobutyrate and ammonia. Thus, the sulfur atom of methionine is transferred to cysteine in mammals. Because of this sequence, cysteine is not an amino acid which must be supplied by the diet in man. Methionine is, however. The cleavage of cystathionine is catalyzed by cystathionine γ-lyase [L-cystathionine cysteine-lyase (deaminating), EC 4.4.1.1], which is a pyridoxal phosphate–dependent enzyme which has been isolated from rat liver as a tetrameric protein which has a molecular weight of 160,000. The reaction mechanism of the formation of cysteine, 2-oxobutyrate, and ammonia is initially similar to that by which orthophosphate is eliminated from aspartyl 4-phosphate; i.e., a substituent bonded to C(4) of the amino acid moiety of the Schiff base is eliminated. In the present case the L-cysteine anion (rather than the orthophosphate anion) is eliminated, and the Schiff base remaining behind then accepts a proton at C(4) and is subsequently cleaved to yield 2-iminobutyrate plus the pyridoxal phosphate. Iminobutyrate is converted into 2-oxobutyrate and ammonia nonenzymatically.

Consider now the catabolic fates of cysteine in mammals. One of these entails the conversion of cysteine into pyruvate, hydrogen sulfide, and ammonia. This takes place in mammalian liver, kidney, and pancreas, and it is apparently catalyzed by cystathionine γ-lyase. Also, cysteine can undergo a transamination reaction catalyzed by cysteine aminotransferase (L-cysteine:2-oxoglutarate aminotransferase, EC 2.6.1.3). The resulting 3-mercaptopyruvate can subsequently be converted into pyruvate and sulfur. The latter is readily reduced to hydrogen sulfide under most circumstances. Sulfide is converted into sulfite and then sulfate in mammals. Sulfate is the principal end product of sulfur metabolism in man with approximately 60 percent or more of the sulfur that is excreted existing in this form. The mechanism by which sulfide is oxidized to sulfite in man is unknown. The oxidation of sulfite to sulfate, on the other hand, is catalyzed by the heme-protein enzyme sulfite oxidase (sulfite:oxygen oxidoreductase, EC 1.8.3.1), which catalyzes the reaction

$$SO_3^{2-} + O_2 + H_2O \rightleftharpoons SO_4^{2-} + H_2O_2 \qquad (14\text{-}20)$$

In man cysteine can also be oxidized to cysteine sulfinate by a reaction catalyzed by cysteine dioxygenase (L-cysteine:oxygen oxidoreductase, EC 1.13.11.20). The dioxygenase requires molecular oxygen, ferrous iron, and NADH or NADPH. Cysteine sulfinate can in turn undergo transamination to yield 3-sulfinylpyruvate. Sulfinylpyruvate is readily converted into pyruvate and sulfite. Alternatively, cysteine sulfinate can be further oxidized to cysteate, or it can undergo decarboxylation to yield hypotaurine. The decarboxylation is catalyzed by aspartate 4-decarboxylase, a pyridoxal phosphate–dependent enzyme that primarily catalyzes the conversion of aspartate into alanine. The decarboxylation product, hypotaurine, can then be oxidized to taurine in the presence of the enzyme hypotaurine dehydrogenase (hypotaurine:NAD$^+$ oxidoreductase, EC 1.8.1.3). As mentioned in Chap. 12, taurine reacts with CoA derivatives of the bile acids to form, for example, taurocholate or taurochenodeoxycholate, the forms of these bile acids that occur in the bile.

**Glutathione** Another metabolic fate of cysteine is its incorporation into glutathione, a tripeptide (more specifically, γ-L-glutamyl-L-cysteinylglycine).

$$\text{}^-\text{O}-\overset{\overset{\displaystyle O}{\|}}{\text{C}}-\overset{\overset{\displaystyle H}{|}}{\underset{\underset{\displaystyle NH_2}{|}}{\text{C}}}-CH_2CH_2-\overset{\displaystyle O}{\underset{\displaystyle \diagdown}{\text{C}}}\overset{\displaystyle \diagup}{\underset{\displaystyle N-H}{}}$$

$$HS-CH_2-\overset{\overset{\displaystyle H}{|}}{\underset{\underset{\displaystyle N-H}{|}}{\text{C}}}-\overset{\displaystyle O}{\underset{\displaystyle \diagdown}{\text{C}}}$$

$$CH_2-\overset{\displaystyle O}{\underset{\displaystyle \diagdown O^-}{\text{C}}}$$

Glutathione (γ-L-glutamyl-L-cysteinylglycine)

Note that in this instance the carbonyl carbon atom of the peptide bond that joins the glutamyl and cysteinyl units is derived from C(5) of glutamate, rather than from C(1). Glutathione, which is synthesized by virtually all living cells, has a variety of functions. It can protect sulfhydryl groups of proteins and participate in the detoxification of hydrogen peroxide; it can function as a cofactor in several enzymatic reactions, a component in an amino acid transport system in the kidney, and a reducing agent, since it readily donates electrons to an appropriate acceptor and is concomitantly oxidized to a disulfide. Glutathione is synthesized as a result of the two reactions

L-Glutamate + L-cysteine + ATP $\rightleftharpoons$

$\gamma$-L-glutamyl-L-cysteine + ADP + $P_i$ (14-21)

$\gamma$-L-Glutamyl-L-cysteine + glycine + ATP $\rightleftharpoons$

glutathione + ADP + $P_i$ (14-22)

Reaction (14-21) is catalyzed by $\gamma$-glutamyl-cysteine synthetase [L-glutamate:L-cysteine $\gamma$-ligase (ADP-forming), EC 6.3.2.2], and reaction (14-22) is catalyzed by glutathione synthetase [$\gamma$-L-glutamyl-L-cysteine:glycine ligase (ADP-forming), EC 6.3.2.3]. $\gamma$-Glutamylcysteine synthetase has been isolated from rat kidney as a protein which has a molecular weight of 92,000. The synthesis of the dipeptide is thought to involve the formation of an enzyme-bound glutamyl 5-phosphate, which is derived from ATP and glutamate. In view of the observation that when the C(5) carboxylate group is labeled with $^{18}O$, labeled orthophosphate is obtained, the following minimal mechanism can be formulated.

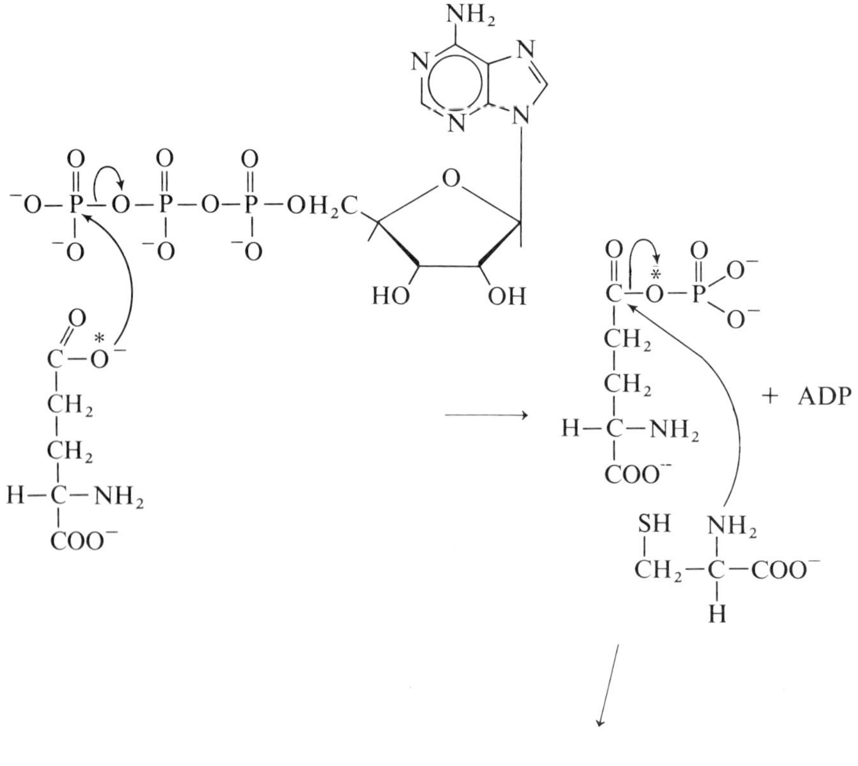

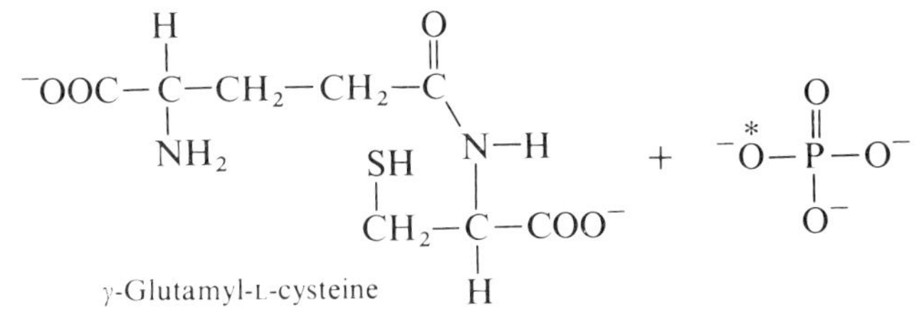

$$\text{}^-\text{OOC}-\underset{\underset{\text{NH}_2}{|}}{\overset{\overset{\text{H}}{|}}{\text{C}}}-\text{CH}_2-\text{CH}_2-\overset{\overset{\text{O}}{\|}}{\text{C}}\diagdown_{\underset{\underset{\underset{\text{H}}{|}}{\text{CH}_2-\text{C}-\text{COO}^-}}{\overset{|}{\text{SH}}\quad \text{N}-\text{H}}} \quad + \quad \text{}^-\overset{*}{\text{O}}-\overset{\overset{\text{O}}{\|}}{\underset{\underset{\text{O}^-}{|}}{\text{P}}}-\text{O}^-$$

γ-Glutamyl-L-cysteine

The mechanism of the formation of the tripeptide, as catalyzed by glutathione synthetase, parallels that shown above.

The activity of γ-glutamylcysteine synthetase (from rat kidney) is inhibited by the ultimate product, glutathione, which binds at the glutamate (substrate) binding site and possibly also at the cysteine binding site.

The principal pathways for the utilization and degradation of methionine and for the synthesis, utilization, and degradation of cysteine as it occurs in mammals are summarized in Fig. 14-3.

**Anabolism of cysteine in microorganisms** Cysteine is synthesized from the carbon atoms of serine and the sulfur atom of methionine in mammals, as described above. In microorganisms and plants, however, the synthesis of cysteine does not entail the use of existing organically bound sulfur; rather, inorganic sulfur in the form of hydrogen sulfide is incorporated. Since the environment provides sulfur primarily in the form of sulfate, this is first reduced to sulfide. This process begins with the formation of adenylylsulfate from ATP and sulfate. The reaction

$$\text{ATP} + \text{SO}_4^{2-} \rightleftharpoons \text{adenylylsulfate} + \text{PP}_i \qquad (14\text{-}23)$$

is catalyzed by sulfate adenylyltransferase (ATP:sulfate adenylyltransferase, EC 2.7.7.4). Adenylylsulfate in fact functions as an acylating agent in microorganisms and in mammals. Saccharides and phenolic compounds are among the biochemical intermediates that can be converted into the corresponding sulfate esters in the presence of adenylylsulfate. In addition, adenylylsulfate can react with ATP in the presence of adenylylsulfate kinase (ATP:adenylylsulfate 3'-phosphotransferase, EC 2.7.1.25) to form 3'-phosphoadenylylsulfate. In microorganisms this compound can subsequently undergo a reductive cleavage reaction which yields AMP and sulfite, although little is known concerning this reaction. The conversion of sulfate into sulfite in microorganisms is summarized below.

Sulfite undergoes a six-electron reduction to yield sulfide. In *E. coli* this process is catalyzed by a soluble NADPH-dependent sulfite reductase (hydrogen sulfide:NADP$^+$ oxidoreductase, EC 1.8.1.2). The reaction can be written

$$5\text{H}^+ + \text{SO}_3^{2-} + 3\text{ NADPH} \rightleftharpoons \text{H}_2\text{S} + 3\text{ NADP}^+ + 3\text{H}_2\text{O} \qquad (14\text{-}24)$$

As isolated from *E. coli* the reductase is a rather complex system which has a molecular weight of 700,000 and comprises eight subunits of one type (designated as α) and four of a second type (designed as β). The α subunit is a flavoprotein which has a molecular weight of 59,000 while the β subunit is a heme protein which also contains nonheme iron and "acid-labile" sulfur. Its molecular weight

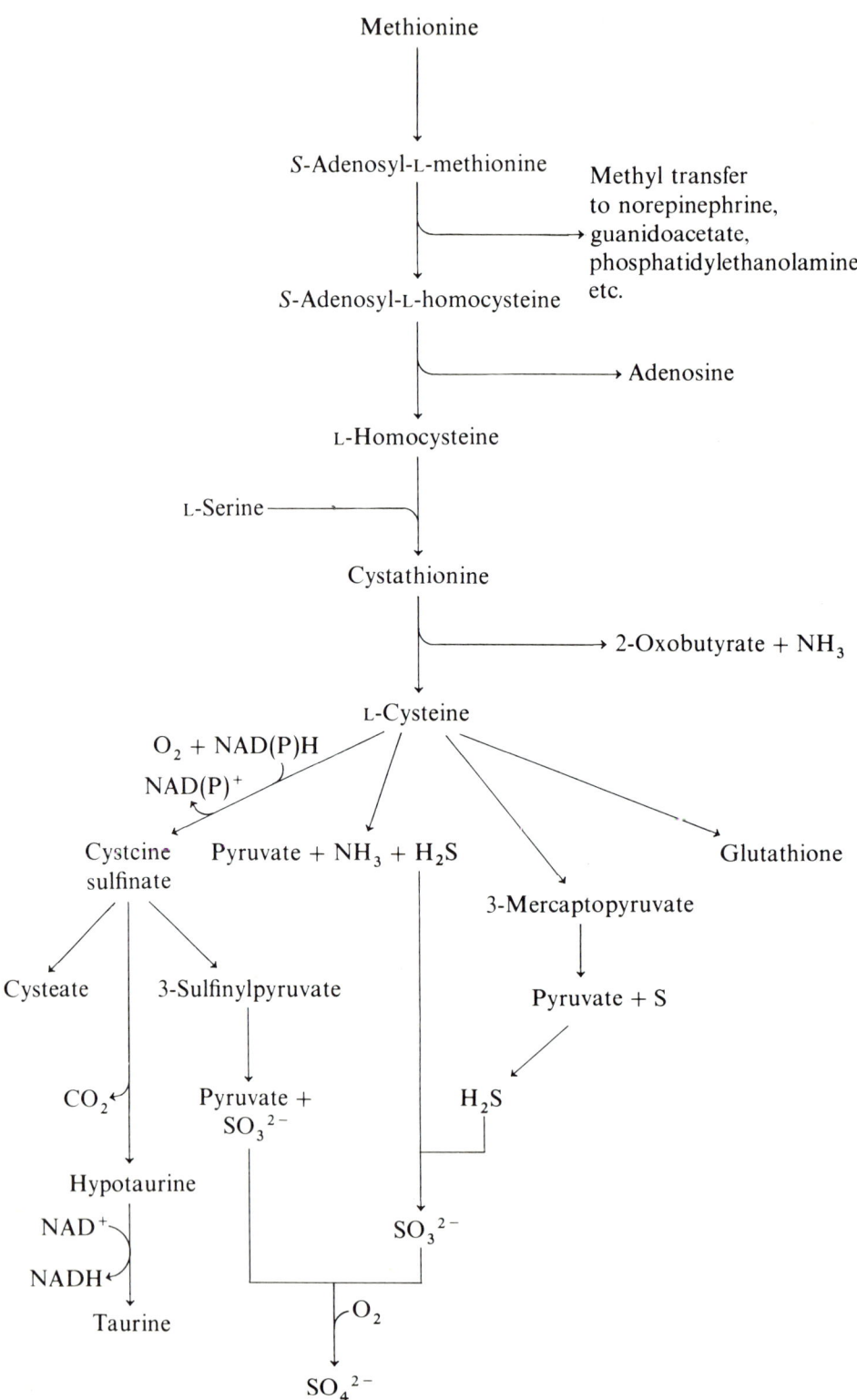

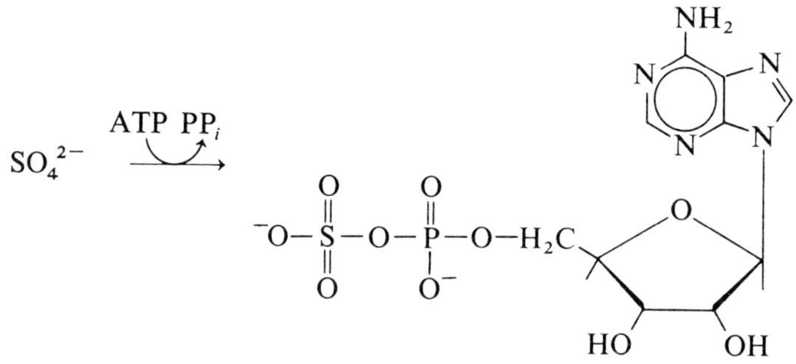

METABOLISM OF AMINO ACIDS AND PROTEINS **647**

$SO_4^{2-}$ →(ATP, PP$_i$)→

Adenylylsulfate

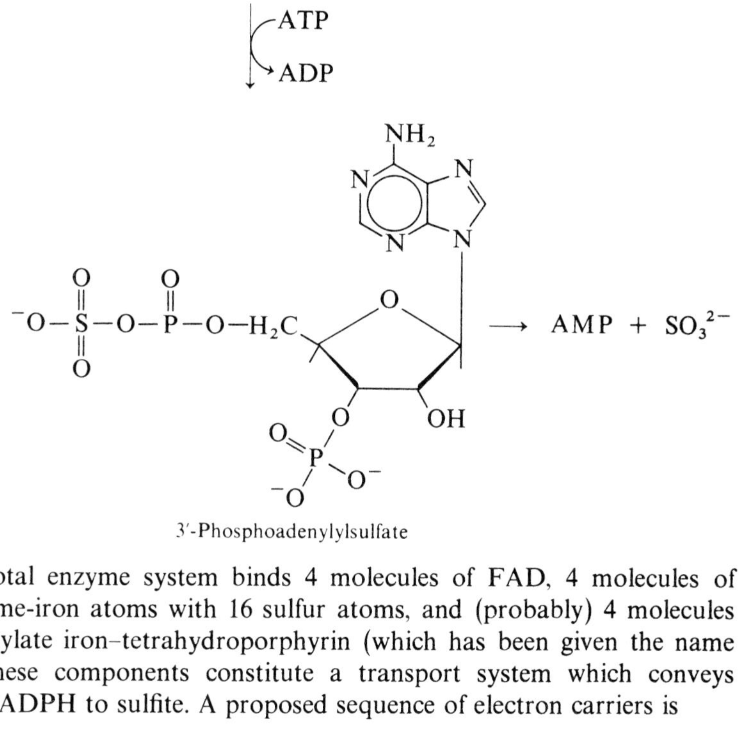

↓ (ATP → ADP)

3'-Phosphoadenylylsulfate  →  AMP + $SO_3^{2-}$

is 56,000. The total enzyme system binds 4 molecules of FAD, 4 molecules of FMN, 16 nonheme-iron atoms with 16 sulfur atoms, and (probably) 4 molecules of an octacarboxylate iron–tetrahydroporphyrin (which has been given the name of siroheme). These components constitute a transport system which conveys electrons from NADPH to sulfite. A proposed sequence of electron carriers is

$$\text{NADPH} \longrightarrow \text{FAD} \longrightarrow \text{FMN} \longrightarrow \text{heme} \longrightarrow SO_3^{2-} \quad (14\text{-}25)$$

Sulfide can be incorporated into cysteine as follows. Initially, serine undergoes acetylation, as catalyzed by serine acetyltransferase (acetyl CoA:L-serine O-acetyltransferase, EC 2.3.1.30). The reaction utilizes acetyl CoA:

$$\text{L-Serine} + \text{acetyl CoA} \rightleftharpoons O\text{-acetyl-L-serine} + \text{CoA} \quad (14\text{-}26)$$

---

**Figure 14-3** A summary of reactions involved in the metabolism of methionine and cysteine as it occurs in mammalian systems.

O-Acetylserine then reacts with hydrogen sulfide to yield L-cysteine and acetate. This reaction is catalyzed by the pyridoxal phosphate–dependent cysteine synthase [O-acetyl-L-serine acetate-lyase (adding hydrogen-sulfide), EC 4.2.99.8]. Mechanistically, the reaction involves the elimination of acetate from O-acetylserine, followed by the addition of the elements of hydrogen sulfide across the C(2)—C(3) olefinic bond generated in the wake of the elimination. In *Salmonella typhimurium* these two enzymes that, together, catalyze the synthesis of cysteine, can exist as a bifunctional complex which has a molecular weight of 300,000 and comprises one molecule of the O-acetyltransferase (which has a molecular weight of 160,000) and two molecules of the synthase (which each have a molecular weight of 70,000).

**Anabolism of methionine in microorganisms** In microorganisms the synthesis of methionine requires the sulfur atom of cysteine, in contrast to the situation pertaining in mammals, where the sulfur atom of methionine is required for the synthesis of cysteine. In microorganisms, the initial step in the anabolic pathway entails the acylation of homoserine. In *Neurospora crassa* and in the yeast *Saccharomyces* homoserine undergoes acetylation. In *E. coli* and *Salmonella typhimurium*, on the other hand, homoserine undergoes succinylation. In this latter case the reaction is catalyzed by homoserine succinyltransferase (succinyl-CoA: L-homoserine O-succinyltransferase, EC 2.3.1.46) and is

$$\text{L-Homoserine} + \text{succinyl CoA} \rightleftharpoons O\text{-succinyl-L-homoserine} + \text{CoA}$$
(14-27)

An acylhomoserine can then react with cysteine to form cystathionine. This formation of cystathionine is catalyzed by cystathionine γ-synthase [O-succinyl-L-homoserine succinate-lyase (adding cysteine), EC 4.2.99.9]. Cystathionine γ-synthase, like cystathionine β-synthase, is a pyridoxal phosphate–dependent enzyme; it catalyzes the elimination of succinate from C(4) of homoserine followed by the addition of the sulfhydryl group of cysteine across the C(3)—C(4) olefinic bond. As isolated from *S. typhimurium* cystathionine γ-synthase is a tetrameric protein which has a molecular weight of 160,000.

Next, the cystathionine can undergo a hydrolytic cleavage reaction which yields homocysteine plus pyruvate and ammonia. This is catalyzed by cystathionine β-lyase [cystathionine L-homocysteine-lyase (deaminating), EC 4.4.1.8], which, as might be expected, is pyridoxal phosphate–dependent. The reaction entails the elimination of homocysteine from C(3) of cystathionine followed by the release of 2-iminopropionate, which undergoes hydrolysis to yield pyruvate and ammonia. All that now remains is for the homocysteine to undergo S-methylation to form methionine. The S-methylation of homocysteine in fact occurs in both bacterial and mammalian systems. In mammals this does not represent *de novo* synthesis, however, since the homocysteine is derived from methionine in this case.

The methylation of homocysteine is a complex process involving 5-methyltetrahydrofolate, cobalamin, catalytic concentrations of S-adenosylmethionine, and a reducing system. An enzyme system that performs this methylation reaction has been isolated from *E. coli* K-12; the system consists of a protein that binds cobalamin and has a molecular weight of 186,000 and two flavoproteins that are components of the reducing system required in order for the reductive methylation of the cobalamin to occur. One of these flavoproteins has a molecular weight of 19,000 and binds FMN. The other flavoprotein has a molecular weight of 27,000 and binds FAD. NADPH, which is also required for the reaction, functions as the electron source, and the following sequence of components in the electron-transfer process has been proposed:

$$\text{NADPH} \longrightarrow \text{flavoprotein (FAD)} \longrightarrow \text{flavoprotein (FMN)} \longrightarrow \text{cobalamin} \quad (14\text{-}28)$$

The function of the catalytic amount of S-adenosylmethionine is that of activating the system. Initially, the methyltransferase is inactive. Then in conjunction with the reducing system a methyl group is transferred from S-adenosylmethionine to the cobalamin moiety. In the process, the cobalt of this moiety is reduced from $Co^{2+}$ to $Co^+$, and a methylcobalamin is formed. The methylcobalamin can now transfer its methyl group to homocysteine, thus forming methionine and generating a cobalamin containing $Co^+$. This cobalamin moiety can now accept a methyl group from 5-methyltetrahydrofolate and transfer it to the next molecule of homocysteine. The utilization of the methyl group of 5-methyltetrahydrofolate can presumably continue as long as the cobalt atom of the cobalamin moiety is maintained in the reduced ($Co^+$) state.

Most strains of *E. coli* also contain a similar but less complex enzymatic system that can convert homocysteine into methionine in the absence of cobalamin. This system also differs from that described above in that 5,10-methylenetetrahydrofolyl-γ-glutamate participates in the reaction rather than 5-methyltetrahydrofolate.

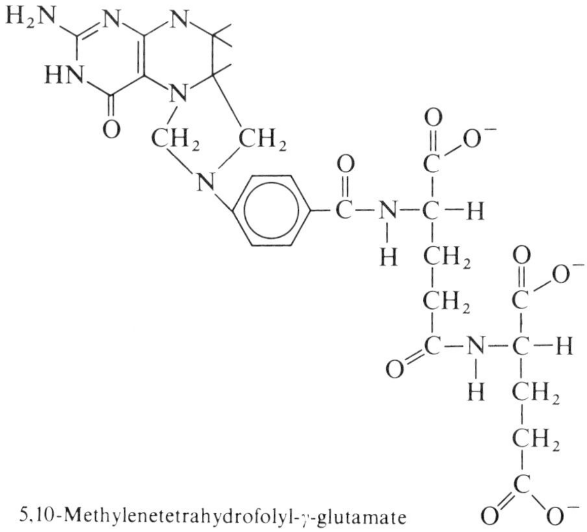

5,10-Methylenetetrahydrofolyl-γ-glutamate

The formation of cysteine and its utilization in forming methionine as they occur in *E. coli* are summarized below.

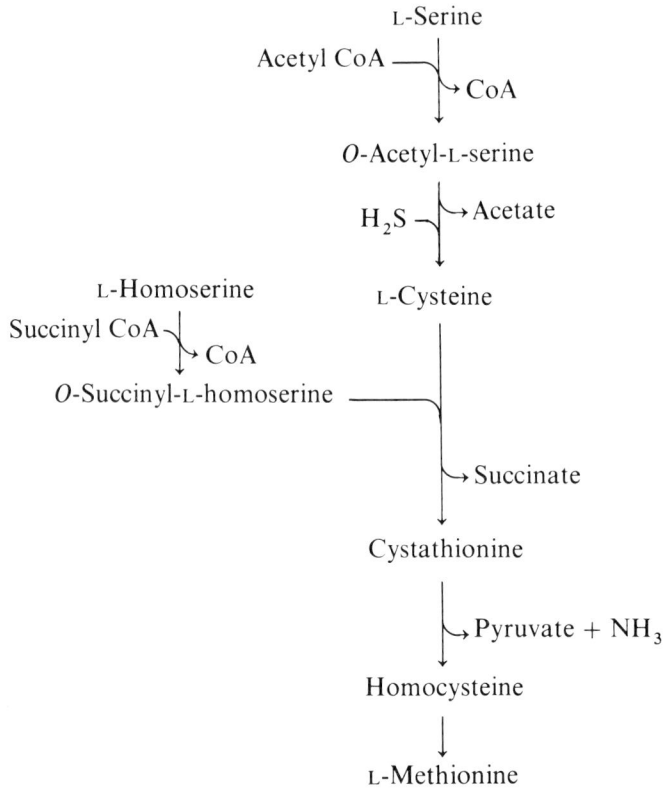

## METABOLISM OF ALANINE AND ASPARTATE

The removal of the nitrogen atom of alanine or aspartate yields pyruvate or oxaloacetate, respectively. Both can enter the tricarboxylic acid cycle. Alanine aminotransferase (L-alanine:2-oxoglutarate aminotransferase, EC 2.6.1.2) has been isolated from rat liver, among many sources, and crystallized. This enzyme is a dimer which has a molecular weight of 114,000. Asparate aminotransferase (L-aspartate:2-oxoglutarate aminotransferase, EC 2.6.1.1) has also been isolated from a variety of sources and purified. A cytoplasmic enzyme from porcine heart is a dimer which has a molecular weight of 93,500. Each of these enzymes catalyzes a reaction that proceeds by a ping pong kinetic mechanism, a characteristic shared by many aminotransferases. In these reactions, the amino acid substrate binds the enzyme initially, and then the corresponding oxo acid product is formed and released. This generates the pyridoxamine phosphate form of the enzyme, which binds the oxo acid substrate; the corresponding amino acid product is formed and released; and the original pyridoxal phosphate form of the enzyme is regenerated, as represented diagrammatically below.

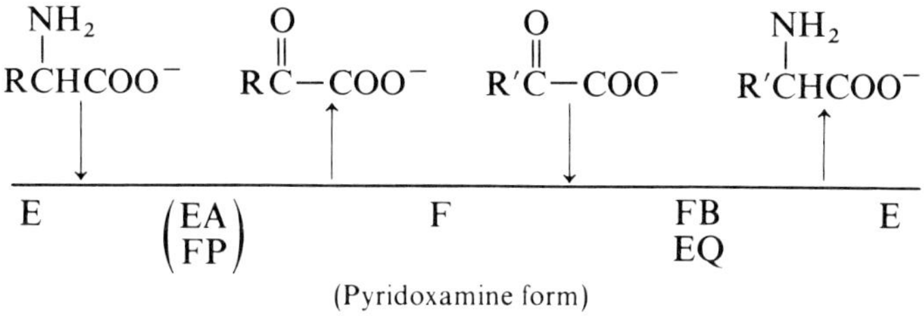

```
        NH₂              O                  O                NH₂
         |               ||                 ||                |
      RCHCOO⁻         RC—COO⁻            R'C—COO⁻          R'CHCOO⁻
         |               ↑                  |                 ↑
         ↓              (EA)                ↓                 |
─────────────────────────────────────────────────────────────────────
         E              (EA)                F                FB          E
                        (FP)                                 EQ
                              (Pyridoxamine form)
```

Aspartate can be converted into alanine by undergoing a decarboxylation reaction catalyzed by aspartate 4-decarboxylase (L-aspartate 4-carboxy-lyase, EC 4.1.1.12). These pyridoxal phosphate–dependent enzymes have been isolated from a variety of microorganisms and are generally quite large. That from *Alcaligenes faecalis* has a molecular weight of 700,000 and is an oligomer comprising twelve subunits which each have a molecular weight of 58,000. A minimal mechanism for the decarboxylation is shown below.

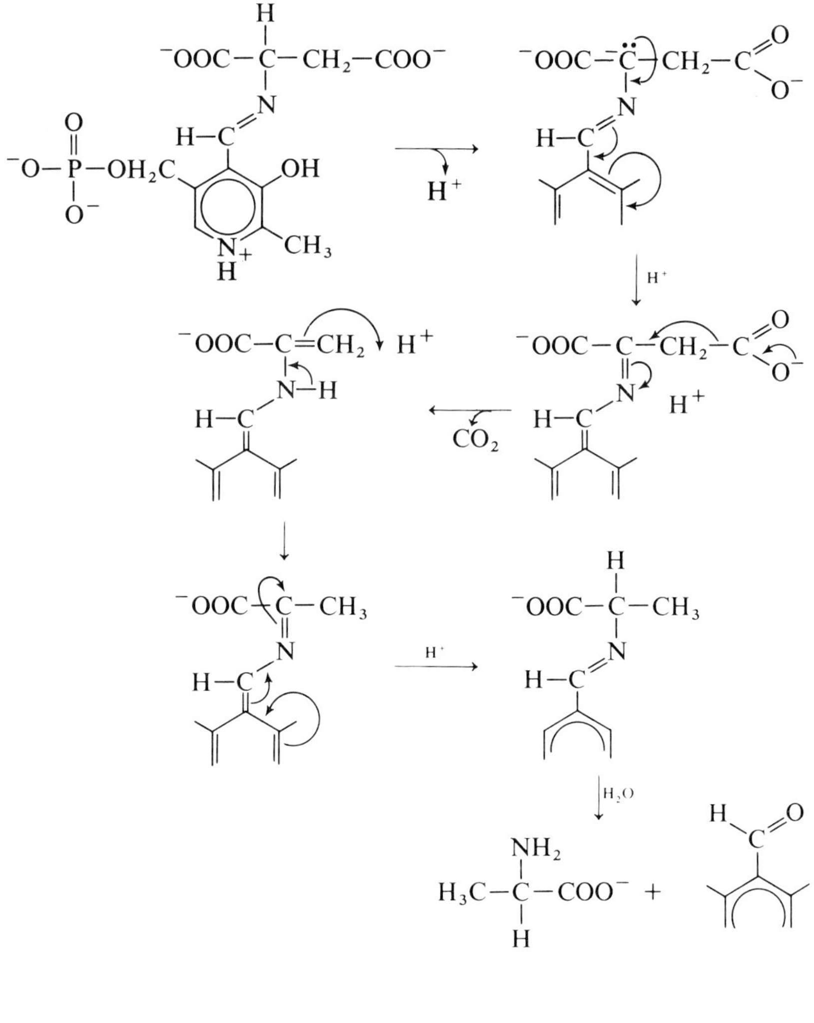

In this reaction, following the loss of a proton from C(2) of the aspartate moiety of the Schiff base, the resulting carbanion undergoes an aldimine-to-ketimine rearrangement which creates a structure analogous to a 3-oxo acid. Therefore this species readily undergoes decarboxylation. Following a 1,3-prototropic rearrangement, the Schiff base derived from alanine is generated, and hydrolysis releases the amino acid.

The anabolism of alanine and aspartate involves transamination since pyruvate is the principal precursor of alanine and oxaloacetate is the principal precursor of aspartate.

The anabolism of asparagine, which is a component of many proteins, is more complex. In certain microorganisms, including *E. coli*, *Streptococcus bovis*, and *Lactobacillus arabinosus*, the formation of asparagine occurs by the reaction

$$\text{L-Aspartate} + \text{ATP} + \text{NH}_3 \rightleftharpoons \text{L-asparagine} + \text{AMP} + \text{PP}_i \quad (14\text{-}29)$$

which is catalyzed by asparagine synthetase [L-aspartate:ammonia ligase (AMP-forming), EC 6.3.1.1]. In mammals since glutamine is generally the nitrogen donor, the reaction is

$$\text{L-Aspartate} + \text{L-glutamine} + \text{ATP} \rightleftharpoons$$
$$\text{L-asparagine} + \text{L-glutamate} + \text{AMP} + \text{PP}_i \quad (14\text{-}30)$$

Asparagine synthetase from *E. coli* K-12 has been isolated as a protein having a molecular weight of 82,000. This enzyme cannot utilize glutamine. Kinetic studies have suggested that aspartate and ATP bind the enzyme in a random manner and that pyrophosphate is then released from the enzyme prior to the binding of the ammonia. Subsequently, asparagine is formed, and this and AMP are released from the enzyme—again, in a random manner:

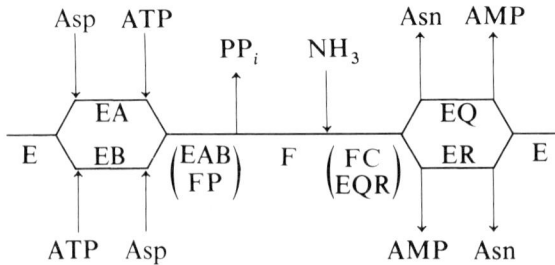

This kinetic mechanism is compatible with a reaction mechanism in which there is the formation of an enzyme-bound aspartyl 4-adenylate intermediate which then reacts with ammonia to yield asparagine and AMP.

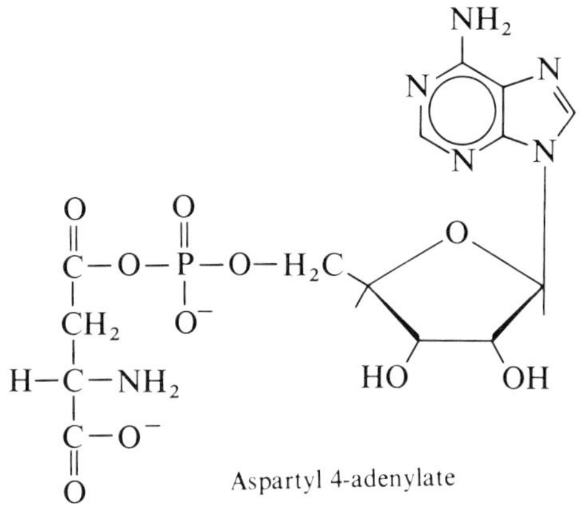

Aspartyl 4-adenylate

## METABOLISM OF LEUCINE, ISOLEUCINE, AND VALINE

The degradation of the three branched-chain amino acids follows a common pathway for the first three steps. First, each of the amino acids undergoes a transamination reaction catalyzed by a specific enzyme, known as the branched-chain–amino-acid aminotransferase (branched-chain-amino-acid:2-oxoglutarate aminotransferase, EC 2.6.1.42). A cytoplasmic branched-chain–amino-acid aminotransferase from porcine heart has a molecular weight of approximately 75,000 and catalyzes the transamination of all three amino acids. The velocities of the reactions with leucine or isoleucine or valine as the substrate are in the ratio 66 : 100 : 90. The 2-oxo acid derived from leucine is 2-oxoisocaproate, that derived from isoleucine is 2-oxo-3-methylvalerate, and that derived from valine is 2-oxoisovalerate.

The second step of this degradative process is the oxidative decarboxylation of each of the oxo acids in reactions reminiscent of the conversion of pyruvate into acetyl-CoA. They are catalyzed by enzyme complexes that utilize thiamine diphosphate, lipoate, FAD, and $NAD^+$. The body of available evidence indicates that these reactions parallel those catalyzed by the pyruvate dehydrogenase complex or the 2-oxoglutarate dehydrogenase complex. Thus, as a result of the reaction catalyzed by the 2-oxoisocaproate dehydrogenase component [2-oxoisocaproate: lipoate oxidoreductase (decarboxylating and acceptor-isovalerylating), EC 1.2.4.3] of the 2-oxoisocaproate dehydrogenase complex, 2-oxoisocaproate, from leucine is converted into a dihydrolipoamide-bound isovaleryl moiety. This component also converts 2-oxo-3-methylvalerate, from isoleucine, into a dihydrolipoamide-bound 2-methylbutyryl moiety. The isovaleryl and the 2-methylbutyryl moieties are subsequently converted into isovaleryl CoA and 2-methylbutyryl CoA, respectively, as in the reactions catalyzed by the pyruvate dehydrogenase complex or the 2-oxoglutarate dehydrogenase complex. A second enzyme complex, the 2-oxoisovalerate dehydrogenase complex, catalyzes the conversion 2-oxoisovalerate, from valine, into isobutyryl CoA. In a similar manner, 2-oxoisovalerate is initially converted into a dihydrolipoamide-bound isobutyryl moiety by the 2-oxoisovalerate

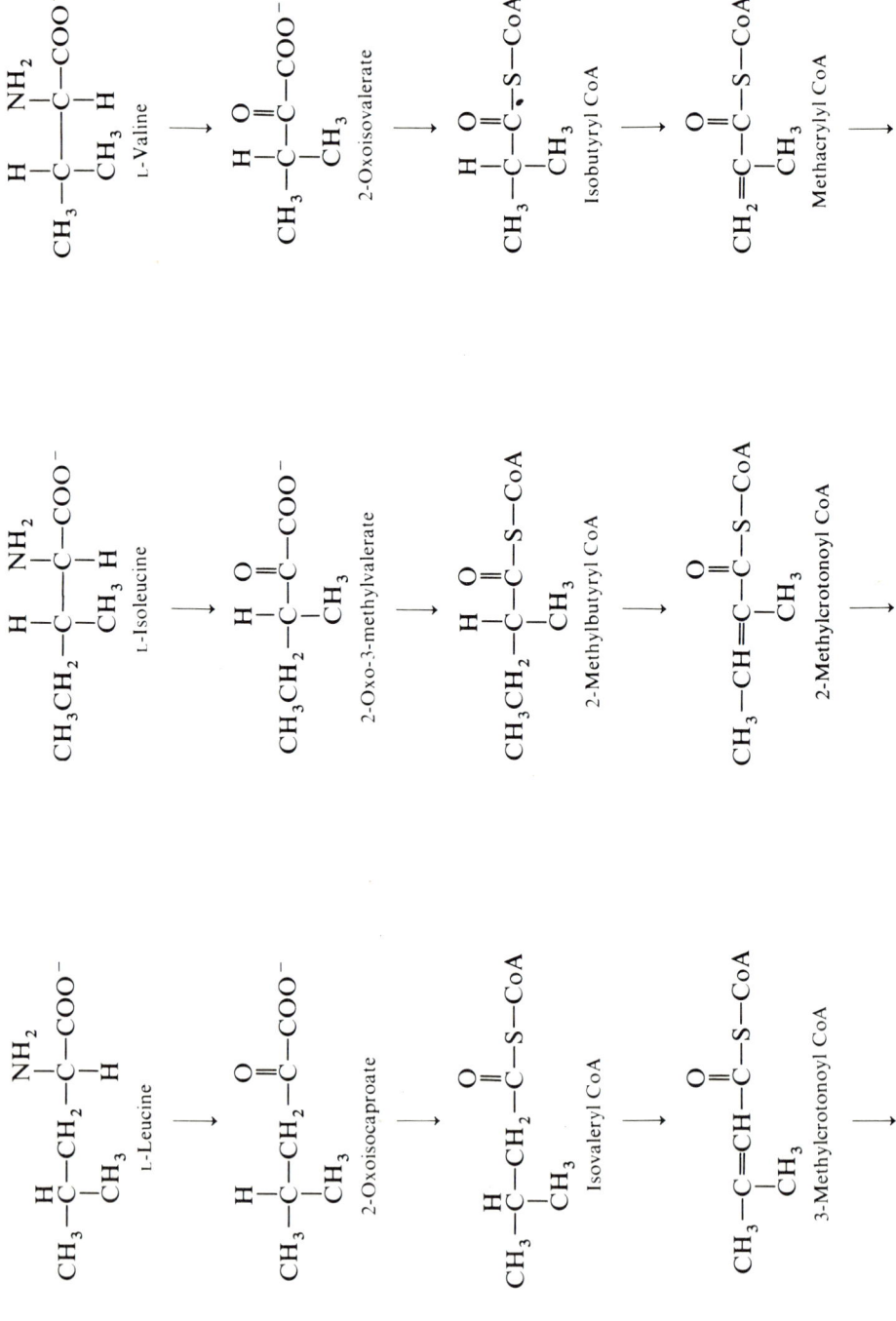

dehydrogenase component [2-oxoisovalerate:lipoate oxidoreductase (decarboxylating and acceptor-2-methylbutyrylating), EC 1.2.4.4] of the system and, subsequently, the CoA ester is formed. Each of these enzyme complexes has been isolated from the inner membrane of bovine-liver mitochondria.

Generally, either the transamination of the branched-chain amino acids or the decarboxylation and oxidation of the corresponding 2-oxo acids is rate-determining with respect to the degradative pathway. Aberrations involving one or the other of these steps are the cause of certain pathological conditions. Specifically, hypervalemia results from the failure of valine to undergo transamination with the result that the patient (usually an infant) exhibits abnormally high concentrations of valine in the blood, hyperkinesia, and mental retardation. The *maple syrup urine disease* (so named because of the characteristic odor of the urine that is voided by the patients) is caused by the failure of the branched-chain 2-oxo acids to undergo decarboxylation and oxidation. In conjunction with the voiding of urine that contains abnormally high concentrations of the branched-chain oxo acids, these patients (again infants), exhibit muscular hypertonicity and may have convulsions. If the infant lives for several months or a year, brain damage becomes evident, but generally death occurs during the first year. An autopsy usually reveals that myelination has not taken place in the normal manner, in addition to other abnormalities.

The third step of the degradative pathway, and the last one that is common to the individual pathways used by leucine, isoleucine, and valine, is the dehydrogenation of the acyl moiety of the acyl-CoA intermediate. A $\Delta^2$-acyl moiety is produced, as in the $\beta$-oxidation pathway. Dehydrogenation of the leucine derivative, isovaleryl CoA, yields 3-methylcrotonoyl CoA. The 3-methylcrotonoyl moiety then undergoes carboxylation (as catalyzed by methylcrotonoyl-CoA carboxylase) to yield 3-methylglutaconyl CoA, which is converted into 3-hydroxy-3-methylglutaryl CoA as the result of undergoing hydration (catalyzed by methylglutaconyl-CoA hydratase). The 3-hydroxy-3-methylglutaryl CoA can now undergo a cleavage reaction (catalyzed by hydroxymethylglutaryl-CoA lyase), which yields acetoacetate plus acetyl-CoA. The reader will recognize that acetyl-CoA can enter the tricarboxylic acid cycle and that acetoacetate can be converted to acetoacetyl-CoA in many tissues or to the ketone bodies in the mammalian liver. These reactions are the same as those undergone by the appropriate branched-chain fatty acid.

Dehydrogenation of the isoleucine derivative, 2-methylbutyryl CoA, yields 2-methylcrotonoyl CoA. Hydration of this unsaturated acyl moiety yields 3-hydroxy-2-methylbutyryl CoA. Oxidation of the secondary alcohol group of the acyl moiety yields 3-oxo-2-methylbutyryl CoA. Cleavage of the 3-oxo-2-methylbutyryl moiety in the presence of CoA and the appropriate acyltransferase yields propionyl CoA plus acetyl-CoA. Remember that propionyl CoA can undergo a carboxylation reaction to yield methylmalonyl CoA, which in turn can undergo a cobalamin-dependent rearrangement to yield succinyl CoA. The latter enters the tricarboxylic acid cycle. These reactions are the same as those which occur when a branched-chain fatty acid is degraded to the stage at which it has a branch point at C(2) of the acyl moiety.

When the valine derivative, isobutyryl CoA, undergoes dehydrogenation, methacrylyl CoA is formed. The hydration of this unsaturated acyl moiety produces 3-hydroxyisobutyryl CoA, which is then hydrolyzed to yield 3-hydroxyisobutyrate and CoA. Hydrolysis is catalyzed by 3-hydroxyisobutyryl-CoA hydrolase (3-hydroxyisobutyryl-CoA hydrolase, EC 3.1.2.4). Now the 3-hydroxyisobutyrate can undergo oxidation at C(3) to yield methylmalonate semialdehyde. The oxidation of the primary alcohol group is catalyzed by 3-hydroxyisobutyrate dehydrogenase (3-hydroxyisobutyrate:$NAD^+$ oxidoreductase, EC 1.1.1.31). Oxidation of the aldehyde group to the level of a carboxylic acid and formation of the corresponding CoA ester generate methylmalonyl CoA. This intermediate can undergo a cobalamin-dependent isomerization to yield succinyl CoA, which can enter the tricarboxylic acid cycle.

The degradation of the branched-chain amino acids is summarized on pages 654–655.

## Anabolism of the Branched-Chain Amino Acids in Microorganisms

As in the degradative pathways, the initial steps of the anabolic pathways for these three amino acids involve the same reactions. The first of these is the reaction of a 2-oxo acid with the two-carbon species derived from the decarboxylation of pyruvate in the presence of thiamine diphosphate. When isoleucine is to be synthesized, the 2-oxo acid that reacts with the two-carbon species is 2-oxobutyrate, which under most circumstances is derived from threonine by the reaction catalyzed by the biosynthetic threonine dehydratase. The activity of this enzyme is inhibited by the ultimate product, isoleucine. Isoleucine causes plots of the reaction velocity vs. threonine concentration to change from hyperbolic to sigmoidal. This effect of isoleucine is countered by valine. When leucine or valine is to be synthesized, the 2-oxo acid that reacts with the two-carbon species is pyruvate. Both reactions are catalyzed by acetolactate synthase [acetolactate:pyruvate-lyase (carboxylating), EC 4.1.3.18], a flavoprotein which binds thiamine diphosphate. The product of the reaction when pyruvate is the recipient oxo acid is 2-acetolactate. When 2-oxobutyrate is the recipient oxo acid, the product is 2-aceto-2-hydroxybutyrate. A minimal mechanism for these reactions is:

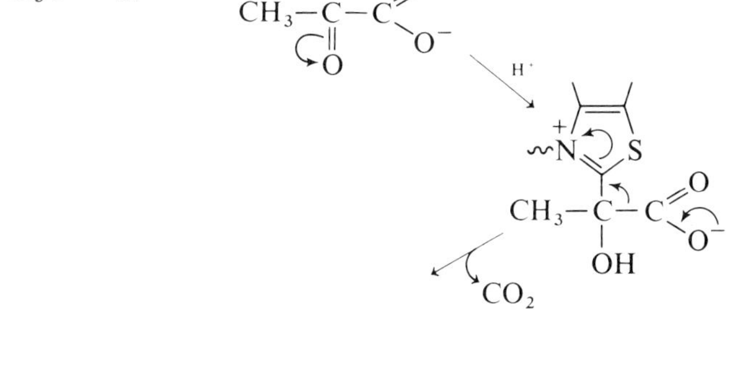

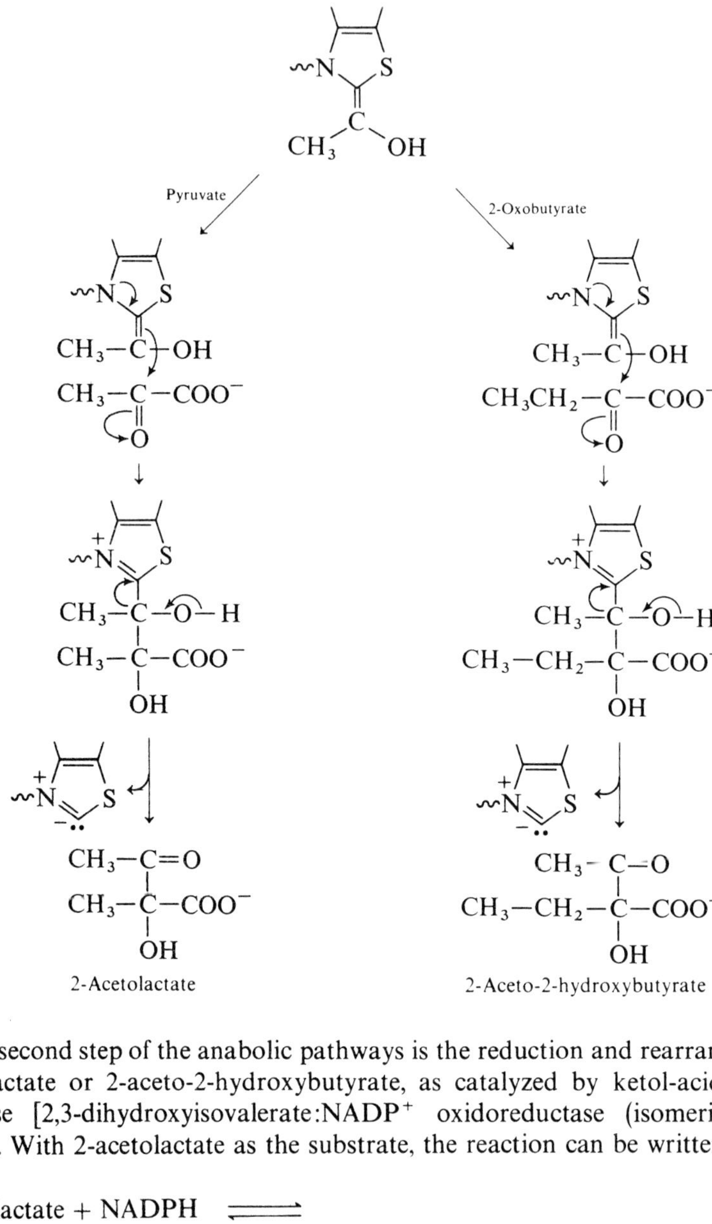

[Scheme showing thiamine-dependent condensation: Pyruvate and 2-Oxobutyrate branches leading to 2-Acetolactate and 2-Aceto-2-hydroxybutyrate respectively.]

2-Acetolactate

2-Aceto-2-hydroxybutyrate

The second step of the anabolic pathways is the reduction and rearrangement of 2-acetolactate or 2-aceto-2-hydroxybutyrate, as catalyzed by ketol-acid reductoisomerase [2,3-dihydroxyisovalerate:NADP$^+$ oxidoreductase (isomerizing), EC 1.1.1.86]. With 2-acetolactate as the substrate, the reaction can be written

2-Acetolactate + NADPH $\rightleftharpoons$ 2,3-dihydroxyisovalerate + NADP$^+$ (14-31)

The enzyme also utilizes 2-aceto-2-hydroxybutyrate as a substrate, in which case, 2,3-dihydroxy-3-methylvalerate is the product. In these reactions the transfer of an electron pair from the oxidation-reduction cofactor to C(2) of the substrate promotes the migration of an alkyl group, as shown in the minimal reaction mechanism.

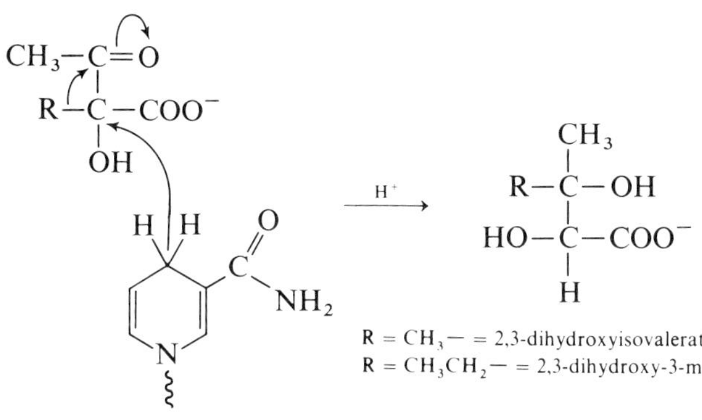

$$CH_3-C=O$$
$$R-C-COO^-$$
$$\quad OH$$

$\xrightarrow{H^+}$

$$CH_3$$
$$R-C-OH$$
$$HO-C-COO^-$$
$$\quad H$$

R = CH$_3$— = 2,3-dihydroxyisovalerate
R = CH$_3$CH$_2$— = 2,3-dihydroxy-3-methylvalerate

The ketol-acid reductoisomerase has been isolated from *Salmonella typhimurium* as a tetrameric protein which has a molecular weight of 220,000. This enzyme can catalyze the reduction and the rearrangement of 2-aceto-2-hydroxybutyrate at a rate over 4 times that at which the reduction and rearrangement of 2-acetolactate occur.

The third step of the anabolic pathway is the dehydration of the diols, which leads to the formation of oxo groups. Dihydroxyacid dehydratase (2,3-dihydroxy-acid hydro-lase, EC 4.2.1.9) catalyzes the reactions, which can be formulated mechanistically as shown.

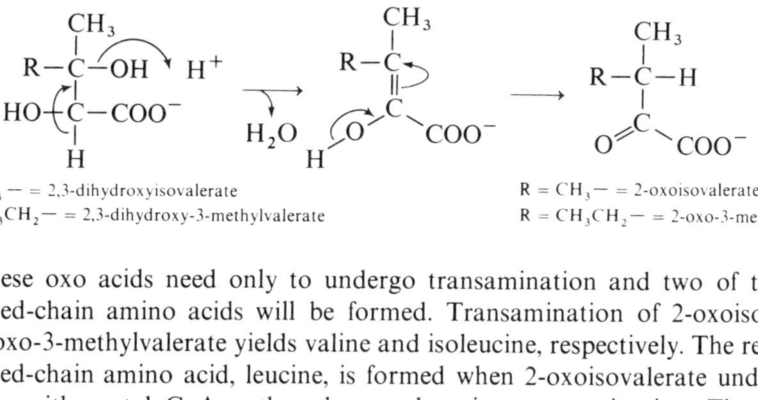

R = CH$_3$— = 2,3-dihydroxyisovalerate
R = CH$_3$CH$_2$— = 2,3-dihydroxy-3-methylvalerate

R = CH$_3$— = 2-oxoisovalerate
R = CH$_3$CH$_2$— = 2-oxo-3-methylvalerate

These oxo acids need only to undergo transamination and two of the three branched-chain amino acids will be formed. Transamination of 2-oxoisovalerate and 2-oxo-3-methylvalerate yields valine and isoleucine, respectively. The remaining branched-chain amino acid, leucine, is formed when 2-oxoisovalerate undergoes a reaction with acetyl CoA, rather than undergoing transamination. The reaction with acetyl CoA yields 3-hydroxy-4-methyl-3-carboxyvalerate, sometimes called 2-isopropylmalate. The reaction, which is an aldol-type condensation, is catalyzed by 2-isopropylmalate synthase [3-hydroxy-4-methyl-3-carboxyvalerate 2-oxo-3-methylbutyrate-lyase (CoA-acetylating), EC 4.1.3.12]. The reaction can be written

2-Oxoisovalerate (2-oxo-3-methylbutyrate) + acetyl CoA $\rightleftharpoons$

3-hydroxy-4-methyl-3-carboxyvalerate + CoA    (14-32)

It is mechanistically analogous to that catalyzed by citrate synthase. Here the C(2) of the acetyl moiety of acetyl CoA adds to the C(2) oxo group of 2-oxoisovalerate rather than that of pyruvate.

Isopropylmalate synthase has been isolated from *Salmonella typhimurium* and from *Neurospora crassa*, among other microorganisms. The synthase from the *Salmonella* has a molecular weight of 150,000, which is decreased to 100,000 as the result of the binding of the ultimate product, leucine. Since this binding also decreases the activity of the enzyme, leucine functions as an inhibitor of isopropylmalate synthase activity. The synthase from *N. crassa* is a trimer which has a molecular weight of 143,000. Leucine also inhibits the activity of this enzyme, although an accompanying change in molecular weight has not been reported.

In the next step of the anabolic pathway 3-hydroxy-4-methyl-3-carboxyvalerate undergoes a dehydration reaction that is followed by a hydration reaction, just as citrate is converted into aconitate and then into isocitrate. This reaction is catalyzed by 2-isopropylmalate dehydratase (2-hydroxy-4-methyl-3-carboxyvalerate hydrolyase, EC 4.2.1.33). As the systematic name of the enzyme implies, the product is 2-hydroxy-4-methyl-3-carboxyvalerate, sometimes called 3-isopropylmalate.

Again, in parallel with the reactions of the tricarboxylic acid cycle, 2-hydroxy-4-methyl-3-carboxyvalerate now undergoes oxidation and decarboxylation. Oxidation is catalyzed here by 3-isopropylmalate dehydrogenase (2-hydroxy-4-methyl-3-carboxyvalerate: $NAD^+$ oxidoreductase, EC 1.1.1.85). The product, 2-oxo-4-methyl-3-carboxyvalerate then undergoes decarboxylation and 2-oxo-4-methylvalerate is formed. The latter needs only to undergo transamination and leucine is formed. The anabolism of leucine, isoleucine, and valine is summarized below.

Considering some of the regulatory influences exerted upon the anabolism of the branched-chain amino acids, it has already been mentioned that the activity of the biosynthetic threonine dehydratase, which converts threonine into 2-oxobutyrate, is modulated by the relative concentrations of isoleucine and valine. Also, in *Salmonella typhimurium* at least, the synthesis of the enzyme catalyzing the second

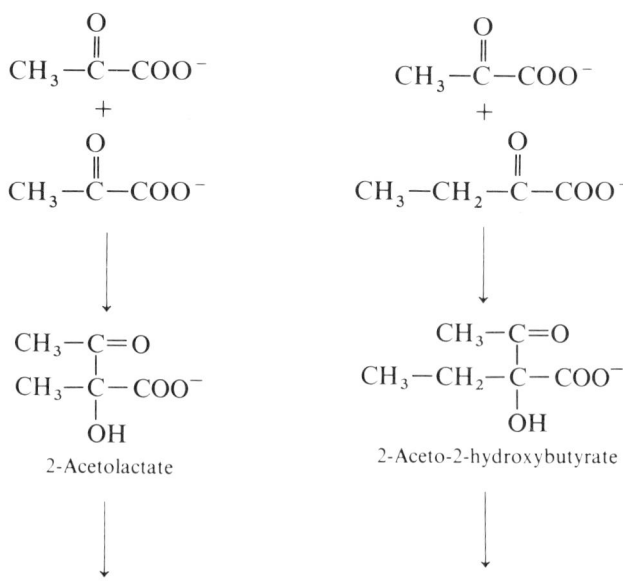

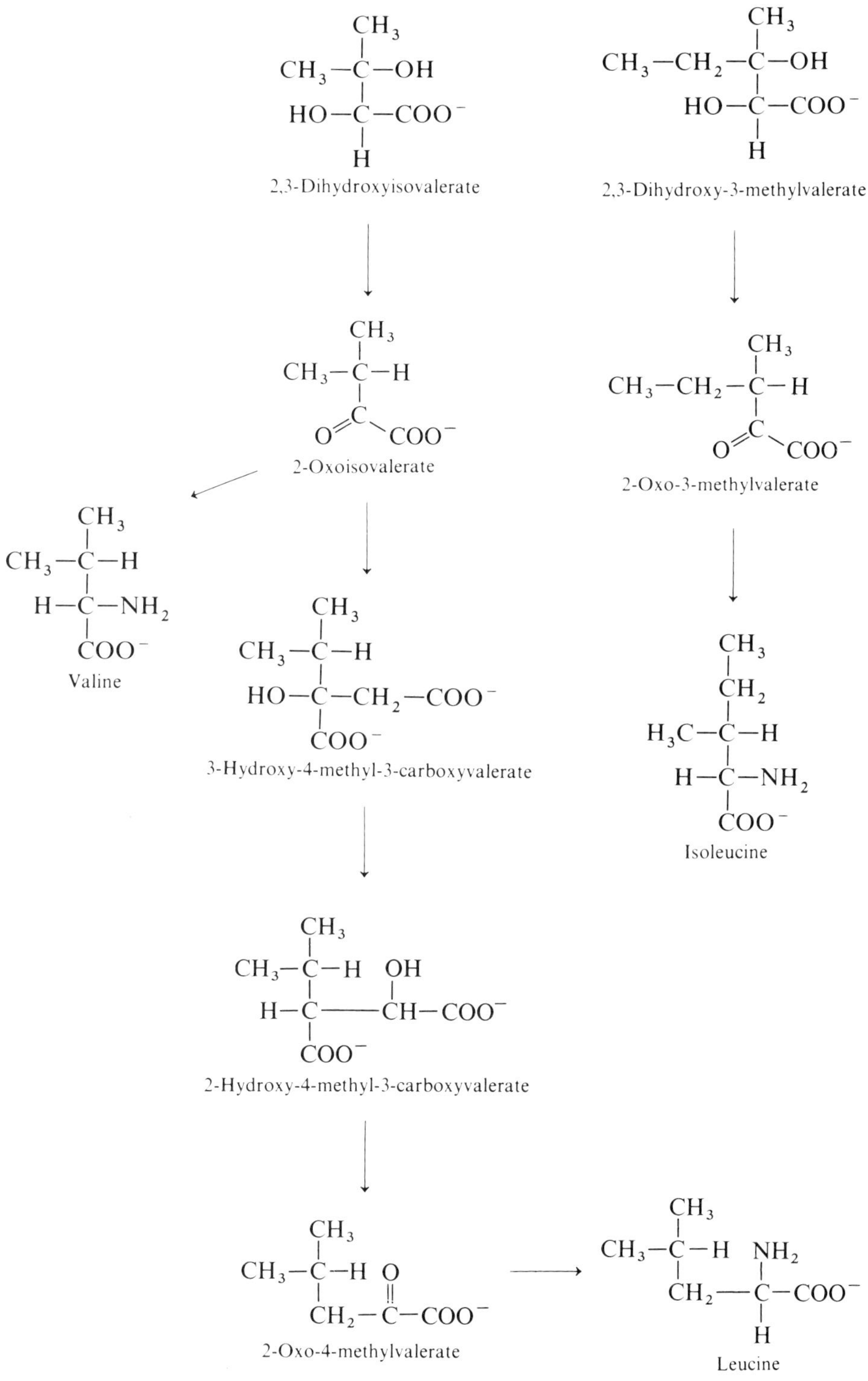

$$\underset{\text{2,3-Dihydroxyisovalerate}}{\overset{\overset{\displaystyle CH_3}{\underset{\displaystyle H}{\overset{\displaystyle |}{CH_3-C-OH}}}}{HO-C-COO^-}}$$

$$\underset{\text{2,3-Dihydroxy-3-methylvalerate}}{\overset{\overset{\displaystyle CH_3}{\underset{\displaystyle H}{\overset{\displaystyle |}{CH_3-CH_2-C-OH}}}}{HO-C-COO^-}}$$

$$\underset{\text{2-Oxoisovalerate}}{\overset{\overset{\displaystyle CH_3}{\underset{\displaystyle}{CH_3-C-H}}}{\overset{C}{\underset{O}{\diagup\diagdown}}COO^-}}$$

$$\underset{\text{2-Oxo-3-methylvalerate}}{\overset{\overset{\displaystyle CH_3}{\underset{\displaystyle}{CH_3-CH_2-C-H}}}{\overset{C}{\underset{O}{\diagup\diagdown}}COO^-}}$$

$$\underset{\text{Valine}}{\overset{CH_3}{\underset{COO^-}{\overset{|}{CH_3-C-H}\atop\overset{|}{H-C-NH_2}}}}$$

$$\underset{\text{3-Hydroxy-4-methyl-3-carboxyvalerate}}{\overset{CH_3}{\underset{COO^-}{\overset{|}{CH_3-C-H}\atop\overset{|}{HO-C-CH_2-COO^-}}}}$$

$$\underset{\text{Isoleucine}}{\overset{CH_3}{\underset{COO^-}{\overset{|}{CH_2}\atop\overset{|}{H_3C-C-H}\atop\overset{|}{H-C-NH_2}}}}$$

$$\underset{\text{2-Hydroxy-4-methyl-3-carboxyvalerate}}{\overset{CH_3}{\overset{|}{CH_3-C-H}\;\;\overset{OH}{|}\atop\overset{|}{H-C\;\;\;\;\;\;\;CH-COO^-}\atop\overset{|}{COO^-}}}$$

$$\underset{\text{2-Oxo-4-methylvalerate}}{\overset{CH_3}{\overset{|}{CH_3-C-H}\;\;\overset{O}{\|}\atop\overset{|}{CH_2-C-COO^-}}}$$

$$\underset{\text{Leucine}}{\overset{CH_3}{\overset{|}{CH_3-C-H}\;\;NH_2\atop\overset{|}{CH_2\;\;\;\;\;\;C-COO^-}\atop\overset{|}{H}}}$$

step of the pathway, the ketol-acid reductoisomerase, is induced by either one of its two substrates, 2-acetolactate or 2-aceto-2-hydroxybutyrate. Leucine, on the other hand, inhibits the activity of isopropylmalate synthase, the first enzyme specifically involved in its synthesis.

## METABOLISM OF THE BASIC AMINO ACIDS: LYSINE, ARGININE, AND ORNITHINE

### Lysine Catabolism

Several pathways for the degradation of lysine have been described. Not only are there different pathways in different living organisms, but sometimes there is more than one pathway in a given organism. In man the principal pathway for the degradation of lysine involves the formation of saccharopine and ultimately acetyl CoA.

In man L-lysine is converted into $N^6$-(glutar-2-yl)lysine, or saccharopine, in the presence of 2-oxoglutarate and reducing conditions. This reaction is catalyzed by saccharopine dehydrogenase (NADP$^+$, lysine-forming) [$N^6$-(glutar-2-yl)-L-lysine: NADP$^+$ oxidoreductase (L-lysine-forming), EC 1.5.1.8]. The reaction can be written

$$\text{L-Lysine} + \text{2-oxoglutarate} + \text{NADPH} \rightleftharpoons$$
$$N^6\text{-(glutar-2-yl)lysine} + \text{NADP}^+ + \text{H}_2\text{O} \quad (14\text{-}33)$$

In the next step of the degradative pathway saccharopine is converted into 2-aminoadipate 6-semialdehyde and glutamate under oxidizing conditions. This is catalyzed by a glutamate-forming saccharopine dehydrogenase [$N^6$-(glutar-2-yl)-L-lysine:NAD$^+$ oxidoreductase (L-glutamate-forming), EC 1.5.1.9], and the reaction is

$$N^6\text{-(glutar-2-yl)lysine} + \text{NAD}^+ + \text{H}_2\text{O} \rightleftharpoons$$
$$\text{2-aminoadipate 6-semialdehyde} + \text{L-glutamate} + \text{NADH} \quad (14\text{-}34)$$

The result of these two reactions is that the $\epsilon$-amino group of lysine is removed, and C(6) of this amino acid is oxidized to the level of an aldehyde—precisely that which would have been accomplished if the $\epsilon$-amino group of lysine had undergone transamination. However, in this case the conversion is catalyzed by an NADP$^+$-dependent, lysine-forming saccharopine dehydrogenase and an NAD$^+$-dependent, glutamate-forming saccharopine dehydrogenase.

Now 2-aminoadipate 6-semialdehyde can be oxidized to 2-aminoadipate by a reaction catalyzed by aminoadipate-semialdehyde dehydrogenase [L-2-aminoadipate semialdehyde:NAD(P)$^+$ oxidoreductase, EC 1.2.1.31]. 2-Aminoadipate, in turn, undergoes a transamination reaction, catalyzed by 2-aminoadipate aminotransferase (L-2-aminoadipate:2-oxoglutarate aminotransferase, EC 2.6.1.39), to yield 2-oxoadipate. The 2-oxoadipate is then converted into glutaryl CoA in a reaction that parallels the conversion of pyruvate into acetyl CoA. Glutaryl CoA then undergoes dehydrogenation to yield glutaconyl CoA, which is then decarboxylated

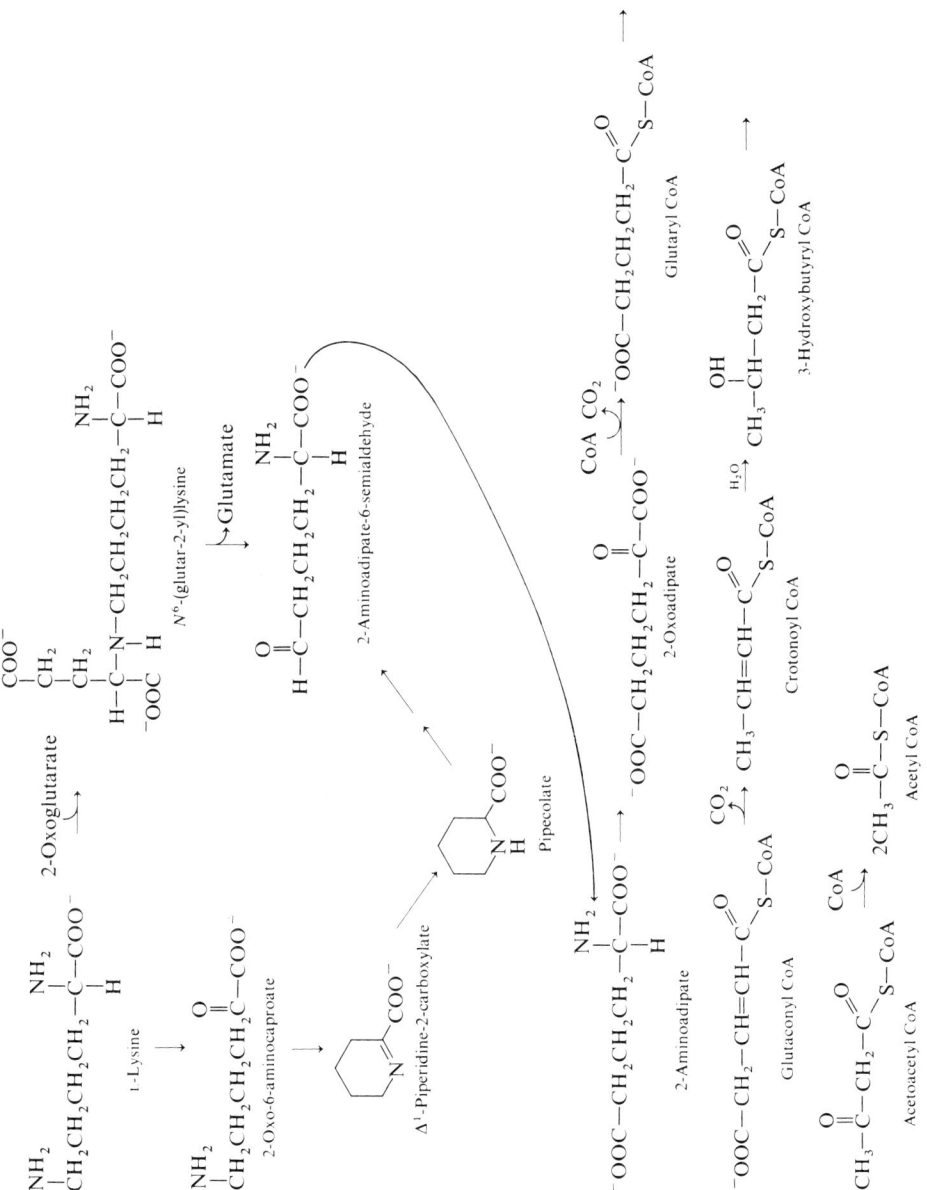

to yield crotonoyl CoA. Crotonoyl CoA undergoes hydration and then oxidation at C(3) of the acyl moiety to yield acetoacetyl CoA. This is converted into two molecules of acetyl CoA under most circumstances. Thus, the degradation of lysine in man entails the removal of the two nitrogen atoms and the conversion of two of the six carbon atoms into carbon dioxide, while the remaining four are converted into two acetyl moieties of acetyl CoA. The latter can ultimately be oxidized to carbon dioxide also.

An alternate pathway for the degradation of lysine (quantitatively of much less importance in man) entails the formation of the intermediate L-pipecolate. This pathway is also shown along with the major pathway on page 663.

Yet another variation of the pathways shown above occurs in certain yeasts, in which the $\epsilon$-amino group of lysine initially undergoes acetylation. The N-acetyl-lysine is then converted into the corresponding 2-oxo derivative, which in turn is reduced to yield a hydroxy derivative. This can be converted into glutarate and subsequently into glutaryl CoA, which is then degraded as in the pathway shown above.

In certain aerobic bacteria, e.g., *Pseudomonas putida* or *Pseudomonas fluorescens*, lysine is degraded by being initially converted into 5-aminovaleramide and carbon dioxide. This reaction requires molecular oxygen and is catalyzed by the flavoprotein lysine 2-monooxygenase [L-lysine:oxygen 2-oxidoreductase (decarboxylating), EC 1.13.12.2]. The reaction can be written

$$\text{L-Lysine} + O_2 \rightleftharpoons \text{5-aminovaleramide} + CO_2 + H_2O \qquad (14\text{-}35)$$

Lysine monooxygenase from *P. fluorescens* is a tetrameric protein which has a molecular weight of 246,000. The enzyme binds four molecules of FAD and utilizes no other oxidation-reduction cofactor. From an overview, the reaction entails the two-electron reduction of a flavin moiety by the amino acid, followed by the introduction of one of the oxygen atoms of molecular oxygen into the amino acid and the transfer of two electrons from the reduced flavin to the second oxygen atom. Decarboxylation then generates the amide, which contains one of the oxygen atoms of the molecular oxygen, and a water molecule, which contains the second oxygen atom. This is represented schematically below.

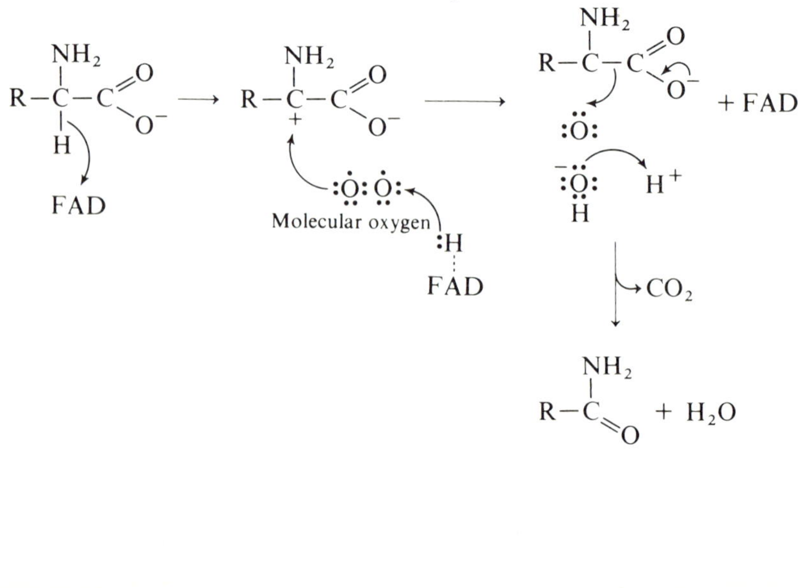

Note that at the conclusion of the reaction the oxidized flavin has been regenerated.

The 5-aminovaleramide thus formed next undergoes hydrolysis to yield 5-aminovalerate. Thus, as a result of these two reactions both C(1) and the nitrogen atom at C(2) have been removed. 5-Aminovalerate now undergoes transamination, and glutarate semialdehyde is formed. This in turn can be converted into glutarate, glutaryl CoA, and ultimately, acetyl CoA.

In the anaerobic clostridia L-lysine is degraded to butyrate, acetate, and ammonia. Initially, L-lysine is converted into 3,6-diaminohexanoate, sometimes called $\beta$-lysine. The rearrangement is catalyzed by lysine 2,3-aminomutase (L-lysine 2,3-aminomutase, EC 5.4.3.2). As isolated from *Clostridium* SB4, the mutase has a molecular weight of 285,000 and is thought to be a hexamer. The enzyme is yellow because of the bound pyridoxal phosphate which participates in the reaction, as does S-adenosylmethionine.

Next, 3,6-diaminohexanoate undergoes a second rearrangement reaction which results in the formation of *erythro*-3,5-diaminohexanoate. The rearrangement is catalyzed by $\beta$-lysine 5,6-aminomutase (L-3,6-diaminohexanoate aminomutase, EC 5.4.3.3), which has been isolated from *Clostridium sticklandii* as a red-orange tetrameric protein that has a molecular weight of 170,000. The enzyme binds both pyridoxal phosphate and cobalamin. A second, smaller sulfhydryl protein (60,000) is also required for the rearrangement.

Following the rearrangement reactions, *erythro*-3,5-diaminohexanoate undergoes an oxidative deamination reaction that results in the formation of 3-oxo-5-aminohexanoate. Enzymes that catalyze this reaction, which is

*erythro*-3,5-Diaminohexanoate + NAD(P)$^+$ $\rightleftharpoons$

3-oxo-5-aminohexanoate + NH$_3$ + NAD(P)H    (14-36)

have been isolated from several clostridia. The enzyme from *Clostridium* SB4 is a tetramer which has a molecular weight of 140,000 and is relatively specific

$$\underset{\text{L-Lysine}}{CH_2CH_2CH_2CH_2-\underset{H}{\overset{NH_2}{C}}-COO^-} \longrightarrow \underset{\text{3,6-Diaminohexanoate}}{\overset{NH_2}{CH_2CH_2CH_2}-\overset{NH_2}{CH}-CH_2-COO^-} \longrightarrow$$

$$\underset{\textit{erythro}\text{-3,5-Diaminohexanoate}}{CH_3-\underset{H}{\overset{NH_2}{C}}-CH_2-\underset{H}{\overset{NH_2}{C}}-CH_2-COO^-} \xrightarrow{NH_3} \underset{\text{3-Oxo-5-aminohexanoate}}{CH_3-\underset{H}{\overset{NH_2}{C}}-CH_2-\overset{O}{\overset{\|}{C}}-CH_2-COO^-}$$

$$\downarrow$$

$$\underset{\text{Butyrate}}{CH_3CH_2CH_2-C\overset{O}{\underset{O^-}{\diagup}}} + \underset{\text{Acetate}}{CH_3-C\overset{O}{\underset{O^-}{\diagup}}} + \underset{\text{Ammonia}}{NH_3}$$

for NAD$^+$. The enzymes from the other clostridia exhibit less specificity with respect to the oxidation-reduction cofactor, however. The 3-oxo-5-aminohexanoate can subsequently be converted into acetate [which is thought to be derived from C(1) and C(2) of lysine] and butyrate [which is thought to be derived from C(3), C(4), C(5), and C(6) of lysine], and a second molecule of ammonia. These reactions are summarized on page 665.

## Lysine Anabolism

Lysine is synthesized by bacteria, fungi, green plants, and green algae. There are two principal pathways for this synthesis. One, which has been demonstrated in bacteria and higher plants, entails the utilization of aspartate semialdehyde. The second, which has been demonstrated in yeasts and in *Neurospora*, begins with the condensation of acetyl CoA and 2-oxoglutarate to form homocitrate and continues along a path that parallels the initial reactions of the tricarboxylic acid cycle.

Recall that aspartate 4-semialdehyde is derived from aspartyl 4-phosphate, which in turn is derived from aspartate. Also recall that in *E. coli*, the formation of aspartyl 4-phosphate is catalyzed by three distinct enzymes. The one providing the aspartyl 4-phosphate that is to be utilized in the synthesis of lysine constitutes almost 80 percent of the total aspartate kinase activity in this cell. The activity of this kinase is inhibited by the ultimate product, lysine, and the inhibitory effect appears to involve the conversion of an active dimer into a subactive tetramer. Thus, the rate at which lysine is synthesized by this pathway can be influenced by the existing concentrations of the end product.

The initial step of this anabolic pathway is the condensation of aspartate semialdehyde and pyruvate, which results in the formation of dihydropicolinate. This reaction, which involves both an aldol-type condensation and the addition of an amino group across an oxo group, is catalyzed by dihydropicolinate synthase [L-aspartate 4-semialdehyde hydro-lyase (adding pyruvate and cyclizing), EC 4.2.1.52]. The reaction can be depicted as

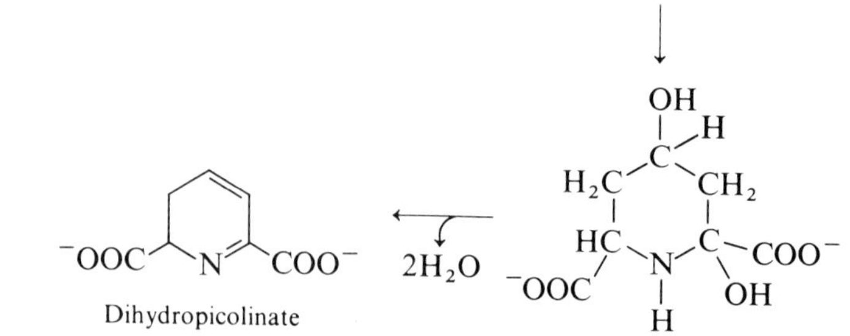

Dihydropicolinate is then reduced to 2,6-dicarboxy-$\Delta^1$-piperideine, which undergoes ring cleavage to yield 2-amino-6-oxopimelate. The latter undergoes succinylation to form $N$-succinyl-2-amino-6-oxopimelate, which is converted by transamination into $N$-succinyl-2,6-diaminopimelate. The transamination introduces the nitrogen atom that will become the $\epsilon$-amino group of lysine and is catalyzed by succinyl-diaminopimelate aminotransferase ($N$-succinyl-L,L-2,6-diaminopimelate:2-oxoglutarate aminotransferase, EC 2.6.1.17). Removal of the succinyl group by succinyl-diaminopimelate desuccinylase ($N$-succinyl-L,L-2,6-diaminopimelate amidohydrolase, EC 3.5.1.18) produces L,L-2,6-diaminopimelate. The enzyme diaminopimelate epimerase (L,L-2,6-diaminopimelate 2-epimerase, EC 5.1.1.7) then converts L,L-2,6-diaminopimelate into *meso*-diaminopimelate, which subsequently undergoes decarboxylation to yield L-lysine. The decarboxylation is catalyzed by the pyridoxal phosphate–dependent diaminopimelate decarboxylase (*meso*-2,6-diaminopimelate carboxy-lyase, EC 4.1.1.20). The pathway is summarized on page 668.

In some yeasts and in *Neurospora*, lysine is synthesized by a pathway that begins with the condensation of acetyl CoA and 2-oxoglutarate. The reaction is analogous to the reaction between acetyl CoA and oxaloacetate, as catalyzed by citrate synthase. In the present case, homocitrate synthase [3-hydroxy-3-carboxyadipate 2-oxoglutarate-lyase (CoA-acetylating), EC 4.1.3.21] catalyzes the reaction, and the product is 3-hydroxy-3-carboxyadipate, or homocitrate. The 3-hydroxy-3-carboxyadipate formed has specifically the $R$ configuration at C(3) although the citrate formed in animals has the pro-$S$ configuration at C(3); however, the citrate synthase of certain anaerobic bacteria catalyzes the formation of citrate which has the pro-$R$ configuration at C(3).

In the second step of this synthesis of lysine, 3-hydroxy-3-carboxyadipate undergoes a dehydration reaction followed by a hydration reaction, to form 2-hydroxy-3-carboxyadipate. As one might guess, this reaction is catalyzed by an enzyme called homoaconitate hydratase (2-hydroxy-3-carboxyadipate hydro-lyase, EC 4.2.1.36).

The third step of the pathway entails the oxidation and decarboxylation of 2-hydroxy-3-carboxyadipate. The product is 2-oxoadipate, and the reaction is analogous to the conversion of isocitrate into 2-oxoglutarate. In the present case, the enzyme 2-hydroxy-3-carboxyadipate dehydrogenase [2-hydroxy-3-carboxyadipate:NAD$^+$ oxidoreductase (decarboxylating), EC 1.1.1.87] catalyzes the reaction. Now 2-oxoadipate undergoes transamination, as catalyzed by 2-aminoadipate aminotransferase (L-2-aminoadipate:2-oxoglutarate aminotransferase, EC 2.6.1.39), and 2-aminoadipate is formed. In the fifth step of the sequence, 2-aminoadipate is converted into 2-aminoadipate 6-semialdehyde by a reaction catalyzed by aminoadipate-semialdehyde dehydrogenase [L-2-aminoadipate-6-semialdehyde:NAD(P)$^+$ oxidoreductase, EC 1.2.1.31]. The reaction is

L-2-Aminoadipate + NAD(P)H $\rightleftharpoons$

$\qquad$ L-2-aminoadipate 6-semialdehyde + NAD(P)$^+$ + H$_2$O $\qquad$ (14-37)

At this point in the pathway, saccharopine is formed. Recall that saccharopine and 2-aminoadipate 6-semialdehyde are also intermediates in the degradative pathway

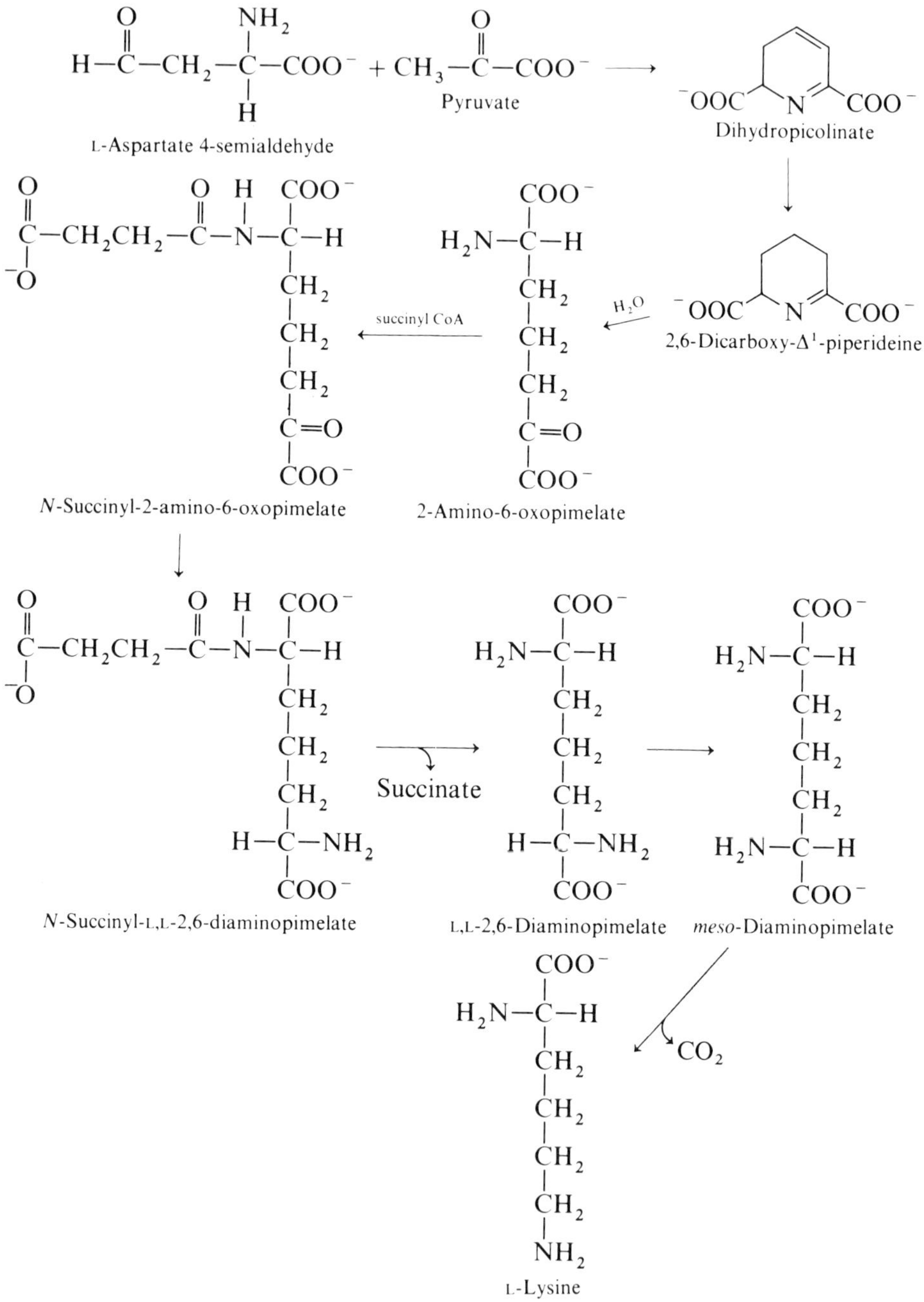

by which lysine is converted into acetyl CoA and carbon dioxide. Here 2-aminoadipate 6-semialdehyde and glutamate react to form saccharopine in the presence of an $NADP^+$-dependent saccharopine dehydrogenase [$N^6$-(glutar-2-yl)-L-lysine: $NADP^+$ oxidoreductase (L-glutamate-forming), EC 1.5.1.10]. The saccharopine is then converted into L-lysine and 2-oxoglutarate in a reaction catalyzed by a lysine-forming saccharopine dehydrogenase [$N^6$-(glutar-2-yl)-L-lysine:NAD$^+$ oxidoreductase (L-lysine-forming), EC 1.5.1.7].

This anabolic pathway is summarized below.

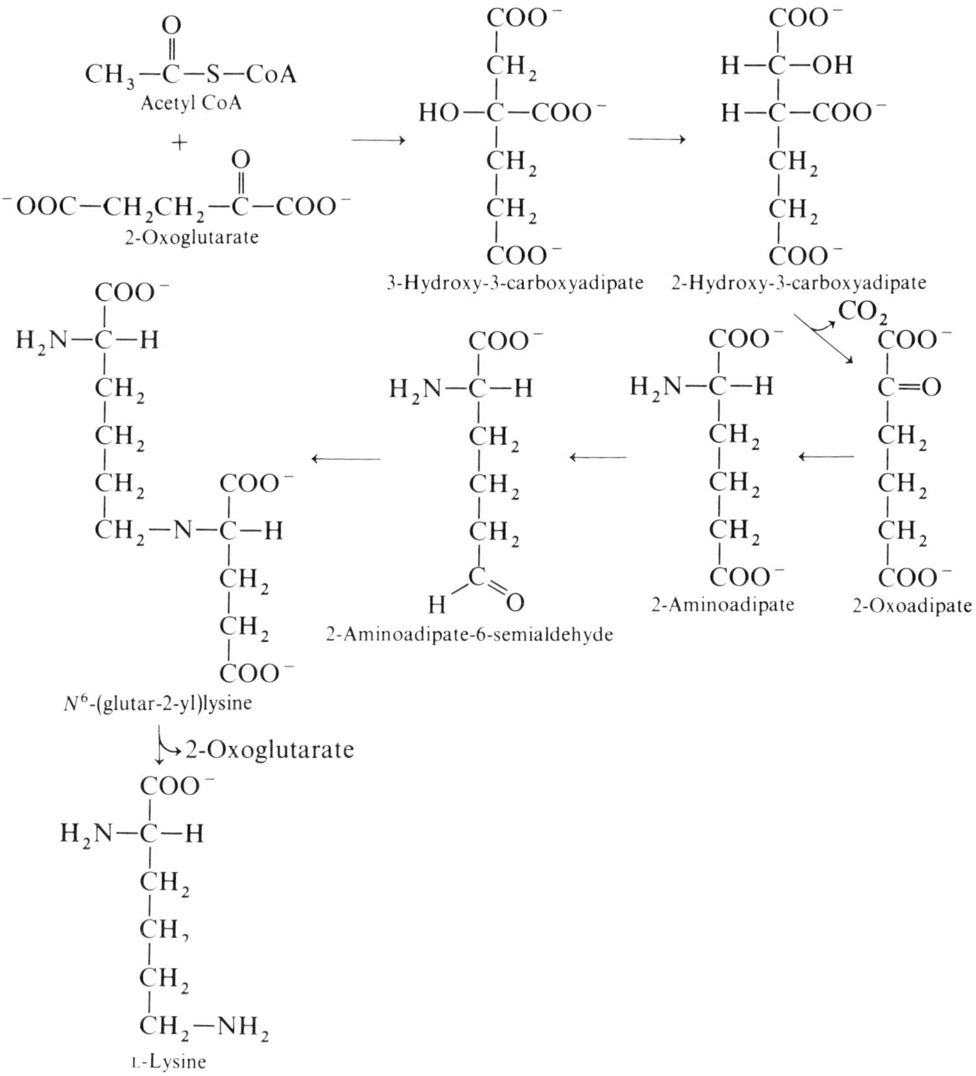

$$CH_3-\overset{O}{\underset{\|}{C}}-S-CoA$$
Acetyl CoA
+
$$^-OOC-CH_2CH_2-\overset{O}{\underset{\|}{C}}-COO^-$$
2-Oxoglutarate

→

$$\begin{array}{c} COO^- \\ | \\ CH_2 \\ | \\ HO-C-COO^- \\ | \\ CH_2 \\ | \\ CH_2 \\ | \\ COO^- \end{array}$$
3-Hydroxy-3-carboxyadipate

→

$$\begin{array}{c} COO^- \\ | \\ H-C-OH \\ | \\ H-C-COO^- \\ | \\ CH_2 \\ | \\ CH_2 \\ | \\ COO^- \end{array}$$
2-Hydroxy-3-carboxyadipate

↘ CO$_2$

$$\begin{array}{c} COO^- \\ | \\ C=O \\ | \\ CH_2 \\ | \\ CH_2 \\ | \\ CH_2 \\ | \\ COO^- \end{array}$$
2-Oxoadipate

←

$$\begin{array}{c} COO^- \\ | \\ H_2N-C-H \\ | \\ CH_2 \\ | \\ CH_2 \\ | \\ CH_2 \\ | \\ COO^- \end{array}$$
2-Aminoadipate

←

$$\begin{array}{c} COO^- \\ | \\ H_2N-C-H \\ | \\ CH_2 \\ | \\ CH_2 \\ | \\ CH_2 \\ | \\ \underset{H}{C}\!\!=\!\!O \end{array}$$
2-Aminoadipate-6-semialdehyde

←

$$\begin{array}{c} COO^- \\ | \\ H_2N-C-H \\ | \\ CH_2 \\ | \\ CH_2 \\ | \\ CH_2 \\ | \\ CH_2-N-C-H \\ \phantom{CH_2-N-}| \\ \phantom{CH_2-N-}CH_2 \\ \phantom{CH_2-N-}| \\ \phantom{CH_2-N-}CH_2 \\ \phantom{CH_2-N-}| \\ \phantom{CH_2-N-}COO^- \end{array}$$
$N^6$-(glutar-2-yl)lysine

↘ 2-Oxoglutarate

$$\begin{array}{c} COO^- \\ | \\ H_2N-C-H \\ | \\ CH_2 \\ | \\ CH_2 \\ | \\ CH_2 \\ | \\ CH_2-NH_2 \end{array}$$
L-Lysine

## Catabolism of Arginine

In mammals, arginine is degraded primarily by being converted into urea and ornithine. This process is a part of the urea cycle, discussed later in this chapter. Also, arginine can be converted into agmatine and then putrescine in the human intestine. The formation of these compounds, which can be excreted, is catalyzed by bacterial enzymes; e.g., *E. coli* contains a pyridoxal phosphate–dependent arginine decarboxylase (L-arginine carboxy-lyase, EC 4.1.1.19) which catalyzes the conversion of arginine into agmatine. Agmatine can then undergo a hydrolytic cleavage which yields 1,4-diaminobutane (sometimes called putrescine) and urea. The hydrolysis is catalyzed by agmatinase (agmatine amidinohydrolase, EC 3.5.3.11). These reactions are shown below.

$$\text{L-Arginine} \xrightarrow{CO_2} \text{Agmatine} \longrightarrow \text{Urea} + \text{1,4-Diaminobutane (putrescine)}$$

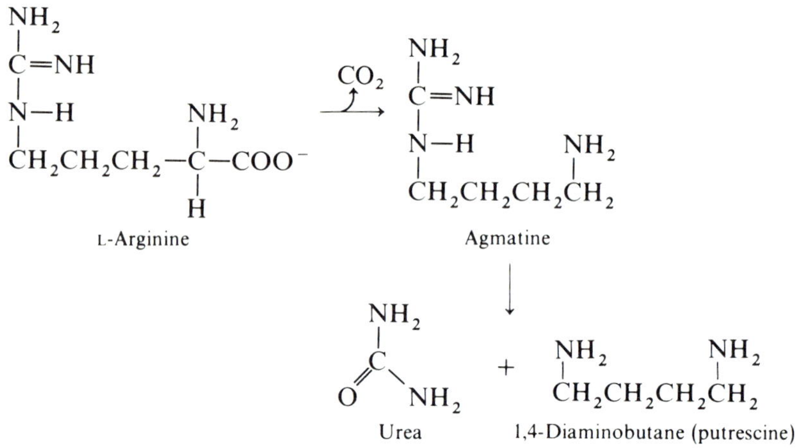

In certain other microorganisms, such as *Bacillus subtilis*, arginine is converted into ornithine by a reaction catalyzed by arginase (L-arginine amidinohydrolase, EC 3.5.3.1):

$$\text{L-Arginine} + H_2O \rightleftharpoons \text{L-ornithine} + \text{urea} \qquad (14\text{-}38)$$

Other microorganisms convert arginine into citrulline and then ornithine and carbamoyl phosphate. The enzyme arginine deiminase (L-arginine iminohydrolase, EC 3.5.3.6) catalyzes the conversion of arginine into citrulline, and ornithine carbamoyltransferase (carbamoylphosphate L-ornithine carbamoyltransferase, EC 2.1.3.3) catalyzes the formation of ornithine and carbamoyl phosphate. The latter can be converted into ATP, carbon dioxide, and ammonia in the presence of carbamate kinase (ATP:carbamate phosphotransferase, EC 2.7.2.2). These reactions are shown below.

$$\text{L-Arginine} \longrightarrow \text{L-Citrulline} + NH_3$$

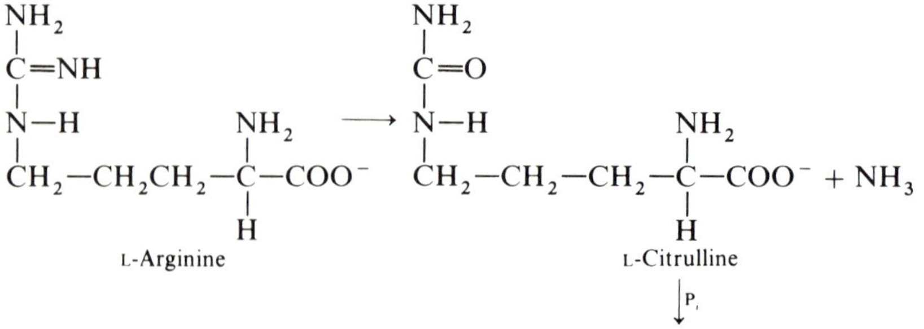

$$\begin{array}{c} \text{ATP} \\ + \\ \text{CO}_2 \\ + \\ \text{NH}_3 \end{array} \xrightarrow{\text{ADP}} \underset{\text{Carbamoyl phosphate}}{\text{NH}_2-\text{C}(=\text{O})-\text{O}-\text{P}(=\text{O})(\text{O}^-)\text{O}^-} + \underset{\text{L-Ornithine}}{\text{NH}_2-\text{CH}_2-\text{CH}_2\text{CH}_2-\overset{\text{NH}_2}{\underset{\text{H}}{\text{C}}}-\text{COO}^-}$$

Various other pathways for the degradation of arginine have been described, including one, demonstrated in *Pseudomonas putida*, that entails the conversion of arginine into 4-aminobutyrate, urea, ammonia, and carbon dioxide.

## Anabolism of Arginine in Mammals

In man the synthesis of arginine entails the conversion of carbamoyl phosphate and ornithine into citrulline, followed by the reaction of citrulline and aspartate to yield argininosuccinate, which is then cleaved to yield arginine and fumarate. These reactions are also involved in the synthesis of urea, which is derived from arginine. When arginine or urea is to be synthesized in mammals, the carbamoyl phosphate is formed in the mitochondria (primarily, the liver mitochondria) as the result of the reaction catalyzed by the ammonia-dependent carbamoyl-phosphate synthase [ATP:carbamate phosphotransferase (dephosphorylating), EC 2.7.2.5]. The synthesis of carbamoyl phosphate has been mentioned previously within the framework of pyrimidine synthesis, but the carbamoyl-phosphate synthase that catalyzes the formation of carbamoyl phosphate to be utilized for pyrimidine synthesis is a cytoplasmic enzyme which utilizes glutamine as a nitrogen donor. The cytoplasmic synthase exists in association with several other enzymes also involved in pyrimidine synthesis. The mitochondrial synthase, on the other hand, does not utilize glutamine as a nitrogen donor although it does utilize $N$-acetylglutamate as an activator. The formation of carbamoyl phosphate in the mitochondria occurs as follows:

$$2 \text{ ATP} + \text{NH}_3 + \text{HCO}_3^- + \text{H}_2\text{O} \rightleftharpoons \text{carbamoyl phosphate} + 2 \text{ ADP} + \text{P}_i \qquad (14\text{-}39)$$

Carbamoyl phosphate can now react with ornithine to yield citrulline and orthophosphate. The reaction is catalyzed by ornithine carbamoyltransferase, which, as mentioned above, also participates in the degradation of arginine in certain microorganisms. The reaction of citrulline and aspartate then yields argininosuccinate. The enzyme argininosuccinate synthetase [L-citrulline:L-aspartate ligase (AMP-forming), EC 6.3.4.5] catalyzes the reaction

$$\text{ATP} + \text{L-citrulline} + \text{L-aspartate} \rightleftharpoons \text{L-argininosuccinate} + \text{AMP} + \text{PP}_i \qquad (14\text{-}40)$$

As a result of this reaction the nitrogen atom of aspartate is utilized to convert the ureido group of citrulline into a guanidino group. The conversion is completed as a result of the cleavage catalyzed by argininosuccinate lyase (L-argininosuccinate arginine-lyase, EC 4.3.2.1). Parallel with the formation of AMP from IMP, argininosuccinate is cleaved to yield arginine and fumarate.

As isolated from bovine liver, argininosuccinate lyase has a molecular weight of 200,000 and is probably a tetramer. The enzyme has also been isolated from bovine kidney, in which it is present in approximately one-half the concentration found in the liver. The kidney and liver enzymes appear to have similar characteristics.

The synthesis of arginine in mammals is summarized below.

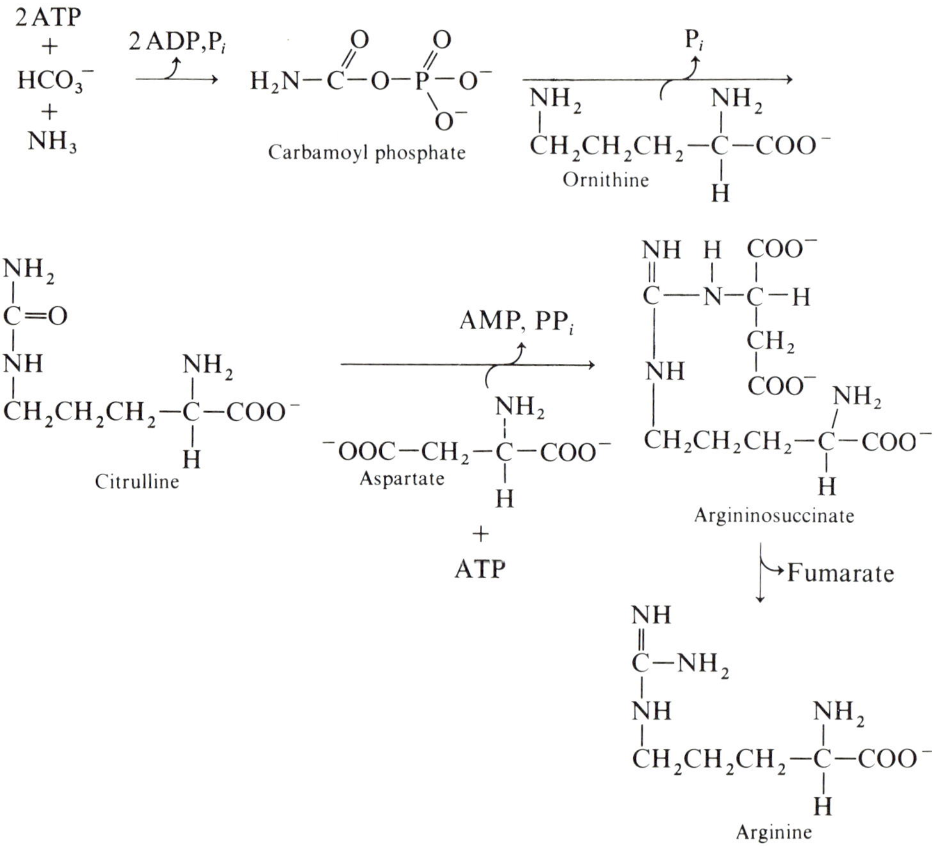

## Anabolism of Ornithine and Arginine in *E. coli*

In *E. coli* the synthesis of ornithine from glutamate and its utilization in the synthesis of arginine are catalyzed by eight enzymes. The expression of the genes that specify these eight enzymes is regulated in a coordinate manner although only four of the eight genes are closely linked on the genome. (Three of these specify enzymes involved in the synthesis of ornithine, while one specifies an enzyme involved in the formation of arginine from ornithine.) The expression of all eight is subject to repression in the presence of adequate concentrations of arginine.

The initial reaction of the conversion of glutamate into ornithine and arginine is the formation of N-acetylglutamate as catalyzed by amino-acid acetyltransferase (acetyl CoA:L-glutamate N-acetyltransferase, EC 2.3.1.1). The reaction is

$$\text{Acetyl CoA} + \text{L-glutamate} \rightleftharpoons N\text{-acetyl-L-glutamate} + \text{CoA} \quad (14\text{-}41)$$

Next, N-acetylglutamate undergoes phosphorylation in the presence of ATP and the enzyme acetylglutamate kinase (ATP:N-acetyl-L-glutamate 5-phosphotransferase, EC 2.7.2.8). The products of the reaction are N-acetylglutamyl 5-phosphate and ADP. Conversion of the acyl phosphate into the corresponding aldehyde is catalyzed by N-acetylglutamyl-5-phosphate reductase [N-acetyl-L-glutamate-5-semialdehyde:NADP$^+$ oxidoreductase (phosphorylating), EC 1.2.1.38]. The reaction parallels the formation of aspartate 4-semialdehyde from aspartyl 4-phosphate. In the present case, the product is N-acetyl-L-glutamate 5-semialdehyde. Transamination, as catalyzed by acetylornithine aminotransferase ($N^2$-acetyl-L-ornithine:2-oxoglutarate aminotransferase, EC 2.6.1.11), generates N-acetylornithine. Deacylation yields ornithine. Acetylornithine deacetylase ($N^2$-acetyl-L-ornithine amidohydrolase, EC 3.5.1.16) catalyzes the hydrolytic cleavage. Ornithine is then converted into citrulline; this in turn is converted into argininosuccinate, which is then converted into arginine, as described above.

It might be mentioned at this point that in *E. coli* the formation of the carbamoyl phosphate that is to be used in the synthesis of arginine or the pyrimidine ring is catalyzed by a single carbamoyl-phosphate synthase. The activity of this synthase is modulated by ornithine, ammonium ion, IMP, and UMP. The first three induce an enhancement in enzymatic activity while UMP inhibits the enzymatic activity. The synthesis of ornithine and arginine in *E. coli* is summarized below.

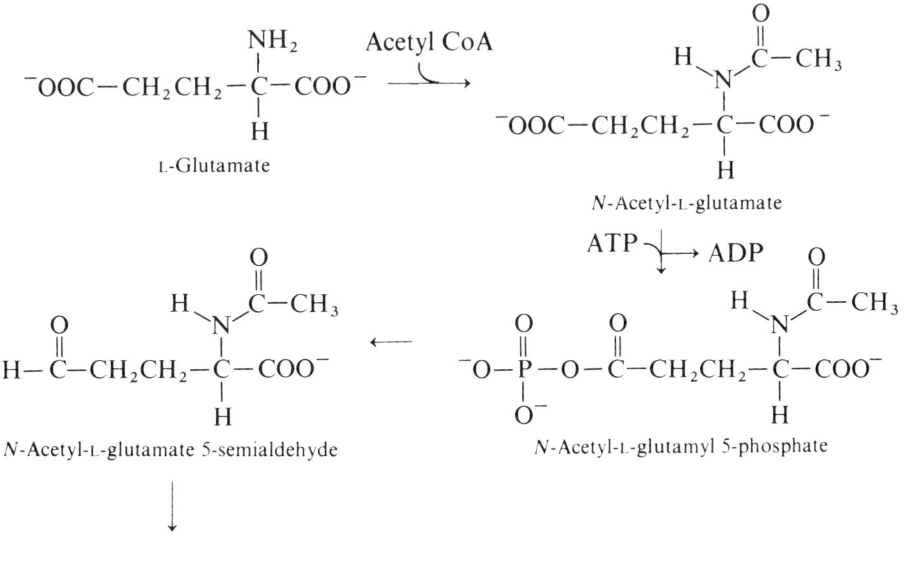

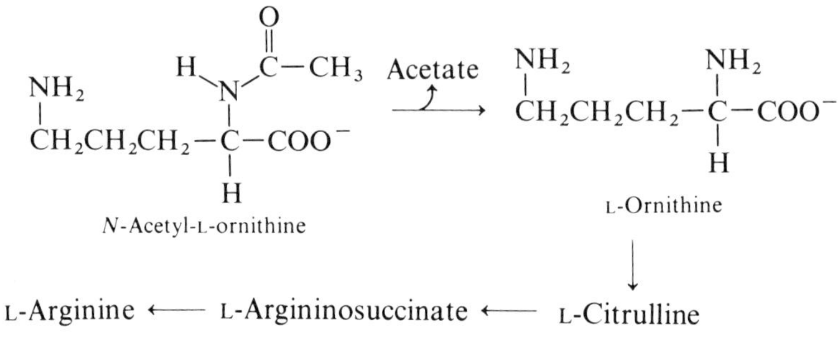

$$\text{N-Acetyl-L-ornithine} \quad \xrightarrow{\text{Acetate}} \quad \text{L-Ornithine}$$

N-Acetyl-L-ornithine: $\text{NH}_2\text{—CH}_2\text{CH}_2\text{CH}_2\text{—C(H)(NHC(O)CH}_3\text{)—COO}^-$

L-Ornithine: $\text{NH}_2\text{—CH}_2\text{CH}_2\text{CH}_2\text{—C(H)(NH}_2\text{)—COO}^-$

L-Arginine ⟵ L-Argininosuccinate ⟵ L-Citrulline ⟵ L-Ornithine

## Catabolism and Utilization of Ornithine

In eukaryotic cells ornithine undergoes decarboxylation to yield 1,4-diaminobutane, or putrescine, which is not only a degradation product but also a precursor of the polyamines spermidine and spermine. In mammals the decarboxylation of ornithine appears to be the only route to spermidine and spermine. The precise functions of the polyamines in eukaryotic cells have not been defined although these polycationic species are implicated in the process of protein synthesis. They can bind not only DNA and RNA but also the ribosomes. Spermidine and spermine also enhance the activity of a ribonuclease from human plasma.

The conversion of ornithine to 1,4-diaminobutane, which can be considered the initial step in the synthesis of spermidine and spermine, is catalyzed by the pyridoxal phosphate–dependent ornithine decarboxylase (L-ornithine carboxy-lyase, EC 4.1.1.17). Ornithine decarboxylase and the other enzymes that participate in the synthesis of the polyamines are localized in the cytoplasm of the mammalian cell. The extent to which ornithine is converted into 1,4-diaminobutane is regulated primarily by influences upon the synthesis of ornithine decarboxylase. Hormones and other factors promote this synthesis, and in view of the fact that the half-life of ornithine decarboxylase is less than 22 min, this mode of regulation is very effective.

To form spermidine and spermine, 1,4-diaminobutane must react with the decarboxylation product of S-adenosylmethionine, i.e., the 5'-deoxyadenosyl-(5'),3-aminopropyl-(1),methylsulfonium ion. This decarboxylation is catalyzed by S-adenosylmethionine decarboxylase (S-adenosyl-L-methionine carboxy-lyase, EC 4.1.1.50). The activity of this decarboxylase is not affected by pyridoxal phosphate although it is enhanced by 1,4-diaminobutane, the component with which the reaction product reacts.

The sulfonium ion and 1,4-diaminobutane react to yield spermidine and 5'-methylthioadenosine. This reaction is catalyzed by aminopropyltransferase [5'-deoxyadenosyl-(5'),3-aminopropyl-(1),methylsulfonium-salt:1,4-diaminobutane (putrescine) 3-aminopropyltransferase, EC 2.5.1.16]. It is analogous to reactions in which S-adenosylmethionine donates a methyl group to an acceptor. In the present case, however, rather than a methyl group, a 3-aminopropyl group is donated to one of the amino nitrogen atoms of 1,4-diaminobutane. The product is N-(3-aminopropyl)-1,4-diaminobutane, or spermidine. Spermidine is then converted into spermine by a similar N-alkylation reaction involving the remaining primary amine group. These reactions are illustrated below.

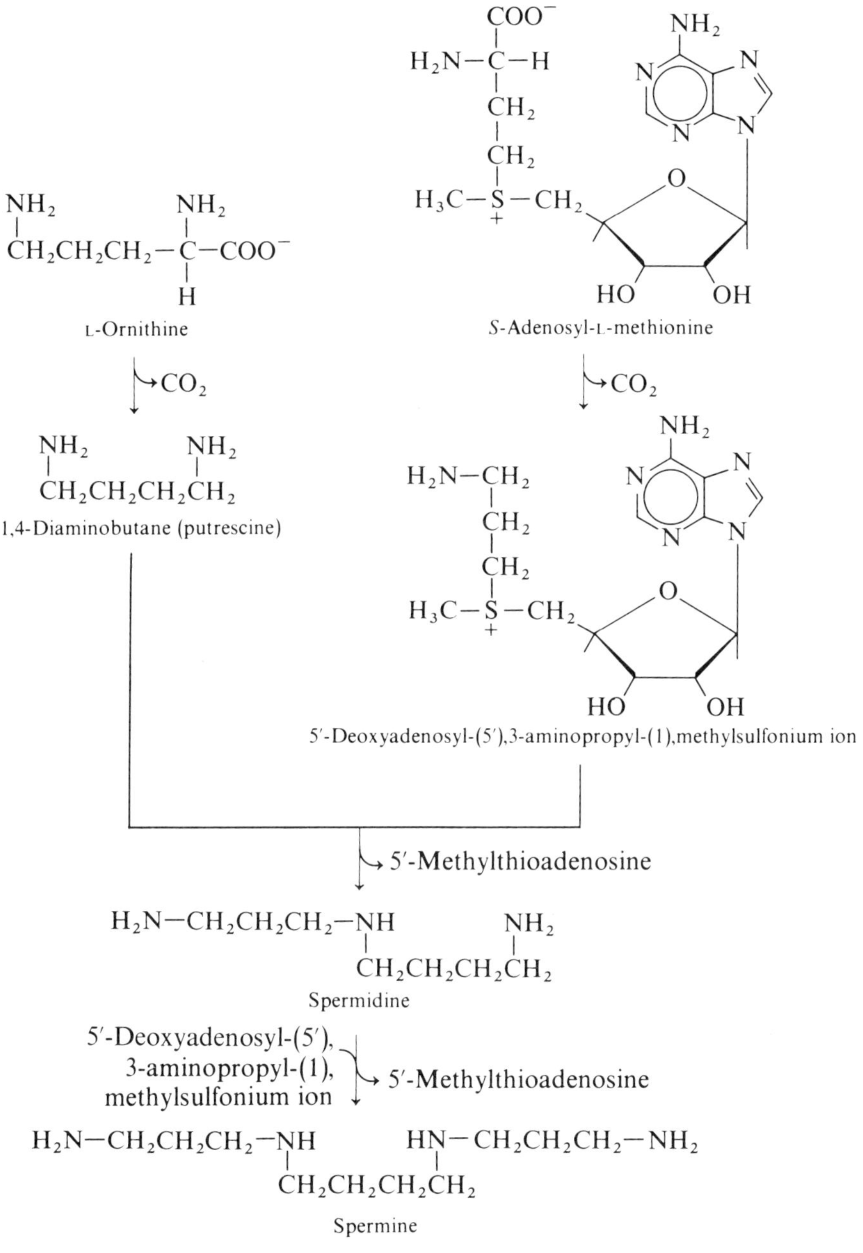

This sequence of reactions also occurs in bacteria such as *E. coli*. In this case the S-adenosylmethionine decarboxylase has been purified and found to have a molecular weight of approximately 113,000. The purified enzyme binds pyruvate covalently and utilizes the oxo acid as a cofactor. It has been suggested that the function of the pyruvate is that of forming a Schiff base in conjunction with the substrate.

Ornithine can also undergo transamination to yield glutamate 5-semialdehyde. This reaction is catalyzed by ornithine–oxo-acid aminotransferase (L-ornithine: 2-oxo-acid aminotransferase, EC 2.6.1.13). Glutamate 5-semialdehyde in turn can be converted into glutamate and then into 2-oxoglutarate, which enters the tricarboxylic acid cycle.

In the anaerobic bacterium *Clostridium sticklandii* ornithine can undergo epimerization, catalyzed by ornithine racemase (ornithine racemase, EC 5.1.1.12) and then a rearrangement reaction, catalyzed by a pyridoxal phosphate– and cobalamin-dependent D-ornithine 4,5-aminomutase (D-ornithine 4,5-aminomutase, EC 5.4.3.5). The product is D-*threo*-2,4-diaminopentanoate. A subsequent oxidative deamination reaction produces 2-amino-4-oxopentanoate. The latter is ultimately degraded to acetate, carbon dioxide, and ammonia.

# METABOLISM OF GLUTAMATE, PROLINE, AND HISTIDINE

Both proline and histidine can be degraded to glutamate. Glutamate can then be converted into 2-oxoglutarate, which can enter the tricarboxylic acid cycle. Thus, the carbon atoms of glutamate, proline, and histidine can be oxidized ultimately to the level of carbon dioxide. These reactions are discussed in the paragraphs that follow.

## Catabolism of Proline

In mammals the degradation of proline is initiated with its conversion into $\Delta^1$-pyrroline 5-carboxylate. This dehydrogenation reaction is catalyzed by a cytochrome-linked enzyme that is a component of the mitochondrial inner membrane. The pyrroline is then hydrolyzed to yield glutamate 5-semialdehyde, which in turn is oxidized to glutamate:

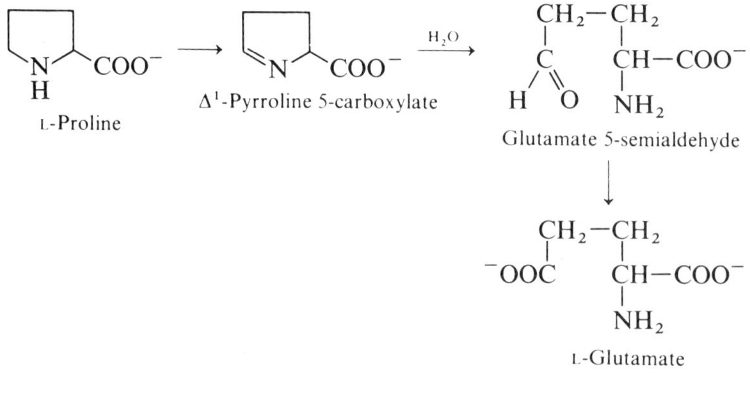

Proline can also undergo a dehydrogenation reaction catalyzed by L-amino-acid oxidase. The product in this case is $\Delta^1$-pyrroline 2-carboxylate. Note that in this case the amino acid substrate has undergone oxidation but not deamination. The $\Delta^1$-pyrroline 2-carboxylate is subsequently converted into 2-oxo-5-aminovalerate.

## Anabolism of Proline

In bacteria proline can be derived from ornithine, which in turn is derived from glutamate. The conversion of glutamate into ornithine (and then into arginine) in *E. coli* has been described above. When proline is to be formed, rather than reacting with carbamoyl phosphate, ornithine undergoes transamination, as catalyzed by ornithine–oxo-acid aminotransferase, and glutamate 5-semialdehyde is formed. This then undergoes ring closure to yield $\Delta^1$-pyrroline 5-carboxylate, which is converted into proline as the result of the reaction catalyzed by pyrroline-5-carboxylate reductase [L-proline: NAD(P)$^+$ oxidoreductase, EC 1.5.1.2], as shown below.

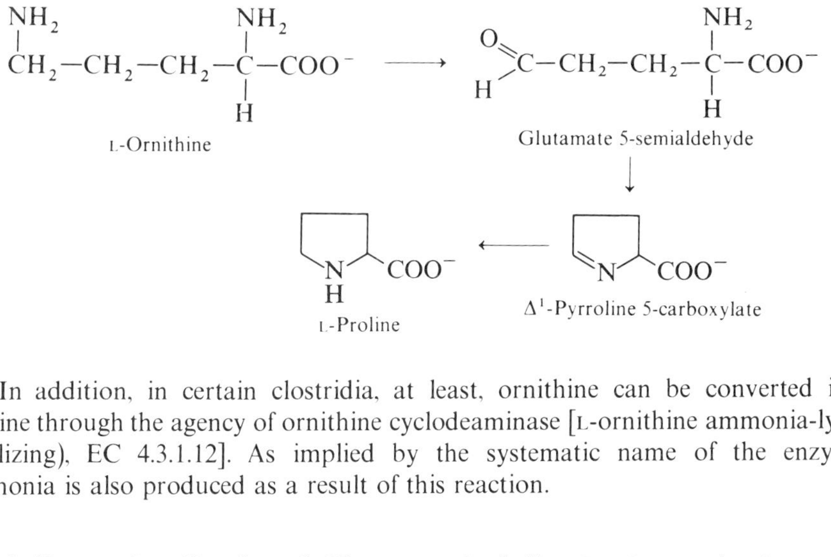

$$\underset{\text{L-Ornithine}}{\text{CH}_2\text{--CH}_2\text{--CH}_2\text{--}\underset{\text{H}}{\overset{\text{NH}_2}{\text{C}}}\text{--COO}^-} \longrightarrow \underset{\text{Glutamate 5-semialdehyde}}{\underset{\text{H}}{\overset{\text{O}}{\text{C}}}\text{--CH}_2\text{--CH}_2\text{--}\underset{\text{H}}{\overset{\text{NH}_2}{\text{C}}}\text{--COO}^-}$$

$$\underset{\text{L-Proline}}{\boxed{\text{N--COO}^-}} \longleftarrow \underset{\Delta^1\text{-Pyrroline 5-carboxylate}}{\boxed{\text{N--COO}^-}}$$

In addition, in certain clostridia, at least, ornithine can be converted into proline through the agency of ornithine cyclodeaminase [L-ornithine ammonia-lyase (cyclizing), EC 4.3.1.12]. As implied by the systematic name of the enzyme, ammonia is also produced as a result of this reaction.

## Catabolism and Utilization of Glutamate, Including Its Conversion into Glutamine

Glutamate, in fact, has several metabolic fates. As mentioned, the carbon atoms of glutamate can be oxidized to the level of carbon dioxide following the conversion of glutamate into 2-oxoglutarate. Glutamate can also undergo decarboxylation to yield 4-aminobutyrate. The decarboxylation is catalyzed by pyridoxal phosphate-dependent glutamate decarboxylase. The 4-aminobutyrate can then undergo transamination, and succinate semialdehyde is formed. The transamination is catalyzed by aminobutyrate aminotransferase (4-aminobutyrate:2-oxoglutarate aminotransferase, EC 2.6.1.19). Finally, succinate semialdehyde can be oxidized to succinate in the presence of the enzyme succinate-semialdehyde dehydrogenase [succinate semialdehyde:NAD(P)$^+$ oxidoreductase, EC 1.2.1.16]. Thus, four of the five carbon atoms of glutamate can enter the tricarboxylic acid cycle as succinate.

Glutamate is also a substrate in the synthesis of the glutathione intermediate, glutamyl-L-cysteine. In addition to being an intermediate in the formation of glutathione, this intermediate can be cleaved to yield cysteine and 5-oxo-L-proline. The latter then undergoes an energy-dependent reaction in which glutamate is regenerated.

An important metabolic fate of glutamate is its conversion into the C(5) amide, glutamine, which is itself a participant in a variety of metabolic reactions. In mammals, for example, the amido nitrogen atom of glutamine is utilized in the synthesis of the purine ring system, the synthesis of carbamoyl phosphate (and hence of the pyrimidine ring), the introduction of the amino groups of GMP and CTP, the formation of the amide group of $NAD^+$ and $NADP^+$, and the synthesis of glucosamine, among other uses. Glutamine is present in virtually all mammalian tissues, the highest concentrations being found in the brain, the liver, and the heart. Glutamine is also the amino acid present in the highest concentration in the blood.

The amidation of glutamate to form glutamine requires ammonia, ATP, and the enzyme glutamine synthetase [L-glutamate:ammonia ligase (ADP-forming), EC 6.3.1.2]. The reaction is.

$$\text{L-Glutamate} + \text{ATP} + \text{NH}_3 \rightleftharpoons \text{L-glutamine} + \text{ADP} + P_i \quad (14\text{-}42)$$

Glutamine synthetase has been isolated from several mammalian sources, including bovine, porcine, rat, and human brain and rat liver. These synthetases have molecular weights of 350,000 to 400,000, and, in those cases in which the subunit structure has been determined, they are octomers. Each subunit from the rat-brain enzyme has a molecular weight of 49,000.

It has been proposed that the formation of glutamine involves the participation of a glutamyl 5-phosphate intermediate, which is subsequently converted into the 5 amido compound in the presence of ammonia. A minimal reaction mechanism which includes this intermediate is shown at top of page 679.

The activity of the mammalian glutamine synthetase is subject to regulation, although this is not so complex a process as it is in the bacterial enzyme. In mammals, the activity of glutamine synthetase is enhanced in the presence of 2-oxoglutarate, and it is suggested that this provides a means of preventing excessive concentrations of ammonia resulting from the oxidative deamination of glutamate.

By contrast, the activity of glutamine synthetase from *E. coli* is subject to an intricate system of controls. As isolated from this microorganism, glutamine synthetase has a molecular weight of 600,000 and is composed of twelve subunits which each have a molecular weight of 50,000. These subunits are arranged in two hexagonal rings which are associated face-to-face. The activity of this synthetase is modulated by several different processes. For example, enzyme synthesis is repressed in the presence of high concentrations of ammonia. From a teleological viewpoint this may reflect the fact that in bacteria ammonia can function as the nitrogen donor in many of the reactions that utilize glutamine. Also, the activity of glutamine synthetase can be inhibited by CTP, AMP, carbamoyl phosphate, histidine, tryptophan, glucosamine 6-phosphate, glycine, and serine. The synthesis of all these components except glycine and serine involves glutamine. The activity of glutamine synthetase from *E. coli* is also modulated as a result of covalent modification. In the presence of ATP each of the enzyme's 12 subunits can undergo adenylylation. A specific tyrosyl unit of the subunit is the acceptor of this adenylyl moiety. The covalently modified tyrosyl unit has the structure

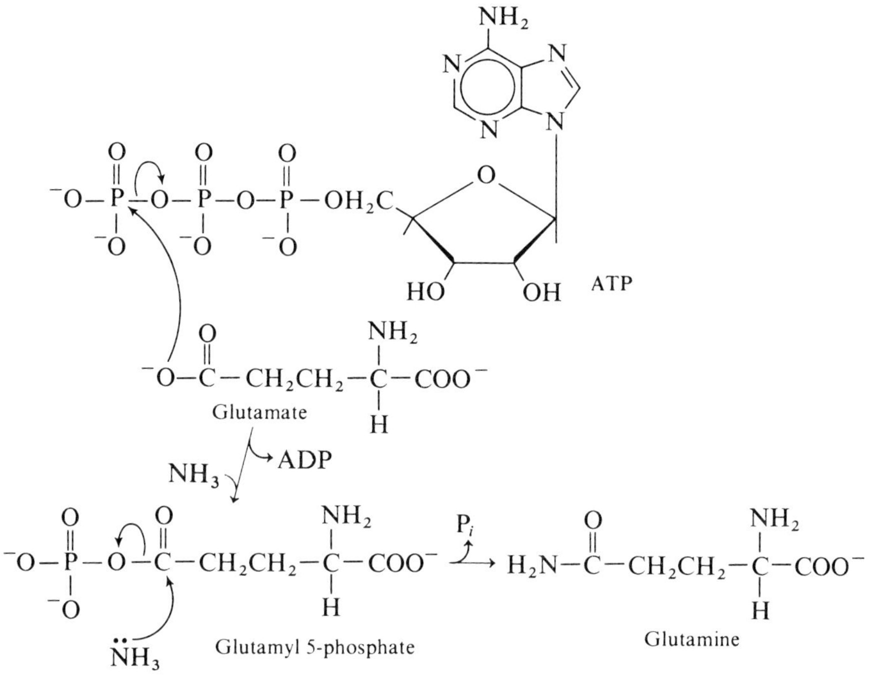

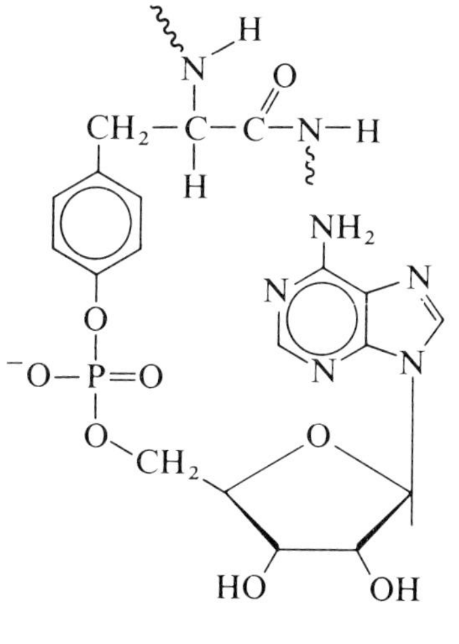

As a result of this modification, the activity of glutamine synthetase is inhibited. The adenylylation is catalyzed by glutamine-synthetase adenylyltransferase {ATP:[L-glutamate:ammonia ligase (ADP-forming)] adenylyltransferase, EC 2.7.7.42}. The reaction is

$$\text{ATP} + \text{glutamine synthetase} \rightleftharpoons \text{adenylyl-glutamine synthetase} + \text{PP}_i \tag{14-43a}$$

The adenylyltransferase, which has a molecular weight of 130,000, catalyzes both the adenylylation and the deadenylylation of glutamine synthetase. It does so, however, in conjunction with a smaller, noncatalytic regulatory protein. The regulatory protein, in fact, determines whether adenylylation or deadenylylation takes place. This regulatory protein, which has a molecular weight of 44,000 also exists in two forms. One is unmodified, while the other has undergone uridylylation. The nonmodified form promotes adenylylation of glutamine synthetase. The uridylylated form promotes deadenylylation of glutamine synthetase. Conversion of the unmodified form into the modified form is catalyzed by a uridylyltransferase which has a molecular weight of 160,000. As a result of the reaction catalyzed by this enzyme, one uridylyl moiety can become covalently bonded to each of the four identical subunits of the tetrameric regulatory protein.

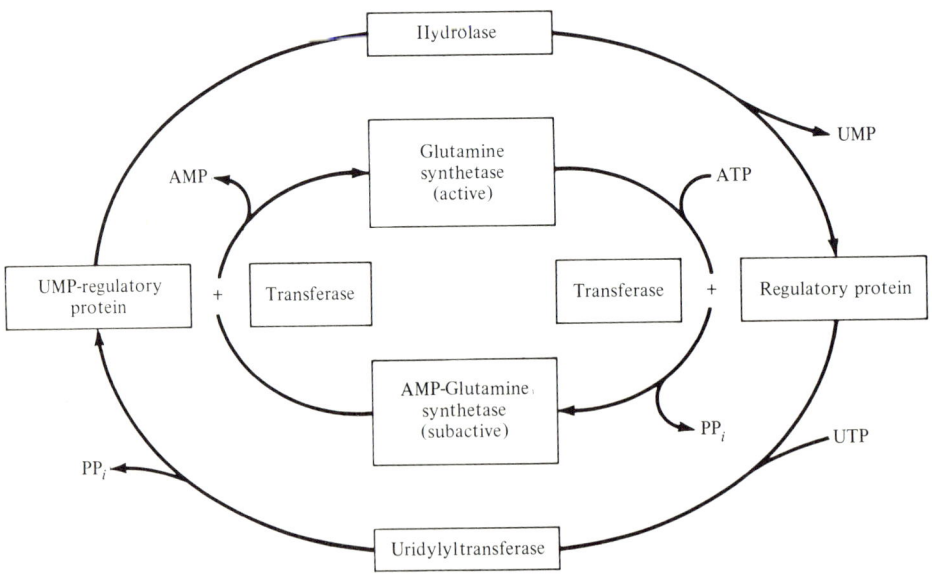

**Figure 14-4** A summary of the regulation of glutamine synthetase by means of covalent modification.

METABOLISM OF AMINO ACIDS AND PROTEINS **681**

Again, it is the tyrosyl units that undergo modification. The reaction can be written

UTP + regulatory protein $\rightleftharpoons$ uridylyl–regulatory protein + PP$_i$   (14-43b)

The deuridylylation of the regulatory protein is catalyzed by a hydrolase that converts the modified regulatory protein back into its nonmodified form. These events are summarized in Fig. 14-4. The inactivation process begins with the action of the hydrolase upon the uridylyl-regulatory protein which generates the non-

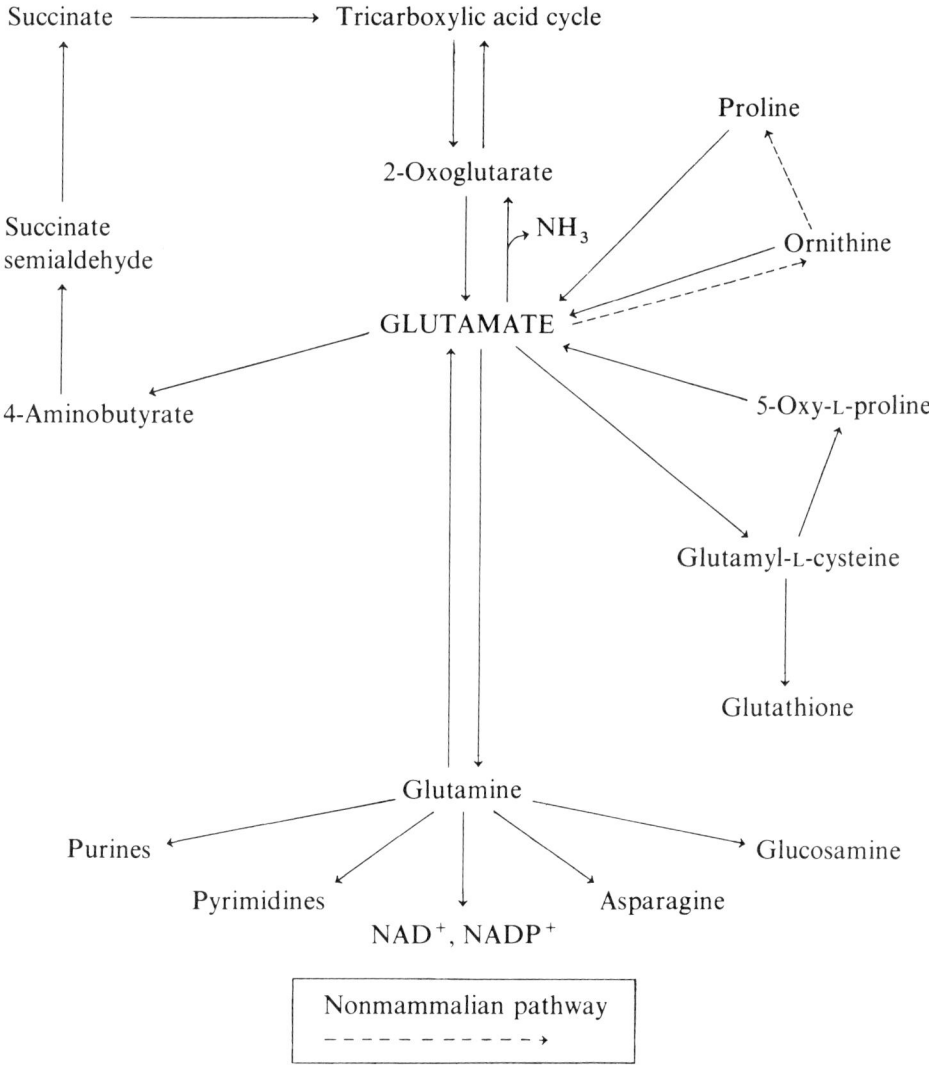

**Figure 14-5** A summary of the reactions involved in the metabolism of glutamate.

modified regulatory protein. This can now interact with the adenylyltransferase to yield a species that catalyzes the adenylylation of glutamine synthetase. As a concomitance of this adenylylation the active form of glutamine synthetase is converted to a subactive form. On the other hand, the activation process begins with the reaction that is catalyzed by the uridylyltransferase. This results in the formation of the uridylyl-regulatory protein which can then interact with the adenylyltransferase to yield a species that catalyzes the deadenylylation of the modified, subactive synthetase. As a concomitance of the deadenylylation the subactive form of the enzyme is converted to the active form.

As is frequently the case when a reaction is energy-dependent and subject to regulatory influences, the reverse reaction, here the deamidation of glutamine, is catalyzed by a distinctly different enzyme. This enzyme is glutaminase (L-glutamine amidohydrolase, EC 3.5.1.2). As a result of the reaction catalyzed by glutaminase glutamine is cleaved to yield glutamate and ammonia. The principal pathways involving the metabolism of glutamate are summarized in Fig. 14-5.

## Catabolism of Histidine

In mammals and certain microorganisms the principal route for the degradation of histidine begins with its deamination to yield urocanate. Subsequently, the remainder of the histidine molecule is converted into glutamate and a one-carbon unit in mammals or into glutamate and formamide or glutamate, formate, and ammonia in the microorganisms. The initial deamination reaction is catalyzed by histidine ammonia-lyase (L-histidine ammonia-lyase, EC 4.3.1.3). The reaction is

$$\text{L-Histidine} \rightleftharpoons \text{urocanate} + NH_3 \qquad (14\text{-}44)$$

The lyases that have been isolated from mammalian sources and purified generally have molecular weights of approximately 2.4 to $2.5 \times 10^5$. These lyases are presumably tetramers. On the other hand, most of that which is known concerning the reaction catalyzed by histidine ammonia-lyase has come from studies on enzymes from various microorganisms. For example, studies on the deamination reaction conducted using the lyase from *Pseudomonas* sp. (ATCC 112996) have indicated that the Schiff base of dehydroalanine participates in the elimination reaction:

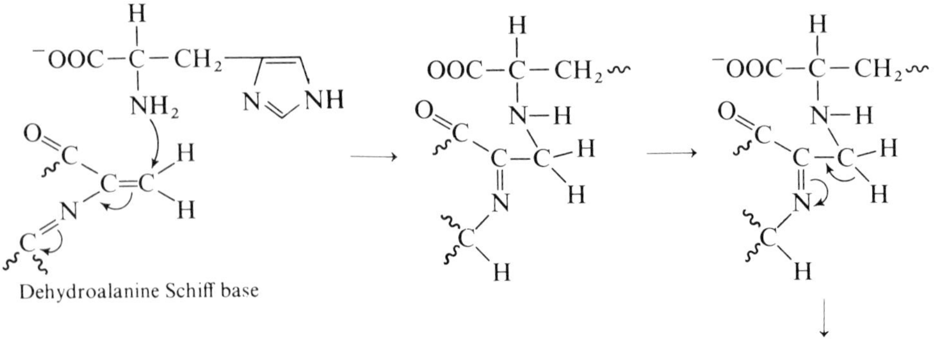

Dehydroalanine Schiff base

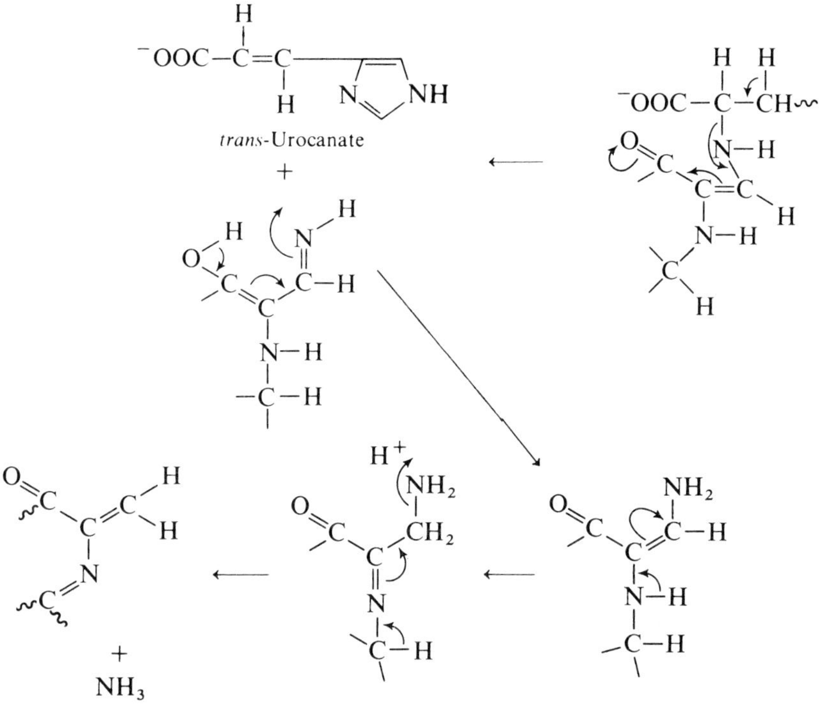

[Scheme showing mechanism with trans-Urocanate + NH₃]

There is an initial 1,4-addition of the histidine amino group across the conjugated system of the dehydroalanine Schiff base. The 1,3-prototropic rearrangement that follows generates a species in which the breaking of the C(2)—N bond of the histidine moiety is facilitated by the presence of the adjoining conjugated system. This is, in fact, the function of the dehydroalanine. Now it only remains for the ammonia to be eliminated from the cofactor. This is accomplished by the prototropic rearrangements shown above.

In the second step of the degradative pathway urocanate undergoes a hydration reaction that yields 4-imidazolone 5-propionate. Urocanate hydratase (4-imidazolone 5-propionate hydro-lyase, EC 4.2.1.49) catalyzes the reaction. Again, little is known concerning the mammalian hydratases, although the hydratase from the *Pseudomonas* has been isolated and purified and its catalytic reaction investigated. This hydratase is a dimer and it exhibits molecular weight of 110,000. The purified enzyme contains covalently bound 2-oxobutyrate, which participates in the reaction in the following manner:

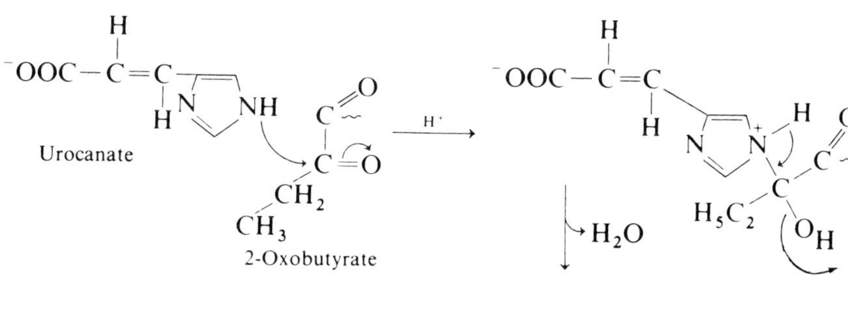

[Scheme showing Urocanate + 2-Oxobutyrate reaction with H⁺ and H₂O]

4-Imidazolone 5-propionate

Initially, a Schiff base is formed from a urocanate nitrogen atom and the oxo group of 2-oxobutyrate. This generates an extended conjugated system to which water is added. Again, the function of the cofactor, in this instance 2-oxobutyrate, is that of facilitating the reaction by providing a conjugated electron-accepting system. Now a proton is removed from the imidazole ring, and subsequently a proton is introduced at C(3) of the side chain. Hydrolysis of the Schiff base releases an enol product, which spontaneously undergoes tautomerism to yield the oxo form. A second tautomerism allows the oxo group to become conjugated with an olefinic bond, thus generating the product.

Next, 4-imidazolone 5-propionate undergoes a ring cleavage that is catalyzed by imidazolonepropionase (4-imidazolone 5-propionate amidohydrolase, EC 3.5.2.7). The reaction product is formiminoglutamate. A minimal mechanism for its formation is

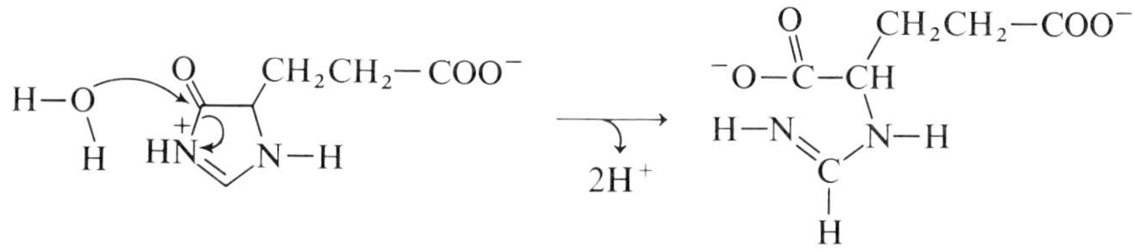

*N*-Formimino-L-glutamate

In mammals the final step of the degradative pathway entails the transfer of the formimino group of formiminoglutamate to N(5) of tetrahydrofolate. The enzyme glutamate formiminotransferase (5-formiminotetrahydrofolate:L-glutamate *N*-formiminotransferase, EC 2.1.2.5) catalyzes the reaction. The cofactor tetrahydrofolate is not involved in the terminal step or steps of the pathway in microorganisms, however. In *Salmonella typhimurium*, *Bacillus subtilis*, and *Aerobacter aerogenes*, for example, formiminoglutamate undergoes hydrolysis to yield glutamate and formamide, as catalyzed by formiminoglutamase (*N*-formimino-L-glutamate formiminohydrolase, EC 3.5.3.8). In *Pseudomonas* sp., on the other hand, formiminoglutamate is converted into ammonia and *N*-formylglutamate. The latter can subsequently be converted into glutamate and formate.

The major pathway for the degradation of histidine in mammals and in some microorganisms is summarized below, together with a secondary pathway which has also been demonstrated in mammals.

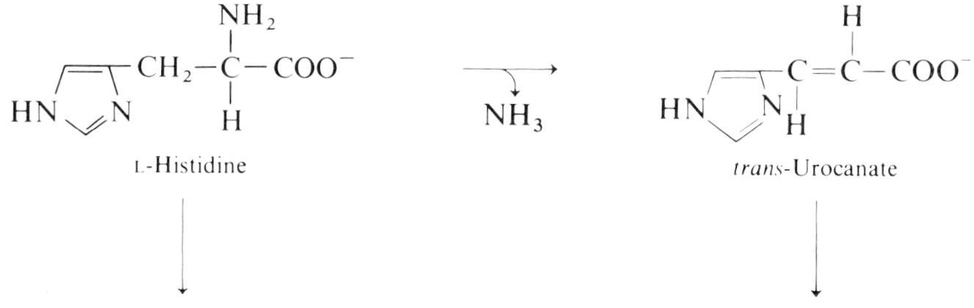

L-Histidine

*trans*-Urocanate

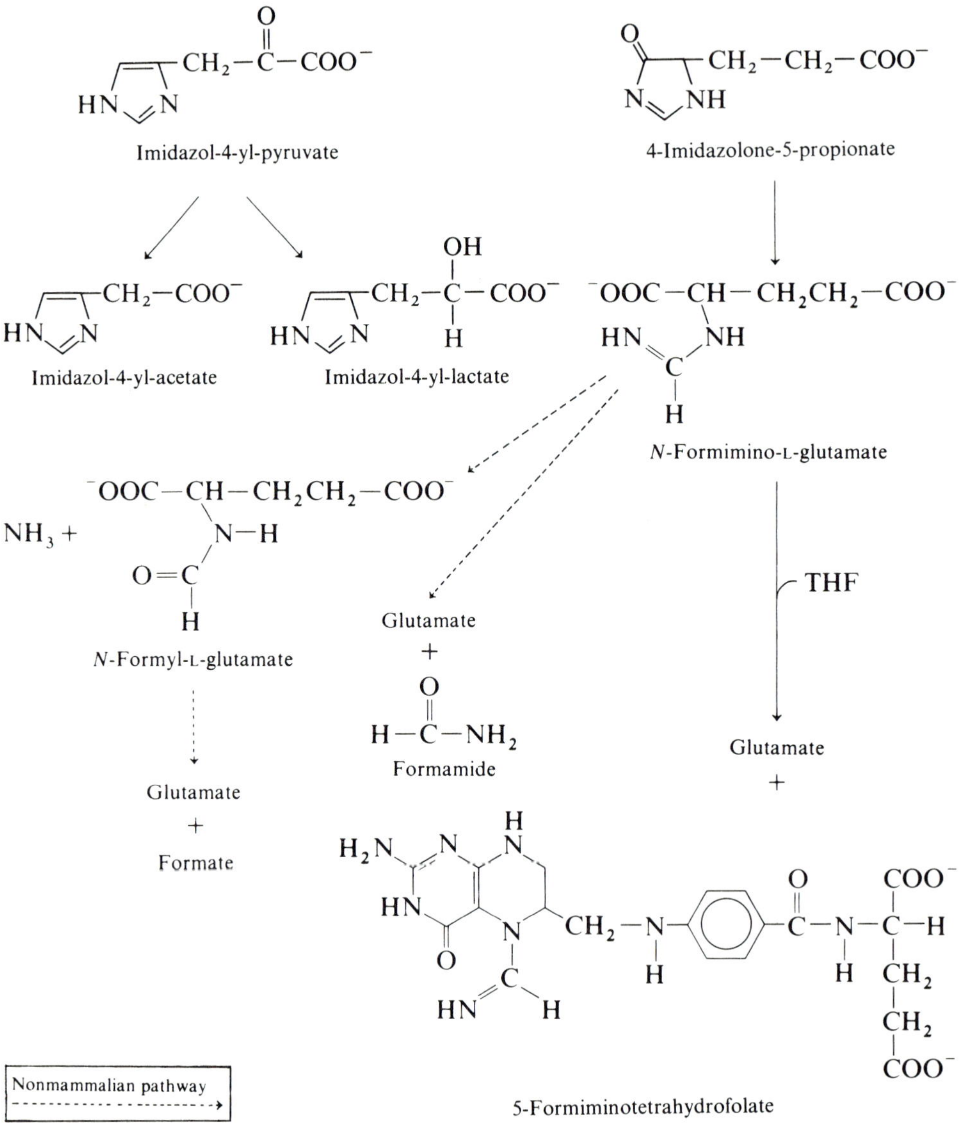

## 686 MECHANISMS OF METABOLISM

[Structures shown:]

Imidazol-4-yl-pyruvate

4-Imidazolone-5-propionate

Imidazol-4-yl-acetate

Imidazol-4-yl-lactate

N-Formimino-L-glutamate

N-Formyl-L-glutamate

Glutamate + Formamide

Glutamate + Formate

Glutamate

THF

Glutamate

5-Formiminotetrahydrofolate

Nonmammalian pathway

In several microorganisms, including *Salmonella typhimurium*, the synthesis of the enzymes involved in the degradation of histidine is subject to coordinate regulation. More specifically, the synthesis of the histidine ammonia-lyase, the urocanate hydratase, the imidazolonepropionase, and the formiminoglutamase is induced by histidine and repressed by glucose. The structural genes that specify these four enzymes plus the associated controlling elements constitute the *hut* (*h*istidine-*ut*ilization) operon.

## Anabolism of Histidine

The synthesis of histidine has not been demonstrated in man. In microorganisms, however, histidine is synthesized by a sequence of 10 reactions.

**Step 1: Formation of 1-(5′-phosphoribosyl)-ATP** The initial step of this anabolic pathway involves the utilization of ATP although not as an energy source. In this case, ATP undergoes an $N$-substitution reaction which subsequently allows N(1) and C(2) of the purine moiety of ATP to be incorporated into the histidine molecule.

The enzyme which catalyzes the initial reaction of this anabolic pathway is ATP phosphoribosyltransferase [1-(5′-phosphoribosyl)-ATP:pyrophosphate phosphoribosyltransferase, EC 2.4.2.17]. The reaction can be written

ATP + 5-phospho-α-D-ribose 1-diphosphate $\rightleftharpoons$

$$1\text{-}(5'\text{-phosphoribosyl})\text{-ATP} + \text{pyrophosphate} \quad (14\text{-}45)$$

As isolated from *Salmonella typhimurium* the phosphoribosyltransferase is a hexamer which has a molecular weight of 216,000. A minimal mechanism for the formation of the reaction products is shown below and on page 688.

**Step 2: Conversion of 1-(5′-phosphoribosyl)-ATP into 1-(5′-phosphoribosyl)-AMP** In the presence of a pyrophosphohydrolase, phosphoribosyl-ATP undergoes hydrolytic cleavage to yield phosphoribosyl-AMP.

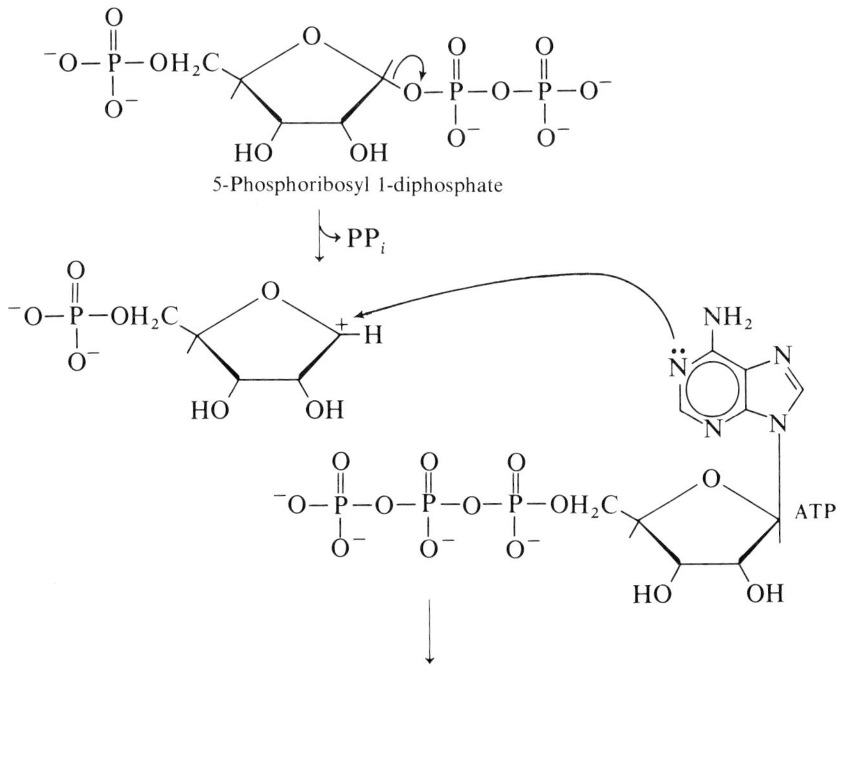

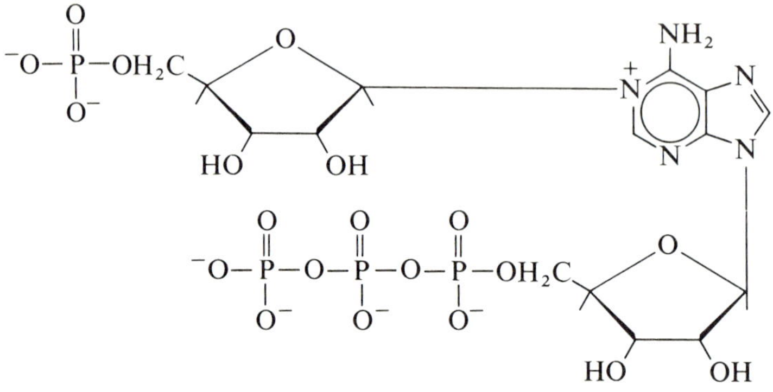

1-(5'-Phospho-β-D-ribosyl)-ATP

**Step 3: Cleavage of purine moiety** As mentioned above, two atoms of the purine ring system of ATP are subsequently incorporated into histidine. In preparation for this, the pyrimidine moiety of the purine ring system undergoes a ring-cleavage reaction catalyzed by phosphoribosyl-AMP cyclohydrolase [1-(5'-phospho-D-ribosyl)-AMP 1,6-hydrolase, EC 3.5.4.19]. This could come about in the following way.

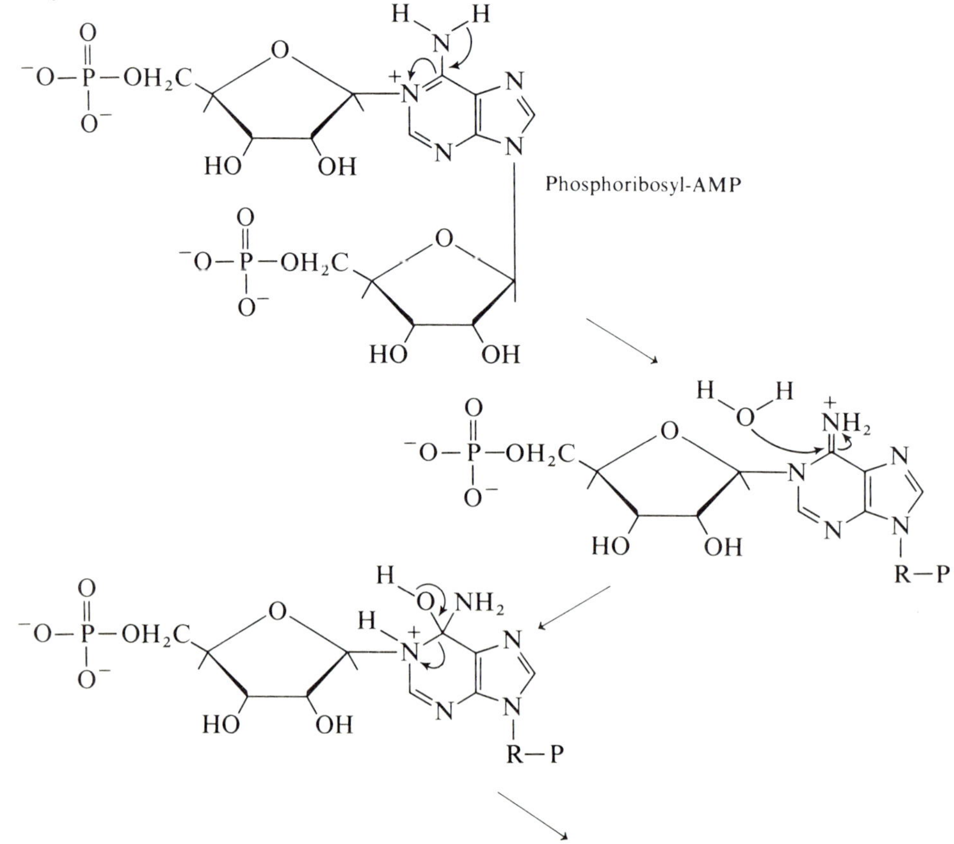

Phosphoribosyl-AMP

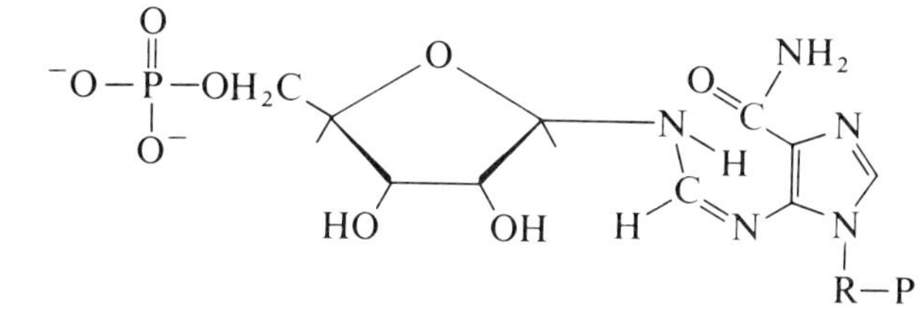

5-(5'-Phospho-D-ribosyl-aminoformimino)-1-(5''-phosphoribosyl)-4-imidazolecarboxamide

### Step 4: Cleavage of the ribose moiety derived from phosphoribosyl 1-diphosphate

Next, the ribosyl moiety bonded to the nitrogen atom that was N(1) of ATP undergoes hydrolytic cleavage and tautomerization. This is catalyzed by 5-(5'-phospho-D-ribosyl-aminoformimino-1-(5''-phosphoribosyl)-4-imidazolecarboxamide isomerase [5-(5''-phospho-D-ribosyl-aminoformimino)-1-(5''-phosphoribosyl) 4-imidazole carboxamide ketol-isomerase, EC 5.3.1.16]. The reaction is formulated as follows.

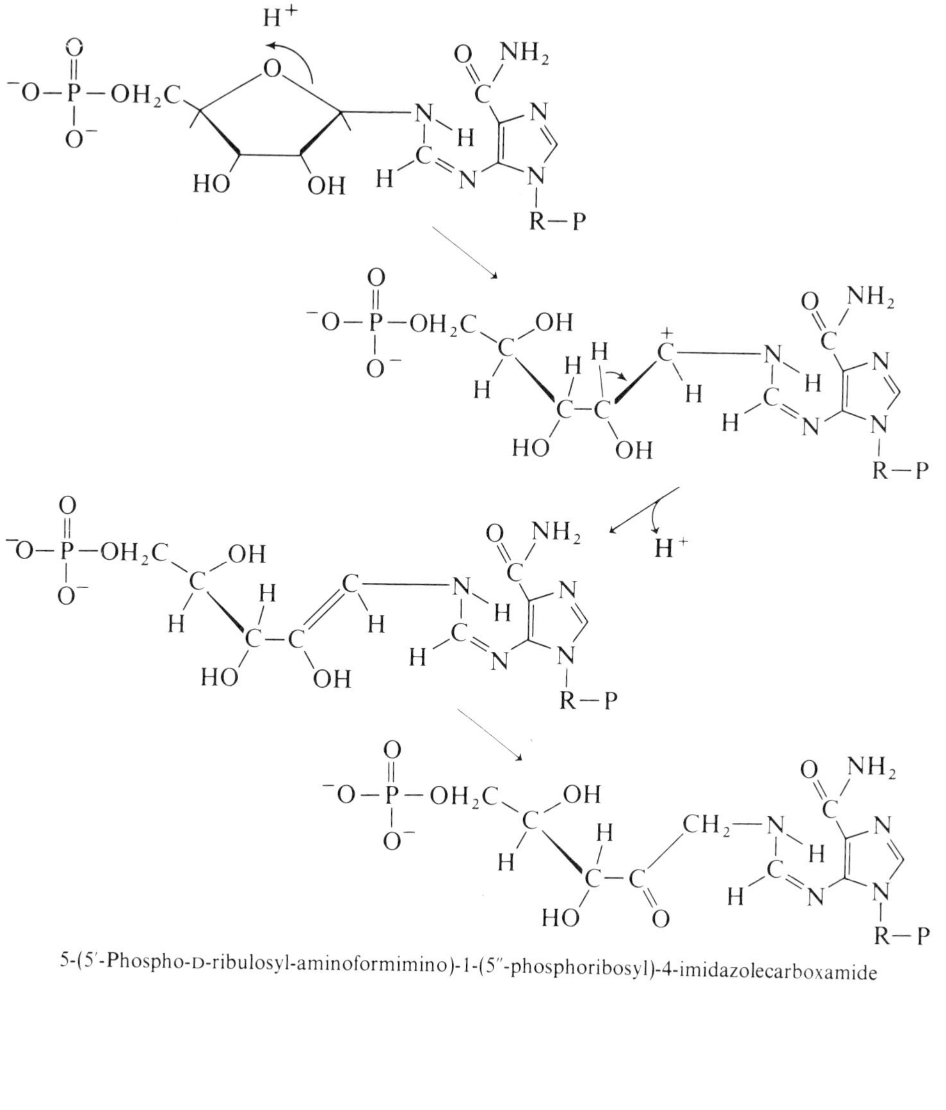

5-(5'-Phospho-D-ribulosyl-aminoformimino)-1-(5''-phosphoribosyl)-4-imidazolecarboxamide

**Steps 5 and 6: Introduction of a nitrogen atom of glutamine and ring closure** At this point, the three carbon atoms and one of the nitrogen atoms of the imidazole moiety of histidine are in place. The second nitrogen atom is now introduced, followed by ring closure. The nitrogen atom that is introduced is derived from glutamine, and although little is known concerning this reaction and the accompanying ring closure, a minimal reaction mechanism for these processes is suggested.

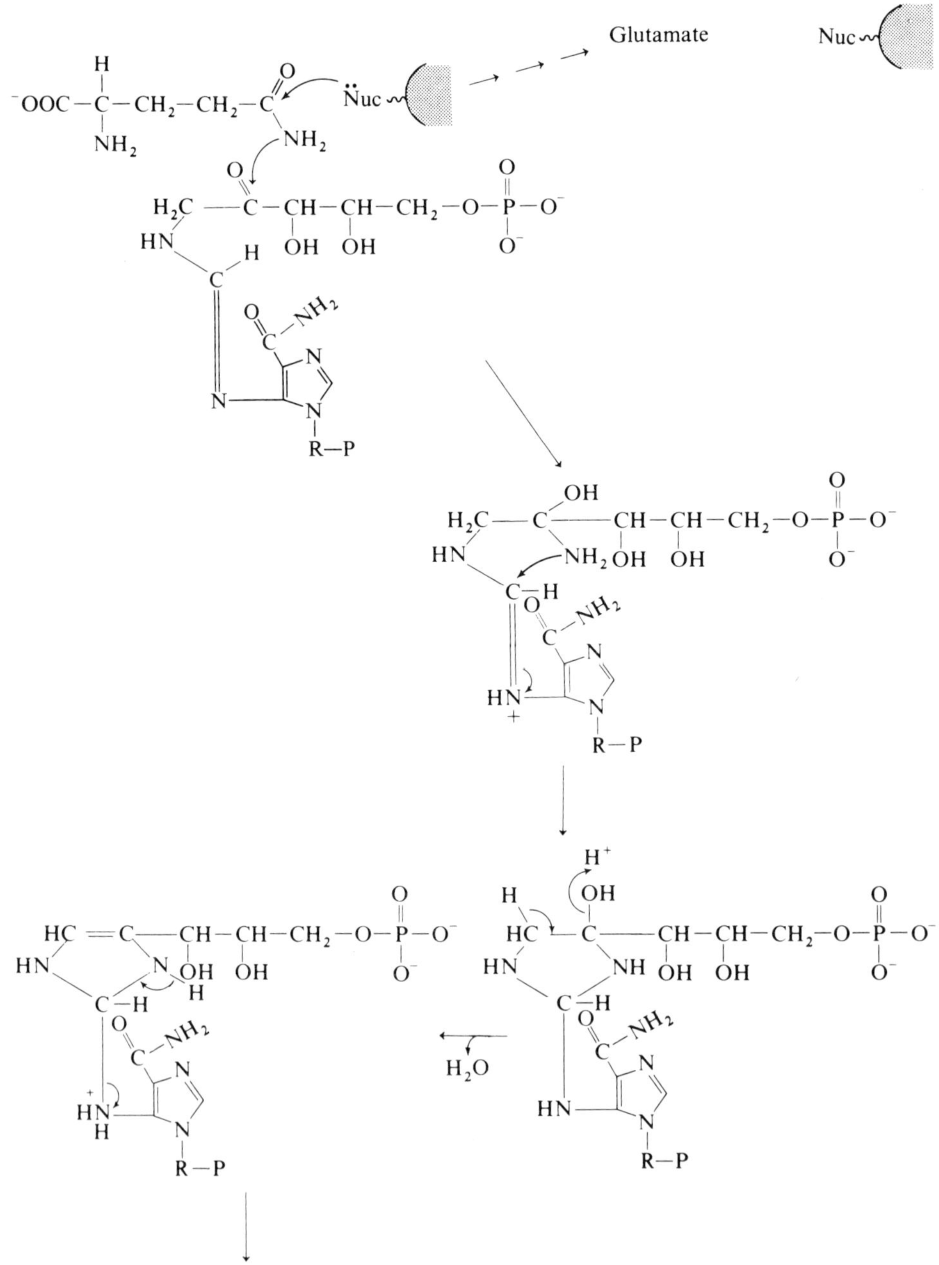

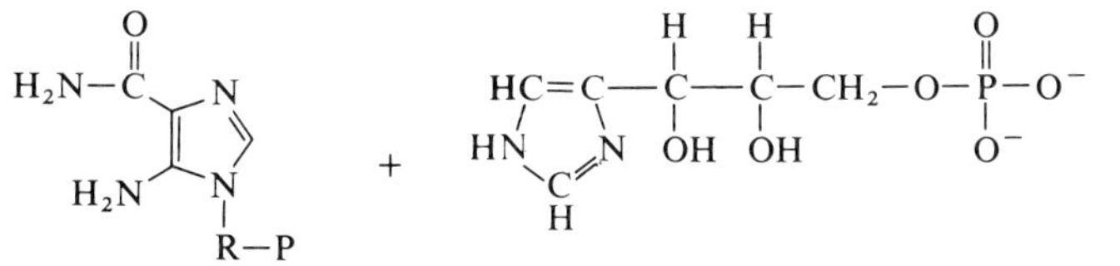

5′-Phosphoribosyl-5-amino-4-imidazolecarboxamide + D-*erythro*-Imidazoleglycerol phosphate

As a result of these reactions the imidazole moiety and the three-carbon side chain of histidine have been formed, along with an intermediate in the *de novo* synthesis of the purine ring system, 5′-phosphoribosyl-5-amino-4-imidazolecarboxamide.

**Step 7: Conversion of imidazoleglycerol phosphate into imidazoleacetol phosphate** In the next step of the pathway the elements of water are removed from the glycerol phosphate side chain. This is catalyzed by imidazoleglycerolphosphate dehydratase (D-*erythro*-imidazoleglycerolphosphate hydro-lase, EC 4.2.1.19). In *Salmonella typhimurium* a single protein exhibits both imidazoleglycerolphosphate dehydratase activity and histidinolphosphatase activity. The latter catalyzes the ninth step of this pathway. The bifunctional enzyme has a molecular weight of 75,000 and is thought to comprise two proteins of approximately equal size (37,000 and 38,000), one of which exhibits dehydratase activity while the other exhibits phosphatase activity. The dehydration of imidazoleglycerol phosphate, which is a diol, yields imidazoleacetol phosphate, as shown below.

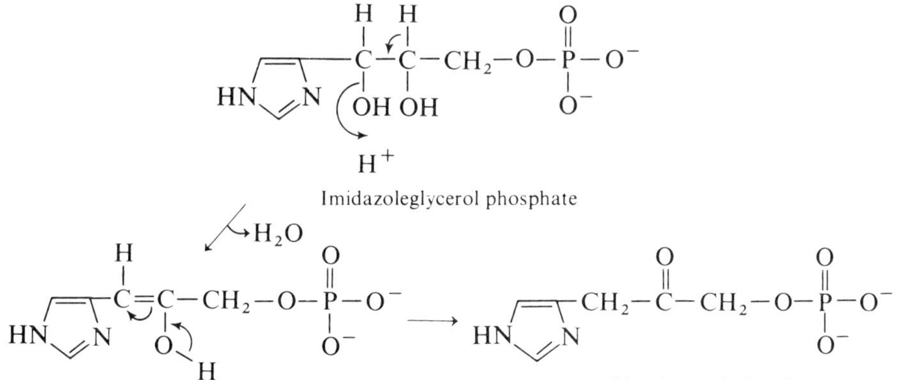

Imidazoleglycerol phosphate

Imidazoleacetol phosphate

**Steps 8 and 9: Transamination and dephosphorylation** Imidazoleacetol phosphate can now undergo transamination, as catalyzed by histidinol-phosphate aminotransferase (L-histidinol-phosphate:2-oxoglutarate aminotransferase, EC 2.6.1.9). This is followed by the removal of the phosphoryl group in the presence of the histidinolphosphatase (L-histidinol-phosphate phosphohydrolase, EC 3.1.3.15), mentioned above. Now all that remains is for the primary alcohol group of histidinol to be oxidized to a carboxylate group. This is accomplished in the tenth and final step of the anabolic pathway.

**Step 10: Formation of histidine** The final step of this pathway is catalyzed by histidinol dehydrogenase (L-histidinol:NAD$^+$ oxidoreductase, EC 1.1.1.23). The enzyme catalyzes both the oxidation of histidinol to the aldehyde histidinal and the oxidation of histidinal to histidine.

**Regulation of the synthesis of histidine** The synthesis of the enzymes that catalyze the 10 reactions involved in the synthesis of histidine is subject to coordinate regulation in *Salmonella typhimurium* and certain other prokaryotic organisms. The structural genes and the associated controlling elements constitute the *his* operon. Expression of these structural genes occurs only when the *his* repressor is not bound at the operator locus. The *his* repressor comprises the aporepressor, which is a protein specified by the regulator gene, and a corepressor, which has been identified as the aminoacylated histidyl transfer RNA; the latter reacts with the aporepressor, and the resulting active repressor can then bind appropriately at the operator locus of the *his* operon. Under these circumstances the anabolic pathway is "turned off." However, a low histidine concentration in the cell will be reflected by the inability to form the aminoacylated histidyl transfer RNA and hence the repressor. Under these circumstances, the anabolic pathway will be "turned on."

In addition to the mode of regulation described above, which constitutes a means of long-term control, another mode of regulation can provide a rapid response to fluctuations in histidine concentration. This is the inhibitory effect of the ultimate product, histidine, upon the activity of the enzyme that catalyzes the initial step of the reaction, ATP phosphoribosyltransferase. The synthesis of histidine in microorganisms is summarized below.

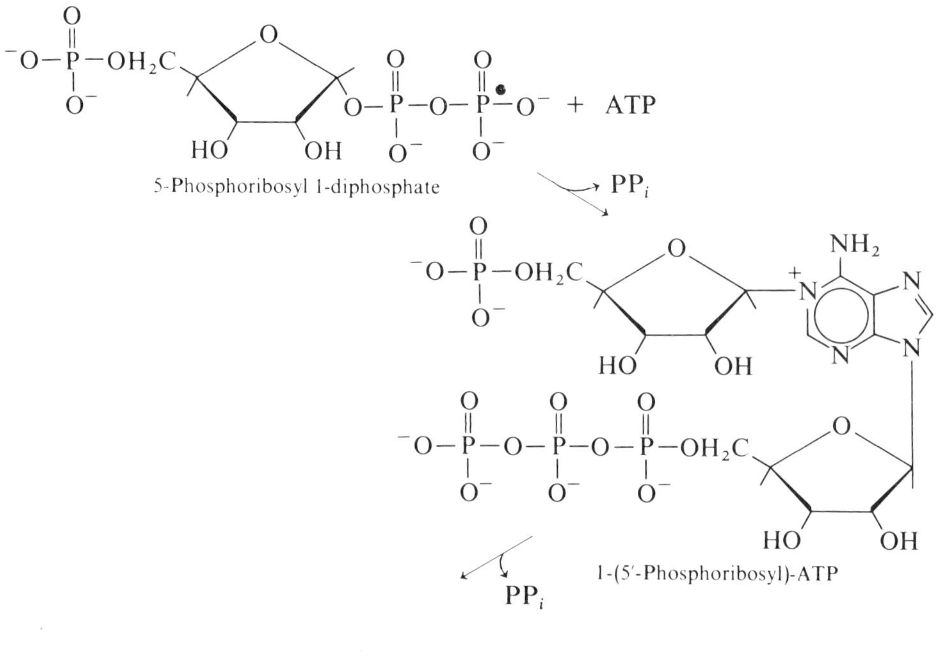

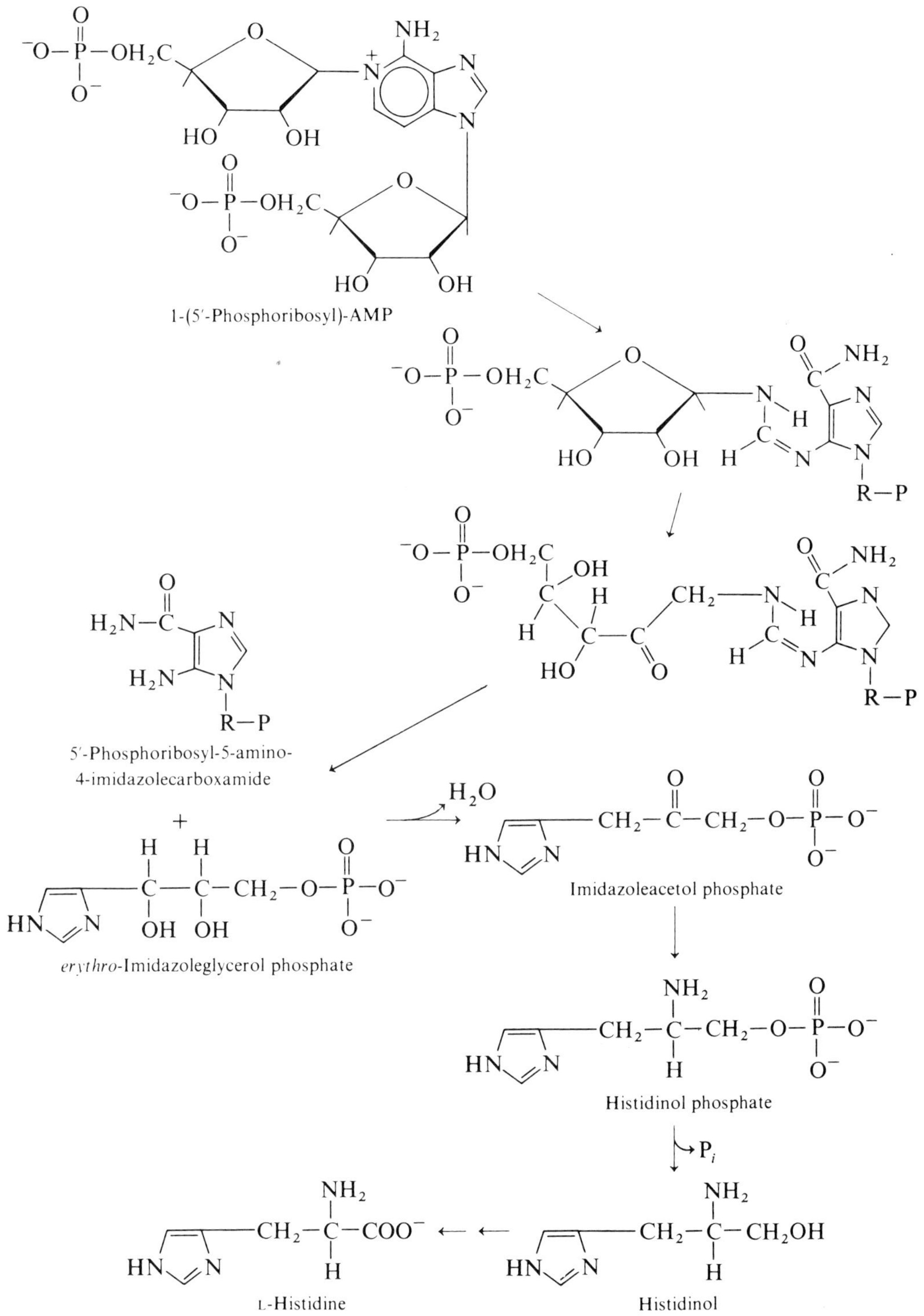

## METABOLISM OF AMINO ACIDS AND PROTEINS 693

1-(5'-Phosphoribosyl)-AMP

5'-Phosphoribosyl-5-amino-4-imidazolecarboxamide

erythro-Imidazoleglycerol phosphate

Imidazoleacetol phosphate

Histidinol phosphate

L-Histidine

Histidinol

# METABOLISM OF PHENYLALANINE, TYROSINE, AND TRYPTOPHAN

Phenylalanine, tyrosine, and tryptophan are the aromatic amino acids. Their metabolism includes some rather complex reactions involving the degradation or synthesis of the aromatic nucleus.

## Catabolism of Phenylalanine and Tyrosine

A single pathway is responsible for the degradation of phenylalanine and tyrosine since phenylalanine is readily converted into tyrosine. This pathway results in the formation of fumarate, which can enter the tricarboxylic acid cycle, and acetoacetate, which can be converted into two acetyl moieties of acetyl CoA in some tissues and into ketone bodies in the liver.

The conversion of phenylalanine into tyrosine is considered first. This reaction, which provides tyrosine for the living organism as long as there are adequate concentrations of phenylalanine and the other necessary components, entails the introduction of a hydroxyl group at C(4). The hydroxylation is catalyzed by phenylalanine 4-monooxygenase [L-phenylalanine, tetrahydropteridine:oxygen oxidoreductase (4-hydroxylating), EC 1.14.16.1]. The reaction can be written

$$\text{L-Phenylalanine} + \text{tetrahydropteridine} + O_2 \longrightarrow \text{L-tyrosine} + \text{dihydropteridine} + H_2O \quad (14\text{-}46)$$

As indicated, the tetrahydropteridine cofactor is oxidized as a concomitance of the hydroxylation reaction. It is subsequently reduced back to its initial oxidation level as a result of the following reaction, catalyzed by dihydropteridine reductase (NADPH:6,7-dihydropteridine oxidoreductase, EC 1.6.99.7):

$$\text{NADPH} + 6{,}7\text{-dihydropteridine} \rightleftharpoons \text{NADP}^+ + 5{,}6{,}7{,}8\text{-tetrahydropteridine} \quad (14\text{-}47)$$

As isolated from rat liver, phenylalanine 4-monooxygenase is a dimer which has a molecular weight of 100,000. The enzyme binds (high-spin $d^5$) iron, which is thought to interact either directly or indirectly with the molecular oxygen. The reaction mechanism proposed for the hydroxylation of phenylalanine involves the formation of an epoxide as a transient intermediate. This mechanism, shown below, takes into consideration the observation that a hydrogen atom migrates from C(4) to C(3) as a concomitance of the hydroxylation.

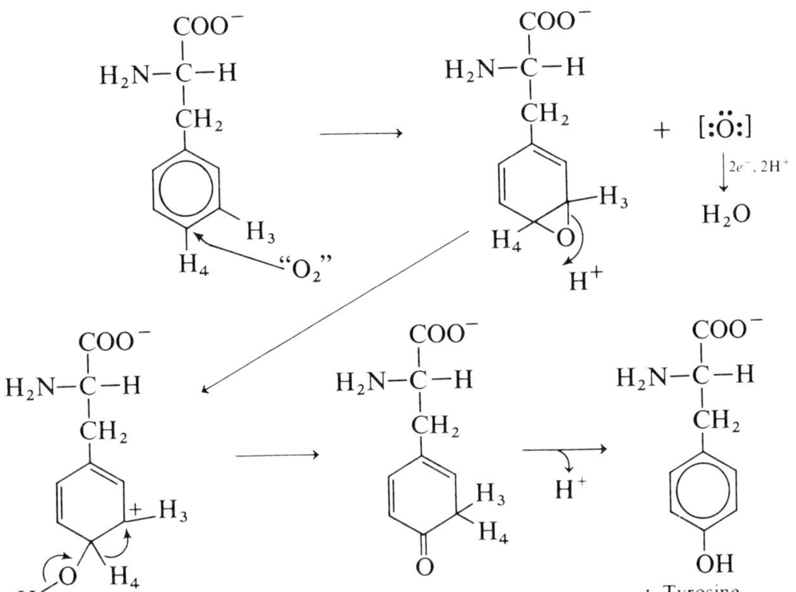

According to this mechanism, molecular oxygen, in an activated form, interacts at C(4) of the aromatic ring with the result that one oxygen atom is incorporated into the amino acid substrate and thereby reduced. The other oxygen atom also becomes reduced, as it is converted into an oxygen atom of water, with NADPH as the ultimate electron donor. The epoxide is subsequently opened, and an oxo intermediate is formed. This is then converted into the product, tyrosine, as the aromaticity of the ring is reestablished. Of the four electrons required to reduce molecular oxygen completely, two are provided by the amino acid substrate and two are ultimately provided by the reduced pyridine nucleotide cofactor. The tetrahydropteridine which has been shown to be specifically 5,6,7,8-tetrahydrobiopterin, participates in the hydroxylation reaction as a component of an electron-transport system, that conveys reducing equivalents from NADPH to an oxygen atom. During the transport process the tetrahydropteridine donates two electrons to an acceptor and is thereby converted into a quinoid form of dihydropteridine.

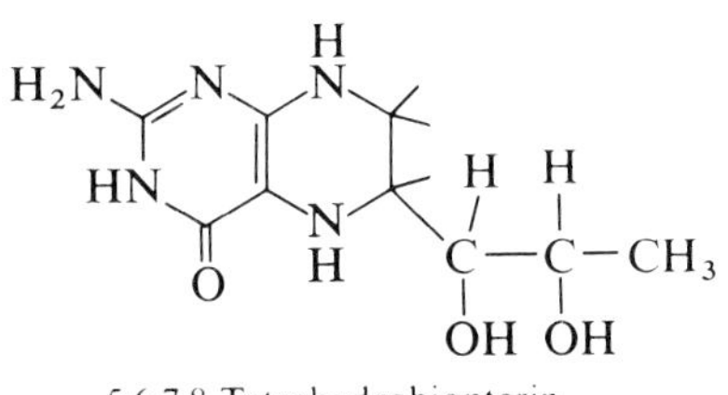

5,6,7,8-Tetrahydrobiopterin
(a tetrahydropteridine)

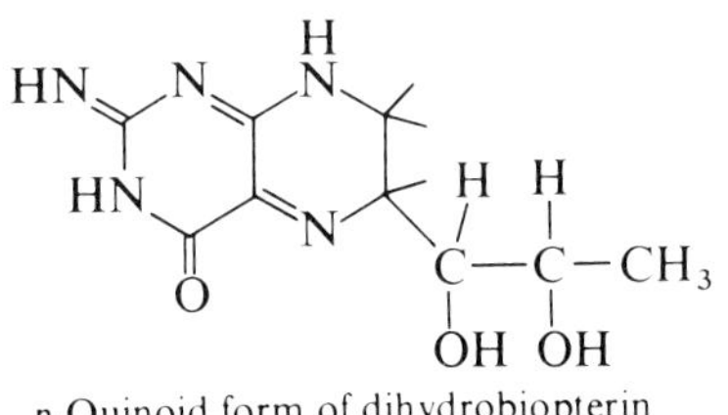

$p$-Quinoid form of dihydrobiopterin
(a dihydropteridine)

This is converted back into the tetrahydro compound by the dihydropteridine reductase. Only the quinoid form of dihydropteridine can serve as a substrate for this reductase. (The tetrahydropteridine cofactor is derived initially from 7,8-dihydrobiopterin

$$\text{H}_2\text{N}\begin{array}{c}\text{N}\\\text{HN}\end{array}\begin{array}{c}\text{H}\\\text{N}\\\text{N}\end{array}\begin{array}{c}\text{H H}\\|\ \ |\\\text{C}-\text{C}-\text{CH}_3\\|\ \ |\\\text{OH OH}\end{array}$$

7,8-Dihydrobiopterin

through the agency of a distinctly different enzyme which is probably tetrahydrofolate dehydrogenase. The conversion of the 7,8-dihydropteridine into the tetrahydropteridine can be viewed as an initiating step. Once the hydroxylation reaction is occurring, the cofactor oscillates between the tetrahydro form and the quinoid dihydro form.)

**Phenylketonuria** Phenylketonuria is a hereditary disease characterized by an elevation in the concentration of phenylalanine in the blood, the excretion of phenylpyruvate, phenyllactate, $N$-acetylphenylalanine, and abnormal quantities of phenylalanine, and neurologic damage. The disease results from a virtual absence of phenylalanine monooxygenase activity. Under these conditions phenylalanine undergoes transamination, catalyzed by tyrosine aminotransferase, to yield phenylpyruvate, which in turn can undergo reduction to yield phenyllactate. Some of the symptoms of phenylketonuria are manifested a few weeks after birth, and generally by the sixth month mental retardation is evident. Most patients afflicted with phenylketonuria are severely retarded although some are only moderately or even mildly retarded. Normal intellectual development at even a low level is rare. The disease is transmitted by an autosomal recessive gene.

**Conversion of tyrosine into homogentisate** The degradation of tyrosine is initiated by its conversion into 4-hydroxyphenylpyruvate as catalyzed by tyrosine aminotransferase (L-tyrosine:2-oxoglutarate aminotransferase, EC 2.6.1.5). In man and other mammals the enzyme tyrosine aminotransferase exists in both cytoplasmic and mitochondrial forms. The activity of the former is subject to diurnal variation as well as certain hormonal controls. (As an example of the latter, the synthesis of the enzyme can be induced by hydrocortisone and certain other adrenocorticosteroids.) Also, an absence of cytoplasmic tyrosine aminotransferase activity is responsible for one type of tyrosinemia.

Continuing with the degradative process, 4-hydroxyphenylpyruvate can undergo decarboxylation, hydroxylation, and rearrangement to yield homogentisate. This reaction is catalyzed by another oxygenase, this time, a dioxygenase, 4-hydroxyphenylpyruvate dioxygenase [4-hydroxyphenylpyruvate:oxygen oxidoreductase (hydroxylating, decarboxylating), EC 1.13.11.27], and is

$$\text{4-Hydroxyphenylpyruvate} + O_2 \rightleftharpoons \text{homogentisate} + CO_2 \quad (14\text{-}48)$$

This dioxygenase has been isolated from several mammalian sources, including human liver.

As implied by the name of the enzyme, the conversion of 4-hydroxyphenylpyruvate into homogentisate entails the incorporation of both atoms of molecular oxygen into the product. Also, in this case, all four of the electrons that are required for the complete reduction of the molecular oxygen are derived from the oxo acid substrate, as illustrated below.†

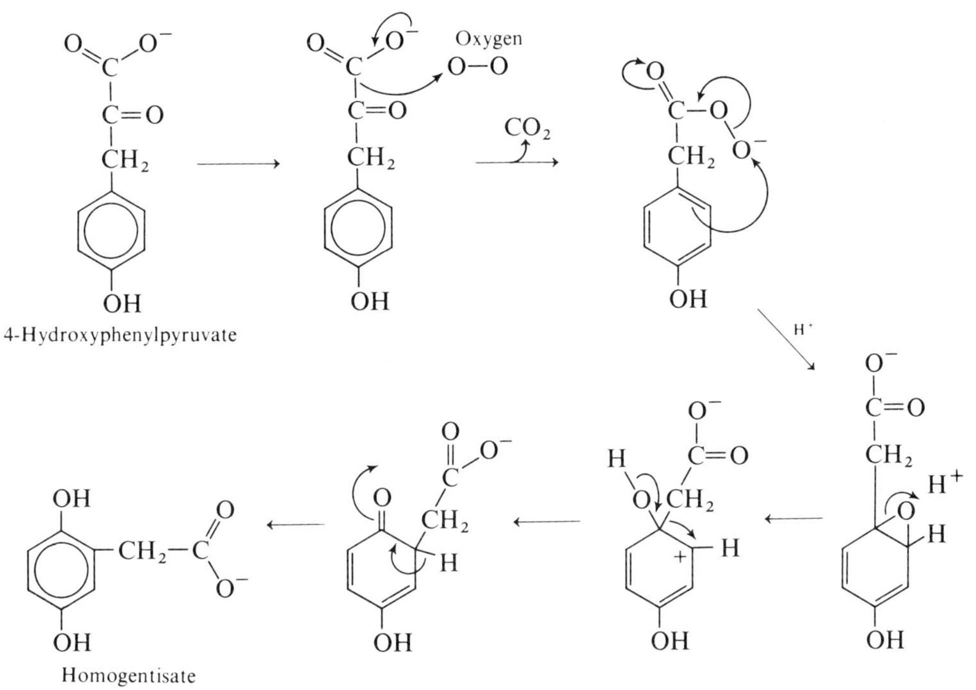

The reaction can thus be formulated in a manner similar to the hydroxylation of phenylalanine but with an additional pair of electrons being derived from the oxo acid substrate as a result of the decarboxylation reaction.

**Formation of fumarate and acetoacetate** Homogentisate undergoes an oxidative ring cleavage which results in the formation of maleylacetoacetate. This is catalyzed by another dioxygenase, homogentisate 1,2-dioxygenase [homogentisate:oxygen

---

† Based on data from Hamilton, G. A. (1971) in *Progress in Bioorganic Chemistry* (Kaiser, E. T., and Kezdy, F. J., eds.), vol. 1, pp. 83-157, Academic, New York. See also Abbott, M. T., and Udenfriend, S. (1974) in *Molecular Mechanisms of Oxygen Activation* (Hayaishi, O., ed.), pp. 167-214, Academic, New York.

1,2-oxidoreductase (decyclizing), EC 1.13.11.5]. Homogentisate 1,2-dioxygenase has been obtained from mammalian sources, e.g., bovine liver, as well as from microorganisms, e.g., *Pseudomonas fluorescens*, and in all cases the enzyme requires ferrous iron in order to be catalytically active. This dioxygenase reaction is somewhat less complicated than the previous one. A minimal reaction mechanism in effect entails the addition of the oxygen molecule across the carbon-carbon bond that is to be severed.

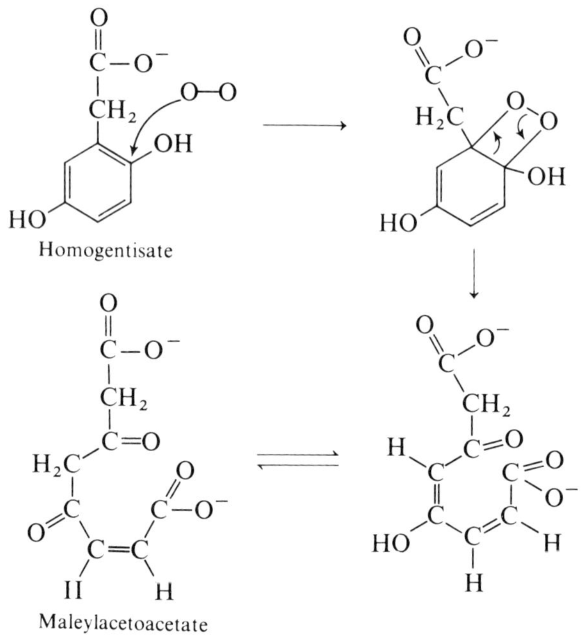

**Alcaptonuria.** A rare hereditary disease known as alcaptonuria has been shown to be a manifestation of the absence of homogentisate 1,2-dioxygenase activity. Under these circumstances homogentisate accumulates in the body and is voided in the urine, which may turn black upon standing as a result of the oxidation and polymerization of the homogentisate to yield a dark-colored polymer. In addition, the person generally exhibits ochronosis, or pigmentation of the cartilage and other connective tissues. This pigmentation is probably due to deposits of the same polymeric material that is responsible for the darkening of the urine. In the later years, the person with alcaptonuria usually develops arthritis. The disease is thought to be transmitted as a recessive trait.

**Conversion of maleylacetoacetate into fumarate and acetoacetate** Maleylacetoacetate readily undergoes cis-trans isomerization to yield fumarylacetoacetate. This reaction is catalyzed by maleylacetoacetate isomerase (4-maleylacetoacetate *cis-trans*-isomerase, EC 5.2.1.2). It has been suggested that the cis-trans isomerization results from the addition of a sulfhydryl anion (or radical) to the double bond, thus generating a species in which there can be rotation about the C(6)—C(7) olefinic bond.

Finally, fumarylacetoacetase (4-fumarylacetoacetate fumarylhydrolase, EC 3.7.1.2) catalyzes the hydrolytic cleavage of fumarylacetoacetate to yield fumarate and acetoacetate. The cleavage has been formulated in terms of the participation of a nucleophilic functional group that can react with the C(5) oxo group of the substrate.

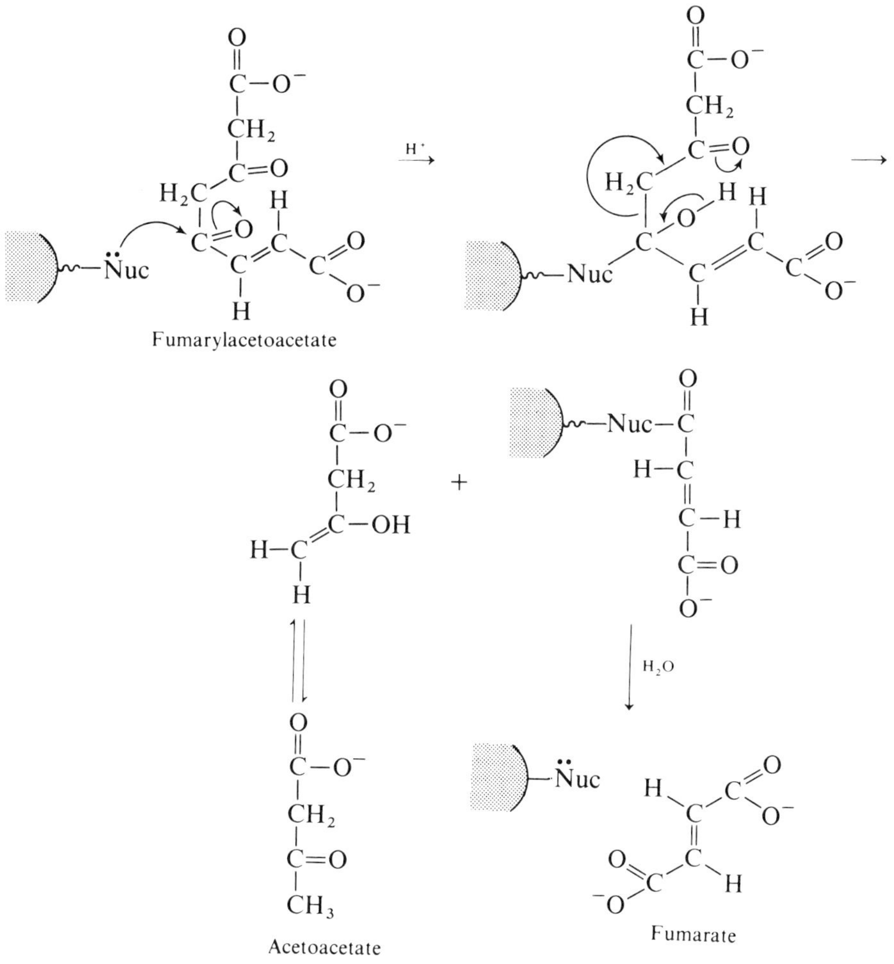

**Summary of phenylalanine and tyrosine catabolism** The degradation of these two aromatic amino acids is summarized below.

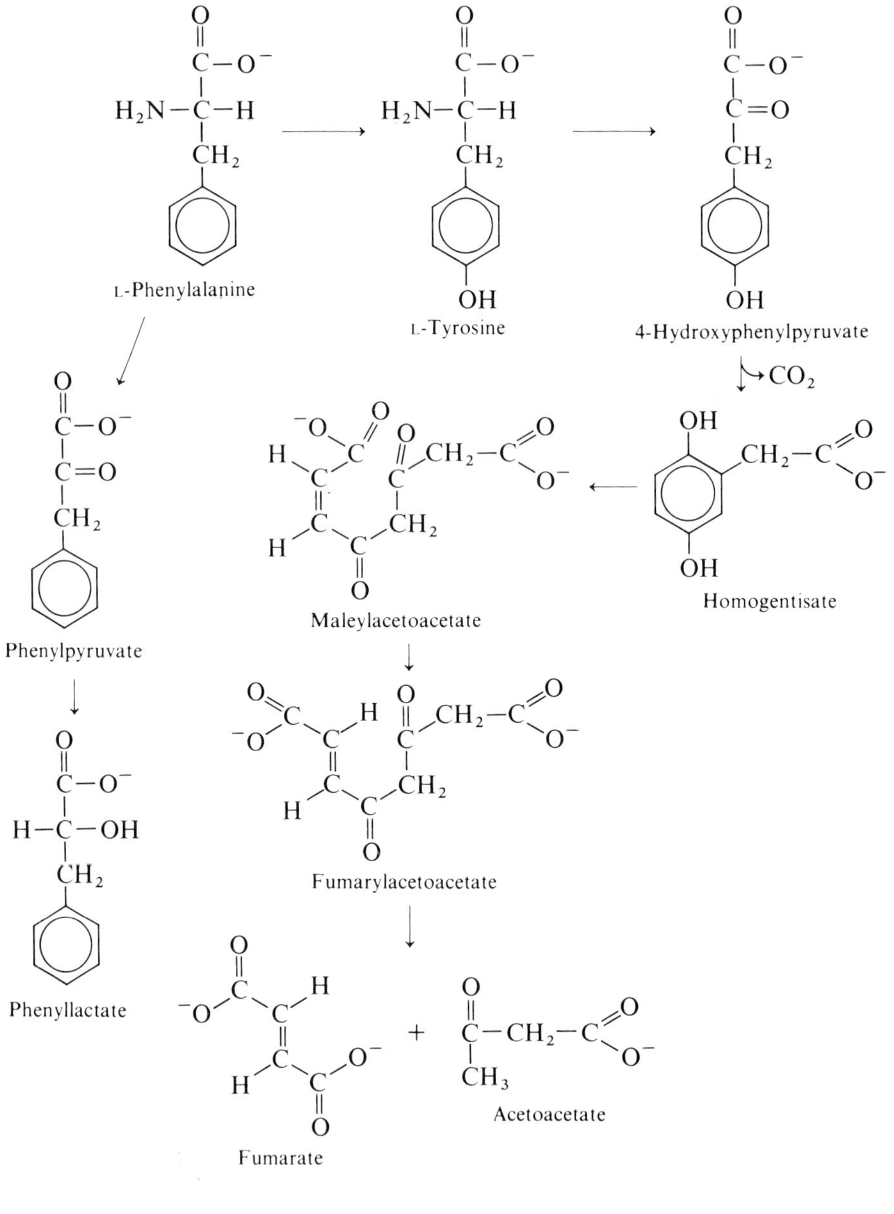

## Utilization of Tyrosine in the Synthesis of Catecholamines

Tyrosine is a precursor of the catecholamines norepinephrine and epinephrine. When tyrosine is to be converted into the catecholamines, it initially undergoes a hydroxylation reaction catalyzed by tyrosine 3-monooxygenase [L-tyrosine, tetrahydropteridine:oxygen oxidoreductase (3-hydroxylating), EC 1.14.16.2]. The product of the reaction is 3,4-dihydroxy-L-phenylalanine (also known as dopa). This hydroxylation reaction parallels that by which phenylalanine is converted into tyrosine. Thus, the reaction requires molecular oxygen and a tetrahydropteridine, which is probably the same as that participating in the reaction catalyzed by phenylalanine 4-monooxygenase.

Since the conversion of tyrosine into 3,4-dihydroxyphenylalanine is the rate-determining step in the synthesis of the catecholamines, it is not surprising that the activity of tyrosine 3-monooxygenase is subject to modulation. More specifically, the activity of the monooxygenase from mammalian peripheral adrenergic tissues and from the brain is subject to inhibition by the ultimate product, norepinephrine. The activity of tyrosine 3-monooxygenase from rat brain is also enhanced in the presence of 3′,5′-AMP, ATP, and a protein kinase. Thus, there is the possibility of modulation as a result of chemical modification.

Dihydroxyphenylalanine undergoes decarboxylation in the presence of aromatic-L-amino-acid decarboxylase (aromatic-L-amino acid carboxy-lyase, EC 4.1.1.28). The enzyme, in fact, catalyzes the decarboxylation reactions involved in the syntheses of several biogenic amines, including tryptamine and serotonin, in addition to the catecholamines. In the latter case, the decarboxylation product is 3,4-dihydroxyphenylethylamine.

Next, 3,4-dihydroxyphenylethylamine undergoes hydroxylation at C(2) of the side chain to yield norepinephrine. The hydroxylation is catalyzed by dopamine (or dihydroxyphenylethylamine) monooxygenase [3,4-dihydroxyphenylethylamine, ascorbate:oxygen oxidoreductase (hydroxylating), EC 1.14.17.1], a copper-containing protein which utilizes ascorbate as an electron donor. The activity of the monooxygenase is subject to modulation under certain circumstances. For example, activation of the splanchnic nerves to the adrenal medulla by reserpine induces synthesis of the enzyme. The rate at which the enzyme is degraded, on the other hand, is thought to be subject to hormonal control.

The conversion of norepinephrine into epinephrine entails an S-adenosyl-methionine-dependent N-methylation that is catalyzed by norepinephrine N-methyltransferase (S-adenosyl-L-methionine:phenylethanolamine N-methyltransferase, EC 2.1.1.28). The formation of the catecholamines from tyrosine is summarized below.

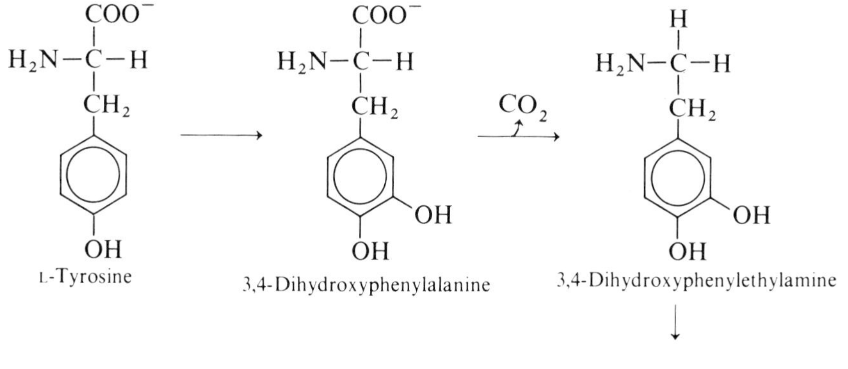

$$\underset{\text{Epinephrine}}{\begin{array}{c} \text{H} \\ | \\ \text{H}_3\text{C}-\text{N}-\text{CH}_2 \\ \text{HO}-\text{C}-\text{H} \\ | \\ \text{C}_6\text{H}_3(\text{OH})_2 \end{array}} \longleftarrow \underset{\text{Norepinephrine}}{\begin{array}{c} \text{H}_2\text{N}-\text{CH}_2 \\ | \\ \text{HO}-\text{C}-\text{H} \\ | \\ \text{C}_6\text{H}_3(\text{OH})_2 \end{array}}$$

## Utilization of Tyrosine in the Synthesis of Melanin

Melanin is a macromolecular species that imparts color to the epidermis. In the absence of melanin the isolated epidermis is a transparent grayish-white membrane. The range of human skin colors is a manifestation of the variations in the number, arrangement, and distribution throughout the epidermis of melanosomes, the granular organelles containing the chromoprotein melanin. In human tissues melanin occurs as a melanoprotein complex, which is formed from the melanin macromolecule and a protein matrix.

The synthesis of melanin begins with tyrosine. Although a detailed pathway has not been completely formulated, it is known that initially tyrosine is converted into 3,4-dihydroxyphenylalanine, which is then further oxidized to a quinoid species, dioxophenylalanine. The enzyme monophenol monooxygenase (monophenol, dihydroxyphenylalanine:oxygen oxidoreductase, EC 1.14.18.1) catalyzes the formation of dioxophenylalanine, which is formed in accordance with the equation

L-Tyrosine + dihydroxyphenylalanine + $O_2$ $\rightleftharpoons$

dihydroxyphenylalanine + dioxophenylalanine + $H_2O$ (14-49)

It has been speculated that dioxophenylalanine can be converted into certain dihydroxyindole derivatives which together with their precursors form the pigment melanin.

A hereditary metabolic defect in the synthesis of melanin results in albinism, which occurs in man, other mammals, fishes, amphibians, reptiles, and birds. In man the metabolic aberration affects the skin, the mucous membranes, the eye, e.g., the retinal pigment epithelium, the hair, and certain portions of the nervous system, e.g., the piarachnoid.

## Anabolism of Phenylalanine and Tyrosine in Microorganisms

The syntheses of the three aromatic amino acids are interrelated, just as is their catabolism. The syntheses of phenylalamine, tyrosine, and tryptophan begin with the condensation of 2-phosphoenolpyruvate and erythrose 4-phosphate and proceeds through seven steps to the formation of chorismate. At this juncture, there is a bifurcation of the pathways with one route leading to the synthesis of phenylalanine or tyrosine while the other leads to that of tryptophan. Here the formation of phenylalanine and tyrosine will be discussed.

**Step 1: Condensation of phosphoenolpyruvate and erythrose 4-phosphate** The initial and generally rate-determining step of the pathways is the condensation reaction catalyzed by phospho-2-oxo-3-deoxy-heptonate aldolase [7-phospho-2-oxo-3-deoxy-D-*arabino*heptonate D-erythrose 4-phosphate-lyase (pyruvate-phosphorylating), EC 4.1.2.15], which can be written

2-Phosphoenolpyruvate + D-erythrose 4-phosphate + $H_2O$ ⇌

$\qquad$ 7-phospho-2-oxo-3-deoxy-D-*arabino*heptonate + $P_i$ (14-50)

Most bacteria, yeasts, and molds contain three distinct enzymes that catalyze this reaction. The activity of one is modulated by phenylalanine, that of the second, by tyrosine, and that of the third by tryptophan. Among the aldolases which have been isolated and purified is a tyrosine-sensitive enzyme from *Salmonella typhimurium* which has a molecular weight of 100,000. The kinetic studies on this aldolase indicate that a sequential mechanism is operative and that phosphoenolpyruvate is the initial substrate that binds while 7-phospho-2-oxo-3-deoxy-D-*arabino*heptonate is the final product released. These conclusions are based upon the observation that the seven-carbon acid is a competitive product inhibitor when phosphoenolpyruvate is varied while it is a noncompetitive product inhibitor when erythrose 4-phosphate is varied. Orthophosphate is a noncompetitive product inhibitor vs. each substrate. With respect to the reaction mechanism, it was demonstrated that the elimination of orthophosphate entails C—O, rather than P—O, cleavage since when phosphoenolpyruvate labeled with $^{18}O$ in the monoester bond was used, the label was recovered in the orthophosphate. A minimal mechanism which takes this into consideration is shown below.

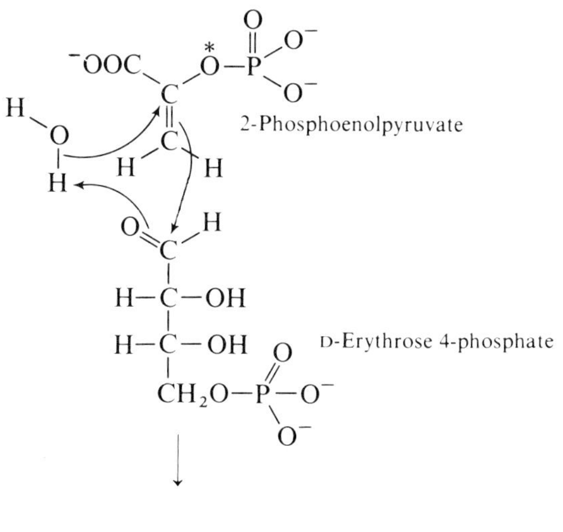

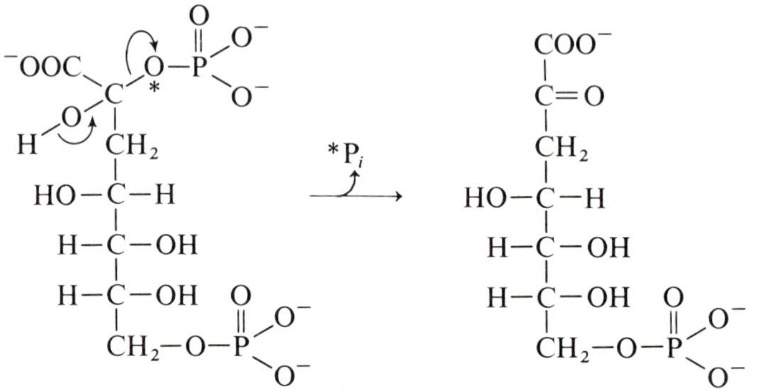

[Structural formulas showing conversion to 7-Phospho-2-oxo-3-deoxy-D-*arabino*-heptonate, with *P_i* released]

In some bacteria at least, e.g., *Bacillus subtilis*, the aldolase exists as a part of an aggregate which includes other enzymes also involved in the synthesis of the aromatic amino acids. In *B. subtilis* the aggregate also contains shikimate kinase and chorismate mutase.

**Step 2: Cyclization to form 3-dehydroquinate** In the next step of the pathway the six-membered ring, which is to become the benzene ring, is formed. The initial cyclic compound in the pathway, 3-dehydroquinate, is formed as the result of a reaction that may be considered an internal aldol condensation, as illustrated below.

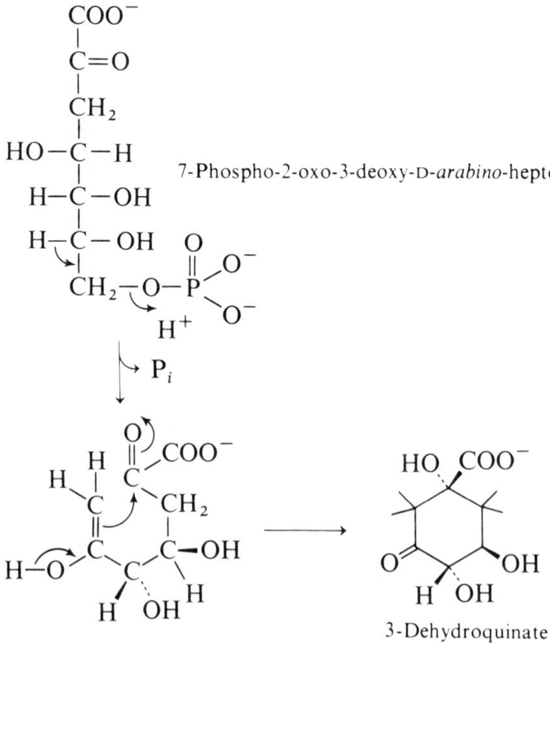

[Reaction scheme showing 7-Phospho-2-oxo-3-deoxy-D-*arabino*-heptonate losing $P_i$ and cyclizing to form 3-Dehydroquinate]

**Step 3: Formation of 3-dehydroshikimate** Next, as the result of a reaction that is catalyzed by 3-dehydroquinate dehydratase (3-dehydroquinate hydro-lyase, EC 4.2.1.10) the elements of water are removed from 3-dehydroquinate, and 3-dehydroshikimate is formed. This can be considered part of the process of converting the saturated ring into the unsaturated aromatic ring.

**Step 4: Conversion of dehydroshikimate into shikimate** In this step, the C(3) oxo group is reduced to an alcohol group. The reduction is catalyzed by shikimate dehydrogenase (shikimate:$NADP^+$ 3-oxidoreductase, EC 1.1.1.25). The introduction of this hydroxyl group is in preparation for the introduction of a second olefinic bond into the ring.

**Step 5: Phosphorylation of shikimate** Next, the C(3) hydroxyl group of shikimate undergoes a phosphorylation reaction catalyzed by shikimate kinase (ATP:shikimate 3-phosphotransferase, EC 2.7.1.71). This produces shikimate 3-phosphate, which has an even better leaving group at C(3).

Shikimate kinase has been isolated from *Bacillus subtilis*, in which, as mentioned, it exists as a part of an aggregate which also contains the aldolase and chorismate mutase. As isolated, the kinase is a small polypeptide having a molecular weight of 10,000. Dissociation of the kinase from the aggregate results in the loss of 99 percent of its catalytic activity.

**Step 6: *O*-Alkylation of shikimate 5-phosphate by phosphoenolpyruvate** A second molecule of phosphoenolpyruvate is utilized in the sixth step of the anabolic pathway. Whereas the first molecule contributed two carbon atoms to the six-membered ring, this second molecule contributes the three carbon atoms that will become the side chain of phenylalanine or tyrosine. The alkylation can come about by the displacement of the phosphoryl group of phosphoenolpyruvate by the C(5) hydroxyl group of shikimate 3-phosphate. The reaction is catalyzed by 3-phospho-5-enolpyruvoyl-shikimate synthase (phospho*enol* pyruvate: shikimate-3-phosphate *enol*pyruvoyl-transferase, EC 2.5.1.19) and the product is 3-phospho-5-enolpyruvoylshikimate.

**Step 7: Formation of chorismate** In the final step of this phase of the synthesis the C(3) phosphoryl group is eliminated, and a second olefinic bond is established, thus generating the intermediate, chorismate. The reaction entails a trans-(or anti-)1,4 elimination of orthophosphate, as shown below.

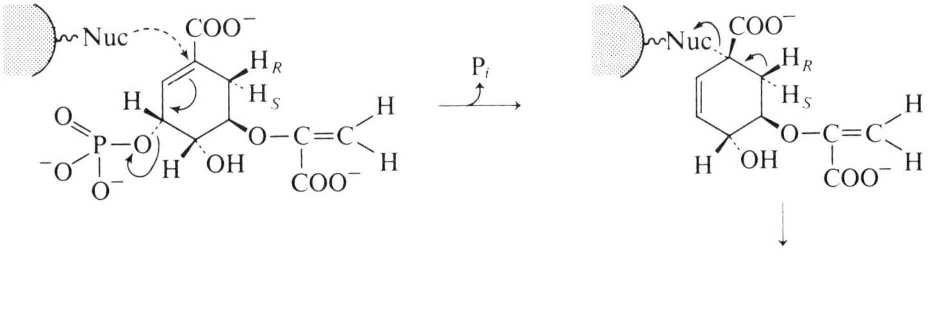

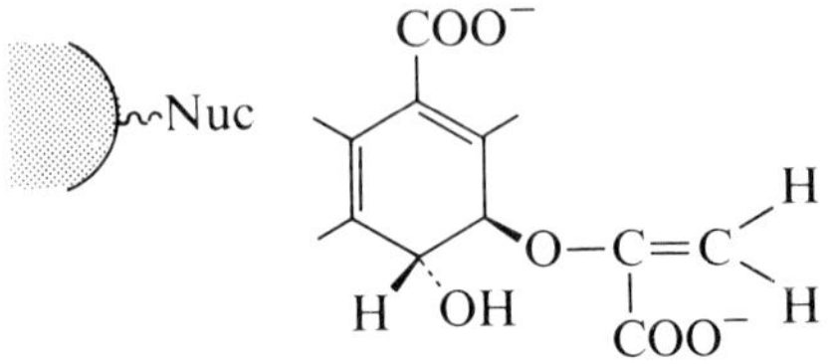

Chorismate

Chorismate stands at the bifurcation of the anabolic pathway. When tryptophan is to be synthesized, chorismate is converted into anthranilate. When phenylalanine or tyrosine is to be synthesized, chorismate is converted into prephenate, as discussed in the paragraphs that follow.

**Step 8: Rearrangement of chorismate to prephenate** As the result of an alkyl-migration reaction, the three-carbon moiety bonded to the oxygen atom at C(5) of chorismate becomes bonded at C(1). This is catalyzed by chorismate mutase (chorismate pyruvatemutase, EC 5.4.99.5). In *E. coli*, *Salmonella typhimurium*, and certain other bacteria, a single protein catalyzes the eighth and ninth reactions in the synthesis of phenylalanine. As isolated from *E. coli* K-12, the chorismate mutase-prephenate dehydratase is a single protein which has a molecular weight of 85,000. The ultimate product, phenylalanine, inhibits both activities. Another similar species (which has a molecular weight of 109,000) has been isolated from *Salmonella typhimurium*. Each of its two enzyme activities is also subject to inhibition by phenylalanine. There is also evidence that in these bacteria a single protein or a tightly associated complex is responsible for the eighth and ninth steps in the synthesis of tyrosine. In this case, chorismate mutase activity and prephenate dehydrogenase activity are involved. Thus, it would seem that either the substrate chorismate binds chorismate mutase-prephenate dehydratase, whereupon it will ultimately be converted into phenylalanine, or it binds chorismate mutase-prephenate dehydrogenase, whereupon it will ultimately be converted into tyrosine. The alkyl-migration reaction that results in the synthesis of prephenate can be formulated as shown.

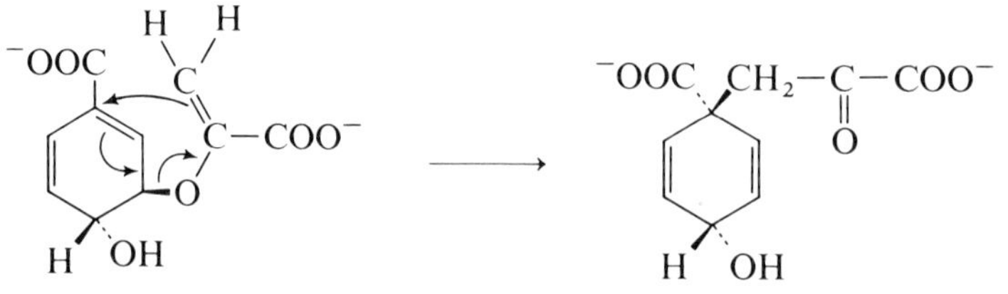

Chorismate → Prephenate

**Step 9: The aromatization of the ring** In the ninth step of the synthesis of phenylalanine or tyrosine the dihydrobenzene ring is converted into a benzene ring. This occurs by two different processes, depending upon whether phenylalanine or tyrosine is to be formed. When phenylalanine is to be formed, the enzyme prephenate dehydratase [prephenate hydro-lyase (decarboxylating), EC 4.2.1.51] catalyzes a decarboxylation reaction in which the electron pair that is left behind is utilized in the accompanying elimination of the C(4) hydroxyl group. When tyrosine is to be formed decarboxylation also occurs, but in this instance rather than the residual electron pair being eliminated with the C(4) hydroxyl group, a hydride ion is eliminated at C(4). Elimination of the hydride ion requires an oxidation-reduction cofactor and thus prephenate dehydrogenase [prephenate:$NAD^+$ oxidoreductase (decarboxylating), EC 1.3.1.12] is an $NAD^+$-dependent enzyme. These reactions are shown below.

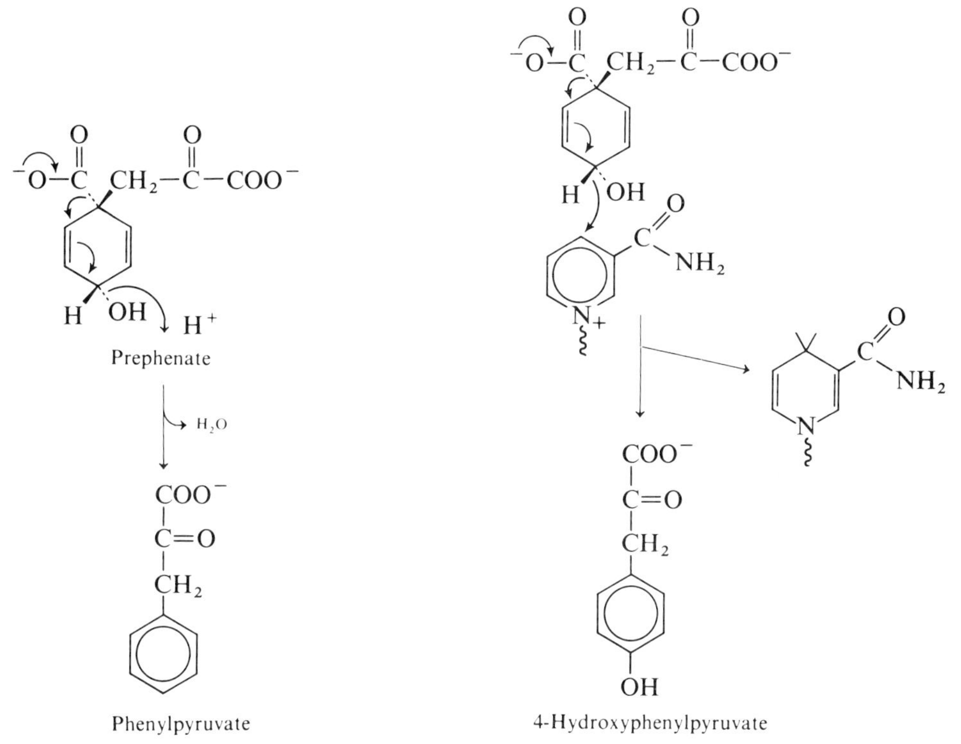

**Step 10: Transamination and the formation of phenylalanine or tyrosine** All that now remains is for these oxo acids to be converted into the corresponding amino acids in the presence of tyrosine aminotransferase and glutamate.

## Summary of the Anabolic Pathways

The synthesis of phenylalanine and tyrosine is summarized on page 708.

## Catabolism of Tryptophan

The principal route for the degradation and catabolism of tryptophan in man and other mammals results in the conversion of the eleven carbon atoms of this molecule into three molecules of carbon dioxide, a molecule of alanine (which can be converted into pyruvate and then into an acetyl moiety of acetyl-CoA plus another molecule of carbon dioxide), a molecule of formate (which can enter the one-carbon pool by becoming bonded to tetrahydrofolate), and the acetyl moieties of two molecules of acetyl-CoA. These reactions are discussed next.

The degradation of tryptophan begins with the cleavage of the pyrrole ring of the indole moiety and the formation of $N$-formylkynurenine. This is catalyzed by tryptophan 2,3-dioxygenase [L-tryptophan:oxygen 2,3-oxidoreductase (decyclizing), EC 1.13.11.11] and the reaction can be written

$$\text{L-Tryptophan} + O_2 \rightleftharpoons N\text{-formyl-L-kynurenine} \qquad (14\text{-}51)$$

Tryptophan 2,3-dioxygenase has been isolated from rat liver, among other sources, and purified to homogeneity. This enzyme, which is localized in the cytoplasm, has a molecular weight of 167,000 and it is composed of two different subunits which have similar molecular weights. The catalytically active enzyme consists of two of each of these subunits and thus has an $\alpha_2 \beta_2$ subunit structure. The dioxygenase binds two heme b moieties noncovalently and also two copper atoms. The latter must be in the cuprous form, $Cu^+$, for the enzyme to be catalytically active.† However, both the cuproferroheme form and the cuproferriheme form of the enzyme appear to be active. The kinetic mechanism of the formation of formylkynurenine is a sequential one, in which the cuproferroheme form of the enzyme preferentially binds tryptophan first while the cuproferriheme form preferentially binds molecular oxygen first. It is speculated that molecular oxygen binds $Cu^+$ in the case of the cuproferriheme enzyme.

With respect to reaction mechanism, the conversion of tryptophan into formylkynurenine can be formulated similar to the conversion of homogentisate into maleylacetoacetate. Such a minimal mechanism is shown below and on page 710.

This initial reaction of the degradative pathway is essentially irreversible, and, as might be expected, the activity of tryptophan 2,3-dioxygenase is subject to modulation. Glucocorticoids, such as hydrocortisone, induce the synthesis of the enzyme, while the substrate, L-tryptophan, inhibits the rate at which the enzyme

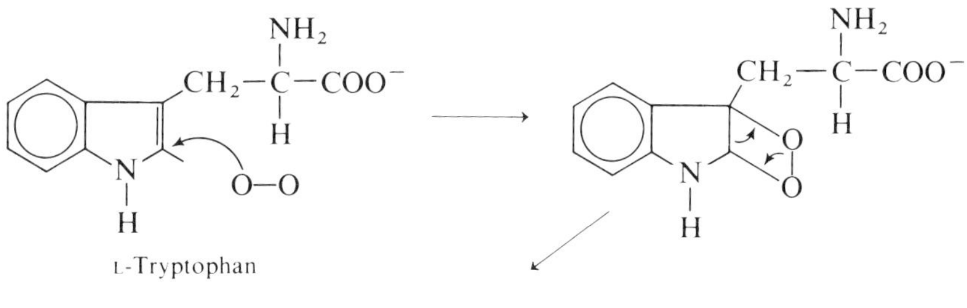

† Brady, F. O., and Feigelson, P. (1975) *J. Biol. Chem.* **250**, 5041–5048.

N-Formyl-L-kynurenine

undergoes degradation. In addition, 3-hydroxyanthranilate, an intermediate in the degradative pathway, causes plots of the reaction velocity vs. tryptophan concentration to change from hyperbolic to sigmoidal. Hence, this intermediate functions as an inhibitor.

As a result of the second step of the degradative pathway, N-formylkynurenine is hydrolyzed to kynurenine and formate in the presence of the enzyme formamidase (aryl-formylamine amidohydrolase, EC 3.5.1.9). The formate thus liberated can become a one-carbon unit bonded by tetrahydrofolate as a result of the reaction

$$\text{ATP + formate + tetrahydrofolate} \rightleftharpoons \text{10-formyltetrahydrofolate + ADP} + P_i \quad (14\text{-}52)$$

The enzyme that catalyzes this reaction, formyltetrahydrofolate synthetase [formate: tetrahydrofolate ligase (ADP-forming), EC 6.3.4.3], is present in both mammalian and bacterial cells.

There are several metabolic fates for kynurenine. In the mammalian liver kynurenine can undergo transamination, it can undergo a cleavage reaction which results in the formation of anthranilate and L-alanine, or it can undergo hydroxylation to yield 3-hydroxykynurenine. The aminotransferase that catalyzes the transamination of kynurenine is localized in the mitochondrial inner membrane, the enzyme that catalyzes the cleavage is localized in the cytoplasm, and the monooxygenase that catalyzes the hydroxylation reaction is localized in the mitochondrial outer membrane. The principal pathway for the degradation of tryptophan entails the hydroxylation of kynurenine as a result of the reaction catalyzed by kynurenine 3-monooxygenase [L-kynurenine, NADPH:oxygen oxidoreductase (3-hydroxylating), EC 1.14.13.9]. The reaction is

$$\text{L-Kynurenine + NADPH} + O_2 \rightleftharpoons \text{3-hydroxy-L-kynurenine + NADP}^+ + H_2O \quad (14\text{-}53)$$

Kynurenine 3-monooxygenase is a flavoprotein, and it has been speculated that the aromatic hydroxylation reaction catalyzed by this enzyme is mechanistically similar to the aromatic hydroxylation reactions catalyzed by phenylalanine 4-monooxygenase or tyrosine 3-monooxygenase but with a dihydroflavin participating rather than a tetrahydropteridine.† If this is the case, the function of NADPH is to

---

† Massey, V., and Hemmerich, P. (1975) in *The Enzymes* (Boyer, P. D., ed.), 3rd ed., vol. 12, pp. 191–252, Academic, New York.

convert the oxidized flavin (FAD in this case) to a dihydroflavin. Although this is an attractive hypothesis, it has by no means been established.

The principal metabolic fate of 3-hydroxykynurenine is its conversion into 3-hydroxyanthranilate and L-alanine as catalyzed by kynureninase (L-kynurenine hydrolase, EC 3.7.1.3). Kynureninase is a pyridoxal phosphate–dependent enzyme which catalyzes a cleavage reaction which can be formulated mechanistically as shown (the reaction is similar to that which converts fumarylacetoacetate into acetoacetate and fumarate).

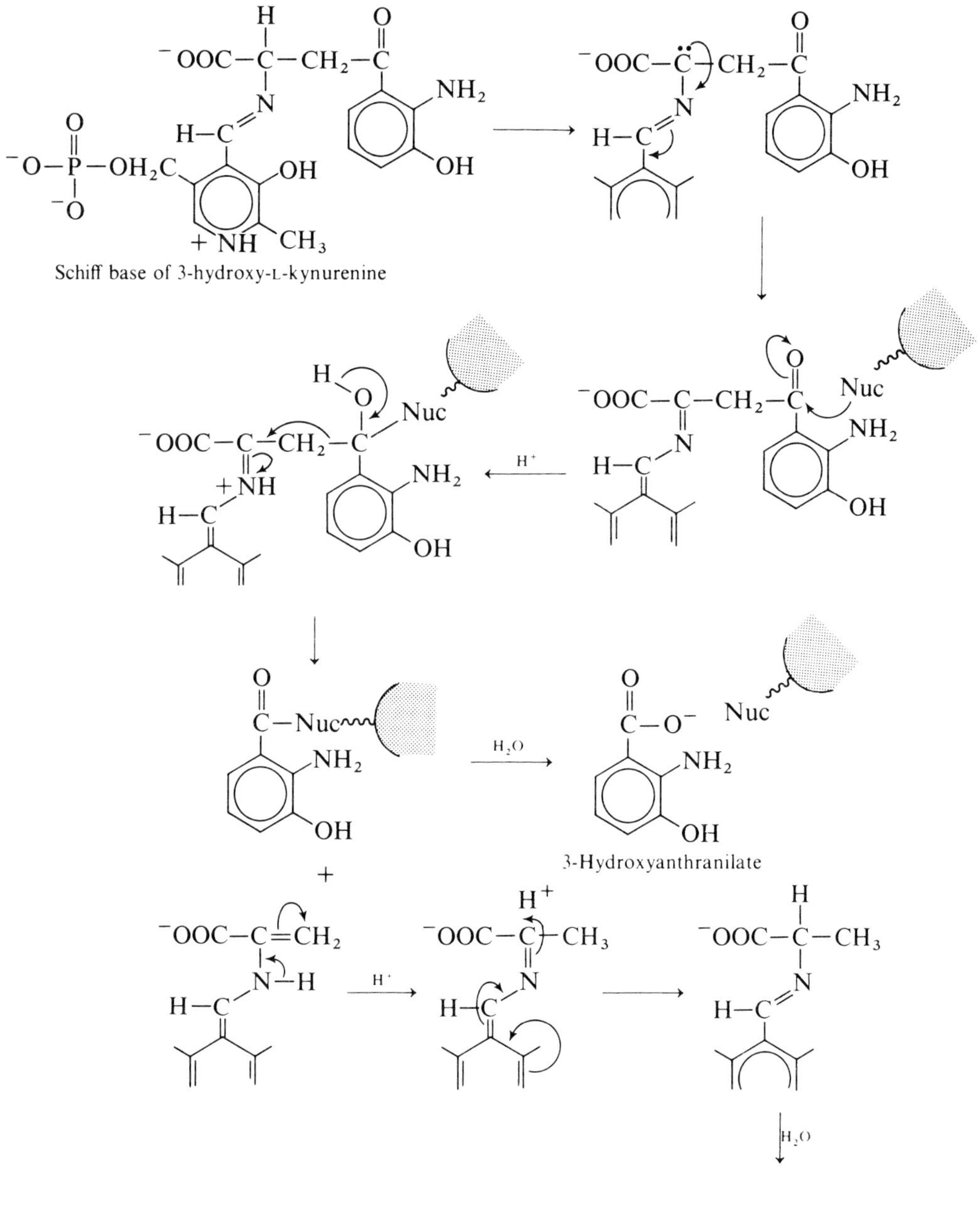

Schiff base of 3-hydroxy-L-kynurenine

3-Hydroxyanthranilate

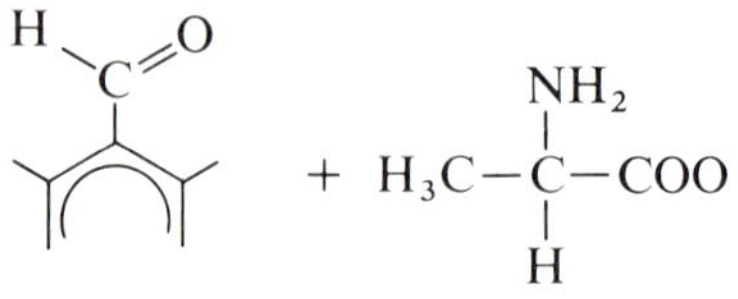

[Structure: aldehyde-bearing ring intermediate] + $H_3C-\underset{H}{\underset{|}{C}}(NH_2)-COO$
Alanine

In the present case, the function of the pyridoxal phosphate appears to be that of converting C(2) of kynurenine into a methenyl carbon atom, which then allows the electron pair that is generated as a result of the bond breaking to be relayed to the positively charged nitrogen.

Kynureninase also catalyzes the cleavage of kynurenine to yield anthranilate and alanine.

Continuing with the principal pathway for the degradation of tryptophan in mammals, 3-hydroxyanthranilate now undergoes an oxidative ring cleavage that results in the formation of 2-amino-3-carboxymuconate 6-semialdehyde. The ring cleavage utilizes molecular oxygen and is catalyzed by 3-hydroxyanthranilate 3,4-dioxygenase [3-hydroxyanthranilate: oxygen 3,4-oxidoreductase (decyclizing), EC 1.13.11.6]. As isolated from bovine kidney, the enzyme has a molecular weight of 34,000. The enzyme consists of a single polypeptide chain. The dioxygenase requires ferrous iron in order to be catalytically active. A minimal mechanism for this aromatic ring cleavage is shown below.

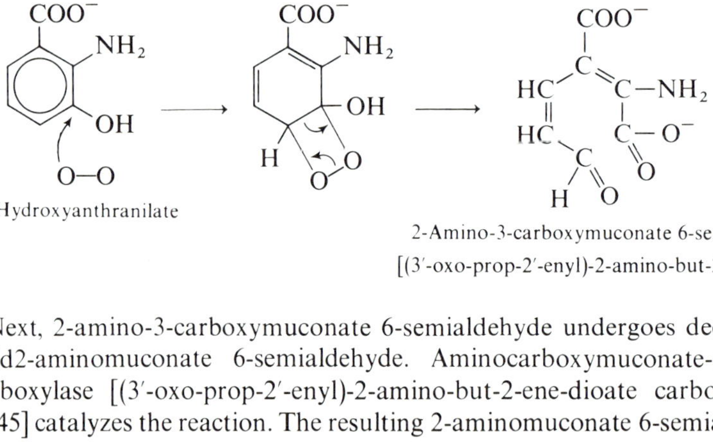

3-Hydroxyanthranilate → [intermediate] → 2-Amino-3-carboxymuconate 6-semialdehyde
[(3'-oxo-prop-2'-enyl)-2-amino-but-2-ene-dioate]

Next, 2-amino-3-carboxymuconate 6-semialdehyde undergoes decarboxylation to yield 2-aminomuconate 6-semialdehyde. Aminocarboxymuconate-semialdehyde decarboxylase [(3'-oxo-prop-2'-enyl)-2-amino-but-2-ene-dioate carboxy-lyase, EC 4.1.1.45] catalyzes the reaction. The resulting 2-aminomuconate 6-semialdehyde then undergoes oxidation at C(6), as catalyzed by aminomuconate-semialdehyde dehydrogenase (2-aminomuconate-6-semialdehyde: $NAD^+$ oxidoreductase, EC 1.2.1.32), and 2-aminomuconate is formed. Deamination and reduction of this intermediate yield 2-oxoadipate. The fate of 2-oxoadipate has been discussed previously since it is also formed when lysine is degraded in man. Thus, these six carbon atoms are converted into two molecules of carbon dioxide and two acetyl moieties of acetyl CoA. The latter, of course, are also ultimately converted to carbon dioxide.

The principal pathway for the degradation of tryptophan in mammals is shown below. Included are some of the alternative reactions which the intermediates of the major pathway undergo.

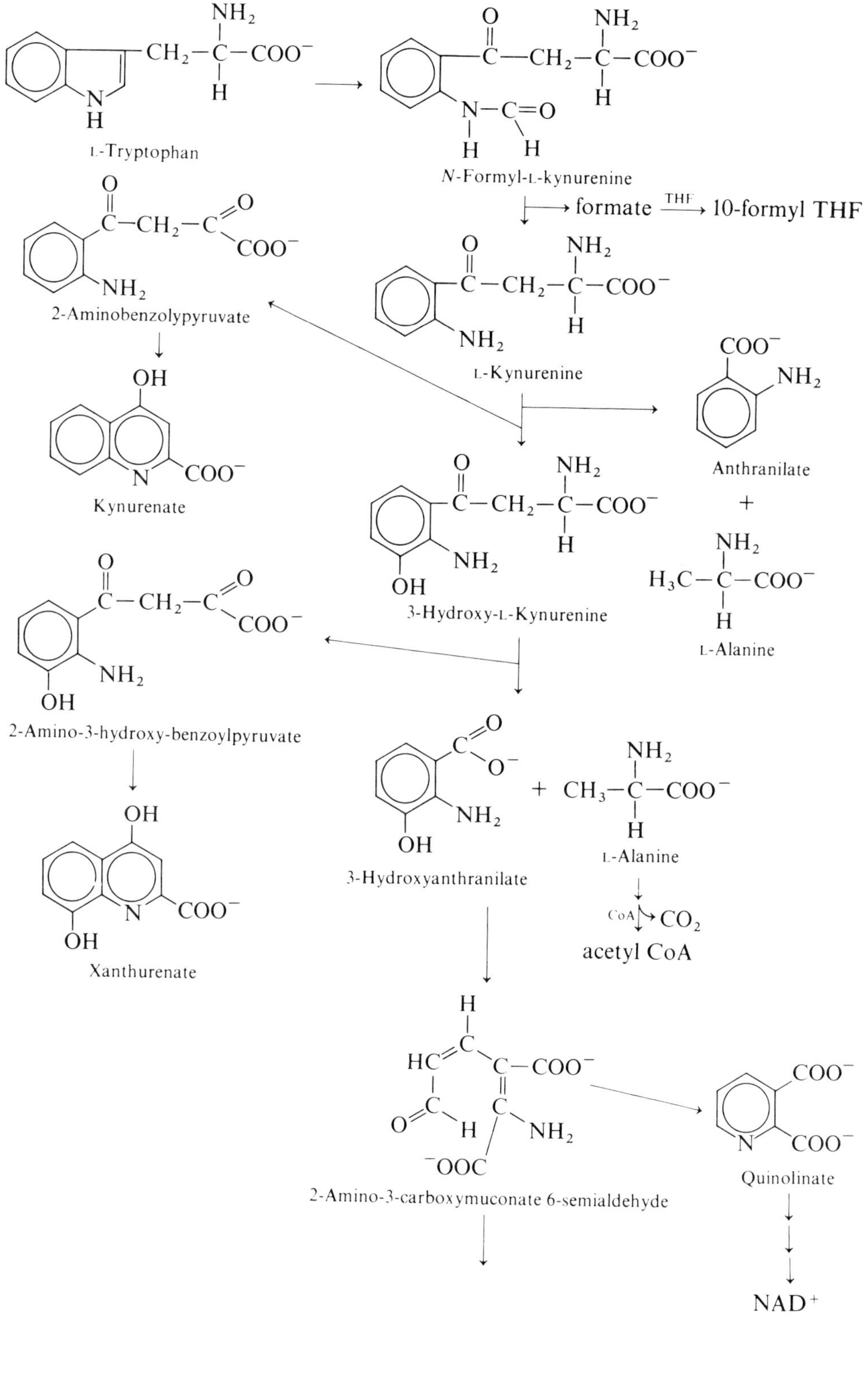

METABOLISM OF AMINO ACIDS AND PROTEINS 713

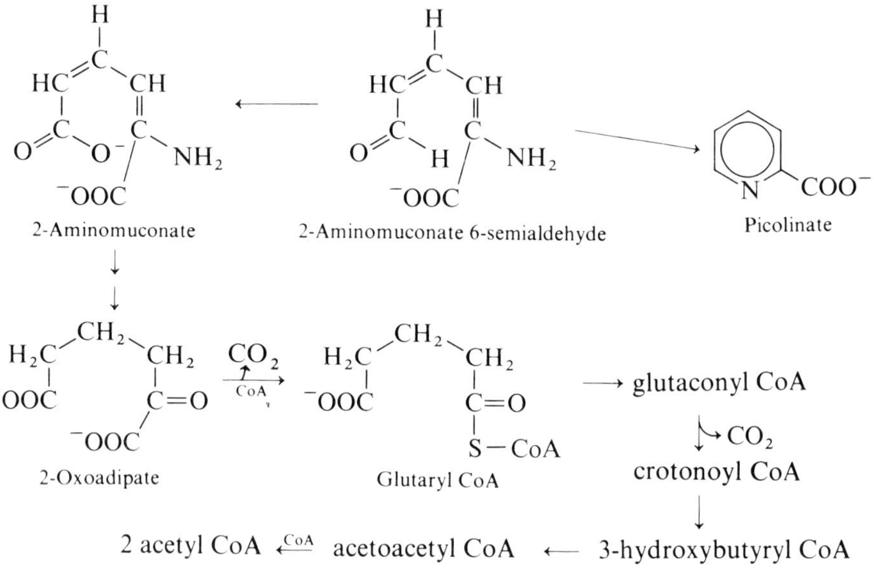

[Diagram showing metabolic pathway: 2-Aminomuconate ← 2-Aminomuconate 6-semialdehyde → Picolinate; 2-Aminomuconate → 2-Oxoadipate —CO₂, CoA→ Glutaryl CoA → glutaconyl CoA → (−CO₂) crotonoyl CoA → 3-hydroxybutyryl CoA → acetoacetyl CoA —CoA→ 2 acetyl CoA]

## Conversion of Tryptophan into Serotonin

Serotonin (5-hydroxytryptamine) is a powerful vasoconstrictor and a putative neurotransmitter which is found in certain areas of the brain and in other neural tissue in mammals. It is derived from tryptophan by a two-step sequence which begins with the hydroxylation of tryptophan. This hydroxylation is catalyzed by tryptophan 5-monooxygenase [L-tryptophan, tetrahydropteridine: oxygen oxidoreductase (5-hydroxylating), EC 1.14.16.4]. The reaction is

L-Tryptophan + tetrahydropteridine + $O_2$ $\rightleftharpoons$
$\qquad$ 5-hydroxy-L-tryptophan + dihydropteridine + $H_2O$ $\qquad$ (14-54)

and is rate-determining with respect to the synthesis of serotonin.

Tryptophan 5-monooxygenase has been isolated from rabbit hindbrain and purified. This enzyme has a molecular weight of 234,000 and comprises two subunits which each have molecular weights of 57,000 and two which each have molecular weights of 60,000. Thus, the enzyme has an $\alpha_2\beta_2$ subunit structure. The hydroxylation of tryptophan parallels that of phenylalanine and tyrosine mechanistically, and, in fact, the same tetrahydropteridine is thought to participate in the formation of 5-hydroxytryptophan.

Purified tryptophan 5-monooxygenase catalyzes the hydroxylation of phenylalanine with approximately 10 percent the efficiency with which it catalyzes the hydroxylation of tryptophan, and it has been suggested that this is of particular significance in the phenylketonuric patient in that it permits the synthesis of tyrosine, at least in the brain.

The decarboxylation of 5-hydroxytryptophan yields 5-hydroxytryptamine, or serotonin. The decarboxylation is catalyzed by the aromatic L-amino acid decarboxylase, which also participates in the synthesis of the catecholamines. The conversion of tryptophan into serotonin is illustrated below.

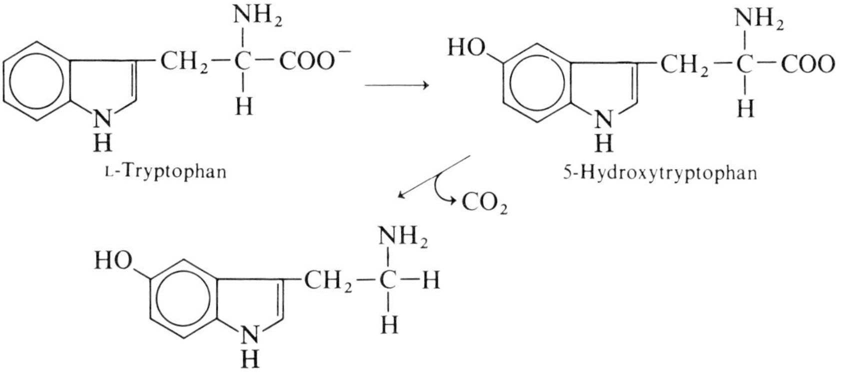

L-Tryptophan → 5-Hydroxytryptophan → (−$CO_2$) → 5-Hydroxytryptamine (serotonin)

## Formation of Nicotine Adenine Dinucleotide

The oxidation-reduction cofactor $NAD^+$ can be derived from quinolinate, an intermediate in the degradation of tryptophan. Although this sequence occurs to only a limited extent in man (and therefore nicotinate or nicotinamide must be ingested), it occurs to an appreciable extent in microorganisms.

When $NAD^+$ is to be synthesized, quinolinate, a nonenzymatic cyclization product of 2-amino-3-carboxymuconate 6-semialdehyde, undergoes a reaction with 5-phosphoribose 1-diphosphate which yields nicotinate ribonucleotide. This is catalyzed by (carboxylating) nicotinate-D-ribonucleotide pyrophosporylase [nicotinate-D-ribonucleotide: pyrophosphate phosphoribosyltransferase (carboxylating), EC 2.4.2.19] and the reaction is

Quinolinate + 5-phospho-α-D-ribose 1-diphosphate ⇌
nicotinate D-ribonucleotide + $PP_i$ + $CO_2$ (14-55)

Next, in the presence of ATP, nicotinate ribonucleotide undergoes adenylylation and deamido-$NAD^+$ is formed. The adenylylation reaction is catalyzed by nicotinate-D-ribonucleotide adenylyltransferase (ATP: nicotinate-D-ribonucleotide adenylyltransferase, EC 2.7.7.18) and is written

ATP + nicotinate D-ribonucleotide ⇌ deamido-$NAD^+$ + $PP_i$ (14-56)

In the third step of the sequence, the nicotinate moiety is converted into a nicotinamide moiety, the nitrogen atom being donated by glutamine. The reaction, which is catalyzed by $NAD^+$ synthetase [deamido-$NAD^+$: L-glutamine amido-ligase (AMP-forming), EC 6.3.5.1], is

ATP + deamido-$NAD^+$ + L-glutamine + $H_2O$ ⇌
$NAD^+$ + L-glutamate + AMP + $PP_i$ (14-57)

Finally, $NAD^+$ can be converted into $NADP^+$ as the result of a reaction catalyzed by $NAD^+$ kinase (ATP:$NAD^+$ 2′-phosphotransferase, EC 2.7.1.23). This sequence of reactions is shown below.

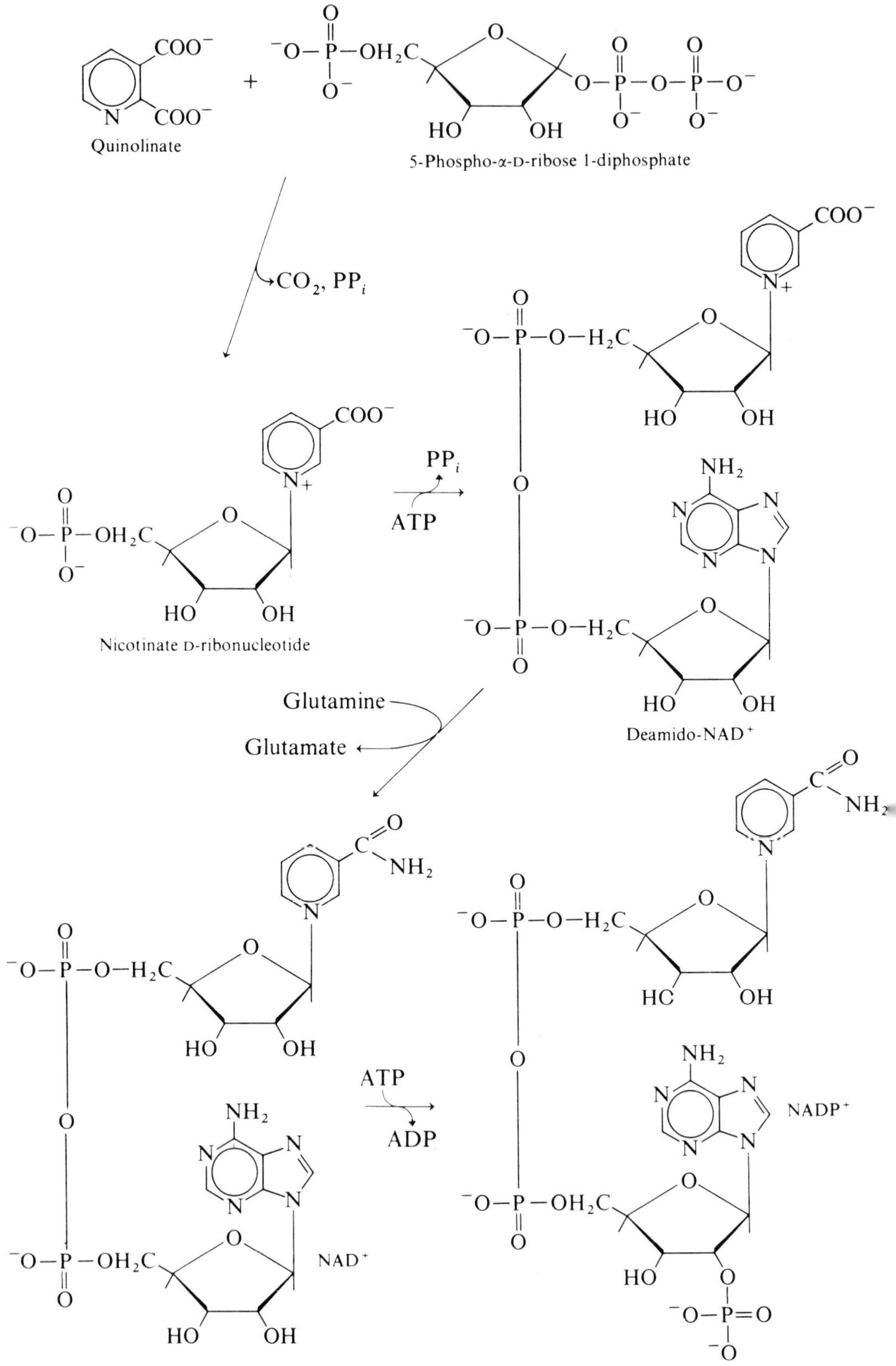

Quinolinate + 5-Phospho-α-D-ribose 1-diphosphate

→ CO$_2$, PP$_i$

Nicotinate D-ribonucleotide

ATP → PP$_i$

Deamido-NAD$^+$

Glutamine → Glutamate

NAD$^+$

ATP → ADP

NADP$^+$

## Bacterial Degradation of Tryptophan

Certain microorganisms, including *E. coli* and *Bacillus alvei*, contain an enzyme that catalyzes the cleavage of tryptophan to yield indole, pyruvate, and ammonia. This enzyme is the pyridoxal phosphate–dependent tryptophanase [L-tryptophan indole-lyase (deaminating), EC 4.1.99.1]. Tryptophanase from *E. coli* or from *B. alvei* is a tetramer which binds four molecules of pyridoxal phosphate. The molecular weight of the enzyme from *E. coli* is approximately 220,000 while that from the bacillus is approximately 210,000. The cleavage of tryptophan might be formulated as shown below. This reaction can occur in the human intestinal tract although it is catalyzed by bacterial enzymes.

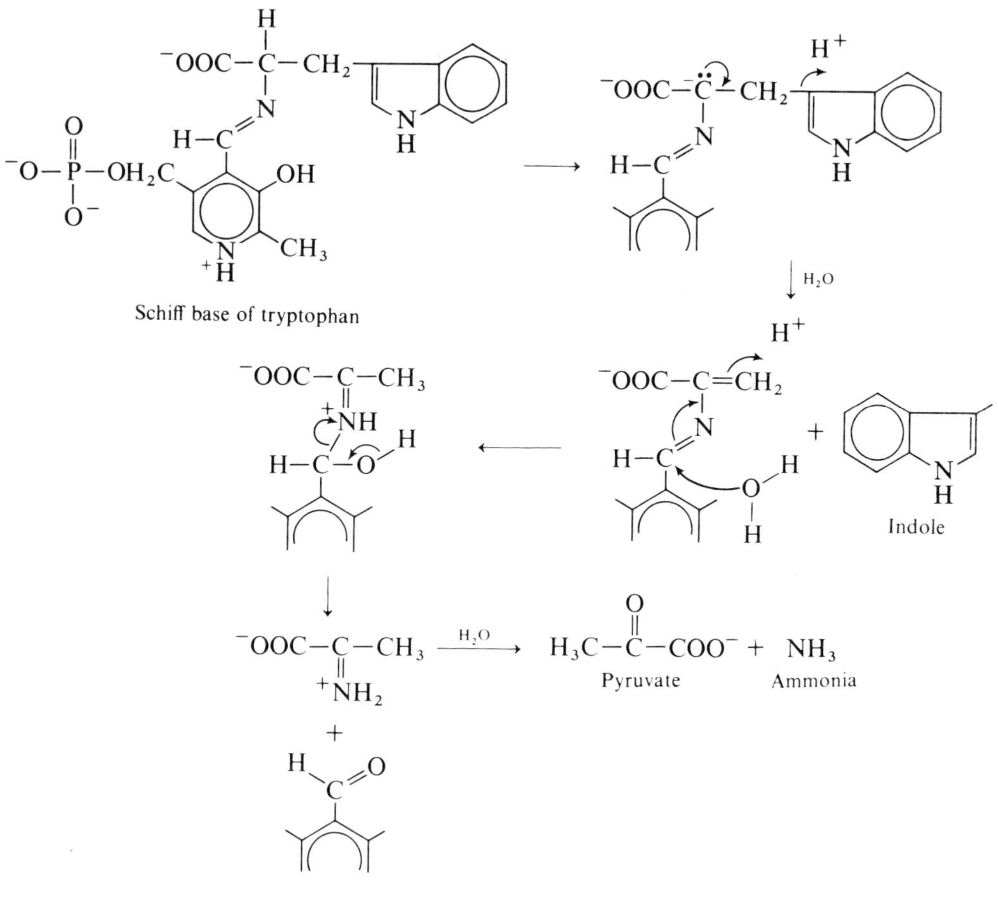

## Anabolism of Tryptophan in Microorganisms

Man does not synthesize tryptophan. In microorganisms, tryptophan is derived from chorismate, which is also an intermediate in the synthesis of phenylalanine and tyrosine, as discussed previously. The conversion of chorismate into tryptophan requires a sequence of five steps.

**Step 1: Formation of anthranilate** Anthranilate is formed from chorismate and glutamine by a reaction catalyzed by anthranilate synthase [chorismate pyruvate-lyase (amino-accepting), EC 4.1.3.27]:

$$\text{Chorismate} + \text{L-glutamine} \rightleftharpoons \text{anthranilate} + \text{pyruvate} + \text{L-glutamate} \tag{14-58}$$

The enzymes that catalyze this reaction have been grouped into three categories: (1) those which exist in association with the enzyme that catalyzes the second step of this anabolic pathway, (2) those which exist in association with some other enzyme of the anabolic pathway, and (3) those which apparently exist in a nonaggregated form. Synthases from *E. coli*, *Salmonella typhimurium*, and *Aerobacter aerogenes* are in the first category; synthases from many fungi and yeasts are in the second category; and synthases from certain other microorganisms, including *Serratia marcescens*, *Pseudomonas putida*, and *Chromobacterium violaceum*, are in the third category.

Of the enzymes of the first category, that from *S. typhimurium* is perhaps the most completely characterized. The enzyme from *S. typhimurium* has a molecular weight (or aggregate weight) of approximately 255,000 and it comprises two different subunits. The subunit stoichiometry is apparently $\alpha_2 \beta_2$. One subunit component, which has a molecular weight of 64,000 catalyzes the formation of anthranilate from chorismate but only if ammonia, rather than glutamine, is the nitrogen donor. The second subunit component, which has a molecular weight of 63,000 confers the ability to utilize glutamine as the nitrogen donor upon the first component and also exhibits anthranilate phosphoribosyltransferase activity. Anthranilate phosphoribosyltransferase catalyzes the second step of the anabolic pathway. Thus, the two associated components constitute a bifunctional enzyme that catalyzes the first two steps of the anabolic pathway. Furthermore, it has been shown that glutamine, a substrate in the first reaction of the pathway, in fact, binds a subunit which catalyzes the second reaction of the pathway and that in addition to its anthranilate phosphoribosyltransferase activity this subunit can also transfer the amide nitrogen atom of glutamine to the appropriate locus on the catalytic site of a synthase subunit. (This is the same locus at which ammonia binds.)

Kinetic studies on the formation of anthranilate catalyzed by the enzyme from *S. typhimurium* show that the reaction has an ordered sequential mechanism, in which chorismate is the initial substrate that binds, followed by the nitrogenous fragment derived from glutamine. Anthranilate is released first and then pyruvate.

The activity of anthranilate synthase is inhibited by the ultimate product, tryptophan, as might be expected since the formation of anthranilate is the first reaction that is unique with respect to the anabolism of tryptophan. Tryptophan causes plots of the reaction velocity vs. chorismate concentration to be converted from hyperbolic to sigmoidal.

The synthesis of anthranilate in *E. coli* and other enteric bacteria is catalyzed by an enzyme aggregate similar to that derived from *S. typhimurium*, described above.

An enzyme that catalyzes the formation of anthranilate in *Neurospora crassa* has been isolated as an aggregate which has a weight of 240,000. This species comprises two subunits that catalyze the formation of anthranilate from chorismate and ammonia and four subunits that catalyze the third and fourth steps of the anabolic pathway. These subunits each have a molecular weight of 40,000. The subunits that catalyze the formation of anthranilate with ammonia as the nitrogen donor require the association of an additional subunit, which has a molecular weight of 30,000 in order to utilize glutamine as a substrate. Thus, it appears that an aggregate which has a molecular weight of almost 300,000 catalyzes the glutamine-dependent synthesis of anthranilate along with the third and fourth reactions of the anabolic pathway.

The anthranilate synthase from *P. putida* provides an example of the non-aggregated enzyme. In this case, the synthase comprises two nonidentical subunits the larger of which has a molecular weight of 64,000 while the smaller has a molecular weight of 18,000. The larger catalyzes the synthesis of anthranilate with ammonia as the nitrogen donor, and the smaller confers the ability to utilize glutamine while exhibiting no other activity.

The formation of anthranilate from chorismate and glutamine (or ammonia) entails the introduction of an amino group and the elimination of a hydroxyl group and an *enol*pyruvoyl moiety. A minimal mechanism for this reaction follows.

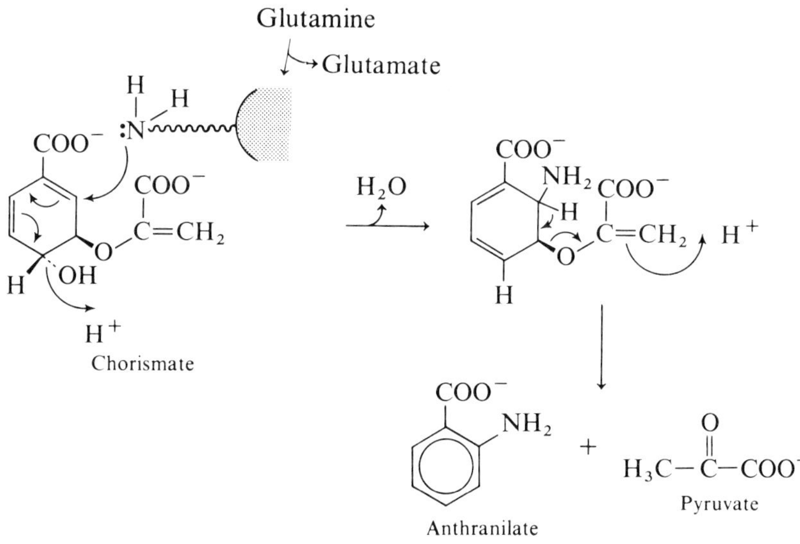

**Step 2: Conversion of anthranilate into N-(5′-phosphoribosyl)-anthranilate** The second step of the anabolic pathway entails the introduction of a phosphoribosyl moiety which will provide the five carbon atoms needed to form the pyrrole moiety and the three-carbon side chain of tryptophan. (This is reminiscent of

the synthesis of histidine.) The reaction, catalyzed by anthranilate phosphoribosyltransferase [*N*-(5′-phosphoribosyl)-anthranilate:pyrophosphate phosphoribosyltransferase, EC 2.4.2.18], is

Anthranilate + 5-phospho-α-D-ribose 1-diphosphate $\rightleftharpoons$

*N*-(5′-phospho-D-ribosyl)-anthranilate + $PP_i$ (14-59)

The reaction mechanism parallels that of the synthesis of 1-(5′-phosphoribosyl)-ATP.

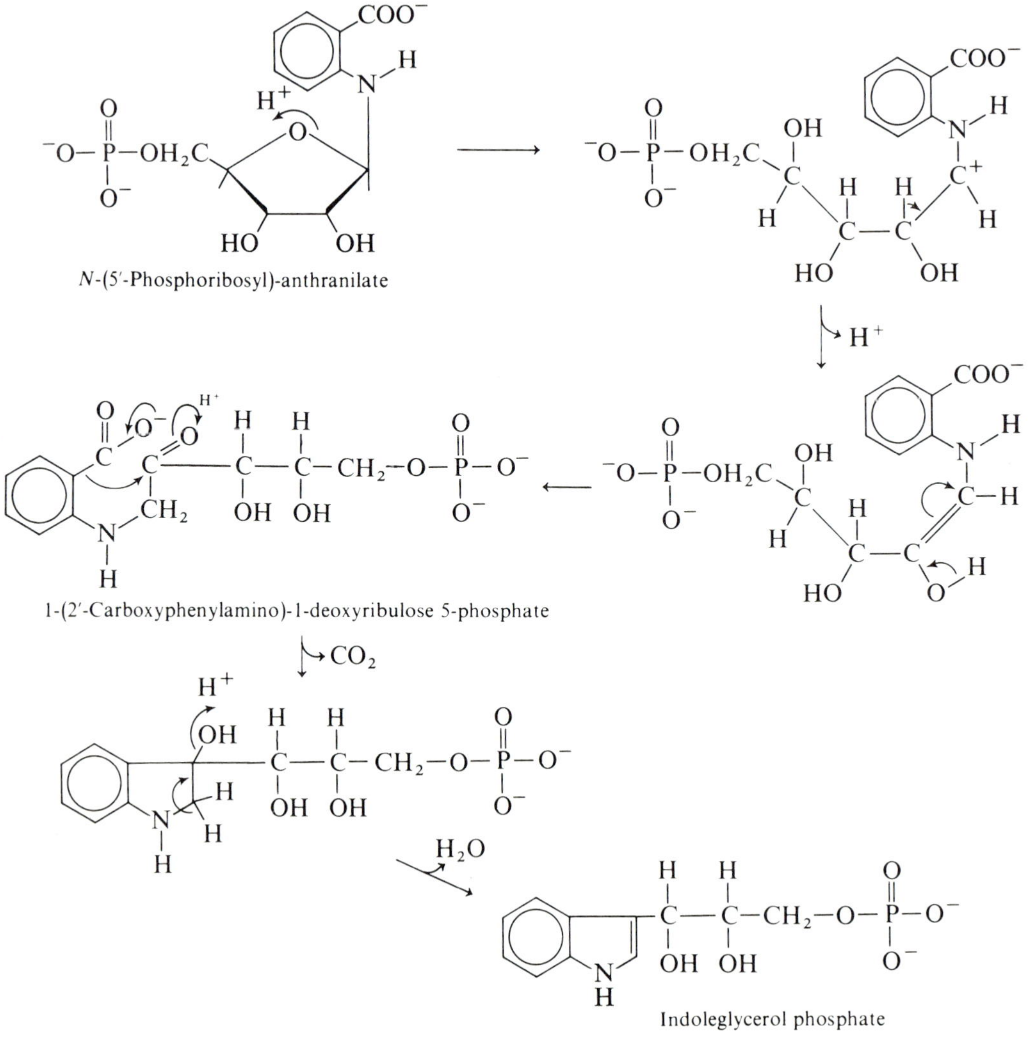

**Steps 3 and 4: Conversion of *N*-(5′-phosphoribosyl)-anthranilate into indoleglycerol phosphate** As in the synthesis of histidine, the ribosyl moiety of *N*-(5′-phosphoribosyl)-anthranilate undergoes hydrolytic ring cleavage and tautomerization which

*N*-(5′-Phosphoribosyl)-anthranilate

1-(2′-Carboxyphenylamino)-1-deoxyribulose 5-phosphate

Indoleglycerol phosphate

result in the formation of 1-(2'-carboxyphenylamino)-1-deoxyribulose 5-phosphate. The latter undergoes decarboxylation and ring closure to yield indoleglycerol phosphate. The enzyme that catalyzes the decarboxylation and ring closure, indole-3-glycerol-phosphate synthase [1-(2'-carboxyphenylamino)-1-deoxyribulose-5-phosphate carboxy-lyase (cyclizing), EC 4.1.1.48], has been isolated from *E. coli*. A minimal mechanism for the conversion of *N*-(5'-phosphoribosyl)-anthranilate into indoleglycerol phosphate is shown on page 720.

**Step 5: Formation of tryptophan** The final reaction of the anabolic sequence is an elimination and replacement reaction catalyzed by the pyridoxal phosphate–dependent tryptophan synthase [L-serine hydro-lyase (adding indoleglycerol-phosphate), EC 4.2.1.20]. Tryptophan synthase is a multifunctional enzyme comprising two different subunits. The $\alpha$ subunit has a molecular weight of approximately 29,000 as obtained from several sources (including *E. coli, Salmonella typhimurium,* and *Aerobacter aerogenes*) and is capable of catalyzing the elimination of glyceraldehyde 3-phosphate from indoleglycerol phosphate (albeit with a reaction velocity that is only 1 percent that which is observed when the native synthase catalyzes the reaction). The $\beta$ subunit has a molecular weight of 44,000 and binds pyridoxal phosphate. The $\beta$ subunit provides the catalysis for the reaction involving the indole moiety and serine which yields tryptophan. The native synthase has an $\alpha_2\beta_2$ subunit structure and catalyzes the reaction

Indoleglycerol phosphate + L-serine $\rightleftharpoons$

$$\text{tryptophan} + \text{glyceraldehyde 3-phosphate} \quad (14\text{-}60)$$

A minimal reaction mechanism for the formation of tryptophan from indoleglycerol phosphate and serine is depicted below.

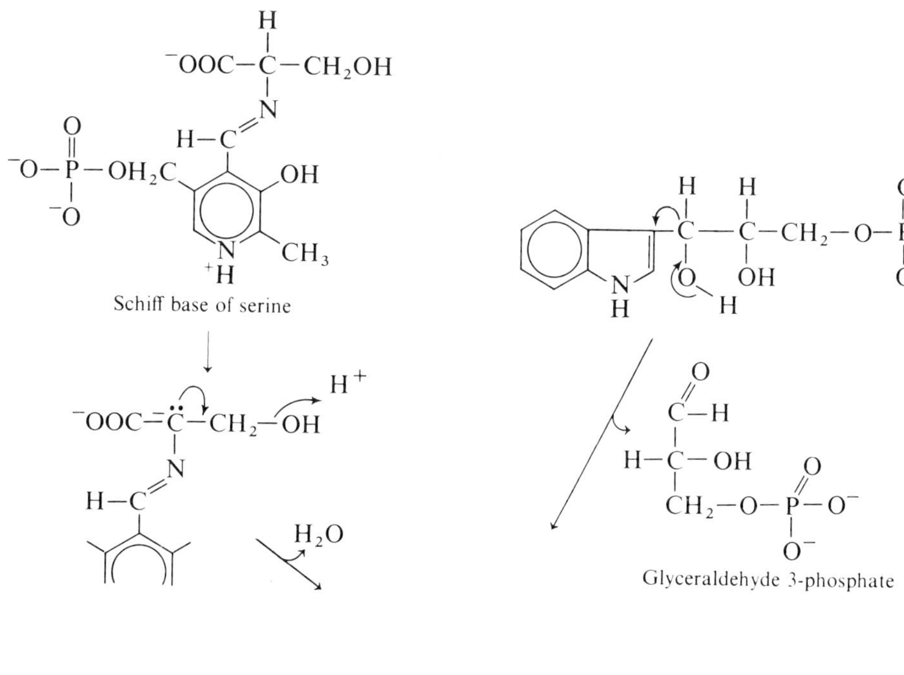

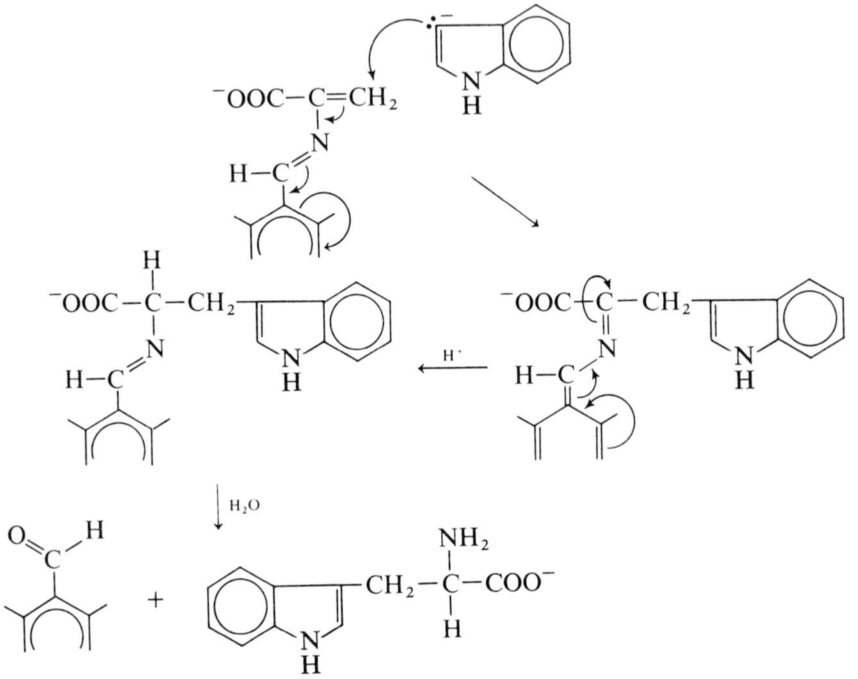

[Scheme showing mechanism of tryptophan synthase reaction producing L-Tryptophan]

Tryptophan synthase catalyzes several other reactions involving an elimination or an elimination and replacement, e.g., the conversion of serine and indole into tryptophan and water and that of indoleglycerol phosphate to indole and glyceraldehyde 3-phosphate.

## Summary of Tryptophan Anabolism and Its Regulation

The synthesis of tryptophan as it occurs in microorganisms is summarized below.

In several microorganisms, including *E. coli* and *Salmonella typhimurium*, the genes that specify the enzymes that participate in the conversion of chorismate into tryptophan are located contiguously on the genome and are expressed coordinately. These structural genes and their associated controlling elements constitute the *trp* operon. Expression of the structural genes occurs only when the operon is derepressed, i.e., only when the repressor is not bound at the operator locus. The

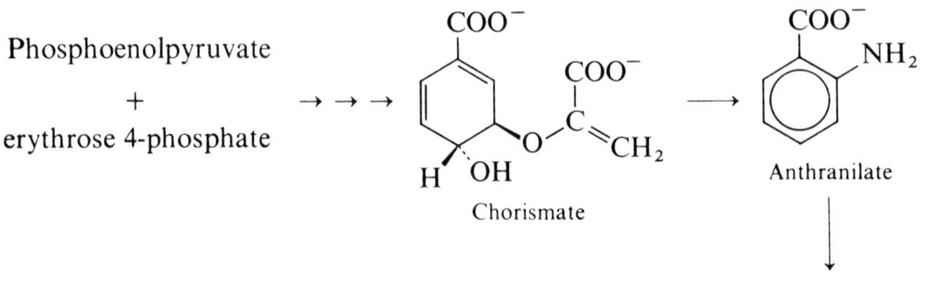

Phosphoenolpyruvate + erythrose 4-phosphate → → → Chorismate → Anthranilate →

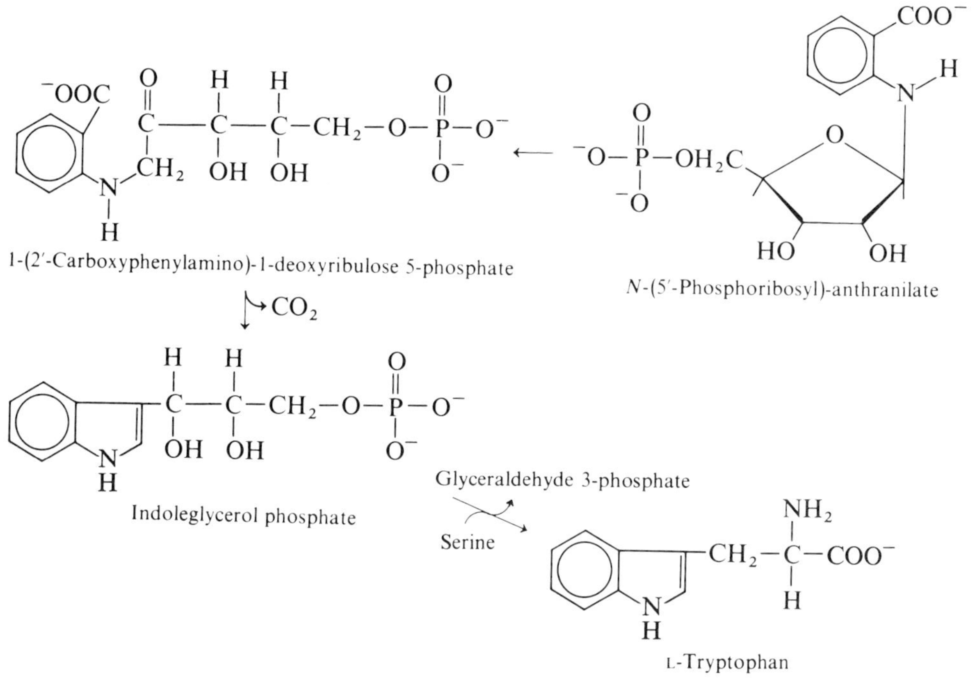

[Chemical structures:

1-(2'-Carboxyphenylamino)-1-deoxyribulose 5-phosphate ← N-(5'-Phosphoribosyl)-anthranilate

↓ CO₂

Indoleglycerol phosphate

Glyceraldehyde 3-phosphate ↗ ↘ Serine

L-Tryptophan]

repressor comprises the aporepressor, a protein that is specified by the regulator gene, plus the ultimate product of the pathway, tryptophan. In this respect, the *trp* operon is similar to the *his* operon.

## SYNTHESIS OF UREA

At the beginning of this chapter it was stated that the catabolism of the amino acids generally entails the removal of the nitrogen atom (or atoms) followed by the degradation of the resulting carbon skeleton by means of an appropriate pathway. These pathways have been the focus of many of the discussions in this chapter. The nitrogen atoms removed from the amino acids can be utilized in the synthesis of other biochemical intermediates, e.g., other amino acids or purines or pyrimidines, or they can be incorporated into urea, the form in which nitrogen is excreted by man. This incorporation into urea is the focus of the discussion here.

### Formation of Carbamoyl Phosphate

The synthesis of urea in man and other mammals occurs primarily in the liver. The first reaction of this process is the formation of carbamoyl phosphate as catalyzed by the mitochondrial ammonia-dependent carbamoyl-phosphate synthase. This enzyme was discussed earlier in this chapter within the framework of the synthesis of arginine in mammals, and it is to be distinguished from the cytoplasmic glutamine-dependent carbamoyl-phosphate synthase that participates in the *de novo* synthesis of the pyrimidine ring. The mitochondrial synthase also differs from the cytoplasmic enzyme in that the former requires $N$-acetyl glutamate to be catalytically active. The reaction catalyzed by the ammonia-dependent carbamoyl-phosphate synthase is the rate-determining step in the synthesis of urea.

## Carbamoylation of Ornithine

As also discussed previously, carbamoyl phosphate can react with ornithine to yield citrulline in a reaction that is catalyzed by ornithine carbamoyltransferase. As a result of this reaction a nitrogen atom derived from ammonia becomes a nitrogen atom of the ureido group of citrulline.

## Formation of Argininosuccinate

The third reaction in the synthesis of urea is the conversion of citrulline into argininosuccinate in the presence of aspartate and ATP. The enzyme argininosuccinate synthetase catalyzes this reaction, which utilizes the energy derived from the cleavage of ATP (to yield AMP and pyrophosphate) to facilitate the bond-making process. This reaction introduces the second nitrogen atom that will become a nitrogen atom of urea.

## Cleavage of Argininosuccinate

Next, argininosuccinate is cleaved to yield arginine and fumarate. This reaction is catalyzed by argininosuccinate lyase. Now all that remains is the cleavage of arginine to yield urea and ornithine.

## Formation of Urea

The final reaction in the synthesis of urea (and the only reaction not previously discussed within the framework of the mammalian synthesis of arginine) is the cleavage of arginine to yield urea and ornithine. The enzyme arginase (L-arginine amidinohydrolase, EC 3.5.3.1) catalyzes this reaction, which is

$$\text{L-Arginine} + H_2O \rightleftharpoons \text{urea} + \text{L-ornithine} \qquad (14\text{-}61)$$

Arginase has been isolated from several mammalian sources including bovine, rabbit, and rat liver. The enzyme from the latter source is a tetramer which has a molecular weight of 120,000.

A minimal mechanism for the formation of urea and ornithine from arginine is shown on page 725.

Since ornithine is the other product formed along with urea, the synthesis of urea is, in effect, a cyclic process. A nitrogen atom from ammonia and a nitrogen atom from aspartate plus a carbon atom from bicarbonate are utilized for the synthesis of urea, with ornithine functioning as the foundation upon which the construction of the urea molecule takes place.

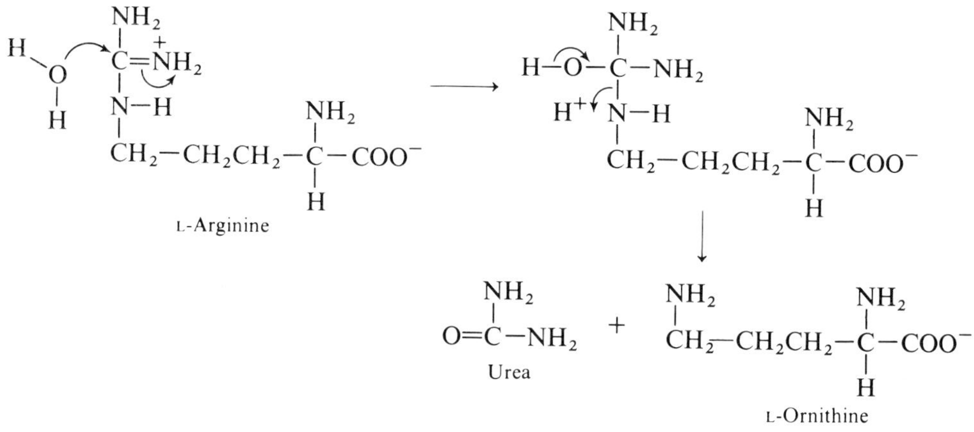

## SUMMARY OF UREA SYNTHESIS AND ITS REGULATION

The synthesis of urea is summarized in Fig. 14-6.

From an overview, in ureotelic species (such as man and the other mammals) most of the amino acids that are to be degraded in the liver undergo transamination with 2-oxoglutarate, and glutamate is formed. Glutamate can then enter the mitochondrion, where (by the reaction catalyzed by glutamate dehydrogenase) the nitrogen atom that was the amino nitrogen of the amino acid becomes the nitrogen of an ammonia molecule. This nitrogen atom can now be incorporated into carbamoyl phosphate and subsequently into the ureido group of citrulline. Citrulline can then pass out of the mitochondrion and into the cytoplasm, where it can be converted into argininosuccinate. This reaction allows the nitrogen atom of any amino acid that undergoes transamination with oxaloacetate to be incorporated into urea. Finally, urea is formed along with ornithine, and the latter enters the mitochondrion, where the cycle can begin again.

It has been proposed that the regulation of the synthesis of urea is accomplished primarily by the effect of $N$-acetylglutamate upon the activity of carbamoyl-phosphate synthase. In support of this proposal is the observation that concentrations of $N$-acetylglutamate increase in parallel with increased protein intake and increased urea excretion in animals. The proposed regulatory mechanism is envisaged as follows. As amino acid concentrations increase in the body, more and more amino acids will undergo transamination with 2-oxoglutarate and increased concentrations of glutamate will be formed. Increased concentrations of glutamate in turn will enter the mitochondrion, where not only oxidative deamination but also the synthesis of $N$-acetylglutamate (from glutamate and acetyl-CoA) can take place. This intramitochondrial synthesis of $N$-acetylglutamate promotes the activity of the ammonia-dependent carbamoyl-phosphate synthase just when an increase in this activity is required.

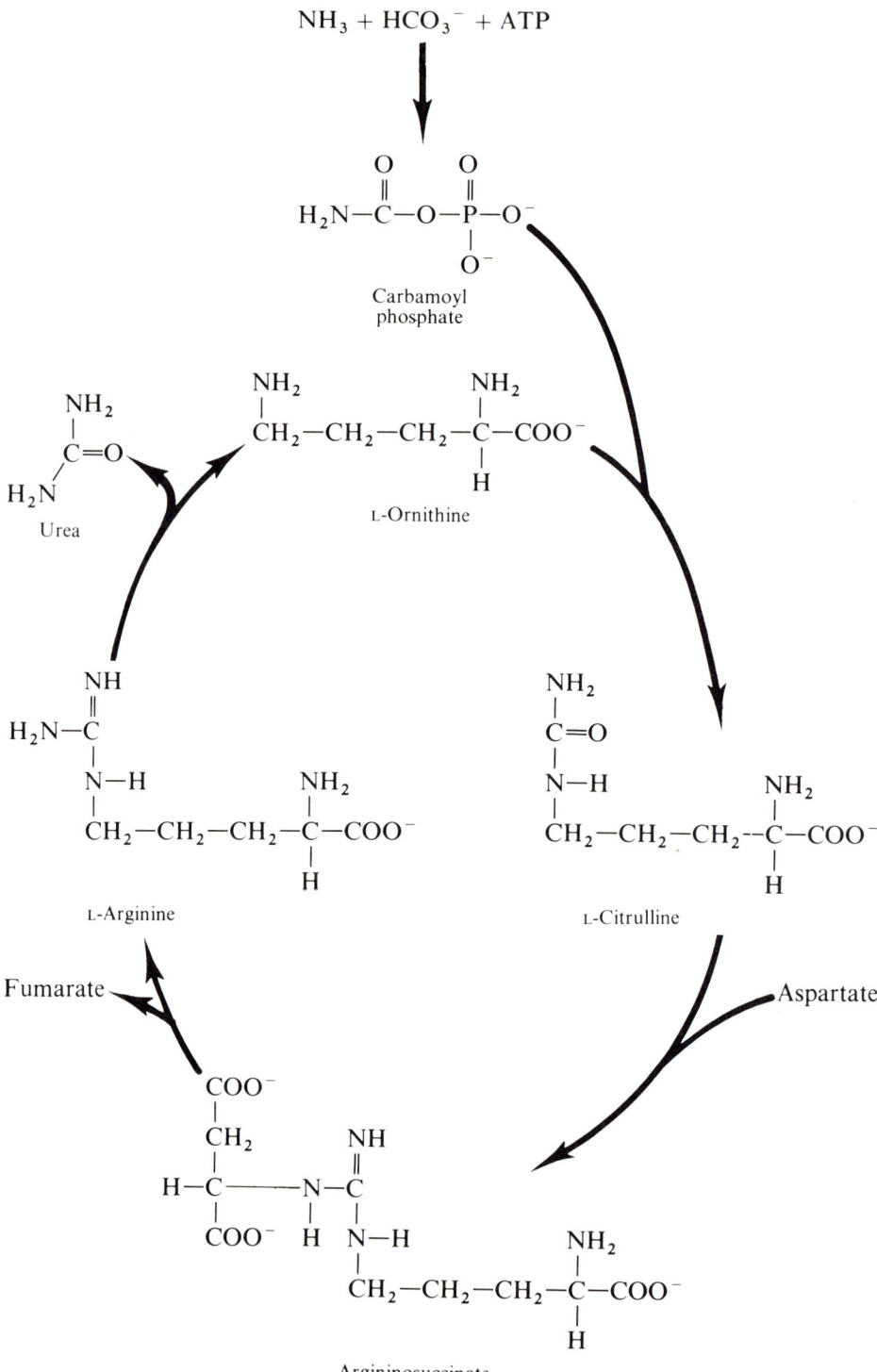

**Figure 14-6** The urea cycle.

# PROTEIN SYNTHESIS

The biosynthesis of proteins is a complex process which entails the interaction of both nucleic acids and proteins. Nucleic acids are involved in preparing an amino acid to be incorporated into a protein, in determining the order in which aminoacyl units are incorporated into the protein, and in the incorporation process itself. Proteins, on the other hand, function as enzymes and as supporting factors in the bond-making processes. From an overview, the synthesis of proteins entails three phases, operationally, namely, initiation, elongation, and termination.

## Initiation

Most of the pioneering studies on protein synthesis were conducted on prokaryotic systems (mainly, *E. coli*), although much is now known and understood concerning this process in eukaryotic systems. Many of the latter studies have focused upon synthesis in rat liver and in rabbit reticulocytes. Our discussion begins with a consideration of the initiation process in eukaryotic cells. Discussion of the process in prokaryotic systems will follow.

In order for protein synthesis to be initiated an initiation complex must be formed. The principal constituents of this complex are the ribosome or polysome, the messenger RNA, the aminoacylated initiator transfer RNA, and the initiation factors.

**Ribosomes** Protein synthesis takes place on the surface of cytoplasmic cell organelles known as ribosomes, which are nucleoprotein aggregates comprising two major subunits. In eukaryotic cells the smaller subunit has a sedimentation coefficient of 40 S and is referred to as the 40-S subunit. The larger subunit has a sedimentation coefficient of 60 S and is referred to as the 60-S subunit. The monomeric ribosome, which can be formed by the association of the 40- and 60-S subunits, has a sedimentation coefficient of approximately 80 S. Rat-liver ribosomes consist of approximately 53 percent protein and 47 percent RNA. The protein component can be resolved to yield approximately 70 proteins. Of these, approximately 30 are components of the 40-S subunit and approximately 40 are components of the 60-S subunit. The RNA component is usually resolved to yield three species, i.e., the 28-S RNA, the 18-S RNA, and the 5-S RNA. (In some eukaryotic cells at least, the 28-S RNA can be further resolved to yield a 25- and a 5.8-S RNA.) The 28-S RNA and the 5-S RNA are components of the larger ribosomal subunit; the 18-S RNA is contained in the smaller subunit. The 40-S subunit (from rat liver) is a prolate ellipsoid, while the 60-S subunit is rounded on the bottom and flattened on the top, as represented by the model shown in Fig. 14-7.

**Messenger RNA** The function of messenger RNA in protein synthesis is that of dictating the primary structure of the protein being synthesized. The messenger RNA that prescribes the sequence of aminoacyl groups in a given protein has been synthesized, i.e., transcribed, using a DNA or RNA genome as the template.

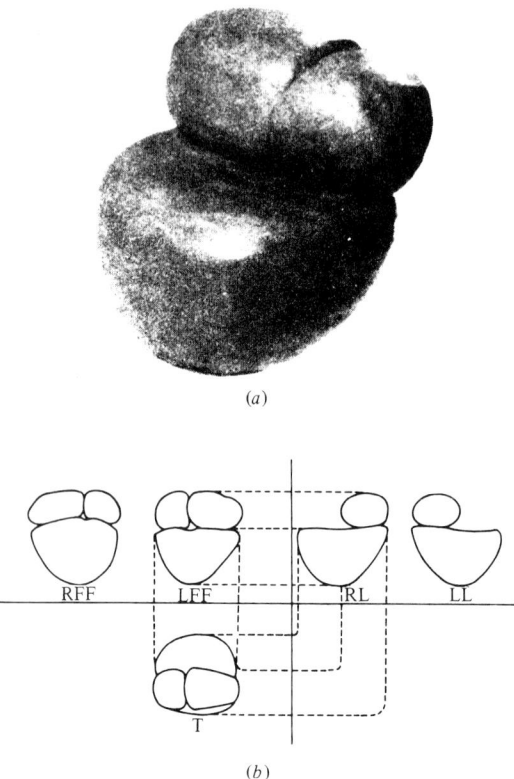

**Figure 14-7** (a) Reproduction of a plastic model of the monomeric ribosome along with (b) representations of various perspectives of this model; RFF, right-featured frontal, LFF, left-featured frontal; RL, right lateral, LL, left lateral; T, top. [*From Sabatini, D., Nonomura, Y., Morimoto, T., and Blobel, G. (1972) in Functional Units in Protein Biosynthesis (Cox, R. A., and Hadjiolov, A. A., eds.), pp. 147–173 (see p. 157), Academic Press, New York. With permission.*]

Thus, the genetic information contained in that genome is passed to the messenger RNA. The messenger RNA in turn utilizes this information to direct the synthesis of the appropriate protein.

The means by which a nucleic acid prescribes the synthesis of a protein entails the translation of the *genetic code*. The primary structure of a messenger RNA molecule is, in fact, a sequence of nucleotidyl triplets which constitute a nonoverlapping, commaless code. Each triplet sequence, such as cytidylyl-uridylyl-adenylyl (CUA), designates a particular aminoacyl unit. (In the present case, a leucyl unit is specified.) The triplet sequence that specifies a given aminoacyl unit is referred to as a *codon*. Since there are four different nucleotidyl units present in the genome, $4^3 = 64$ different triplet sequences, or codons, are possible. In most instances, as one can see in Table 14-1, a given aminoacyl unit is designated by more than one codon. Hence, the genetic code is said to be *degenerate*.

With respect to the mechanism by which a sequence of three nucleotidyl units

## Table 14-1 The genetic code

| First position (5' end) | Second position | | | | Third position (3' end) |
|---|---|---|---|---|---|
| | U | C | A | G | |
| U | Phe | Ser | Tyr | Cys | U |
| | Phe | Ser | Tyr | Cys | C |
| | Leu | Ser | Stop | Stop | A |
| | Leu | Ser | Stop | Trp | G |
| C | Leu | Pro | His | Arg | U |
| | Leu | Pro | His | Arg | C |
| | Leu | Pro | Gln | Arg | A |
| | Leu | Pro | Gln | Arg | G |
| A | Ile | Thr | Asn | Ser | U |
| | Ile | Thr | Asn | Ser | C |
| | Ile | Thr | Lys | Arg | A |
| | Met | Thr | Lys | Arg | G |
| G | Val | Ala | Asp | Gly | U |
| | Val | Ala | Asp | Gly | C |
| | Val | Ala | Glu | Gly | A |
| | Val | Ala | Glu | Gly | G |

dictates the incorporation of a given aminoacyl unit, a specific recognition process between the messenger RNA and the aminoacyl transfer RNA is involved and this can be described more effectively following a brief discussion of transfer RNA.

**Transfer RNA** Transfer RNA is a relatively small ribonucleic acid which generally comprises 75 to 85 nucleotidyl units. Transfer RNA molecules have molecular weights in the range of 30,000. They have a sedimentation coefficient of 4 S. These nucleic acids are also characterized by the presence of a spectrum of modified purine and pyrimidine moieties. These include 2-thiocytosine, 5-carboxymethyluracil, 2-thiouracil, $N^6$-($\Delta^2$-isopentenyl) adenine, $N^2$-dimethylguanine, 7-methylguanine, dihydrouracil, and the 5-ribofuranosyluracil (pseudouridine) moiety. The transfer RNA molecule assumes an unusual three-dimensional structure which is represented schematically in Fig. 14-8. Several structural characteristics of the transfer RNA molecule should be mentioned. For example, in (a), on the left there is a nonpaired region which is referred to as the *dihydrouridine loop*. The nonpaired region on the right is called the *pseudouridine loop* on the other hand. This region frequently includes the trinucleotide sequence T $\psi$ C, which includes a *ribo*thymidyly unit. The nonpaired region at the bottom is the anticodon. It is the anticodon of an aminoacylated transfer RNA that must be recognized by a given codon of the messenger RNA during protein synthesis. There is at least one specific transfer RNA for each amino acid, and this transfer RNA reacts specifically with its amino acid. During protein synthesis the recognition of a given transfer RNA anticodon by a messenger RNA codon translates into the incorporation of the aminoacyl group of that transfer RNA into the protein. This is the mechanism by

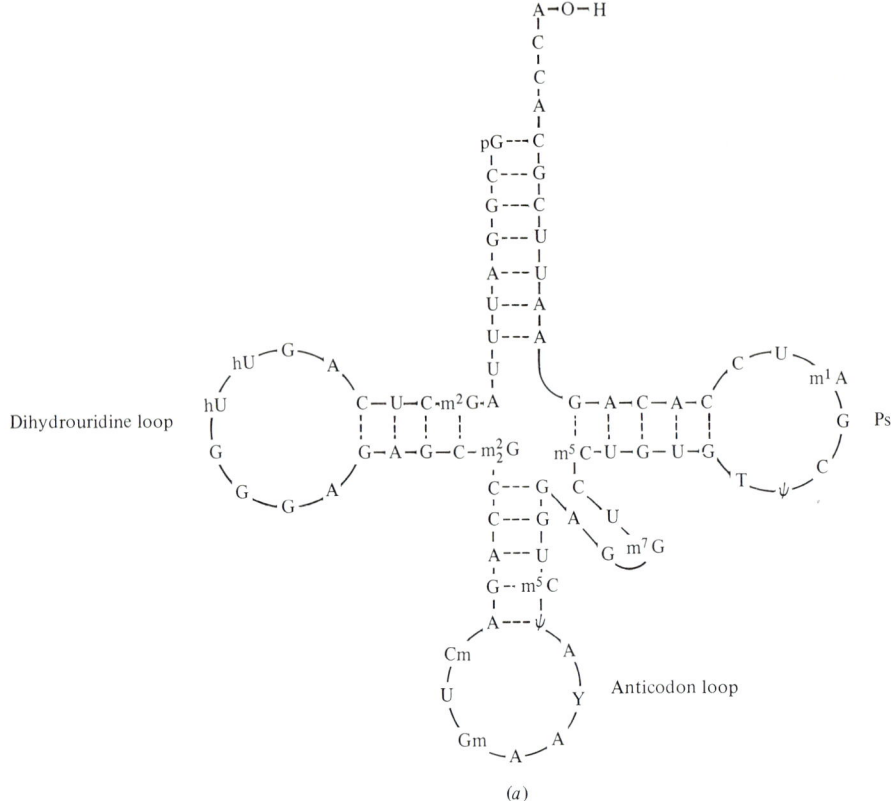

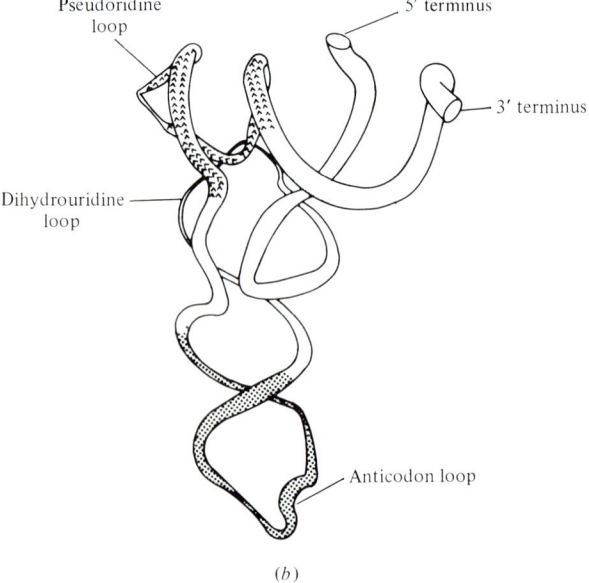

which a sequence of three nucleotidyl units of messenger RNA dictates the insertion of a specific aminoacyl unit into the protein being synthesized.

As mentioned above, the reaction between an amino acid and its cognate transfer RNA is highly specific. It results in the amino acid becoming covalently bonded to the transfer RNA. All transfer RNA molecules have the sequence cytidylyl-cytidylyl-adenylyl at their 3' terminus, and it is the 3'-hydroxyl group of the terminal adenylyl moiety with which the amino acid reacts to form an ester. This esterification of the amino acid, or aminoacylation of the transfer RNA, is catalyzed by an aminoacyl-transfer RNA synthetase. There is a specific synthetase for each aminoacyl unit incorporated into proteins, and the general reaction that these enzymes catalyze is

$$\text{L-Amino acid} + \text{ATP} + \text{transfer RNA} \rightleftharpoons \text{aminoacyl-transfer RNA} + \text{AMP} + \text{PP}_i \quad (14\text{-}62)$$

Several aminoacyl-transfer RNA synthetases have been isolated from mammalian sources. For example, a tryptophanyl-transfer RNA synthetase [L-tryptophan: transfer RNA ligase (AMP-forming), EC 6.1.1.2] has been isolated from bovine pancreas as a protein that comprises four subunits and has a molecular weight of 110,000. This enzyme has an $\alpha_2 \beta_2$ subunit structure. A seryl-transfer RNA synthetase [L-serine: transfer RNA ligase (AMP-forming), EC 6.1.1.11] from rat liver has a molecular weight of 90,000 on the other hand. Generally, the molecular weights of the aminoacyl-transfer RNA synthetases tend to cluster around 100,000.

With respect to reaction mechanism, studies on threonyl-transfer RNA synthetase [L-threonine:transfer RNA ligase (AMP-forming), EC 6.1.1.3] from rat liver have indicated that an aminoacyladenylate intermediate can be formed during the course of the reaction. In fact, threonyladenylate has been isolated in the presence of this enzyme—although this of itself does not prove that such an intermediate is formed on the primary reaction pathway. Certainly, the function of the ATP required is that of facilitating the formation of the ribose ester of the amino acid, but such facilitation could come about either through the formation of an intermediate such as an aminoacyladenylate or by means of a concerted mechanism. A concerted mechanism is, in fact, shown on page 732 although the participation or nonparticipation of an aminoacyladenylate remains to be established.

---

**Figure 14-8** (*a*) Sequence of nucleotidyl units and (*b*) a reproduction of a three-dimensional model of yeast phenylalanine transfer RNA. In (*a*), A, G, C, and U have their usual meanings (adenylyl, guanylyl, cytidylyl, and uridylyl, respectively) and

| | |
|---|---|
| $m^2G = N^2$-methylguanylyl | Y = Unidentified |
| hU = dihydrouridylyl | $\psi$ = 5'-phospho-5-ribofuranosyluracil |
| $m_2^2G = N^2,N^2$-dimethylguanylyl | $m^7G$ = 7-methylguanylyl |
| Cm = 2'-O-methylcytidylyl | T = ribothymidylyl (5-methyluridylyl) |
| Gm = 2'-O-methylguanylyl | $m^1A$ = 1-methyladenylyl |

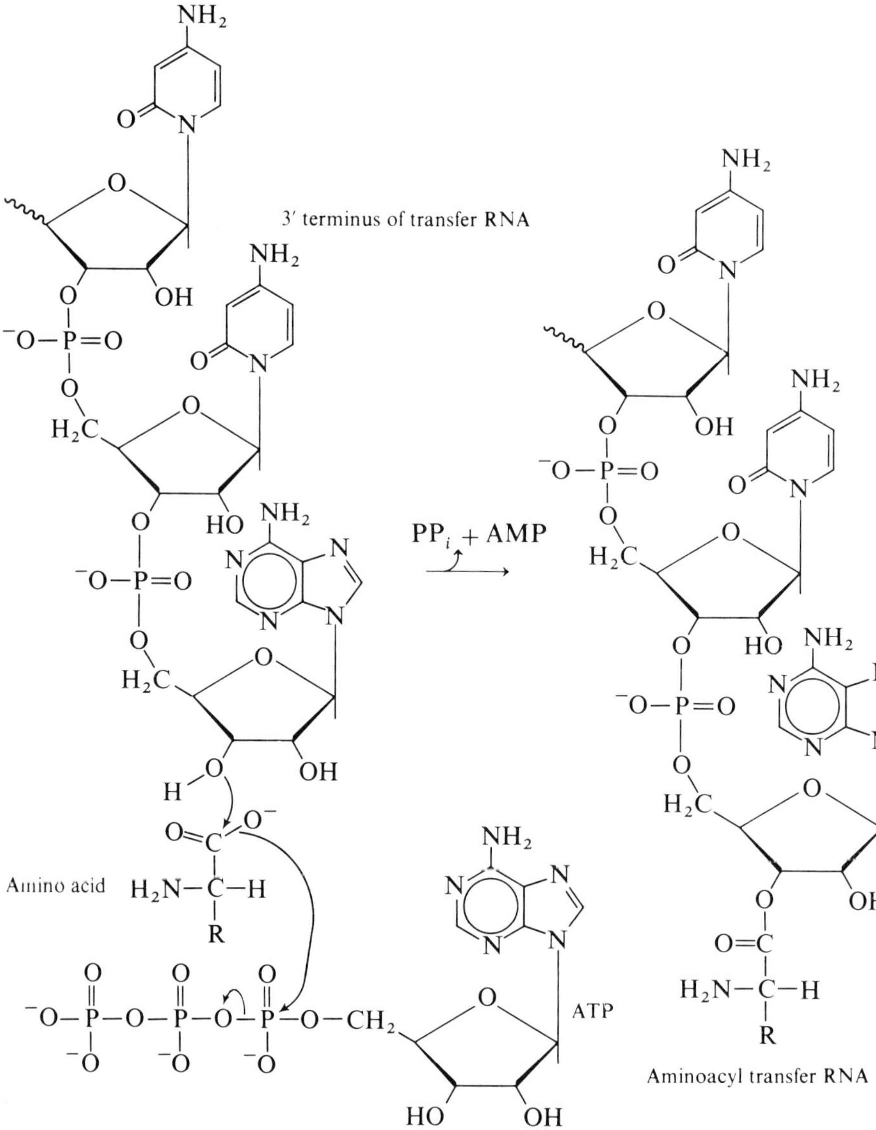

Studies on several mammalian and bacterial aminoacyl-transfer RNA synthetases have suggested that this Ter Ter reaction has a random sequential mechanism. Again, however, the data are less than conclusive.

An important aspect of the formation of the aminoacyl transfer RNA is the specificity of the reaction, since the bonding of the wrong aminoacyl moiety by a transfer RNA could result in the incorporation of the wrong aminoacyl unit into a protein. As mentioned above, the principal recognition processes that occur when an aminoacyl unit is incorporated into a protein involve interactions between the transfer RNA moiety and the system (rather than the aminoacyl moiety and the system). Studies designed to delineate these recognition processes have indicated that there are probably two levels of recognition. First, there appears to be a general, nonspecific recognition between an aminoacyl-transfer RNA synthetase and any transfer RNA. In addition, however, there is a precise recognition process that takes place between a synthetase and its particular transfer RNA. The structural features of the transfer RNA that are involved in the second process are unknown, although the accumulated data suggest that the loci of these recognition sites may vary from one nucleic acid molecule to another. According to one hypothesis, a given synthetase may recognize several bases located at different points on the surface of the transfer RNA. It has also been suggested that the specificity of the aminoacylation process does not rest solely upon the recognition and binding process but rather, that the reaction velocity in the presence of the appropriate and an inappropriate transfer RNA may serve as a means of discrimination.

**Initiation factors** In addition to the components described above, i.e., the ribosome, the messenger RNA, and the aminoacylated transfer RNA, several proteins are required to form an initiation complex. Their functions will be described as the formation of the initiation complex is described.

**Initiation in eukaryotic systems** Studies on the initiation process as it occurs in rabbit reticulocytes, as well as in other mammalian systems, have demonstrated that specific proteins called *initiation factors* are required for the formation of the initiation complex.[†] These studies have also demonstrated that the formation of the initiation complex can occur by two different routes. In one, the messenger RNA for the protein to be synthesized first binds the noncomplexed 40-S ribosomal subunit. This requires the participation of a protein factor, designated the mammalian initiation factor 3 (IF-M3). Now, in the presence of two other proteins, the mammalian initiation factor 1 (IF-M1) and the mammalian initiation factor 2B (IF-M2B), a specific initiator aminoacyl transfer RNA is bound to the 40-S subunit–messenger RNA complex. It has been shown that IF-M1 is primarily responsible for promoting the binding of this aminoacylated transfer RNA. The initiator aminoacyl transfer RNA is a unique methionyl transfer RNA which must participate in the formation of the eukaryotic initiation complex. In fact, the methionyl unit initially becomes the N-terminal aminoacyl unit of all eukaryotic proteins although it is generally removed before completion of the protein sequence. The initiator aminoacyl transfer RNA is usually designated methionyl transfer $RNA_f$ to distinguish it from the methionyl transfer RNA that participates in the introduction of a methionyl unit into the protein sequence at some point other than at the amino terminus. As one might expect, a recognition process is involved in the binding of the initiator aminoacyl transfer RNA by the 40-S subunit–messenger RNA complex in that the messenger RNA codon adenylyl-uridylyl-guanylyl (AUG) must be

---

[†] Merrick, W. C., and Anderson, W. F. (1975) *J. Biol. Chem.* **250**, 1197–1206; Safer, B., Anderson, W. F., and Merrick, W. C. (1975) *J. Biol. Chem.* **250**, 9067–9075; Safer, B., Adams, S. L., Anderson, W. F., and Merrick, W. C. (1975) *J. Biol. Chem.* **250**, 9076–9082; Adams, S. L., Safer, B., Anderson, W. F., and Merrick, W. C. (1975) *J. Biol. Chem.* **250**, 9083–9089.

properly positioned on the complex in order for the initiator aminoacyl transfer RNA to become bound. The codon AUG is, in effect, punctuation. This triplet sequence signals the beginning of a message, i.e., the beginning of a series of nonoverlapping, commaless triplet sequences which are to be translated into the primary structure of a given protein. Thus, the codon AUG serves somewhat the same function as the capital letter at the beginning of a sentence. The formation of the initiation complex continues as a 60-S ribosomal subunit becomes associated with the 40-S complex, i.e., the 40-S subunit–messenger RNA–initiator aminoacyl transfer RNA complex. This step requires the presence of an additional protein, the mammalian initiation factor 2A (IF-M2A). In addition, GTP is required. With the association of the 60-S subunit the 80-S initiation complex (consisting of the 40-S subunit, messenger RNA, initiator aminoacyl transfer RNA, and the 60-S subunit) is formed. At this stage, the initiation factors involved have dissociated from the complex or are dissociated from the complex as a concomitance of the formation of the 80-S complex. Also as a concomitance of the formation of the 80-S complex, GTP is cleaved to yield GDP and orthophosphate.

The alternative process for the formation of the eukaryotic initiation complex entails the participation of a protein designated IF-MP. This protein factor has been purified to homogeneity and found to have a molecular weight of 86,000. This protein factor comprises two types of subunits, one type which has a molecular weight of 34,000 and one type which has a molecular weight of 52,000. The factor IF-MP can react with GTP and the initiator aminoacyl transfer RNA to form a soluble ternary complex, which in turn can bind the 40-S subunit. In this case, IF-MP facilitates the binding of the initiator aminoacyl transfer RNA by the 40-S subunit. Next, the messenger RNA becomes bound by the 40-S subunit–initiator aminoacyl transfer RNA complex in the presence of IF-M3. Now, in the presence of IF-M2A, IF-M2B, and GTP the 60-S subunit becomes associated with the 40-S complex, and the 80-S initiation complex is formed. These pathways are summarized on page 735.

**Initiation in prokaryotic systems** In general, the initiation processes in eukaryotic and prokaryotic systems are analogous, although there are some significant differences. First, in the prokaryote the two ribosomal subunits have sedimentation coefficients of 30 and 50 S (rather than 40 and 60 S) and they are therefore referred to accordingly. The 30-S subunit comprises a 16-S ribosomal RNA plus 21 proteins, while the 50-S subunit comprises a 23-S ribosomal RNA, a 5-S ribosomal RNA, and 34 proteins. Formation of the initiation complex is generally considered to begin with the association of a protein designated as IF-3 with the noncomplexed 30-S subunit. Then, in the presence IF-2, IF-1, and GTP the messenger RNA and the initiator aminoacyl transfer RNA become bound by the 30-S subunit. In this process IF-3 promotes the binding of the messenger RNA, and IF-2 promotes the binding of the initiator aminoacyl transfer RNA by the 30-S subunit. Thus, the prokaryotic factor IF-3 is analogous to the mammalian (or eukaryotic) IF-M3, while the prokaryotic factor IF-2 is analogous to the mammalian (or eukaryotic) IF-M1 or IF-MP. It must be pointed out, however, that in prokaryotic systems the specific initiator aminoacyl transfer RNA is $N$-formylmethionyl transfer RNA, rather than methionyltransfer RNA, which serves in this capacity in eukaryotes.

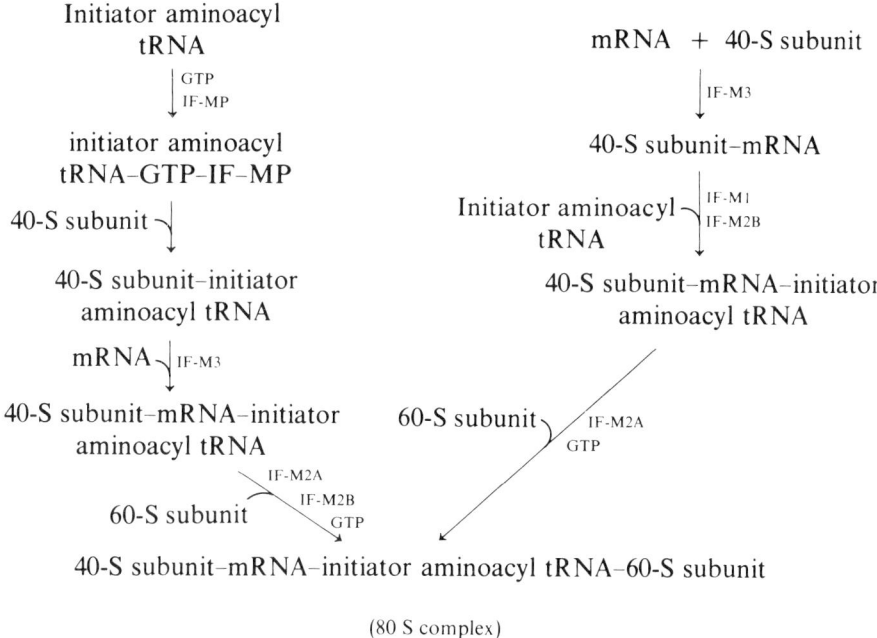

(80 S complex)

Following the association of the 30-S subunit, the messenger RNA, and the initiator aminoacyl transfer RNA, IF-3 dissociates from the complex. Next, the 50-S subunit becomes associated with the 30-S complex, i.e., the complex comprising the 30-S subunit, messenger RNA, and the initiator aminoacyl transfer RNA, as IF-1 dissociates. Association of the 50-S subunit is accompanied by the cleavage of the GTP to yield GDP and orthophosphate and as a concomitance of the dissociation of the GDP, orthophosphate, and IF-2, the 70-S complex is formed.

## Elongation

The bond-making process in protein synthesis is referred to as elongation. Basically, elongation entails three steps:

1. The GTP-dependent binding of an aminoacyl transfer RNA at a locus on the catalytic site, called the *acceptor site*
2. The formation of a peptide bond derived from the carboxyl group of the aminoacyl moiety at a locus on the catalytic site called the *donor site* and the amino group of the aminoacyl moiety at the acceptor site
3. The GTP-dependent translocation of the peptidyl transfer RNA from the acceptor site to the donor site

The formation of the peptide bond is catalyzed by an enzyme activity associated with the larger ribosomal subunit. This activity is referred to as peptidyltransferase activity, although it is thought that rather than a single enzyme, the formation of the peptide bond requires several enzymatic activities associated with several ribosomal proteins. The catalytic site at which peptide-bond formation takes place has two bonding sites: one of these, the *acceptor site*, is the site at which the aminoacyl moiety being introduced becomes bound, while the other, the *donor site*, is the site at which the existing peptidyl moiety is bound. When the first, i.e., the N-terminal, aminoacyl unit of a protein is to be incorporated the methionyl (or *N*-formylmethionyl) moiety of the initiator, aminoacyl transfer RNA occupies the donor site.

When the initiation complex has been formed, and with the initiator aminoacyl moiety at the donor site the binding of the aminoacyl moiety of the first aminoacyl transfer RNA takes place at the acceptor site. This binding requires GTP, as mentioned above, and also a protein which in mammalian (or eukaryotic) systems is called EF-1. (If the nomenclature were consistent, this mammalian elongation factor would be designated EF-M1.) The factor EF-1 can reportedly be resolved to yield EF-1A and EF-1B. The individual functions of these components are unknown, however. As a concomitance of the binding of the aminoacyl moiety at the acceptor site, GTP is cleaved to yield GDP and orthophosphate.

Once both the acceptor and donor sites are appropriately occupied, peptide-bond formation takes place. A minimal mechanism for this bond-making process is shown on page 737.

With the new peptide bond formed, it now remains for the transfer RNA to dissociate from the ribosome and for the peptidyl transfer RNA to be translocated from the acceptor site to the donor site as the ribosome moves along the messenger RNA in such a manner that the next codon of the message is properly positioned to recognize the anticodon of the next aminoacyl transfer RNA. In mammalian systems the translocation process requires GTP and a protein designated as EF-2. The elongation factor has been isolated from rabbit reticulocytes and purified to homogeneity. Its molecular weight is 100,000. As a concomitance of translocation, GTP is cleaved to yield GDP and orthophosphate.

Elongation in bacterial cells is analogous. With the initiation complex formed and the peptidyl or *N*-formylmethionyl moiety at the donor site, the incoming aminoacyl moiety becomes bound at the acceptor site through the agency of GTP and the prokaryotic elongation factor, designated EF-Tu. The GTP is cleaved; GDP, orthophosphate, and EF-Tu dissociate; and the peptide bond is formed. Translocation in this case requires the prokaryotic protein EF-G and GTP. Thus, the bacterial protein EF-Tu is analogous to the mammalian EF-1, similarly the bacterial protein EF-G is analogous to the mammalian EF-2. In addition, in the bacterial system it has been shown that a protein which is associated with EF-Tu and designated EF-Ts is required in order for EF-Tu to be recycled and used again. (The designations Tu and Ts were made when it was erroneously believed that these proteins possessed peptidyl*t*ransferase activity and it had been observed that one was relatively *u*nstable while the other was more *s*table.) Another observation made with respect to the bacterial system is that while GTP is required for the binding of the elongation factors by the ribosomal subunit, the cleavage of GTP is required in order for the elongation factor to dissociate from the ribosomal subunit.

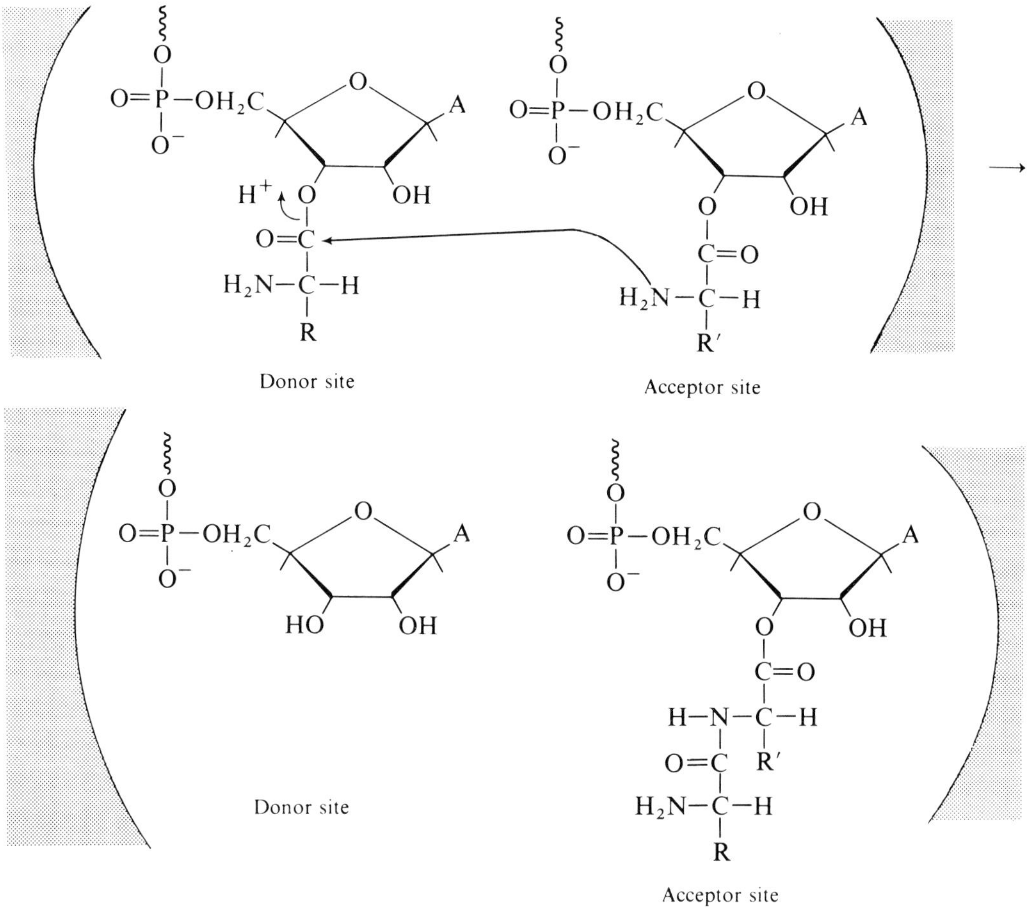

## Termination

Perhaps less is known concerning the termination of protein synthesis than the other phases of this process. However, it is known that each of the messenger RNA codons UAA, UAG, and UGA can signal the end of a given message. It is also known that specific proteins, called *release factors*, participate in the termination process. These factors are required in order for the newly synthesized protein to be released from the ribosome. Studies on the termination of protein synthesis in rabbit reticulocytes have shown that GTP is also required during termination, and it is speculated that the nucleoside triphosphate is required for the binding of the release factor (RF) by the ribosomal subunit and that its cleavage to GDP and orthophosphate is required in order for RF to dissociate from the system after it has facilitated the release of the completed protein. The catalytic activity needed to release the completed protein from the transfer RNA is thought to be provided by the larger ribosomal subunit.

As a part of the termination process it has also been shown that the messenger RNA dissociates from the ribosomal complex and that the monomeric ribosome

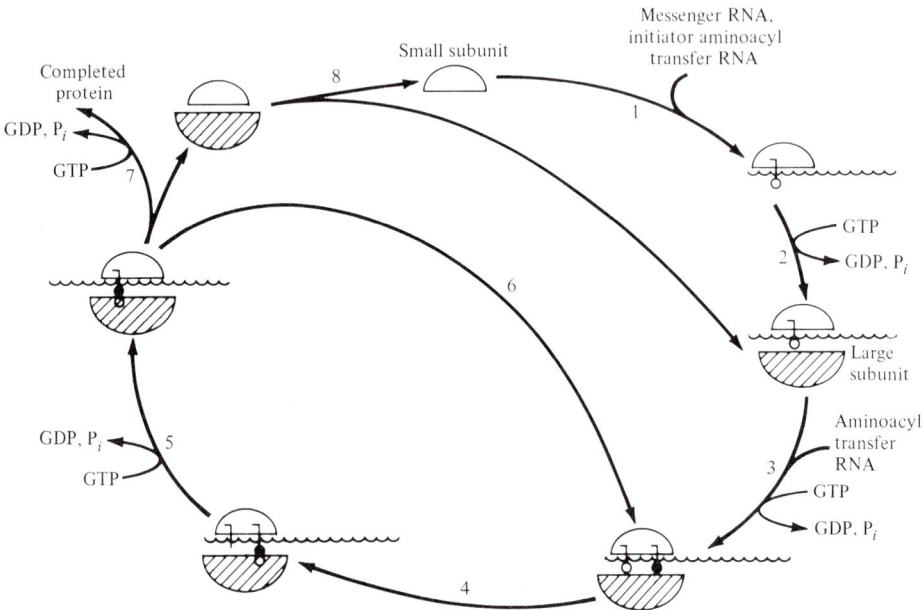

**Figure 14-9** Schematic representation of the sequence of events in protein synthesis. (1) Messenger RNA, initiator aminoacyl transfer RNA, and the small subunit form a complex in the presence of the appropriate supporting factors. (2) Large subunit becomes associated with the complex containing the small subunit. GTP undergoes cleavage as a concomitance of this association. (3) Through the agency of the cleavage of GTP the aminoacyl transfer RNA that is stipulated by the messenger RNA becomes bound at the acceptor site. (4) Peptide-bond formation occurs. (5) Through the agency of the cleavage of GTP the peptidyl transfer RNA is translocated from the acceptor site to the donor site. (6) When another aminoacyl unit is to be incorporated, the appropriate aminoacyl transfer RNA becomes bound at the acceptor site and steps 4 and 5 follow. (7) When the synthesis has been completed, the product dissociates from the ribosomal complex. The cleavage of GTP is also required at this stage. (8) The ribosomal complex dissociates yielding the noncomplexed subunits which, thus, become available for the formation of a polysome which will support the synthesis of another protein molecule.

dissociates to yield the noncomplexed smaller subunit and larger subunit. These are required for the next cycle of events. (The associated 70- or 80-S ribosome monomer is inactive.) In bacterial systems, at least, the dissociation of the ribosome monomer is promoted by IF-3.

## Summary of Protein Synthesis

Figure 14-9 summarizes the process of protein synthesis.

## Mitochondrial Protein Synthesis

In eukaryotic cells protein synthesis takes place not only on the ribosomes or polysomes (multiple pairs of ribosomal subunits associated with a messenger RNA) in the cell cytoplasm but also in the mitochondria. However, even most mitochondrial proteins are in fact specified by nuclear DNA and synthesized on cytoplasmic ribosomes. Actually, no more than 8 to 10 hydrophobic polypeptides, which have the function of interdigitating certain components in the mitochondrial inner membrane, are synthesized by the mitochondrion. Three of these polypeptides are components of the cytochrome *c* oxidase complex, four are a part of the oligomycin-sensitive ATPase complex, one is associated with cytochrome *b*, and the identities of any others remain to be established.

Mitochondrial protein synthesis also takes place on ribosomal subunits which are smaller than those of the eukaryotic cell cytoplasm. As isolated from mammalian mitochondria, the associated monomeric ribosome has a sedimentation coefficient of 55 S, while its larger and smaller subunits have sedimentation coefficients of 40 and 30 S, respectively. The larger subunit contains a 16-S RNA and the smaller a 12-S RNA. A component that is comparable to the 5-S RNA has not been found in the mitochondrial ribosome.

Few details of the mitochondrial synthesis of proteins are known although it has been shown that the specific initiator aminoacyl transfer RNA in this case is *N*-formylmethionyl transfer RNA. This observation is one of several which has caused speculation that the mitochondrion of the eukaryotic cell evolved from the prokaryotic bacterial cell.

It has also been speculated that mitochondrial and cytoplasmic protein synthesis must somehow be coordinated in order to prevent the accumulation of a large excess of the proteins of either cytoplasmic or mitochondrial origin that must interact to form, for example, the cytochrome *c* oxidase complex. There is now some evidence that the accumulation of the participating proteins of cytoplasmic origin can stimulate the synthesis of those of mitochondrial origin and that this entails the increased dissociation of ribosome monomers to yield the noncomplexed ribosomal subunits, which can then function in protein synthesis.

## INHIBITORS OF PROTEIN SYNTHESIS

A number of components that inhibit protein synthesis and have been found useful in studying the mechanisms involved in this complex process are discussed briefly.

### Puromycin

The antibiotic puromycin is, in fact, a structural analog of the 3′ terminus of an aminoacyl transfer RNA. However, it lacks the remainder of the transfer RNA molecule, including the anticodon region, and hence it does not interact with messenger RNA. It does bind at the acceptor site on the larger subunit, however, and, once bound, its amino group can react at the carbonyl carbon atom of the aminoacyl moiety at the donor site with the result that a peptide bond is formed. Once this has occurred, the aminoacyl- or peptidylpuromycin cannot undergo translocation from the acceptor site to the donor site, and consequently protein synthesis stops.

Puromycin has been used in many studies in which only the initiator transfer RNA and the inhibitor are available to form the peptide bond, and thus with the formation of methionylpuromycin (or *N*-formylmethionylpuromycin) synthesis stops.

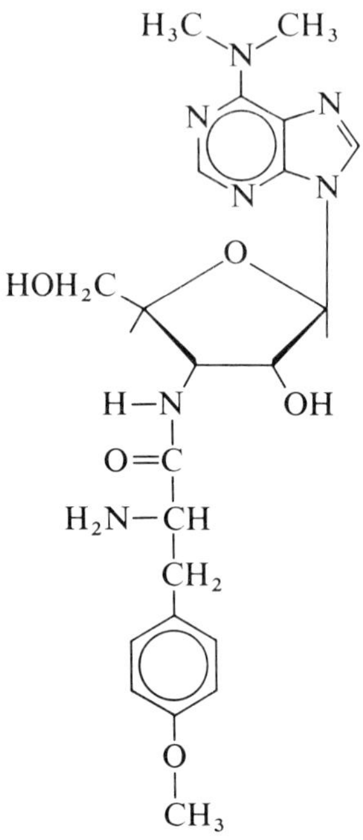

Puromycin

This has proved a useful technique for exploring some of the processes of protein synthesis in a greatly simplified system.

## Inhibitors of Peptidyltransferase Activity

Several antibiotics inhibit protein synthesis by inhibiting the peptide bond-making process. Included in this category are chloramphenicol and erythromycin,

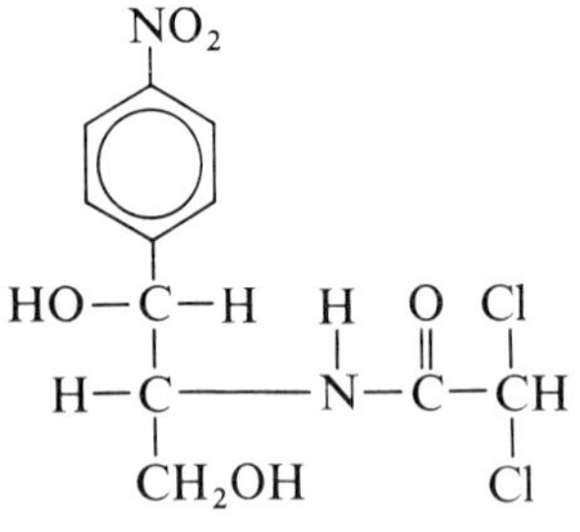

Chloramphenicol

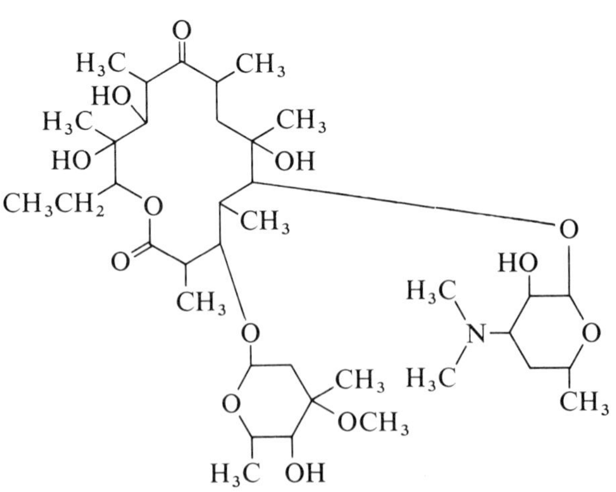

Erythromycin

which interact specifically with the larger subunit of a bacterial or mitochondrial ribosome. Since cytoplasmic protein synthesis in eukaryotic cells is not affected by these agents, their use provides a means for observing cytoplasmic protein synthesis while blocking mitochondrial protein synthesis in mammalian cells.

## Inhibitors of the Actions of Elongation Factors

The steroidal antibiotic fusidate

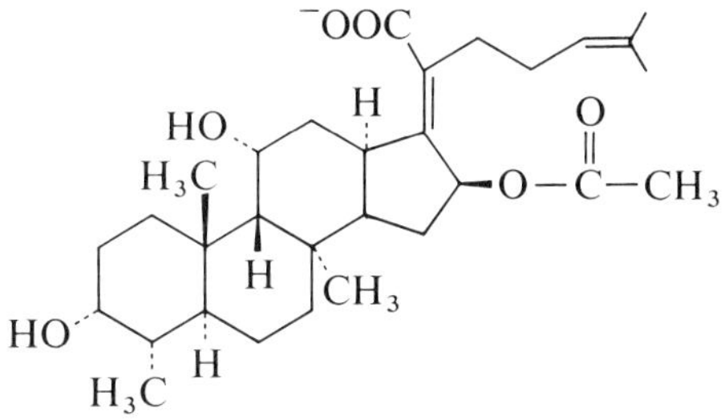

Fusidate

inhibits the release of the GDP-EF-2 complex from the ribosome. This inhibits the translocation process, and protein synthesis stops.

Yet another effect upon EF-2 is that imposed by an active principle of diphtheria toxin. In the presence of catalytic amounts of the toxin, EF-2 can undergo a reaction with $NAD^+$ which results in the ADP-ribosylation of the factor. This renders the factor inactive.

## Cycloheximide

Cycloheximide and the other glutarimide antibiotics

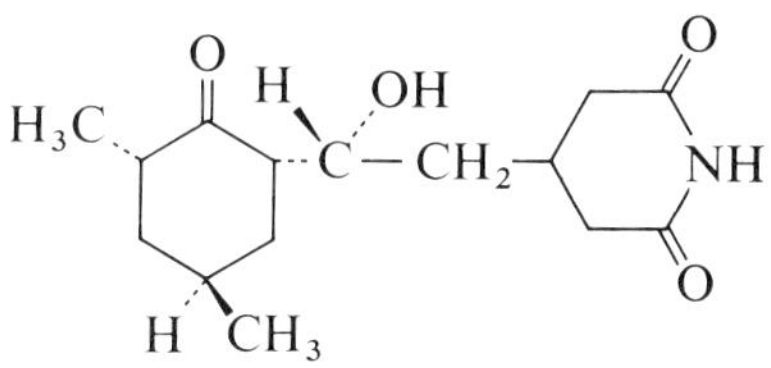

Cycloheximide

are specifically inhibitors of protein synthesis in the cytoplasm of eukaryotic cells. These agents bind the 60-S ribosomal subunit, and as a result the dissociation of the deacylated transfer RNA from the donor site and the translocation of the peptidyl transfer RNA from the acceptor site to the donor site are prevented. Through the use of either cycloheximide, which inhibits cytoplasmic protein synthesis in eukaryotic cells, or chloramphenicol (or erythromycin), which inhibits mitochondrial protein synthesis, these two processes can be examined individually and compared and contrasted.

# APPENDIX A

# KINETIC EQUATIONS

## VELOCITY EQUATION FOR ORDERED SEQUENTIAL BI BI REACTION

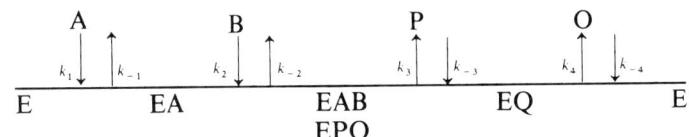

Since there are four enzyme forms, E, EA, EAB-EPQ, and EQ, the King-Altman polygon has four vertices:

The four nonspecific patterns can be written

The reaction velocity of this ordered sequential Bi Bi process is given by

$$v = k_4[\text{EQ}] - k_{-4}[\text{Q}][\text{E}]$$

Note that this is *not* an initial-velocity equation but the complete velocity equation.

743

The *steady-state* concentrations of EQ and E, required by this equation, are equal to the appropriate distribution equations multiplied by the total enzyme concentration $[E]_0$. The numerators of distribution equations are derived from the specific King-Altman patterns which relate to the enzyme forms concerned. The denominator of a distribution equation is the sum of the numerator expressions for all of the enzyme forms involved.

Written below are the numerator expressions for E, EA, EAB-EPQ, and EQ, followed by their common denominator. The complete velocity equation for an ordered sequential Bi Bi reaction is then derived.

E:

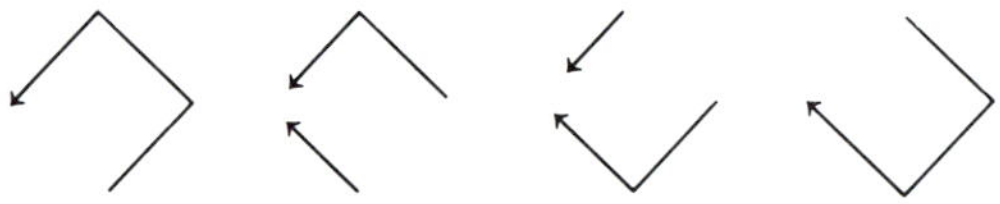

$$E = k_{-1}k_{-2}k_{-3}[P] + k_{-1}k_{-2}k_4 + k_{-1}k_3k_4 + k_2k_3k_4[B]$$

EA:

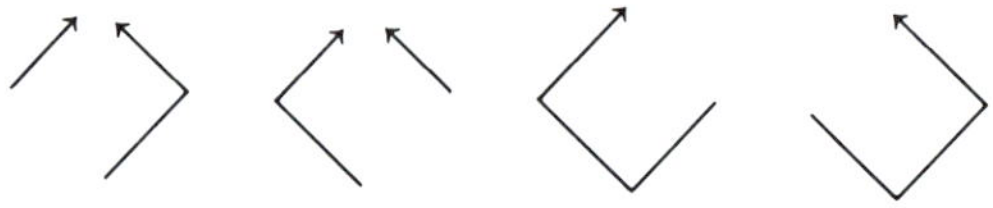

$$EA = k_1k_{-2}k_{-3}[A][P] + k_1k_{-2}k_4[A] + k_1k_3k_4[A] + k_{-2}k_{-3}k_{-4}[P][Q]$$

EAB-EPQ:

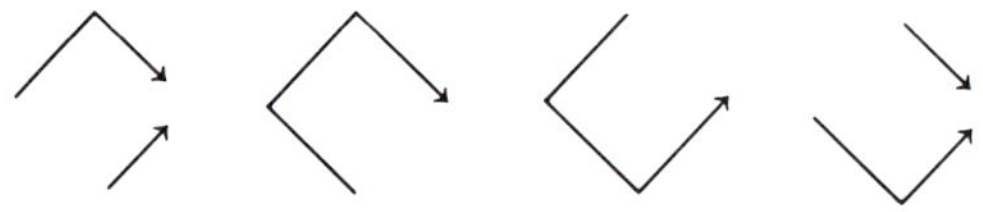

$$EAB\text{-}EPQ = k_1k_2k_{-3}[A][B][P] + k_1k_2k_4[A][B] + k_{-1}k_{-3}k_{-4}[P][Q]$$
$$+ k_2k_{-3}k_{-4}[B][P][Q]$$

EQ:

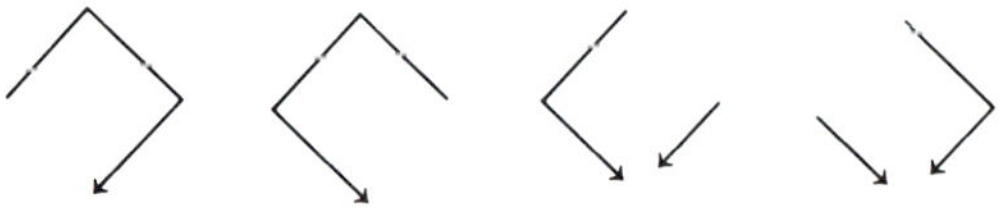

$$EQ = k_1k_2k_3[A][B] + k_{-1}k_{-2}k_{-4}[Q] + k_{-1}k_3k_{-4}[Q] + k_2k_3k_{-4}[B][Q]$$

The sum of these four terms gives the denominator term. Thus,

$$\begin{aligned}\text{Denominator} = & (k_1k_{-2}k_4 + k_1k_3k_4)[A] + k_2k_3k_4[B] + k_{-1}k_{-2}k_{-3}[P] \\ & + (k_{-1}k_{-2}k_{-4} + k_{-1}k_3k_{-4})[Q] + (k_1k_2k_4 + k_1k_2k_3)[A][B] \\ & + k_1k_{-2}k_{-3}[A][P] + k_2k_3k_{-4}[B][Q] + (k_{-1}k_{-3}k_{-4} \\ & + k_{-2}k_{-3}k_{-4})[P][Q] + k_1k_2k_{-3}[A][B][P] \\ & + k_2k_{-3}k_{-4}[B][P][Q] + k_{-1}k_{-2}k_4 + k_{-1}k_3k_4\end{aligned}$$

Now, since $v = (k_4[EQ] - k_{-4}[Q][E])[E]_0$

$$\begin{aligned}v = & \{k_4(k_1k_2k_3[A][B] + k_2k_3k_{-4}[B][Q] + k_{-1}k_{-2}k_{-4}[Q] \\ & + k_{-1}k_3k_{-4}[Q]) - k_{-4}[Q](k_2k_3k_4[B] + k_{-1}k_{-2}k_{-3}[P] \\ & + k_{-1}k_{-2}k_4 + k_{-1}k_3k_4)\}[E]_0/\text{denominator (sum of E, EA, EAB-EPQ, and EQ terms)}\end{aligned}$$

$$v = (k_1 k_2 k_3 k_4 [A][B] + k_2 k_3 k_4 k_{-4}[B][Q] + k_{-1} k_{-2} k_4 k_{-4}[Q]$$
$$+ k_{-1} k_3 k_4 k_{-4}[Q] - k_2 k_3 k_4 k_{-4}[B][Q] - k_{-1} k_{-2} k_{-3} k_{-4}[P][Q]$$
$$- k_{-1} k_{-2} k_4 k_{-4}[Q] - k_{-1} k_3 k_4 k_{-4}[Q])[E]_0/\text{denominator}$$

Cancelling the appropriate terms,

$$v = (k_1 k_2 k_3 k_4 [A][B] - k_{-1} k_{-2} k_{-3} k_{-4}[P][Q])[E]_0/\text{denominator}$$

or

$$v = (k_1 k_2 k_3 k_4 [A][B] - k_{-1} k_{-2} k_{-3} k_{-4}[P][Q])[E]_0/\{(k_1 k_{-2} k_4 + k_1 k_3 k_4)[A]$$
$$+ k_2 k_3 k_4 [B] + k_{-1} k_{-2} k_{-3}[P] + (k_{-1} k_{-2} k_{-4} + k_{-1} k_3 k_{-4})[Q]$$
$$+ (k_1 k_2 k_4 + k_1 k_2 k_3)[A][B] + k_1 k_{-2} k_{-3}[A][P] + k_2 k_3 k_{-4}[B][Q]$$
$$+ (k_{-1} k_{-3} k_{-4} + k_{-2} k_{-3} k_{-4})[P][Q] + k_1 k_2 k_{-3}[A][B][P]$$
$$+ k_2 k_{-3} k_{-4}[B][P][Q] + k_{-1} k_{-2} k_4 + k_{-1} k_3 k_4\}$$

Now making the following substitutions

$$K_b = \frac{\text{coef A}}{\text{coef AB}} = \frac{k_1 k_{-2} k_4 + k_1 k_3 k_4}{k_1 k_2 k_3 + k_1 k_2 k_4} = \frac{k_4}{k_2} \frac{k_{-2} + k_3}{k_3 + k_4}$$

$$K_a = \frac{\text{coef B}}{\text{coef AB}} = \frac{k_2 k_3 k_4}{k_1 k_2 k_3 + k_1 k_2 k_4} = \frac{k_4}{k_1} \frac{k_3}{k_3 + k_4}$$

$$K_{ia} = \frac{\text{const}}{\text{coef A}} = \frac{k_{-1} k_{-2} k_4 + k_{-1} k_3 k_4}{k_1 k_{-2} k_4 + k_1 k_3 k_4} = \frac{k_{-1}}{k_1}$$

$$K_{ib} = \frac{\text{coef PQ}}{\text{coef BPQ}} = \frac{k_{-1} k_{-3} k_{-4} + k_{-2} k_{-3} k_{-4}}{k_2 k_{-3} k_{-4}} = \frac{k_{-1} + k_{-2}}{k_2}$$

$$K_p = \frac{\text{coef Q}}{\text{coef PQ}} = \frac{k_{-1} k_{-2} k_{-4} + k_{-1} k_3 k_{-4}}{k_{-1} k_{-3} k_{-4} + k_{-2} k_{-3} k_{-4}} = \frac{k_{-1}}{k_{-3}} \left[\frac{k_{-2} + k_3}{k_{-1} + k_{-2}}\right]$$

$$K_q = \frac{\text{coef P}}{\text{coef PQ}} = \frac{k_{-1} k_{-2} k_{-3}}{k_{-1} k_{-3} k_{-4} + k_{-2} k_{-3} k_{-4}} = \frac{k_{-1}}{k_{-4}} \frac{k_2}{k_{-1} + k_{-2}}$$

$$K_{ip} = \frac{\text{coef AB}}{\text{coef ABP}} = \frac{k_1 k_2 k_3 + k_1 k_2 k_4}{k_1 k_2 k_{-3}} = \frac{k_3 + k_4}{k_{-3}}$$

$$K_{iq} = \frac{\text{coef B}}{\text{coef BQ}} = \frac{k_2 k_3 k_4}{k_2 k_3 k_{-4}} = \frac{k_4}{k_{-4}}$$

and

$$V_{\max}^f = \frac{k_1 k_2 k_3 k_4 [E]_0}{\text{coef AB}}$$

$$V_{\max}^r = \frac{k_{-1} k_{-2} k_{-3} k_{-4} [E]_0}{\text{coef PQ}}$$

the velocity equation assumes the following form:

$$v = V^f_{max} V^r_{max} \bigg( [A][B] - \frac{K_{ia}K_b}{K_p K_{iq}}[P][Q] \bigg) \bigg/ \bigg\{ K_b[A] + K_a[B] + [A][B]$$

$$+ \frac{K_{ia}K_bK_q}{K_p K_{iq}}[P] + \frac{K_b K_q}{K_p K_{iq}}[A][P] + \frac{K_{ia}K_b}{K_{iq}}[Q] + \frac{K_{ia}K_b}{K_p K_{iq}}[P][Q]$$

$$+ \frac{K_a}{K_{iq}}[B][Q] + \frac{1}{K_{ip}}[A][B][P] + \frac{K_{ia}K_b}{K_{ib}K_p K_{iq}}[B][P][Q] + K_{ia}K_b \bigg\}$$

## INITIAL-VELOCITY EQUATION FOR RANDOM SEQUENTIAL BI BI REACTION

A random sequential Bi Bi reaction can be represented diagrammatically as shown:

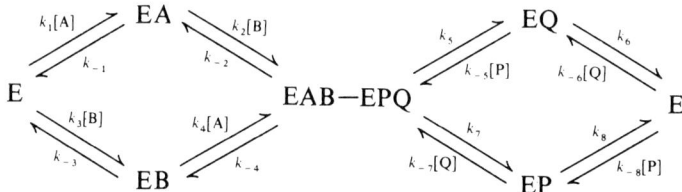

In this case, the King-Altman polygon below can be used to represent the reaction as it occurs under initial-velocity conditions. Since the reaction involves two substrates and two products but with alternate pathways, the figure is, in fact, two four-sided polygons appropriately arranged.

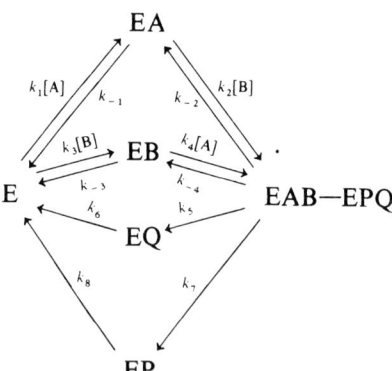

The total number of possible patterns each having $n - 1$ lines (when $n$ is the number of enzyme forms) can be derived by the formula

$$\text{Total patterns possible} = \frac{m!}{(n-1)!(m-n+1)!}$$

in which $m$ is the number of interconversion steps in the reaction. In a random sequential Bi Bi reaction, $m = 8$. Therefore,

$$\text{Total patterns possible} = \frac{8!}{(6-1)!(8-6+1)!} = 56$$

However, some of these patterns contain *closed loops*, i.e.,

```
    EA                    EB                    EA
   /  \                  /  \                  /  \
  E    EAB–EPQ         E    EAB–EPQ          /    \
   \  /                  \  /                /  EB  \
    EP                    EQ                E――――EAB–EPQ

  E\   /EAB–EPQ
    EQ                    EA                    EB
   /  \                  /  \                  /  \
  /    \               E    EAB–EPQ         E    EAB–EPQ
    EP                    \  /                  \  /
                           EQ                    EP
```

Patterns containing closed loops must be eliminated since patterns used must represent a unique pathway by which one enzyme form is converted into another. Hence, the number of patterns to be used is given by the total number of patterns possible minus patterns that contain closed loops. A closed loop having $r$ sides will occur

$$\frac{(m-r)!}{(n-1-r)!(m-n+1)!}$$

times. Since these closed loops have 4 sides, each will occur 4 times. Therefore, 24 patterns of the possible 56 patterns are not to be used. The 32 to be used are represented below.

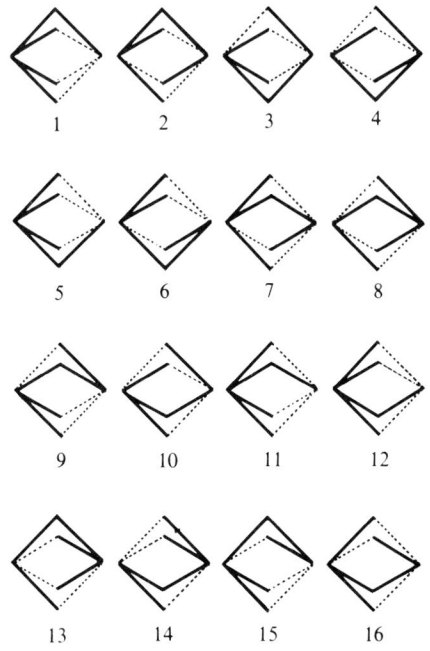

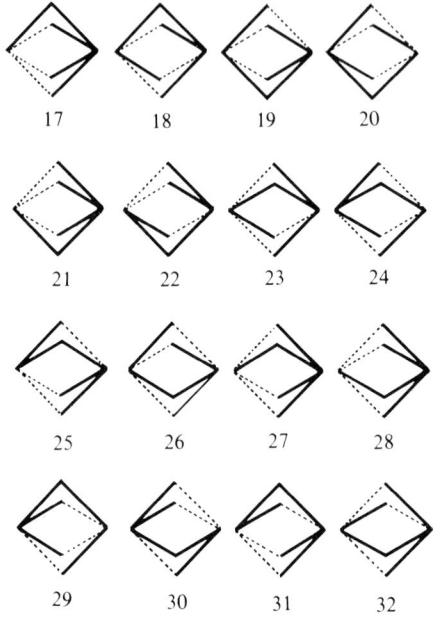

When these patterns are used as described previously, the following terms are obtained:

$$E = k_{-1}k_{-2}k_{-3}k_6k_8 + k_2k_{-3}k_6k_7k_8[B] + k_{-1}k_{-3}k_6k_7k_8$$
$$+ k_2k_{-3}k_{-4}k_6k_8[B] + k_2k_{-3}k_5k_6k_8[B] + k_{-1}k_{-3}k_{-4}k_6k_8$$
$$+ k_{-1}k_{-3}k_5k_6k_8 + k_2k_4k_5k_6k_8[A][B] + k_{-1}k_{-2}k_4k_6k_8[A]$$
$$+ k_{-1}k_4k_5k_6k_8[A] + k_{-1}k_4k_6k_7k_8[A] + k_2k_4k_6k_7k_8[A][B]$$

$$EA = k_1k_{-2}k_{-3}k_6k_8[A] + k_1k_{-3}k_6k_7k_8[A] + k_{-2}k_3k_4k_6k_8[A][B]$$
$$+ k_1k_{-3}k_{-4}k_6k_8[A] + k_1k_{-2}k_4k_6k_8[A]^2 + k_1k_4k_5k_6k_8[A]^2$$
$$+ k_1k_4k_6k_7k_8[A]^2 + k_1k_{-3}k_5k_6k_8[A]$$

$$EB = k_{-1}k_{-2}k_3k_6k_8[B] + k_2k_3k_6k_7k_8[B]^2 + k_{-1}k_3k_6k_7k_8[B]$$
$$+ k_2k_3k_{-4}k_6k_8[B]^2 + k_2k_3k_5k_6k_8[B]^2 + k_{-1}k_3k_{-4}k_6k_8[B]$$
$$+ k_{-1}k_3k_5k_6k_8[B] + k_1k_2k_{-4}k_6k_8[A][B]$$

$$EAB\text{-}EPQ = k_1k_2k_{-3}k_6k_8[A][B] + k_2k_3k_4k_6k_8[A][B]^2 + k_{-1}k_3k_4k_6k_8[A][B]$$
$$+ k_1k_2k_4k_6k_8[A]^2[B]$$

$$EQ = k_1k_2k_{-3}k_5k_8[A][B] + k_{-1}k_3k_4k_5k_8[A][B] + k_2k_3k_4k_5k_8[A][B]^2$$
$$+ k_1k_2k_4k_5k_8[A]^2[B]$$

$$EP = k_{-1}k_3k_4k_6k_7[A][B] + k_2k_3k_4k_6k_7[A][B]^2$$
$$+ k_1k_2k_{-3}k_6k_7[A][B] + k_1k_2k_4k_6k_7[A]^2[B]$$

KINETIC EQUATIONS  **749**

The initial velocity of this reaction is given by
$$v_i = (k_6[EQ] + k_8[EP])[E]_0$$
Therefore
$$v_i = k_6\{(k_1k_2k_{-3}k_5k_8 + k_{-1}k_3k_4k_5k_8)[A][B] + k_1k_2k_4k_5k_8[A]^2[B]$$
$$+ k_2k_3k_4k_5k_8[A][B]^2\}[E]_0 + k_8\{(k_1k_2k_{-3}k_6k_7 + k_{-1}k_3k_4k_6k_7)[A][B]$$
$$+ k_1k_2k_4k_6k_7[A]^2[B] + k_2k_3k_4k_6k_7[A][B]^2\}[E]_0/\text{denominator (sum of E, EA,}$$
EB, EAB-EPQ, EQ and EP terms)

or

$$v_i = \{(k_1k_2k_{-3}k_5k_6k_8 + k_1k_2k_{-3}k_6k_7k_8 + k_{-1}k_3k_4k_5k_6k_8$$
$$+ k_{-1}k_3k_4k_6k_7k_8)[A][B] + (k_1k_2k_4k_5k_6k_8$$
$$+ k_1k_2k_4k_6k_7k_8)[A]^2[B](k_2k_3k_4k_5k_6k_8 + k_2k_3k_4k_6k_7k_8)[A][B]^2\}[E]_0/$$
$$\{(k_1k_{-2}k_{-3}k_6k_8 + k_1k_{-3}k_{-4}k_6k_8 + k_1k_{-3}k_5k_6k_8 + k_1k_{-3}k_6k_7k_8$$
$$+ k_{-1}k_{-2}k_4k_6k_8 + k_{-1}k_4k_5k_6k_8 + k_{-1}k_4k_6k_7k_8)[A] + (k_{-1}k_{-2}k_3k_6k_8$$
$$+ k_{-1}k_3k_{-4}k_6k_8 + k_{-1}k_3k_5k_6k_8 + k_{-1}k_3k_6k_7k_8 + k_2k_{-3}k_{-4}k_6k_8$$
$$+ k_2k_{-3}k_5k_6k_8 + k_2k_{-3}k_6k_7k_8)[B] + (k_1k_{-2}k_4k_6k_8 + k_1k_4k_5k_6k_8$$
$$+ k_1k_4k_6k_7k_8)[A]^2 + (k_2k_3k_{-4}k_6k_8 + k_2k_3k_5k_6k_8 + k_2k_3k_6k_7k_8)[B]^2$$
$$+ (k_1k_2k_{-3}k_5k_8 + k_1k_2k_{-3}k_6k_7 + k_1k_2k_{-3}k_6k_8 + k_1k_2k_{-4}k_6k_8$$
$$+ k_{-1}k_3k_4k_5k_8 + k_{-1}k_3k_4k_6k_7 + k_{-1}k_3k_4k_6k_8 + k_2k_4k_5k_6k_8$$
$$+ k_2k_4k_6k_7k_8 + k_{-2}k_3k_4k_6k_8)[A][B] + (k_1k_2k_4k_5k_8 + k_1k_2k_4k_6k_7$$
$$+ k_1k_2k_4k_6k_8)[A]^2[B] + (k_2k_3k_4k_5k_8 + k_2k_3k_4k_6k_7$$
$$+ k_2k_3k_4k_6k_8)[A][B]^2 + (k_{-1}k_{-2}k_{-3}k_6k_8 + k_{-1}k_{-3}k_{-4}k_6k_8$$
$$+ k_{-1}k_{-3}k_5k_6k_8 + k_{-1}k_{-3}k_6k_7k_8)\}$$

This equation can be simplified to some degree as follows:
$$V_{max} = \frac{(\text{coef } AB^2 \text{ numerator})[E]_0}{\text{coef } AB^2 \text{ denominator}}$$

or
$$V_{max} = \frac{k_6k_8(k_5 + k_7)[E]_0}{k_5k_8 + k_6k_7 + k_6k_8}$$

With further mathematical manipulations, one can obtain
$$v_i = V_{max}(K_1[A][B] + K_2[A]^2[B] + [A][B]^2)/K_3[A] + K_4[B] + K_5[A]^2$$
$$+ K_6[B]^2 + K_7[A][B] + K_2[A]^2[B] + [A][B]^2 + K_8$$

Here $K_1$ to $K_8$ are complex combinations of rate constants.

# INDEX

# INDEX

Acetolactate synthase, 657–658
Acetyl-CoA acetyltransferase, 491
Acetyl-CoA acyltransferase, 481–482
Acetyl-CoA carboxylase, 495–496
Acetylglutamate kinase, 673
Acetylglutamyl-5-phosphate reductase, 673
$N$-Acetylneuraminate, structure of, 12
Acetylornithine aminotransferase, 673
Acetylornithine deacetylase, 673
Aconitate hydratase, 424–425
Actinomycin D, 603
Acyl-CoA dehydrogenases, 479–480
Acyl-CoA desaturase, 503
Acyl-CoA synthetase, 477–478
Acylglycerols:
 assimilation of, 474–477
 biosynthesis of, 503–505
 hydrolysis of: acid-catalyzed, 120–122
  base-catalyzed, 122–124
 laboratory synthesis of, 113–118
 structures of, 20–21
Adenine phosphoribosyltransferase, 565
 Lesch-Nyhan syndrome and, 565
Adenosine deaminase, 561
Adenosine kinase, 565
Adenosine monophosphate (AMP):
 catabolism of, 561–564

Adenosine monophosphate (AMP):
 from inosine monophosphate (IMP), 557–558
Adenosine monophosphate deaminase, 560
Adenosine-triphosphate phosphoribosyltransferase, 687–688
Adenosylhomocysteinase, 641
$S$-Adenosyl-L-methionine, formation of, 641
 in formation of epinephrine, 701
 in formation of methionine, 648–649
 in formation of phosphatidylcholine, 508
 in formation of phosphocreatine, 630
 in lysine catabolism, 665
 structure of, 508
$S$-Adenosyl-L-methionine decarboxylase, 674–675
Adenylosuccinate lyase, 554–555
Adenylosuccinate synthetase, 557–558
Adenylylsulfate kinase, 645
Adrenodoxin, 531
Agmatinase, 670
Alanine aminotransferase, 650
Albinism, 702
Alcaptonuria, 698
Alcohol dehydrogenase, 405
Aldehyde dehydrogenase, 405

Allantoicase, 566
Allantoinase, 566
Allosteric transitions, 322–327
Amidophosphoribosyltransferase, 546–547
Amine oxidases, 614–615
Amino-acid acetyltransferase, 673
Amino-acid oxidases, 611–614
Amino acids:
   acid-base properties of, 154–161
   laboratory synthesis of, 152–154
   optical rotation of, 151–152
   reactions of, 161–164
   removal of nitrogen from:
      by amine oxidases, 614–615
      by amino-acid oxidases, 611–614
      by aminotransferases, 619–622
      by glutamate dehydrogenase, 615–619
   structures of, 149–151
Aminoacyl-transfer ribonucleic acid synthetases, 731–733
Aminoacyl units, conformation of, 41–44
Aminoadipate aminotransferase, 662, 667
Aminoadipate-semialdehyde dehydrogenase, 662, 667
Aminobutyrate aminotransferase, 677
Aminocarboxymuconate-semialdehyde decarboxylase, 712
5-Aminolevulinate, formation of, 625–627
5-Aminolevulinate synthase, 625–627
Aminomuconate-semialdehyde dehydrogenase, 712
Aminopropyltransferase, 674–675
Amytal, structure of, 460
Anabolism:
   of acylglycerols, 503–505
   of androgens, 534–536
   of arginine, 671–674
   of cholesterol, 519–531
   of cysteine, 645–648
   of deoxyribonucleic acids, 585–597

Anabolism:
   of estrogens, 536–537
   of fatty acids, 494–503
   of heme, 624–629
   of histidine, 687–693
   of isoleucine, 657–662
   of leucine, 657–662
   of lysine, 666–669
   of methionine, 648–650
   of phenylalanine, 702–708
   of phospholipids, 506–513
   of prostaglandins, 515–517
   of proteins, 727–739
   of purines, 543–556
   of pyrimidines, 568–574
   of ribonucleic acids, 597–601
   of sphingolipids, 513–515
   of threonine, 637–641
   of tryptophan, 717–723
   of tyrosine, 702–708
   of valine, 657–662
Anaplerotic enzymes, 371
Androgens, biosynthesis of, 534–536
Anthranilate phosphoribosyltransferase, 720
Anthranilate synthase, 718–719
Antigens:
   blood-group, 16
   homoglycans as, 11
   pneumococcal polysaccharide, 20
Antimycin, 461
Arginase, 670, 724
Arginine:
   biosynthesis of, 671–674
   catabolism of, 669–671
Arginine decarboxylase, 670
Arginine deiminase, 670
Argininosuccinate lyase, 671–672, 724
Argininosuccinate synthetase, 671, 724
Aromatic-L-amino-acid decarboxylase, 701
Arrhenius complex, 284–285, 290–291
Asparagine, formation of, 652–653
Asparagine synthetase, 652–653
Aspartate aminotransferase, 650

Aspartate carbamoyltransferase, 570–572
Aspartate 4-decarboxylase, 651–652
Aspartate kinase, 637, 666
Aspartate-semialdehyde dehydrogenase, 637–638
Asymmetric syntheses, 77–79

Bacterial cell envelope, polysaccharides of, 18
Baeyer-Villiger rearrangement, 141–142
Bile acids, 539–542
   conjugation of, 542
Biological membranes, diffusion across, 277–281
Biotin as a cofactor, 366–369, 484–486, 489, 495–496
   structure of, 366
Blood coagulation, 195–198
Bongkrekic acid, structure of, 465
Branched-chain-amino-acid aminotransferase, 653
Buffers, 160–161
Butyryl-CoA dehydrogenase, 479
Butyryl-CoA synthase, 477

Cahn and Ingold, priority rules of, 72–73
Carbamate kinase, 670–671
Carbamoyl-phosphate synthase:
   ammonia-dependent, 723–724
   glutamine-dependent, 568–570
   in prokaryotic cells, 569–570, 673
Carbon dioxide in purine anabolism, 553
Carboxypeptidase A, 53
Cardiac glycosides, 30–31
Cardiolipin:
   biosynthesis of, 511
   structure of, 24
Carnitine, 479
Carnitine palmitoyltransferase, 479

Catalase, 564
Catecholamines, biosynthesis of, 700–702
Cellulose, structure of, 9
Chenodeoxycholate from cholesterol, 539–541
Chitin, structure of, 9
Chloramphenicol, 740
Chloroplasts, 466
Cholate from cholesterol, 539–541
Cholestenol $\Delta$-isomerase, 528–529
Cholesterol:
   biosynthesis of, 519–531
   catabolism of, 539–542
   structure of, 29
Cholinephosphotransferase, 507–508
Chondroitins, structures of, 15
Chorismate mutase, 706
Chromosomes, 202
Circular birefringence, 67
Circular dichroism, 68
Citrate lyase, 438–440
Citrate synthase, 423–424
Cobalamin:
   5′-deoxyadenosyl-, structure of, 487
   in fatty acid catabolism, 487–489
   in lysine catabolism, 665
Collagen helix, 39
Complex I, 444–445
Complex II, 445–446
Complex III, 447–449
Complex IV, 449–450
Cooperativity:
   Hill coefficient and, 326–327
   negative, 326
   positive, 326
Coordination complexes:
   high-spin, 45$n$.
   low-spin, 45$n$.
Coproporphyrinogen oxidase, 628
Corticosteroids, biosynthesis of, 532–534
Corticosterone 18-monooxygenase, 534
Cotton effect, 69
Creatine kinase, 630–631

Crotonoyl-[acyl-carrier-protein] dehydratase, 498
Cycloheximide, 741
Cystathionine, formation of, 641-642
Cystathionine β-lyase, 648
Cystathionine γ-lyase, 642-643
Cystathionine β-synthase, 642
Cystathionine γ-synthase, 648
Cysteine:
   biosynthesis of, in microorganisms, 645-648
   catabolism of, 643-645
   formation of, in mammals, 642-643
Cysteine aminotransferase, 643
Cysteine dioxygenase, 643
Cytidine deaminase, 583
Cytidine diacyldiphosphoglycerol, 508-509
Cytidine diphosphodiacylglycerol-inositol phosphatidyltransferase, 509
Cytidine triphosphate (CTP) from uridine monophosphate (UMP), 575-576
Cytidine triphosphate synthetase, 575-576
Cytochrome $b_5$ reductase, 503
Cytochrome $c$ oxidase, 449-450
Cytochrome P-450, 492-493
Cytochromes:
   $a$ family, 449-450
   $b$ family, 448-449
   $c$ family, 448-449

Dalton, definition, 246
Dehydroalanine in catabolism of histidine, 682-683
7-Dehydrocholesterol reductase, 529
3-Dehydroquinate dehydratase, 705
Dehydrosphinganine reductase, 514
Deoxycholate, formation of, 542
Deoxycytidine kinase, 582
Deoxycytidine-monophosphate (dCMP) deaminase, 580-581
Deoxycytidylate hydroxymethyltransferase, 581
Deoxyribonucleases:
   bacterial, 606-607
   pancreatic, 603-605
   spleen, 605-606
Deoxyribonucleic-acid nucleotidyltransferases, 585-589
Deoxyribonucleic acid polymerase I, 587-588
Deoxyribonucleic acid polymerase II, 588
Deoxyribonucleic acid polymerase III, 588-589
Deoxyribonucleic acid Polymerases, ribonucleic-acid-dependent, 596-597
Deoxyribonucleic-acid-unwinding protein, 591
Deoxyribonucleic acids:
   biosynthesis of, 585-597
   hydrogen bonding of, 240-244
   hydrophobic bonding of, 244-246
   replication of, 589-597
      elongation, 592-594
      in eukaryotic cells, 595
      initiation, 590-592
      in mitochondria, 595-596
      termination, 595
   structure of, 238-246
Deoxyribonucleotides from ribonucleotides, 576-578
Deoxythymidine kinase, 582
Deoxythymidine monophosphate (dTMP) from uridine monophosphate (UMP), 576-580
Deoxyuridine monophosphate (dUMP) from deoxycytidine monophosphate (dCMP), 580-581
Diacylglycerol acyltransferase, 505
Diaminopimelate decarboxylase, 667
Diaminopimelate epimerase, 667
Dienone-phenol rearrangement, 140-141
Dihydroorotase, 573
Dihydroorotate oxidase, 573

Dihydropicolinate synthase, 666
Dihydropteridine reductase, 694, 696
Dihydropyrimidinase, 583
Dihydrouracil dehydrogenase, 583
Dihydroxyacetone-phosphate acyltransferase, 503-504
Dihydroxyacid dehydratase, 659
Dihydroxyphenylethylamine monooxygenase, 701
Dimethylallyltransferase, 522
Diphosphomevalonate decarboxylase, 521
Disaccharides, structures of, 6-7
Dopamine monooxygenase, 701

Eadie plot, 292
Eicosasphingenine:
  biosynthesis of, 513-515
  structure of, 24
Electron paramagnetic resonance (EPR), 275n.
Electron-transferring flavoprotein, 479-480
Endodeoxyribonucleases, 606-608
Enolase, 353-354
Enoyl-[acyl-carrier-protein] reductase, 498-499
Enoyl-CoA hydratase, 480
Enzyme activation, 311
Enzyme inhibition:
  analogs and, 310
  competitive, 305
  hyperbolic, 311-312
  noncompetitive, 306
  parabolic, 312
  product, 306-309
  substrate, 309-310
  uncompetitive, 306
  velocity equations for, 310-312
Enzymes, classification of, 327-329
Ergosterol, 30
Erythrocytes, glycolysis in, 360
Erythromycin, 740

Estradiol 17 $\beta$-dehydrogenase, 537
Estrogens, biosynthesis of, 536-537
Ethanolaminephosphotransferase, 508
Eukaryotic cells, 202
Exodeoxyribonucleases, 606-607


Farnesyl diphosphate, 523
Farnesyltransferase, 523-525
Fatty acid catabolism, 477-494
  branched-chain acids, 489-491
  $\alpha$-hydroxylation, 493-494
  $\omega$-hydroxylation, 492-493
  nonbranched acids, 477-489
  regulation of, 494
  unsaturated acids, 492
Fatty acid synthase complex, 496-500
Fatty acids:
  biosynthesis of, 494-503
  boiling points, table, 113
  elongation of, 501-502
  melting points, table, 113
  unsaturated: hydration of, 137-139
    oxidation of, 136-137
    reduction of, 133-135
Ferredoxin, 470
Ferredoxin-nicotine-adenine-dinucleotide-phosphate (NADP$^+$) reductase:
  in formation of pregnenolone, 531
  in photosynthesis, 471
Ferrochelatase, 629
Fischer projection formula, 70-71
Flavin semiquinone, 274-276, 418, 445
Formamidase, 710
Formiminoglutamase, 685
Formiminotetrahydrofolate in catabolism of histidine, 685
Formyltetrahydrofolate:
  in biosynthesis of purines, 555
  structure of, 548
Formyltetrahydrofolate synthase, 710
Free-energy changes, 259-261
  calculation of, 266-269

Free-energy changes:
  ionization and, 264
  nonstandard, 269
  oxidation-reduction reactions and, 270–272
  reactive molecules and, 261–266
Fructosebisphosphate aldolase, 342–344
Fumarate hydratase, 434–435
Fumarylacetoacetase, 699
Fusidic acid, 527, 741

Galactokinase, 402
β-Galactosidase, 601
Galactoside acetyltransferase, 601
Gametes, 201
Gangliosides:
  biosynthesis of, 514–515
  structure of, 26, 514
Gel electrophoresis, molecular weight determination and, 179–180
Genetic code, 728–729
Genotype, 201
Geranyl diphosphate, formation of, 521–522
Geranyltransferase, 523
Glucokinase, 334
Gluconeogenesis, 365–380
  regulation of, 377, 379–380
Glucose-6-phosphatase, 375–377
Glucose-6-phosphate dehydrogenase, 392–393
Glucose-1-phosphate uridylyltransferase, 381–383, 402–403
Glucosephosphate isomerase, 336–338, 375
Glutamate dehydrogenases, 615–619
Glutamate formiminotransferase, 685
Glutaminase, 682
Glutamine in purine biosynthesis, 546–547, 550–552, 559–560
Glutamine synthetase, 678–682
Glutamine-synthetase adenylyltransferase, 680

Glutamyl-cysteine synthetase, 644–645
Gluthathionine synthetase, 644
Glyceraldehydephosphate dehydrogenases 345–350, 408
Glycerate kinase, 635
Glycerol kinase, 503
Glycerolphosphate dehydrogenases, 457–458
Glycerophosphate acyltransferases, 503
Glycerophosphate phosphatidyltransferase, 509
Glycine:
  catabolism of, 622–624
  incorporation into heme, 624–625, 627
  incorporation into phosphocreatine, 630–632
  incorporation into serine, 633–634
Glycine amidinotransferase, 630
Glycine aminotransferase, 622
Glycine dehydrogenase, 623
Glycine synthase, 623–624
Glycogen:
  bacterial, 386–387
  metabolism of, 380–391
  structure of, 11
Glycogen synthase, 383–386
Glycolysis, 334–365
  regulation of, 362–365
N-Glycosides:
  hydrolysis of, 100–101
  laboratory synthesis of, 99
O-Glycosides:
  hydrolysis of, 95–99
  laboratory synthesis of, 93–95
N-Glycosidic bonds, torsion angles of, 55–56
O-Glycosidic bonds:
  α-configuration, 6
  β-configuration, 6
  torsion angles of, 12
Glycosphingolipids, 24
Glyoxalate, metabolism of, 622–623
Gout, 566
Guanidinoacetate methyltransferase, 630
Guanine deaminase, 564

Guanosine monophosphate (GMP):
  from inosine monophosphate (IMP), 558–560
  from xanthosine monophosphate (XMP), 558–560
Guanosine-monophosphate reductase, 560
Guanosine-monophosphate synthetase, 558–560
Gummiferin, 465

Heme a, 449
Heme b:
  biosynthesis of, 624–629
  structure of, 447
Heme c, 448
Hemoglobin, structural characteristics, 44–49
Hemoglobin S, 49
Heparin, 14–16
Heterotropic effect, 324
Hexokinase, 334–336
Hexose interconversions, 402–404
Hexosediphosphatase, 374–375
Hexose-1-phosphate uridylyltransferase, 402
Hill coefficient, 326–327
*His* operon, 692
Histidine:
  biosynthesis of, 687–693
  catabolism of, 682–686
Histidine ammonia-lyase, 682–683
Histidinol dehydrogenase, 692
Histidinolphosphatase, 691
Histidinol-phosphate aminotransferase, 691
Hofstee plot, 292
Homoaconitate hydratase, 667
Homocitrate synthase, 667
Homogentisate 1,2-dioxygenase, 697–698
Homoserine dehydrogenase, 638
Homoserine kinase, 638

Homoserine succinyltransferase, 648
Homotropic effect, 324
*Hut* operon, 686
Hyaluronic acid, 13
Hybrid nuclease, 609
Hydrazones as saccharide derivatives, 89
3-Hydroxyacyl-CoA dehydrogenase, 480
3-Hydroxyanthranilate 3,4-dioxygenase, 712
3-Hydroxyaspartate aldolase, 623
3-Hydroxyaspartate dehydratase, 623
2-Hydroxy-3-carboxyadipate dehydrogenase, 667
D-3-Hydroxydecanoyl-[acyl-carrier-protein] dehydratase, 500–501
3-Hydroxyisobutyrate dehydrogenase, 657
3-Hydroxyisobutyryl-CoA hydrolase, 657
Hydroxymethyldeoxycytidylate, formation of, 581
Hydroxymethylglutaryl-CoA lyase, 489–490, 656
Hydroxymethylglutaryl-CoA reductase, 519–520
Hydroxymethylglutaryl-CoA synthase, 491
2-Hydroxy-3-oxoadipate carboxylase, 622
4-Hydroxyphenylpyruvate dioxygenase, 696–697
15-Hydroxyprostaglandin dehydrogenase, 517–518
Hydroxypyruvate reductase, 635
$\beta$-Hydroxysteroid dehydrogenase, 532
Hypervalemia, 656
Hypotaurine dehydrogenase, 643
Hypoxanthine phosphoribosyltransferase, 565


Imidazoleglycerolphosphate dehydratase, 691
Imidazolonepropionase, 685

Immunoglobulins, 198–200
Indole-3-glycerol-phosphate synthase, 721
Initiation factors, 733–735
Inosine monophosphate (IMP):
  from adenosine monophosphate (AMP), 560
  from guanosine monophosphate (GMP), 560
Inosine-monophosphate cyclohydrolase, 555–556
Inosine-monophosphate dehydrogenase, 558
Isocitrate dehydrogenase, 425, 428–429
Isoleucine:
  biosynthesis of, 657–662
  catabolism of, 653–657
Isopentenyl diphosphate, 521
Isopentenyldiphosphate Δ-isomerase, 521–522
3-Isopropylmalate dehydratase, 660
3-Isopropylmalate dehydrogenase, 660
2-Isopropylmalate synthase, 659–660
Isotope exchange, 313–322


Ketohexokinase, 404
Ketol-acid reductoisomerase, 658–659
Ketone bodies, 490–492
Kinetic equations:
  for bisubstrate, ordered sequential reactions, 295–300
  for bisubstrate ping pong reactions, 300–301
  for bisubstrate random reactions, 301
  Cleland's terminology and, 294–295
  for inhibited reactions, 310–312
  for isotope exchange reactions, 314–322
Kinetic isotope effect, secondary, 354$n$.
Kinetics, laws of, 282–284
Kynureninase, 711
Kynurenine 3-monooxygenase, 710–711

*Lac* operon, 601–602
Lactate dehydrogenase, 357–360
Lanosterol:
  conversion of, into cholesterol, 528–529
  formation of, 525–527
Lathosterol oxidase, 529
Lesch-Nyhan syndrome, 565
Leucine:
  biosynthesis of, 657–662
  catabolism of, 653–657
Light scattering, 247–251
Lineweaver-Burk plot, 291–292
Lipoamide dehydrogenase, 418–419
Lipoate, 415
Lipoate acetyltransferase, 418
Lipoproteins:
  apoproteins of, 475–477
  classification of, 475–477
Lithocholate, formation of, 542
Lysine:
  biosynthesis of, 666–669
  catabolism of, 662–666
Lysine 2,3-aminomutase, 665
β-Lysine 5,6-aminomutase, 665
Lysine monooxygenase, 664–665
Lysophospholipase, 506
Lysozyme, 52–53


Malate-aspartate shuttle, 458–459
Malate dehydrogenase, 435–436
Malate dehydrogenase (decarboxylating), 440–441
Maleylacetoacetate isomerase, 699
Mannokinase, 403
Mannosephosphate isomerase, 403
Maple-syrup-urine disease, 656
Meiosis, 203–204
Membranes, cell: characteristics of, 144–146
  components of, 143–146
  Singer model for, 144–145

Messenger ribonucleic acid, 727–728
Methenyltetrahydrofolate:
   in purine biosynthesis, 549–550
   structure of, 548
Methionine:
   biosynthesis of, in microorganisms, 648–650
   catabolism of, 641–643
Methionine adenosyltransferase, 641
Methylcrotonoyl-CoA carboxylase, 489, 656
Methylenetetrahydrofolate:
   in deoxythymidine monophosphate (dTMP) formation, 578–580
   in glycine catabolism, 623–624
   in glycine-serine interconversion, 633–634
   structure of, 549
Methylglutaconyl-CoA hydratase, 656
Methylmalonyl-CoA mutase, 484–489
Methylmalonyl-CoA racemase, 485–486
Methylsterol monooxygenase, 528
Methyltetrahydrofolate:
   in formation of methionine, 648–649
   structure of, 549
Mevalonate, formation of, 519–520
Mevalonate kinase, 520
Michaelis constant, 291
Mitochondria, 411–414
   localization of enzymes in, table, 414
Mitochondrial electron-transport system, 444–453
   inhibition of, 460–463
   variable midpoint potentials of components of, 459–460
Mitochondrial inner membrane:
   asymmetry of, 443
   permeability of, 438–441, 456–459
Mitosis, 202–203
Monophenol monooxygenase, 702
Monosaccharides:
   laboratory synthesis of, 86–88
   reactions of, with carbonyl reagents, 89–92

Monosaccharides:
   structures of, 83–85
Mutorotation, 74

Nicotinate-D-ribonucleotide adenylyltransferase, 715
Nicotinate-D-ribonucleotide pyrophosphorylase, 715
Nicotine adenine dinucleotide (NAD$^+$), formation of, 715–716
Nicotine adenine dinucleotide dehydrogenase, 444–445
Nicotine adenine dinucleotide kinase, 715
Nicotine adenine dinucleotide synthetase, 715
Nicotine adenine dinucleotide ubiquinone reductase, 444–445
Nonheme iron-sulfur centers in mitochondrial electron-transport system, 445–446
Norepinephrine $N$-methyltransferase, 701
Nuclear magnetic resonance (NMR), 90$n$.
Nucleic acids:
   biosynthesis of, 585–601
   degradation of, 603–610
   hypochromism of, 253–254
   laboratory synthesis of, 233–238
   molecular weight determinations of, 246–253
   molecular weights of, table, 58
   mutagenic modification of, 255–258
   primary structure of, 58
   quaternary structure of, 58
   secondary structure of, 58
   structural characteristics of, 57–58
   tertiary structure of, 58
   thermal melting of, 254–255
Nucleosidase, 561
Nucleoside diphosphates from monophosphates, 560–561

Nucleoside triphosphates from diphosphates, 560–561
Nucleosidediphosphate kinase, 432
Nucleosidemonophosphate kinase, 560–561
Nucleosides:
　hydrolysis of N-glycosidic bonds of, 228–229
　laboratory synthesis of, 221–223
　ribosyl ring conformations of, 56
　structures of, 54
5'-Nucleotidase, 561
Nucleotides:
　laboratory synthesis of, 223–227
　ribosyl ring conformations of, 56
　structures of, 55

Octant rule, 139–140
Okazaki fragments, 592
Operon, 601–602
Optical rotatory dispersion (ORD), 68
Ornithine, catabolism of, 674–676
D-Ornithine 4,5-aminomutase, 676
Ornithine carbamoyltransferase, 670–671, 724
Ornithine cyclodeaminase, 677
Ornithine decarboxylase, 674
Ornithine-oxo-acid aminotransferase, 676
Ornithine racemase, 676
Orotate phosphoribosyltransferase, 573
Orotidine-5'-phosphate decarboxylase, 573
Osazones, formation of, 90
$\beta$-Oxidation, 477–483
Oxidation-reduction cofactors, 273–277
Oxidative phosphorylation, 451–454
　inhibitors of, 464–466
　mechanism of, 453–454
　uncouplers of, 463–464
Oxidative photophosphorylation, 472
Oximes, formation of, 89–90
3-Oxoacid CoA-transferases, 490–491

3-Oxo-[acyl-carrier-protein] reductase, 498
3-Oxo-[acyl-carrier-protein] synthase, 497–498
2-Oxobutyrate in histidine catabolism, 683–685
2-Oxoglutarate dehydrogenase complex, 429–430
2-Oxoisocaproate dehydrogenase, 653


Palmitoyldihydroxyacetone-phosphate reductase, 504
Pentose phosphate pathway, 392–402
　regulation of, 399–402
Peptide bonds, torsion angles of, 43
Phenotype, 201
Phenylalanine:
　biosynthesis of, 702–708
　catabolism of, 694–700
Phenylalanine 4-monooxygenase, 694–696
Phenylketonuria, 696
Phosphate esters, cyclic, 126–128
Phosphatidate cytidylyltransferase, 509
Phosphatidate phosphatase, 505
Phosphatidylcholine, formation of, 507–508
Phosphatidylethanolamine, formation of, 507–508
Phosphatidylglycerophosphatase, 511
Phosphatidylinositol-bisphosphate phosphatase, 511
Phosphatidylinositol kinase, 509–510
Phosphatidylinositol-phosphate kinase, 510–511
Phosphatidylinositols:
　formation of, 508–511
　structure of, 23
Phosphatidylserine, formation of, 508
Phosphocholine cytidylyltransferase, 507–508
Phosphocreatine, biosynthesis of, 630–632

Phosphodiesters, hydrolysis of: acid-catalyzed, 128–130
base-catalyzed, 131–133
Phosphoenolpyruvate carboxykinase, 371–373
3-Phospho-5-*eno*lpyruvoylshikimate synthase, 705
Phosphoethanolamine cytidylyltransferase, 507
Phosphofructokinase, 339–341
Phosphoglucomutase, 380–381
Phosphogluconate dehydrogenase, 393–395
Phosphoglycerate dehydrogenase, 636
Phosphoglycerate kinase, 350–351
Phosphoglyceromutase, 352–353
Phospholipase $A_1$, 505
Phospholipase $A_2$, 505
Phospholipase C, 506
Phospholipase D, 506
Phospholipids:
 biosynthesis of, 506–513
 catabolism of, 505–506
 structures of, 21–23
Phosphomevalonate kinase, 521
Phosphomonoesters, hydrolysis of, 125–126
Phospho-2-oxo-3-deoxy-heptonate aldolase, 703–704
Phosphoribosyl-adenosine-monophosphate cyclohydrolase, 688–689
5-(5′-Phospho-D-ribosyl-aminoformimino)-1-(5″-phosphoribosyl)-4-imidazolecarboxamide isomerase, 689
Phosphoribosylaminoimidazole carboxylase, 553
Phosphoribosylaminoimidazole synthetase, 552–553
Phosphoribosylaminoimidazolecarboxamide formyltransferase, 555
Phosphoribosylaminoimidazolesuccinocarboxamide synthetase, 554
Phosphoribosylformylglycinamidine synthetase, 550–552

Phosphoribosylglycinamide formyltransferase, 548–550
Phosphoribosylglycinamide synthetase, 547
5′-Phospho-5-ribosyluracil, reaction with periodate, 231–233
Phosphoribulokinase, 406
Phosphorylase, 387–389
Phosphoserine aminotransferase, 636
Phosphoserine phosphatase, 636
Photosynthesis:
 electron transport in, 466–473
 reductive pentose phosphate cycle of, 406–410
Piericidin, 460
Pinacol rearrangement, 142
Ping pong mechanism, two-site, 368–370, 484–486, 496
Plasma proteins, table, 196
Plastoquinone, 469
Polarized light, 62–64
Polynucleotide synthetase:
 adenosine triphosphate-dependent, 595
 nicotine adenine dinucleotide-dependent, 592–594
Porphobilinogen, formation of, 626–627
Porphobilinogen synthase, 626–627
Porphyrias, 629–630
Pregnenolone, formation of, 531–532
Prephenate dehydratase, 707
Prephenate dehydrogenase, 707
Proline:
 biosynthesis of, 677
 catabolism of, 676–677
Propionyl-CoA carboxylase, 483–486
Prostaglandin synthase, 516–517
Prostaglandins:
 biosynthesis of, 515–517
 catabolism of, 517–518
 structures of, 27, 515–516
Proteins:
 biosynthesis of, 727–739
  elongation phase, 735–737
  inhibitors of, 739–741

Proteins:
   biosynthesis of: initiation phase, 727–735
      termination phase, 737–738
   denaturation of, 184–187
   fluorescence of, 183–184
   laboratory synthesis of, 164–172
   molecular-weight determinations of, 172–180
   optical activity of, 180–182
   primary structure of, 39–41
      determination of, 187–191
   quaternary structure of, 39–41
   reactions of, 191–194
   secondary structure of, 39–41
   tertiary structure of, 39–41
Protoporphyrin IX, 447
Pseudorotation, 128
Pseudouridine (*see* Ribosyluracil)
Purine-nucleoside phosphorylase, 565
Purine nucleotide cycle, 568
Purine salvage pathways, 565
Purines:
   alkylation of, 209–210
   biosynthesis of, 543–556
   catabolism of, 561–567
   laboratory synthesis of, 208–209
   metabolism of, regulation of, 567–568
   reactions of: with carbonyl compounds, 210–211
      with nitrous acid, 213–214
   structures of, 53–54
   tautomerism of, 206–207
Puromycin, 739–740
Putrescine, formation of, 670
Pyridoxal 5-phosphate:
   in biosynthesis of heme, 625–627
   in biosynthesis of threonine, 638–641
   in biosynthesis of tryptophan, 721–722
   in catabolism of arginine, 670
   in catabolism of lysine, 665
   in catabolism of tryptophan, 711–717
   in cleavage of cystathionine, 642–643, 648

Pyridoxal 5-phosphate:
   in decarboxylation reactions, 623–627, 651–652, 670, 674–675, 677
   in formation of 5-aminolevulinate, 625–627
   in formation of cystathionine, 641–642, 648
   in formation of cysteine in mammals, 642–643
   in formation of cysteine in microorganisms, 648
   in formation of $N$-succinyl-2,6-diaminopimelate, 667
   in formation of putrescine, 674–675
   in formation of pyruvate from serine, 634–635
   in formation of threonine, 639, 641
   in formation of tryptophan, 721–722
   in glycine-serine interconversion, 633–634
   structure of, 619
   in transamination reactions, 619–622
Pyrimidine salvage pathways, 582–583
Pyrimidines:
   biosynthesis of, 568–574
   catabolism of, 583–584
   dimerization of, 215–217
   excimers derived from, 215–216
   ionizing radiation and, 217–219
   laboratory synthesis of, 207
   metabolism of, regulation of, 584–585
   structures of, 53–54
   tautomerism of, 206–207
   ultraviolet radiation and, 214–217
Pyrroline-5-carboxylate reductase, 677
Pyruvate carboxylase, 366–371
Pyruvate decarboxylase, 404–405
Pyruvate dehydrogenase complex, 414–422
   kinetic studies on, 420–421
   regulation of activity of, 422
Pyruvate dehydrogenase component, 415–417
Pyruvate kinase, 355–357

R, S nomenclature for optically active centers, 72–73
Reaction mechanisms, denotement for, 95n.
Refsum's syndrome, 493–494
Replication of deoxyribonucleic acids, 589–597
Replication fork, 591
Replots:
  intercept, 304
  slope, 304
Restriction endonucleases, 607–608
Ribonuclease, bovine pancreatic, 608–609
Ribonuclease II, 609–610
Ribonucleases, bacterial, 609–610
Ribonucleic-acid nucleotidyltransferases, 597–600
Ribonucleic acids, biosynthesis of, 597–601
  elongation phase, 600
  initiation phase, 599–600
  termination phase, 600–601
Ribonucleoside-diphosphate reductase, 576–578
Ribonucleoside-triphosphate reductase, 578
Ribosephosphate diphosphotransferase, 543–546
Ribosephosphate isomerase, 395–396
Ribosomes, 727–728
Ribosyluracil:
  laboratory synthesis of, 229–230
  reactions of, 230–231, 233
  structure of, 229
Ribulosebisphosphate carboxylase, 406–408
Ribulosephosphate 3-epimerase, 395–396
Rifampicin, 600, 602
Ring conformation:
  alternative form, 4
  boat form, 3–4
  chair form, 3

Ring conformation:
  envelope form, 3
  half-chair forms, 3, 29
  normal form, 4
Ring substituents:
  axial, 4
  dihedral angle between, table, 5
  equatorial, 4
Rings, carbocyclic, properties of, table, 3
Rotenone, 460
Rubredoxin, 493

Saccharides:
  laboratory synthesis of, 86–88
  periodate oxidation of, 92–93
  phophoryl derivatives of: hydrolysis of, 104–108
    laboratory synthesis of, 102–103
  reactions of, with carbonyl reagents, 89–92
Saccharopine dehydrogenase:
  nicotine-adenine-dinucleotide-dependent: glutamate-forming, 662
    lysine-forming, 669
  nicotine-adenine-dinucleotide-phosphate-dependent: glutamate-forming, 668
    lysine-forming, 662
Sedimentation equilibrium, 176–179
Sedimentation velocity, 173–176
Semicarbazides, formation of, 89–90
Serine:
  formation of: from glycine, 633–634
    from 3-phosphoglycerate, 636
Serine acetyltransferase, 646
D-Serine dehydratase, 635
L-Serine dehydratase, 634–635
Serine hydroxymethyltransferase, 633–634
Serine-pyruvate aminotransferase, 635
Serotonin, formation of, 714–715
Shikimate dehydrogenase, 705

Shikimate kinase, 705
Sickle-cell anemia, 49–51
Spermidine, formation of, 674–675
Spermine, formation of, 674–675
Sphingenine:
   biosynthesis of, 513–515
   structure of, 24, 513
Sphingolipids, glyco-, 24–25
Squalene:
   cyclization of, 525–527
   formation of, 520–525
Squalene monooxygenase, 525–527
Starch, structure of, 10
Steady-state assumption, 284–285, 293
Stereoselectivity, 75
Stereospecificity, 75
Steroid hormones:
   formation of, 531–539
   functions of, 537–538
Steroid Δ-isomerase, 532
Steroid 11β-monooxygenase, 534
Steroid 17α-monooxygenase, 534
Steroid 21-monooxygenase, 534
Steroids, 518–542
   Cotton effect exhibited by, 139–140
   ring structure of, 28–29
Succinate dehydrogenase, 433–434, 446
Succinate-semialdehyde dehydrogenase, 677
Succinate-ubiquinone reductase, 445–446
Succinyl-CoA synthetase:
   adenosine-diphosphate-dependent, 430–431
   guanosine-diphosphate-dependent, 430–432
Succinyl-diaminopimelate aminotransferase, 667
Succinyl-diaminopimelate desuccinylase, 667
Sulfate adenylyltransferase, 645
Sulfite oxidase, 643
Sulfite reductase, 645–646
Superoxide anion, 562
Superoxide dismutase, 562, 564

Testosterone 17β-dehydrogenase, 536
Tetrahydrobiopterin in formation of tyrosine, 694–696
Tetrahydrofolate, "one-carbon" derivatives of, 548–549
Tetrahydrofolate dehydrogenase, 580
Thiamine diphosphate:
   in biosynthesis of branched-chain amino acids, 657–658
   in catabolism of branched-chain amino acids, 653
   in decarboxylation of 2-oxoglutarate, 430
   in decarboxylation of pyruvate, 404–405, 414–417
   in formation of sedoheptulose 7-phosphate, 396–397
Thioredoxin, 577
Thioredoxin reductase, 577
Threonine:
   biosynthesis of, 637–641
   catabolism of, 636–637
Threonine dehydratase, 636, 657
Threonine 3-dehydrogenase, 637
Threonine synthase, 638–641
Thylakoid membrane, asymmetric arrangement of components of, 466–468
Thymidine phosphorylase, 582
Thymidylate synthase, 578–580
Transaldolase, 396, 398–399
Transamination, 619–622
Transcription, 598
   inhibitors of, 602–603
   regulation of, in *E. coli,* 601–602
Transfer ribonucleic acids, 729–733
   structural characteristics of, 58–59
Transhydrogenation, 456–457
Transketolase, 396–397
Triacylglycerols, 474–505
   digestion of, 474–477
Tricarboxylic acid cycle, 422–437
Triglycerides (*see* Triacylglycerols)
Triokinase, 404
Triosephosphate isomerase, 345

Trisaccharides, 8
*Trp* operon, 722–723
Tryptophan:
   biosynthesis of, 717–723
   catabolism of, 709–714
Tryptophan 2,3-dioxygenase, 709–710
Tryptophan 5-monooxygenase, 714
Tryptophan synthase, 721–722
Tryptophanase, 717
Tyrosine:
   biosynthesis of, 702–708
   catabolism of, 694–700
Tyrosine aminotransferase, 696
Tyrosine 3-monooxygenase, 700–701

Ubiquinone, 446–447
   structure of, 444
Ubiquinone-cytochrome *c* reductase, 447–449
Uracil phosphoribosyltransferase, 585
Urate oxidase, 566
Urea, biosynthesis of, 723–726
Urea cycle, 723–726
Urease, 566
3-Ureidopropionase, 583–584
Uridine-diphosphoglucose 4-epimerase, 402

Uridine kinase, 582
Uridine phosphorylase, 582
Urocanate hydratase, 683–685
Uroporphyrin decarboxylase, 628
Uroporphyrinogen I synthase, 628

Valine:
   biosynthesis of, 657–662
   catabolism of, 653–657
van't Hoff complex, 284–286, 292–293
Vitamin $B_{12}$ cofactor, 487–489
   in rearrangement reactions, 487–489, 665
Vitamin $D_2$, formation of, 142–143

Xanthine oxidase, 561–562
Xanthosine monophosphate (XMP) from inosine monophosphate (IMP), 558
X-ray diffraction, 34–37

Zygote, 201